Introduction to Game Development

Introduction to Game Development

Edited by
Steve Rabin

CHARLES RIVER MEDIA, INC.

Hingham, Massachusetts

Editor: David Pallai
Cover Design: Tyler Creative

CHARLES RIVER MEDIA, INC.
10 Downer Avenue
Hingham, Massachusetts 02043
781-740-0400
781-740-8816 (FAX)
info@charlesriver.com
www.charlesriver.com

This book is printed on acid-free paper.

Steve Rabin. *Introduction to Game Development.*
ISBN: 1-58450-377-7

Library of Congress Cataloging-in-Publication Data
Introduction to game development / edited by Steve Rabin.
    p. cm.
 Includes bibliographical references and index.
 ISBN 1-58450-377-7 (hardcover with cd-rom : alk. paper)
 1. Computer games—Design. 2. Computer games—Programming. 3. Video games—Design. I. Rabin, Steve.
 QA76.76.C672I58 2005
 794.8'1536—dc22
             2005007512

Printed in the United States of America
05 7 6 5 4 3 2 First Edition

CHARLES RIVER MEDIA titles are available for site license or bulk purchase by institutions, user groups, corporations, etc. For additional information, please contact the Special Sales Department at 781-740-0400.

Requests for replacement of a defective CD-ROM must be accompanied by the original disc, your mailing address, telephone number, date of purchase, and purchase price. Please state the nature of the problem, and send the information to CHARLES RIVER MEDIA, INC., 10 Downer Avenue, Hingham, Massachusetts 02043. CRM's sole obligation to the purchaser is to replace the disc, based on defective materials or faulty workmanship, but not on the operation or functionality of the product.

Contents

Acknowledgments

Many dedicated people helped create this book. First and foremost, I want to thank the authors. This book is a tribute to their hard work and dedication to sharing their knowledge with others. As leaders in their respective fields, it takes a great deal of sacrifice and goodwill for them to spend their free time distilling their wisdom for others to benefit from. For this effort, I thank them.

This book started out as a dream to bring top industry veterans together to create an unparalleled tome of knowledge and wisdom. Dave Pallai of Charles River Media strongly believed in this project from the start and entrusted me with bringing it to fruition. I want to thank him for his guidance, support, and faith. The staff of Charles River Media was also very helpful and skilled in putting this book together quickly, and they deserve many thanks as well.

I want to thank Jason Della Rocca, executive director of the IGDA, not only for his encouragement for this project, but also for his support and contribution to the IGDA and the IGDA Curriculum Framework, which inspired and guided this book. Thanks also to the other Curriculum Development Committee members: Doug Church, Robin Hunicke, Warren Spector, and Eric Zimmerman.

I want to extend additional thanks to Rob Bakie, Isaac Barry, Hal Barwood, Jim Charne, Henry Cheng, Miguel Gomez, Jeff Lander, Eric Lengyel, Tito Pagan, and Graham Rhodes for help recruiting authors as well as reviewing many of the chapters.

Finally, I want to thank my wife Leslie and my children Aaron and Allison for supporting me during this endeavor, as well as my parents, Diane and Barry Rabin, and my in-laws, Jim and Shirley Stirling.

Preface

Welcome to *Introduction to Game Development*. This is a unique book in that it combines the wisdom and expertise of over 25 games industry professionals to give you an unprecedented view of game development—from game design, to programming, to production and business issues.

The greatest challenge in creating this book was to cover virtually all of game development, while still maintaining the depth necessary to truly understand and appreciate state-of-the-art processes. The solution was to gather some of the brightest and most respected experts in the industry and allow each author to go into the detail that he or she felt was necessary to cover his or her field of expertise. While this resulted in a very large book by most standards, it was critical to maintaining all of the key concepts and ideas, while giving practical insight into the problems of real game development.

The background of the respective authors is most impressive. Most have more than a decade of experience in the games industry and are leaders in their respective fields, speaking regularly at the annual Game Developers Conference, instructing college-level game development classes on the side, or having written books of their own. What sets this book apart is the incredible insight and experience that each author brings to his or her chapter, with the entire gamut of game development explored. No one person could write a book like this, since it requires lifetimes of specialization and experience to understand and distill the issues. However, don't take my word; browse through each author's biography in the following pages.

Book Structure and Inspiration

The structure of this book is largely based on the International Game Developers Association (IGDA) Curriculum Framework proposed by the IGDA Curriculum Development Committee. Through cooperation between respected games industry professionals and academia, this committee was able to define a framework that would give guidance to schools and universities working to create their own academic programs in game development. While the IGDA Curriculum Framework is an ongoing process, it provided the guidance and inspiration for this book.

It is not the intention that every topic and every chapter of this book be taught thoroughly within a single class on game development. Rather, this book contains an assortment of topics, broken up in parts, which can be mixed and matched to create a custom, yet focused curriculum for a particular academic program.

While this book can be customized to create a particular focus, there is immense value to understanding all elements of game development and how they interact. Game development isn't just about game design or programming or creating 3D models. It is about the entire process and how each element interacts and impacts the others. Experts on graphics programming will be ineffective if they don't understand the motivations of the game designer, artists, or producer. Artists will create useless art if they don't appreciate the programming limitations of the hardware and don't create art that works to meet the game design. Finally, it would clearly be detrimental to a project if the business professionals failed to understand the technical challenges with both programming and art generation. Game development is a cooperative process that depends on each discipline understanding the motivations, requirements, and constraints placed by the others. This book strives to create a mutual respect and teamwork attitude toward game development.

Game Development in the Twenty-First Century

Gone are the days of the lone game developer single-handedly crafting the game design, code, and art for a game. Game development in the twenty-first century is about large teams striving toward a common goal over a period of several years. The games industry is a "hits-driven" business, and it takes incredible talent, expertise, creativity, marketing, and luck to make the next blockbuster game. However, in this innovative and evolving industry, there is an enormous opportunity to break new ground and push the state of games further.

As this book was being assembled, the games industry witnessed the introduction of the Nintendo DS. This portable handheld game system is a perfect example of how innovation continues to spring forth around us, year after year. This system supports multiple screens, a microphone, a touchpanel, wireless connectivity, and wireless download play. Each of these elements has existed for some time in one form or another, but by putting it into one package that millions of people will buy, developers can depend on these features being present and can explore new ways of play. Hundreds of companies are now dedicating their most talented developers to creating games that exploit this new interactivity.

At roughly 30 years old, the videogames industry is still young and expanding at an amazing clip. According to Pricewaterhouse Coopers, the industry will continue to globally grow at about a 20 percent compound annual growth rate through 2008. This far exceeds the projected growth rate of any other media, including Internet advertising and access, TV, movies, radio, music, magazines, books, or newspapers. The games industry's 2003 global revenues of $22.3 billion are projected to reach $55.6 billion by 2008.

This incredible growth means opportunity for new ideas, new ways to play, and the need for new talent within the industry. This book hopes to inspire, motivate, and guide future generations of game developers to create innovative games that continue to push the boundaries of what has come before.

www.IntroGameDev.com

With the publication of this book is the debut of a new Web site to support aspiring game developers with learning everything there is to know about game development. This Web site will hold the corrections for this book, and will serve as a guide for where to find articles and information on game development that aren't indexed anywhere else. Use it as a tool and a resource when exploring available information on game development.

How to Use this Book

At first glance, the comprehensive nature of this book can be daunting to any student, instructor, or aspiring game developer. Clearly, it is not the intention that every single chapter be taught in-depth within a single academic quarter, but rather it is encouraged that various parts are used to create a customized educational experience. By tailoring the content of this book, many academic programs with slightly different purposes can be well served. The parts and chapters are largely independent, which facilitates customization by omitting certain parts or shuffling around chapters as needed. The following provides guidance and examples for how to use this book in an educational setting.

Understanding the various parts of this book is key to creating a custom curriculum. As shown in Figure 1, the parts can be divided into four main categories: understanding games, game programming, art/asset creation, and business/management. For any given curriculum, the goal is to find a suitable balance among these four categories.

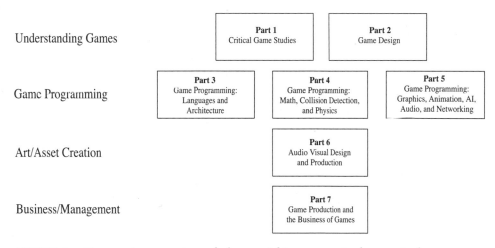

FIGURE 1 *Four main categories to balance within any particular curriculum.*

As a game development course within a computer science department, it is undoubtedly important to focus on game programming aspects (Parts 3, 4, and 5). However, it is essential to motivate what is being built (Parts 1 and 2), what constraints exist with regard to integrating assets (Part 6), as well as how a game project is managed (Part 7). Within a 10-week course, it would be appropriate to spend seven or eight weeks on game programming, while interspersing the core topic with roughly two or three weeks of understanding games, art/asset creation, and business/management issues.

Increasingly among universities, special interdisciplinary courses are being offered in game development, bringing together students from several different majors such as computer science, art, music, and business. In such a rich, dynamic environment, this book can serve many different purposes ranging from game design, programming, art creation, and management of group projects. Within this type of course, students adopt a role and interact with each other as if they were part of a real game development team. The class lectures can consist of an even split among the four main categories, staying fairly high level with respect to programming topics. The book then provides enough depth for students in each discipline to delve deeper and explore individual topics.

Narrow curriculums, such as game design, can benefit greatly from exploring the interrelationships of all aspects of game development that this book offers. While most of the programming topics would be lightly or sparsely covered, there is a great deal of material to explore within Parts 1, 2, 6, and 7. A course on game design would dedicate about three weeks to looking at the history of games and game studies, another two or three weeks on core game design, then the remaining four weeks looking at how programming, asset creation, and business issues (such as content regulation) relate to game design. For example, topics such as artificial intelligence or audio can have a large impact on game design by affording many interesting gameplay opportunities.

In summary, three sample curriculums are given in Table 1 for each of the three types of courses presented. Interestingly, each covers most of the chapters in this book, but the difference is in focus and depth. By spending the appropriate amount of time on each topic, students are guaranteed to delve deeply into a particular subject, yet stay well-rounded and appreciate the technological, artistic, and business issues that are integral to game development. Also note that the parts and chapters are mostly independent and can be omitted, shuffled, or paired as needed.

Table 1 Three Sample Curriculums Based on a 10-week College-level Course

Week	Programming-oriented Course	Interdisciplinary Course	Game Design Course
1	Overview and Design of Video Games (1.1, 1.2, 2.1, 2.2)	Overview of Video Games (Ch 1.1, 1.2, 1.3)	History of Video Games (Ch 1.1)
2	Game Production and Teams (Ch 3.1, 7.1)	Game Production and Teams (Ch 3.1, 7.1)	Societal and Cultural Game Issues (Ch 1.2)
3	Language and Architecture (Ch 3.2 – 3.7)	Game Industry Roles and Economics (Ch 7.2, 7.3, 7.4)	Studying Games from an Academic Perspective (Ch 1.3)

Week	Programming-oriented Course	Interdisciplinary Course	Game Design Course
4	Mathematics, Collision Detection, and Physics (Ch 4.1, 4.2, 4.3)	Game Design (Ch 2.1, 2.2)	Game Design (Ch 2.1, 2.2)
5	Graphics, 3D Models, Textures (Ch 5.1, 6.2, 6.4, 6.7)	Art and Asset Creation (Ch 6.1–6.7)	Game Design (Ch 2.1, 2.2)
6	Animation Programming and Creation (Ch 5.2, 6.7)	Programming Languages and Architecture (Ch 3.2–3.7)	Influence of Artificial Intelligence and Audio on Game Design (Ch 5.3, 5.5, 6.8)
7	Graphics and Animation Continued (Ch 5.1, 5.2)	3D Math and Physics Concepts (Ch 4.1, 4.3)	Game Production and Teams (Ch 3.1, 7.1)
8	Artificial Intelligence (Ch 5.3, 5.4)	Graphics and Animation Overview (Ch 5.1, Ch 5.2)	Art Asset Creation Overview (Ch 6.1–6.7)
9	Audio and Networking (Ch 5.5, 5.6)	Artificial Intelligence, Audio, and Networking Overview (Ch 5.3, Ch 5.5, Ch 5.6)	Game Industry Roles and Economics (Ch 7.2, 7.3, 7.4)
10	Business and Legal Issues (Ch 7.2–7.6)	Intellectual Property and Content Regulation (Ch 7.5, 7.6)	Intellectual Property and Content Regulation (Ch 7.5, 7.6)

PowerPoint Slides on the CD-ROM

ON THE CD

As a feature of this book, each chapter has an accompanying PowerPoint presentation that is included on the CD-ROM. The benefit of such a resource is that the key points of each chapter have been distilled in a manner that closely follows the text. In addition, almost all charts, figures, and screenshots from the book have been incorporated into the presentations, allowing students to explore the material in class as well as on their own. This also reduces the burden on the instructor by making it easier to prepare for class lectures that complement the book.

Contributor Bios

Robert T. Bakie

slinkie@serv.net

Rob Bakie has been a games industry professional for the past seven years and an avid game player for the last two decades. Currently, he works at Nintendo of America as Webmaster for the developer support group. Previously, he worked at Sierra Entertainment's online multiplayer division WON.net. He has written game reviews for national magazines and game walkthroughs for Web sites. Rob holds a B.A. in Communications Broadcast Journalism from the University of Washington with a minor in Computer Music.

Isaac Barry

isaac.barry@gmail.com

Isaac Barry is a game designer at Radical Entertainment. He began working in game development as a tester with Monolith Productions and began designing at Surreal Software. He has spoken at the Game Developers Conference and as a guest at the University of Washington Extension. He reflects on brains and games at *http://play-cube.org/*.

Ed Bartlett

ed@hivepartners.com

During a career in the video games industry spanning over a decade, Ed Bartlett has worked in a wide range of roles, from managing a team of 13 product analysts, through senior production and design roles, to his most recognized role with infamous UK developer The Bitmap Brothers as their business development director. In August 2003, Ed set up Hive Partners, an exciting new creative communications consultancy helping developers and publishers to commercially exploit their portfolios, and helping brands to use interactive digital entertainment to engage consumers more effectively. Recently noted as one of 30 key individuals in the games sector, Ed has already established Hive Partners as market leader in the burgeoning interactive product placement market, with exciting plans for global expansion and diversification.

James Boer

author@boarslair.com

James Boer has been in the games industry since 1997, working on such titles as *Deer Hunter*, *Deer Hunter II*, *Trophy Hunter*, *Pro Bass Fishing*, *Microsoft Baseball 2000*, *Tex Atomic's Big Bot Battles*, and *Digimon Rumble Arena 2*. He has also contributed prolifically to the games industry's printed media, having written several articles for *Game Developer* magazine, coauthoring *DirectX Complete*, authoring *Game Audio Programming*, and contributing to four volumes of *Game Programming Gems*. He is currently employed at Amaze Entertainment, where he is working on current and next-generation console titles.

Sue Bohle

sue@bohle.com

Sue Bohle is a senior-level PR professional. The Bohle Company was Microsoft's first PR agency. Sue also launched Epson America, handling all marketing and corporate PR work for eight years, and steered Packard Bell's PR for nine years, from the time the company was $10 million in sales to over $5 billion. She has worked in the videogames industry for more than 20 years, serving Atari, Eidos, Electronic Arts, Activision, and many developers. More than a decade ago, Sue was elected to the College of Fellows, an honor bestowed on less than 1 percent of all PR professionals. She later served as chair of this organization, one of the few women to hold that honor. In 1999, Sue was named one of the "Top 50 Most Powerful Women in PR" by *PR Week* magazine. Sue currently serves on the National Board of the Public Relations Society of America (PRSA), the dominant professional organization in the public relations field, internationally.

Todd M. Fay

todd@audiogang.org

Todd M. Fay is the director of development for the Game Audio Network Guild (*www.audiogang.org*). Todd has worked with Creative Labs ATC, Blizzard Entertainment, THQ, Vivendi Universal, Black Ops Entertainment, G4 Media, and Tommy Tallarico Studios. His work has appeared in *Game Developer Magazine*,

Gamasutra.com, Music4Games.net, and on *G4: Television for Gamers*, the 24-hour network dedicated to games and the gaming lifestyle. While at G4 Media, Todd oversaw the development of the shows *Filter* and *Cheat!: Pringle's Gamer's Guide*, as well as the *Icon's Special: Splinter Cell*. While working with Creative Labs, Todd contributed to the development of EAX 3.0 as well as authoring the designer's guide for that technology. Todd produced his first book, *DirectX 9 Audio Exposed: Interactive Audio Development* for Wordware Publishing in 2003, which captured him a G.A.N.G. Award in 2004. Todd holds a bachelor of music degree from the University of Massachusetts Lowell's award-winning Sound Recording Technology Department.

Noah Falstein

nf@theinspiracy.com

Noah Falstein has been a professional game developer since 1980. He was one of the first 10 employees at LucasArts, The 3DO Company, and DreamWorks Interactive. Among his best-known designs or codesigns are *Sinistar*, *Strike Fleet*, *Indiana Jones and the Fate of Atlantis*, and *Chaos Island*. Since 1997, Noah has headed The Inspiracy as a freelance game designer and producer, working with startups and established companies in the games industry, corporate training, and games for health. He is the design columnist for *Game Developer* magazine, and his Web site is at *www.theinspiracy.com*.

Tom Forsyth

Tom.Forsyth@eelpi.gotdns.org

Tom Forsyth has been working on 3D rendering and games since the mid-1980s, and professionally since 1991. He has contributed many articles to the *Game Programming Gems* and *Shader X* series of books, given a number of talks at the Game Developers Conference, Microsoft Meltdown, and other game development conferences, and has a master of arts in computer science from Cambridge University. He has worked in the past at Microprose, Sega, 3Dlabs, and Muckyfoot, where he wrote rendering engines for three published games. He currently works at RAD Game Tools in Seattle writing the "Granny" suite of animation and rendering middleware.

Jussi Holopainen

jussi.holopainen@nokia.com

Jussi Holopainen is currently heading the Game Design Group at Nokia Research Center. The group's primary research area is on models and methods for game design, evaluation, and playtesting. Jussi has presented his work in several conferences and journals, including SIGGRAPH and the Game Developers Conference. He is also the coauthor of *Patterns in Game Design* published by Charles River Media, and a member of the executive board of Digital Games Research Association.

Aki Järvinen

aki.jarvinen@veikkaus.fi

Aki Järvinen has promoted ludology in both academic and industry contexts. He has worked for the Game Research Lab at University of Tampere, Finland, and as a designer of mobile games for Fathammer. Presently, he is employed by Veikkaus, the Finnish National Lottery Company, where he produces and designs electronic games of chance, and coordinates game research. Järvinen is finishing his Ph.D. about game analysis and design methods in 2005. As a case study of his thesis, he is designing *The Game Game*, a card game about game design that illustrates the thesis' ludological theory. *The Game Game* design diary can be followed at his Weblog *www.gameswithout-frontiers.net*.

David Johnson

undertone_dj@yahoo.com

David Johnson started his career as a colorist at CST technology in 1994 colorizing cartoons and film. After studying animation and special effects at Santa Monica College's Academy of Entertainment Technology, David became a 3D modeler. He worked as a professional modeler at 3Name3D and Viewpoint Digital. David has one film credit, several game credits, and has created models for several Web sites and TV commercials. David is currently employed by WildTangent as an art lead, where he is responsible for creating models, effects, levels characters, and leading other artists on various game titles.

Eric Lengyel

lengyel@terathon.com

Eric Lengyel has been dedicated to 3D graphics research for over 10 years and is the author of the bestselling book *Mathematics for 3D Game Programming and Computer Graphics*. He also the author of *The OpenGL Extensions Guide* and has written many articles for industry publications ranging from gamasutra.com to the *Game Programming Gems* series.

Peter Lewis

peterlewis@primitive-eye.com

Peter Lewis has been working in computer graphics since the mid-1980s, when he started programming motion control cameras for the film industry. He began working in the videogames industry in 1991 with Dynamix, Sierra Online, where he created Cinematics and 3D graphics for games. Since 2000, he has been a senior art lead at WildTangent, developing games with their Web-based real-time 3D game engine. Peter has been an instructor at the DigiPen Institute of Technology, where he taught computer animation to art and programming students and is currently an instructor for the Computer Animation certificate program through the University of Washington Extension.

Noel Llopis

llopis@convexhull.com

Noel Llopis is the lead technical architect at High Moon Studios where he spearheads the research and development of their internal technology for next-generation platforms. Before that, he architected and developed the technology behind the games *MechAssault 1* and *2* at Day 1 Studios. He is very enthusiastic about agile development, automated testing, and test-driven development. He is the author of the book *C++ for Game Programmers* and has contributed several articles to the *Game Programming Gems* series and *Game Developer Magazine*. He obtained a B.S. from the University of Massachusetts Amherst and an M.S. from the University of North Carolina at Chapel Hill.

Syrus Mesdaghi

syrusm@hotmail.com

Syrus is the lead AI engineer at Dynamic Animation Systems where he works on gaming and simulation technologies. Previously, he was the course director for the AI course that is part of Full Sail's Game Design & Development curriculum. He has been researching and developing AI techniques for many years. Besides his immeasurable passion for AI, he has put forth many efforts in improving, demonstrating, and promoting Java technology. He has developed and exhibited cutting-edge game technology demos for DAS, Full Sail, and Sun Microsystems at various conferences such as GDC, SIGGRAPH, QuakeCon, and I/ITSEC. The projects include genres such as FPS, RTS, fighting, and racing games. He has also presented at GDC03, GDC04, and GDC05. He is one of the authors of *Practical Java Game Programming* and has contributed to *AI Game Programming Wisdom 2*. Syrus is also on the AI Interface Standard Committee, which aims to develop standards for game developers. He holds a degree in computer science and hopes to pursue his Ph.D. as soon as days become longer than 24 hours.

Tito Pagan

www.titopagan.com

Art director Tito Pagan is a veteran game developer and writer with 13 years of industry experience and dozens of published game titles to his credit. His professional experiences range from texture artist, level designer, animation lead, character modeler, concept artist, motion capture director, and technical director. Presently at Screenlife LLC in Seattle, he leads the effort in creating rich and compelling 3D art content for their new technology that turns a DVD player into an interactive gaming device. Previously for WildTangent, Tito led the art direction of client branded Internet game titles as well as custom published Internet retail games. The aggressive development cycles at WildTangent taught Tito a great deal about streamlining game art production and outsourcing with an average of three games per year during his five years of service. With the startup Gas Powered Games, he led the animation effort charged with the task of making the character movement elements in the game *Dungeon Siege*. Tito is currently the proud owner of a motion capture studio called Paganimation.

Mark Peasley

mp@pixelman.com

Mark Peasley is a games industry veteran with over 15 years of experience producing artwork, scheduling, managing teams, and herding cats. During his tenure, he's been an artist, art director, producer, and project director. He has worked on over 25 PC, 3DO, and Xbox titles. He has spent the past two years working on the racing simulation *Forza Motorsport* at Microsoft Games Studio. His work can be seen at *www.pixelman.com*.

Steve Rabin

steve_rabin@hotmail.com

Steve Rabin has worked in the games industry for more than a decade and is currently a senior software engineer at Nintendo of America. He has written AI for three published games and was a significant contributor to the *Game Programming Gems* series, as well as the founder and chief editor of the *AI Game Programming Wisdom* series. He has spoken at the Game Developers Conference and is an instructor in the Game Development Certificate Program through the University of Washington Extension. Steve holds a B.S. in computer engineering from the University of Washington and is pursuing a master's degree in computer science.

Glen Rhodes

glen@glenrhodes.com

During the day, Glen Rhodes is the CTO of Crash!Media Corp. located in Toronto, Canada. At night, he is a Flash game developer and author, having written such books as *Macromedia Flash MX Game Development*, *Flash MX Games Most Wanted*, *The Actionscript Designer's Reference*, and at least six other titles. He is also a regular writer for several computer magazines, including *Web Developer Magazine* and *Practical Web Projects*. Glen has developed dozens of games since the early 1990s for many platforms, including Windows® PC, PlayStation®, Sega® Saturn, and these days, Macromedia Flash. He has developed many Flash games, including *Honda Racing* for *www.civicnation.ca*, *Domino Dementia* at Shockwave.com, *W.R.A.X.* at Superdudes.net, and *Catch the Train* for Nike.com. Glen's Web site is *www.glenrhodes.com* and he is the founder of and currently runs the Flash game development community Web site, *www.flashgamecoders.com*.

Graham Rhodes

WillieTheKing@gsrhodes.com

Graham Rhodes is a principal scientist at the Southeast Division of Applied Research Associates, Inc., in Raleigh, North Carolina. He has been creating software for interactive and real-time 3D graphics, gaming, and physical simulation for many years. Graham has been the lead software developer for a variety of game projects, including arcade-style games developed on Commodore VIC-20 and Atari 400 home computers as a teen; a series of sponsored educational minigames for the *World Book Multimedia Encyclopedia*; and more recently, first/third-person action games for commercial industrial safety training, built on a state-of-the-art 3D game engine. He is currently involved in developing software that provides physics-based solutions for military and homeland defense simulation and training. Graham previously contributed articles for *Game Programming Gems 2* and *Game Programming Gems 5*, and was the Physics section editor for *Game Programming Gems 4*. He is the moderator of the math and physics section of the gamedev.net game development Internet portal, has presented at the annual Game Developer's Conference (GDC), regularly attends GDC and the annual ACM/SIGGRAPH conference, and is a member of ACM/SIGGRAPH and the International Game Developer's Association (IGDA). Graham holds an M.S. in aerospace engineering from North Carolina State University.

Stephen Rubin, Esquire

rubinesq@aol.com

Steve Rubin represents video and mobile game developers and distributors, from startups to brand names, in such matters as intellectual property protection and enforcement, contracts and licenses, litigation, employment law, and business formation, acquisitions, and financings. Before establishing his own firm, Steve was in the Antitrust Division of the Department of Justice, professor of law at the University of Florida, and partner at a national firm where he headed the antitrust and intellectual property practices. He has served as special master and as a mediator in federal court patent litigation. He is the author of several books and a number of articles on antitrust and intellectual property, and is a presenter on law and business topics at the annual Game Developers Conference.

Kathy Schoback

kathy@igda.org

As the vice president of content strategy for the Phantom gaming service at Infinium Labs, Kathy Schoback oversees relationships with game publishers and developers worldwide, including title selection, prioritization, negotiations, and lifecycle management. She has spent previous lifetimes at Eidos and Sega, as well as at the Game Developers Conference as part of the show management team. In addition to serving on the board of the International Game Developers Association, Kathy is cochair of the IGDA Business Committee.

Jeff Selbig

crfdigital@mailcity.com

Jeff Selbig has worked in the games industry for five years and is currently a lead artist with WildTangent, Inc. Jeff has published over 10 games as lead artist, and 5 more as production artist while at WildTangent. Jeff holds a B.S. in geology, another B.S. in geological engineering, and finally an M.S. in geotechnical engineering, and gave it all up for some reason . . . oh yes, love of games and game art!

Tom Sloper

tomster@sloperama.com

Tom Sloper is a 25-year veteran of the games industry. As a game designer, he's been involved in the development of 60 games. As a producer, he has led external and internal teams in 135 projects. He's now a consultant and freelance game designer, doing business in Los Angeles as Sloperama Productions.

Tommy Tallarico

www.tallarico.com

Tommy Tallarico has been writing music for videogames for more than 15 years. In 1994, he founded Tommy Tallarico Studios, the multimedia industry's largest audio production house. Tommy was the first to use 3D audio in a game (*Q-Sound*) and was instrumental in bringing true digital interactive surround 5.1 (six-channel) to the gaming industry. Tommy has worked in the games industry as a games tester, product manager, producer, writer, designer, and heads of both music and video departments. He is the founder and president of G.A.N.G. (Game Audio Network Guild), which is a nonprofit organization educating and heightening the awareness of audio for the interactive world (*www.audiogang.org*). Tommy is an advisory board member for the Game Developers Conference, a proud member of the International Game Developers Association, and a nominating committee member for the Academy of Interactive Arts & Sciences. He has won over 20 industry awards for best videogame audio and has worked on more than 200 game titles; to date, they total sales of more than 75 million units and 2 billion dollars.

Bretton Wade

Bretton_Wade@acm.org

Bretton Wade is a 10-year veteran of the games and graphics industries currently working as a manager on the Xbox system software team and as an instructor in the highly praised University of Washington Extension Game Development course. Previous game development roles include title lead for an independent studio contracted by Blizzard Entertainment, development lead on Microsoft's *Flight Simulator*, and individual contributor roles in a variety of titles published by Microsoft Game Studios. Bretton worked on VR authoring tools at SGI, and was a research engineer for Advanced Rendering Technology and for Microsoft Research. He is a graduate of Virginia Tech, and holds a master's degree from the Cornell University Program of Computer Graphics.

Chuck Walters

chuck@zugig.com

Chuck Walters is a game development contract engineer and an instructor for the Multiplayer Game Architecture course at the University of Washington Extension.

Chuck is currently working on *Magic: The Gathering Online* at Wizards of the Coast and is developing cell phone games for Tooned In. During his seven years at Electronic Arts, he worked on multiple versions of *The Need for Speed*, *Motor City Online*, and provided support engineering for several EA Sports titles. He has also worked for the Microsoft Research Group, Manley & Associates, Tektronix, Attachmate, and has written for *Game Developer Magazine*.

CRITICAL GAME STUDIES

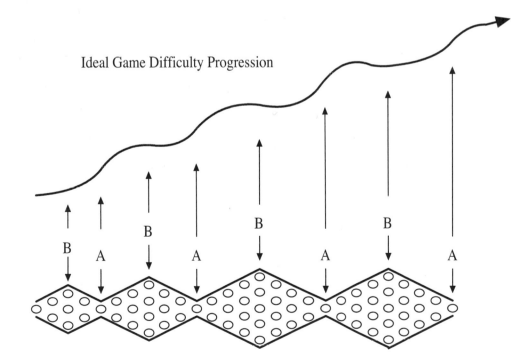

Ideal Game Difficulty Progression

1.1 A Brief History of Video Games

In This Chapter

- Overview
- The First Video Games
- Games for the Masses
- The Console Kings
- Home Computers
- The Designers
- The Phenomenons
- The Studios
- A Brief Overview of Genres
- Summary
- Exercises
- References

Overview

In the quest to learn about the video games industry and how state of the art games are made, it helps to start with some perspective. How did it all begin? Who were the people who drove the business and what were their inspirations? What significant games of yesteryear shaped the way games are made today?

While a student of filmmaking will study legendary directors like Orson Welles and groundbreaking films like *Citizen Kane*, there is equal reason for game developers to study the work and techniques of Shigeru Miyamoto and influential games like *Donkey Kong* and *The Legend of Zelda*. It is certainly true that games have not reached the status of films as works of art, but this is slowly changing. The skill and artistry involved in making games will soon rival motion pictures, with typical game production budgets skyrocketing upwards of 10 to 20 million dollars with no end in sight.

This chapter travels through time from the first recorded video game in 1958 all the way to the present. There are many ways to view and compare history, so we'll start with a timeline approach, and then break out specific platforms, studios, people, and genres to effectively understand specific lines of innovation.

The First Video Games

The first video games can be attributed to two key people: William Higinbotham and Steve Russell. While William Higinbotham would be credited as the first to design and implement a video game, Steve Russell would be the first to create a game that would inspire the multibillion-dollar video games industry.

William Higinbotham and Tennis for Two

Who invented the first video game? As far as historians can tell, it was the United States Department of Energy. Specifically, it was a man named William Higinbotham who was the head of the Instrumentation Division for Brookhaven National Laboratory. Before Brookhaven, William had previously worked on the Manhattan Project at Los Alamos and had witnessed the very first atomic blast. However, in the 1950s, people were wary of atomic power, and Brookhaven tried to present a friendly image by hosting an annual visitor's day. Hundreds of people would visit the laboratory every fall to see the various exhibits that were set up in their gymnasium. In 1958, William had a brainstorm. On previous visitor days, people weren't very interested in static exhibits, so for this year he came up with the idea for an interactive display. The display would be a video tennis game.

In a matter of three weeks, the very first video game was assembled. William, who drew up the original design in only a couple of hours, worked closely with Robert V. Dvorak, a technical specialist, who wired up the patchboard. Between the two of them, they spent about two days debugging and tuning the game, getting it done just in time for the first tour. *Tennis for Two* was the result and it was a big hit with the visitors.

Running on an analog computer and hooked up to an oscilloscope, the first video game looked sharp and ran fast. Surprisingly, this game was not a top-down perspective like *Pong*, but rather a side view of a tennis court. Two players would smash a ball back and forth, with the ball realistically bouncing off the ground and net, apparently under the influence of gravity. While the game kept no score, clearly there was a winner and loser after each volley. Even without audio speakers of any kind, the game had its own distinct sound effects, even if they were somewhat unintentional. The relays that enabled the device to operate made loud clicking noises with every hit and bounce of the ball.

This game was truly an impressive first attempt, even by today's standards. Yet to William, the fact that he had invented something unique didn't occur to him. The analog computer that he used actually came with examples in the instruction book, showing how to simulate many things on an oscilloscope, such as missile/bullet trajectories as well as a bouncing ball. Therefore, when William made the leap allowing two people to volley a bouncing ball back and forth, he didn't consider it a major breakthrough.

Although several hundred people saw the Brookhaven exhibit in 1958 and 1959, it failed to inspire future video games. The exhibit simply didn't reach the right people to make an impact, and thus is recorded in history as an isolated incident. It was as if the airplane was invented, but nobody recognized the significance or possessed the interest to push the idea further. After the autumn of 1959, *Tennis for Two* was dismantled and replaced with newer exhibits the following year.

Steve Russell and *Spacewar*

In 1961, computers were scarce, but they could be found at the most prestigious schools, such as MIT. Steve Russell was a student at MIT, and over the course of six months and roughly 200 hours he created a two-player video game called *Spacewar* on a DEC PDP-1 computer. The goal of the game was for each player to maneuver his spaceship while trying to shoot the other player's spaceship with torpedoes. Using four separate switches, each player could rotate clockwise and counterclockwise, thrust, or fire a torpedo.

Spacewar was created in 1961, but by the spring of 1962, the game had been expanded. Pete Sampson added an accurate starfield in the background by integrating an existing program called *Expensive Planetarium*. Next, Dan Edwards optimized the game to allow gravitational computations to be performed. Thus, a flickering sun was added to the center of the display that would influence the spaceships and destroy any that flew too close. Finally, J. Martin Graetz added the concept of hyperspace: the ability for a panicked player to warp his spaceship from its current location to a new randomly generated location. With these additions, interesting tactics began to develop, such as slingshotting oneself around the sun to quickly overtake a slow moving opponent. Within MIT, the game was a huge success and created quite a sensation at MIT's annual Science Open House.

Steve Russell never made any money off *Spacewar*, but he did briefly consider the possibility. Unfortunately, the cost of a PDP-1 computer in the early 1960s was about $120,000, and the feasibility of commercially recouping that cost was out of the question. *Spacewar* become a public domain program and quickly spread to other colleges over ARPAnet, an early version of the Internet. In addition, DEC ended up using *Spacewar* as a diagnostics program that shipped with new PDP machines, therefore distributing the game to its customers for free. A re-creation of *Spacewar* in Java can be played at *http://lcs.www.media.mit.edu/groups/el/projects/spacewar/*.

Games for the Masses

While *Tennis for Two* and *Spacewar* were amazing first games, they only reached a select group of people. During the early 1970s, two key people, Ralph Baer and Nolan Bushnell, would bring video games into the home and the arcades for the masses to enjoy. Thus, these two visionaries gave birth to the video games industry as we know it today.

The Advent of Home Video Games:
Ralph Baer and the Magnavox Odyssey

The next significant chapter in video games centers on Ralph Baer. Ralph's background was in TV design, but in the early 1960s he was a division manager at Sanders Associates, a military defense contractor based in New Hampshire. While on a business trip to New York in the summer of 1966, he came up with the idea of making games for a home TV. Since Ralph had more than 500 people under him, along with a payroll of almost $8 million, he was able to allow a couple of engineers, Bob Tremblay and Bob Solomon, to work on his ideas without anyone noticing.

When Ralph finally presented his project to the executive board at Sanders, his new invention garnered a cold reception. Most on the board thought Ralph was wasting the company's money and wanted to kill the project. Despite this poor showing, Ralph's boss, Bill Rusch, was impressed, primarily by the rifle game. Rusch was quite adept at shooting the target spot on the television from the hip with the plastic rifle. With a champion in his corner, the project remained alive.

In 1967 and 1968, better games started to take shape with the help of Bill Rusch. Soon, the small group had a respectable ping-pong game working. With a little refinement—removing the net and adding a blue "ice" color for the background—it became known as a hockey game. The game featured three controls: an up/down control for protecting the goal, a left/right control for moving close to the centerline, and an "English control" to put a spin on the puck.

Since Sanders wasn't in the TV or toy business, the next step was to sell the home video game system to a large manufacturer. After several failed attempts with General Electric, Zenith, and Sylvania, the television company Magnavox finally signed contracts with Sanders in late 1971. By 1972, Magnavox dealerships showed the new device, marketed as the Magnavox Odyssey. Unfortunately, the machine was badly overpriced at $100 and went largely unnoticed by the public due to limited marketing.

Breaking into the Amusement Business:
Nolan Bushnell and Atari

William Higinbotham was a scientist, Steve Russell was a programming prodigy, and Ralph Baer was a determined inventor. However, for the video games industry to really take off, it needed a salesperson and entrepreneur. Enter Nolan Bushnell. As an engineering major at the University of Utah from 1962 to 1968, Nolan was lucky enough to be at one of the very few colleges experimenting with computer graphics. He learned to program in FORTRAN and became an avid player of Steve Russell's *Spacewar*. Being a charismatic man, he convinced several senior students to help him create video games of their own. He ended up creating seven computer games with the help of his friends.

While the university and *Spacewar* were huge influences, an equal influence was Nolan's experience during those same years working at an amusement park north of Salt Lake City. Starting out on the midway selling balls to knock over milk bottles, Nolan became an expert at convincing people to part with their quarters. Later, he would work at the park's pinball and electromechanical game arcade, learning how the devices worked and how the business operated. These experiences would later prove invaluable. Nolan was an engineer who loved video games, understood the amusement business, and had the charisma to sell his passion. All he needed was a product.

With *Spacewar* on his mind, in 1969 Nolan worked to re-create a *Spacewar*-inspired game as a coin-operated device. Since cheap computers lacked the computational power to make the game work, he resorted to building a custom device that would only play his single game. Once the prototype was completed after a few months, he found a partner to manufacture it: Nutting Associates. Nutting was already in the amusement business with a successful trivia game called *Computer Quiz*, but the company saw promise in the new action space game, *Computer Space*. Nutting licensed the game from Nolan and hired him as their chief engineer.

Soon there were 1,500 *Computer Space* machines manufactured in wildly curvy futuristic cabinets—but the public reaction to the game was poor. Although Nolan personally demonstrated the game at the 1971 Music Operators Association show in Chicago, few arcade operators bought the machines. In the end, the game was too complex and intimidating for early audiences. Thinking that he could do a better job of marketing, Nolan set out to start his own company to produce arcade games. That company would be Atari.

Bringing Games to the Masses

The Atari name is synonymous with video games. However, in 1972, it was a tiny startup with Nolan Bushnell as its visionary leader. While Nolan worked on plans to combine the physics of *Computer Space* with a racetrack concept, he hired an engineer named Al Alcorn. Al's first warm-up assignment was to make a game based on ping-pong with one ball and two paddles. After three months, a working prototype was finished. Al wasn't sure the end product would be successful as an arcade game, but Nolan was impressed and dubbed the game *Pong*. After two weeks of testing at a local tavern, it seemed clear that *Pong* would be a hit.

Soon after Atari started marketing *Pong*, Magnavox took Atari to court. Unfortunately for Atari, Ralph Baer kept impeccable records of his inventing process and had filed numerous patents during the late 1960s. Magnavox alleged that Atari had violated many of Ralph's patents and even more critically had copied Ralph's ping-pong concept. In depositions, witnesses had also alleged that Nolan Bushnell had been given a demonstration of the Magnavox Odyssey at a large trade show in May of 1972.

In the end, Atari settled with Magnavox in 1976 for a one-time license payment of $700,000. After that, Atari was free to produce video games without paying any more money to Magnavox—"a sweetheart deal" as Nolan would later put it. As part of the settlement, Magnavox agreed to aggressively go after other video game makers, demanding royalties on every video game produced. Nolan escaped from this predicament with Atari still intact and still on top.

Pong became the first well-known video game and helped launch the entire video games industry. Atari struggled to keep up with orders for *Pong*, while other companies imitated it and exploited Atari's success. Atari became the premier video game company; however, it was forced to innovate to keep competitors at bay. During the 1970s, this innovation led to Atari creating the first racing game, *Trak 10*, and the first maze chase game *Gotcha*.

The Console Kings

After the success of *Pong*, the next stage in the evolution of video games in the home was the cartridge-based console. Atari was an important player, but was soon joined by other companies with a mark to make of their own.

Atari and the 2600

In 1977, Atari entered the cartridge-based home console market with the Atari Video Computer System (later redubbed the Atari 2600). Despite their reputation for innovation, they were not the first company to release a cartridge-based home system, having been beaten to the punch by two short-lived consoles, the Fairchild VES and the RCA Studio II. While they weren't the first to market, after a rocky Christmas, they became the first giant success (selling well for the next 10 years) and the name of the system became nearly synonymous with video games. Initially released with nine games, it was an innovative system based on the idea of moving costly functionality out of the hardware and into the software. In addition to having brightly colored graphics, and selector switches that selected the games and changed difficulty settings, it also introduced the joystick to the home market.

Part of the reason for its success was the huge variety of games that could be made for it—an unintended consequence of having an architecture built around saving costs in the hardware. Third-party companies formed to take advantage of the open architecture and create games without Atari's blessing. The most famous of these is Activision, which was formed by four ex-employees of Atari. Atari initially tried to stop third-party companies from making games for its system, but later relented and charged royalties on the games instead. This is standard practice in the home console market these days, with massive sums of money in the form of royalties exchanging hands for games to be "licensed" by the console manufacturers.

Video Game Crash of 1983

In 1983, a great shakeup occurred in the video games industry that would have serious repercussions on the fledgling market. There were several factors leading to the crash: a poor economy, natural market cycles, and consumer perception that video games were just a fad. Two of the largest factors leading to the crash were the role of the Atari and the 2600, and the introduction of cheap home computers to the market.

In addition to a glut of poor third-party games released for the Atari 2600 at that time, two infamously bad high-profile first-party titles were released for the system that year. The home console version of *Pac-Man* was a disappointing rendition of its video arcade counterpart, featuring poor graphics and differing far too much from the beloved original. The game *E.T.*, a tie-in with the blockbuster Spielberg movie, was created in a frantically rushed five weeks by Atari programmer Howard Scott Warshaw. The game rights were purchased for $20 million, with the expectation that the game would be a big Christmas hit. Gameplay was poor, the programming was understandably buggy, and the game was another disappointment for Atari, who had produced more copies of the game than there were 2600s in homes at the time (leading to now-substantiated rumors of New Mexico landfills being filled with millions of cartridges). These two games, given other factors, did irreparable damage to Atari's reputation. Moreover, while Atari alone had created more game cartridges than could be absorbed by the market, the oversupply of third-party game cartridges for the 2600 exacerbated the issue.

Another factor was the influx of inexpensive home computers into the market—particularly the Commodore Vic-20, Commodore 64, and Atari 400. Where computers had long been expensive and the province of specialty stores, the early 1980s saw computers being sold from department stores, toy stores—everywhere that video game consoles were selling. The computers offered a compelling sales pitch, duplicating many of the popular games from the consoles, while also offering software such as word processing and accounting programs. In addition, companies like Commodore offered trade-in deals on used game machines, further encouraging people to abandon their consoles.

As a result of increased competition, the lack of a next-generation console being ready, the huge glut of poor first and third-party games, and a bad economy—the market crashed. The third-party companies, unable to sell their product, were also unable to pay their distributors and had to close doors. Atari, a bulwark against the panic that was setting in, eventually began to dump its product cheaply on the market and then collapsed as well. The consumers, seeing this, began to believe that it all was a fad, and lost confidence in the industry. Companies like Mattel, Magnavox, and Coleco, as well as a host of others, got out of the video game business. The slump lasted for years, until the introduction of the NES console from the Japanese company Nintendo.

Nintendo and Shigeru Miyamoto

Nintendo helped shape the video games industry and pull it out of the slump of 1983, and continues to be a major force and innovator. Surprisingly, Nintendo was founded over 100 years ago, in 1889, and started out making hanafuda cards (Japanese playing cards). By the middle of the twentieth century, Nintendo had done well with Disney-licensed Western-style cards and later expanded into toys. During the late 1970s, toys began to move toward electronic video games, and Nintendo joined the fray with the introduction of the *Game and Watch* series.

The *Game and Watch* series, created by the visionary Gunpei Yokoi in 1980, was a line of over 50 handheld games that featured one or two LCD screens. As the name implies, each unit had one simple game along with the functionality of a digital watch. Gunpei invented the D-Pad (the plus-shaped directional pad found on most modern-day controllers), and would later go on to create the handheld Game Boy and the groundbreaking NES game *Metroid*.

Around the same time as the *Game and Watch* series, another visionary creator within Nintendo began designing the arcade game *Donkey Kong*. Nintendo had shipped 3,000 *Radarscope* games to the United States, but only 1,000 sold. Desperate to sell the remaining inventory, a young Shigeru Miyamoto was given the task of creating a new game that could be put within the *Radarscope* cabinets. Shigeru started out by creating an elaborate story about a gorilla that had stolen a carpenter's girlfriend. This carpenter, simply named Jumpman (but later known as Mario), would be forced to avoid barrels and flames, while jumping around on steel girders to reach his girlfriend. The converted *Radarscope* units quickly sold out in 1981 and orders continued to roll in. *Donkey Kong* would become one of the most influential arcade games ever, selling more than 65,000 units in the United States, and launching Mario as the enduring corporate mascot of Nintendo.

Shigeru Miyamoto's Mario character has now appeared in more than 80 games, selling a combined total of roughly 200 million games. The most notable are *Mario Brothers*, the *Super Mario Brothers* series, *Super Mario 64*, *Super Mario Kart*, and the *Mario Party* series. In 1983, *Mario Brothers* first introduced Mario's brother, Luigi. The 1985 game *Super Mario Brothers*, which first appeared in arcades and later on the Nintendo Entertainment System (NES), is recognized, next to Tetris, as the bestselling game of all time, with approximately 40 million copies sold in North America alone. In 1996, *Super Mario 64* on the *Nintendo 64* console would again innovate by bringing the platform genre into 3D. For the first time, players could explore Mario's world, running, jumping, swimming, flying, and tiptoeing wherever the player wished.

Although retailers were reluctant to stock home video games after the 1983 video game crash, in 1985 Nintendo was able to position the NES in a manner that made it more palatable to risk-averse retailers. The unit was bundled with a light gun and a robot named R.O.B. (Robotic Operating Buddy), and was labeled as an "entertainment system" rather than a "video game system." Nintendo also guaranteed to retailers that they would buy back all unsold systems, to further put them at ease. This unique positioning worked, and the NES snuck onto retailer shelves and soon became a remarkable success.

During the late 1980s, Nintendo's success was so extreme that at times they owned more than 90 percent of the video game market. As a result of being too successful, internally Nintendo was worried that they might lose their "Nintendo" trademark since it was becoming synonymous with "video game" and "video game machine." However, this fear would fade and by the late 1990s, it was more common to hear "PlayStation" used to obliquely refer to video game machines.

Today, Nintendo remains a fierce competitor in the video games industry. Given the Game Boy Advance, Nintendo GameCube, Nintendo DS, and consistent top 10 franchises like *Pokémon* and *Mario*, Nintendo easily owns the biggest piece of the video games business. Whether Nintendo can hold onto this dominance will depend on how much market share Sony can pull away by entering the handheld arena with the introduction of their PlayStation Portable (PSP). So far, Nintendo has beaten back almost a dozen handheld competitors over the last 15 years, with the latest being Nokia's N-Gage, but Sony has a good reputation and has beaten Nintendo before.

Sega

Japanese company Sega started life in 1952 as Service Games. Seeing a viable market supplying jukeboxes and other amusement devices to U.S. military bases, American creators Dick Stewart and Ray Lemaire soon grew the company beyond their modest ambitions. Changing their name to Sega (the first two letters of each word in their previous company name), they proceeded to take advantage of the recovering Japanese economy. In 1965, they merged with Dave Rosen's Rosen Enterprises, a company formed by another American in 1953 to import arcade machines from the United States into Japanese arcades. They became Sega Enterprises Ltd., and created many of the finest mechanical arcade games ever built.

In the 1970s, they began working on arcade video games, acquiring California company Gremlin, and soon expanding by creating games for the home console market. In the early 1980s, Sega briefly became part of Hollywood moviemaker Paramount, until the video game crash saw them parting ways. Rosen, his head of Japanese operations H. Nakayama, and Japanese investor Mr. Ohkawa bought the company back. Rosen became head of U.S. operations, with Nakayama the president and Ohkawa the chairperson back in Japan.

Sega had been developing a home console during this time, the Sega Master System. After seeing Nintendo's NES revive the video games market, Sega made a distribution deal with Tonka Toys and released the Master System nearly a year after the NES proved that there was still a viable market. Sega had trouble securing third-party software for its new system (Nintendo had locked many developers in with exclusive contracts), and mostly ported its arcade properties to the system.

While the Master System was not a great success, it allowed Sega time to create a 16-bit console to fuel the next generation. By Christmas 1990, Sega had released the Genesis (inspired by a sense of rebirth and the Genesis Project from *Star Trek II: The Wrath of Khan*). Its main competition was the aging NES and NEC's PC Engine (released in the United States as the TurboGrafx-16). Sega won the Christmas battle with its combination of well-known arcade titles and sports games. Ultimately, Sega gained some important support with a third-party deal with Electronic Arts, and the 16-bit console race was on between Sega, Nintendo, and NEC, with all three parties remaining viable throughout.

In 1994 in Japan, Sega released its next system, the Saturn. While the system did well in Japan on release, the May 1995 U.S. release was more problematic. Consumers had become unhappy with Sega because of the release or failed release of add ons for the Genesis. The Saturn was more expensive than Sony's PlayStation by $100, and because of a rushed introduction had initial supply problems. All of this ultimately contributed to the system's demise by 1998, despite some innovative games such as Yuji Naka's *Nights* and add-ons such as a modem.

The year 1999 saw the release of Sega's last home console to date, the Sega Dreamcast. An innovative console in many ways, it included a built-in 56k modem, 128-bit graphics, and support for graphical memory cards that could display game objects or mini games on the controller. Despite the innovative nature of the system, it was unable to gain a strong foothold. The PlayStation and N64 were still strong in the marketplace, and when Sony announced the specifications of its next-generation system the PlayStation 2, Nintendo revealed the codename of "Dolphin" for its next project, and Microsoft made clear its intentions to join the console market, the Dreamcast fell by the wayside, ultimately being discontinued before its product life-cycle was over. Sega has since shifted business focus, producing quality software for the other consoles.

While Sega employed many talented people, of special note was Yu Suzuki who drove many of Sega's best arcade games. He was responsible for *Hang-On*, *Space Harrier*, *Out Run*, and *Afterburner*, which were all pseudo-3D arcade games. Then in 1992, he began producing the *Virtua* series of games that relied on real 3D hardware. The most notable was *Virtua Fighter*, the first real-time 3D fighting game. The Smithsonian Institute recognized the *Virtua Fighter* series for its contribution to arts and entertainment, and *Virtua Fighter* has become part of the Smithsonian Institution's Permanent Research Collection (the first Japanese game to receive that honor). Later in 2001, Yu Suzuki finished the console game *Shenmue*, which took five years to develop and roughly $50 million, making it one of the most expensive video games ever created. In development, the game was referred to as *Virtua Fighter RPG*, which characterized the game quite nicely with its mix of *Virtua Fighter*-like battles and RPG elements.

Sony's PlayStation

In 1991, consumer electronics giant Sony contracted with Nintendo to design a CD-ROM game system, but the project was prematurely abandoned. As a result of the knowledge gained, Sony took their newly honed expertise and decided to pursue their own video game console. In December 1994, Sony released the PlayStation in Japan, and in September 1995 released it in both the United States and Europe. Lacking good first-party games, Sony relied on third-party publishers to provide the lion's share of games. While not a huge success at first, the PlayStation increased in popularity and slowly became the dominant home console of its time. This was largely due to exclusive games such as the *Final Fantasy* series, but was also influenced by the cheaper CD game format, which resulted in faster manufacturing times and less money tied up in inventory—both critical factors in getting third-party support.

The year 2000 saw the release of the Sony PlayStation 2 in Japan and the United States (a year before Nintendo's GameCube and Microsoft's Xbox were released).

Incorporating a DVD player, strong third-party support, and maintaining backward compatibility with the PlayStation, the PlayStation 2 dominated the home console market of the early 2000s. Sony hopes to extend that dominance into the handheld market in 2005 with the release of the disc-based PlayStation Portable (PSP), a device that has comparable 3D power to the PlayStation 2, as well as being an MP3 and movie player. Sony's next step after that is the release of the PlayStation 3, in a bid to maintain their hold on the home console market.

Microsoft and the Xbox

Founded in 1975 by Bill Gates and Paul Allen, Microsoft's modest beginnings creating and selling BASIC interpreters have lead to them becoming the largest software development company in the world. The Windows operating system is nearly ubiquitous in the world of personal and business computers. Before 2001, Microsoft was somewhat less known for their games, although they have two strong franchises in *Age of Empires* and *Microsoft Flight Simulator*.

In 1999, they decided to enter the home console market, going head to head against Sony and Nintendo. Released on November 15, 2001, the Xbox has become a very popular system with a strong software lineup topped by the first-person shooters *Halo* and *Halo 2*. Based on the PC architecture, the Xbox is the most powerful of like-generation consoles, and the most expensive to produce (with Microsoft taking a substantial loss on each console sold). Perhaps the Xbox's strongest feature is Xbox Live, a subscription-based online service connecting Xbox users nationwide. Microsoft has sunk billions of dollars into the Xbox and Xbox Live, and is not expecting to make a profit on it for years to come, instead sacrificing money in a long-term bid to gain a foothold in living rooms worldwide.

Home Computers

Simultaneous to the advent of the home consoles is the introduction of inexpensive home computers into the marketplace. Where before, computers had been the purview of universities and businesses, the introduction of the home computer had serious implications for the budding electronic games business.

Apple Computer

Formed on April Fools Day, 1976, Apple Computer began life as a partnership between two California whiz kids and Hewlett-Packard employees, Steve Wozniak and Steve Jobs. "Woz," as he has become known, was a homebrew computer genius. Jobs was a fellow electronics enthusiast and former Atari employee with an abundance of confidence and a strong vision. Woz showed his latest creation at the Homebrew Computing Club, dubbed the Apple I, and Jobs convinced him to start a company together. Seeing some success with the Apple I in local shops, Jobs made a gutsy move and went to Atari's Nolan Bushnell to ask for advice. Bushnell's advice eventually led

Jobs to Mike Markkula, a former Intel employee who had retired as a millionaire. Markkula invested his money in the young dreamers and the company was born.

Their next computer, the Apple II, was released in 1977 and started a revolution. Featuring an integrated keyboard and TV or monitor support, the Apple II was the first computer to gain a real foothold in the home market and found huge support with software publishers. With its open design and hardware slots, the Apple II also allowed the use of a plethora of third-party devices that could improve its capabilities. Various models of the Apple II came out during its lifetime, each improving on its predecessor—the most famous being the Apple IIe. The Apple IIc Plus was the last new computer in the Apple II series, and was produced in 1988. A popular staple in school classrooms, however, the Apple IIgs was produced and sold until 1993. Many classic games were created or ported to the Apple II, including *The Bard's Tale*, *Castle Wolfenstein*, *Choplifter*, the Infocom games, *Karateka*, *Prince of Persia*, *Swashbuckler*, the *Ultima* series, and *Wizardry*. All told, somewhere in the neighborhood of 366 games were produced for the Apple II series.

Commodore

Founded in 1954 by Auschwitz survivor Jack Tramiel, Commodore Business Machines started life as a typewriter manufacturer. Switching from typewriters to adding machines and then calculators before settling on computers in 1977, the company's motto became "Computer for the masses, not the classes." In 1977, they released the Commodore PET, a simple computer with a monochrome monitor, keyboard, tape drive, and metal case. The PET was not a huge success (finding its best market in classrooms because of its durable metal construction). Their next computer would change all that.

The Commodore Vic-20 debuted in 1981 with an ad campaign starring William Shatner that posed the question, "Why buy just a video game?" Although the computer was fairly low-powered for the time, its $299 price point, and placement in department stores and toy stores helped it become the first computer to sell more than 1 million units. Eventually, the Vic-20 would sell 2.5 million units before being discontinued.

The follow-up to the Vic-20 was a significant improvement, with its 64K of memory and a customized sound chip. Selling for $595, the Commodore 64 was released in 1982 in an effort to compete more directly with the Apple II. A three-way battle erupted between Texas Instruments, Atari, and Commodore. Tramiel reduced the price of the C64 to compete with the lowered prices of the TI-99/4a. The plan worked and the Commodore 64 became the best-selling computer in history, moving 22 million units in 1983 alone. The battle did serious damage to the competition, with Texas Instruments dropping out entirely and Atari being seriously hurt. The price war also had consequences at Commodore, though, and Tramiel left the company in 1984.

Commodore tried to pick up the pieces by buying a design for a new computer from a group of ex-Atari designers. In 1985, they released this design as the Amiga. The Amiga was an innovative machine that ultimately had trouble finding its niche in a market dominated by Apple's Macintosh and cheap PC clones. In 1992, the last Amigas, the A4000 and A1200, were released. The third-generation Amigas were powerful computers, offering a compelling alternative to PCs, but were more expensive—dooming them to failure.

IBM

In August 1981, the venerable computer manufacturer IBM introduced the IBM PC (short for "personal computer"). The PC represented a departure for IBM, which had failed to bring an affordable computer to market once before with the IBM 5100. This time around, IBM committed a small team of engineers headed by William Lowe to the project, and gave them free reign for their design. The team came up with the IBM 5150 within a year, deciding to use parts bought from OEMs (Original Equipment Manufacturers) instead of IBM-designed components. Another important aspect of the PC, one that would have important ramifications for IBM, was the use of an open architecture—allowing other companies to create compatible machines or "clones." IBM's goal with the PC was to license their BIOS and keep innovating to dominate the competition.

The PC was released with a price tag of $1,565.00, placing it outside the price range of most homes. However, it made important inroads with business users when the *VisiCalc* spreadsheet program was ported to it. More PC models followed, offering expanded capability (such as internal hard drives). Eventually, the PC and its compatibles would become a significant player in the home market, with most games being ported to it or developed for it.

IBM's plan to license their BIOS and keep an open architecture ultimately backfired when the BIOS was reverse-engineered by several companies that then came to market with compatible clones that were cheaper. Even then, IBM did great business because consumers felt they could trust them. This trust started to erode when IBM released computers that did not maintain 100 percent compatibility with their own specification. Largely, consumers wanted a computer that could run programs branded as IBM PC software right out of the box. When they began to feel that other manufacturers could provide them that security cheaper, IBM's more expensive computers fell by the wayside.

Today, the term *PC* has become a generic term for personal computers, and IBM has completely removed itself as a player in the home market. The modern PC architecture is still very similar to that originally created by William Lowe's team, although more powerful by leaps and bounds. The IBM-Compatible PC (running some variant of Windows or Linux) largely dominates the personal computer market, with only Apple providing a significant alternative.

The Designers

In addition to the companies that create the hardware for games to run on, someone must create the games themselves—enter the designers.

Maxis and Will Wright

Will Wright has created one of the most enduring software legacies around. In 1984, Wright created the successful game *Raid on Bungeling Bay* for Brøderbund. His next project, inspired by the books *Urban Dynamics* and *System Dynamics* by Jay Forester, was a Commodore 64 game initially called "City Builder" or "Micropolis." Eventually, teaming with fledgling company Maxis (created by Jeff Braun, Ed Kilham with a desire to develop video games that adults would enjoy), the game would be renamed *SimCity*.

In February 1989, it was released for the Apple® Macintosh® and Commodore™ Amiga. An article in *Newsweek* and good press all around helped the innovative city simulation game become a success. People loved the game, in which you managed many aspects of a city's development. The "Sim" appellation, suggested by Maxis writer Michael Bremer, helped defined a brand.

Wright followed *SimCity* with a somewhat less successful game called *SimEarth* in which you guided the ecosystem, geology, and climate of Earth. The follow-up to that was a somewhat more playful game called *SimAnt*, an ant colony simulation. Wright's next project was *SimCopter*, an ambitious simulation that allowed you to fly a helicopter through *SimCity 2000* cities. Maxis published other *Sim* titles (including *SimTower*, *SimFarm*, and *SimLife*), but Wright's next project wouldn't debut for a few years. When it did, it would cement the *Sim* name in popular culture.

While working on *SimAnt* and *SimCopter*, Wright was inspired by books once more—*Understanding Comics* by Scott McCloud provided the idea for a level of abstraction in representation that would allow players to put more of themselves into a game; the architecture book *A Pattern Language*, by Chris Alexander, led to the idea of making placement of household elements fun. The game, codenamed *Project X* for much of its early life, was eventually called *The Sims*.

The Sims, a "God game" of sorts, is a simulation of the lives of virtual people. You guide them in many of the daily elements of their lives—cooking, eating, hygiene, jobs, learning, sleeping, and so forth—while outfitting their house based on the money they earn. The game has become a phenomenon—selling more than 6 million copies since its January 2000 debut. It has an unprecedented number of expansion packs, as well as an outright sequel, and has become one of those rare video games played by people who traditionally do not purchase or play video games.

MicroProse and Sid Meier

MicroProse began life as something of a dare. On a company trip to Las Vegas, Sid Meier and J. W. "Wild Bill" Stealey met over a game of *Red Baron*, an arcade dogfight machine. Wild Bill had been beating all comers until Sid Meier plugged in his quarter. Meier impressed Stealey by trouncing the game—one that Meier had never played before. Meier followed up his impressive performance with a boast, telling Stealey that he could program a better game in just one week. Stealey countered by saying that if Meier could program it, he could sell it.

It took Meier two months, but he created a game called *Hellcat Ace*. Stealey followed up on his end of the bargain and successfully sold 50 copies right away, so they joined forces and created a company. They named it MicroProse as a nod to the microprofessionals working on the games and the idea that they would be creating works of art. More games were created and the money started coming in. They quit their jobs at the Baltimore defense contractor that had sent them on that fateful Vegas trip, and started working on MicroProse projects full time.

Solo Flight (1984) was their first national success, and its combination of fun and realistic gameplay helped to define what the company was shooting for. More strategic simulations followed, games putting the player in planes, submarines, or in control of armies in hex-based board game conversions as in 1985's *Decision in the Desert*.

Then, in 1987, came the first game to bear Sid's name right on the cover—*Sid Meier's Pirates!* A clever mix of role-playing, action, and swash-buckling adventure, *Pirates!* is largely regarded as one of the best games of all time (demand for a visit back to the sun-splashed Caribbean game world was so strong that Meier even remade it in 2004 with updated graphics and modifications to a few gameplay elements). More signature games would follow, the next being *Railroad Tycoon*—a "God game" where you controlled the nation's budding transportation system and economy during the golden age of railroads.

In 1991, Sid expanded on ideas from *Railroad Tycoon*, threw in a little *SimCity* and *Empire*, and came up with *Sid Meier's Civilization*. The game was an instant classic, with gameplay that inspired many a late-night session with its addictive "one more turn" style. In the game, the player guided a budding civilization through all the technologies of the ages—from bronze working and pottery to computers and nuclear power. The ultimate goal of the game was adaptable to the style of the player, with peaceful strategies and gameplay being just as viable as ones that were more warlike. The game has sponsored numerous sequels; some with Meier's guiding hand, and others that just carried the name and spirit. In 2001, Sid's new company Firaxis obtained the rights to the series and created *Civilization III*, expanding and updating the classic game with new elements while retaining the same addictive play.

MicroProse had many hits with other talented game designers in their stable. Particularly of note are the games *Master of Orion*, a space exploration game created by Steve Barcia's SimTex group, and 1994's turn-based UFO-inspired squad combat game *X-Com* by Mythos Gaming.

Spectrum Holobyte acquired MicroProse in 1993, with Sid leaving to form Firaxis games some time after. In 1998, Hasbro Interactive purchased MicroProse, closing both California and North Carolina studios in 1999. In 2001, French company Infogrames (which later purchased Atari and renamed itself to the classic brand) acquired Hasbro Interactive and discontinued the MicroProse label, eventually closing the Maryland offices where MicroProse started.

Sierra and Ken and Roberta Williams

One of the most enduring computer game companies of all time, Sierra literally got its start on a kitchen table. Programmer Ken Williams had created a company named On-Line systems in 1979, doing odd programming jobs for the financial sector. His wife, Roberta, with newborn in tow and too much time on her hands, played a computer game called *Colossal Cave* on a mainframe through a connection from Ken's TRS-80. Inspired by this simple line-text adventure, she started planning a computer adventure game of her own, mapping it out with pieces of paper strewn across their kitchen table. One romantic dinner later, Roberta convinced Ken to help her with the project and a legacy was born.

Mystery House, the world's first graphical adventure game, was their first product. Released in 1980—and distributed by hand to stores in Ziploc® bags—*Mystery House* eventually sold 80,000 copies. Their output was prolific in those first few years; making a variety of re-creations of arcade games, graphical adventures, and licensed titles. Their real claims to fame, though, were the graphical adventure titles that Roberta scripted, such as *The Princess and The Warrior*. Ken was also an innovator, doing things with graphics that hadn't been done before, drawing complex scenes programmatically, rather than relying on premade graphics stored on the disk (a technique that saved tremendous amounts of space).

In 1982, they changed their name to Sierra On-Line and moved their offices to Oakhurst, California. IBM approached them soon after to create a computer game that would show off its new computer, the PCjr. Roberta made an important leap at this point. With the advanced capabilities of the PCjr, she saw a way to place the player on the computer screen, rendered in third-person. Given the change in focus, her story writing took off, and the IBM-commissioned game became the now-classic *King's Quest*.

Released in 1984, *King's Quest* was a huge success, eventually spawning seven sequels. Other *Quest* titles by other designers followed, including *Space Quest* and *Police Quest*. Each started a successful franchise and Sierra became hugely profitable. In addition to the *Quest* lineup, Sierra had success with several other franchises as well, including the adult-aimed comedy series *Leisure Suit Larry*, supernatural detective *Gabriel Knight's* adventures, *Phantasmagoria* (a mature horror series), the futuristic *EarthSiege*, and the blockbuster first-person shooter *Half-Life*.

In 1994, they moved their headquarters to Bellevue, Washington in an effort to place themselves in more of a technological hub. In the 1990s, Sierra started acquiring other studios to add to its growing stable of talent (Impressions and Dynamix being the most notable). In 1996, they were acquired themselves by CUC, later merging with HFS to become Cendant Software. Cendant was, in turn, purchased by French publisher Havas Interactive, and then eventually became part of the Vivendi empire.

Today, Sierra Entertainment exists only as a brand of Vivendi Universal games. Ken left Sierra a year after the sale to CUC. Roberta's last production credits were in 1999, although she has not ruled out coming back to computer games. The Bellevue offices were closed in 2004.

Origin Systems and Richard Garriott

Inspired by *Dungeons & Dragons*, J. R. R. Tolkien's *The Lord of the Rings*, and his love of computers, Richard Garriott built an RPG empire. Garriott created his first commercial game, *Akalabeth*, as a teenager working one summer at a Computerland store. Based on a game he had created at school, *Akalabeth* was a first-person dungeon crawl where players received quests from a character named "Lord British" to kill progressively harder monsters. The Ziploc-bagged adventure caught the attention of California Pacific Computer, who struck a deal with Garriot that gave him $5 per game sold. Garriott made $150,000 and then started work on a game called *Ultimatum*.

Ultima I, as it was later called, was published in 1981, and put the player on a quest to bring down the evil wizard Mondain. *Ultima I* was later republished by Sierra On-Line when California Pacific went out of business. In 1982, Sierra published *Ultima II*, a grand time-traveling adventure sending the player on a quest to thwart Mondain's lover, Minax. A signature element of the *Ultima* series was a cloth map contained in each box (one of the reasons Garriott went with Sierra as a publisher was their willingness to include the map). By the time *Ultima III* came out, though, Garriott had become disenchanted with the deal with Sierra and created his own company, Origin Systems.

While the early *Ultima*s were good games, with *Ultima IV*, Garriott (or "Lord British" as he was known in and out of his games) raised the bar. Garriott has acknowledged that the first three games were really a process of him learning to program, and that with *Ultima IV* he concentrated on the story for the first time. It contained an element of morality and ethics to it, an element that Lord British worried would ruin the game's chances for success, but *Ultima IV* went to the top of the software charts. In the game, the player's goal was to become a prophet, the paragon of the Eight Virtues of the Avatar. This was a departure from most previous RPGs, in which the goal was to dispose of some evildoer. The next two *Ultima*s continued the story started in *Ultima IV*.

EA acquired Origin Systems in 1992, around the time that production was started on *Ultima VII*. In 1997, *Ultima Online*, one of the first massively multiplayer online role-playing games (MMPORPGs), was released. The game was enough of a success that EA decided in 1999 that Origin would become an online-only company. Garriott left soon after. While many expansion packs to *Ultima Online* were released, that last single-player *Ultima*—*Ultima IX: Ascension*—was released in 1999. *Ultima IX: Ascension* was released before it was finished, and was notorious for its bugs and incomplete storyline. Origin Systems was disbanded in 2004 by EA, although they still retain rights to the brand.

Origin's Other Blockbuster: *Wing Commander*

Ultima was not the only famous series to come out of Origin Studios. In 1990, Chris Roberts created *Wing Commander*. The games featured an epic storyline based on intergalactic war. The story was told through a series of starfighter missions and cut-scenes.

Later installments of the game featured full-motion video cut-scenes starring Holly-wood actors such as Mark Hamill and Malcolm McDowell. In 1996, Chris Roberts left Origin to form his own studio, Digital Anvil (although EA has continued to produce *Wing Commander* games). He revisited the *Wing Commander* universe in 1999 when he directed a live-action movie version set during the timeline of the first game.

The Phenomenons

While there are many success stories in the history of video games, there are a few breakouts that reach above and beyond the status of mere success. These phenomenons speak to the incredible innovation and spirit of discovery that has defined the industry.

Space Invaders

In 1978, the Japanese company Taito, with distribution partner Midway, introduced the U.S. market to the arcade machine *Space Invaders*. While not the first Japanese import, *Space Invaders* was the first big Japanese success. The game, created by Taito's Toshihiro Nishikado, featured a never-ending stream of airborne alien invaders attacking the player's lone base on the ground. The player used three destructible shields for cover while firing at the rows of aliens as they descended. All levels were essentially the same, but the aliens got progressively faster as the game went on, thus ensuring that the player would ultimately never win. The music was simple, but effective, keeping pace with the aliens' attack and increasing the tension. The graphics were simple—black and white with a color overlay on top of the video screen.

Despite its seemingly simple premise, presentation, and gameplay, the game was a huge success, creating a shortage of 100-yen coins in Japan when it was released. The game later went on to be successfully reproduced on a variety of home consoles, including the Atari 2600. Perhaps its most notable contribution to the world of video games is its introduction of the High Score, a saved list of the highest scores achieved during gameplay that was then displayed while the game was in attraction mode.

Pac-Man

Inspired by the Japanese folk hero Paku (who was known for his large appetite) and a pizza with one slice missing, Namco's Toru Iwatani created the most popular arcade game of all time. Originally dubbed "Puckman," the game was Iwatani's attempt to create a completely nonviolent arcade game, one that would appeal to both men and women.

In the game, players use a simple four-position joystick to guide the yellow protagonist around the mazelike playing field. Pac-Man's mission is to eat all the little white dots, while trying to avoid four ghosts (named Inky, Blinky, Pinky, and Clyde) that chase him around the screen. On each screen are four larger dots that Pac-Man can eat to turn the tables—the ghosts become blue for a brief period, during which Pac-Man can eat them. The game was a huge hit in Japan, and with a slight name change to prevent vandals from easily turning the hero's name into something improper, *Pac-Man* debuted on American shores in 1981.

The Bally/Midway-distributed *Pac-Man* was a huge success in arcades, generating some $100 million worth of sales during its lifetime. The *Pac-Man* craze was not limited to arcade coin-ops, however, as a fevered nation bought everything from *Pac-Man* cereal and t-shirts to albums featuring songs about the hungry fellow. To date, there have been 10 sequels to the game, with likely more to follow that feature the enduring yellow hero, as well as Ms. Pac-Man and the ghosts Inky, Blinky, Pinky, and Clyde.

The Tangled History of *Tetris*

In 1985, Russian programmer Alexey Pajitnov created the game *Tetris*, based on a puzzle game called *Pentominoes*. Pajitnov decided to take the concept onto the computer (specifically an Electronica 60 in the Computer Center at the Academy of Sciences in Moscow), making some important alterations to the concept in the process. Pajitnov first limited the blocks on his pieces to four instead of five, which reduced the number of shape permutations to seven. He then made the playing field two dimensional and vertical, allowing the pieces to drop into place. While writing the code that rotated pieces, Pajitnov was impressed with the speed he was getting and decided the game needed to be in real time. Lastly, Pajitnov solved the problem of what to do when lines were filled in by removing the finished lines completely, allowing play to continue and new plays to open up. Renaming it to *Tetris* (from the Greek word for four, "tetra"), he had Vadim Gerasimov port it to the PC. Gerasimov's port started spreading across Moscow, and then on to Budapest, Hungary. From there, things got more complicated.

Hungarian programmers had ported Pajitnov's game to the Apple II and Commodore 64. One of these ports caught the attention of Robert Stein of Andromeda, a British software company. Stein started working with Pajitnov to get the rights, but sold the PC rights to Mirrorsoft UK—and its U.S. affiliate Spectrum Holobyte (a subsidiary of Pergamon, headed by Robert Maxwell)—before the deal was inked. The deal with Pajitnov fell through and Stein contacted the Hungarian programmers, attempting to license it through them. Spectrum Holobyte's PC version was released and quickly became a hit.

Stein later went to Russia and eventually came back with home computer rights to *Tetris*—but no contract. Before Stein could work his other angle and secure rights from the Hungarian programmers, the *CBS Evening News* did a piece on *Tetris* that firmly established Pajitnov as the inventor of the program. Stein's negotiations with the Russians then started going through ELORG (Electronorgtechnica), the trade organization of the Soviet government. ELORG threatened to cancel any deals with Stein when they learned about his involvement with the Hungarian programmers. Eventually, they reached terms, with Stein getting the rights to do computer versions of *Tetris*, but specifically not arcade or handheld versions.

Things got further complicated, however, when Spectrum Holobyte sublicensed Japanese computer game rights to Bullet-Proof Software (under the leadership of

Henk Rogers), and its UK division Mirrorsoft licensed home console and arcade rights to Tengen (an Atari company). These were rights that they did not actually possess. In November 1988, Bullet-Proof software released *Tetris* for the Nintendo FamiCom in Japan.

Rogers contacted Stein at the request of Nintendo of America president Minoru Arakawa. The Game Boy was in development and Nintendo wanted to offer *Tetris* as a bundle with the new handheld. Months passed and Stein failed to get the rights for Rogers, so Rogers flew to Moscow to try to secure the rights directly. Stein flew to Moscow as well, having guessed that Rogers had lost faith in his ability or willingness to secure the handheld rights and was attempting to take matters into his own hands. Spectrum Holobyte approached Nintendo at the same time, wanting to develop *Tetris* for the Game Boy. Kevin Maxwell, Robert Maxwell's son, flew to Moscow to attempt to gain the rights so they could create their handheld version.

Maxwell, Rogers, and Stein converged on Moscow at the same time. Rogers met with ELORG before the others, and secured the handheld rights. In the process of meeting with ELORG, the Russians were surprised to realize that a console version had already been developed (*Tetris* for FamiCom). Stein had never discussed with ELORG that he had sold console rights he didn't possess to Atari. Rogers pushed on, thinking he might be able to secure all console rights with Nintendo's muscle behind him.

Stein met with ELORG after Rogers and signed a document with the Russians that slightly altered his contract—a brief passage defining a computer in such a way that consoles and arcade games were clearly not covered by his contract. ELORG then told Stein that he could not get the handheld rights, but could get the arcade rights— so he did just that.

Maxwell made his way to ELORG. Maxwell was shown the FamiCom cartridge and, not realizing that his company had licensed it, told ELORG that it must be a fake. He didn't get the handheld rights he came for, and was then offered the chance to bid on any Tetris rights remaining.

When all was said and done, Rogers had secured the handheld rights for Nintendo, and had opened a door so Nintendo could bid on the console rights; Stein had secured the arcade rights, and signed a contract that defined very specifically what a computer was; and Maxwell had asserted that no legal console version existed, and secured for his company the opportunity to bid against Nintendo for console rights.

Nintendo's bid was too high for Maxwell's company to match, and Nintendo secured the home console rights. A lawsuit ensued, with Tengen suing Nintendo, alleging that a version of *Tetris* would violate their copyright. Nintendo countersued Tengen. Tengen then released *Tetris* for the NES, despite the legal issues. Tengen's contention was that the FamiCom was a computer, and a *Tetris* version on the platform violated their rights. Nintendo's assertion was that the Russians had never planned to give out video game rights until Nintendo had bid on them.

Nintendo won the lawsuit after many years, but an initial injunction favored them strongly. Tengen was forced to pull its version of *Tetris* for the NES off the shelves. Nintendo released *Tetris* for the NES, and then as a bundle with the Game

Boy. Both versions sold phenomenally well, with the Game Boy pack-in version helping to sell Game Boys in the 10s of millions.

In 1996, Pajitnov partnered with Rogers to form The Tetris Company LLC, which maintains and controls *Tetris* rights worldwide, allowing Pajitnov to see money from his sensational game—nearly 17 years after its creation.

Capcom and *Resident Evil*

Founded in 1979, Japanese Capsule Command (Capcom for short) is one of the premiere Japanese video game developers and game publishers. Over the years, they have created many memorable games, appearing on virtually every video game platform and in arcades, and have created three series of special note. First is the *Street Fighter* series of fighting games, immortalized in arcades and feature film. Second is the immensely popular platformer series *Mega Man*. Finally, is the series that popularized a genre, *Resident Evil*.

Resident Evil (known as *Biohazard* in Japan) coined the term "survival horror" in describing the genre it has come to define. In *Resident Evil*, you are part of an elite commando team sent in to retrieve another team that was lost investigating a series of gruesome murders outside Raccoon City. The game throws all manner of puzzles, zombies, and other undead things at the player, with the player's goal being to stay alive and solve the mystery of what's happened. The game has spawned 15 variations, updates, and sequels since its release on the Sony PlayStation in 1996, as well as two Hollywood movies (2002's *Resident Evil* and 2004's *Resident Evil: Apocalypse*).

Square and *Final Fantasy*

In 1987, in a last ditch effort to stave off bankruptcy, Japanese software company Square Co., Ltd. released what they thought would be their last game. They were wrong, and happily so—their next game was *Final Fantasy*, a console role-playing game for the FamiCom. Created by Hironobu Sakaguchi, the game proved successful enough that Square sought a distribution deal with Nintendo for the North American market.

Fifteen games later, and 40 million copies sold so far, the *Final Fantasy* series is the king of the console RPG. Games from the *Final Fantasy* series have appeared on nearly every platform since the NES (despite a feud between Nintendo and Square that saw no *Final Fantasy* games on the N64). Although most games in the series are not sequels as such, the complex stories, graphic quality, and superb art direction clearly define games with the *Final Fantasy* name. The *Final Fantasy* series is so popular that a computer-animated motion picture was released in 2001, called *Final Fantasy: The Spirits Within*. In 2004, *Final Fantasy: Advent Children*—a computer animated movie like *The Spirits Within*—was produced as a sequel to the most popular game in the series, *Final Fantasy VII*.

Final Fantasy is not the only popular series from Square; the series *Dragon Quest* (known as *Dragon Warrior* in the United States) is incredibly popular in Japan, with each installment setting sales records over the previous ones. The *Kingdom Hearts* series, featuring a mix of Square and Disney characters, has also proven very popular.

Cyan and *Myst*

Working from their studios in Spokane, Washington, the brothers Robyn and Rand Miller created one of the most popular games of the 1990s. The Millers had made a couple of modestly successful games when Japanese company Sunsoft approached them to create a game for adults. Anticipating a CD-ROM add-on for the N64 (that was never released in the United States), Sunsoft was only interested in the console rights. The Miller's budgeted $400,000 and paid for the overages themselves. Starting work in 1991, the game *Myst* was created on Macintosh computers as a very large *HyperCard* stack, with each card being a 3D-rendered scene of atmospheric, ethereal beauty. The scenes were punctuated with short live-action video clips that helped move the story along. The user clicked through each screen, navigating the world and solving puzzles that lead to unraveling the mystery of the island.

Released in 1993 on the Macintosh, and then on the PC quickly thereafter, *Myst* became a critical darling and the kind of game that everyone had to own in the beginning of the CD-ROM age. The immense success of *Myst* led to the sequels *Riven*, *Myst III: Exile*, *Uru: Ages Beyond Myst*, and *Myst IV: Revelation* as well as remakes, three books, and a host of clones attempting to capture the essence of the groundbreaking adventure-puzzle game.

Pokémon

When avid insect hunter Satoshi Tajiri earned the nickname Dr. Bug from his friends as a boy, little did he know that he would create one of the most lucrative video games franchises ever. Satoshi would search the ponds and fields near his home in a suburb of Tokyo for any insects he could find, classifying them as he caught them. Sometimes he would trade them with friends and they would let them fight. As a teen, he went to technical school to become an electrician at his father's request, but haunted the local arcades in his spare time. In 1982, he formed a magazine called *Game Freak* with his friends. In 1991, Satoshi bought a Game Boy and, seeing a Link Cable, imagined insects crawling along them between the Game Boys. The idea for *Pokémon* was born. Striking a creation deal for initial funding from the studio Creatures, and then bringing his idea to Nintendo, Tajiri worked for the next six years to create his game.

Originally called *Pocket Monsters* (*Pokketo Monsuta* in Japanese), the name was shortened to *Pokémon* when it was discovered that there already existed a Pocket Monsters toy in the United States. *Pokémon Red* and *Green* were released in 1996 in Japan and localized as *Pokémon Red* and *Blue* for the North American release. In the game, the player sets about collecting the mythical monsters and having them battle each other. Each version (*Red* and *Blue*) features different subsets of the entire collection of *Pokémon* monsters. This aspect has added to the addictiveness of the games—indeed, the first motto for *Pokémon* was "Gotta catch 'em all!" Since its debut, each version of

Pokémon has broken the sales records set by the previous versions. The game has become hugely popular, and has branched out into several other forms of media, including comic books, cartoons, anime, movies, manga, and collectible card games.

The Rise and Fall of the Video Game Mascot

Shortly after the dawn of video game history came the mascots. Pac-Man and Frogger were popular, but the first real breakout character was Mario. Starring as "Jumpman" in the arcade game *Donkey Kong*, Mario soon starred in titles of his own. *Super Mario Bros.*, which came as a pack-in with the NES, rocketed Mario to the heights of popularity—the Italian plumber even became more well-known to kids of the era than Mickey Mouse.

Others mascots would follow, first up being Sega's Sonic the Hedgehog. Conceived as competition for Mario, Sonic became the flagship character for Sega. Soon after its release, *Sonic the Hedgehog* replaced *Altered Beast* as the Sega Genesis pack-in title. Sonic was the first of the anthropomorphic animal characters such as Crash Bandicoot, Spyro the dragon, and Blinx.

As Mario was to Nintendo, and Sonic was to Sega, Crash Bandicoot became the original mascot for the Sony PlayStation. Featured in a variety of games and humorous commercials, Crash was never quite as popular as his competing console hawkers were. In recent years, long since making the leap from the PlayStation (Vivendi Universal currently owns the rights to the character), Crash has been seen on Nintendo's systems and Microsoft's Xbox.

Another mascot of mythic proportions (no pun intended) is Lara Croft, the braided heroine of the *Tomb Raider* games. She has appeared in six *Tomb Raider* games covering the various platforms and PC. She is a strong female character that nevertheless comes under a lot of criticism for her overtly sexualized persona. Despite the criticism, she has become immensely popular, and has had two live-action movies (*Tomb Raider*, and *Tomb Raider: Cradle of Life*) that chronicle her adventures as well as books and comic books.

Other mascots have become popular to varying degrees over the years. Nintendo has the lion's share with Samus Aran, star of the *Metroid* series (and one of the few non-sexualized females in video games); Link, the yellow-haired hero of Hyrule in the *Zelda* series; Kirby, the pink ball-shaped creature who stars in his own cartoon now; Donkey Kong, the original arcade ape; and Pikachu, the electrifying yellow hero of the *Pokémon* games, movies, and cartoon series. Sony has had their own sets of heroes with *Jak and Daxter* (now in their third video game appearance); Solid Snake from *Metal Gear Solid*; *Ratchet and Clank* (also in their third game appearance); and Spyro the dragon. It is worth noting that many of Sony's once-exclusive mascots have since appeared on other systems. Microsoft has just a few mascots for its relatively recent system, including the Master Chief from *Halo* and *Halo 2* and Blinx the time sweeping cat.

Many consider the heyday of the mascots to be over. There are several reasons why mascots may not be as popular as they once were. One is the possible over-saturation of existing characters. At the apex of a character's popularity, there seems to be no upper limit to how much attention a mascot can garner and sustain, but when a character is not at its apex, this same attention level can appear to be far too much. In the 1980s, after the initial introduction of characters such as Sonic and Mario, everyone jumped on board the mascot bandwagon. Everything from soft drink to pizza chain mascots made it into video games, creating an influx of characters without much depth to them that the public didn't get behind (cheapening all mascots as a result).

Another possibility is the advancing age of the audience: the audience that first fell in love with Mario's adventures in 1985 has had roughly two decades to grow up and move on to other concerns. An audience not present for a character's defining games may not view the character in the same light as those present for the character's introduction (as in the case of *Tomb Raider* where Angelina Jolie's movie representation of Lara Croft may far overshadow the games that made the character popular in the mid-1990s).

Marketing can also be a factor in the popularity of the mascots. If a particular console is skewed toward an older audience and doesn't possess any strong mascots, it benefits them to characterize the mascots and other consoles using them as "kiddy." Calling a system "kiddy" is a disingenuous way of denigrating a particular system, as it has no technological basis in the ability of the console.

Perhaps the largest factor in the perceived decrease in popularity of the video game mascot is the increased realism and immersion level in video games. Most mascots have appeared as brightly colored third-person characters manipulated within the games, while the trend is toward games where the player is the main character in the game, seeing through the eyes of an on-screen persona (as in most first-person shooters) or treating the character as a sort of alter ego (*Grand Theft Auto*). As technology advances, the opportunities for immersion increase as the game playing field becomes far more realistic. The president of Nintendo, Satoru Iwata, underlined the problem at his E3 2003 speech when he pledged that Mario would never start shooting hookers. While on the one hand, this promise takes a stand in addressing the trend of increasing violence in games, it also points to the idea that the video game mascot might just be of a different era—an era now gone.

The Studios

In the games industry, hits, innovation, and great design do not necessarily mean that a company will experience long-term success. Indeed, the history of video games is littered with once-successful companies that no longer exist. It takes a particular combination of success and business savvy to last.

Activision and Infocom

Formed by four former Atari programmers and Jim Levy, a former music industry executive, Activision was the first third-party game developer. David Crane, Larry Kaplan, Bob Whitehead, and Alan Miller were among Atari's best and brightest, but they'd become disillusioned with practices at Atari. The new company created some of the best-known Atari 2600 games ever, including such hits as Bob Whitehead's *Chopper Command*, Carol Shaw's *River Raid*, and David Crane's *Pitfall!* (Activision prided itself on giving its designers credit, featuring them in much of its marketing—a practice that Atari had eschewed). A lawsuit from Atari resulted in Activision and all other third-party companies agreeing to pay royalties on each game sold, but Activision had become so successful that this hardly damaged their bottom line.

After Activision's initial success, they merged with popular text adventure creator Infocom. Infocom had created the beloved *Zork* franchise, as well as other popular text-based games, but had fallen on difficult financial times. The merger soon created issues for the combined companies, however, when new CEO Bruce Davis took over. Davis had been against the merger and made changes that eventually led to the closing of Infocom's studios in Massachusetts, losing most of the Infocom staff in the process.

A name change to Mediagenic, a change in focus to business software, an eventual bankruptcy, a merger, and a name change back to Activision leads us to the present day, where Activision continues to make and distribute popular PC and console game titles like *Doom 3*, *Tony Hawk's Underground*, and *Spider-Man*.

Electronic Arts

Originally starting life as Amazin' Software, Electronic Arts (EA) was founded in 1982 by former director of product marketing for Apple Computer, Trip Hawkins. Acquiring $2,000,000 in venture capital and putting up $200,000 of his own money, Hawkins was able to bring to life ideas he'd had for seven years. The business plan developed by Trip was visionary and had three key elements: first, that the creative talent at the company would be treated like artists, involved in the marketing, and generally revered more than at other companies in the industry; second, that they would develop proprietary tools and technology that would enable them to quickly develop their titles cross-platform; and third, that they would handle the distribution to stores. Hawkins brought many of his former colleagues at Apple onboard and the company was off and running. Nobody liked the name Amazin' Software, though, and at an early company retreat—and inspired by Hollywood's United Artists—the company was renamed to Electronic Arts.

In May 1983, Electronic Arts released its first five titles: *Hard Hat Mack* for the Atari 800 and Apple II; *Archon* for the Atari 800; *Pinball Construction Set* for the Atari 800 and Apple II; *Worms* for the Atari 800; and *M.U.L.E.* for the Atari 800. The last four of these are seminal titles in the history of video games. *Archon* was an innovative chess-like game with action elements to it. *Pinball Construction Set* allowed you to create your own pinball playing fields. *Worms*, the first entry in the venerable series, was a strategic war game with worms as your troops. *M.U.L.E.* was an economic simulation set on a space colony that was masquerading as a game.

While EA wouldn't develop their own internal games until 1988's *Skate or Die!*, they had a knack for finding external development houses with great ideas. Some other early classic EA titles include *One on One: Dr. J vs. Larry Byrd* (1983), *The Seven*

Cities of Gold (1984), *The Bard's Tale* (1984), *Mail Order Monsters* (1985), Bullfrog's *Populous* (1989), and Maxis' *SimCity* (1991). True to Trip's business plan, these titles were developed for multiple computer platforms and eventually consoles.

Trip Hawkins left EA in 1991 to help found the 3DO company, a console and game maker that eventually filed for bankruptcy in 2003. Larry Probst became the next CEO of EA, guiding it to reach profits of $1 billion in 1994—the first for a video game publisher. The outspoken Probst has been criticized for his reluctance to create games such as Take Two Interactive's ultraviolent (but ultrasuccessful) *Grand Theft Auto* Series. Despite that, in 2005 EA is expected to reach $3 billion in profit.

Under Probst's leadership, EA has found a knack for acquiring external development houses that rivals Microsoft's. In 1992, they acquired Richard Garriot's Origin Studios, creators of the *Ultima* series. In 1995, they added Peter Molyneux's Bullfrog (makers of *Populous, Dungeon Keeper,* and *Magic Carpet*) to their list of studios. In 1997, Maxis (all things *Sims*) joined their stable. Finally, in 1998, Westwood Studios (creators of the *Command and Conquer* series) came on board. Consolidating their external studios, EA now publishes some of the most famous franchises in games through their three brands (EA Games, EA Sports, and EA Sports Big). Some of these franchises include *James Bond 007, The Lord of the Rings, Madden NFL, Tiger Woods Golf, Need for Speed, Medal of Honor, Battlefield 1942, Harry Potter,* and *The Sims.*

Interplay

Formed in 1983, Interplay Productions created a few odds-and-ends game products and ports until striking it big with *The Bard's Tale* in 1985. *The Bard's Tale* was a dungeon crawl similar to the *Wizardry* series, but featured innovative quasi-3D graphics. Two sequels followed in the immensely popular series, further expanding on adventures in the town of Skara Brae.

In 1987, Interplay created one of the finest entries ever into the CRPG (Computer Role-Playing Game) genre using the *Bard's Tale* engine. *Wasteland* was set in a post-apocalyptic desert world, the universe created by the tabletop role-playing game *Mercenaries, Spies, and Private Eyes*. The innovative game allowed players to solve problems in the game based on their variety of skills, not just brute force. *Wasteland* has become a steady staple of "best of" lists since its release.

Founder Brian Fargo realized around that time that they could make more money by publishing their own games. The company released *William Gibson's Neuromancer* and *Battle Chess* on their own label in 1988. In 1990, amidst financial troubles, they released *Castles*, which did well enough that they could release their next hit—*Star Trek: 25th Anniversary. 25th Anniversary* broke the curse of licensed *Star Trek* games, and became very successful, eventually being rereleased in a CD-ROM version with voiceovers recorded by the original actors.

In 1997, they released *Fallout*, the spiritual successor to *Wasteland. Fallout* showcased a retro-futuristic style that was a marvel of art direction. Coupled with a combination of real-time and turn-based gameplay and a strong dash of humor, *Fallout* was a classic CRPG that, in turn, spawned its own sequel (*Fallout 2*). Like *Wasteland* before it, *Fallout* has become a steady fixture in lists of the best games of all time.

One of Interplay's most important and lucrative partnerships was with a Canadian company called BioWare. Formed by three medical doctors, BioWare has specialized in creating superb CRPGs, including the *Baldur's Gate* series, *Neverwinter Nights*, and *Star Wars: Knights of the Old Republic*—the latter two published by Infogrames and LucasArts, respectively. The *Baldur's Gate* series, in particular, spawned several immensely popular games, including *Baldur's Gate: Tales of the Sword Coast*, *Baldur's Gate II: Shadows of Amn*, and *Baldur's Gate II: Throne of Baal*.

In the late 1990s, despite the success of *Baldur's Gate*, Interplay's fortunes began to wane. After becoming a public company in 1998, Interplay then announced losses covering several years. The company divested itself of its publisher duties and signed with Vivendi Universal. Soon after, Titus Interactive gained control of the company, prompting the departure of founder Fargo. The company has since been de-listed from the NASDAQ, threatened with eviction from their offices, and, for all intents and purposes, become defunct.

LucasArts

LucasArts started in 1982 as the Games Group, an offshoot of Lucasfilm Ltd. Using $1 million in seed money from Atari, they set to work on creating two games, *Ballblazer* and *Rescue on Fractalus*. The games were completed, but before they could be released, they were pirated. In the meantime, Jack Tramiel had taken over at Atari, and the Games Group didn't like the terms he was offering. In 1984, Epyx published the games, and Lucasfilm Games (as they were now known) had its unique and innovative product on the shelves.

While their early games were creative and well made, it wasn't until 1987, with the release of *Maniac Mansion*, that LucasArts began to define themselves. *Maniac Mansion* was essentially the first point-and-click adventure game. All the game verbs were located on the screen, so interaction was accomplished by clicking on combinations of on-screen items and words—no typing was needed. The engine used to create the game was called SCUMM (Script Creation Utility for *Maniac Mansion*), and typified the sense of humor that went into the games themselves. SCUMM was used for the next 10 years in every adventure game by LucasArts until *The Curse of Monkey Island* was produced in 1997. With SCUMM, LucasArts built a powerful reputation as a maker of witty and original adventure games.

LucasArts wasn't known only for its adventure games, though. In the early years, they had produced a few strategic simulations, and, after working on adventure game ports, programmers Larry Holland and Noah Falstein were anxious to return to their roots. In 1988, they released *Battlehawks 1942*, the first in a series of World War II air combat games. They followed up with *Their Finest Hour: The Battle of Britain* and then the classic *Secret Weapons of the Luftwaffe*.

In 1992, rights to produce games set in the *Star Wars* universe reverted to LucasArts from Brøderbund, and Holland seized the opportunity to apply his combat simulation experience to a new genre. *Star Wars X-Wing* was the result of this first effort—a space combat game that skillfully captured the feel of the beloved movies and put you in the pilot's seat of an X-Wing fighter. *Star Wars TIE Fighter* followed, which told the story from the Empire's point of view, providing shades of gray to the evil Empire. The next game in the series, *Star Wars X-Wing VS. TIE Fighter*, brought the series to the Internet in an ambitious multiplayer experience—complete with death match and co-operative missions. The final game in the venerable series was *Star Wars X-Wing Alliance*, which allowed the player to pilot the Millennium Falcon for the first time.

LucasArts has had other notable games in other genres. They brought The Force to the first-person shooter with *Dark Forces*, released in 1995. Sequels to *Dark Forces* followed in the form of the *Jedi Knight* series and saw the lead character, Kyle Katarn, go from mercenary to Jedi Knight to Jedi Master, adding light sabers and force powers to his arsenal along the way. The 1998 *Grim Fandango* saw them revisiting familiar territory with an amazing 3D adventure game featuring skeletal Manny Calavera on his journey through the land of the dead. Finally, the popularity of the action game *Star Wars Rebel Assault* (which was released only on CD-ROM) is credited with helping bring CD-ROM drives to the masses. LucasArts has continued to produce many great games over the years, many of which are set in the *Star Wars* universe.

Blizzard

Starting life in 1991 as Silicon & Synapse, the company later to be known as Blizzard Entertainment was founded by Mike Morhaime, Allen Adham, and Frank Pearce. Using ties with Brian Fargo at Interplay, they spent their first three years creating console games like *The Lost Vikings* and *Rock & Roll Racing*. They were acquired in 1994 by Davidson & Associates and soon thereafter released the game *Warcraft*—their first big hit. *Warcraft* was one of the first real-time strategy games (along with Westwood's *Command & Conquer*), and helped to define the genre.

The development house Condor had been shopping around a game idea called *Diablo*—and finding no takers—when they talked to their old friends at Blizzard. Blizzard liked the idea, and contracted Condor to make it happen. While Condor was working on *Diablo*, Blizzard was applying the finishing touches on the sequel to their biggest success. *Warcraft II* was released in 1995, and was a blockbuster hit. In 1996, they purchased Condor and renamed it Blizzard North. Blizzard has had an unprecedented number of blockbuster hits since then, each game outselling the last; their latest game, the MMORPG *World of Warcraft* has become the fastest selling PC game in history.

id Software

id Software formed on February 1, 1991, when the game development group at Softdisk (a monthly software newsletter) quit nearly en masse.

John Carmack, Adrian Carmack (no relation), John Romero, and Tom Hall had created a shareware game called *Commander Keen*. *Keen* was distributed by Apogee, who had figured out that splitting a game into three parts and charging for the second and third parts was a way to make shareware pay off well. Seeing the success of *Keen*, Scott Miller of Apogee encouraged the id team to create a 3D game. In December 1991, they completed some final obligations to Softdisk and began work on a 3D game. The game was *Wolfenstein 3D*, a first-person shooter based on *Castle Wolfenstein*. Within the first month after release, Miller paid the id team $100,000 in royalties on the smash hit.

Inspired by the movies *Evil Dead* and *Aliens*, id parted ways with Apogee and created the phenomenon *DOOM*. While not the first first-person shooter (Carmack's contributions to Softdisk earning that place in history), *DOOM* became the ultimate expression of it. Featuring a state-of-the-art graphics engine, *DOOM* was a compelling combination of action, puzzle-solving, art, multiplayer LAN play, and inspired level design. Like their previous products, *DOOM* was distributed using the shareware model that had helped make *Commander Keen* and *Wolfenstein 3D* lucrative.

Each successive product since *DOOM* has been a showcase of genius programming and 3D engine design, with id making massive profits licensing their engines to other game companies. On the heels of *DOOM* followed success with *DOOM II*, *Quake*, *Quake II*, *Quake III: Arena*, and their latest, *DOOM III*, a dark, atmospheric return to the demon and zombie-filled world of their first giant success.

A Brief Overview of Genres

Most modern video games can be assigned to a particular genre, or classified as a hybrid of two or more genres. These genres have come about over the years, often as a result of trial-and-error, but more often as an evolution. The following is a description of some important genres and the games that either introduced or popularized them.

Adventure

In the adventure game genre, there have been two important subgenres: the text-based adventure and the graphical adventure. For text-based breakouts, one need look no further than *Zork* by Infocom. On the graphical adventure side, one of the series that defined the genre was the *King's Quest* series from Roberta Williams at Sierra.

Action

The action game is the superset of many other genres. First-person shooters, action-adventure, combat simulations, fighting games, even platform games are all parts of the action genre. Games in the action genre are typified by fast-paced combat and movement. Some of the earliest examples of video games such as *Spacewar*, *Pong*, and *Space Invaders* defined the genre and were also its earliest successes.

Action-Adventure

Action-adventure games are similar to adventure games, but incorporate action elements. Nintendo's *The Legend of Zelda* was the first breakout hit of the genre, but there have been many more since. Recent games like *Jak 3*, *Metroid Prime 2 Echoes*, and *Resident Evil 4* continue the tradition of action with strong puzzle solving.

Platformer

The original platform games involved the character running and jumping in a side-scrolling playing field. While the definition has been expanded now to include 3D playing fields, the genre is still fairly true to its roots. Some of the most famous platformers have been *Super Mario Bros.*, *Sonic the Hedgehog*, *Pitfall!*, and *Super Mario 64*.

Fighting

In fighting games, the player fights other players or the computer with martial arts or swordplay. These games originated in the arcades, where players could signify their intent to challenge one another by placing quarters on the top of the cabinet. *Double Dragon* is one of the most famous games from the genre, allowing players to fight side by side through a scrolling landscape. *Street Fighter* and *Mortal Kombat* are two of the most famous of the 2D fighting games in which players choose characters and fight against each other (called a "versus fighter"), while *Virtua Fighter*, *Soul Calibur*, and *Tekken* are the leading examples of the 3D version of this subgenre.

First-Person Shooter

The first-person shooter is an action game that places the player "behind the eyes" of the game character. In the games, the player is able to wield a variety of weapons, and dispatches enemies by shooting them. The genre took hold with id Software's *Wolfenstein 3D* and *Doom*.

Real-Time Strategy (RTS)

In a typical RTS, the goal is for the player to collect resources, build an army, and control his units to attack the enemy. The action in these games is fairly fast-paced and because of the continuous play, strategic decisions must be made quickly. While 1984's *The Ancient Art of War* and 1989's *Herzog Zwei* were early examples of the genre, the games that popularized it were Westwood's *Dune 2* and *Command and Conquer*, and Blizzard's *Warcraft*.

Turn-Based Strategy

These games are similar to real-time strategy games (indeed, they were the precursors to them), but the players take turns in which they make their moves. For example, most board games (like Chess and Checkers) are turn based. In the era of the RTS, turn-based games are less frequently made, but there are some notable games in the genre, namely *Civilization*, *X-COM*, *Master of Orion*, and *Jagged Alliance*.

Role-Playing Game (RPG)

The video game version of pen and paper games like *Dungeons & Dragons* differs from its tabletop counterpart mostly in its ability to create a world that doesn't require imagination. Most differentiations from the formula are hybrids with other genres. Some of the most famous RPGs to grace computer and TV screens are the *Final Fantasy* series, the *Baldur's Gate* series, and *Wasteland*.

Massively Multiplayer Online Role-Playing Game (MMORPG)

The MMORPG is a role-playing game set in a persistent virtual world populated by thousands of players simultaneously connected over the Internet. The MMORPG was predated by text-based games called Multi-User Dungeons/Dimensions (MUDs), but in modern times is largely graphical. In the games, the player is represented by an on-screen character called an "avatar." The first modern MMORPG was *Meridian 59* in 1996. The first popular implementation, however, was *Ultima Online* in 1997.

Stealth

Stealth games (sometimes called "sneakers") are characterized by their focus on subterfuge and their planned-out, deliberate gameplay. They are generally similar to first-person or third-person shooters, but are less action-oriented and more methodical in nature. The first stealth game was the original *Metal Gear* in 1987, but other notable stealth games include the *Thief* series, the *Metal Gear* series, and the *Splinter Cell* series.

Survival Horror

Survival horror is a subgenre of action-adventure and first-person shooter games. Typically, they involve exploring abandoned buildings or towns where various monsters and undead creatures lurk. The survival elements are stressed by never giving the player quite enough bullets or health, thus increasing the tension. The horror aspect defines the theme and pacing, commonly directing the player to explore quiet, deserted, bloodstained hallways until a monster comes crashing through a window, or a seemingly lifeless corpse begins to stir. Players are often startled and can become visibly shaken from the experience, much like a good horror movie. While 1992's *Alone in the Dark* is recognized as the first in the genre, *Resident Evil* in 1996 popularized the "survival horror" term and set the bar for subsequent games.

Simulation

Simulation games are based on the simulation of a system. This system can be anything from the workings and economy of the railroads (such as in *Railroad Tycoon*) to a combat scenario where the player controls large movements of troops, or even single fighter craft. *SimCity* is one of the breakout simulation games, allowing you to micromanage a city. *Wing Commander* and *X-Wing* are two of the defining space combat simulation games. *Microsoft Flight Simulator* is one of the most famous airplane simulation games. In recent years, *The Sims* is one of the more popular games in the genre, with its complex simulation of human life and social interactions.

Racing

Racing games involve competing in a race in vehicles ranging from racecars to motorcycles to go-karts. This genre is a little different from others in that the games essentially try to re-create as best they can a real-world activity. The first breakout racing game was *Pole Position* from Atari.

Sports

The sports game genre covers the myriad of games that simulate the sporting experience. As with racing games, sports games are mostly an attempt to re-create the complex interactions in a real sport. Some of the breakout series in the genre have been *John Madden Football* and *Tiger Woods Golf*.

Rhythm

Rhythm games gauge a player's success on his ability to trigger the controls in time to the beat of music. Some games, such as Konami's *Dance Dance Revolution (DDR)*, require the player to step on floor pads in time to music, while Nintendo's *Donkey Konga* for the Nintendo GameCube comes with a specialized bongo drum controller—although not all rhythm games require specialized controllers. For example, *PaRappa the Rapper* is regarded as the first significant rhythm game, appearing on the PlayStation in 1996, and only required the standard controller. However, *DDR* is the most recognized and enduring game in the genre, appearing in both arcades and on home consoles.

Puzzle

Puzzle games combine elements of pattern matching, logic, strategy, and luck—often with a time element. *Tetris* is easily the most popular puzzle game ever, and serves as a fine example of the genre with its frenetic pattern-matching action.

Mini-Games

Mini-games are typically short, simple games that exist within a larger traditional game. They are sometimes used as a reward for completing a challenge or unlocked by discovering a secret. Alternately, the larger game can be a thin veil for a collection of mini-games, as in the *Mario Party* series or the *Wario Ware* series. The *Wario Ware* series is of special note since each title contains more than 100 games, with each lasting only several seconds. Many games on the Internet used for advertising purposes could also be described as mini-games.

Traditional

Traditional games include computerized versions of card games and board games. The first traditional game implemented on a computer screen was *Noughts and Crosses* (tic-tac-toe) by A. S. Douglas at the University of Cambridge in 1952. Throughout the years, chess has long been a staple of traditional video games, with *Chessmaster* being the most recognized series. In 1988, Interplay developed *Battle Chess*, which was just normal chess, but when each piece took another, there was a unique (and often humorous) animation of the "battle." Sierra's *Hoyle* series is one of the most dedicated efforts to bring traditional games to a computer format, with its faithful translations of card, board, casino, word, table, and puzzle games.

Educational

Educational games are designed to teach grade-school concepts to children and young adults in an entertaining manner. The first notable educational game was *Oregon Trail*, originally designed in 1971 for teletype machines at Carleton College, but made popular in the 1980s and 1990s by a version running on Apple computers in the public schools. Other notable games in this genre include the *Carmen Sandiego* series and *Mavis Beacon Teaches Typing*.

Serious

The serious game genre has emerged in the past couple of years as a cheaper and more entertaining way of teaching real-world events or processes to adults. These games are usually privately funded for specific uses, with the U.S. government and medical professionals being the largest users. For example, game developers can develop training simulators relatively cheaply, while infusing the simulation with entertainment value. The fun value is important so that users are motivated to replay the game often and thus become better trained. The Game Developers Conference has recognized the strong interest in serious games and in 2004 added a two-day Serious Games Summit as part of their annual event, focusing on "the intersection of games, learning, policy, and management." [GDC]

Summary

While the history of video games tells a story of men and women driven by innovation and creativity, it as often tells the story of bad business moves and failure to capitalize on opportunities. Innovation doesn't necessarily lead to success, and success doesn't necessarily lead to longevity. True success and longevity in the video game world often rely on a combination of creativity, business acumen, and luck. Just as in any emerging media, there is an evolution that takes place, as genres are defined and capabilities are explored. The consoles and computers of the year 2000 enable ways of game playing that weren't possible in the early 1980s, while some classic games still remain classic games despite featuring outdated technology. Ultimately, as advanced as video games have become, the medium must still be considered in its infancy. This does not invalidate the lessons learned from the designers and companies that have made a success in it, but serves to inform the future.

 ## Exercises

1. A graphical computer version of tic-tac-toe (*Noughts and Crosses*) was developed by A. S. Douglas at the University of Cambridge in 1952. Why do many historians not consider this the first video game? Research the game on the Internet and make an argument why it should be regarded as the first video game.
2. Why was Atari successful with the 2600 while Fairchild and RCA both bowed out of the console race early?
3. Do you believe that the video game mascot is in decline? If so, why? If not, why not?
4. Having read stories of companies that were both successful and unsuccessful, what are some of the elements that would lead to having a successful video game company and some pitfalls to watch out for?

References

[Burnham03] Burnham, Van, "Supercade: A Visual History of the Videogame Age 1971–1984," The MIT Press, 2003.

[DeMaria03] DeMaria, Rusel, and Wilson, Johnny L., *High Score!: The Illustrated History of Electronic Games*, Second Edition, McGraw-Hill, 2003.

[GDC] Game Developers Conference, *www.gdconf.com*.

[Kent01] Kent, Steven L., *The Ultimate History of Video Games*, Three Rivers Press, 2001.

[Sellers01] Sellers, John, *Arcade Fever: The Fan's Guide to the Golden Age of Video Games*, Running Press, 2001.

[Wikipedia04] Wikipedia, 2004, *http://en.wikipedia.org*.

1.2 ░ Games and Society

Overview

Twenty years ago, the study of video games might have been greeted with scorn or derision. After all, who would have considered simplistic games like *Pong* and *Breakout* anything more than a novelty? At most, they were perceived as primitive extensions of board and card games. However, in the two plus decades since then, what was seen as a mildly diversionary collection of dots on a TV screen has become a cultural phenomenon of massive proportions and certainly one worth examining in greater detail.

Clearly, the enormous fiscal and cultural success of video and computer games is too long-lived to be a fluke or fad. The presumption has to be that they fulfill some social or personal need, and that this fulfillment has enabled their enduring success. However, what is this social or personal need, and what power does it have? Are video games merely a reflection of culture and society, or do they exert undue influence on that culture and society? Surely, the answer is somewhere in between, but the answer to this question is critical in determining how societies reconcile their relationships with video games. Are they to be feared or embraced? What laws, if any, should regulate them? Are children or adults susceptible to violent content within video games? How do particular societies and cultures view games and react to their content, and how does that change when that game has been produced by a different culture or society?

Moreover, the classification of video games can be a tricky business. Clearly, they are intended to be entertainment, but what kind of entertainment? Are they an art form, like paintings or literature? Or are they an entertainment medium like television or movies? Are they to be considered an activity or sport, like tennis or ping-pong, because of their capability to sharpen reflexes and improve hand-eye coordination? Or does the interactive nature of the gaming experience require a new classification? Whatever the classification, do video games constitute speech, and thus fall subject to the protections and laws governing speech? How should a society reconcile these very different portrayals of video games? While consumers, lawmakers, and judges hammer out these thorny issues, society keeps humming along, and the consumption and integration of video games into daily life continues, often creating or highlighting newer and thornier issues.

At the extreme of this absorption into daily life is the phenomenon of massively multiplayer online games (MMOGs) such as *EverQuest* or *Lineage*. The nature of these games is such that they can be remarkably immersive and time consuming. Because of this, within these MMOGs, video games and society combine to form a completely new environment with its own unique cultural flavor and its own set of societal rules. People will play, chat, cooperate, compete, and argue with other humans in a place that knows no borders or time zones. No study of games and society could be complete without the acknowledgment and study of how these societies form and operate, and the view that this "blank slate" provides into the inner workings of more traditional societies.

Why Do People Play Video Games?

An examination of this question could easily fill a book, and, in fact, UCLA psychology professor Patricia Marks Greenfield wrote a book in 1984 that addresses it, amongst others [Green01]. Her approach was anthropological in nature because research into this emerging field was nearly nonexistent at the time. In *Mind and Media: The Effects of Television, Video Games, and Computers*, she concluded that video games are appealing to people, in part, because they provide real-time gameplay, goals, and stages. Additionally, they encourage communication by facilitating cooperation. Even this very brief summary of her work yields some important insights. As the games themselves have evolved, however, the concept of these fundamental appealing elements should evolve as well. Greenfield anticipated these potential changes by suggesting that every game will offer different things to different players in terms of their appeal. In this spirit, "real-time gameplay" will be expanded to "real-time interaction," and "facilitating cooperation" will be expanded to "facilitating community." These expanded elements and their varied implementations provide a basis for the rest of this chapter.

Audience and Demographics

At this point, it is useful to determine who in society is playing games and how this information is known. While video games are ostensibly about fun and entertainment, every published video game is, at its core, a business venture designed to make money. As such, it is targeted toward a particular audience or demographic. The demographics within a society can guide what kinds of games are financially feasible to produce. For example, in the late 1990s, several game development companies were created to capitalize on what was seen as a rapidly emerging preteen female market, despite evidence that only a small percentage of these individuals had previously sought out video games aimed at their age group and gender. Unfortunately for these companies, they could not grow the demographic and were forced to close doors after conceding that there wasn't a viable market there.

However, sometimes it is possible to create a new video game genre and thus capture a previously unknown or untapped demographic. In 1997, the game *Deer Hunter* showed that it was possible to make game players out of people who normally did not play games. This game was produced exclusively for Wal-Mart, at their request. Wal-Mart understood the demographics of their customers and was confident that there would be demand for a hunting game that ran on lower-end computers. The game was developed in a mere three months and went on to sell several million copies and spawn a whole genre of hunting games. For a short time, the games industry was baffled and dumbfounded, but came to accept the new demographic.

Demographics can give you the broad strokes of who is out there buying and playing games. Of course, there will be exceptions (the soccer mom who plays nothing but first-person shooters), but, in general, demographics can show informative trends. For instance, a broad brushstroke view of gamers indicates that games with cute, cartoony images tend to be geared toward children. If a game features violent gameplay or sexual innuendos in the context of cute, fuzzy creatures, there might be some demographic issues.

Interestingly, this exact situation occurred in 2001 with the Nintendo 64 game *Conker's Bad Fur Day*. The UK company that developed the game, Rare, originally designed a cute, harmless platform game centered on a bushy-tailed squirrel named Conker. An early version of the game was demonstrated at a trade event, but the press angrily derided the developer for making another happy-go-lucky children's game. As a result, the team at Rare took the criticism to heart and retooled the game to make it adult-oriented; however, they retained the main character and the cartoonish style. Using English wit, sexual innuendos, and a gratuitous amount of toilet humor, the final game spoofed such R-rated movies as *The Terminator*, *Saving Private Ryan*, *The Godfather*, *Reservoir Dogs*, and *The Matrix*. In one of the most demented gameplay moments, the player would direct Conker to drink from a beer keg so that he could then urinate on fire demons. While the game was applauded by critics for being extremely innovative and well done, the cartoony main character failed to appeal to an older demographic and sales were dismal. In the end, Nintendo also had to go to considerable effort to ensure that parents did not accidentally purchase the game for someone under 17. By an odd twist of fate, Nintendo later sold the development company Rare to Microsoft, and now a remake of the game, *Conker: Live and Reloaded*, is scheduled to appear on the Xbox (which has a considerably older demographic than the Nintendo 64).

Understanding what (beyond some very basic elements) will appeal and be desirable to particular demographics and societies can be tricky. Demographics research is one tool that can shed light on how a society uses and interacts with games. It also provides answers to the question of who within society is currently playing games.

The Entertainment Software Association

Where can demographic data be found? The Entertainment Software Association, which is comprised of many leading gaming industry companies and professionals, performs a yearly survey of representative U.S. households to determine gaming and purchasing habits [ESA04]. These numbers provide some insight into who is buying and playing video games.

ESA Statistics for the United States in 2003

- The average game player's age is 29.
- The average game buyer's age is 36.
- 39 percent of gamers are women.
- 40 percent of online game players are women.
- 54.7 percent of online casual game players are women.
- 50 percent of all Americans play video games.

While it's important to remember that these are generalities of a particular market (U.S.) during a particular year, it is remarkable that 50 percent of all Americans play video games. Markets do fluctuate, and certainly, the statistics were very different five years before this survey, but just as certainly, video games have achieved great mainstream acceptance within society. Also of note is that while video games have typically been targeted toward a male audience, clearly games must now target a healthy mix of genders to truly reach the mass market. Massively multiplayer online games (a fairly recent and popular addition to the market) have been particularly adept at providing compelling entertainment for both males and females.

ESRB

The Entertainment Software Rating Board [ESRB04], a self-regulatory body created in 1994 for the interactive software industry by the ESA, provides ratings for video games much like the Motion Picture Association of America provides ratings for movies. Recently, they've significantly expanded their ratings system, so in addition to a rating geared toward ages (EC for Early Childhood, E for Everyone, T for Teen, M for Mature, and AO for Adults Only), they've provided Content Descriptors to describe particular kinds of activity in games, as well as more specifics on the kinds of violence a game may contain (e.g., Cartoon Violence, Mild Violence, Violence). An ESRB rating, while technically voluntary, is always required by console manufactures, the majority of game publishers, and most large retail stores within the United States.

More 2003 ESRB Statistics

- 57 percent of all games rated received an E for Everyone rating.
- 32 percent of all games rated received a T for Teen rating.
- 10 percent of all games rated received an M for Mature rating.
- 1 percent of all games rated received an EC for Early Childhood rating.
- In 2003, 70 percent of the top 20 best-selling console games were rated E or T, while 90 percent of the top 20 best-selling computer games were rated either E or T.

So, how does one interpret the ESRB and ESA data? Does the fact that 57 percent of all games were rated E mean that these are necessarily the most popular games, or just the most frequently made? The *Grand Theft Auto* series of games is a huge success—despite its M for Mature rating. Of course, looking at the average age of game buyers from the ESA data (36 years old) versus the average age of game players (29 years old), one might reasonably conclude that parents make up a significant portion of the game-buying public. Consequently, of course, games are going to be made to appeal to everyone from the young to the old.

Societal Reaction to Games

Societal reaction to games is often not favorable. Even given the $7 billion the industry experienced in sales in 2003, there is a prevailing idea that games are just kid stuff. Even gaming industry professionals, pulling down close to six-figure salaries, have a difficult time explaining what they do for a living to those not in the industry (fighting the idea that all they do is play games all day). Clearly, the numbers support the fact that it's primarily adults buying and playing games, but there are significant issues that arise because of this perception of games as child's play.

In addition, violence in video games has garnered an incredible amount of attention because of concerns with youth violence. As with television and movies, parents are concerned with their children being exposed to violent images in video games. Throw several school shootings (where the assailants were known to play video games) into the mix, and the perception is formed that games are detrimental to children in our society. Is this perception well deserved or unfair? If part of the popularity of games is because they have goals and stages, what happens when those goals and stages are violent in nature?

Legal Issues

An exhaustive history of controversial video games is beyond the scope of this chapter (and has been done very well on the Web in at least two places: an article on the Gamespot Web site [Gonzalez03] and one by University of Bucknell computer science student Jason Yu [Yu01]). However, a few "notorious" games spurred Congress or community to action, and we'll briefly survey some of them here.

In 1992, Sega released a game called *Night Trap* to a largely unaware public. The game, likely destined for the bargain bin on its own merits, gained a certain celebrity for its "mature" content. Although the game featured nothing more controversial than your average B-grade movie, it was pulled from stores. In the game, you were tasked with saving the lives of five coeds living in a house haunted by vampires (and not cast in the role of the killer as was often mistakenly reported). Through a series of closed-circuit cameras, you were able to view events in the house, spring traps on the vampires, and catch the occasional lingerie pillow fight. Certainly, the game achieved notoriety far beyond what was warranted by the crude gameplay and vaguely titillating content.

Segue to another 1992 game called *Mortal Kombat*. Between its gruesome "fatalities" and the virtual gouts of blood, this fighting game was notable for its gameplay, but notorious for its quasi-realistic depictions of violence. While the arcade debut didn't garner much negative attention, the decision to bring it into the home shined a harsh spotlight on the game.

As a reaction to games like *Mortal Kombat* and *Night Trap*, Senator Joseph Lieberman (D-Connecticut) started hearings in late 1993 to call the video games industry on the carpet. The ultimatum to video game manufacturers was delivered: regulate yourselves or the government will do it for you. Lieberman, joined in March 1994 by Senator Herbert Kohl (D-Wisconsin), held a meeting attended by top video game officials where video game companies presented the senators with a 12-point plan for self-regulation. This was the birth of the ESRB.

In late 1994, another game destined for notoriety was created in Texas by (now legendary) id Software. The game *Doom* featured fast-paced action as you wandered around a demon-infested space station destroying the zombified former occupants (as well as various hell-spawned monsters) with a variety of armaments littering the hallways. It, and its predecessor, *Wolfenstein 3D*, were some of the earliest entries into the first-person shooter genre of games. It was a hugely successful game, and was one of the first to popularize a method of distribution where the first "chapter" of the game was free and players purchased the game only if they wanted to play the subsequent two chapters. It skated by the 1993–1994 hearings without mention, but was the subject of controversy a few years later.

On April 20, 1999, one of the most devastating school shootings in U.S. history occurred at Columbine High School, just west of Denver, Colorado. The two teenage gunmen were known to play *Doom*. Once more, video games were at the forefront of controversy. Several lawsuits followed, against id Software and other video game companies, alleging that their games had influenced the two perpetrators. Since then, all lawsuits have been dropped [AP0302].

Finally, another game that has been the focus of legal issues is Rockstar's *Grand Theft Auto: Vice City*. Set in Miami, this first-person action/adventure game puts you in the role of a lackey driver for the mob. A sequel to the equally controversial *Grand Theft Auto III*, the game's innovative brand of gameplay has made it a huge success.

The game series is not without its detractors, however. In November 2003, the Haitian Centers Council and Haitian Americans for Human Rights, two Haitian-American rights groups, protested the game in New York City. In *Vice City*, during one of the missions, the player is instructed to "Kill the Haitians." The context of the game places this in the midst of a gang battle between a Cuban gang and a Haitian gang, where to score points with one gang, you are to eliminate members of the other. In early December 2003, Rockstar announced that they would remove the offending line from the game. This didn't really quell the controversy, however, when in January 2004 a Federal case against Rockstar Games, Take-Two Interactive, Sony, Wal-Mart, Microsoft, Best Buy, and Target was dropped, only to be taken up again in a Florida court where the plaintiff group, headed by the Haitian-American Coalition of Palm Beach County, hoped to get a more stringent ruling than they would by leaving it at the Federal level.

Finally, in the year 2000, in the state of Missouri, a St. Louis County ordinance was passed that regulated access of video games in the home and arcades. The ESA (then called the Interactive Digital Software Association) filed a lawsuit in response. In April 2002, Senior U.S. District Judge Stephen N. Limbaugh rejected the Association's argument [AP0402]. After viewing gameplay from *Resident Evil*, *Mortal Kombat*, *Doom*, and *Fear Factor*, he wrote in his decision, "This court reviewed four different video games and found no conveyance of ideas, expression, or anything else that could possibly amount to speech. The court finds that video games have more in common with board games and sports than they do with motion pictures." The 8th Circuit Court of Appeals in St. Louis eventually overturned the decision stating, "Whether we believe the advent of violent video games adds anything of value to society is irrelevant; guided by the first amendment, we are obliged to recognize that 'they are as much entitled to the protection of free speech as the best of literature'" [USDCOA03].

Games and Youth Violence

As you will have noticed, most of the legal battles and threatened legislation in these few, brief examples revolved around fears about the potential effects of violent video games on youth. Is this a reasonable concern? What are the effects of violent video games on children? That's a tricky question, as often anecdotal or skewed evidence is pointed to as definitive.

In the same St. Louis court case mentioned previously, an amicus scholars' brief was filed by 33 media scholars, games researchers, historians, and psychologists. The scholars' brief quoted British psychologist Guy Cumberbatch, who claimed that it was puzzling that anyone could look at the research evidence and be so confident and passionate that harm was caused by the violence on television, film, and video games. While tests of statistical evidence are important, Cumberbatch worried they were being used to torture the data until it confessed to something that could secure publication in a scientific journal. He further claimed that lynch mob mentality has surrounded the debate on media violence with almost any evidence used to prove guilt [FEP02]. There are studies that point to such things as heightened heart rates after playing violent video games or watching violent television programs or movies, but these studies also point to those physical effects quickly fading. If the amicus scholars' brief is correct, then clearly, more thoughtful research needs to be done to determine the effects of violent video games on children.

It begs the question: What exactly is violence as portrayed in video games? Does a violent action correspond exactly with what would be considered a violent action in society? There are many games for children where the on-screen character hits other characters or is hit in cartoonlike fashion, and they are largely not considered violent. Games that depict just the strategic elements of war in *Risk*-like fashion are largely not considered violent either, although war is, by its very nature, unavoidably violent. Is whether an action is violent or not determined in some sense by the realism of the depiction? How does this change over time? Games like *Mortal Kombat* were controversial for their "realistic" depictions of blood, but that 1992 depiction is now laughable compared to any modern depiction of blood.

Root of All Evil, or Good, Old-Fashioned Fun?

On the one hand, the argument by one St. Louis judge concludes that games don't constitute speech (much less protected speech), while on the other hand, the fear in violent games is that they are essentially indoctrinating our youth into violent behavior. Is there a disconnect there, in the idea that games are simultaneously seen as meaningless entertainment, and yet as a source of potentially violent behavior? These arguments would seem opposed to each other, for wouldn't games have to be more than meaningless entertainment to have a lasting effect? If a game currently considered speech is stripped of elements one by one (art, story, gameplay, sound, etc.), which element or elements would need to be stripped away to not consider it speech anymore? Moreover, at what point would it not be able to be considered a game anymore? How would that change depending on the culture you were in, and their particular values?

Cultural Issues

Cultural issues are an important consideration during game creation. Things that may be commonplace in one culture can have an entirely different connotation in another culture. If a game is going for a global release versus a domestic release, many things might have to be changed to appeal to or even simply not offend another culture. Even within a culture, there might be people in an intended demographic who don't get the in-jokes, or find the content of a game outright offensive. It's not always clear from the outset what these issues might be, either. History can provide important guideposts in this area, while not necessarily providing all the answers.

Worst . . . Stereotype . . . Ever

Humor is subjective, as anyone who's listened to eggnog-inspired, bad holiday jokes can tell you, and some cultures are a little more sensitive to depictions within games than others (as evidenced by the Haitian-American response to *Grand Theft Auto: Vice City*). Sometimes, when a cultural stereotype is played for humorous effect, the effects may just not hit everyone's funny bone. It's easy to rationalize it away or say, "Well, they just don't get the joke," but a significant uproar can have detrimental effects on a games sales and community standing.

See the case of the 1997 3D Realms game *Shadow Warrior* and its humorously (but perhaps insensitively) named hero "Lo Wang." The game was riddled with send-ups of cultural stereotypes and rife with politically incorrect references. The Japanese-American community didn't appreciate the lampooning of their culture, and didn't see it as the good-natured jab it was intended to be. Sales for the game weren't huge, and the controversy didn't last long, but it could be argued that the culture that might have found the most fun with the game was offended instead of amused.

Even the TV show *The Simpsons*, which has a long history of poking fun at literally everything and everyone, got in some trouble when Bart pretended to have Tourette's Syndrome in one episode. *The Simpsons* has had umpteen years with millions and millions of viewers to build a strong case of being an equal-opportunity offender to all creeds, cultures, races, and religions. However, games don't have that long to establish exactly where they stand, and it can be dangerous and insensitive to be seen as singling out one culture for ridicule.

Foreign Diplomacy

A global release brings its own set of issues. Games can be banned outright in some countries for seemingly arbitrary reasons, sometimes even after great lengths have been taken to be culturally sensitive to that specific country. Other times, a game that would seem on its face to be offensive to a particular country can be a huge success, leaving befuddled producers and marketers scratching their heads.

Germany

Germany, sensitive to its past, has stringent regulations on the violent content in its video games. In Germany, there exists a list called *the index* or banned list. With restrictions more stringent than most other European countries (or most countries in general), many violent video games have some hoops to jump through upon German release. Some games can avoid being placed on the list by changing a few controversial elements (red blood to green blood, for example). Games depicting Nazi iconography have avoided the list by switching those images to less controversial ones. In cases like *Return to Castle Wolfenstein* (where in addition to changing the Nazi flags to a generic symbol, a Nazi song played by a phonograph within the game was changed to a piece of classical music), that may not be enough, and the game may be placed on the index despite extensive measures taken to be sensitive to the culture. Ultimately, a banned list game cannot be advertised, displayed in stores, or be sold to people under 18, which can make a game incredibly hard to market and sell.

China

China has a long history of banning video games as well. In May 2004, the 2002 PC game *Hearts of Iron* by Swedish company Paradox was banned by China's Ministry of Culture for "distorting history and damaging China's sovereignty and territorial integrity" [CD04]. In part, the game supposedly misrepresented historical facts regarding Japan, Germany, and Italy's participation in World War II. In addition, the game made "Manchuria," "West Xinjiang," and "Tibet" sovereign countries in the in-game maps. All of these are big no-nos according to China's gaming and Internet service regulations. As a result, Web sites were prohibited from releasing the game, sellers were prohibited from selling the game (under threat of legal punishment), and all CD-ROM copies of the game were to be confiscated. This is just one example from a very long list.

Japan

While Japan has in the past banned games for sexual content, and, in general, they eschew the more violent games, a recent game caused a curious reaction. EA's *Medal of Honor: Rising Sun* depicts, among other things, the Japanese attack on Pearl Harbor. The game covers the Pacific campaign of World War II from 1941–1945. The player's basic goal, as outlined on EA's Web page, is to "stop Japanese forces from achieving control of the Pacific Theatre." The game sold 200,000 copies in Japan in its first two weeks. The game did a good job of depicting nonstereotyped Japanese soldiers as real human beings in an armed conflict, but still, one wouldn't necessarily expect a game depicting this particular conflict to be a huge success in Japan. Japanese gamers were unconcerned with the idea that they were killing their grandfathers, and concentrated instead on the gameplay.

Cultural Acceptance

It's not a simple thing to make clear-cut rules about what will find acceptance within others' cultures. Sometimes, the preemptive tailoring of a game to a specific culture's mores helps, and sometimes it doesn't. Certain cultures will ban a game specifically for a depiction of history that disagrees with what they believe; others will ignore culturally sensitive issues in favor of strong gameplay. Cultural sensitivity is a minefield, where only the strongest instances of offense are clearly problematic.

Society within Games

Take any subset of society and you'll see much of what that superset of that society has to offer—the good, the bad, and the ugly of human behavior, if you will.

Online Behavior: The Good

The hugely popular massively multiplayer online role-playing game (MMPORPG) *EverQuest* has seen many different kinds of behavior since its release in 1999. One phenomenon of note, though, is *EverQuest* Weddings, where characters "wed" other characters in online ceremonies (complete with virtual food, drink, and avatars of their virtual friends). In some ways, this might seem to represent stunted social interaction, but that would be a somewhat pessimistic view. It can be seen as representing the natural culmination of society—the joining of people together in bonds that, to the people involved, can be serious and genuine. What can be better than the mutual expression of love between two people, virtual or otherwise? Societally speaking, we are built around that very premise.

Online Behavior: The Bad

Online play is not always representative of the best society has to offer, though. More serious than simple antisocial behavior (which we will discuss next), online games can become so involving to people that their real lives are neglected or they can't separate the virtual world from the real. Take the case of South Korea's Kim Kyung-Jae, a 24-year-old who collapsed and died after playing online games nearly nonstop (taking breaks only to use the restroom and buy cigarettes) for 86 straight hours [Gluck02]. In another disturbing online gaming-related death, a 17-year-old British Columbia boy was killed after repeatedly trouncing three men in a game of *CounterStrike* at an Internet café. After one too many wins, the three men physically beat the 17-year-old, then left the café, returned with a handgun, and shot him [Devitt03]. Lastly, there is the case of a mentally troubled Wisconsin man who took his life with a shotgun after many months of a 12-hour-a-day *EverQuest* habit. His mother claimed to have found him with an *EverQuest* login screen up on his computer, and started a lawsuit against Sony, wanting warning labels placed on the games. Her belief is that some event online caused him to take his own life, and that Sony should be held partially responsible [Fox02]. While online gaming can't reasonably be held responsible for the behavior of a few emotionally troubled individuals, as more and more online games get more and more popular, statistically speaking, there will be an increase of these types of incidents.

Online Behavior: The Ugly

An interesting psychological phenomenon that has taken root in the online gaming world and in gaming forums is that of *deindividuation*. This is the phenomenon where anonymity allows the person to demonstrate behaviors that he would not be able to exhibit if he were known. A somewhat insidious noncomputer example of this is that of the Ku Klux Klan. Essentially, the white hoods and robes rob the individuals of their identity and thus their compunction to follow societal norms, allowing them to commit acts outside the bounds of accepted behavior. In online games, this behavior, taken to a far less extreme than in the KKK example, nonetheless allows people a certain anonymous "bravado" with which to fuel antisocial desires. In games, this often exhibits as rude or disruptive behavior to other players (excessive taunting, swearing, racial and homophobic epithets, etc.). In real life, these people almost universally would not be able to act this way, but in the anonymity of an online world, they have few perceptible limits on their behavior.

Tools

Society in the online world has come up with ways to deal with these issues. Just as the police in nonvirtual society enforce socially acceptable behavior, moderators and game wardens can help create a sense of stronger community within a game by encouraging social behavior and discouraging disruptive behavior. A game is not going to be fun to members of a particular ethnicity if that particular ethnicity is the target of the invective of some anonymous gamer. Gamers also like the ability to take control of their own destinies, as it were, so tools that allow them to ignore other users or report bad behavior are also a standard in most modern games with online capability.

Some of the more positive tools are those that facilitate communication. Often, games come with multiple tiers of communication. The MMPORPG *World of Warcraft* contains the ability to talk on a zone channel (where players can conduct general, game, or nongame chat to players within the same zone); a trade channel (to facilitate the buying and selling of player-created/found goods); a "say" channel with a limited range so players can communicate with those directly near them; a "yell" channel (a larger ranged "say" channel); a group channel (for communication within a joined party); a whisper channel (for private communication between players); and a guild channel (for discussion within player-created guilds). That's quite a few ways that people can do something seemingly simple, like talk with each other, but this reflects the myriad ways in which societal communication works (whispers, private phone calls, interaction with small groups, garage sales, yelling in a public place, social groups and clubs, etc.). In addition, the game features mailboxes where players can send each other messages, money, or goods (for when players are not on simultaneously), further enhancing the societal interaction and sense of cooperation.

In-game tools are only the start, though. There are many *EverQuest* fansites on the Internet, with seemingly more popping up every day. These sites contain elements like fan-created stories, game information, forums, newsletters, and fan-created art. Liken it to, for example, golfers, who purchase golfing magazines, wear golfing paraphernalia, spend time reading books about and discussing their favorite hobby. People like to spend time immersed in their favorite hobbies, even when they're not directly doing them. It's not hard to tie this into two of the fundamental reasons posited why people play video games, namely communication and interactivity.

Summary

The tremendous popularity of games can be attributed, in part, to characteristic elements of games that fulfill certain societal and personal needs. Some of these elements are real-time interaction, goals, and stages. Increasing audience and expanding demographics point to the further evolution of video games in their ability to incorporate these elements in a way that fulfills players' needs. Different game elements appeal differently to people. Culture and society have a major impact on the success of games because of this variability.

The success of video games as a fiscal and cultural entity is not without controversy, though, as people struggle to understand this emerging media's effect on society. In some cases, a game may find a niche within a particular culture or society; in others, a game element may inadvertently cause offense. In particular, concerns over the effects of violent games on youth are prevalent, with few comprehensive studies done that can point to clear answers. Lawmakers and judges will continue to hammer out issues of what regulations and restrictions should apply to games, while attempting to answer questions about whether games constitute speech or merely mechanical action.

Ultimately, the evolution and sophistication of games has led to a point where the communities that spring up within and around games act as a microcosm for the larger society. In-game tools and extra-game elements like fansites enable these in-game societies to function at a high level, and increase the absorption of video games into society. This absorption is also not without controversy, as some individuals are unable to successfully separate their online lives from their real lives.

Exercises

1. Take the statement: The ultimate measure of a video game's success is the absorption of its characters and symbols into other forms of media, such as television or movies. Defend or refute this statement.
2. Do you agree with the list of appealing video game elements (interactive play, goals, community facilitation, stages)? What would you change, remove, or add to this list?
3. What elements of a game need to be taken away before it can no longer be considered speech? At what point does it no longer become a game?
4. Discuss which is more violent, a game that uses very graphic, but cartoon-like violence, or a game that has mild, but incredibly realistic violence? Is realism the only key, or are there others?
5. Consider your culture and society. What aspects of your culture and society might be offensive to you if lampooned in a game? Would it depend on the overall presentation, or are there always taboo elements despite the presentation?

References

[AP0302] Associated Press, *Columbine lawsuit against makers of video games, movies thrown out, www.firstamendmentcenter.org/news.aspx?id=4161*, 2002.

[AP0402] Associated Press, *Federal judge backs limits on kids' access to violent video games, www.firstamendmentcenter.org/news.aspx?id=3977*, 2002.

[CD04] China Daily, *Swedish video game banned for harming China's Sovereignty, www.chinadaily.com.cn/english/doc/2004-05/29/content_334845.htm*, 2004.

[Devitt03] Devitt, Ron, *Coquitlam teen killed at Internet café*, *www.thenownews. com/issues03/013203/news/013203nn1.html*, 2003.

[ESA04] Entertainment Software Association, *Essential Facts About the Computer and Gaming Industry*, *www.theesa.com/pressroom.html*, 2004.

[ESRB04] Entertainment Software Rating Board, *www.esrb.com*, 2004.

[FEP02] The Freedom of Expression Policy Project, *Media Scholars' Brief in St. Louis Video Games Censorship Case*, *www.fepproject.org/courtbriefs/stlouissummary.html*, 2002.

[Fox02] Fox, Fennec, *Mother blames 'EverQuest' for son's suicide*, *http://archives.cnn. com/2002/TECH/industry/04/05/everquest.suicide.idg/*, 2002.

[Gluck02] Gluck, Caroline, *South Korea's gaming addicts*, *http://news.bbc.co.uk/ 2/hi/asia-pacific/2499957.stm*, 2002.

[Gonzalez03] Gonzalez, Lauren, *A History of Video Game Controversy*, *www.gamespot. com/features/6090892/index.html*, 2003.

[Green01] Greenfield, Patricia Marks, *Mind and Media: The Effects of Television, Video Games, and Computers*, Harvard University Press, 1984.

[USDCOA03] U.S. District Court of Appeals for the 8th Circuit, *No. 02-3010*, *www.ca8.uscourts.gov/opndir/03/06/023010P.pdf*, 2003.

[Yu01] Yu, Jason, *The Online Guide to Controversial Video Games*, *www.boilingpoint. com/~jasonyu/cs240/*, 2001.

1.3 ■ Ludology for Game Developers—An Academic Perspective

In This Chapter

- Overview
- Introducing Ludology
- Ludology as an Attitude
- Design Research: Ludology for Game Developers
- Two Ludologists: A Dialogue
- Summary
- Exercises
- References

Overview

There has been a recent rise in academic studies of games, and the term *ludology* has been coined to characterize this new discipline. In truth, *ludology* is a term for a host of different methods with which to study, teach, and even design games. This chapter introduces various aspects of ludology, and suggests means to apply ludology for practical game-development purposes. Numerous references and pointers to ludological resources encourage the reader to become familiar with ludology and make his or her own interpretation of the field.

The authors have experience from both industry and academic contexts, and have employed ludological methods in their own game design and concept evaluation tasks. The chapter concludes with a dialogue where various aspects and applications of ludology are discussed through concrete examples.

Introducing Ludology

Game scholar and editor-in-chief of the online journal *Game Studies*, Espen Aarseth has named 2001 as the inaugural year of academic game studies [Aarseth01]. This academic approach has been referred to as *ludology*. The word is a neologism resulting from the combination of the Latin word *ludus*, meaning game, and Greek term *logos* referring to reason and science. In similar fashion as "narratology" refers to a set of theories on narratives and narration, ludology is a general term for studies and theories focusing on games [Frasca99].

For a game developer interested in broadening his or her understanding of games across different media and technology, the general rise in interest toward games presents fresh opportunities to get familiar with both early and contemporary contributions to ludology and feed off their findings. Thus, the neologism that constitutes our topic is not just a buzzword to promote academic activities in the present, but also a tool to give new worth and usefulness to earlier theoretical discussions on games.

Defining Ludology, Defining Game Studies

The heart of the matter is in first asking, what kind of research is possible to do on games? Second, if games are the object of study, we must understand what distinguishes games from nongames.

Descriptions of Games, Play, and Gameplay

We all have an instinct that tells us if something is a game or not, but, as most probably have noticed, we do not seem to agree with everyone else about specific cases. Providing a definition to solve these differences is difficult for two reasons. First, games are a very diverse category of artifacts and activities where the challenge is to pinpoint characteristics that appear in all games. Second, people have different opinions of what a game is, so any possible definition would either have to be based on popular opinion or based on a narrower definition of some form of an expert group.

The meaning of the word *game* also has many, sometimes radically different meanings ranging from animals that are hunted to concepts of social manipulation ("game of love"), making it even more difficult to define. Some people, such as analytical philosopher Ludwig Wittgenstein, have even proposed that it is futile to try to define what a game is [Wittgenstein58].

The word *play*, which is closely linked to the word *game*—for example, in the concepts of "to play a game" and "gameplay"—is likewise difficult to define (see Brian Sutton-Smith's *Ambiguity of Play* for further discussion on the meaning of *play* [Sutton-Smith97]).

What does it mean to play a game? How is playing a game different from other activities such as watching television, participating in politics, or taking a stroll in the park? Games and play have been studied, and defined, in many different fields from economics to anthropology. The descriptions presented here range from definitions to models and have been selected from a myriad of other descriptions because they represent views from different fields of study and together show the complexity of games and the activity of gameplay. The fields of practice of these descriptions range from rigorous scientific fields to practical game design, which, of course, have an effect on their level of rigor. Some are based on ethnographical and anthropological studies, some on analytical examinations, some on personal design experiences, and some on a combination of different fields of expertise. The studies and methods presented here have different intended readers and therefore provide different views on the subject.

Historical and Contemporary Studies of Games

Early landmarks of academic game studies have been documented by Elliot M. Avedon and Brian Sutton-Smith [Avedon71 pp. 19–26]. This work consists largely of anthropological and historical perspectives to games in a particular culture or period of time. These studies testify for the lasting presence of games as an everyday part of the various people and their cultures.

Probably the most well-known "early" study of games is Johan Huizinga's cultural critique *Homo Ludens: A Study of the Play-Element in Culture* originating from 1938. Huizinga sketches out a concept called "magic circle," which refers to the particular enchantment of games as something detached from everyday activities, and governed with make-believe rules. Magic circle is a powerful metaphor for games, and it has sustained its explanatory power to this day: it has been promoted in contemporary game studies and writings on game design, especially by Katie Salen and Eric Zimmerman in their influential book *Rules of Play* [Salen04].

However, Huizinga's book was preceded by a number of anthropological and/or historical approaches, such as Stewart Culin's studies on the games of Native Americans, Chinese, and so forth [Culin93a, Culin93b; see also Avedon71]. H.J.R. Murray was another prominent figure of game studies in the early twentieth century. He was a historian of board games, studying both chess and other forms [Murray51]. These studies can be recommended to those who want to learn about the origins of classic game genres.

A notable modern entry into ludology is Roger Caillois' *Les Jeux et les Hommes* from 1958 (translated into English as *Man, Play and Games* in 1961). Caillois looks into various sorts of games from a socio-anthropological viewpoint, and introduces the four categories of *agon*, *alea*, *mimicry*, and *ilinx*, which account for different game and play activities. Caillois also introduced an axis that describes the players' attitude to the game. According to him, it ranges from free-form *paidia* to rule-bound *ludus* [Caillois01]. If we adapt Caillois' thinking to contemporary games, then *The Sims*, with its loose goals and winning conditions fosters a paidia type of attitude, whereas an *Unreal Tournament* death match clearly demands a ludus type of attitude. The *Grand Theft Auto* series, with its seemingly open mission structure, would reside somewhere in between these two extremes.

Game theory is another discipline that warrants attention when discussing the roots of ludology as we know it today. John von Neumann and Oskar Morgenstern wrote their *Theory of Games and Economic Behavior* (1944), which gained prominent status and was applied to various applications. Game theory mainly discusses so-called zero-sum games where the players are making rational and informed decisions. As such, a number of game design problems (e.g., balancing a game's resources evenly, etc.) are indebted to game theory and theories on mathematical probability.

It also needs to be noted that there is a rich field of play theory, of which especially the work of Brian Sutton-Smith and his colleagues is recommended reading for game developers [Avedon71]. Studies on simulations present another field of relevance: there is a rich literature that discusses simulations in the form of games. The work of theorists and designers such as Cathy Stein Greenblat are of interest for contemporary ludology as well [Greenblat88].

Ludology as an Attitude

To be precise, we understand ludology as an *academic attitude to games*; in other words, a specific interest for knowledge concerning games. This is an inclusive definition, rather than an exclusive one.

There is evidence that the academic world tends to opt for exclusive definitions. A debate on a particular subject has shadowed the early steps of contemporary ludology: the so-called narrativist-ludologist debate has been going on in the field even though Gonzalo Frasca has argued that the "debate never took place" [Frasca03]. The supposed conflict was between scholars investigating games with an emphasis on their narrative aspects (i.e., the "narrativists") and ones dedicated to studying "games as games" (i.e., the "ludologists"). Essentially, this meant that the former were interested in games with strong narrative aspirations (e.g., *Myst* and many similar adventure games), whereas the latter liked to throw the "*Tetris* card" onto the table, promoting games with no narrative or characters.

The stance of *radical ludology* came to be known and articulated via Finnish game scholar and writer Markku Eskelinen who argued that stories are unimportant features of games and putting effort into studying these would not be worthwhile [Eskelinen01].

This debate between stories and "pure" game mechanics is something that we've found to exist among discussions between game developers as well, whether or not with the same terms and concepts (see [Scholder03]). Regardless of the terms and contexts, the interest for knowledge is similar, we believe: to better understand what games are, how they work, why people play them, and how to design better, or at least more diverse, games.

This equals the inclusiveness that we argued for a couple of paragraphs earlier. Seeing ludology as an attitude with which to conduct detailed inquiries into games and their players allows us to regard many development-oriented activities as ludological. For instance, it is quite clear that the Game Tuning Workshops held at the Game Developer Conferences for a number of years have displayed a very evident ludological attitude, and yes, the "L" word has even been voiced aloud in this context.

Some counter-examples include market research, for instance. Seldom do you see market researchers, or the ones taking advantage of the figures produced, conducting their business with a ludological attitude; their interest for knowledge regarding games is quite different and very case specific. We do not see background research focusing on a specific technological solution or, for example, finding out facts for a game concept that has a historical setting as particularly ludological activities. In conclusion, ludology as an attitude requires a more generic approach to games.

Design Research: Ludology for Game Developers

Is there a form of "applied" ludology, especially geared toward practical applications for game design and development? Could or should there be? One answer to these questions would be to put ludology in context with another discipline of research introduced and articulated recently: design research.

What is design research? In general, it is research that is particularly interested in methods and results of the different stages of the design process. Thus, we see design research as the means to apply ludology as an attitude to practical game development tasks.

In the preface to the anthology *Design Research* [Laurel03], Peter Lunenfeld discusses the various attempts to define design research from Bauhaus to date. He cites Sir Christopher Frayling's threefold identification of key areas of design research:

1. Research *into* design
2. Research *through* design
3. Research *for* design

Research into design covers aesthetics and history of art and design. Research through design is done for particular projects and includes, for example, research of materials. Finally, the goal of research for design, even though the most difficult to formulate, is to come up with systems and models that showcase and validate the results of the research [Laurel03].

The three approaches are useful also for situating ludological activities into the contexts of design research. The most traditional aspect is "research into design," which consists of ludological analyses of existing games (i.e., their designs) and how players engage with those designs (i.e., play the games). Research into creating methods for these kinds of endeavors is something that the ludological attitude is able to contribute as well. The representatives of "research into game design" mostly equal the academic papers found in the online journal *Game Studies* and conferences of Digital Games Research Association [DiGRA].

"Research through design" is characteristically research that builds prototypes of games or game-related products as its results. These kinds of tasks may be built on specific ludological findings or theories that thus constitute research for design, possibly even for highly specific design purposes. Moreover, the documentation of the prototyping process and reflecting its solutions and outcomes becomes part of ludological study.

Research for Design

For the purpose of this chapter, we feel that the ludological attitude as research for design is the most fruitful area to cover in more detail, even though generally research for design has to borrow heavily from assumed history of design processes for games.

Games can be said to have been around as long as tales, mythologies, and rituals have been, while play predates these since it does not require a language and can be found in many animal species [Sutton-Smith97]. It can be assumed that these early games were designed in a similar way as folk tales are authored: the game elements and rules evolve over time by the effort of countless, and nameless, "designers." Physical games, including sports, contests, and children games have been around even longer than games based on the use of symbols.

The difference between the gameplay in these activities can be divided into four main groups:

- Somewhat codified gamelike interaction spontaneously arising from normal play behavior.
- Physical contests and tests with codified rules to determine the conduct and the outcome.
- Evolved symbolic games such as dice games and early board games.
- Games that have been designed on purpose.

The focus of analyzing gameplay in games (i.e., research into their designs) covers all these four categories, while the discussion of the problem of designing games focuses on the last category. All these categories are somewhat overlapping and share the common ground of gameplay activity, but all games in all categories can also be seen as artifacts that are the result of conscious design choices. For the last categories, this can be obvious as there may be records of the intentions the game designers had before starting the design process. Activities in the first three categories do not have initial design goals, but have been changed by the participants themselves while performing the activity, so that the activity suits their current intentions. As the activity has been repeated, the rules for the activity have developed in an evolutionary way where every change has been the adjustment to a local context.

The similar distinction can be made in general between craft and design [Jones92]: the characteristics of a craft product can be understood as a combination of the methods and materials available as well as the situations in which the product has been used over a longer period of time; and the characteristics of a designed product can be understood as the result of trying to reach a design goal, which is often at least partly implicitly defined, by using methods and materials available. A product can, however, be the result of movement between the categories. For example, an initial design can be the starting point for how a product develops through craft practice, and an already crafted product can be the inspiration for a designer to create new designs.

This view of craft and design can be found in Herbert A. Simon's *Sciences of the Artificial* [Simon96], where he states that any activity with an intention to devise a course of action to change the existing situations to preferred ones can be classified as design. In other phrasing, things created by people can be treated as if they were designed when analyzing them, even if the people who created the things did not perform the actions, specifically setting design goals, normally associated with design.

Some argue that designing games is an art, knack, or a mystical craft that cannot by analyzed, and that the attempt to create methods and models of game design is futile. We believe that there is some truth to this claim, at least that it is impossible to come up with a cookbook or a set of instructions that can automatically create beautiful designs without any other insight, talent, or skill. However, we also feel that it is possible, even desirable, to find and describe the basic features, elements, and patterns that can assist, guide, and inspire design work. Visual artists have to know the methods and techniques of visual composition, novel writers benefit greatly from understanding the principles of drama such as foreshadowing and climax points, and architects have to know the basic elements of how to construct buildings. Making the principles of how to design explicit gives designers a conscious layer of self-evaluation, and makes it easier to consciously break the principles and to seek new forms of expression. These are all practical aspects of a ludological attitude that game developers can embrace.

Tools, Methods, and Models

As seen previously, many of these definitions and models with ludological attitude come from professional designers as well as researchers who do experimental designs as part of their method to explore the design space of games. It is no wonder that many of these researchers and practitioners also have developed methods and models to design games.

The following methods and models are all recently proposed with an intention of supporting design of games and, obviously, the ludological attitude is evident in each of them.

Chris Crawford

Chris Crawford's *The Art of Computer Game Design* [Crawford84] may well be the first contemporary treatise with a strong ludological attitude. In the book, Crawford identifies representation, interaction, conflict, and safety as the four common factors in all games. Although he does not give a definition based on these factors, he elaborates the meaning of game through exploring the factors. According to Crawford, all games are constructed representations, since games are closed formal systems that represent parts of reality [Crawford84, p. 9]. The terms *closed* and *formal* are used to signify that there is a clear distinction between what constitutes the game state, and what does not, and that the system is mechanically deterministic respectively. Based on this perception of a game as representation of a selection of reality, Crawford then claims that the most fascinating thing about reality is the relationships of cause and effect, and that these are best explored through interaction as he states that interactive representations are the most complete kinds of representations and that interactivity is the most important aspect of games as such [Crawford84, p. 10]. Crawford has also written numerous articles on this area and his newest book on game design [Crawford03] is also worth noting because of his distinctive attitude toward games.

Greg Costikyan

Greg Costikyan in his "I Have No Words & I Must Design" article [Costikyan94] identifies design choices that have to be made when games are designed. He lists decision making, goals, opposition, managing resources, game tokens, and information as the main features that are necessary for games and that should be taken into account by game designers when making games. After identifying these categories, he continues to describe them and explain why each is necessary, but does not provide specific details on how the features can be created.

Decision making is, according to Costikyan, the most integral feature of games. The players have a choice between different courses of action in the game and have to weigh the pros and cons of these alternatives. Regarding goals, Costikyan argues that they are what make players stay interested in playing the game. If there are no goals, no objectives in the game, the players eventually lose interest, as there is no purpose for their actions. Opposition is something that the players have to overcome to reach their goals. Opposition provides struggle, and Costikyan claims that a game without a struggle will fail as a game. Having the players manage resources in the game avoids the pitfall that the decisions are eventually trivial. If the player has to make trade-offs between using different resources, the choices are both more complex and interesting. The players have to have some methods to change the game state, and this is done through game tokens. The last feature, information, governs that the players should have enough, but not too much, information available about the factors that have an effect on decision making. The information itself can also be used as a resource, especially in games based on exploration. In the article, Costikyan also mentions some other features that strengthen games, from diplomacy between the players to narrative tension.

MDA: Mechanics, Dynamics, and Aesthetics

Robin Hunicke, Marc LeBlanc, and Robert Zubek have developed a formal approach to understanding games, which they call the Mechanics, Dynamics, and Aesthetics (MDA) framework. It has been employed in the Game Tuning Workshops held in Game Developers Conferences since 2001 [LeBlanc]. The MDA framework consists of three main components: mechanics that describe particular components of the game (e.g., how data is represented and what kind of algorithms are used); dynamics that describe how player inputs affect the game system's behavior over time; and aesthetics that describe players' emotional responses while interacting with the game system. The goal of MDA is to provide a framework for bridging the gap between game studies, game design, and game development [Hunicke04].

These three components can be thought as three separate, but causally linked aspects of the game. The design of mechanics gives rise to the dynamic behavior of the system, which finally creates the aesthetic responses for the player. The aesthetics can be broken up into more distinct components; what the authors call *Eight Forms of Fun*:

- Sensation, game as sensory pleasure
- Fantasy, game as make-believe
- Narrative, game as drama
- Challenge, game as obstacle course
- Fellowship, game as social framework
- Discovery, game as uncharted territory
- Expression, game as self-discovery
- Submission, game as pastime

The framework supports designers by showing how the one design goal regarding one part of the framework can be achieved by making specific design choices in other parts of the framework. They do not provide a detailed model for the possible ways the different parts can affect each other, but do offer some examples. For example, the authors argue that *fellowship* can be encouraged in a game's design by goals that require cooperation or information that becomes more valuable when shared among players.

That is, different dynamics create different aesthetic experiences, and it is the designer's task to determine the aesthetic forms he wants and develop dynamics that create these forms. Finally, the actions, behaviors, and control mechanisms available to the players create and support these dynamics.

Formal Abstract Design Tools

Doug Church in his "Formal Abstract Design Tools" article [Church99] argues that in current computer game development, the lack of common design vocabulary has slowed the evolution of game design in a considerable way. He then proposes a framework to overcome this problem, the Formal Abstract Design Tools (FADT), stressing abilities to communicate design ideas and shifting the focus on underlying ideas rather than specific implementations. This would lead the way for a common vocabulary.

One of his ways to approach the problem is to look at current good games and first identify and collect some key elements and aspects that make those games work. These concrete elements are then abstracted and formalized into a FADT. For example, his analysis of *Super Mario 64* led to two FADTs: *Intention* (forming a plan in response to one's understanding of the gameplay options and the current situation), and *Perceivable Consequence* (a clear reaction from the game as a result of the player's action).

FADTs give designers concepts to use when describing ideas and choices, and different collections of FADTs can be identified and created independent of each other, allowing them to be tailored for specific use. However, they do not have relationships to other FADTs as part of their definition, so designers are not helped in understanding the effect of using a FADT to change a game design where other FADTs have already been used.

The 400 Project

The 400 Project is an attempt to formalize what Falstein perceived as the basic rules of game design in an accessible way [Falstein02]. The rules consist of five parts:

- An imperative statement of the rule.
- A description of the domain of the rule.
- Rules that take precedence over the rule.
- Rules over which the rule takes precedence.
- A description of examples and counter-examples.

The rules are meant to be tools, which can be used in different phases of the design process, from problem solving during the design to fine-tuning an existing design. The target of the project is to come up with, as the name implies, 400 such rules.

The rules in the 400 Project differ from FADTs in that they are more structured and contain relationships to each other. However, they are not concepts that designers can use in their designs, but rather instructions on how the design process should be done. That is, they are *imperative*, and can be seen as a way of codifying best practice.

Ernest Adams and Andrew Rollings

In their book, *Ernest Adams and Andrew Rollings on Game Design*, the authors divide game design into three different areas: core mechanics, interactivity, and storytelling and narrative [Adams03]. Adams and Rollings continue to separate other elements of games, such as setting, interaction model, perspective, the player's role, and define gameplay as a series of challenges that are causally linked and take place in a simulated environment [Adams03, p. 201].

Adams and Rollings support design by showing how gameplay can be constructed from what they call "pure challenges," or combinations of these pure challenges, which they call "applied challenges." Their pure challenges are based on physical, mental, or social challenges with the following categories: logic and inference, lateral thinking, memory, intelligence based, knowledge based, pattern recognition, moral, spatial awareness, coordination, reflex/reaction time, and physical. Examples of the applied challenges that are based on the pure challenges include races, puzzles, exploration, conflict, economies, and conceptual challenges. The authors further provide descriptions of game design elements specific to different genres that can be used when creating the pure or applied challenges.

Game Design Workshop

Tracy Fullerton, Christopher Swain, and Steven Hoffman in *Game Design Workshop: Designing, Prototyping, and Playtesting Games* [Fullerton04] discuss the structure of games and identify eight basic formal elements: players, objective, procedures, rules, resources, conflicts, boundaries, and outcomes. These formal elements are the basis for their further elaboration and refinement of the method and structure to design games. The main theme in their design methods is to use the formal elements, and specific instances of them, to describe the current design and make sure that all aspects of a game design are taken into consideration. By doing this, an initial game idea can be described in a format that maintains the key elements as the idea is transformed into a concept, paper prototype, alpha release, and so on.

Steffen P. Walz

Steffen P. Walz has proposed and elaborated an approach to game design based on applying the classic rhetoric models and rhetorical figures of, for example, Aristotle, Quintilianus, and Burke [Walz03]. The main thrust of Walz's approach is to explore how rhetoric, defined as the science of persuasion, can be applied to the design and analysis of games. Walz takes the triadic relationship between game designer, game, and players as the starting point for his further analysis of digital game rhetoric. This relationship is similar to the classic rhetoric relationship between the communicator (or orator); the performance and the message to be conveyed; and the receiving audience. Further, Walz argues that identification, a concept adopted from Kenneth Burke's work on rhetoric, is the key for the use of rhetoric in game design. The three dimensions of identification—systemic, symbolic, and structural coupling—define the processes and strategies of how the game designer persuades the players to play the game. The most interesting dimension for this discussion is the structural coupling, where the game designer can modulate the player's expectations, motives, needs, and actions in the game by structuring the levels of offers and demands the game provides to the player. For example, *Tetris* contains several levels of these offer-demand pairs. The basic level is that of the demand of the block moving down and the offer of rotating and moving it left and right. The highest level is the demand of keeping the screen as clear as possible and the offer of removing several rows at one time. The interplay of these offer-demand pairs then creates the flow of the gameplay experience.

Game Design Patterns

The first article about game design patterns was Bernd Kreimeier's "Case for Game Design Patterns" [Kreimeier02], in which he formulates the four basic aims of game design methods: they should relate to game design, have utility as a tool, be abstract, and be formalized. Inspired by Christopher Alexander's pattern approach to architecture, Kreimeier [Kreimeier03] developed an approach to game design based on the concept of game design patterns. Parallel and inspired by Kreimeier's work, Björk and Holopainen started their ambitious Game Design Patterns Project [GDPP]. Björk and Holopainen have a slightly different approach than Kreimeier. They follow the basic principles of Alexander to describe invariant and recurrent characteristics of game design. These are expressed as interdependent semiformal pattern descriptions. Their collection of almost 300 patterns can be found in the book *Patterns in Game Design* [Björk04].

Katie Salen and Eric Zimmerman

Salen and Zimmerman's book *Rules of Play* [Salen04] introduces a formidable set of theories and schemas for game design and studies: theoretical groundings run from psychology to game theory, information theory, systems theory, semiotics, mathematics, and so forth. The book testifies to the wide number of different backgrounds on which game design and game studies can potentially draw. The authors' goal is to see the actual conceptual tools that are relevant regarding games, and thus better understand the uniqueness of game design as design practice.

Salen and Zimmerman promote "meaningful play," which refers to actions and outcomes within a "magic circle" (see Johan Huizinga previously) that add to the emotional and psychological experience of playing the game. Creating meaningful play is a complex process, and Salen and Zimmerman address different aspects of analyzing and designing systems that facilitate the emergence of meaningful play. They articulate a number of game design schemas that are intended to provide frameworks for understanding formal, experiential, and cultural aspects of games.

Discussion

The use of what we call ludological methods and models is also dependent on the different intuitive approaches the designers already have. Some designers prefer the structured, sometimes even rigorous approach to game design, while some are more comfortable with the feeling of playful freedom of the design process. The methods and models, however, are developed to assist the design process, not to straightjacket it into following step-by-step cookbook instructions. According to both anecdotal evidence from designers and personal experiences of the authors, the use of a method is not always conscious. During the design process, there are phases when the design falls into place intuitively, without conscious reflection on the choices. The methods and models are then used consciously and with rigor to evaluate and sometimes validate these intuitive design choices. The explicit and structured models of games are also good for understanding the role of games in larger cultural context and analyzing games in general.

Two Ludologists: A Dialogue

To close the discussion, the authors engage in a dialogue to highlight some aspect of ludology and its uses in their own design and research tasks.

AJ:　By naming our chapter "Ludology for Game Developers," we offer a particular interpretation of what ludology is and, more or less, what it should be, right?

JH:　That is correct, although I am a bit hesitant to offer interpretations, as they tend to be regarded as definitions and this can lead to much confusion later. So, I stress here that what we offer is just our interpretation of what ludology means in this particular context; i.e., "Ludology of Game Developers." The focus is on shedding light on the ludological issues that are, in our opinion, the most important ones for those who are in the trenches of game development. Ludology itself is still a slightly vague and sometimes far too encompassing discipline. For example, one definition presented previously, "the study of games, particularly computer games" [Frasca99], is not really useful in this context, as it could also include specific technical topics such as rendering techniques, which, again in my opinion, are not part of ludology as I understand it. Following the discussion in the first part of the chapter and also my own research interests, I would like to make the area of ludology focusing on the structures of gameplay as the most important one for game developers.

AJ: In your experience, how do people working in the industry find ludology? Do they embrace or resist it? To put the question in context, I've had a couple of opportunities to witness how people react to your and Staffan Björk's ideas and methods about using game design patterns, and there seems to always be someone from the "not invented here, or by me" camp. Any thoughts on this?

JH: This depends quite a lot on what kinds of developers there are in the audience. Some of them are obviously interested in all kinds of things related to games, and they usually carefully listen to our argumentation and take bits and pieces which fit in their work and choose to ignore or criticize the rest. The resistance, however, is widespread, and we have heard many, many times that the models we have presented are useless because 1) they are too complex, 2) they do not reflect the actual work done by the designers, and last but not least, 3) we are not working in the games industry (as it is).

AJ: I believe this has to do with a more general perception of theory. For theorists, theory is a means to produce order from chaos and thus reduce complexity, but theorists (myself included) often fail in communicating this intent with their complex figures, concepts, etc. Do you agree?

JH: Yes, pretty much. The first issue, the models being too complex, is something we are trying to address in our future work by somehow making it easier to access the complex models. This issue, however, has two sides: on the one hand, we do not believe that it is possible to have a simple model of game design without sacrificing way too much, and on the other, there might be flaws in the model if it is impossible to use it in a practical way. This issue is, I feel, ubiquitous in every theoretical approach to creative work. Just looking at, for example, the models of narrative and drama by French semioticians: the models are complex and beautiful, but it is almost impossible to use them in a fruitful way without revising the presentation heavily. The second issue, that the models do not reflect how real designers do real designs, is a slightly more subtle problem to tackle. However, after discussing this in more detail with those people, it usually turns out to be that the model does not fit their intuitive view on their work process, and by making the mappings between their implicit conceptual models and our model more explicit there are surprising similarities. The last issue with us being outsiders to the games industry often turns out to be a case of "Not Invented Here" syndrome, which in one sense is understandable. The last two complaints are also based on mutual misunderstanding about the reason for presenting the model. Developers sometimes take these theoretical models as outright and blunt criticism of their own work, and I have to admit that sometimes our style of presentation fits this view quite well ("here we are presenting a model which describes the design process in a structured and clear way…"). These models, however, should not be taken as facts or normative guidelines, but rather as tools which can be modified and added to the developers' toolboxes based on their needs.

AJ: So what about this idea of ludology as an attitude rather than some clearly distinguishable design or research method?

JH: I feel that this is a beneficial approach for both the people working in game development and the ludologists themselves, especially for helping them understand each other better. The ludologist (well, I might be a good example) storming into a development studio to present these fancy new research results as *the* design method is going to be ignored or, in the worst case, smeared in tar and rolled in feathers. The key issue is first to create a mutual understanding of the approach, in this case ludology as an attitude, and then start to investigate what is useful and what is not. Somehow, I have this feeling that we as academics have a tendency to "preach," and I fully understand the developers who resist these kinds of approaches. What about your experiences? You are working in the Finnish National Lottery company as a games researcher. What kinds of experiences have you had with ludology as an attitude there?

AJ: Well, I have tried to pursue it within the company, with varying results. There is definitely the challenge of incorporating formal methods with the "silent knowledge" and routinized practices of experienced designers. But I've had some successful steps in introducing board game workshops, systematic analysis methods, etc., into the design process. Overall, my own work divides into two branches: one, I am working on my academic thesis on game analysis and design methods, and two, I am trying to adapt those methods to the practical design and evaluation tasks that I am responsible for. The thing is that I am working within an industry that has long traditions (gambling in all its forms) and this presents quite specific and rather ruthless requirements for new games, such as luck being a near-absolute deciding factor regarding outcomes, and so on. I believe the formalistic approach has helped enormously to better see the formal structures and their configurations—rules, draws, game mechanics—that one has to have in a game in order for it to be operated as a lottery or a betting game. After distinguishing those, it is easier to focus your attention to how the game appears and how you "thematize" the game, to use a theoretical term from my own theory. Also, it has enabled us to experiment with completely new forms of lottery and gambling games and focus on the player's experience. To emphasize this point, I've found game design patterns very useful and tried to adapt them for games of chance in particular. In the context of my academic pursuits, I've taken the MDA approach as a starting point and tried to reformulate it by giving its ad hoc nature a more detailed groundings in psychological theories on emotions, moods, and cognition.

JH: That is quite similar to my work at Nokia Research Center. I also feel that the ludological view we are pursuing is quite different from research done on games, for example, in media culture and philosophy just because we both have to apply the research to our daily work.

AJ: Exactly. It doesn't mean that research that remains on a descriptive level is useless, but rather that it has to be filtered or remodeled into tools that one needs in everyday work. In practice, though, there has to be someone who has the means and the time to do it. For this, having one foot—or at least a couple of toes—in the academia helps a lot, as one can use general knowledge of research methods in seeing what kind of research and theory is applicable for design and product development. This is definitely a benefit of general interest in ludological matters, I believe!

Let's move on to discuss more examples of ludological attitude or ludological method. I find many kinds of self-reflective approaches to design processes or fundamentals of game design (Game Tuning Workshops, *Rules of Play*, etc.) quite lucid examples of ludological attitude. But how about less formalistic approaches, such as studies of player behavior, do you see them representing ludology? How do you see "culturalist" ludology and the questions it would be interested at?

JH: As I previously mentioned, for this particular context I feel that the formalist ludology focusing on structures of gameplay and design processes is more appropriate than cultural issues. Even though this is the case, I really, really do not want to say that the cultural issues are irrelevant for game developers, far from it. I just feel that the issues of "culturalist" ludology might be more difficult to use in the day-to-day work in game development. Of course, it would be beneficial if at least the producers, designers, and marketing people would be familiar with issues such as the cultural history of representation in games and game advertisements.

AJ: We both were involved in a study where psycho-physiological player responses (heart rate, skin conductance, etc.) were measured in relation to specific events in games such as *Tetris* and *Super Monkey Ball* [Ravaja04]. I believe ludology played a part in that study in the sense that we tried to analyze and distinguish those particular events as general patterns that exist in a wide array of games...you agree?

JH: Sure. I guess that this study was an excellent example of ludology as an attitude approach within the research itself. Both parties (we as ludologists and the other researchers as media psychologists) had the "ludological attitude" and the first results were cautiously optimistic about the relevance of this research to playtesting methods in general, even though the conclusions were not done with proper ludological rigor. However, in the later phases of the study we are starting to look at how this attitude can be expanded to making the method available and accessible also to the developers by automating the now cumbersome testing methods. I strongly believe that the results of this kind of research can, in the end, validate and guide otherwise intuitive design choices by making explicit the patterns of player responses to different gameplay structures. In conclusion, the study confirmed, to certain extent, our initial hypothesis that a ludological approach can produce results that are useful to game developers, and I think that is, or at least should be, one of the drivers for ludology: to provide research results to be able to make better games!

AJ: True! In general, I believe ludology as an attitude tries to question the tug-of-war between theory and practice by trying to show that the ends of the rope, so to speak, are not necessarily clearly demarcated in the first place. Also, why won't we ask, "How does practice inform theory" for a change? This is where ludology and design research are able to provide examples and answers, and compete on both ends of the rope!

Summary

Ludology is an attitude toward game design and development that is driven by a need to understand games in general terms. Ludology finds practical applications both in academic studies of games, and in developing formal methods for game design. The generic nature of ludological attitude means that it is interested in learning and developing interdisciplinary methods for making better games: ludologists want to learn from psychology, architecture, play theory, design theory, information theory, semiotics, rhetoric, and so forth, and adapt them for the purposes of game analysis and development. Ludological attitude can also point the way for finding common vocabularies and practices for game scholars and developers, even though there doesn't need to be a division between "thinkers" and "doers." Rather, it is the ludological attitude that builds bridges between the two, with methods such as Formal Abstract Design Tools, Game Design Patterns, and Meaningful Play presenting concrete ways of how to build them.

Exercises

1. What is ludological attitude? Describe at least four different dimensions of ludology as an attitude.
2. Select one of the approaches listed in the *Tools, Methods, and Models* section and describe how it could be used in a real-life game development project. It is recommended that you go through the source material in more detail than is done in the chapter itself.
3. What are the perceived benefits of ludology for game development? What issues would hinder using ludological approaches in game development? Make a short pros and cons analysis of ludology for game developers.
4. Give concrete examples of the three key areas of design research as applied to game development.

References

[Adams03] Adams, Ernest, and Rollings, Andrew, *Andrew Rollings and Ernest Adams on Game Design*, New Riders Publishing, 2003.

[Avedon71] Avedon, E. M., and Sutton-Smith, Brian (eds.), *The Study of Games*, Wiley, 1971.

[Björk04] Björk, Staffan, and Holopainen, Jussi, *Patterns in Game Design*, Charles River Media, 2004.

[Caillois01] Caillois, Roger, *Man, Play and Games*, University of Illinois Press, 2001.

[Church99] Church, Doug, "Formal Abstract Design Tools," *Game Developer Magazine*, August 1999, available at *www.gamasutra.com/features/19990716/design_tools_01.htm*, July 9, 2004.

[Costikyan02] Costikyan, Greg, "I Have No Words and I Must Design: Toward a Critical Vocabulary for Games," *Proceedings of Computer Game and Digital Cultures Conference*, edited by F. Mäyrä, Tampere University Press, 2002.

[Costikyan94] Costikyan, Greg, "I Have No Words and I Must Design," *Interactive Fantasy 2*, Hogshead Publishing, 1994, available online at *www.costik.com/nowords.html*.

[Crawford03] Crawford, Chris, *Chris Crawford on Game Design*, New Riders Publishing, 2003.

[Crawford84] Crawford, Chris, *The Art of Computer Game Design*, McGraw-Hill Osborne Media, 1984, available online at *www.vancouver.wsu.edu/fac/peabody/game-book/Coverpage.html*.

[Culin92] Culin, Stewart, *Games of the North American Indians: Games of Chance vol. 1*, University of Nebraska Press, 1992.

[Culin93] Culin, Stewart, *Games of the North American Indians: Games of Skill vol. 2*, University of Nebraska Press, 1993.

[DiGRA] Digital Games Research Association, *www.digra.org*.

[Eskelinen01] Eskelinen, Markku, "The Gaming Situation," *Game Studies vol. 1*, 2001, *www.gamestudies.org/0101/eskelinen/*.

[Falstein02] Falstein, Noah, "Better By Design: The 400 Project," *Game Developer Magazine*, vol. 9, Issue 3, March 2002, p. 26.

[Frasca03] Frasca, Gonzalo, "Ludologists Love Stories, Too: Notes From a Debate that Never Took Place," Level Up Digital Games Research Conference 4–6 November 2003 Proceedings, Universiteit Utrecht, 2003. Available online at *http://ludology.org/articles/Frasca_LevelUp2003.pdf*.

[Frasca99] Gonzalo Frasca, "Ludology Meets Narratology. Similitude and Differences Between (Video)Games and Narrative," *www.ludology.org/articles/ludology.htm*.

[Fullerton04] Fullerton, Tracy; Swain, Christopher; and Hoffman, Steven, *Game Design Workshop: Designing, Prototyping, and Playtesting Games*, CMP Books, 2004.

[GDPP] Game Design Patterns Project, available online at *www.gamedesignpatterns.org*.

[Greenblat88] Greenblat, Cathy Stein, *Designing Games and Simulations: An Illustrated Handbook*, Sage Publications, 1988.

[Hunicke04] Hunicke, Robin; LeBlanc, Marc; and Zubek, Robert, *MDA: A Formal Approach to Game Design and Game Research*, available at *www.cs.northwestern. edu/~hunicke/pubs/MDA.pdf*, July 9, 2004.

[Jones92] Jones, J. C., *Design methods*, 2nd ed., John Wiley & Sons, 1992.

[Kreimeier02] Kreimeier, Bernd, "The Case for Game Design Patterns," available online at *www.gamasutra.com/features/20020313/kreimeier_03.htm*, March 2002.

[Kreimeier03] Kreimeier, Bernd, "Game Design Patterns," *Game Developers Conference*, International Game Developers Association, San Jose, 2003.

[Laurel03] Laurel, Brenda (ed.), *Design Research: Methods and Perspectives*, MIT Press, 2003.

[LeBlanc] The collected game design rantings of Marc "MAHK" LeBlanc, *http://algorithmancy.8kindsoffun.com/*.

[Murray51] Murray, H.R.J., *A History of Board-Games Other than Chess*, Oxford University Press, 1951.

[Ravaja04] Ravaja, Niklas; Saari, Timo; Salminen, Mikko; Laarni, Jari; Holopainen, Jussi; and Järvinen, Aki, "Emotional Response Patterns and Sense of Presence During Video Games: Potential Criterion Variables for Game Design," Proceedings of the NordiCHI 2004, available at *http://doi.acm.org/10.1145/1028014. 1028068*.

[Salen04] Salen, Katie, and Zimmerman, Eric, *Rules of Play: Game Design Fundamentals,* MIT Press, 2004.

[Scholder03] Scholder, Amy, and Zimmerman, Eric (eds.), *Replay: Games Design and Game Culture,* Peter Lang, 2003.

[Simon96] Simon, Herbert A., *The Sciences of the Artificial*, 3rd ed., The MIT Press, 1996.

[Sutton-Smith97] Sutton-Smith, Brian, *The Ambiguity of Play*, Harvard University Press, 1997.

[Walz03] Walz, Steffen P., "Delightful Identification and Persuasion: Towards an Analytical and Applied Rhetoric of Digital Games," In Proceedings of Level Up Digital Games Research Conference, edited by M. Copier and J. Raessens, University of Utrecht, 2003.

[Wittgenstein58] Wittgenstein, Ludwig, *Philosophical Investigations*, Oxford: Basil Blackwell, 1958.

GAME DESIGN

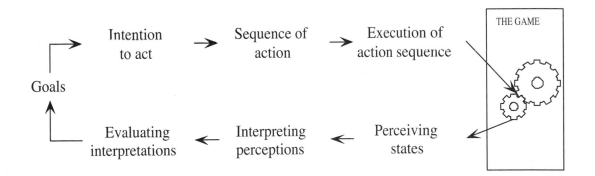

2.1 ▐ Understanding Fun— The Theory of Natural Funativity

Overview

This chapter delves into a theory called "Natural Funativity" that explains why people enjoy entertainment in general and games in particular. Understanding the natural basis for fun provides an important tool that helps game designers craft more effective games. Supporting this theory is an analysis of Classic Game Structure, some rules for structuring the sequence of choices in a game to maximize players' enjoyment, and a discussion of The Flow Channel, a concept from psychology that is particularly useful in creating popular games. The chapter concludes with a discussion of Story and Character in Games, extending the previous topics to provide practical guidance for game designers and writers.

Throughout these sections, useful tips and quotes about how the theory can be applied to practical aspects of game design are highlighted like this:

Game design is both a logical and an intuitive process. Learning to use these tips consciously will, over time, foster an instinctive sense of how to apply them to future game designs.

Are We Having Fun Yet?

According to most dictionaries, *fun* is a synonym for *enjoyment*, or a source of amusement. However, on a deeper level, asking what is the underlying nature of fun, or more precisely, why we human beings find some things entertaining and others not, is a critical question that is rarely addressed when considering game design. Certainly, the ultimate test of a game's worth is often summed up in the question, "how much fun is it?" If we don't consciously know what fun is, then we are doomed to try to evoke it in our games by trial and error, or by copying successes of others and forever lurking in their shadows.

In the early 1980s when computer games were just starting to catch on with the public, the new manager of the Lucasfilm Games Division (which later became the LucasArts Entertainment Company) was Dr. Stephen Arnold. Steve had come to Lucasfilm from Atari, and had been a practicing child psychologist for years before that, training that qualified him to understand the game audience, and helped him to ride herd over a group of 20-something game developers. Steve's first question about any new proposal brought to him was, "what is the funativity quotient?" By coining this term, he prompted the designers to consider precisely what elements of the game contributed to the feeling of fun, and the degree to which each part of the design was important in that process.

However, the question of Fun (with a capital F) transcends game design. To get at the heart of what makes video games fun, we have to begin by looking at entertainment in general. Therefore, we'll explore the realm of all things that fall into the domain of entertainment as we look at its underlying foundations.

Evolutionary Antecedents

When dealing with practical answers to fundamental questions about human behavior and preferences, the logical place to start is with evolution. The basic drives for all creatures are survival and reproduction, and (with mammals like ourselves in particular) the social skills that let us interact successfully with others of our species. And to understand human evolution, it's necessary to look farther back than our current society, because from an evolutionary standpoint the last few thousand years of civilization are just a thin veneer on the millennia that have shaped our species, and the last few hundred years of technology have hardly affected our evolutionary heritage at all. Most of that legacy is in genes that helped our ancestors survive and reproduce in the hunter-gatherer societies that prevailed from the time they began to walk upright until the recent present. Therefore, we have to look at the way humans must have lived tens of thousands of years ago to see the survival significance of some of our evolutionary traits [Pinker97].

How does this relate to games? Games are an organized form of play, and the roots of play go deep into human history, and even further, beyond our species. Everyone has seen kittens or puppies playing with their littermates, stalking and pouncing, rolling and nipping. Their play focuses on practicing basic survival skills while also establishing social dominance and learning to live with their peers [Wills93]. People share much of that foundation, but our much larger brains and more complex social structures have caused us to extend play into adulthood. Human entertainment is also at its heart all about learning about survival and reproduction and associated social rules.

Marshall McLuhan, a communications theorist, proposed that there is little difference between education and entertainment. On its surface, that may seem like an extreme belief. However, examine the underlying assumptions. People tend to divide their lives into time spent doing what is necessary for survival, inactivity, and leisure time. In short, work, rest, and fun. It's easy to see why we have evolved to attend to our basic survival needs—our potential ancestors who weren't willing to do so didn't survive to become our ancestors in the first place. Moreover, even though in general people make a strong distinction between work and entertainment activities, their origins are very similar.

Consider our ancestor who has just come back from a successful hunt. He can go right back out and try to hunt some more, or attend to other basic survival needs. That has the benefit of keeping the larder full, but runs the danger of being hurt or even killed on a hunt that isn't strictly necessary. There are some people who are "wired" that way—today we might call them diligent workers or even workaholics. Alternatively, our ancestor might have just rested, conserving his strength and not being motivated to do much more until an empty belly forced him out again—also a personality type familiar today. Such a person would have the advantage of staying safer while resting, but runs the risk of running out of food if game is scarce when he finally goes to hunt, or if he's out of shape when running after an elk—or away from a sabertooth tiger. However, there's a third alternative. It turns out that foraging is a very efficient mode of subsistence, leaving many hours for other tasks [Leakey94].

If one of those early humans' brain and emotions happened to be structured to provide pleasure from practicing and perfecting survival skills or learning new ones in a comparatively safe way that did not endanger his life to the same degree as the actual survival tasks, he would be likelier than his fellows to survive to become our ancestor. After many entertainment-related activities, people's brains release chemicals known as enkephalins and endorphins that resemble opiates like opium and morphine, creating effects like the well-known "runner's high" [Dunbar96]. Moreover, it is because of that evolutionary innovation that modern humans seek entertainment and derive pleasure from it, including video games as one of the latest examples.

These games, as with all play and entertainment in general, involve learning new things. When people stop learning from a game, they stop playing it. Multiplayer games can extend the learning process as players learn to top each other's strategies and adapt, which helps explain their long-term play value. In addition, the skills are taught in a context that is safer than real life, particularly for some of the fighting, hunting, and war games, because if they were just as dangerous as the real thing, there would be no evolutionary advantage to learning from a game instead of the actual activities. Consider when emotions flare and a playful game between friends suddenly becomes serious and confrontational—it might evoke the protest, "relax, it's only a game." This may well explain why the groundbreaking EA game *Majestic* failed to catch on—it managed to evoke actual real-world fear by generating threatening e-mails and phone calls to the player (and had the unfortunate timing of coming out around September 2001). Its highly touted innovation of being "the game that plays you" by intruding into the real world apparently backfired. The great majority of people want to feel safe in their entertainment, even (especially) when it involves violent conflict.

Consider what skills and information the player learns over the course of your game, and emphasize skills important to the player's survival in the game.

TIP

Sometimes the connection between a specific game or form of entertainment and learning survival skills is hard to see. For one thing, there can be many levels of abstraction present in games. For example, the modern game of chess is about moving pieces across a board, but its origins are in a simulation of war. Or a game might seem trivial on the surface, but evoke our hunter/gather ancestors' priorities, like *Pac-Man* that managed to combine both gathering (eating berrylike dots while avoiding dangerous predators) and hunting (turning the tables and chasing down—and consuming—those very predators). This very simple game was a huge hit in its era, even though there were more elaborate and sophisticated games available at the time.

So, is the secret to success to make games about hunting and gathering? Actually, that's not a bad place to start. Consider all the games that are directly or indirectly about those basic topics. Certainly, first-person shooters and games like flight sims, wargames, most fantasy role-playing games, and most real-time strategy games are very much about a violent kill-or-be-killed world, with a huge amount of gathering thrown in—gathering the tools, weapons, and armor to survive, gathering resources or information critical to prosper, even in some cases gathering in the sense our ancestors did it, finding food in the wilderness. The most popular PC game of all time is *The Sims*, which has very little to do with hunting, but much to do with both gathering and, unusual in games, the social rituals of mating and even reproduction that obviously fascinate a large number of people and are vital to our genes' survival.

Natural Funativity

This theory of how entertainment in general and how games in particular relate to learning about survival skills is known as Natural Funativity. Natural, as in natural selection, because it is based on evolutionary principles, and Funativity from the Lucasfilm Games anecdote, and because it elevates the simple term *fun* to one that seems more worthy of serious analysis—and because a theory about fun should sound a little silly and fun itself. However, to learn to apply these theoretical concepts to practical theory for game design, it helps to break the theory down into manageable pieces.

Everything that people do to entertain themselves falls into one of three categories. The first category is physical things that people do for fun.

Physical Fun

The physical realm has obvious and direct connections between our evolutionary past and what people do for fun. One of the strongest urges in people, and indeed in most animals, is the survival instinct. Anything that directly threatens our immediate survival will instantly capture our total attention. We have become hardwired to enjoy practicing physical activities that enhance our survival for the simple evolutionary logic that our potential ancestors, who were not that interested in practicing those skills, were less likely to survive to *become* our ancestors. If one looks at entertainment in general, activities that involve threats to survival and the means to deal with those threats have always been tremendously popular—think of the success of movies, books, TV shows, and even news features about violent criminals, soldiers, doctors, and police. Even when the point of the entertainment is abstracted—for example, scoring more points than another team at football—there are obvious concrete advantages to survival in a hunter-gatherer society of having the muscular development and coordination of an athlete.

Sports are in general another big area of physical fun. Solitary sports like running and bodybuilding have obvious survival advantages for the individual, while team sports also incorporate cooperative strategies that mimic group hunting expeditions of early humans—as well as tribal competitions and even war. For that matter, actual hunting and fishing have remained popular even when no longer directly necessary for survival. In 1997, the computer game *Deer Hunter* and its sequels were big hits, selling millions of units even though their technology and gameplay were fairly simplistic. This surprised many in the industry who had assumed that the tastes of computer game players were fixed solely on elaborate science fiction and fantasy themes along with state-of-the-art graphics.

Gathering is a component of many forms of entertainment. Pick almost any obscure item from buttons to Beanie Babies, and there are people who collect them. Gambling is an incredibly popular kind of gathering, showing that when people see the potential for a payoff that can actually help them survive, their interest in the activity goes way up. In video games, *Pac-Man* was probably the first hugely successful gathering game—with an element of "the hunted becomes the hunter" as well—and *Pokémon*'s slogan "Gotta catch 'em all!" points to its gathering roots. Many very successful games, from *Pokémon* to *Creatures* to various real-time strategy games include the idea of training and even breeding creatures with various helpful qualities—and not surprisingly, evidence suggests that the first domestication of animals goes back at least as far as 70,000 years ago, and learning to survive among potentially hostile creatures goes back much farther.

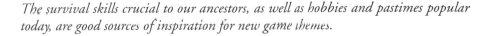

The survival skills crucial to our ancestors, as well as hobbies and pastimes popular today, are good sources of inspiration for new game themes.

TIP

In addition to these basic survival skills, one physical activity many people enjoy is exploring places—some like to travel to exotic locations, others prefer to stick to their own neighborhoods until they are extremely familiar with every home and store, but either way they gain pleasure from improving their knowledge of their surroundings, which is also a major feature of many games of almost every genre. There are obvious survival advantages to knowing where to find "good stuff" and what areas to avoid because of danger or of a lack of anything worthwhile.

Establishing a safe, familiar territory and then inviting players to explore its mysterious boundaries is a proven feature of many successful games.

Consider dancing, an activity popular across a wide range of human cultures, going back into prehistory. A skilled dancer develops strength, coordination, and stamina, all basic physical survival advantages. In addition, dancing is a way to demonstrate those advantages to others, and therefore has become an important social skill, a way for people to flirt, show off, and even attract possible mates. For many years, video games seemed almost the antithesis of dance, encouraging players to become solitary couch potatoes. However, the popularity of *Dance Dance Revolution* has shown that all that was necessary to extend dance into the video game realm was a good user interface device and some clever game design. Surely, there are other undiscovered opportunities where an understanding of the basis of one form of entertainment will help extend it into the video game field.

It makes sense that practicing physical activities gives people pleasure, particularly those that involve hand-eye coordination, as one of the key things that makes us human is our upright posture and the associated freedom we have had to develop tools and use our hands. Many important entertainment activities involve tool use, from the aggressive nature of something like hitting a fast-moving ball with a bat, to the more sedate things people do to use or create tools, from knitting to fencing to tying flies for fly-fishing. All of these involve hand-eye coordination. Since the vast majority of video games use hand-controlled inputs and video displays, this is particularly interesting for the games industry. And it's not only the direct actions of practicing survival skills that fascinates people, but even the indirect experiences of observing others in the process, or even reading about them, talking about them, or seeing them in movies or on TV.

Video games are about doing, not telling. Let the players control or initiate actions so they can learn physical skills instead of making them into a passive observer.

Reproduction and all the associated aspects of meeting and attracting a possible mate are also of course critical to evolution and part of our heritage, but until the rise of multiplayer gaming there was little opportunity for that dynamic to be central to video games. Recently, innovations like Internet gaming and games on cell phones have made it possible to integrate games with actual meetings with other people, as friends—or more.

Social Fun

That brings us to the diverse area of social fun. People organize themselves in groups and like to watch other people do things—other qualities we share with our primate relatives. However, we go one better than chimps and gorillas, and spend large amounts of time talking to each other—and about each other. There are many nongame entertainment activities that are based on social fun. These include cooperative gathering-type activities like shopping or trading collectibles (anything from stamps to plush toys to beer cans), talking about where to find the best bargains or the hottest dance club, or social bonding activities like chatting with friends in small groups or at parties. Language has allowed us to add levels of indirection to our participation in survival activities. We don't have to see something firsthand to learn a valuable survival lesson, we can hear about it from someone else who was there. With the development of storytelling, we were able to spread stories many times removed from the original teller, and what we know of early stories and epic poems suggests that matters of survival and finding mates have been of great interest as long as there have been storytellers. Storytelling is our first "virtual reality"—so much a part of all human cultures that it is taken for granted, and yet our unique ability to hear a story and learn important physical, moral, and social lessons has been one of humanity's most valuable mental tools. And it doesn't stop there—with the invention of writing we can experience stories without storytellers, painting pictures in our minds, while movies and related technologies have let us literally see someone else's story. Whether it's an interactive drama delivered over the latest high-tech platform or just one person recounting his day to another, storytelling has become one of people's favorite entertainment activities. A quick test of the basic principles of Natural Funativity shows that these too are methods for learning about how to deal with situations critical to survival, reproduction, and their social equivalents. There's more on this in the upcoming *Story and Character* section.

In games, social fun manifests itself in several ways. Many games have associated stories or story contexts, particularly including first-person action/adventure games and role-playing games, and of course older text and graphic adventure games. More recently the rise of multiplayer and massively multiplayer games has transformed video games from an often solitary pursuit to a true social experience, creating virtual communities, tribes, and even resulting in some marriages. Other games like *The Sims*, *EverQuest*, and *Ultima Online* have proven very popular as inspiration for storytelling about in-game adventures in Internet chat rooms, and it is common for people to play even single-player games together, competing or cooperating. This is an area that is subject to a great deal of expansion in the future through improved technology. Broadband connections are making multiplayer gaming easy and more prevalent, cell phone games allow people to play with others anywhere and any time. Better AI may even expand the social game space with more realistic and involving virtual people.

What is *The Sims* if not an opportunity to observe and interact with the social and basic survival and mating choices familiar to us in the real world? Some of the most popular networked computer games by "number of users" are not the immensely complex massively multiplayer online games, but rather simple video versions of card games like hearts and poker—but with the ability for people to use text chat or even voice chat with their opponents. Many popular board games have similar social components that transcend their core game rules, serving mainly as an opportunity for social interaction.

Just as physical fun is associated with the unusual human qualities of an upright posture and the associated ability to use our hands and tools, social fun is associated with another major human quality, that of language. So, does that cover all types of fun? Some things we do for fun mix physical and social fun. Team sports are an obvious blend. People participate in sports, and turn them social by watching others participate, and by talking about them to their friends. Likewise, people can spend as much time talking about shopping and where to find bargains as actually going out and participating in this modern form of gathering. Dancing, going out to dinner, and dating in general blends physical and social fun (and sometimes that other pillar of evolution, reproduction!). Massively multiplayer online games also tend to be a seamless blend of active physical (simulated) hunting and gathering, and (actual) social interaction and conversation.

Adding secrets, Easter eggs, tradable objects, or characters to games that players can share with friends adds social aspects that can extend gameplay opportunities.

In analyzing video games and fitting them into this theory of fun, one apparently exceptional game is *Tetris*, one of the most successful games of all time, and unusually popular with a wide range of ages and with both men and women. There is not much physical fun in *Tetris*—some hand-eye coordination of course—but the main action doesn't resemble hunting or gathering like so many other very successful games, and neither is there a significant social or story-oriented component. In fact, *Tetris* is about as story free as a game can be. The answer to this riddle can also be found in our evolutionary past, with an organ that shows a major difference between us and the rest of the animal kingdom. Have you figured it out? You're using it right now.

Mental Fun

Our brains are the key. For although we use our intelligence with physical fun and social fun, there is a whole class of entertainment activities, including quite a few video games, which focus primarily on mental fun, improving our mental skills and intelligence just as physical fun improves our physical skills and social fun improves our social skills. This fits in well with the ideas that physical fun is often related to a human's ability to use tools, and that social fun is often related to language. The third, and arguably the most important unique human quality is the relative size of our brains compared to the rest of our bodies. Some animals like blue whales have much larger brains—but proportionate to our body size, our brains are by far the biggest. Of course, our intelligence, hands and tool use, and language all complement each other. Our larger brains and higher intelligence allowed our ancestors to make and use more sophisticated tools, and to carry on more complex and useful conversations. Our tool use and our ability to talk and coordinate activities made our ancestors more efficient hunters and gatherers so they could find enough food to fuel their large brains (which consume as much as 25 percent of the food and oxygen despite taking up 5 percent of the body weight). Moreover, the ability to describe the use of tools and pass on tricks for the construction of those tools benefited both tool use and the intelligence and dexterity necessary to make them.

The essence of intelligence is the ability to perceive and use patterns. *Tetris* is one example of mental fun. So are other puzzle-related games like *Bejewelled*, or nonvideo games, toys, and pastimes like jigsaw puzzles, crossword puzzles, and physical puzzles like *Rubic's Cube*. Listening to music is a form of mental fun, for music is patterned sound, just as poetry and song are patterned words. By the logic of Natural Funativity, playing these mental games should teach us something useful for survival—so of what use to our ancestors was the ability to quickly recognize patterns and act on them? The literal theme of *Tetris* is hard to apply to our hunter/gatherer ancestors and see how it helps build survival skills. However, the abstract quality of simply training people to recognize patterns and manipulate them instantly and accurately is applicable to a huge range of survival skills. Even basic hunting and gathering benefits from being able to, for example, recognize the shape and meaning of tracks in the ground quickly and accurately, or recognize and grab only the ripe berries quickly while avoiding thorns. This also helps explain some *Tetris*-like hobbies that seem to have little survival use like stamp or coin collecting, as well as other pattern-appreciation activities like collecting and viewing art, or listening to music. Aside from the gathering aspects, these hobbies have a lot to do with identifying patterns in common items that make them rare and valuable—and the survival benefit is not in the actual collecting, but in the mental fun of training to recognize those patterns. It's like exercise for the brain.

TIP

Making underlying play patterns in games consistent and predictable makes them easier to learn, but adding new patterns as the game progresses keeps it fresh and fun.

Multipurpose Fun

It is rare for any form of entertainment to be purely in one of these three categories. Usually, they have aspects of all three, sometimes one or two most strongly. Table 2.1.1 shows how four diverse real-world entertainment activities and four video games each have physical, social, and mental learning aspects.

Table 2.1.1   Deconstructing Fun

Fun Activity	Physical Aspects	Social Aspects	Mental Aspects
Hunting	Using senses, weapons, tools, living off the land.	Cooperative hunting, discussing or reading about how to hunt.	Tracking, recognizing patterns in prey behavior.
Football	Gaining strength, practicing throwing, catching, blocking, running.	Team play, working effectively with others, intimidating other teams.	Game strategies, recognizing split-second opportunities, choosing responses.
Shopping	Finding best merchandise at lowest prices, learning to judge quality.	Discussing quality of purchases, trading information on good sales, stores.	Evaluating bargains, monetary or social value of purchases.
Dancing	Gaining agility, stamina, learning popular dance moves.	Meeting others, showing off prowess, style, flirting.	Choreography, memorizing best moves, synchronizing to music.
Playing *Quake*	Mastering mouse and keyboard, practicing moves.	Playing in teams or against other players, discussing game.	Developing tactics, applying strategies, adapting to others.
Playing *Halo*	Mastering controls, buttons, hand-eye coordination.	Following story, playing with or against humans.	Choosing weapons, tactics to use against different enemies.
Playing *The Sims*	Mastering interface, learning most efficient placement of furniture to provide pathways.	Sharing stories about *Sims*, playing with others, reading about tips and hints online.	Choosing most efficient skills, actions to grow family or meet player-set goals.
Playing *Grand Theft Auto*	Learning to move, fight, drive, and navigate through the world.	Dealing with game characters, discussing tactics, tips with friends.	Choosing and planning strategies, selecting routes.

Harnessing Natural Funativity

Does Natural Funativity explain the reason behind all sorts of fun? The jury is still out, but certainly it covers the core aspects that are of interest to game designers. It also explains the appeal of jokes, puns, and slapstick, as well as more serious areas like art, music, and religion—but that's beyond the scope of this chapter. Other game designers are expanding on this theory or proposing their own overlapping ones, such as Raph Koster [Koster05], Chris Crawford, Nicole Lazzaro, and Jesse Schell. It's an exciting area that promises much more in the future.

How does this theory help us make better games? There are several ways:

- By understanding why some activities are fun, it helps us to know what aspects of popular games can be best adapted to make new ones.

- It helps us analyze concepts and proposals, and could save a lot of trouble. For example, this theory helps show why *The Sims* and *Tetris* were successful, both games that almost didn't get published. It can also show why *Majestic* was not, which might have saved a lot of money.
- It suggests new areas for designers to consider for game design, particularly in the social area on new interpersonal technologies like cell phones or instant messaging.
- It gives game designers a mutual language to use to discuss the concept of fun.

The next section, *Classic Game Structure and the Flow Channel*, demonstrates how understanding of Natural Funativity can help designers craft better games by influencing the player's natural rhythms of learning and perception.

Classic Game Structure and the Flow Channel

Natural Funativity shows us how games entertain by teaching us survival skills in the physical, social, and mental arenas. However, the theory by itself doesn't say much about how a game should be structured to maximize its effectiveness (and hopefully consequently its popularity as well!). This next section focuses on what constitutes a classic game; classic in the sense of serving as the established standard and having great significance or worth.

What Are the Essential Elements of a Great Game?

Here is a working definition of a great game (with thanks to the legendary designer Sid Meier for inspiration):

"A great game is a series of interesting and meaningful choices made by the player in pursuit of a clear and compelling goal."

Let's analyze that sentence carefully, starting with the idea of a series of choices leading to a goal. A game must consist of choices or it is not interactive, and a single choice, like the flip of a coin, may be interactive but is too simple to be called a game. A series of scenes without choice would be a movie, not a game. Likewise, a series of choices without a goal would be a toy. Will Wright has designed many games that lack explicit goals, including his best-known hits *Sim City* and *The Sims*. He has in fact referred to them not as games but as software toys. When the subjects of these software toys have been abstract and beyond the everyday knowledge of players, their appeal has been limited, as with ecology in *Sim Life* or cosmology and geology in *Sim Earth*. However, in the cases of *Sim City* and *The Sims* where their respective settings of a city or a household are part of everyone's common experience, players bring their own goals to the process and in doing so create a game out of the toy. It is not a coincidence that these particular titles have been big hits.

TIP

Make sure the player is aware of both short-term and long-term goals at all points of the game.

Next, consider the qualifiers *interesting and meaningful*. It may seem obvious that the choices in a good game need to be interesting, but many games allow the player to make deadly dull choices just because it is easy to program or because the designer lacks imagination. The previous section *Natural Funativity* suggests some ways to select topics or actions that are inherently interesting. The psychologist Csikszentmihalyi, who figures prominently later in this chapter, defines an experience as meaningful "when it is related positively to a person's goals" [Csikszentmihalyi90]. If a player believes that to reach a goal, one alternative is better than another, it is a meaningful choice.

On the other hand, if the player can choose from among three weapons but they all work equally well to accomplish his goal, the choice is functionally meaningless. It is also meaningless if there is an opportunity to insult, flatter, or ignore a game character, but the response from the character is identical in each case. However, "meaningful" in this definition requires only that the player perceives the choices subjectively as meaningful. If a gnarled tree branch and a polished mahogany club are functionally identical in a game, with the same availability, weight, and combat results, but a player mistakenly thinks the club is more effective, or has a goal of carrying only the most aesthetically pleasing weapons, that may be a meaningful choice *to that player*. The meaning is in the mind of the player, and it is the game designer's job to provide cues to put it there. Conversely, if two different objects in a world have different functions but the player does not notice the difference, the choice between them is not meaningful for that player.

Finally there is the point of having *clear and compelling* goals. Having clear goals for the player to pursue is greatly preferable to indistinct or confusing ones. Players who have no idea what to do next in a game can quickly become bored or frustrated. Making sure those goals are compelling and not arbitrary or disagreeable is also a very useful principle that somehow gets left by the wayside in poor games. Natural Funativity is a good tool for picking goals that appeal to players and compel them forward.

Test your game regularly with people who have never seen it before. Periodically ask them what they think they are supposed to accomplish next, and why it is important. That will tell you if your goals are clear and compelling.

Game Structure Basics

Let's delve deeper into the concept of a game being a series of choices. There are quite a few possible ways to structure that series, but after many years of experimentation and trial and error, only a few variations of one basic structure have proven to be most effective and popular. Many different designers have converged on a few basic structures that are present in the skeletons of most successful games.

It's helpful to look at game structures visually. The following figures use circles to show possible actions or decisions the player may take.

Theoretically, the simplest structure for a game would involve no choice at all, as shown in Figure 2.1.1.

FIGURE 2.1.1 *No choice.*

In this case, each player action results in a single possibility, with no choice involved. Many first-time designers who come from linear fields, like novelists or screenwriters, have made the mistake of proposing games like this. Let's pick on a hypothetical designer named Phil. A narrative section of Phil's game design document description might go something like this:

The player is confronted by two demons. He attacks the left demon with his sword, cutting him on the leg and sending him sprawling to the ground. Then he whirls to the right and beheads the second demon. But the first demon is just close enough to swipe at the player with a claw, so the player jumps just in time and stabs downward to impale his attacker.

Sounds exciting, just like a movie! However, a designer always has to ask, "what if?" In this case, what if the player goes after the demon on the right first, or attacks the first demon on the left but misses, or runs away instead of fighting at all?

Our friend Phil considers this. Perhaps his suggestion is that no matter what the player tries to do, the demon on the left will jump in front of him and confront him first, and the player will be forced to swing his sword. If he aims high, the demon will jump, ensuring that his leg is always hit. The game structure would look like Figure 2.1.2.

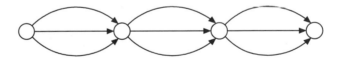

FIGURE 2.1.2 *Meaningless choices.*

Although the player may seem to have choices, they are actually meaningless. Some early experiments in interactive movies used this format—no matter what the viewers chose, the storyline folded back to the same place. They were not successful.

Another common mistake is the opposite approach going from no choice to an infinite number of choices, which can look like Figure 2.1.3.

Here, each choice the player makes leads to new ones. At first, this sounds pretty good. After all, life is full of similar infinite variety. However, the problems pop up when we study Phil's game design document that uses this structure:

The player is confronted by two demons. She can flee or attack, and if she attacks, she can choose either demon, and attack low or high, and if attacking low, strike the leg or the foot, and if the leg, aim at the thigh or shin, striking with the flat of the sword, or throwing it point first, or hilt first, or tossing it end over end, or melt it down to use the metal to make a plowshare instead...

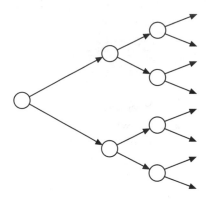

FIGURE 2.1.3   *Infinite choices.*

The problem of course is that the game must have code and artwork to support each variation that the player can choose, and the interface must also be capable of incorporating an infinite variety of moves. This is just not possible, and in fact, all games are severely restricted in the range of things the player can do compared to real life. The artistry in game design consists of structuring the restrictions so that they seem natural and even transparent to the player. How can such restriction be accomplished? One way was often used in early adventure games and "choose your own adventure" books (see Figure 2.1.4).

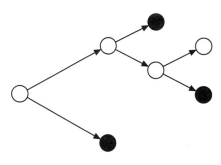

FIGURE 2.1.4   *Choose wisely.*

The solid circles in Figure 2.1.4 indicate choices that kill the player off, requiring her to start again. Phil's game design document says:

The player is confronted by two demons. She can flee or attack, but if she flees, she is killed immediately. She can attack either demon, but if she starts with the one on the right, the one on the left will kill her immediately. If she attacks the one on the left and aims high, it will duck below her blade and kill her immediately. If she aims low...

It's easy to see that this quickly becomes a frustrating version of the Figure 2.1.1 "no choice" option. Yet it's not hopeless; it does do the job of restricting the player's choices to a subset that can actually be developed, and it's very easy to implement so that developers can afford to put more choices into the game. One of its biggest drawbacks is that it rubs the player's nose in the fact that this is just a game. If you've designed an elaborate world intended to capture the player's imagination, it erodes the illusion of reality by constantly saying, "You're dead, but since this is just a game, you can try again." Over the years, players have become accustomed to this, yet all but the most hard-core game players resent having to start over again and again. The arcade game *Dragon's Lair* was infamous for using this structure. The novelty of this first videodisc-based game with full-screen video cartoons brought players to the arcades, only to send them away again in frustration over the task of memorizing an often arbitrary series of joystick moves and button presses.

Classic Game Structure

So, what is the ideal structure? After much experimentation, designers around the world have all converged on some similar configurations. At the heart of most games is a structure where the player starts with just a few choices that in turn lead to more. Then the inherent rules of the design and the physical setting cause the choices to gradually narrow back down again to a few, and often down to a single choice or action the player must accomplish. This core structure can be called a *convexity* because of its outwardly curving shape, as shown in Figure 2.1.5.

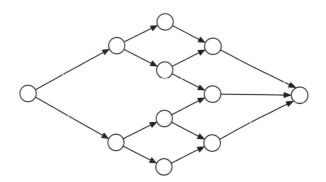

FIGURE 2.1.5 *A single convexity.*

The best way to limit player choices is to design the world or environment so that the limitations seem natural, perhaps even inevitable. For example, one convexity of choices would be made in the exploration of a small island. The player starts at one end, gradually moves to the middle as more places to explore become visible, and at some point most of the island has been explored, leaving only a few places to look, and finally only one. In this case, the physical layout of the island roughly matches the shape of Figure 2.1.5, but that's not necessary to form a convexity. The domain of the choices can be shapeless, or even abstract. The build trees in real-time strategy games or the skill trees in role-playing games are often shaped as convexities, with one or two initial choices growing to several or many, but eventually all the new possibilities are exhausted and the choices shrink back to one. The key thing is to be creative enough to come up with game rules or settings that make the player's limitations seem logical, or better yet, seem inevitable or even imperceptible. Other examples of limited settings might be a limited number of enemies to fight in a building, or a quest to collect several key items and bring them back to a character.

Change the story, setting, or interface if necessary to make limitations invisible.

Many classic games like checkers, chess, and backgammon have the structure of a single large convexity, with a limited number of movies at first opening to many and finally converging back down toward the end of the game. Often, these games are played repeatedly, so one play session may include a series of games linked together. Successive games or challenges require the same basic set of skills, but offer variations on the central theme of the game to allow the players to gradually increase their skill level as they play.

Video games often use that structure too, calling the individual games "levels," "episodes," "acts," or "worlds," whatever is appropriate for the game setting. Figure 2.1.6 is a diagram of such a series, with the arrows removed to keep the size manageable, but the choices as in Figure 2.1.5 are still implied.

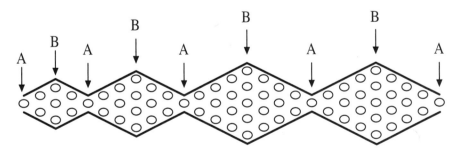

FIGURE 2.1.6   *A series of convexities.*

This structure, consisting of narrow points of a single decision (A) alternating with wide points with many decisions (B) is at the core of nearly all successful games. And each of the circles shown in Figure 2.1.6 can be single action or decision points but are more likely to be entire convexities of such choices, resembling Figure 2.1.5.

For instance a large-scale decision in a level of a game like *Age of Empires* may be "take a defensive stance" or "attack aggressively." The decision "take a defensive stance" is not a single action, but a convexity of smaller actions, including "create a small squad to defend the left flank," which in turn may consist of convexities like "gather enough resources to build an archer unit" and so on. Big, complex games often have this shape (mathematically known as *fractals*) where the large-scale structure is repeated on progressively smaller scales as well. In addition, often the first levels, missions, or regions of a game are smaller than later ones to give the player a simpler task to accomplish and get used to the game. Similarly, sometimes the final levels are small as well to speed up the pace of the game near the end so the player does not bog down in an ever-lengthening series of challenges.

As an example, consider the game *Diablo II*. On the largest scale, it is organized into four acts, much like Figure 2.1.6. Each act is set in a new part of the world, and the player can choose from among a handful of regions to explore in each act. A circle on Figure 2.1.6 might represent the player's choice to enter a region in the game. However, that region is a convexity too, with multiple areas to explore in turn. Moreover, each of those areas has multiple enemies. Even the decision to attack a single enemy can result in a convexity of choices for the player, ending in defeat of one of the combatants. *Diablo II* also layers in other kinds of convexities of choices, in the form of skills a character can use, quests the character can undertake in each act, and so on. These convexities overlap, so that when the player is reaching a narrow point (A) in enemies (e.g., fighting Andariel, a boss monster who must be defeated to end the first act), the character may be at a widening point (B) in the skill tree, having just reached experience level 18 where a set of new skills can now be selected when investing experience points. Even that apparent single choice of fighting the boss monster is not a true bottleneck, as the player can always choose to go back to an earlier level and refight the same monsters as before—and this is a meaningful choice because the player's character will grow stronger and the player will gain skill, both of which may make the defeat of Andariel easier.

> *Give players alternatives to tough challenges that let them improve their skills or gather new resources to avoid frustrating bottlenecks.*

TIP

Sid Meier's *Civilization* series of games also use the idea of overlapping convexities on many levels. It is typical in those games to be finishing up one task, like completing a wonder of the world, in the middle of a second task like assembling an army to invade a neighboring company, and just beginning a third task, researching the discovery of gunpowder. Each of these tasks conveys clear advantages to the player as well. This type of structure ensures that the player always has a compelling short-term goal as a reason to keep playing, and plenty of meaningful choices to make at all times.

This same classic structure of overlapping series of convexities is present in just about every popular video game. It is critical to both PC and console games, including *Halo*, *Fable*, *Super Mario 64*, and the *Zelda* games (indeed, almost all of Shigeru

Miyamoto's wildly popular Nintendo games use this structure or variations). Many other designers have endorsed this structure. Bob Bates, game designer and former head of Legend Entertainment compares this to a series of sideways hourglasses [Bates01].

Why Is the Classic Structure So Effective?

There are several practical reasons why this structure works well. It gives the player choice, but limits the choice so that the developer does not have an infinitely expanding job. It provides places where things can happen in any order (the B points) so the player has freedom to choose, as well as places where things happen strictly sequentially (the A points) where the designer can add time-critical narrative or introduce new technologies, tools, or weapons in a specific order. This is particularly useful for story-based games, where major plot points almost always occur at the A points.

Some designs require the player to eventually select most or all of the choices in a wide part of a convexity before moving on to the next section, while others require completion of only a small subset. A player may need to defeat a tough enemy at the end of a level at a narrow A point, but is free to collect as many resources as she wishes in the wide B section to do it. In general, the larger the budget of the game, the more latitude the designer has to relax the requirement of seeing every part of the level before moving on. A big-budget game in *The Sims* or *Grand Theft Auto* franchises can spend enough overall to ensure that a player who only plays a subset of characters or completes a fraction of the missions can still have a satisfactory experience. That in turn means the game can include a wider range of such characters and missions to appeal to various types of players instead of having to shoot for the lowest common denominator.

TIP

The smaller your budget, the more critical it is for you to make sure the player sees and uses everything you can afford to put into the game.

A series of convexities is also a great way to allow for a gradual increase in difficulty, with each successive level or area having slightly tougher challenges for the player to master—and as we saw in the "Natural Funativity" section, mastering these new challenges is at the heart of what makes games fun.

That in turn brings up an interesting psychological reason why this structure is so universal. Since Natural Funativity shows us that we play to master new skills and knowledge, it follows that a game must be accessible to new players, and then must provide continuing fresh challenges for players to learn. This is the idea behind the old truisms, "Easy to learn, difficult to master," and the directive of Trip Hawkins, founder of Electronic Arts, to make games simple, hot, and deep.

Flow

A more specific analysis of the enjoyment we get from mastering skills in games can be found in the life work of the psychologist and University of Chicago professor

Mihaly Csikszentmihalyi, particularly in his book *Flow, The Psychology of Optimal Experience*. He uses the term *flow* to refer to a kind of optimal experience, which includes a sense of exhilaration along with a deep sense of enjoyment [Csikszentmihalyi90]. This is a state familiar to most avid game players, and is something that designers strive to provide to players. Further, he claims that the best moments occur when the body or mind is willingly stretched to accomplish a difficult and worthwhile task. This is an accurate description of what goes on in any popular game, and is certainly a major source of that popularity.

Csikszentmihalyi provides a chart to describe the transformation in consciousness of a person in a flow state, choosing the example of someone learning to play the game tennis. He shows that a player begins with a low set of skills and seeks an appropriately low level of challenge, but as time progresses and his skills improve, he is driven to seek progressively higher levels of challenge. If the challenge becomes too difficult too quickly, the player experiences anxiety—although "frustration" is a more typical and accurate term for computer games. If the challenge does not increase over time, boredom can set in. He calls the path between these extremes "The Flow Channel," as demonstrated in Figure 2.1.7.

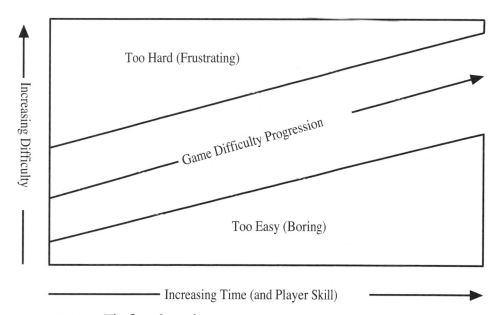

FIGURE 2.1.7   *The flow channel.*

A good game is carefully designed to have its difficulty increase over time so that as the player gains skill, he or she does not drift into boredom or frustration. A game that starts and ends with the same degree of difficulty quickly becomes boring and unappealing, as with tic-tac-toe. However, while it is better to have a straight-line increase in difficulty over time than no increase at all, it is better still to impose some variety on the slope of the line so there are periods of fast difficulty increase alternating with slower increase, or even a slight decrease. This gives players a chance to catch their breath between tougher challenges, and in fact, learning improves with the rhythm of challenging the players and providing immediate feedback on the results of their efforts [Ratey01].

Csikszentmihalyi also reinforces the basic assumptions of Natural Funativity, noting that the flow state can help develop physical and sensory skills, relationship skills, and symbolic skills (e.g., poetry and mathematics) [Csikszentmihalyi90], echoing the three basic areas that entertainment addresses of physical, social, and mental fun.

Many great games also make sure to introduce skills one or two at a time; for example, letting the players master a long jump before requiring them to make three long jumps in quick succession to get across a crumbling bridge. Professor James Paul Gee calls this a "cycle of expertise," one of the many ways games encourage learning [Gee03].

This staggered increase in difficulty could look like Figure 2.1.8.

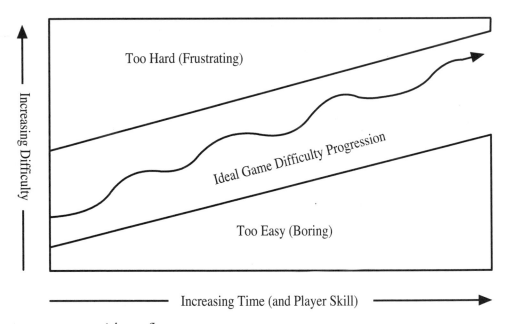

FIGURE 2.1.8   *A better flow.*

By periodically including particularly tough sections, a game adds excitement and challenge, increasing the player's exhilaration when the challenge is overcome. In addition, by alternating those sharp increases with flatter, easier, or quieter sections, it gives the player a chance to learn new skills or review older ones without the potentially frustrating threat of imminent failure.

Introduce new skills to master one at a time, and give players a chance to enjoy their sense of mastery (if they so choose) before challenging them with a tough obstacle or opponent and then moving on to the next skill and challenge.

When we compare Figure 2.1.6's series of convexities with this curving difficulty progression, we can see another reason why the classic structure works so well, as shown in Figure 2.1.9.

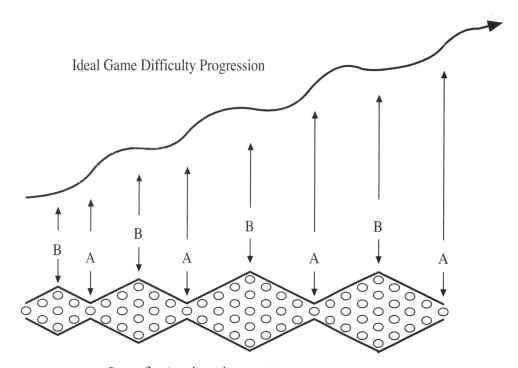

FIGURE 2.1.9 *Better flowing through convexities.*

The narrow decision points (A) in the convexities where players' choices are limited can be set to correspond to the difficult parts of the game. Designers have come up with many game mechanisms to make this happen, tough boss monsters or climactic battles or quest resolutions being common ones for many games. The wider points (B) where there are many alternatives give the player more discretion, and typically difficulty increases more slowly, or even decreases a bit to provide a break for the player and let him or her rehearse new skills. There are proven game mechanisms for that too, like bonus levels, unlocking new treasure-rich areas, or even simply providing more resources to gather or a succession of easy enemies to overcome.

This variable difficulty curve can arise interactively simply because of the structure of the convexities. Assume a stereotypical mission where a player is sent off into a city to find the five crystal shards, so that they can be brought together to form the legendary gem of power. The five shards can be found in any order, and are defended by guardians with different qualities that are, as far as the designer can manage, roughly equally easy to find and defeat. In fact, this will create a convexity where the player gradually explores the city and finds the locations of the shards (widening out in choices), and then one by one defeats the guardians until only one is left (narrowing down). There is tremendous variation between players, and each person will have his or her own particular strengths and weaknesses that will show up in the way he or she approaches challenges in games. The player will naturally find some guardians easier to locate and some easier to defeat, so as the choices widen, the game may feel subjectively easier, but the last to be defeated will, through human nature, quite likely be the hardest *in the subjective opinion of the player*. This can create a self-adjusting game that tunes itself to adapt to the skills of the player. The player gains experience and perhaps weapons or information defeating the first guardians, and uses those to help defeat the final guardian, left for last at the choice of the player. Many game designers don't leave this to chance and make sure that the ends of levels or regions have the toughest bosses or biggest battles, and that the explicit placement of challenges allows players to alternate between tough challenges and easier sections of consolidation. In either case, this structure manages to match the natural human rhythms and encourage the flow state by matching increasing challenge to increasing skills.

Always include variations in type and difficulty of challenges and actions the player must accomplish to account for the range of players' skills and abilities to make your games accessible and popular to a wide audience.

This important element of classic game structure—intense pieces alternating with quieter sections, organized sequentially into a series of variations on a theme—applies to many other forms of human endeavor, notably popular songs, classical symphonies, even theater, novels, and films, which are relevant to our next section.

Story and Character

If we go back to the definition of a great game at the start of the last section, some of the key points are that the choices in the game must be interesting, and that the eventual goal be compelling to the player. *Interesting* and *compelling* are subjective, emotional terms. Natural Funativity gives us some ideas about the kind of conflicts, themes, and challenges that players find interesting and compelling, but the question remains, how can a game designer incorporate those themes in a game? Often the answer lies in story and character.

To do sufficient justice to the study of storytelling requires a lot more than a few pages of text. Unlike video games, storytelling has been a part of our culture for tens of thousands of years, and even the specific use of storytelling for entertainment can be traced back at least 2500 years to the ancient Greeks and beyond. Therefore, instead of trying to provide a complete examination of the broad nature of story-telling, this section covers only some of the most essential things a game designer should know about story and character.

Don't Try This at Home!

Storytelling is difficult, and the art of writing takes years to perfect. Game developers often forget that, sometimes with disastrous results. Game designers are particularly prone to fall in love with their own prose and to try to turn games into their chance to prove themselves as a great novelist or screenwriter. However, games are not books or movies. If your game requires writing, work with a professional writer who has already invested time learning the craft, preferably someone who has experience with the par-ticular challenges of writing for the interactive medium. And don't bring the writer in to the process late in the course of development. The very best examples of games with strong storytelling elements invariably have incorporated the expertise of profes-sional storytellers right from the early stages of design, when it is still possible to let the gameplay and story shape each other. *Halo* does a nice job of integrating the sto-ryline into the need to teach the player how to control his character in the first act of the game. The designers made that character a soldier freshly unfrozen from sus-pended animation and suggested that he might have some difficulty remembering things upon being thawed.

TIP

Designers should work with experienced writers (and vice versa) to take advantage of the best integration of gameplay and story.

Do, Don't Show

Beginning writing classes always include the admonishment to "Show, don't tell." Inexperienced writers have a tendency to write long sections telling the readers what they should know; for example, saying, "Largo LaGrande was an evil man, the type who would trip a blind man and laugh or steal candy from a baby." It's better to show the action and let the readers form their own conclusions, letting them read, "LaGrande watched the blind beggar hobble slowly down the sidewalk, and stuck out his foot at just the right instant to send the graybeard sprawling on the pavement. LaGrande chuckled and grabbed a lollipop from a little boy who had stopped to gape in horror."

However, games are not stories, and with games the adage is "Do, don't show." It's much better to accomplish your storytelling by letting the player experience the events interactively. In fact, Largo LaGrande is a character from Ron Gilbert's game *Monkey Island 2: LeChuck's Revenge*. LaGrande is a henchman of the chief villain of the game, and Gilbert wanted the player to actively resent him. He arranged for the player to begin the game stranded on an island, having to strive to collect the elements necessary to get a boat to escape (the first convexity). Then, LaGrande abruptly takes the boat away from the player, through his action directly imperiling the player's hard-won gains. In the parlance of Hollywood, "this time it's personal!" *Starcraft* also does a great job of integrating storytelling into gameplay, and even uses a similar mechanism, having a General in the game betray not only the character the player controls but to directly affect the player by leaving him to fend for himself at a critical early point in the game.

Whenever possible, reveal character and advance the storyline through gameplay, not exposition.

It's All about Interactivity

The previous example illustrates the point that games are about choices and interactivity. In a movie or book, the interesting choices are the ones that the protagonist makes, unaffected by anything the moviegoer or reader does. However, in a game, the player becomes the protagonist, and so the interesting choices are the ones given to the player. It's critical for a designer to remember to give the player the chance to make those interesting choices, and not make them for him. Storytelling and character can add an emotional context to those choices, and if done well, that context can greatly enhance or even provide essential meaning to them, but ultimately it's all about the gameplay and choices that the player makes. Over the years, the trend has been to incorporate storytelling more and more into the gameplay and the choices the player can make, as in the *Monkey Island* example. Long cinematic scenes that take control away from the player have been giving way to shorter in-game scenes. There is still a place for these noninteractive scenes (in fact, Gilbert himself coined the term "cut-scenes" to refer to these sequences in his first game, *Maniac Mansion*), but they are like strong spices in cooking—best used sparingly lest they overwhelm the final result. Hal Barwood, a game designer who can claim both multiple game design and screenwriting credits, has a useful rule of thumb about the length of noninteractive cinematic scenes in games. His advice is to cut, edit, and cut some more until the writing is just as brief and concise as possible—and at that point, the scene is probably about twice as long as it should be. Often, it can be helpful to have someone else do the final edit on a scene to condense it even further, or better yet, replace it with an interactive equivalent. It has been shown that designers can greatly increase player's emotional involvement in a scene by breaking up a long, noninteractive scene into a dialog where the player triggers half of the responses, *even when the player has just a single option to choose*. This apparent contradiction of the desirability of providing meaningful choices to the player shows how destructive to the players' attention a noninteractive scene can be.

Let the player play. Delete nonessential cut-scenes, and minimize those that cannot be deleted.

The Relevance of Characters

Another element from the realm of storytelling that has bearing on games is the use of characters and characterization. Game designers make a distinction between the *player character* (PC), a character the player controls, and the *nonplayer characters* (NPCs) that are controlled by the computer. Both types of characters serve in a game to provide emotional context to the choices the player makes [Ratey01]. NPCs are the antagonists, allies, and inhabitants of the setting of the game, and can increase the player's enjoyment by making the game world feel more real and consequential. The PC is the player's alter ego, and often represents an idealized or exaggerated hero to provide an attractive avatar to control, or to provide the player with a chance to experience a virtual role in life that is impossible or too dangerous or difficult to pursue in real life. Often, game characters are bold stereotypes, taking the shortcut of building on common exaggerated preconceptions to convey character with as little exposition as possible. One reason why games based on movie licenses have been so popular is that the exposition and character development has already happened in the players' minds when they watch the movie, letting them dive right into choices in the game while benefiting from their emotional associations with the established character.

Make your PCs and NPCs memorable, and give them colorful and fun qualities.

Gameplay Trumps Story

To summarize these points, when a designer has to choose between serving the choices or gameplay a player can make, or the needs and requirements of a story, it's important to let the gameplay win. Often, the best solution is to find some other way to structure the game so that the story elements complement and reinforce the choices the player can make, instead of fighting against them. Story is often more malleable than gameplay, too, and from a practical standpoint it can be much cheaper to modify story elements to fit gameplay or technical requirements. For example, it is often better to restrict the size of the game world by changing the story setting than to try to create the technology to show an immense world, or to use most of the available computer memory sustaining that large world dictated by the story requirements alone.

If faced with a conflict between a design decision that will favor gameplay or story, first look for a compromise that favors both, and failing that, favor gameplay.

Fundamental Incompatibility

In conclusion, it is apparent that some elements of storytelling and gameplay are fundamentally incompatible. The main function of storytelling in all its forms is to let us know of the events that happened to someone else, the choices they made, and the consequences of those choices. A movie character who stops and turns to the audience to ask, "What would you do next?" is shattering not only the audience's absorption in the story, but their very enjoyment of the process. Conversely, a game is about the choices the player makes firsthand. A game that abruptly wrests control away from the player to show the character the player has been controlling suddenly acting autonomously can be just as jarring to the player's enjoyment of the game.

When making the transition between interactive and narrative modes, be sure to warn the player with visual and auditory cues, and try to minimize or eliminate those transitions.

Summary

Game design is still a blend of science and art, of accepted convention and mystery. It's a bit like the art of seafaring navigation a few hundred years ago. Back then, there was knowledge of how to steer by the stars, but a lack of reliable clocks and the vagaries of storms and tides made each voyage uncertain. Like those early navigators, game designers today find their way through the shoals and hazards by following in the path of earlier successful explorers, and gradually establish a map of the world that shows useful destinations. Gradual improvements in technology and craft make the process safer and more reliable, and better understanding of the underlying processes helps as well.

With an understanding of the principles behind fun, the most successful structures for games and some of the psychological reasons for their success, and a careful application of story and character, game design may eventually become as predictable as modern navigation. However, for now there are still some uncertainties, and happily also some wonderful discoveries awaiting us. With the lore and tips in this chapter and a little luck, aspiring game designers may be able to chart the course to those new lands and avoid the reefs and rocks along the way.

Exercises

1. Pick a popular video game (not shown in Table 2.1.1) and list five various actions it makes available to the player, breaking them down into areas of physical, social, and mental fun (or combinations of two or all three).
2. Choose an activity or hobby that people do for fun that is rare or nonexistent in current video games. Write a two- or three-paragraph description of a new game that uses that activity as a basis. Be sure to describe the choices

the player makes, and what the player actually does to progress through the game.

3. Suggest three ways that good-quality speech-recognition software coupled with sophisticated artificial intelligence might aid in creating a new game based on principles of social fun.

4. Many sequels improve on the original titles by adding more choices for the players, and often those new choices form convexities where the original game had a straight line of progression with no choice. Take an existing game that is linear in some aspect of its design and describe how that aspect could be made into a convexity by adding choices.

5. Identify a popular video game that introduces a new skill for the player to master at a slow-paced point of the game and then requires mastery of the skill at a climactic moment later in the game.

6. Take a common, popular card game like solitaire, blackjack, bridge, or something else, and write a few paragraphs of description to give it a story context with the objective of providing an emotional significance the game currently lacks.

7. Pick one of your favorite characters from a book or movie who has not yet been featured in a video game, and list 10 interesting choices or actions that would be available to a player controlling that character.

References

[Bates01] Bates, Bob, *Game Design: The Art and Business of Creating Games*, Prima Press, 2001: Chapter 3.

[Csikszentmihalyi90] Csikszentmihalyi, Mihaly, *Flow, The Psychology of Optimal Experience*, Harper Perennial, 1990: pp. 3, 74, 244.

[Dunbar96] Dunbar, Robin, *Grooming, Gossip, and the Evolution of Language*, Faber and Faber Ltd, 1996: pp. 36–37.

[Gee03] Gee, James Paul, *What Video Games Have to Teach Us About Learning and Literacy*, Palgrave Macmillan, 2003.

[Koster05] Koster, Raph, *A Theory of Fun*, Paraglyph Press, 2004.

[Leakey94] Leakey, Richard, *The Origin of Humankind* Science Masters, 1994: p. 60.

[Pinker97] Pinker, Steven, *How the Mind Works*, W.W. Norton & Co. 1997: p. 207.

[Ratey01] Ratey, Dr. John J., *A User's Guide to the Brain*, Pantheon Books, 2001: pp. 179, 186.

[Wills93] Wills, Christopher, *The Runaway Brain: The Evolution of Human Uniqueness,* Basic Books 1993: p. 249.

2.2 Game Design

Overview

Although the practice of designing games has existed for centuries, recognition as a field to be studied has been late in coming. The fashioning of games seems to have traditionally been the work of communities and societies, evolving as cultural products over decades and centuries. These cultural products of antiquity may be conveniently referred to as "folk" games [Costikyan04], and would include most of the classic games we grew up with, such as chess, checkers, Parcheesi, snakes and ladders, and the like.

It is almost certain that the ability for people to sustain themselves purely by means of the design and construction of games is a historically recent development. There is little in the way of practical history or treatment of game design method until we come to the latter half of the twentieth century.

In this chapter, you will study an introduction to computer game design. More precisely, you will be introduced to a simplified view of some practices that will prepare you for future study in the field. Upon completing this chapter, you should be able to communicate effectively with a wide audience of designers, developers, and enthusiasts and be able to understand a technical approach to solving game design problems.

First, you will be introduced to a superficial caution on the subject of forms and models, which will give way to brief reviews of a term or two. Next, we will describe games in general, as artifacts of human design constructed for the purpose of arousing emotions via structured play. A feature-based approach will be suggested, along with three domains into which features (or at least their aspects) can be roughly categorized. In other words, we will get a handle on a technical view of games. Later, our attention turns to the constraints that define typical problems facing game designers; the workaday world of game design, execution, and testing. After surveying a few models of creativity and decision-making and suggesting methods for managing and communicating vision, we will wind things up with a review of some work in psychology relevant to the work of game designers.

There is no one "right" way to design games, but there are many successful approaches. However, do not assume that this brief chapter will be able to teach you any of them. Instead, it will provide context and direction for your future studies. If you are left excited and a bit more conversant, we could ask for no more.

The Language of Games

The professional game development industry is still quite young, and its standards in theory, practice, and terminology are still being formed. As odd as it may first seem, debates even remain over the definition of *game*. However, for the most part, differences between one organization's culture and another's are related to use of terminology and workflow. In this chapter, care will be taken to define terms where they may be new to the reader, as well as when differences in use exist.

The beginning:

Play: An activity engaged for the purpose of eliciting emotions.
Game: An object of rule-bound play.

The reason why we and other animals play is not fully understood, although there are plenty of theories and potential answers. In fact, one of the only safe assumptions may be that animals, like people, are motivated to play because it's found to be pleasurable [Grier92]. Indeed, studies have begun suggesting similarities in brain activity that may ultimately lead to understanding the impulses in animal and human play [Siviy98]. They, just like us, may play because it's "fun."

Games, one would assume, seem easier to define. On the contrary, there are probably more diverse opinions on what constitutes a game than on the nature of play. In this chapter, we prefer to treat both terms lightly.

The previous definitions are easy to modify, fitting the culture of any organization. For example, if it is believed that all proper games must include conflict, amend the definition here to accommodate. Likewise, add "win" or "challenge" or whatever your needs demand. By being reductive to start, we stay focused on more rudimentary matters.

After offering two simple definitions for game and play, we come to the third term we will oversimplify into something easy to work with:

Aesthetics: The emotional responses evoked during play [LeBlanc04].

Classical aesthetics is a philosophical discipline that deals with understanding beauty and the ways in which objects appeal to and affect our senses. It is a deep subject worthy of serious study and well outside the scope of this chapter.

Our use of aesthetics, inspired by designer/programmer Marc LeBlanc, simply correlates the experiences of playing with the emotional responses generated as a result. As we did with play and game before it, we leave our term general and easy to work with.

The scope of aesthetics can vary at all levels. At the component level, we can describe *tension, surprise, fear, wonder*, and others that work together to form larger aesthetics such as *adventure, challenge*, and *fantasy*. Eventually, we reach the scope of the whole, the experience of a game in its entirety.

Aesthetics needn't be restricted to those feelings we would at first think desirable. Just as the experience of a tragic drama can be as moving and satisfying as a light comedy, we cannot so simply claim they are "fun." It is easy to use common sense to understand the appeal of comedy: laughing feels good. Tragedy, on the other hand, is less explainable this way; sadness and loss hardly seem appropriate to fun. However, when the interests of the audience are safe—that is, that the experiences of the entertainment will not have lasting or *real* effects—then people freely experience all sorts of feeling, many of which are no more desirable than a stubbed toe. However, even fear and anger can be part of satisfying experiences.

That play occurs within a context of safety is one recurrent theme in the study of games. Players know that the experiences they will have are free from potential harm [Crawford03]. This environment is frequently referred to as a *frame* and indicates to players that the actions taken within it are not part of "real life" [Salen04]. In this setting, players allow themselves to experience emotions that might otherwise not be considered pleasurable, and it resembles the contexts of other arts. However, humans aren't the only species to establish a safe context for play; many others (mammals and nonmammals alike) are known to signal each other their intent to engage and remain in play [Beckoff01].

Feelings within the context of the game's frame are considered safe—they can be experienced without real repercussions. However, when a player experiences a feeling such as frustration, he is being disengaged from the safety of the frame; it affects the player in the real world.

So, while a frequent assumption made while talking about games is that they are "fun," nailing this down has proven very tricky. Our goal, as designers, is to make games that people will like to play, which we do by creating opportunity for experiences. These can stimulate a variety of emotions (including those that arise during problem solving) and do not have to be restricted to those ordinarily recognized as typical of games.

Approaching Game Design

Computer game design and creation is an art form that, like most others, requires good technical discipline to be applied successfully and consistently. Most of the early claims that neither the "art" nor "science" of design could be taught or instructed have been slowly set aside in favor of more reasonable attitudes. (That it may not be taught to you *here* is the fault of the author.) Contrary to these early views, game designers do not require special inborn sensitivities that can only be nurtured and refined through years of toil and experience. There is nothing "magic" about the practice of game design, just as there is nothing mystical about playing and composing fine music. Desire and dedication, practice, and the willingness to work methodically are all that are truly required.

Technical skills are essential, and it is easy to draw analogies to other arts such as music, wherein the "art" is an application of these skills to emotionally affect ("move") the audience. If works of art are seen in such terms, then it's easy to argue that the designs of games are artistic expressions in the form of dynamic models.

Models, Forms, and Paradigms

Science is neat but tricky stuff. A common sense view typically assumes that the goal of science is to pursue knowledge or truth through the careful and objective use of experimental observation [Chalmers94]. This "naïve inductivist" approach assumes that observations are conducted independently from theoretical assumption. Theories then arise from considering the experimental results and integrating new findings into the context of previous knowledge. In other words, knowledge is seen as something based on objective evidence, in turn based on other prior knowledge that we might refer to as "facts." Presumably, the foundation of these facts runs deep, for each is supported by yet more and more layers of fact. While popular, this view doesn't fill well to the history of scientific development. It would be better (although by no means wholly "true" either) to view given periods of scientific thought and approach as describing and testing formal models within paradigms.

A *model* is a representation of something else [Chartrand77]. As you may imagine, models are fundamental to our daily lives. Each day, each of us looks to countless models for guidance and understanding in our relationships to and with the world around us.

Suppose that a new acquaintance invites you to dinner. Driving to his address, you use a road map that models the geographic area and its roads. You consult the back of an envelope where you have written a model of your route—the directions. Along the way, the velocity of your car is modeled on a speedometer, while the fuel gauge models the level of gasoline in the tank. To determine if you should stop to fill up, you invent a mental model of the car's fuel economy; you factor the reported level of fuel and distance of the trip that remain. At dinner, your host offers a choice of several frozen dinner packages, each showing a picture that models the food inside. You can probably see where this is going.

A *mental model* (first suggested in 1943 by Kenneth Craik) is a psychological representation, a "small-scale" conceptual model, of something [Johnson99]. People construct these models after experience, training, and instruction and use them to represent the structure of situations, reason, and explain the world they live in [Norman88]. Will Wright has described games as running on a "coprocessor system" where player's mental models are half of the experience. [Wright03]

Abstract models are another type of conceptual model useful for investigating specific questions about a subject. They are idealized, where the process of abstraction has been taken to the extreme, and, because of this may even include some assumptions known to be false. These inaccuracies are allowed, provided the important questions can be investigated more clearly as a result.

For example, linguist Noam Chomsky created an abstract model, the ideal speaker-hearer, to investigate the way language communicates meaning. To avoid the distraction of issues concerning a given person's ability to use his language (competence), Chomsky proposed an imaginary situation wherein both participants in a conversation could communicate between one another perfectly (i.e., every utterance from one person would be perfectly understood by the other).

For example, we can use an abstract model to help simplify our thinking about basic topics. Figure 2.2.1 shows a simple game. The game equipment is a board (1 × 2) and a *piece* (or *token*) that will be used for indicating.

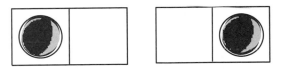

FIGURE 2.2.1 *Two views of an abstract model.*

We begin with a single rule:

- *The piece is moved to the open square.*

Remember that we are working in the abstract and can allow assumptions that would be unacceptable under ordinary circumstances: Figure 2.2.1 won't be any "good" or "fun"; it will barely be a game at all, but will be "game enough" for our needs (observing the results of modification).

Form refers to the shape and structure of anything [MICRA98], and *formal models* are models that attempt to represent this. The basis of modern science is founded on formalizing regularities, both in the structure of things and their transformations [Fauconnier02]. Talk about "scientific" understanding—whether of stars and quarks, neurons and networks, cultural signs and economics, or whatever—refers to knowledge of forms.

Paradigms are like overarching, high-level models; they present a way of thinking about a system [Chalmers94]. They might consist of fundamental laws, theoretical assumptions, standard application of fundamental laws, instrumentation and instrumental techniques, a general metaphysics, and other shared outlooks on one or more fields. They set the way in which questions are asked and how the results of observation are to be interpreted. In other words, paradigms are a way of understanding something, a pattern of beliefs and experiences through which new experiences and beliefs are filtered.

Understand that formal constructs (models, paradigms, theories, etc.) are not reality. Forms may underlie our knowledge of the universe, but just as the photo of the food is not the food [Fauconnier02], they only represent the meaning of that universe.

There are many reasons to be well acquainted with models, but for designers, some are of particular importance. First, our game designs are formal models of the game. Second, we need to understand ways people will create their mental models of the system; much of what we think of as the game experience is better understood as the player experience. Therefore, the game designer is a modeler working within these two spheres: games and minds.

To make the most from our models, we must be ever mindful of scopes and limits. Good models contain details that are appropriate to the purpose at hand. Models with lots of useless data are usually more trouble than they are worth. Ideally, everything significant to its purpose is included within the model boundaries, and all else is abstracted or cut away. For example, a set of blueprints to a house would include details such as architecture (walls, doors, windows, etc.), plumbing, and electrical diagrams. The process of trimming away factors is *abstraction*. Abstracted components might include the exterior paint, location of your wallet, or the nearest shoe store. Even though, at some time, any of these other factors may be important to the resident, regarding the construction of the home they are simply not needed.

Video games not only exploit the latest developments in digital technologies (in turn based on advancements in physical and logical sciences), but are designed and constructed in accordance with paradigms and models of human nature—we need to understand people and how they play. Yet the models of player perception we often work with are not always well accepted by serious scientists working in the fields of psychology and neuroscience. However, game designers are free to accept compelling and applicable models as long as they work.

Designer Jay Minn uses a conceptual model of player reward and reinforcement. His "potato chip loop" operates on an analogy between a player's desire for food and desire for entertainment. Each reward is imagined as a potato chip that, in all of its salty and fatty glory, is given to the player periodically to encourage him to continue progressing through the game. The chip might be a reward to the player for completing a stage or collecting an object or having performed some interesting feat. At times, the chip may be bigger or smaller, but the most important factor is the temporal spacing between chips—the timing between one reward and the next. Too few, and the player gets too hungry and looks for food elsewhere. Too many, and the player gets full and wants to take a break. Minn's simple idea doesn't attempt to establish formal account of behavior conditioning, but an easily understood, communicated, and remembered device.

Game Artifacts

Games can be described and defined within many paradigms, some more straightforward than others. We can make elaborate, sometimes awkward conceptual models such as games are "stories" or "conversations" or "hallucinations." However, with each attempt to construct new analogies, we risk distancing ourselves from understanding games in simple terms. The typical consumer has little trouble understanding what a game is. Professional developers also know what they are making, more or less; they like to ponder the subject but prefer working to worrying about it. "At the end of the day, all I care about are results."

From a common-sense perspective, it is useful to discuss games simply as *artifacts* [LeBlanc04], objects made by people. For most of us, talk about artifacts is natural; we live in a world surrounded by the products of human invention. The shoes and clothing you are wearing are artifacts. This book you hold as well as cars, diapers, lawnmowers, pennies, golf clubs, and pencils are all examples of artifacts. In the case of each, we understand them as wholes of form and function where identity is tied to physical makeup of the object and its *affordances*—the properties that determine how people believe the artifact is to be used [Norman88].

The idea of treating games as artifacts isn't radical or new. Most developers have been doing this implicitly all along. However, another tradition in cognitive studies has described artifacts used to aid thinking as *cognitive artifacts* [Hutchins99]. Lists, maps, and string tied around a finger are examples, as well as mental artifacts like mnemonics, maxims, and rules of thumb. We might even presume to describe games as cognitive artifacts, but for the time being it's safest to distinguish them as game artifacts; games stimulate the emotions of the players rather than improve their cognition.

Game Frames and Rules

The *frame* of a game is the understood context of play—the time and space that distinguishes play activities from nonplay activities. The moves chess players make are within the frame of the game but their entrance into the room is not.

Rules are the predominant aspect of a game construct. They are often what people refer to by use of the word *game*. Rules provide the formal description of a game's structure within its frame. The basic purpose of a rule is to contribute organization and context to play. They can be categorized into *procedures* and *delimiters*—two sides of the same coin.

Procedures: The processes and techniques players use to reach goals. As a set of instructions, they describe the methods players may use to perform actions, including:
- Who is eligible to perform the action?
- When is the action to be performed?
- How is the action performed?

Delimiters: Restrictions placed on possible actions. They work, as Chris Crawford describes, to prevent the player from subverting a game's challenges [Crawford03]. Certainly, the experience of challenge is widely seen as critical to building enjoyment.

Without predefined rules, play is an unregulated and nebulous activity. Personal creativity and social skills are used to express and negotiate acceptable behavior. The fantasy play of children (e.g., *House*, *War*, *Cops and Robbers*, etc.) is one common example. Rules for these games exist on a moment-to-moment basis, inconclusive and ephemeral; rules are "made up" while the game is being played. Ad hoc rules such as these force players to make an effort to simply understand the boundaries of the game. By clarifying the manner of play, formal rules allow players to concentrate on exploring different strategies in the system rather than on understanding and interpreting the system itself.

Explicit rules are a basic formal structure of any game artifact. These are sometimes called the "laws" of the game—binding, nonnegotiable, and unambiguous [Huizinga55]. In nonelectronic games, the explicit rules are written into rule books or formed by the playing equipment and moderated by either the players or a separate referee. In electronic games, they exist within the hardware and software architecture.

For example, the rule we described for Figure 2.2.1 is an explicit rule—a procedure; *the piece is moved to the open square*. While this is easy to understand, it is also necessary to recognize that both the piece and board are explicit rules as well. Rather than provide them with a handsome illustration, we could have described them in two more written rules.

Ideally, explicit rules are clear, every player sharing the same interpretation of their meaning. Vagueness is often harmful to the system, leading to confusion, exploitation, or a breakdown in the play. If ambiguity is revealed, the players must agree, among themselves, to clarifications.

It's safe to say that, as it exists, Figure 2.2.1 has some problems. For one, the rules fail to define the number of players allowed in a game. In addition, we don't indicate when the piece is to be moved. Interestingly, if we specify that Figure 2.2.1 is a one-player game, our job is finished; there's only one player and he may move the piece whenever he so chooses. However, if we allow more than one player, the players may run into some confusion; "When do *I* go?" So, we might add "Each turn…" to the wording of our first written rule to clear up any confusion.

Implicit rules [Salen04] are unlike explicit rules in two important ways: they are unwritten and are not necessarily binding. To players, implicit rules may appear as critical to the game's enjoyment as are the explicit rules. For example, implicit rules often include an agreement between the players not to exploit certain weaknesses in the game system [Sniderman99].

Robert Fulghum tells of his experience of childhood hide-and-seek games with another player that "hid too well" [Fulghum89]. After looking for a very long time, the other children would give up and continue playing without him. Eventually, he would appear upset about being abandoned and arguments over the rules would erupt. Disagreements about the rules would then turn into disagreements about who made up the rules and so on.

Implicit rules are broad assumptions made in the "spirit" of the game, not amendments to explicit rules. For example, if Fulghum's playmates agreed to a new rule prohibiting hiding in a certain spot (e.g., "no hiding under leaves"), that rule would not be implicit but explicit, known and accepted by the players. However, it would still fall short of the implicit rule under which most of the children were operating: *you shouldn't hide so well that it is impossible to be found.*

We have to leave certain matters up to the implicit rules. In fact, most matters in nondigital games are governed by implicit rules. Few games instructions specify, "You shall not pelt your opponent with rocks and garbage," or, "Pouring a milkshake over the board is not allowed while the game is in play." These countless rules do not need to be stated explicitly because players are expected to have a *lusory attitude*—the willingness to submit to the conventions of the game [Suits90]. At the most basic level, the lusory attitude demands that the explicit rules will be followed. However, at its fullest, the lusory attitude is the willingness to abide by the cultural conventions common to those with which you are playing [Salen04].

Some rules only come into effect at given times or in particular circumstances. These often serve to create variation, govern game progress, and ensure the system remains within preordained limits [Fullerton04].

Rules in electronic games are formed by the platform and software architectures. The first advantage is that no ambiguity in explicit rules is possible; the computer referees the game, and players are forced to abide if they are to continue playing. Second, the rule systems can be modeled in much greater detail because players are not required to process all of the rules themselves. The richness and responsiveness of computer simulation can operate at a level of sophistication impractical by other means.

Features

In software development, a *software methodology* (*method*) is a set of procedures and practices developers use to create programs. There are many of them, each representing a given philosophy on the best way to get software built. Most of these methods are *feature-based*: they describe a paradigm of software architecture as organizations of small, functional units. In this paradigm, a software application (e.g., word processor, game, virus, etc.) is expected to perform one or more tasks. The application performs a sequence of operations to complete each task. This set of operations, that performs a given task, collectively forms a *feature*.

As with all systems, features vary in size and complexity according to their job. When several features are being discussed as a whole, they are a *feature set*.

How do we determine what is a single feature and what is a set? How fine an approach should we take when describing these units? For example, we think of a map in a game as a feature. However, looking closer, we see that there are smaller features in there. Unit locations are displayed. The color of each unit reflects its team. The terrain is colored. How do we know when to stop? The level of detail that goes into feature descriptions will depend on the development method being used and the culture of the organization.

In this chapter, we discuss the aspects of game features framed in terms of three major domains shown in Figure 2.2.2: *mechanics*, *interface*, and *system*. It is an *approximate model*: one that puts us in the ballpark of form. This starts us with an easy way to conceptualize a structure that we can build up.

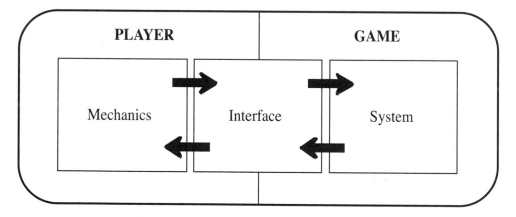

FIGURE 2.2.2   *A model of the player-game relationship.*

The model isn't complicated:

Mechanics: Things the player does.
Interface: The way the player and game communicate.
System: How the game structure behaves.

In our model, the relationship between player and game is shown. Players experience the game through the interface, which processes the inputs and outputs of the system. Back and forth, back and forth, information is moved along the structure.

Players act in the game by manipulating the values of *control variables*, such as changing the angle of a joystick or the pressing of a key. In turn, these inputs affect the various *state variables*, which describe, by their values, the current state of the game [Isaacs65]. If the game were halted at any particular moment, only the values of the state variables would be needed to resume play; this is the data written in a game save file or a character record.

However, there is a problem: we can't build players! All we can do is design the structures of the game. Considering that a player's imagination can be half the experience, we must design systems and interfaces to produce play mechanics.

Play Mechanics

Gameplay was once the term du jour; to refer to an experience in a game, it was handy. Gameplay usually indicates either the feeling of playing a game or the activities engaged in a game [Costikyan02]. However, a lack of precision in its definition has led gameplay to fall on hard times; now it seems out of style. Being hip is probably not worth the effort, but clarity is useful.

Here, when discussing specific player activities within a game, we will use *play mechanics*, *game mechanics*, and *mechanics* synonymously. *Aesthetics* will be used for the feelings experienced during play. If you, however, prefer to use gameplay, please do.

Play mechanics are the activities in which a player participates during the game; what the player does. This can include actions and strategies as well as the player's construction of a mental model of the game.

It might be easy to consider play mechanics as a version of Donald Norman's Seven Stages of Action applied to game playing. Donald Norman describes a model of action, as shown in Figure 2.2.3, in the world at large; it works the same way when applied to games [Norman88]. He structures the action in three aspects: *goal*, *execution*, and *evaluation*.

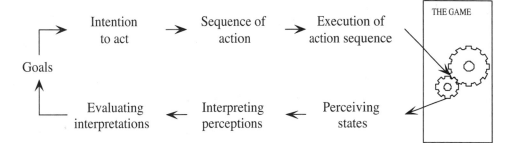

FIGURE 2.2.3 *The Seven Stages of Action [Norman88].*

A *goal* is first formed that models a desired state. This goal does not describe how something is to be done, but what is desired as a result of an action. During the *execution* phase, the goal must be turned into an *intention* to act, what Norman calls the *specific statements of what is to be done.* Intentions are put into an *action sequence*, the order in which the internal commands will be performed. At last, this mental processing is turned into a physical manipulation of the controller: the *execution*.

The evaluation stage begins as we *perceive* the state of the game through the interface. Perceptions of the game states are *interpreted*—understood according to our mental model of the system—and *evaluated* by comparing the current states with our intentions and goals.

As our model of a game (in Figure 2.2.1), this is an approximate model. Most actions do not occur in discrete stages. Not all action needs to progress through every stage in the sequence. Most doings in the real world are made up of many steps, each an action in itself.

We can understand a game mechanic, at the finest level of detail, as an action leading to a result in the game system—one complete turn of the seven stages of action that produce a perceived change in the game state. These *primary elements* [Cousins04] can be things such as "move forward" or "jump" or "select item," depending on their context within the game.

In a way, to design games is to devise model systems that create opportunities for player action. We attempt to satisfy the basic desire of players to do something, whether engaging, intriguing, or otherwise significant.

Mechanics must be able to fit into the players' mental model of the game—they must have the opportunity to understand it through their relationship to the system. Often, players are not *aware* of mechanics in the sense that they understand how they are being affected by the results of their actions.

Game designers do well when they remember that mental models in their mind differ from those inside the players' minds. The designer consults a mental model when the game artifact is being built, but the reality of the *system image*—the portion of system that can be perceived from the outside, including documentation and other available information—does not always correlate perfectly to that intention. Users form their mental models based on insights received while interacting with the system image (see Figure 2.2.4). Player and designer are not in direct dialog with each other; the player is not told by the designer how the game is supposed to operate, play, or feel [Norman88].

Designers often spend time visualizing the actions within the spaces of the game. They imagine that players will do certain activities and enjoy them, while fearing and avoiding others. To help understand the player's viewpoint and strategy, designers imagine themselves playing the game. "What would I do?" These thought experiments are crucial to designing well; a cheap and quick way to test ideas. However, you must remember that the player is not you and will not understand the game as you do. Player strategies will *always* be based on their unique conceptual model of the game. Be cautious of relying on too many assumptions about these understandings. We can only expect players to know what they have been told or shown by the game; sometimes a solution that seems painfully obvious to the designer is painfully frustrating to a player.

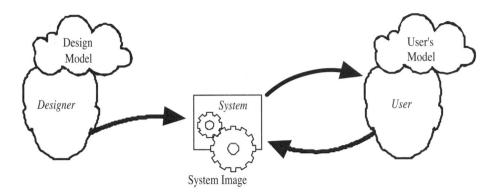

FIGURE 2.2.4 *Conceptual models, ours and theirs [Norman86].*

For every game, there is one or more *core mechanics*—the fundamental action (or set of actions) that characterizes the typical activities engaged by the player. Core mechanics are patterns of behavior where the player cycles through the same kind of same actions repeatedly. In a first-person shooter, core mechanics might be "run, shoot, and explore"; in a strategy game, "harvest, build, expand, and conquer." Finding the proper set of activities to make up the core mechanic will depend on the type of game and audience intended. Balancing those will rely, as the other mechanics, on prototyping, testing, and tuning the system to satisfy the needs of that audience.

Premise—Analogies and Metaphors

The *premise* (or *fiction*) of a game refers to the metaphors of action and setting [Fullerton04]. This premise directs the players' experiences and gives them a context within which their experiences fit. Through the course of play, users *map* the states of the game and their actions to the premise, actively participating in the metaphor.

Consider aspects typically related to the *story* of a game: setting (time and place), characters, motivations, relationships, and so forth. It is easy to see how these all work together to help form the premise. In fact, this method of establishing premise has existed for centuries in narrative forms.

The Legend of Zelda background story forms the backdrop against which play will occur. From the moment players engage the game, they control Link in his quest to save Princess Zelda and the land of Hyrule. Likewise, the terse introduction to *Robotron: 2084*, describing how superior robots decided to eliminate humans, also establishes the backdrop action, even if only to elaborate on the imperative given to the player to save the last humans.

Game premises can be complex, as in the case of character and story-based games. Alternatively, they may be little more than an abstract metaphor that allows people to manipulate agents in some understandable way, like arranging shapes in *Tetris* or stacks of colored balls in *Magical Drop*.

Premise extends beyond the story's canonical narrative. It encompasses all game activities. Link's sword and shield, his abilities to store items in an inventory, and his ability to interact with the inhabitants of Hyrule are all part of the game's fiction. In fact, all of the actions available to Link during his adventure are members of its premise.

Discussing actions in a game, players are rarely using literal terms to depict the performance. Recounting a game session, they will use the language of the premise, primarily describing actions, perceptions, and strategies experienced within its context. The portrayal is largely symbolic, representing activities such as fighting, buying, building, and so forth. All of this conduct occurs within the boundaries of the game's premise. The vocabulary used by players in describing play reflects the metaphors evoked by the game [Crawford03].

Understand the distinction between the model (the game) and the activity being modeled. Playing a typical basketball video game, for example, is no more playing the physical sport than is reading a comic book the same as having superpowers. The goal of the video game is to make the players *feel* as though they were controlling athletes on court. Those without interest in sports might still enjoy sports games, just as people do not play *The Sims* because of an increased interest in taking their own garbage out. Model and reality are different.

Premise is more than just about simply establishing a setting or a tone; it can significantly alter the players' mental model and the way in which they develop strategies. Consider a classic example, a selection task designed by psychologist Peter Wason. Four cards are set before you, each having a letter on one side and a number on the other. You are told that a card with a "D" on one side must have a "3" on the other.

In Figure 2.2.5, which card(s) do you need to turn over to see if this is true?

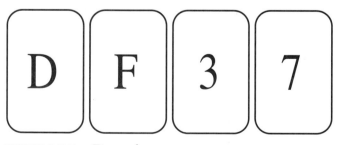

FIGURE 2.2.5   *First task.*

Make a quick note of your answer. Now, imagine that you are working in a restaurant and must make sure that no one under legal age (18) is drinking. You can check what a person is drinking and how old he is.

In Figure 2.2.6, which person(s) do you need to check to make sure no law is being broken?

FIGURE 2.2.6 *Second task.*

These tasks have been featured in several studies, and over 90 percent of people, when faced with the first task, answer incorrectly [Pinker97]. Yet most people are quick to give the correct answer for the second task. (Leda Cosmides and James Tooby proposed that people possess an innate capacity for detecting "cheats.") The illustration indicates that people may fail to choose a successful strategy (checking "D" and "7") while operating within one premise, while another allows them to readily discover the solution (checking "Drinking Beer" and "16 Years Old").

One last point worth making on the subject of premise is regarding its content. Writers are often taught to distinguish *plausibility* from *possibility*. When something is considered possible, it is capable of happening in the real world; planes may fly, but muscular men in cape and tights alone cannot. However, in creative writing, you are free to suggest any kind of truth as long as it is plausible within the rules of the universe you've described in your fiction; there must be an explanation that *makes sense* in the particular context of the environment. As it relates to a player's map of the premise, we can view plausibility as the domain (area) of the player's map; when an object or situation is implausible, it is beyond the border of what the player can (or is willing to) map acceptably.

The limits of plausibility are subjective, understanding what audiences will and will not allow being essential to pushing those boundaries. For example, games that attempt to blend science fiction and fantasy universes together have to account for the segment of their audience that cannot accept the two fictional conventions in the same space. Similarly, it is common for fantasy massively multiplayer online games (such as *Dark Age of Camelot*) to have to provide special *role-playing* (RP) servers for their customers who find the implausibility of a wizard named "MonsterTruck," since it shatters their enjoyment of the game.

Choices and Outcomes

Choice—the act of choosing—lies close to the root of how we understand our game experiences. Sid Meier, an industry legend responsible for *Civilization* among other titles, is credited with observing that a game is largely a series of interesting choices. This quickly became one of the earliest and most popular maxims to be adopted by other designers. It gave direct and succinct articulation to an experience everyone understood firsthand: satisfying play.

A choice may be known as a question asked of the player. What unit would you like to build? Which ally will you betray? Which door will you choose? And so on.

Through the course of a game, player choices create imperatives for actions. These actions by the player result in *outcomes*, a result or consequence. If choices are felt at the root of our experiences, then outcomes are the fruits we taste—sweet or bitter—as results from the system are interpreted.

One way to describe the landscape of potential choice is as a *possibility space*. This space represents the set of possible actions in a given environment. We might refer to a game as having a wide possibility space, indicating that there are many possible choices for the player to make. A narrow or small possibility space indicates there are very few options available. Many games, especially those depending on a predetermined narrative sequence, will have possibility spaces that change during the course of play; many things to do and ways to do them at one point, building to momentous, key decisions at others.

The *consequence*, or *weight*, of a choice might be called the "significance of its outcome." This is one of the most important factors in designing choices. We can understand the scale of consequence by relating it to the alteration of the game; the greater the consequence of a choice, the more significant its outcome will be to the course of the game. A well-designed choice will often feature both desirable and undesirable effects [Fullerton04].

Choices that your players must deal with should involve their desire to achieve their goals. Insignificant or irrelevant decisions are almost always detrimental to the experience. The more decisions the players must make outside of this scope, the weaker their connection to the experience will be. While particular distributions will differ for each particular style of game, play should be a progression of actions periodically marked by significant decisions.

Excitement, anticipation, and tension are created when the player is faced with weighty choices. On the other hand, if every choice is too melodramatic (i.e., life and death, save the universe, etc.), then the experience risks violating plausibility.

In keeping players engaged, you try to enable an experience that oscillates within an ever-rising balance of challenge and ability. You will often want the weight of choice to behave similarly—more significant on average as the game progresses.

One way to make decisions more significant is to keep the available choices *orthogonal*—distinctive by nature of quality and property [Smith03]. With a set of orthogonal choices, the desirable and undesirable effects of each choice are different from each other. This difference is not just in scale, but also in kind.

To help assess how effective a choice is, the book *Game Design Workshop* offers eight qualities to characterize [Fullerton04]. These are a starting place; add your own qualities as you need—we add "orthogonal" here.

Hollow: Lacking any real consequence.
Obvious: A decision that leaves no choice to be made.

Uninformed: An arbitrary decision.
Informed: Describes a deciding player with sufficient information.
Dramatic: Strongly connects to the player's feelings.
Weighted: Positive and negative outcomes with each choice.
Immediate: Effects of the decision are immediate.
Long-term: Effects of the decision manifest over an extended period.
Orthogonal: Distinct among other choices.

A hollow choice lacks measurable outcome, while an obvious choice leaves nothing to be decided—a player would be either stupid, self-destructive, or both to choose the nonobvious option. Uninformed choices are those made without enough information to support meaningful judgment; the player selects a strategy at random. Informed choices are those the players can make, confident they know all they need to about the decision. Dramatic choices produce emotional responses within the premise, such as when players must abandon a companion to save themselves. Weighted choices have significant desirable and undesirable outcomes. The outcomes of immediate choices are produced close to the decision event, while long-term choices have lasting results. Lastly, the orthogonal choice is one that is distinctive relative to other potential choices.

Goals and Objectives

Few words are so intimate or have such a history with games as the word *goal*. There are many meanings one might consider, each depending on the context in which it is used. These can be generalized into two of the most common:

- An objective
- An intentional outcome

Objectives are designed requirements that players must satisfy to accomplish a particular outcome [Fullerton04]. Encoded into the structure of the system itself, objectives are formal properties of the game, gating player progress.

Goals (or *incentives*) are subjective notions that direct action toward outcomes [LeDoux02]. Put another way, a goal is "what the player *wants* to do." All games involve goals, even those rare few in which we are unable to define clear high-level objectives (i.e., *software toys*). Goals are personally created and maintained rather than formally structured by the system.

Goals are subject to player discretion and not just those intended by the game's designers. Every opportunity for choice or action is an opportunity for goal setting. Goals provide motivation and direction to the player. These goals most often include reaching game objectives; if players aren't motivated to reach the game's objectives, they usually stop playing.

Typically, objectives are set at many levels—from major requirements to minor steps unessential or unrelated to the main objectives. In keeping with the competitive nature of most games, winning is the most common objective. So common that it is frequently cited as a formal requirement for games. Even in those games that lack victory conditions, most players will expect objectives by which their progress can be measured. Although there are a growing number of examples that demonstrate players are more than happy to dispense with high-level objectives when system interactions are compelling enough without them (e.g., *The Sims*).

Objectives are key elements to establishing a fixed challenge. When goals are self-directed, players are free to overcome adversity by changing or modifying their goals. For most games relying on challenge to provide dramatic aesthetics, the result is a breakdown in motivation.

Objectives may be the same for each player, or they may differ. Usually, when a game provides objectives that differ for the players, they depend on conditional roles (such as in team sports where a role might be distinguished as *offense* and *defense*).

Just as with other aspects of the mental model, users will not always have the same set of goals the designer has intended, as in Figure 2.2.7. Choices are invented by the player in light of the system's *affordances*—the apparent ways something can be used [Norman88]. Forcing player goals to align to specific intentions requires the use of objectives. Players may still have their own notions, but must make adjustments when they cannot achieve them. Balance your need for players to behave within the system with their desire for *expression*—the latitude for them to set and achieve their own goals.

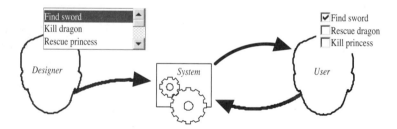

FIGURE 2.2.7 *Objectives and goals aren't always the same.*

Measurable outcomes require objectives. Without them, players become solely responsible for generating their own goals. This is the hallmark of the *software toy*.

Resources and Economies

Whether in games or in the world at large, *resources* are things that are used in support of some activity (such as manufacturing) and are drawn from an available supply—they are the factors of production and the bases of development. Resources needn't only be physical things: for example, entrepreneurship and education are viewed as important resources in capitalist systems. In games, resources are the things used by players and other agents to reach goals [Fullerton04].

Resources may exist within the premise of the game or without. Within the game's premise, we might expect resources such as materials, people, magic power, or health.

Outside of the premise, we might consider functional components as resources, such as save games or lives; these can be provided in limited supply to build tension, challenge, and provide opportunity for further strategy but without necessarily being understandable within the game's premise.

To be meaningful, a supply of resources must not only be useful, but also limited in some way. To limit a resource, we can restrict the total supply to a finite amount, or restrict the rate. We might instead provide special conditions for their use or employment, or create penalties for their consumption.

The relative value of a given resource can be determined by looking at the relationship between its utility and its scarcity. Expect problems to arise if a resource is either useless or readily and infinitely available. To consider these issues in the context of systems, it is helpful to view resources in *economies*—closed systems of supply, distribution, and consumption.

Some typical questions regarding resource economies include:

- What resources exist in the game?
- How and when will a player use the resources?
- How and when are the resources supplied?
- What are their limits?

Player Strategy

People are unlikely to apply formal logic in the course of making everyday decisions; they may not be necessarily "rational" in the sense of computing likely outcomes based on statistical assessments. Instead, we tend to let experience and common sense guide most of our actions and reactions [Norman88]. Why not? What has served evolution probably remains sufficient to serve us in our daily lives. (We will have more to say on economics and game theory later.)

From our experiences with simple systems, we acquire a common-sense world view of linear causation (see Figure 2.2.8); every event has a cause preceded by an infinite history of causes before it. Likewise, the standard approach to strategizing tends to be linear, appropriate to this general outlook. As we will see later, most systems of any complexity, including games, do not often behave in a linear fashion.

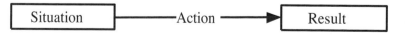

FIGURE 2.2.8   *A linear outlook/strategy.*

Strategic challenges do not need obvious or simplistic solutions, but you must be aware of what assumptions you expect the player to have about the way in which the game works.

Game Theory

Game theory (sometimes known as *multiperson decision theory*) is a branch of economics that studies decision making. It asks questions about optimal strategy in a variety of situations, especially those where outcomes are dependent on the choices of others. Originally developed by mathematicians working on economic problems, it was soon applied in sociology, biology, and many other fields.

Many designers, at first, expect game theory to help them create systems and find themselves quickly disappointed; game theory is concerned with numerical analyses of strategy. In other words, game theory studies playing games, not making them.

In a nutshell, game theory uses models, in the form of games, to study how decisions produce outcomes. The *utility* (a measure of desire) of an outcome is represented by numeric *payoffs*. Higher payoffs correspond to higher utility. The bias of players to utility is known as their *preference*.

Game theory games are played by *rational players*, abstract models with one goal: to maximize their potential utility. Rational players solve problems using pure logic, with complete awareness of the game's state. At any point during a game, they understand every option available given the information they have been allowed. We use these conceptual models to avoid worrying about individual intelligence or ability and to focus on understanding how the optimal strategies can be determined.

Three categories of games describe of how decisions are afforded [Baillie-de Byl04]:

Games of skill: One-player games where outcomes are determined solely by their choices.
Games of chance: One-player games with the outcome determined, in whole or in part, by probability (or as a two-player game with *nature* as one of the players).
Games of strategy: Competitions between two or more players.

In a game of skill, every choice is a *decision under certainty*: the player knows the outcome of any decision beforehand. It is up to the player to select the best available strategy.

Choices made during games of chance are known by two types. In cases where the probabilities are known—such as 1 in 37 for ("European") Roulette—the strategy made by the player is a *risky decision*. When probabilities are unknown, the player makes *decisions under uncertainty*.

Games of strategy model competitions between two or more players, with outcomes determined by their collective decisions. Of these games, there are three types:

Zero-sum: Players' outcomes are directly opposed.
Pure coordination: The best outcome is the same for all players.
Mixed-motive: Payoffs between players do not correspond to each other.

Zero-sum games are two-player games of strategy where the payoffs, when added together, equal zero. Player preferences are directly opposed. This is the classic win-lose arrangement of many popular two-player games: chess, checkers, go, and so forth.

One elementary tool in game theory is the *decision tree* (or *game tree*). Each node on the tree represents a choice made by a player; other nodes along the same row represent alternate choices available in the same turn; games that resolve simultaneously are still discussed in turns. Games start as a single node: the initial condition of the game. From there, lines branch out to nodes representing possible moves that the first player could select. In each successive row, lines branch to more nodes representing moves available to the next player in the sequence.

The biggest limitation with decision trees, as tools, is their complexity. With a very small range of potential moves, they can be useful diagrams. However, with any real game, they quickly become so complicated that they are rendered impractical. In Figure 2.2.9, for example, with only three choices possible at any point, the Rock-Paper-Scissors game has nine potential outcomes. Consider chess, with its 20 possible openings and 25×10^{115} distinct 40-move games (while the number of electrons in the universe is 10^{79}) [Parr02], it is all but practically impossible to map such a tree.

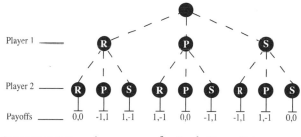

FIGURE 2.2.9 *A game tree for Rock-Paper-Scissors.*

(Outcomes for zero-sum games are usually shown with just one figure, since the other player's score is assumed known. We show both first and second players' scores to introduce the notation for multiple players—each is given in order.)

Cake-cutting is a zero-sum game that we can use to wet our feet. Imagine two children are sharing a piece of cake. Their father has decided, to avoid an argument, that one child will cut the piece and the other will select their pieces.

We can use the *payoff matrix* in Figure 2.2.10 to examine the strategies available to each player and the outcomes that will result. On the left is a friendly version that lists, explicitly, the outcomes possible during our game. On the right, each pair of outcomes is represented with a payoff value signifying utility. Read payoffs left to right, the first value corresponding with the first player and so on.

In *coordination games*, the best outcome for the game is the same for all players. When a condition of perfect information exists, the choices are trivial. When the information is imperfect, with players unable to communicate with one another, a greater challenge arises.

In some of these games, however, there exists a quasi solution—it isn't a proper formal solution, but a very strong tendency toward a particular intuitive choice. As

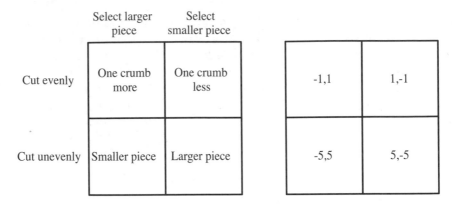

FIGURE 2.2.10   *Cake-cutting payoff matrix.*

Roger Schelling found, some strategies emerge more strongly than others [Baillie-de Byl04]. For example, Schelling asked a series of paired people to select heads or tails (as in coin tossing). They were told that, should both pick the same side, they would win; otherwise, they would lose—86 percent of those questioned chose heads [Schelling60].

In another experiment, Schelling gave people a scenario where they would pick the place and date to meet someone they hadn't met. Then they were told that, without being able to communicate to the stranger, they would have to pick the time to arrive at the meeting place, within a minute of the other person. Almost every participant chose 12 P.M., noon.

These points of prominent strategy are "Schelling points" and the strategies are known as "salient." Because these strategies seem to be based on a broad spectrum of cultural knowledge, a zeitgeist, it is almost impossible to calculate.

Many designers reconsider game theory once they begin to understand how it can be useful to their needs. At a higher level, it can be useful for analyzing mechanics—game theory can help you design and tune choices and outcomes. At a low level, it can be useful within the behaviors of game objects (AI strategies, etc.). Lastly, game theory provides a language that we can use for describing and discussing our games and the kinds of choices they make available.

Interface—Player and System Communication

The interface is the set of components by which players interact with the game system. Both input and output features work together, establishing a link between player execution and system reports. Any information passed from user to system, or vice versa, is channeled through interface components. Players *experience* the game by interpreting their perceptions of these transactions. From a player's perspective, the interface is the form of the game, while the system content is its function [Crawford03].

The interface contains both hardware and software elements. For example, in Figure 2.2.11, the interface consists of display, sound, keyboard, and mouse. The player receives information from the game system by seeing and hearing it, and executes actions by manipulating the keyboard and mouse.

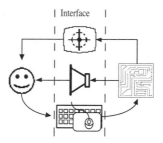

FIGURE 2.2.11 *A typical PC interface.*

The parts are easy to categorize, as most of us are already familiar with the types:

Output: Communicating information to the player
Input: Communicating information to the system

With the technologies currently available to most consumers, players can get information from video games in three ways: seeing (visual), hearing (audio), and feeling (haptic). Of these, only the visual and audio systems can be taken for granted; it's safe to assume that a general audience will be able to see and hear the game. Many platforms have peripherals with *haptic* features available, but these we cannot always rely on to be engaged.

States in video games can be staggeringly complex, but poorly understood systems can risk confusing players. When every consequence is unexpected, every decision misunderstood, players feel cheated. You must constantly consider how the players will understand the system and events and get them the information they need through the interface.

Output—Video

Vision is the dominant sense to inform us of the world beyond our bodies. As well as having large and mobile eyes, we have a large amount of the cerebral cortex associated with visual processing, much greater than any other sense [Goodale99]. Understandably, the most salient features in a video game are usually represented visually.

A *graphical user interface* (GUI) was first known as a paradigm of computer control, a friendly metaphor: files and folders that could be managed with a mouse. In games, the term "GUI" still tends to be applied to those graphic features that either present control metaphors (buttons, etc.) or labels. However, for purely practical reasons, it can be helpful to understand the graphical interface as encompassing all graphical elements, including those within the game environment itself.

Every scene in a game is viewed in two dimensions, through the physical screen (LCD, CRT, etc.). Even 3D games are still limited to rendering scenes onto the plane of the video screen. We identify, collectively, the set of features directly involved in rendering the game environment as the *graphics engine*.

The engine is one of the most significant parts of a game's user interface, determining how scenes will appear. The *camera* represents the vantage from which the current scene is drawn, the viewpoint. We described cameras by their perspective or a combination of perspective and behavior.

Typical perspectives are:

First-person: Camera views from a character's (or object's) point of view in 3D; controls are usually direct, moving camera and avatar together.
Over-the-shoulder (OTS):   Camera views from above and behind the subject in 3D.
Overhead (or **top-down**):   Camera views from directly above the scene.
Side: Camera views from directly to one side of the scene.
Isometric (or **three-quarter**):   3D view from a fixed perspective, usually high above, giving a view of roughly three-quarters of any given object in the scene.

Powerful 3D engines are now commonplace, both on the desktop and in gaming consoles. The level of detail and variation that can be displayed on the average gaming PC is beginning to approach photo-realism—in real time. New technologies make presentations more compelling and certain perspectives easier to manage than before. These advances enable us to model activities in ever-greater detail and effectiveness, but do not necessarily change *what* we can model. Indeed, many current games are *translations* of earlier mechanics to new interfaces.

The *Grand Theft Auto* (*GTA*) series presents a great opportunity for examining play mechanics translated from one mode of presentation to another. The core mechanics of the original, which was set in 2D, have been retained in each installment, even though the latest titles are in 3D. Players move a character freely about an environment populated by numerous agents (characters and vehicle objects). Agents each follow simple behavioral rules describing how to act in the environment and with other agents. Each title introduces more behaviors and more choices for the player, but the core model—stealing cars and performing mission objectives in an "open" world—is present from the beginning to the end of the series.

First-person perspectives are often assumed to connect the players closely to their character. In fact, it can actually create distance between them because the players revert to assuming their own identity: they play as themselves rather than as the character. This can be overcome with persistent reinforcement of the premise, such as in *Half Life 2*.

Other issues common to FPS games are the nuances of world and object interactions. Without a clear frame of reference, scale can be difficult to judge, and presenting believable world interaction is tricky. Navigating through game spaces often first requires that players acquaint themselves with the dimensions of the game, testing widths, heights, and depths to discover how their virtual body fares. Designers and artists in these circumstances have to make sure they follow some standard system of scale to help clearly indicate to players when something can be navigated or not.

Third-person perspectives present avatars more plainly. As a result, it is easier for players to identify strongly with them. A typical problem of third-person perspectives is the lack of connection to the character's focus or aim; the camera is usually over the shoulder. This makes action games more difficult to tune, especially those featuring ranged combat. In addition, the avatars can obscure a fair portion of screen real estate when the camera is close.

Output—Audio

Because our vision is so dominant, it is easy to underestimate the importance of sound to compelling experiences. Proper use of sound effects can reinforce the premise, evoke emotions and moods, and inform the player when significant events of the game change.

Our sense of hearing is remarkably sensitive, capable of detecting a wide dynamic range of sounds, both in pitch—*frequency*—and in loudness—*intensity*. Despite this range, our hearing remains finely tuned—we can detect a difference in frequency as fine as 0.2 percent and a difference in intensity as small as one decibel (dB) [Richards99]. Our ability to locate sounds in the world is astonishing: we can detect differences between each ear as small as a few microseconds.

Game audio is typically broken into in three categories: *music, sound effects*, and *dialog*. Production pipelines for audio work vary between organizations, but, from a designer's perspective, considering the subject within these three should work well enough.

Sound effects are sounds triggered by game events. They range from the simple feedback of a mouse click to a chiming alert signal to bloodcurdling screams of the murderous War Beast! To a greater extent than the other types of sounds, the effects serve to inform the player of game states. Often they are used to provide information when the player's eyes may be to busy to look away from their current focus.

Table 2.2.1 is a list that designers might supply to the audio team. Categories provide context for the event so the audio designer understands how the sound is to be used. The game designer will often describe the kind of sound he imagines working, to give the audio team a starting place, a reference.

Table 2.2.1 Sound Effect List

Category	Condition/Event	Type
System	Menu select	Soft tap
System	Overflow warning	Short siren call
Action	Flush	Swooshing water
Action	Flush	Swooshing water—loop
Environment	Large pipe	Tight echoes
Power-up	Toilet duck	Brief quack-quack

Dialog is any voice recording that the player will need to understand during play. Occasionally, dialog will be used for warnings and announcements ("Orange alert!"), but the most common use is to give game characters a voice. Although technically dialog can be seen as a sound effect, its unique challenges often require separate studio and production schedules. Game designers must work closely with audio designers to ensure that the intent and meaning behind the words is clearly understood so that they may properly direct the *voice talent* (actors) during recording.

Music is a powerful tool for establishing moods and reinforcing themes, arguably more potent than narrative at tying players to the attitude and tension of the environment. It can motivate, frighten, and transport the imagination.

The unique needs of games have given rise to new technologies and compositional techniques known collectively as *interactive music*. Producing good interactive music requires forethought and planning on the part of the designers, who then work with an interactive music producer. Fortunately, your game's aesthetic objectives will often help determine the basic music categories. From there it is a process of refining the detail and mapping the meanings to events. Table 2.2.2 shows an example of how certain places or events might trigger particular music.

Table 2.2.2   An Example List of Interactive Music Needs

Category	Condition/Event	Aesthetic/Feeling/Meaning
Self	Combat victory	Triumphant
Party	Companion death	Sorrow
Location	Toy shop	Hospitality, friendliness
Environment	Woodlands	Safety, idleness
Environment	The Editor's Lair	Danger, impending doom

Because the aesthetic goals of your game are not likely to change, it is best to begin planning for music early. This will allow time to refine goals, and nail the themes exactly as you want.

Input—Controls

The *controls* are the physical input devices players use to communicate to the system.

Most platforms will have a standard controller layout that designers will map to their game actions, usually some combination of keyboard, mouse, joystick, or game pad. Other, nonstandard controllers are available, but the expense in production and distribution can make these products unappealing to publishers.

Control inputs are the manipulations, by the user, of the game's controls—the way the controls are used. These are patterns of presses, clicks, and movements performed to initiate actions. These inputs are detailed in a *key map* or *control table*—see Figure 2.2.12, a diagram showing control input, action, and context for the event.

Action	Control	Context
Left	←	all
Right	→	all
Forward	↑	all
Backward	↓	all
Sprint	✕	all
Pass	◯	Offense
Lob	▲	Offense
Shoot	☐	Offense
Steal	◯	Defense
Block	▲	Defense
Hit	☐	Defense

FIGURE 2.2.12 *A simple control diagram.*

For example, in a fighting game we might assign a button (X) to trigger a punch. Each time the player presses X, his fighter hits an opponent for one unit of damage. If the player taps X in a special pattern, rather than a single punch, the fighter performs a three-punch combination that deals five units of damage. The same button on the controller was used, but the control inputs determined which attack was initiated.

Control inputs are not strategies; they are controls. The ability to perform a combo in a fighting game is not a strategic decision—it is not a choice, as such. Deciding *when* to perform moves is the strategy.

The ability for players to express themselves, to do what they want, must be balanced against the intuitiveness of the control design. Generally, the more diverse the actions allowed in the play mechanics, the more demands will be made of your controls.

When a given set of controls needs to be accessible at the same time, try to keep their layout and activations as orthogonal as can be practical: players appreciate clear, understandable mappings between their controls and actions. In other words, controls should be immediately distinct from each other. You should only mix mappings when contexts can be apparent to the player.

Controls are one of the most difficult aspects to innovate in games. For every known style of game, there already exist schemes of control that are accepted as norms. However, if your controls simply mirror the function of all other games in the genre, it is possible that your design may not be creating any new experiences [Dietrich02]. Designers should not be discouraged from inventing control systems that break with common conventions when the new scheme is better suited.

We might look for inspiration in a recent boxing game. Despite having been one of the earliest and most well-known subjects in sports video games, controls in boxing games have been similar among all of the various titles in the genre. Punches are triggered by pressing buttons corresponding with the type of punch (jab, hook, uppercut, etc.), and whether it was thrown with the left or right arm. However, Electronic Arts'

Fight Night 2004 introduced a new scheme—shown in Figure 2.2.13—that uses the right analog joystick to give players better command of their boxers' fists. The result is an interesting device, and a fighting experience unmatched in other boxing games because of the *natural mapping* between control input and action.

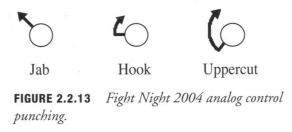

Jab   Hook   Uppercut

FIGURE 2.2.13   *Fight Night 2004 analog control punching.*

When creating control designs, look to your hands frequently. Evaluate your ideas for control mappings by keeping your attention tuned to your hands rather than the game's display. *How* your fingers are moving is just as or more important than to *where* they are moving. In this way, controls reveal a lot about the nature of the model you are making; they can indicate where player attention is being spent.

Current games offer a wide range of actions for the player, and moderating this complexity is a challenge for designers. In a single game, they may need to interact with characters, open containers, push crates, search under beds, or unlock a door. Rarely, however, are these actions performed at the same time, so orthogonal mappings don't necessarily make the most sense.

Contextual controls allow games to map any number of actions to common (i.e., shared) controls. This is done by relating the player's current situation (position in the environment, relationship to nearby agents, etc.) to the actions available. Football games, for example, commonly map multiple functions to the same buttons. The game uses the current context of play—the possession of the ball—to determine which mapping is currently active. In games where the characters are in complex 3D environments, the difficulty of determining context becomes more complex. Even so, the "action" button has fast become a staple of many games.

HUDs and Front-Ends

In application software, the *front-end* is a façade, the visible portion of the product with which the user interacts, while the *back-end* is the portion that processes data. In games we typically use *front-end* to refer to GUI elements not set directly within the environment—in other words, not rendered as part of the scene. Front-ends may include menus, buttons, HUD, help text, and the like.

Some typical elements of a front-end:

- Title
- Main Menu

- New Game
- Load/Save Game
- Options
- Credits
- Quit Game
- Pause Menu
- Map
- Log/Journal
- Game Stats
- Exit to Main Menu

Where possible, strive for thematic consistency, using the style of decoration to support and enhance the game premise. The layout and design of your interface should support the experiences you are trying to create.

The *HUD* (Head-Up Display) overlays the camera display during play, most often to show important information that can't be visualized directly in the game. The HUD elements border the game view.

Some typical information displayable in HUD:

Progress/Scores: Kills, points, levels, etc.
Resource levels: Health, ammunition, money, etc.
Map: Geography, agent locations, etc.
Alerts: Warnings, help, information, etc.
Chat: Dialog from the system, players, team, etc.

Designing an effective HUD requires an artist's skill with visual communication. As Figure 2.2.14 will no doubt attest, a game designer does not a graphic designer make. The duty of a game designer is to understand what information needs to be presented, not necessarily *how* it is best presented.

FIGURE 2.2.14   *A head-up display.*

Human-Computer Interaction and Cognitive Ergonomics

A relationship between two things is called a *mapping* [Norman88]. Consider how we navigate by using a (literal) map: looking at a two-dimensional bird's eye view of the world, we relate positions on the map to positions in the three-dimensional space around us. Similarly, we may map a light switch to a lamp, relating one position to "on" and the other to "off."

Human-Computer Interaction (HCI) is a study concerned with creating and enhancing communication between users and computers: it examines the ways in which people design, build, and use interfaces [Hollan99]. HCI is concerned with using current models of perception and cognition to create better interfaces, move beyond the current metaphors of icon and desktop, and develop better support for cooperative work. *Cognitive ergonomics* is a discipline that analyzes the cognitive representations and processes involved with performing tasks to better understand how we interact with systems to achieve goals [Cara99]. Many of the goals and methods of HCI and cognitive ergonomics overlap, as do many of the practitioners.

In the *Design of Everyday Things* (formerly *The Psychology of Everyday Things*), Donald Norman specifies five principles of design [Norman88]:

Visibility: Making the relevant parts visible
Mappings: Understandable relationships between controls and actions
Affordances: The perceived use of an object
Constraints: Prevent the players from acting in ways they shouldn't
Feedback: Reporting to the user what has been done and accomplished

As a set, these principles offer us clues to designing better interfaces, and better games. We can design challenges that are less focused on feats of dexterity or perplexing logic puzzles and more focused on managing the flow of information to the player.

Significant controls should not be obscure, and their functions in hardware should map, as naturally as possible, the functions in-game. The function of our game objects should be intelligible—their use and behavior knowable. Player actions need to be constrained, guided by the game and the interface so that there is no confusion *how* players are able to play the game.

Even as players signal their intent through buttons, keys, mice, and sticks, they need feedback from the interface—reassurance that they have been heard. In many styles, feedback can be managed solely within the mechanics—a button is pressed and a character jumps, for example. If the state of the game will change noticeably and immediately, additional cues are not needed. However, if player actions do not produce outcomes until a measure of time has passed (such as in strategy games), it's good to provide feedback with sound and visual effects.

Players are often ignorant of much of the internal structure of the games they play. In nonelectronic games, players must arbitrate the rules themselves; they develop a direct familiarity with the systems at work. However, when the system is maintained by a computer, the players are no longer required to be even familiar with the formal organization. They know what they can glean through their experience through their relationship to the play mechanics and interface. This puts the onus on us to make our systems clear. By applying Norman's principles to your design, you can increase the player's comprehension of the system without having to provide lengthy tutorials, training sessions, or frustrating trial-and error-sessions to do so.

Systems

Game systems have one purpose: to enable play mechanics. At the end of the day, a player will be unimpressed by beauty and sophistication that isn't experienced. If creating better games were simply a matter of adding more technology or more complexity, design would be a much simpler practice.

A *system* is a set of components structured in such a way that their properties and relationships to each other form a whole [Salen04]. It is a set of pieces that work together. In our daily experience, it is impossible to find anything that is not both a system and a part of a system itself.

Consider a cellular phone, one small piece of a cellular network. In a nutshell, it is a tiny, low-power radio transmitter/receiver, operating among base stations and switching offices. This system connects one caller to another. A closer view of that phone reveals that it is, itself, a system: a circuit board, microphone, speaker, display, and antenna. Further down, each of those parts are systems of yet smaller pieces, and so on and so on.

Conceptually, we seem to prefer dealing with wholes rather than parts, viewing each system as a coherent body. In other words, we think and talk about each system, as well as each of its pieces, as a *thing*. We know a sock is a system of threads, but do we think of this when trying to find the lost mate?

Systems depend on the particular arrangement of their objects, their *architecture*, for their function. Relationships between their pieces determine how they work to produce results. If the architecture of the system changes, so does the operation; it needs every one of its elements for it to work properly. This doesn't mean that a change must appear significant for it to have an effect: sometimes, the smallest adjustment leads to metamorphosis. Generally speaking, however, if objects of a system can be added, removed, or otherwise altered without affecting the relationships of the other objects or the behavior of the whole, then you are working with a *collection* rather than a system [Fullerton04].

Familiarity with modeling an object-oriented *modeling language*—a collection of standardized symbols and techniques for designing software architecture—(e.g., UML) can be helpful when designing systems. Conceptualizing and describing game objects becomes easier and more productive with training.

Objects and Relations

The pieces of a system are *objects*. These can represent just about anything: items, agents, places, and so forth. Just as in the real world, objects can be described by their *attributes*—the properties that determine what they are—and *behaviors*—the things that they do. Additionally, *relationships* are used to describe the ways in which their behavior and influence will change as contexts within the system change.

Once you understand the *requirements*—the things your system must accomplish—list the objects that will make up the system, including everything that seems important. Don't worry about the details when beginning: you will have plenty of time to review and revise the particulars.

Imagine we are working on a game where children run their own businesses, *Child Tycoon*. They can sell lemonade, popsicles, lawn mowing, or whatever we feel is appropriate. We might begin with a list of objects: characters, businesses, goods, services, and locations.

Each of these top-level objects is a new *class*—a basic type—of object. Once the objects are known, you begin to define what they are and what they do. Of course, the moment you begin deciding what objects will be in the system, you have already begun considering their attributes and behaviors. This is one of the reasons why working with objects is so useful: we already know how to think about them!

Each of our businesses will be operated by characters that sell either goods or services to other characters. Each business is operated at a location that is capable of supporting it. These are relationships between the game objects that will solidify as we describe the rules defining the object behaviors.

When creating a list of behaviors, you are asking, "What can this object do?" Each behavior is therefore an action a character might do in the game. Potential character behaviors might include buys goods, sells goods, performs service, hires characters, and befriends characters. For example, characters can buy items and services or they can hire other characters for help. These behaviors will help define the potential relationships between objects in the system.

Determining attributes is providing answers to more questions about your objects. What are the important qualities of an object? What distinguishes one from another? How do similar objects differ? How are they the same? These object properties will be used to determine which behaviors are appropriate and under what conditions.

At the highest level is an attribute that differentiates one kind of object from another, it is the very type of object at hand (e.g., characters, locations, etc.). From there we begin to describe properties in finer detail. For example, character attributes might include name, organization, ethic, charisma, and money.

Objects are distinguished further by the value of their attributes, which describe the state of the object. These determine which of its potential behaviors are relevant or available at any given moment and how behaviors involving these objects will produce results. Table 2.2.3 shows some different values for our childhood entrepreneurs.

Table 2.2.3 Example Values

Name	Chris Clifford	Jesse Lopez	Michel Christy
Organization	5	8	4
Ethic	10	3	4
Charisma	3	7	10
Money	0.00	4323.75	12278.00

Our object behaviors have to be given rules that define when and how the behavior is supposed to work. For example, it is clear that a character cannot buy goods or hire other characters if it has no money (such as poor Chris Clifford). These conditions will be defined along with the rule itself.

Attributes can also be used to determine the result of a behavior. For example, we might have the sale price of goods increased when a character has a high charisma. Alternatively, we might have a similar increase in pay when the character performing a service has a high ethic—the character puts more effort into the work.

The relationships between objects are manifest in their behaviors. In Figure 2.2.15, we see a diagram of two characters during a service exchange. One character hires a service that the other performs. We include, in the illustration, the attributes of each character that are relevant to the outcome of this behavior.

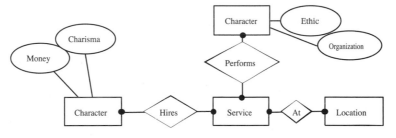

FIGURE 2.2.15 *An entity relationship diagram.*

System designs usually begin at a high level, starting with an intended play mechanic, and then get broken down into more specific details. With each pass, you refine your questions and answers. How does a character trade? What can be traded? When can trade of this object occur? Where? As you go, it is likely the complexity of your system will deepen. It is difficult to predict the behavior of all but the simplest systems. You need to periodically observe the behavior and make adjustments. In other words, you design, prototype, test, and tune. You *iterate*—perform the steps repeatedly—until the level of detail you need has been reached.

Emergence and Systemic Design

Every year, gaming audiences grow savvier. As they become versed in the conventions typical of a style, they demand more novelty as a result. Experienced players can quickly map boundaries of environment and expression, plumb the depth of the simulation, and expose limitations. Our customers grow ever hungrier for larger and larger possibility spaces [Wright03]. In the past, industry has responded by delivering products with more elaborate technology and more content. However, in attempting to add more of everything, the size and expense of the typical project have ballooned and are becoming more difficult to sustain. As a result, most small development studios are having difficulty continuing to operate successfully as independents.

However, many developers are discovering that, perhaps, "more" isn't the only approach. At the 2002 Game Developers' Conference, Harvey Smith delivered a popular lecture contrasting *special case* with *systemic* design. His distinction between *special case*—creating gameplay for a specific, localized occurrence in a game—and *systemic*—creating gameplay out of mixing existing game elements which consist of globally consistent behaviors and characteristics—contrasts two approaches to the demands of players.

Special case refers to game interactions that have been designed by anticipating game states and player actions [Smith02]. The designer visualizes each scene of play as he imagines a user will experience it. Unique events, encounters, and challenges are designed and created for each of these interactions and the emphasis is placed on a "micro" approach; the implementation addresses each special case directly and specifically. Events are mainly prescripted—the sequence and nature of the interaction fully determined beforehand. Player strategies are often concerned with discovering the intentions of the designer.

The *systemic* approach refers to approaches where the structure of the game system provides a set of consistent, universal behaviors. Rather than create many individual and unique problems and solutions throughout the game, the basic rules are generalized and structured into a system. The player experiences the game by working freely within the established rules and premise, as in *Grand Theft Auto* or *SimCity*. Key events and encounters may still be sequenced and scripted on a case-by-case basis, but the *core mechanics* work as part of a rule-based environment. Player strategies are most usually concerned with better understanding the behavior of the world and inventing novel solutions.

Systemic approaches to design often lead to *emergent complexity*—behaviors that cannot be simply predicted from the rules of a system [LeBlanc00]. Player immersion intensifies when the system behaves unexpectedly while remaining self-consistent—events of the game are plausible within its own rules.

In 1843, John Stuart Mill wrote *Systems of Logic* and distinguished "mechanical" from "chemical" modes of producing effects [McLaughlin99]. In the mechanical mode, two or more causes produce results that would be the same had each cause happened on its own rather than together. Imagine pushing a ball in two directions—

once straight-ahead and once to the side. The final position of the ball would be the same regardless of the order in which the pushes were applied. Mill suggested that in the chemical mode (so named because of the way in which chemical reactions seemed to produce results), the resulting product could not be achieved by the effects of each cause independently. For example, methane reacts with oxygen to produce carbon dioxide and water, a process that would not occur with each reactant on its own. Mill called the mechanical products "homopathic" and the effects of the chemical mode "heteropathic." Mill's work would spawn the tradition of British Emergentism. In 1873, George Henry Lewes coined the term "emergence" when he labeled effects that were heteropathic as *emergents* and homopathic as *resultants*.

Emergence is used today in many scientific disciplines to refer to unexpected, novel, and nontrivial phenomena that arise from the behavior of complex systems over time. Indeed, many games exhibit this type of emergence as well. However, some controversy has arisen regarding which are *really* examples of emergent phenomena and which are not. To avoid confusion, you may choose to use *rule combinations* to refer to a game's heteropathic effects, and reserve *emergence* for describing behaviors arising unexpectedly in complex multiagent systems (such as John Conway's *Game of Life*) [Juul02]. When all else fails, Lewes' definition seems broad enough to accommodate everyone.

Uncertainty and Probability

The mathematical study of *probability*, measuring the likelihood a given even will occur, is rooted in the study of games. Italian mathematicians had first solved some specific problems regarding games of chance, but no general theory of probability emerged until the seventeenth century [Apostol69]. A French nobleman consulted Blaise Pascal on a gambling question. In where a pair of dice was thrown 24 times, was it profitable to wager that 12 ("double 6") would be rolled at least once? The discussion that would follow on this and other related matters, between Pascal and mathematician Pierre de Fermat, would develop into the basis of probability theory.

When a system always responds in the same way to a set of conditions and inputs, that system is called *deterministic* [Ledin01]. Assuming the state and control variables remain the same, multiple runs will produce the same result again and again. However, if there is variation from one run to another, while the state and control variables have remained constant, that system is called *stochastic*—in other words, random.

When we discuss *uncertainty*, we are referring to an aesthetic—not knowing what's to come. This lack of foreknowledge, when regarding the outcomes of play, is vital to all games. Without uncertainty, player motivation flattens into a weak signal. When every decision is obvious, every outcome known, people lack the desire to play.

There are four main causes of uncertainty:

- Incomplete information
- Inaccurate information
- Linguistic imprecision
- Disagreement between sources of information

Any of these causes can increase the degree of uncertainty players experience (we support the argument that intentionally introducing linguistic imprecision is not usually fair). The most common method in computer games is to present the player with incomplete information. Some state or aspect of the system is not revealed explicitly to the player. In economics and in game theory, this is referred to as *imperfect information* and is in contrast with *perfect information*—when all players know all there is to know about the state of the game. Both types have existed for a long time: games such as chess and go are of perfect information, nearly all card games are of imperfect information, and so on.

Although uncertainty and probability are related, they are not synonymous. Uncertainty is a psychological experience, probability a mathematical likelihood. While we can make use of probability to generate player uncertainty, we must be careful. "Added randomness" can be easier for a player to detect than one might, at first, suspect, and players tend to resent suffering at the hands of fate rather than by their own actions.

Deterministic systems can still elicit a high degree of uncertainty. One approach is to make outcomes dependent on player performance as well as strategy, similar to sports. For example, first-person shooters are usually deterministic: the variability in player performance and strategy maintains uncertainty. Another method, the most common in video games, is to occlude portions of the system structure or function so that the players operate from a position of imperfect information. They must understand and strategize from knowledge at hand and allow the rest of their decision making to be based on estimates and deductions.

Stochastic systems, on the other hand, can be very difficult to implement and their influences should rarely reach the outcomes of major objectives. When used to introduce variety or in some other way "fuzz" a system to seem more natural (e.g., when propagating environments), stochastic systems can be very useful. Nevertheless, it is usually best to avoid letting pseudorandom fate seal the player's doom.

Dynamics

In game design, we discuss the behavior of systems over time as *dynamics*. Specifically, we are concerned with understanding and generalizing the ways relationships between components of a system can change [Wright03]. However, this has proven difficult to do beyond a case-by-case basis.

The player experiences the game system as a dynamic structure. Figure 2.2.16 shows a model, first used at the 2001 Game Developers' Conference, created by game designer Marc LeBlanc for understanding games [Hunicke04]. *Mechanics, Dynamics, Aesthetics* (MDA) ties the players' emotional responses to the body of a game. The players' view of the game is the result of their interaction with the system over time. (In MDA, *mechanics* refers to the game components, at the level of data representation and algorithms; it encompasses the *system* and *interface* of our model.)

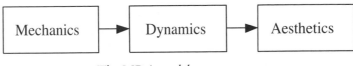

FIGURE 2.2.16 *The MDA model.*

Game dynamics result from continued interactions between the players and the game system. It is hard to determine general behaviors of dynamic systems—each is dependent on their particular structure of objects, properties, and the relationships between the member elements. You can appreciate the complexity of dynamics by reflecting on the problems of creating decision trees.

Feedback and Feedback Loops

Established in the late 1940s, *cybernetics* is a study of communication, control, and regulation in organisms and machines. An early paradigm for modeling systems, it designed and analyzed mechanisms that affect control. Some typical examples of cybernetic systems are governors, thermostats, and autopilots [Wright03].

Figure 2.2.17 shows the elementary cybernetic systems consisting of a *sensor* detecting a condition and reporting to a *comparator*, which evaluates the information, potentially triggering an *activator*, which makes a change in the system that alters the monitored condition [Salen04].

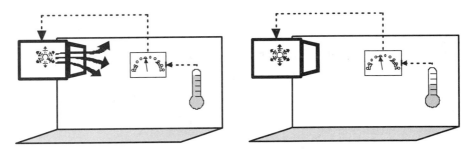

FIGURE 2.2.17 *A climate control system [LeBlanc04].*

When a portion of output from a system is returned back into the same system as an input, the returned portion is known as *feedback*. Literally, this output has been "fed back" into the system from which it came, resulting in further output being altered by the returned input.

The path that is taken by the returned portion is called a *feedback loop*. Feedback is a central concept in cybernetics, control theory, and many other systems disciplines. By connecting several of these simple systems together, more complex systems and behaviors are created.

As Jay Forrester illustrates in Figure 2.2.18, filling a glass with water is more complex than just the flow of water into a container [Forrester96]. The volume of water is being controlled by a feedback loop that spans from the level of water to eye to hand to faucet controlling the water flow.

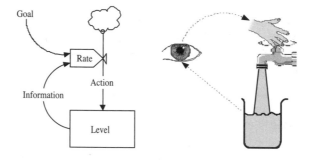

FIGURE 2.2.18   *Simple feedback loops [Forrester97].*

Feedback comes in two basic types:

Negative feedback: Leads to goal seeking
Positive feedback: Leads to runaway behavior—explosion or standstill

Although the name can be a bit misleading, *positive feedback* can be rather difficult to make use of. It either increases an already increasing rate of an accumulation (as in Figure 2.2.19), or it decreases an already decreasing rate. In Figure 2.2.17, a positive feedback on the left would turn the room into an icebox.

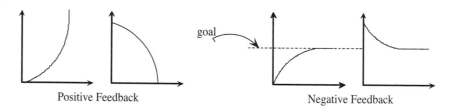

FIGURE 2.2.19   *Curves representing basic feedback types.*

The best-known kind of positive feedback is audio feedback, the Larson effect. A microphone is positioned too near a speaker connected to the microphone's amplifier. The system rapidly overloads itself and a piercing screech threatens all eardrums within range.

Negative feedback can be described as a *goal-seeking* behavior: as it nears a target level, its rate is restricted more and more (Figure 2.2.19). In Figure 2.2.18, a negative feedback loop from water level to eye to hand turns the spigot off as the water reaches the "full" mark. In Figure 2.2.17, a negative feedback loop turns the climate control systems off when the ideal temperature is reached.

LeBlanc has generalized some of the feedback behaviors as they relate to games [LeBlanc99]:

- Negative feedback stabilizes the game.
- Positive feedback destabilizes the game.
- Negative feedback forgives the loser.
- Positive feedback rewards the winner.
- Negative feedback can prolong the game.
- Positive feedback can end the game.
- Negative feedback magnifies late successes.
- Positive feedback magnifies early successes.

System Dynamics—A Modeling Tool

As we've mentioned, it is very difficult to make assumptions about the behavior of a system over time. A variety of tools allows us to simulate system structure and behavior—useful if we will need to be testing and changing this structure frequently. One such tool was started in 1956 at MIT. *System dynamics* is a modeling and simulation discipline created by Dr. Jay Forrester to study how systems change over time.

At first, system dynamics was a tool for policy analysis in organizations. Why would some decisions produce expected results while others catastrophic failure? Since then it has been a popular tool for observing system behavior in urban planning, biology, economics, and a wide variety of other fields. For game designers it provides an easy tool for quickly prototyping systems—object relationships and behaviors can be taken for a trial run.

System dynamics describes everything in two aspects: *stocks* (or *levels*) and *flows* (or *rates*):

Stock: A level; an accumulation of something
Flow: A change in the quantity of an accumulation

Figure 2.2.20 shows a basic system-dynamics model. The clouds on either end symbolize the *boundaries* of the model—factors beyond the current scope. In this model, we are looking at a population of peasants.

We begin with 10 peasants and, each month, we will add to this a number of new peasants equal to the value of "births"; currently 10. Therefore, each month, 10 new peasants are born. Likewise, a number equal to "deaths" will expire each month; 2. When we run the simulation over a period of several months, we get a graphed result like that on the left of Figure 2.2.21.

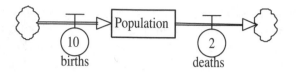

FIGURE 2.2.20   *A simple system-dynamics model of a peasant population.*

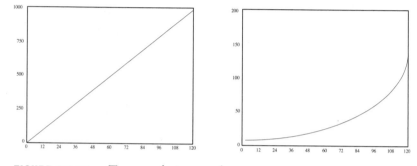

FIGURE 2.2.21   *Two population graphs.*

Every year 10 peasants are added to the town's population and 2 are removed, for a net gain of 8 peasants. By the end of 10 years, there are 970 peasants living in the town. To turn this linear relationship into something more interesting, we change the birth and death numbers into rates that are fractions of the population.

Figure 2.2.22 shows how a diagram of our improved simple system might look. Now, rather than a fixed rate of births and deaths, we have a "birth rate" and a "mortality rate" that are based on the total peasant population—5 and 2.8 percent, respectively. Now, when the simulation is run, we see a population graph (Figure 2.2.21, right) that appears to rise more naturally. Our fictional peasants are prospering nicely.

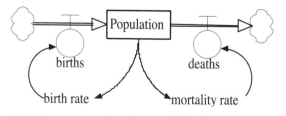

FIGURE 2.2.22   *Population feedback.*

Remember that a positive feedback loop produces change in the same direction, which may be either a rate of increase or of decrease. It is also known as a *reinforcing loop*. Negative feedback, on the other hand, produces change in the opposite direction. Negative feedback is goal oriented, in that it attempts to modify a condition to some target level (indicated in Figure 2.2.19 by the horizontal line).

Other types of behaviors result from a compound of positive and negative feedback types—oscillations and S-shaped curves. When a delay is introduced to a negative feedback loop, oscillations are produced as in Figure 2.2.23. The system responds to a condition, but, because the results of that response aren't immediate, the condition passes the goal in the other direction and the system has to compensate. Typically, the oscillations will diminish as the policy directs the system closer and closer to its goal.

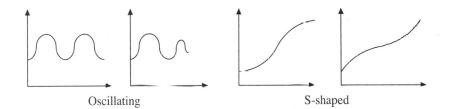

Oscillating   S-shaped

FIGURE 2.2.23   *Compound feedback curves.*

You've probably had, at some time or another, the experience of filling a bathtub where the water is, at first, too cold and then, after adjusting the spigot to compensate, too hot. You may have had to trade too hot and too cold back and forth a few times until the temperature was comfortable enough to step into the tub. The delay in that system would have been the time it took for heat to be exchanged through the volume of water in the tub, at which point your testing (with a finger or a toe perhaps) would indicate when the goal temperature had been reached.

S-shaped behaviors (Figure 2.2.23, right) occur when a system changes from a positive to a negative feedback loop, or vice versa. Objects might use a given behavior until a certain condition is reached, at which point another behavior takes over.

Constraints

At first glance, a topic on *constraints*—the condition of being restricted within fixed bounds—doesn't promise to be very exciting. However, constraints are at the kernel of game design and most veteran designers would probably agree that working within them often leads to the best features [Hecker02]. In fact, it could be said that design is, itself, a process of dreaming within constraints. Most of this chapter has already been addressing constraints implicit in our work; this topic will clean up a few we have not yet addressed.

When designing, think of constraints as *parameters* rather than as *limitations—measurable factors that define a system* versus *a restriction.* The semantic difference may seem slight, but constraints are easier to appreciate when seen as a help to understanding, rather than as an obstacle to progress.

Consider an analogy to motorcycle riding: When riding a motorcycle, it's good not to run into things. People, however, tend naturally to look at threats. They also tend to steer their body and vehicle in the direction they look. Because, to a motorcycle, any object larger than a poodle is a potential threat, these two behaviors lead to "undesirable" results; in a car, a fender-bender, but on a motorcycle an emergency room. New riders must be taught to look away from obstacles, finding paths that avoid rather than paths that collide into them. Game designers deal with constraints by creating solutions that move around and within, rather than against them.

This approach to constraints is similar across the various roles designers fill, from senior to associate, game to level. Each of these differ more by scale and context than by kind. Whether you are designing systems, interfaces, or placing interactive props in a scene, you are inventing solutions to problems within constraints. What does the player do within these constraints? How do the objects relate within these constraints? Where should I position these crates within these constraints?

Platforms

A computer game *platform* is a general description of hardware and software that collectively determine how the device will function, applications will operate, and how the user will interface with the appliance. It is no surprise that the capabilities of these devices are frontline concerns to designing games.

Typical platform categories include:

Personal computer (PC):   A multipurpose system supporting applications ranging from spreadsheets and Web browsers to games (e.g., Windows PC).
Console: A dedicated gaming system designed to integrate with consumer audio/video appliances (e.g., PlayStation 2).
Handheld (console):   Dedicated handheld gaming devices with integrated controller, display, and sound (e.g., Game Boy Advance).
Mobile device: Handheld multipurpose devices; cell phones, PDAs, etc.
Arcade: Proprietary coin-operated systems, for public use (e.g., *Asteroids!*).

From a production perspective, the PC is the easiest platform for which to develop games. Most of the tools used in production run on the same machine as the game being developed. The memory and storage capacities of the average desktops outstrip that of even the most powerful console systems currently available; dedicated gaming machines built by hardcore PC gamers push that technology to extremes.

Developing for console and handheld systems, on the other hand, can be technically challenging. First, proprietary development kits are required. These range from special development environments, such as Sony's TOOL for PlayStation 2 development, to more generic "homebrew" solutions that require a fair amount of patience to accommodate.

Next, console performance and capacity limitations mean that designers must watch resources to a much larger extent than on a similar PC project. Limited system RAM leads to careful asset loading management, and limited memory card storage resulting in careful use of state variables and persistent data. Being judicious with space is not as unwelcome a constraint as it sounds; often, what is left out of the model is unimportant.

Mobile devices suffer similar technical constraints to handhelds, although they are typically easier to develop for. Distribution is often from the Internet so costs can be lower. Typically, the problem has been finding the consumers. However, over the past few years, the mobile market has taken hold, and millions are spending more time playing games on their phones than talking into them.

Arcades have been in steady decline since the end of the 1980s and beginning of the 1990s. There are any number of reasons why this may be so, the most significant being that the technology, once far superior to that available in home consoles, has been met and sometimes outmatched by consumer devices. The main advantage left to arcade machines is the integration of unique, specialized controllers such as the mock cockpits for racing games.

So why doesn't the personal computer dominate the video game market? Several advantages to consoles make them attractive to game developers. First, they are dedicated systems with controllers tuned to game playing; in contrast, keyboard-mouse interfaces are often unwieldy for many types of games. Consoles are known as *lean-back* devices—designed to work either in the hand or with entertainment systems that afford comfortable seating positions and relaxed environments—you play them while lounging in an easy chair or on the couch. In contrast, PCs are known as *sit-forward* devices where one sits upright at a desk—a position more usually associated with work than with play.

During development, testing a console title can be more focused and productive because there is one standard hardware configuration; in testing PC games, QA teams may have to test over 100 different configurations and *still* not cover more than a portion of those configurations possible.

Lastly, although PCs may have an *installed base*—the estimated number of units out in the world—of over 700 million [Shiffler04], only a small portion of those are capable of playing the latest games. The PS2, however, currently has an installed base of over 70 million units, *all* of which are capable of playing the latest games. As a result, the typical *hit* PC title might sell several hundred thousand copies, while hit console titles sell in the millions.

Game Saves

The ability to save progress is expected in nearly all digital games outside of the arcade, but raises many challenges for designers. The subject is somewhat controversial, as there are many personal philosophies, biased by negative experiences with one system or another.

Save triggers automatically save the game state when the player performs a particular action such as reaching a location or overcoming a challenge. They can make it easier to tune the pace of the game; players cannot "game" the save system by frequent, incremental saving. Objections to this scheme often cite the lack of control this affords the players to moderate their own progress and play session length—sometimes, the real world does interrupt our gaming. Pitfall to avoid: the risk of saving players' progress at inopportune moments, leaving them vulnerable to events immediately following a reload.

Save-anywhere systems (a hallmark of PC games) allow players to maintain safety in the most challenging of situations—each encounter can be replayed with little effort and the outcomes will tend toward minimal losses and maximal gains [Imlach02b]. Balancing difficulty with these systems can be challenging, as even unintentional overuse of the system can make the most difficult game a cakewalk.

Save points allow users to save progress at any time they wish, while mandating set locations to save. Most consoles are known for this type of system in lieu of the more resource-intensive save-anywhere schemes. Save points allow the system to write a smaller set of state variables when storage space is at a premium.

Coded-text or *password* systems may be similar to triggered or save points systems. Rather than use hardware storage, an algorithm codes relevant state variables into a text string (a password) that the player must write down and remember. Because it must be relatively easy to record, the amount of data these systems encode is usually quite limited. These days, even the simplest systems can afford a few bytes of storage, so coded-text saves are becoming rare. They still find occasional use when it is desirable for players to share saves with each other.

Genres

The entertainment arts are classified first by media (film, literature, games, etc.) and then further into *genres*—categories describing generalities of conventions, style, and content. Genres are commonly criticized for loose definitions. Most games fit more than one at the same time, sometimes leading to designation as a *hybrid*—a blend of two or more genres—such as the ubiquitous *action-adventure*.

A few examples:

Action: Emphasize a fast pace, quick reactions, and motor coordination.
Adventure: Players engage in story-driven exploration and puzzle solving.
Arcade: A type of action game where mechanics vary little during play.
Casual: Gradual learning curves, short play sessions, and broad appeal.
Educational: Teaches real-world knowledge or skills to the player.
Fighting: Typically fast and short one-on-one bouts with elaborate controls.
First-person shooter (FPS): Emphasize quick reactions and precision targeting.
Platform: Players performing feats in an environment; jumping, swinging, etc.

Puzzle: Solve logical or geometric puzzles as the core mechanic.
Racing: Driving along a track, trying to achieve shorter (i.e., faster) times.
Rhythm: Emphasis on matching rhythms through the controls.
Role-playing (RPG):   Adventure games focusing on character development.
Simulation: Games that emphasize model detail (i.e., perceived realism).
Sports: Emulate contests of physical sport.
Strategy: Core mechanics focus on strategy and managing resources.
Traditional: Digital renditions of nondigital games.

Audiences

During design, we frequently consult mental models of our *target audience*—the group of consumers expected to buy and play our game—to make judgments. We imagine their preferences, abilities, and habits. The accuracy of these intuitions can vary wildly; mappings between mental models and the real world are strongest when the population in question resembles our own. Unfortunately, it is difficult to make good decisions on the sole basis of intuition.

One tool to appreciate audiences objectively is *demographics*, the study of relevant economic and social statistics about a given population. The relevant factors are called *demographic variables* (e.g., age, gender, income, etc.) and are used to segment consumers into groups known as *markets* and smaller groups known as *market segments*. The attributes of a typical market member are known as a *demographic profile*.

For game designers, demographics provide a starting point to defining the audience, but typical demographic techniques (e.g., polling, surveys, etc.) do not always produce the information most interesting to us: understanding the play preferences of the segments. Knowing *what* a market segment likes is not as valuable to designers as understanding *why* it likes something.

For a long time, game genres themselves have been used to classify player preferences. For example, the preference for detailed realism is often attributed to fans of the simulator genre (typified by *Microsoft Flight Simulator*). However, these models are informed by the product, not the players, and are really a kind of folk demographic—a guesstimate by nonspecialists.

Various efforts have been made to typify players' behavior and preference by their motivation to play. Most of these studies rely on personal experience and anecdote to form categories such as *explorers, collectors, competitors, jokers, storytellers*, and so forth [Fullerton04].

Similarly, the industry has long divided consumers into two broad groups: *hardcore* (core) and *casual*. While it is generally acknowledged that this distinction is no better than any other arbitrarily invented scheme, it follows that it is no worse.

Some typical attributes of the hardcore gamer include [Ip02]:

• Playing games over many long sessions
• Discussing games frequently and at length

- Being knowledgeable about the industry
- Having a higher threshold for frustration
- Desire to modify or extend games creatively
- Have the latest game systems
- Engage in competition with themselves, the game, and others

Casual gamers, it is implied, are everyone else. As you may imagine, this type of distinction's usefulness can be somewhat minimal when the largest potential audience is left essentially undefined.

Recently, there have been more rigorous attempts to understand player motivations and types. In particular, Nicole Lazzaro (XEODesign) has presented the *Four Keys*, a breakdown of what players like best about games [Lazzaro04]. Successful games contain elements of two or more of these keys simultaneously:

The Player: The Internal Experience Key
Hard Fun: The Challenge and Strategy Key
Easy Fun: The Immersion Key
Other Players: The Social Experience Key

Internal experience: Refers to the enjoyment from visceral activities—resulting sensations such as excitement or relief.
Hard fun: Encompasses challenging aesthetics such as strategy and problem solving.
Easy fun: Comes from intrigue and curiosity—stimulated by exploration and adventure and moved by wonder, awe, and mystery.
Social experience: Involves stimulating our social faculties. Experiences range from competition, teamwork, bonding, and recognition.

"What surprised us most was the dramatic contrast in emotional displays between one vs. several people playing together. Players in groups emote more frequently and with more intensity than those playing on their own. Group play adds new behaviors, rituals, and emotions that make games more exciting."—Nicole Lazzaro, *Why We Play Games* [Lazzaro04].

Iterating

One long-standing approach to software development is the *waterfall method*. In this paradigm, software design and production are broken down into distinct phases. First, the needs of the customer are assessed and documented as *requirements*. These are then analyzed and a plan for the software functionality is designed. After design, the product is developed and tested before finally being released.

There are strengths and weaknesses to any methodology, and waterfall development does put an emphasis on planning, which can be useful. However, it also works best when the needs of the customer (and therefore the form of the product) are reasonably well understood. Because games are dynamic, it is difficult to predict formal requirements with great precision. What is needed is a structured way to adjust the design of the product as it takes shape.

Iterative development refers to the practice of producing things incrementally, by refining and rerefining the product. This approach to building games is marked by use of *prototypes* and frequent *play-testing* in repeated cycles of designing, building, and tuning. Rather than attempting to design the game in complete detail, before production, designers produce a framework—a fundamental organization of features—around which the rest of the game can be built.

Prototyping

Prototypes are early models of the finished product, used to test ideas and techniques. They can be used during all phases of design; you don't have to wait until production is underway [Fullerton04]. All prototypes, whether built in software or from physical material, serve the same purpose: to present a rough, working model that can be evaluated and tuned. Sometimes they may approximate the whole of the game, but more often they are used as disposable test beds—an idea or feature is mocked up and taken for a test drive.

Physical prototypes are nonelectronic models made from paper, cards, chips, tokens, dice, and other common items. Use pens to draw figures, words, and numbers on playing surfaces while concentrating on the utility of the art, not its aesthetics; it needs to be effective while play-testing, not pretty. Make changes quickly as testing and tuning demand and do not let romantic attachments to features get in your way.

Software prototypes are implemented in code. These are the prototypes that, once in production, you are most likely to make use of regularly. They may be separate from the main body of the game's code, or they may be implemented within the main *branch* but in a discrete location where they are easy to remove. Often, prototypes are written in a scripting language (such as Lua or Python) where performance concerns are secondary to ease of development.

Testing

Software testing, also known as *quality assurance* (QA), is the process of verifying the performance and reliability of a product. Expected behaviors are verified by a *tester*, a person trained in the methods of evaluating quality in software products. When a *bug*—a discrepancy between what should and what is happening—is found, a *problem report* or *bug report* (also called a *bug*) is written. The bug describes the current behavior and the steps to be followed to reproduce it.

Play-testing is akin to software testing, but focuses on detecting problems in the play mechanics. *Play-testers* are individuals who play the game, in either directed play or freely, and report feedback on the experience. Designers will often observe play-testers, taking notes and occasionally asking questions of them [Federoff03].

Some considerations:

- Can the players use the controls? Do they understand them?
- Is the GUI clear? Menus navigable?
- Can the levels be completed? With how much effort?
- Can the needed skills be learned? In how long?
- Are they entertained? In what ways?

A *focus test* is a particular kind of testing session, when a group of play-testers (a *focus group*) representing the target audience is brought to a single location to play-test. These sessions are good for getting lots of feedback at once, but the social dynamics among testers in a group often add noise to the data that compromises its usefulness. On the subject of user feedback, Nathaniel Borenstein recommends listening to the concerns of the users but ignoring what they say in favor of determining what they really mean [Borenstein94].

It is an easy thing, during the course of creating a game, for developers to become blinded to the actual experience of play. Some aspects of the game may have undergone several revisions and, with each change, the risk that the player experience is overlooked is increased. In *Game Design Perspectives*, Sim Dietrich offers the following list of warning signs for faulty game design [Dietrich02]:

- New players can't play the game without assistance.
- New players don't enjoy the game without assistance.
- Excessive saving and loading.
- Unpopular characters.
- The all-offense syndrome.
- Players frequently reconfigure controls.

Tuning

Problems found in the play mechanics during testing must be solved by the designers. *Tuning* refers to the process of developing solutions by adjusting the properties and behavior of systems and interface.

Balance is a property of relationships, usually characterized by equilibrium. In classical aesthetics, it is a harmonious relationship of elements—like the distribution of shape and form in a painting or the movement of dancers on a stage. In games, balance is used in a few ways, all indicating a similar relationship to the preceding definitions.

We might seek to balance:

Player relationships: A lack of bias toward one player versus another.
Mechanics: Keeping the player in the flow channel.
System: Game objects are balanced amongst each other.

Rock-Paper-Scissors (RPS) is the common name of a balancing approach that uses *intransitive relationships*—three or more elements offer weakness and strengths relative to each other as a whole, so that balance is reached [Rollings00]. Figure 2.2.24

shows the relationship in RPS and its counterpart between light infantry (archers), heavy infantry, and cavalry. Table 2.2.4 shows a payout matrix.

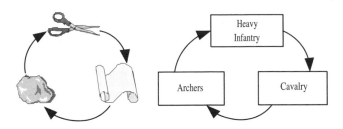

FIGURE 2.2.24 *Two simple intransitive relationships.*

Table 2.2.4 Rock-Paper-Scissors Payoffs

	Rock	Paper	Scissors
Rock	0	−1	1
Paper	1	0	−1
Scissors	−1	1	0

Intransitive relationships are common in multiplayer games because they allow each group of players to feel powerful in a given set of circumstances. They can also provide incentive for players to form groups; one character's abilities are not enough for it to perform a task on its own.

Creativity

Creativity is the ability or power to create. In psychology it is specifically understood as the ability to produce an idea, action, or object that is considered new and valuable within the context of the culture at hand [Csikszentmihalyi99]. To the work of a designer, however, the novelty and acceptance of a creative idea are secondary to its effectiveness. In other words, it's more important that the solution *work* for the game and not as important that it be widely recognized as a creative approach. Think of the creative approach as a mode of decision making.

Most people believe creativity to be a talent or an aptitude. People inherit creativity through the luck of the gene pool, and you either have it or you don't. If you're of the unlucky majority, so the wisdom goes, you may as well pack it in. The truth is that anyone can learn to be creative.

A Classic Approach

In 1926, Graham Wallas proposed a general form for creative thought. It described the creative process in four distinct stages, and later work on the subject of creativity commonly looks to this early framework for guidance [Wallas26]. Later versions of this model would integrate a fifth stage, elaboration, to appear as follows:

Preparation: The background of research and comprehension of a subject, preparation is an intentional effort to become immersed in a symbolic system or domain. You read, study, and consider every lesson on the subject you encounter. Known and common solutions are reviewed or deconstructed in a process typical of reverse engineering.

Incubation: "Mulling things over," is the thinking and reflection applied to an idea. This work may or may not occur consciously and can continue during unrelated activities [Campbell85]. During this time, ideas are subjected to broad censorship and discrimination, most of which occurs either too subtly or too rapidly to be noticed.

Insight: Whole answers that are resistant to unconscious censorship become revealed to awareness in a moment of sudden illumination. These revelations are the "Eureka!" or "Aha!" experience, hallmarks of the creative process. This is the "one percent inspiration" of Edison's famous quote: "Genius is one percent inspiration and ninety-nine percent perspiration."

Evaluation: Validating the revealed insight. Strive for balance in the evaluation of your ideas, as there are equal tendencies to be overly critical or not critical enough. Solutions should be discarded if a lack of significant novelty is revealed.

Elaboration: Although Wallas did not include this phase in his first description of the creative process, it is a common addendum. Elaboration is the transformation from concept to object; transforming the idea into substance.

These phases are recursive, to be repeated in part or in full as many times as necessary. Failure at any given stage often returns creative thinkers back to the preparation phase where they incorporate what has been learned by the failure into their assessments.

Brainstorming Techniques

By far, the most popular and common approach to stimulating creative thoughts is *brainstorming*. Nearly all brainstorming involves forcing ideas to be driven through the incubation stage to insight by eliminating discrimination during early stages. Instead, thinkers are encouraged to evaluate only after a wide catalog of ideas have been noted.

This technique works both for groups and alone; the practice remaining essentially the same.

Start with a board or piece of paper with a clear view of the goals and constraints that define the problem. Write a single sentence summary of the brainstorm's purpose. Follow this with cycles of free association ("saying whatever comes into your head") and elaboration on these ideas, writing down key words and statements along the way. Once the participants are satisfied with the volume of ideas or overcome with exhaustion, the processes of normal review and selection can begin.

Critics point out that brainstorming is often unproductive because the process is not directed. Participants are encouraged *not* to think critically and time is wasted elaborating on plainly bad ideas.

Six Thinking Hats

Edward de Bono created a mnemonic thinking tool for assuming different perspectives when engaged in the decision process [deBono85]. These modes of thought are described as colored hats that one "puts on" in order to consider other viewpoints that may not be natural to his or her default outlook. When a given hat is on, the thinker role-plays from the perspective represented by the color:

White Hat: Neutral and objective, wearing this hat involves analyzing known facts and detecting gaps to fill in with information. The emphasis is on assessing the decision.

Red Hat: Intuition, gut reaction, and emotion are all qualities of the red hat. Use your feelings and anticipate those of your audience. Allow views to be presented without justification or explanation.

Black Hat: Dark and gloomy, the naysayer's hat is worn when judging and criticizing ideas. Identify all the bad points of a proposed decision cautiously and defensively and actively play the part of devil's advocate.

Yellow Hat: Pollyannaish attitude typifies this hat. Optimistic logic is applied, looking for benefits and profitable outcomes that could result from an idea.

Green Hat: Symbolizing vegetation, growth and creative possibilities are explored. New ideas or modifications to earlier suggestions are offered with an emphasis on novelty.

Blue Hat: The cool mediating influence of organization is symbolized by blue sky. Wearing this hat, you maintain a process and control-oriented perspective, organizing and reviewing the work of the other hats.

Inspiration

Countless new ideas are littering the world at large. To find them you have only to maintain a mind receptive to playfulness and the structure of games. For game designers, play is the thing. Look for opportunities to play at all moments. Look at elements of life around you and reconfigure them into amusements. Play with your friends. If you lack friends, learn how to have them; a number does not matter—one is enough—but the ability to relate to people is coupled with anticipating their feelings.

Other media types are another endless source of inspiration. Don't just consume passively, but take joy in analyzing them: deconstruct their signs and techniques.

A few sources of inspiration:

Board games: Spatial relationships
Card games: Resource management strategies
Paper and dice role-playing games: Dynamic narratives

Books: Fantasy and agency
Film: Continuity techniques
Television: Serializing stories
Music: Rhythm and temporal relationships
Martial arts: Disciplined competitive sport
Children: Endless invention and capacity for play

Communication

One of the most important roles played by game designers is that of communicators; many describe communication as their primary duty. As part of a team, they must liaise for many groups within the organization, helping build and maintain a shared vision for the game. Often this vision is formed in documentation that may include written specification, asset lists, and diagrams.

Documentation

The subject of documentation is controversial. Each developer will have a set of opinions on the proper form and function documents should have. Each organization will have preferred ways to create, manage, and share documentation among its members; a "treatment" here is a "high-concept document" there. Furthermore, each project will have its own specific needs and challenges.

Remember that documentation is a written, descriptive model of the game you are to build. The depth of detail needed will vary in accordance with the depth and complexity of the feature sets you will be creating as well as the culture of the organization. In general, you should not concern yourself with page counts, but with content, clarity, and usefulness to the situation.

A *treatment* (also *high-concept document* (HCD) or *general overview document* (GOD) or *proposal*) is a brief, general description of the game and the fundamental concepts. François Laramée writes: "A treatment is a document containing the smallest amount of data that can allow a reader to make a reasoned decision on whether he wants to be involved with a project," [Laramée02].

Organizational needs will vary, but a treatment may include:

Concept statement: Two- or three-sentence summation of the game
Goals and objectives: List of the overall purpose of the game
Core mechanics and systems: Overview of all *significant* features
Competitive analysis: Situation of other games and the profile of the market
Licensing and IP information: Intellectual property ownership/requirements
Target platform and audience: Who the customers will be, how they will play it
Scope: Overall budget and timeline estimates
Key features: A "back-of-the-box" list of prominent features

Depending on the particular organization, other documents may include a preliminary design document (PDD) or initial design document (IDD), a revised design document (RDD) or general design document (GDD), an expanded design document (EDD) or technical design document (TDD), and a final design document (FDD). Each of these works within a similar paradigm: the documentation begins at a general scope, and then describes the product in finer and finer detail.

One approach that is growing in popularity is the use of intranet *Wikis*—Web site systems that allow users to contribute content (including new pages, links, and formatting) from within standard Web browsers. Often freely available, they have many of the attributes of commercial documentation management systems while being easier to edit from any machine on the local network because no special client installs are required.

Be careful of letting documentation take on a life and a game of its own. In particular, do not mistake the volume or complexity of the documentation as an indication of the thoroughness of the design. Instead, measure how the documentation is being used as a reference and how relevant its material during production. If it is largely unused or inaccurate, the time spent writing might have been better spent prototyping.

Some developers have proven that it is possible to produce good games consistently using lightweight documentation methods. Notably, Mark Cerny (of Cerny Games) is known for his *antidocumentation* stance as manifest in his process dubbed "The Method" [Cerny02]. Cerny's *macro design* is a short document that forms a roadmap for production. For example, a typical five-page macro design may include:

- Character and move sets
- Any exotic mechanics described
- Description of level structure size and count
- Level contents
- Overall structure—level, progression, etc.
- A "macro chart"—showing dependencies and distribution of mechanics

No other general document is created. Instead, the *micro design* that follows is the day-to-day work of the designers. Using lessons being continually learned through production (including prototypes), the level maps, enemy descriptions, mini games, and other elements are designed "on the fly."

It bears mentioning that many *stakeholders*—directly responsible for or otherwise directly interested in a work—may be reluctant to entrust such a degree of responsibility upon someone lacking Mr. Cerny's 20+ years of proven experience.

Flowcharts

Flowcharting is a very typical technique for diagramming steps in a process. Most developers will be familiar with flowcharting to some degree. This wide familiarity is one of their largest benefits. Once the basic conventions are understood, they can be "read" without needing to understand technical details. Figure 2.2.25 shows the four most common steps in a flowchart.

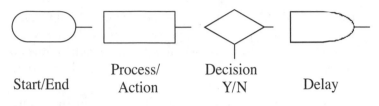

FIGURE 2.2.25   *Common steps in a flowchart.*

Flowcharts are commonly used to describe a series of events ranging from player actions to system behaviors. Because flowcharts are put together step by step, they are helpful for working through sequencing problems. Figure 2.2.26 shows the start of an adventure in a multiplayer game, where party members split up to gather resources and then regroup before heading off to the main encounter.

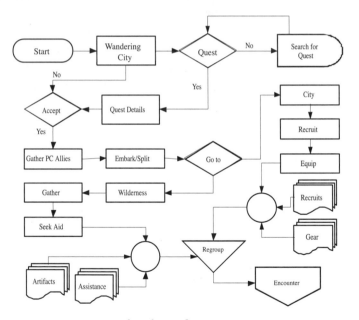

FIGURE 2.2.26   *Flowchart of a game sequence.*

Flowcharts have a downside: as detail and complexity increase, the diagram can become complicated to read. Because of this, flowcharts are most often used to illustrate constrained examples, not detailed accounts of an entire game.

Associative Diagrams

An *associative diagram*, such as the Mind Map in Figure 2.2.27 [Buzan96], is a drawing that helps us manage and organize complex networks of information visually. Elements are linked together illustrating their relationships and context. There is a variety of techniques for creating associative diagrams, all of which can be useful both in creative exercises and in organizing. As documentation tools, they are most useful when those who will be using the diagram are involved in making it.

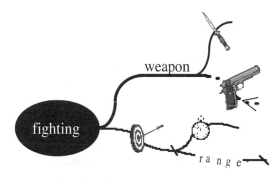

FIGURE 2.2.27 *A Mind Map.*

A central word (or image) begins each diagram, and around this, arms are drawn with key words representing related ideas written along their length. From each of these, more associations are drawn, and the process continues iteratively.

Psychology

Because so much of games and play occurs at the mental level, it is natural that game designers need a basic appreciation for the systems that produce and support the activities inside peoples' minds. For most of us, this is tricky business because we begin with an amazing amount of bad information.

For example, have you heard that people use less than 10 percent of their brain at any particular moment? However, natural selection isn't known for favoring large, complex organs that don't work but 10 percent of the time; especially not when over 50 percent of all genes in our bodies are believed to be in the brain [LeDoux02]. The brain, during periods of relative inactivity, isn't sitting idly by, waiting for something interesting to come along. It is actively processing stimuli, regulating bodily functions (including its own), and producing all kinds of cognitive activity—only a small portion of which is conscious.

So much is happening inside our heads, it's difficult to choose a reasonable starting point to discuss. Fortunately, as designers we need only a basic, approximate model that will be more or less relevant to building opportunities for play.

Working Memory and Attention

Working memory, or short-term memory, is one of our most important cognitive systems. It allows us to keep a limited amount of information, roughly 7 ± 2 items at any one time [Zimbardo92], for a few seconds, while other portions of the brain perform computations on it. When a new task is begun, the old information is bumped out to make room [LeDoux02], and if we aren't done with the first, too bad.

Attention (also known as *selectivity* or *selective attention*) is the method in which our perceptions of certain stimuli are enhanced relative to other stimuli in the same environment when granted lesser immediate priority [Duncan99]. In other words, it's how we turn our focus on things that seem to matter and how we prioritize some goals over others.

Some of the most important studies of selectivity were conducted in the 1950s and involved people listening to two simultaneous messages. These studies formed the basis of much subsequent research.

These studies produced several findings:

Limited capacity: Identifying both messages at once is difficult.
Conditions for selectivity: One message can be identified and the other ignored if the messages differed in physical property (pitch, location, etc.).
Consequences of selection: Listening to one message while ignoring the other resulted in only the crudest recollection of the ignored message.

Any professional dealing with the abilities and capacities of others must respect both of these precious capacities; don't squander or abuse them. As a designer, you must balance the decisions and choices you ask of your players at any given moment so as not to frustrate them. This includes overwhelming them with information or requiring that their attention be spread over too many areas at the same time.

Conditioning

Arguably, Behaviorism's most significant contributions to psychology are its insights into the type of learning known as *conditioning*. The best known of these is *classical conditioning*. In classical conditioning, one stimulus that does not elicit a particular response naturally is paired with another that does until the subject learns to respond to both in the same manner.

Three states are shown in Figure 2.2.28: before conditioning, during conditioning, and after conditioning. Before conditioning, a tone (sound) heard by the dog produces no salivation, but meat (the *unconditioned stimulus* or UCS) in the dog's mouth does (the *unconditioned response* or UCR). During conditioning, the tone (the *conditioned stimulus* or CS) is played while meat is put into the dog's mouth, causing salivation as normal. After conditioning, the dog needs only to hear the tone for salivation (the *conditioned response* or CR) to begin [Zimbardo92].

Operant conditioning (or *instrumental conditioning*) describes learning where an action is encouraged or discouraged by the consequences of the action. The *operant* is a response behavior (e.g., smashing a crate) that produces observable effects in the environment. A *reinforcement contingency* is a consistent relationship between the operant and a change in the environment that results (e.g., get health). The resulting

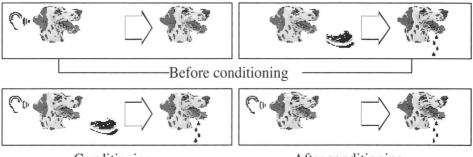

FIGURE 2.2.28 *Classical conditioning.*

changes in the environment are *reinforcers*—they increase the probability the operant behavior will be repeated, in the future and in similar circumstances.

There are two types of reinforcers—*positive reinforcers* and *negative reinforcers*—both of which increase the probability of the behavior. Positive reinforcers (e.g., more health) present a positive stimulus, and negative reinforcers present a negative stimulus (e.g., death). In Figure 2.2.29, the positive reinforcer, staying dry, is contingent upon the use of an umbrella in the rain. Getting wet negatively reinforces the use of an umbrella. In both cases, the user is being trained to use an umbrella.

FIGURE 2.2.29 *Positive and negative reinforcers.*

The process of *operant extinction* withholds positive reinforcement so that an existing operant may be eliminated. Operant extinction is most successful when, in addition to withholding reinforcers, another operant is reinforced by producing the player's desired result. For example, if we wish to train the player to stop smashing crates to find health, we would first stop placing health kits in crates. Then we would use another device for the player to interact with that would result in an increase in health (medics, robot nurses, etc.).

Punishers decrease the probability of an operant when made contingent [Zimbardo92]. *Punishment* is the application of the punisher. The classic example of punishment is being burned by touching a hot stove, the resulting pain being the punisher.

It is easy to get confused by negative reinforcement and punishment. They are related, but work differently:

Punisher: Reduces the likelihood of a behavior

Negative reinforcer: Increases the likelihood of a behavior

Be judicious regarding the use of punishment to eliminating undesired behaviors. Psychologist Philip Zimbardo suggests reinforcing alternative behaviors rather than punishing the undesired. Punishment, as an aesthetic, is not one that will appeal to most players. The punished response will be suppressed grudgingly and a negative attitude toward the game can result.

Keep conditioning in mind when considering player *training*—introducing the player to new mechanics. In the past it was common to instruct the players using tutorials or user manuals, but these methods tend to get set aside; even when the players know they *should* go through the process of learning how to play the game properly, they would rather spend their time actually engaged in the game.

More recently, games have been dispensing with tutorials in favor of training the player in-game. Objectives can be structured to present the player with one or two new features, allowing the player to become acquainted with them before moving on. By tying the outcomes to the actual game progression, players are more easily motivated to go through the training scenarios and less likely to feel as though time is being wasted.

Summary

This chapter surveyed a broad spectrum of vocabulary, tools, methods, and practicalities of game design. We began by describing games as artifacts of play. Much as with other forms of entertainment, we interact with these to experience feelings within a safe frame, removed from repercussions in the real world. Viewing games like this, we began to explore their different aspects through a feature-based lens.

We examined play mechanics as the models experienced by the players: premise, choices, outcomes, goals, strategies, and other interactions with the game. These actions are mediated by the interface, which we discussed in terms of input and output systems, governed by principles being explored by human-computer interaction and cognitive ergonomic practitioners.

Our examination of game artifacts proper ended with an introduction to game systems. We touched on systemic design and emergence and introduced a few basic examples of modeling systems with objects. We briefly discussed positive and negative feedback systems as well as probability and uncertainty and their relationship to gaming experiences.

We touched on some common constraints that designers must work with on a day-to-day basis (especially those of platforms, genres, and audiences) and followed this with a quick introduction to iterative development—honing through repeated testing, prototyping, and balancing.

To help direct our creative efforts, we reviewed a few views of creativity itself. This was followed by discussing methods by which communication is propagated in a development organization using documents, flowcharts, and associative diagrams.

Our final topic scratched the surface of some issues in psychology that are immediately relevant to designing games, including working memory, attention, and conditioning.

As the game development industry matures, so too do the approaches and techniques of design. Traditional methods for creating media artifacts, which first inspired a broadening of the game design field, now seem to be reaching the end of their usefulness. Game designers are beginning to explore new forms of interactive expression that do not fit well within the earlier paradigms of art. Our art requires that designers develop not only aesthetic sensibilities, but also a technical capacity for defining and tuning systems. Our talents lie in the ability to model activities, both imagined and real, in dynamic simulations that are understandable through the lens of screen and game pad.

Exercises

1. Select a game with which you are familiar. Create a list of objectives in the game. Next to each, describe how a player might structure goals to reach that objective.
2. Find a volunteer to observe at play. For 20 minutes, create an exhaustive list of mechanics down to primary elements. For 10 minutes, ask the player to describe immediate goals; correlate these self-reports with mechanics you have observed.
3. Describe six qualities of choice. Provide examples of each from a released game. Do the same for all of Norman's principles of design.
4. Plan a level in a horror-themed game. Provide at least one diagram of a successful player experience, beginning to end, and one diagram of a failure.
5. Design a small game system of no fewer than five object classes. Detail each type of object, its attributes, behaviors, and relationships.
6. Plan a save game feature for *Pac-Man*. Choose between save-anywhere and triggered schemes. Explain how it functions and what state variables will need to be stored.
7. Build a physical prototype of a game; it may be an original design or a translation of a video game of your choice [LeBlanc04].
8. Create a treatment for a video game version of traditional marbles.

9. Design a "catch-up" feature for a racing game; explain how feedback would be used.
10. Describe the control scheme for a barbershop game where players cut hair.

References

[Apostol69] Apostol, Tom, *Calculus, Volume II*, 2nd ed., John Wiley & Sons, 1969.

[Baillie-de Byl04] Baillie-de Byl, Penny, *Programming Believable Characters for Computer Games*, Charles River Media, 2004.

[Borenstein94] Borenstein, Nathaniel S., *Programming as if People Mattered*, Princeton University Press, 1994.

[Buzan96] Buzan, Tony, *The Mind Map Book*, Plume 1996.

[Campbell85] Campbell, David, *Take the Road to Creativity and Get off Your Dead End*, Center for Creative Leadership, 1985.

[Cerny02] Cerny, Mark, John, Michael, "Game Development: Myth vs. Method," *Game Developer Magazine*, June 2002: pp. 32–36.

[Chalmers94] Chalmers, A. F., *What is this thing called science?* 2nd ed., University of Queensland Press, 1994.

[Chartrand77] Chartrand, Gary, *Graphs as Mathematical Models*, Prindle, Webber & Schmidt, 1977.

[Cosmides99] Cosmides, Leda and Tooby, John, "Evolutionary Psychology," *The MIT Encyclopedia of the Cognitive Sciences*, The MIT Press, 1999: pp. 295–297.

[Costikyan02] Costikyan, Greg, "Talk Like a Gamer," available online at *http://costik.com/gamespek.html*, 2002.

[Costikyan04] Costikyan, Greg, "Pastimes and Paradigms," available online at *http://costik.com/weblog/2004_06_01_blogchive.html*, June 18, 2004.

[Cousins04] Cousins, Ben, "Elementary game design," *Develop*, October 2004.

[Crawford03] Crawford, Chris, *Chris Crawford on Game Design*, New Riders, 2003.

[Csikszentmihalyi96] Csikszentmihalyi, Mihalyi, *Creativity: Flow and the Psychology of Discovery and Invention*, Harper Collins, 1996.

[Csikszentmihalyi99] Csikszentmihalyi, Mihalyi, "Creativity," *The MIT Encyclopedia of the Cognitive Sciences*, The MIT Press, 1999: pp. 205–206.

[Damasio94] Damasio, Antonio, *Descartes' Error*, Gosset/Putnam, 1994.

[deBono85] de Bono, Edward, *Six Thinking Hats*, Little, Brown, and Co., 1985.

[Duncan99] Duncan, John, and Hollan, James D., "Attention," *The MIT Encyclopedia of the Cognitive Sciences*, The MIT Press, 1999: pp. 39–40.

[Fauconnier02] Fauconnier, Gilles, and Turner, Mark, *The Way We Think*, Basic Books, 2002.

[Forrester97] Forrester, Jay, "System Dynamics and K-12 Teachers," Jay Forrester, 1997.

[Fulghum89] Fulghum, Robert, *All I Really Need to Know I Learned in Kindergarten*, Random House, 1989.

[Fullerton04] Fullerton, Tracy, et al, *Game Design Workshop*, CMP, 2004.

[Goodale99] Goodale, Melvyn, "Visual Processing Streams," *The MIT Encyclopedia of the Cognitive Sciences*, The MIT Press, 1999: pp. 873–874.

[Grier92] Grier, James W., and Burk, Theodore, *Biology of Animal Behavior*, 2nd ed., Mosby Year Book, 1992.

[Hecker02] Hecker, Chris, "Jay Stelly: Technically Speaking," *Game Developer Magazine,* January 2002.

[Hollan99] Hollan, James D., "Human Computer Interaction," *The MIT Encyclopedia of the Cognitive Sciences*, The MIT Press, 1999: pp. 379–380.

[Huizinga55] Huizinga, Johann, *Homo Ludens: A Study of the Play Element in Culture*, Beacon Press, 1955.

[Hunicke04] Hunicke, Robin, LeBlanc, Mark, Zubek, Robert, "MDA: A Formal Approach to Game Design and Game Research," available online at *http://algorithmacy.8kindsoffun.com/MDA.pdf*.

[Ip02] Ip, Barry, and Adams, Ernest, "From Casual to Core: A Statistical Mechanism for Studying Gamer Dedication," Gamasutra.com, June 2002.

[Isaacs65] Isaacs, Rufus, *Differential Games: A Mathematical Theory with Applications to Warfare and Pursuit, Control and Optimization*, Addison Wesley, 1965.

[Johnson99] Cara, Francesco, "Cognitive Ergonomics," *The MIT Encyclopedia of the Cognitive Sciences*, The MIT Press, 1999: pp. 130–131.

[Johnson99] Johnson-Laird, Philip N., "Mental Models," *The MIT Encyclopedia of the Cognitive Sciences*, The MIT Press, 1999: pp. 525–526.

[Juul02] Juul, Jesper, "The Open and the Closed: Games of Emergence and Games of Progression," Computer Games and Digital Cultures, 2002.

[Laramée02] Laramée, François, "Writing Effective Design Treatments," *Game Design Perspectives,* Charles River Media, 2002.

[Lazzaro04] Lazzaro, Nicole, "Why We Play Games: 4 Keys to More Emotion in Player Experiences," XEODesign® Inc., available online at *www.xeodesign.com/whyweplaygames*, 2004.

[LeBlanc00] LeBlanc, Marc, "Formal Design Tools: Emergent Complexity, Emergent Narrative," (Game Developers Conference), available online at *http://algorithmancy.8kindsoffun.com/gdc2000.ppt*, 2000.

[LeBlanc04] LeBlanc, Marc, "Game Design and Tuning Workshop Materials," (Game Developers Conference), available online at *http://algorithmacy.8kindsoffun.com/GDC2004/*, 2004.

[Ledin01] Ledin, Jim, *Simulation Engineering*, CMP, 2001.

[LeDoux02] LeDoux, Joseph, *Synaptic Self: How Our Brains Become Who We Are*, Penguin, 2002.

[McLaughlin99] McLaughlin, B. P., "Emergentism," *The MIT Encyclopedia of the Cognitive Sciences*, The MIT Press, 1999: pp. 267–268.

[MICRA98] MICRA Inc, *Webster's Revised Unabridged Dictionary*, MICRA Inc., 1998.

[Norman86] Norman, D. A., *The Psychology of Everyday Things*, Basic Books, 1988.

[Norman88] Norman, D. A., and Draper, S. Eds., *User Centered System Design: New Perspectives in Human-Computer Interaction*, Erlbaum Associates, 1986.

[Pinker97] Pinker, Steven, *How the Mind Works*, W. W. Norton & Co., 1997.

[Richards99] Richards, Virginia M., and Kidd, Gerald D. Jr., "Audition," *The MIT Encyclopedia of the Cognitive Sciences*, The MIT Press, 1999: pp. 48–49.

[Rollings00] Rollings, Andrew, and Morris, Dave, *Game Architecture and Design*, Coriolis, 2000.

[Salen04] Salen, Katie, and Zimmerman, Eric, *Rules of Play: Game Design Fundamentals*, The MIT Press, 2004.

[Shiffler04] Shiffler, George III, "Global PC Installed Base Reaches 716 Million," Gartner, 2004, available online at *www4.gartner.com/DisplayDocument?doc_cd=125049*.

[Siviy98] Siviy, S. M., "Neurobiological Substrates of Play Behavior: Glimpses into the Structure and Function of Mammalian Playfulness," *Animal Play: Evolutionary, Comparative, and Ecological Perspectives*, Cambridge University Press, 1998: pp. 221–242.

[Smith02] Smith, Harvey, "Systemic Level Design for Emergent Gameplay," Game Developers Conference, 2002, available online at *www.gamasutra.com/features/slides/smith/index.htm*.

[Smith03] Smith, Harvey, "Orthogonal Unit Differentiation," Game Developers Conference, 2003, available online at *www.gdconf.com/archives/2003/Smith_Harvey.ppt*.

[Sniderman99] Sniderman, Stephen, "Unwritten Rules," *The Life of Games*, No. 1 1999, available online at *www.gamepuzzles.com/tlog/tlog2.htm*.

[Suits90] Suits, Bernard, *Grasshopper: Games, Life, and Utopia*, David R. Godine, 1990.

[Wallas26] Wallas, Graham, *The Art of Thought*, Harcourt-Brace, 1926.

[Wright03] Wright, Will, "Models Come Alive," *PC Forum 2003*, EDventure Holdings Inc., 2003.

[Zimbardo92] Zimbardo, Philip, *Psychology and Life, Thirteenth Edition*, Harper-Collins, 1992.

PART 3

GAME PROGRAMMING: LANGUAGES AND ARCHITECTURE

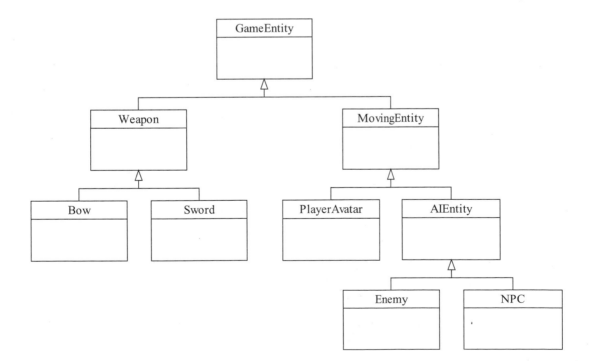

3.1 ▍ Teams and Processes

Overview

There is more to programming a game than sitting in front of a computer equipped with your favorite editor and compiler and banging away at the keyboard all night long. Most commercial games are created by large teams of people, ranging from just a handful to hundreds of programmers, depending on the team size and scope of the program. This chapter explains how programming teams are organized and what techniques they commonly use to effectively coordinate the work of all the team members and create a great game.

Programming Teams

Years ago, all the way to the early 1990s, programmers were often at the center of game development and were the vision behind the game. However, as team sizes and budgets grew and the focus of game development shifted from technical improvements to gameplay itself, people realized that just because someone was a brilliant programmer, it didn't mean that he or she was a good game creator.

The role of programmers today is very different from what it was a few decades ago. Today, the game is created by the content creators (artists and designers) with full support from the programmers. Programmers are responsible for creating some of the game code (following designers' input), the technology on top of which the game will run (usually called the "game engine"), and the tools that the artists and designers will use to create the content for the game itself.

This is by no means a less interesting or prestigious role, but it's more oriented toward servicing the rest of the development team and providing them with the means to create an amazing game. The fate of the entire team rests in the programmers' hands, and it's their responsibility to make sure everything runs smoothly and reliably.

Programming Areas

There are three distinct areas of programming involved when creating a game.

Game Code

Game code is the main body of code that people think about when referring to game programming. This includes everything directly related to the game itself: how the camera behaves when the controller is pushed, how the score is kept for a particular game type, or how the AI entities in the world react to certain situations.

This type of programming often involves writing a large amount of code in scripting languages (as opposed to the main language the rest of the game is written in, such as C++). The purpose of using scripting languages at this level is to:

- Produce faster iteration by avoiding time-consuming compile, link, run cycles
- Allow technically inclined designers and artists to change behaviors in the game directly
- Present a more appropriate language to deal with the problem domain (e.g., a high-level custom language to deal with AI issues is probably much easier to use than C++)

Game Engine

Programming the game engine involves all the code that goes into the final game that is not game specific. You can think of it as all the support code necessary to have the game run on top of it. Sometimes, people erroneously think of a game engine as being what draws the pretty 3D graphics, but that is only the graphics renderer (also called the "graphics engine," which adds to the confusion), which is one of the many parts of the game engine.

One of the goals of a game engine is to isolate the game from the hardware on which it's running. It does that by creating an abstract layer between the game and the hardware. That way, the game doesn't have to worry about the details of the platform and can concentrate exclusively on the game logic itself. Examples of this type of abstraction are gathering input from the controller, putting graphics on the screen, or playing back sounds.

The engine also provides common functionality that is needed by different parts of the game. For example, the game engine will provide support for serialization (reading and writing the state of objects), network communication and synchronization for multiplayer games, pathfinding functionality for the AI, or collision detection and response for physical simulation of objects in the world.

As we'll see in a later section, effective use of middleware can reduce, or even completely remove, the need for this type of programming.

Tools

Tools programming is an extremely important but often overlooked area. The more data-driven game development becomes, the more crucial tools become, and the more of a difference they make in the quality of the final game.

The primary type of tools involves content creation: level editors, particle effect editors, sound editors, and so forth. These tools are often written in the form of plug-ins for existing, off-the-shelf tools, so the functionality of existing tools is extended to provide exactly what the team requires. This has the huge advantage of allowing the content creators to use robust, mature tools they're already familiar with instead of quirky in-house tools without any documentation. Some of the most popular tools used in game development extended through the use of plug-ins are modeling tools such as Alias' Maya and Autodesk's 3ds max, and bitmap-editing tools such as Adobe® Photoshop®.

If a tool to create a certain type of content is not available, or extending it through a plug-in is not feasible, then it is written from scratch. This is usually the case with very specialized types of editors, such as particle effects, or editing of game unit attributes (number of hit points, speed, animations, etc.). These tools are written in C++ or any other high-level language that allows for quick GUI development and still interfaces reasonably well with the primary language in which the engine is written.

Other types of tools that are often necessary in game development are scripts to automate repetitive tasks, converters to optimize and package data into efficient formats, and testing code to verify everything is working as expected. All these are usually command-line tools without a GUI.

Team Organization

The bulk of the programming team is comprised of programmers (or software engineers). These are the people who actually design and implement all the different systems and bring the game art and design to life.

Game programming is a very technically challenging activity, so programmers usually come from a computer science, engineering, or mathematics background.

Other nontechnical backgrounds are not uncommon if they were complemented with a lot of self-instruction and independent game-related projects.

Because games are so large and they encompass so many different areas, programmers often specialize in specific areas, allowing them to concentrate on a subset of problems and work on solutions beyond what any generalist could do. You will often find specialists in graphics, networking, AI, sound, and so forth. An advanced degree can be very useful for programmers who want to specialize in a particular area.

In contrast to the specialists, some programmers are able to understand most areas of game programming without mastering any of them. These generalists are often crucial to a project because they're the glue that binds all the specialists. Their global view of the project gives them a unique perspective to pinpoint bugs and narrow down unexpected interactions between different systems. Generalists with a lot of experience often make great lead programmers.

As soon as the number of programmers goes over three or four, some form of organization is usually needed. At this point, the role of lead programmer is introduced. A lead programmer coordinates the efforts of the rest of the programmers and makes sure they all work toward the same goal. Someone in that role usually spends a lot of his time with management duties, and can only devote part of his time to actual programming.

If a team grows even larger (over 10 programmers or more), it is common to also have several programmers as leads for specific parts of the game. Some common positions are graphics lead, AI lead, and so forth.

Blurring the line between programming and design are the people in charge of writing the scripts that control the behavior of most things in the game. In some companies, they're called "technical designers," while in others they are "gameplay programmers."

Skills and Personalities

Some people might think that the ideal team is comprised of very experienced senior programmers who have all worked with each other in many projects before. However, teams comprised of team members from a variety of backgrounds and with different levels of experience can be much more effective.

It is true a seasoned, senior programmer with many battles under his belt can bring a lot of experience and wisdom to the team. However, a smart junior programmer straight out of college will bring a new perspective, question decisions, and bring a certain degree of enthusiasm to the entire team. Hopefully, all members of the team can contribute to the project and learn from each other.

The same can be said for having different personalities. Some people are very methodical and organized, preferring to proceed slowly and with sure footing. They are the reliable workhorses that the team can depend on to get from point A to point B. Other people are much more impulsive and visionary, and tend to think outside of the established customs. They can be the spark that takes the game in new directions, opens new doors, or inspires other people with their ideas.

Having a team with diverse levels of experience and different personality types can present some management challenges, but with the right management, a diverse team can accomplish truly outstanding results.

Methodologies

A "methodology" is just a fancy name for what procedures will be followed during development to create the game. It can range from something completely informal, to something very structured with very specific steps. The choice of methodology will have a great effect on how smoothly the development comes along. The larger the team, the more important it is to have a well-defined methodology to allow everybody to work side by side without tripping over each other.

Code and Fix

Unfortunately, the most common development methodology in game development today is the lack of one—often referred to as a "code-and-fix" environment. It involves very little or no planning, diving straight into implementation, and fixing problems as they come, also referred to as "fire fighting." Such environments are mostly reactive, not proactive, because they're always dealing with the latest emergency situation in a hurried way as opposed to meeting new challenges head-on with full knowledge of what's coming ahead.

Poor quality and unreliability of the finished product are a consequence of a code-and-fix environment. Looking at the number of games with technical problems, incompatibility issues, or crash bugs, this is quite common in the industry today. What is worse, the poor reliability of the game also affects the development of the game itself. If the game and the tools are often crashing or are difficult to work with, iteration and experimentation by content creators is going to be reduced, leading to poorer quality of the final product.

Things can get even worse for code-and-fix environments, though. The entire development process can quickly spiral out of control as bug counts mount faster than they can be fixed and the creation of game content crawls to a halt. This is called the "death spiral." Projects at this stage are often cancelled by the publisher and put out of their misery.

The lucky projects that manage to make it to the end usually had to survive significant "crunch" times of extended work hours. Even though game companies often like to boast about their long crunch times, the result is burned-out employees who either leave the company or become far less productive in future projects.

If a code-and-fix environment has so many problems, why does the industry continue to go down that path? Mostly because of inertia. That's the way things were done 15 or 20 years ago, and back then they probably worked fine with a team size of four people and a project that only lasted from six months to a year. With modern team sizes, budgets, and development cycles, such an environment is clearly not adequate. Projects aren't getting any smaller—quite the contrary—so things will continue to get worse.

On the positive side, many companies are concerned about this state of affairs and are starting to look beyond code-and-fix environments for new solutions, so there is hope that the industry will pull itself out of this rut.

Waterfall

A waterfall approach tries to combat the uncertainties of game development by planning all the details ahead of time. Teams create detailed technical documents (and usually thick design documents and art bibles) explaining all the details of how they're going to go about implementing the game.

The benefits of this approach is that it does force the team to think ahead of time about what it's going to do, what the challenges are going to be along the way, and how they're going to solve them. If done well, such an approach can also create an accurate schedule, come up with a set of milestones for the publisher, and estimate the delivery date of the finished game. As long as the planning was done correctly and nothing unexpected happens, everything will go smoothly and the game will ship on time. This approach might work well for sequels or games that attempt very little innovation from both a technical and a gameplay point of view, like sports sequels or expansion packs.

However, in most situations, game development is just too unpredictable to plan in such detail ahead of time. If there's one thing you're guaranteed in game development, it is that something unexpected is going to happen: you have to support new hardware in the middle of development, some of the most challenging technology is delayed, or simply your game is not turning out to be as fun as you hoped for at the beginning. As soon as that happens, the entire plan usually goes out the window. Managers and producers might try to bring it back on track, or to come up with new schedules, but usually this schedule is always behind the realities of development. In the worst situation, a waterfall environment can degenerate into code-and-fix environments as the team fumbles to try to catch up with some initial schedule and meet the publisher's milestones.

Iterative

Iterative methodologies encompass many different approaches. The basic idea is to do development for a period of time (a month or two), accomplish a set of goals, get the game to a reasonable state, and then start again with another period and add new features to it. Each of the periods is usually made to coincide with publisher milestones.

This approach has the benefit that some planning is possible, it can be a proactive environment instead of a reactive one, and it allows the flexibility of changing course in midproject if it's necessary or adjusting things based on how the development progresses.

Iterative methods can vary from extremely informal approaches to much more formalized methodologies like the *unified process*, which is still iterative but recommends that the team follows a set of phases and produces a set of specific documents and deliverables for each iteration.

Agile Methodologies

Agile methodologies attempt to deal with an unpredictable environment, not by trying to plan for every possible contingency, but by admitting that things will change and adapting to those changes. The general strategy is to avoid looking too far into the future. Instead, they plan for short periods of time (a few weeks), work based on that plan, and iterate constantly on their product. They value simplicity and the ability to change course at any time.

These characteristics allow agile methodologies to adapt to any unexpected events, or even to what they learn as they develop the game. If a competitor comes up with a must-have feature, they can easily incorporate it in their game halfway through development; if the team loses a key member, things can be scaled back or adapted and still allow the game to ship on time.

The team is always very aware of the current state of their game, where they are with respect to where they want to be, and what the highest-priority tasks are at any moment. This visibility and flexibility give agile methodologies an edge in this industry. When the strong winds of change blow, agile methodologies bend and follow the wind instead of being rigid and eventually breaking under pressure.

The main drawback of agile methodologies is convincing the publishers or stakeholders in the project that this is a reasonable development methodology, because it's still relatively new in game development. Agile methodologies also require that everyone involved has a flexible mindset and is ready for things to change as necessary. Unfortunately, some people are much more comfortable planning hard milestone dates set months in advance even though the probability of that plan remaining unchanged is virtually zero.

Common Practices

Every team does things differently, but the following are some of the common practices you're bound to find in just about every development team.

Version Control

In a nutshell, a version control program is a database that contains any number of files and, possibly, the past history for each of them. Every team nowadays has all their source code under version control. This has several main benefits:

Team collaboration. This is the main benefit of version control. By having all source code files under source control, it is possible for team members to work on a related set of files without overwriting each other's work. The version control program acts as an arbiter, and takes care of avoiding conflicts between different changes people make.

Centralized location. By using version control, there is one clear, central point that contains all the source code for the game and tools.

History for each file.   The history of each file in the project is preserved in the version control database. This can be extremely useful to track down problems that started happening at a particular date, to look at implementation decisions made in the past, or to undo some recent changes and go back to how a certain part of the code was a few days ago.

Branching and merging.   Finally, version control programs allow you to branch a set of files. Branching a set of files means that a new copy of those files is created. The original files are called the "main line," and the new files are the "new branch." The key part is that the version control program "remembers" when and where they were branched from, and then uses that information to allow merging changes made to the branch or to the main line relatively easily. Branching can be used to separate code that is almost ready to ship, to work on complex subtasks without affecting the rest of the team, or to split the work among several functional subteams by giving each of them a working branch.

Version control is not limited to source code. It is very common now for game companies to put their game assets in version control as well. This includes all the assets that artists and designers create: textures, models, shaders, levels, characters, animations, sounds, effects, and so forth.

Coding Standards

Programming is, above anything else, a team activity. You don't write code for the computer to understand, you write it for other team members to understand. They'll need to read, modify, or debug your code at some point in the future, and you'll probably have to do the same with theirs. It's for this reason that many companies establish a coding standard to facilitate collaboration between programmers.

The coding standard is a document that describes the guidelines that programmers must follow when writing code. It can cover layout issues such as where to put the braces and the amount of indentation, naming conventions for variables and classes, or even design aspects, such as when to use interface classes and what to expose to the users of a library.

The actual coding standard varies from company to company. Its contents vary, since everybody seems to have a different way of doing things, and even the length of the document itself varies from a quick one-page document to a massive 50+ page volume detailing every guideline. Another difference is how strict the contents of the standard are. Some companies treat it as a suggested set of guidelines that people might want to follow, while others treat it as the ultimate law, and code will have to be modified to comply with those standards before it is checked in to version control.

Daily Automated Builds

Teams will often have a dedicated automated build machine. At fixed times of the day (and night), it will automatically get the latest code from source control, build the game, tools, and any other programs, and report success or failure by sending an e-mail to the team. If an error was encountered, the list of errors is included in the e-mail so they can be fixed right away. If the build was successful, the code is usually labeled in source control so programmers know about a set of source code that built successfully and can use it as a starting point for their work.

These builds are crucial to the progress of the project. As long as the game builds successfully, progress is being made. If the game enters a period when it fails to build for several builds in a row, there is no visible progress. Additionally, as long as the game cannot build and run correctly, programmers can't run the game to test their changes. Having the build always pass and the game always run should be a high priority for any team.

In addition to building code, the automated build machine (or another dedicated machine) can also build game assets: convert assets to efficient binary formats, check for asset validity, build levels, run expensive lighting calculations, and pack the resources into large resource files. Additionally, it can also take it one step further and run a set of tests on the game with the code and resources that were just built to make sure all the levels can be loaded and nothing crashes.

Quality

As projects become larger and more complex, more programmers are needed to write code, and the resulting codebases are larger and more complicated than ever before. At this point, the main challenge is not to do some clever hardware trick, but to make sure all the code works as expected, reliably and robustly. This section presents some techniques to help with the quality and reliability of the code.

Code Reviews

Two pairs of eyes are better than one: that's the principle behind code reviews. It is very easy for the programmer who implemented a certain feature to get too close to the code and miss obvious mistakes or potential problems. Having another programmer look at the code can catch many things the original author missed.

Code reviews can vary a lot in how they're implemented. On one end of the spectrum, they can be a very formal affair, presenting the code to a group on an overhead projector and having everybody contribute comments and point out pitfalls. On the other end, it can be very informal, with just one other programmer quickly looking over the code on the author's workstation.

Code reviews can also differ in when they're conducted. Some teams prefer to review a different section of code once a week after it has been added to the code base, while others prefer to do it frequently for small sections of code, often before the code even makes it in to source control.

A side benefit of code reviews is that they make programmers aware that team members will be reading their precious code, so they're going to think twice before taking any ugly shortcuts or becoming sloppy. Don't underestimate the positive power of peer pressure in a situation like this.

Asserts and Crashes

For all the care you put into making sure your game is as bug-free as possible, it's almost sure that it will crash at some point or another during development (hopefully not after it ships!). What's important is that you quickly learn the reason it crashed and that it's fixed right away so it never crashes again. How can we do that?

The main tool at our disposal is the use of *assert statements* (or the language equivalent if you're not using C++). An *assert* is simply a statement that checks a certain condition. If the condition is valid, then nothing happens and the program continues executing as normal. However, if the condition is not valid, the program is halted, printing as much information as possible about the failed assert: what the condition that failed was, where in the code the assert was, and any other relevant information. If the game (or tool) was running from a debugger, a breakpoint is hit so that the programmer can quickly determine the sequence of events that led to the failed assert.

In a way, we're crashing the program ourselves in a controlled way to prevent a total disaster. Think of it as an emergency landing of a plane that is running out of fuel: we cut our trip short and try to land in a controlled way instead of continuing our flight to spectacularly crash to the ground once all the fuel is used up. Fortunately, hitting an assert statement is much less life threatening than an emergency landing, so programmers can use them liberally all over the code base.

Probably the most common use of asserts is to check that pointers are not NULL before using them. Otherwise, if we attempt to use a NULL pointer, the program will crash right away. Other uses of asserts including checking the range of parameters passed into a function (e.g., that an index into an array is not larger than the array itself), or even that the results of a calculation make sense (e.g., that the number of hit points of an entity is never negative).

It is important that asserts are only used for detecting errors caused by code bugs, not by unexpected things the user of the game or tool could do. So, while it's fine to assert if we run out of memory (clearly a technical problem that needs to be fixed), we should avoid asserting if the user tries to open a file that doesn't exist. Instead, we should report those user errors in a meaningful way without stopping the program, and let the user try again. This is particularly important to improve the efficiency of the content creators in the team; it will make them more confident in what they're doing, and they'll be much happier and productive in the long run.

However, in spite of all our best efforts, we should still be ready for the game to crash (hopefully not very often though). In this situation, the objective is not to recover from the crash, but to give us as much information as possible to fix the bug that caused it right away. To do that, we should write some code that gets called whenever our program crashes and try to collect as much information as possible about what led us here: where in the code the crash happened, what the call stack looked like, a dump of the CPU registers, and perhaps even a full dump of some of the hardware state that can be used to diagnose the problem with a debugger.

Keep in mind that you might only want to use asserts and crash notifications like these during development. Especially in the case of console games, which can't easily be patched, once the game is shipped and out of your hands it's usually best to remove all that code, hope all the bugs have been ironed out, and hope for the best. On the other hand, if you're working on a PC game or a massively multiplayer game that is expected to be fixed and upgraded over time, you might want to leave the option in for users to report any fatal errors they encounter.

Unit Tests

When you have a codebase as large as the one for modern games, consisting of hundreds of thousands or even millions of lines of code, created by an entire team of programmers, no single person can keep all the details in his or her head. How can anybody be sure that whatever changes they just made aren't going to break or interfere with existing code? Sure, we can run the game and make sure that it runs OK. However, what if we broke a different section of code that we're not testing? What if we broke it in a nonobvious way? What if we broke a tool? Are we going to test them all every time we make a change?

Unit tests are small tests that verify that a single bit of functionality is working correctly. They are usually written at a very low level and test single systems in isolation. For example, we can have a set of unit tests that verify that our math library works correctly: a matrix transpose does what we expect, and a vector-matrix multiplication produces the correct result.

The real power of unit tests is that the computer is running the tests, we're not. It can run thousands of such tests in no time, it never gets tired of running them repeatedly, and it lets us know as soon as any test fails. That means that we can run all the unit tests every time we make a change. Assuming our unit tests cover most of the functionality in our code, if we ever cause something else to break, we'll know it right away, even before we run the game. Otherwise, if everything passes, we can confidently go ahead and commit our changes to source control.

Two factors are crucial in how useful unit tests become for a particular project. First, they have to be easy to write. The harder or more complicated they are to write, the less programmers will use them. The second factor is how easy they are to run. Ideally, they should run automatically every time any change is made to the source code, maybe as a post-build step. If that's not practical, then they should at least run during the automated daily build.

People have already written test harnesses that greatly simplify the process of adding new unit tests and running them. You should start looking at the freely available xUnit test framework, which is almost sure to have a version for the language you're using. Two popular C++ frameworks are CppUnit and CppUnitLite.

Acceptance Tests

Unit tests are able to verify that low-level functionality is working correctly. That's very useful, but it doesn't tell us much about the game itself. We know that the math library is doing all the calculations correctly, but can the player reach the end of a level by completing all the objectives? Does the AI respond correctly to a certain path through the dialog tree?

Acceptance tests verify that the game is working correctly at a very high level and answer some of the previous questions. As with unit tests, the power of acceptance tests comes from the fact that they're automated, so they can be executed over and over without any direct supervision and we'll know as soon as anything breaks.

These tests are usually implemented in a simple scripting language that drives the game. The scripts also need to interact with the game and retrieve some state to verify the results of the test. For example, an acceptance test can be as simple as making sure that every level loads correctly. It iterates through the list of levels, attempts to load each, and checks that they loaded correctly. If any errors are encountered, information is collected and e-mailed to the relevant team members.

A different, more advanced acceptance test could automatically move the player through all the objectives in a level and make sure the mission is completed with a success state. Clearly, to implement this type of functionality, we need to provide enough hooks in our game to allow all those actions to be driven from the test script. Any time and effort spent adding such a system will pay for itself many times over during the development cycle of the game.

Bug Database

Using a bug database is one of the most established techniques in game development. Hardly any game development team will be without a bug database, and most publishers require that their developers use them.

The idea of a bug database is to document all the bugs, any steps that led to that bug, and what the expected behavior of the game was instead. These bug reports are filled by the QA department, other programmers, the publisher, or anybody who plays the game during development. Bugs are usually classified based on their severity, so it's possible to quickly find and fix crash bugs, and put off purely cosmetic bugs until later. As programmers fix the bugs, they are marked as resolved but remain in the database as a record of what was done.

The bug database serves a dual purpose. The primary purpose is to make sure all bugs are listed and that everybody is aware of them. Otherwise, in a large team, it's far too easy for bugs to fall through the cracks by forgetting to tell people about them or incorrectly assuming that someone else is already working on a certain bug.

The secondary purpose of the bug database is to get an idea of how the game is progressing. If the goal is to meet the ship date without any important bugs left, but bugs aren't being fixed fast enough, we can immediately tell that the target ship date is in jeopardy and something should be done about it.

Unlike the other techniques for improving code quality listed in this section, a bug database doesn't prevent bugs from being created in the first place, it just keeps a record of them and makes sure they get prioritized and fixed. The bug database is an invaluable tool that no project should be without, but it should not be used in isolation, and preventive quality techniques such as unit testing or code reviews should be used in conjunction with it.

Leveraging Existing Code

Of the three programming areas we mentioned earlier (game code, engine code, and tools), only the game code (and maybe a small part of the tools) is unique to each project. The game engine, by definition, is mostly game-independent. The tools are also, for the most part, independent of the game itself since models, textures, sounds, and most content are created in similar ways across different games.

Isn't it a waste of time and resources for every game project to write an engine from scratch before writing the game? Engine development is a very complicated and challenging part of programming, and experts in the fields of graphics, physics, or networking are often required to create production-quality game engines. Tools are also very time consuming, and it can take years for a team of experienced programmers to come up with robust, mature tools that the content creators can use effectively. Consequently, not only is it duplicated effort to do that every time, but it's also very costly.

If you're working for a large company, you might be able to reuse the tools and engine from earlier games, especially if you have a dedicated technology group in charge of maintaining that code and making it available to each game group. However, what if you're in a small company or you're starting from scratch?

One possibility is to try to adopt existing code that is freely available on the Internet. A bit of searching will usually reveal lots of source code already written for the most general tasks, and this code will often be free for anyone to use (be sure to check the license for any restrictions on commercial use, such as contacting the author or having to release the source code to your product). Good examples of existing code that is ready to be used are Boost (a set of general templated C++ libraries), or Zlib (a popular compression library). However, be aware that free code usually doesn't come with any technical support other than mailing lists with other users, so be sure you can handle any unforeseen problems by yourself or you have a backup plan.

If the code you wanted wasn't freely available, or if you're uncomfortable with the lack of support, you may be able to buy both. Some companies specialize in providing solutions for specific subsystems of game engines. This is called "middleware," because it sits in the middle between the hardware of your target platform and the game itself. Middleware is usually available for very specific, well-defined subsystems. For example, you'll be able to find companies offering middleware for graphics rendering, collision detection and physics, animation, sound, AI, video playback, or network connectivity. You have to pay for middleware, but it usually comes with technical support to help you in your development so it is usually well worth the money.

If you license middleware, you're just buying parts of an engine. You get a renderer or a network layer, but that's not sufficient to write a full game. You still need to write the rest of the game engine and tools to bind all the middleware together with your own custom technology into a coherent game engine, so plan ahead for that time.

You can go further than that and license a full game engine. Unlike middleware, game engines are a full package: they include all the game engine code, tools, and often game code that you can use as a starting point for your own game. You only have to modify the engine code if you need to implement something unique to your own game. Otherwise, you can use it right away to start creating your own game. Full engines are usually tailored to specific game genres (such as FPS, RTS, massively multiplayer, etc.), so as long as the engine is targeted at your type of game, it'll make your development much easier.

The benefits of leveraging existing code are clear. You don't need to spend any time designing, implementing, and debugging that code. Most of the time, even if you have to pay to license middleware or an engine, the licensing cost is often less than what it would have cost to pay a team of programmers to develop that same technology (assuming you even had access to programmers with that skill set). Therefore, not only do you often save time, you also save money. Keep in mind that programmers will still need some time to become familiar with the new code and how to use it, so there will still be a certain amount of ramp-up time.

On the other hand, there are some reasons not to use existing code. One of them is monetary. If you're in the rare situation of having unlimited time but not unlimited budget, then developing the technology yourself might make more sense. In addition, if you're looking ahead and planning multiple titles, developing the technology yourself might save you money in the long run.

However, the most compelling argument for not using existing code is that you need more control over the code or that it's not capable of supporting the features you want in your game. Beware of this situation, though. Programmers are notorious for having a huge NIH (Not Invented Here) syndrome, and they will criticize and reject any code they didn't write. Fight that tendency and try to analyze objectively whether the existing code will fit your needs or will be easier to modify than writing it from scratch. That decision can have tremendous consequences for the project and even the entire company down the line.

Some of the areas where existing code can fall short are dealing with new platforms (it might take a few months or years before it fully takes advantage of new hardware), or integration with other tools or pieces of code (such as interfacing with your own content pipeline). Finally, always keep in mind the possibility of the middleware company going out of business, and be ready with a backup plan or at least make sure you can have access to the full source code.

There is no doubt that the focus of game development is moving to a higher level. We're already seeing a trend of middleware being much more common than it was a few years ago. Few teams today consider writing their own physics system, and more and more teams are considering licensing sound, graphics, or networking middleware. In the future, expect licensing of middleware and full engines to become much more common, so start getting comfortable with the idea of using other people's code.

Platforms

Games have always been developed for a wide variety of platforms. Any type of electronic device that could support games usually did. However, it seems that today, more than ever, there is an enormous variety of different platforms with extremely varied capabilities. Your choice of platform can profoundly affect how you decide to program the game.

Personal Computers (PCs)

PCs have been a very popular platform for games for many years. Currently, the most popular operating system for games is Microsoft® Windows®, but there are games for other operating systems as well such as Linux or Macintosh.

Games on PCs are just another application that runs on the computer, so they have to behave and play nice with the operating system and other applications. For example, games will often have an install program, must deal with switching focus between applications, or have to put up with a virus scanner running in the background. Unlike most applications, games will often push those limits and take over as much of the PC as possible by using the entire screen, using every hardware resource, and possibly even requiring that other programs not be running in the background.

There is a unique characteristic to PC games that becomes both one of its most important draws and one of its main problems: changing hardware. PC games are the first ones to push the limits of the hardware. New video and sound cards are developed exclusively for games, and a top-of-the-line PC can usually sport amazing audio-visuals that dwarf anything else out there.

The downside is that not everyone has the latest hardware, and PC games need to make sure they run on a wide range of hardware, from several years old to the newest thing on the market. The wider the audience the game aims for, the wider the hardware range it needs to support. The problem is not only having to deal with quirky drivers and unusual hardware combinations, but also supporting a wide range of performance and functionality. It takes a lot of effort to make a game look good on the latest hardware and on an outdated CPU with an old video card at the same time, because the new system is easily an order or two of magnitude more powerful. Because of that, PC games always have a set of minimum hardware requirements and they do not support anything less powerful than that.

Currently (late 2004), a typical high-end PC is a Pentium 4 CPU running at 3.6 GHz with 800 MHz FSB, 1 GB of RAM, a large 10,000 rpm SATA hard drive, and an NVidia GeForce 6800 or ATI RADEON X800 video card with 256 MB of RAM. In contrast, some games are being released with minimum recommended systems of a Pentium 3 CPU at 866 MHz, 256 MB of RAM, and an NVidia GeForce 2 or better video card. The performance and capability gap between the two specs is enormous. This forces developers who want to fully support both ends of the spectrum to treat them as separate platforms.

Another strength of PC games is the ability to create and distribute user-created content. Many games ship with the tools necessary to create new content and sometimes with the source code of the game itself, so users can modify it to create new variations of the game and redistribute them (usually called "mods").

Network connectivity used to be the exclusive domain of PC games, but game consoles have been making some inroads in this area in the last few years. Access to a network and the Internet allows for new types of multiplayer gameplay (anything from a network link between two computers to a persistent massively multiplayer game). It also allows for easier patching from the game companies, since the program can be updated after it has been shipped. This can be a boon or a curse depending on whether companies improve the game with new content after it ships, making it more valuable to the players, or they ship it before it's ready and fix bugs with patches.

Game Consoles

Game consoles are closed, proprietary systems with a fixed set of hardware. The primary purpose of consoles is to play games, so there will be no issue of other programs interfering with the games in any way. Consoles have a typical life cycle of about five years, after which time they're usually replaced by a newer model.

From a programming point of view, having a fixed set of hardware makes a world of a difference. Programmers don't have to worry about supporting dozens or hundreds of video cards, or about incompatibilities with different input devices. They can count on one set of hardware being there and making sure their game does the best it can with it.

Consoles will often have a different set of APIs than those on PCs. Those APIs are customized to the console itself and are not found anywhere else, which means programmers need to become familiar with the new hardware and the APIs themselves. In addition, because of the fixed hardware, console games can often do some programming at a lower level than their PC counterparts.

Overall, PCs and consoles are fairly well matched in power and capabilities, so other than the low-level code that interfaces with the hardware, games for both platforms can often be written using the same language (usually C++) and same set of techniques. Moreover, it is usually possible to release a game on both PCs and consoles that uses the same high-level code and very similar game assets.

The flipside of having fixed hardware is that the console manufacturer tries to keep the costs down to a minimum, so programmers are often constrained by not having enough memory, having slow memory access, or having quirky video hardware. Games aimed at consoles should take into account the limitations of the specific console and deal with them from the beginning.

Handhelds and Mobiles

The game market for handhelds and mobiles has seen a huge boom in the last few years. Devices for this platform trade very limited hardware capabilities for lightweight mobility and low power consumption. Programming games for this platform is nothing like dealing with a PC or a game console. Rather, it's more akin to game programming in the mid-1980s: memory is counted in KBytes rather than in MBytes, graphics often consist of 2D sprites, and screen resolutions are usually very low.

This has a large impact on the programming side. C++ is not automatically the language of choice, and if it is, it's usually extremely pared down to keep it manageable in such limited hardware. More common choices are plain C or even straight assembly. It also becomes almost impossible to reuse code or game assets between game consoles and handhelds.

However, games for handhelds are developed in a much smaller time frame (months instead of years), with a much smaller team, and consequently a much smaller budget. Some people are attracted to this type of development because it brings back the "simplicity" of game development from 20 years ago. Of course, we can expect handheld hardware to continue improving, so it will soon reach levels comparable to the game consoles of just a few years ago.

Some of the latest handhelds to hit the market are starting to bridge that gap already. Both the Nintendo DS and the Sony PSP are very powerful machines, comparable to full game consoles from just a few years ago. With enough memory and CPU power available, development more closely resembles regular game consoles, and many developers and libraries opt to make full use of C++.

Browser and Downloadable Games

The fourth major "platform" for game development is browser or downloadable games. This is not a true hardware platform like the other three categories we have seen, but it's so different that it makes sense to think of it as a separate platform.

As with handheld games, these are often small, simple games, sporting 2D graphics and simple gameplay. Instead of running on a phone or a mobile game console, they run on the user's Web browser on the PC and are downloaded "on the fly" every time they're played.

These games can count on having the hardware of a full PC behind them, but they have to keep their size to a minimum to be quickly downloaded. This is particularly important to attract casual gamers who prefer not to wait around for a large download. These games are also different from regular PC games in that they do not try to take over most of the PCs resources. Instead, they try to play nice with the rest of the applications and the operating system, and are often confined to running in a window instead of taking over the full screen.

Browser games aim to be able to run in any browser, independent of the hardware or the operating system. Some of the most popular languages for these games are Java and Macromedia Flash, and all they need is a specific browser plug-in to be installed. These languages can't compete with C++ in terms of performance, but they allow games to be developed at a higher level of abstraction, which allows for faster development. The emphasis of these games is on gameplay, not technical innovation.

Multiplatform Development

Releasing the same game on multiple platforms has its unique set of challenges. On paper, it sounds like a very good deal. The plan usually goes something along these lines: we make the effort of writing one game, and then we ship it on four different platforms, effectively making four times the money for the same development effort. In practice, things are not so straightforward.

First, you have to make sure that all platforms you're targeting have roughly equal capabilities. The more they vary, the harder it's going to be to do effective multiplatform development. Typically, this means targeting several consoles and PCs, or several handhelds and maybe a downloadable version. The hardware gap between consoles and handhelds is more of a chasm and makes multiplatform development between them extremely difficult.

Then there's the fact that each platform will cost you a certain amount of time and effort, even if all the high-level code and the game assets are the same. You will have to write the low-level engine code for each platform (unless you license it), debug and test your game in each platform separately, create custom code for each platform to meet the expected standards in that platform (an installer for a PC game, special standard menu icons for consoles, etc.), and deal with a variety of hardware, including different input devices (keyboard and mouse versus different gamepads) and storage devices (hard drive, memory cards, DVDs, CD-ROMs, etc.).

In practice, if everything goes smoothly, an experienced team won't use twice the resources to release a game on two platforms, but it might take one and a half times the resources of just aiming at a single platform. Each new platform after that becomes a bit easier, so releasing it for three platforms should require a bit under twice the effort of doing it for a single platform.

To make multiplatform development as effective as possible, we should try to maximize the amount of shared source code between the different platforms. There is nothing worse than having the same code duplicated for each platform and having to fix the same version of a bug in each. Ideally, we should have a low-level hardware abstraction layer that unifies the access to the hardware for all our platforms. That means we can access files in the same way, play sounds the same way, and put graphics on the screen in the same way. Then, we can build the rest of the engine and game code on top of that layer.

Choosing exactly where that layer is and what operations it presents is a very delicate decision. It has to strike a balance between being low-level enough to minimize the amount of platform-specific code, and high enough to maximize performance and the ability to take advantage of each platform's hardware. For example, if we added a graphics-abstraction layer where the main operation was to render a single triangle, we would be heading for disaster because most platforms would have horrendous performance. Instead, we want to have a higher level abstraction that allows us to render entire meshes at once.

Another important aspect of multiplatform development to consider is what to do if the platforms have slightly different capabilities, as is usually the case. One approach is to aim for the lowest common denominator. That is, if one platform can only deal with screen resolutions of 640×480, then we make our game only use that resolution even though our other platforms could use a higher, better looking resolution. This approach has the advantage that it minimizes development cost and resources, but is usually much derided by players and developers alike, and it's one of the reasons why multiplatform development has a reputation for creating mediocre games.

A better approach is to try to take advantage of the capabilities of each platform. Sometimes this will require extra programming, and sometimes extra game content. It also requires that the engine be flexible enough to be able to easily replace or enhance specific systems for specific platforms. In the end, unless you're aiming for a budget production, the resulting game will be much better received by the players.

Summary

In this chapter, we learned that there is much more to making a game than just coding. The composition and organization of a team has a great impact on the final product. Equally important is the methodology that the team chooses to employ for the development of the game: code-and-fix environments are common but not very effective, waterfall development can be useful for very well-known genres with little risk involved, and iterative and agile development environments are probably the best match for the ever-changing games industry.

When it comes to writing code, we saw how some common practices such as coding standards or use of source control can greatly help a team to work together. In particular, techniques that help improve the quality of the code—such as code reviews, good use of asserts, or unit and acceptance tests—will have a direct impact on the game itself.

Finally, it is very important to research what code can be reused instead of writing your own. The game middleware industry is growing and becoming more important every year. That, combined with our choice of platform, will determine how development should be done and the areas on which the team should concentrate.

Exercises

1. Write a one-page coding standard document on your language of choice based on your preferences and style.
2. Swap coding standards with another student and discuss the choices you made. Where do you disagree? Why? Write a revised coding standard that both of you can agree on.
3. Choose one of the major areas of middleware (graphics, AI, networking, sound, movie, animation, physics). Research the major middleware providers for that area and come up with a table highlighting their features, differences, and licensing costs. Which would you choose, and why?

4. Compile a list of the major commercial game engines available to be licensed. List any games released or currently in development that are using each engine. Do any of those engines offer an editor and capabilities for end users to mod the game?

5. Pick a game console of your choice. Find out as many hardware specs as you can about it: CPU, memory, bus speed and/or bandwidth, graphics capabilities, and so forth. How does it compare to a current PC? Why do you think that console games manage to look almost as good (if not better) than many current PC games?

References and Further Reading

[Beck00] Beck, Kent, *Extreme Programming Explained*, Addison-Wesley, 2000.

[Beck03] Beck, Kent, *Test-Driven Development*, Addison-Wesley, 2003.

[Bethke93] Bethke, Erik, *Game Development and Production*, Wordware Publishing, 2003.

[Hunt00] Hunt, Andrew, and Thomas, David, *The Pragmatic Programmer*, Addison-Wesley, 2000.

[Jacobson99] Jacobson, Ivar; Booch, Grady; and Rumbaugh, James, *The Unified Software Development Process*, Addison-Wesley, 1999.

[Larman03] Larman, Craig, *Agile and Iterative Development: A Manager's Guide*, Addison-Wesley, 2003.

[Llopis03] Llopis, Noel, "By the Books: Software Engineering in the Games Industry Roundtable," Game Developers Conference 2004, available online at *www.gamesfromwithin.com/articles/0403/000015.html*.

[Maguire94] Maguire, Steve, *Debugging the Development Process*, Microsoft Press, 1994.

[McConnell93] McConnell, Steve, *Code Complete*, Microsoft Press, 1993.

[McConnell96] McConnell, Steve, *Rapid Development*, Microsoft Press, 1996.

[McConnell98] McConnell, Steve, *Software Project Survival Guide*, Microsoft Press, 1998.

[Rabin00] Rabin, Steve, "Squeezing More Out of Assert," *Game Programming Gems*, Charles River Media, 2000.

[Rollings03] Rollings, Andrew, and Morris, Dave, *Game Architecture and Design: A New Edition*, New Riders, 2003.

[Schwaber02] Schwaber, Ken, and Beedle, Mike, *Agile Software Development with Scrum*, Prentice Hall, 2002.

3.2 C++, Java, and Scripting Languages

In This Chapter

- Overview
- C++ and Game Development
- Java
- Scripting Languages
- Summary
- Exercises
- References and Further Reading

Overview

You should always choose the right tool for the job, and a programming language is just that, a tool. Apart from a few physical limitations, you can almost get the job done with any language you want. However, if you choose the most appropriate language, the development will go much smoother and you will get done faster.

This chapter outlines the major languages used in game development, explains their strengths, and helps you decide which one to choose in which situation.

C++ and Game Development

Just a few years ago, in the mid-to-late 1990s, C was the language of choice for game development. Today, C++ has clearly stepped into the limelight and taken its place as the preferred language for games.

Strengths

Why use C++? What is the reason for the language's popularity? There are four main reasons.

Performance

Traditionally, performance has been king in anything related to game development. Games often push hardware to the limits and try to do the unexpected. Today, with the advent of powerful hardware in the form of modern PCs and game consoles, this is not as much of an issue except for a few performance-critical sections of the game. Even so, most games must perform many computations in the time it takes to display one frame. For games trying to maintain a constant 60 or 30 frames per second, they need to do everything in about 16 ms or 33 ms, respectively, so performance is always an issue. We simply can't afford for an operation to suddenly take 100 ms, because it would affect our constant frame rate and shatter the player's involvement in the game.

C++ is a very efficient language, and its constructs map very closely to low-level operating system functionality and even hardware operations. With some knowledge of assembly language and hardware architecture, it's relatively easy to guess what the hardware is going to be doing for a given section of C++ code.

C++ also makes the performance cost for each operation very explicit. The general philosophy behind the C++ design is not to force people to pay for performance of functionality they are not using. For example, using virtual functions adds a small performance cost, but programmers can choose not to use them whenever they are not necessary, and avoid any extra cost.

Memory management is left up to the programmer, so there is no automated garbage collection (the process that takes care of releasing memory that is no longer used). Garbage collection is one of the most common causes for performance woes in high-level languages and its potential for unexpected performance spikes makes it a problematic match with near real-time applications such as games.

In the rare situation where the performance provided by C++ is not enough, we always have the option to drop to C, or even straight assembly language. It is a trivial matter to integrate C and assembly with C++ on most platforms. That way, we can always squeeze that extra bit of performance necessary in a few critical parts of the code.

High-Level

What makes C++ particularly well suited for games is that, in addition to sporting top-notch performance, it is also a language rich in high-level features. C++ has the concept of classes with different levels of encapsulation, single and multiple inheritance, polymorphism, metaprogramming (templates), and exception handling. These features allow programmers to deal with the problem at hand at a higher level than with assembly or C, and they can be used to easily apply development techniques such as object-oriented programming.

Using high-level language features is especially important today as project complexity keeps skyrocketing. When teams are working on code bases that exceed a million lines of code, and involve dozens of programmers, any features that help programmers work at a higher level are well worth it. That way, programmers can concentrate more on solving the problem and dealing with the architecture, and less with bit-twiddling, poking registers directly, and managing memory by hand. As a result, the code will be much less error prone and productivity will be significantly higher.

Usually, high-level languages are associated with poor performance. In the case of C++, though, all of the high-level features are implemented efficiently (sometimes at the cost of clarity or simplicity), so the added performance cost for those features is minimal.

C++ also provides some language features that improve code reliability and minimize errors at compile time instead of at runtime. C++ is a strongly typed language, which means the compiler is going to be very attentive that we always try to use parameters of the correct type when passing them on to functions. Such a simple concept can catch many potential errors that would go unnoticed otherwise and waste everybody's time chasing after the problems in the debugger.

Another compile-time feature that C++ introduces is const correctness. Member functions can be marked as being constant (with the keyword const), which means that they will not modify the contents of an object, or call any non-const functions on them. Again, this is a simple concept that adds more information to the source code about our intent and allows the compiler to catch any errors in our programs right away at compile time.

C Heritage

C++ is not the only high-level language with promises of good performance out there, but it's the only one with backward compatibility with C. Since C was the main programming language during the late 1980s and early 1990s, it is natural that the industry transitioned to C++ since it was such a small and gradual step. Companies were able to carry over some code from previous projects, and, most importantly, programmers were able to carry over their expertise and past knowledge. This also meant that C++ was mostly used as a simple "C with classes" at first, but it was enough to hook the entire industry very quickly.

It also meant that compiler makers only had to improve their existing C compiler to deal with C++ (not a trivial task by any means, but better than creating a whole new compiler or development environment). As a result, C++ compiler support was quickly widespread, even for some of the game consoles' spotty tool support.

Finally, the C backward compatibility also meant that library writers had an easy time with the transition. Any existing libraries for C could be used from within C++, and as the language became more popular, new libraries specifically written in C++ started to appear.

Libraries

Most of the major middleware providers offer C++ (and sometimes plain C) libraries, which makes using them for C++ a trivial matter. All of the major graphics APIs, such as OpenGL and DirectX, also provide C++ libraries.

In addition to commercial libraries, C++ has a very comprehensive set of standard libraries, the STL (Standard Template Library). The STL attempts to provide all the major high-level functionality needed by most programs. Specifically, it provides two major types of functionality:

Containers: A set of common data structures that can be used with any type. Some of the ones included are vectors (resizable arrays), lists, deques (queues), and sets. All containers use the concept of iterators to access the elements inside the containers.

Algorithms: A set of basic algorithms that work on containers. Some of the most popular are sorting algorithms, search algorithms, or copying algorithms.

Using the STL will save you lots of time and resources creating (and debugging!) some of that code from scratch, and because it's part of the C++ standard, programmers will already be familiar with it, and other third-party code could be written to easily interface with it.

Another, very popular library is Boost. Even though it's not an official library like the STL, its usage is very extended and it's written in a way to seamlessly integrate with the STL. Boost contains a wider variety of functionality than STL, and is a bit more esoteric and specialized. You're not likely to use all of it, but there probably are a few sections that are perfectly suited for your current project. Just a few of the highlights from Boost include a graph container and set of algorithms to manipulate graphs, a set of matrix manipulation functions, several smart pointers, and a regular expression library.

What's not to like about these libraries? For starters, sometimes they are overkill for the task at hand. Perhaps that's not an issue when writing a GUI tool, but it might be if we try to add it to the game engine. While the performance of most of these libraries is top-notch, it sometimes surprises people who are not familiar with the libraries by causing many copies of an object or creating many dynamic memory allocations. It is important to become familiar with the inner workings of the most common parts of these libraries to use them effectively.

These libraries also make heavy use of templates and some very advanced compiler features. Even though every C++ compiler should ideally fully implement the entire C++ standard specification, the truth is that few do. These libraries will not always compile in every platform, and even if they do, the code generated might be less than optimal, so you might be limited by your choice of platforms and compilers.

Debugging can be difficult when using these libraries because their code is templated and sometimes debuggers have a hard time peeking at the contents of some of the containers. This can usually be solved with a few debugger tricks or by making the code that uses them take smaller steps, each of which can be examined in the debugger more easily.

Weaknesses

C++ might be the most popular language for game development today, but it is far from perfect. The following are some of the major weaknesses of C++ as it applies to game development.

Too Low-Level

Although C++ has many high-level features, it still forces the programmer to deal with too many low-level issues. C++ programmers have to constantly worry about how memory is allocated and freed, they need to deal with memory pointers and check whether they're NULL and worry about them pointing to an invalid memory location, or they have to manipulate texts with char * instead of using the higher level concept of a string.

Both the STL and Boost attempt to alleviate this problem by providing high-level ways of dealing with those issues. For example, the STL provides the std::string class, which is a huge step forward from dealing with char *. Boost provides a set of smart pointers that help remove some of the burden of memory allocation from the programmer.

This is mostly the flipside of one of the main benefits of C++: performance and good mapping to hardware operations. C++ was designed foremost as a systems language, so performance was chosen at the expense of high-level features. When using C++, much of the programming effort goes into the nitty-gritty, low-level details without providing any performance benefits. Considering that over 90 percent of the code that goes into a game is not performance critical, C++ might not be the best match for game development. A higher-level language would allow the programmer to ignore many of those features and concentrate his or her efforts on writing a great game or engine instead. Later in this chapter, we'll see how scripting languages can be used to complement C++ in this respect.

Too Complicated

C++ is not just too low level, it's way too complicated. A programmer might use C++ full time for years before he can claim to be somewhat competent, and even then, there will be many aspects of the C++ standard of which he will have no knowledge.

The main reason why C++ is so complicated is because of its C heritage. Not surprisingly, that was one of its major benefits. At the time, the designers of C++ preferred to have a more complicated, backward-compatible language, than a clean, totally new one that nobody was going to use and support. Looking at all the casualties left along the road in the evolution of programming languages in the last few decades, it looks like their decision was the right one.

In any case, what we're left with now is a language much more complicated than it could have been, and we need to put up with it. Other languages, like Java or C#, take most of the good concepts of C++ without any of the historical baggage and present a clean, relatively simple, high-level language.

Lacking Features

The more you use C++ for modern game development, the more you realize how many features C++ is lacking. You will probably spend a surprisingly large amount of time trying to implement and shoehorn features into the game engine that should have been readily available in the programming language itself.

Any serious, data-driven design will want to have reflection or introspection features in its entities (meaning, the objects themselves are aware of their structure and the type of data they contain and can query it at runtime). Implementing that in C++ usually involves a mess of preprocessor macros or other complicated trickery that gets in the way of writing the game or the engine itself.

Object serialization (writing to and reading from some media the state of an object) is another perfect example. Every game has to come up with some way to serialize its state to create saved games or send its status across the network. Invariably, every game engine implements a different custom solution, wasting time and resources.

The same is the case with message passing. Many game engines want to pass messages between objects, but since C++ doesn't natively support that feature, they each need to implement it from scratch. The result is a different system in every game engine, and it's usually not as efficient as it could have been.

Other languages offer those features and many more right out of the box, and can be applied to a game engine right away.

Slow Iteration

The last of the big problems with C++ is that it is often very slow for programmers to iterate and try different things. C++ is very efficient, and because of that, it's fully compiled into native binary format from source code. That means that for every change, the program needs to be compiled and linked against any other modules.

When you're dealing with just a handful of source files and a couple of libraries, build times are probably blazingly fast. However, hundreds of thousands or even millions of lines of code go into making a game. Compiling all those files takes a significant amount of time, even upwards of an hour or two in some cases, depending on the amount of code, how it is structured, and what features it uses.

Even if you only make a few changes and only one file needs to be compiled, the link time could easily take 30 seconds to a full minute or more. Perhaps not very much in the long scheme of things, but it certainly puts a damper on really fast iteration times.

Some compiler vendors are attempting to get around this problem by providing special features, such as precompiled headers, incremental linking, or distributed builds. Unfortunately, these features are not supported across all the platforms, and they still don't reduce iteration times to an acceptable amount.

Waiting for faster hardware is not likely to help because program size and complexity will continue growing as the hardware improves. It's even possible that this problem will worsen because program complexity is an exponential problem that is going to outpace any hardware improvements.

When to Use It?

After it's all said and done, when does it make sense to use C++?

C++ is a very good match for any code where performance is crucial. This used to be all the game code just over a decade ago. Today, it's limited to some of the low-level code in the engine along with things like graphics, physics, or low-level, CPU-intensive AI functions. Most of the other code could be better written in a higher level language, even at the expense of some performance.

Tools is another area in which C++ is not a perfect fit. There are higher level languages that are better suited to the development of GUI tools, including Java, C#, or Python. Writing them in C++ is a bit like painting a wall with a paintbrush instead of a roller: you can do it, but it'll be more time consuming and you'll probably do a worse job, even though you have more control over every stroke and can reach the corners better.

On the other hand, if your current code base is mostly C and C++, it makes sense to continue using C++. Perhaps consider alternatives whenever you rewrite sections of it, but don't fix what's not broken.

In addition, if you have a lot of C++ expertise in-house, you might be able to be as productive in C++ if you make good use of high-level libraries, as you would with other languages. You'll certainly be more productive if you count the time it would take to get up to speed with a new language. Again, plan to look at alternatives in the near future since your team composition is likely to change, and bring in some people who are not quite so experienced with C++.

Java

Java has been knocking at the door of game development for several years now with its promises of rapid development and platform independence. It seems that with the latest features added recently, Java is finally ready to enter the big time in game development.

Why Java?

On the surface, Java is simply a high-level language that borrows many concepts from C++ but simplifies things greatly because it doesn't have to worry about maintaining any backward compatibility with C. Not only did it avoid many of the low-level features present in C, such as pointers and explicit memory management, but it also sidestepped some of the overly complicated features of C++, such as templates or multiple inheritance.

In addition to presenting a very clean language, Java also introduced several high-level features that are very useful in game development. Java has a serialization mechanism through which objects can easily save and restore their state to the disk or even the network. It is also possible for a Java object to query its own structure through the functionality provided by reflection.

However, there is much more to Java than a simplified C++. One of Java's most noticeable features is that it is not compiled into a native binary format and executed directly on the hardware. Instead, Java is compiled into a special bytecode, which is then interpreted "on the fly" by the Java Virtual Machine (JVM), which is not a real hardware machine, but rather an abstract computing machine. An implementation of the JVM is a program that supports all the features present in the JVM specification and can execute the Java bytecode directly on the platform on which it runs.

A consequence of being compiled into an intermediate bytecode is that, at least in theory, we can run compiled Java programs on any platform that has an implementation of the JVM. This was originally touted as "develop once, run everywhere." In practice, this is not always true because of slight variations between platforms, different capabilities, screen resolutions, and input devices. In any case, it is a large step forward for multiplatform development over C++.

Because Java programs run directly on the JVM, they are completely isolated from the actual hardware on which they run. This has the advantage of freeing programs from having to deal with the low-level details of the hardware. However, it also means that programs have very little control over how they run on the hardware, and might not be able to take advantage of platform-specific optimizations. We'll look at performance in more detail in the next section.

Java came surrounded by a very comprehensive set of libraries that made developing applications in Java very convenient from the very beginning. Some examples of Java libraries are I/O, graphics, both low-level networking (sockets) and high-level networking (e.g., HTTP and FTP protocols), and even libraries for writing GUI applications (AWT and Swing). New libraries continue to be created for Java, and in recent years we have seen the introduction of libraries that bind Java to OpenGL (graphics) or OpenAL (sound), which opened the door for developing high-performance games in Java.

Performance

Performance has traditionally been Java's Achilles heel when it comes to game development. Even if performance wasn't very close to what could be achieved with C++, it was usually good enough for other types of programs, such as traditional GUI applications or Web-based programs. Over the years, many simple, Web-based games for which performance wasn't critical were created in Java because of the relative ease of development and the simple deployment to many platforms. However, Java wasn't able to make it into the big leagues of commercial, shrink-wrapped games because developers couldn't afford to take a 4x to 10x performance hit across the board.

However, things have rapidly changed over the last few years, and, while Java performance is still not up to the level of C++, it is close enough that it has turned many heads and made developers reconsider their choice of development language. Many optimization techniques have been applied to the JVM, including Just-In-Time (JIT) compiling, which takes the next section of code that is going to be executed and compiles it "on the fly" to native binary format, and, more recently, HotSpot virtual machines, which look at particularly critical sections of the code and optimize them "on the fly."

Years ago, Java was very strict about only using platform-independent code that could run on any Java platform. The result was that programs were easy to port, but performance was often lacking. Now, Java has taken a more open approach, and allows access to native binary code. Java can now use hardware-accelerated 3D graphics through OpenGL bindings, or have access to sound hardware operations through OpenAL. It is also possible to write some of the high-performance parts of the code in C++ or other language that compiles natively, and use that code from within a Java program through the Java Native Interface (JNI). Clearly, using native code that way restricts the range of platforms we can develop for, but it makes it possible to write programs that would be impossible to write otherwise.

We can expect the trend of providing better and faster access to native code to continue in the future. Java is also about to introduce some features that are crucial to commercial game development, such as access to high-resolution timers.

One area in which Java is still lacking is memory management. Because it doesn't allow for explicit memory management on the part of the programmer, it needs to do automatic garbage collection. The problem with garbage collection is that it can have unexpected performance hits, causing unexpected pauses in the middle of the game. There are programming techniques that people can apply to minimize the amount of dynamic memory allocation that is going on and to try to smooth out the costs of garbage collection. However, doing so comes with the cost of extra complexity, which starts to detract from the original simplicity of the language in the first place.

When you consider everything together, Java can now very seriously compete with C++ as a game development language. It can't quite compete with C++ in pure raw power, but it more than makes up for it with a shorter learning curve, and its ease of development and maintenance. Especially now that games are so complex, trading some performance for robustness and easier development seems like a move in the right direction.

Platforms

Java can be used on a wide range of platforms, but unfortunately, it's not available for every major gaming platform yet.

Java has a strong presence in downloadable or browser games. It is very well suited to that platform because Java programs can be delivered very easily to many platforms using a Web browser, and also because Java runs entirely inside its virtual machine, which reduces the security risk of running downloadable programs.

Java started its life targeting embedded systems, so it's not a surprise to find that it's a major contender in the mobile and handheld arenas. Even though the hardware in those platforms is not nearly as powerful as full-blown PCs, Java is still a good choice because it abstracts out all the different hardware and allows developers to write games that can be used in many different mobile phones or handheld consoles.

Java is also well suited to create full commercial PC games, but so far, there haven't been many PC titles using Java as their primary language. Especially for simpler games that concentrate more on gameplay rather than pushing the limits of the hardware, Java would be a very good fit. One area in which Java has contributed to PC games is as an embedded scripting language. Several high-profile titles have chosen Java to implement most of the high-level game behavior to reap the benefits of ease of development.

However, the one area in which Java is conspicuously absent is game consoles. None of the major game consoles for this generation has an official implementation of the JVM. It doesn't mean that developers can't write their own since the specifications for the virtual machine are widely available, but it's yet another obstacle for Java's adoption in these platforms.

It looks like Java has the game platforms very well covered, except for the notable exception of game consoles. Unfortunately, game consoles are currently the most popular gaming platform for full, commercial games, so that tends to put Java into a secondary role behind C++. However, Java dominates the handheld development, and has a strong presence in downloadable games. Do not be surprised if Java's influence soon spreads to game consoles and PCs.

WHAT GAMES USE JAVA?

The proof, as they say, is in the pudding. When all is said and done, what commercial games are using Java?

First, we have all the downloadable games aimed at the casual market. Probably the most successful company is PopCap Games, with games fully written in Java, such as *Mummy Maze*, *Seven Seas*, and *Diamond Mine*.

A very different market segment that also uses Java, because of its downloadable potential, are online card games. Yahoo Games is one of the most popular portals for card games, most of which use a Java client. Many online casinos also provide Java clients to play Poker or Blackjack.

In the commercial PC games arena, we have some very popular titles that use Java as their main scripting language. One of the first to incorporate Java was *Nihilistic's Vampire: The Masquerade*. The postmortem in Gamasutra gives more details about how they integrated Java into their game [Huebner00].

A more recent example of a game making good use of Java is *Star Wars Galaxies*. They also use a slightly simplified version of Java as their scripting language.

This is even more meaningful because *Star Wars Galaxies* is a massively multiplayer online game, so it is interesting to see they were willing to go in this direction.

What about games that were fully written in Java? Some of the most popular are Jellyvision's *You Don't Know Jack* and *Who Wants to Be a Millionaire*. Both of them were extremely popular games aimed at the casual market. A game aimed at a more hardcore gamer market that made heavy use of Java technology was EA's now defunct game, *Majestic*, whose back end was completely implemented using Java.

Scripting Languages

It is usual for many games today to rely on scripting languages to implement some part of their high-level game code. Some use scripting languages just for triggering a few events and perhaps controlling a sequence during an in-game cinematic, while others use them for all their game logic and behavior. This section looks at the role of scripting languages in games, and the choices we have when using a scripting language in our own projects.

Why Scripting Languages?

There are many reasons why games use scripting languages.

Ease of Development

Ease of development is one of the reasons cited most often for using scripting languages. They're certainly easier to use than C++, but unfortunately, that thought is often followed by saying that the designers can take care of writing in the scripting language themselves, but that is hardly ever a good idea. True, designers can make some changes to existing code, and even some designer-programmers (also called "technical designers") are often up to the task without any problems. The majority of the time, though, script code still needs to be written by a programmer, even if a less experienced one.

It should also be faster and less error prone writing code in a scripting language than doing it in C++. Because scripting languages are often higher level than C++, many things are taken care of behind the scenes for us. For example, scripting languages often take care of memory allocation, freeing the programmer from dealing with pointers and managing object lifetimes.

In the end, we're trading some performance (because scripting languages are usually significantly slower than C++) for ease and speed of development. Since high-level game code is not usually performance critical, but it's very feature rich and involves a lot of programming, this is a very worthwhile tradeoff in most situations.

Iteration Time

Perhaps the most important reason for using a scripting language is iteration time, the time elapsed between the moment we make a change to the code and the moment we see the results in the game. If we were doing our programming in C++, the iteration time involves compiling the code, linking it with all the libraries, and running the game. With a scripting language, we usually don't need to compile anything, and we sometimes can reload scripts "on the fly" while the game is running. Iteration time can easily go down from 1 to 2 minutes to about 10 seconds.

Code Becomes an Asset

One interesting consequence of writing some code in a scripting language is that it becomes possible to treat that code as a game asset instead of being part of the program. For a data-driven game, this means it's much easier to keep game code and the rest of the game content in sync, since they can be modified and updated together.

For example, consider a peon unit in a real-time strategy game. Without using a scripting language, the behavior for the peon would be specified in code, so it would be part of the game executable, and the rest of the peon would be game assets (textures, sounds, animations, etc.). If we implement all of the peon's behavior in a scripting language, we can add those scripts to the rest of the data and have a self-contained set of assets that fully describes how the peon looks and behaves in the game.

Another consequence of treating code written in a scripting language as a game asset is that it can be easily modified, updated, and redistributed by end users who want to make modifications to the game. If all code were written in C++ and compiled as part of the program, users would be limited to providing new textures, models, or levels. If they wanted to write new behaviors or overwrite existing ones, they would either not be able to do it, or would need to write C++ code in the form of DLLs, compile them, and redistribute them. This requires that people have a full development environment, and also creates important security problems by redistributing full DLLs and executables. However, if the game code uses a scripting language, users can edit existing scripts or write new ones and redistribute them with the rest of their new assets as part of their mod without any difficulty.

Features

Scripting languages are easier and simpler than C++, but that doesn't mean they are a crippled language. Quite the contrary; many scripting languages offer features that are not found in C++. For example, scripting languages often provide functionality to save and restore the state of objects (serialization), ways to examine the contents and structure of an object (reflection), or even lightweight versions of threads. If we were writing the game purely in C++ and wanted to use some of those features, we would be forced to write them from scratch.

Apart from some general language features, scripting languages can be highly customized to the way they're used in the game, so they might provide a lot of high-level functionality for those tasks. For example, a scripting language that is mainly intended to be used for AI behaviors might support finite-state machines or fuzzy decision trees. On the other hand, a scripting language intended to sequence events for in-game cinematics and other scripted events might have very good support for events on a timeline. Trying to write code like that in straight C++ would be fairly cumbersome and not very intuitive.

Drawbacks of Scripting Languages

Not everything is greener on the other side of the fence of scripting languages. For all their advantages, they have their share of drawbacks.

Performance

You pay for all the nice features of scripting languages with performance. You just can't expect to achieve the same performance writing some code in a scripting language as you would in C++. Depending on the scripting language, the performance hit could be as much as 10 times or more the performance of an equivalent C++ program. Don't despair, though, because the primary use of scripting languages is high-level game logic code, and most of the time this should not be performance-critical code and we can afford the extra performance hit.

Why are scripting languages so slow? Because they are usually not compiled into a native, binary format as C++ programs are. Many scripting languages are purely interpreted languages, which means that they are parsed and executed "on the fly," while the game is running. Being interpreted means that there is no need for a compile step between changing the code and running it; it can also mean that we can reload scripts even while the game is running, which might not have been possible with a purely compiled language.

Some scripting languages take an intermediate approach and compile their source code into an intermediate bytecode (much like Java does), and execute that bytecode instead. The results are usually much better performance at the cost of having a short compilation step after modifying the program.

Another area that can greatly affect performance is automatic memory management (also referred to as "automatic garbage collection"). Unlike C++, most scripting languages try to avoid forcing the programmer to deal with managing memory manually, so they have to take care of releasing memory whenever it's not used anymore. It sounds like a great idea because it frees the programmer from dealing with low-level details, but it can sometimes cause unacceptable stalls and performance problems in a real-time application such as a game.

Dynamic memory utilization is another problematic area that can affect performance. Some scripting languages are not very careful about limiting how much memory they use as they parse and execute the script code. That might be fine on a PC with large amounts of RAM and virtual memory, but will be completely inadequate on a game console with very limited amounts of RAM.

Tool Support

It's an unfortunate reality that tool support for most existing scripting languages is severely lacking when compared to C++. You will find that if you have a debugger at all, it will be rather primitive. Profiling tools might be nonexistent. Even finding an integrated development environment with syntax highlighting and a good code browser could be a challenge. So, count on the fact that your tools will not be as sharp as the C++ ones.

Unless you have many resources, writing your own scripting language is not going to help either. It is hard enough to implement a scripting language that does exactly what you want, but writing all the supporting tools on top of that is a huge effort that most teams can't afford to do. Usually, home-brewed scripting languages end up having the worst set of tools, if any at all, unless they are reused and improved in subsequent projects.

Catching Errors

Most scripting languages are dynamically typed. In theory, this is a good thing because it frees the programmers from having to explicitly declare variable types and then use them, so productivity should be higher by allowing programmers to write the program and forget about language rules. Unfortunately, dynamic typing combined with how scripting languages are often interpreted also means that scripts can contain errors that won't be detected until that code is executed. With strongly typed, compiled languages like C++, the compiler is merciless and catches many mistakes at compile time, saving much time and effort in the long run.

Interfacing with the Rest of the Game

The scripting language code sits on top of all the engine and game code, which was probably written in C++. For those scripts to do anything useful, they need to communicate with the game code. It should be possible to trigger actions from the scripts, create new objects, run calculations, or read the game state. The interfacing between the scripting language code and the C++ code is not a trivial matter.

Different languages handle this differently, but it usually involves having to explicitly flag C++ functions as being "exported" to the scripting language. This is usually done with a lot of macro or template trickery to avoid all the typing involved if it were to be done manually. Often, these functions are limited to having basic data types for their parameters, such as integers, floats, Booleans, and strings, and very rarely can they pass around full objects. The functions themselves are also usually required to be global functions, so scripting languages can't always access objects and their member functions directly.

All of these restrictions make the interface between the scripting language and the rest of the game more awkward than it should be, and leave script programmers wishing for more functionality and a better interface.

Popular Scripting Languages

These are some of the most popular scripting languages in game development. You can use this section as a starting point to finding out more about each language.

Python

Python is an interpreted, object-oriented scripting language. It has a host of libraries covering just about any functionality. The syntax is clear and easy, but it stands out from a C-like syntax in that white space determines the structure of the program. Because it's a mature language and has been around for a while, it has a lot of available documentation, tutorials, and reference materials. Tool support is also fairly good, with an interactive shell, and even a remote debugger.

On the flipside, Python is quite large, so using it in memory-limited environments might not be an option. There is a variant of Python called "Stackless Python" that attempts to remedy this situation and is better suited for embedded systems or game consoles.

Lua

Lua is a very lightweight scripting language, designed to be embedded in other programs. It is not natively object oriented, but it can be extended to use many object-oriented concepts. Lua sports a small memory footprint and very good performance, which makes it a very good candidate to embed in games, even for game consoles with more limited hardware.

On the negative side, Lua has some performance issues with garbage collection, causing pauses in execution at inopportune moments. Unlike Python, Lua uses only one number type, a C double format, which causes numerical computations to be quite slow, so those are best left to the code written in C++. In addition, Lua is a small and simple language, but because of that, it doesn't necessarily scale well to large projects written exclusively in Lua.

Other Off-the-Shelf Languages

Lua and Python are currently the two most popular scripting languages used in games, but the world of scripting languages doesn't end there. Other less popular languages that are sometimes used in a game include Ruby, Perl, and JavaScript. Before jumping into your next project, it might be worth evaluating those languages to see if they have some advantages given your project requirements.

GAMES USING PYTHON

In recent years, as computing power has increased, we have seen more and more games turn to Python for their scripting language. Table 3.2.1 contains some of the most popular titles. Notice the remarkable variety of genres present in the list, but how the great majority of the titles were released for the PC only.

→

Table 3.2.1   Games Using Python

Title	Company	Genre	Platforms	Year
Blade of Darkness	Rebel Act Studios	Action	PC	2001
Frequency	Harmonix Music	Puzzle, music	PS2	2001
Freedom Force	Irrational Games	Role-playing, strategy	PC	2002
Earth & Beyond	Westwood Studios	Massively multiplayer	PC	2002
Star Trek: Bridge Commander	Totally Games	Simulation	PC	2002
Backyard Sports series	Humongous Games	Sports	PC	2002–2004
Toontown Online	Disney Interactive	Massively multiplayer	PC	2003
Eve Online	CCP	Massively multiplayer	PC	2003
Temple of Elemental Evil	Troika Games	Role-playing	PC	2003
Uru: Ages Beyond Myst	Cyan Worlds	Adventure	PC	2003
Civilization IV	Firaxis Games	Strategy	PC	2005

Games Using Lua

Lua is perhaps even more extended than Python, as far as integration in games. Because of its smaller memory footprint and faster performance, it was used in commercial games as early as 1998. Also, notice in Table 3.2.2 that, unlike Python, games using Lua run on a large variety of platforms, including all the major game consoles.

Table 3.2.2   Games Using Lua

Title	Company	Genre	Platforms	Year
Grim Fandango	LucasArts	Adventure	PC	1998
Baldur's Gate	Bioware	Role-playing	PC	1998–2001
Escape from Monkey Island	LucasArts	Adventure	PC, Mac, PS2	2000
MDK 2	Bioware	Action	PC, PS2, Dreamcast	2000–2001
Impossible Creatures	Relic	Strategy	PC	2002
Defender	7 Studios	Action	PS2, Xbox, GCN	2002
Homeworld 2	Relic	Strategy	PC	2003
Far Cry	Crytek	Action	PC, Xbox, PS2	2004–2005
Darkwatch	Sammy Studios	Action	PS2, Xbox	2005

Custom Languages

Many games take the route of writing their own scripting language from scratch. You won't be able to use those languages in your game (unless you're working with their engine), but it is worthwhile to familiarize yourself with some of the most popular languages and learn their advantages and drawbacks.

Some of the most popular custom scripting languages are UnrealScript (Unreal engine), QuakeC (Quake engine), and NWNScript (*Neverwinter Nights*). These languages are used heavily in the creation of mods (modifications) of those programs by gamers who want to provide their own content and new games on top of those engines. You'll be able to find extensive documentation online, both from the companies that wrote those engines, and the users themselves.

One word of warning before you decide to write your own scripting language: writing a robust, efficient scripting language is extremely difficult. Unless you have a lot of experience creating languages, compilers, and interpreters, it's going to take much longer than you thought and it's going to be much slower and less effective than you hoped for. Make sure that you need to do something unique that you can't do with an existing language. In the end, many teams that attempt to write their own language end up regretting it, and they're left with a general scripting language very similar to Python or Lua, but much less effective and without any of the support from existing tools and documentation.

Choosing a Scripting Language

As discussed earlier, scripting languages are not without their set of problems. Selecting the wrong scripting language will do more harm to a project than any benefits it will provide. This section raises some questions you should answer before choosing what scripting language (if any) you should use for your next project.

Do You Need a Scripting Language?

We've been assuming all along that we want a scripting language, but this is the very first question you should ask yourself. A scripting language is a great tool for rapid iteration, experimentation, and future modifications. However, if you don't need any of those features or you can't give up a bit of performance, a scripting language might not be for you. If you're working on a very well-defined genre, you know exactly what you're going to write, and you don't plan to make many changes along the way, writing all the game code in C++ might even save you time.

However, most games of a reasonable complexity will greatly benefit from the use of a scripting language to implement most of their high-level game code.

What Features Do You Need?

What do you want out of the scripting language? Do you want a general scripting language that replaces C++ for the high-level game code, or do you want something much more specialized? The wider the range of tasks you want to do with it, the more general the scripting language should be. Alternatively, you could use several types of scripting languages in the same game; for example, one for the animation system, one for the AI decisions, and one general one for the user interface and any other miscellaneous code. However, you will need to go to the effort of integrating and supporting each scripting language in your game.

What Kind of Performance Do You Need?

Do you need to write code in a scripting language that is going to be almost as fast as C++, or are you willing to give up some performance? Usually, the more performance you're willing to give up, the more features and ease of development you'll get in return.

Before you answer that you need top performance, keep in mind that most games only have a few areas that are true performance bottlenecks (graphics, physics, collision), and high-level code is not usually one of them. However, if you're planning to move thousands of units simultaneously on the screen, you might want to use a scripting language with high performance.

In addition to pure execution speed, you should also consider memory footprint and the performance of garbage collection if the language you're considering has it.

What Debugging Facilities Does the Language Have?

If all the scripting language is going to do is drive the front-end GUI, you probably don't need much in the way of debugging facilities. Whenever you need to verify something, you can rely on the old-fashioned method of printing something to the console output whenever an event happens. However, if most of your high-level game code is written in a scripting language, you will definitely want to have a full-blown debugger for that language. You will want to set breakpoints, step into code, see the state of the game, and so forth. You will also want to have robust error handling to prevent the scripts from crashing at the first sign of trouble.

This very important aspect is often overlooked when evaluating scripting languages. Having adequate debugging facilities in a game that makes heavy use of scripting can make the difference between shipping a great game or not shipping at all.

On What Platforms Does the Scripting Language Need to Run?

If you're using an off-the-shelf scripting language, you might be limited to the platforms to which it has already been ported. Specifically, that means you might find it difficult to find languages to run on game consoles. Sometimes, the source code for the scripting language itself will be available and you'll be able to port it to your platform of choice, but that might be a challenging task (depending on how different your target platform is). Also, keep in mind that by porting it to a new platform, you might lose some of the other benefits already available such as high-performance, debuggers, platform-specific libraries, and so forth.

What Expertise and Resources Do You Have Available?

Look around you and think about what expertise you have in your team. If everybody is already comfortable with a certain scripting language, that is a big point in its favor, as the team will be able to start using it effectively from the first day. On the other hand, if you're just putting a team together or nobody has any previous experience, you're free to choose a language based on other factors. In addition, if you have a language guru on the team with a lot of previous experience, and you want to do something unique, maybe putting together a new scripting language is a possibility.

Summary

C++ is the current language of choice for most game development. It combines the low-level control and high performance of C with the object-oriented approach and higher productivity of high-level languages. Knowing the language well is essential to take full advantage of it and avoid common pitfalls that are all too frequent in C++.

Java has been making some inroads in game development in the last few years. With some of the recent updates to the Java language and libraries, the performance of Java programs has become much better. Combined with the fact that Java is easier and much cleaner than C++, as well as slightly higher level (which implies more productivity), it is easy to see why it has become a more attractive alternative.

More games every day are using scripting languages to write much of the high-level game code. Whether it's done by designers or programmers, it allows for very fast development and iteration of game features. When using a scripting language, we can use one of the popular off-the-shelf ones (Python or Lua), adopt one for an existing game, or write our own.

Exercises

1. Some of the more complicated features of C++ not present in Java are multiple inheritance and templates. How does Java provide similar functionality?
2. List all of the containers available in the STL and give an example of how you would use each.
3. Select two libraries from Boost (*www.boost.org/*) and explain how they can be applied to any aspect of game development.
4. Serialization and reflection are two features found in Java that are not present in C++. Write some code that uses both features. Explain specific uses for those features in a game.
5. Look at the top-10 list of PC games sold this month or year. For every game, list whether it has a scripting language exposed to the end user, and if so, which one. What conclusions can you draw from looking at the list? Is any one language dominant?
6. Choose any PC game of your choice with a custom scripting language. Analyze its scripting language and compare it to Python or Lua. Is it faster or simpler? Does it have any radically different features? What kind of tool support does it have (editors, profilers, debuggers, etc.)?

References and Further Reading

C++

[Alexandrescu01] Alexandrescu, Andrei, *Modern C++ Design*, Addison-Wesley, 2001.

[Boost] Boost C++ Libraries, *www.boost.org/*.

[Josuttis99] Josuttis, Nicolai M., *The C++ Standard Library*, Addison-Wesley, 1999.

[Llopis03] Llopis, Noel, *C++ for Game Programmers*, Charles River Media, 2003.

[Meyers96] Meyers, Scott, *More Effective C++*, Addison-Wesley, 1996.

[Meyers98] Meyers, Scott, *Effective C++ Second Edition*, Addison-Wesley, 1998.

[Meyers01] Meyers, Scott, *Effective STL*, Addison-Wesley, 2001.

[Stroustrup97] Stroustrup, Bjarne, *The C++ Programming Language Third Edition*, Addison-Wesley, 1997.

Java

[Bloch01] Bloch, Joshua, *Effective Java Programming Language Guide*, Addison-Wesley, 2001.

[Clingman04] Clingman, Dustin; Kendall, Shawn; and Mesdaghi, Syrus, *Practical Java Game Programming*, Charles River Media, 2004.

[Eckel02] Eckel, Bruce, *Thinking in Java, 3rd Edition*, Prentice Hall, 2002.

[Flanagan02] Flanagan, David, *Java in a Nutshell, Fourth Edition*, O'Reilly & Associates, 2002.

[GameJUG] Game Developers Java Users Group (GameJUG), *https://gamejug.dev.java.net/*.

[Huebner00] Huebner, Robert, "Postmortem of Nihilistic Software's Vampire: The Masquerade—Redemption," Gamasutra, 2000, available at *www.gamasutra.com/features/20000802/huebner_01.htm*.

[JavaTech] Java Technology, *http://java.sun.com/*.

Scripting Languages

[Beazley01] Beazley, David, *Python Essential Reference, 2nd Edition*, SAMS, 2001.

[Burns04] Burns, Jonathan, "Lua in the Gaming Industry Roundtable," Game Developers Conference 2004, available online at *www.gdconf.com/archives/2004/burns_jon.doc*.

[Ierusalimschy03] Ierusalimschy, Roberto, *Programming in Lua*, Roberto Ierusalimschy, 2003.

[Lua] Lua Programming Language, *www.lua.org/*.

[LuaUsers] Lua Users Wiki, *http://lua-users.org/wiki/*.

[Martelli03] Martelli, Alex, *Python in a Nutshell*, O'Reilly & Associates, 2003.

[Python] Python Programming Language, *www.python.org/*.

3.3 ▪ Macromedia Flash

Overview

Macromedia Flash has emerged over the past few years as one of the leading platforms on which to develop games for the Web. Flash has grown in scope and breadth over the past few versions, from a mildly game-friendly Flash 4 in 2000, to the latest, Flash MX 2004, which has all of the power and strength of most professional (non-Web) programming languages.

Advantages of Flash

Flash provides the aspiring game developer with several immediate advantages.

Wide Audience

The number of people across the globe who now have access to the Internet is huge, and is growing daily. In late 2004, the estimate was that approximately 800 million people were Internet users, with over 200 million in North America and over 200 million in Europe [IWS04]. Imagine that; the ability to reach hundreds of millions of people within seconds of finishing a Flash game. Granted, not all of them will be looking for online games, or even be interested in games, but this is the potential audience.

Online games are extremely popular on the Internet today; in fact, a recent study from the Nielsen Net Ratings showed that online games sites were the "stickiest" Web sites; that is, the sites where users visited most frequently, and stayed the longest. During the month of May 2004, more than 46 million Americans visited online game sites; that's one in three online Americans [Nielsen04]. This is extremely promising for the aspiring Flash game developer, and extremely enticing for clients who would want to *hire* a Flash game developer.

Flash is in the unique position of being supported by nearly all computers and operating systems. The Flash player has been developed by Macromedia to run on the PC, Mac, and Linux, and is constantly being ported to new operating systems. This gives Flash game developers the ability to develop games across multiple platforms at once. In an industry in which companies are investing millions to develop console, handheld, and PC versions of their games, Flash provides an immediate incentive in its cross-platform compatibility.

The number of users on the Internet who have the Flash player installed on their computer is huge, and growing. Given the small download size of the Flash player, and the ease with which it is installed, it is no wonder that 98 percent of Web viewers have the Flash player installed. The number varies by version, but at last check, over 93 percent of worldwide users had the Flash 6 player, with the Flash 7 player approaching 75-percent penetration [Macromedia04]. Most game sites at this point are requiring users to have the Flash 7 player, which means that although it's 75-percent penetration worldwide, it's closer to 100-percent penetration among the Flash-gameplaying population.

Rapid Development

When going from design, to prototype, to final game, nothing allows us to do this faster than Flash. This is one of Flash's key selling points. Within the Flash development environment, we can draw our graphics, create our game code, and attach our sounds. In fact, it is possible to create a rudimentary game from scratch—in less than 10 minutes if we know what we're doing.

Take, for example, creating a simple tic-tac-toe game. The first thing we would do is draw a background grid, and then create the X and O pieces as *movie clips*. Movie clips are the basic graphic building block of Flash. All assets that appear on screen, move around, and have code attached to them are extensions of the basic movie clip object. Do not confuse the Flash movie clip (usually referred to as an "MC") with the actual film concept of a movie clip.

Once we had created our grid background, and our X and O movie clips, we would then attach code to the Flash project to handle player interaction, game logic, and opponent AI. All coding in Flash is done in the Flash code language, Action-Script. Assuming that we knew how to "code" the AI for a tic-tac-toe game, we could build this entire game in less than half an hour.

Easy Deployment

Once we've finished a Flash game, it is extremely easy to deploy it to the world. All we need to do is use the built-in export engine of Flash. When we're done programming the game, we simply choose the Export option from the File menu, to create an HTML page and corresponding SWF file. The SWF file is the compiled Flash game itself, and the HTML page is the page that is automatically programmed to embed that SWF. Once this pair of files has been created, we simply launch the HTML in a browser, and the game is now playable on the Web.

The next step would be to take the HTML file and the SWF file and upload them to a Web server. Then, by giving out the URL of the newly uploaded HTML file, anyone can play the game. For example, if we uploaded the tic-tac-toe game to the root folder of *www.mytictactoe.com*, and our game HTML was called "mytictac.html," we would simply tell players to go to (or click on a link to) *http://www.mytictactoe.com/mytictac.html*.

Usually, Flash names the HTML and SWF file the same name as the FLA file you've made. The FLA file is, of course, the game source file itself. Therefore, if you create mygame.fla, your export will be mygame.html and mygame.swf. It is possible to specify the export names manually (to override the defaults), but we must be careful not to just manually *rename* the SWF file itself, because it will be embedded in the HTML file under the exported name. Look at the following HTML:

```
<object classid="clsid:d27cdb6e-ae6d-11cf-96b8-444553540000" code-
base="http://fpdownload.macromedia.com/pub/shockwave/cabs/flash/swfla
sh.cab#version=7,0,0,0" width="550" height="400" id="mytictac"
align="middle">
<param name="allowScriptAccess" value="sameDomain" />
<param name="movie" value="mytictac.swf" />
<param name="quality" value="high" />
<param name="bgcolor" value="#ffffff" />
<embed src="mytictac.swf" quality="high" bgcolor="#ffffff"
width="550" height="400" name="mytictac" align="middle" allowScrip-
tAccess="sameDomain" type="application/x-shockwave-flash"
pluginspage="http://www.macromedia.com/go/getflashplayer" />
</object>
```

This code would embed the game mytictac.swf into html. Notice that the text in bold shows the actual filename, mytictac.swf. If we were to rename the SWF file, we would have to manually edit this HTML to reflect the name. Also notice the parameters "width" and "height." This is the size of the Flash player window, in pixels, that the game will take up on the page. (See Figure 3.3.1.)

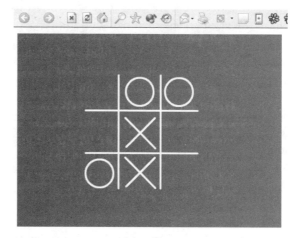

FIGURE 3.3.1   *A Flash game in an embedded Flash player in an HTML page.*

Fast Learning Curve

One of the nicest things about Flash is how fast it can be learned. A novice programmer with little experience can be up and running in Flash in a matter of hours. An artist with no programming experience whatsoever can be creating graphics within minutes, and adding code to those graphics with only a small amount of study. Once a new Flash game developer learns the concepts of motion, collision, and interaction, he or she can turn anything into a game element. The fact that everything in Flash is based on simple x and y positions means that we have everything we need to move objects around on screen. In addition, since Flash has all of the basic keyboard and mouse input routines associated with other game development platforms, we immediately have the ability to interact with our on-screen elements.

To learn how to make games in Flash, we must learn a few fundamental concepts:

• Creating graphics in Flash, or importing external graphics into Flash
• Converting graphics to movie clips
• Placing code on the main Flash timeline
• Adding code to movie clips

We'll be covering these concepts later in this section, but all can be learned relatively quickly, allowing new game developers to start creating their games in no time.

Easily Applicable to Designers and Programmers

Flash game developers tend to be two different types of people. There are programmers, who have sought to bring their programming skills into Flash, and there are designers and artists, who would like to learn how to add programming to their Flash graphics. No matter which direction you come from, you will have *some* learning to do.

Programmers can rapidly learn the ActionScript language because it very similar to most standard ECMA programming languages. If you know C, C++, or Java, you'll be able to directly apply most of the things you know into Flash. The ActionScript language follows all of the same basic conventions for logic, conditions, loops, classes, and functions.

Designers and artists will be very familiar with the basic Flash drawing tools, as they are similar to those found in most popular graphics packages. In addition, adding code to Flash can be as simple or as complex as we want. With three lines of code, we can make a movie clip move across the screen. Add a few more lines of code, and we can make this same movie clip bounce around. Add a few more, and it can appear to follow the laws of gravity. Add a few more lines of code, and the object can start reacting to user interaction. Designers can learn these concepts in a step-by-step manner, enabling them to know as little or as much about ActionScript as they wish. Many code concepts can be copied and reused from ActionScript found in books and tutorials, and don't require a large amount of understanding to make use of.

How Flash Works

What exactly is Flash at its core? What's going on "under the hood?" Flash has many integrated and interlocking parts to create the entire experience. Let's look at them now.

Timeline Based

Flash works based on a system of frames. This is now things take place, temporally speaking. When we say "frames," we're literally talking about the same concept as the frames of a motion picture. Flash renders an entire frame and then displays that frame, and this happens at a specific rate known as the *frame rate*.

For example, if we've created a new Flash game and have set the frame rate to 30 frames per second (FPS), that means the screen will be updated and refreshed 30 times each second. That also means that our game code will be executed 30 times in one second. If we have game code that moves a ball on the screen, we'll be moving the ball a certain number of pixels *per frame*.

The frame-based timeline also means that our user interaction will only take place on a frame, meaning that user input will be reflected on screen 30 times per second. If the user is holding down the right arrow key to move a superhero, then every frame our game is checking to see if the right arrow key is being pressed. If it is, the superhero is moved to the right. We move the superhero graphic, render the frame, and repeat.

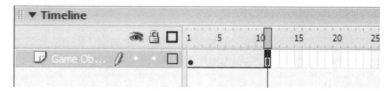

FIGURE 3.3.2   *The timeline in the Flash IDE.*

The timeline in Flash is a visual guide available at design time, and a conceptual resource available for code at runtime. In the Flash integrated development environment (IDE), we see a timeline that looks like Figure 3.3.2.

Figure 3.3.2 shows what is known as the *main timeline*. Each vertical division corresponds to a single frame. Each frame can contain graphics, movie clips, or ActionScript code.

Designers and artists will be more likely to make use of this timeline to draw and animate character animations, motion graphics, and so forth. This type of timeline development is visually powerful, but tends to leave little room for interactivity because the animations are all *canned*; predrawn and set at design time. If we draw a different image on each frame, Flash will play them one at a time, at the desired frame rate, creating animation.

Programmers, on the other hand, will tend to place all of their ActionScript on one single frame, and keep their timeline only one frame long. The timeline requires no more than one frame because all of the frame-based animation is done with code, at the frame rate set in the IDE. Look at the following code:

```
beachball.onEnterFrame = function()
{
    this._x += 3;
}
```

That code would be placed on Frame 1 of the main timeline. All this code does is attach an onEnterFrame event to the movie clip called beachball. This simply moves the beachball movie clip to the right by three pixels, every frame. By taking the value

FIGURE 3.3.3 *A timeline that is only one frame long, with all code attached to it.*

of the _x property (horizontal position), and increasing it by three, every frame, the beach ball will move to the right at three pixels per frame. A timeline with this code would look like Figure 3.3.3.

When we use this approach, we will usually attach *all* of our game's code to one single frame, and this is where we'll set events, user feedback, motion, and so forth. In Figure 3.3.3, we can see that all our ActionScript is entered into a window known as the Actions window.

Vector Engine

The base graphics engine behind Flash is a vector engine. This means that all graphics and shapes are defined in terms of mathematical shapes such as lines, spline curves, vertices, circles, and stroke/fill information. All graphics, movie clips, and other objects are placed on the area known as the *stage*. This is the central area of the Flash IDE, where we can use the drawing tools to draw, and where we can move and position movie clips. The stage shows up as the background color, width and height specified in the movie properties. The movie properties are edited with Ctrl+J.

The advantage of using a vector engine is that a game can be scaled to any size, and its graphics will continue to look sharp and crisp.

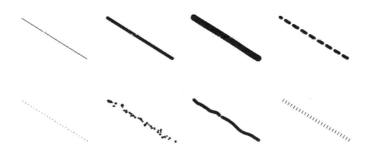

FIGURE 3.3.4 *The various line styles of Flash.*

The most basic shape in Flash is the line. This consists of a stroke that is defined by two points, and has associated with it a specific line style. A line may be thinner or

FIGURE 3.3.5   *Various curves.*

thicker and may be any color. It may also be solid, dashed, dotted, and so forth. Figure 3.3.4 shows a simple line in several different styles.

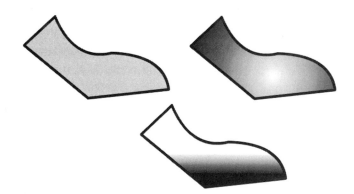

FIGURE 3.3.6   *Various shapes.*

These lines are straight, and are simply defined by two points. If we want, we can take any line and drag it into a curve, thus adding curve information to the line shape, as shown in Figure 3.3.5.

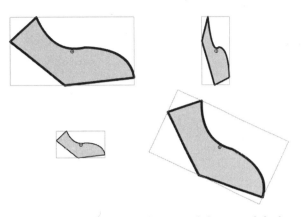

FIGURE 3.3.7 *Clockwise from top-left: unmodified, squashed horizontally, rotated clockwise, and squashed equally (shrunk).*

The curves are defined by a hidden point that "pulls" the line in a certain direction. This style of curve is known as a *spline curve*. Several lines can be connected together to form a complete shape that then has fill information associated with it, making solid shapes, as shown in Figure 3.3.6.

Shapes can be filled with solid colors, radial gradients, linear gradients, and even a tiled bitmap. Once a shape is defined, it can then be converted into a movie clip by selecting it and pressing F8. Once converted to movie clips, objects can be stretched, squashed, rotated, and skewed (see Figure 3.3.7).

The vector engine in Flash is very powerful, and vector images can also be imported from external vector graphics programs such as Adobe® Illustrator®. There is no real limit to the complexity that vectors can contain when imported into Flash. There are a

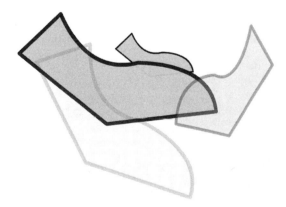

FIGURE 3.3.8 *Using alpha to define semitransparency.*

few things to be aware of, though. The more complex the vector, the slower it will be rendered in Flash, and the more it will be likely to slow the game performance.

The colors in Flash are based on the RGBA system, where you specify red, green, blue, and alpha values for each color. The red, green, and blue are the standard colors of light combined to make millions of different color combinations. The alpha value is used to specify semitransparency; how "see through" a color is. The alpha value can also be set on an individual movie clip from 0 percent (invisible) to 100 percent (opaque), creating some terrific effects, as shown in Figure 3.3.8.

In ActionScript, we can set the alpha value of a movie clip to 50 percent just by writing:

```
myMovieClip._alpha = 50;
```

We must be careful with alpha as well. In many cases, it's better to import a bitmap rather than use a vector or alpha image, because Flash can draw bitmaps very quickly. Flash treats bitmaps as rectangular areas that are filled with a pixel-based image. We can convert bitmaps into movie clips as well. As a rule of thumb, if we have a vector image that uses thousands of vector points, it's probably better to use a bitmap representation of that image rather than the vector image itself, because Flash will try to rerender the vector image every frame in which it moves.

The Audio Engine

On top of all of its graphics capabilities, Flash also has the capability to handle audio. We can easily create sound effects, music, or voice-overs in an audio application, and then import these sounds into Flash. When imported, they can be embedded directly into the timeline, or set up to be accessible at runtime only with code. This is called setting up the sound for *linkage*.

When a sound is set up for linkage (and thereby given a *linkage id*), we can use this linkage id to create an instance of the Sound object in ActionScript, and then trigger this sound every time we need it. Take, for example, the sound of a laser gun, imported to Flash and set for linkage with the id "laser." The following code shows how we would set up an instance of the Sound object:

```
laserSound = new Sound();
laserSound.attachSound("laser");
```

Then, whenever we wanted to start the sound of the laser, we would write:

```
laserSound.start();
```

Using this method, we can place sound effects within the game, driven by user interactions and game events.

Flash can import a large number of audio formats, and can embed the sounds in the SWF file as RAW, ADPCM, or MP3 encoding. Using the MP3 encoding allows us to embed large sound effects with minimal SWF file size impact, and even allows us to embed musical soundtracks.

If the music is created so that it loops seamlessly, it's possible to tell Flash to loop a sound any number of times, so that the soundtrack will go on for as long as we want.

Flash also has the capability to load MP3 files directly, so that we can create a game SWF that has no music embedded, but rather streams MP3 files at runtime. This allows the file size to be very small, and allows us to code the game to only load sounds that it needs. For example, we may not want a particular song to play until a certain level is reached.

The Flash audio engine also has the capability to play up to eight stereo sounds at once. This means that we can mix multiple sound effects such as background ambiance, foreground actions, and even various musical elements. It's possible to mix pieces of music so that we create a seamless soundtrack that seems to react to the game. The music could get more intense during scary moments, and be calm the rest of the time.

The Scripting Environment

As mentioned earlier, all coding and scripting is done in Flash in a language known as ActionScript. ActionScript is very similar to JavaScript, and uses all of the basic ECMA coding conventions.

Curly Braces for Code Blocks

In ActionScript, the code of all functions, loops, and conditions are enclosed in curly braces: { and }.

Semicolon for Statement Line Endings

All statements must end with a semicolon.

```
p = 0;
i ++;
```

if Logic

Code conditions are based on the if statement, where we say:

```
if (condition)
{
    do something
}
```

Loops

Loops are accomplished with the standard for, do or while:

```
for (j = 0; j < 100; j++)
{
    do something 100 times;
```

```
}
or
do
{
    something;
} while (condition)
or
while (condition)
{
    do something;
}
```

Variable Types

Flash supports all sorts of standard variable types, including `Number`, `String`, `Array`, and `Boolean`. It also supports many of its own built-in types such as `Object`, `MovieClip`, `Color`, `Date`, `Camera`, `Microphone`, `Sound`, `TextField`, and more.

Classes

In Flash MX 2004, Macromedia introduced ActionScript 2.0, which introduced the ability to create true classes with all of the standard class elements available to other OOP ECMA languages. Classes are created in their own files called "class files," with the format *classname*.as. The following example would be in ball.as:

```
class Ball
{
        var radius:Number;
        var weight:Number;

        function Ball(newRadius:Number, newWeight:Number)
        {
                this.radius = newSize;
                this.weight = newWeight;
        }

        function getRadius():Number
        {
                return radius;
        }

        function getWeight():Number
        {
                return weight;
        }
}
```

The class file would then be included in the game by setting up the movie's class path to point to the location of the ball.as file. To create a new instance of a `Ball` class, we would write:

```
var beachball:Ball = new Ball(24, 10);
```

This would create a new instance of the `Ball` class `beachball`, with a radius of 24 and a weight of 10.

The Draw API

Flash has a series of ActionScript commands that are available to use at runtime called the Draw API. The Draw API allows us to draw shapes and graphics at runtime by using a few routines:

`myMC.moveTo(x, y):`   Moves the invisible cursor to a screen position.

`myMC.lineTo(x, y):`   Draws a line to a point, from the last `moveTo` or `lineTo` position.

`myMC.lineStyle(thickness, color, alpha):`   Sets the style of the line to draw in subsequent calls to `lineTo`.

`myMC.beginFill(color, alpha):`   Sets the color and alpha value of the fill to start filling in the shape defined by `lineTo`.

`myMC.endFill():`   Fills in the shape that has been defined by the preceding calls to `lineTo` made after `beginFill`.

There are several other functions useful to draw curves and gradients, but at its core, we can see that the Draw API provides a powerful interface for us to use when developing games in Flash, where we want dynamically created graphics.

The Integration of Graphics and Code

When it comes time to add code to games created in Flash, there are several options as to where to place the code. The decision depends on the goal.

The Main Timeline

The main timeline was introduced earlier. This is where we have several movie clips on the stage, and we place ActionScript on frame one of the main timeline. All movie clips on the stage can be referred to in this frame by simply addressing their instance names:

```
beachball._alpha = 10;
beachball._rotation = 90;
beachball._x = 214;
beachball._y = 12;
beachball._xscale = 50;
beachball._yscale = 50;
beachball.onPress = function()
{
    this._y++;
}
```

All of this code would apply to the movie clip `beachball`, and would do several things. First, it would set the `_alpha` transparency to 10 percent, making the beachball almost invisible. Then, it would set its _rotation to 90 degrees, its _x position to 214, _y position to 12, and then set its scale to 50 percent by adjusting _xscale and _yscale to 50. Finally, this would create an onPress function on the beachball, which would be triggered whenever the user clicked the mouse on the beachball. When triggered, this would move the beachball down by one pixel, by incrementing _y.

The Movie Clip Timeline

Alternatively, it's also possible to place code on the first frame of a movie clip itself. Once a movie clip has been created, we can go into its timeline and place code on any of its frames, just like the main movie. In fact, it can almost be thought of as a "mini" main timeline. In the beachball example, we would use this code instead, on frame one of the beachball's timeline:

```
this._alpha = 10;
this._rotation = 90;
this._x = 214;
this._y = 12;
this._xscale = 50;
this._yscale = 50;
this.onPress = function()
{
    this._y++;
}
```

This is not much different, except we're referring to this instead of beachball. The advantage of using this method is that if we were to make several copies of the beachball movie clip on stage, they would all inherit the exact same behavior. Generally, however, the first method (code on the main timeline) is considered the ideal method because it keeps all game code in one location, and therefore makes things easier to read. When we have hundreds of movie clips, all with code inside them, it can become a challenge to update and edit all this code, much less remember where all the code is.

Backend and Server Connectivity

One of the other powerful features of Flash is its capability to load external files and resources at runtime, from a URL. We saw that Flash could load audio from an external source, but it can also be used to load data from a server through ASP, JSP, PHP, or any other scripting language.

loadMovie

The design of Flash is so modular that we can actually load other SWF movies into other SWF movies. We could have a SWF in which we have an empty movie clip on stage. Into that movie, we could then load another SWF file, essentially allowing us to have a "game within a game." The loadMovie method can also be used to load JPEG images at runtime.

getURL

We can use the getURL command to open a link in a browser. For example, if we have a movie clip that displays the text "Click here to open somenewsite.com," we could write:

```
myMC.onRelease = function()
{
    getURL("http://www.somenewsite.com", "_blank");
}
```

This would open the site *www.somenewsite.com* in a blank window.

LoadVars

The loadVars object is an ActionScript object that is capable of sending and receiving data to and from a URL. The URL would normally contain an ASP, JSP, or PHP script that we had written.

We can use the loadVars object to send and load variables to and from a backend script. We could use this to load game data such as a list of online users or a list of high scores. Alternatively, we could use the loadVars object to send data to a script and allow our Flash games to do things like save high scores or log in users.

Where Flash Struggles

As of Flash MX 2004, Flash does not have the capability to do serious real-time 3D graphics. The Draw API could be used to create simple, flat-color 3D images, but with the complexity required by most 3D games, Flash would fall short, with slow mathematical computations, and then large overhead in rendering the 3D vector images in real time. Flash is best used for 2D: flat background and foreground graphics.

Flash also struggles when we have too many things going on at once. When we have hundreds of movie clips, all running their own onEnterFrame code, with user interaction and sound, Flash will have difficulty keeping all of this going, and still maintain our desired frame rate. This has to do with the fact that Flash doesn't actually compile the ActionScript to a low-level machine language form. Instead, Flash converts the ActionScript into codes that are several bytes in size (bytecode), and then parses them at runtime. In essence, a SWF file still contains scripted code, even though it has been compressed.

Where Flash Excels

With respect to games, the following are some areas in which Flash excels.

Physics and Motion

Given the x, y grid-based design of the Flash stage, we can apply all sorts of standard physics concepts to Flash games. We can easily do things like translation (movement), collision, gravity, bounce, and friction. With just a few simple formulas, we can create a world that appears to be as realistic as our own.

Bitmap-based Tile Games

With a few careful tricks, Flash can be used to recreate all of the bitmap games of the 1980s and early 1990s. Recreating a *Super Mario Brothers* type of platform game is relatively easy using bitmap tiles, and it will run very, very fast.

"Old School" Games

We can use Flash to easily re-create all of the games of the early 1980s, like *Pac Man*, *Galaga*, *Asteroids*, and so forth. These games were all based on simple graphics and minimum processor overhead. Flash can duplicate this perfectly.

Popular Puzzle Games

Flash excels at puzzle games, such as the ones found online at *shockwave.com*. These are games that people can play easily and quickly, and tend to have very addictive gameplay. In fact, Flash can even be used to create simple games that are actually used in banner advertisements for the Web, essentially creating interactive, playable advertisements online.

Games for Devices

Because the Flash player is available on dozens of platforms, we can technically create games that work on all of these platforms. It's possible to create games that play on devices such as the Pocket PC, and soon even cell phones and watches. This capability opens up Flash as a viable game development platform for hundreds of different devices.

Summary

Flash has emerged as one of the most powerful development tools for making Web games, and indeed games in general. In this chapter, we learned that:

- Flash games have an instant potential audience of millions.
- Flash games can be rapidly and easily developed.
- Flash games can be deployed easily and quickly.
- Both programmers and artists can learn Flash quickly and easily.
- Flash moves along based on a timeline that proceeds at a specified frame rate.
- Flash is a vector-based graphics engine that supports lines, fills, gradients, and bitmaps.
- Flash has strong support for audio, including MP3, ADPCM, and RAW compression.
- Flash uses a powerful scripting language called ActionScript to program the game.

- ActionScript 2.0 has a powerful class structure.
- Graphics and code are integrated into one unit in the Flash IDE.
- The Draw API can be used to create graphics at runtime.
- Flash can communicate with external servers to retrieve files and data.

Exercises

1. What series of Draw API instructions would be used to create a solid black square, with a white outline, one pixel thick, that is 50 x 50 in size, with its upper-left corner at position (0,0)?

   Answer:

   ```
   myMC.lineStyle(1, 0xFFFFFF, 100);
   myMC.beginFill(0, 100);
   myMC.moveTo(0,0);
   myMC.lineTo(50, 0);
   myMC.lineTo(50, 50);
   myMC.lineTo(0, 50);
   myMC.lineTo(0, 0);
   myMC.endFill();
   ```

2. Use the Web to research more differences between Macromedia Flash ActionScript versions 1.0 and 2.0.
3. Research what graphic file formats Flash can import?
   Answers: FreeHand (*.fh, *.ft), All PostScript (*.AI, *.PDF, *.EPS), PNG File (*.png), Adobe Illustrator (*.eps, *.ai), AutoCAD DXF (*.dxf), Bitmap (*.bmp, *.dib), Enhanced Metafile (*.emf), Flash Movie (*.swf, *.spl), GIF Image (*.gif), JPEG Image (*.jpg), Windows Metafile (*.wmf), Macintosh PICT Image (*.pct), MacPaint Image (*.pntg), PhotoShop 2.5, 3 Image (*.psd), QuickTime Image (*.qtif), Silicon Graphics Image (*.sgi), TGA Image (*.tga), TIFF Image (*.tif, *.tiff)
4. What are some of the most popular Flash games on the Internet today?
5. Research how much a Flash game developer typically charges for the development of a medium-sized game for a corporate client.

References

[IWS04] Internet World Stats, 2004, available at *www.internetworldstats.com/ stats.htm*.

[Macromedia04] "Macromedia Flash Player Version Penetration," Macromedia, 2004, available at *www.macromedia.com/software/player_census/flashplayer/version_ penetration.html*.

[Nielsen04] "Online Games Claim Stickiest Web Sites," Nielsen//NetRatings, 2004, available at *www.nielsen-netratings.com/pr/pr_040616.pdf*.

3.4 Programming Fundamentals

In This Chapter

- Overview
- Data Structures
- Object-oriented Design in Games
- Component Systems
- Design Patterns
- Summary
- Exercises
- References

Overview

A firm understanding of programming fundamentals is required to program video games. This includes rudimentary data structures, object-oriented techniques, and a healthy repertoire of design patterns. While these topics are covered in many introductory programming books, this chapter will directly address how they apply to games, providing many useful insights along the way.

Data Structures

Game programming, like any other type of programming, involves using data structures for just about everything. The fundamental data structures are the same as for any other type of programming, but this section will highlight which ones are used the most, when they are typically used, and what unusual twists you may come across.

Arrays

Arrays are a sequence of elements occupying adjacent positions in memory. It is possible to access any element of an array from its index very quickly (in constant time). You can't insert new elements in an array, but you can replace existing ones by copying over them.

Arrays are very attractive for their simplicity: they never grow, they don't fragment memory, and elements never move to a different memory location. In addition, arrays are extremely cache-friendly because all their elements lie contiguously in memory and, as long as you're traversing them in order, you will get great cache coherence. These properties make them a good choice for situations with limited memory or where dynamic memory allocations are not possible, and we know the number of elements we want to store is fixed. Arrays were probably the most used data structure in game development during the 1980s, when memory was counted in KB instead of MB or GB.

However, those same properties make arrays unsuitable for a variety of applications. Arrays can't really be used if the number of elements is not known ahead of time (unless you want to check for running out of space, reallocating a new array, copying all the elements, and fixing up any pointers—not a trivial task). In addition, inserting or deleting elements in a specific place in the sequence requires copying all the elements after that place and shifting them over by one. That copy operation can be very costly, so it's better to avoid it as much as possible.

One of the main problems with arrays is trying to access an element out of bounds. It is very easy to set up a `for` loop that is off by one and tries to read or write one element past the last one in the array. In C and C++, the program will silently try to access that element without any warnings or errors, although other languages handle this situation better. If you are lucky, this will result in a crash and you'll know something is wrong right away. Otherwise, the program could go on having read garbage data from the nonexistent slot, causing all sorts of weird behavior, or, even worse, could write data to a location in memory that is used by something else, causing the game to crash at a later time or behave in very strange ways. Bugs like that are very difficult to track down, and have haunted programmers for many a night. There are commercial products that check your code for out-of-bounds errors, but not everybody is using them.

A better alternative to arrays is to use a higher level data structure with many of the same performance properties but better error checking and even the possibility for growth. The `std::vector` data structure in the C++ STL is one very good alternative to arrays: it is just as fast as an array, it has some error checking (in debug mode) to prevent the program from accidentally going out of bounds, and it can grow if needed. Just keep in mind that if the vector ever grows, it needs to copy all its elements over to the new location. This means that the type of object you store in the vector must be able to be copied (if they're objects, they need to have a valid copy constructor), any pointers or iterators you had from before the copy will be invalidated, and the copy operation itself might be a significant expense. You should consult the documentation or a good book on STL for the exact behavior of the std::vector data structure.

Linked Lists

Lists are extremely common in game programming. It seems that just about everything ends up stored in a list at one point or another: game entities in the world, projectiles in the air, players in the game, items in the inventory, and so forth. Their main advantage is that, unlike arrays, it's really fast to add or remove any element. The drawbacks are that lists require a bit more memory (a pointer or two per element), and they're not stored consecutively in memory, so we won't get as good a cache consistency as with arrays.

Linked lists can be either singly linked or doubly linked. Singly linked lists only have one pointer per node, going from each element to the next one in the list. This reduces the memory overhead of the list, but prevents us from efficiently traversing the lists backwards, or adding an element at any arbitrary point in the list unless we already have a pointer to the previous element. Doubly linked lists don't have any of those problems, but require two pointers per element.

Since linked lists are used so frequently, there is no excuse to write code for a new linked list in every situation. Even though lists are a very simple data structure, it's always a bit tricky to get all the cases right when removing elements from the end or the beginning of a list, and it's easy to introduce bugs. You should be using an existing linked-list implementation, such as std::list in C++ STL (or std::slist for a singly linked list). Java and other languages all offer a version of a linked list in their libraries. If those implementations of linked lists for some reason are not acceptable, consider rolling your own once and using it everywhere you need it.

Dictionaries

It might come as a surprise that dictionaries are one of the most common data structures used in games, but that's due to the interactive nature of games. In a modern game, game entities are constantly interacting with each other: they send messages to other entities (as they collide or as the result of a trigger), they create new entities (spawning new enemies or creating debris during an explosion), and they are on the lookout for the presence of other entities (AI scanning for enemy presence or a trap waiting for the player to walk into). During these interactions, we often need a way to go from some sort of unique entity ID to the actual game entity it represents, and that's exactly what a dictionary does.

A dictionary efficiently maps one set of keys to a set of data. This can be implemented in many different ways: as a balanced tree, as a hash table, or as an ordered list of pairs. The important part is that the translation from key to data happens efficiently. The C++ STL provides several types of dictionaries: std::map, std::multimap, and, in some versions, `std::hash`. Which one you use will depend on your data set and your performance and memory requirements.

These dictionary structures will often have an algorithm complexity of $O(\log n)$ or even $O(1)$. However, don't be lured by the algorithmic complexity alone; keep in mind that for small data sets (less than one hundred or even a few hundred), it is often faster to do a linear search through all the elements in an array than try to use a fancy dictionary data structure. When in doubt, run some tests to decide if you should be using a dictionary for your queries.

Dictionary data structures are not limited to mapping entity IDs to pointers. Other frequent uses of dictionaries in games are mapping between entity names and their code definition, between filenames for resources and the actual loaded resource, or between sound names and their offset in the sound bank.

Other

Other types of data structures often crop up in game development. Some of the most common are stacks and queues. As you can imagine, the C++ STL provides templated implementations for both of them: `std::stack`, which is an adapter that sits on top of another container, and `std::deque` or `std::queue`.

Stacks are used for anything that needs to be processed in first-in, last-out order. They will often be used internally with functions that traverse a hierarchy of elements, using a stack to store information about each level visited and then unwinding the stack to combine the results (e.g., updating rotations and translations through a hierarchy of nodes). Other uses of stacks could involve applying damage or effect rules if the design requires them to be added all at once and then resolved in reverse order.

Queues, which implement a first-in, first-out order, are perhaps used more frequently than stacks. The most common use of a queue is to store messages between entities for a frame. In one phase, all messages are stored, and then they're distributed in the same order in which they were received. Queues are also used for network packets (incoming and outgoing), to store all collisions affecting an object, and so forth.

A variation on a queue is a priority queue, in which the exit order is not determined just by the order in which it was added, but by some other factor. Priority queues are extremely useful for optimizing access to a set of elements. For example, if there were 1,000 entities in the world, it would be a waste of performance to visit every entity every frame and ask it if it needs to update anything for this frame. Even if they did nothing, traversing all entities that way would slow things down significantly because of the constant cache misses. A better strategy would be to store all the entities in a priority queue, and the priority factor would be at what time in the future they need to be executed. The sooner they have to be executed, the more toward the front of the queue they are. That allows us to pop entities from the top, execute them, and put them back in the queue until we find that the top entity does not need to execute this frame, which can mean that maybe we only executed a handful of entities and didn't touch the rest.

There are many other types of data structures used in game development, but they're usually very specialized ones that apply to a specific domain. For example, one of the most crucial ones to the performance of a game is a spatial data structure; that is, a data structure that gives us good performance in spatial queries such as "what entities are nearby," "what am I seeing in front of me," "what am I colliding against," and so on. Some types of spatial data structures are hierarchical grids, quadtrees, or octrees, and you would pick which one to use based on the requirements for your particular game. Computer graphics also has its share of specialized data structures, such as BSP trees for visibility, or adjacency data structures to quickly traverse the edges of a mesh and create shadow volumes.

Bit Packing

Bit packing is one of those very useful tricks that are not usually taught in computer science courses. Perhaps it's not all that necessary for general software development, but it certainly comes up a lot in game development and embedded systems programming.

Basic data types, such as integers or floats, are of a fixed size, independent of the value of the number they represent. For example, an unsigned integer could be represented with 32 bits, and have values ranging from 0 to $2^{32}-1$. Bit packing allows you to use less space when you know you don't have the need for so many bits to represent the range of values in which you are interested.

Flags

Let's look at a simple example. Imagine that every item in the game has a set of flags indicating some of its properties. Since each property is just a true or false, we can use Boolean variables to represent each state. The corresponding C++ code could look like this:

```
bool isWearable;
bool isMagical;
bool isCursed;
bool isPoisoned;
bool isLightSource;
//... more properties here
```

In theory, we just need one bit to represent each Boolean: it can only be either true or false. However, if you actually look at the memory layout of such a structure, you will find that the compiler probably set aside more bits than that for each variable. In most current platforms, it probably used up 32 bits for each Boolean, although sometimes, depending on the platform and the compiler, it will allocate as few as 8 bits, and as many as 64 bits. Why would it do that? In the name of optimization. Because processors deal in sets of multiple bits at a time, it is usually much faster to access a set of data if it's aligned on a certain bit boundary.

However, in our case, this is unnecessary. Not only does the compiler layout take up more memory than we want, but by making each object larger, it can significantly reduce performance by increasing the amount of data cache misses, which is one of the major bottlenecks with today's hardware architectures.

How much memory are we wasting? Let's say each Boolean is 32 bits, so we're using 160 bits instead of only 5 bits that we need to represent five states. That's not much memory at all, so why all the fuss? Now imagine we have 30 different states. Also, remember that each game entity in the world is going to have all those 30 states. If we have a world with 5,000 of those entities, the Booleans will take 585 KBytes. That's over half a megabyte! Now it starts being significant.

The most common way to bit pack those flags is to put all the bits in the same 32-bit value, and use a series of bit masks to query whether a certain bit is present. Even though this sounds low level and very error prone, it's actually very readable:

```
#define IS_WEARABLE      0x0001
#define IS_MAGICAL       0x0002
#define IS_CURSED        0x0004
#define IS_POISONED      0x0008
#define IS_LIGHTSOURCE   0x0010
// other flags 0x0020, 0x0040, 0x0080, 0x0100, etc
int flags;
if (flags & IS_MAGICAL) //... do something
```

In this case, we managed to pack all the Booleans into a single integer value that is 32 bits. We could have packed up to 32 of these Booleans before needing another integer variable. Notice the value we've assigned to each of the constants. The numbers are represented in the hexadecimal system, but are chosen so each is just a single bit so there is no overlap between them.

Going back to our previous example, all the status bits of a single entity would fit in 32 bits, and with 5,000 entities in the world makes for a grand total of about 20 KBytes. We have saved over 550 KBytes of memory by doing this bit-packing operation on the flags alone.

It is worth becoming familiar with this approach to storing flags because you will see it used everywhere in game programming. However, it has its share of disadvantages. The first one is that you lose any pretense of being type safe. Anyone could assign any integer to the flags variable and the compiler wouldn't know there was anything wrong. In addition, we could accidentally check the flags variable against other sets of constants intended to be used in another context and the program would continue to work fine. This is a significant problem with libraries that rely on this type of mechanism for many different things, such as Direct3D, and sometimes it's too easy to get two sets of constants confused.

A better implementation for bit packing flags in C++ would take advantage of the bit fields feature of the language itself. This is a possible way of implementing the previous example using bit fields:

```
union EntityFlags {
    int isWearable : 1;
    int isMagical : 1;
    int isCursed : 1;
    int isPoisoned : 1;
    int isLightSource : 1;
}
EntityFlags flags;
if (flags.isMagical) // ... do something
```

By using bit fields, we still achieve the same memory savings, but we remain type safe and don't have any constants that can be mixed up. The optimized code generated by the compiler should be exactly the same as the one produced with the previous approach, so it should have the same efficiency.

Network Communication

Another common use for bit packing is network communication. In online games, network bandwidth is usually a scarce resource. Even with broadband becoming more popular, the uplink bandwidth remains very limited, and we want to keep it as small and constant as possible to avoid hiccups in the game.

A common approach is to use bit packing even for types other than Booleans. For example, when passing messages around, we'll constantly need to pass entity IDs. These IDs are unique to each entity in the world. Normally, the ID would be stored in an integer and we would send all 32 bits down the network. However, if we know that an ID number can never get any larger than 20,000, we can bit pack it to 15 bits, to give us a range between 0 and 32,768. That leaves us with 17 bits to use for other purposes in every message that contains an entity ID.

Clearly, the code on the receiving side needs to be aware of exactly how we're packing our values and needs to go through the reverse process to unpack them and interpret them correctly.

The following code packs three values and a status bit into a single 32-bit integer:

```
unsigned int packed = ID; // This uses up 15 bits
packed |= ((int)coordX << 15); // This uses up 8 bits
packed |= ((int)coordY << 23); // This uses up another 8 bits
packed |= ((int)status << 31); // Last bit
// send packed value over the network
```

The following code unpacks them at the receiving end:

```
int ID = (packed & 0x7FFF); //Get the lower 15 bits
packed = packed >> 15;
int coordX = (packed & 0xFF); // Get the next 8 bits
packed = packed >> 8;
int coordY = (packed & 0xFF); // Get the next 8 bits
packed = packed >> 8;
bool status = (packed & 0x01); // Last bit
```

You can apply the same principle to any value that you know is going to be bounded: maximum health, hit points, velocity, world coordinates, and so forth. Considering how many messages are sent every second, and how many of those fields we can be transmitting over the network, the savings can add up very rapidly.

Floating-Point Numbers

Packing other numerical data types such as floats is more complicated. We can't reduce the number of bits like we did with integers because floats typically use the IEEE-754 floating-point format, which involves a sign bit, a mantissa, and an exponent. However, if we're willing to accept a smaller range of numbers and some possible loss of precision, we can store them using fewer bits.

One such technique uses *fixed-point* numbers, and is different from floating-point numbers in that it has a fixed number of bits that represent the integer part of the number, and a fixed number of bits that represent the fractional part of the number. For example, a 16-bit fixed point could use 4 integer bits and 12 fractional bits. That would allow us to represent numbers from 0 to almost 16 in increments of 0.00024 units. It's not a very large number, and it doesn't have great precision, but it fits nicely in 16 bits. Depending on your requirements, you could try using a different fixed-point format, such as using 6 integer bits and 10 fractional bits. The important part is that, as long as those restrictions don't affect the results of what we're trying to accomplish, we have reduced the amount of memory required by those numbers by half.

Fixed-point numbers used to be extremely popular to perform fast arithmetic operations back when floating-point operations used to be very slow compared to integer operations. For example, id's popular game *Doom* made heavy use of fixed-point arithmetic. Nowadays, floating-point operations are often faster than integer operations, and they can be parallelized better with the rest of the program, so there would be no benefit in trying to perform arithmetic operations directly on the fixed-point numbers, but they still remain a viable solution to store fractional numbers in fewer bits.

Other Uses

If bit packing is so great and saves so much memory, should we use it everywhere? The answer is a resounding "No." Bit packing should be saved as a last resort to get some significant memory or bandwidth savings. Other than the case of flags, we should avoid using it in everyday programming as much as possible.

A drawback of bit packing is that accessing packed values is generally slightly slower than accessing nonpacked values. However, that's not the big problem. The real reason to avoid bit packing as much as possible is that it is error prone, it prevents the compiler from doing type-safety checks, and is highly dependent on the exact size of each data type. You can reap significant gains by packing flags, and you can even make it fairly safe to use. Anything else is usually not worth the effort and the complication unless it's something so common that you'll save significant amounts of memory.

Object-Oriented Design in Games

Games are often all about interacting with objects or entities in some virtual world: you control an avatar, pick up keys, smash crates, slay monsters, and open doors. Look at the previous sentence and count the number of nouns we used there: avatar, keys, crates, monsters, and doors. The rest of the sentence is made up of the actions we can perform on those objects: control, pick up, smash, slay, and open. It is no wonder that so many games today are developed using object-oriented design, since it maps very closely to the concepts we're trying to represent.

Object-Oriented Concepts

Back in the 1980s and early 1990s, games were mostly implemented using procedural programming. The emphasis of procedural programming is on the code itself: on the scope of the code (divided in modules), and on the procedures (or functions) provided in each module. Conceptually, a procedural program is simply a sequence of procedure calls that perform some operations, which might change some data in some parts of the system.

Object-oriented programming, on the other hand, emphasizes the concept of the object, which is a collection of data along with a set of operations that work on that data. The key to object-oriented programming is that the data and the code are treated as a unit, as opposed to the data just being a consequence of running the code as was the case with procedural programming. That data is usually encapsulated and can only be accessed through the defined operations on the object itself.

Before we go any further, it's important to define some basic terms that are going to be used constantly when talking about object-oriented development:

Class: The abstract specification of a user-defined type. It includes both the data and the operations that can be performed on that data.

Instance: A region of memory with associated semantics used to store all the data members of a class. There can be multiple of these for each class.

Object: Another name of an instance of a class. Objects are created by *instantiating* a class.

Inheritance

Inheritance allows us to easily create new classes that extend the behavior of existing classes, just by adding a bit of code, and without having to modify the original class in any way.

This ability comes in handy to represent concepts in a very intuitive way. For example, we might have just finished creating a class that represents a normal enemy character in our game. The class takes care of animating the character on the screen, keeping track of its hit points, running the AI for that character, and so forth.

```
class Enemy
{
public:
    void SelectAnimation();
    void RunAI();
    // Many more functions
private:
    int m_nHitPoints;
    // Many more member variables here
};
```

At the end of the level, we'd like to add a "boss" enemy. Bosses are going to have much of the basic functionality in common with a regular enemy unit: they have hit points, they move around and play animations, they shoot, they take damage, and they (hopefully) die. However, they're going to have very different AI to make them much smarter and tougher to kill.

How do we go about implementing a boss enemy? We have already written much of the functionality for the enemy that can be used in the bosses. One possible solution is to cram any extra functionality in the Enemy class and ignore it when it's a regular enemy unit. This approach leads to bloated classes that are hard to maintain and understand because we end up adding everything and the kitchen sink. An alternative would be to refactor many of the functions out of the Enemy class and have a new Boss class that also used them. Unfortunately, that would mean breaking up the nice, encapsulated class that we just created, which will result in more maintenance headaches down the line.

Fortunately, there's a better way—using inheritance. We can create a new Boss class that inherits from the Enemy class. That means that it's going to adopt all the functionality of the Enemy class by default, but in addition, we can override particular sections to give the boss the unique behavior we want. In this case, we can override the AI to do something completely different and give the boss his unique character. This is how the Boss class would look using inheritance:

```
class Boss : public Enemy
{
public:
    void RunAI();
};
```

In a situation like this, Enemy would be called a "parent" class, and Boss would be a "child" class, because it inherits from Enemy.

You can continue inheriting from a child class to create a new child class. For example, we might want to create a special boss for the end of the game, so we create the SuperDuperBoss. A derived class is not limited to overriding functions from its immediate parent class; it can override public and protected functions from any of its parent classes. In this case, we will override another function from the `Enemy` parent class:

```
class SuperDuperBoss : public Boss
{
public:
    void RunAI();
};
```

It quickly becomes cumbersome to talk about classes inheriting from each other and from other classes in turn just by trying to describe how they are connected. Sentences quickly become a mouthful of the words *parent*, *child*, and *derived* mentioned over and over making very little sense. Not much different from trying to explain a distant family relation: "it was my step-sister's twice-removed cousin's brother who . . ." Just like a good family tree, class diagrams can be used to give the same information in a much more concise way. The diagram in Figure 3.4.1 shows the relation between the three classes we have constructed so far.

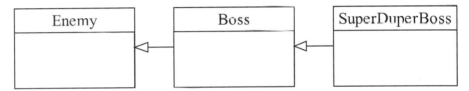

FIGURE 3.4.1 *Inheritance relationship between our three enemy classes.*

We'll be using that type of diagram throughout this chapter. You'll also find similar diagrams used extensively in game development and in general software development.

Polymorphism

Inheritance might be the most popular trait of object-oriented development, but polymorphism is what really allows us to make good use of object-oriented design in our programs.

Consider the following situation. We have a game with units as described in the previous section, but we have 20 different types of enemies and 5 different bosses, and we want to call the `ExecuteFrame()` function once for all the enemies currently in the level. To do so, we need to keep track of the type of each enemy unit, so we have to keep a list for each type of enemy and boss, and then iterate through each list. Every time we add a new unit type, we have to remember to add a new list, iterate through it, and so on. This sounds quite cumbersome. Wouldn't it be nice if there were a way to just keep a list of enemy units and call the `RunAI()` function in all of them independently of what type they really are?

That is exactly what *polymorphism* gives us: the ability to refer to an object through a reference or a pointer of the type of a parent class of the object itself. That is quite the mouthful, but it sounds far scarier than it really is. Read it again and you will see it starts to make sense. It is a fundamental concept and it is extremely important you understand it to be able to follow this chapter and the rest of the book, as well as for any game development work.

Here is a quick example of what polymorphism allows us to do:

```
class A {
    //...
};
class B: public A {
    //...
};
// We create an object of type B
B * pB = new B;
// But now we use a pointer of type A to refer to it
A * pA = pB;
```

Polymorphism allows us to forget about the true type of the object we are manipulating, and decouple the code that deals with those objects from the specific implementations of each derived class. For instance, we could have a function that takes an enemy as a parameter and figures out whether we can shoot at it. This function could look something like this:

```
bool CanShootAt (const Enemy & enemy) const;
```

As soon as we add a boss to the game, we want to know whether we can shoot at it. Without polymorphism, we are either forced to write a similar function taking an object of type Boss as a parameter, or do something very dangerous like passing a void pointer and a flag indicating what type of variable it is. Things can only get worse once we add new types of enemy classes. Polymorphism helps us with that by allowing us to have only one function that takes a reference to an enemy class independently of exactly what type of enemy it is.

Going back to the enemy example, we can take advantage of polymorphism to make our program much simpler by keeping all the enemy units in one array, independently of whether they are plain enemies, bosses, or the final special boss. That way, we can treat them all the same way.

In C++, we have to remember to flag functions that are going to be used polymorphically as *virtual*. A function marked as virtual indicates that the type of the object, not the type of the reference, should be used to determine which function should be called in case inherited classes override that function. Otherwise, the type of the pointer or reference will always be used.

In our example, we want the bosses running the boss AI, and each enemy running the correct type of AI based on its object type, so we should make the RunAI() function virtual. Here is the revised Enemy class:

```
class Enemy
{
public:
    void SelectAnimation();
    virtual void RunAI();
    // Many more functions
private:
    int m_nHitPoints;
    // Many more member variables here
};
```

Now we can finally treat all the enemies with the same code, independently of whether they are a boss:

```
Enemy * enemies[256];
enemies[0] = new Enemy;
enemies[1] = new Enemy;
enemies[2] = new Boss;
encmies[3] = new FlyingEnemy;
enemies[4] = new FlyingEnemy;
// etc...
{
    // Inside the game loop
    for ( int i=0; i < nNumEnemies; ++i )
        enemies[i]->RunAI();
}
```

Multiple Inheritance

Not all object-oriented languages support multiple inheritance, but since it's a feature of C++, it is important to know when to use it, and, even more importantly, when not to use it.

Multiple inheritance, as the name indicates, allows a class to inherit from more than one base class at the same time. As in the case of single inheritance, the derived class adopts all the public and protected functionality of all the base classes. It can also be treated polymorphically as if it were of the type of any of its base classes.

Logically, it should be used just like single inheritance since it still models the "is a" relationship. For example, when we design our game entity class, we want to make sure that it can receive messages (so it must be a MessageReceiver), and that it can be inserted in any tree (so it must be a TreeNode). We could use multiple inheritance to model that relationship.

This is how we would do it in code:

```
class GameEntity : public MessageReceiver, public TreeNode {
public:
    // Game entity functions...
};
```

The corresponding inheritance diagram is shown in Figure 3.4.2.

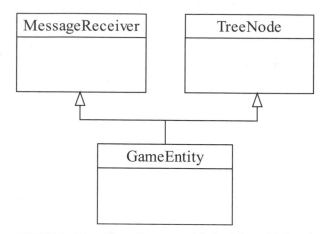

FIGURE 3.4.2   *GameEntity modeled with multiple inheritance.*

Even though multiple inheritance sounds great on paper, it has its fair share of problems and limitations. The C++ language attempts to solve some of these problems by providing new features in the language itself, but at the cost of further complicating things.

The first problem introduced by multiple inheritance is ambiguity. What happens if two classes we inherited from contain a member function with the exact same name and parameters? In our previous example, imagine that both MessageReceiver and TreeNode have a public member function called IsValid(), used for debugging, that checks whether the object is in a correct state. What is the result of calling IsValid() on a GameEntity object? It turns out that you need to explicitly disambiguate the call by saying which parent class you want to call.

An even larger problem is the topography of some of the possible inheritance trees that can be created with multiple inheritance. It is possible for a class D to inherit multiply from classes B and C, and have those classes in turn inherit from class A. This arrangement is what is often called the DOD (Diamond Of Death), and it has all sorts of problems: the contents of base class A will appear twice in the structure of class D, it will be ambiguous to try to use any of the contents of class A from class D, and so forth. C++ attempts to solve this by introducing *virtual inheritance* (not to be confused with virtual functions), but it just complicates matters further. You're better off avoiding the diamond inheritance hierarchy at all costs. Usually, it is the sign of a bad class design, and will cause more problems in the long run than it will solve.

There is one situation in which multiple inheritance is more acceptable and less error prone: when we multiply inherit from *interface* classes (also known as *pure virtual* classes). Interface classes are classes that declare a set of member functions but don't have any implementation of their own. A class that inherits from an interface class commits to implementing the interface by providing implementations to all the member functions.

Why would you want to inherit from an interface without implementation? So you can treat a class polymorphically on any of the interfaces from which it inherits. However, since those interface classes have no implementation of their own, it side-steps some of the most serous problems of general multiple inheritance.

In C++, you can create a pure virtual function by adding = 0 to the end of its declaration. That tells the compiler that you're not providing an implementation and that other classes that inherit from it must implement it. Here is an example of an interface class in C++:

```
class MessageReceiver {
public:
    bool HandleMessage(const Message & msg) = 0;
};
```

The Java designers made the wise decision to leave multiple inheritance out of the language to avoid complicating things too much. However, since inheriting from interface classes is very useful, they provided the Interface type and the implements keyword, so a class can inherit from one full-blown parent class, and implement as many interfaces as necessary.

Component Systems

Using object-oriented design doesn't mean that everything needs to be represented as part of a large inheritance class hierarchy. A component system is a different approach that uses independent components and aggregation to create complex behavior and reuse common code while retaining flexibility and the ability to change properties dynamically at runtime.

Limitations of Inheritance

When all you have is a hammer, everything looks like a nail. It is easy for programmers who started using object-oriented design recently to be carried away with enthusiasm. Usually, it results in complicated tangles of class hierarchies that use inheritance for everything.

Yes, inheritance is very useful, there's no denying that, but it is also easy to overuse and it's not particularly flexible. Let's examine the potential problems of using inheritance before we present some alternative approaches.

Tight Coupling

The first problem with inheritance is the *coupling* it introduces between classes. Coupling is a measure of how much two classes know about and depend on each other. You should always strive to have very loose coupling between classes, which means they're very modular and easy to change, and modifications to one don't affect the other. Tight coupling, on the other hand, means that two classes are very tied together and it's hard to do anything with one class without affecting the other. In real life, you need to strike a compromise between low coupling and efficiency and ease of development, but it should always be a concern. The larger and more complicated the project, the more important loose coupling becomes.

Inheritance happens to be the tightest form of coupling between two classes. The base class knows about all the public and protected members of its parent class and relies on them being exactly the way they are. Changes to the parent class often result in changes to the derived classes as well.

Unclear Flow of Control

The main reason for using inheritance is to be able to override a few functions to provide new functionality for a base class without affecting its parent class. This is a great solution for simple situations, but quickly becomes unmanageable for deep and complex class hierarchies.

All too often, you'll find a class hierarchy that has many different levels. Not only is class B inheriting from A, but C inherits from B, D from C, E from D, and so on. If you now make a call to a virtual function, which one will be called? B might override A's function, but so might C, and perhaps E as well. Trying to find the flow of execution can be very tricky.

Things get even more complicated when the base class just wants to add some functionality instead of completely overriding it, so it implements a virtual function, does some computations, and then calls the parent's version of that function. For every class, you need to remember whether it calls the parent function before or after its own code, and whether it calls it at all. The code eventually becomes completely dependent on the order in which it's executed, and attempting to make a small change to a class toward the top of the hierarchy often results in the program's behavior changing completely.

Not Flexible Enough

This is a particularly important drawback for game development. Say you've decided to model all the entities in your world using inheritance. After all, it makes sense this way. Figure 3.4.3 shows part of the class hierarchy of this organization.

In this example, the Sword class inherits from Weapon. However, what if later on, the designers wanted to make a talking sword? To be able to have dialogue, and allow normal interactions, it would have to be an AIEntity, which is in a separate branch of the hierarchy. Multiple inheritance is not the correct solution because it introduces the dreaded DOD and will cause more problems than it solves in the long run. We could add a new Weapons class under AIEntity or a new AI class under Weapons, but that would have a lot of duplicated code that would be hard to maintain and easy to get out of date, and have slightly different behaviors than the corresponding code on the other branch of the tree.

This is not just a contrived example; it happens all the time. There are many different ways to organize a class hierarchy given a set of object types, so that means there

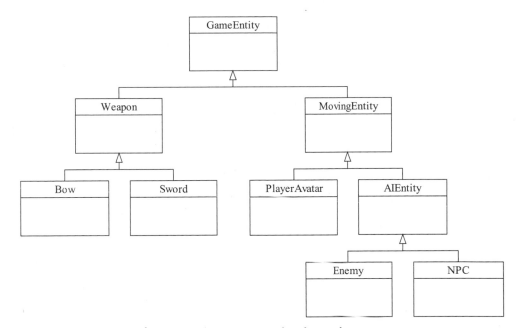

FIGURE 3.4.3 *Part of a potential game entity class hierarchy.*

are many different ways of looking at the same set of data. Having a single, static class hierarchy is just too inflexible for what we're trying to accomplish in games.

Static Hierarchy

A class inheritance hierarchy is completely static, at least in most commonly used languages in game development such as C++ and Java.

The Dragon class is under AIEntity, but what if you get to tame the dragon and you can ride on its back later? At that point, the Dragon would need to be under Vehicles. Using class inheritance, you'll probably have to have a DragonVehicle class, create a DragonVehicle object, transfer all the data from the Dragon to the DragonVehicle before you ride it, and destroy the original Dragon while making sure that everything on the screen looks exactly the same so the player is under the impression that nothing changed. Hardly a clean solution, and it introduces a very tight coupling between the Dragon and DragonVehicle classes, which will make future maintenance a headache.

Component System Organization

By now, you should be starting to question how wise it is to model all your game objects using inheritance. What is the alternative? After all, isn't inheritance the "object-oriented way" of doing it? That's the first concept we need to get rid of. Just because something is object-oriented, it doesn't mean it needs to use inheritance everywhere.

A component system is an alternate, much more flexible solution that relies on composition (or aggregation) rather than inheritance for most of its modeling. The idea is that we don't create a separate class for every game object type. Instead, we just have one class, called GameEntity, which represents every object in the game. This entity contains a series of components, each of which adds a new type of behavior or functionality to the entity itself. For example, we can have a RenderComponent, which displays the representation of the entity on the screen; a BrainComponent, which takes care of doing AI decision making; or a HealthComponent, which keeps track of how many hit points an entity has left.

Figure 3.4.4 shows a possible organization for a sword entity. Notice how easy it is to make changes to it without affecting any other entities. If we want the sword to talk, we add a BrainComponent to it. And if we want to be able to ride it like a witch on a broom, we just have to add a special VehicleComponent without having to twist the inheritance hierarchy in any way.

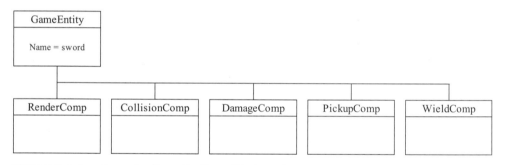

FIGURE 3.4.4   *Organization of a SwordEntity using a component system.*

The sword itself could be created in C++ this way:

```
GameEntity * pSword = new GameEntity;
pSword->AddComponent(new DamageComponent(...));
pSword->AddComponent(new RenderComponent(...));
pSword->AddComponent(new CollisionComponent(...));
//... and any other components necessary
```

Notice that we can even add and remove components at runtime, so it is possible to radically modify an entity's properties without affecting the rest of the game or having to make copies of the object and substitute references to it everywhere as we had to do before.

Since the entity class knows nothing about what it is trying to represent, its execution code will just give each of its components a chance to execute. The animation component will move the animations one frame forward, the render component will render the object to the screen, and so forth.

Interactions between entities are a bit more difficult to handle than they were in the case of the static class hierarchy, because entities know nothing about what they are, and all the logic is in the components themselves, so interaction needs to happen at the component level as well. Conceptually, it is easiest to think of the interactions as messages being passed around (although they could be implemented as functions calls or some other method that might be more efficient).

For example, consider the situation in which a bullet is flying through the air. The bullet itself might be an entity (again, as an optimization, if you have many bullets as in the case of a machine gun, you could model the "stream" of bullets as a single entity instead). In this frame, the bullet collides with a crate, so when we execute the bullet this time, a CollisionComponent executes and detects the collision. The bullet also has a DamageComponent that, as it learns about the collision, sends a package of damage to the entity it collided with, including information such as type of damage, amount of damage, location, and so forth.

On the receiving end, the crate will receive a damage message from the entity bullet. It turns out the crate has a HealthComponent, so it accepts that message and starts processing it. If it didn't have a HealthComponent, the message would have been ignored and nothing would have happened. The component parses the content of the message and realizes that the bullet dealt so much damage that the health is brought to zero, so it sends a death message to the other components in the entity. The DestructionComponent catches that message, and plays an effect of the crate being shattered and replaces the mesh from the RenderComponent with the destroyed state.

Data-Driven Composition

We can take the idea of the component system even further and actually define the structure of each of our game entities in a data file instead of in the code itself. This gives us extreme flexibility and pushes the entity structure to be a piece of data instead of part of the code. That means that many changes to the entity structure will not affect the code and will not require us to do full recompiles of the game and tools. We have effectively decoupled the code from the data.

For example, here is how the data for the sword entity might look like in an XML file:

```
<entity name="sword" full_name="Great sword of Pelayo">
    <component type="weapon"
               damage="slashing"
               damage_range="5-10"
               magical="true"
               range="1.5" />
    <component type="render"
               mesh="meshes/weapons/great_sword.mesh"
               attributes="glow"/>
```

```
    <component type="collision"
              collision_type="tight_volume"
              attributes="standard"/>
    <!- Any other components go here ->
</entity>
```

If you write a tool to represent the different components as visual units, you can give the designers in your team the power to create totally new entity types without any intervention from a programmer. You will most likely be surprised at the creative uses they come up with given the freedom of experimenting with such a flexible, data-driven system.

Drawbacks and Analysis

Even though we have been singing the virtues of a component-based system in this section, it has its share of drawbacks, and you should be aware of them before deciding what approach to take for your next game.

The first drawback of a component-based system is that it's hard to debug. If you break in the middle of a game with the debugger, in the case of a class hierarchy, you will see things like a Sword class in your debugger, and you can easily access all its member variables and examine their contents. On the other hand, with a component system all you'll see are lists of entities, each with a set of components. It will take more work to dig into each of them and find out what they represent. That arrangement also makes it harder to use breakpoints, since the only unique code you have is the one in the components, not in the entities themselves.

Performance can also be a problem if you're not careful. Instead of having straight function calls within a class, we are passing messages around, both within the entity and to other entities. This is the price we pay for decoupling the parts of an entity. Also, keep in mind that a deep class hierarchy might pass function calls up and down the hierarchy tree, so it's not just the components that are having chains of messages and function calls. With a bit of care and a good eye toward optimizations, it should be possible to have performance very close to that of a static class hierarchy.

If you use a data-driven approach and move the structure of the entities to a data file, it can be difficult at times to keep the code and the data in sync. Ideally, they should be completely independent of each other, but in practice, they will depend on specific variables or functions being there. What happens if the code relies on a variable that is not defined in the data file? Conversely, what if there's a variable in the data file that the code knows nothing about? Deciding what to do in those situations and handling it well is key to having an efficient workflow and avoid breaking the game.

Finally, a problem with the component-based design is its own flexibility. For larger systems, an entity could have several dozen components. They have been so modularized and decoupled that it's hard to see at a glance how they're going to interact with each other. Sometimes, even the order in which messages are processed could affect the result of operations and the behavior of the entities in the game, so it is important to try to keep things simple and enforce some strict order rules if this becomes a problem.

Having said all that, which approach should you use for your next game? A class-inheritance structure or a component-based one? The answer, as it is often the case, depends on the exact nature of your game and how you're planning to use it.

Imagine you're writing the fourth iteration of a successful tennis franchise. You know you're going to have a court, net, players, rackets, and a ball. You know how the games will be scored, what type of matches you'll have, and what the multiplayer games will involve. You also know that the designers aren't going to ask for a net that starts talking in the middle of the match, or a racket that can be ridden like a vehicle on the court during the game. Since everything in the game is known ahead of time and you know exactly how you're planning to deal with it, a class-inheritance structure might be perfectly adequate.

However, if you're writing a game where the player will visit a variety of environments (only a few of which are known ahead of time), and will have to interact with many different characters and items, a component-based approach will probably give you the best results. It'll let designers experiment with new entity types and create new and challenging situations much more easily than if they were constricted by a static class hierarchy.

Design Patterns

Design patterns are general solutions to specific situations and problems that come up often in software development. Because design patterns deal with high-level concepts of organization and architecture, they are not usually presented by providing libraries of code that can be dropped straight into a project, but are defined instead in more abstract terms of classes, objects, and their interactions.

There are many design patterns listed and cataloged in books and on the Internet. In this section, we will see some of the most important patterns that come up frequently in game development. Patterns are often listed as having four elements: pattern name, problem they solve, solution, and consequences. In addition, here we will describe how each pattern applies to game development and what some of its most common uses are. Refer to some of the references listed at the end of the chapter for a more detailed discussion of each pattern.

Singleton

Problem

Some classes need to have exactly one instance and be globally available to all parts of the program. For example, hardware resources such as a graphics device or a file system are unique and need to be used from many different parts of the program. How can we create such an organization?

Solution

Singletons are usually implemented so they have a single point of creation and access. That gives us the control to just create a single instance and make it available to the rest of the code.

Some implementations have a set of separate creation and destruction functions, while others automatically create the instance the first time it's requested. The advantage of having separate creation and destruction functions is that it is easier to control the lifetime of a singleton object, which allows us to create it after other systems are initialized or to destroy it before reporting memory leaks. A class diagram for the singleton pattern is shown in Figure 3.4.5.

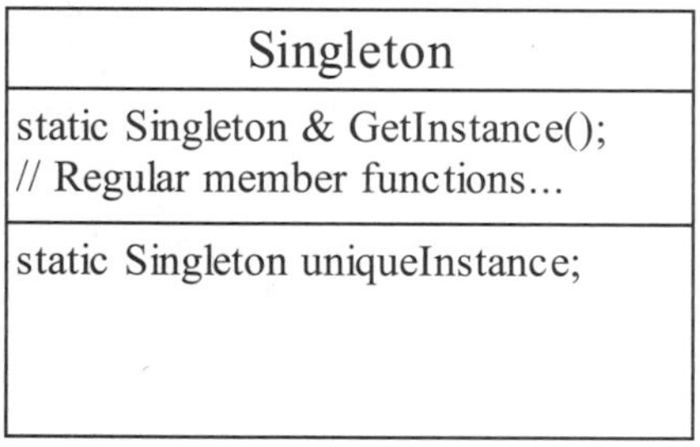

Singleton
static Singleton & GetInstance(); // Regular member functions...
static Singleton uniqueInstance;

FIGURE 3.4.5   *Class diagram of a singleton.*

Application to Game Development

There are plenty of opportunities in game development to use singletons. Unique hardware resources are a clear target for singletons: graphics devices, sound systems, file and memory managers, network interfaces, and so forth. However, not all hardware resources are unique, such as gamepads or memory cards, so they would be best implemented as regular objects.

There are also plenty of other unique objects in the game that can benefit from having global access, even if they're not related to hardware resources: a logging system to keep a log of all activity, warnings, and errors in the game; a messaging queue to distribute messages between game entities; or even an object that represents the game itself.

Consequences

Singletons give us two main things: a single instance, and global accessibility. How is that different from a global variable? It's not very different. Actually, the only benefit over a global variable is that we retain more control over how it is created and destroyed. As far as everything else goes, it can be considered a global variable.

What do we know about global variables? They don't lead to modular code, and can be a serious problem in large code bases to understand and maintain existing code. The same warnings about global variables apply to singletons, so don't use them unless you have to.

Overuse of singletons is a common situation in teams that recently switched to C++ and started using design patterns. Singletons are unique patterns and it's easy to see everything as a singleton. Resist that temptation as much as possible. Avoiding singletons will produce more modular code, better logical and physical structure of the program, and will make the code easier to test and maintain.

Some things, such as a logging system, might make sense as a singleton, but other things such as a messaging queue should probably be implemented as member variables of the game object system. The game object system can ensure that only one instance of the messaging queue is created, but it restricts access to it to only the code that deals with the game object system directly instead of exposing it to the entire game engine.

Object Factory

Problem

Sometimes we need to create an object of a class we don't know at compile time. We need a way to defer the decision of what type of object to create until runtime.

Solution

Instead of dynamically creating instances of a class by using new (or whatever mechanism your favorite language uses), we use a factory object that takes care of creating other objects. We call a member function with a parameter to specify which type of object to create, and it returns a new object of that type. A class diagram for the object factory pattern is shown in Figure 3.4.6.

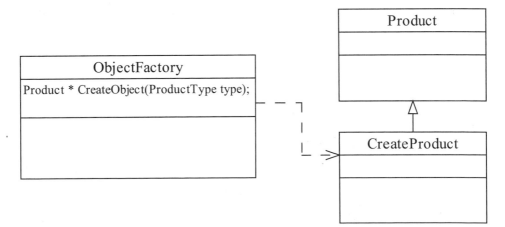

FIGURE 3.4.6 *Class diagram of an object factory.*

Application to Game Development

Object factories play a crucial role in game development and are essential to data-driven programming, as we are constantly creating new objects of all sorts of different types that we can't predict ahead of time.

For example, when we first load a level in a game, we need to know what type of objects are in the world, where they are located, and what their initial properties are. Clearly, we're not going to have a function called PopulateLevel1() that explicitly creates every object in the level. Instead, we typically have a data file that contains all that information. The level-loading code parses that file, and for every object, it determines what type of object it needs to be, calls the object factory with that type, reads all its data from the file, and adds it to the world.

We often use the object factory when we create objects at runtime as well, since many of the decisions about what objects are created are stored in data, not in the code itself. So, for example, the type of creature a spawn point creates is stored in a data file, and the type is fed to the object factory, which creates a creature of the desired type.

Object factories can also be used to easily extend the game and add new object types by making minor modifications, or even no modifications at all if we load code dynamically. Once we have an object factory in place, it is very easy to add new object types, which can be created just by supplying new data.

Consequences

A straightforward implementation of an object factory could be done like this:

```
enum GameObjectType {
    PLAYER,
    ENEMY,
    POWERUP,
    WEAPON,
    // ... rest of the objects...
}
GameObject * ObjectFactory::Create(GameObjectType type) {
    switch (type) {
        case PLAYER: return new Player();
        case ENEMY: return new Enemy();
        case POWERUP: return new Powerup();
        case WEAPON: return new Weapon();
    }
    return NULL;
}
```

That would work fine, but has the drawback that the object factory class needs to know ahead of time about all the object types it can possibly create. Adding new object types requires adding another enum and another entry in the Create() function. Worse, it makes it impossible to add new object types without modifying the code, so it restricts the power available to users who want to "mod" the game.

A good solution is to use an *extensible* object factory. Instead of having the object types hardwired in a code file, every class that wants to be created through an object factory needs to register itself with a unique ID and a way to create the object. The factory itself is just a dictionary that associates type IDs with object creators, and looks up that dictionary every time a request for a new object comes in. The companion CD-ROM contains an example of an extensible object factory that you can start using in your projects right away.

ON THE CD

Observer

Problem

Objects often need to know when certain things happen or when the state of other objects changes. We want to have a way to notify objects of different types with minimal coupling.

Solution

The observer pattern involves two classes: a subject, and many observers. Observers register themselves with a subject at runtime and the subject adds all the observers to a list. Whenever any event that would trigger a notification happens, the subject iterates through all the observers in the list and calls their Update() function. A class diagram for the observer pattern is shown in Figure 3.4.7.

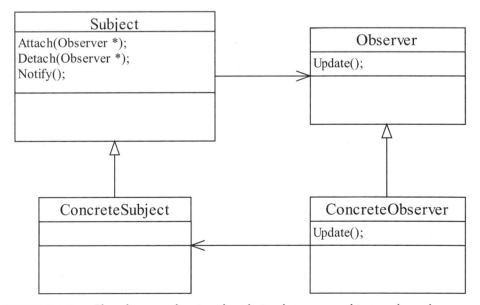

FIGURE 3.4.7 *Class diagram showing the relation between a subject and an observer.*

Application to Game Development

It is extremely common in games to need to notify other objects when certain events happen. For example, if the graphics device changes color depth or resolution, we probably want to notify all the objects that hold some graphics buffer so they can update themselves.

This situation is even more common at a higher level, among game entities. Entities don't live isolated from each other; rather, they interact with each other as they would in the real world. If a knight drops a sword on the ground, the sword might need to be notified so it can update its status. If the player steps on a pressure plate, the trapdoor should be notified so it can open.

We can hardwire those situations by having the knight explicitly update the sword after he drops it, but that is tedious and error prone. How many things should be notified in each event? It's much better to let each object decide what events it is interested in, and subscribe itself as an observer in the subjects it cares about.

Another common use of observers in game development involves notifying other objects that a certain object was destroyed. For example, the player might keep a pointer to the enemy that is currently locked in the weapons targeting system. If that enemy is destroyed for some other reason, we want to make sure the player knows it right away so it can reset its pointer. Otherwise, it might still try to access the invalid pointer and cause the game to crash.

Consequences

The observer pattern is great because it allows the subject to be completely decoupled from the observers, so it seems like an excellent solution for most object interactions. However, you need to be careful with performance and memory utilization.

If the subject has a long list of observers it needs to notify, it needs to traverse it linearly, call the update function in each observer, and let them deal with the update. For events that occur multiple times per frame, this can be a considerable performance drain, especially because traversing through the list and accessing a set of unrelated objects is very cache unfriendly.

A possible improvement, if you have large lists of observers and many different types of notifications (so only a small subset of the observers actually cares about a specific update), is to have the observers register themselves for specific update changes. For example, one observer can be notified every time an object moves, but another one just wants to know when the object is destroyed.

Memory use can also be an issue. Each subject is going to store a list of pointers to objects. As a plain linked list, that's going to take two pointers per node, plus whatever overhead there is for a dynamic memory allocation. If we plan to have thousands of these subjects with thousands of possible observers, the memory count is going to add up rapidly.

In cases of very frequent events or very large numbers of them, we might want to consider not using the observer pattern, and use tighter coupling by integrating the subject and the observer more closely and obtain better performance and less memory overhead.

Composite

Problem

We often want to group a set of objects and treat that set as a single object everywhere in the code. We want to avoid having special cases for a set of objects and for a single object.

Solution

We can create a new type of object that is a collection of objects. We then implement all the functions the regular object type would expose by iterating through all its objects and performing that operation. A class diagram for the composite pattern is shown in Figure 3.4.8.

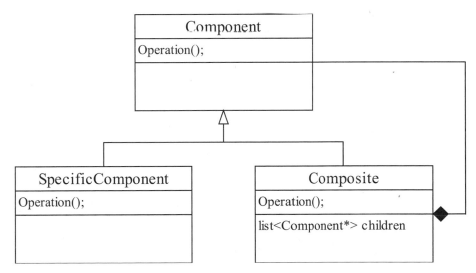

FIGURE 3.4.8 *Class diagram of the composite pattern.*

Application to Game Development

The composite pattern shows up frequently in game development. The most common example happens in the user interface of the menus for the game and the elements of the in-game HUD. For example, we have a widget class, and we inherit from it and create a button class, a text pane class, and a picture class. Now we can group sets of those widgets together and treat it as any other widget, which means it can be moved on the screen, can have focus, and so forth.

We also use the composite pattern on game entities and scene nodes. That way, any operations performed on the set of nodes are applied to all of them. If they are arranged hierarchically, the operation can be performed in a specific order while we traverse the tree. For example, if we have a set of nodes arranged hierarchically, and we used the composite pattern to make the set of nodes look like a single node to the rest of the code, when we apply a transform, the composite node will traverse the tree hierarchically and update the matrices correctly as it combines the transform down the tree.

Consequences

Composite patterns are all around very useful and have very few drawbacks. Probably the largest drawback is that you need to manually write code for every function exposed in the base class and create a new implementation that iterates through the set of objects applying the same operation.

To use the composite pattern, the functions need to be virtual, which can have a slight performance impact, but if you were using polymorphism they were already virtual anyway, so it shouldn't cause any performance penalties.

Other Patterns

Many more design patterns are used in game development. Some of them are more applicable to certain areas than others, so you'll find that some patterns are more used in the high-level game code than in the engine, and some are used in the physics calculations, but not in AI.

The best way to learn about patterns is to learn some of the most popular patterns and then read through existing source code for games and see how many you find. Sometimes, just doing a search for a particular pattern name will be enough to find them because they'll be named that way or there will be a comment explaining what pattern is implemented.

Here are some of the other patterns you will likely come across in game development:

Decorator: Provides a way to attach new functionality to existing objects "on the fly" without the need to inherit from the original class.

Facade: Combines a complex set of interfaces involving many objects and functions into a single, unified interface.

Visitor: Allows us to define new operations to be performed on a set of objects without having to modify any existing code.

Adapter: Lets classes work together that would not be able to communicate otherwise.

Flyweight: Allows sharing of memory among a large number of small objects.

Command: Encapsulates a request or message, which can then be stored, passed around between objects, and so forth.

Summary

To become an effective programmer, you need to know more than the specifics of a computer language. Data structures are fundamental to any structured program, and every game programmer should be well acquainted with the basics: arrays, lists, dictionaries, stacks, queues, and so forth. Additionally, a firm grasp of the object-oriented fundamentals should be considered essential in today's game development, with object-oriented languages such as C++ and Java being the norm.

Being familiar with the basics of object-oriented programming is not enough. It is important to apply it correctly and know when to choose a class inheritance hierarchy and when to use composition. Correctly identifying and using design patterns will also lead to faster development and a clearer architecture.

Exercises

1. Exactly how much memory is required by an `std::list` with N elements? Look through the header files for your implementation of STL or write a program to verify it. Make sure to take into account both the memory for the list itself and the memory used up by the nodes.
2. The STL provides several types of associative containers: sets, maps, and, in some implementations, hashes, as well as their "multi" counterparts. Explain what each container does, how they differ from each other, and give one example of how each could be used.
3. Write a program that adds 20 integers (values 1 through 20) to a vector using `std::vector`. Search the vector linearly for each of the elements. Time how long all the searches took (if you don't have a high-resolution timer, loop the searches several times). Now add the same set of integers to an `std::set` and search for all of them. Which approach was faster? What about for 100 or 1000 integers? Make sure you compile your program with all optimizations turned on.
4. Draw a class diagram of a possible class hierarchy for a game like *Pac-Man*.
5. Organize the same game using a component-based approach. Draw a diagram showing what components some of the major entities would have (player, enemy, pill, power-up).
6. Choose two patterns from a patterns catalog (other than singleton, object factory, observer, and composite) and explain how they can be applied to game development.

References

[Alexandrescu01] Alexandrescu, Andrei, *Modern C++ Design*, Addison-Wesley, 2001.

[Bilas02] Bilas, Scott, "A Data-Driven Game Object System," *Game Developers Conference 2002,* available online at *www.drizzle.com/~scottb/gdc/game-objects.htm*.

[Gamma95] Gamma, Eric, et al, *Design Patterns*, Addison-Wesley, 1995.

[Josuttis99] Josuttis, Nicolai M., *The C++ Standard Library*, Addison-Wesley, 1999.

[Llopis03] Llopis, Noel, *C++ for Game Programmers*, Charles River Media, 2003.

3.5 ▪ Debugging Games

In This Chapter

- ▪ Overview
- ▪ The Five-step Debugging Process
- ▪ Expert Debugging Tips
- ▪ Tough Debugging Scenarios and Patterns
- ▪ Understanding the Underlying System
- ▪ Adding Infrastructure to Assist in Debugging
- ▪ Prevention of Bugs
- ▪ Summary
- ▪ Exercises
- ▪ References

Overview

Debugging a game, or any other piece of software, can be an arduous task. For the most part, an experienced programmer can quickly identify and correct even the most difficult bug, but for the novice, it can become a frustrating and insurmountable task. To make matters worse, when you start looking for the source of a bug you never know how long it will take to find. The trick is not to panic and instead be disciplined and remain focused on the bug-finding process. Once you are armed with the techniques and knowledge presented in this chapter, you will be able to beat back even the toughest bugs and regain control of your game.

The difficult chore of debugging can be made simpler by using the *Five-step Debugging Process* described in this chapter. The disciplined use of such a process will ensure that you spend a minimal amount of time searching for and identifying each bug. It is also important to have some expert tricks up your sleeve when approaching an especially tough bug, so this chapter includes some valuable time-tested tips. We will also present a list of tough debugging scenarios explaining what to do when dealing with particular bug patterns. Since good tools are essential to debugging any game, we will discuss specific tools that you can embed within your game to help debug situations that are unique to game programming. Finally, we will review some simple techniques for preventing bugs in the first place.

The Five-Step Debugging Process

Expert programmers have the uncanny ability to quickly and masterfully track down even the toughest bugs. The magical way in which they instinctively know where to find the flaw can be awe-inspiring. While experience plays a significant role in this apparent talent, they have also internalized a disciplined method for investigating and narrowing down possible causes. The following five-step process aims to reproduce that discipline and will help you track down bugs in a methodical and focused manner.

Step 1: Reproduce the Problem Consistently

No matter what the bug, it is important that you know how to reproduce it consistently. Trying to fix a bug that shows up randomly is frustrating and usually a waste of time. The fact is, almost all bugs will consistently occur given the right circumstances, so it is the job of either you or your testing department to discover those circumstances.

Given a fictional game bug, a tester might report, "Sometimes the game crashes when the player kills an enemy." Unfortunately, this type of bug report is too vague, especially since the problem doesn't seem to happen consistently. The player might regularly blast away enemies, so there must be some other correlation to when the game crashes.

For bugs that are nontrivial to reproduce, the ideal situation is to create a set of "repro steps" that show how to reproduce the bug every time. For example, the following steps greatly improve on the previous bug report:

Repro steps:

1. Start a single-player game.
2. Choose Skirmish on map 44.
3. Find the enemy camp.
4. From a distance, use projectile weapons to attack the enemies at the camp.
5. Result: 90 percent of the time the game crashes.

Obviously, repro steps are a great way for a tester to help others reproduce a bug; however, the process of narrowing down the chain of events that lead to a bug is also critical for three other reasons. First, it provides valuable clues as to why the bug is happening in the first place. Second, it provides a systematic way to test that the bug has been fixed. Third, it can be used in regression testing to ensure that the bug doesn't reappear.

While this information doesn't tell us the direct cause of the bug, it does let us reproduce it consistently. Once you are sure of the circumstances that cause the bug to occur, you can comfortably move forward to the next step and begin to gather useful clues.

Step 2: Collect Clues

Now that you can reliably force the bug to occur, the next step is to put on your detective hat and collect clues. Each clue is a chance to rule out a possible cause and narrow the list of suspects. With enough clues, the source of the bug will be obvious, so it's worth the effort to keep track of every clue and understand its implications.

One word of caution: in the back of your mind you should always consider that a gathered clue may be misleading or incorrect. For example, maybe we were told that a particular bug always followed an explosion. While it might be a vital clue, it could be a red herring. Be prepared to discard clues that end up conflicting with other information you gather.

Continuing with the example bug report, we now know that the game crashes during a projectile attack on a particular enemy camp. What is so special about projectiles or fighting from a distance? These are important points to ponder, but don't spend too much time doing so. Get in there and observe exactly how it fails. We need more hard evidence, and mulling over superficial clues is the least efficient way to get it.

In the example, when we get into the game and actually watch the failure, we will notice that the crash occurs in an arrow object when it references a bad pointer. Further inspection shows that the pointer should point to the character that shot the arrow. In this case, the arrow was trying to report back that it hit an enemy and that the shooter should receive experience points for the successful attack. While it might appear that we found the cause, the real cause is still unknown. We must discover what made the pointer bad in the first place.

Step 3: Pinpoint the Error

When you think you have enough clues, it's time to focus your search and pinpoint the error. There are two main ways to do this. The first is to propose a hypothesis for what is causing the bug and try to prove or disprove that hypothesis. The second more methodical way is to use the divide-and-conquer method.

Method 1: Propose a Hypothesis

With enough clues, you will begin to suspect what is causing the bug. This is your hypothesis. Once it is clearly stated in your mind, you can begin to design tests that will either prove or disprove it.

In the game example, our detective work has produced the following clues and information about the game design:

- When an arrow is shot, it is given a pointer to the character who shot it.
- When an arrow hits an enemy, it gives credit back to the shooter.
- The crash occurs when an arrow tries to use a bad pointer to give credit back to the shooter.

Our first hypothesis might be that the pointer becomes corrupted sometime during the arrow's flight. Armed with this hypothesis, we now need to design tests and collect data to prove or disprove this cause. One method might involve having every arrow register the shooter's pointer in a backup location. When we catch the crash again, we can check the backup data to see if the pointer is different from when it was originally given to the arrow.

Unfortunately in this particular game example, this hypothesis turned out not to be correct. The backup pointer was equal to the pointer that caused the game to crash. Thus, we have to make a decision. Do we want to come up with another hypothesis and test it, or revert to looking for more clues? Let's try one more hypothesis.

If the arrow's shooter pointer never became corrupted (our new clue), perhaps the shooter was deleted after the arrow was shot but before the arrow hit an enemy. To check for this, let's record the pointer of every character who dies in the enemy camp. When the crash occurs, we can compare the bad pointer to the list of enemies who died and were deleted from memory. With a little work, it turns out that this was the cause. The shooter died while his arrow was in midflight!

Method 2: Divide and Conquer

The two hypotheses that led to finding the bug also demonstrate the concept of "divide and conquer." We knew the pointer was bad, but we didn't know if it actually changed values as a result of being corrupted, or if the pointer became invalid at some earlier point. By testing the first hypothesis, we were able to rule out one of the two possibilities. As Sherlock Holmes once said, ". . . . when you have eliminated the impossible, whatever remains, however improbable, must be the truth."

Some people might describe the divide-and-conquer method as simply identifying the point of failure and backtracking through the inputs to discover the error. Given a noncrashing bug, there is a certain point at which an initial error cascaded and eventually caused the failure. Identifying the initial error is usually accomplished through setting breakpoints (conditional or not) at all of the input paths until you find the input that breaks the output, thus causing the bug.

When backtracking from the point of failure, you are looking for any anomalies in local variables or in functions higher in the stack. With a crash bug, you should be looking for NULL values or values with extremely high numbers. If it's a bug with floating-point numbers, look for NANs or really large numbers further up on the stack.

Whether you make educated guesses at the problem, test a hypothesis, or hunt down the culprit through a methodical search, eventually you *will* find the problem. Trust yourself and keep your wits about you during this stage. Further sections in this chapter will elaborate on specific techniques that can be used during this step.

Step 4: Repair the Problem

Once the true cause of the bug has been identified, a solution must be proposed and implemented. However, the fix must also be appropriate for the particular stage of the project. For example, in the latter stages of development, it's generally not reasonable to change the underlying data structures or architecture to fix a bug. Depending on the stage of development, the lead or system architect should make the decision about what type of fix should be implemented. At critical times, often individual engineers (junior or midlevel) can make poor decisions because they aren't looking at the big picture.

Another important issue is that the programmer who wrote the code should ideally fix the bug. When this is not possible, try to discuss the fix with the original author before implementing any remedies. This will give you insight into what might have been done in the past about similar problems and what might break as a result of your proposed solution. It is dangerous to change other people's code without thoroughly understanding the context.

Continuing along in our game example, the source of the crash was a bad pointer to an object that didn't exist anymore. A good solution for this type of game pattern is to use a level of indirection so that this type of crash can't happen. Often, games use handles to objects instead of direct pointers for this very reason. This would be a reasonable fix.

However, if the game must be ready for a milestone or an important demo, you might be tempted to implement a more direct fix for this special situation (like having the shooter invalidate his pointer in the arrow when he gets deleted). If this kind of quick hack is made, be sure to make a note of it so that it can be reevaluated after the deadline. It's a common problem to see quick fixes forgotten only to cause trouble months later.

While it seems we've found the bug and identified a fix (using handles instead of pointers), it is crucial to explore other ways that might make the same problem occur. This can take extra time, but it's worth the effort to make sure that the underlying bug was fixed, and not just one particular manifestation. In our game example, it's probably the case that other types of projectiles will also cause the game to crash, but other nonweapons or even character relationships might also be vulnerable to the same design flaw. Find these related cases so that your solution addresses the core problem and not just one symptom.

Step 5: Test the Solution

Once the solution has been implemented, it must be tested to verify that it actually repaired the bug. The first step is to make sure that the original repro steps no longer cause the bug. It is also a good idea to have someone else, like a tester, independently confirm that the bug is fixed.

The second step in fixing the bug is making sure that no other bugs were introduced. You should run the game for a reasonable amount of time and ensure that nothing else was affected by the fix. This is very important since many times a bug fix, especially toward the end of the development cycle, will cause other systems to break. At the very end of a project, you'll also want every bug fix to be reviewed by the lead or another developer as an additional sanity check that they won't adversely affect the build.

Expert Debugging Tips

If you follow the basic debugging steps, you should be able to find and repair most bugs. However, when you attempt to come up with a hypothesis, prove/disprove a cause, or try to find the point of failure, you might want to consider the following tips.

Question Your Assumptions

It is important to keep an open mind when debugging and not make too many assumptions. If you assume that the simple stuff works, you could be prematurely narrowing down your search and missing the cause completely. For example, don't always assume that you are running with the most up-to-date software or libraries. It often pays to make sure your assumptions are valid.

Minimize Interactions and Interference

Sometimes, systems interact with each other in ways that complicate debugging. Try to minimize this interaction by disabling subsystems that you believe are not related to the problem (e.g., disable the sound system). Sometimes, this will help identify the problem since the cause might be in the system that you disable, thus indicating that you should look there next.

Minimize Randomness

Often, bugs are hard to reproduce because of variability introduced by the frame rate or from actual random numbers. If your game has a variable frame rate, try locking the "time elapsed per frame" to a constant. For random numbers, either disable your random number generator or seed your random number generator with a constant so that it always produces the same sequence. Unfortunately, the player introduces a significant source of randomness that you can't control. If the player randomness must be controlled, consider recording player input so that it can be fed back into your game in a predictable manner [Dawson01].

Break Complex Calculations into Steps

If a particular line of code combines many calculations, perhaps breaking the line into multiple steps will help identify the problem. For example, perhaps one piece of the calculation is being cast badly, a function doesn't return what you thought it did, or the order of operations is different from what you expected. This also allows you to examine the calculation at each of the intermediate steps.

Check Boundary Conditions

The classic off-by-one problem has bitten all of us at one time or another. Check algorithms for these boundary conditions, especially in loops.

Disrupt Parallel Computations

If you suspect a race condition, serialize the code to check if the bug disappears. In threads, add extra delays to see if the problem shifts. The problem can be narrowed down if you can identify it as a race condition and use experiments to isolate it.

Exploit Tools in the Debugger

Understand and know how to use conditional breakpoints, memory watches, register watches, stack, and assembly/mixed debugging. Tools help you to find clues and the hard evidence that are key to identifying the bug.

Check Code that Has Recently Changed

It's amazing the debugging that can be done with source control. If you know a date when it worked and the date when it stopped working, you can look at which files changed and quickly find the offending code. This will at least narrow your search to particular subsystems or files.

Another way to exploit source control is to create a build of the game before the bug was introduced. This is helpful if you can't eyeball the problem. Running the old and new versions through a debugger and comparing values might be the key to finding the problem.

Explain the Bug to Someone Else

Often, when explaining a bug to someone else, you'll retrace your steps and realize something you missed or forgot to check. Other programmers are also great for suggesting alternate hypotheses that can be explored. Don't underestimate the power of talking to other people, and never be embarrassed to seek advice. The people on your team are your allies and one of your best weapons against truly difficult bugs.

Debug with a Partner

This usually pays off since each person carries different experiences and tactics for dealing with bugs. You'll often learn new techniques and attack the bug from an angle you might not have tried. Having someone looking over your shoulder can be one of the very best ways to track down a bug.

Take a Break from the Problem

Sometimes, you're so close to the problem that you can't look at it clearly anymore. Try removing yourself from the situation and take a stroll outside of your environment. When you relax and come back to the situation, you will have a fresh perspective.

Once you've given yourself permission to take a break, sometimes your subconscious mind will work on the problem and the solution will simply dawn on you.

Get Outside Help

There are many great resources for getting assistance. If you are making a game for a console, each console manufacturer has a full team of people ready to assist you when you run into trouble. Know their contact information. The big three console makers all provide phone support, e-mail support, and newsgroups where developers can help each other.

Tough Debugging Scenarios and Patterns

Bugs often follow patterns in which they give themselves away. In tough debugging scenarios, the patterns are the key. This is where experience pays off. If you've seen the pattern before, you have a good chance of quickly finding the bug. The following scenarios and patterns will give you some guidance.

The Bug Exists in Release But Not Debug

A bug that only exists in a release build usually points toward uninitialized data or a bug in optimized code. Often, debug builds will initialize variables to zero even though you wrote no code to do so. Since this invisible initialization doesn't happen in release builds, the bug shows up.

Another tactic for tracking down the cause is to take your debug build and slowly turn on optimizations one by one. By testing with each optimization, you can sometimes find the culprit. For example, in debug builds, functions are usually not inlined. When they become inlined for optimized builds, sometimes a bug will show up.

It is also important to note that debug symbols can be turned on in release builds. This allows limited (albeit often frustrating) debugging of optimized code and even allows you to keep some debugging systems enabled. For example, you could have your exception handlers perform a full-blown stack trace (which requires symbols) to the crash site. This can be especially helpful for when testers must run an optimized version of the game, yet are able to trace crashes.

The Bug Exists on Consumer Console Hardware But Not on the Dev Kit

When developing games for consoles, the hardware manufacturers (Sony, Microsoft, and Nintendo) provide developers with dev kits. These dev kits are almost identical to the consumer production hardware that sells in stores, but they usually have added memory for debugging, extra hardware for communicating to a PC, and emulate the disc-based media access times (since all loads off the disc actually come from the PC). These differences are important when the game has a bug or crashes on consumer hardware but not on the dev kit. This usually points toward a problem with using too much memory, a timing problem involving loading data off the disc, or some other esoteric difference between the dev kit and the production hardware.

The Bug Disappears When Changing Something Innocuous

If a bug goes away by changing something completely unrelated, like adding a harmless line of code, then it is likely a timing problem or a memory overwrite problem. Even if it looks like the bug has disappeared, it probably has just moved to a different part of your code. Don't lose this opportunity to find the bug. It's still there and it will most certainly bite you in the future in a subtle or nearly undetectable way.

Truly Intermittent Problems

As mentioned previously, most problems will occur reliably given the correct circumstances. If you truly can't control the circumstances, you must catch the problem when it rears its ugly head. The key here is to record as much information as you can when you do catch the problem so that you can examine the data later, if needed. You won't get many chances, so make the most out of each failure. Another helpful tip is to compare the data collected from the single failure case to data collected from when it worked properly and then identify the differences.

Unexplainable Behavior

There are cases when you will step through code and variables will change without anything touching them. Truly bizarre behavior such as this usually points toward the system or debugger becoming out of sync. The solution is to try to resync the system with "increasing levels of cache flushing."

The following four Rs of cache flushing are courtesy of Scott Bilas:

- Retry (flush the current state of the game and run again)
- Rebuild (flush the intermediate compiled objects and do a full rebuild)
- Reboot (flush the memory of your machine with a hard reset)
- Reinstall (flush the files and settings of your tools/OS by reinstalling)

Of these four Rs, the most important is rebuild. Sometimes, compilers don't properly track dependencies and will fail to recompile affected code. The symptoms are usually general weirdness. A complete rebuild often fixes the problem.

When dealing with unexplainable behavior, it is important to second-guess the debugger. Verify the real value of variables with `printf`s, since sometimes the debugger becomes confused and won't accurately reflect the true values.

Internal Compiler Errors

Every once in a while, you'll run into a situation in which the compiler itself has given up on your code and complains of an internal compiler error. These errors could signal a legitimate problem in your code, or they could be entirely the fault of the compiler software (e.g., if it exceeded its memory limit or can't deal with your fancy templates). When faced with an internal compiler error, here's a good series of first steps to follow:

1. Perform a full rebuild.
2. Reboot your machine and then perform a full rebuild.
3. Check that you have the latest version of the compiler.
4. Check that you have the latest version of any libraries you're using.
5. Check if the same code compiles on other machines.

If these steps don't fix the problem, attempt to identify what piece of code is causing the error. If possible, use the divide-and-conquer technique to pare down the code until the internal compiler error goes away. Once it's identified, examine the code visually and ensure that it looks correct (it might help to have several different people look at it). If the code looks reasonable, the next step is to try rearranging the code to see if you can get a more meaningful error message from the compiler. One last step you might want to try is compiling with older versions of the compiler. It's quite possible that a bug was introduced into the newest compiler version, and an older compiler will compile the code correctly.

If none of these solutions helps, search Web sites for similar problems. If nothing turns up, contact the compiler maker for additional assistance.

When You Suspect It's Not Your Code

Shame on you—you should always suspect your own code! However, if you're convinced it's not your code, the best course of action is to check Web sites for patches to libraries or compilers that you're using. Study the readme files or search Web sites for known bugs with your libraries or compiler. Often, other people have run into similar problems, and workarounds or fixes exist.

However, there is always a remote possibility that your bug is a result of someone else's library or even faulty hardware (and you happen to be the first person to find it). While this is usually not the case, it certainly happens. The fastest way to deal with this is to make a tiny sample program that isolates the problem. You can then e-mail that program to the makers of the libraries or the hardware vendor so that they can investigate the problem further. If it really is someone else's bug, you can get it fixed the fastest by helping these other people identify and reproduce the problem.

Understanding the Underlying System

To find really tough bugs, you must understand the underlying system. Thoroughly knowing C or C++ simply isn't enough. To be a really good programmer, you must understand how the compiler implements higher level concepts, you must understand assembly, and you must know the details of your hardware (especially for console development). It's nice to think that high-level languages mask all of these complexities, but the truth is that when something *really* breaks, you'll be clueless unless you understand what lies beneath the abstractions. For more discussion on how high-level abstractions can *leak*, see "The Law of Leaky Abstractions" [Spolsky02].

So, what underlying details should you know? For games, you should understand the following:

Know how a compiler implements code. Be familiar with how inheritance, virtual function calls, calling conventions, and exceptions are implemented. Know how the compiler allocates memory and deals with alignment.

Know the details of your hardware. For example, understand a particular hardware's caching issues (when memory in the cache might differ from main memory), address alignment constraints, endianness, stack size, and type sizes (such as int, long, and bool).

Know how assembly works and be able to read it. This can help track down problems with optimized builds where the debugger has trouble tracing through the source.

Without a firm grasp of these issues, you will have an Achilles heel when it comes down to fighting the really tough bugs. You must understand the underlying system and intimately know its rules.

Adding Infrastructure to Assist in Debugging

Debugging in a vacuum without the right tools can be very frustrating. The solution is to swing the pendulum in the other direction and build great debugging tools directly into your game. The following tools will help greatly when tracking down bugs.

Alter Game Variables During Gameplay

A valuable tool in debugging and reproducing bugs is the ability to change game variables at runtime. The classic interface for doing this is to use a keyboard to alter variables through a debug command-line interface (CLI) in your game. With the press of a button, debug text is overlaid onto your game screen and a prompt lets you enter input via the keyboard. For example, if you want to change the weather in your game to stormy, you might type "weather stormy" at the prompt. This kind of interface is also great for tuning and checking the value of variables or particular game states.

Visual AI Diagnostics

Good tools are invaluable to debugging, and standard debuggers are simply inefficient for diagnosing AI problems. Debuggers give great depth at a moment in time, but they are lousy at showing how an AI system evolves during gameplay. They are also poor at showing spatial relationships in the game world. The solution is to build visualization diagnostics directly into the game that can monitor any given character. By using a combination of text and 3D lines, important AI systems like pathfinding, awareness boundaries, and current targets can be easily tracked and checked for errors [Tozour02, Laming03].

Logging Capability

Often, in games, we make dozens of characters interact and communicate with each other, resulting in very complex behavior. When these interactions break down and a bug arises, it becomes crucial to be able to log the individual states and events from each character that led to the bug. By creating separate logs for each character, with key events time-stamped, it becomes possible to track down the failure by examining the logs [Rabin00a, Rabin02].

Recording and Playback Capability

As mentioned before, the key to tracking down bugs is reproducibility. The ultimate in reproducibility would entail recording and playing back player input [Dawson01]. For very rare crashes, this can be a key tool in pinpointing the exact cause. However, to support this capability, you must make your game predictable so that an initial state coupled with player input produces the same result each time. That doesn't mean your game is predictable to players, it just means that you have to carefully deal with random number generation [Lecky-Thompson00, Freeman-Hargis03], initial state, input, and be able to save the input when a crash happens [Dawson99].

Track Memory Allocation

Create memory allocators that can perform a full stack trace on every allocation. By keeping records of exactly who is requesting memory, you'll never again have to chase down memory leaks.

Print as Much Information as Possible on a Crash

Postmortem debugging is very important. In a crash situation, ideally you'll want to capture the call stack, registers, and any other state information that might be relevant. This information can be printed to the screen, written to a file, or automatically e-mailed to a developer's mailbox. This kind of tool will help you find the source of the crash in a couple of minutes instead of a few hours. This is especially true if the crash happens on an artist or designer's machine and they don't remember how they triggered the crash.

Educate Your Entire Team

While this is not infrastructure that you can program, it's mental infrastructure that must be in place so that your team uses the tools you've created. Train them to not ignore error dialogs, and make sure they know how to gather information so that a found bug is not lost. Spending the time to educate testers, artists, and designers is well worth the investment.

Prevention of Bugs

A discussion of debugging wouldn't be complete without a small guide on how to avoid bugs in the first place. By following these guidelines, you'll either avoid writing some bugs, or stumble upon bugs you didn't know you had. Either way, this will help you eliminate bugs in the long run.

Set your compiler to the highest warning level and enable warnings as errors.
Try to fix as many of the warnings as possible, and then #pragma the rest away. Sometimes, automatic casts and other warning-level issues will cause subtle bugs.

Make your game compile on multiple compilers. If you make sure your game builds with multiple compilers and for multiple platforms, the differences between the warnings and errors of both compilers will usually ensure better code all around. For example, people writing Nintendo Game Cube games can also make sure a crippled version also runs in Win32. This can also allow you to see if a bug is platform specific.

Write your own memory manager. This is crucial for console games. You must understand what memory you're using and shield against memory overruns. Since memory overruns cause some of the toughest bugs to track down, it is important to make sure they never happen in the first place. Using overrun and underrun guard blocks in debug builds can make bugs show up before they can manifest themselves. For PC developers, writing your own memory manager is not really necessary since the memory system in VC++ is quite powerful, and good tools like SmartHeap can be exploited to identify errors with memory.

Use asserts to verify your assumptions. Add asserts to the beginning of functions to verify assumptions about arguments (such as non-NULL pointers or ranges). In addition, if the default case of a switch statement should never be reached, add an assertion for that case. Additionally, the standard assert can be expanded to give you much more debugging power [Rabin00b]. For example, it can be extremely helpful if your assertions print out a call stack.

Always initialize variables when they are declared. If you can't assign a variable a meaningful value when it's declared, then assign it something recognizable so that you can spot that it was never properly set. Some ideas for values are 0xDEADBEEF, 0xCDCDCDCD, or simply zero.

Always bracket your loops and if statements.   This keeps you honest by making you explicitly wrap the intended code, making it more obvious what was intended.

Use variable names that are cognitively different.   For example, m_objectITime and m_objectJTime look almost the same. The typical example of this problem is the use of "i" and "j" as loop counters. The characters "i" and "j" are very similar looking and you could easily mistake one for the other. As an alternative, you could use "i" and "k" or simply use more descriptive names. More information on cognitive differences in variable naming can be found in [McConnell93].

Avoid having identical code in multiple places.   Having the same code in several different places is a liability. If the code is changed in one place, it is unlikely it will also be changed in the other locations. If it seems necessary to duplicate code, then rethink the core functionality and try to centralize a majority of the code in one place.

Avoid magic (hardcoded) numbers.   When a unique number appears in code, its meaning and significance can be completely lost. If there is no comment, it is unclear why that particular value was chosen and what it represents. If you must use magic numbers, declare them as constants or defines that give a meaningful label to the number.

Verify code coverage when testing.   When you write a piece of code, verify that it executes correctly down every branch. If you have never seen it execute a particular branch, there's a good chance it contains a bug. One possible bug that you might catch from this process is discovering that it's impossible to take a particular branch. The sooner this is discovered, the better.

Summary

This chapter gave you the tools you need to effectively debug games. Debugging is sometimes described as an art, but that's only because people get better at it with experience. As you internalize the *Five-step Debugging Process*, learn to spot bug patterns, integrate your own debugging tools into your game, and build up your repertoire of debugging techniques, you'll quickly become adept at methodically tracking down and squashing tough bugs. With an ounce of prevention, hopefully your game will be smooth sailing and nary a bug will bite you.

 ## Exercises

1. Recount a tough bug that took several hours to track down and fix. What steps did you take to find it? What steps could you have taken to find the problem more quickly?
2. A release version of a console game only crashes when it is burned to disc and played on consumer hardware. What steps should be taken to trou-

bleshoot this problem? Propose several hypotheses of what the problem might be.

3. When debugging game AI, it helps to visually represent what game agents are thinking or moving toward. What graphical drawing services must be in place to support this functionality?

4. Why might it be a poor choice to use the variable names `distanceSquared-ToObject` and `distanceSquaredToOrigin` within the same function?

5. How might a profiler help find bugs you didn't know about?

6. Write a tutorial on how to use conditional breakpoints in your debugger. How is a conditional breakpoint better or worse than testing for the condition directly in the code (using an if statement and a normal breakpoint)?

References

[Agans02] Agans, David, *Debugging: The 9 Indispensable Rules for Finding Even the Most Elusive Software and Hardware Problems*, Amacom, 2002.

[Dawson99] Dawson, Bruce, "Structured Exception Handling," *Game Developer Magazine* (Jan 1999), pp. 52–54.

[Dawson01] Dawson, Bruce, "Game Input Recording and Playback," *Game Programming Gems 2*, Charles River Media, 2001.

[Freeman-Hargis03] Freeman-Hargis, James, "The Statistics of Random Numbers," *AI Game Programming Wisdom 2*, Charles River Media, 2003.

[Laming03] Laming, Brett, "The Art of Surviving a Simulation Title," *AI Game Programming Wisdom 2*, Charles River Media, 2003.

[Lecky-Thompson00] Lecky-Thompson, Guy, "Predictable Random Numbers," *Game Programming Gems*, Charles River Media, 2000.

[McConnell93] McConnell, Steve, *Code Complete: A Practical Handbook of Software Construction*, Microsoft Press, 1993.

[Rabin00a] Rabin, Steve, "Designing a General Robust AI Engine," *Game Programming Gems*, Charles River Media, 2000.

[Rabin00b], Rabin, Steve, "Squeezing More Out of Assert," *Game Programming Gems*, Charles River Media, 2000.

[Rabin02], Rabin, Steve, "Implementing a State Machine Language," *AI Game Programming Wisdom*, Charles River Media, 2000.

[Spolsky02] Spolsky, Joel, "The Law of Leaky Abstractions," Joel on Software, 2002, available online at *www.joelonsoftware.com/articles/LeakyAbstractions.html*.

[Telles01] Telles, Matt, and Hsieh, Yuan, *The Science of Debugging*, The Coriolis Group, 2001.

[Tozour02] Tozour, Paul, "Building an AI Diagnostic Toolset," *AI Game Programming Wisdom*, Charles River Media, 2002.

3.6 Game Architecture

Overview

The code necessary to create modern games is anything but simple. Gone are the days when the source code for a full game was just a couple of files and we didn't have to worry about overall structure and architecture. In today's games, with code bases exceeding a million lines of code, it is vitally important to have a well-defined architecture in order to understand the source code, add new features, and ship the game on time.

Main Structure

Most games make a distinction between *game-specific code* and *game-engine code*.

Game-specific code is, as the name implies, tailored to the current game being developed. It involves the implementation of specific parts of the game domain itself, such as the behavior of zombies or spaceships, tactical reasoning for a set of units, or the logic for a front-end screen. This code is not intended to be generically reused in any other game in the future other than possibly direct sequels.

Game-engine code is the foundation on top of which the game-specific code is built. It has no concept of the specifics of the game being developed, and deals with generic concepts that apply to any project: rendering, message passing, sound playback, collision detection, or network communication.

Both game-specific code and game-engine code are large enough that they are often split into several modules. Depending on how the project is organized, these modules can be static libraries, dynamically linked libraries (DLLs), or sometimes simply subdirectories in a project.

Architecture Types

When discussing different architectures, we will often talk about *coupling*. Coupling is a measure of how tightly two parts of the code are connected to each other. Loose coupling means that there's only a slight connection between the two sets of code, which is the ideal situation because it makes it possible to change one without affecting the other. The greater the coupling, the harder it is to modify or replace one without affecting the other. Really tight coupling means that the two sets of code are highly dependent on each other.

Game code is often organized in one of the following ways, which are discussed in order of increasing structure and complexity:

Ad-Hoc Architecture

Code bases developed this way don't have any apparent organization. They often grow organically, with code being added as needed without looking at the big picture. Different subsystems are not identified, let alone isolated, which leads to extremely tight coupling between all parts of the code. This approach works fine for projects with very small code bases (a few dozen files), but is very limiting in large projects, making development difficult and costly, and makes it virtually impossible to reuse the code in future projects (see Figure 3.6.1).

Modular Architecture

In a modular architecture, specific subsystems are clearly identified and separated into modules or libraries. Modules can vary in how they interface with the rest of the game. On one extreme, they can just be a group of related objects or functions that anybody can use, and on the other extreme, they can present a unified facade to the rest of the system.

Reuse and maintainability of code are greatly improved over an ad-hoc architecture. This approach also allows easier integration of middleware packages since modules can be more easily replaced or even wrapped to present a unified interface to the rest of the engine. However, dependencies between modules are not controlled, so over time, things often degenerate into a situation where every module communicates directly with almost every other module, leading to tighter coupling than we would ideally want (see Figure 3.6.2).

FIGURE 3.6.1 *Code base with an ad-hoc architecture.*

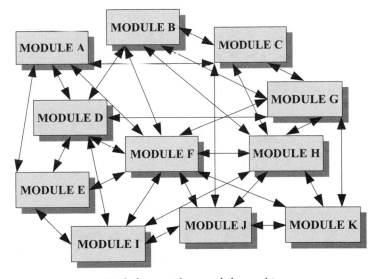

FIGURE 3.6.2 *Code base with a modular architecture.*

Directed Acyclic Graph (DAG) Architecture

A DAG architecture is a modular architecture in which the dependencies between modules are tightly controlled. Think of modules as nodes in a graph, and their dependencies as the edges. A DAG architecture requires that there be no loops in the dependencies. Therefore, if Module A depends on Module B, Module B cannot depend on any module that directly or indirectly depends on Module A.

This arrangement allows us to classify some modules as being higher or lower level than others, and has the advantage that it keeps modules ignorant of any modules that are higher level than they are, which reduces the overall coupling between modules. Typically, the game-specific code will be the highest level module since it depends on all of the high-level engine modules. It also makes it easy to decide to use only part of the code base, since by selecting any branch of the DAG we're guaranteed to get all the necessary modules. This is particularly useful when creating tools that only need specific parts of the engine, or that are completely game independent and don't need any game code.

Ideally, we'd like the DAG to be as wide (or as shallow) as possible, which means that the chain of dependency between modules is relatively short. That makes it easier to add, replace, or remove modules without affecting the rest of the program. The worst case is when all the modules are lined up, each of them depending on the previous one (see Figure 3.6.3).

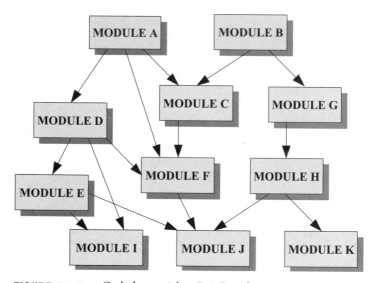

FIGURE 3.6.3   *Code base with a DAG architecture.*

Layered Architecture

A layered architecture is an arrangement like the DAG architecture in that there cannot be any cyclic dependencies between modules, but it takes a step further. While the DAG architecture allowed a module to access any other module underneath itself, here modules are arranged in rigid layers, and a module can only interact with modules in the layer directly below.

This type of architecture is more heavyweight than a simple DAG arrangement, and it can sometimes lead to duplication of code or interfaces in order to expose certain functionality available in a lower layer to a layer that is several levels above. Some domains are very well suited to a layered architecture, such as network communication, because, by their nature, they perform many serial operations from layer to layer. However, the code base of a game is not as rigidly structured, so it might not be a perfect match for a layered approach.

This type of architecture is more desirable when the number of modules grows to be quite large, and keeping track of individual dependencies between modules becomes too difficult. At that point, the layers can act as another level of organization on top of the DAG arrangement of the modules within each layer (see Figure 3.6.4).

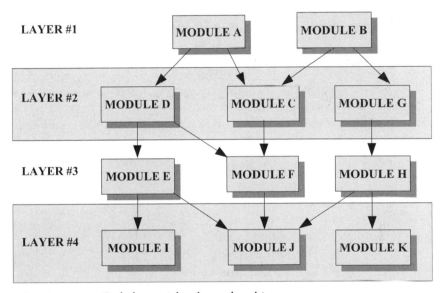

FIGURE 3.6.4 *Code base with a layered architecture.*

In-House Tools

The in-house development tools always warrant special consideration. These are the tools we create for the artists and developers so they can create awesome worlds and fill them with amazing content. How do these tools fit into the overall architecture?

One of the first things we need to decide is how much functionality will be in common between the game engine and the tools. Perhaps the only way the tools and the game interact is by creating a series of XML files that can be parsed in the game. In that case, they don't need to have any common code, and keeping them as two separate code bases would be a good idea.

Another possibility is that tools require some of the game functionality, but not all of it. For example, they might need to load resources and write files back out. Or, they might need to render some 3D graphics, but they have no need for any of the AI, collision, or networking code. In that case, ideally we should use only the parts of the game code that are necessary for the tool. If we have a DAG or layered architecture, it should be very easy to grab only the parts in which we're interested. After all, nobody wants to initialize the graphics renderer just to run a command-line tool.

Finally, our last option is full integration. If the tools need full access to all areas of the game (which is a suspicious situation that might indicate an ad-hoc or modular architecture), then we can make it so the tools use all of the game code. Or, take it even further, and make it so the tools are part of the game engine itself and you just have one executable for everything.

As with the overall architecture, thinking about this ahead of time and deciding which approach to use will make it easier to develop the tools and ensure they integrate well with the game engine itself.

Bird's-Eye View of a Game

Before we go any further and start getting into details, let's have a quick look at what the game does at the highest level.

Here is a sequence of events that a typical game will go through from the moment it starts until the moment it exits:

1. Game initialization
2. Main game loop
    a. Front-end initialization
    b. Front-end loop
        i. Gather input
        ii. Render screen
        iii. Update front-end state
        iv. Trigger any state changes
    c. Front-end shutdown
    d. Level initialization
    e. Level game loop
        i. Gather input
        ii. Run AI
        iii. Run physics simulations
        iv. Update game entities
        v. Send/receive network messages
        vi. Update time step
        vii. Update game state
    f. Level shutdown
3. Game shutdown

As you can see, there are some patterns in this sequence of events. We repeatedly see initialization and shutdown events for a variety of phases. These events are always paired together, and there's a matching shutdown for each initialization. We also see several game loops that run through a sequence of operations every frame. The next two sections cover each of these features in detail.

Initialization/Shutdown Steps

Initialization and shutdown of different systems and phases of the game is a very important step, yet it is often overlooked. Without a clean and robust way of initializing and shutting down different parts of the game, it becomes very difficult and error prone to switch between levels, to toggle back and forth between the game and the front end, or to even run the game for a few hours without crashes or slow downs.

Overview

The purpose of an initialization step is to prepare everything that is necessary to start a certain part of the game. For example, the front-end initialization step could take care of initializing the GUI system, loading some common art resources, and setting the correct state into the player profile.

```
void FrontEnd::Initialize() {
    GUI::Initialize();
    LoadCommonResources();
    PlayerProfile::Set(LoadPlayerProfile());
}
```

The shutdown step usually has a set of statements to undo everything the initialization step did, but in the exact reverse order they were listed in the initialization step. Every system that was initialized is shut down, every object that was created is destroyed, and every resource that was loaded is freed.

It is very important that the shutdown step undoes everything that was done in the initialization step. Failure to do so will result in memory leaks, subsystems that are never shut down, and plenty of other subtle bugs. In addition, to minimize the potential for bugs, it is recommended that it does everything in the opposite order than the initialization step. That way, we can be sure that we don't free a resource or shut down some system that is required by a later part of the program.

```
void FrontEnd::Shutdown {
    // Nothing to free for the player profile
    ReleaseCommonResources();
    GUI::Shutdown();
}
```

This is how the initialization and shutdown functions would be called from the game program:

```
{
    FrontEnd frontEnd;
    frontEnd.Initialize();
    frontEnd.Loop();
    frontEnd.Shutdown;
}
```

Notice the conspicuous absence of any error handling in the previous functions. In practice, you will want to check for errors in initialization and loading and deal with them following the game's policy for error handling: perhaps displaying the error, logging it and continuing as normal, trying to recover gracefully, or just by using the assert() function and letting a programmer fix it right away.

Resource Acquisition Is Initialization

A good rule to follow to minimize mismatch errors in initialization and shutdown steps is to use the *Resource Acquisition Is Initialization* philosophy (often abbreviated as RAII). That means that creating an object will acquire and initialize all the necessary resources, and destroying it will take care of destroying and shutting down all those resources. The advantage of this approach is that the initialization and shutdown calls are automatically called as the objects themselves are created and destroyed, so there's no potential to forget to call them, or to have mismatched calls.

Continuing the previous example, if we used RAII with the FrontEnd class, its initialization will be done in its constructor, and all its shutdown operations in its destructor. The functions Initialize() and Shutdown() shouldn't even be listed as public because nobody should call them directly. If an object of the class FrontEnd is around, we can be sure it has gone through the initialization phase successfully. Now we can use the FrontEnd class in the following way, and all the bookkeeping happens behind the scenes:

```
{
    FrontEnd frontEnd;
    frontEnd.Loop();
}
```

How do we check for errors now? Earlier we could just have the Initialize() function return a Boolean variable indicating whether it had succeeded or failed. Now we're doing the initialization in the constructor, which doesn't return any values. The shutdown step happens in the destructor and can't return any values.

The cleanest way of handling it is to use exception handling. Instead of cluttering all the source code with statements checking for errors, and returning out of a function as soon as they find a problem, we can just wrap the previous front-end creation into a try-catch statement:

```
try {
    FrontEnd frontEnd;
    frontEnd.Loop();
}
catch (...) {
    // Handle any problems here
}
```

It's a clean solution, but unfortunately not always practical. Dealing with exceptions can be a tricky issue, especially in C++. It requires writing exception-safe code, which requires that all resources are freed correctly whenever an exception is triggered, even if it happens in the middle of a constructor. At the very least, it will require the use of smart pointers (which is mostly a good thing) and that some programmers brush up on the consequences of dealing with exceptions.

Another issue is the support for exception handling in different languages and compilers. Unfortunately, in C++ not every compiler will deal with exceptions very well. Some of them will generate very inefficient code that might affect the performance of the game. Some console manufacturers even admit that their compiler doesn't really generate good exception-handling code and that you shouldn't count on it for your games.

Even if you can't use exception handling, it's still worth using the RAII approach whenever possible. You will have to check manually whether the initialization was successful, but you will still benefit from knowing that the object is always in a well-known state and not having to worry about calling the matching shutdown step by hand.

Optimizations

The following are some techniques sometimes used in games to make the shutdown phase faster or more reliable.

Fast Shutdown

Ideally, we want to be able to transition between levels or between the game and the front end as quickly as possible. During the initialization step we need to load some resources, so we try to do that as quickly as possible, but sometimes, you'll be surprised to see that you spend a second or two in the shutdown step for the game level before we start loading anything. Reducing that time to a minimum would definitely improve the user experience and keep players happier and more engaged in your game.

What exactly are we doing that takes so long? Usually, the shutdown step for the game is not trivial; after all, we need to destroy the entire world we had loaded in memory and bring everything back to its initial, pristine state. Games will usually iterate through all the game entities in the world and free them one at the time. Then they will do the same with each of the resources that were loaded (textures, geometry, etc.). They'll reset or destroy complicated data structures with many nodes and edges, and do a lot of general cleanup, most of which involves freeing memory that was allocated dynamically.

If we're just going to wipe the entire level, do we really need to be so careful and meticulous by deleting each little piece one bit at the time? It's like taking down a house by carefully removing each brick and placing it neatly in a pile. An alternative is to make sure all dynamic memory allocations for the game level happen in a set of memory pools dedicated exclusively to that level. At the end, when it's time to shut down the level, all we have to do is to reset those memory pools to an empty state, which is a very fast operation. As long as no code ever tries to access any objects or memory that was allocated in those memory pools, we have safely reduced the shutdown time for a level from a second or two to virtually nothing.

Warm Reboot

Your game should be able to run for hours on end without crashing. That's more difficult than it sounds. Just because it runs fine for a few levels doesn't mean that it can last for three days of nonstop play (some publishers require that the game runs for that long without any problems before they approve a game). Even if the game doesn't crash after several days of play, it often develops annoying side effects, such as a choppy frame rate caused by memory leaks, memory allocation problems caused by memory fragmentation, or jittery animations produced by loss of precision in the game timer.

One drastic but very effective way to avoid these problems is to do a warm reboot of the machine after each level. Clearly, this is not something we can do on a PC, but it will work fine on a game console since it's fully dedicated to the game. As long as the warm reboot is fast enough and the game loads immediately and preserves all its state, the player won't notice the difference, but the machine will be reset to its initial state, without developing any long-term problems. To make this even more seamless for the player, some game consoles provide functions to display an image on the screen while the machine is rebooting instead of going blank or flickering.

Main Game Loop

At their heart, games are driven by a game loop that performs a series of tasks every frame. By doing those tasks every frame, we put together the illusion of an animated, living world. Sometimes, games will have separate loops for the front end and the game itself, since the front end usually involves a smaller subset of tasks than the game. Other times, games are organized around a unified main loop. This section describes in detail the different tasks done during a game loop and ways of implementing them.

Tasks

The tasks that happen during the game loop perform all the actions necessary to have a fully interactive game, such as gathering player input, rendering, updating the world, and so forth. It is important to realize that all of these tasks need to run in one frame. In the case of a game that runs at 30 frames per second, that means all the tasks for a frame have to be done in less than 33.3 ms. If we choose to run the game at 60 frames per second, then we have half that amount of time: 16.6 ms. A task can't decide to take an unusually long time in one frame and run over its allotted time, because it would affect the overall frame rate and detract from the game experience. If a task really needs a long time to complete, it has to be broken down into multiple steps and executed across several frames. Even in games that allow for a variable frame rate, it is desirable to avoid sudden changes in frame rate to provide smooth gameplay.

The following are the main tasks just about every game needs to perform in its game loop at one point or another:

Time Step

Once upon a time, in the dark ages of game development, games didn't bother using clocks. They just did as many things as they could in one frame (which was determined either by how much the CPU could do, or until the next vertical synch signal of the monitor). That worked fine as long as the game only ran on that exact same hardware. As soon as somebody with a faster CPU tried to run it, the game became faster. Not only did the game run at a faster frame rate, but everything actually moved faster on the screen, causing the game to quickly become unplayable.

Today, things are different. Most contemporary games use some form of clock to drive the game and make it independent of the speed of the system on which they are run. Even console games that can always count on running on the same hardware usually benefit from using a clock to deal with updating the game at different video frequencies for PAL and NTSC video systems.

Most of the computations done during the game loop involve updating objects to reflect all the changes that happened since the last frame (or since the last time they were updated). Since we want to avoid our game changing speed depending on the actual frame rate, we use the duration of time since the last pass through the game loop as the amount of time to move our simulation forward for this frame.

The time step in the game loop updates the game clock to match the hardware clock and computes how many milliseconds elapsed since the last time step. These are the only two sources of time information we will use during this frame. If we went back and read the hardware clock every time we needed to know the time elapsed, we would get slightly different readings throughout the frame because the hardware clock never stops. Instead, we just read the time values once at the beginning of the frame, and use them throughout the entire simulation for this frame.

There are two ways of handling time in games: *variable frame duration* and *fixed frame duration*. Most games on PCs, as well as many console games, use variable frame duration. That means that frames can last any amount of time depending on what is displayed on the screen, what the player is doing, or any number of factors. Sometimes, frames will be blazingly fast and only take 10 ms (100 frames per second), and sometimes they can slow down and take 50 ms (20 frames per second). This approach has the advantage that it scales very well to different hardware configurations, different content, and different game loads. It also lets players tweak the game settings to achieve a quality versus speed tradeoff.

Fixed-frame duration games are most commonly found on consoles, where the hardware is unchanging and frames can always be assumed to be of the exact same duration (which will usually coincide with a multiple of the vertical synch signal on the display). Fixed-frame duration has some nice properties, such as more predictable behavior, easier physics simulation, and more reliable network behavior. Even if you plan to have fixed-frame duration, it's still a good idea to make sure your game measures and uses the actual time duration of each frame for its simulation instead of assuming a fixed time per frame. That way, the game will be able to react correctly to a hitch in the frame rate (a much bigger explosion than you had anticipated, for example), and it will make it easier to run at a different fixed frame rate, such as on a PAL video system (which runs at 25 frames per second instead of 30 frames per second on an NTSC system).

Input

A game is an interactive experience, so one of the most important tasks is to gather the player input and react accordingly. We get input through a variety of input mechanisms: gamepad, mouse, keyboard, driving wheel, video camera, or any of a myriad of custom input devices. The important thing is that the input be consistent and as close as possible to instantaneous.

To provide the user with consistent input, it is best to sample the input device once per frame and save those values for the rest of the frame. Otherwise, if we sample the input device every time we need to know its state, we could end up with very inconsistent results within the same frame.

It is important to minimize the amount of time elapsed between the moment we sample the input from the device and the moment our game reacts to the input. This will give the player a better impression of responsiveness and control. To minimize that time, we typically get the input at the beginning of the game loop, right before the simulation step. Otherwise, if we left the input task for the end of the loop, we would be reacting to the player a frame behind, and everything would feel lagged by about 30 ms (or less in the case of higher frame rates).

Networking

Another aspect of input is the input we receive from the network. At some point in the game loop, we need to collect all the new messages we received from the network, and deal with them accordingly, by updating game entities or providing new input.

Simulation

This is a huge task that encompasses all sorts of subtasks, and it is where the world really comes alive. The simulation step takes care of running any AI behavior code so AI entities decide what to do next and where to go. It runs any game code or scripts that update the game state or trigger new events. It runs physics simulations to make sure objects move correctly on the screen. It updates particle systems to make the misty waterfalls and the fiery explosions come alive. It moves the animations forward for all the visible characters. It updates the player's position and camera based on the input recorded in an earlier task.

Because of the sheer number of computations to do and the entities to update, this is often the most expensive of all the tasks we do in a game loop. So much, that for a game to run at a reasonable frame rate, it is important that we limit the number of entities and the type of updates we do every frame. We don't need to waste any time with an AI entity that isn't activated, and we don't need to continually update an enemy that is moving inside a building three blocks down the street. Deciding what to update and when to update it is one of the largest performance boosts we can do in some of today's games with large worlds filled with lots of game entities.

Collision

In the previous task, when we did the simulation step, we just moved everything to the position where it would ideally like to be. In this phase, we check for collisions between entities and deal with them accordingly. This is done in two separate phases: *collision detection* and *collision response*.

Collision detection is the simpler of the two phases. For each entity, we need to detect whether it's colliding with another entity. By *entity*, we really mean anything in the world: another character, an arrow, or even the ground. This is relatively straightforward, but it's not a cheap operation. We usually try to speed it up by providing simplified volumes to collide against, and we only check for collisions for the entities we care about (the ones that are directly in view or nearby).

The second phase is collision response. This can be much more complicated than the detection part. The response phase deals with correctly updating the entities that have collided (*correct* being defined by the consistent laws of the game, not necessarily by reality). If a character collides with an arrow, we need to assign damage and notify the character that it has been hit. If a car collides with a wall, we need to crumple the car, and change its position and velocity to account for the collision. Making sure that those things look realistic requires a solid physics simulation and some good game tuning.

Object Updates

Now that we have run the simulation and dealt with any collision issues, it's time to update the objects to their desired position. Here we're applying the correct transform to the objects, updating all their children, applying animations to a skeleton, and so forth.

If we have our world structured as a scene graph, this is when we propagate states up and down the tree such as render or game states.

Rendering

Finally, the moment we've been waiting for during this entire frame. Now that everything is in place, we finally get to display it on the screen.

Again, because of the large worlds in today's games, we can't just throw the entire world at the graphics hardware and expect to have decent performance. We first need to identify all the objects that could be potentially visible, and then pass down only those objects to the graphics hardware. To do that, we can use a variety of spatial partitioning techniques, such as portals or BSP trees, and perhaps combine them with a simple frustum cull against the frustum defined by the camera.

This operation needs to be repeated once for every camera we're displaying on the screen, as would be the case in a split-screen game, or for a rear-view mirror in a driving game. Sometimes we need to render the scene more times if we have any real-time reflections or environment maps.

Many techniques are applied at this time to achieve realistic shadows, complex lighting models, full-screen processing, and so forth. Rendering is an active area of research, and every year new techniques are being developed to create new effects and more realistic visuals. The graphics hardware also keeps advancing at a breakneck pace, which contributes to the improvement of game visuals every year.

Other

There are plenty of miscellaneous tasks that have to be done during each frame, so it's important that they are included in the game loop. For example, we might need to tend to the sound system and update it once per frame to keep all the sounds loading and mixing correctly, or perhaps we batched all the outgoing network packets created during the frame and we need to send them at once at the end.

Structure

We now know what a game loop does, but how exactly is it structured? The most straightforward approach is to simply have a `while` loop with all the steps included in the loop. The following code is a typical game loop:

```
while (!IsDone()) {
    UpdateTime();
    GetInput();
    GetNetworkMessages();
    SimulateWorld();
    CollisionStep();
    UpdateObjects();
    RenderWorld();
    MiscTasks();
}
```

Such a game loop has the virtue that it's simple, straightforward, and very clear. The steps are clearly spelled out, and it's very easy to add new steps or remove existing ones. However, the steps are hardwired in the loop itself, so what if we want to have different steps depending on the state of the game? For example, if we're not playing a game on the network, we don't need to have a network step. We can easily fix that by doing a check at the beginning of the `GetNetworkMessages()` function itself, but there might be other similar situations.

One of the most common places where we need a very different game loop is the front end. Conceptually, it is very similar: we want to loop, get player input, update the state of the menus, and render them, but unless we have some sort of 3D front end, we probably don't want to do collision detection, network updates, or many other game-specific tasks. The same applies for other game states such as the loading screen while we're loading level data, or special transitions between levels.

A possible solution is to have multiple game loops, one for each major game state. However, that solution involves duplicating a lot of code, and is error prone and hard to maintain. Every time we make a change to one of the game loops, we need to think about how it should affect all the other loops, or suffer subtle bugs that could be hard to track down.

A more flexible alternative is to consider each of the steps in a game loop as generic tasks, and have the game loop simply iterate through all the tasks and call the Update() function in each:

```
while (!IsDone()) {
    for (Tasks::iterator it=m_tasks.begin();
        it != m_tasks.end(); ++it) {
        Task * task = *it;
        it->Update();
    }
}
```

Now we can control exactly what steps we want to perform in the game loop from the game code itself. That means that we can have a single game loop for all the states of the game, including the front end itself. Whenever we transition from the front end to the game, we just add the correct tasks to the main loop and continue running as usual.

Coupling

So far, the game loop we have seen has been extremely simple. Every pass through the loop corresponds to a frame, and at every frame, we perform the same set of operations. Not all game loops are structured like this, however. A common technique is to decouple the rendering step from the expensive simulation and update steps. This technique allows a game to run the simulation at a fixed rate (e.g., 20 times per second), while still rendering as fast as possible. It combines the advantages of a fixed time step simulation with the scalability and improved frame rates of a variable time step game.

For a decoupled main loop to work effectively, we can't just run the simulation 20 times per second and render the graphics 100 times per second. If we did that, many of the frames we would render on the screen would be duplicates of the previous frame because the game state didn't change. To solve this problem, before rendering the screen, we interpolate any position and rotation values based on their previous position and known velocity. This arrangement can result in higher frame rates, smoother animation, and better overall responsiveness than a fully coupled game loop.

We can implement a decoupled game loop by using two threads: one for the simulation, and one for the rendering. It seems like a good idea on paper, but unfortunately, multithreading programming can be a tricky business, and it's much more prone to errors than single-threaded approaches are. The performance cost of context switches between the threads and synchronization to the same set of data can also add up and become a significant drain on performance.

Since we have a tight game loop that repeats every 30 ms or so, we can do the scheduling ourselves without much trouble. The main loop would look something like this:

```
while (!IsDone()) {
    if (TimeToRunSimulation())
        RunSimulation();

    InterpolateState();
    RenderWorld();
}
```

The function `RunSimulation()` could be implemented using the flexible task approach described in the previous section. `RunSimulation()` only gets executed at fixed intervals, and the rest of the loop runs as fast as possible.

Execution Order

When we talked about the different steps involved in a game loop, we didn't really address the order in which they were executed. For the most part, it doesn't matter too much, and the game will run fine whether we do network message gathering at the beginning or toward the end. We're going around the game loop constantly anyway. However, there are a few situations in which execution order of the different tasks is important.

In a game, the player is constantly interacting with the world. One of the goals we want to achieve is to keep that interaction as seamless as possible, which means reducing the delay between the time the player interacts with the world and the time the game is updated to reflect that interaction. For example, if the player moves the mouse, we want to move the camera as soon as possible, not 100 ms from now. If we waited that long, the game would feel sluggish even if it had a very high frame rate.

To achieve this, we want to minimize the time between the input gathering step and the time the rendering happens with those changes taken into account. A natural arrangement would be to gather input, perform simulations, and render the frame in that order. After rendering, we can take care of noncritical tasks such as updating the sound system.

We also want to reduce the time between receiving network messages and the time we process them in the game. If we were to delay them for a few frames, we would add another 30–60 ms delay to the messages, which is a significant percentage of the 100–200 ms that they spent traveling through the network already.

Another reason to be careful with the execution order of the different steps in the game loop is to maximize the parallelism we can achieve between the graphics hardware and the CPU. Most video cards in PCs nowadays, and all modern game consoles, have dedicated graphics hardware. This hardware can work in parallel without affecting the CPU, so we want to maximize this parallelism.

The best ordering of steps will depend on your specific hardware. Most graphics hardware have buffers to queue instructions, so they can be somewhat forgiving about when the data was sent to them, and they'll work at full efficiency as long as this buffer is always full. Ideally, we want to keep this buffer full while the CPU is busy working on the simulation for the next frame. This is represented in Figure 3.6.5a. Contrast that with the worst situation shown in Figure 3.6.5b, where the CPU sends a bunch of graphics data to the graphics hardware, and then waits until it's all done before continuing on to the next frame. In the first case, our game will run twice as fast and smoothly as in the second one.

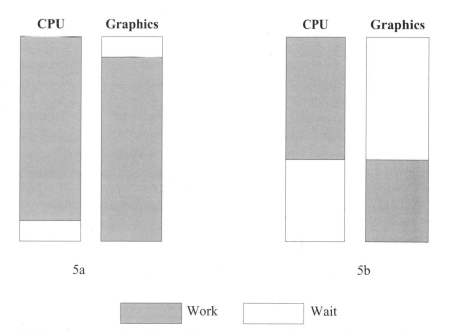

FIGURE 3.6.5   *a) A well parallelized game loop. b) A game loop not taking advantage of the parallelism between the graphics hardware and the CPU.*

As we move into the next generation of game consoles and modern PC hardware, the presence of multiple CPUs will become increasingly common. Games architected today will need to take advantage of the parallelism between the different CPUs to achieve the best performance. How exactly to achieve this while minimizing the amount of communication between threads in different CPUs will be an active area of research for the next few years.

Game Entities

A game is all about interacting with the world, but it's the smelly orcs and telepathic aliens, the faster-than-light spaceships and the all-terrain vehicles, the rocket launcher and the magical sword that inhabit the world and make it an unforgettable experience for the player. Those are the game entities and those are what ultimately make a game. This section describes how game entities are handled in a game: how they are organized, how they interact with each other, and how they can be put together to create a full game.

Definition

Up until now, we've been talking about game entities without ever defining them rigorously. We have been relying on an intuitive understanding of what a game entity is. Frankly, that's because a game entity is a very fuzzy and slippery beast. It can really refer to anything in a game world that can be interacted with.

Some examples of game entities are obvious: an enemy unit is a game entity, a sword you can pick up is a game entity. Others are a bit fuzzier, because we don't think of interacting with them so much, but the sky dome is probably a game entity as well since it needs to be rendered, animated, and moved along with the player. In addition, possibly so are effect-rich objects like fires and waterfalls; even the level geometry or heightfield itself might be considered a game entity. Other game entities that people sometimes forget about include triggers that generate some action when the player enters an area, or even the camera that is controlled by the player; they don't have any physical representation in the world, but they're still an essential part of the game.

Looking back over those examples, a good definition of game entity might be "a self-contained piece of logical interactive content." It is broad enough to cover all the previous examples, but fuzzy enough to deal with just about any type of game entity. The most important part of that definition is the self-contained aspect. A piece of clothing might be a game entity if it can be picked up in the world and equipped, but it wouldn't be considered a game entity if it's just decoration on a player avatar and can't be changed.

Deciding what is and what is not a game entity is not an arbitrary decision. As we'll see in the rest of this section, a game entity has a certain memory footprint and performance cost associated with updating it and traversing it. Only those things that we really are going to interact with should become game entities.

Organization

Conceptually, all the game entities in the world are stored in a list. We then iterate through the list to update the entities every frame, to render them, or to perform any other operations. It is important that entities be stored in a list, and not in an array or vector, because some game entities tend to be very volatile and new entities are constantly being created (bullets, spawned enemies, dropped items), while others are being destroyed (fading corpses, finished explosions, and projectiles after hitting a target).

In practice, keeping all of the entities in a list and traversing them linearly is probably too much of a naive and slow approach for anything but games with just a handful of entities in the world. We usually want some better organization that allows the game to perform its simulation and rendering steps as quickly as possible.

Here's where games vary a lot. A real-time strategy game will have a very different organization of game entities than an indoor first-person shooter or a fighting game. In general, entities will be stored in data structures that allow the game to do whatever operations it needs to do most efficiently. For example, a real-time strategy game could use a grid structure to quickly have access to all entities in a particular region of the world since the world can be easily projected on a 2D plane. However, a first-person shooter might use BSP trees or portals as a more efficient method given the type of environments it has to deal with.

However, we might want to perform different operations with conflicting requirements on the game entities. One interesting approach to solving this is not to limit ourselves to a single arrangement of game entities, but to use as many data structures as is necessary for the different operations we want to perform. That way, collision detection can use a type of data structure that is highly optimized to find contact between objects, but the rendering code can use one that can quickly cull objects that are outside of the camera frustum and occluded by other objects. To do that, we would go back to the original idea of keeping all entities in a single list, and then each type of data structure would keep a reference to an entity in the list.

If we're going to have the same entity referenced in many different data structures, it is crucial that all data structures remain in sync. If the entity is moved or deleted, all data structures need to be automatically updated. The observer design pattern is a very clean solution to this situation.

Updating

One of the operations we want to perform very frequently on game entities is to update them. Normally, we give each game entity a chance to do all the updates it needs to do once a frame during the simulation step. This involves running any AI, scripts, physics simulations, triggering events, or sending messages to other entities.

We usually want every entity to have a chance to run its update code once per frame, but unfortunately, that is often too expensive with large worlds and complex entities. Instead, we can try being smart about what entities we update, and only deal with those that are near the player or are important to the game in some way. The ones that are out of sight and not currently having a direct effect on the game can be left for later when we have a few CPU cycles to spare.

Game entities are sometimes organized hierarchically, so instead of storing them in a straight list, we store them in a tree structure. This allows us to impose some type of hierarchy on the entities: if the parent entity doesn't need to be updated, we can skip updating all the children. This can cut down the number of updates we need to do per frame if the tree is deep and well populated. Sometimes, this approach will be mixed with a logical spatial partitioning, by having all entities in a room or sector in one branch of the tree, so we can ignore them if we're nowhere near the room.

A more general technique involves using a priority queue of game entities to decide which ones to update every frame. The idea is that entities are added to the priority queue and sorted based on the time when they next need to be updated. Therefore, an entity that is right in front of the player would be sorted toward the front of the queue, while an entity that is very far away would remain at the back. The importance of the entity would also affect the time of update, so a very important entity would be updated frequently, even if it is far away.

The key concept is that now we can just start popping entities off the front of the queue, calling their update functions, and putting them back in the queue. Whenever the entity at the front of the priority queue doesn't need to be updated this frame, we can stop all the processing of entities. The biggest win is not so much reducing the number of entities that are updated, but not even having to traverse the full list of entities asking them one at the time whether they need to be updated or not. In modern hardware, traversing a list with many elements and accessing each can be painfully slow due to the constant cache misses. In contrast, the priority queue method only needs to access the exact number of entities we updated this frame and not one more.

Creation

There's more to creating game entities than meets the eye. At first, we might think it's a trivial operation: there is a class that corresponds to every game entity, and we simply do a new on that class to create an object of that time. That was easy.

It turns out that things aren't that simple. Depending on how you structure your game entities, you might not have one class per game entity (see the "Component Systems" section in Chapter 3.4), so you can't new an object whenever you want. In addition, we will need to create game entities by name (or ID) when we initially load a game level or a saved game, so using new directly is out of the question.

From the requirements we just listed, the creation of game entities is a perfect match for an object factory. An object factory will take care of creating the correct game entity on request. It is not limited to simply creating one specific object, but can create any other objects it needs if it uses a component approach.

In Chapter 3.4, we presented a simple object factory that created game entities. Here we will describe a more complex version, called an *extensible object factory*, which allows us to register new object types to be created at runtime. The advantages of an extensible object factory are many. One of the immediate consequences is that the factory itself doesn't have to know about every item it can create, so the coupling (and physical dependencies) between the factory and the items it produces is greatly reduced.

A second consequence is that it is much easier to add new object types to the factory, just by registering them at runtime. This makes it easier to add new objects during development, and opens the door to extending our game after it ships by having DLLs or some other dynamically loaded code register any new object types with the factory.

Let's start with a simple implementation of an extensible object factory. Our factory needs a `Create()` call, and a way to have the program register (and unregister) new object types:

```
class ExtensibleGameFactory {
public:
    GameObject * Create(GameObjectType type);
    void Register (FactoryMaker * pMaker, GameObjectType type);
    void Unregister (GameObjectType type);
private:
    typedef std::map<GameObjectType,FactoryMaker*> TypeMap;
    TypeMap m_makers;
};
```

Every time we register a new maker type, we add it to the map structure that gives us very fast mapping between the type of an object and a pointer to its maker. Creating new objects is just a matter of looking up the map and calling the creation function on the maker if we find one:

```
GameObject * ExtensibleGameFactory::Create(GameObjectType type) {
    TypeMap it = m_makers.find(type);
    if (it == m_makers.end())
        return NULL;
    FactoryMaker * pMaker = (*it).second;
    return pMaker->Create();
}
```

As you can see, the game factory knows absolutely nothing about what object types it is creating this time around. That detail is totally left up to the maker itself.

What steps do we have to take to add a new object to this factory?

1. Define a new object type (which is just an enum at the moment).
2. Create a maker class that creates the object we want.
3. Register it with the factory at the beginning of the program.
4. Unregister it at the end of the program.

So, there's a fair amount of work involved. If we're going to have hundreds of such object types, it could get cumbersome taking all those steps every time we need to add a new object type. It turns out that we can automate quite a few things in that process.

First, the object type can be changed so it's not an enum, but a unique ID that every object type has. This avoids having to explicitly add an entry to an enum list, and also means we don't have to have a centralized list of all object types, which would make it harder to extend from other sections of the code or from a DLL.

If we have some sort of runtime type identification in our engine, we could use a unique ID from that system for every class. Otherwise, we could simply create a class static variable in the classes we're interested in, and use its memory address as the unique ID into the map since it would never change and would be guaranteed to be unique. The only drawback is that it might not be the same between different executions of the program, so we should make sure we use a type ID that will not change for saved games and level files.

Another approach is to simply use a unique string for every new object type. It won't be as efficient as a 32-bit unique ID, but it will be easy to debug and can be saved to disk without any problems because it will never change.

If all the objects are going to be created in more or less the same way, taking the same type and number of parameters in their constructors, and performing the same set of operations, we can wrap the `maker` class in a template so they're automatically generated.

Finally, since the game factory doesn't know anything specific about the type of objects it creates, other than their base type, we can also create a template for the factory and reuse it in other places of the game where we need to create objects by type. The companion CD-ROM includes the source code for a fully templated extensible factory you can start using right away in your projects.

ON THE CD

This is how we would use the templated extensible factory in the game:

```
ExtensibleObjectFactory<GameObject> m_factory;
m_factory.Register(new FactoryMaker<GameClass_1>);
m_factory.Register(new FactoryMaker<GameClass_2>);
m_factory.Register(new FactoryMaker<GameClass_3>);
//... etc...
```

As you can see, it takes virtually no effort to register new objects with the factory.

One technique you might come across is the automatic registration of object types with factories. Automatic registration makes it unnecessary to register object types by hand, or even to have any sort of registration step. All that happens behind the scenes for you, taking advantage of constructors and global object creation. The idea is to create a global object that deals with the registration in its constructor when it's first created. Since it's a global object, its constructor will be called during the static initialization phase, which happens even before `main()` is called.

You could create a template to make creating registration objects as simple as possible:

```
template <class Factory, class Type>
class Registrar {
    Registrar(Factory & factory) {
```

```
            factory.Register(new FactoryMaker<Type>);
    }
};
```

Now, all you need to do to register your object types automatically is create a global `Registrar` object:

```
Registrar<ExtensibleObjectFactory<GameObject>, GameClass_1> regis-
trarGameClass_1;
```

If that's too cumbersome to type every time, just wrap it up in a macro (or combine it in a class definition macro if you already have one), so you can just type:

```
FACTORY_REGISTER(GameClass_1)
```

However, as convenient as this technique might sound, it has its share of drawbacks. One of the most annoying ones you're bound to run into sooner or later is that the compiler could very well strip out the registration code when optimizations are turned on. We're creating a global object for the sole purpose of executing its constructor, but nothing in the rest of the program references it anywhere. Consequently, many compilers with aggressive dead-code reduction will remove it from the final executable, and none of our object types will be registered.

You might be able to trick the compiler into not stripping that code, but there are other drawbacks as well. One of the biggest problems with this approach, and with anything that relies on static initialization, is that you don't have much control over exactly when it happens. You can't control the order of initialization (unless the objects are in the same file), and you can't ensure that other subsystems have been initialized before. What if we wanted to initialize the factory before we register anything? We're out of luck, or we have to check in the `Register()` function whether it's already initialized, and do it if it isn't, which is just ugly and asking for trouble. What if we need to call a different function, or a totally different subsystem?

As if that weren't enough, automatic registration doesn't allow us to customize which objects get registered at runtime. For example, if a tool is running in "artist mode," we might want to only register and make available certain object types, but if it's running in "programmer mode," we might register a different set of objects. Even in the game, we might have different object types for a mod than for the regular game.

Once we consider what we gain by automatic registration of types and all the possible drawbacks, explicit registration sounds more and more appealing. Especially if you can get it down to one line as we did in the previous example, there's very little reason not to do it that way and save ourselves many headaches down the line.

Level Instantiation

Before we can play a level, we need to load it from disk. We aren't just loading the assets, but the actual game state. Whether this is our first time playing the level, or we're loading a previously saved state, we need to create the game entities that are in the world at this point, and set the correct state for each.

The creation part is easy now that we have an extensible object factory that creates game entities. The level file will contain a list of entities in the world, listed by name or ID. All we have to do is read through that list and repeatedly call the object factory with each of the object types, and we'll end up with the correct amount and type of game entities.

What we haven't talked about is the state of the game entities themselves. Just creating a game entity of the class Orc isn't enough. We need to set its correct position, orientation, amount of health, what weapons it is carrying, and so forth. Otherwise, we would have many, completely identical orcs in the world, and that's probably not what we want.

This situation is even clearer if we have more general classes like Enemy. It's not enough to just create an enemy; we need to load the correct textures, geometry, animation, AI state, scripts, and so forth for each type of enemy that we want to create.

One straightforward way of doing this is to store all necessary state data with each entity in the level file, so it can be restored as we create each entity. This approach will work, but it has one major drawback: similar entities will have the same data loaded repeatedly, and, even worse, they will take the extra memory to store all that information. If we have 200 orcs in our level, all 200 orc objects are going to contain most of the same data (geometry, animations, etc.), and are only going to differ in a handful of values (current health, position, and state). So, not only are our load times slower, but we're wasting memory in the game. Figure 3.6.6 shows this situation with several similar entities that have a lot of data in common.

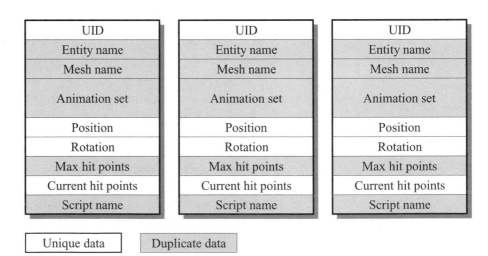

FIGURE 3.6.6 *Several similar entities with a lot of duplicate data.*

To solve this, we divide the data that is associated with each entity into instance data versus template data. Instance data are the values that differ from entity to entity: position, rotation, current AI state, current health, and so forth. Template data are the values that apply to all entities of that type: animation, textures, geometry, scripts, and so forth. Notice that we're using the word *template* in the general sense of a template to create a particular entity with some specific attributes, not in the C++ sense of code template. With this approach, we can load the template data just once, and have the entities themselves contain only the instance data, which should be much smaller. Figure 3.6.7 shows several entities sharing the same template data.

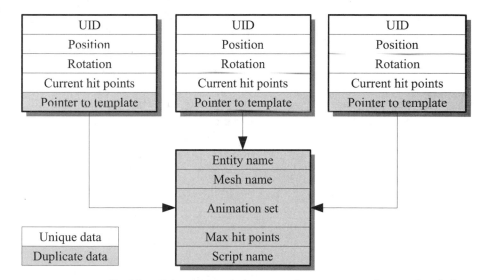

FIGURE 3.6.7 *Entities of the same template type share common data and only have per-instance data.*

This is a particularly powerful approach because it means we can have multiple entity templates that use the same C++ class, but have different sets of template data. Expose these values to your designers, and they'll be able to create a large variety of entities with minimal code changes. For example, we could have the regular "Orc" template, which loads the standard orc values. However, it would be trivial to add an "OrcChieftain" template that uses values very similar to the Orc, but has twice the health, better armor, a slightly different appearance, and perhaps a different weapon. All those values are part of the template, not of the instance, and a designer could create them just by editing a text file or through the game editor.

Identification

Before we can deliver a letter, we need to know the name and address of the person to whom we're sending it. It's the same thing with interaction between game entities. Before two entities can interact with each other, they need to know how to find each other and address each other by name.

A naive approach would be to use strings to identify game entities. We could make sure entities are created with a unique string based on their template or class name plus a timestamp or a sequential number. However, strings will take too much memory and be too slow to process at runtime unless you have a tiny level with just a handful of entities.

Another approach is to use pointers to the entities themselves. Unfortunately, pointers are error prone, and there's no way to know if the entity referred to by the pointer is still there. This is a particularly insidious problem because of how dynamic most modern games are. You can interact with many objects in the environment, move them, pick them up, and even destroy them. Things are constantly being created and destroyed, so there are no guarantees that just because you have a pointer to something that you saw a few frames ago, that object is still around now.

Consider the following example: Right after a turret fires a volley of projectiles in the air, it is destroyed by a nearby tank. A few seconds later, the projectiles land and destroy some other unit. Usually, when a projectile hits, we want to notify the entity that shot that projectile so it can gain experience, or get upgrades, or simply keep stats of hit ratios and accuracy. If the projectiles had a pointer to the turret that generated them, the game is about to crash as they try to access an invalid pointer since the turret doesn't exist anymore. Clearly, we need a better approach.

Most games use a system of unique IDs (often referred to as UIDs) or handles. This means that entities refer to each other not through pointers, but through some value that uniquely represents each entity in the world. When necessary, the game itself takes care of translating between handles and pointers. The advantage of this approach is that if somebody tries to communicate with an entity after it has been destroyed, the game will detect that the handle is no longer valid and ignore the message or even indicate that the entity is no longer around.

Many schemes allow us to map handles to game entities. The only requirement is that each handle maps uniquely to a game entity, and that the translation is as efficient as possible because it could be done hundreds or even thousands of times per frame. The most straightforward approach is to create a hash table in which the handles are the keys, and the buckets contain pointers to game entities.

As for generating unique handles, usually a globally increasing 32-bit integer will do the job nicely. Every time a new entity is created, the entity is given the next larger number. This approach will work fine for most games. However, if your game is expected to come close to generating 2^{32} entities in one run (as a persistent online world might do), then you need to use more bits, or come up with a way to reuse old, unused IDs.

Communication

We have created a bunch of entities to populate the level, we update them every frame, and they do their own thing. Even though it might be fun to wander aimlessly through the world for a bit, in order to have a full game we need some way to interact with those entities (and have them interact with each other). Communication between entities allows that interaction.

Communication between entities can be very straightforward through the use of function calls, or can be slightly more complicated by using a full messaging system.

In the simplest case, when an entity needs to communicate with another entity, it gets the pointer to the entity it wants to talk to (through the handle to pointer translation we discussed in the previous section), and calls a function directly on the receiving entity. This approach is simple and straightforward, but it has several drawbacks.

The first problem is that it might require that the sending entity know a fair amount of things about the receiving entity in order to know what functions to call. For example, if entity A attempts to pick up entity B, it first needs to find out if B can be picked up, and then it needs to know what sequence of functions to call in B to make sure its status is updated to reflect that it has been picked up. Much of this type of code leads to entities finding out what specific type of entity other entities are, casting them to their real type, and doing conditional operations on them based on their type (usually with a long switch statement). This leads to brittle code that is hard to maintain, with lots of potential for bugs with entity interactions.

The second problem is that if we call a function on an entity directly, the entity will deal with it right away. This is fine sometimes, but other times we want to make sure we update entities in a certain order, or that we update them all in lockstep (i.e., we first run the simulation in all of them, and only when they're all finished do we want them to deal with any messages they received this frame). To do that, we need to buffer the communication between them.

A common approach in many games is to use a messaging system. Entities, instead of calling functions directly, send messages to each other. An entity then creates a message, fills it with the information it wants to pass to another entity, and sends it to the messaging delivery system. The message is queued there until we want to deliver it, and only then do we pass it to the receiving entity (assuming it's still around).

This approach solves the problem of being able to buffer messages (since they can stay in the queue as long as we want), and minimizes the coupling between entities. Now an entity can send a message to another entity without knowing anything about it. If the other entity doesn't know how to handle that message, nothing happens. For example, entity A can go around sending "pick-up" messages to entities it encounters without knowing what they are. An enemy unit will ignore a pick-up message, but a weapon entity will react correctly and initiate a pick-up sequence.

The messages themselves can be implemented in a variety of ways. If you're planning on only having about half a dozen different messages, you might want to consider coming up with a single struct that can hold all the data you need, along with a type ID that indicates what type of message this is. As long as you manage to keep your message size small (since it's going to have to be filled, passed around, and read), this has the advantage of making all your messages exactly the same type and exactly the same size, which means you can easily optimize how they get created and passed around.

If you're going to have many different types of messages, and modern games can easily have hundreds of different messages to model all the different ways entities and players can interact with each other, then a different approach might be beneficial. We could create an interface Message class that can be used to send and receive any type of message, and then implement specific messages as classes (or structs) that inherit from Message and add their own set of data. This allows us to have very different messages, requiring completely different sets of data, without bloating the size of the message or having to resort to reusing the same memory space with multiple variables (through unions or by casting directly). With this approach, you don't even need to have a type ID indicating what type of message it is. Instead, you can use your system's runtime type identification (either the standard C++ one or a custom-made one) to find out the type of a particular message and handle it accordingly.

Messages are being created and destroyed constantly. For every interaction between a pair of entities, there will be at least one message created and sent. It can easily be followed by a response message, or perhaps the message itself triggers a cascade of events that create more messages. In any case, we should be ready for potentially hundreds or even thousands of messages per frame.

What does all this mean to us? We should be very careful about how we pass these messages. The messages themselves usually aren't very large, but they aren't a plain 32-bit number either. We should avoid copying them as much as possible, and instead prefer to create them once and then pass pointers (or references) to them during their lifetime.

We also need to be careful about how we allocate these messages, especially in game consoles. If we simply did a new/delete every time we wanted to create or destroy a message, performance would be suboptimal (new is hardly a fast operation that you want to do thousands of time per frame), and it can potentially fragment memory in no time. To solve this, we should take care to allocate messages from a set of memory pools, which avoids fragmentation and makes allocation faster. By overriding operators new and delete, we make it so the fact that we're using memory pools is totally transparent to the rest of the program, which keeps the code cleaner and allows us to change how we implement it. However, if we take the approach of using several different message classes, message objects are going to be of all different sizes, which makes using a memory pool a bit less straightforward. See Chapter 3.7 for more details on memory pools.

One word of caution: just because we're passing messages between entities, it doesn't mean that we can pass those messages across the network and implement an online game that way. Usually, we only want to pass a subset of those messages across the network, and they often need to contain different data (using timestamps, special network IDs, etc.) and be treated in different ways (they might need to be compressed, or their results might need to be interpolated or ignored). For these reasons, it is usually better to have a completely different set of messages for network communication.

Summary

As projects grow in size and complexity, carefully considering the architecture of a game code base is becoming increasingly important, especially if you plan to reuse some of the code in future projects.

At the highest level, games are usually a set of initialization/shutdown steps and one or more game loops. Each initialization step takes care of setting up any resources or systems needed by the game, and the corresponding shutdown step cleans up anything done by the initialization step. The game loop is executed once per frame, and it does all the tasks that have to be done each frame to make the game respond to the player: input gathering, simulation, collision, rendering, and so forth.

Every game has some form of game entity. These are self-contained units of gameplay logic. They can be enemy units, animated scenery, the player avatar, or even just a trigger. Creating, managing, and updating these entities efficiently is very important for the smooth functioning of the game.

Exercises

1. Why exactly does the shutdown phase need to mirror the order in which items were initialized? Write a program with an initialization and a shutdown phase that demonstrates why using a different shutdown order can cause problems.

2. Most game engines will have a memory manager that, among many other things, will report memory leaks. However, many C++ libraries provide special functions to display memory leaks. Learn what functions are available in your platform and write a quick program with memory leaks to demonstrate all the information you can gather about them. Are you able to display the number of memory leaks? Their address? What part of the code allocated them? Their content?

3. Implement a simple main game loop that calls each of the tasks described in this chapter. Each task function simply prints out its name to the screen and returns. Now, modify the game loop to decouple simulation and rendering. Run it again and compare the outputs.

4. Reimplement the game loop from the previous exercise by using tasks that are registered in a generic game loop. Set up two sets of tasks: one set for the front end, and one set for the main game loop. Add the ability to toggle between the two sets of tasks by pressing a key.

5. Choose a game you have played recently. Create a list with all the possible game entities you see and interact with in the first few minutes of play. Remember to look out for entities without physical representations such as triggers or timers.

References

[Alexandrescu01] Alexandrescu, Andrei, *Modern C++ Design*, Addison-Wesley, 2001.

[Bilas02] Bilas, Scott, "A Data-Driven Game Object System," *Game Developers Conference 2002,* available online at *www.drizzle.com/~scottb/gdc/game-objects.htm.*

[Duran03] Duran, Alex, "Building Object Systems: Features, Tradeoffs, and Pitfalls," *Game Developers Conference 2003*, available online at *www.gdconf.com/archives/2003/Duran_Alex.ppt.*

[Lakos96] Lakos, John, *Large-Scale C++ Software Design*, Addison-Wesley, 1996.

[Laramée01] Laramée, François, "A Game Entity Factory," *Game Programming Gems 2*, Charles River Media, 2001.

[Llopis04] Llopis, Noel, "The Clock: Keeping Your Fingers on the Pulse of the Game," *Game Programming Gems 4*, Charles River Media, 2004.

[Rabin00] Rabin, Steve, "The Magic of Data-Driven Design," *Game Programming Gems*, Charles River Media, 2000.

[Ranck00] Ranck, Steven, "Frame-Based Memory Allocation," *Game Programming Gems*, Charles River Media, 2000.

[Rollings03] Rollings, Andrew, and Morris, Dave, *Game Architecture and Design: A New Edition*, New Riders, 2003.

[Sutter00] Sutter, Herb, *Exceptional C++*, Addison-Wesley, 2000.

3.7 Memory and I/O Systems

In This Chapter

- Overview
- Memory Management
- File I/O
- Game Resources
- Scrialization
- Summary
- Exercises
- References

Overview

Every game needs to deal with the low-level details of the platform on which it runs. It needs to decide how memory will be used, how to load data from some type of storage, how to deal with the game resources, and so forth. Usually, that type of functionality is buried deep in the low-level systems of the game engine itself. Knowing how those systems work and the tradeoffs involved will make you a much more effective game programmer, even if you never have to implement them yourself. In this chapter, we'll look at memory management, handling file I/O, organizing game resources, and the process of saving and loading game states.

Memory Management

High-level languages such as Java or Python take care of the memory management for the programmer. In C++, it is completely up to us to manage the memory we use. Having full control over memory management gives us an extremely powerful tool that, when used well, can improve a program's performance by an order of magnitude. It also allows us to take control over all available memory in game consoles to make sure our game uses every available byte, but no more than that.

On the flipside, explicit memory management is an area where errors are constantly introduced, causing bugs, crashes, and unexpected behaviors. The problems caused by errors in memory management can also be very difficult and time consuming to debug.

This section will explain how we can best use memory management in C++ while still remaining as safe as possible and minimizing the number of problems. Later in the section, we will see these ideas in action as we develop a custom memory manager.

Working with Memory

We have three main objectives when managing our own memory: safety, knowledge, and control.

Safety

Safety should always be the number-one priority when dealing with memory. It is too easy to make mistakes and cause the entire program to crash in ways impossible to reproduce or debug, or to slow down over time and fail after hours of play.

We always want to keep an eye out for *memory leaks* and fix them right away. A memory leak is an allocation of memory that is "forgotten" by the program and never used again. One small memory leak by itself is no big deal. The problem is that when some part of our program starts creating memory leaks, it means there is a logic error, and chances are it is going to happen again, and again, and again. Before you know it, a good chunk of your overall memory will be used up by leaked memory and you won't have room for your game. In a console, you will simply run out of memory and crash (although it could be after many hours of playing, depending on the severity of the leak); on a PC with virtual memory, performance will slowly get worse as memory starts being swapped to the hard drive more and more frequently. Keeping on top of memory leaks and fixing them as soon as they occur should be a top priority.

The other safety issue is dealing with corrupt memory. This situation happens when some part of the program starts overwriting memory locations that it's not supposed to. This can be one of the hardest problems to debug since the cause (program overwriting memory) and the effect (crash or strange behaviors) can be very far removed from each other. Immediately detecting when a program starts corrupting memory will save many hours down the line.

Knowledge

If we're going to take it upon ourselves to manage memory (not like we have much choice in C++), we'd better have a good idea where that memory is, what parts of the program are using it, exactly how it is being used, and how much memory is left at all times. This knowledge will allow us to decide what to trim when it comes time to squeeze in all the content for the game, as well as to tune our memory allocation strategies.

Knowing how much memory we have allocated, and possibly how much memory we have left, is also crucial in case we want to do some emergency feedback to avoid using too much memory. For example, if particles cause memory allocations, we could throttle back the particle effect systems if we know we're running dangerously low on memory.

Control

Finally, we want control over memory allocations. That control can give us a big performance boost.

One aspect of control is to determine where something is allocated. If we have full control, we can choose to allocate closely related objects together in memory. That will give us much better cache efficiency because both objects might be in the data cache at the same time. This is the perfect strategy to apply to long lists of objects that will be traversed sequentially by the program, and it can net us a very significant performance boost.

The other aspect of control comes from how memory is allocated. For some specific types of objects, we might want to allocate memory in a much faster but also more limited way. This is particularly true for small objects of the same size that are allocated during runtime. In that case, the performance gained over those fast allocations can also add up to a very noticeable improvement.

Memory Fragmentation

Memory fragmentation is an insidious problem that rears its ugly head on most platforms with a limited amount of memory. This is one thing that PC developers don't usually have to worry about, but it is an issue in most other game platforms.

Let's look at what happens in memory as a game starts allocating dynamic memory. At first, before any allocation takes place, all memory is one big block of contiguous free memory. No matter what allocation size we request (as long as it is under the memory total), it will be almost trivial to allocate. As more memory is allocated and freed, things start looking a bit uglier. Blocks of memory of wildly different sizes are allocated and freed in almost random order. After a while, the large, contiguous memory block has been shredded to pieces, and while there might be a large percentage of free memory, it is all scattered in small pieces.

Eventually, we might request an allocation for a single block of memory, and the allocation will fail, not because there isn't enough free memory, but because there is no single block large enough to hold it. Because of the random nature of memory fragmentation, there is no easy way to predict when this will happen, so it could cause one of those really hard to track down bugs that are almost impossible to reproduce when you need to.

A *virtual addressing* system will greatly help reduce this problem. Virtual addressing is an extra level of indirection offered by the operating system or the memory allocation libraries, usually relying on hardware features to make its performance cost almost free. Physical memory is divided into equally sized blocks (4 KB, for example), and each block is given a different virtual address, which is what the program sees. Any time we try to use a virtual address, it is translated into a real physical address by looking it up in a table. All that is done transparently to the user of the memory allocation functions. The key point is that, under such a scheme, two separate memory blocks, in completely different parts of the physical memory, could be made to map to two contiguous blocks in the virtual address (see Figure 3.7.1). All of a sudden, one of the major problems with memory fragmentation has almost disappeared, since we can always piece together a larger memory block from several scattered ones.

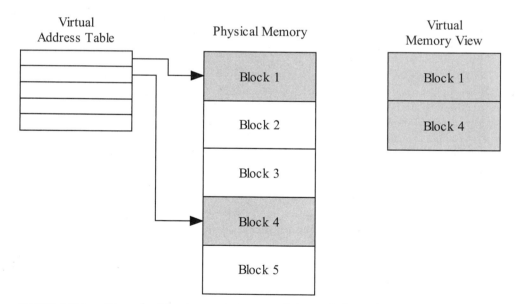

FIGURE 3.7.1   *Virtual addressing mapping two disjointed physical memory blocks into one consecutive virtual address block.*

Both the PC and the Xbox have virtual addressing as part of their standard OS and libraries. In the PC, it is taken a step further, and, when memory is tight, some of the least recently used memory blocks are saved to the hard drive to make room for new allocations. This is called a "virtual memory system." Needless to say, that is usually not an acceptable situation for games, because it causes major slowdowns in the game while memory is being read from or written to the hard drive.

The rest of the major gaming platforms don't have virtual addressing to rely on, so they need to deal with the issue of memory fragmentation explicitly.

Static Allocation

One of the oldest solutions to all memory allocation problems is to avoid it altogether. A program could be designed so it never uses new and delete (or malloc and free), and relies exclusively on statically allocated objects or objects created on the stack.

Here are some examples of static allocation:

```
// Create a fixed number of AI path nodes
#define MAX_PATHNODES      4096
AIPathNode  s_PathNodes[MAX_PATHNODES];
// Create a fixed-size buffer for geometry
// 8 MB
#define GEOMSIZE       (8*1024*1024)
byte *  s_GeomBuffer[GEOMSIZE];
```

This approach has some definite advantages. Clearly, memory allocation performance is not an issue since it never happens during runtime. In addition, since everything is statically allocated by the compiler and nothing changes during the execution of the game, neither memory fragmentation nor the potential to run out of memory is an issue.

Another advantage of static initialization is that it is very straightforward to keep track of where memory goes and how much each type of data takes. We explicitly decide how large each array and buffer will be at compile time, and we know they will never grow, so just glancing at the source code is enough to know the memory distribution. In the previous example, it is clear we are reserving 8 MBytes for geometry, and 4096 times the size of a path node of pathfinding memory.

So far, we have addressed all the safety, knowledge, and control issues we mentioned earlier. Does that mean that static allocation is the answer we were looking for? Perhaps, but it also has its share of drawbacks.

The first major drawback of static allocation of memory is wasted memory. We are forced to decide ahead of time how much memory will be dedicated to each aspect of the game, and all that memory is allocated at once. This means that, for a game with many things happening on the screen and changing over time, we are wasting large amounts of memory. Think of all the explosions, particle effects, enemies, network messages, projectiles in the air, temporary search paths, and so forth. All those things would have to be created ahead of time, while with dynamic memory allocation only the ones that we currently need would be allocated, and we would allocate more only as we require them. It is unlikely we would ever need as much memory at once as with static allocation.

It is important to note that it is not enough to decide ahead of time how many objects of a whole hierarchy branch we want allocated. We must decide exactly how many we need of each individual class type. For example, if we have a game object hierarchy, from which other more concrete object types derive (such as enemy, player, projectile, trigger, etc.), it is not enough to say that we will have 500 game objects; instead, we need to decide exactly how many enemies, how many projectiles, and so forth. The more detailed the class hierarchy, the more difficult it becomes, and the more wasteful of memory it becomes. On the other hand, having a complex inheritance hierarchy is probably not the best of designs, so it is not such a bad thing that static allocation discourages that approach.

One apparent advantage of static allocation is that it seems to reduce the chances of dangling pointers, since the memory referred to by a pointer will never be freed. It is very possible, though, to have the contents of that memory become invalid (e.g., after a projectile explodes and its object is marked invalid), at which point the pointer will still be valid, but it will access meaningless data. That is an even more difficult bug to track down than a dangling pointer to an invalid memory location, because using the dangling pointer would most likely result in an immediate access violation exception with dynamic memory allocation, but under this scheme the program will silently continue to run with bad data and possibly crash at a later point.

Finally, another disadvantage of static allocation is that objects need to be prepared to be statically initialized, with all its consequences. When dealing with dynamic allocation of objects, it is a good practice to make sure the object is fully initialized when it is first constructed, and it is correctly shut down when it is destroyed. With static allocation, objects will be constructed ahead of time, but will not be initialized until some time later. This means we need to add extra logic to all our objects to initialize and shut down correctly multiple times without ever being freed.

In addition, we need to be extremely careful with any initialization done in the constructor. We are planning to create static arrays of those objects, and, as you may recall, static initialization is a sticky issue with C++. The long and the short of it is, you have very little control in what order things become initialized, so we cannot rely on our pathfinding data being ready when the enemy objects are initialized, or the effects system being ready when the special effects objects are created. In fact, in a situation like this, it is probably best to leave all initialization until later, and not do anything at all in the constructor, other than set default values and mark the object as uninitialized.

Dynamic Allocation

When static allocation is not enough, we need to turn to the flexibility offered by dynamic allocation. We want to find a solution that is safe, and gives us enough knowledge of how memory is allocated and the control necessary to optimize allocations when we decide it's necessary.

Dynamic memory allocation can be a messy business. Allocations happen at seemingly random times, for random amounts of memory. Our first goal is to gather enough information about the memory allocations of our program to understand how we're spending our memory and what we can do to improve it.

Before we can come up with a solution, we need to understand what happens as a result of a memory allocation request.

1. Everything starts with an innocent-looking object creation in the code:

   ```
   SpecialEffect * pEffect = new SpecialEffect();
   ```

2. The compiler, internally, substitutes that call with two separate calls: one to allocate the correct amount of memory, and one to call the constructor of the SpecialEffect class:

   ```
   SpecialEffect * pEffect = __new (sizeof(SpecialEffect));
   pEffect->SpecialEffect();
   ```

3. The global operator new must then allocate the amount of requested memory. In most of the standard implementations, the global operator new simply calls the malloc function:

   ```
   void * operator new ( unsigned int nSize ) {
       return malloc(nSize);
   }
   ```

The call sequence does not end there; malloc is not an atomic operation. Instead, it will call platform-specific memory-allocation functions to allocate the correct amount from the heap. Often, this can result in several more calls and expensive algorithms to search for the appropriate free block to use.

Global operator delete follows a similar sequence, but calls the destructor and free instead of the constructor and malloc. Fortunately, the amount of work needed to return memory to the heap is usually much less than the work done allocating it, so we will not look at it in detail.

Custom Memory Manager

To take full advantage of dynamic memory allocation, we need to create our own custom memory manager. When we're done with it, we will have addressed the issues of safety, knowledge, and control, and it will be ready to drop straight into a commercial game.

Global Operators New and Delete

We need to start by overriding the global operators new and delete. We won't change the allocation policy yet, so we will continue calling malloc and free. However, we will add some extra logic to allow us to keep track of what system the allocated memory belongs to.

To specify our memory allocation preferences, we will create a Heap class. For now, this Heap does not correspond to a fixed amount of memory, or even to a set of contiguous memory. It is just a way for us to logically group some memory allocations together. To start, all the Heap class needs is a name:

```
class Heap {
public:
    Heap (const char * name);
    const char * GetName() const;
private:
    char    m_name[NAMELENGTH];
};
```

Now we are ready to provide our first version of the global new and delete operators:

```
void * operator new (size_t size, Heap * pHeap);
void operator delete (void * pMem);
```

In addition to those, we will need one version of operator new that does not take a Heap parameter. That way, all the code that does not explicitly pass a heap will still work correctly. Because there is only one operator delete, it always needs to correctly free the memory allocated by any of the different operator new functions. In effect, that means that if we create any operator new, we need to override all of them and the operator delete:

```
void * operator new (size_t size) {
    return operator new (size,
        HeapFactory::GetDefaultHeap() );
}
```

Before we look at how operator new will be implemented, let's see how it will be used first. To call our special version of operator new, we need to explicitly pass a heap reference as a parameter to the new call:

```
GameEntity * pEntity = new (pGameEntityHeap) GameEntity();
```

Our implementation of operator new is going to start very simply. For now, all we want is to keep the association between the heap it was allocated from and the allocated memory itself. Notice that the delete operator only takes a parameter as a pointer, so, somehow, we need to be able to go from a pointer to its information.

For now, we will allocate a little bit more memory than was requested, enough to fit a header for each memory allocation with the information we need. For simplicity, this header will just contain a pointer to the correct heap:

```
struct AllocHeader {
    Heap * pHeap;
    int    nSize;
};
```

The functions operator new and operator delete now look something like this:

```
void * operator new (size_t size, Heap * pHeap) {
    size_t nRequestedBytes = size +
        sizeof(AllocHeader);
    char * pMem = (char *)malloc(nRequestedBytes);
    AllocHeader * pHeader = (AllocHeader *)pMem;
    pHeader->pHeap = pHeap;
    pHeader->nSize = size;
    pHeap->AddAllocation (size);

    void * pStartMemBlock = pMem +
        sizeof(AllocHeader);
    return pStartMemBlock;
}

void operator delete (void * pMem) {
    AllocHeader * pHeader =
        (AllocHeader *)((char *)pMem -
            sizeof(AllocHeader));
    pHeader->pHeap->RemoveAllocation (pHeader->nSize);
    free(pHeader);
}
```

These two functions are doing the bare minimum to get the job done. Even so, they are already quite useful. At any point in time, we can look at how much memory we have allocated in each heap, which gives us a good idea of the overall memory usage.

So far, we have been purposefully ignoring the close relatives of operator new and operator delete: operator new[] and operator delete[]. Their job is to allocate and free memory for a whole array of objects. For the moment, we can just treat them like their nonarray counterparts and call operator new and operator delete from them.

Class-Specific Operators New and Delete

Even though this system starts being useful, it is still quite cumbersome to have to explicitly pass the heap to every allocation we care about. Overriding the class-specific new and delete operators will automate this task and finally make it useful enough to use in our game and tools.

We can use the class-specific operator new to automate some of the complexities of our memory management scheme. Since we usually would like to put all objects from a certain class in a particular heap, we can have the class operator new deal with calling the global operator new with the extra parameters:

```
void * GameObject::operator new (size_t size) {
    return ::operator new(size, s_pHeap);
}
```

Now, every time an object of the class GameObject is created with new, it will automatically be added to the correct heap. That certainly starts making things easier.

What exactly do we need to add to each class to support that? An operator new, an operator delete, and a heap static member variable:

```cpp
// GameObject.h
class GameObject {
public:
    // All the normal declarations...

    static void * operator new(size_t size);
    static void operator delete(void * p,
        size_t size);

private:
    static Heap * s_pHeap;
};


// GameObject.cpp
Heap * GameObject::s_pHeap = NULL;

void * GameObject::operator new(size_t size) {
    if (s_pHeap==NULL) {
        s_pHeap = HeapFactory::CreateHeap(
            "Game object");
    }
    return ::operator new(size, s_pHeap);
}

void GameObject::operator delete(void * p,
    size_t size)
{
    ::operator delete(p);
}
```

By the third time we add those same functions to a class, we realize that there has to be an easier way instead of doing all that error-prone typing—and there is. We can easily provide the same functionality with two macros, or even with templates if you really must. Here we will show the simpler macro version. The same GameObject class would now look like this:

```cpp
// GameObject.h
class GameObject {
    // Body of the declaration
private:
    DECLARE_HEAP;
};

// GameObject.cpp
DEFINE_HEAP(GameObject, "Game objects");
```

One important observation: any derived classes from a class that has custom new and delete operators will use its parent operators unless it has its own. In our case, if a class `GameObjectTrigger` inherited from `GameObject`, it will also automatically use `GameObject`'s heap.

Now it is really simple to use, to the point that it should be worthwhile adding it to all the most important classes.

An object could also do raw memory allocation from the heap during execution. A raw memory allocation means allocating a certain amount of bytes straight from memory, not allocating new objects. If that is the case, the allocation can be redirected to point to that object class' heap to keep better tabs on memory usage:

```
char * pScratchSpace;
pScratchSpace = new (s_pLocalHeap) char[1024];
```

At this point, we have the basis for a simple, but fully functional memory management system. We can keep track of how much memory is used by each class or each major class type at any time during the game execution, as well as some other useful statistics (peak memory consumption, etc.). With a few more features, it will be ready for use in a commercial game.

Error Checking

To make the memory manager truly something that can be used in commercial software, we need to consider the possibility of error and misuse. The way the memory manager was described in the last two sections, there was no provision for any errors: we couldn't detect memory leaks, we could attempt to delete a pointer that wasn't allocated by us, and we didn't have any mechanism to trap memory corruptions.

The first thing to do is make sure the memory we are about to free was allocated through our memory manager. The way `operator new` and `delete` are implemented, it should always be the case, but there is the possibility of another library allocating the memory, or perhaps some part of the code calling `malloc` directly. In addition, this check will catch any stray pointers that are referring to other parts of memory, as well as problems with memory corruption, where allocated memory was later overwritten by something else.

To accomplish all that, we will add a unique signature to our allocation header:

```
struct AllocHeader {
    int     nSignature;
    int     nSize;
    Heap * pHeap;
};
```

Of course, there is no "unique" number we can add, or even combination of numbers. There is always the possibility that somebody will allocate memory with that exact same number, but the possibility of it occurring at exactly the place we are looking at is pretty slim. Depending on how paranoid we want to be, we can add more than one integer at the cost of higher overhead, but one will be enough for this example and for most purposes.

What should that unique number be? Anything that is not a common occurrence. For example, using the number zero is not a good idea, as it happens too much in real programs. Same thing with 0xFFFFFFFF, common assembly opcodes, or addresses to virtual memory. Just typing any random hexadecimal number will usually be good enough. One of the old favorites is 0xDEADCODE.

One common mistake when dealing with dynamically allocated memory, especially in the form of an array, is to write past the end of the allocated block. To check for this situation, we can add a guard number at the end of the allocated memory. Just another magic number will do for now. Additionally, we will also save the size of the allocated memory block to double check against it when we attempt to free the memory:

```
void * operator new (size_t size, Heap * pHeap) {
    size_t nRequestedBytes = size +
        sizeof(AllocHeader) + sizeof(int);
    char * pMem = (char *)malloc (nRequestedBytes);
    AllocHeader * pHeader = (AllocHeader *)pMem;
    pHeader->nSignature = MEMSYSTEM_SIGNATURE;
    pHeader->pHeap = pHeap;
    pHeader->nSize = size;

    void * pStartMemBlock = pMem +
        sizeof(AllocHeader);
    int * pEndMarker = (int*)(pStartMemBlock + size);
    *pEndMarker = MEMSYSTEM_ENDMARKER;

    pHeap->AddAllocation (size);

    return pStartMemBlock;
}

void operator delete ( void * pMemBlock ) {
    AllocHeader * pHeader =
        (AllocHeader *)((char *)pMemBlock -
        sizeof(AllocHeader));
    assert (pHeader->nSignature ==
        MEMSYSTEM_SIGNATURE);
    int * pEndMarker = (int*)(pMemBlock + size);
    assert (*pEndMarker == MEMSYSTEM_ENDMARKER);

    pHeader->pHeap->RemoveAllocation(pHeader->nSize);
    free (pHeader);
}
```

Finally, as another safeguard, a good strategy is to fill the memory we are about to free with a fairly distinctive bit pattern. That way, if we accidentally overwrite any part of memory, we will immediately see that it was caused by attempting to free a pointer. As an added advantage, if that pattern is also the opcode for an instruction indicating a halt of program execution, our program will automatically stop if it ever tries to run in a section that was supposed to be freed.

All these safety features are great, but they come at a price. Doing all that extra bookkeeping takes some time, especially filling freed memory with a certain bit pattern. One of the original goals of creating our custom memory-management system was to achieve better performance, so we do not seem to be heading in the right direction. Fortunately, most of what we are doing here will only be enabled for debug builds, and we can turn it off in release builds for optimal performance.

Detecting Memory Leaks

The concept of finding memory leaks is simple: at one point in time, we take a bookmark of the memory status, and then later we take another bookmark, and report all memory allocations that were present the second time but not the first time. Surprisingly, the implementation will be almost trivial.

All we have to do is keep an allocation count. Every time we have a new allocation, we increase the allocation counter and mark that allocation with its corresponding number. In this example, let's assume that we will never have more than 2^{32} allocations. If that is a problem, we need to keep 64 bits for the allocation count, or device a scheme to wrap around. In either case, it is reasonably easy to implement.

Our allocation header now looks like this:

```
struct AllocHeader {
    int             nSignature;
    int             nAllocNum;
    int             nSize;
    Heap *          pHeap;
    AllocHeader *   pNext;
    AllocHeader *   pPrev;
};
```

And operator new is just like before, except that it fills in the nAllocNum field.

Next, we create a trivial function, GetMemoryBookmark. All it does is return our current allocation number.

```
int GetMemoryBookmark () {
    return s_nNextAllocNum;
}
```

Finally, the function that will do a bit more work is ReportMemoryLeaks. It takes two memory bookmarks as parameters, and reports all memory allocations that are still active that happened between those two bookmarks. It is implemented simply by traversing all allocations in all heaps, looking for allocations that have a number between the two bookmarks. Yes, it is potentially very slow to traverse all allocations in all heaps, but this is a luxury we can permit ourselves this time since this function is used purely for debugging, and we do not really care how fast it executes.

Notice that we also added a pPrev and pNext field to the allocation header. Those pointers are going to allow us to traverse all the allocations for a certain heap. Operators new and delete will take care of correctly updating the list pointer for each allocation and each free call. Since we are maintaining a doubly linked list, the performance overhead for maintaining the list is trivial.

The memory leak reporting function is shown next in pseudocode form.

```
void ReportMemoryLeaks (int nBookmark1,
    int nBookmark2)
{
   for (each heap) {
      for (each allocation) {
         if (pAllocation->nAllocNum >= nBookmark1 &&
            pAllocation->nAllocNum < nBookmark2) {
            // Print info about pAllocation
            // Print its alloc number, heap, size...
         }
      }
   }
}
```

Memory Pools

So far, we have addressed two of the goals for a memory management system: safety and knowledge. We still haven't seen how to gain control over memory allocations to improve performance. The solution to most allocation performance problems is memory pools.

Recall that the expensive part of the default implementation of heap memory allocation was finding the block of memory to return. Especially when the memory is heavily fragmented, the search algorithm might have to look through many different blocks before it can return the appropriate one.

Conceptually, a memory pool is a certain amount of preallocated memory that will be used to allocate objects of a particular size at runtime. Whenever one of those objects is released by the program, its memory is returned to the pool, not freed back to the heap.

This approach has several advantages:

No performance hit.   As soon as somebody requests memory from the pool, we return the first free preallocated block. There are no calls to malloc and no searching.

No fragmentation.   Those memory blocks are allocated once and never released, so the heap does not get fragmented as program execution progresses.

One large allocation.   We can preallocate those blocks in any way we want. Typically, this is done as one large memory block, from which we return small subsections. This has the advantage of reducing even further the number of heap allocations, as well as providing spatial coherence for the data being returned (which might improve performance even more by improving data cache hits).

The only disadvantage is that pools will usually have some unused space (slack space). As long as the pools are reasonably sized and only used for dynamic elements, the extra space is well worth the benefits we will reap.

The first thing that the memory pool needs to know is how large the allocated objects are going to be. Since that will never change, we will pass it to the constructor. In addition, the two fundamental operations we will perform on a pool will be allocating and freeing memory. Here is the first, bare-bones version of a memory pool class declaration:

```
class MemoryPool {
public:
    MemoryPool (size_t nObjectSize);
    ~MemoryPool ();

    void * Alloc (size_t nSize);
    void   Free (void * p, size_t nSize);
};
```

We need to come up with a scheme to be able to manage many similarly sized memory blocks, return one in the `Alloc` call, and put it back to be managed when it is returned in the `Free` call.

We could preallocate all those memory blocks, and keep a list of pointers to them; get the first one in the list in the `Alloc` call, and return it back to the list in the `Free` call. Conceptually, that is very simple, and it avoids doing dynamic heap allocations at runtime, but it also has several problems. The main one is that we are increasing the memory overhead per allocation. Now an allocation requires an entry in the list of free objects. It also means that all the preallocated objects are allocated individually, not as a large memory block, so we also incur whatever overhead the operating system requires for multiple, small allocations.

There is a solution that solves all these problems, but it requires that we get our hands a bit dirty: handling memory directly, casting memory addresses to specific data, and other unsightly things. It is well worth the trouble, though, and in the end, it will require no extra overhead, and all the memory will be allocated out of large, contiguous memory blocks—exactly what we were looking for. Besides, all that complexity will be hidden under the memory pool class, so nobody using it will have to know how it is implemented to use it correctly. In fact, once we are done, if we have done our job correctly, nobody will even need to know there is a memory pool class at all.

Let us start by allocating one large memory block. Conceptually, we will think of that block as made up of contiguous, similarly sized slices of memory. Each slice will be exactly the size of the allocations we will be requesting from this pool (see Figure 3.7.2a).

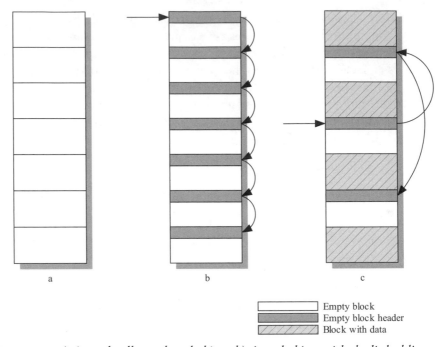

Empty block
Empty block header
Block with data

FIGURE 3.7.2   *a) A newly allocated pool object. b) A pool object with the linked list connections. c) A pool object after being used for a while.*

At the start, before any allocations are done, all memory in the block is available, so all slices can be marked as free. To do that, we will create a linked list of free slices. Since the memory block has already been allocated, but we have not given any of that memory to the program, we have a lot of unused memory lying around, so we might as well put it to good use. Instead of wasting memory with a separate list, we will double up the first two double words from each slice as the next and previous pointers for a list element, and we will link all the slices in one doubly linked list (see Figure 3.7.2b).

The rest is simple. Any time a new request comes to the pool class, we grab the first element in the free slice list, fix up the list, and return a pointer to that slice. Whenever memory is freed, we add that memory to the head of the free slice list. After a few allocations, the slices will be out of order in the list, but it does not matter. We are not causing any memory fragmentation, and we allocate and free memory blazingly quick (see Figure 3.7.2c).

What if we need more memory than the original amount we allocated? That's up to you. Perhaps you want to make sure that memory pools never grow beyond a certain size, in which case, if they ever get filled up, you can throw an assert and stop. Otherwise, if you want them to grow, you can allocate another memory block and link them together along with the rest of the free blocks.

How big should those memory blocks be? It will totally depend on the type of allocations we are performing, and on the behavior of the program that uses the memory pool. On one hand, we do not want to waste lots of space by having a really large block that will never be completely used, but on the other hand, we do not want to have lots of little memory allocations all the time.

The best course of action is to pick some default. For example, each pool will create a block that can hold 512 slices. Once we have memory pools hooked up to our memory manager, we can report how much wasted space there is, and tweak them accordingly. We might also want to make sure that the allocated blocks of memory are multiples of the size of a memory page size or some other significant size that might make our life easier and the allocations faster. In Win32, it makes sense to make each block a multiple of 4 KB and allocate that memory directly, bypassing `malloc` and all its overhead.

To make sure all objects of a particular class use the pool for their allocation, we need to create a static member variable that holds the memory pool, and then override `operator new` and `operator delete` to use the memory pool to allocate the memory they need.

```
// MyClass.h
class MyClass {
public:
    // All the normal declarations...

    static void * operator new(size_t size);
    static void operator delete(void * p,
        size_t size);

private:
    static MemoryPool * s_pPool;
};


// MyClass.cpp
MemoryPool * s_MyClass::pPool;

void * MyClass::operator new(size_t size) {
    if (s_pPool==NULL) {
        s_pPool = new MemoryPool(sizeof(MyClass));
    }
    return s_pPool->Alloc(size);
}

void MyClass::operator delete(void * p, size_t size) {
    s_pPool->Free(p, size);
}
```

We can clean this up as well and wrap it up in a couple of macros (see macro definition in source code on the companion CD-ROM). Now we can write the class as follows:

ON THE CD

```
// MyClass.h
class MyClass {
public:
    // All the normal declarations...
    MEMPOOL_DECLARE(MyClass)
};

// MyClass.cpp
MEMPOOL_IMPLEMENT(MyClass)
```

Finally, to integrate pools with the memory manager, each pool can contain a heap, and register all its allocations through the heap. Now all the allocations, pooled or not, will appear correctly in the pool display.

File I/O

Every language comes with its own standard set of library calls to open files, and to read and write data, so why do we need to worry about file I/O in game development? There are several reasons.

One of the most important reasons is that we want to load files very quickly. There are few things more frustrating than having to wait a long time for a level to load, so we need to make sure we can minimize load times, and loading files one at a time from the default file system usually doesn't cut it. In addition, if we do any type of multiplatform development, we want to be able to access and manipulate files in the same way across all different platforms.

Creating our own custom file system lets us address those issues. It also gives us the opportunity to extend the file system to access files in different media, such as a DVD drive, a memory card, or even the network, in a uniform way, further simplifying any file I/O operations in our game and tools.

Unified, Platform-Independent File System

Before we can manipulate any files, we need to find them and open them. At the very least, our platform-independent file system should let us open a file and retrieve a handle or an object to do any further operations on it. The declaration for this minimalist file system looks like this:

```
class FileSystem {
public:
    File * Open (cons std::string & filename);
};
```

However, for a full game, we probably want to add more operations. For instance, we might want to check whether a file exists before we open it (for performance reasons and to avoid cluttering the log with errors if we're just checking to see if a file exists and we have no intention of opening it).

We might also want to be able to mount and unmount parts of the file system, such as a memory card or the contents of a game pack file (which we'll cover in detail in a moment). If we're going to mount parts of the file system, we might also treat the local file system just like any other type of file and explicitly mount it. This gives us the extra flexibility of being able to have different mappings in our game and tools than the exact paths in our computers, which will come in handy during development.

It may also be useful to manipulate the concept of current path. Some file systems support this concept natively, whereas some of the minimalist ones in some game consoles don't. If you decide that you'd like to support it, you should add functions to retrieve and set the current directory, as well as internal functions to translate relative directories and incomplete path names into full paths. Otherwise, you can just make sure you deal with absolute paths, which might take some getting used to, but might save a few headaches down the line by making things easier to debug.

A more fleshed-out file system interface might look like this:

```
class FileSystem {
public:
    File * Open (const std::string & filename);
    bool DoesFileExist (const std::string &
        filename) const;

    bool Mount (const std::string & src,
        const std::string & dest);
    bool Unmount (const std::string & src);
};
```

To start implementing this file system, we need a way to map filenames to the files themselves so they can be queried and opened. We also want this operation to be very efficient because we will probably be opening thousands of files during a level load.

The other major requirement is to minimize the amount of memory used by the file system itself, so we want to avoid keeping a list of all the files' full names. This might seem like a trivial memory optimization, but filenames can quickly add up to significant amounts of memory. Imagine that our game has 10,000 files, and on the average, each of those files is about 60 characters long (because we're keeping full paths with the filenames): we'd be spending about 600 KB on the filenames alone. On a console with just 32 or 64 MB of RAM, that's a luxury we can't afford.

A hash table is the perfect data structure to meet our needs. We can achieve very efficient (constant time) access to any file in a large set, and we don't need to store the filenames themselves. Every time we ask for a filename, we run the string through the hash function, and then access the hash table itself. A CRC function does the job nicely by allowing us to map an arbitrary string into 32- or 64-bit numbers very efficiently.

Files

We'll operate on the files themselves through a `File` class. We could have chosen to use a handle system, where the `Open()` call returns a handle instead of a pointer to an object, but the resulting code is less readable and more cumbersome. Instead, we can use the nice object-oriented syntax to treat a file as an object. As an added benefit, whenever a file object is destroyed, we can automatically close the file, so there's no need to explicitly close it.

The basic operations we want to perform on a file are to read from it, write to it, and possibly seek to some other part of the file. Here is the basic interface for a `File` class:

```
class File {
public:
    File (const std::string & filename);
    int Read(byte * pData, int bytesToRead);
    int Write(byte * pData, int bytesToWrite);
    int Seek(int desiredPosition);
};
```

Internally, the read, write, and seek functions just call the native platform functions pretty much straight.

With a simple file class like that, we're ready to start reading and writing data:

```
int number;
if (pFile->Read((byte *)&number, sizeof(number)) !=
    sizeof(number))
{
    return false;
}
```

That's some pretty ugly code with all that casting and `sizeof()` calls everywhere. We can make it much easier to use and understand using the following member function templates:

```
class File {
public:
    File (const std::string & filename);
    int Read(byte * pData, int bytesToRead);
    int Write(byte * pData, int bytesToWrite);
    int Seek(int desiredPosition);

    template<typename T>
    int Read (T * pData, uint nCount = 1) {
        uint nRead = ReadRaw((byte *)pData,
            uint(nCount * sizeof(T)));
        return nRead/sizeof(T);
    }
};
```

Now we can write the same example in a much simpler way:

```
int number;
if (!pFile->Read(&number))
    return false;
```

Buffering

One of the goals we had for creating our own file system was to achieve great performance. Buffering is a key element toward achieving that goal.

Consider the following innocent-looking code that simply tries to read a sequence of numbers from a file:

```
int attribute[NUM_ATTRIBUTES];
for (int i=0; i<NUM_ATTRIBUTES; ++i)
    if (!pFile->Read(&attribute[i]))
        return false;
```

We're just reading a series of numbers sequentially in the same file. Ideally, the preceding code should execute very quickly, only requiring one or two actual reads from the physical disk that buffers all the results. In the worst case, a system with no buffering will hit the disk for every value read, bringing the loading code to its knees.

A similar situation happens if we want to read from many different parts of the file. Our code would seek to different locations and read some data, but that could cause horrible performance. In this situation, we might want to buffer the entire file into memory before we start reading from different parts of it. Having control over the buffering, the file system gives us the ability to improve our loading performance and memory consumption by tweaking it to fit what we know we're about to do.

The cleanest way to implement a buffering scheme is by using a layered approach. Once we start thinking about it, we realize that buffering and file reading/writing are totally orthogonal concepts. Buffering describes what we do with the data we just read (or we're about to write), nothing else.

If we could add a buffering layer on top of a file, and make it look like a regular file to the rest of the world, we could achieve control over the buffering while still looking like the same file interface. We can achieve exactly this effect by using polymorphism, creating an interface class DataStream, and a set of derived classes, FileSource and BufferingLayer. Figure 3.7.3 shows the class inheritance diagram that describes this arrangement.

The BufferingLayer class looks like this:

```
class BufferingLayer : public DataStream {
public:
    BufferingLayer (DataStream & sourceStream,
                    int bufferSize);
    virtual int Read(byte * pData, int bytesToRead);
    virtual int Write(byte * pData, int bytesToWrite);
    virtual int Seek(int desiredPosition);
```

```
private:
    DataStream & m_stream;
    byte * pBuffer;
};
```

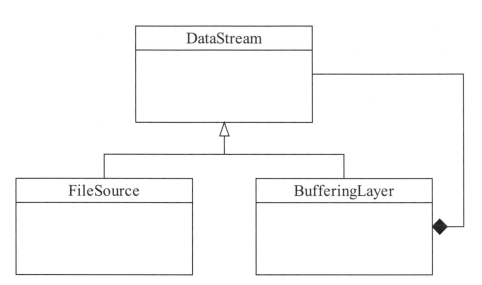

FIGURE 3.7.3   *Class inheritance diagram for some* `DataStream` *classes.*

Notice that `BufferingLayer` needs a `DataStream` passed to it in its constructor. That is where it gets all the data to buffer since the buffer itself doesn't read data from any physical device. That's the job of the `FileSource` class. We also need to specify how big a buffer we want to use. Sometimes, we don't know how big we want the buffer to be, we just want to make sure that the entire file is buffered into memory. In that case, we could pass −1 as the size of the buffer and we would interpret that to be of the correct size.

By default, for optimal performance, we should make our buffer size match some multiple of the sector size of the physical media we're reading from. That way, one buffer read corresponds exactly to one (or several) whole sector read. We also have to take some care to always start the buffer at multiples of that physical sector size to avoid straddling two physical sectors and causing two physical reads for every single one of our own reads.

We also need to change the `FileSystem Open` function to take an optional buffer size parameter. So, if we know we're going to need a buffer of at least 32 KB for a particular file, we can call it this way:

```
DataStream * pStream =
    fileSystem.Open("myfile.txt", 32);
```

And if we wanted to fully buffer the file's contents into memory, we could call it this way:

```
DataStream * pStream =
    fileSystem.Open("myfile.txt", FULL_BUFFER);
```

Pack Files

So far, this custom file system looks like a fairly generic reimplementation of the file systems in most platforms. It's nice to have the added flexibility over the buffering aspect, but we can sometimes achieve the same effect by using platform-specific file I/O functions. However, pack files are what makes this file system unique and extremely useful to game development.

If you were to develop a game without worrying about the file system, you would probably notice excruciatingly slow loading times, especially if you were loading directly from a CD-ROM or a DVD like many of the game consoles. We would then take our profiler to try to find out what was causing the poor performance, and after some investigation we would see that most of our time was spent seeking to different places on the disc. "Seeking? But we took care to not do any seeking during the loading of each file," you might say. This seeking comes not from moving around during a single file load, but from loading files that are located in different physical locations on the disc.

Usually, when we use the default file system, we have no control over where files are physically located. Most applications don't need to know that, so that would be a useless complication. Unfortunately, games do need to know, and this is where pack files come in.

Another large performance hit would probably show up in the form of file open and close operations. File systems in most platforms have a fairly large overhead for opening and closing files. If we're planning on 1,000 files during a level load, even an extra 10 ms per file adds up to 10 more seconds.

A pack file is simply a large file that contains other files. It probably contains some header information with a list of all the files contained inside and where they are located (their offset from the origin of the file), plus a large chunk of data with the contents of every file. Because we created this file ourselves, we have full control over where different files are located, so we can minimize seek times. In addition, because it is a single, large file, we also completely remove the overhead associated with opening and closing files as long as we keep reading from this pack file.

The actual format of the pack file doesn't really matter. We can adopt an existing format and get the benefit of existing tools to create and view their contents. Some of the popular pack file formats are cab files, or even zip files (with or without compression). If for some reason an existing format doesn't meet our needs, we can always roll our own very easily, but keep in mind that it will also require writing several support tools.

Before we can use a pack file, we need to mount it on our file system, so the FileSystem needs to be extended to handle pack files. Whenever a pack file is mounted, we can hand it over to the PackFileSystem object, which takes care of parsing its contents and adding all the entries to the file system map.

What happens when we try to open a file that is contained in a pack file? Clearly, we can't use the standard file open and close calls we used for files in the local file system. Instead, we pass the request to the PackFileSystem, and it creates a DataStream that starts at the correct offset into the large pack file. We also have to take care that the length of this new DataStream matches the file we are opening and not the length of the pack file itself. The cleanest way to implement this is to add a new layer to use a smaller range from an existing stream.

```
class RangeLayer : public DataStream {
public:
    RangeLayer (DataStream & sourceStream, int offset,
                int length);
    virtual int Read(byte * pData, int bytesToRead);
    virtual int Write(byte * pData, int bytesToWrite);
    virtual int Seek(int desiredPosition);

private:
    DataStream & m_stream;
    int m_offset;
    int m_length;
};
```

The pack file system can return the new data stream this way, and the rest of the code will just see a normal DataStream with the correct data and length.

```
return new RangeLayer(packFileStream,
    file.Offset, file.Length);
```

Now that we have a working pack file, load times should already be faster because we only make one native open call to open the pack file itself, and all other open operations on the contents of the pack file are very fast. At this point, we can also try to rearrange the contents of the pack file so that files that are read consecutively are positioned next to each other. This will further reduce load times by avoiding seeks as much as possible.

Other possible optimizations we can do are to align files on some particular boundary (such as 4 KB), which wastes a bit of space, but might give us even faster load times by aligning the files with sectors on the physical medium where the pack file is stored. Some other media have strict requirements on read operation alignments, especially for asynchronous, low-level read calls, so we can change the alignment of our files to match those requirements very easily.

Extensions and Advanced Uses

With a custom file system like this in place, you can add any features that you need for the game or even during development.

You will probably want to offer a file-like interface to a section of memory instead of a physical file on disk. All you need to do is implement a new `DataStream` class that reads to and writes from a section of RAM. You can even make it so the area of RAM can grow as you write to it, just as a real file would. The ability to read from RAM as if it were a file will come in very handy if we attempt to do any asynchronous loading, in which we first load the contents of a file asynchronously into memory, and then we create the appropriate objects from the contents of that file.

Another extension that can be very useful, especially during development, is a `DataStream` that accesses files over the network. It lets you operate on any file over the network just as if it were local, and it makes it really convenient to work with the latest game resources stored on a network drive, or, in the case of a game console, to get files directly off a PC to make iteration time even faster for artists and designers.

Compression can be an extremely useful feature to add to our file system. Especially in hardware with slow data access (CD or DVD drives) and relatively fast CPUs, a reasonable compression algorithm could cut the data size in half while having little impact on the CPU, which could translate into almost halving load times. We could easily add compression by implementing a new `DataStream` layer that would sit between the file layer and the game. As in the case of the buffering layer, it would be totally transparent, but it would take care of doing all the decompression. If we also want to save out compressed data (e.g., to fit in a small memory card), we can also implement the write operations in this layer and make it work both ways. If we use a standard compression algorithm, we get a lot of source code that we can use when implementing that layer, and also get tools to compress and uncompress files. Some popular compression algorithms are gzip (zlib library) and bzip2. Both of them are very effective, lightweight algorithms, and they're free, so you can use them in any commercial game.

It is important that all file I/O calls be handled by our custom file system. If parts of our program use the regular OS file I/O calls, and the other half uses the custom file system, we're headed for disaster. We can easily control what we do in our code, but we have to be particularly careful about middleware and third-party libraries. Any decent middleware should have file I/O hooks, so we can point them to our custom functions to ensure all operations are done through the same file system. Otherwise, the middleware library wouldn't be able to take advantage of all the great features we implemented, such as pack files or custom buffering.

Game Resources

A game resource, also called a "game asset," is anything that gets loaded from a disc and could be shared by several parts of the game: a texture, an animation, a sound, and so forth. Game resources are created by artists and designers; they are usually quite big and take up a large percentage of all available memory in modern games. This section explains how to organize resources effectively in the game engine.

Working with Game Resources

Let's imagine for a moment that we don't have any particular system in place to deal with game resources. Do we really need one? What happens if we don't?

We're in the middle of loading a game level. From the level description file, we are told we need to create an orc and place it in the corner of the dungeon. That should be easy. We look up the definition of an orc and we load its mesh, textures, animations, and sounds from a disk. So far, so good. As we keep loading the level, we encounter that there's another orc that needs to be placed nearby. This orc is exactly like the previous one: same textures, same animations, same everything. Unfortunately, our dumb loading code doesn't know how to take advantage of that, and simply hits the disk again and loads and creates all those resources. Imagine that there are not just two orcs, but dozens. It will take forever to load the level, and it's a monumental waste of memory, which is one of the most precious resources game developers have.

As if that were not enough, imagine that we go ahead and load the level anyway. The player starts going through the dungeon and kills some orcs. At some point, the game logic decides that it wants to spawn a few more orcs. How can we do that? All the information we have are the filenames of the different resources of the orc, so we go to the disk again and load those resources. However, this time the load happened during gameplay, causing the game to freeze for a short period of time, or maybe stutter badly over several frames.

Clearly, this is not an acceptable situation. We definitely need a system to deal with game resources more effectively.

Resource Manager

We could try being a bit smarter about how we load resources. For example, the code that loads textures could try to remember each texture that was loaded. If we try to load the same texture again, we just return a reference to the one we have in memory. The game code will get the resource it needs, and we don't even have to hit the disk.

It seems perfect, except that then we realize we need to write the same code for animations (and for meshes, and sounds, and movies, and level geometry, etc.). We're likely to have dozens of different types of resources, so writing the same code everywhere doesn't seem like an appealing idea.

The solution was a good one; we just need a way to generalize it into something that can be used with any type of resource. The first thing that we need is to create the concept of a generic game resource. That's the perfect use for an interface class. Any specific resources that we need to deal with will inherit from this interface class. Additionally, there are probably a few operations we want to do on any type of resource, so we can add them to the interface class.

```
class IResource {
public:
    virtual ~IResource() {};
    virtual const std::string & GetName() const = 0;
    virtual ResourceType GetType() const = 0;
};
```

Now we can finally create a resource manager, which will be in charge of loading resources, remembering all resources currently loaded, and returning references to them whenever anybody asks. A first pass at the resource manager looks like this:

```
class ResourceManager {
public:
    Texture * CreateTexture(const std::string &
        filename);
    Animation * CreateAnimation(const std::string &
        filename);
    Mesh * CreateMesh(const std::string & filename);
    //...

private:
    IResource * CreateResource(const std::string &
        filename);
    typedef std::map<std::string, IResource *>
        ResourceMap;
    ResourceMap m_resources;
}
```

Each of the creation functions simply calls CreateResource() and does some simple error checking. The heart of the resource manager is in the CreateResource() function. It first looks to see if the resource is in the map, and if so it returns it right away. Otherwise, it creates it, and adds it to the map. That's all there is to it.

```
IResource * ResourceManager::CreateResource(
    const std::string & filename)
{
    ResourceMap::iterator it =
        m_resources.find(filename);

    if (it != m_resources.end())
        return (*it).second;

    IResource * pResource = LoadResource(filename);
    if (pResource == NULL)
        return NULL;

    m_resources[filename] = pResource;
    return pResource;
}
```

The resource manager will work fine as implemented so far, but there's a certain ugliness about it. Having to create a function for every resource type is rather cumbersome. It also means that if the game needs to load custom resource types, it needs to modify the resource manager itself, which is part of the low-level systems of the game engine.

A much better approach is to use a registering system, just like the registering object factories we saw in Chapter 3.6. For any resource type we want our resource manager to support, we need to create a class that derives from the interface IResourceMaker, and register it with the resource manager. The manager then keeps the association between file extensions (or header bytes or however you prefer to identify your resources) and resource makers. Whenever the game tries to load a resource of one of those types, if it hasn't already been loaded, it lets the ResourceMaker itself load it and return a pointer to it. Otherwise, we return the pointer to the one that was already loaded in memory. See the low_level_memory_mgr files on the companion CD-ROM for a full implementation of a registering resource manager.

ON THE CD

Resource Lifetime

So far, we've been completely glossing over the issue of what happens when resources are destroyed. Is the resource manager notified so it can remove the resource from its list? What happens if we then try to create the same resource again? Before we answer those questions, we really should think about how we want to deal with resources in our situation.

All at Once

For many games, we simply want to load all the resources for a level at the beginning of that level, and keep them around until we exit the level. We don't want to destroy or create any resources while the level is being played. The simplest way to handle that is to destroy all resources and wipe the resource manager clean at the end of every level. Then we load any new resources needed for the front end or the next level.

This approach has the advantage of being very simple: there is no dynamic creation of resources, and we never need to worry about a resource not being there when we need it or having to keep track of how many places are using a particular resource at the moment.

It is also very limiting because it doesn't allow us to implement any type of on-demand loading to bring in high-resolution models or textures when needed during gameplay. It also makes it difficult to update individual resources during development, which would really improve iteration time for artists and designers. Finally, throwing away all resources at the end of each level might be a bit too much. There might be resources that we want to reuse from level to level, or maybe some front-end resources that we simply never want to unload. It also requires that all parts of the code that held pointers to resources be aware that those resources are gone. This approach seemed very appealing due to its simplicity, but now it's starting to appear too limiting.

Explicit Lifetime Management

We could take it upon ourselves to manage the lifetime of each resource manually. Whenever we don't want a resource anymore, we make an explicit call to delete it.

This solves some of the drawbacks of the previous approach in that we can easily swap resources and load new ones "on the fly."

However, we have to be extremely careful with how we destroy existing resources. The whole point of resources is that they can be shared. If we're destroying an orc and we decide to destroy all its textures and animations, what happens if there is another orc out there that is using the same resources? We could try to keep track of everybody that holds a pointer to resources and notify them when a resource is destroyed, but that could take a lot of memory and it wouldn't solve the problem of what other parts of the code will do when a resource is destroyed out from under them.

Reference Counting

Reference counting attempts to address the problem of shared ownership of resources. Each resource keeps track of how many parts of the code are holding a reference to it. As long as that reference is greater than zero, the resource is needed somewhere. Whenever it reaches zero, it means that nobody is using it and it can be safely deleted if we want to.

Reference counting can be done explicitly. That is, every time something holds a new reference to a resource, it has to call the AddRef() function, which simply increments the current reference count. Whenever something doesn't need a resource anymore, it calls the Release() function, which decrements the reference count. This approach works reasonably well for dealing with shared resources, but having to call AddRef() and Release() manually is usually too error prone, and it's common for resources to get mismatched calls, which throws off reference counting completely.

A safer approach is to use smart pointers. These smart pointers can be used almost like a regular pointer by the rest of the code, but they take care internally of calling AddRef() and Release() on the resource as they are created or deleted. When dealing with smart pointers, we have many choices: intrusive or nonintrusive reference counting, deletion policy, copy on write, and so forth. Refer to the references at the end of the chapter for a detailed discussion of smart pointers applied to game resources as well as several off-the-shelf implementations.

Reference counting is very convenient. It deals neatly with the sharing problem, the previous objections about swapping resources in and out, and updating single resources during development. However, sometimes we need to be careful how we use reference counting inside a game. We want to make sure that if we kill the last of the orcs, the resources needed by the orc aren't released, because we might create a few more orcs just in the next dungeon room. In situations like these, we might want to have the game itself hold an extra reference to each resource needed in the level, and release them when the level is over to prevent any resources from being freed ahead of time.

Resources and Instances

When dealing with resources, it's important to make a clear distinction between resources and instances. *Resources* are all the data that could be shared among different parts of the game. An *instance* is any data associated with the resource that is unique for each occurrence of the resource in the game. Keeping the two concepts clearly separated will help us use resources correctly.

Sometimes, the distinction between resources and instances is very clear. For example, a skeletal mesh is a resource, but its position and orientation are part of the instance. We usually don't even think about this because position and orientation are often associated with a higher level concept of the entity rather than with the resource itself.

Other times, the distinction between resources and instances is not as clear-cut. Consider a texture with multiple frames (depicting the flame of a torch, for example). The resource contains the number of frames and the data in each of the frames themselves. However, the speed at which these frames animate and the current frame is probably part of the instance data. Otherwise, all meshes in the world that use this texture would cycle through the frames at the same time.

Similar situations happen with parameters that are initially part of the resource, but that we end up wanting to modify during gameplay. For example, consider the transparency value of a material applied to a force field. Unless we move it to the instance part, whenever we change it to make it more or less opaque, all the force fields in the game will change at the same time.

If you find that most of your resources have some data that has to change per instance, you might want to consider dividing resources into two parts: an instance and the resource itself. The instance would be a very lightweight object, with just the values necessary to describe the instance, and a pointer to the expensive resource. Every time we use the resource in the game, we create a new resource instance with the default instance values.

Resource Precaching

We've been assuming that to load all resources necessary for a particular game level, all we have to do is go through the file that describes the level and load all the resources for all the entities that appear in that level. It turns out this is not enough. We also need to deal with the resources of the objects that will be spawned during gameplay, but are not necessarily part of the original layout of the level. This is called "precaching."

Precaching involves loading resources for objects that we don't need right away, but we know we will need later. For example, an explosion needs a set of sounds and textures, but we certainly don't want to wait until an explosion happens for the first time to actually load those resources, or we risk having our game pause for several frames while we access the disk, totally disrupting the player's experience.

How do we know what resources we'll need in the future? We certainly don't want to hardwire any resource names in the code itself. Otherwise, every time we need a new resource, designers or artists would have to come to the programmers to ask them to add or change a resource.

An important observation is that any resources that will be needed in the middle of the game are going to be requested by entities that are already in the level. For example, a barrel containing flammable gases knows that if it explodes, it will need to play certain explosions. A spawn point knows that it might need to create new orcs if triggered. Or a player avatar knows about all possible weapons it can cycle through. The cleanest way of dealing with precaching, then, is to simply allow every entity a chance to precache anything it will need to use later. The entity doesn't need to hold on to the resource, it simply needs to tell the system to keep it around in case we use it later. The game can keep a list of all the precached resources for the level, which, if we use reference counting, will also keep the reference count positive, so we know they won't be destroyed before the end of the level.

During gameplay, we can create new resources as we would do with any other resource, through the resource manager itself. In this case, however, resources will already be loaded in memory so we won't hit the disk and disrupt the game. We might want to take the extra precaution of disabling disk access, during the level itself. At the least, we can print an obvious warning or error if any entity in the game attempts to create a resource that hasn't already been precached; that way, we'll get a notification right away and we'll know to fix it by adding it to the precache list.

Serialization

Just about every game needs to deal with saving and loading game states. Even if your game only supports checkpoint saving, you probably still need to implement a full save feature to export the initial state of the level from the level editor, or at least a simplified version of a game state for each checkpoint save and load.

Saving

When it comes time to save game entities, it is best if each entity decides for itself how to best save itself to the stream. To this end, we will make a pass through all the entities we are interested in saving, and give them the chance to serialize themselves.

ISerializable *Interface*

We can call the Write function for each entity we want to serialize. We could just make that function part of the base GameEntity class and everything would work fine. Entities that did not want to be serialized could just leave it blank, and everybody else would implement the function depending on their contents.

A better approach is to make the serialization-related functions part of an abstract interface, ISerializable. Then, the GameEntity base class can inherit from it and everything would work the same way. However, splitting those functions into a separate interface allows us to easily serialize other types of objects that are not necessarily game entities. The ISerializable interface is very simple:

```
class ISerializable
{
public:
    virtual ~ISerializable() {};
    virtual bool Write(IStream & stream) const = 0;
    virtual bool Read(IStream & stream) = 0;
};
```

As you can see from the Read function, we'll also use the ISerializable interface during the load process.

Implementing Write

Implementing the Write function for each entity is a straightforward task. We need to decide what exact data we want to save. Then, for each member variable that we want to save, we serialize it to the stream.

For integers, floats, and other standard data types, we just stream them directly. However, what if our entity contains a member variable of its own that we need to serialize? Easy. We have to ensure that the variable also implements the ISerializable interface, and we just call its Write function, which in turn will be implemented in the same way. That way, we can save any amount of nested objects without any difficulty.

If the entity contains pointers or references to other objects instead of the object itself, we need to deal with them in a different way. We will see how in the next section.

If our entity classes use inheritance, we might want to let the parent classes deal with the serialization for their own data. Derived classes only have to worry about the new variables they add.

Here is some potential code for the Write function of a camera class:

```
bool GameCamera::Write(IStream & stream) const
{
    // Let the parent class write common things like
    // position, rotation, etc.
    bool bSuccess = GameEntity::Write(stream);

    // These are basic data types, serialize
    // them directly
    bSuccess &= WriteFloat(stream, m_FOV);
    bSuccess &= WriteFloat(stream, m_NearPlane);
    bSuccess &= WriteFloat(stream, m_FarPlane);

    // This is an object that needs to be
    // serialized in turn
    bSuccess &= m_lens.Write(stream);

    return bSuccess;
}
```

What we have implemented so far is a pure binary format—no headers, no extra information, just the raw data. It might be a fine format for whenever we need to load entities as fast as possible, as in the released game, but it is not a very friendly format with which to develop the game. As soon as a minor change is made to an entity class, all the previously saved games become unusable. Worse, there is no way to detect when something is wrong and we will most likely read garbage data.

For this reason, it is a good idea to implement at least two types of formats: a fast, binary format like the one we saw previously, and a slower, text-based one that is easier to debug, and will still work when the format changes.

Unique Identifiers

We still have not solved one of the major problems: what to do about saving pointers. It turns out we have several choices.

The first possibility is to completely avoid pointers, or at least pointers to other game entities. Instead of a pointer, we could refer to any other game entities through unique IDs (or UIDs). If every game entity has a UID that is guaranteed never to be repeated, then we can just keep that number. Any time we need to work directly with the entity, we ask the game entity system to give us a pointer to the entity corresponding to that number. As we saw in Chapter 3.6 about game entities, this is a reasonable approach that we might want to adopt just to make it easier to communicate between game entities.

For example, the following code updates the position of a homing projectile that has locked on to some target, all using the UID method.

```
void HomingProjectile::Update()
{
    if (!m_bLocked)
        return;

    GameEntity * pTarget =
        GetEntityFromUID(m_targetUID);

    if (pTarget == NULL) {
        m_bLocked = false;
        return;
    }

    // Do whatever course correction
    // is necessary here...
    // ...
}
```

This is exactly like the solution to the shared-object problem using handles that we saw in Chapter 3.6. The same comments about the construction of handles and how the translation is implemented applies.

Resources

What about pointers to game resources instead of entities? Usually, that is less problematic. Entities point to resources because they were created that way, and their data was set up that way from the beginning. For example, one of the properties of a certain player avatar entity is the mesh it will use to be rendered, along with all its animations and textures. Usually, entities will refer to resources by filename, or by some resource ID, and that is all we need. If the resource it points to is going to change during the program, the entity should save that filename or ID to be restored later. Otherwise, it will always remain the same so there is no need to save it.

Saving Pointers

What if we decided not to use UIDs to identify our game entities and we just use straight pointers instead? Changing an existing code base from using pointers to using UIDs can be quite a task. Imagine wading through hundreds or thousands of classes changing all the pointers and the code that uses them to UIDs. If all we want is a quick way of serializing entities, there is a better alternative: we can save the pointers straight to disk.

We know that the memory address contained in the pointer will not point to the correct memory location when we load the game again. Clearly, something has to be done when we load the game entities to solve that problem. For now, we will save the raw pointers and leave it at that. The next section covers what needs to be done at load time to get everything to work.

Loading

Here comes the moment of truth. All we have done so far are preparations for loading the game entities and restoring the game state.

Creating Objects

A requirement when restoring different types of objects is to be able to create any object type based on the data we read from the stream. It is not enough to be able to read the data that should go in a GameCamera class; we need to know that it belongs to a GameCamera class and we need to actually create an object of that type.

If that problem sounds familiar, it is because it should. We covered it in detail when we talked about object factories. A good game entity factory should be able to create any entity type we want just by passing the class name or a type identifier. Then, we can call Read on the object we just created to load all its data from the stream.

```
string strClassName = ReadString(stream);
GameEntity * pEntity =
    EntityFactory::Create(strClassName);
// ... Some bookkeeping here ...
pEntity->Read(stream);
```

Depending on what type of factory system we have, we can save full strings for the class name of our entities and create them again by passing the strings to the factory system. Using strings has the usual tradeoffs: it is easy to debug and clear to see what we are trying to do, but it is slower and takes more memory than using simpler identifiers. 32-bit identifiers will be more efficient, but it will not be immediately obvious what type of object we are trying to create by looking at the identifier in the debugger.

Loading Pointers

How do we deal with the thorny issue of pointers? We mentioned earlier that we could just save them straight and we would restore them correctly. Here is how to do it.

We know that every memory address is unique. By storing the memory address of the entity we are interested in, we are uniquely identifying it. If, along with every entity, we also store its memory location when it was saved, we can construct a translation table at load time that can allow us to go from the old memory addresses to the new memory addresses.

For the translation to work correctly, it will need to be done once all the entities are loaded; otherwise, we might try to look up a memory address that we have not loaded yet. The load process is as follows: First, we load all the entities and construct a table mapping old addresses to new ones; then we make a "fix-up" pass through all the entities and give them a chance to fix any pointers they have to point to the new, correct memory locations.

To accomplish this fix-up of addresses, we need a bit more support from the loading system and the `ISerializable` interface itself, so we extend the `ISerializable` interface to include a `Fixup` function.

```
class ISerializable
{
public:
    virtual ~ISerializable() {};
    virtual bool Write(IStream & stream) const = 0;
    virtual bool Read(IStream & stream) = 0;
    virtual void Fixup() = 0;
};
```

Just as the entities implemented their own `Write` and `Read` functions, they will implement a `Fixup` function that takes care of translating old pointer addresses to correct addresses for each pointer they saved. If an entity saved no pointers, it does not need to implement the `Fixup` function, since the base `GameEntity` class implemented an empty one. As with the other serialization functions, an entity must call its parent's version of `Fixup` in addition to doing its own pointer translations.

To make this fix-up step possible, each entity needs to be associated with its old address when it is loaded back in memory. We can do that simply by saving the address of each entity when it is written out to the stream.

With all this information in hand, we are ready to deal with pointers correctly. Whenever an object is created from the stream, we also read what its old address was, and enter it in the translation table along with the new address. The class `AddressTranslator` will be in charge of keeping track of all the addresses and providing us with a translation during the fix-up pass.

```
GameEntity * LoadEntity(IStream & stream)
{
    string strClassName = ReadString(stream);
    GameEntity * pEntity =
        EntityFactory::Create(strClassName);
```

```
        void * pOldAddress = (void *)ReadInt(stream);
        AddressTranslator::AddAddress(pOldAddress,
            pEntity);

        pEntity->Read(stream);
        return pEntity;
    }
```

The `AddAddress` function puts the new address in a hash table, indexed by the old address, so it will be very efficient to translate from old address to new address.

To implement the `Fixup` function, we need to use the other function provided in the `AddressTranslator`, `TranslateAddress`. That function will look through the hash table for an old pointer value, and fetch the new value. Here is how the `Fixup` function for our `HomingProjectile` class might look:

```
        void HomingProjectile::Fixup()
        {
            m_pTarget = (GameEntity *)
                AddressTranslator::TranslateAddress(
                    m_pTarget);
        }
```

After the loading is complete and all the pointer fix-ups are done, we should reset the translation table to save memory since it will not be needed any longer.

One important thing to notice is that this method will only work for pointers that we explicitly saved and then added to the table. In this case, it happens automatically for all game entities. If we were to attempt to do this with a pointer that had not been added to the translation table, it should assert or print a big warning to let us know something went wrong in the translation process. Otherwise, the problem might go unnoticed, and the bug might not be found until after exhaustive testing.

There's a fair amount of typing involved for every variable that we want to serialize. We need to add it to the `Write()` function, to the `Load()` function, and perhaps to the `Fixup()` function. It's easy to forget to add it to one of those places, and then the serialization will fail in subtle ways. What we have seen is the basic way of doing serialization. A full game engine should have a way to automate all that typing with a few simple macros or templates that do the same thing under the hood as our serialization functions.

ON THE CD

Refer to the companion CD-ROM for the full source code for a serialization system with all the features described in this section.

Summary

In this chapter, we saw what to expect from low-level systems such as memory management and file I/O.

Memory allocation is often the cause of many bugs and crashes in games. In this chapter, we implemented a dynamic memory allocation system that gave us knowledge, safety, and control over memory allocations.

We then saw how naive file I/O could really slow down game loads with lots of file open and seek calls. We created a full file management system that allowed us to access different resources in a consistent way, as well as give us enough control to allow for much faster performance.

Game resources are large sections of data that are loaded from disk and shared among different parts of the game. We saw different strategies to deal with that sharing, how to separate resources and instances, and how to precache resources to avoid pauses in the middle of the game as new entities are created.

Finally, we looked at a simple serialization system that allowed us to save and load the game state at any point. Such a system can be used for in-game saves, or even to export the initial level state from the level editor.

Exercises

1. Consider the situation in which you have to manage a contiguous block of RAM to allocate textures at runtime. You can't rely on virtual addressing because it's either not supported, or because you need to ensure that the memory is physically contiguous (this is often the case with memory that the graphics processing unit accesses directly). Research the topic in the references and describe a good and simple algorithm you can use to minimize memory fragmentation.

2. Look at three or more PC games from the last couple of years (you can use demos that you can download for free). Install them and look at the files they're using. Do they use pack files, or do they have thousands of single files? Time how long it takes to load a level in each of those games. Is there any correlation between load times and pack-file usage?

3. Implement a `MemoryDataStream` class that works by getting data from a memory location instead of a file. Make sure it remains fully compatible with the `DataStream` interface and the rest of the stream layers.

4. Implement a simple reference-counted class that other classes can derive from. Implement the following member functions: `AddRef()`, `Release()`, and `GetRefCount()`. Write a simple program that shows how the reference class works.

5. Rewrite the same program you wrote in the previous exercise, but instead of using the reference-counting class, use the `boost::shared_ptr` pointers from the Boost library, which use nonintrusive reference counting (the reference count is in the smart pointer itself, not in the object being reference counted).

References

Memory Management

[Hixon02] Hixon, Brian, et al, "Play by Play: Effective Memory Management," *Game Developer Magazine*, February 2002.

[Llopis03] Llopis, Noel, *C++ for Game Programmers*, Charles River Media, 2003.

[Meyers98] Meyers, Scott, *Effective C++ Second Edition*, Addison-Wesley, 1998.

[Ravenbrook01] Ravenbrook Limited, *The Memory Management Reference*, *www.memorymanagement.org/*, 2001.

File I/O

[Gailly03] Gailly, Jean-loup, "Zlib," *www.gzip.org/zlib/*, 2003.

[PKWARE04] PKWARE, "Application Note: .ZIP File Format Specification," *www.pkware.com/company/standards/appnote/*, 2004.

[Sousa02] Sousa, Bruno, "File Management Using Resource Files," *Game Programming Gems 2*, Charles River Media, 2001.

Resource Management

[Bilas00] Bilas, Scott, "A Generic Handle-Based Resource Manager," *Game Programming Gems*, Charles River Media, 2000.

[Boer00] Boer, James, "Resource and Memory Management," *Game Programming Gems*, Charles River Media, 2000.

[Colvin02] Colvin, Greg; Dawes, Beman; and Adler, Darin, "Boost: Smart Pointers," *http://boost.org/libs/smart_ptr/smart_ptr.htm, 2002.*

[Hawkins03] Hawkins, Brian, "Handle-Based Smart Pointers," *Game Programming Gems 3*, Charles River Media, 2003.

[Llopis04] Llopis, Noel, "The Beauty of Weak References and Null Objects," *Game Programming Gems 4*, Charles River Media, 2004.

Serialization

[Brownlow03] Brownlow, Martin, "Save Me Now!" *Game Programming Gems 3*, Charles River Media, 2003.

[Eberly00] Eberly, David H., *3D Game Engine Design*, Morgan Kaufmann, 2000.

GAME PROGRAMMING: MATH, COLLISION DETECTON, AND PHYSICS

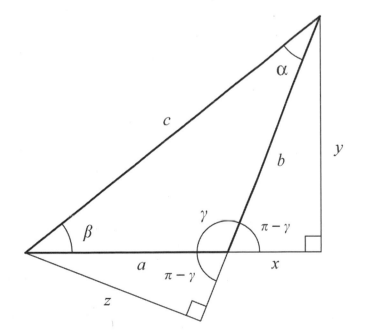

4.1 Mathematical Concepts

In This Chapter

- Overview
- Applied Trigonometry
- Vectors and Matrices
- Transformations
- Geometry
- Summary
- Exercises
- References

Overview

Mathematics has become an essential component of modern game development. As both the main processors and graphics processors in our gaming hardware become more powerful, the complexity of the mathematics used to model realistic environments and physical simulations increases without bound. This chapter provides an introduction to several fields of mathematics that are vital to today's game engines.

Trigonometry is a ubiquitous tool used extensively by game programmers and serves as this chapter's opening topic and prerequisite for the indisputably important topic of linear algebra. The bulk of this chapter discusses vectors and matrices, the indispensable tools of linear algebra with which every 3D game developer needs to be familiar. We also introduce mathematical representations of geometrical entities, such as lines and planes, and describe how to perform certain routine calculations with them.

Applied Trigonometry

Modern game development usually involves a considerable amount of geometrical computation. A 3D environment and the objects that reside within it are composed entirely of vertices, edges, and faces that all carry the geometrical information necessary to produce a rendered image. Furthermore, visibility determination, collision detection, physics, and many more components of a game rely on the ability to perform useful calculations with geometrical data. Many of such calculations depend either directly or indirectly on trigonometric relationships.

Trigonometric Functions

Consider the right triangle shown in Figure 4.1.1. For the angle labeled α, we call the side whose length is x the *adjacent* side, and we call the side whose length is y the *opposite* side. The side opposite the right angle, whose length satisfies the Pythagorean Theorem $h^2 = x^2 + y^2$, is called the *hypotenuse*. The six trigonometric functions are defined for the angle α as the ratios of side lengths shown in Table 4.1.1.

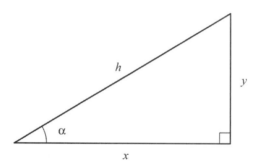

FIGURE 4.1.1   *The trigonometric functions are defined as ratios of side lengths in a right triangle.*

Table 4.1.1   Trigonometric Functions

Function Name	Symbol	Definition
sine	sin	$\sin\alpha = \dfrac{y}{h}$
cosine	cos	$\cos\alpha = \dfrac{x}{h}$
tangent	tan	$\tan\alpha = \dfrac{y}{x} = \dfrac{\sin\alpha}{\cos\alpha}$
cosecant	csc	$\csc\alpha = \dfrac{h}{y} = \dfrac{1}{\sin\alpha}$
secant	sec	$\sec\alpha = \dfrac{h}{x} = \dfrac{1}{\cos\alpha}$
cotangent	cot	$\cot\alpha = \dfrac{x}{y} = \dfrac{1}{\tan\alpha}$

The cosecant, secant, and cotangent functions are rarely used in computer programming and don't even have standard library implementations. We will therefore focus exclusively on the sine, cosine, and tangent functions, which are available to C and C++ programs as the `sin()`, `cos()`, and `tan()` functions.

What makes the trigonometric functions useful is that for a given angle α, the ratios of side lengths in a right triangle containing the angle α are always the same. Thus, the sine, cosine, and tangent functions depend only on the angle α, and not on the actual size of the triangle. The values of these functions are listed in Table 4.1.2 for several common angles.

Table 4.1.2 Values of Trigonometric Functions for Common Angles

Angle α, in radians	Angle α, in degrees	$\sin \alpha$	$\cos \alpha$	$\tan \alpha$
0	0°	0	1	0
$\pi/6$	30°	1/2	$\sqrt{3}/2$	$\sqrt{3}/3$
$\pi/4$	45°	$\sqrt{2}/2$	$\sqrt{2}/2$	1
$\pi/3$	60°	$\sqrt{3}/2$	1/2	$\sqrt{3}$
$\pi/2$	90°	1	0	undefined

The standard `sin()`, `cos()`, and `tan()` functions require that the angle be specified in radians. One *radian* is the angle α for which the circular arc subtended by α in a circle of radius r has a length equal to r itself, as shown in Figure 4.1.2. Since the circumference C of a circle of radius r is given by $C = 2\pi r$, there are precisely 2π radians in a full circle, and this corresponds to 360 degrees. We thus have the following formulas for converting between radians and degrees.

$$radians = \frac{\pi}{180}(degrees) \qquad\qquad degrees = \frac{180}{\pi}(radians) \quad (4.1.1)$$

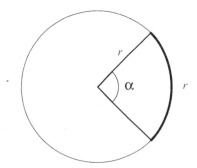

FIGURE 4.1.2 *In a circle of radius r, one radian is the angle α for which the circular arc subtended by α has a length equal to r itself.*

The trigonometric functions are often used to decompose a line segment having a known length and making a known angle with the x-axis into components that are aligned with the coordinate axes. Consider the line segment shown in Figure 4.1.3 that begins at the origin and extends to some point **P** a distance r from the origin. Given that this line segment forms an angle α with the x-axis, we can treat it as the hypotenuse of a right triangle whose remaining two sides are aligned to the x- and y-axes. Using the definitions of the sine and cosine functions, we can calculate the x and y coordinates of the point **P** as follows:

$$x = r\cos\alpha$$
$$y = r\sin\alpha \tag{4.1.2}$$

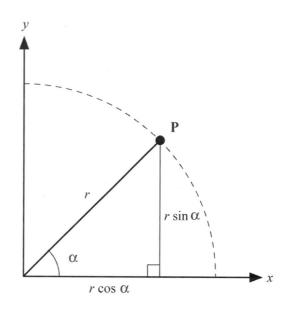

FIGURE 4.1.3 *The sine and cosine functions can be used to decompose a point on a circle into its x and y components.*

The relationships given by Equation 4.1.2 also allow us to make a natural extension of the trigonometric functions to angles beyond 90 degrees. The cosine function is associated with the x-coordinate of a point on a circle centered at the origin, and thus is negative for angles between 90 degrees and 270 degrees, or in quadrants II and III. The sine function is associated with the y-coordinate, and thus is negative for angles between 180 degrees and 360 degrees, or quadrants III and IV. This is summarized in Figure 4.1.4. Note that the tangent function is positive in quadrants I and III where the sine and cosine functions have the same sign, and is negative in quadrants II and IV where the sine and cosine functions have opposite signs.

Trigonometric Identities

There is a multitude of relationships among the trigonometric functions that allow calculations involving them to be simplified in many situations. These relationships are expressed as formulas called *identities*. Some of the simplest identities come from recognizing symmetries in the trigonometric functions. The cosine function is an *even* function, meaning that it is symmetric about the y-axis. The sine and tangent functions are *odd* functions, meaning that they are symmetric about the origin. These symmetries provide us with the following identities:

$$\sin(-\alpha) = -\sin\alpha$$
$$\cos(-\alpha) = \cos\alpha$$
$$\tan(-\alpha) = -\tan\alpha \qquad (4.1.3)$$

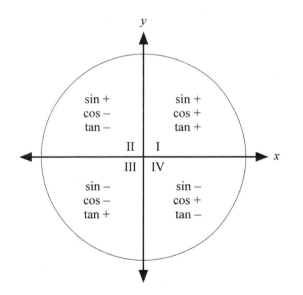

FIGURE 4.1.4 *The sine, cosine, and tangent functions change sign only at the angles 0, 90, 180, and 270 degrees, where a point on a circle centered at the origin moves from one quadrant to another.*

A few more identities can be found by recognizing that the sine and cosine functions have the same shape and that one is simply offset by $\pi/2$ radians relative to the other. The cosine function produces the same value at an angle α that the sine function produces at the angle $\alpha + \pi/2$. This allows us to formulate the following identities:

$$\cos\alpha = \sin\left(\alpha + \pi/2\right)$$
$$\sin\alpha = \cos\left(\alpha - \pi/2\right) \tag{4.1.4}$$

Using the symmetry properties given by Equation 4.1.3, we can further deduce the following identities:

$$\cos\alpha = -\sin\left(\alpha - \pi/2\right)$$
$$\sin\alpha = -\cos\left(\alpha + \pi/2\right) \tag{4.1.5}$$

Shifting the sine or cosine function by a value of π simply negates the values of the function. This property gives us several more simple identities.

$$\sin\alpha = -\sin\left(\alpha + \pi\right) = -\sin\left(\alpha - \pi\right)$$
$$\cos\alpha = -\cos\left(\alpha + \pi\right) = -\cos\left(\alpha - \pi\right) \tag{4.1.6}$$

A more powerful set of trigonometric identities can be derived from the simple fact that $x^2 + y^2 = h^2$ in the right triangle shown in Figure 4.1.1. Dividing both sides of this equation by h^2 gives us

$$\frac{x^2}{h^2} + \frac{y^2}{h^2} = 1 \tag{4.1.7}$$

Replacing the ratios x/h and y/h with the functions that they define, we have

$$\sin^2\alpha + \cos^2\alpha = 1 \tag{4.1.8}$$

This identity is true for any angle α. We can also solve for the sine or cosine function in terms of the other as follows, but we must be careful to account for sign when we take square roots.

$$\sin\alpha = \begin{cases} \sqrt{1-\cos^2\alpha}, & \text{if } 0 \le \alpha \le \pi \\ -\sqrt{1-\cos^2\alpha}, & \text{if } \pi \le \alpha \le 2\pi \end{cases}$$

$$\cos\alpha = \begin{cases} \sqrt{1-\sin^2\alpha}, & \text{if } 0 \le \alpha \le \frac{\pi}{2} \text{ or } \frac{3\pi}{2} \le \alpha \le 2\pi \\ -\sqrt{1-\sin^2\alpha}, & \text{if } \frac{\pi}{2} \le \alpha \le \frac{3\pi}{2} \end{cases} \tag{4.1.9}$$

Inverse Trigonometric Functions

It is sometimes the case that we know certain lengths in a geometrical arrangement, and we need to determine an angle. If we can establish a trigonometric relationship, such as $\sin\alpha = z$, then we can solve for the angle α by applying the appropriate *inverse* trigonometric function. The inverses of the sine, cosine, and tangent function are called the *arcsine*, *arccosine*, and *arctangent* functions, respectively, and are available in C and C++ as the asin(), acos(), and atan() functions.

The inverse trigonometric functions are often written using the superscript -1 notation. For example, arcsine can be written $\sin^{-1}$, arccosine can be written $\cos^{-1}$, and arctangent can be written $\tan^{-1}$. In these cases, the -1 denotes an inverse function and not an exponent. Applying an inverse trigonometric function to its ordinary counterpart undoes the trigonometric operation. For instance, in the equation $\sin\alpha = z$, we solve for α by applying the arcsine function to both sides to obtain $\alpha = \sin^{-1} z$. Because the trigonometric functions are periodic, there are always infinitely many angles that satisfy an equation such as $\sin\alpha = z$. The inverse functions return the angle that is closest to zero, preferring the positive angle for the cosine function. This results in the ranges listed in Table 4.1.3.

Table 4.1.3 Domains and Ranges of Inverse Trigonometric Functions

Function	Domain	Range (radians)
$\sin^{-1}z$	$[-1, 1]$	$[-\pi/2, \pi/2]$
$\cos^{-1}z$	$[-1, 1]$	$[0, \pi]$
$\tan^{-1}z$	R	$[-\pi/2, \pi/2]$

The Laws of Sines and Cosines

Everything that we have discussed so far has pertained only to right triangles, but many problems do not lend themselves to the construction of right triangles. In this section, we examine two trigonometric laws that apply to arbitrary triangles, not just those that contain a right angle.

Consider the triangle with side lengths a, b, and c shown in Figure 4.1.5 and observe the following relationships derived directly from the definition of the sine function.

$$\sin\alpha = \frac{z}{c}$$

$$\sin\beta = \frac{y}{c} \qquad (4.1.10)$$

Solving both of these for c allows us to form the equality

$$\frac{z}{\sin\alpha} = \frac{y}{\sin\beta} \qquad (4.1.11)$$

The following observations may also be made.

$$\sin(\pi - \gamma) = \frac{z}{a}$$

$$\sin(\pi - \gamma) = \frac{y}{b} \tag{4.1.12}$$

Thus, $z/a = y/b$. Multiplying the left side of Equation 4.1.11 by a/z and the right side of Equation 4.1.11 by b/y yields the *law of sines*.

$$\frac{a}{\sin\alpha} = \frac{b}{\sin\beta} \tag{4.1.13}$$

The same relationship can be derived for the pair of angles α and γ or the pair of angles β and γ, so we can write

$$\frac{a}{\sin\alpha} = \frac{b}{\sin\beta} = \frac{c}{\sin\gamma} \tag{4.1.14}$$

What this means is that the ratio of a side's length to the sine of the angle opposite that side is the same for all three sides of any particular triangle.

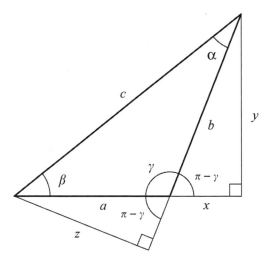

FIGURE 4.1.5   *For the triangle having sides of lengths a, b, and c, the law of sines is given by Equation 4.1.14, and the law of cosines is given by Equation 4.1.19.*

Now observe the following Pythagorean relationships existing within the triangle shown in Figure 4.1.5:

$$x^2 + y^2 = b^2$$
$$(a+x)^2 + y^2 = c^2 \qquad (4.1.15)$$

Solving the first equation for y^2 and substituting into the second equation gives us:

$$c^2 = (a+x)^2 + b^2 - x^2$$
$$= a^2 + b^2 + 2ax \qquad (4.1.16)$$

The value of x can be replaced by observing:

$$\cos(\pi - \gamma) = \frac{x}{b} \qquad (4.1.17)$$

Since $\cos(\pi - \gamma) = -\cos\gamma$, we have

$$x = -b\cos\gamma \qquad (4.1.18)$$

Plugging this into Equation 4.1.16 produces the *law of cosines*.

$$c^2 = a^2 + b^2 - 2ab\cos\gamma \qquad (4.1.19)$$

The law of cosines is a generalization of the Pythagorean Theorem to arbitrary triangles. When γ is a right angle, Equation 4.1.19 reduces to the Pythagorean Theorem, since $\cos\pi/2 = 0$.

Vectors and Matrices

Numerical quantities arising in geometry, physics, and many other fields employed by game developers generally fall into two broad categories. Quantities such as distance, time, and mass can be fully described using a single numerical value, and these types of quantities are called *scalars*. Other quantities can only be fully described by associating a direction with an ordinary magnitude, as illustrated by the following examples:

- The difference between two points in space is represented by both the distance between the points (the magnitude) and the direction pointing from one of the points to the other.
- The velocity of a projectile is represented by both its speed (the magnitude) and the direction in which it is traveling.
- A force acting on an object is represented by both its magnitude and the direction in which it is applied.

Such quantities, carrying information about both a magnitude and a direction, are called *vectors*. Vectors are used extensively throughout many facets of modern game development, particularly 3D graphics, 3D audio, physics simulation, and artificial intelligence.

Vector Arithmetic

A vector is often visualized by drawing a line segment with an arrowhead at one end, as shown in Figure 4.1.6. The length of the line segment corresponds to the magnitude of the vector, and the angle at which the line segment is drawn corresponds to the direction of the vector. Multiplying a vector **V** by a scalar quantity *a* changes the length of the line segment by the factor *a*, thus modifying its magnitude by the same factor. If the quantity *a* is negative, then the direction in which the vector **V** points is also reversed by the multiplication, which amounts to moving the arrowhead to the opposite end of the line segment representing **V**.

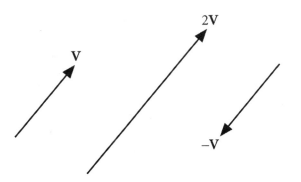

FIGURE 4.1.6   *Vectors can be visualized using line segments whose lengths correspond to their magnitudes, and whose angles correspond to their directions.*

Two vectors **V** and **W** are added by placing the beginning of **W** at the end of **V** and forming a new vector that begins where **V** begins and ends where **W** ends as shown in Figure 4.1.7. If we think of each vector as a distance and direction along which we can travel, then the sum represents the cumulative distance and direction that we would travel if we first traveled along the vector **V** and then traveled along the vector **W**. If one vector is subtracted from the other, then we travel along the subtracted vector in the opposite direction.

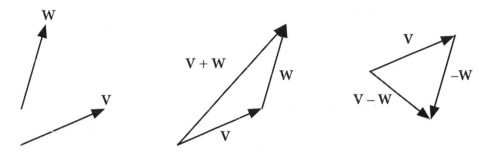

FIGURE 4.1.7   *The sum* **V + W** *is formed by concatenating W and V and drawing a new vector that points directly from the beginning of V to the end of W. The difference* **V − W** *is formed by reversing the direction in which W points.*

Whereas a scalar is represented by a single numerical value, a vector requires a representation composed of multiple numerical values called *components*. The number of components corresponds to the *dimension* of a vector, and we write the components of an *n*-dimensional vector as an ordered *n*-tuple. For example, a three-dimensional vector **V** whose components are 1, 2, and 3 is written as

$$\mathbf{V} = \langle 1, 2, 3 \rangle \tag{4.1.20}$$

The first, second, and third components of a vector are usually referred to as the *x*, *y*, and *z* components of the vector. We represent an individual component of a vector by writing *x*, *y*, or *z* as a subscript following the symbol representing the vector. For the vector **V** shown in Equation 4.1.20 we have

$$V_x = 1$$
$$V_y = 2$$
$$V_z = 3 \tag{4.1.21}$$

Notice that the symbol for the vector is now written in italics instead of the boldface type used earlier. To distinguish between scalars and vectors, the widely adopted convention is to print scalars in italic type and vectors in boldface type. This convention extends to the case in which we are referring to individual components of a vector, as in Equation 4.1.21 The vector **V** by itself is printed in boldface type, but a component of **V** is a scalar, so we print the subscripted symbol in italic type as done in Equation 4.1.21.

We add or subtract two vectors **V** and **W** by simply adding or subtracting their individual components. (To do this, the two vectors must have the same dimension.) If **V** and **W** are both *n*-dimensional, then we can write their sum and difference as:

$$\mathbf{V} + \mathbf{W} = \left\langle V_1 + W_1, V_2 + W_2, \ldots, V_n + W_n \right\rangle$$
$$\mathbf{V} - \mathbf{W} = \left\langle V_1 - W_1, V_2 - W_2, \ldots, V_n - W_n \right\rangle \tag{4.1.22}$$

Here, we use an integer subscript to refer to each component of the vector $\mathbf{V}$ as a notational necessity. In three dimensions, the subscripts 1, 2, and 3 have the same meaning as the subscripts x, y, and z.

The magnitude, or length, of an n-dimensional vector $\mathbf{V}$, written $\|\mathbf{V}\|$, is defined as:

$$\|\mathbf{V}\| = \sqrt{\sum_{i=1}^{n} V_i^2} \tag{4.1.23}$$

For a three-dimensional vector $\mathbf{V}$, this becomes

$$\|\mathbf{V}\| = \sqrt{V_x^2 + V_y^2 + V_z^2} \tag{4.1.24}$$

If we consider the components of a vector $\mathbf{P} = \left\langle x, y, z \right\rangle$ to be the coordinates of a point in three-dimensional space, then the magnitude of $\mathbf{P}$ can be thought of as its distance from the origin. The formula given by Equation 4.1.24 is simply the Pythagorean Theorem in three dimensions. The distance between two points $\mathbf{P}$ and $\mathbf{Q}$ is equal to the magnitude of $\mathbf{P} - \mathbf{Q}$, since this difference is the vector whose direction and magnitude represent the direct path starting at $\mathbf{P}$ and finishing at $\mathbf{Q}$.

As mentioned before, multiplying a vector $\mathbf{V}$ by a scalar a changes its magnitude by the factor a. To make this work with the definition of magnitude given by Equation 4.1.23, we define the product of an n-dimensional vector $\mathbf{V}$ and a scalar a so that each component of $\mathbf{V}$ is multiplied by a as:

$$a\mathbf{V} = \mathbf{V}a = \left\langle aV_1, aV_2, \ldots, aV_n \right\rangle \tag{4.1.25}$$

A vector whose magnitude is exactly 1 is said to be *normalized* or to have *unit length*. (The term *normal vector* also exists and refers to the unrelated property that a vector's direction is perpendicular to a surface.) A normalized vector is often treated as if it no longer carries information about magnitude, but only represents a pure direction. Any vector $\mathbf{V}$ can be normalized by simply dividing it by its magnitude as:

$$\hat{\mathbf{V}} = \frac{\mathbf{V}}{\|\mathbf{V}\|} \tag{4.1.26}$$

The hat added to the $\mathbf{V}$ on the left side of the equation is a common notation used to indicate that a vector has unit length.

The vectors $\hat{\mathbf{i}}$, $\hat{\mathbf{j}}$, and $\hat{\mathbf{k}}$ are often used as a shorthand notation for the unit vectors aligned to the three coordinate axes. They are defined by the following equalities:

$$\hat{\mathbf{i}} = \langle 1,0,0 \rangle$$
$$\hat{\mathbf{j}} = \langle 0,1,0 \rangle$$
$$\hat{\mathbf{k}} = \langle 0,0,1 \rangle \qquad (4.1.27)$$

This notation allows us to write any three-dimensional vector $\mathbf{V} = a\hat{\mathbf{i}} + b\hat{\mathbf{j}} + c\hat{\mathbf{k}}$ in the form

$$\mathbf{V} = a\hat{\mathbf{i}} + b\hat{\mathbf{j}} + c\hat{\mathbf{k}} \qquad (4.1.28)$$

Matrix Arithmetic

A *matrix* is a rectangular array of individual numerical quantities arranged as a set of rows and columns. When describing the size of a matrix, the number of rows comes first and the number of columns follows. Thus, a matrix having n rows and m columns is called an $n \times m$ matrix. For example, the following matrix is a 2×3 matrix.

$$\mathbf{M} = \begin{bmatrix} 1 & 2 & 3 \\ 4 & 5 & 6 \end{bmatrix} \qquad (4.1.29)$$

If $n = m$ (i.e., the number of rows equals the number of columns), then the matrix $\mathbf{M}$ is called a *square* matrix.

The individual components of a matrix are called *entries*. The single entry of a matrix $\mathbf{M}$ residing in row i, and column j is denoted by M_{ij}. Note that we have again used the convention that the matrix itself is printed in boldface type, and an entry of the matrix is printed in italic type. For the matrix shown in Equation 4.1.29, we can write

$$M_{11} = 1 \quad M_{21} = 4$$
$$M_{12} = 2 \quad M_{22} = 5$$
$$M_{13} = 3 \quad M_{23} = 6 \qquad (4.1.30)$$

The entries M_{ii} are called the *main diagonal* entries of the matrix $\mathbf{M}$. A square matrix having nonzero entries only on the main diagonal is called a *diagonal* matrix.

The *transpose* of a matrix $\mathbf{M}$, denoted by $\mathbf{M}^{\mathrm{T}}$, is the matrix for which the entry residing at the (i, j) position is equal to M_{ji}. That is, the transpose of a matrix is obtained by exchanging the meanings of rows and columns and effectively reflecting the entries through the main diagonal. The transpose of the matrix $\mathbf{M}$ shown in Equation 4.1.29 is

$$\mathbf{M}^{\mathrm{T}} = \begin{bmatrix} 1 & 4 \\ 2 & 5 \\ 3 & 6 \end{bmatrix} \tag{4.1.31}$$

A matrix that is equal to its own transpose (and therefore must be square) is called a *symmetric* matrix.

Two matrices of the same size can be added or subtracted component wise, although the need for doing so does not often arise. As with vectors, multiplying an $n \times m$ matrix $\mathbf{M}$ by a scalar a simply distributes the factor a to each of the entries of the matrix as follows:

$$a\mathbf{M} = \mathbf{M}a = \begin{bmatrix} aM_{11} & aM_{12} & \cdots & aM_{1m} \\ aM_{21} & aM_{22} & \cdots & aM_{2m} \\ \vdots & \vdots & \ddots & \vdots \\ aM_{n1} & aM_{n2} & \cdots & aM_{nm} \end{bmatrix} \tag{4.1.32}$$

An n-dimensional vector $\mathbf{V}$ can be considered an $n \times 1$ matrix, so we could write

$$\mathbf{V} = \langle V_1, V_2, \ldots, V_n \rangle = \begin{bmatrix} V_1 \\ V_2 \\ \vdots \\ V_n \end{bmatrix} \tag{4.1.33}$$

When a vector is written as a single column of entries like this, we usually call it a *column* vector. Sometimes, it will be convenient to write the components of a vector as a single row of entries, in which case we can transpose the matrix shown in Equation 4.1.33 to obtain

$$\mathbf{V}^{\mathrm{T}} = \begin{bmatrix} V_1 & V_2 & \cdots & V_n \end{bmatrix} \tag{4.1.34}$$

When a vector is written as a matrix having a single row, we usually call it a *row* vector. Whether a vector is written as a column vector or row vector really depends on how we want to transform it using matrix multiplication.

Two matrices $\mathbf{A}$ and $\mathbf{B}$ can be multiplied together whenever the number of columns of $\mathbf{A}$ is equal to the number of rows of $\mathbf{B}$. If $\mathbf{A}$ is an $n \times m$ matrix, then it can be multiplied by $\mathbf{B}$ only if $\mathbf{B}$ is an $m \times p$ matrix, where m is the same for both $\mathbf{A}$ and $\mathbf{B}$. The product $\mathbf{AB}$ is an $n \times p$ matrix for which the entry in the (i, j) position is given by the following equation.

$$\left(\mathbf{AB}\right)_{ij} = \sum_{k=1}^{m} A_{ik} B_{kj} \tag{4.1.35}$$

The (i, j) entry of $\mathbf{AB}$ is derived only from the entries in the i-th row of $\mathbf{A}$ and the j-th column of $\mathbf{B}$. What Equation 4.1.35 tells us is that to calculate the (i, j) entry of $\mathbf{AB}$, we multiply every k-th entry in row i of $\mathbf{A}$ by the k-th entry in column j of $\mathbf{B}$ and add all of the individual products together. For example, consider the following product of two 2×2 matrices.

$$\mathbf{M} = \begin{bmatrix} 2 & 3 \\ 1 & -1 \end{bmatrix} \begin{bmatrix} -2 & 1 \\ 4 & -5 \end{bmatrix} = \begin{bmatrix} 8 & -13 \\ -6 & 6 \end{bmatrix} \tag{4.1.36}$$

The individual entries of $\mathbf{M}$ were calculated using Equation 4.1.35 as follows:

$$\begin{aligned}
M_{11} &= 2 \cdot (-2) + 3 \cdot 4 &&= 8 \\
M_{12} &= 2 \cdot 1 + 3 \cdot (-5) &&= -13 \\
M_{21} &= 1 \cdot (-2) + (-1) \cdot 4 &&= -6 \\
M_{22} &= 1 \cdot 1 + (-1) \cdot (-5) &&= 6
\end{aligned} \tag{4.1.37}$$

Matrix multiplication is not generally a commutative operation. Not only might it be the case that $\mathbf{AB} \neq \mathbf{BA}$, but it may not even be possible to form one of the products $\mathbf{AB}$ or $\mathbf{BA}$ because the numbers of rows and columns do not match correctly. We will almost always be working with square matrices, so it will always be possible to form both the products $\mathbf{AB}$ and $\mathbf{BA}$, but it should be noted that the order of multiplication is important.

It is often the case that we need to multiply an $n \times n$ matrix $\mathbf{M}$ by an n-dimensional vector $\mathbf{V}$. As we will see later, such an operation is used to transform a vector from one coordinate system to another. If $\mathbf{V}$ is expressed as an $n \times 1$ column vector, then we can only form the product $\mathbf{MV}$, and we say that $\mathbf{V}$ is multiplied by the matrix $\mathbf{M}$ on the left. If we express $\mathbf{V}$ as the $1 \times n$ row vector $\mathbf{V}^{\mathrm{T}}$, then we can form the product $\mathbf{V}^{\mathrm{T}}\mathbf{M}$, and we say that $\mathbf{V}^{\mathrm{T}}$ is multiplied by the matrix $\mathbf{M}$ on the right. Ordinarily, either column vectors or row vectors are chosen to be the convention and are consistently used throughout a project. In this chapter, we use column vectors as the convention, and in three dimensions, we thus have the following product between a 3×3 matrix $\mathbf{M}$ and a three-dimensional vector $\mathbf{V}$.

$$\begin{bmatrix} M_{11} & M_{12} & M_{13} \\ M_{21} & M_{22} & M_{23} \\ M_{31} & M_{32} & M_{33} \end{bmatrix} \begin{bmatrix} V_x \\ V_y \\ V_z \end{bmatrix} = \begin{bmatrix} M_{11}V_x + M_{12}V_y + M_{13}V_z \\ M_{21}V_x + M_{22}V_y + M_{23}V_z \\ M_{31}V_x + M_{32}V_y + M_{33}V_z \end{bmatrix} \tag{4.1.38}$$

An $n \times n$ square matrix having entries of 1 along the main diagonal and entries of 0 everywhere else is given a special name, the *identity* matrix, and is sometimes denoted by $\mathbf{I}_n$. When the matrix $\mathbf{I}_n$ is multiplied by another matrix $\mathbf{M}$ on the left or right, the result is $\mathbf{M}$ itself. Multiplying by the identity matrix in the context of matrix multiplication is the analog of multiplying by one in the context of ordinary scalar multiplication.

The importance of the identity matrix lies in our ability to take a square $n \times n$ matrix $\mathbf{M}$ and find another matrix, that we denote $\mathbf{M}^{-1}$, whose product with $\mathbf{M}$ produces the identity matrix. The matrix $\mathbf{M}^{-1}$ is called the *inverse* of the matrix $\mathbf{M}$ and satisfies both $\mathbf{M}\mathbf{M}^{-1} = \mathbf{I}_n$ and $\mathbf{M}^{-1}\mathbf{M} = \mathbf{I}_n$. Using the inverse matrix allows us to solve equations such as $\mathbf{MV} = \mathbf{W}$ for which we know the values of $\mathbf{M}$ and $\mathbf{W}$, and we need to determine the value of $\mathbf{V}$. If we multiply both sides of the equation by $\mathbf{M}^{-1}$ on the left, we have $\mathbf{V} = \mathbf{M}^{-1}\mathbf{W}$.

Not every matrix has an inverse, and those that are noninvertible are called *singular*. Whether a matrix $\mathbf{M}$ is singular can be determined by examining a quantity called the *determinant* of $\mathbf{M}$, denoted by $\det \mathbf{M}$ or $|\mathbf{M}|$. The determinant of a 2×2 matrix is defined as

$$\det \begin{bmatrix} a & b \\ c & d \end{bmatrix} = \begin{vmatrix} a & b \\ c & d \end{vmatrix} = ad - bc \tag{4.1.39}$$

and the determinant of a 3×3 matrix is given by:

$$\begin{vmatrix} m_{11} & m_{12} & m_{13} \\ m_{21} & m_{22} & m_{23} \\ m_{31} & m_{32} & m_{33} \end{vmatrix} = m_{11} \begin{vmatrix} m_{22} & m_{23} \\ m_{32} & m_{33} \end{vmatrix} - m_{12} \begin{vmatrix} m_{21} & m_{23} \\ m_{31} & m_{33} \end{vmatrix} + m_{13} \begin{vmatrix} m_{21} & m_{22} \\ m_{31} & m_{32} \end{vmatrix}$$

$$= m_{11}\left(m_{22}m_{33} - m_{23}m_{32}\right) - m_{12}\left(m_{21}m_{33} - m_{23}m_{31}\right)$$
$$+ m_{13}\left(m_{21}m_{32} - m_{22}m_{31}\right) \tag{4.1.40}$$

Determinants of larger matrices can be found by using a recursive formula, as described in [Lengyel04].

A matrix is invertible if and only if its determinant is not zero. There are numerous methods for calculating matrix inverses, but we restrict ourselves to explicit formulas for the types of matrices commonly used during game development. (Descriptions of more general algorithms can be found in [Press92].) The inverse of a 2×2 matrix $\mathbf{M}$ is given by

$$\mathbf{M}^{-1} = \frac{1}{\det \mathbf{M}} \begin{bmatrix} M_{22} & -M_{12} \\ -M_{21} & M_{11} \end{bmatrix} \tag{4.1.41}$$

and the inverse of a 3×3 matrix $\mathbf{M}$ is given by

$$\mathbf{M}^{-1} = \frac{1}{\det \mathbf{M}} \begin{bmatrix} M_{22}M_{33} - M_{23}M_{32} & M_{13}M_{32} - M_{12}M_{33} & M_{12}M_{23} - M_{13}M_{22} \\ M_{23}M_{31} - M_{21}M_{33} & M_{11}M_{33} - M_{13}M_{31} & M_{13}M_{21} - M_{11}M_{23} \\ M_{21}M_{32} - M_{22}M_{31} & M_{12}M_{31} - M_{11}M_{32} & M_{11}M_{22} - M_{12}M_{21} \end{bmatrix} \quad (4.1.42)$$

In computer graphics, a special type of 4×4 matrix is commonly used to transform between coordinate systems. Such matrices have the form

$$\mathbf{M} = \left[\begin{array}{ccc|c} R_{11} & R_{12} & R_{13} & T_x \\ R_{21} & R_{22} & R_{23} & T_y \\ R_{31} & R_{32} & R_{33} & T_z \\ \hline 0 & 0 & 0 & 1 \end{array} \right] \quad (4.1.43)$$

where the entries R_{ij} correspond to a 3×3 rotation matrix $\mathbf{R}$, and the vector $\mathbf{T}$ represents a translation. The fourth row of the matrix is always $\langle 0,0,0,1 \rangle$. The inverse of this matrix is given by

$$\mathbf{M}^{-1} = \left[\begin{array}{c|c} \mathbf{R}^{-1} & -\mathbf{R}^{-1}\mathbf{T} \\ \hline \mathbf{0} & 1 \end{array} \right] = \left[\begin{array}{ccc|c} R_{11}^{-1} & R_{12}^{-1} & R_{13}^{-1} & -\left(\mathbf{R}^{-1}\mathbf{T}\right)_x \\ R_{21}^{-1} & R_{22}^{-1} & R_{23}^{-1} & -\left(\mathbf{R}^{-1}\mathbf{T}\right)_y \\ R_{31}^{-1} & R_{32}^{-1} & R_{33}^{-1} & -\left(\mathbf{R}^{-1}\mathbf{T}\right)_z \\ \hline 0 & 0 & 0 & 1 \end{array} \right] \quad (4.1.44)$$

The Dot Product

The *dot product* of two vectors, also known as the *inner product* or *scalar product*, is arguably one of the most important vector operations used in computer game development. The dot product gets its name from the symbol used to denote the operation—a single dot between two vectors. (In the next section, we examine the cross product, which is denoted by a crosslike symbol.) The dot product is also called the "scalar product" because is combines two vector quantities to produce a scalar result.

The dot product $\mathbf{V} \cdot \mathbf{W}$ between two n-dimensional vectors $\mathbf{V}$ and $\mathbf{W}$ produces the scalar quantity given by the formula

$$\mathbf{V} \cdot \mathbf{W} = \sum_{i=1}^{n} V_i W_i \quad (4.1.45)$$

That is, we calculate the n products of corresponding components of the two vectors and add them all together. In three dimensions, the dot product becomes

$$\mathbf{V} \cdot \mathbf{W} = V_x W_x + V_y W_y + V_z W_z \tag{4.1.46}$$

The dot product $\mathbf{V} \cdot \mathbf{W}$ can also be expressed as the matrix product

$$\mathbf{V} \cdot \mathbf{W} = \mathbf{V}^{\mathrm{T}}\mathbf{W} = \begin{bmatrix} V_1 & V_2 & \cdots & V_n \end{bmatrix} \begin{bmatrix} W_1 \\ W_2 \\ \vdots \\ W_n \end{bmatrix} \tag{4.1.47}$$

which yields a 1×1 matrix (that we treat as a scalar) whose single entry is equal to the sum given by Equation 4.1.45.

The dot product earns its place of importance through the following equation:

$$\mathbf{V} \cdot \mathbf{W} = \|\mathbf{V}\|\|\mathbf{W}\|\cos\alpha \tag{4.1.48}$$

Here, the angle α is the planar angle between the two directions in which the vectors $\mathbf{V}$ and $\mathbf{W}$ point. If both $\mathbf{V}$ and $\mathbf{W}$ are normalized, the dot product yields the cosine of the angle between the two vectors. This fact is particularly useful for lighting and shading calculations performed by 3D graphics applications.

Equation 4.1.48 can be verified by applying the law of cosines to the triangle shown in Figure 4.1.8 to obtain

$$\|\mathbf{V} - \mathbf{W}\|^2 = \|\mathbf{V}\|^2 + \|\mathbf{W}\|^2 - 2\|\mathbf{V}\|\|\mathbf{W}\|\cos\alpha \tag{4.1.49}$$

Using the definition of magnitude given by Equation 4.1.23, we can rewrite this as

$$\sum_{i=1}^{n}(V_i - W_i)^2 = \sum_{i=1}^{n}V_i^2 + \sum_{i=1}^{n}W_i^2 - 2\|\mathbf{V}\|\|\mathbf{W}\|\cos\alpha \tag{4.1.50}$$

After expanding the left-hand side of the equation, all of the V_i^2 and W_i^2 terms cancel, and we have

$$\sum_{i=1}^{n}-2V_i W_i = -2\|\mathbf{V}\|\|\mathbf{W}\|\cos\alpha \tag{4.1.51}$$

Dividing both sides by -2 brings us to Equation 4.1.48.

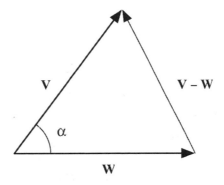

FIGURE 4.1.8 *The dot product is related to the angle between two vectors V and W by the equation* $\mathbf{V} \cdot \mathbf{W} = \|\mathbf{V}\|\|\mathbf{W}\|\cos\alpha$. *This can be verified by applying the law of cosines to the angle* α.

A couple of important facts follow immediately from Equation 4.1.48. The first is that two vectors $\mathbf{V}$ and $\mathbf{W}$ are perpendicular if and only if $\mathbf{V} \cdot \mathbf{W} = 0$. This follows from the fact that the cosine function is zero at an angle of 90 degrees. Vectors whose dot product yields zero are called *orthogonal*. We define the *zero vector*, $\mathbf{0} \equiv \langle 0,0,\ldots,0 \rangle$, to be orthogonal to every vector $\mathbf{V}$, since $\mathbf{0} \cdot \mathbf{V}$ always equals zero.

The second fact is that the sign of the dot product tells us how close two vectors are to pointing in the same direction. For any vector $\mathbf{V}$, we can construct a plane that passes through the origin and is perpendicular to the direction that $\mathbf{V}$ represents, as shown in Figure 4.1.9. Any vector lying on the same side of the plane as $\mathbf{V}$ yields a positive dot product with $\mathbf{V}$, and any vector lying on the opposite side of the plane from $\mathbf{V}$ yields a negative dot product with $\mathbf{V}$.

The dot product of a vector with itself always produces a positive number that is equal to the squared magnitude of the vector. Because the angle between a vector and itself is zero, the cosine term in Equation 4.1.48 is 1, and we have

$$\mathbf{V} \cdot \mathbf{V} = \|\mathbf{V}\|\|\mathbf{V}\| = \|\mathbf{V}\|^2 \tag{4.1.52}$$

The shorthand notation V^2 is often used in place of $\mathbf{V} \cdot \mathbf{V}$ or $\|\mathbf{V}\|^2$, and all three expressions have identical meanings. In the shorthand case, the vector is printed in italics because its square is a scalar quantity.

The situation often arises in which we need to decompose a vector $\mathbf{V}$ into components that are parallel and perpendicular to another vector $\mathbf{W}$. As shown in Figure 4.1.10, if we think of the vector $\mathbf{V}$ as the hypotenuse of a right triangle, then the perpendicular projection of $\mathbf{V}$ onto the vector $\mathbf{W}$ produces the side adjacent to the angle α between $\mathbf{V}$ and $\mathbf{W}$.

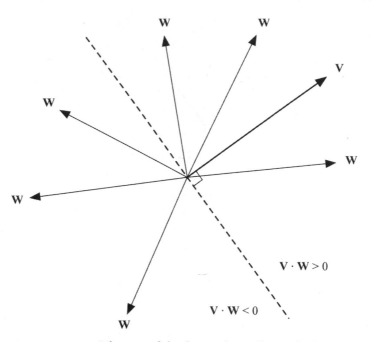

FIGURE 4.1.9   *The sign of the dot product tells us whether two vectors lie on the same side or on opposite sides of a plane.*

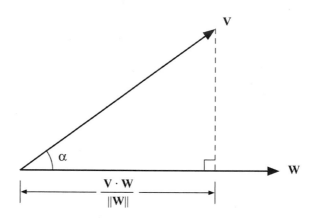

FIGURE 4.1.10   *The length of the projection of the vector V onto the vector W is given by $\mathbf{V} \cdot \mathbf{W}/\|\mathbf{W}\|$ because $\mathbf{V} \cdot \mathbf{W} = \|\mathbf{V}\|\|\mathbf{W}\|\cos\alpha$.*

Basic trigonometry tells us that the length of the side adjacent to α is given by $\|\mathbf{V}\|\cos\alpha$. Equation 4.1.48 gives us a way to calculate the same quantity without knowing the angle α.

$$\|\mathbf{V}\|\cos\alpha = \frac{\mathbf{V}\cdot\mathbf{W}}{\|\mathbf{W}\|} \qquad (4.1.53)$$

To obtain a vector that has this length and is parallel to $\mathbf{W}$, we simply multiply by the unit vector $\mathbf{W}/\|\mathbf{W}\|$. We now have the following formula for the projection of $\mathbf{V}$ onto $\mathbf{W}$, which we denote by $\mathrm{proj}_{\mathbf{W}}\,\mathbf{V}$.

$$\mathrm{proj}_{\mathbf{W}}\,\mathbf{V} = \frac{\mathbf{V}\cdot\mathbf{W}}{\|\mathbf{W}\|^2}\mathbf{W} \qquad (4.1.54)$$

The projection of $\mathbf{V}$ onto $\mathbf{W}$ is a linear transformation of $\mathbf{V}$ and can thus be expressed as the following matrix product. In three dimensions, $\mathrm{proj}_{\mathbf{W}}\,\mathbf{V}$ can be computed using the alternative formula

$$\mathrm{proj}_{\mathbf{W}}\,\mathbf{V} = \frac{1}{\|\mathbf{W}\|^2}\begin{bmatrix} W_x^2 & W_x W_y & W_x W_z \\ W_x W_y & W_y^2 & W_y W_z \\ W_x W_z & W_y W_z & W_z^2 \end{bmatrix}\begin{bmatrix} V_x \\ V_y \\ V_z \end{bmatrix} \qquad (4.1.55)$$

The perpendicular component of $\mathbf{V}$ with respect to $\mathbf{W}$, denoted by $\mathrm{perp}_{\mathbf{W}}\,\mathbf{V}$, is simply the vector left over when we subtract the parallel component given by Equation 4.1.54 from the original vector $\mathbf{V}$.

$$\mathrm{perp}_{\mathbf{W}}\,\mathbf{V} = \mathbf{V} - \mathrm{proj}_{\mathbf{W}}\,\mathbf{V}$$
$$= \mathbf{V} - \frac{\mathbf{V}\cdot\mathbf{W}}{\|\mathbf{W}\|^2}\mathbf{W} \qquad (4.1.56)$$

This operation is the basis for an algorithm called *Gram-Schmidt orthogonalization*. At various points in game development, there arise situations in which a set of vectors that is almost pairwise orthogonal needs to be corrected so that each vector in the set is orthogonal to all of the other vectors in the set. Gram-Schmidt orthogonalization performs this correction by putting the vectors in a particular order and then subtracting from each vector the projection of that vector onto all of the preceding vectors. For example, the set of three vectors $\{\mathbf{U},\mathbf{V},\mathbf{W}\}$ is orthogonalized by leaving $\mathbf{U}$ alone, subtracting $\mathrm{proj}_{\mathbf{U}}\,\mathbf{V}$ from $\mathbf{V}$, and subtracting both $\mathrm{proj}_{\mathbf{U}}\,\mathbf{W}$ and $\mathrm{proj}_{\mathbf{V}}\,\mathbf{W}$ from $\mathbf{W}$ (where the projection of $\mathbf{W}$ onto $\mathbf{V}$ uses the already orthogonalized vector $\mathbf{V}$). For many applications, it is further necessary to renormalize each of the vectors to unit length.

The Cross Product

The *cross product* of two vectors, also known as the *vector product*, produces a vector that is perpendicular to both of the vectors being multiplied together. This product has many uses in computer graphics and physics, and one such application is the calculation of a surface normal at a particular point by evaluating the cross product of two distinct tangent vectors. The cross product between two vectors $\mathbf{V}$ and $\mathbf{W}$ is written $\mathbf{V} \times \mathbf{W}$, and therein lays the source of its name—the crosslike symbol placed between the two operands.

The cross product applies only to three-dimensional vectors and is defined as:

$$\mathbf{V} \times \mathbf{W} = \langle V_y W_z - V_z W_y, V_z W_x - V_x W_z, V_x W_y - V_y W_x \rangle \tag{4.1.57}$$

A tool that is often used to remember this formula is to calculate the cross product by evaluating the following expression, which resembles a matrix determinant:

$$\mathbf{V} \times \mathbf{W} = \begin{vmatrix} \hat{\mathbf{i}} & \hat{\mathbf{j}} & \hat{\mathbf{k}} \\ V_x & V_y & V_z \\ W_x & W_y & W_z \end{vmatrix} \tag{4.1.58}$$

The symbols $\hat{\mathbf{i}}$, $\hat{\mathbf{j}}$, and $\hat{\mathbf{k}}$ represent the unit vectors aligned to the coordinate axes as defined by Equation 4.1.27. This expression is sometimes called a *pseudodeterminant* since it is not technically a real matrix (because the entries in the top row are vectors). Nevertheless, the usual method for evaluating the determinant does produce the correct value for the cross product, as shown here:

$$\begin{vmatrix} \hat{\mathbf{i}} & \hat{\mathbf{j}} & \hat{\mathbf{k}} \\ V_x & V_y & V_z \\ W_x & W_y & W_z \end{vmatrix} = \hat{\mathbf{i}}(V_y W_z - V_z W_y) + \hat{\mathbf{j}}(V_z W_x - V_x W_z) + \hat{\mathbf{k}}(V_x W_y - V_y W_x) \tag{4.1.59}$$

The cross product $\mathbf{V} \times \mathbf{W}$ can also be expressed as the following matrix product:

$$\mathbf{V} \times \mathbf{W} = \begin{bmatrix} 0 & -V_z & V_y \\ V_z & 0 & -V_x \\ -V_y & V_x & 0 \end{bmatrix} \begin{bmatrix} W_x \\ W_y \\ W_z \end{bmatrix} \tag{4.1.60}$$

As mentioned previously, the cross product $\mathbf{V} \times \mathbf{W}$ produces a vector that is perpendicular to both $\mathbf{V}$ and $\mathbf{W}$. For this to be true, it must be the case that $(\mathbf{V} \times \mathbf{W}) \cdot \mathbf{V} = 0$ and $(\mathbf{V} \times \mathbf{W}) \cdot \mathbf{W} = 0$. We can verify these equations by simply writing out the individual components, as we do for the dot product with $\mathbf{V}$ here:

$$(\mathbf{V} \times \mathbf{W}) \cdot \mathbf{V} = \langle V_y W_z - V_z W_y, V_z W_x - V_x W_z, V_x W_y - V_y W_x \rangle \cdot \mathbf{V}$$

$$= V_y W_z V_x - V_z W_y V_x + V_z W_x V_y - V_x W_z V_y + V_x W_y V_z - V_y W_x V_z$$

$$= 0 \tag{4.1.61}$$

Like the dot product, the cross product has trigonometric significance. The magnitude of the cross product between two vectors satisfies the following equation:

$$\|\mathbf{V} \times \mathbf{W}\| = \|\mathbf{V}\|\|\mathbf{W}\|\sin\alpha \qquad (4.1.62)$$

As with the dot product, the angle α corresponds to the planar angle between the two directions in which the vectors $\mathbf{V}$ and $\mathbf{W}$ point. Equation 4.1.62 can be proven by first recognizing that the square of $\|\mathbf{V} \times \mathbf{W}\|$ can be written as:

$$\|\mathbf{V} \times \mathbf{W}\|^2 = \left(V_x^2 + V_y^2 + V_z^2\right)\left(W_x^2 + W_y^2 + W_z^2\right) - \left(V_x W_x + V_y W_y + V_z W_z\right)^2$$
$$= V^2 W^2 - (\mathbf{V} \cdot \mathbf{W})^2 \qquad (4.1.63)$$

Replacing the dot product with the right side of Equation 4.1.48, we have

$$\|\mathbf{V} \times \mathbf{W}\|^2 = V^2 W^2 - V^2 W^2 \cos^2\alpha$$
$$= V^2 W^2 \left(1 - \cos^2\alpha\right)$$
$$= V^2 W^2 \sin^2\alpha \qquad (4.1.64)$$

Taking the square root of both sides brings us to Equation 4.1.62.

As shown in Figure 4.1.11, Equation 4.1.62 demonstrates that the magnitude of the cross product $\mathbf{V} \times \mathbf{W}$ is equal to the area of the parallelogram whose sides are formed by the vectors $\mathbf{V}$ and $\mathbf{W}$. As a consequence, the area A of an arbitrary triangle whose vertices are given by the points $\mathbf{P}_1$, $\mathbf{P}_2$, and $\mathbf{P}_3$ can be calculated using the formula

$$A = \frac{1}{2}\|(\mathbf{P}_2 - \mathbf{P}_1) \times (\mathbf{P}_3 - \mathbf{P}_1)\| \qquad (4.1.65)$$

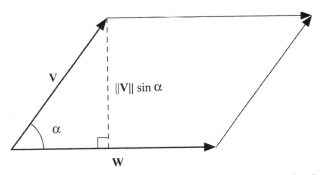

FIGURE 4.1.11 *This parallelogram has base width $\|\mathbf{W}\|$ and height $\|\mathbf{V}\|\sin\alpha$. The product of these two lengths is equal to $\|\mathbf{V} \times \mathbf{W}\|$ and gives the area of the parallelogram.*

We know that any nonzero result of the cross product must be perpendicular to the two vectors being multiplied together, but two possible directions satisfy this requirement. It turns out that the cross product follows a pattern called the *right-hand rule*. As shown in Figure 4.1.12, if the fingers of the right hand are aligned with a vector **V**, and the palm is facing in the direction of a vector **W**, then the thumb points along the direction of the cross product **V** × **W**.

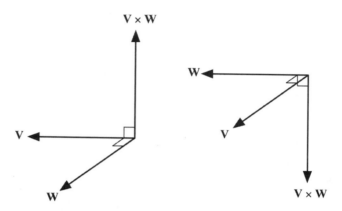

FIGURE 4.1.12   *The right-hand rule provides a way for determining in which direction the cross product points. When the vectors V and W are interchanged, their cross product is negated.*

The unit vectors $\hat{\mathbf{i}}$, $\hat{\mathbf{j}}$, and $\hat{\mathbf{k}}$, which point in the directions of the positive x-, y-, and z-axes, behave as follows. If we order the axes in a circular fashion so that $\hat{\mathbf{i}}$ precedes $\hat{\mathbf{j}}$, $\hat{\mathbf{j}}$ precedes $\hat{\mathbf{k}}$, and $\hat{\mathbf{k}}$ precedes $\hat{\mathbf{i}}$, the cross product of two of these vectors *in order* yields the third vector as:

$$\hat{\mathbf{i}} \times \hat{\mathbf{j}} = \hat{\mathbf{k}}$$
$$\hat{\mathbf{j}} \times \hat{\mathbf{k}} = \hat{\mathbf{i}}$$
$$\hat{\mathbf{k}} \times \hat{\mathbf{i}} = \hat{\mathbf{j}}$$

$$(4.1.66)$$

The cross product of two of the vectors *in reverse order* yields the negation of the third vector as:

$$\hat{\mathbf{j}} \times \hat{\mathbf{i}} = -\hat{\mathbf{k}}$$
$$\hat{\mathbf{k}} \times \hat{\mathbf{j}} = -\hat{\mathbf{i}}$$
$$\hat{\mathbf{i}} \times \hat{\mathbf{k}} = -\hat{\mathbf{j}}$$

$$(4.1.67)$$

In general, the cross product is not a commutative operation, but it is always true that reversing the order of the operands negates the result. That is,

$$\mathbf{W} \times \mathbf{V} = -\mathbf{V} \times \mathbf{W} \qquad (4.1.68)$$

For this reason, the cross product is referred to as an *anticommutative* operation. Additionally, it should be noted that the cross product is not an associative operation. For any three vectors $\mathbf{U}$, $\mathbf{V}$, and $\mathbf{W}$, it may be the case that $(\mathbf{U} \times \mathbf{V}) \times \mathbf{W} \neq \mathbf{U} \times (\mathbf{V} \times \mathbf{W})$.

Transformations

Game engines usually need to perform calculations involving an array of different types of objects such as geometrical models, light sources, and cameras. It is often convenient to perform these calculations in a coordinate system that is aligned to the object in a natural way. For example, a camera may possess a local coordinate system in which the origin coincides with the camera's position, one axis is aligned along the direction in which the camera is facing, and the other two axes are aligned to the viewer's horizontal and vertical directions. Since different objects can use different coordinate systems, a game engine needs to be able to transform vectors from one coordinate system to another.

Coordinate System Transformations

Suppose that the coordinate axes in three-dimensional coordinate system A correspond to the directions given by the vectors $\mathbf{R}$, $\mathbf{S}$, and $\mathbf{T}$ in coordinate system B. That is, the coordinate axes are different in coordinate system B, so even though the vector $\hat{\mathbf{i}}$ in system A and the vector $\mathbf{R}$ in system B point in the same direction, they have different x, y, and z coordinates. A vector $\mathbf{V}$ specified in the coordinates of system A is transformed into a vector $\mathbf{W}$ that has coordinates in system B by performing the matrix multiplication

$$\mathbf{W} = \begin{bmatrix} \mathbf{R} & \mathbf{S} & \mathbf{T} \end{bmatrix} \mathbf{V} = \begin{bmatrix} R_x & S_x & T_x \\ R_y & S_y & T_y \\ R_z & S_z & T_z \end{bmatrix} \begin{bmatrix} V_x \\ V_y \\ V_z \end{bmatrix} \qquad (4.1.69)$$

This operation simply replaces the vectors $\hat{\mathbf{i}}$, $\hat{\mathbf{j}}$, and $\hat{\mathbf{k}}$ with the vectors $\mathbf{R}$, $\mathbf{S}$, and $\mathbf{T}$. In coordinate system A, we can write any vector $\mathbf{V}$ as

$$\mathbf{V} = a\hat{\mathbf{i}} + b\hat{\mathbf{j}} + c\hat{\mathbf{k}} \qquad (4.1.70)$$

After transforming into coordinate system B, the vector $\mathbf{W}$ can be written as

$$\mathbf{W} = a\mathbf{R} + b\mathbf{S} + c\mathbf{T} \qquad (4.1.71)$$

We transform in the reverse direction from system B to system A by inverting Equation 4.1.69 to obtain the following:

$$\mathbf{V} = \begin{bmatrix} R_x & S_x & T_x \\ R_y & S_y & T_y \\ R_z & S_z & T_z \end{bmatrix}^{-1} \mathbf{W} \qquad (4.1.72)$$

A certain subset of invertible matrices satisfies the property that $\mathbf{M}^{-1} = \mathbf{M}^{\mathrm{T}}$. Such matrices are called *orthogonal*. If a matrix is orthogonal (which is often the case in computer graphics), its inverse is equal to its transpose, and the matrix that transforms vectors from system B to system A is the one whose rows are simply the vectors $\mathbf{R}$, $\mathbf{S}$, and $\mathbf{T}$. In this case, we can express the vector $\mathbf{V}$ as $\langle \mathbf{R} \cdot \mathbf{W}, \mathbf{S} \cdot \mathbf{W}, \mathbf{T} \cdot \mathbf{W} \rangle$.

Equation 4.1.69 can reorient the coordinate axes in any manner we wish, but it leaves the origin fixed. To move the origin, we need to incorporate an additional vector $\mathbf{D}$ that represents the difference between the origin in coordinate system A and coordinate system B. The general transformation from one three-dimensional system to another now becomes

$$\mathbf{W} = \begin{bmatrix} R_x & S_x & T_x \\ R_y & S_y & T_y \\ R_z & S_z & T_z \end{bmatrix} \begin{bmatrix} V_x \\ V_y \\ V_z \end{bmatrix} + \begin{bmatrix} D_x \\ D_y \\ D_z \end{bmatrix} \qquad (4.1.73)$$

Homogeneous Coordinates

There are two significant drawbacks to the form of Equation 4.1.73. The first is that the full transformation is represented by two different parts: the 3×3 matrix that reorients the coordinate axes, and the vector $\mathbf{D}$ that offsets the origin. The second drawback is that the full transformation cannot make a distinction between a vector $\mathbf{V}$ that represents a point in space and a vector $\mathbf{V}$ that represents a direction. In the case that $\mathbf{V}$ is a direction, we do not want to add the offset $\mathbf{D}$ because doing so changes the direction in which $\mathbf{V}$ points.

Fortunately, there is an elegant solution that allows us to represent the transformation in Equation 4.1.73 as a single matrix and to make a natural distinction between position vectors and direction vectors. Most 3D graphics systems in use today employ what are called *four-dimensional homogeneous coordinates*. Three-dimensional vectors are expressed in homogeneous coordinates by adding a fourth component labeled w. For vectors representing a direction, the w-coordinate is zero. A nonzero w-coordinate indicates that a vector represents a position instead of a direction. Normally, a position vector is given a w-coordinate of 1.

In homogeneous coordinates, the 3×3 matrix and offset vector in Equation 4.1.73 are combined into a single 4×4 matrix so that the transformation assumes the following form:

$$\mathbf{W} = \begin{bmatrix} R_x & S_x & T_x & D_x \\ R_y & S_y & T_y & D_y \\ R_z & S_z & T_z & D_z \\ 0 & 0 & 0 & 1 \end{bmatrix} \begin{bmatrix} V_x \\ V_y \\ V_z \\ V_w \end{bmatrix} \tag{4.1.74}$$

The w-coordinate of $\mathbf{V}$ determines whether the offset vector $\mathbf{D}$ takes part in the transformation because it is the coordinate by which each of the entries in the fourth column of the matrix is multiplied. If $V_w = 1$, the vector $\mathbf{D}$ is added to the transformed vector, but if $V_w = 0$, the vector $\mathbf{D}$ is effectively ignored.

It is possible for a vector $\mathbf{V}$ to have a w-coordinate that is neither 0 nor 1. Such a vector may be explicitly specified or may be produced by a 4×4 transformation matrix whose fourth row is not $\langle 0,0,0,1 \rangle$. The corresponding three-dimensional vector is always determined by dividing the x-, y-, and z-coordinates by the w-coordinate as follows:

$$\mathbf{V}_{3D} = \left\langle \frac{V_x}{V_w}, \frac{V_y}{V_w}, \frac{V_z}{V_w} \right\rangle \tag{4.1.75}$$

Thus, in homogeneous coordinates, the vectors $\langle V_x, V_y, V_z, V_w \rangle$ and $\langle aV_x, aV_y, aV_z, aV_w \rangle$ both represent the same point in three-dimensional space.

Common Transformations

Some common transformations, such as translations, scales, and rotations, have simple matrix representations. A translation simply moves the origin of the coordinate system without reorienting or stretching the axes in any way. As a 4×4 transformation matrix, a translation has the form

$$\mathbf{M}_{\text{translate}} = \begin{bmatrix} 1 & 0 & 0 & T_x \\ 0 & 1 & 0 & T_y \\ 0 & 0 & 1 & T_z \\ 0 & 0 & 0 & 1 \end{bmatrix} \tag{4.1.76}$$

where the vector $\mathbf{T}$ is the difference between the old origin and the new origin. A scale stretches or shrinks each of the coordinate axes and is represented by a matrix having the form

$$\mathbf{M}_{scale} = \begin{bmatrix} a & 0 & 0 & 0 \\ 0 & b & 0 & 0 \\ 0 & 0 & c & 0 \\ 0 & 0 & 0 & 1 \end{bmatrix} \tag{4.1.77}$$

The scalars a, b, and c are the factors by which each of the x-, y-, and z-axes are scaled, respectively. If all three scale factors are the same, the matrix $\mathbf{M}_{scale}$ is called a *uniform* scale; otherwise, it is a *nonuniform* scale.

For rotations, we first examine a general method for rotating a point about the origin in two dimensions. Let $\mathbf{P} = \langle x, y \rangle$ be a point lying in the x-y plane. As shown in Figure 4.1.13a, the point $\mathbf{P}$ is rotated counterclockwise through an angle of 90 degrees by exchanging its x- and y-coordinates and negating the new x-coordinate to construct the point $\mathbf{Q} = \langle -y, x \rangle$. The result of rotating $\mathbf{P}$ through any other angle can be expressed as a linear combination of the original $\mathbf{P}$ and its 90-degree rotation $\mathbf{Q}$. As illustrated by Figure 4.1.13b, the result $\mathbf{P}'$ of rotating the point $\mathbf{P}$ through an angle θ is given by

$$\mathbf{P}' = \mathbf{P}\cos\theta + \mathbf{Q}\sin\theta \tag{4.1.78}$$

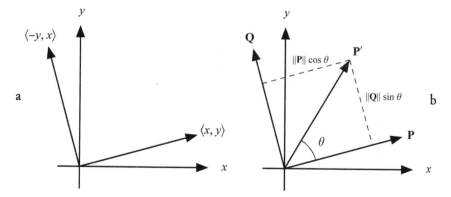

FIGURE 4.1.13   *(a) A point is rotated counterclockwise by 90 degrees in the x-y plane by exchanging its coordinates and negating the new x-coordinate. (b) The result $\mathbf{P}'$ of rotating the point through an arbitrary angle θ is expressed as a linear combination of the original point $\mathbf{P}$ and the 90-degree rotation $\mathbf{Q}$.*

Using the fact that $\mathbf{Q} = \langle -P_y, P_x \rangle$, the two components of $\mathbf{P}'$ can be written as

$$P'_x = P_x \cos\theta - P_y \sin\theta$$
$$P'_y = P_y \cos\theta + P_x \sin\theta \tag{4.1.79}$$

This can also be written as the equivalent matrix product

$$\mathbf{P'} = \begin{bmatrix} \cos\theta & -\sin\theta \\ \sin\theta & \cos\theta \end{bmatrix} \mathbf{P} \tag{4.1.80}$$

The rotation performed by the matrix in Equation 4.1.80 occurs in the x-y plane and is thus equivalent to a rotation in three dimensions about the z-axis. We can express this rotation using the following 4×4 transformation matrix:

$$\mathbf{M}_{z\text{-rotate}} = \begin{bmatrix} \cos\theta & -\sin\theta & 0 & 0 \\ \sin\theta & \cos\theta & 0 & 0 \\ 0 & 0 & 1 & 0 \\ 0 & 0 & 0 & 1 \end{bmatrix} \tag{4.1.81}$$

Rotations about the x- and y-axes have the following similar forms:

$$\mathbf{M}_{x\text{-rotate}} = \begin{bmatrix} 1 & 0 & 0 & 0 \\ 0 & \cos\theta & -\sin\theta & 0 \\ 0 & \sin\theta & \cos\theta & 0 \\ 0 & 0 & 0 & 1 \end{bmatrix} \tag{4.1.82}$$

$$\mathbf{M}_{y\text{-rotate}} = \begin{bmatrix} \cos\theta & 0 & \sin\theta & 0 \\ 0 & 1 & 0 & 0 \\ -\sin\theta & 0 & \cos\theta & 0 \\ 0 & 0 & 0 & 1 \end{bmatrix} \tag{4.1.83}$$

A rotation through the angle θ about an arbitrary axis $\mathbf{A}$ is given by the following transformation matrix, in which we have made the abbreviations $c = \cos\theta$ and $s = \sin\theta$. (For a derivation of this matrix, see [Lengyel04].)

$$\mathbf{M}_{\text{rotate}} = \begin{bmatrix} c+(1-c)A_x^2 & (1-c)A_xA_y - sA_z & (1-c)A_xA_z + sA_y & 0 \\ (1-c)A_xA_y + sA_z & c+(1-c)A_y^2 & (1-c)A_yA_z - sA_x & 0 \\ (1-c)A_xA_z - sA_y & (1-c)A_yA_z + sA_x & c+(1-c)A_z^2 & 0 \\ 0 & 0 & 0 & 1 \end{bmatrix} \tag{4.1.84}$$

Plugging in the values $\mathbf{A} = \langle 1,0,0 \rangle$, $\mathbf{A} = \langle 0,1,0 \rangle$, and $\mathbf{A} = \langle 0,0,1 \rangle$ brings us back to the matrices $\mathbf{M}_{x\text{-rotate}}$, $\mathbf{M}_{y\text{-rotate}}$, and $\mathbf{M}_{z\text{-rotate}}$, respectively.

Transforming Normal Vectors

In addition to its position in space, a vertex belonging to a polygonal model usually carries additional information about how it fits into the surrounding surface. In particular, a vertex may have a tangent vector and a normal vector associated with it that represents a direction parallel to the surface and a direction perpendicular to the surface, respectively. When we transform a model, we often need to transform not only the vertex positions, but the tangent and normal vectors as well.

A tangent vector can usually be calculated by taking the difference between one vertex and another, and thus we would expect that a transformed tangent vector could be expressed as the difference between two transformed points. If $\mathbf{M}$ is a matrix with which we transform a vertex position, the same matrix $\mathbf{M}$ can be used to correctly transform the tangent vector at that vertex. Some care must be taken when transforming normal vectors, however. Figure 4.1.14 shows what can happen when a nonorthogonal matrix $\mathbf{M}$, such as a nonuniform scale, is used to transform a normal vector. The transformed normal can often end up pointing in a direction that is no longer perpendicular to the transformed surface.

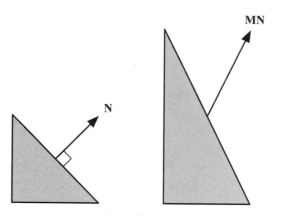

FIGURE 4.1.14   *Transforming a normal vector using a nonorthogonal matrix can cause the vector to no longer be perpendicular to the transformed surface.*

Since tangents and normals are perpendicular, the tangent vector $\mathbf{T}$ and the normal vector $\mathbf{N}$ associated with a vertex must satisfy the equation $\mathbf{N} \cdot \mathbf{T} = 0$. We must also require that this equation be satisfied by the transformed tangent vector $\mathbf{T}'$ and the transformed normal vector $\mathbf{N}'$. Given a transformation matrix $\mathbf{M}$, we know that $\mathbf{T}' = \mathbf{MT}$. We would like to find the transformation matrix $\mathbf{G}$ with which the vector $\mathbf{N}$ should be transformed so that

$$\mathbf{N}' \cdot \mathbf{T}' = (\mathbf{GN}) \cdot (\mathbf{MT}) = 0 \qquad (4.1.85)$$

Recall that the dot product $\mathbf{V} \cdot \mathbf{W}$ can also be written as the matrix product $\mathbf{V}^{\mathrm{T}}\mathbf{W}$. Applying this to Equation 4.1.85, we can write

$$(\mathbf{GN}) \cdot (\mathbf{MT}) = (\mathbf{GN})^{\mathrm{T}}(\mathbf{MT})$$
$$= \mathbf{N}^{\mathrm{T}}\mathbf{G}^{\mathrm{T}}\mathbf{MT} \qquad (4.1.86)$$

Since $\mathbf{N}^{\mathrm{T}}\mathbf{T} = 0$, the equation $\mathbf{N}^{\mathrm{T}}\mathbf{G}^{\mathrm{T}}\mathbf{MT} = 0$ is satisfied if $\mathbf{G}^{\mathrm{T}}\mathbf{M} = \mathbf{I}$. We therefore conclude that $\mathbf{G} = (\mathbf{M}^{-1})^{\mathrm{T}}$. This tells us that a normal vector is correctly transformed using the *inverse transpose* of the matrix used to transform points. Vectors that must be transformed in this way are called *covariant* vectors, and vectors that are transformed in the ordinary fashion using the matrix $\mathbf{M}$ (such as points and tangent vectors) are called *contravariant* vectors.

If the matrix $\mathbf{M}$ is orthogonal, then $\mathbf{M}^{-1} = \mathbf{M}^{\mathrm{T}}$, and thus $(\mathbf{M}^{-1})^{\mathrm{T}} = \mathbf{M}$. Therefore, the inverse transpose operation required to transform normal vectors can be avoided when $\mathbf{M}$ is known to be orthogonal, as is the case when $\mathbf{M}$ is equal to one of the rotation matrices discussed earlier in this section.

Geometry

Games nearly always need to provide some kind of virtual environment in which all of the action occurs. This environment and the objects that interact with it are represented inside the computer as geometrical structures. Game engines invariably need to be able to mathematically manipulate these structures as well as create additional geometrical objects during gameplay. In this section, we examine the basic mathematical properties of lines and planes in three-dimensional space because they are fundamental geometrical entities upon which many game engine calculations are based.

Lines

In three-dimensional space, a line is usually described by two quantities: any point $\mathbf{S}$ lying on the line and the direction $\mathbf{V}$ along which the line runs. The set of all points belonging to the line is then generated by the parametric function

$$\mathbf{P}(t) = \mathbf{S} + t\mathbf{V} \qquad (4.1.87)$$

A line can be thought of as the path traced out by starting at the point $\mathbf{S}$ and traveling along the direction $\mathbf{V}$ over time t. (Allowing t to be negative enables us to travel both directions.)

Two lines $\mathbf{S}_1 + t\mathbf{V}_1$ and $\mathbf{S}_2 + t\mathbf{V}_2$ are parallel if their directions $\mathbf{V}_1$ and $\mathbf{V}_2$ are parallel (i.e., $\mathbf{V}_1 = a\mathbf{V}_2$ for some scalar a). In three dimensions, lines that are not parallel do not necessarily intersect, as they must in two dimensions. Nonparallel lines that do not intersect are called *skew* lines.

Planes

Given a 3D point **P** and a normal vector **N**, the plane passing through the point **P** and perpendicular to the direction **N** can be defined as the set of points **Q** such that $\mathbf{N} \cdot (\mathbf{Q} - \mathbf{P}) = 0$. As shown in Figure 4.1.15, this is the set of points whose difference with **P** is perpendicular to the normal direction **N**. The equation for a plane is commonly written as

$$Ax + By + Cz + D = 0, \tag{4.1.88}$$

where A, B, and C are the x-, y-, and z-components of the normal vector **N**, and $D = -\mathbf{N} \cdot \mathbf{P}$. As shown in Figure 4.1.16, the value $|D|/\|\mathbf{N}\|$ is the distance by which the plane is offset from a parallel plane that passes through the origin.

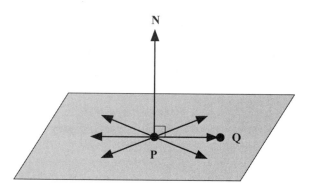

FIGURE 4.1.15   *A plane is defined by the set of points Q whose difference with a point P, known to lie in the plane, is perpendicular to the normal direction N.*

The normal vector **N** is often normalized to unit length because in that case the equation

$$d = \mathbf{N} \cdot \mathbf{Q} + D \tag{4.1.89}$$

gives the signed distance from the plane to an arbitrary point **Q**. If $d = 0$, then the point **Q** lies in the plane. If $d > 0$, we say that the point **Q** lies on the positive side of the plane since **Q** would be on the side in which the normal vector points. Otherwise, if $d < 0$, we say that the point **Q** lies on the negative side of the plane.

It is convenient to represent a plane using a four-dimensional vector. The shorthand notation $\langle \mathbf{N}, D \rangle$ is used to denote the plane consisting of points **Q** satisfying $\mathbf{N} \cdot \mathbf{Q} + D = 0$. If we treat our three-dimensional points instead as four-dimensional homogeneous points having a w-coordinate of 1, Equation 4.1.89 can be rewritten as $d = \mathbf{L} \cdot \mathbf{Q}$, where $\mathbf{L} = \langle \mathbf{N}, D \rangle$. A point **Q** lies in the plane if $\mathbf{L} \cdot \mathbf{Q} = 0$.

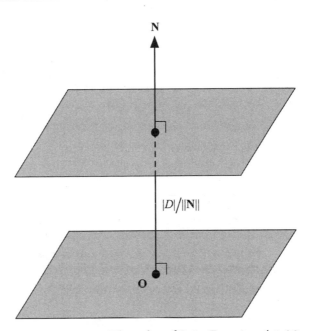

FIGURE 4.1.16 *The value of D in Equation 4.1.88 is proportional to the perpendicular distance from the origin to the plane.*

Like normal vectors, planes are covariant vectors that must be transformed from one coordinate system to another using the inverse transpose of the matrix ordinarily used to transform points. If the matrix $\mathbf{M}$ is the 4×4 transformation matrix used to transform points, a plane $\mathbf{L}$ is transformed by $\mathbf{M}$ using the formula

$$\mathbf{L}' = \left(\mathbf{M}^{-1}\right)^{\mathrm{T}} \mathbf{L} \qquad (4.1.90)$$

Distance from a Point to a Line

The distance d from a point $\mathbf{P}$ to a line defined by the endpoint $\mathbf{S}$ and the direction V can be found by calculating the magnitude of the component of $\mathbf{P} - \mathbf{S}$ that is perpendicular to the line, as shown in Figure 4.1.17.

Using the Pythagorean Theorem, the squared distance between the point $\mathbf{P}$ and the line can be obtained by subtracting the square of the projection of $\mathbf{P} - \mathbf{S}$ onto the direction $\mathbf{V}$ from the square of $\mathbf{P} - \mathbf{S}$. This gives us

$$d^2 = \left(\mathbf{P} - \mathbf{S}\right)^2 - \left[\operatorname{proj}_{\mathbf{v}}\left(\mathbf{P} - \mathbf{S}\right)\right]^2$$

$$= \left(\mathbf{P} - \mathbf{S}\right)^2 - \left[\frac{\left(\mathbf{P} - \mathbf{S}\right) \cdot \mathbf{V}}{V^2} \mathbf{V}\right]^2 \qquad (4.1.91)$$

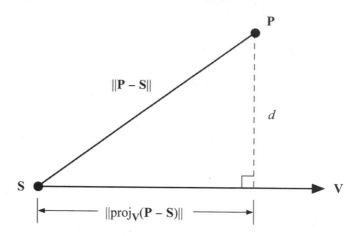

FIGURE 4.1.17   *The distance d from a point* **P** *to the line* **S** $+ t$**V** *is found by calculating the length of the perpendicular component of* **P** $-$ **S** *with respect to the line.*

Simplifying a bit and taking the square root gives us the distance d that we desire:

$$d = \sqrt{(\mathbf{P}-\mathbf{S})^2 - \frac{[(\mathbf{P}-\mathbf{S})\cdot\mathbf{V}]^2}{V^2}}$$

(4.1.92)

If the vector **V** is normalized, the division by V^2 can be removed.

Intersection of a Line and a Plane

Let $\mathbf{P}(t) = \mathbf{S} + t\mathbf{V}$ represent a line containing the point **S** and running along the direction **V**, and let $\hat{\mathbf{j}}$ be a plane with normal direction **N**. For any point **P** lying in the plane **L**, we must have $\mathbf{L}\cdot\mathbf{P}=0$, so to find the point at which the line $\mathbf{P}(t)$ intersects the plane, we simply need to solve the equation $\mathbf{L}\cdot\mathbf{P}(t)=0$ for t and plug it back into the equation for the line. The value of t is given by

$$t = -\frac{\mathbf{L}\cdot\mathbf{S}}{\mathbf{L}\cdot\mathbf{V}}$$

(4.1.93)

We must be careful when evaluating four-dimensional dot products in this expression. Since **S** represents a point, its w-coordinate is 1, and since **V** represents a direction, its w-coordinate is 0. Thus, Equation 4.1.93 should be expanded into the following form:

$$t = -\frac{L_x S_x + L_y S_y + L_z S_z + L_w}{L_x V_x + L_y V_y + L_z V_z}$$

(4.1.94)

If $\mathbf{L}\cdot\mathbf{V}=0$, the line is parallel to the plane, and no intersection occurs. Otherwise, the point of intersection is given by

$$\mathbf{P}(t)=\mathbf{S}-\frac{\mathbf{L}\cdot\mathbf{S}}{\mathbf{L}\cdot\mathbf{V}}\mathbf{V}\qquad\qquad(4.1.95)$$

Summary

This chapter introduced several mathematical aspects of computer game development, including trigonometry, vector and matrix arithmetic, coordinate transformations, and basic three-dimensional geometry. These concepts represent the foundations of many more advanced mathematical applications in game programming. Because they are so heavily relied upon in modern game making, a familiarity with such concepts can benefit both programmers and all members of a game development team.

Exercises

1. Convert the following radian angle measurements to degrees: (a) $7\pi/8$, (b) $3\pi/2$, (c) $\pi/10$, (d) 4π, (e) $7\pi/6$.

2. Convert the following degree angle measurements to radians: (a) $135°$, (b) $18°$, (c) $330°$, (d) $-315°$, (e) $3°$.

3. Calculate the measurements of the acute angles of a right triangle whose side lengths are 3, 4, and 5.

4. Let $\mathbf{V}=\langle 2,2,1\rangle$ and $\mathbf{W}=\langle 1,-2,0\rangle$. Calculate (a) $\mathbf{V}\cdot\mathbf{W}$, (b) $\mathbf{V}\times\mathbf{W}$, and (c) $\text{proj}_{\mathbf{V}}\,\mathbf{W}$.

5. Find the planar angle between the vectors $\mathbf{V}=\langle 0,1,2\rangle$ and $\mathbf{W}=\langle -1,2,0\rangle$.

6. Show that $\|a\mathbf{V}\|=a\|\mathbf{V}\|$ for an n-dimensional vector $\mathbf{V}$ and a scalar a.

7. Calculate the area of the triangle whose vertices lie at the points $\langle 2,3,4\rangle$, $\langle -1,3,5\rangle$, and $\langle 8,-7,1\rangle$.

8. Calculate the determinants of the following matrices.

   (a) $\begin{bmatrix} 2 & 7 \\ -3 & \frac{1}{2} \end{bmatrix}$
   (b) $\begin{bmatrix} 0 & 0 & 1 \\ 0 & 1 & 0 \\ 1 & 0 & 0 \end{bmatrix}$
   (c) $\begin{bmatrix} \frac{1}{2} & -\frac{\sqrt{3}}{2} & 0 \\ \frac{\sqrt{3}}{2} & \frac{1}{2} & 0 \\ 0 & 0 & 1 \end{bmatrix}$

9. Show that the set of all 4×4 matrices whose fourth row is $\langle 0,0,0,1\rangle$ is closed under matrix multiplication. That is, show that the product of any two such matrices is also a matrix whose fourth row is $\langle 0,0,0,1\rangle$.

10. Construct 4×4 matrices that represent a rotation of $\pi/4$ radians about (a) the x-axis, (b) the y-axis, (c) the z-axis, and (d) the axis $\mathbf{A} = \left\langle \frac{\sqrt{2}}{2}, \frac{\sqrt{2}}{2}, 0 \right\rangle$.

11. Determine a plane $\mathbf{L} = \langle \mathbf{N}, D \rangle$ that contains the three points $\langle 1,2,0 \rangle$, $\langle 2,0,-1 \rangle$, and $\langle 3,-2,1 \rangle$.

12. Classify the following points with respect to the plane $\mathbf{L} = \langle 1,1,0,5 \rangle$ and tell whether each lies on the positive side of the plane, the negative side of the plane, or in the plane: (a) $\langle 1,2,3 \rangle$, (b) $\langle -5,0,8 \rangle$, (c) $\langle 6,-12,6 \rangle$.

13. Let $\mathbf{S} = \langle 2,2,2 \rangle$ and $\mathbf{V} = \langle -1,2,3 \rangle$. Calculate the perpendicular distance between the line $\mathbf{P}(t) = \mathbf{S} + t\mathbf{V}$ and the point $\mathbf{Q} = \langle 3,4,5 \rangle$.

14. Let $\mathbf{S} = \langle 1,0,3 \rangle$ and $\mathbf{V} = \langle 2,1,-1 \rangle$. Find the point at which the line $\mathbf{P}(t) = \mathbf{S} + t\mathbf{V}$ intersects the plane $\mathbf{L} = \langle 1,1,0,5 \rangle$.

References

[Lengyel04] Lengyel, Eric, *Mathematics for 3D Game Programming and Computer Graphics,* 2nd ed., Charles River Media, 2004.

[Press92] Press, William H., et al, *Numerical Recipes in C,* 2nd ed., Cambridge University Press, 1992.

4.2 Collision Detection and Resolution

Overview

In the virtual world of a game, physical simulation must be painstakingly added through programming. Initially there is no gravity, no inertia, no friction, and most disconcerting, no concept of solidness. Objects will pass through each other without any hesitation, as if they were ghosts drifting through walls. Solidness is the property that is missing, and it is implemented through *collision detection* and *collision resolution*.

Collision detection will determine if and when two objects collide. Since it is not enough to merely detect the collision, collision resolution will figure out where each object should be once a collision is detected. Effectively, collision detection and resolution together will make objects solid so that they will never pass through each other. Calculating how objects move after the collision is the job of the physics, which is described in Chapter 4.3, "Real-Time Game Physics."

Collision Detection

Determining if and when two objects collide is not as simple as it might initially seem. Some objects can move very fast (e.g., bullets), and some objects can have very complicated geometry (e.g., characters). In addition, collision detection is very costly because, fundamentally, every object should be tested against every other object for a possible collision, which is $O(n^2)$ time complexity (in that for n objects, the amount of work is $n*(n-1)$, which is proportional n^2). Because of these difficulties, many strategies have been devised to perform collision detection in real-time during gameplay.

For detecting a collision, there are basically two techniques that can be employed: *overlap testing* and *intersection testing*. The main difference is that overlap testing detects whether a collision has already occurred, and intersection testing predicts if a collision will occur in the future.

Overlap Testing

Overlap testing is the most common technique, yet exhibits the most error. The idea is that at every simulation step, each pair of objects will be tested to determine if they overlap with each other. If two objects overlap, they are in collision. This is known as a *discrete test* since only one particular point in time is being tested.

Overlap testing is actually a containment problem. The goal is to test if any part of an object is inside any part of another object. This can be simple with volumes, such as spheres and boxes, but with polygons, it can be more difficult. One imperfect technique for polygons is to test whether the vertices of one object lie in the area of the other object, and vice versa. At some point, the volume of polygonal objects must be approximated by simpler geometric shapes to make the problem tractable in real time.

Results

If a collision is detected, two helpful results can be calculated. The first is the time the collision took place. The second is the collision normal vector. This normal vector is needed to later compute the collision response that prevents the objects from further interpenetrating. Depending on the technique used, the accuracy of the results may not be important as long as the objects are separated so that a collision doesn't occur again on the next simulation step.

To determine exactly when the collision took place, the two objects must be moved back in time to the last simulation step when they were not in collision. Using a technique called *bisection*, the simulation should be moved forward or backward by half of the last simulation step, in order to converge on the exact time of collision. For example, once the collision is detected, the simulation is moved back to the last simulation time. Then, the simulation should be moved forward by half. If that is in collision, the simulation should be backed up and moved forward by one-quarter. If that's not in collision, the simulation should be moved forward by one-eighth, and so on.

This is demonstrated in Figure 4.2.1. In practice, a reasonably close solution will be found within five iterations. By calculating the exact time before collision, we know the correct, nonoverlapping positions where the objects should be placed for collision resolution.

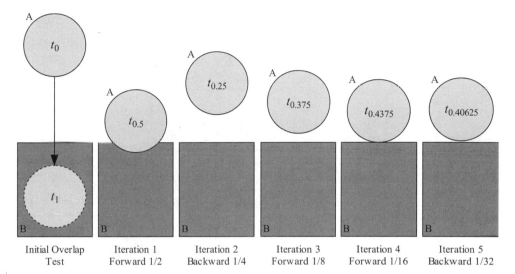

| Initial Overlap Test | Iteration 1 Forward 1/2 | Iteration 2 Backward 1/4 | Iteration 3 Forward 1/8 | Iteration 4 Forward 1/16 | Iteration 5 Backward 1/32 |

FIGURE 4.2.1   *Using overlap testing, it has been detected that the moving object A collides with the stationary object B at time t_1. To find the exact time before intersection, five iterations of bisection are performed in order to converge on the time right before collision.*

Limitations of Overlap Testing

Overlap testing seems reasonable, but it fails horribly when objects move a little too fast. For example, imagine that a bullet is fired at a glass window. We want to detect this collision, but since the bullet is small and traveling very fast, it is unlikely the bullet will ever overlap the thin window during one of the simulation steps. The result is that the bullet will fly right through the window without a collision being detected, as shown in Figure 4.2.2.

For overlap testing to always work, the speed of the fastest object in the scene multiplied by the time step must be less than the size of the smallest collidable object in the scene. This implies a design constraint on the game to keep objects from moving too fast relative to the size of other objects. Optionally, the simulation step size can be reduced to satisfy the constraint, but this might result in stepping the simulation dozens or hundreds of times a frame. Since both of these options might be undesirable, there is an alternative collision detection technique called "intersection testing."

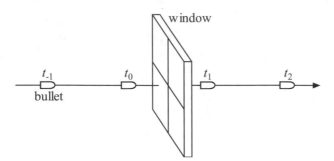

FIGURE 4.2.2   *Overlap testing is problematic for small, fast-moving objects such as bullets.*

Intersection Testing

The defining characteristic of intersection testing is that it predicts future collisions before they happen. They are predicted and thus the simulation can be carefully moved forward to the time of impact, often more accurately and efficiently than overlap testing. For example, if two objects will collide in $1/60^{th}$ of a second and the simulation step size is $1/30^{th}$ of a second, the simulation can be moved forward by $1/60^{th}$ of a second (up to the time of collision), the collision can be resolved, and then the remaining $1/60^{th}$ of a second can be simulated. If multiple collisions occur within a simulation step, each must be resolved with the clock advancing in time for each of those intervals.

If overlap testing can be viewed as a containment problem, intersection testing can be viewed as a visibility problem. Intersection testing must test the geometry of an object *swept* in the direction of travel against other swept geometry. Whatever geometry the object is composed of, it must be extruded over the distance of travel during the simulation step and tested against all other extruded geometry. For example, an extruded sphere becomes a capsule shape (a sphere on each end of a cylinder), as shown in Figure 4.2.3.

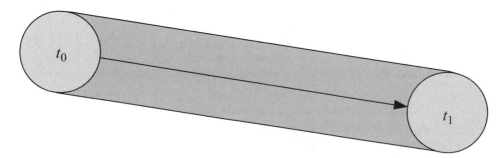

FIGURE 4.2.3   *A sphere extruded over the distance of travel becomes a capsule shape, between the simulation time t_0 and t_1.*

In the specialized case of a sphere-sphere collision, there is a direct formula that will provide the exact time of impact, as shown in Equations 4.2.1 and 4.2.2 [Lengyel04]. The sphere of radius r_P moving from the point $\mathbf{P}_1$ at time $t=0$ to the point $\mathbf{P}_2$ at time $t=1$ collides at time t with another sphere of radius r_Q moving from the point $\mathbf{Q}_1$ to the point $\mathbf{Q}_2$ (see Figure 4.2.4).

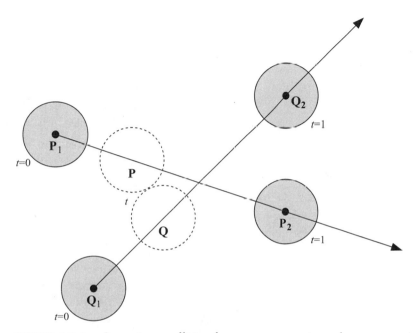

FIGURE 4.2.4 *Detecting a collision between two moving spheres.*

A collision occurs if t falls into the interval $(0,1)$. However, two special cases also indicate no collision. If the value inside the radical is negative, there is no collision. Additionally, in the case that $B^2 = 0$, either both spheres are stationary or both are traveling in the same direction at the same speed and cannot collide.

(As a reminder from Chapter 4.1, "Mathematical Concepts," bolded variables are vectors and italicized variables are scalars. For example, $\mathbf{A} \cdot \mathbf{B}$ is the dot product of the vectors $\mathbf{A}$ and $\mathbf{B}$, while B^2 is the squared magnitude of vector $\mathbf{B}$.)

$$t = \frac{-\left(\mathbf{A} \cdot \mathbf{B}\right) - \sqrt{\left(\mathbf{A} \cdot \mathbf{B}\right)^2 - B^2\left(A^2 - \left(r_p + r_Q\right)^2\right)}}{B^2}, \tag{4.2.1}$$

where

$$\mathbf{A} = \mathbf{P}_1 - \mathbf{Q}_1$$
$$\mathbf{B} = \left(\mathbf{P}_2 - \mathbf{P}_1\right) - \left(\mathbf{Q}_2 - \mathbf{Q}_1\right) \qquad (4.2.2)$$

As a simpler test of whether the spheres collide at all, Equation 4.2.3 can be used to determine the smallest distance ever separating the centers of the two spheres.

$$d^2 = A^2 - \frac{\left(\mathbf{A} \cdot \mathbf{B}\right)^2}{B^2} \qquad (4.2.3)$$

If $d^2 > \left(r_P + r_Q\right)^2$, we can quickly know if there is a collision.

Finally, note that there is a numerically stable method to solve the quadratic equation detailed in the book *Numerical Recipes in C* (available for free on the Internet) [Press92].

Limitations of Intersection Testing

Initially, it appears that intersection testing might not have any design constraints other than striving to use simple collision detection geometry. However, one important problem arises in networked games. The issue is that future predictions rely on knowing the exact state of the world at the present time. Due to packet latency in a networked game, the current state is not always coherent, and erroneous collisions might result. Therefore, predictive methods aren't very compatible with networked games because it isn't efficient to store enough history to deal with such changes and, in practice, running clocks backward to repair coherency issues rarely works well.

One more potential problem for intersection testing is that it assumes a constant velocity and zero acceleration over the simulation step. This might have implications for the physics model or the choice of integrator, as the predictor must match their behavior for the approach to work.

Dealing with Complexity

Regardless of which technique is used, overlap testing or intersection testing, there are two significant challenges in performing these calculations in real time. The first problem is that testing complex geometry for containment or visibility is complicated and computationally costly. The potential solution is to substitute simpler geometry, and initially test rough approximations of each object. The second problem is that a naïve collision-detection implementation is $O(n^2)$ time complexity, since every object must be tested with every other object. Fortunately, there are techniques that can achieve nearly linear time complexity in the number of objects. We will take each of these problems in turn.

Simplified Geometry

The first way of dealing with complexity is to simplify the geometry. If a complex object can be roughly approximated with a simpler shape, testing will be cheaper. For example, Figure 4.2.5 shows how a spiky object can be simplified as an ellipsoid. Note that the ellipsoid does not encompass the object; it just approximates its shape. Using this rough approximation, some parts of the object might come into collision without being able to detect it, but for a given game, this might be acceptable.

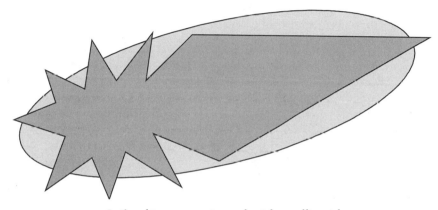

FIGURE 4.2.5 *Spiky object approximated with an ellipsoid.*

Minkowski Sum

In an effort to simplify geometry for cheaper overlap and intersection testing, there is a powerful geometric operation called the *Minkowski sum* [VanDerBergen03]. By taking the Minkowski sum of two convex volumes and creating a new volume, it is possible to determine overlap by testing if a single point is within this new volume. Equation 4.2.4 shows the Minkowski sum.

$$X \oplus Y = \{A + B : A \in X \text{ and } B \in Y\} \tag{4.2.4}$$

The Minkowski sum of X and Y can be created by sweeping the origin of X over all points within Y. This can best be visualized in Figure 4.2.6. If one convex volume is a circle and the other is a square, the Minkowski sum appears to be a "bloated" square.

Once the new volume is created, we can determine overlap by taking the origin of the sphere and testing if it is within the new volume. If it is, the sphere is in collision with the box. To perform the intersection test, the point becomes a line, going from the center of the sphere at time t_0 to the center of the sphere at time t_1. We then test this line to see if it intersects with the new volume, as shown on the right side of Figure 4.2.7.

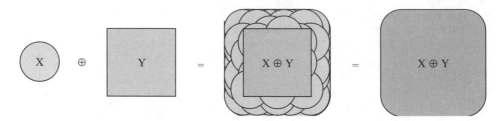

FIGURE 4.2.6   *The Minkowski sum of a circle and a square.*

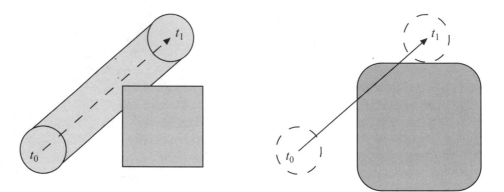

FIGURE 4.2.7   *Performing an intersection test as a sphere moves during the simulation step. On the left, the swept sphere is tested against a stationary box. On the right, the line from the center of the sphere at t_0 to the center of the sphere at t_1 is tested against the Minkowski sum of the sphere and box.*

In the case that all moving objects in a game can be approximated by their bounding spheres, this method can serve as the main collision test for objects with a static polygonal environment [Lengyel04]. Once these bounding volumes are determined to be in collision, a secondary test can be activated on more detailed geometry.

Bounding Volumes

Containment and visibility testing can be costly if the geometry is complex. In modern 3D games, each game object is constructed with hundreds or thousands of polygons. Consequently, an object's volume is defined by these polygons, but testing this complex volume is too expensive in most cases. The solution is to use bounding volumes when approximate collision detection suffices, or use increasingly complex bounding volumes when accuracy matters.

A *bounding volume* is a simple geometric shape, like a sphere, that fully encapsulates an object. In this way, the bounding volume is an approximation of the object's shape. The advantage is that if there is no collision with the bounding volume, it is known that there is no collision with the object. Since the test with the bounding volume is cheaper, and since most objects are not in collision, many potential collisions can be dismissed with little computational work.

If the bounding volumes of two objects collide, this indicates that there *could* be a collision. If the bounding volumes are very good approximations of the objects, this might suffice for determining that the objects collided. Otherwise, more detailed tests can be performed on tighter fitting bounding volumes until you get down to the level of testing individual polygons.

The simplest bounding volume is a sphere. What makes spheres convenient is that they are represented by a position and a radius, with no need for an orientation. This makes containment and visibility calculations particularly simple to perform. For example, two spheres overlap each other if the distance between their centers is less than the sum of their radii. In the case of visibility, an extruded sphere is a capsule, as mentioned before. A capsule is composed of two spheres and one cylinder, so each of these objects can be tested against the other extruded objects to determine overlap.

The next most common bounding volume is a box. There are two types: an axis-aligned bounding box (AABB) and an oriented bounding box (OBB). An AABB is built so that the faces line up with the three axes. This restriction usually results in a loose fit around an object, but the resulting tests against the box are simplified and cheaper to perform. An OBB is a tighter fitting box that is oriented in a manner to best encapsulate the object. Figure 4.2.8 shows examples of each.

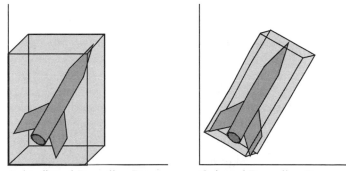

Axis-aligned Bounding Box   Oriented Bounding Box

FIGURE 4.2.8 *An axis-aligned bounding box and an oriented bounding box.*

If an object is complex, it is often possible to fit several bounding volumes around its unique parts. For example, a character model might have individual OBBs around its arms, torso, and legs, while its head might be encapsulated by a sphere. In addition, there might be several levels of bounding volumes. For example, the character model with multiple OBBs and spheres around its parts might have a higher level bounding volume of a single sphere around the entire character. Therefore, the first collision test is with the large sphere, and if that indicates a collision, the individual bounding volumes can be tested next.

Achieving O(*n*) Time Complexity

Collision detection can be fairly complex simply because every object must be checked against every other object. One solution to this $O(n^2)$ time complexity is to partition space. Figure 4.2.9 shows an example. If there are 15 objects and the world is partitioned with a simple grid, each object must only be tested against objects in the same or neighboring grid cells.

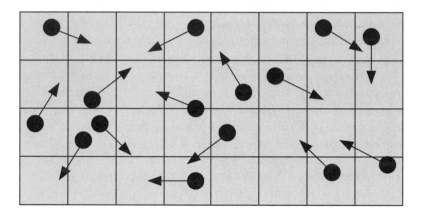

FIGURE 4.2.9   *Partitioning space with a simple grid.*

While this seems to have greatly reduced the complexity, there are some problems. First, what if objects vary in size and don't fit inside a single grid cell? In this case, the grid cell size might need to be increased or more grid cells "further out" must be tested. A second problem is if all of the objects move into the same grid cell, then the time complexity has reverted back to $O(n^2)$, since each object must be tested against all others. Depending on the game, this worst-case condition might not be probable or even possible.

If there are *N* collidable objects, a 2D grid will need to be at least $\sqrt{N} \times \sqrt{N}$ in size, and a 3D grid will need to be at least $\sqrt[3]{N} \times \sqrt[3]{N} \times \sqrt[3]{N}$. This will on average result in one object per grid cell, which should support linear time complexity (on average).

Plane Sweep

The *plane sweep* algorithm is an alternative method for reducing the time complexity of collision detection between objects. This method leverages the temporal coherence of objects to roughly stay in the same location from frame to frame, thus reducing the problem to linear $O(n)$ time complexity.

The idea is to record the bounds of every object on each of the three axes, as illustrated in two dimensions in Figure 4.2.10. Any objects that have overlapping bounds in all axes should be examined more closely for a collision. However, the time-consuming aspect of this algorithm is collecting and then sorting the bounds on each axis every frame. The best sorting algorithm, *quicksort*, will sort a list in $O(n\log(n))$ time, but it turns out we can do much better. Since objects display coherence from frame to frame, we can sort each axis boundary list once, and then use *bubblesort* to quickly repair any of the bounds that became slightly out of order during the last frame. The result is nearly linear time collision detection.

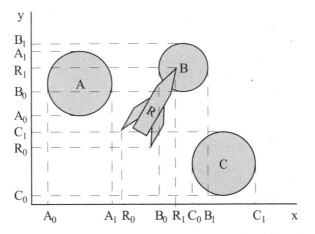

FIGURE 4.2.10 *Marking boundaries of objects for the plane sweep algorithm. In this example, the rocket R and object B are the only two objects whose boundaries overlap in both axes, indicating they might be in collision.*

Terrain Collision Detection

Collision detection with terrain is often a special case. Particular objects, like characters, must usually stay in contact with the terrain, so detecting the collision of each foot with the ground is very important. However, there are many opportunities to simplify the problem.

First, let's start with a flat plane as the ground. This is the simplest type of terrain, since it is defined by a single y height coordinate. If the character is standing, the bottom of each foot should rest at the terrain's y coordinate. If the character jumps into the air and falls to the ground, the character will hit the ground when his foot attempts to go below the terrain height, thus piercing the terrain. If it does go below, the foot is in collision with the terrain and should be placed at the terrain height.

In most games, the terrain is defined as a polygonal mesh, sometimes represented as a *height field*. A height field is a uniform triangle mesh where the x- and z- coordinates of each vertex are fixed in a grid, but the y-(height) coordinate of each vertex can vary, thus creating 3D terrain in a simple manner. Figure 4.2.11 shows an example of a height field.

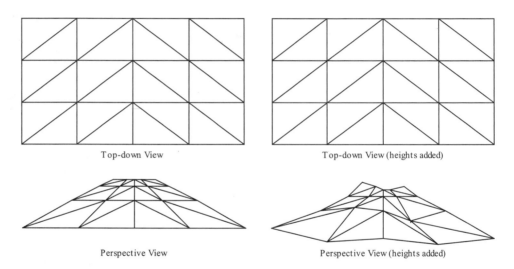

Top-down View   Top-down View (heights added)

Perspective View   Perspective View (heights added)

FIGURE 4.2.11   *A height field before and after the heights have been added. Notice how the surface is essentially 2D. Also, notice how it is not possible to represent vertical walls, overhanging ledges, or caves with this representation.*

In the case of a height field, it is fairly trivial to determine which triangle the character is standing on, since it is essentially a 2D problem. First, we must represent the colliding object with a single point **Q** that represents the point of the object that should rest on the terrain. For a character's foot, this might be the heel or tip of the foot. We then treat the terrain mesh as a 2D planar mesh and use the nature of the 2D uniform grid (uniformly spaced rows and columns) to locate the exact rectangular cell that contains point **Q**.

Once we have identified the rectangular cell, we must determine which triangle contains point **Q**. The point can be on one of two triangles depending on the triangulation, but a simple comparison with the dividing line can give us the exact triangle. This is shown in Figure 4.2.12.

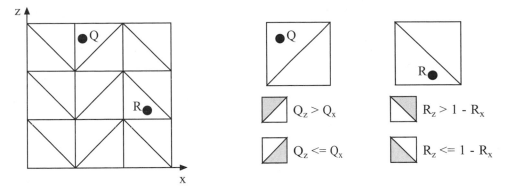

FIGURE 4.2.12 *Finding the colliding triangle on a height field.*

With the triangle known, the height inside the triangle at the point $\mathbf{Q}$ must be found. This can be done by creating the plane equation for the triangle, plugging in the x- and z-components of point $\mathbf{Q}$ and solving for y. Let's begin with the plane equation

$$Ax + By + Cz + D = 0 \qquad (4.2.5)$$

where A, B, and C are the x-, y-, and z-components of the plane's normal vector $\mathbf{N}$, $D = -\mathbf{N} \cdot \mathbf{P}_0$, and $\mathbf{P}_0$ is one of the triangle's vertices. This gives us

$$\mathbf{N}_x(x) + \mathbf{N}_y(y) + \mathbf{N}_z(z) + \left(-\mathbf{N} \cdot \mathbf{P}_0\right) = 0 \qquad (4.2.6)$$

The normal $\mathbf{N}$ of the triangle can be constructed by taking the cross product of two sides, as follows:

$$\mathbf{N} = \left(\mathbf{P}_1 - \mathbf{P}_0\right) \times \left(\mathbf{P}_2 - \mathbf{P}_0\right) \qquad (4.2.7)$$

Given Equation 4.2.6, we can solve for y and insert the x- and z-components of point $\mathbf{Q}$, obtaining the final equation for the height of point $\mathbf{Q}$ within the triangle,

$$\mathbf{Q}_y = \frac{-\mathbf{N}_x \mathbf{Q}_x - \mathbf{N}_z \mathbf{Q}_z + \left(\mathbf{N} \cdot \mathbf{P}_0\right)}{\mathbf{N}_y} \qquad (4.2.8)$$

Triangulated Irregular Networks (TINs)

If the terrain is a *nonuniform* polygonal mesh, built by displacing vertically the vertices of a 2D mesh, we can still simplify the problem by treating the terrain as a 2D mesh projected into the xz plane. Given a point $\mathbf{Q}$ with a fixed x- and z-component, it can only lie on a single triangle of the terrain. The problem is identifying the correct triangle. Once the correct triangle is found, Equation 4.2.8 can be used to determine the height at that point.

Using spatial partitioning techniques, such as octrees, it is possible to narrow down what part of the terrain we're interested in, producing a subset of candidate polygons. Given this bag of polygons that represent the terrain, we have no choice but to test each polygon until one is found that contains point **Q**. An efficient method of testing if point **Q** lies in a triangle is to compute the *barycentric coordinates* of the point. The barycentric coordinates represent point **Q** in terms of a weighted sum of each triangle vertex. Figure 4.2.13 shows an example.

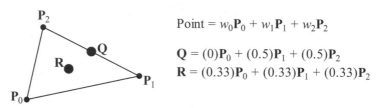

$$\text{Point} = w_0\mathbf{P}_0 + w_1\mathbf{P}_1 + w_2\mathbf{P}_2$$

$$\mathbf{Q} = (0)\mathbf{P}_0 + (0.5)\mathbf{P}_1 + (0.5)\mathbf{P}_2$$

$$\mathbf{R} = (0.33)\mathbf{P}_0 + (0.33)\mathbf{P}_1 + (0.33)\mathbf{P}_2$$

FIGURE 4.2.13   *An example representing points in terms of barycentric coordinates. The values w_0, w_1, and w_2 are the barycentric coordinate weights. Note that a negative weight would indicate the point is not inside the triangle.*

Equations 4.2.9 and 4.2.10 show how to calculate the barycentric coordinates for a point **Q** that is in the triangle's plane [Lengyel04]. In the case of nonoverlapping terrain, we can ignore the *y*-coordinate and make point **Q** and all triangles lie in the same plane. Otherwise, Equation 4.2.8 could be used to obtain point **Q** in the triangle's plane.

$$\begin{bmatrix} w_1 \\ w_2 \end{bmatrix} = \frac{1}{V_1^2 V_2^2 - \left(\mathbf{V}_1 \cdot \mathbf{V}_2\right)^2} \begin{bmatrix} V_2^2 & -\mathbf{V}_1 \cdot \mathbf{V}_2 \\ -\mathbf{V}_1 \cdot \mathbf{V}_2 & V_1^2 \end{bmatrix} \begin{bmatrix} \mathbf{S} \cdot \mathbf{V}_1 \\ \mathbf{S} \cdot \mathbf{V}_2 \end{bmatrix} \tag{4.2.9}$$

where

$$\mathbf{S} = \mathbf{Q} - \mathbf{P}_0$$

$$\mathbf{V}_1 = \mathbf{P}_1 - \mathbf{P}_0$$

$$\mathbf{V}_2 = \mathbf{P}_2 - \mathbf{P}_0 \tag{4.2.10}$$

Since the three weights must add up to 1.0, w_0 can be calculated with $w_0 = 1 - w_1 - w_2$. If any of the weights are negative, point **Q** does not lie within the triangle.

Once the weights are calculated, they can be used to determine the texture coordinate of point Q. This might be valuable if the terrain triangles are very large and part of the texture implies special conditions, such as water. For example, a check can be performed whether point Q translates to a water pixel or a land pixel. If the texture coordinates $\langle s_0,t_0 \rangle$, $\langle s_1,t_1 \rangle$, and $\langle s_2,t_2 \rangle$ are associated with vertices P_0, P_1, and P_2, the texture coordinates $\langle s,t \rangle$ at the point Q are given by

$$s = w_0 s_0 + w_1 s_1 + w_2 s_2$$
$$t = w_0 t_0 + w_1 t_1 + w_2 t_2. \tag{4.2.11}$$

Collision Resolution

Once a collision is detected, some action must be taken to resolve the collision. This collision resolution can take on many forms.

In the simplistic case of two billiard balls striking each other, the position of the balls at the time of collision must be calculated, to place them in the correct location at the time of impact. In addition, new resulting velocities must be imparted onto the balls, and a "clinking" sound effect would likely be played.

However, consider a second collision scenario: If a rocket slams into a wall, the rocket should disappear, an explosion with sound effect should be spawned at the point of impact, the wall should be charred, and area damage should be inflicted on all game characters that are near. In a third collision scenario, perhaps a character can walk through a particular wall triggering a magical sound effect, in which case the detection of certain wall collisions must be recognized, but the positions and trajectories of the objects should not be affected.

For collision resolution to meet these very different needs, there must be a procedure for the resolution. This procedure has three parts: a prologue, the collision, and an epilogue.

Prologue

When collision resolution begins, the collision is known to have occurred, but there is a chance that it should be ignored. This is verified in a prologue callback function. If the prologue determines that the collision shouldn't affect the position or trajectories of the objects, the function will return `false` so that the collision resolution doesn't continue. The prologue may also trigger other events, such as sound effects, by sending a collision notification to the objects themselves. In true object-oriented style, the objects would deal with the prologue collision notification as they see fit.

Collision

In the collision step of the procedure, the objects will be placed at the point of impact and new velocities will be assigned using physics or some other decision logic. The exact steps will depend on which method, overlap testing or intersection testing, was employed. This will be discussed shortly.

Epilogue

In the epilogue, any post-collision affects must be propagated. These might include destroying one or both objects, playing a sound effect, inflicting damage, and so on. This can generally be done by sending a collision epilogue event notification to each object, with the object determining what effects to trigger. Whether these effects take place in the prologue or epilogue is somewhat arbitrary and will depend on the game design and circumstance.

Resolving Overlap Testing

Moving back to the collision step of the procedure, there are four steps to resolving the collision when overlap testing is used:

1. Extract the collision normal.
2. Extract the penetration depth.
3. Move the two objects apart to a penetration depth of zero, if needed.
4. Compute the new velocities.

The first step is to extract the collision normal. One method that works particularly well is to first find the position of each object immediately before collision (preferably with the bisection technique as previously discussed). Knowing the object positions prior to contact, the collision normal can be constructed using the two closest points on each surface. This technique is shown in Figure 4.2.14. As long as the objects can be located very close before impact and neither has a large angular momentum, the results will be fairly good.

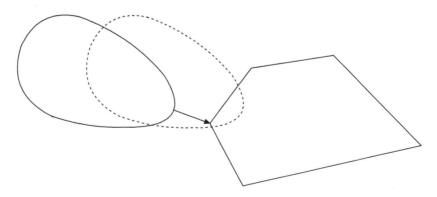

FIGURE 4.2.14   *A collision normal constructed using the two closest points immediately before impact.*

Calculating the two closest points on the surface of each object can be tricky. Lin-Canny is an incremental algorithm that can find the two closest features for general convex polygonal volumes [VanDerBergen03]. With spheres, the collision normal can be directly defined as the difference between the centers of each sphere at the point of impact, as shown in Figure 4.2.15.

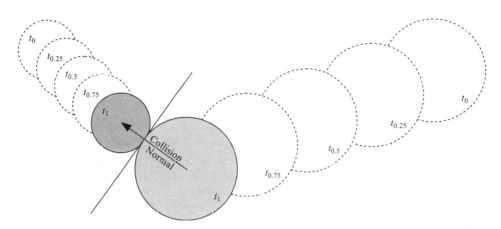

FIGURE 4.2.15   *In a sphere-sphere collision, the difference between the centers of each sphere, at the point of collision, can be used as the collision normal.*

In the second step of resolving a collision, the penetration depth must be calculated to move the objects apart. For this purpose, an alternate algorithm to that of bisection is Gilbert-Johnson-Keerthi (GJK), which is particularly good at extracting the penetration depth from convex objects [VanDerBergen03]. GJK builds dividing planes between the objects using what are known as the Minkowski supporting lines. An example is shown in Figure 4.2.16.

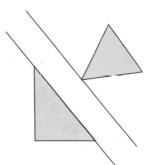

FIGURE 4.2.16   *GJK dividing planes between two objects, used to extract penetration depth.*

With the collision normal vectors and the penetration depth in hand, the third step is to move the objects apart (i.e., move them to their locations at the time of collision when there is zero interpenetration depth). Once this is done, the fourth step is to compute each object's new velocity using Newtonian physics, as discussed in Chapter 4.3, or using some other decision logic.

Resolving Intersection Testing

Collision resolution with intersection testing is much simpler since the objects never actually penetrate. Without overlap, there is no need to detect the penetration depth and move the objects apart (steps 2 and 3). All that is required is to extract the collision normal vector at the time of collision and then calculate the new velocities of each object.

Summary

Collision detection and collision resolution enable game objects to behave as solid masses. Through either overlap testing or intersection testing, collisions can be detected. When a collision is detected, there is a prologue, collision, and an epilogue that help produce the many different behaviors of colliding objects. Once a collision has been detected, collision resolution corrects each object's position and imparts appropriate velocities based on physical simulation.

The complexity in collision detection comes from two primary sources. First, collisions between arbitrarily complex polygonal models are expensive to test. Second, each object could potentially collide with any other object. Fortunately, using simplified geometry, bounding volumes, and the partitioning of space, these complexities can be mitigated.

Exercises

1. Compute the time of collision for two spheres, each of radius 0.25, that start at $t = 0$ at the positions $(0,0)$ and $(1,1)$, respectively, and both end up at $(1,0)$ at $t = 1$.
2. For the collision in the preceding exercise, compute the collision normal for each sphere.
3. Draw the Minkowski sum of a circle and a triangle.
4. Devise three levels of bounding volumes for a character model.
5. Given a triangle with vertices at $(1,0,0)$, $(0,0,1)$, and $(0,1,0)$, find the point where a character's foot located at $(0.2,0,0.2)$ should be placed.
6. Given a triangle with vertices at $(0,0,0)$, $(1,0,0)$, and $(0,0,1)$, calculate the barycentric coordinates of the points $(0.5,0,0)$ and $(1,0,1)$. Please show your work.

7. In games, collisions between characters are usually not very precise, as often times the arm or leg of one character will penetrate another character. If precise collision detection is employed, what problems or issues might arise? What advantage does modeling character-character collisions with spheres or cylinders offer?

References

[Lengyel04] Lengyel, Eric, *Mathematics for 3D Game Programming & Computer Graphics*, 2nd ed., Charles River Media, 2004.

[Press92] Press, William H.; Flannery, Brian P.; Teukolsky, Saul A.; and Vetterling, William T., *Numerical Recipes in C: The Art of Scientific Computing*, 2nd ed. Cambridge University Press, 1992, available online at *www.nr.com/*.

[VanDerBergen03] Van Der Bergen, Gino, *Collision Detection in Interactive 3D Environments*, Morgan Kaufmann, 2003.

4.3 ■ Real-Time Game Physics

In This Chapter

- ■ Overview
- ■ Rewind: A Fresh Look at Basic Physics
- ■ Introduction to Numerical Rigid-body Simulation
- ■ Generalized Translational Motion
- ■ Rotational Motion
- ■ Collision Response Revisited
- ■ Bringing It All Together
- ■ Commercial and Freeware Physics Engines
- ■ Summary
- ■ Exercises
- ■ References

Overview

Physics is part of our life experience. Our brains are conditioned through life to recognize physically based motion as being correct motion. It makes sense, then, that game players become more immersed in some types of games when objects move in a realistic manner. When appropriate, there are a number of ways to create realistic motion for a game. One common approach is for artists to author keyframe animations that give the appearance of being physically based. Another common approach, which is popular for character animation in particular, is to use motion capture technology to record real-life motions and then apply those recorded motions to game models. Both of these approaches are extremely labor intensive, and expensive.

Simulation of physics represents a third approach to generating realistic motion for games. Physics simulation can provide at least two benefits that are significant to publishers, developers, and game players. The first benefit is a cost savings to developers and publishers. Physics simulation has the potential to be far less expensive than keyframe or motion capture animation, since (ideally) the artist only needs to configure the physical properties of a game model. The simulation rather than an artist or actor determines the actual motion, and does so without charging an hourly rate!

In game physics simulation, there is the possibility of simulating an object's motion within digital content creation software, thus creating a preprocessed solution that is fixed at runtime, just as with keyframe or motion capture animation. There is also the possibility of simulating motion at runtime. The latter case provides the second benefit of physics simulation. By simulating physics at runtime, the game engine can create emergent behavior, leading to a richer game experience for the game player.

This chapter contains a whirlwind introduction to physics simulation, with a focus on techniques that can run in real time. The concepts presented herein are not comprehensive, but are intended to provide sufficient information to implement a wide variety of realistic behaviors. The entire chapter can be useful in generating physics simulation within a runtime game engine, as well as within digital content creation tools.

Rewind: A Fresh Look at Basic Physics

Let's begin slowly. Chances are good that you've already attended a science course, perhaps in high school or during the first year at a university, that introduced you to the fundamentals of physics. It makes sense to reflect back on what you may already know. Those basic equations are easy to code, and can actually be useful in real games. Further, they are a building block upon which we will develop more generalized rigid body physics that can make simulated 3D worlds come to life.

The Importance of Consistent Units

Throughout this chapter, as new variables or quantities are introduced, we will identify units in which the quantity can be measured, from the International System of Units (SI). For example, position can be measured in meters, and time can be measured in seconds. You can choose to use a different system of units, such as the English System of Units, if you wish. However, make no mistake about this: it is *necessary* that you use consistent units in your equations. *Equations will produce the wrong results if you use values with inconsistent units!* An example of using inconsistent units would be to use a force measured in pounds (English Units) and an object mass measured in kilograms (SI Units) in the same equation. To correct the inconsistency, convert the force to Newtons, which is consistent with a mass measured in kilograms. Conversion factors are readily available on the Internet, and can be found using any search engine.

Particle Kinematics

Every introduction to physics begins by defining several fundamental properties of motion. It is likely that you already understand these properties implicitly, and find them to be second nature. Nevertheless, we begin our review by formally defining the properties of particle motion, or *particle kinematics*. They are the basis for everything that follows.

From the point of view of theoretical physics, a particle is an object that has no volume; for example, a particle is a mass concentrated into an infinitely small sphere. For our purposes, however, we define a particle to be a perfectly smooth, frictionless sphere with a finite radius. We choose this definition solely to avoid the need to consider rotational motion, an advanced topic, until later. Perfectly smooth, frictionless spheres will never begin to rotate due to normal interactions with other objects. Figure 4.3.1 illustrates a particle in motion along a curved path.

At any moment in time, t, the particle is located at a position, $\mathbf{p}$, measured in an *inertial reference frame*. We won't worry about the formal definition of an inertial reference frame (it has to do with the relative position of the stars in space). For games, we simply choose a game's world coordinate system to be the inertial reference frame. The position, $\mathbf{p}$, is the location of the particle, measured in world space, $\mathbf{p} = \langle p_x, p_y, p_z \rangle$. *Position is measured in units of type distance or length. The SI units for position are meters (m).*

If the particle is moving, its position is a function of time, $\mathbf{p}(t)$. Figure 4.3.2 illustrates the particle at time t and at a later time, $t + \Delta t$. The symbol, Δ, is the Greek letter Delta, commonly used to indicate a change in value. The quantity, Δt, indicates an incremental change in time. *The SI units for time are seconds.*

The vector quantity, velocity, is defined to be the change in position over time. The magnitude of velocity is the particle's *speed. Velocity and speed are measured in units of type distance over time. The SI units for velocity and speed are meters per second (m/s).* Given the position of a particle at two different times, the average velocity between the start and end time can be computed as $\mathbf{V}_{avg} = \big(\mathbf{p}(t + \Delta t) - \mathbf{p}(t)\big)/\Delta t$. It is possible that the particle's velocity changes significantly between time t and $t + \Delta t$. The average velocity is not necessarily the particle velocity at time t. From calculus, the true, *instantaneous velocity* at time t is the time derivative of position, shown in Equation 4.3.1. Note also that the inverse is true: position is the integral of velocity over time. (If you are unfamiliar with calculus, and the meaning of the terms *derivative* and *integral*, please refer to any introductory calculus text, such as [Munem78].)

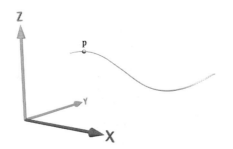

FIGURE 4.3.1 *Position of a particle in a world coordinate system.*

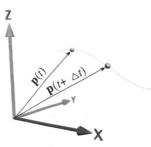

FIGURE 4.3.2 *Time-dependent position of a particle moving along a path.*

$$\mathbf{V}(t) = \lim_{\Delta t \to 0} \frac{\mathbf{p}(t + \Delta t) - \mathbf{p}(t)}{\Delta t} = \frac{d}{dt} \mathbf{p}(t) \qquad (4.3.1)$$

There is one more fundamental property of particle kinematics that we require. The vector quantity, *acceleration*, defined in Equation 4.3.2, is the time derivative of velocity. Note that the inverse is also true: velocity is the integral of acceleration over time. Acceleration can also be defined as the second time derivative of position. *Acceleration is measured in units of type distance over the square of time. The SI units for acceleration are meters per second squared (m/s²).*

$$\mathbf{a}(t) = \frac{d}{dt} \mathbf{V}(t) = \frac{d^2}{dt^2} \mathbf{p}(t) \qquad (4.3.2)$$

Newton's Famous Laws

We begin our review of basic physics by considering Sir Isaac Newton's First and Second Laws of Motion. *Newton's First Law of Motion*, paraphrased, states that an object will move at a constant velocity until compelled to change its velocity by forces imposed upon the object. From this, we can make a profound observation from the history of video games: the classic arcade and console game, Atari's *Breakout*, actually had a realistic physics model.

Newton's Second Law of Motion is important to us, as we can use it to implement physics simulations in the presence of forces that cause an object's velocity and position to change in interesting ways. This law, paraphrased, states that an object's change in velocity is proportional to an applied force. Stated in equation form, the law is the infamous $\mathbf{F} = m\mathbf{a}$, shown in vector form as Equation 4.3.3 (assumes mass is constant).

$$\mathbf{F}(t) = m\mathbf{a}(t) \qquad (4.3.3)$$

Here, the force, $\mathbf{F}(t)$, may change over time, resulting in an acceleration that changes over time. The quantity, m, is called the *mass* of the object. *The SI units for mass are kilograms (kg). Force is measured in units of type mass times distance over the square of time. The SI units for force are called Newton's (N).* By definition, 1 Newton is equal to 1 kg-m/s² (note the consistency). Note that mass is not the same as the object's weight (which is a force)!

The Cycle of Motion

You should be able to see a cycle of motion in Equations 4.3.1 through 4.3.3. A force causes acceleration. Acceleration causes a change in velocity. Velocity causes a change in the position of a particle. By integrating the equations in reverse order from 4.3.3 to 4.3.1, we can determine the motion of the particle. This is what physics simulation is all about.

The Effect of a Constant Force on Particle Motion

As described by *Newton's First Law of Motion*, the simplest possible motion is that of a particle experiencing no force and therefore continuing to move at a constant velocity (zero for a particle at rest). We continue our review by analyzing a slightly more complex case: a particle experiencing a constant force. Consider Equation 4.3.3, when **F** is constant. Since the right-hand side is constant in time, acceleration also is a constant, **a**. Constants are easy to integrate (even vector constants), and by integrating Equation 4.3.3, we derive Equation 4.3.4, a closed-form equation for the velocity of a particle experiencing a constant force. Note that the integration was performed using a change of variable, $\tau = t - t_{init}$. The equation is valid for a force that is applied to the particle beginning at time t_{init}, but not before. The velocity, $\mathbf{V}_{init}$, is the velocity of the particle at time t_{init}.

$$\mathbf{V}(t) = \int \mathbf{a}\, d\tau = \int \frac{\mathbf{F}}{m}\, d\tau = \mathbf{V}_{init} + \frac{\mathbf{F}}{m}\tau = \mathbf{V}_{init} + \frac{\mathbf{F}}{m}\left(t - t_{init}\right) \qquad (4.3.4)$$

From here, we can derive a closed-form equation for position by integrating Equation 4.3.4. This is shown in Equation 4.3.5, in which $\mathbf{p}_{init}$ is the initial position of the particle, at time t_{init}.

$$\mathbf{p}(t) = \int \mathbf{V}(\tau)\, d\tau = \int \left(\mathbf{V}_{init} + \frac{\mathbf{F}}{m}(\tau) \right) d\tau = \mathbf{p}_{init} + \mathbf{V}_{init}\left(t - t_{init}\right) + \frac{\mathbf{F}}{2m}\left(t - t_{init}\right)^2 \quad (4.3.5)$$

It is important that you recognize one fact about Equations 4.3.4 and 4.3.5. *This equation is exact and will produce a correct, realistic result for any time t > t_{init}, as long as the applied force remains a constant.* Further, you can use these equations in a piecewise fashion, applying them as long as the applied force remains constant, and then restarting them when the force changes to a different, constant value by updating the values t_{init}, $\mathbf{p}_{init}$, and $\mathbf{V}_{init}$ to be the current values of t, $\mathbf{p}(t)$, and $\mathbf{V}(t)$, respectively, at the moment the force changes. It is only valid to restart the equations when **F** remains constant for some time after every change.

Consistency of Units, Still Important

Let us revisit, for a moment, the important issue of consistency of units. It is insufficient to simply ensure all of the values used in an equation are measured in a consistent system of units such as SI. It is also crucial that all of the terms in an equation measure the same *type* of unit. For example, as presented previously, velocity is measured in units of the type distance over time. You can verify the consistency of unit types in the rightmost term of Equation 4.3.4, $\frac{\mathbf{F}}{m}\left(t - t_{init}\right)$, by substituting the unit types for the variables and simplifying algebraically, as though the unit types were variables. This verification is shown in Equation 4.3.6, which proves that the units of the rightmost term are, correctly, the unit type for velocity. Note that the difference of two values of time, $(t - t_{init})$, does not result in a cancellation of the units of time. The value represented by $(t - t_{init})$ is a change in time, which also has units of type time. *If you have reason to derive new equations yourself, make it your standard practice to analyze the unit types in your derived equation to be sure they are consistent. If you discover that one or more of the terms in your equation are inconsistent, you will know that there is an error in your equation.*

$$\text{Units of } \frac{\mathbf{F}}{m}(t - t_{init}) = \frac{(mass)(dist)/(time^2)}{mass} time = \frac{(mass)(dist)}{(mass)(time^2)} time = \frac{dist}{time} \quad (4.3.6)$$

Projectile Motion

It is actually possible to use Equation 4.3.5 to achieve meaningful physics simulations in games. We continue the review by looking at simple projectile motion in 3D. One approximately constant force acts on all real objects near the surface of a planet. That force is, of course, the force due to gravity. This force is the *weight* of the object, equal to the object's mass times a constant acceleration due to gravity, acting in the direction of a vector from the object's position toward the center of the planet. The acceleration due to gravity is commonly represented by the variable g. In SI units, the value of g on Earth is 9.81 m/s² toward the center of the Earth, or the vector, $\mathbf{g} = \langle 0.0, 0.0, -9.81 \rangle$. Here, we've chosen the up direction to be the positive z-axis in world space. We can rewrite Equation 4.3.5 for a simple projectile on Earth, as Equation 4.3.7.

$$\mathbf{p}(t) = \mathbf{p}_{init} + \mathbf{V}_{init}(t - t_{init}) + \frac{1}{2}\mathbf{g}(t - t_{init})^2 \quad (4.3.7)$$

If $\mathbf{V}_{init}$ is not parallel to $\mathbf{g}$, the path will be parabolic, as illustrated in Figure 4.3.3.

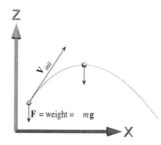

FIGURE 4.3.3   *Particle undergoing simple projectile motion.*

Listing 4.3.1 is a fragment of pseudocode that can be used to simulate a particle undergoing simple projectile motion on Earth, using Equation 4.3.5.

Listing 4.3.1   Pseudo-code for simulating projectile motion of a particle on Earth.

```
void main()
{
    // Initialize variables used in the simulation.
    Vector3D V_init(10.0, 0.0, 10.0);
    Vector3D p_init(0.0, 0.0, 100.0), p = p_init;
    Vector3D g(0.0, 0.0, -9.81);
    float t_init = particle launch time;

    // The game simulation/rendering loop
    while (game simulation is running)
    {
        float t = current game time;
        if (t > t_init)
        {
            float tmti = t - t_init;
            p = p_init + (V_init * tmti);
            p = p + 0.5 * g * (tmti * tmti);
        }
        render particle at location p;
    }
}
```

Complete Exercise 1 to translate this pseudocode into a simple targeting game.

Frictionless Collision Response

We conclude our review of basic physics with a detailed analysis of classical particle-collision response. First, a definition. *Linear momentum* is defined to be the vector quantity mass times velocity, or *m*$\mathbf{V}$. *Linear momentum is measured in units of type mass times distance over time. The SI units of linear momentum are kilogram-meters per second (kg-m/s).*

Linear momentum is related to the force being applied to an object. In fact, its relationship with force is more fundamental than the relationship between force and acceleration shown in Equation 4.3.3. Equation 4.3.3 is actually an approximation to Equation 4.3.8, a more general relationship that defines the first time derivative of linear momentum as being equal to the net force applied to an object.

$$\frac{d}{dt}\left(m\mathbf{V}(t)\right) = \mathbf{F}(t) \tag{4.3.8}$$

For most objects, mass is constant, and this enables us to derive Equation 4.3.3 by noting $\frac{d}{dt}\left(m\mathbf{V}(t)\right) = m\frac{d}{dt}\mathbf{V}(t)$ when mass is constant. Equation 4.3.8 is called the *Newtonian Equation of Motion*, since when integrated over time it determines the motion of an object. By integrating the force applied to an object over time, we obtain the change in linear momentum and velocity over time.

Consider two colliding particles, 1 and 2. For the duration of the collision, each particle exerts a force on the other. The duration of most collisions is an extremely short period of time, and yet the change in velocity of the objects is often dramatic. For example, think about the collision response of billiard balls. Large, nearly instantaneous changes in velocity can only occur if the collision forces are large. Collision forces are usually so large that they dominate during the collision. It is usually acceptable to ignore other forces entirely, assuming their effect is negligible for the duration of the collision. By integrating Equation 4.3.8 over the duration of the collision, we obtain the *linear impulse-momentum equation*, given as Equation 4.3.9.

$$m_1 \mathbf{V}_1^+ = m_1 \mathbf{V}_1^- + \mathbf{\Lambda} \qquad (4.3.9)$$

Here, $m_1 \mathbf{V}_1^-$ is the linear momentum of particle 1 just before the collision, and $m_1 \mathbf{V}_1^+$ is the linear momentum just after the collision. The superscripts, – and +, indicate quantities before and after collisions, respectively. The vector $\mathbf{\Lambda}$ is called the *linear impulse*, defined to be the integral of the collision force over the duration of the collision.

Newton's Third Law of Motion states that for every action there is an equal but opposite reaction. This law tells us that the collision forces, and the impulses, on the two objects are equal in magnitude but opposite in direction. From this result, we can immediately write the linear impulse-momentum equation for particle 2, as Equation 4.3.10. Note that impulse is negated on the second object—equal but opposite.

$$m_2 \mathbf{V}_2^+ = m_2 \mathbf{V}_2^- - \mathbf{\Lambda} \qquad (4.3.10)$$

Our goal is to find the velocities of the two objects after the collision response is complete. We can solve Equations 4.3.9 and 4.3.10 for the after-collision velocities if we are able to compute the impulse. The fact that we are assuming a frictionless collision allows us to simplify the situation somewhat. Without friction, the impulse will always act purely along the unit surface normal vector at the point of contact. In this case, $\mathbf{\Lambda}$ can be defined by Equation 4.3.11, where Λ is the scalar value (positive or negative) of the impulse and $\hat{\mathbf{n}}$ is the unit surface normal vector. A collision detection algorithm determines $\hat{\mathbf{n}}$ and the point of contact, as detailed in Chapter 4.2, "Collision Detection and Resolution."

$$\mathbf{\Lambda} = \Lambda \hat{\mathbf{n}} \qquad (4.3.11)$$

By substituting Equation 4.3.11 into Equations 4.3.9 and 4.3.10, we obtain two vector equations that together contain three unknowns: the two vectors $\mathbf{V}_1^+$, $\mathbf{V}_2^+$, and one scalar Λ. We require a third equation before we can solve for all three unknown values. We can generate the third equation by observing the physical behavior of real objects during collisions. Observe the behavior when two objects in real life collide, as shown in Figure 4.3.4. Here, just prior to impact, the objects exhibit their natural geometric shapes. During the initial impact, both objects experience a *period of deformation* in which their shapes change in response to the collision force. After the initial impact, the objects experience a *period of restitution*, in which they are restored to their natural shapes and accelerate to their after-collision velocities.

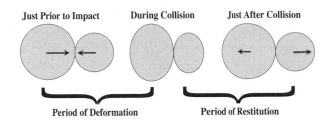

FIGURE 4.3.4 *A realistic view of collision response.*

The third equation is chosen to be an approximation to the material response of real objects during a collision. Before we present the equation, observe that objects do not always collide while traveling toward each other along collinear paths. The more general situation is illustrated in Figure 4.3.5.

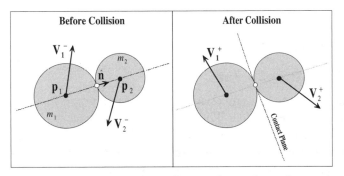

FIGURE 4.3.5 *Frictionless collision of two spherical particles.*

Equations 4.3.9 and 4.3.10, being vector equations, can be represented in a variety of coordinate systems. One valid choice is the world coordinate system; however, it is more convenient if we consider them in a coordinate system that includes $\hat{n}$ and the contact plane that is tangent to the object surfaces at the point of contact. In the general case, with friction, a collision will affect the object velocity components parallel to the contact plane and the component parallel to the contact normal direction. For a frictionless collision, however, the velocity components in the contact plane do not change. Our third equation, given as Equation 4.3.12, reflects this fact and defines the relationship between the normal components of the velocities of the objects, before and after a collision.

$$\left(\mathbf{V}_1^+ - \mathbf{V}_2^+\right) \cdot \hat{\mathbf{n}} = -\varepsilon\left(\mathbf{V}_1^- - \mathbf{V}_2^-\right) \cdot \hat{\mathbf{n}} \qquad (4.3.12)$$

Here, the scalar ε is called the *coefficient of restitution*. This coefficient is related to the conservation or loss of *kinetic energy* during a collision. Due to space constraints, we will not discuss the concept of energy in detail here; however, you should know that *total energy*, equal to kinetic energy plus *potential energy*, is a physical quantity that is conserved similar to linear momentum. If ε is equal to 1, the collision is perfectly elastic, representing objects that rebound fully so that the sum of the particles' kinetic energies is the same before and after the collision. If ε is equal to 0, the collision is perfectly plastic, representing objects that experience no period of restitution and a maximum loss of kinetic energy. In real life, ε is a function of the material properties of the objects involved in the collision. For example, the coefficient of restitution for a collision between a tennis ball and tennis racket is approximately 0.85, and that for a deflated basketball colliding with the court surface is nearly 0.

Using Equations 4.3.9 through 4.3.12, we can solve for the linear impulse, given in Equation 4.3.13. To compute the after-collision velocities, apply the result of Equation 4.3.13 into Equations 4.3.9 and 4.3.10, and divide by m_1 or m_2, respectively, to find the after-collision velocities.

$$\Lambda = -\left(\frac{m_1 m_2 \left(1+\varepsilon\right)\left(\mathbf{V}_1^- - \mathbf{V}_2^-\right) \cdot \hat{\mathbf{n}}}{m_1 + m_2}\right)\hat{\mathbf{n}} \qquad (4.3.13)$$

The Story So Far

To this point, we have revisited a few basic concepts in kinematics and physics that you may have seen before. The concepts have been generalized to three dimensions and are ready to use in certain types of games. Depending on the game you are developing, you may not need to read any further. Listing 4.3.2 is a fragment of pseudocode that you can use to simulate a collection of N spherical particles experiencing gravitational acceleration in a game, with occasional frictionless collisions.

Listing 4.3.2 Pseudocode for simulating a collection of N spherical particles under gravity with frictionless collisions.

```
void main(
{
    // Initialize variables needed by the simulation.
    Vector3D V_init[N] = initial velocities;
    Vector3D p_init[N] = initial center positions;
    Vector3D g(0.0, 0.0, -9.81);
    float mass[N] = particle masses;
    float time_init[N] = per particle start times;
    float eps = coefficient of restitution;
```

```
// Main game simulation/rendering loop.
while (game simulation is running)
{
    float t = current game time;
    detect collisions and collision times;

    // Resolve collisions.
    for (each colliding pair i, j)
    {
        // Calc before collision position and
        // velocity of obj i (Equations 4 and 5).
        float tmti = time_collision - time_init[i];
        pi = p_init[i] + (V_init[i] * tmti);
        pi = p + 0.5 * g * (tmti * tmti);
        vi = V_init[i] + g * tmti;

        // Calc before collision position and
        // velocity of obj j (Equations 4 and 5).
        tmti = time_collision - time_init[j];
        pj = p_init[j] + (V_init[j] * tmti);
        pj = p + 0.5 * g * (tmti * tmti);
        vj = V_init[j] + g * tmti;

        // For spherical particles, surface normal
        // is just the vector joining their centers.
        normal = Normalize(pj - pi);

        // Compute the impulse (Equation 13).
        impulse = normal;
        impulse *= -(1 + eps) * mass[i] * mass[j];
        impulse *= normal.DotProduct(vi - vj);
        impulse /= (mass[i] + mass[j]);

        // Restart particles i and j immediately
        // after the collision. (Equation 9 and 10).
        // Since the collision occurs instantaneously,
        // the after-collision positions are pi, pj,
        // the same as the before-collision positions.
        V_init[i] += impulse / mass[i];
        V_init[j] -= impulse / mass[j];
        p_init[i] = pi;
        p_init[j] = pj;

        // Reset the start times since we updated
        // initial velocities.
        time_init[i] = time_collision;
        time_init[j] = time_collision;
    }

    // Update particle positions (Equation 5) and
    // render particles
    for (k = 0; k < N; k++)
    {
```

```
        float tmti = t - time_init[k];
        p = p_init[k] + (V_init[k] * tmti);
        p = p + 0.5 * g * (tmti * tmti);

        render particle k at location p;
    }
  }
}
```

Complete Exercise 5 to determine how to handle particle collisions with an immovable object (terrain or a wall).

Introduction to Numerical Rigid-Body Simulation

The presentation in the prior section provides you with simple equations that you can use to put projectile physics into real games. If your game needs only to simulate spherical objects that do not rotate and that experience only gravity plus an occasional frictionless collision, you can use the pseudocode in Listing 4.3.2 as a basis for your physics system.

In many games, as in real life, the most interesting motion involves forces other than constant and collision impulse forces. Unfortunately, for the general case, closed-form solutions, such as those presented in the prior section as Equations 4.3.4 and 4.3.5, rarely exist. We assign the term *numerical simulation* to a series of techniques that allow us to approximate the motion of objects for which there is no closed-form solution. This section provides a brief introduction to numerical simulation, along with some implementation suggestions.

Numerical Integration of the Newtonian Equation of Motion

We will consider a family of numerical simulation techniques called *finite difference methods*. Most finite difference methods are derived using the *Taylor series* expansion of the properties we are interested in. We begin in a generic way. Equation 4.3.14 shows the Taylor Series expansion of a vector property, $\mathbf{S}(t)$. Equation 4.3.14 is valid, *and exact*, when $\mathbf{S}(t)$ is continuous and differentiable on the closed domain, $[t, t + \Delta t]$. In this context, Δt is called the *time step*, and it represents the incremental intervals at which we will update $\mathbf{S}(t)$ over time.

$$\mathbf{S}(t+\Delta t)=\mathbf{S}(t)+\Delta t\frac{d}{dt}\mathbf{S}(t)+\frac{\left(\Delta t\right)^2}{2!}\frac{d^2}{dt^t}\mathbf{S}(t)+\sum_{n=3}^{\infty}\frac{\left(\Delta t\right)^n}{k!}\frac{d^n}{dt^n}\mathbf{S}(t) \quad (4.3.14)$$

In general, we will not know the values of any of the higher order time derivatives of a property. We can convert Equation 4.3.14 into a *truncated Taylor series*, shown in Equation 4.3.15, by simply removing the terms involving $d^2\mathbf{S}/dt$ and higher order derivatives. In some cases, the truncation may occur beyond $d^2\mathbf{S}/dt$, but it is always the higher order terms that are eliminated.

$$\mathbf{S}(t + \Delta t) = \mathbf{S}(t) + \Delta t \frac{d}{dt}\mathbf{S}(t) + O(\Delta t^2) \qquad (4.3.15)$$

By removing the higher order terms, we introduce numerical error into the equation that is equal in magnitude, opposite in sign to the higher order terms. This error is called the *truncation error*. The largest component of truncation error is usually the term with the smallest exponent on the time step. The last term in Equation 4.3.15, $O(\Delta t^2)$, indicates the order of magnitude of the truncation error, based on the time-step exponent of the largest error term, in "big-O" notation. The truncation error term is never evaluated, and there is never any need to verify its units. It is simply used to annotate the accuracy of the equation. Since the truncation error of Equation 4.3.15 is second order in time, the truncated series must be accurate to something less than second order; for example, this truncated series is first-order accurate. Formally, this is determined by solving the truncated series for $d\mathbf{S}/dt$ and algebraically showing that the truncation error of the derivative equation is $O(\Delta t)$. (Note that $O(\Delta t^2)/\Delta t = O(\Delta t)$.)

Equation 4.3.15 is our first example of a finite difference equation that can be used for numerical simulation. The process of updating properties using this particular truncated Taylor series is called "simple" or "explicit" Euler integration. Explicit Euler integration is called a one-point method, because we can solve it using properties stored at exactly one point in time, t, which is prior to the update time, $t + \Delta t$. It is called an explicit method since the property $\mathbf{S}(t + \Delta t)$ is the only unknown value, which we can explicitly update without solving a system of simultaneous equations. An important characteristic of explicit Euler integration is that every term of the right-hand side of the equation is evaluated at time t, the time step immediately prior to the new time $t + \Delta t$.

Let's take a closer look at Equation 4.3.15. We take the view that the variable that we are numerically integrating, $\mathbf{S}$, is the state of an object, and that $d\mathbf{S}/dt$ is the state derivative.

$$\underbrace{\mathbf{S}(t + \Delta t)}_{\text{new state}} = \underbrace{\mathbf{S}(t)}_{\text{prior state}} + \Delta t \underbrace{\frac{d}{dt}\mathbf{S}(t)}_{\text{state derivative}} \qquad (4.3.16)$$

This view enables us to conveniently write a *numerical integrator* that can integrate arbitrary properties as they change over time. We can, in fact, write an integrator that can integrate a collection of properties for a collection of objects in a single function call. Listing 4.3.3 is a fragment of pseudocode for an explicit Euler integrator that integrates a state vector of arbitrary length.

Listing 4.3.3   Pseudocode for an explicit Euler integrator that integrates a state vector of arbitrary length. Here, N is the number of states, *new_S* is $\mathbf{S}(t + \Delta t)$, *prior_S* is $\mathbf{S}(t)$, *S_derivs* is $d\mathbf{S}(t)/dt$, and *delta_t* is Δt

```
void ExplicitEuler(N, new_S, prior_S, S_derivs, delta_t)
{
    for (i = 0; i < N; i++)
    {
        new_S[i] = prior_S[i] + delta_t * S_derivs[i];
    }
}
```

For a single particle, one choice (but not the only choice) for the state vector is quite simply $\mathbf{S} = \langle m\mathbf{V}, \mathbf{p} \rangle$. The corresponding vector of state derivatives follows directly from Equations 4.3.1 and 4.3.8: $d\mathbf{S}/dt = \langle \mathbf{F}, \mathbf{V} \rangle$. Note that for three-dimensional motion, the state and state derivative vectors contain six real values each, since the linear momentum, position, force, and velocity are all three-component vectors. For a collection of N particles, we can expand these states to include properties for all of the particles.

$$\mathbf{S}(t) = \langle m_1\mathbf{V}_1, \mathbf{p}_1, m_2\mathbf{V}_2, \mathbf{p}_2, \cdots, m_N\mathbf{V}_N, \mathbf{p}_N \rangle \qquad (4.3.17)$$

$$\frac{d}{dt}\mathbf{S}(t) = \langle \mathbf{F}_1, \mathbf{V}_1, \mathbf{F}_2, \mathbf{V}_2, \cdots, \mathbf{F}_N, \mathbf{V}_N \rangle \qquad (4.3.18)$$

Using Numerical Integration to Simulate a Collection of Particles

Listing 4.3.4 is pseudocode for implementing explicit Euler integration for a collection of particles. This code is a straightforward implementation of the state vector shown in Equation 4.3.17 and the state derivative vector shown in Equation 4.3.18, and makes use of the integrator shown in Listing 4.3.3. Note that the CalcForce function called by the pseudocode is a placeholder for a function that can determine the force applied to a given particle. For example, if the only force applied is that due to gravity, CalcForce will simply return the weight of the given particle, since the particle's weight is the force due to gravity.

Listing 4.3.4   Pseudocode for explicit Euler integration for a collection of N particles that move without colliding

```
void main()
{
    // Initialize variables needed by the simulation.
    Vector3D cur_S[2*N];    // S(t+delta_t)
```

```
Vector3D prior_S[2*N];   // S(t)
Vector3D S_derivs[2*N];  // dS/dt at time t
float mass[N];           // Mass of particles
float t;                 // Current simulation time
float delta_t;           // Physics time step

// Set current state to initial conditions.
for (i = 0; i < N; i++)
{
    mass[i] = mass of particle i;
    cur_S[2*i] = particle i initial linear momentum;
    cur_S[2*i+1] = particle i initial position;
}

// Game simulation/rendering loop
while (game simulation is running)
{
    DoPhysicsSimulationStep(delta_t);
    for (i = 0; i < N; i++)
        Render particle i at position cur_S[2*i+1];
}
}

// Update the physics
void DoPhysicsSimulationStep(delta_t)
{
    copy cur_S to prior_S

    // Calculate the state derivative vector.
    for (i = 0; i < N; i++)
    {
        S_derivs[2*i] = CalcForce(i);
        S_derivs[2*i+1] = prior_S[2*i] / mass[i];
    }

    // Integrate the equations of motion.
    ExplicitEuler(2*N, cur_S, prior_S, S_derivs, delta_t);

    // By integrating the equations of motion, we have
    // effectively moved simulation time forward by
    // delta_t.
    t = t + delta_t;
}
```

Collision Response in the Simulation Loop

You can adapt the code in Listing 4.3.4 to a real game without modification as long as there are no collisions; however, in general the code must be modified somewhat to handle collisions.

In theory, if collisions all happen to occur at the beginning of a time step (e.g., at time *t* before the equations of motion are integrated), the modification is quite simple. The collisions should be resolved before copying cur_S to prior_S at the top of

DoPhysicsSimulationStep. For each colliding pair, simply use Equation 4.3.13 to compute the impulse, and then compute the after-collision linear momentums using Equations 4.3.9 and 4.3.10. The after-collision linear momentums should replace the corresponding values in cur_S. When the algorithm continues, these after-collision linear momentums are copied into prior_S, and after S_derivs is set up, the call to ExplicitEuler will use the after-collision velocities to update the positions of the particles.

In practice, collisions will rarely occur at the beginning of a time step. It is far more likely that collisions will occur at some time, t_c, between t and $t + \Delta t$. Further, the collision time t_c is likely to be different for every pair of colliding objects. Observe what must happen in the simulation in this case, if we are to be strictly correct in our handling of collision response using the impulse-momentum approach. For a pair of colliding objects, we know that from time t until time t_c, the two objects obey the equations of motion. Then, at time t_c, the objects exhibit an instantaneous change in velocity due to the collision event. Finally, from time t_c until time $t + \Delta t$, the objects again obey the equations of motion. We must, then, integrate the equations of motion twice in a given physics update for objects in collision: once to obtain the object states at t_c, and again to obtain the state at the end of the time step following the collision, $t + \Delta t$.

Listing 4.3.5 illustrates a modification to the DoPhysicsSimulationStep function to allow for collisions and the two-step integration. Note that this modified function has been written for clarity, not efficiency. For example, although not shown here, the code will run must faster if you batch objects not involved in collisions and integrate their states in a single call to ExplicitEuler, as illustrated in Listing 4.3.4.

Listing 4.3.5 Modification to the DoPhysicsSimulationStep function to support collisions

```
// Update the physics
void DoPhysicsSimulationStep(delta_t)
{
    // Detect collisions using methods described in
    // the Collision Detection and Resolution Chapter 4.2.

    ...

    // Integrate the equations of motion to update
    // the physics.
    for (each object i NOT involved in a collision)
    {
        copy cur_S[2*i] and cur_S[2*i+1] to
        prior_S[2*i] and prior_S[2*i+1]
```

```
                    // Calculate the state derivative vector.
                    S_derivs[2*i] = CalcForce(i);
                    S_derivs[2*i+1] = prior_S[2*i] / mass[i];

                    // Integrate equations of motion, for object i only.
                    ExplicitEuler(2, &current_S[2*i],
                                &prior_S[2*i], &S_derivs[2*i], delta_t);
                }

                for (each pair of objects i, j, involved in a collision)
                {
                    // tc is the time of the collision, which
                    // occurs between t and t + delta_t.

                    // Copy current state to prior state.
                    copy cur_S[2*i] and cur_S[2*i+1] to
                    prior_S[2*i] and prior_S[2*i+1]

                    copy cur_S[2*j] and cur_S[2*j+1] to
                    prior_S[2*j] and prior_S[2*j+1]

                    // Calculate the state derivative vector.
                    S_derivs[2*i] = CalcForce(i);
                    S_derivs[2*i+1] = prior_S[2*i] / mass[i];

                    S_derivs[2*j] = CalcForce(j);
                    S_derivs[2*j+1] = prior_S[2*j] / mass[j];

                    // First integration: prior to collision.
                    ExplicitEuler(2, &cur_S[2*i], &prior_S[2*i],
                                &S_derivs[2*i], tc - t);

                    ExplicitEuler(2, &cur_S[2*j], &prior_S[2*j],
                                &S_derivs[2*j], tc - t);

                    // current_S now has the position and velocity of
                    // objects i and j at tc, the time of collision.

                    // Use Equations 13, 9, and 10 to compute the
                    // after-collision linear momentums. The updated
                    // momentums should be placed in cur_S[2*i] and
                    // cur_S[2*j] for objects i and j, respectively.

                    // Once cur_S reflects the after-collision
                    // momentums, perform the after-collision
                    // integration step, using the pseudo-code below.

                    copy cur_S[2*i] and cur_S[2*i+1] to
                    prior_S[2*i] and prior_S[2*i+1]

                    copy cur_S[2*j] and cur_S[2*j+1] to
                    prior_S[2*j] and prior_S[2*j+1]
```

```
        // Calculate the state derivative vector.
        S_derivs[2*i] = CalcForce(i);
        S_derivs[2*i+1] = prior_S[2*i] / mass[i];

        S_derivs[2*j] = CalcForce(j);
        S_derivs[2*j+1] = prior_S[2*j] / mass[j];

        // Second integration: after collision.
        ExplicitEuler(2, &cur_S[2*i], &prior_S[2*i],
                      &S_derivs[2*i], t + delta_t - tc);

        ExplicitEuler(2, &cur_S[2*j], &prior_S[2*j],
                      &S_derivs[2*j], t + delta_t - tc);
    }

    // Now all objects, including those in collision, have
    // been updated to time t + delta_t.

    // By integrating the equations of motion, we have
    // effectively moved simulation time forward by
    // delta_t.
    t = t + delta_t;
}
```

To be strictly correct, the algorithm used to discover the time of collision t_c, should use the physics integrator to advance the motion from t to t_c until a converged solution for t_c is found. For example, the bisection method discussed in Chapter 4.2 should use the physics integrator to compute the position of objects for each estimate of t_c until the bisection iterations are stopped. However, when object accelerations are zero or moderate and the physics time step is small, depending on the game, it may be perfectly acceptable to assume velocity is constant from t until t_c during collision discovery. If you make this assumption, the position of the objects at time t_c is trivially determined using Equation 4.3.5, with $\mathbf{V}_{init}$ set to the velocity at the start of the time step, and $\mathbf{p}_{init}$ set to the position at the start of the time step, and dropping the gravitation term. Note that swept-volume intersection tests are usually based on this assumption of constant velocity from time t to t_c before a collision. The swept-sphere intersection test discussed in Chapter 4.2, for example, makes this assumption, and only produces the exact result for t_c when the velocity of both spheres is constant prior to the collision.

Complete Exercise 6 to create a simple marbles game that implements frictionless particle collision response.

Complete Exercise 7 to create a projectile particle system based on explicit Euler integration.

Numerical Stability Issues and Alternatives to Explicit Euler Integration

Truncation error is always present in numerical integration. Since the result of one numerical integration step feeds the next numerical integration step, the truncation error at each step accumulates into a total error in the state vector that may grow or shrink over time. A critical goal in numerical simulation is to ensure that the total error is bounded; that is, the total error does not grow large without limits. A numerical simulation in which the total error is bounded for all time is said to be *numerically stable*. Unfortunately, in some circumstances the truncation error can interact with the properties that drive the motion in such a way that the simulation is *numerically unstable*. In this case, the total error is unbounded and will eventually grow as large as possible, ultimately resulting in floating-point overflow. Numerical integration techniques are said to be *conditionally stable* if they can be made stable by reducing the time step, Δt, below some threshold, a *stability bound*. The references [Rhodes01], [Eberly04], and [Anderson95] provide a more detailed introduction to these concepts.

It happens that explicit Euler integration, while simple, even intuitive, is one of the worst possible choices for numerical rigid-body physics simulation. It is conditionally stable at best, and unconditionally unstable when used to simulate physical systems that include spring forces (described in the next section), unless damping forces are added.

One alternative to explicit Euler integration, which is often a better choice for rigid-body physics simulation is *Verlet integration*. There are several variations, and we present the velocityless version here, as Equation 4.3.19, without proof. It is called "velocity-less" since the first time derivative of the state, the velocity of state, does not appear. The references [Porcino04], [Eberly04], and [Jakobsen03] provide a more in-depth look at the derivation of the Verlet integrator. Note that in this case, you must track the state vector for two prior time steps and that the state derivative is actually the second time derivative. Listing 4.3.6 provides pseudocode for a velocityless Verlet integrator.

$$\underbrace{\mathbf{S}\left(t+\Delta t\right)}_{\text{new state}} = 2 \underbrace{\mathbf{S}\left(t\right)}_{\text{prior state 1}} - \underbrace{\mathbf{S}\left(t-\Delta t\right)}_{\text{prior state 2}} + \left(\Delta t\right)^2 \underbrace{\left(\frac{d^2}{dt^2}\mathbf{S}(t)\right)}_{\text{state derivative}} \qquad (4.3.19)$$

Listing 4.3.6 Pseudocode for a velocityless Verlet integrator

```
void VelocityLessVerlet(N, new_S, prior_S1, prior_S2,
                        S_2nd_derivs, delta_t)
{
    for (i = 0; i < N; i++)
    {
        new_S[i] = (2.0 * prior_S1[i]) - prior_S2[i] +
                   (delta_t * delta_t * S_2nd_derivs[i]);
    }
}
```

In the case of velocityless Verlet integration, the natural choice for the state vector of a particle is simply $\mathbf{S} = \langle \mathbf{p}_1, \mathbf{p}_2, \cdots, \mathbf{p}_N \rangle$, with the corresponding second state derivative being $d^2\mathbf{S}/dt^2 = \langle \mathbf{F}_1/m_1, \mathbf{F}_2/m_2, \cdots, \mathbf{F}_N/m_N \rangle$.

In some cases, we shall see, the force applied to an object depends on velocity. In this case, you will need to integrate velocity in addition to position. It is often acceptable to use a mixture of different techniques; for example, explicit Euler integration to update the velocity states needed to compute forces that are dependent on velocity, and velocityless Verlet integration to update the position states.

There are a great many alternatives to explicit Euler and Verlet, which can be derived by manipulating truncated Taylor series expansions at different offsets from time *t*. Each method exhibits its own precision and stability characteristics. In terms of game physics, the *Runge-Kutta* series of integrators is quite popular, with the fourth-order Runge-Kutta method being a robust general-purpose, explicit integrator.

The most stable numerical integration methods are called *implicit methods*. These require solving a system of linear equations for each time step. If you must implement a general-purpose physics engine, it will be well worth your time to explore implicit methods. The so-called *A-Stable* implicit methods are stable for any time step size, Δt, meaning you will never have to reduce your physics time-step size to achieve a stable simulation, although you may need to adjust Δt to achieve good accuracy. (There is an exception to this. A-Stable and other implicit methods usually are at best conditionally stable when simulating situations that are physically unstable. See [Rhodes01] or [Eberly04] for more details on physical vs. numerical instability.)

There are many, many resources on numerical integration. Details on implementing the Runge-Kutta and implicit methods can be readily found in a library.

Complete Exercise 8 to demonstrate the difference between velocityless Verlet integration and explicit Euler integration.

The Importance of Frame-Rate Independence

Given the tendency of numerical simulation to be sensitive to the time step, it is rather important that you strive to create a physics engine that is frame-rate independent. By implementing a frame-rate independent system, you gain two significant benefits. First, your results will be repeatable, every time you run a simulation with the same inputs, regardless of computer CPU or GPU performance. Second, you will have maximum control over the stability of your simulation. Listing 4.3.7 is a fragment of pseudocode that illustrates a simple way to ensure that your physics simulation is updated using a constant time step that is independent of your actual game frame rate.

Listing 4.3.7   Pseudocode for updating the physics simulation at fixed time steps.

```
void main()
{
    float delta_t = 0.02;    // Physics time step, seconds
    float game_time;         // Current game time, seconds
```

```
float prev_game_time;   // Game time at previous frame
float physics_lag_time=0.0; // Time since last update

// Simulation/rendering loop
while (main game loop)
{
    update game_time;
    physics_lag_time += (game_time - prev_game_time);
    while (physics_lag_time > delta_t)
    {
        DoPhysicsSimulationStep(delta_t);
        physics_lag_time = physics_lag_time - delta_t;
    }
    prev_game_time = game_time;

    render scene;
}
}
```

Generalized Translational Motion

With the basics of numerical physics simulation in place, we will now consider a variety of nonconstant forces that contribute to the generalized motion of an object. Any combination of these forces might be acting on an object at a given time. You can obtain the net force acting on an object, $\mathbf{F}_{net}$, by simply adding all applied forces together. $\mathbf{F}_{net}$ is exactly the value of $\mathbf{F}$ to be used in the state derivative vector for numerical integration. If $\mathbf{F}_{net}$ has zero magnitude, the object has zero acceleration and is said to be in *translational equilibrium*, although it may still be moving at a nonzero velocity.

General Rigid Bodies versus Spherical Particles

We will now generalize our discussion to include arbitrary sized and shaped rigid bodies, rather than perfectly smooth spherical particles. There is exactly one reason for the smooth sphere restriction so far: we were able to completely avoid considering the issue of rotational motion. This is important: *all of the equations presented previously are perfectly valid for rigid bodies of any shape that are of finite size.*

Despite the fact that the previous equations support arbitrarily shaped objects, they describe the translational physics of a single point on the object (e.g., the center of a sphere). Rigid body objects fill a volume in space, and so we must find an appropriate point on the object for use in a simulation. It is standard practice to choose the object's *center of mass* to be the reference point for translational motion. The reason for this choice is that it removes *inertial coupling* that would otherwise make the translational equations dependent on rotation and the entire system more difficult to solve.

Equation 4.3.20 defines the location of the center of mass for a rigid body.

$$\mathbf{p}_{center-of-mass} = \frac{1}{mass} \iiint_{Vol} \rho \mathbf{r} dxdydz \qquad (4.3.20)$$

The density, ρ is the mass per unit volume, with units of type mass per the cube of distance. *The SI units for density are kilograms per meter cubed (kg/m³).* The variable, **r**, is the vector from a known reference point to the location of a differential element of the object's mass. The resulting center-of-mass location is calculated relative to the same reference point. Note that density might be a constant, but in general it might also vary with the differential element position, **r**. For example, if you are computing the center of mass of an object made partly of steel and partly of plastic, the integration over the plastic parts would use a different density from the integration over the steel parts. For arbitrarily shaped objects, Equation 4.3.20 can be difficult to evaluate. Brian Mirtich [Mirtich96] and David Eberly [Eberly03] have documented robust techniques for evaluating the center of mass of triangle mesh objects, which are extremely useful for game development.

Figure 4.3.6 illustrates a rigid body and its center of mass, and shows the standard symbol for center of mass. For physics simulation, we normally choose a local object-aligned coordinate system with its origin located at the center of mass. This same local coordinate system can be used for collision detection and rendering, as well as physics simulation.

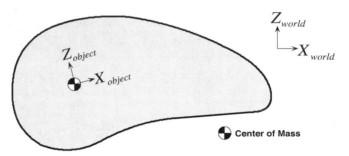

FIGURE 4.3.6   *The center of mass of an object.*

Linear Springs

The first generalized force that we will consider is due to a spring connecting two objects. Figure 4.3.7 illustrates a spring that is connecting two objects.

The spring is connected to one of the objects at location $\mathbf{p}_{e1}$, and to the other object at location $\mathbf{p}_{e2}$, the endpoints of the spring. The length of the spring is simply the Euclidian distance between the two endpoints. A spring has a so-called *rest length*, l_{rest}, which defines the length of the spring when it is neither compressed nor stretched. The spring exerts zero force when its length is its rest length. When the spring is stretched to be longer than l_{rest}, it applies an attraction force to each of the objects. When the spring is compressed to be shorter than l_{rest}, it applies a repulsion force to each of the objects. Equation 4.3.21 presents the simplest realistic model of

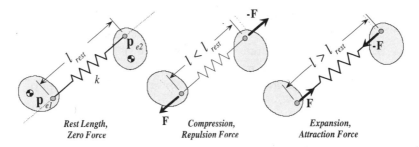

FIGURE 4.3.7 *The linear spring.*

spring force, *Hooke's Law*, in which the force is a linear function of the displacement from l_{rest}.

$$\mathbf{F}_{spring} = k\left(l - l_{rest}\right)\hat{\mathbf{d}} \qquad (4.3.21)$$

The variable, k, is the *spring stiffness,* a measure of the strength of the spring. *The stiffness is measured in units of type force per unit length. The SI units for spring stiffness are Newtons per meter.* The variable, l, is the current length of the spring, and the vector variable, $\hat{\mathbf{d}}$, is a unit length vector in the direction from $\mathbf{p}_{e1}$ to $\mathbf{p}_{e2}$. The spring force, $\mathbf{F}_{spring}$, is applied to object 1 at location $\mathbf{p}_{e1}$. An equal but opposite force, $-\mathbf{F}_{spring}$, is applied to object 2 at location $\mathbf{p}_{e2}$.

Viscous Damping

Viscous damping is a dissipative force (one that reduces kinetic energy) acting on objects moving at low speeds through fluids such as air, water, and oil. Mechanical damping devices called *dashpots* generate viscous damping forces, and are often used to reduce vibrations in machines, vehicle suspension systems, and so forth. Dashpots apply a damping force to the objects to which they are connected, as shown in Figure 4.3.8.

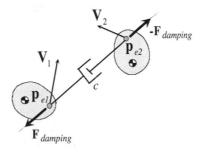

FIGURE 4.3.8 *The dashpot damper. If objects approach each other along the line between the points where the damper is connected, the damping force is repulsive.*

The viscous damper applies forces along the damper axis. The magnitude of the forces is related to the relative velocity of the objects along the damper axis. Equation 4.3.22 defines the force. The parameter, c, is the damping coefficient, *measured in units of type mass per unit time. The SI units for damping coefficient are kilograms per second.* The parameter, $\hat{\mathbf{d}}$ is a unit vector in the direction from $\mathbf{p}_{e1}$ to $\mathbf{p}_{e2}$.

$$\mathbf{F}_{damping} = c\left(\left(\mathbf{V}_{ep2} - \mathbf{V}_{ep1}\right) \cdot \hat{\mathbf{d}}\right)\hat{\mathbf{d}} \tag{4.3.22}$$

The damping force, $\mathbf{F}_{damping}$, is applied to object 1 at location $\mathbf{p}_{e1}$. An equal but opposite force, $-\mathbf{F}_{damping}$, is applied to object 2 at location $\mathbf{p}_{e2}$.

Aerodynamic Drag

An object traveling through a fluid, such as air or water, experiences a drag force that acts in the opposite of the object's velocity through the fluid. Equation 4.3.23 provides a simple approximation for this aerodynamic drag. Here, C_D is the drag coefficient, which has no units. Typical values for nonstreamlined objects range from 0.1 to 0.4. The variable S_{ref} is a representative front-projected area of the object. For game objects, other than aircraft, choose S_{ref} to be the cross-section area of a bounding sphere for the object, and assume the drag force acts at the center of mass of the object. In Equation 4.3.23, the variable ρ is the mass density of the fluid through which the object is traveling. [Rhodes05] provides a comprehensive overview of aerodynamic forces.

$$\mathbf{F}_{drag} = -\frac{1}{2}\rho|\mathbf{V}|^2 C_D S_{ref} \frac{\mathbf{V}}{|\mathbf{V}|} \tag{4.3.23}$$

Surface Friction

When two objects make contact, either during a collision, while in resting contact, or during sliding contact, the objects potentially exert a force on each other within the contact plane. This tangential force is called *friction*. The behavior of the friction force is rather complex. Observe that if you apply a horizontal force to an object at rest on a surface, the object does not begin moving unless the force exceeds a threshold. Once the force exceeds the threshold, the object begins moving, often abruptly. When the object is moving, the force required to keep the object moving is less than the force required to cause the initial motion. This observation illustrates the presence of a variable *static friction* when the object is at rest, and a *dynamic friction* when the object is in motion.

Coulomb developed the most common model of friction in the year 1781. You may be familiar with *Coulomb friction* from your prior studies. Using the Coulomb model, the magnitude of static friction is equal to the component of an external force, $\mathbf{F}_{applied}$, applied between the objects in the contact plane up to a maximum magnitude of $\mu_s|\mathbf{F}_n|$, where μ_s is a *static friction coefficient*, and $\mathbf{F}_n$ is the component of the applied force parallel to $\hat{\mathbf{n}}$, given by $\mathbf{F}_n = \hat{\mathbf{n}}\left(\mathbf{F}_{applied} \cdot \hat{\mathbf{n}}\right)$. The magnitude of dynamic friction, generated when there is relative motion in the contact plane between the two objects, is given by $\mu_d|\mathbf{F}_n|$. Here, μ_d is the *dynamic friction coefficient*. The friction coefficients are functions of the material properties of the two objects that are in contact. For example, the value of μ_s between two objects made of wood ranges from around 0.2 to around 0.75. The value of μ_d is usually smaller than μ_s. The difference between the coefficients leads to a discontinuity in the magnitude of friction force at the moment the objects begin to slide past one another, and this discontinuity can cause a difficulty in numerical simulations. *The friction coefficients have no units.*

There are three basic scenarios for two objects in contact with each other, shown in Figure 4.3.9. The following are the conventions used in the figure and equations to follow: $\mathbf{F}_{applied}$ is the total force, less friction, applied by object 1 onto object 2; $\mathbf{V}_t$ is the tangential component of the relative velocity of object 1 moving past object 2; $\hat{\mathbf{n}}$ is the contact normal measured outward from object 2; the resulting friction force, $\mathbf{F}_{friction}$ as calculated is applied on object 1, so that the net force on object 1 becomes $\mathbf{F}_{net} = \mathbf{F}_{applied} + \mathbf{F}_{friction}$. By *Newton's Third Law of Motion*, $-\mathbf{F}_{friction}$ is applied on object 2, so there is no need to calculate the friction force twice. The tangential relative velocity, $\mathbf{V}_t$, is given by $\mathbf{V}_t = \left(\mathbf{V}_1 - \mathbf{V}_2\right) - \hat{\mathbf{n}}\left(\left(\mathbf{V}_1 - \mathbf{V}_2\right) \cdot \hat{\mathbf{n}}\right)$.

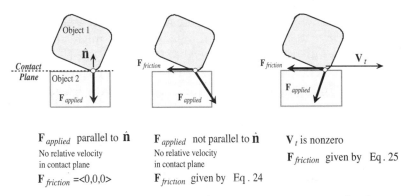

FIGURE 4.3.9   *Friction acting on object 1 at a contact point for three scenarios. The force, $\mathbf{F}_{applied}$, is applied by object 1 onto object 2.*

An intuitive example of an external force, $\mathbf{F}_{applied}$, applied by one object onto another is simply the weight of an object resting on a horizontal surface. The resting object applies a force equal to its weight on the surface in the direction $-\hat{\mathbf{n}}$, and from *Newton's Third Law of Motion*, the surface applies an equal but opposite force back on the object. If you exert an additional horizontal force on the object, attempting to slide the object, $\mathbf{F}_{applied}$ would be the sum of the object's weight plus the additional horizontal force.

If $\mathbf{V}_t$ is zero, the friction force is given by Equation 4.3.24. Note that this equation guarantees that the magnitude of static friction never exceeds the Coulomb maximum of $\mu_s |\mathbf{F}_n|$. The tangential component of the applied force, $\mathbf{F}_t$, is given by $\mathbf{F}_t = \mathbf{F}_{applied} - \mathbf{F}_n$.

$$\mathbf{F}_{friction} = -\frac{\mathbf{F}_t}{|\mathbf{F}_t|} \min\left(\mu_s |\mathbf{F}_n| \, , \, |\mathbf{F}_t|\right) \qquad (4.3.24)$$

If $\mathbf{V}_t$ is zero, and $\mathbf{F}_t$ exceeds $\mathbf{F}_{friction}$ in magnitude, the objects will begin to accelerate tangentially past one another. For the case when $\mathbf{V}_t$ is nonzero, the friction force is given by Equation 4.3.25. Note that here, $\mathbf{F}_{applied} \cdot \hat{\mathbf{n}}$ is always negative, and so friction acts in a direction opposite $\mathbf{V}_t$. Friction is a dissipative force when the objects are in relative motion, and acts to reduce the kinetic energy of the two objects.

$$\mathbf{F}_{friction} = \frac{-\mathbf{V}_t}{|\mathbf{V}_t|} \mu_d |\mathbf{F}_n| \qquad (4.3.25)$$

It is interesting to note that it is possible for dynamic friction to act in the same direction as the tangential applied force, rather than always against it. For example, consider a passenger train headed on a deadly course toward a bridge recently destroyed by a villain. Our hero has managed to set the brakes so that the wheels are no longer turning. Sliding, Coulomb friction acts to slow the train down. However, friction is insufficient to stop the train in time. Our hero might tie one end of a chain to the train, and then hold the other end of the chain while bracing herself against a building, or a perhaps a mountain. The force that the chain applies to the train acts opposite the train's velocity, in the same direction as the friction force. Thus, the applied force and the friction force act in the same direction, both contributing to the deceleration of the train and saving of lives.

A Simple Spring-Mass-Damper Soft-Body Dynamics System

To understand better how you might go about using these various forces, consider a fun example. Using the results of this section and the prior section, you can construct a simple soft-body dynamics simulator. Simply create a polygon mesh with an interesting shape. You can create the mesh in code or use a digital content creation modeling package. For this system, you will use physics to update the position of the vertices of the mesh. For the physics system, create a particle at the location of each vertex of the mesh, and assign a mass to the particle. Then, create a spring and a damper between unique pairs of particles. The spring rest lengths should be equal to the initial distance between particles. Figure 4.3.10 illustrates this configuration, for a 2D model; the arrangement extends naturally to 3D. It is important that you include springs that connect particles on opposite sides of the mesh, to prevent the shape from collapsing; however, for complex meshes you don't necessarily have to have springs between every unique pair.

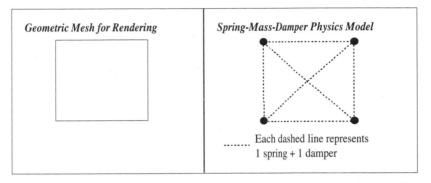

FIGURE 4.3.10 *A simple soft-body model of a mesh, represented by a collection of particles connected by springs and dampers.*

As a way of experimenting with this type of simple soft-body model, consider the pseudocode in Listing 4.3.8, which initializes the object in midair, with an initial velocity of zero. The forces acting on the particles include gravity, as well as the spring and damper forces.

Listing 4.3.8 A simple spring-mass-damper soft-body dynamics system.

```
void main()
{
    N = number of particles;    // # verts in visual model
    Vector3D cur_S[2*N];        // S(t+delta_t)
    Vector3D prior_S[2*N];      // S(t)
    Vector3D S_derivs[2*N];     // dS/dt
    Vector3D g(0.0,0.0,-9.81);  // Gravity
    float mass[N];              // Mass of particles
    float k[N][N];              // Spring constant between particles
    float lrest[N][N];          // Spring rest lengths
    float c[N][N];              // Damper constant between particles
    float delta_t = 0.02;       // Physics time step, seconds
    float game_time;            // Current game time, seconds
    float prev_game_time;       // Game time at previous frame
    float physics_lag_time=0.0; // Time since last update
    float init_height;          // Initial height above the ground
```

```
// Initialize the particles.
for (i = 0; i < N; i++)
{
    mass[i] = 1.0f;          // mass = 1 kg

    // Set initial linear momentum to be zero.
    cur_S[2*i] = Vector3D(0,0,0);

    // Assign initial position from visual model.
    cur_S[2*i+1] = position of model vertex i;

    // Update the initial position to reflect init_height.
    cur_S[2*i+1].z += init_height;
}

// Initialize a spring and damper between every pair
// of particles.

for (i = 0; i < N; i++)
{
    for (j = 0; j < N; j++)
    {
        // Configure the spring.
        k[i][j] = 10.0f;    // stiffness = 10 N/m

        // Configure the damper.
        c[i][j] = 0.1f;      // damping coef = 0.1 kg/s

        // Configure the rest length.
        lrest[i][j] = length of vector
                    (cur_S[2*j+1] - cur_S[2*i+1]);
    }
}

// Runtime loop, derived from Listing 6.
while (main game loop)
{
    update game_time;
    physics_lag_time += (game_time - prev_game_time);
    while (physics_lag_time > delta_t)
    {
        DoPhysicsSimulationStep(delta_t);
        physics_lag_time = physics_lag_time - delta_t;
    }
    prev_game_time = game_time;

    // Once physics has updated the particle
    // positions, we must transfer these to the
    // visual model for rendering.
    for (i = 0; i < N; i++)
    {
```

```
                        update visual model vertex i position to
                        be cur_S[2*i + 1];
                }

                render the visual model;
        }
}

void DoPhysicsSimulationStep(delta_t)
{
        Use Listing 5.

        For better stability, modify Listing 5 to use
        velocity-less Verlet integration for the position
        updates and explicit Euler to update particle
        velocities.
}

Vector3D CalcForce(i)
{
        Vector3D d, SForce, DForce, RelativeVel;
        Vector3D Force_Net = 0.0f;

        // Initialize the net force by calculating the
        // force due to gravity, the particle's weight.
        Force_Net += mass[i] * g;

        // Compute the spring and damper forces.
        for (j = 0; j < N; j++)
        {
                // Compute unit vector from particle i to
                // particle j, and the current length of the spring.
                d = cur_S[2*j+1] - cur_S[2*i+1];
                length = d.Length();

                d.Normalize();     // Make d unit length.

                // Compute the spring force using Equation 20.
                // i is attracted to j if the current length is
                // greater than the rest length, repelled from j
                // if the current length is less than rest length.
                SForce = k[i][j] * (length - lrest[i][j]) * d;

                // Compute the damping force. First we need the
                // relative velocity.
                RelativeVel = (cur_S[2*j]/mass[j]) -
                              (cur_S[2*i]/mass[i]);

                // From here, we calc the damping force using
                // Equation 21. If object j is moving away from
                // object i, the force on object j draws i
```

```
                // towards j, otherwise the force repels i away
                // from j.
                DForce = c[i][j] * RelativeVel.DotProduct(d) * d;

                // Increment the net force.
                Force_Net += SForce;
                Force_Net += DForce;
        }

        return(Force_Net);
    }
```

Complete Exercise 10 to implement a soft-body simulation based on Listing 4.3.7. Note that for this exercise, you should initially implement collision detection and response between the particles and a solid, immovable ground surface. Use the results of Exercise 5 to determine the results of an impulsive collision with an immovable object. Jeff Lander [Lander99] has created a simple demo program based on the approach outlined in Listing 4.3.7. Jeff's code is available for download on the Internet at *www.gdmag.com/src/mar99.zip*. This demo can serve as a nice reference for Exercise 10.

Rotational Motion

The physics of rotational motion are analogous to the kinematics of particle or center-of-mass translational motion. Torque, the analog of force, causes an angular acceleration. Angular acceleration causes a change in angular velocity. Angular velocity causes a change in orientation, the rotational analog of position. We begin our analysis of rotational motion with Equation 4.3.26, the rotational analog to Equation 4.3.8.

$$\frac{d}{dt}\mathbf{L}(t) = \boldsymbol{\tau}(t) \tag{4.3.26}$$

Here, the vector $\boldsymbol{\tau}(t)$ is the *torque,* sometimes called the *moment,* or *moment of force. Torque is measured in units of type force times distance. The SI units for torque are Newton-meters.* Torque is calculated at a point about which an object is expected to rotate, and is related to a force applied to the object. Torque is nonzero when the force acts along a line that does not intersect the point where torque is being calculated. Equation 4.3.27 gives the mathematical definition of torque, where $\mathbf{r}$ is the vector from the point about which torque is being calculated to the point where the force causing torque is being applied. From the equation, note that torque has a direction that is perpendicular to the force vector and $\mathbf{r}$.

$$\boldsymbol{\tau} = \mathbf{r} \times \mathbf{F} \tag{4.3.27}$$

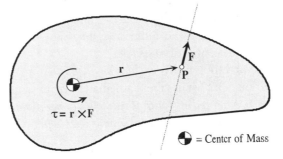

FIGURE 4.3.11 *The relationship between force and torque. The arc arrow indicates that the torque due to* **F** *causes a counterclockwise rotation, (e.g., a positive rotation about a vector pointing out of the page, the direction of the torque vector).*

Figure 4.3.11 illustrates the generation of torque about the center of mass of a rigid body, due to a force, **F**, applied at a point, **P**, on the body. Here, **r** is the vector from the center of mass to the point **P**.

Before continuing, let's consider the effect of torque on an object. We would like the concept to be somewhat intuitive. The effect of torque is fairly intuitive when it acts on an object that initially is not rotating, and so we will consider that case here. Consider the classic children's outdoor play toy, the seesaw. A seesaw in play rotates back and forth about the center fulcrum. If you approach a seesaw that is not in use, it will be resting, not rotating. When you sit on the end of the seesaw, your weight acts straight down near one end, and the vector **r** from the fulcrum to your body points in a generally horizontal direction. Your weight results in a torque about the center of the fulcrum that acts to one side, parallel to the ground and perpendicular to the seesaw and your weight vector. It happens that the torque applied is exactly parallel to the axis of rotation about the fulcrum. This, in a nutshell, is the effect of torque on an object that is not initially rotating: the torque causes the object to begin rotating about the torque axis. For objects that are rotating with fairly small angular velocities, the result is similar: large torques change the axis of rotation to be approximately the torque axis. Objects with large angular momentum exhibit behavior that is less intuitive, called *gyroscopic precession*, in response to an applied torque, and even respond in a nonintuitive fashion when no torque is being applied (*torque-free precession*). We will not discuss these high angular momentum behaviors here.

If an object is moving freely in space, torque is calculated at the center of mass, and rotation is about the center of mass. If an object is constrained in some way, torque should be calculated about some other point that represents the possible axis of rotation. For example, if an object is constrained by a hinge, torque should be measured at a point along the hinge axis. In this chapter, we are only concerned with torque about the center of mass.

The vector, $\mathbf{L}(t)$, is called *angular momentum*, the rotational analog to linear momentum. Equation 4.3.28 states the mathematical definition of angular momentum. *Angular momentum is measured in units of type mass times distance squared per unit time. The SI units for angular momentum are kilogram-meters-squared per second (kg-m²/s).*

$$\mathbf{L} = \mathbf{J}\omega \tag{4.3.28}$$

The variable $\mathbf{J}$ is a symmetric 3×3 matrix called the *inertia tensor*, the analog of mass. The terms of the inertia tensor describe the distribution of mass throughout the volume of a rigid body. ($\mathbf{J}$ is represented by the variable $\mathbf{I}$ in many texts; however, we use $\mathbf{J}$ here to avoid confusion with the identity matrix.) Equation 4.3.29 defines the inertia tensor, which is measured in world coordinates.

$$\mathbf{J} = \begin{bmatrix} J_{xx} & J_{xy} & J_{xz} \\ J_{xy} & J_{yy} & J_{yz} \\ J_{xz} & J_{yz} & J_{zz} \end{bmatrix} \tag{4.3.29}$$

The diagonal components of the inertia tensor are called *moments of inertia*, and the off-diagonal elements are called *products of inertia*. *The inertia tensor is measured in units of type mass times distance squared. The SI units for the inertia tensor are kilogram-meters-squared (kg-m²).* Equations 4.3.30 and 4.3.31 define the moments of inertia and products of inertia, respectively. Here, the variables r_x, r_y, and r_z are the components of a vector $\mathbf{r}$ from the object's center of mass to a differential element of mass in the object.

$$J_{xx} = \iiint_{Vol} \rho\left(r_y^2 + r_z^2\right)dxdydz \ ; \ J_{yy} = \iiint_{Vol} \rho\left(r_x^2 + r_z^2\right)dxdydz \ ; \ J_{zz} = \iiint_{Vol} \rho\left(r_x^2 + r_y^2\right)dxdydz \tag{4.3.30}$$

$$J_{xy} = \iiint_{Vol} \rho r_x r_y dxdydz \ ; \ J_{xz} = \iiint_{Vol} \rho r_x r_z dxdydz \ ; \ J_{yz} = \iiint_{Vol} \rho r_y r_z dxdydz \tag{4.3.31}$$

As with center of mass, for general-shaped objects these equations can be tedious to evaluate. Table 4.3.1 provides equations for the inertia tensor elements for a few simple shapes. The products of inertia for these objects are zero. [Mirtich96] and [Eberly03] provide methods for robustly evaluating the inertia tensor and center of mass for the arbitrary triangle meshes that are common to game development.

Table 4.3.1 Inertia Tensor Values and Center-of-Mass Locations for Primitive Shapes with Constant Density

Cylinder	Rectanguloid	Cone	Sphere
r = radius $J_{xx} = \dfrac{1}{12} m\left(3r^2 + h^2\right)$ $J_{yy} = J_{xx}$ $J_{zz} = 0.5mr^2$	d = depth $J_{xx} = \dfrac{1}{12} m\left(d^2 + h^2\right)$ $J_{yy} = \dfrac{1}{12} m\left(w^2 + h^2\right)$ $J_{zz} = \dfrac{1}{12} m\left(d^2 + w^2\right)$	$J_{xx} = \dfrac{3}{20} m\left(r^2 + \dfrac{h^2}{4}\right)$ $J_{yy} = J_{xx}$ $J_{zz} = \dfrac{3}{10} mr^2$	$J_{xx} = J_{yy} = J_{zz} = \dfrac{2}{5} mr^2$

For physics simulation, as presented herein, the inertia tensor must be represented in the inertial reference frame, or the game's world coordinate system. If the object is rotating, the inertia tensor in this coordinate system will change as the object rotates. To avoid an expensive recomputation for every numerical integration step, it is best to compute the inertia tensor, and its inverse, $\mathbf{J}^{-1}$, in the object's local coordinate system, and then transform that tensor into world space at every integration step using Equation 4.3.32. Note that the same transformation is applied to both the tensor and its inverse, where $\mathbf{R}$ is the 3×3 object-to-world rotation matrix.

$$\mathbf{J} = \mathbf{R}\mathbf{J}_{object\_space}\mathbf{R}^T \; ; \; \mathbf{J}^{-1} = \mathbf{R}\mathbf{J}^{-1}_{object\_space}\mathbf{R}^T \qquad (4.3.32)$$

The orientation of an object can be represented by either $\mathbf{R}$ or by a unit quaternion, q. Each of these is an analog to position. The angular velocity of an object, $\omega = \left\langle \omega_x, \omega_y, \omega_z \right\rangle$, measured in world space, is the analog of velocity. The direction of angular velocity is the direction of the object's rotation, and its magnitude is the rate of rotation. *Angular velocity is measured in units of type angle per unit time (angle/time). The SI units for angular velocity are radians per second (rad/s).*

We can use Equations 4.3.26 through 4.3.32 to perform the rotational portion of our numerical physics simulation. For a single rigid body, the state vector for explicit Euler integration, with both translational and rotational states included, can be $\mathbf{S}_i = \left\langle m_i\mathbf{V}_i, \mathbf{p}_i, \mathbf{L}_i, \mathbf{R}_i \right\rangle$, or $\mathbf{S}_i = \left\langle m_i\mathbf{V}_i, \mathbf{p}_i, \mathbf{L}_i, q_i \right\rangle$ if you choose a unit quaternion to represent the object's orientation state. The state derivative entries for $m_i\mathbf{V}_i$ and $\mathbf{p}_i$ are the same as for the no-rotation case. The state derivative entry for $\mathbf{L}$ is given by Equation 4.3.26; it is the net torque, $\boldsymbol{\tau}_{net}$, calculated as the sum of torques due to the applied forces in Equation 4.3.33.

$$\boldsymbol{\tau}_{net} = \left(\sum_{i=1}^{N_{springs}} \mathbf{r}_{spring,i} \times \mathbf{F}_{spring,i} \right) + \left(\sum_{i=1}^{N_{dampers}} \mathbf{r}_{dmp,i} \times \mathbf{F}_{dmp,i} \right) + \mathbf{r}_{contact} \times \mathbf{F}_{friction} + \cdots \quad (4.3.33)$$

Equation 4.3.34 defines the value of the state derivative of $\mathbf{R}$ when the orientation state is represented as an object-to-world rotation matrix, and Equation 4.3.35 defines the state derivative of q when the orientation state is represented by a unit quaternion. Take care to note the special representation of the angular velocity as a quaternion with its real component equal to 0.0.

$$\frac{d}{dt}\mathbf{R}(t) = \begin{bmatrix} 0 & -\omega_z & \omega_y \\ \omega_z & 0 & -\omega_x \\ -\omega_y & \omega_x & 0 \end{bmatrix} \mathbf{R}(t) \quad (4.3.34)$$

$$\frac{d}{dt}q(t) = \frac{1}{2}\omega(t)q(t), \quad \text{with} \quad \omega = 0 + i\omega_x + j\omega_y + k\omega_z \quad (4.3.35)$$

With the state vector and state derivative vector in place, you can use your favorite numerical integrator to solve for the updated state vector.

There are two postprocessing steps that you must perform to properly simulate rotation. First, since the state derivative of orientation, given by Equation 4.3.34 or 4.3.35, requires that we know the angular velocity, it is necessary to compute the angular velocity *after* the integration step, by solving Equation 4.3.28 for the angular velocity and transforming the object space inertia tensor into world space using the second part of Equation 4.3.32. This step is given here as Equation 4.3.36.

$$\omega(t + \Delta t) = \mathbf{R}(t + \Delta t)\mathbf{J}_{object\_space}^{-1}\mathbf{R}^T(t + \Delta t)\mathbf{L}(t + \Delta t) \quad (4.3.36)$$

Once the updated angular velocity is known, you will be able to prepare for the next integration step.

Second, a correction step must be applied to $\mathbf{R}$ or q every few frames. When simulating rotation, $\mathbf{R}$ is expected to be orthogonal and q is expected to be unit length. Floating-point round off and truncation error will cause these to drift over time. Every few frames, you must ensure that $\mathbf{R}$ is orthogonal by performing a Gram-Schmidt orthonormalization ([Eberly04], [Golub96]) or perform a Euclidian normalization of q.

The Simulation Loop with Support for Rigid Body Rotation

As discussed previously, the simulation loop for rigid body dynamics with rotational motion is somewhat more complex than pure translational motion. Listing 4.3.9 outlines the steps required to configure such a system, and illustrates the simulation loop without collision detection and response. As in prior code listings, comments within the code clarify the process. Note that in practice, collisions must be handled in a manner similar to Listing 4.3.5.

Listing 4.3.9 Simulation loop with rotation

```
void main()
{
    N = number of rigid bodies
    Matrix33 JObj[N];        // Inertia tensors in object space
    Matrix33 JObjInv[N];     // Inverse inertia tensors in
                             // object space
    Matrix33 J;              // Temporary inertia tensor
                             // in world space
    float mass[N];           // Rigid body masses
    Vector3D cur_S[3*N];     // Velocity, position, and
                             // angular momentum states
    Quaternion cur_q[N];     // Orientation states as
                             // quaternions
    Vector3D prior_S[3*N];   // Prior vel, position,
                             // angular momentum states
    Quaternion prior_q[N];   // Prior orientation state
    Vector3D S_derivs[3*N];  // dS/dt for vel, pos,
                             // angular mom
    Quaternion q_derivs[N];  // dS/dt for orientation
    Vector3D cur_w[N];       // Current angular velocities
    Matrix33 R;              // Temporary rotation matrix
    int iCounter = 0;        // Counter to tell us when to
                             // renormalize the
                             // orientation quaternion

    // Initialize the rigid bodies
    for (i = 0; i < N; i++)
    {
        mass[i] = mass of rigid body i;

        // The initial center-of-mass position and
        // linear momentum are the same as the
        // translational only case.
        cur_S[3*i] = initial linear momentum of i
        cur_S[3*i+1] = initial position of i's center-of-mass;

        // The rotational state variables are dependent
        // on the inertia tensor, so we calculate that here.

        JObj[i] = compute inertia tensor of rigid body i,
                  in the local object space of i;

        // Since we need it later, compute and store the
        // inverse inertia tensors.
```

```
        JObjInv[i] = JObj[i].Inverse();

        // Set the initial orientation of object i. This
        // is a quaternion represented in world space.

        cur_q[i] = current orientation as a unit quaternion;

        // The initial angular velocity is here assumed
        // to be zero, but it might be nonzero.

        cur_w[i] = Vector3D(0,0,0);

        // Compute initial angular momentum given angular
        // velocity using Equation 28 and 32. This
        // requires that we first compute a 3x3 rotation
        // matrix cur_q[i].

        R = cur_q[i].ConvertToRotationMatrix();

        // From here we can compute the initial world
        // space inertia tensor using Equation 32.

        J = R * JObj[i] * R.Transpose();

        // Now we can compute the initial angular
        // momentum using Equation 28.
        cur_S[3*i+2] = J * cur_w[i];
}

// Game simulation/rendering loop
while (game simulation is running)
{
    update game_time;

    // Update the physics.
    physics_lag_time += (game_time - prev_game_time);
    while (physics_lag_time > delta_t)
    {
        DoPhysicsSimulationStep(delta_t);
        physics_lag_time = physics_lag_time - delta_t;
    }
    prev_game_time = game_time;

    // Occasionally renormalize the orientation
    // quaternion.
    if (++iCounter == 5)
    {
        iCounter = 0;
        for (i = 0;  i < N;  i++)
            cur_q[i].Normalize();
    }
```

```
            // Render the scene.
            for (i = 0; i < N; i++)
            {
                render rigid body i at position
                cur_S[3*i+1], and orientation cur_q[i];
            }
        }
    }

    // Update the physics
    void DoPhysicsSimulationStep(delta_t)
    {
        copy cur_S to prior_S
        copy cur_q to prior_q

        // temp_w is a temporary quaternion version of the
        // angular velocity, as shown in Equation 35.
        Quaternion temp_w;

        // Calculate the state derivative vectors.
        for (i = 0; i < N; i++)
        {
            // State derivative for translational linear
            // momentum and position are the same as for
            // the non-rotation case.
            S_derivs[3*i] = CalcForce(i);
            S_derivs[3*i+1] = prior_S[3*i] / mass[i];

            // State derivative for angular momentum is the
            // net torque, given by Equations 26 and 33.
            S_derivs[3*i+2] = CalcTorque(i);

            // State derivative for the orientation
            // is given by Equation 35.
            temp_w.Set(0, cur_w[i].x, cur_w[i].y, cur_w[i].z);

            q_derivs[i] = 0.5 * temp_w * cur_q[i];
        }

        // Integrate the equations of motion. Vector states first.
        ExplicitEuler(3*N, cur_S, prior_S, S_derivs, delta_t);

        // Followed by the quaternion orientation state.
        ExplicitEuler(N, cur_q, prior_q, q_derivs, delta_t);

        // We are not done yet. We have the updated state, but
        // we need to compute the new angular velocity using
        // Equation 36. We do this in a loop since it has to
        // be done for all objects.
        for (i = 0; i < N; i++)
        {
            // We need a rotation matrix for time t + delta_t.
            R = cur_q[i].ConvertToRotationMatrix();
```

```
        // We next compute the inverse inertia tensor
        // in world space, which is used in Equation 36.
        J = R * JObjInv[i] * R.Transpose();

        // We are now in a position to update the
        // angular velocity using Equation 36.
        cur_w[i] = J * cur_S[3*i+2];
    }

    // Now we're done with the integration!

    // By integrating the equations of motion, we have
    // effectively moved simulation time forward by delta_t.
    t = t + delta_t;
}
```

A Brief Word about Integrators and Different State Variable Types

If you look carefully at Listing 4.3.9, you will see that the call to ExplicitEuler looks identical regardless of whether the state vectors and derivatives contain Vector3D objects or Quaternion objects. In addition, you may wonder how you can actually create a single integrator function that can integrate state variables of different types. There are a couple of ways to accomplish this. One approach is to flatten all state variables (e.g., vectors and quaternions) into an array of floating-point values, and use an integrator that simply integrates an array of floating-point state values. Another approach, using object-oriented programming, is to derive all state variables from a base State class, and ensure that all concrete state classes overload the operators required by the integrator: −, +, and *.

Let's look at the first approach, in which the state variables are flattened to an array of floats. A Vector3D object can be represented as an array of three floats, and a Quaternion object can be represented as an array of four floats. Listing 4.3.10 shows how you might represent a collection of object states that follow this approach, along with the call to ExplicitEuler. The state variable vector includes $m\mathbf{V}$, $\mathbf{p}$, $\mathbf{L}$, and q in a single floating-point array.

Listing 4.3.10   Object states flattened into an array of floating-point values

```
    float cur_S[13*N];      // Current state
    float prior_S[13*N];    // Prior state
    float S_derivs[13*N];   // State derivatives

    // for object i
    cur_S[13*i + 0] = linear momentum x component;
    cur_S[13*i + 1] = linear momentum y component;
    cur_S[13*i + 2] = linear momentum z component;
    cur_S[13*i + 3] = position x component;
```

```
cur_S[13*i + 4] = position y component;
cur_S[13*i + 5] = position z component;
cur_S[13*i + 6] = angular momentum x component;
cur_S[13*i + 7] = angular momentum y component;
cur_S[13*i + 8] = angular momentum z component;
cur_S[13*i + 9] = orientation real component;
cur_S[13*i + 10] = orientation imaginary i component;
cur_S[13*i + 11] = orientation imaginary j component;
cur_S[13*i + 12] = orientation imaginary k component;

prior_S[13*i + 0] through prior_S[13*i + 12] is similar;

S_derivs[13*i + 0] = Net force x component;
S_derivs[13*i + 1] = Net force y component;
S_derivs[13*i + 2] = Net force z component;
S_derivs[13*i + 3] = Velocity x component;
S_derivs[13*i + 4] = Velocity y component;
S_derivs[13*i + 5] = Velocity z component;
S_derivs[13*i + 6] = Net torque x component;
S_derivs[13*i + 7] = Net torque y component;
S_derivs[13*i + 8] = Net torque z component;
S_derivs[13*i + 9] = 0.0;
S_derivs[13*i + 10] = angular velocity x component;
S_derivs[13*i + 11] = angular velocity y component;
S_derivs[13*i + 12] = angular velocity z component;

// The following call integrates the vector values and
// quaternion values all in one call.
ExplicitEuler(13*N, new_S, prior_S, S_derivs, delta_t);
```

Using an object-oriented approach, the integrator parameters would be specified as arrays of a base object class type, and then derive all state variable types from the base class. The base class in this case must define pure virtual functions for the basic mathematical operators $-$, $+$, and $*$, and the state variable classes must each provide concrete implementations of those operators. If you choose to use C++, and store the states in STL vectors, the state variable classes will also need to provide assignment operators and copy constructors to make the STL container classes happy. Listing 4.3.11 shows example code in pseudo-C++.

Listing 4.3.11 Object-oriented state classes and integrator

```
class State
{
    const State &operator+(const State &Other) = 0;
    const State &operator-(const State &Other) = 0;
    const State &operator*(const State &Other) = 0;
    const State &operator*(const float fFactor) = 0;

};
```

```cpp
class Vector3D : public State
{
    const Vector3D &operator+(const Vector3D &Other);
    const Vector3D &operator-(const Vector3D &Other);
    const Vector3D &operator*(const Vector3D &Other);
    const Vector3D &operator*(const float fFactor);

    float m_fX, m_fY, m_fZ;     // Components of vector
};

class Quaternion : public State
{
    const Quaternion &operator+(const Quaternion &Other);
    const Quaternion &operator-(const Quaternion &Other);
    const Quaternion &operator*(const Quaternion &Other);
    const Quaternion &operator*(const float fFactor);

    float m_fR;                 // Real component
    float m_fi, m_fj, m_fk;     // Imaginary components
};

void main()
{
    ArrayContainer<State> cur_S;
    ArrayContainer<State> prior_S;
    ArrayContainer<State> S_derivs;
    for (i = 0; i < N; i++)
    {
        cur_S.Add(Vector3D(linear momentum of i));
        cur_S.Add(Vector3D(position of i));
        cur_S.Add(Vector3D(angular momentum of i));
        cur_S.Add(Quaternion(orientation of i));

        // prior_S and S_derivs follow similarly.
    }

    // In the simulation loop, just call the integrator by
    // passing references to cur_S, prior_S, and S_derivs.
}

void ExplicitEuler(ArrayContainer<State&> &new_S,
                const ArrayContainer<State&> &prior_S,
                const ArrayContainer<State&> &S_derivs,
                delta_t)
{
    unsigned int N = new_S.size();
    for (i = 0; i < N; i++)
    {
        new_S[i] = prior_S[i] + delta_t * S_derivs[i];
    }
}
```

There certainly are other ways in which you might build an object-oriented numerical simulator; however, one strong benefit of the approach shown in Listing

4.3.11 is that the numerical integrator method need only exist in one location in your source code. This makes the code fairly easy to maintain.

Collision Response Revisited

Now that we understand how to simulate the motion of objects undergoing rotational motion, it is worth revisiting impulse-momentum-based collision response. Figure 4.3.12 illustrates a generalized, frictionless rigid-body collision. Because there is no friction, the collision impulse acts through the point of impact in the direction of a unit normal vector at the point of impact. As shown in Figure 4.3.12, the line of action of the impulse does not necessarily intersect the centers of mass of the objects involved, resulting in an impulsive torque that changes the rotational motion state of the objects.

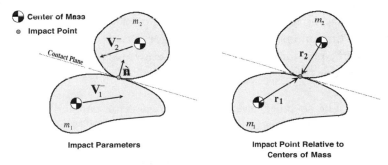

FIGURE 4.3.12   *Generalized frictionless collision.*

The rotational analog to the linear impulse-momentum equation is the *angular impulse-momentum equation*, given by Equation 4.3.37 for frictionless collisions between two objects.

$$\mathbf{L}_1^+ = \mathbf{L}_1^- + \Lambda\left(\mathbf{r}_1 \times \hat{\mathbf{n}}\right) \quad ; \quad \mathbf{L}_2^+ = \mathbf{L}_2^- - \Lambda\left(\mathbf{r}_2 \times \hat{\mathbf{n}}\right) \tag{4.3.37}$$

To compute generalized frictionless collision response, we must solve Equations 4.3.9 through 4.3.12 and 4.3.37 for the impulse. Equation 4.3.38 gives the resulting impulse value, which models both translational and rotational effects. The impulse vector is given by Equation 4.3.11.

$$\Lambda = \frac{-\left(1+\varepsilon\right)\left(\hat{\mathbf{n}}\cdot\left(\mathbf{V}_1^- - \mathbf{V}_2^-\right) + \omega_1^- \cdot\left(\mathbf{r}_1 \times \hat{\mathbf{n}}\right) - \omega_2^- \cdot\left(\mathbf{r}_2 \times \hat{\mathbf{n}}\right)\right)}{\dfrac{1}{m_1} + \dfrac{1}{m_2} + \left(\left(\mathbf{r}_1 \times \hat{\mathbf{n}}\right)^{\mathrm{T}} \mathbf{J}_1^{-1}\left(\mathbf{r}_1 \times \hat{\mathbf{n}}\right) + \left(\mathbf{r}_2 \times \hat{\mathbf{n}}\right)^{\mathrm{T}} \mathbf{J}_2^{-1}\left(\mathbf{r}_2 \times \hat{\mathbf{n}}\right)\right)} \tag{4.3.38}$$

To compute the postcollision linear and angular momentums, simply apply the impulse from Equations 4.3.38 and 4.3.11 to Equations 4.3.9, 4.3.10, and 4.3.37. Note that Equation 4.3.38, when substituted into Equation 4.3.11, simplifies to Equation 4.3.13 when the line joining the two centers of mass intersects the impact point and is parallel to the contact normal, since all the cross products in Equation 4.3.38 become zero. This is to be expected, since there is no impulsive torque in this case.

A Brief Word on Alternative Collision Response Methods

The impulse-momentum approach to resolving collision response is robust, realistic, and reliable. However, in practice, it is no panacea. Case in point: as illustrated earlier, the numerical integration of state can be difficult to manage efficiently since collisions usually occur between t and $t + \Delta t$, requiring a two-part integration—before and after the collision—with time steps that differ from the noncollision time step. Further, as discussed in Chapter 4.2, an expensive iteration may be required to determine the time and position of collision prior to computing the response. In some cases, this can be prohibitively slow when there are many simultaneous collisions between pairs or groups of objects. Alternative methods exist, and we briefly mention some of them here.

The so-called *penalty force methods* represent one alternative to impulse-based collision response. In the classical penalty force-based collision response, rather than calculate instantaneous changes in velocity and angular velocity in response to a collision, stiff springs are applied between objects that impact each other, with a displacement based on interpenetration depth. As the objects interpenetrate, the spring stretches, creating a force that attempts to reduce the interpenetration depth to approximately zero over a few integration steps. As with the impulse-momentum method, penalty force methods have a basis in reality. The spring force is a model of the real-life forces generated as two colliding objects deform and rebound. The effect of the spring force applied over a few physics integration steps is an approximation to the collision impulse. In a sense, penalty force methods are more realistic than the impulse-momentum method. Whereas the impulse-momentum approach models deformation and restitution as occurring instantaneously, the penalty-force methods approximately model deformation and restitution over a finite period of time, which is, of course, what happens in the real world.

The use of penalty-force methods is often problematic, for two reasons. First, to achieve reasonable-looking collision response, the springs must have a large stiffness, and this greatly increases the likelihood of numerical instability. (In particular, the explicit Euler integrator will often fail dramatically.) Second, if the spring stiffness is relaxed to avoid instability, significant interpenetration is likely, which is both physically and visually inconsistent. Implicit methods are highly recommended if you choose to implement penalty-based collision response, since they will be stable even for stiff penalty forces.

Despite the difficulties, state management is quite elegant with penalty methods, which do not require a two-part time integration for objects in collision. All objects can be updated with a single integration step and no iterative discovery of the exact time and location of collision, although a collision detection technique that can estimate interpenetration depth is required. Many real-world games use penalty force methods because of their elegance and simplicity. David Wu of Pseudo Interactive has demonstrated good success using penalty methods for collision response, using implicit Euler integration (a one-step implicit numerical integrator) and potential functions rather than springs to model the penalty force that keeps colliding objects separated [Wu00].

Jakobsen [Jakobsen03] presents a novel approach to collision response, which he implemented with good success in IO Interactive's game, *Hitman: Codename 47*. In this approach, all objects are represented as collections of particles, rigidly connected together via a series of constraints designed to maintain the shape of the object and prevent articulating components from exceeding rotation limits. Rather than handle collision response in a physically based manner, when two or more objects are detected to interpenetrate, Jakobsen projects particles of each object such that they lie on the boundary of the other object involved in the collision. He then adjusts the positions of all of the particles of the objects involved such that the rigid connection constraints are satisfied. This process is performed iteratively, for a few repetitions, until the rigid connection constraints are satisfied and no particles of a given object remain inside the other object(s) involved in the collision. Jakobsen's method can readily support simulation of rigid bodies, particles, cloth, and characters.

Baraff [Baraff] has written a number of papers, available online, that present various collision-response techniques and issues, including comprehensive discussions of the impulse-momentum approach summarized in this chapter.

Bringing It All Together

You now should have a good understanding of the major factors that cause and affect the motion of general rigid bodies, and a basic understanding of the numerical integration techniques that can be used to approximately solve for the motion of a collection of objects over time. Whether you are implementing simple spherical particle physics or general rigid-body physics, your basic process is rather straightforward, as outlined here:

1. Choose a numerical integrator (or integrators), which will determine the state vector and the number of prior states you must track.
2. Choose a representation for the state vector, $\mathbf{S}$, and derivative vector, $d\mathbf{S}/dt$ and/or $d^2\mathbf{S}/dt^2$.
3. Choose a set of initial conditions for your rigid bodies, and assign these into $\mathbf{S}$.
4. If your selected numerical integrator requires more than one prior state, use explicit Euler integration to initialize the entire set of prior states. Alternatively, initially set all prior states equal to the initial conditions.

5. During the simulation for each physics step, if collisions are detected and you are using impulse-momentum-based collision response, resolve them using the instantaneous impulse-momentum equations and update the state properties for the objects involved before continuing with the general update of all objects. Alternatively, if you are using penalty-force-based collision response, compute the penalty force on objects involved in collisions based on current interpenetration depths at the time t, and add the penalty force to the net force applied to each object. Then, update all objects in one step, including those in collision.

6. During the simulation for each physics step:
   a. Copy the current state $\bar{S}$ into a temporary state array to be given to the integrator as one of the prior states. Copy other prior states if necessary.
   b. Calculate or copy the state derivative vector for each object.
   c. Call the integrator(s) to update the state vector.
   d. If simulating rotational motion, update the angular velocity every frame, and renormalize the orientation matrix and/or orientation quaternion every few frames.

Commercial and Freeware Physics Engines

Currently, there is a handful of ready-made rigid-body physics engines available for games. Many of them include their own collision detection, and many also run on both game consoles and PCs. These engines can save you the trouble of actually writing your own comprehensive and robust physics code; however, you still need a good understanding of physics to use the engines properly. You will not obtain good results, for example, if you do not provide inputs that use consistent units, or if you provide an incorrect inertia tensor.

The following is a list of several physics engines that are available as of 2005.

Commercial Physics Engines

Game Dynamics SDK by Havok.com, Inc. (*www.havok.com*)
Renderware Physics by Renderware, Inc. (*www.renderware.com*)
NovodeX SDK by NovodeX, Inc. (*www.novodex.com*)

Freeware/Shareware Physics Engines

Open Dynamics Engine (ODE) (*www.ode.org*)
Tokamak Game Physics SDK (*www.tokamakphysics.com*)
Newton Game Dynamics SDK (*www.newtondynamics.com*)

Licensing Issues

As with any middleware software, whether labeled as commercial, shareware, or freeware, you should carefully read the license agreement terms before selecting products to use in your games. The licensing terms of these engines may change over time, and may be different for commercial projects, school projects, and hobby or giveaway projects. Freeware engines, for example, often require that you credit the middleware in any binaries, documentation, advertising, or source code you publish or distribute. Be certain that you are willing and able to comply with the license terms before deciding to use any products or tools that you did not develop yourself.

Summary

Closed-form particle physics are extremely practical for games that require only simple physics. One significant benefit of these equations, if they are suitable, is that they are perfectly stable and will never cause floating-point overflow. In practice, these equations are only useful for spherical particles experiencing occasional collisions and at most a constant acceleration, such as that due to gravity.

Numerical integration techniques remove the restriction that an object experiences only a constant force, making these techniques quite useful for implementing a general-purpose physics engine. These techniques are subject to stability concerns that you must consider carefully. Regardless of the stability considerations, these techniques open up a world of opportunity for physics simulation.

In this chapter, we developed the physics and numerical integration techniques that can be used to implement general rigid-body motion. However, the presentation here is by no means comprehensive. If you want to implement a full, rigid-body physics system, your studies have only just begun. For example, one rather obvious effect that we have deliberately ignored is the presence of surface friction during collisions. Impulsive friction is present during collisions, in the real world, and can affect motion. Friction in collisions can, for example, create a torque causing the objects to rotate, even if the vector joining the two objects' centers of mass intersects the contact point. Some of the other important features that we ignored include:

- Multiple contact points between a given pair of objects
- Simultaneous collisions between more than two bodies
- Articulating rigid body chains, in which two bodies are linked for all time via various hinges and joints, with limits
- The friction of rolling objects
- The details of mechanically applied forces, such as motor forces
- Dealing with resting contact and stacking of objects
- Breakable objects

The material presented here is a great starting point. The exercises that follow will solidify your comprehension of the theory and implementation of basic rigid-body physics. Beyond these rigid-body effects, you may need to implement a deformable or soft-body physics system, which can be used to simulate cloth, hair, and objects that wobble. You may also need to implement a fluid physics system, to simulate the motion of bodies of water, such as a raging river. Some of the references listed, and many other sources not listed, provide good introductions to these advanced topics should you wish to explore them.

Exercises

1. Use Equation 4.3.7 to create a simple targeting game in which the player launches a projectile particle at a target particle. You can implement a full 3D game, or a 2D system. Provide the player with the ability to change the launch speed of the particle and the launch direction (thus, setting $\mathbf{V}_{init}$). Provide a "perfect launch" feature that allows the game to automatically choose the proper launch velocity to hit a given target. To do this, use Equations 4.3.4 and 4.3.7 together to solve for $\mathbf{V}_{init}$ and the time of impact, $t_{impact} - t_{start}$, given that the particle position at time of impact is $\mathbf{p}_{particle}(t_{impact}) = \mathbf{p}_{target}$.

2. Verify that the units of linear impulse, defined as $\int_{t-}^{t+} \mathbf{F}_{collision} dt$, are the same as the units of linear momentum. Determine what the units of the coefficient of restitution must be, so that Equation 4.3.12 is consistent.

3. Verify that the velocity in the contact plane for the frictionless collision of two spheres is unchanged during the collision response, using Equations 4.3.9 through 4.3.13.

4. Determine whether the direction of the surface normal is important when computing collision response (e.g., is the result still valid if you choose $\hat{\mathbf{n}} = -\hat{\mathbf{n}}$?).

5. Most game worlds, or simulation worlds, include objects that are immovable; for example, the terrain or structures fixed to the terrain. In physics terms, these immovable objects can be considered to have infinite mass; however, infinite mass is not physically feasible from the point of view of classical dynamics. Because of the infeasibility of infinite mass, conservation of linear momentum is not satisfied, and Equation 4.3.13 is invalid. However, Equation 4.3.12 remains valid. After all, there is still an action and reaction, and they can still be related using a coefficient of restitution. Note, though, that the before-collision and after-collision velocities of the immovable object are identical. Using Equation 4.3.12, derive the velocity of a 0.5 kg ball after a collision with the Earth, with Earth considered immovable. Your goal is to derive an equation that can be used for any valid values of $\mathbf{V}^-$ and ε. Verify that the units of your equation are consistent.

6. Implement a simple top-down view marbles game. The goal of this game should be to allow the player to experiment with different marble collisions. Allow the player to choose two marbles at a time, each with a different mass. The player should be able to launch both marbles toward each other at the same time so that they are moving toward each other. Use Equation

4.3.7 to simulate the motion of the marbles prior to and after the collision, and Equations 4.3.9, 4.3.10, and 4.3.13 to determine the collision response.

7. Implement the projectile system of Exercises 1 and 6 using explicit Euler integration. Ensure that your implementation is frame-rate independent. Compare the results against the exact solutions from the other exercises.

8. Modify your implementation of Exercise 7 to use Verlet integration, and compare the results with the explicit Euler solution.

9. Use Equations 4.3.9 through 4.3.12 to prove Equation 4.3.13. Using Equation 4.3.37 also, prove Equation 4.3.38 (advanced).

10. Linear springs can be used to cheaply approximate soft bodies. Using Listing 4.3.8 as a guideline, create a simulation for a soft-body rectanguloid block (or other shape) being dropped on a hard surface. Use velocityless Verlet integration to update the positions, and use explicit Euler integration to compute velocities for the dashpots. Simulate the block being dropped at a slight angle from some height above an immovable plane, and use the result of Exercise 5 to implement collision of the particles with the immovable plane (choose ε to be 0.75). Experiment with different spring stiffness and dashpot damping coefficients. Observe the difference in behavior when the dashpots are enabled versus disabled.

11. Create a simple bumper-cars simulation, with rotational collisions. To do this, treat the cars as simple rectanguloid geometries. Implement a simple propulsion force that causes acceleration in the forward direction and is proportional to a throttle setting that the player can control with a keyboard or joystick. Implement a simple, constant braking force that acts in the rearward direction and is activated with the keyboard. When resolving collisions, take the point of contact to be at the same height as the center of mass of the car bodies. Implement a friction model that uses only dynamic friction.

12. Springs and dashpots can be used to approximate an automobile suspension. Simulate a vehicle moving at a constant speed over a speed bump. To do this, approximate the vehicle as a rectanguloid. Place a spring and damper at each corner, between the rectanguloid and the ground plane, to model the suspension. Represent the speedbump as a simple constant change in height of the ground plane. As each corner of the vehicle moves over the edge of the speed bump, force the bottom endpoint of the corresponding spring to be at the new ground height. Force the lower endpoint of the spring to remain fixed to the ground (e.g., the vehicle does not bounce) and apply the appropriate spring force to each corner of the vehicle. Use the same integration schemes as Exercise 11. How does the behavior of the vehicle change as you increase or decrease the spring stiffness, and if you change the width and length of the vehicle?

References

[Anderson95] Anderson, John D., Jr., *Computational Fluid Dynamics: The Basics with Applications,* McGraw-Hill, 1995.

[Baraff] Baraff, David, various papers available online at *www-2.cs.cmu.edu/~baraff/nyinfo/research/deb/*, 1989 through 2003.

[Eberly03] Eberly, David, "Polyhedral Mass Properties (Revisited)," *www.magic-software.com/Documentation/PolyhedralMassProperties.pdf,* January 2003.

[Eberly04] Eberly, David, *Game Physics,* Morgan Kaufmann, 2004.

[Golub96] Golub, Gene H., and Van Loan, Charles F, *Matrix Computations,* Third Edition, Johns Hopkins, 1996.

[Halliday78] Halliday, David, and Resnick, Robert, *Physics, Parts 1 & 2,* 3rd ed. or greater, John Wiley & Sons, 1978.

[Jakobsen03] Jakobsen, Thomas, "Advanced Character Physics," *www.gamasutra.com/resource_guide/20030121/jacobson_01.shtml*, Gamasutra.com, January 2003.

[Lander99] Lander, Jeff, "Collision Response: Bouncy, Trouncy, Fun," article in *Game Developer Magazine,* article available online at *www.gamasutra.com/features/20000208/lander_01.htm*; code available online at *www.gdmag.com/src/mar99.zip,* March 1999.

[Mirtich96] Mirtich, Brian, "Fast and Accurate Computation of Polyhedral Mass Properties," *Journal of Graphics Tools,* vol. 1, Issue 2, February 1996, online at *www.cs.berkeley.edu/~jfc/mirtich/massProps.html.*

[Munem78] Munem, Mustafa A., and Foulis, David J., *Calculus with Analytic Geometry,* Worth Publishers, Inc., 1978.

[Porcino04] Porcino, Nick, "Writing a Verlet-Based Physics Engine," *Game Programming Gems 4,* Charles River Media, 2004.

[Rhodes01] Rhodes, Graham, "Stable Rigid-Body Physics," presented at the Game Developer's Conference 2001, available online at *www.gdconf.com/archives/2001/index.htm,* March 2001.

[Rhodes05] Rhodes, Graham, "Back of the Envelope Aerodynamics for Game Physics," *Game Programming Gems 5,* Charles River Media, 2005.

[Shabana94] Shabana, Ahmed A., *Computational Dynamics,* John Wiley & Sons, 1994.

[Shames80] Shames, Irving H., *Engineering Mechanics: Statics and Dynamics,* Third Edition, Prentice-Hall, 1980.

[Wu00] Wu, David, "Penalty Methods for Contact Resolution," Presented at the Game Developer's Conference 2000, available online at *www.pseudointeractive.com/games/penaltymethods.ppt,* March 2000.

PART

5

GAME PROGRAMMING: GRAPHICS, ANIMATION, AI, AUDIO, AND NETWORKING

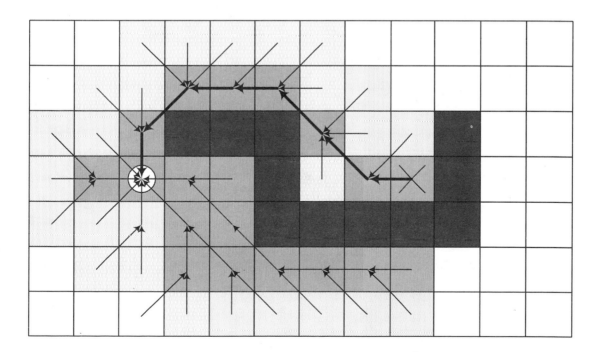

5.1 Graphics

Overview

This chapter focuses on the rendering of three-dimensional scenes onto a flat screen of pixels. There are many ways to do this, but for games, the most common is to use custom hardware to render scenes made out of triangle-based meshes. While there are large differences in the wide range of graphics cards in desktop computers, and the more special-purpose hardware in various consoles, there are also plenty of shared generalizations that travel well between most of the common platforms. Regardless of the low-level interface or API used, these common features tend to remain similar. With care, a developer can use these common features to write a graphics engine that works well on a variety of platforms.

Graphics Fundamentals

Before diving straight in and getting elbow deep in code, it is wise to introduce the shared concepts of most rendering systems and establish a common framework of terminology. As always in any evolving technical field, some of this terminology may be slightly different in various places, and this is a chance to precisely define what is meant by particular terms in this chapter.

Frame Buffer and Back Buffer

At the heart of graphics is the area of memory where the screen is stored, the *frame buffer*. In a standard desktop system with a GUI (graphical user interface), there is only one frame buffer, the visible one, and the computer draws directly to it. However, this means that the user can see the frame being constructed. For a window-based GUI, this is usually not objectionable, but in most games and 3D applications, seeing the frame being constructed is very distracting—the game would like to construct the frame in a nonvisible area, and then show only the finished frame. This is usually done by having two frame buffers, one visible and one hidden.

Rendering is then performed to the hidden frame, called the *back buffer*, and when the frame is finished, everything is displayed in one operation. In some cases, the two frames are simply swapped, so that the frame buffer becomes the back buffer and vice versa. This is done by telling the television or monitor to read data from the other buffer, rather than copying memory. In other cases, the back buffer data is copied to the frame buffer to display it, but their roles are not swapped. In modern systems, the copy happens in a relatively trivial amount of time, and is not visible.

Although the latter method seems inefficient, since it involves copying memory rather than simply swapping some pointers around, there are good reasons why it is currently the more common method. Today's graphics systems have amazing amounts of memory bandwidth, and copying the back buffer to the frame buffer consumes only a small fraction of the available bandwidth. While copying the data, the graphics card can also manipulate it and change its format, instead of merely copying it unchanged. This allows the back buffer to have a different pixel format, such as a *high dynamic range* format, or to be compressed, or for it to be a different size and have more or fewer pixels than the display device. If it has more pixels, the back buffer may be antialiased, or filtered down to smooth the image and reduce some of the visible pixels.

Antialiasing is increasingly important for image quality as the number of pixels on display devices is not increasing very quickly. In fact, as people move from CRT to LCD displays, the average number of pixels on a screen is dropping, although this is probably only temporary as LCD technology improves. Full-screen antialiasing is one way to get the quality improvements of more pixels, without physically having more on the display device.

Visibility and the Depth Buffer

When rendering a 3D scene, the game needs to make sure that only unobscured objects are visible in the finished scene. For simplicity, assume that everything in the world is opaque for now—there is no transparency. The obvious way to do this is simply to not render objects that are hidden, and this is a useful method, mainly for increasing speed. However, it cannot solve the entire problem because sometimes only part of an object is visible.

The next solution is to render objects in a specific sequence, ordering them from far away ("back") to nearby ("front"). That way, when nearer objects are drawn, they will be rendered over the further ones, and hide them. This has been used very successfully in hardware all the way up to the PlayStation 1, and still works to an extent. However, this process of sorting objects is time consuming, and there are many problems. Sometimes, one object is not obviously in front of another—think of a bird in a birdcage. The bird is in front of the back of the cage, but behind the front of the cage. What is more, if the cage is round, there is no obvious way to split the cage into two halves—a back and front half—since if the viewer turns the cage by 90 degrees, the two halves are now side by side, and each of the two halves is again both in front of and behind the bird at the same time.

The solution most commonly used today is to have a second buffer that stores depth values. For each pixel on the back buffer, there is a corresponding pixel in the depth buffer. The depth buffer is never displayed directly on-screen, it simply helps decide which pixels are visible and which are not. Since x and y coordinates are commonly used to refer to screen pixels, the depth buffer is also commonly called a *Z-buffer*, since it stores the third dimension.

The value held in the depth buffer is an indication of how far away the corresponding pixel is. When attempting to render another pixel from a different object over the top, the depths of the existing pixel and the new pixel are compared. If the new depth value is less, the object currently being drawn is closer than the object already drawn, and the new pixel and depth values replace the old. If the new depth value is greater, the object being drawn is farther away, and both the new pixel and depth value are discarded. In this way, the order in which objects are rendered does not matter for the result, so the difficult process of carefully sorting objects can be avoided. Better still, since each pixel is considered separately, objects can be partly in front and partly behind others, as in the example of the bird in the cage. Two objects can even intersect; for example, a spoon in a cup of milky coffee. The surface of the coffee can be drawn as a single flat surface, and because the depth test is done separately at every pixel, the spoon's handle will intersect the coffee in the correct way.

Notice that there is no requirement that the values held in the depth buffer have any actual meaning. They do not need to be in centimeters or light years or furlongs, and they do not even need to be linearly distributed. The only operation performed with them is to compare one with another, so all that is necessary is that they have a consistent ordering, so that if one depth value is larger than another, the distance it represents is further away.

Stencil Buffer

There is often a third buffer paired with the back and depth buffers called the *stencil buffer*. In fact, it is so common that is it usually interleaved with the depth buffer, with the depth buffer occupying 24 bits and the stencil buffer occupying 8 bits of a 32-bit word. The combined buffer is logically called the *depth/stencil buffer*. The stencil buffer does not have a clearly defined role like the other two—it is the "really useful" buffer. It holds an arbitrary value, and like the depth buffer it can be used to reject pixels on the basis of a comparison between the existing value held in the stencil buffer and a value attached to the pixel that the chip is trying to render.

The applications for the stencil buffer are anything that requires pixels to be rejected on a per-pixel basis. One example is rendering a 3D scene to an irregularly shaped window on-screen. Geometrically clipping the scene to this irregular shape would be time consuming, and in some cases almost impossible. However, the stencil buffer can be set to the value 0 for the entire back buffer and the value 1 only inside the window, and then the scene is rendered, setting the stencil buffer comparison to only allow pixels to be written to the back buffer where the stencil value is 1. In this way, the scene does not overwrite any of the pixels outside the window. This is a common technique when rendering mirrors inside scenes, and can be used for more advanced effects such as rendering shadows using stencil volume techniques.

Triangles

Now that the rendering system has buffers to hold the color and depth values, it needs to render things into them. Overwhelmingly, those things are going to be triangles. Some pipelines and APIs have support for other primitives such as *quads* and *point sprites*, but usually both are reduced to triangles for rendering, and the use of other primitives is simply a convenience.

Triangles are so common because they have a number of useful properties. They are the simplest primitive that describes a surface in space, it is simple to linearly interpolate values across them, and as noted, they can be used to construct a number of higher order primitives.

The only other true primitives used with any frequency are lines. While useful for many diagrammatic needs, when rendering real-world scenes, lines are less useful because they often have a width that is fixed in pixels rather than in any real-world units. Some APIs have line primitives that have widths in real-world units, but they too are converted to triangles for actual rendering.

Besides simply defining a surface in space, triangles also have properties associated with them that determine which algorithms are used to determine how they are rendered on the screen. This is frequently called a *material*, and may have associated 2D and 3D surfaces such as textures.

Vertices

A triangle is defined as the connection of three points in space. These points are called *vertices*. Besides a position, each vertex also has a variety of properties that can be fed into the material to determine how that particular vertex, and the triangles that use it, are rendered. These properties include values such as which way its normal points, where on a particular texture it lies, and so on.

In some cases, a single point in space may have multiple properties. For example, consider one corner of a cube. It is a single point, but it has at least three triangles that use it, and each triangle faces in a different direction, one on each adjacent side of the cube (and note that each side of the cube is usually rendered with two triangles). Since, for the purposes of rendering, the normal of a surface is stored at the vertices, not at each triangle, there are three different normals at this point in space. One solution is to store a single vertex with three normals in it, but this gets complex. The solution used by most rendering APIs is to store the vertex three times, each with the same position, but a different normal vector. The same is done wherever attributes such as normals, texture coordinates, and so on need to be different at a single point in space. Although it seems slightly wasteful to process the position of the point three times, in practice, any other method has other complications that make it even less efficient. As the number of triangles in a mesh increases, the proportion of these *coincident* vertices to the number of vertices that are not duplicated tends to drop rapidly, limiting their impact on speed.

Coordinate Spaces

When specifying the position of a point in space, it is standard to use three numbers. However, what do these numbers mean? They need to be defined relative to an origin, where the point (0, 0, 0) is, and the direction and scale of the three axes needs to be defined.

Most coordinate spaces are in turn defined in terms of another coordinate space—their parent space. The definition of a coordinate space is usually done by specifying the position of its origin in the parent space as a three-dimensional vector, and the directions of its three axes in the parent space. These four vectors are usually shown as the columns of a four-column matrix, with the *x*, *y*, and *z* axes listed first, and finally the position of the origin as the fourth vector. For most cases, each column can simply be a three-component vector, giving a total 4×3 matrix to represent a coordinate space relative to its parent coordinate space. Mathematicians dislike this representation because the first three columns simply indicate *directions*, whereas the forth indicates a *position*. Thus, they add a fourth row with a zero in the first three positions (indicating the column is a direction) and a one in the fourth position (indicating that column holds a position). Programmers frequently adopt this convention as well, since although it takes up a little more storage space, it allows the columns of the matrix to be processed in a clean and elegant way, and computers are usually better at processing four things at once than only three things (or at least, no worse). This is a gross simplification of what are called *homogenous coordinates*, but it is a good rule of thumb and a place to start, without delving into the mind-bending complexity of four-dimensional geometry. A discussion of homogenous coordinates is given in Chapter 4.1, "Mathematical Concepts."

However, three-component vectors and matrices are still used where memory is at a premium, despite the additional processing costs. In these cases, the final zero or one is implied by the context. For these and many other reasons, matrices and vectors in most game code are sometimes stored with three components, and sometimes with four, according to the needs of that part of the code. The reader should be fluent in using both 4×3 and 4×4 systems.

It is also a quasi-religious issue whether vectors (whether on their own, or as part of a matrix) are written as columns or rows. The meaning of the representation does not change, it is simply a convention chosen. This chapter chooses to use the vectors-are-columns convention, as it is the one used by most math textbooks. Be aware that different graphics APIs (specifically, Direct3D and OpenGL) use different conventions, and be ready to deal with the "other" convention.

The most fundamental space is *world space*. This is where everything happens, where the game is set, and the space in which most coordinates are defined. World space is not defined in terms of any parent space, and the position and orientation of world space are not particularly special, they are simply a convention decided on by the makers of the game.

The next space is *object space*. This is the space in which the vertices of a model are usually defined. These do not change as an object moves and rotates around the world. What does change is the relationship between world space and object space. Note that each separate object in a game has its own object space, with its own relationship to world space.

When rendering an object, the first step is to transform each vertex from the object space in which it is defined, into world space so that the renderer knows where it is at that instant relative to other objects. This is usually achieved by means of a matrix describing the mapping from object space to world space.

Besides objects in space, a scene needs a camera. A camera also has a position and orientation in world space. To actually render a scene, objects must be moved out of world space and into camera space, so that when the camera turns right, the objects on the screen move left.

A camera has a certain area in front of it that is visible on the screen. This area is called a *frustum*, and it is usually defined by six planes in space. Imagine a scene in a game, and now imagine that the monitor screen that they are going to be rendered on is actually a model of the monitor sitting in the game scene, in front of the camera. Now form four planes, each going through one edge of the screen, and through the center of the camera. These four planes form a pyramid with its tip at the camera, extending out into space. These are four of the planes defining the camera frustum. The frustum has two other planes: the *near plane*, and the *far plane*. Both are parallel to the plane of the screen, and in general, the aim is to move the near clip plane as close as possible and the far clip plane as far away as possible. However, there is only a finite amount of precision in the Z-buffer, and the major controller of how this precision is distributed is the position of the near clip plane. Moving the near clip plane too close to the camera can dramatically affect the precision of the depth testing, leading to severe rendering artifacts. The result is that the near clip plane should only be moved as close as it absolutely has to be, and no further. However, because of the curious way in which projection transformations work, the far clip plane can often be moved to infinity without significant loss of precision.

Before being rendered, triangles are chopped into two parts—the part inside the edges of the frustum, and the parts outside the edges. The part outside is discarded, and only the part inside is rendered. This process is called *clipping*, and is performed by transforming triangles and their vertices into a special space called *clip space*. Clip space is a difficult concept to explain—it is roughly similar to camera space, but it has two strange properties. First, it is four dimensional rather than the usual three (the fourth component is usually given the label w), and second, it does not preserve angles—it is warped. Clip space is warped so that whatever size or shape the screen's frustum is, the edges lay along certain special planes in clip space. These planes are defined mathematically by the six plane equations, Equations 5.1.1 through 5.1.3.

$$x = +w \quad x = -w \tag{5.1.1}$$
$$y = +w \quad y = -w \tag{5.1.2}$$
$$z = +w \quad z = -w \quad \text{or 0 (according to the rendering API)} \tag{5.1.3}$$

This warping simplifies clipping substantially, because hardware finds it easy to clip along these six elegantly defined planes, but much harder to clip along the more complex representation in camera space of the same frustum planes. Naturally, a mapping that distorts the pyramid of the frustum into the above six planes in four-dimensional space is likely to be very strange indeed. Don't worry too much about what clip space "means." In most cases, the calculation is performed by library code and hardware, and attempting to derive any intuition about the values in clip space is tricky at best. Those wishing to investigate the details of perspective transformations in the rendering pipeline are advised to read [Blinn96].

Once clipped, the vertices of a triangle are projected out of this 4D clip space and into screen space. Their positions are now in actual screen pixels, and their depth values are used directly for testing and updating the Z-buffer.

One final space to mention is *tangent space*, sometimes called *surface-local* space. This is a subspace of object space, that follows the surface of a mesh, and each triangle has its own tangent space. One axis of tangent space is the normal of the face, and the other two axes lay along the surface in user-defined directions—usually called the *tangent* and *binormal* vectors. Strictly speaking, each triangle has its own version of tangent space, and it is not the same as any adjacent triangles' tangent space unless they happen to be coplanar and their tangent and binormal vectors point in the same directions. However, in practice it is convenient to define a more continuous tangent space that curves smoothly over a mesh of triangles, defined at each vertex (rather than face), and smoothly interpolated across the mesh. There is more discussion of tangent space later in this chapter.

Textures

A *texture* is a surface that holds fragments of data called *texels* (derived from the words *texture pixel*). Each texel conventionally holds a red, green, and blue value, and sometimes an *alpha* transparency channel (usually abbreviated to R, G, B, A), although with the arrival of highly programmable shaders, these values can actually mean anything the shader-writer wants them to mean. The RGBA names are preserved as a convention for easy reference.

Textures are typically 2D arrays of texels, and conventionally represent a picture that is mapped onto the object and used for shading. However, there are many other formats and types of texture as well. Textures will be discussed in more depth later.

Shaders

A shader is a small program used to determine either the shape or the color of a mesh. In older hardware, fixed-function hardware performed this job, but now the graphics programmer can write these small programs to decide exactly what algorithms to use for parts of the rendering pipeline. Typically, these programs are small and run many times on different bits of data such as vertices and pixels—more like a function that is called than an entire program such as a game or application.

Materials

A *material* is a description of how to render a triangle. Usually, this consists of one or more shaders, associated textures, and data taken from the vertices of the triangles such as normal, tangent, binormals, texture coordinates, various colors, reflectivity, and other information. Materials can also include higher level information such as multiple rendering passes, each with a different shader, and materials usually change the exact rendering algorithm used to take lighting and shadowing into account. Thus a material is simply a grouping of all these items taken together, given a consistent name, and applied to the surface of a mesh.

Higher Level Organization

Now that the lower level components of rendering have been introduced, it is helpful to give an overview of the general structure of most engines. Engines vary widely in their actual structure, according to the demands of the games, and the scenes they will actually be rendering. The requirements of a virtual dollhouse will be very different from the needs of a flight simulator. Yet, there are always concepts that are useful as a starting point for any specialization.

Note that in any discussion of large-scale structure in rendering engines, there are frequently "side-band" channels for tunneling through and working around the structures, used for special purposes. This is doubly true for game engines. These interfaces are frequently used for miscellaneous non-time-critical functions, and especially for rendering objects that are not in the "physical" game world, such as drawing text and the heads-up display (HUD).

Interactions between Game and Render

In general, it is recommended that the game logic and the rendering engine be structured so that they may operate at different rates. This is especially important if the game must run on many different console platforms or on hardware such as the PC or Mac where different users have very different graphics hardware available. On one machine, the graphics may render extremely fast, at hundreds of frames per second. On another machine, the graphics may render more slowly at only 20 frames per second—still playable, but far slower.

If the rendering engine and game logic are locked together, the game logic must be capable of playing the same game, but at these two very different update rates. If, for example, the hero is poisoned and is losing health at the rate of one point every "turn," having 10 times as many turns on one machine means the hero will die in one-tenth the time. This is not an acceptable experience.

Naturally, simple problems such as this can be solved by scaling damage taken, distances traveled, and so on by the number of seconds between rendered frames. However, common experience has shown that in real games, running the complex game logic at a single fixed rate, while allowing only the graphics engine to run at different speeds, vastly simplifies the process of developing a game. This is doubly true for networked games, where multiple machines with different capabilities, and rendering different scenes, may be talking to one another. If they lack a consistent framework of time, the logic is massively complicated.

Render Objects

A *render object*, or sometimes just *object* in the context of rendering, represents the renderable description of one game entity, such as a particular type of person ("henchman #3"). A render object is usually comprised of a single animation skeleton and one or more meshes that share the same skeleton or position in space. However, this has many exceptions, and every game treats its exceptions differently, so this is only a very general concept.

There is only one of each type of render object, so in a flock of a thousand seagulls, there is only one seagull render object.

Render Object Instances

Each game object needs to have an equivalent in the graphics engine that stores all the graphics information that the game logic doesn't care about. This is the *render object instance* (frequently called an *instance*). Each instance points to a single render object that defines how the object is drawn, what shape it is, and so on. However, the instance stores where that object is to be drawn, the animation state, lighting, and so on. In a flock of 1,000 seagulls, there are 1,000 instances, each with its own position and orientation, but they all reference a single render object and a single set of meshes, textures, and shaders that define the shape of a seagull.

Instances typically have a position and orientation, an animation state that is "played" on the render object's skeleton, and various bits of graphics-engine state used in rendering (such as whether it is visible and where in the visibility graph it currently lives). Note that not every render object instance necessarily has an associated game object. Some instances are purely visual effects; for example, a pretty particle system that the game logic does not care about. Conversely, many game objects may not have an instance, either because they do not have a graphical equivalent, or because at the moment they are outside the visible frustum and are incapable of being rendered.

Meshes

A *mesh* is defined differently by many, but a useful definition is that a mesh is a collection of triangles, the vertices those triangles use, and a single material that is used to render all the triangles. A render object may have multiple meshes, which allows it to represent objects with multiple materials. However, since most graphics APIs atomic operation is drawing a set of triangles with a single material, it is useful to have this separate concept of a mesh as the "unit of rendering." A mesh may share its skeleton and lighting context with other meshes in the same render object, but each will usually have a different material. In general, the number of meshes in a render object heavily influences how fast the object can be rendered. With too many meshes, the engine needs to make too many rendering calls, and the game becomes limited by the speed of the CPU. Since most current games are limited by the speed of the CPU and not by the rendering hardware, it is wise to minimize the number of meshes in each rendering object. This typically means minimizing the number of different materials and textures used by each render object. However, this need not be taken to unreasonable extremes.

To give a concrete example, a single person may have a mesh for his face (using a shader optimized for skin rendering), a mesh for his hands (the same skin shader, but a different set of textures), a mesh for his hair (a specialized hair shader and texture), a mesh for his clothes (cloth shader and textures), and a mesh for his hat. Although the hat is also made of cloth, and probably shares the same material as the clothes mesh, the mesh is kept separate so that the game can show or hide the hat mesh at will. When the person is moving the hat around as an independent object (raising it, or holding it), a separate render object will be used for the hat, and the hat mesh attached to the person's head will be turned off. When the person is simply wearing the hat and walking around, the hat mesh is turned on, and the separate render object is discarded. This gives extra speed for the two most common cases—where the hat is either on the head, or off-screen on a hat stand somewhere.

Skeletons

Each render object will typically have a single skeleton, which describes how the bones of that object are connected together. Each render object instance will describe the animation state, which describes the current position of those bones. Both are orthogonal to meshes—a single skeleton and animation state can be used for rendering multiple meshes. More rarely, multiple skeletons may be used to control a single mesh. See Chapter 5.2, "Character Animation," for more details on this concept.

Render Volume Partitioning

The previous concepts are, in combination, sufficient for rendering a scene. However, they are usually not sufficient for rendering it efficiently. The problem is one of culling. Most scenes do not simply draw everything in the entire world because this would take far too long, and most of the world is not visible at any particular time. The depth buffer will hide meshes hidden behind other geometry, and clipping will reject off-screen triangles, but those triangles and pixels will still need to be processed. Ideally, the rendering engine needs to simply avoid rendering the vast majority of the instances in a large world to get reasonable performance. Not drawing instances is known as the process of *culling*.

The most obvious example of culling is to ignore any instance that is behind the camera or outside its frustum, or field of view. This is known as *frustum culling*. More complex forms of culling try to find which of the instances that might be inside the frustum are still not visible—for example, because there is a mountain in the way, or because they are on the other side of a closed door.

The second related concept is that simply culling instances one by one is not sufficient for speed. In some cases, worlds are so big and complex that they may have millions of instances in them. In these cases, going through each instance every frame and asking, "Is this visible?" is inefficient. What is needed is a way to ask the question the other way around—"Which instances are visible?" This avoids even thinking about the vast majority of instances that are not visible, and is far more efficient.

There is a variety of ways to organize scene data to achieve this. All use various forms of graph (or tree, which is a special but common case of a graph) to represent the scene. Instances live in nodes of the graph, and the graph is traversed starting from the node that the camera is in, and going outward until some limit of visibility is reached. This way, nodes of the graph that are not visible are simply never considered, nor are the instances inside them.

The following sections describe some examples of graphs that are in common use today, such as portals, BSPs, quadtrees, octrees, and PVSs, along with their advantages and disadvantages. Different games use different graphs according to their needs, and many games use more than one type of graph for different purposes. These may be combined in various ways; for example, a portal system with each portal having an octree inside it (because nodes may get very large for outdoor scenes). They may also be used in parallel. For example, a PVS system is useful for visibility testing, but an octree may be more useful for sound propagation.

A word of caution: the graphs and trees presented here are not what are referred to by some as the *scene graph*. The scene graph theory proposes that everything in the scene can be placed in a single unifying tree or graph structure. Meshes, vertices, shaders, and textures are all placed inside the scene graph. This graph is then traversed and drawn, and by specially ordering the nodes of the graph, optimal rendering performance is achieved. While a seductive concept, in practice so much time is spent keeping this massive data structure up to date and correctly ordered that any gains are completely erased. Worse still, the structure of the graph frequently needs to be subverted for practical matters, removing many of the (largely theoretical) benefits. The fact is that many successful games and rendering engines have been written without the scene graph concept. Trees and graphs are extremely useful in rendering, but in practice, many different graphs and trees are required for many different purposes, and attempting to unify them is not a particularly useful goal.

Portals

In a *portal* system, the scene is split into nodes, each occupying a given space, usually defined simply by the geometry it contains. Each node is joined to one or more other nodes by a "portal," which is usually represented by a planar convex polygon (although sometimes represented by rectangles or by more complex shapes).

To find which nodes are visible, the renderer starts the graph at the node that the camera is in, and everything in that node that is inside the camera frustum is drawn. For each portal leading out of this node, the shape of the portal on the screen is found. The shape is either found precisely or approximately (by taking a screen-space bounding box of the portal). If the portal is not inside the viewing frustum at all, it is ignored. Any portal that is inside the frustum, and therefore visible, marks the node on the other side of the portal as also visible, and also remembers the screen shape of the portal, which is the only part of the node that will be visible. If multiple portals open onto a given node (a common occurrence), the two shapes are combined. Again, this may be done precisely using a multiple-polygon representation, or it may be approximated by finding the combined bounding box of the portals. For example, a house may have a living room with two windows on the same wall, each of which is a portal from the node that represents that room to the node that represents the outside world.

This new node is now marked as being visible, and its contents are drawn. In turn, the portals leading from it are checked to see if they are visible. Note that they are checked against the existing screen-space shape of the portals that led to the node, not against the entire frustum. If a portal is not visible through an existing portal, it is marked as invisible, and the node beyond is not drawn, nor are its portals checked for visibility. Traversal continues on through the graph of nodes and portals, until all portals that are visible have been rendered.

For example, the house with the two windows (each a portal) that open onto the living room may have an open doorway (another portal) leading to the kitchen. From the outside of the house, the camera may be able to see the living room through the windows, and the kitchen doorway may be in the visible frustum. However, if the camera cannot see the doorway through the windows because of where it is currently situated, the kitchen is not visible, and does not need to be drawn. Similarly, anything visible from the kitchen does not need to be drawn, unless the camera can see it through some other sequence of portals that does not go via the kitchen.

Some portals may change shape or be switched on and off during the game to change the visibility set. For example, if the kitchen door is closed, that portal will still exist, because regenerating the portal network is expensive, but it will be marked as "always hidden," and the kitchen will never be visible from the living room through that portal, even when the door itself is clearly visible.

Some render object instances may live in multiple nodes. For example, the actual door itself (and doorframe) is in both the kitchen and the living room. If either is visible, the door instance needs to be drawn, even if the door itself is closed and the camera cannot see from one node to the other.

The good thing about portal systems is that they are relatively cheap in both processor time and memory, and they are simple and flexible. For indoor environments, portals are an extremely effective way to quickly reduce the number of instances that require drawing.

One annoying problem with a portal system is that the renderer must first know which node to start in (in other words, which one the camera is in). This is usually possible by tracking which node the camera is currently in, as it moves from node to node during gameplay, and tracking which portals it moves through. The problem is that cameras have a habit of moving through areas with no portals (such as traveling through solid walls), or being teleported around, and this can cause the system to lose track of the current portal. This can be solved in a variety of ways, such as starting from a known reference point, or by using some other structure such as an octree to track down which node a given point is in.

The other problem with portals is that they must be generated from the scene geometry so that the game can use it at runtime. There are some automatic portal generation algorithms that can generate nodes and portals from "polygon soups" (unordered collections of triangles), but they tend to be picky about the type of geometry used in the scene, and generate either too few or too many nodes and portals. If there are too few portals, not enough instances will be culled. Too many, and processor time is wasted processing them, but with no extra culling as a consequence. The usual way to generate portals is to simply have level designers or artists lay out portals manually, but it is not a particularly natural concept to some, and effective portal layout can sometimes be rather counterintuitive.

The other problem with portals is that in outdoor settings, even in scenes such as built-up cities with large buildings and skyscrapers, it can be difficult to pick portals that do not result in nearly everything still being marked as visible, without having massive numbers of portals and nodes. Huge numbers of portals take time to process each frame, and remove some of the benefits of culling objects in the first place.

Binary Space Partitioning (BSP)

The BSP is a generalized form of hierarchical space partitioning, of which there are also many more specialized types such as kd-trees, quadtrees, and octrees (although these have special properties that make them interesting as a separate topic). A BSP is a tree structure, and the entire tree represents all of the game space. Each node of the tree represents a section of space that does not intersect with any of its sibling nodes, and can be further subdivided into child nodes.

A node can have no children, in which case it represents a single area of space, just like the nodes in a portal system. These are often called *leaf* nodes (as part of the whole "tree" metaphor). Alternatively, it can have exactly two children, and a single geometric plane. The plane splits the space that the node represents into two halves, each on opposite sides of the plane. Each half is in turn represented by one of the two child nodes. Each of those nodes may in turn have a plane that split the halves into two further pieces, and so on.

By marking each leaf node (one with no children) as either hollow or solid, the code can perform similar traversals through a BSP to determine which nodes are visible from which other node, although it is slightly more complex than for a true portal system. Hollow nodes will have render object instances living in them, and if the node is visible, those instances will be rendered.

The advantage of a BSP system is that all of space is classified. It is simple to pick any point in space, start at the top node, decide which side of the dividing plane it is on, go to that child node, test against its plane, go to one of its children, and so on until a leaf node is hit, and that is the node that the point (e.g., the camera) is in. This is reliable and fast and always computes the right answer, which is far better than the case with portals. Another advantage of BSP trees over portal systems is that they are far easier to generate automatically, rather than requiring construction by hand.

Because portal and BSP systems are similar in structure, but good at different things, many games use a hybrid of the two, using each in different situations.

Quadtrees and Octrees

Quadtrees and *octrees* are the same data structure, except that quadtrees are two dimensional and octrees are three dimensional. For simplicity, quadtrees will be discussed here since the extension to the third dimension is relatively straightforward.

A quadtree is, as the name suggests, a tree. Each node represents a square in space aligned with the x- and y-axes, and has either no children (a leaf node) or four equally sized children, cutting the node into quarters. Typically, the root node of the tree is aligned with the origin, and each node is a power of two in size. This makes it extremely easy to find which nodes a given point intersects. Simply take the x- and y-coordinates of the point, convert them to integers, and start at the root node. At each node, take the top bit of each of the x- and y-coordinates, combine them to create a 2-bit number from 0 to 3, and that is the index of the child node to traverse into. Then, shift the x- and y-coordinates left one bit, and repeat until a leaf node is reached. This makes tree traversal incredibly fast.

In the example shown in Figure 5.1.1, the point of interest has coordinates (3, 6). Although the quadtree is quite large, only the sections that are traversed for this point are shown in solid lines, the rest in dotted lines. Stepping through the search algorithm:

Position (3, 6) in binary is (0̲011, 0̲110)

Step 1:   node (00)=0, new coordinates now   (0̲110, 1̲100)
Step 2:   node (01)=1, new coordinates now   (1̲100, 1̲000)
Step 3:   node (11)=3, new coordinates now   (1̲000, 0̲000)
Step 4:   node (10)=2, which is a leaf node, so this is the node the point is in.

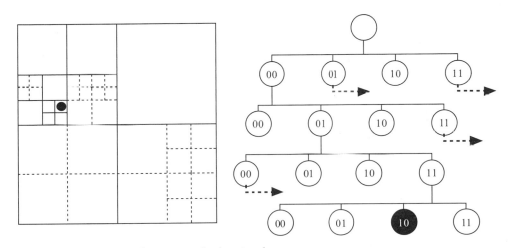

FIGURE 5.1.1   *A quadtree example showing how to traverse.*

Quadtrees are typically used for collision checking and fast frustum culling in outdoor environments. A given node can be checked to see whether it is in the visible frustum, and if it is not, none of its children needs to be checked—by definition they will not be visible, since they are entirely enclosed by the parent node.

Although it seems that almost all games are three dimensional and would use an octree, many games are only "two and a half" dimensional, and their world is mainly flat. Most real-time strategy games show this very clearly. Although the landscape may go up and down, and elevation may be important for strategy, the number of times two render object instances occupy space one above the other is rare, and the extra complexity of an octree does not give any significant culling advantages over the simpler quadtree. As a result, both quadtrees and octrees are equally common in games, according to the type of scenes a particular game will be rendering.

The close relative of the quadtree or octree is the *loose quadtree* or *loose octree*. These are similarly useful for rendering, but are far more practical than the standard quadtree for collision detection.

Potentially Visible Set (PVS)

A PVS is node based like all the other systems, and in fact may be built on top of any of the other graph-based systems. Each node has a PVS, which is a list of links to other nodes that are potentially visible from that node. That is, if the camera is in that node, the PVS lists all the nodes that ever need to be considered for drawing. Some of these nodes may not actually be visible from the current camera position, but it is guaranteed that any nodes not in the list will never be visible from anywhere in the given node.

Although conceptually simple, generating PVS lists is tricky. To do it by brute force, every single possible camera position in each node needs to be checked to see if it can see any other node in the world. Of course, there are many ways to accelerate this process, but none is simple, and many make very specific requirements of the geometry used in the level. PVS systems also do not cope well with changing geometry. For example, if a door can ever be opened during a game, for the purposes of calculating the PVS, it must always be regarded as open.

Because a PVS is a static list, and does not change according to the exact position of the camera inside each node, or the current state of the scene (such as open or shut doors), it must be conservative, and may have many nodes that are not in fact visible for a given frame. For this reason, PVS systems are often combined with other dynamic visibility systems to do further culling of the list of nodes. The most obvious is, of course, to perform standard frustum culling, but any of the other partitioning schemes are common as well.

What a PVS does provide is an extremely quick way to reject nodes. For example, if the PVS says that only 10 nodes are visible, it is guaranteed that at most those 10 are visible, and no others need checking. This information is not found by traversing trees or graphs and performing complex visibility operations (as with other methods here); it is simply given immediately as a list.

Common Uses

Spatial partitioning schemes have many uses, both inside rendering and in general game code. Frequently, the rendering and game code may share the same scheme, but equally often, they do not, or each part of the game may use different algorithms for different purposes. For example, portal systems are not particularly useful for collision detection schemes, because they are frequently imprecise about exactly what space the node occupies.

The most obvious use has already been mentioned—visibility culling. Some spatial partitioning schemes such as quadtrees can really only accelerate frustum culling by providing early culling tests. Others such as portals can directly provide very aggressive visibility culling.

Another principle use of spatial partitioning in graphics rendering is sorting instances according to depth. A well-known problem in graphics is that instances containing translucent parts need to be rendered from back (far from the camera) to front (near the camera); otherwise, the translucency will not work properly, with or without a depth buffer. In contrast, to get good speed from rendering hardware, it is typical to draw opaque instances first, ordered roughly from front to back. In this case, the sort does not need to be as precise as with translucent instances.

Spatial partitioning can accelerate both of these sorts by providing a simple way to traverse the scene in a given order—for example, in a mostly back-to-front or a mostly front-to-back ordering—by visiting each node's children in a specific order. Adding the instances found this way to a list in the order found results in a nearly sorted list, and a nearly sorted list is far easier to sort than a randomly ordered list. In the case of the opaque instances, no further sorting is usually needed anyway, as the image will be correct whatever the order; it is simply a matter of improving speed. Spending more time performing a perfect sort does not usually give significantly better speed, and is wasteful.

Speed and Efficiency

It is clear that some algorithms are faster than others. The previous structures are listed roughly in order of decreasing cost to traverse from one node to another. Portals involve a rather lengthy step of checking arbitrary portal geometry, BSPs involve a check against a single plane, quadtrees simply check 2 bits, and PVS does no tree traversal at all. However, these speed increases arise because of increasing simplicity. Each portal node can describe very complex shapes, so only a few are needed to accurately represent a given scene and obtain efficient culling. BSPs can only describe convex hulls, and may chop areas that are conceptually a single space up into multiple parts (at each point, the plane chosen must split the entire space into two halves), resulting in many more nodes being generated for a given scene. A quadtree or octree can only represent power-of-two-sized axis-aligned squares or cubes, so many require a very large number of nodes to represent a particular scene.

For this reason, careful consideration should be given to which data representation should be used for a particular type of game. Sometimes, the answer may be counterintuitive, and it is wise to try all the options if possible. In many cases, what the partitioning scheme is used for is more important than how efficient it is. It is fairly common to use a portal scheme for visibility checking, but the same game may choose to use an octree for collision detection.

However, in other cases it may not actually matter. It may be advisable to pick the simplest and most robust representation (such as an octree) to implement first. If the profile then shows it using one-quarter of a percent of CPU time and 100 kbytes of memory, there is little point in spending programming time investigating the other options. In most cases, having *any* spatial partitioning scheme is more important than which scheme is used.

Types of Rendering Primitive

Several primitive types are used in rendering. The most common by far is the triangle, with its well-known properties. Also common are lines and points, although they tend to be used more for representational geometry such as HUDs and user inter-faces, as they do not have such inherent "3D"-ness as triangles. For example, lines are typically one pixel wide, no matter how far away they are, which is unlike any real physical object, but perfect for a display such as a targeting reticule. All primitives are constructed as a number of vertices joined together, the main difference being how many vertices are used—three for a triangle, two for a line, and one for a point.

Quadrilaterals, or *quads*, are used by some graphics APIs as a primitive, comprising of a plane (not necessarily a flat one) defined by four vertices. However, in most cases they are rendered by the underlying hardware as a pair of triangles. In theory, there are slight speed advantages to quads, since they are only comprised of four vertices rather than the six used by two triangles. In addition, they are slightly quicker to clip and ras-terize because they have only four edges, not six. However, modern hardware design usually finds that the extra circuitry required to handle quads is better put to use mak-ing triangles go faster. Quads are still extremely useful as higher level concepts in things such as user-interface and font rendering, because they are simpler to deal with, but they are usually converted to triangles by the low-level rendering routines.

Looking at the common uses of any of the primitives, we see that frequently, mul-tiple primitives are used in sequence, one following on from the next. Submitting the primitives one at a time is a waste of processing power. As already noted, two triangles that form a quad require only four vertices, but submitting them as separate triangles requires the processing of six vertices. It also requires two calls to the API instead of one.

One solution to both these problems is to string sequences of primitives together, supplying an explicit topology. Several of these primitives are shown in Figure 5.1.2. One of the common topologies for triangles is a *triangle fan*. These triangles are spec-ified by a single vertex that forms the "base" of the fan, followed by the vertices at the "tips" of the fan. The number of triangles drawn is two less than the number of ver-tices submitted, which is far more efficient than submitting each triangle separately, requiring three times the number of vertices as triangles actually drawn. Fans are use-ful because they can directly represent an arbitrary convex polygon. The vertices are simply fed in, and the fan topology automatically breaks the polygon into triangles for rendering.

Another common topology is that of a *triangle strip* where the triangles form a continuous long strip. Again, the number of vertices is only two more than the num-ber of triangles, rather than needing three times as many. The final common topology is the *triangle list* where each triangle is separate and does require three separate ver-tices, but at least multiple independent triangles can be submitted with one call, rather than calling the rendering API once for each triangle. Lines have similar "list" and "strip" primitives, and although they could have a "fan" equivalent, this is not present in most APIs.

These primitives are a fairly good way to reduce the number of vertices processed, but still not ideal. Most meshes consist of a continuous surface of triangles. Splitting

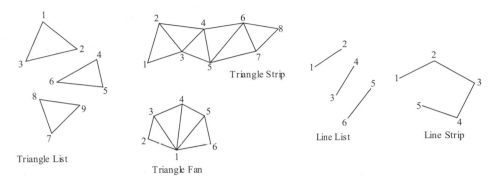

FIGURE 5.1.2 *Primitive types such as a triangle list, triangle fan, triangle strip, line list, and line strip.*

these into fans is possible, but not very efficient. Because all triangles in a fan must share a single vertex, only a certain number of triangles can be rendered before needing to stop and start a new fan. Strips are much more promising, and a large number of triangles of a mesh can be drawn using strips before needing to restart a new strip. The problem is that meshes are not regular, and when forming strips, odd triangles can be left behind, which then requires more strips (or sometimes individual triangle lists) to render them. More fundamentally, the vertices where two strips touch will be processed twice, once for each strip. The best case is a mesh that can be perfectly converted to strips, such as a regular grid. For a concrete example, Figure 5.1.3 shows a regular grid of 5 by 5 vertices, 25 in all. This mesh has 32 triangles in it, and can be divided into 4 strips of 8 triangles each. Each strip processes 10 vertices, so 40 vertices in total are processed. However, there are only 25 vertices in the mesh, so 40 is quite an increase!

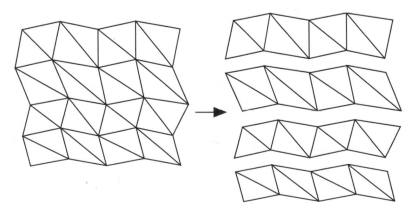

FIGURE 5.1.3 *Example of a mesh divided into triangle strips.*

Increasingly elaborate topologies of triangles could be added to the API to reduce this number, but this would only help in the case of regular grids, not for general meshes. The real solution is to separate the vertices from the topology of the mesh, and supply each separately, with the topology *referring* to the vertices, not being specified by their ordering.

Therefore, there is a list of vertices, which are numbered from zero upwards. This is usually put into an area of memory that is readable by the rendering hardware, commonly called a *vertex buffer*. Then there is the topology of the mesh—the triangles—which is a list of numbers, each referring to the vertex with that array index. This list specifies which vertices each triangle uses, and may itself be specified as a strip, fan, or list topology, just as before. These numbers are called *indices*, and are placed where the hardware can read them, often called an *index buffer*.

The indices in Figure 5.1.4 still form four separate triangle strips, and most vertices are still specified more than once, in different strips. The first strip is 5,0,6,1,7,2,8,3,9,4. The second strip is 10,5,11,6,12,7,13,8,14,9, and so on. However, there are two main advantages with this representation. The first is that total memory use has dropped. Vertices are relatively large—around 32 bytes is not uncommon, and with complex materials and rendering schemes, vertices can easily be twice that size or more. However, indices are small—each is a single number, usually 16 bits (allowing a mesh of 65,536 vertices) or occasionally 32 bits (4 billion vertices). Duplicating indices is extremely cheap compared to storing a vertex twice in memory. In this specific case, with 32 bytes per vertex and 16 bits per index, the memory use has dropped from $(40)(32) = 1280$ bytes to $(25)(32) + (40)(2) = 880$ bytes. A typical mesh in a game has around twice the number of triangles as vertices, so the saving is almost a halving of memory (this example saves less than that because it is such a small mesh, and many vertices lie on the edges of the mesh and so are not referred to more than once).

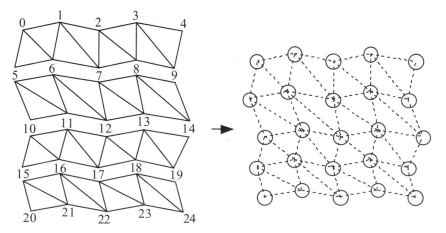

FIGURE 5.1.4   *Triangle strips converted to indexed strips.*

The other advantage of indexing vertices is that when a vertex is referred to more than once by different strips, it is done using the same index value. If the vertex-processing hardware caches the results of its processing, it can tag each processed vertex with its index. For subsequent triangles, the incoming indices are used to look in the cache to see if those vertices have already been processed. If they have, the cached results are used, and the vertices do not need to be processed again. In the previous example, instead of processing 40 vertices, the hardware would process only 25—a considerable reduction in processing.

Most hardware vertex caches are typically 16 to 32 entries in size, which is large enough to prevent reprocessing of approximately 95 percent of the vertices, as long as the triangles are specified in an ordering that is friendly toward the hardware's vertex cache. Exactly what that ordering is depends on the exact size and workings of the vertex cache used by the hardware. If these details are known ahead of time, there are algorithms to optimize the ordering of the triangles for that target; for example, [Hoppe99]. However, in many cases, the exact hardware behavior is unknown, and more heuristic methods must be used. In general, each triangle should be close to the previous triangles, and not scattered all over the mesh. Finding the optimal ordering is still a subject of research, especially when the exact cache size and behavior of the hardware is not known ahead of time—one interesting approach is shown in [Bogomjakov01].

The final primitive commonly used in rendering APIs is the *point sprite*. These are specified similarly to the point primitives, but have one major difference—they have both a position and a size. This is most useful for rendering clouds of particles. Each particle is specified only as a single vertex and a size in world-space units. The hardware performs perspective correction on the world size to produce a size in pixels, and then typically expands the vertex to a screen-aligned quad, which is then assigned automatically generated texture coordinates, and rendered. Rendering a screen-aligned quad is extremely efficient for hardware, and is the one place where quads are still common as a fundamental primitive. However, point sprites currently have many annoying restrictions on different bits of hardware, and can sometimes be troublesome to use efficiently.

Textures

The rendering primitive defines which pixels in the back buffer will be rendered to, but not what colors will be used to render with. The most common way to specify the color of the pixels of a triangle is by mapping a texture onto it. The colors are read out of the texture at each pixel, and used in the lighting algorithms to modify or specify the properties of the surface at that pixel.

Texture Formats

A *texture* is simply an array of colors, each known as a *texel*, and the most common shape of the array is a two-dimensional rectangular grid. Frequently, these are stored on disk as common image formats such a targa (.TGA), bitmap (.BMP), portable network graphics (.PNG), JPEGs, and so on. There is a close similarity between the concept of a texture and the concept of a stored image. In most cases, a texture is simply a picture that is mapped onto the rendered mesh.

The texels that make up a texture come in a wide variety of formats. By convention they each have four values—red, green, blue, and alpha—usually represented by RGBA. The ordering of the letters often represents their ordering in memory, and so may be different for various platforms and formats (ARGB and BGRA are common). Many texel formats have fewer than the full four channels, and many store or compress the different channels in different ways. This gives the graphics programmer a variety of texel formats to choose from, each having a certain trade-off between the precision of the stored data and the memory size of the texture. In most hardware, speed of rendering is directly related to each texel's size in memory. The larger the size, the more precision the texel will have, but the rendering will be slower.

The RGB components usually mean the red, green, and blue components that make up an actual color, and the alpha channel typically represents an opacity value of some sort. However, with the advent of fully programmable shader hardware, this is now just a convention, and the four channels may in fact mean four completely different things with possibly unrelated concepts. A common example of this is given later in the chapter for "normal maps" where the RGB channels now represent the XYZ components of a vector, and not a color at all. When a texture stores values such as a color or vector, it is fairly common to pack another useful value into the alpha channel; for example, a value that represents the shininess of that part of the surface. It is important to think of textures as simply arrays of values, and although the RGBA names do frequently represent colors, they are simply convenient labels. The real meaning of the channels is determined by the shader code that uses them.

Common texel formats that illustrate many of these points include:

ARGB 8-bits-per-channel integer: Four channels, each represented by 8 bits of integer data representing numbers from 0.0 (integer value 0) to 1.0 (integer value 255). Sometimes written as "A8R8G8B8." Total size per texel = 32 bits.

RGB 565:   Three channels of integer data, the red and blue channels using 5 bits and the green channel using 6. All three channels represent the numbers 0.0 to 1.0, with the extra bit in the green channel giving it a little more precision, but the same range. Sometimes written as "R5G6B5." Total size per texel = 16 bits.

ARGB 32-bits-per-channel IEEE754 floating-point: Four channels, each stored as a standard floating-point number with one sign bit, eight bits of exponent and 23 bits of mantissa. Range is roughly −3e38 to +3e38. Total size per texel = 128 bits.

ARGB 16-bits-per-channel floating-point: Four channels, each stored as a floating-point number. A variety of formats exists, but the most common is 1 sign bit, 5 bits of exponent, and 10 bits of mantissa. Range is roughly −32768.0 to +32768.0. Total size per texel = 64 bits.

RG and R versions of the 8-, 16-, and 32-bit-per-channel formats: Used when only two or one channel of data is required. Sizes are respectively one-half and one-quarter of the previous.

8-bit-per-texel palletized texture: Each texel is an 8-bit index into a separately supplied 256-color "palette"—usually composed of A8R8G8B8-format texels. Total size per texel = 8 bits, plus an additional $(32)(256) = 8912$ bits added to the total texture size to store the palette.

RGB 4-bits-per-texel compressed texture format: Each 4×4 block of the texture holds two R5G6B5 colors. Each texel in that block is then represented by a 2-bit code. This gives each texel four possible values, representing either one of the two colors, or one of two intermediate colors formed by interpolation between them. This gives a total size for the 4×4 texel block of $(2)(16) + (4)(4)(2) = 64$ bits. This format goes by many names—"DXT1" and "S3TC" being the most common. Total size per texel = 4 bits.

As mentioned previously, the ordering of the channel names may be permuted in some graphics architectures, and many of the formats listed may not be present in some APIs and on some hardware. For example, although palletized textures were common on early graphics hardware, they are now less efficient to render with than the newer compressed formats, and most newer hardware does not support them directly.

As well as each texel having a format, there are various different ways they can be laid out. The most common, already mentioned, is the two-dimensional rectangular array of texels. There are frequently speed and flexibility advantages to using textures with sizes that are a power of two, and of keeping textures square, or nearly so (e.g., using a 256×128 texel array rather than a 512×64 one, even though they have the same number of texels). It is not uncommon for rendering engines to simply reject textures that are not powers of two, and many complain about textures that are not square. The details of why this is, aside from computers naturally liking powers of two, are related to rendering efficiency and the generation of *mipmaps* (discussed shortly).

Although most textures are 2D arrays, there are also 1D (linear array) and 3D (volume) arrays in common use. Note that although the texture array may be conceptually a volume of texels, the primitive being rendered on the screen is still a flat 2D triangle. The fact that it is reading its colors from a 3D array does not change which pixels it affects on-screen. The triangle has not somehow become a volume itself; it is simply reading a volume of texels for its shading information.

A final common texture format is that of six square (and usually power-of-two) textures assembled in the shape of a hollow cube. This is called a *cube map*, and is useful when representing a spherical shell of data. A true hollow sphere of texels would be hard to represent for a computer, but it is relatively simple to distort a sphere into a cube, which then has the desired rectangular and power-of-two properties, and relatively understandable texel mapping and sampling properties.

In addition, textures may have a *mipmap* chain. A mipmap chain is a sequence of textures (each called "a mipmap level"), each roughly half the size in each dimension of the previous one, until the final mipmap is just one texel. For example, the mipmaps of a 256 × 256 texture are 128 × 128, 64 × 64, 32 × 32, 16 × 16, 8 × 8, 4 × 4, 2 × 2, and 1 × 1. Each mipmap holds the same "picture" as the previous one, but shrunk and filtered down to the smaller size. Mipmapping is used to reduce the aliasing artifacts that occur when textures are rendered very small on-screen.

All the types of textures listed previously (1D, 2D, 3D, and cube maps) may have mipmaps, and in each case, the mipmap of a given type of texture is simply the same texture, but halved in each linear dimension. Thus, a 3D texture may have mipmap levels of 32 × 32 × 32, 16 × 16 × 16, 8 × 8 × 8, 4 × 4 × 4, 2 × 2 × 2, and 1 × 1 × 1 texels, and for a cube map, each mipmap level is itself a cube map of progressively smaller size. The rules for creating mipmap levels for nonsquare and non-power-of-two textures are somewhat tricky to implement, and tend not to work terribly well—especially textures that are not powers of two in size. This is one of the reasons why many rendering engines require textures that are powers of two. Mipmapping is now such a fundamental feature of 3D rendering that having to turn it off for some textures is deemed unacceptable.

Texture Mapping

At rendering time, the hardware must know which texels to read to find the color for a given pixel on the screen. The texture must be mapped over the surface of the mesh by some method. This is generally done in two slightly different ways.

The first is by explicit mapping. Each vertex of the mesh supplies a texture coordinate, comprising of one to three numbers, conventionally labeled u, v, and w. 1D textures require just u, 2D textures require u and v, and 3D textures require all three. The values supplied by each vertex are linearly interpolated across the triangle, and at each rendered pixel, the numbers are used to look up the required texel in the texture map. By convention, most rendering APIs map the 0.0 to 1.0 range to the entire texture, no matter how large in texels the texture is. Thus, u and v values of (0.5, 0.5) always sample the texels in the middle of the texture, whatever size it happens to be. This also makes sense in the context of mipmapping—using a mipmap level with a different number of texels does not change the fact that (0.5, 0.5) samples from the middle of the texture.

Cube maps also require all three values—these represent a vector (but this time, each component has the range −1.0 to +1.0) from the middle of the cube, pointing outward. This vector is projected outward until it hits the side of the cube at a certain point on one of the faces, and that is where the texels are sampled from for that pixel.

Besides explicit mapping, where the coordinates are supplied by each vertex and interpolated over the triangle, the coordinates may also be computed at each pixel. This is under almost total programmatic control by the pixel shader, and is used for things such as looking up the surface normal at a pixel by referring to a texture map (a *normal map*), reflecting the eye vector around that surface normal, and then shooting that reflected ray off to be looked up in a cube map representing the environment around the object being rendered. Because the surface normal is itself represented by a value taken from a texture map, this reflection computation that decides which texel to use from the cube map must be done at each pixel.

In practice, hardware performs a computation at each pixel even if the coordinates are supplied at each vertex. This is because interpolation in screen space does not produce the same results as interpolation in world space, because of the effects of perspective. The results must first be corrected to provide linear interpolation, and the results of this *perspective correction* are then used to sample textures.

What happens when the *u*, *v*, and *w* values go outside the 0.0 to 1.0 range, and therefore off the edge of the texture, is determined by something that is generally referred to as the "wrap/clamp" mode of the texture. A variety of things can happen, as chosen by the renderer, and different things may happen in each direction—for example, the texture may wrap in the *u* direction but clamp in the *v* direction. The following are the common modes:

Wrap: The texture "wraps" or "tiles" so that multiple copies appear side by side. Going off one edge of the texture brings the sampler back to the other side. The texture coordinates (3.2, 5.7) will sample from the texel at position (0.2, 0.3).

Clamp: The coordinates are simply clamped to the range 0.0–1.0. Running off the edge of the texture repeats the same texel over and over in that direction. The texture coordinates (3.2, −5.7) will sample from the texel at position (1.0, 0.0).

Mirror: Similar to wrapping, except that each time, the texture is flipped in the respective direction. The texture coordinates (3.2, −5.7) will sample from the texel at position (0.8, 0.3) (because the 3.0 to 4.0 range is a "flipped" version, and therefore the inverse of the "wrap" result, but the −6.0 to −5.0 range is not, and therefore the same).

Mirror once: Like mirror, but only in the region −1.0 to +1.0. Outside this range, behaves like clamp. Useful for textures that have reflection symmetry, such as round blobs or star flares or some lighting functions—only one-quarter of the memory is required. The texture coordinates (3.2, −5.7) will sample from the texel at position (1.0, 1.0).

Border color: Like clamp, except that instead of repeating the texels at the edge of the image over and over, a specified color is returned instead. The texture coordinates (3.2, −5.7) will not sample any texels; it will instead return the border color.

Texture Filtering

In a standard bitmap image, the texel can be thought of as a solid square of color, entirely filling its box. However, when this bitmap image is used as a texture, and the shader simply picks the color of the nearest texel, this representation looks extremely ugly if the texture is rotated or magnified—the square nature of the texels is immediately obvious. This type of texture sampling is called *point sampling*, and is only used when rendering textures such as fonts that will always be displayed aligned with the screen pixels, with no enlargement or shrinking.

To smooth the sharp edges of the texels, hardware generally picks the nearest few texels to the sampled point and blends them together smoothly, with the amount of blending depending on exactly how close to each texel center the sample is taken. In this representation, texels should be thought of not as square blocks of color, but as single points of color, right in the center of the squares, that influence the surrounding parts of the texture. The closer the sample is to this center point, the more the sample is like the color of that texel. The most common type of filtering is *bilinear filtering*, and each sample uses the nearest four texels to construct its color. The term "bilinear" is because there are two linear interpolations happening—one in the *u* direction, followed by one in the *v* direction. There are larger filter sizes that use more texels in each direction, but these are not supported by current hardware except in special cases such as video rescaling. If needed, it is possible to construct them manually using clever shader programming.

Bilinear filtering improves the look of a texture when it is magnified, by smoothing the edges. However, when the texture is shrunk, or *minified*, bilinear filtering cannot help much. Even though it is still choosing the nearest four texel samples, each adjacent rendered pixel uses very different sets of four texels, and the image "sparkles" as it moves—a sign of *aliasing*. The solution is to create mipmaps of the texture that are essentially prefiltered versions of the texture at different sizes. As the texture is rendered smaller and smaller on-screen, smaller and smaller mipmap levels are chosen to take samples from.

Besides reducing aliasing, using mipmaps also has the side effect of increasing rendering speed considerably. In general, the correct mipmap level is chosen so that the size of one texel is roughly the same size as one screen pixel. This means that when rendering nearby pixels on the screen, nearby texels in the mipmap level are read, and this is fairly easy for the various caches in the rendering system to help optimize. Most rendering engines should always generate mipmaps for all textures, and turn mipmapping on for almost every texture. Not doing so causes visible quality problems, and can severely affect speed—it is one of those rare decisions in rendering where there are few tradeoffs to consider.

However, if the renderer simply turns mipmapping on, a visible change happens when the mipmap level changes. This happens not only over time as triangles move further and closer to the camera, but can happen over the area of a single triangle on a single frame. Perspective correction can mean that part of the texture on a triangle uses a different mipmap level than another part, and the place where the mipmap selection changes is extremely visible as a straight line of change. The solution here is to stop "point sampling" which mipmap level is used, and to instead linearly interpolate between the mipmap levels, smoothly blending from one to the other. When

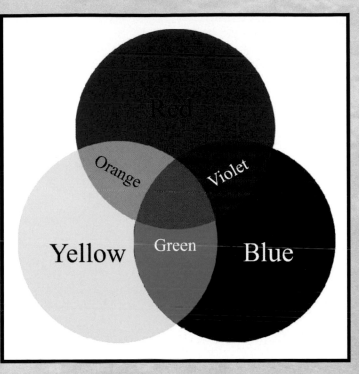

Color Plate 1   An example of subtractive color.

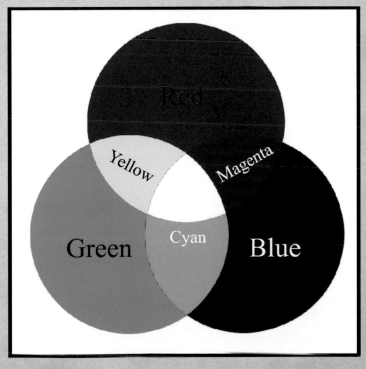

Color Plate 2   An example of additive color.

Color Plate 3   Phoenix Assault before principles of depth and volume.

Color Plate 4   Phoenix Assault after depth principles have been applied.

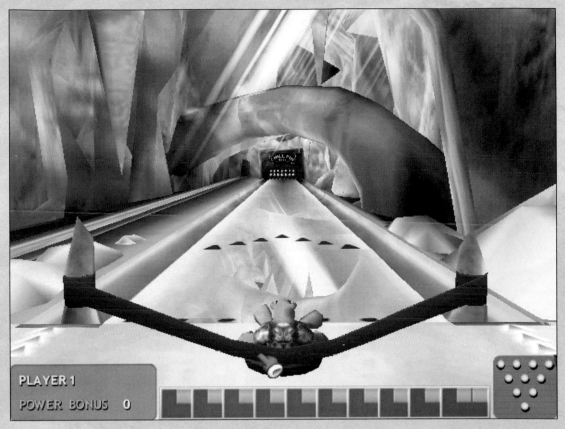

Color Plate 5 Polar Bowler ice walls rely heavily on vertex coloring to add interest to a single tiled texture.

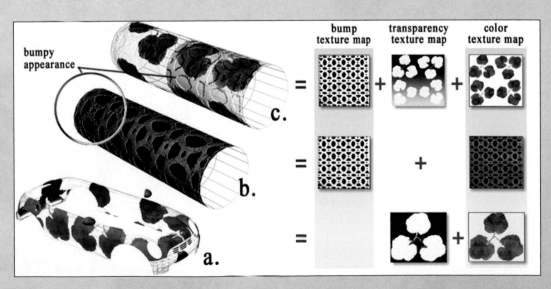

Color Plate 6 Examples of texturing with a bump map, transparency map, and a color texture map.

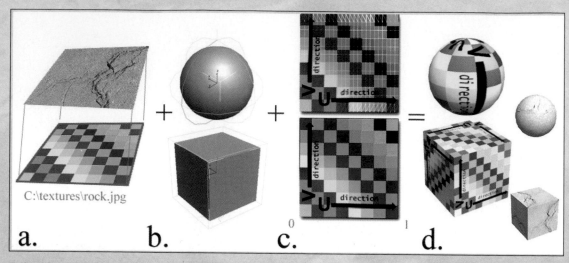

Color Plate 7 Mapping a texture to a surface.

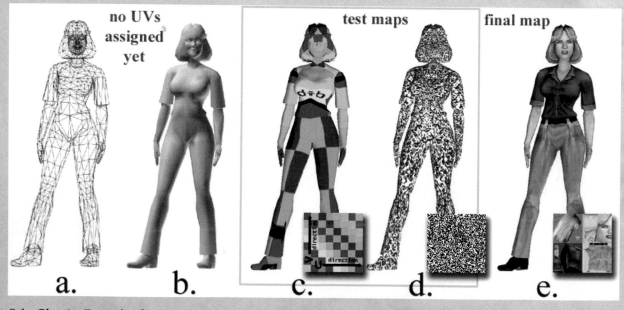

Color Plate 8 Example of using test maps to gauge the quality of the texture mapping, with the final result on the right.

combined with the bilinear filtering happening within each mipmap level, this has three linear interpolations occurring at once, and so is called *trilinear filtering* or *trilinear sampling*. Although trilinear sampling is very slightly more expensive than bilinear sampling with mipmapping, the results are far less objectionable, and usually worth the small cost.

Mipmapping has one major artifact. The mipmapped version of a texture is pre-filtered, but it is prefiltered in both *u* and *v* directions equally. Sometimes, this is not what the graphics hardware needs—sometimes it wants to filter the texture more in one direction than in another. Think of a road with a 512 × 512 texture mapped on it at regular intervals, rendered on a 640 × 480 screen, stretching away to the distance. Looking only at the section of road in the middle distance, in the horizontal direction, the road texture should not be filtered much at all. The texture is 512 texels wide, and it occupies most of the screen width of 640 pixels. Thus, the ratio is nearly even, and very little filtering or mipmapping needs to be done. However, in the vertical direction, the road texture may repeat many times in the space of just a few tens of pixels, because of the effect of perspective correction. If standard mipmapping is used, both directions must be filtered equally, and so the rendering hardware may choose to use the 64 × 64 mipmap level. Vertically, this is fine, but horizontally, the texture is now very fuzzy—those 64 texels have been magnified to occupy nearly 500 pixels of screen space, and turned into a blurry mess.

The solution is to use an even more expensive texture-filtering algorithm called *anisotropic filtering*. "Isotropic" means "the same in all directions," which is what standard mipmapping is. Therefore, "anisotropic" means "not the same in all directions." Rather than take a single filtered sample, anisotropic filtering (in its most common form) takes a sequence of filtered samples from the texture, taking more in the direction of greatest filtering, and then blending them together. Mipmapping is still used, but now it is used for the least-filtered direction, not the most. The details of anisotropic filtering vary from hardware to hardware, and generally speaking, the rendering engine can simply turn it on, and it works. Anisotropic filtering does have a significantly higher cost compared to standard trilinear mipmapping, but it produces a higher quality output, and frequently only needs to be applied to certain textures, particularly those that are often mapped to large, flat surfaces.

Rendering to Texture

Textures are usually supplied to the game by loading them from disk, and originally by artists creating them using art packages. As textures are really just arrays of numbers that map from one set of numbers (the *u*, *v*, and *w* coordinates) to some other set of numbers (the R,G,B,A of the texel), they can also be used to store arbitrary functions; for example, a cosine table, or the amount of reflection a particular surface has in a particular direction. In this case, the CPU may generate the texture.

However, in some cases, the game may want the graphics hardware to generate the texture, by rendering triangles to it. One indirect way to do this is to render to the back buffer and then copy the pixels to the texture's texels with the CPU. Another way is to do the copying with the graphics hardware. However, the most direct way is to have the graphics hardware render directly to the texture's memory. This process redirects rendered primitives from affecting the back buffer so that they hit the texture, and is commonly referred to as "changing the render target." After the texture has been rendered to, the game changes back to the back buffer and renders the scene as usual.

If the texture is a 2D texture with no mipmaps, this is a fairly simple process—there is an obvious way to render to a 2D surface—and the fact that it is a texture and not the back buffer is easy to deal with. If the texture is more complex, the rendering hardware can usually only render to one 2D part of it at once. For example, the hardware can only render to a single "slice" of a 3D texture at a time, but can be directed to different slices at different times. For a cube map, the hardware can render to only a single side at once, but can be directed to render to different sides by the game. Rendering to all six sides of a cube map is becoming more common, and allows dynamically updated environment maps.

For textures that are mipmapped, mipmaps can either be generated automatically from the top mipmap level (usually by an internal render-to-texture process), or less frequently by selecting the mipmap levels themselves as render targets, and rerendering the scene.

When rendering to a texture, a depth buffer may be assigned that is the same size as the texture, and hidden-surface removal performed in the same way.

Rendering to textures is a powerful feature, and allows the graphics hardware to composite many partial renders together in interesting ways not normally possible if always rendering to the back buffer. One of the simplest examples is rendering a television screen. The scene on the television is rendered to a texture with no distortion applied, as if the television was being viewed straight on. This texture can then be used when rendering the scene with the television set in it. If the camera is off to one side, the correct perspective will be applied to the flattened TV image, and artifacts such as light bouncing off the television screen, and (if the TV is an old one, or viewed close up) the image may be split into visible red, green, and blue screen elements, with distortion, blur, and static added. Without render-to-texture functionality, this would be a very difficult effect to re-create.

Lighting

"Lighting" is an umbrella term for the processes of determining the amount and direction of light incident on a surface, how that light is absorbed, reemitted, and reflected from the surface, and which of those outgoing light rays eventually reach the eye. Primarily, a renderer is only concerned with the rays that finally reach the eye. Although there are some interesting effects such as fluorescence that depend on the motion of light rays that do not eventually hit the eye, these are rare, and hard to simulate.

There are three major approaches to solving this problem. The first is called *forward tracing*—take every photon emitted by a light source, trace it through the environment, see what it hits, and decide if it is reemitted and in which directions. Then, ignore all photons that do not eventually hit the eye. This technique is used by nature and our actual eyeballs, and is obviously very accurate. However, it is extremely expensive to calculate, because only a miniscule fraction of the photons in a scene actually reaches the eyeball. However, techniques such as *photon mapping* perform an approximation of this process to achieve high-quality, but extremely slow, results.

The second is *backward tracing*—trace a hypothetical photon that hit the eye backwards from the eye in a particular direction, see which object it came from, and then see the range of places it could have come from, and if so, what their color values would be. This is what traditional *raytracing* does, and is also behind the concept of techniques such as *radiosity*.

In general, both of these techniques are too slow for real-time rendering. Both involve a phase of spreading a bunch of photons out to see either what they hit, or where they could have come from. Real-time rendering must compromise reality for speed, and the way to do this is to only pay attention to the important rays. These are generally those that hit the eye, and those that come from light sources. Additionally, because the hardware is rendering triangles, at any one time, the renderer knows which surface the rays must bounce off—the one currently being drawn. Thus, the question real-time rendering most often asks in lighting is, "Given this bit of surface, how much light came from these sources of light and ended up hitting the eye?" This type of *middle-out* evaluation is very efficient, but uses different mathematical models than the previous two cases.

Note that in practice, all three major rendering techniques use a wide variety of lighting models, because speed is always important in all of them. However, the broad classifications of forward tracing, backward tracing, and middle-out are always useful to bear in mind when thinking about lighting algorithms.

Components

From the previous comments, it should be obvious that there are a few major bits of data that any real-time lighting algorithm needs to generate the correct color for a given pixel.

What lights are shining on the surface? This data is held by the scene in the form of various representations of lights and lighting environments. This is also determined by the positions of those lights relative to other objects, since in many cases they may be fully or partially occluded by other geometry—causing shadows. In more advanced algorithms, the light may also bounce off some surfaces and cause indirect lighting.

How does the surface interact with the incoming (or *incident*) light? This data is held in the material structure of the mesh, the shader code it is composed of, and together with data such as textures and various numerical material values, it answers questions like, "How much of a certain color does the surface reflect? How shiny is it? How bumpy is it?" and so on.

What part of the result of these interactions is visible to the eye?   The data required to resolve this is the easiest to express, and is usually simply represented by the vector pointing from the point on the surface toward the camera. However, it can often be the trickiest part of the algorithm to implement efficiently.

Taken together, these three parts, the position of the eye or camera, the position of the lights in the scene, and the material description all combine to determine the total lighting algorithm in the shaders used to render the instance.

The other question is at what point in the pipeline lighting occurs. Current hardware has two major places, the vertex shader and the pixel shader, and both are capable of performing most of the lighting calculations. Naturally, the vertex shader operates at a coarser granularity than the pixel shader, over more pixels, but a benefit of this is that it operates less frequently, and therefore the cost of performing expensive operations there is lower.

In classic lighting texts, the distinction between performing lighting at vertices or pixels was often termed *Gouraud shading* (performing lighting at each vertex, and interpolating the result over a triangle) and *Phong shading* (interpolating the input to the lighting equations, then evaluating the equations at each pixel). With both vertex and pixel units growing in power, this distinction is now very fuzzy indeed, since a lighting algorithm may be implemented at either vertices or pixels, or parts of it may be moved between the two almost at whim. This is especially true when higher level languages are used to program the shaders. In the following discussions, remember that many of the techniques may be implemented at either level, or parts in one and parts in the other. Future hardware may introduce even further levels of granularity, giving the programmer even more choices for the trade-off between cost and fidelity.

Representation of the Lighting Environment

The first part of the lighting question is, "What lights are shining on the surface?" The game needs a representation of the lighting environment to be able to answer this question for each mesh it renders.

The standard, physically based solution is to regard all lights in a scene as infinitely small points (*point lights*) giving off a certain number of photons per second, of various wavelengths. In practical terms, the light has an *intensity*, a *position*, and a *color*. The intensity is usually measured by the "brightness" of a diffuse white surface illuminated by it at unit distance, and then assuming that the brightness falls off according to the inverse square law. Although "intensity" and "brightness" are technically two very different quantities, in real-time rendering the two are frequently interchanged. The quantity most often being stored and calculated for lights is usually the brightness of a "standard" 100-percent-white object.

While this may offend physicists, this trick is especially helpful on older hardware with limited precision and range, where storing brightness instead of intensity or light flux keeps most numbers in the pipeline in the 0 to 1 range, and is extremely common in practical games programming. However, it should always be noted that this hack is being used, and noticed when it is no longer appropriate to the lighting model. As time goes on, rendering engines may move toward using physically correct units such as lumens, but the old-fashioned "full white" scale is still extremely popular and easy to understand. Fundamentally, all rendering is a hack, and that applies double to real-time rendering in games—the trick is to choose which hacks are useful.

Any surface illuminated by this light takes the brightness value, divides by the square of the distance from the surface to the light, and multiplies by the RGB color value of the light. This is then the amount of incident light on the surface, as shown in Equation 5.1.4.

$$incidentColor = \frac{\left(lightColor\right)\left(lightBrightness\right)}{distanceToLight^2} \tag{5.1.4}$$

The separation of the light's color and brightness into separate components is purely for modeling convenience. Color is frequently chosen using a "color picker" that only displays colors with RGB values in the range 0.0 to 1.0, whereas brightness is a floating-point number with a huge range that is typically adjusted with a slider bar or typed in manually. Keeping them separate simply allows for easier modeling, and a rendering may want to combine the two at whatever stage it wishes.

While this is a clean and efficient representation of light brightness, it actually looks rather poor in practice. Real lights are not infinite points; they have a volume, their light does not only go straight from the light to the surface, they generally have a built-in reflector, or they bounce off nearby objects. The other problem is that computer monitors have a limited *color gamut*—that is, they can only represent a narrow range of intensities. In contrast, lights in the real world have a massive range. Our eyes can adjust to most of this huge range, and "normalize" the images we see, but the monitor simply cannot display this huge range. Actually rendering a scene using inverse square falloff results in many black pixels, many "overbright" white pixels, and very few with any intermediate colors. Useful for a "film noir" effect, but it makes it very difficult for the player of the game to see what is going on.

Thus, the magnitude of the light intensities in a game environment needs to be brought down to a manageable range. A quick inspection of the inverse square falloff curve shows that it generates a huge range of intensities—an object placed 10 centimeters from a light source is 100 times as bright as one placed a meter away, and almost 1,000 times brighter than one placed three meters away. Monitors simply cannot deal with this range, and as noted previously, it's not actually very true to life.

An empirical tweaking of the lighting equation results in a version that is almost as simple, but visually far more pleasing and controllable. Instead of an inverse squared distance falloff, an inverse distance falloff is used, and a clamp is put on the maximum value of the curve to prevent the brightness from exceeding a certain value as an object gets very close to the light. This clamp is typically measured as a "minimum distance" rather than a brightness, but the effect is the same. Equations 5.1.5 and 5.1.6 describe these new equations.

$$clampedDistance = \max\left(distanceToLight, lightMinimumDistance\right) \quad (5.1.5)$$

$$incidentColor = \frac{\left(lightColor\right)\left(lightBrightness\right)}{clampedDistance} \quad (5.1.6)$$

As a further speed optimization, lights are given a "maximum distance" beyond which their effect is so dim that it can be ignored. This maximum distance is usually where the light has very little visible effect, but if the light is simply turned off as the object gets to this distance, there will still be a sharp visible "pop." The (usually small) brightness at this distance can be subtracted from the total, and the result clamped so it never goes negative. Equations 5.1.7 through 5.1.10 describe this new optimization.

$$brightnessAtMaxDistance = \frac{lightBrightness}{lightMaximumDistance} \quad (5.1.7)$$

$$clampedDistance = \max\left(distanceToLight, lightMinimumDistance\right) \quad (5.1.8)$$

$$clampedBrightness = \max\left(0.0, \left(\frac{lightBrightness}{clampedDistance}\right) - brightnessAtMaxDistance\right) \quad (5.1.9)$$

$$incidentColor = \left(lightColor\right)\left(clampedBrightness\right) \quad (5.1.10)$$

In practice, the exact values of the various inputs end up being not particularly meaningful, as artists tend to ignore the actual numerical values and simply play with the numbers until things start to look good. If they have an art package with lighting models they like, it is also a good idea to try to reproduce something close to those behaviors inside the shader.

This is only a very brief look at single-light lighting models. There are many different lighting models, and many are interesting and efficient representations of light sources in particular situations.

Representing Multiple Lights

The next step beyond representing a single light at a time is to represent an entire environment of lights at once. One way to do this is simply to store multiple lights in a list and process them individually, adding up their contributions. However, cost grows linearly with the number of lights, and in an environment with hundreds of lights, can become prohibitive. One important thing to realize is that in most scenes, the lighting environment for a particular object instance can usually be classified into two parts—a few, bright, important light sources, and "all the rest," stored as some type of unified, but possibly not particularly accurate, representation. The major lights that contribute to most of the lighting are processed individually at high quality, and the rest are stored in some other less-precise way, and processed as a whole. However, how do we represent the rest?

The simplest version, and one that has been used since the beginning of computer graphics, is the notion of an *ambient* light. This is simply a constant term that is added to all calculations of incident lighting, and it models the rather tenuous assumption that in any environment, there is a constant number of photons bouncing at random in every direction and illuminating every surface by some chosen amount. This is actually a fairly acceptable model for a small indoor environment with multiple light sources and white-painted matte walls, ceiling and floor, and no external sunlight. The combination of the multiple artificial light sources and the bright matte surfaces does a good job of distributing light fairly evenly around the scene. Add this ambient term to the direct lighting effect of the nearest few lights, and fairly convincing (although not necessarily accurate) results can be obtained.

A better model for an outdoor scene during the day is *hemisphere lighting*. There are three major sources of lighting in this environment. Direct sunlight is the major one, and is modeled as a standard distinct light source. The bright blue sky (the result of diffracted sunlight) is the second, and is modeled as a hemisphere of constant blue. The ground also reflects sunlight shining on it and bounces to illuminate the object from below, although as the ground is not particularly shiny, this is a lesser effect. This latter effect is usually modeled as a brownish hemisphere opposite the blue of the sky, although in some environments it may be a different color—for example, a dark blue for a scene on the open ocean, or a green color rather than brown for a scene set in large meadows during the summer.

The result of being illuminated by two hemispheres, one a bright blue and the other a dark brown, is quite well approximated by taking the dot-product of the normal of the surface with the vector pointing vertically upward, shifting and scaling it into the 0.0 to 1.0 range, and then using this value to interpolate between the two colors, as shown in Equations 5.1.11 through 5.1.13.

$$howUpwards = \text{dotProduct}\left(hemisphereUpVector, surfaceNormal\right) \qquad (5.1.11)$$

$$lerpFactor = \left(howUpwards\right)\left(0.5\right) + 0.5 \qquad (5.1.12)$$

$$incidentColor = \left(lerpFactor\right)\left(hemiColor1\right) + \left(1.0 - lerpFactor\right)\left(hemiColor2\right) \qquad (5.1.13)$$

This, together with the standard direct lighting from the sun, can produce an effective and cheap model of outdoor lighting.

Another very flexible solution is to render, either at runtime or as a preprocess step, a cube map that is a picture of the lighting environment. When used directly, this is called a *reflection map* or *environment map* for shiny surfaces, or it can be heavily blurred and used to look up the diffuse lighting environment.

The latest technology, getting some early adoption in the games industry, is to encode the previous cube map in the frequency domain rather than the spatial domain, as a set of spherical frequencies—much as the movement of a loudspeaker membrane can be encoded as a series of sine waves. There are a few ways to do this, but one of the most common is by using *spherical harmonics* [Ramamoorthi01]. Although mathematically complicated, the actual implementation and use of these representations in a shader are surprisingly simple and powerful [Forsyth03].

All the previous techniques assume that the object is essentially "small"— its size relative to the lighting striking it is trivial, and the only thing that matters is the direction the light falls on it, not how the incident light varies over the surface of the object. For objects up to about the size of humans, such approximations are frequently reasonable for games, but for objects such as walls or houses, it is not. This is especially true if the lights are actually inside the objects; for example, a light mounted on a wall in a house. Even the concept of "which direction is the light from the house" makes no sense. However, a useful property of large objects is that in many games, they do not move, and this is also true of most lights. If the light and object do not move, it is possible to precalculate the incident light directions and brightness and store them in a texture map. If the result of the diffuse lighting equation is also precalculated, the result is a texture with colors in it—known as a *lightmap*, and used by many games over the years. However, there is no need to fully resolve the lighting equation at preprocess time, and the maps may simply store the direction and brightness values for use in later runtime calculations. Some newer variants go further and store not just a single light direction and brightness, but the entire lighting environment—for example, storing a spherical harmonic series at each sample. Note that the frequency of samples, and thus the texture size in memory, can often be surprisingly low and yet still obtain good-quality lighting results. The direction and brightness of incident light does not change particularly quickly over most areas of a scene.

Once the amount and direction of incident light has been established for the surface in the current scene, the interaction of this light with the specific type of surface can be modeled, and the color and number of the light rays that enter the eye from this interaction found. There are two main types of lighting interaction, usually referred to as *diffuse* and *specular* lighting.

Diffuse Lighting

The distinguishing feature of diffuse lighting is that it models how light is absorbed by the material, and then reemitted as new, changed photons. The main feature of these new photons is that they are emitted equally in all directions from the surface. What this means for the purposes of lighting is that the result looks the same from every angle. Since the photons are emitted equally in all directions, it does not matter where the eye is. The only thing that affects the appearance of the surface is the incoming light, and properties such as the normal of the surface.

The most basic diffuse lighting equation, and yet still the most common, is known as Lambert lighting. This says that the number of photons hitting a given area of a surface and being reemitted in all directions is proportional to the dot-product of the surface normal and the incident light vector. If the light is facing directly at the surface, a given area of the surface will receive many photons. However, if the same light shines with a grazing angle, the same photons will be spread out over a much larger patch of the surface, and the same area will receive fewer photons.

Since this is a diffuse lighting formula, the apparent brightness of the surface is directly proportional to the total number of photons striking it, being absorbed, and then being reemitted in a random direction. The proportionality is stored as the "color" of the surface, which actually stores which wavelengths of photons are absorbed completely, and which are absorbed and reemitted, and is only actually a real color when illuminated by white light. Thus:

$$clampedNdotL = \max\left(0.0, dotProduct\left(surfaceNormal, incidentLightVector\right)\right) \quad (5.1.14)$$

$$reflectedColor = \left(surfaceColor\right)\left(incidentColor\right)\left(clampedNdotL\right) \quad (5.1.15)$$

Note that by convention, the incident light vector points away from the surface toward the light, rather than from the light toward the surface. When the surface normal faces in the opposite direction to the incident light, the light is shining on the other side of the object and (unless the object is made of thin paper or other transmissive material, which is not well modeled by Lambert diffuse) the surface will be dark. This is why the dot-product is clamped so that it is always positive or zero.

Normal Maps

The previous lighting operation can be performed at either a vertex or a pixel level. If performed at each pixel, the surface normal may be calculated at each vertex and interpolated over the triangle, or may be read from a texture applied to the object. If read from a texture, that texture is commonly known as a *normal map*, since it is a texture map that holds surface normal vectors. This is one of the most common places where the R,G,B channels of the texture are reinterpreted as arbitrary data rather than a color—in this case, as the *x*, *y*, *z* values of the surface normal vector.

This brings up an important question, "In which space is this calculation being performed?" One possible answer is to perform the entire operation in world space. The light's position is usually stored in world space, the vertex shader will need to transform the vertices into world space at some point to render the triangle on the screen, and so the vertex shader can also calculate the incident light vector in world space. However, the texture cannot store world-space normals—they must be in object space, or they would all have to be recalculated when the instance rotates. One solution is to read the object-space normals from the normal map and then transform them into world space. Once everything is in world space, the previous lighting calculation can be performed and the pixel shaded. In total:

$$worldVertexPosition = \text{transformSpaceObjectToWorld}\left(objectVertexPosition\right) \qquad (5.1.16)$$

$$worldIncidentVector = \text{normalize}\left(worldLightPosition - worldVertexPosition\right) \qquad (5.1.17)$$

$$objectNormal = \text{sampleTexture}\left(normalMap\right) \qquad (5.1.18)$$

$$worldNormal = \text{transformSpaceObjectToWorld}\left(objectNormal\right) \qquad (5.1.19)$$

$$clamped = \max\left(0.0, \text{dotProduct}\left(worldNormal, worldIncidentVector\right)\right) \quad (5.1.20)$$

$$brightness = \left(surfaceColor\right)\left(incidentColor\right)\left(clamped\right) \qquad (5.1.21)$$

The annoying part of this is that the transformation of the surface's object-space normal to world space must be performed at every pixel, since that is where the normal map texture is sampled.

One nice property of the dot-product operation is that if you transform both vectors from one orthonormal space to another, the result of the dot product is unchanged. In games, both object and world space are almost always orthonormal spaces, which means the previous algorithm could be converted to work in object space instead, as follows:

$$worldVertexPosition = \text{transformSpaceObjectToWorld}\left(objectVertexPosition\right) \qquad (5.1.22)$$

$$objectLightPosition = \text{transformSpaceWorldToObject}\left(worldLightPosition\right) \qquad (5.1.23)$$

$$objectIncidentVector = \text{normalize}\left(objectLightPosition - objectVertexPosition\right) \qquad (5.1.24)$$

$$objectNormal = \text{sampleTexture}\left(normalMap\right) \qquad (5.1.25)$$

$$clamped = \max\left(0.0, \text{dotProduct}\left(objectNormal, objectIncidentVector\right)\right) \quad (5.1.26)$$

$$brightness = \left(surfaceColor\right)\left(incidentColor\right)\left(clamped\right) \qquad (5.1.27)$$

Note that the vertex shader still needs to calculate the *worldVertexPosition* of the vertex, because that is what it uses to render the triangle. At first glance, the amount of work has not been reduced. There are still two transformations from one space to another being performed. However, the transformation of the surface normal that was read from a texture has been removed and replaced by the transformation of the light's position from world space to object space. This can be done in the vertex shader rather than the pixel shader. Since the vertex shader is run less often than the pixel shader, this can be a significant speed saver. In fact, in many cases, when rendering rigid bodies such as machinery, it can be done once per instance on the host CPU, and never executed in either the vertex or pixel shaders. This concept of shuffling parts of an algorithm around between the shader stages is important, and very useful when optimizing for speed.

More on Tangent Space

A further refinement of the bump-map technique is to realize that most bump maps do not store normals in object space, but instead store normals in tangent space. Tangent space is defined at any place on the surface of a mesh by three vectors. The first is the normal to the surface, and other two are the tangent and binormal vectors that lie along the surface, and usually at roughly right angles to each other. Note that the "surface normal" that defines tangent space is the one specified at each vertex of the mesh, whereas the surface normal being looked up in the texture is a per-pixel value representing the fine bumps and grain of the surface.

The normal, tangent, and binormal vectors that define tangent space are specified at each vertex of the triangle, usually as an average of the tangent-space vectors of each triangle that meets at that vertex. Since each vertex of a triangle can point the three vectors in different directions, with the directions interpolated across the triangle, this space is only loosely defined. Strictly speaking, all three vectors should be at right angles and unit-length. In other words, they should form an orthonormal basis that defines tangent space. However, this is frequently not quite true in practice, and the vectors may only point at somewhere close to right angles. This is especially true as tangent space is interpolated across a triangle—the interpolated space may be even less orthonormal than at any of the vertices. In practice, this effect can be reduced as needed by adding a few vertices where tangent space distorts too severely over the more curved areas of a mesh.

The result is that calculations in tangent space should be treated with caution—lines are only "mostly straight" and angles are only roughly correct over short distances. Over long distances, because tangent space curves to follow the surface of the mesh, all conventional geometry breaks down completely. This lack of rigor means that most calculations in tangent space are only approximate, but since it is almost entirely used for lighting, some degree of error is usually acceptable, especially for real-time game rendering.

There is a variety of reasons to store normal maps in tangent space, but the main one is to reduce the size of the normal-map texture. Normal maps can consume considerable portions of available memory, and reducing their size is of major importance, even at the cost of some rendering speed.

Notice that in tangent space, almost all the normals of a normal map will point away from the surface. Unless the surface is incredibly bumpy, there is no way that a normal can point back toward the surface, and for all practical purposes this situation can be ignored (remember—the normal map is meant to encode fine surface details—large details should still be represented as actual geometry). The other main point is that surface normals are unit-length vectors, which means that the sum of the squares of the x, y, z components is 1. Because the normals all point away from the surface, that perpendicular component (by convention, the z-component) must be positive. These two facts mean that the z-component can be discarded, because the shader can always compute it by combining these two facts:

$$z = +\text{sqrt}\left(1 - x^2 - y^2\right) \qquad\qquad (5.1.28)$$

Reducing the texture from a three-component x, y, z texture to a two-component x, y texture (or, in more conventional terminology, from RGB to RG) significantly reduces the memory that the texture takes up. Another optimization is that for relatively smooth surfaces, the normal will rarely diverge far from being perpendicular to the surface, which means the x- and y-components will be small. Knowing that the range of possible values is usually small allows several compression tricks, meaning that each texel of the normal map can use fewer bits to store the x- and y-components, further reducing storage requirements.

Precomputed Radiance Transfer

Instead of representing a surface as a geometric construction, such as storing its normal vector, it is possible to represent the diffuse lighting of a surface in terms of its response to external lighting from a variety of directions. This effectively bypasses the question of what the surface is made of, what shape it is, and how it casts shadows on itself. Instead, the representation simply stores what the final brightness of the surface is under lighting from any given direction.

Thus, each texel of the image is effectively just a lookup table. For each light, the incident direction is looked up in the table, and the result is a color—the color response of the surface. This includes all the information about the color of the surface, in which direction that part of the surface faces, and how it responds to light. It can even include slightly more "global" information, such as how well the surrounding surface casts shadows on it from that direction (known as *local self-shadowing*), and whether the light can bounce off another nearby surface and illuminate the surface indirectly.

This is a very powerful technique, but how to store the table? This table stores a color in response to a unit-length vector: the incident light vector. This type of lookup usually requires a cube map, but this would require a cube map per texel, which is an unlikely and memory-hungry concept.

However, maps of the unit sphere can also be stored as spherical harmonics, and if only the lower frequency bands are used, the memory requirements are reasonable. There is also a variety of cunning compression schemes possible for storing the higher frequency spherical harmonics in a memory-efficient way. This technique is called *precomputed radiance transfer* because it stores the transfer of incident radiance to exit radiance toward the eye.

Even cleverer is if the lighting environment is itself represented with a spherical harmonic, as in the previous example. Therefore, a spherical harmonic represents the total incident light from all directions, and a spherical harmonic represents how the incident light from each direction is reflected into the eye. One of the interesting mathematical tricks is that combining these two together (the correct term is *convolving*) is as simple as performing a large dot-product. This is extremely simple for rendering hardware to perform, and the result is the color that is seen by the eye.

Precomputed radiance transfer (PRT) is a fairly new technique, but is extremely powerful [Sloan02]. It does still have some limitations to work through, such as poor support for animated meshes, and relatively large storage requirements, but it and related techniques are already being used by some games to enhance the quality of their diffuse lighting. With some work, PRT can be extended to include specular lighting, although at this point the memory and speed costs are prohibitive for current hardware.

Specular Lighting

There are many *specular lighting* techniques, but they all share one main feature. Whereas photons in diffuse lighting are absorbed and reemitted from the surface, photons in specular lighting bounce off the surface. Because the photon is bouncing, its exit direction is closely related to its incident direction. What this means is that for a light from a particular direction, more photons will bounce off the surface in some directions than others will. However, the rendering engine is interested in only one direction—the one the eye is in.

Contrast this with diffuse lighting, where it is assumed that whatever direction the photon comes in along, it leaves in a random direction. The only reason why diffuse lighting uses the incident light direction is to calculate how many photons strike a given area of the surface—where the actual direction is not in itself important. Because photons leave at random angles, the direction of the eye is unimportant—wherever it is in space, the same number of photons will reach it. However, for specular lighting, photons do not all leave in random directions, and thus the direction of the eye from the surface is a key component of the lighting result.

There are many specular lighting models, all showing slightly different effects or modeling different materials, but in many cases, even simple models can give a good effect. One of the simplest is *Blinn specular lighting*, which takes advantage of a neat insight—to treat the surface as a collection of minute conceptual *microfacets*, each facing in a random direction relative to the visible surface. These microfacets are individually far too small to see, it is the net effect of huge numbers of them that the specular lighting equation is trying to model.

If each microfacet is a perfect specular mirror, then a photon bounces off them with perfect reflection with the angle of exit being the same as the angle of incidence. Naturally, most of these photons miss the eye, and the lighting equation should ignore them. However, how many hit the eye? To hit the eye, the microfacet must be perfectly oriented to reflect the incoming light directly into the eye. Therefore, the normal of the microfacet must point along the average of the eye vector and the incident light vector—exactly halfway. This vector is named the *half vector*. Only then will incoming light bounce into the eye and cause a bright spot.

To determine how bright this part of the surface is, the only question is, "What proportion of the microfacets do in fact point in this particular special direction—the half vector?" The Blinn model assumes that microfacets are randomly oriented, but not in a uniform way. Their average orientation is the same as the overall surface normal. At one extreme, if the surface is a perfect mirror, all the microfacets are oriented in exactly the same direction. As the surface gets rougher, the microfacet orientation gradually diverges from the surface normal, and there is a chance that a certain proportion of them will be oriented along the half vector and bounce light into the eye. The closer the half vector is to the actual surface normal, the higher the number of microfacets that are likely to be oriented correctly, and the brighter the pixel.

If the surface is quite smooth, there is a significant number with this orientation if the half vector and the surface normal are quite close. Conversely, the rougher the surface is, the wider the random distribution of microfacets, which means that even when the half vector is significantly different from the surface normal, a significant number of microfacets are still reflecting light into the eye. This distribution of microfacet orientations may be modeled in various ways, and the standard Blinn method is to take the dot-product between the normal and half vectors and raise it to a certain power.

For a photon to get from the light to the eye, it must bounce off a microfacet oriented toward the half-vector (Figure 5.1.5, left). A rough surface (Figure 5.1.5, middle) has more microfacets oriented in the direction of the half-vector than a smooth surface (Figure 5.1.5, right).

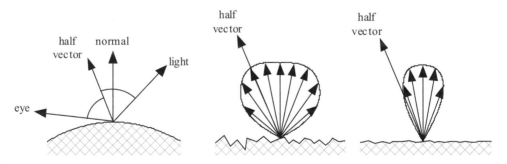

FIGURE 5.1.5   *Left: the relationship between the four vectors in Blinn lighting. Middle and right: the distribution of microfacets in rough and smooth surfaces.*

When put together, Blinn's model of specular lighting is:

$$halfVector = \frac{\left(incidentLightVector + eyeVector\right)}{2} \qquad (5.1.29)$$

$$alignment = \max\left(0.0, \text{dotProduct}\left(halfVector, surfaceNormal\right)\right) \qquad (5.1.30)$$

$$brightness = \left(surfaceColor\right)\left(incidentColor\right)\left(alignment^{materialSmoothness}\right) \qquad (5.1.31)$$

The value *materialSmoothness* is used here because a low value denotes a very rough surface that produces specular reflections in many different directions, while a very high value represents a very smooth surface that only reflects any significant specular light when the surface normal is almost exactly aligned with the half vector.

There are many specular lighting models, each representing a different approximation to a certain set of materials, and the reader is encouraged to try as many as possible. Programmable shader hardware also encourages experimentation with existing algorithms, tweaking them to increase speed or reduce undesirable artifacts.

Environment Maps

The Blinn specular model is useful for moderately smooth surface models such as varnished wood and plastic, where the slight grain in the surface means that the only lights that reflect enough light into the viewer's eyes (to be significant) are large, strong point lights such as the sun or a light bulb.

However, one of the most common specular lighting models is that of a nearly perfect reflector such as well-polished metal or glass. These surfaces are so smooth that nearly everything can reflect an image well enough to be seen. If one of the one-light-at-a-time models were used to render these, all that would be seen would be a few tiny points of light—the perfect reflections of those major light sources. In reality, these surfaces reflect nearly everything, not just strong emitters of light.

For outdoor environments, and objects that are only mildly reflective such as the cars in a racing game, it may be sufficient to simply create a cube map containing some generally dark stuff (i.e., the road) at the bottom, some trees or hills around the middle, and blue sky and clouds at the top. The shader then takes the eye vector, reflects it around the surface normal, and looks up the result in the cube map. This tells the shader the color of the light bouncing off the surface and into the eye. This is an example of a "backward trace" lighting algorithm being used in real-time rendering. The shader may also modify the color according to the color of the surface. For example, gold metal reflects more red and green photons than it does blue, whereas silver metal reflects all three equally well.

As long as the cars are not too highly polished, and the action is moving reasonably quickly, it is rare for people to notice (or care) that the reflected environment does not actually match the rendered environment (e.g., a certain part of the racetrack may not have many trees around it, and yet the environment maps always contains trees). A simple but common trick in this particular case is to have several different environment maps for different parts of the track, but even this goes unnoticed by most people. The same is true if the object being rendered is highly reflective, but also a complex shape, so that no large part of the environment can be seen without severe distortion. The common example of this in many games is the metal parts of weapons or equipment. If the surface normal is read from the normal map at every pixel, the reflected environment map gives the equipment an authentic "shiny bumpy metal" look without it actually being all that important what the environment map actually contains.

Of course, in some cases, it would be nice if the environment map did correctly reflect the surroundings, and in this case the same trick can be used. However, this time the game can render the actual environment to the sides of the cube map one each frame (or, in some cases, every couple of frames), using six render-to-texture operations, one for each side of the cube map. In this case, it is important that each instance in the game has its own cube map. If there is a red car and a blue car racing side by side, the cube map used for the red car should be rendered from the center of the red car, and therefore have a picture of the blue car in it. Conversely, the cube map used for the blue car should be rendered from the center of the blue car and thus show the red car in it. Trying to use the same cube map for both cars will create some odd results. Either one car will not have a reflection of the other car, or both cars will have reflections not only of the other car, but also of themselves!

The Hardware-Rendering Pipeline

The hardware-rendering pipeline presented here is intended as a reference to what to expect from recent graphics hardware. As hardware becomes increasingly programmable, certain parts of this pipeline may become more complex, simpler, mutate, or vanish entirely. However, most of the principles are fairly fundamental, and even when replaced by programmable units, those units will perform similar functions, although presumably with a much higher degree of customizability by the rendering engine.

The part of the pipeline most likely to change significantly in the next few years is that the simple one-in-one-out geometry unit currently embodied by a single vertex shader program stage is likely to become far more complex. Frequently, games want to generate multiple triangles from a single input primitive, and currently this must be performed on the host CPU, with only some of the work possible on the vertex shader. One common example is that of tessellating a higher order surface representation (such as a *Bézier* or *Catmull-Clark surface*) and displacing the new vertices by values from a texture map or noise function. Another example is the generation of shadow volumes. Currently, this is done either on the CPU, or by pregenerating all the possible triangles, and then having the vertex shader cull the ones not needed by various tricks. Neither method is particularly efficient. A final example is the generation of the "fins and shells" of geometry commonly used for rendering fur or grass—another task currently performed by the host CPU.

Since these operations are highly parallel, and in many cases fairly simple, it is likely that hardware will expand to take this extra functionality on-board. However, the exact form this will take is still a matter of conjecture.

Bear in mind while reading that this is mainly a conceptual model, not a physical model of what hardware actually does. In practice, hardware may perform these operations in a completely different order, and perform some operations in different places in the pipeline, or even in multiple places where appropriate. For example, it is not uncommon for hardware to have at least two depth buffers, one the "real" one at the end of the pipeline, and one much earlier in the pipeline to throw pixels away as early as possible, without taking the time to shade them. Although the functional behavior is the same as presented here, the actual implementation of most hardware is far more complex, and it is expected that this will continue in the future. Because of this, the performance characteristics of real hardware are already very different from the conceptual software model most programmers have of the process. It is therefore important when considering the performance implications of using rendering hardware in various ways to always remember this guiding principle—hardware is absolutely nothing like software. Even the programmable shaders that look a bit like software models can have strange and counterintuitive performance implications.

With that in mind, here is the almost entirely fictitious conceptual model.

Input Assembly

The renderer feeds many streams of data to the hardware—buffers of vertices, indices, values to be fed to the shaders in other ways, textures, and various other control data. The data is read, de-indexed as necessary, and assembled into primitives. For simplicity, it is assumed for the rest of this section that the primitives are triangles. These triangles then decide which bits of data they require to be processed before they can be rendered to the screen. Typically, these are the vertices of the mesh.

Vertex Shading

If the vertices required by the triangle have already been processed and are sitting in the postshading vertex cache, they are used directly. Otherwise, the vertex shader's input data is read from the various buffers it lives in, and fed to an instance of the vertex shader program.

The vertex shader typically transforms the vertex's local-space position to clip space using a matrix transformation. If the mesh is animated, this matrix may be a composite of many separately animated matrices (discussed in Chapter 5.2, "Character Animation").

Additionally, the vertex shader may further modify the vertex's position in various ways, such as looking up a displacement map or projecting it in various directions for effects such as fur-rendering "shells." Alternatively, the vertex shader may not use a source position at all—it may simply generate the position directly from mathematical formulae. This is common when rendering particle systems. The vertex shader is told the type of particle system, some details about when and where this particle was created, and calculates the current position by assuming the particle followed a few standard equations of motion (such as parabolic motion under gravity) since it was created. The advantage of this is that the data describing the particle never changes—it always describes the particle's birth. All that changes from frame to frame is the time since the particle's birth.

The vertex shader then calculates any data required by the pixel shader for its shading. Many values can be calculated in either pixel or vertex shader, and which is performed where depends entirely on the performance and quality trade-offs. Some quantities, such as the computation of vectors to lights and the eye, can be performed in the vertex shader and interpolated over the triangle with reasonable fidelity. However, the exact shading of the pixels is usually performed in the pixel shader, because this allows each pixel to have a different normal and color, provided by a texture map.

Note that newer models of vertex shader may sample textures, just like pixel shaders, and in fact, the programming models of the pixel and vertex shader are gradually converging, with similar capabilities in both. Some hardware already uses the same processing units to perform both tasks, and this convergence is expected to continue. This allows further migration of algorithms from one to the other, according to quality and speed requirements.

Primitive Assembly, Culling and Clipping

Once all the vertices for the triangle are shaded, the triangle has the clip-space positions for all its vertices, and can now decide if it is visible, and if so, how much of it is visible. The first thing to happen is *backface culling*. Triangles conventionally have two sides—a clockwise side (the front) and a counterclockwise side (the back). The order in which the vertices are specified by the game is preserved and remembered, and if these vertices appear in a clockwise ordering when rendered on the screen and the triangle is told to render its front side, the triangle will be visible.

When rendering, the renderer can decide if both sides are visible, or only one, and if so, whether it is the clockwise or anticlockwise side that is visible. Note that if the triangle primitive used is a "strip," the ordering of the vertices is reversed for every even-numbered triangle. This is taken into account, so that the entire strip has a consistent side that is visible—the renderer only has to consider the ordering of the first triangle, and the rest follow.

If the game has specified that only one side is to be visible, and that side is not facing the camera, the triangle is discarded and not rendered (i.e., it is *backfaced culled*). There are two main reasons to do this. The first is if the game wants to render each side of a triangle with a different shader, or different properties. For example, when rendering a page of newspaper or a book, one side has one set of writing on it, the other side has another. The simplest way to do this is to render the page twice. The first time, only clockwise triangles are rendered, and the texture on that side is set. The second time, only counterclockwise triangles are rendered, and the texture on the other side is set. Because the same geometry is used each time, and a particular triangle cannot be both clockwise and counterclockwise in a single frame, each triangle is rendered only once, and the correct texture is used.

The other reason to backface cull triangles is efficiency. Most objects being rendered are solid, and have a definite "inside" to them that is never seen. If triangles of the mesh are always ordered so that the clockwise side faces "outward," then they are the only ones that ever need rendering. This is an extremely fast way to discard approximately half the triangles in a typical scene without performing any depth tests at all, and should be used whenever possible.

After this, frustum culling is performed. The three vertices of the triangle are tested against the six planes of clip space, and if all three are off one of the planes, the triangle is quickly rejected. After this, the triangle is clipped to those six planes to remove the invisible parts. If the game has chosen to add in some additional user-defined clip planes, the triangle must be clipped against those as well.

Note that clipping is an expensive operation, as it involves geometric operations, and may involve generating more than one output triangle from a single input triangle. A triangle can potentially be clipped by all six sides of clip space to produce a nine-sided polygon, usually rendered as seven triangles internally. Add user clip planes, and it can be even more. Some hardware can use guard-band regions and other tricks to move some processing down to a per-pixel test to remove some of this geometry-processing cost, but again, this is an implementation detail.

Projection, Rasterization, and Antialiasing

Once the triangle has been clipped, it can be projected from clip space to screen space (where pixels live) by dividing the clip-space x, y, and z values by the w value, some simple scale-and-biasing to fit the result to the screen rendering window (called the *viewport*), and rasterized. *Rasterization* is the process of finding which pixels and samples the triangle hits. This is a relatively simple process, but because of the speed with which it must be performed, there are many tricks and subtleties in this process. Fortunately, most of them are invisible to the renderer.

The distinction between pixels and samples is subtle, but important when using full-screen antialiasing. In this scheme, each displayed pixel on the frame buffer has many "samples" in the back buffer. Each sample has a separate color and Z value, and in fact, the back buffer behaves much like a frame buffer with a much higher resolution. When the back buffer has finished rendering and is displayed, the multiple samples are combined (often using a complex filtering process) to create a single pixel. This allows triangle edges to be smoothed and appear less jagged—this jaggedness is caused by *aliasing*, and therefore the process to smooth them is called *antialiasing*.

So far, this process happens the same way for both current methods of antialiasing—called *multisampling antialiasing* (MSAA) and *supersampling antialiasing* (SSAA). The difference is in the pixel-processing pipeline. For supersampling AA, it is exactly like rendering to a larger back buffer and then filtering down—each sample is shaded individually by the pixel shader, depth tested, and stored.

For multisampling AA, only one screen pixel is sent to the pixel shader. The result is then sent to all the samples for that pixel, and each sample is then individually depth-tested and written. This obviously lowers the amount of work required—only one pixel is shaded, rather than every sample being shaded individually. Additionally, if all the depth tests for all the samples of a single pixel pass, then the color values for all the samples in that pixel will be the same, and some hardware can use this fact to reduce the amount of memory bandwidth it uses, rather than always storing all these identical values. This reduction in memory bandwidth and the number of times the pixel shader is being run gives MSAA a considerable speed advantage over SSAA in most cases.

However, multisampling AA has some artifacts that may be objectionable, and as shaders become more complex, these artifacts may become more of a problem. The details are long and complex, and vary between different hardware, so it is usually sufficient to be aware of the two types of antialiasing, and be aware that although multisampling is considerably faster, there is (as always in graphics) a price to be paid for the extra speed.

To alleviate the confusion between whether a pixel shader is being run on a pixel (MSAA) or a sample (SSAA), the term "fragment" is used to denote whatever unit a pixel shader works on. Therefore, the term "pixel shader" is somewhat inaccurate and it should be called a "fragment shader." Nevertheless, the original name has stuck.

Pixel Shading

The pixel shader is invoked once per fragment (a pixel for MSAA, a sample for SSAA). The various attributes calculated by the vertex shaders at each vertex are interpolated across the triangle, and a single value is given to each invocation of the pixel shader. In some shader architectures, these attributes are assigned specific meanings, such as a set of texture coordinates, a set of colors, an interpolated normal, a depth value, and so on. Other shader programming models simply see an array of attributes generated by the vertex shaders, interpolate them, and feed the results to the pixel shader to be interpreted as the shader writer wishes.

The pixel shader may use the attributes as coordinates for sampling texels from textures, and may generally perform a wide range of standard operations on the results. Since this part of the pipeline is programmable, the limits are defined by the hardware, the speed costs of each shader instruction, and the ingenuity of the programmer.

Each pixel shader outputs one or more color values as its result, and may optionally also output a new depth value for the pixel (although this is currently an expensive option to use, and should be used sparingly). Again, although the outputs are labeled "colors," they are really just a set of numbers, and may represent whatever values the programmer wishes. The pixel shader may also abort the current pixel and decide that it should not be rendered after all. This is useful when rendering translucent objects. If the current fragment comes from a part of the object that is entirely transparent, there is no point in outputting any colors, because the back buffer will not be affected in any way by this fragment. It is often quicker to abort processing of the fragment as soon as this fact is known, rather than going on to shade the fragment that will then have no effect.

Z, Stencil, and Alpha-Blend Operations

Once the pixel shader has generated its fragment color and possibly a new depth value, the fragment becomes one or more samples (again, this only applies to MSAA).

Unless the sample has been killed by the pixel shader, the depth value of the new sample is compared against the current value in the depth buffer. The new sample may also have a stencil reference value, which is compared against the current value in the stencil buffer, if one is present. Both these tests (depth and stencil) have a variety of configurable settings, but the result of a couple of moderately programmable logical operations is that the new sample is either accepted or rejected. Probably the most common setting for these tests is that the new sample is accepted if the new depth value is less than the existing depth value, and rejected otherwise. If the sample is rejected, no further processing takes place, and the existing sample's depth, stencil, and color values are preserved.

If the new sample passes, a number of things may happen. All of these are under the direct control of the renderer and may be enabled or disabled between batches of primitives. First, the new sample's depth value may or may not replace the existing sample's value in the depth buffer (the usual setting is that it does). Second, the existing sample's stencil value may be incremented, decremented, inverted, set to zero, or replaced by the new reference value. Most simple rendering does not involve the stencil buffer at all—it is only used for advanced rendering options. Finally, the new sample's color may replace the existing color in the back buffer, or may be blended with it in a variety of ways. This may also be enabled or disabled on a per-channel basis. For example, the game may choose to preserve the existing alpha channel for a particular rendering operation, and only change the red, green, and blue channels. Currently, the blending operations available are fairly limited, with all blending being of the form $(A \cdot B) \text{ op } (C \cdot D)$, where A, B, C, and D are various values taken from the current sample in the back buffer and the new sample output by the pixel shader, and where "op" is an add, subtract, minimum or maximum operation. Different blending operations may be performed on the color (RGB) and alpha channels.

In the past, this part of the hardware was even more limited, and could perform only a simple "alpha blending" operation. This unit has many names, most of them inaccurate but historical, such as the *alpha blender* (it now does more than simple alpha blends) or the *frame buffer blender* (it technically blends to the back buffer or current render target, not only to the frame buffer).

This largely fixed-function "back end" unit is likely to be a source of considerable innovation over the next few years. It will probably become far more programmable, although there are currently good performance-critical reasons why it is not already fully programmable and simply part of the pixel shader. The most obvious is that most hardware will perform the depth and stencil tests before the pixel shader whenever possible, and reject fragments before they require shading, giving a huge boost to processing speed, since in a typical game scene approximately 80 percent of pixels are rejected by the depth buffer. Of course, if the pixel shader chooses to modify the fragment's depth value, this is no longer possible, and on current hardware, there are considerable performance penalties for doing so. For this reason, the functional diagram shows the depth and stencil tests as conceptually occurring after the pixel shader.

Multiple Render Targets

One modification to the previous pipeline is fairly recent—the capability for the pixel shader to write to more than four channels of data (the RGBA channels of a single back buffer). This is achieved by giving the pipeline multiple render targets, each of which may have a different texel format and up to four channels each (still conventionally named RGBA). The pixel shader may then output one color per render target. However, these multiple render targets must be the same size, and currently must have the same alpha-blend function applied to all of them. There is still only one depth and stencil buffer rather than one per-render target, and the fragment either modifies all the render targets, or none at all.

In total, this feature effectively allows the pixel shader to produce more than four outputs, which can often be useful when combining multiple shaders together for a particularly complex effect—the multiple render targets can be read as separate textures by pixel shaders in later rendering passes and recombined in interesting ways. Again, this area is expected to evolve rapidly in the coming years.

Shader Characteristics

Current shader models place considerable restrictions on what a shader can do and what data it may access. Most of these restrictions are designed to allow the hardware to run many hundreds or even thousands of these shaders in parallel. Parallelism is mainly where graphics hardware gets its immense speed from, because graphics rendering is an inherently highly parallel operation. Although these restrictions might seem annoying and unreasonable in some cases, removing them would often also remove a lot of the possible parallelism, dramatically reducing speed.

Part of the fine art of the graphics programmer is working within the restrictions of this highly parallel framework to produce interesting real-time effects. In many cases, this requires attacking a problem in a different way to maintain this parallel execution as much as possible, even at the cost of some theoretical efficiency. For example, it may be quicker to recompute a value many times over, rather than trying to calculate it once, write it out, and then read it multiple times. Although this latter option sounds faster in theory, it breaks the parallelism—the first operation must be performed, the graphics hardware must wait until that operation is completed, and only then can the second be started. This may result in slower overall speed, because more of the hardware is sitting idle and simply waiting for other parts of the chip to finish their jobs.

The most notable restrictions placed on current shaders are discussed here. Some of these restrictions may be lifted with future shader models and hardware, but in many cases, it is expected that there will be an associated speed penalty, and so these guidelines are still useful.

The most important restriction is that shaders may not write out to anywhere but their assigned output slots, and they may not change where they write to according to program execution. For a vertex shader, this output is the per-vertex position and attribute data. For a pixel shader, this is the fully shaded fragment (pixel or sample, as appropriate). Additionally, shaders may not read the results of any other shader in the current batch of primitives, except for the specific case of a pixel shader reading the output of a vertex shader. This can be achieved in other ways to a certain degree by rendering to a texture and then reading that texture in subsequent passes, but rendering to and reading from the same texture within a single pass is not allowed.

Shaders may not have any persistent data. Each invocation of a shader starts with the same context as every other. Any local data that one shader may have modified is forgotten when that shader finishes, and registers are reset to default values. The only difference is in specific input values. For the vertex shader, these are the attributes of the respective vertex, fetched from various vertex buffers, and for the pixel shader, these are the interpolated attributes of the vertices, and some other contextual information such as the screen coordinate, and which side (clockwise or counter-clockwise) of the triangle is being rendered.

Shaders may not access arbitrary memory. They must declare ahead of time which areas of memory they will access—typically restricted to a set number of "buffers" rather than being arbitrary areas of memory—and because of the previous considerations, they may only read from these buffers, never write to them. This is not only because most shaders lack sufficient integer arithmetic functionality to handle arbitrary 32-bit addresses, but also because attempting to access any memory from both the CPU and a shader at the same time is extremely difficult. Typically, only one of the two may access any part of memory at a single time, and the handover must be carefully synchronized.

Shader Programming Languages

The wide variety of shader capabilities, especially pixel shaders, and the rapid rate of change, has lead to a profusion of shader languages, each targeted for a specific range of hardware.

Most of these appear to be very similar to CPU assembly language, except with the previous restrictions, and the fact that most registers are four components wide (typically and interchangeably named either R, G, B, A or X, Y, Z, W), and most instructions can operate on up to four of those components at a time. The experience of programming these units will be moderately familiar to anyone who has done any SIMD programming on a CPU, although it should be remembered that in most cases, the CPU's integer, arbitrary memory fetch, and looping and branching instructions are not available for most shader hardware, except in the newest examples.

Fortunately, there is also some higher level language support to help hide this complexity behind a veneer of C-like readability. In many cases, the languages look very much like C, but with no pointers or arbitrary arrays, little or no global data, few looping and conditional constructs, and specialized instructions to perform tasks such as texture sampling. In addition, it is extremely common for shaders to fail to compile because of complexity or length limitations, so the programmer is always required to understand and adapt to the underlying hardware capabilities for which his code is being compiled. As time goes on and hardware improves, these will be less and less of a problem, and the difference between high-level shading languages and "real" C will be further eroded. However, it is important to bear in mind that for many algorithms, the performance characteristics of graphics hardware will be radically different from that of a CPU. A change that may double the speed of an algorithm on a CPU may halve the speed of the same algorithm when performed on rendering hardware, and vice versa.

Fixed-Function Pipelines

The pipeline presented so far describes the current state of the art for consumer rendering hardware. However, there is plenty of older hardware still around and being used for playing games, both in console systems and in PCs, and it is worth mentioning some of the places in which the previous model must be modified when dealing with older hardware.

First, internal shading precision can be reduced dramatically. The previous model assumes all shaders run at full 32-bit floating-point precision. Currently, only the latest and greatest hardware does this. Most hardware only performs vertex shading to this precision, while pixel shading is performed at a variety of precisions depending on age, such as 24-bit floating point, 16-bit floating point, 12-bit fixed-point, 9-bit fixed point (8 bits plus a sign bit). The oldest hardware has only 8 bits of precision internally with no sign bit.

Second, the range of programmability drops off rapidly. Even fairly new hardware has tight limits on the functionality exposed. Pixel shaders have limited instruction and texture counts, and may perform no conditional execution or dynamic loops. Slightly older hardware allows only certain combinations of texture sampling and places restrictions on the amount of computation that can be applied to texture coordinates before being used to look up texels, and the maximum number of total instructions drops to around 20. Still older hardware removes any semblance of a "shader program," and instead has only a set number (between two and six) of blend units, each with a limited range of functionality—each equivalent to maybe only two or three shader instructions at best, with less flexibility. The most basic hardware allows only a single texture to be sampled, four possible operations performed on the texel value, a depth-test unit, and a restricted alpha-blend unit.

Vertex shaders have only recently been able to read textures and to perform conditional execution. As hardware gets older, the amount of space available to hold shader "constant" data (such as animation bone matrices or scene lighting information) drops rapidly, as does the number of instructions allowed in a single program. Older hardware has no vertex shaders at all, and instead has a fixed-function unit that transforms vertices by a matrix, lights them according to a variety of standard per-vertex lighting formulae, and projects them into screen space. Older still, there is no vertex processing hardware at all—the host CPU must perform all vertex calculations and supply the rendering hardware with vertices already mapped to screen space with lighting and texture coordinate calculations already performed.

Summary

Writing a full graphics engine for any cutting-edge hardware is extremely challenging. The multitude of speed, memory, and quality tradeoffs required is daunting, and changes every hardware generation. In most games, the rendering engine is a large module taking most of the memory and processing power of the system, and as such will have only a few specialized programmers who truly know how it works and what the performance characteristics are.

However, this chapter should have given the reader a rough guide to the various capabilities and performance characteristics of most engines, and removed some of the unknowns. It should also have established enough of a framework to allow readers to start using most of the common graphics APIs to create their own rendering engine.

Exercises

These exercises are intended to be performed in a shader-editing environment such as DirectX's "Effect Edit" or any of the similar environments available from various graphics card manufacturers, and in most 3D art packages.

1. Perform the Lambert diffuse calculation in both the vertex shader and the pixel shader. Compare the differences between the two (the differences between Phong and Gouraud shading). Which has fewer artifacts? Which has lowest cost? For what type of meshes is either acceptable? Which vectors must be normalized before being used in the pixel shader? Try to amortize the cost of per-pixel shading by moving only parts of the lighting equation into the pixel shader and leaving others in the vertex shader. Do the same with normal-mapped surfaces, rather than surfaces where the normal is provided only at each vertex.

2. Blinn specular lighting was discussed in the text. The other common version of specular lighting is Phong lighting (note that this is not the same as Phong *shading*). Write both versions in a shader, and compare the two in visual appearance, trying to use similar-looking roughness values. Check the appearance at grazing angles of the eye and of the light. Where does each method have problems or artifacts? Which would artists prefer? Would they like different ones for different materials? Which is more flexible? What is the approximate speed difference between the two?

3. Blinn and Phong specular classically use an exponent to model the distribution of microfacets. This has no particular basis in reality; it was simply chosen because (at the time) it was easy to calculate. However, shader hardware can find exponents moderately expensive to perform, but is very good at

multiplies and adds. Try replacing the exponent with various polynomial approximations, such as quadratic or cubic ones. How does this change the appearance? Can you match the exponential model closely enough? Can you produce specular reflection patterns that are not like an exponent at all? Could this extra flexibility be useful to an artist?

4. Try the same Gouraud versus Phong shading tricks with the various forms of specular lighting, moving bits of code between pixel and vertex shader. How much can be moved into the vertex shader and still look acceptable? Could diffuse shading be done in one place while specular is done in the other?

5. Add an environment map to your shading model by reflecting the eye vector in the normal of the surface and looking up the result in a cube map. Very shiny objects do not reflect uniformly; the value changes depending on the incident angle. This is commonly called a "Fresnel term" and there are many ways to approximate it. Add such a term to your environment map reflection. Experiment with different approximations such as exponential and polynomial ones.

References

[Blinn96] Blinn, Jim, *Jim Blinn's Corner*, Morgan Kaufmann, 1996.

[Bogomjakov01] Bogomjakov, Alexander, and Gotsman, Craig, "Universal Rendering Sequences for Transparent Vertex Caching of Progressive Meshes," Proceedings of Graphics Interface, 2001.

[Forsyth03] Forsyth, Tom, "Spherical Harmonics in Actual Games," *Proceedings*, Game Developers Conference, 2003.

[Haines02] Haines, Eric, and Akenine-Möller, Tomas, *Real-Time Rendering*, AK Peters, 2002.

[Hoppe99] Hoppe, Hugues, "Optimization of Mesh Locality for Transparent Vertex Caching," ACM SIGGRAPH 1999, available at *http://research.microsoft.com/~hoppe/tvc.pdf*.

[Ramamoorthi01] Ramamoorthi, Ravi, and Hanrahan, Pat, "An Efficient Representation for Irradiance Environment Maps," *ACM SIGGRAPH 2001*, available at *http://graphics.stanford.edu/papers/envmap/*.

[Sloan02] Sloan, Peter-Pike; Kautz, Jan; and Snyder, John, "Precomputed Radiance Transfer for Real-Time Rendering in Dynamic, Low-Frequency Lighting Environments," *ACM SIGGRAPH 2002*, available at *http://research.microsoft.com/~ppsloan/*.

5.2 ■ Character Animation

Overview

This chapter delves into the details of animating meshes for the purpose of character animation. This includes how to make them move and deform according to an animator's instructions, how to store the animations and replay them efficiently, and how to blend multiple animations together. The primary focus will be on bone-based skeletal animation systems, since they are by far the most widely used systems today, used by most tools and runtime systems.

It is assumed that the reader has a decent grounding in 3D geometry and is familiar with the basics of vector and matrix math, and the transforming of vertex positions and normals by matrices, as covered in Chapter 4.1, "Mathematical Concepts." *Quaternions* are introduced as an essential component of most animation systems, although this is only a brief introduction and readers are urged to read some more comprehensive texts on the subject before using them.

Fundamental Concepts

Many fundamental concepts are important to understanding how to program an animation system. These include understanding the skeletal hierarchy, the concepts of transforms and rotations, and models and instances. We begin with the skeletal hierarchy.

The Skeletal Hierarchy

At the heart of most bone-based animation systems are, of course, bones. Bones are usually (although not always) arranged in a tree hierarchy, where each bone hangs from a single parent bone, which in turn has its own parent bone, and so on. Each bone may have multiple child bones. This matches most real-world skeletal hierarchies. As the song says, "the thigh bone is connected to the hip bone, the hip bone is connected to the back bone," and so forth.

Associated with each bone is a *transform* that determines how that bone's motion differs from its parent. If the transform is the identity transform, the bone will be in exactly the same translation and orientation as its parent. If the bone has no parent, the transform determines how that bone moves relative to some other defined space. This is either the space of the object with the skeleton we are looking at, or just the space of the world in general. The bone at the top of a bone tree has no parent and is usually called the *root bone*. Most skeletons will have a single root bone, and thus only one bone will have no parent. This root bone is often the pelvis or the shoulders, or sometimes halfway down the back. The concept of a *synthetic root bone* will be introduced later that somewhat modifies this arrangement.

Animations change the transforms of each bone over time, and thus create motion. Although you could have animations storing the transform of the bone in world space, encoding the transform of a bone as being relative to its parent is an efficient mechanism in many ways. It also matches the ways people actually move. To move the elbow but not the tip of a finger requires the coordination of many muscles to move the elbow and then move the wrist, hand, and knuckles to compensate and keep the fingertip still. Whereas moving the finger without moving the elbow is trivial.

This type of animation is commonly termed *forward kinematics*, where motion is transmitted "forward" down the hierarchy of bones. The opposite, where an end-bone's position is fixed at a certain place and the bones higher up the hierarchy are moved to keep it there, is called *inverse kinematics* or IK for short. Because motions due to IK are rarer than motions due to forward kinematics, storing most animations using this implicit hierarchy is very efficient.

The organization of bones and how they are joined to each other in a model is usually termed a *rig*. This rig does not determine the animation on its own (it does not change over time), but it does heavily influence what motions are possible, and how easily some motions can be achieved. Although many games will use a single rig for all the motions of a particular character, it is possible to have multiple rigs, each for a different purpose. Some rigs may be designed for walking, some for acrobatics, and some for "acting" work such as delivering dialogue in close-up. Although you can write an animation system without the ability to change skeletons and rigs, and require the use of a single skeleton for all purposes, it can limit what your animators can do with objects.

Not all bones have parents. An example of this in the physical human body (although not usually in the animation rigs used for human animation) is the shoulder blade (scapula), which is not joined to the rib cage in the same way the thigh bone (femur) is joined to the hip bone (pelvis) with a ball-and-socket joint. Instead, the shoulder blade is anchored to the rib cage with many large and small muscles that allow it to move in many different ways that no physical joint would allow. For the same reason, some rigs have bones with no parent bone—they are sometimes constrained in space by a series of rules, but the movement of another bone does not directly cause motion. These systems are termed *multiroot bone systems,* and although not very common, they are again very useful in certain cases.

The Transform

We so frequently talk about a particular bone's orientation, translation, scale, and shear that it is useful to have an umbrella term for this collection: a *transform*. A transform expresses a geometrical transformation, and in almost every animation system, these are linear transforms. That is, a line that is straight before the transform is also straight after the transform. This is obviously a useful property in a rendering system composed of triangles with straight edges and flat planes.

A transform can be represented as a 4×3 matrix, and typically written "widthways," with more columns than rows (this does vary, but the notation does not alter the mathematics performed). The left-hand 3×3 section represents the rotation, scale, and shear, and the three-element right-hand column represents a translation. Mathematical purists will also add a fourth row to the matrix always composed of $\langle 0,0,0,1 \rangle$, but for animation purposes it is usually left as implied, since it never changes (and we certainly wouldn't want to store it anywhere and have it take up space). As we will see, memory use is a major problem with animation systems.

Any 4×3 matrix can be represented as a combination of the four elements: translation, rotation, scale, and shear. It is frequently convenient to perform the *decomposition* of the matrix into these four elements when manipulating animations, since they each have distinct properties and meanings, and can lead to better compression and runtime performance. For example, in a "conventional" hierarchical skeleton that closely mimics the human body, all bones simply rotate in the joint they have with their parent bone. Thus, they have a fixed translation (representing the position of the joint in their parent bone's space) and can only change their orientation. Being made of calcium carbonate and rigid, they cannot normally scale or shear. Thus, the position can be held in the rig as a constant value, scale/shear can be discarded as being always identity (zero shear, scale of one), and only the orientation needs to be stored and played back for the animation.

As we will see, in practice things are more complex, and some bones use all four components. However, the orientation-only and translation-orientation cases are so common that it is worth optimizing both memory and execution speed for them.

Euler Angles

Euler (the name of a Swiss mathematician, pronounced "oi-luh") angles are a set of three angles that can describe any orientation of an object in 3D space. These three angles each describe a rotation around a particular axis. Each rotation is applied to the result of the previous one. Because there are three axes to choose from to apply each rotation to, and because the order of rotations is important (a rotation of 90 degrees around the X followed by 90 degrees around the Y is not the same as 90 degrees around Y and 90 degrees around X), there needs to be an ordering and axis convention that goes along with the three numbers to pick from 1 of the 12 possible axis/order combinations (and of each of these, eight possible sign/rotation direction conventions). Sadly, at least seven of these combinations are used commonly in various places, and probably many more. This means that when using Euler angles, you need to know which convention is being used, and be aware that whichever convention you pick, it may not match anyone else's.

For ease of reference, we will use a common convention for the rotation ordering, *xyz*, which means that we first rotate around the *x*-axis, then around the *y*-axis, and then around the *z*-axis. Although this "seems" the most obvious ordering, it is far from it. In the mathematics world, a far more common ordering is *zxz*. Although this rotates around the *z*-axis twice, because there is another rotation in the middle, it is not the same *z*-axis. All the 12 possible orderings of Euler angles are equally powerful (and have equal problems), mathematically speaking.

Aside from the angle-ordering convention confusion, Euler angles suffer from a more serious problem, often given the term *gimbal lock*. As mentioned, Euler angles are rotations about three angles. However, there are places where the values of these three angles do not specify a unique orientation. Using the *xyz* angle convention, consider the rotation (90,90,–90) performed on an object. Now consider the orientation (0,90,0).

The resulting orientation of the object from these two very different sets of angles is identical (see Figure 5.2.1). Worse still, there are arbitrarily many combinations of three angles that describe the same resulting orientation. The problem is that Euler angles have *poles* in their formulations, where different rotations produce the same result. Different conventions have poles in different places, but they all have poles.

For representing static orientations, this is actually not much of a problem. If you give either of these two orientations to an astronomer (although astronomers use yet another convention, so you may need to translate the values to that system first), he will look at the same place in the sky. The problem comes when you want to store animations this way. Animation systems rely heavily on interpolation. You cannot store every possible orientation between two poses, because as animation programmers we

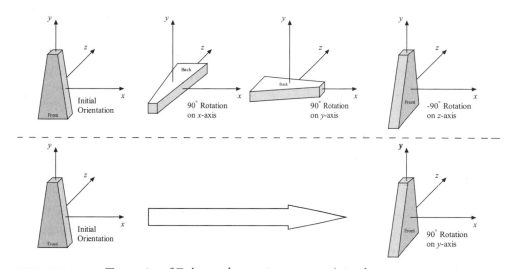

FIGURE 5.2.1 *Two series of Euler angle rotations can result in the same orientation.*

are frequently short of memory, so you must be able to interpolate smoothly between adjacent orientations. If given the orientations (0,88,0) and (2,90,0) to interpolate between, it is fairly obvious that these two are quite close together, and that (1,89,0) might be a fairly reasonable half-way point. However, if given (0,88,0) and (88,90,–90) to interpolate between, a numerical check suggests these are very different orientations, and that the halfway point is somewhere around (44,1,–45). Yet we know that (0,90,0) and (90, 90,–90) are the same orientation, so in fact those two are far closer than they appear, and (44,1,–45) is in fact a terrible midpoint.

There are ways to fix this sort of thing, rather than doing a naïve averaging of the three values, but all these interpolation methods rely on fiendishly complex (and thus expensive) computation, or end up transforming the Euler angles into another representation, doing the interpolation there, and transforming it back. If you are going to do that, it would be better to use one of the other representations all the time, rather than constantly performing conversions.

The 3 × 3 Rotation Matrix

An obvious alternative to Euler angles is describing the orientation as a 3 × 3 matrix. This has the benefits of simplicity. We can use the 3 × 3 matrix directly for our transformations of vertices since we do not need to do any conversions to use it. Moreover, two orientations that look the same will have very similar numbers in their matrices, which means that a simple linear blend between the two will produce a sensible-looking result.

The main problem with storing a 3×3 is, of course, that you have to store it. It is three times as large as the three values required by Euler angles. Since storage space is typically at a premium for animation systems, this is an issue.

The other problem is that a 3×3 can represent a rotation, but it can also represent any combination of rotation, scale, and shear. This is to be expected, since there are three times as many values stored in a 3×3 than in a triplet of Euler angles. In practice, this also means that if two 3×3s are interpolated, the result is not a pure rotation—some types of scale and shear creep in, and the matrix needs to be *orthonormalized*. This is a fairly expensive operation. In addition, the blend between two source rotations will not be completely correct—performing a 30:70 blend between a rotation of zero degrees and one of 100 degrees does not result in a 70-degree rotation, even after orthonormalization.

Quaternions

Quaternions are the best method of representing rotations without the polar problems of Euler angles or the large size and interpolation problems of 3×3 matrices. Quaternions are composed, as the name suggests, of four components, usually referred to as (x, y, z, w); although, sometimes the ordering is given as $(w, x, y, z,)$. The "meaning" of these components is generally that (x, y, z) defines an axis of rotation, and the length of the vector (x, y, z) defines the sine of half the rotation angle. The value of w defines the cosine of half the rotation angle (note that without w, you cannot tell the difference between a rotation of 20° and a rotation of 340°, because both have the same half-angle sine, but different half-angle cosines).

Generally, the only types of quaternions used for representing orientations or rotations are unit-length quaternions. As the name suggests, and by extension from three-dimensional vectors, these are quaternions whose lengths are 1, for whom $x^2 + y^2 + z^2 + w^2 = 1$. A non-unit-length quaternion can be normalized by dividing it by its length, similar to the way a standard 2D or 3D vector is normalized.

Because a quaternion defines an axis and a rotation angle, it shows no preference to any particular orientation. All axes are the same, so there is no "pole" around which orientations slew bizarrely, as there are with Euler angles, and the "distance" between two orientations defined by quaternions is fairly intuitive. If the numbers seem similar, they are very similar. This leads to good interpolation properties. In most cases, interpolation between two orientations always occurs along the path of least rotation, which is a desirable thing when interpolating.

The one exception is that a single rotation can be represented by two different quaternions. If one is the quaternion (a, b, c, d), the other is the quaternion $(-a, -b, -c, -d)$. These both represent the same rotation, and for many (but not all) purposes are interchangeable. When interpolating between two quaternions, it is common to first take their dot-product. If it is negative, one of the quaternions—it does not matter which—is negated before performing the interpolation. If this negation is not done, the interpolation is still sensible, but it goes the "long way around," which is frequently not what is wanted.

For these various reasons, quaternions are almost always the animation programmer's representation of choice for orientations, even though they might not be very intuitive to work with. In practice, artists will author animations using a wide variety of controls, often specialized for a particular joint type. Conversion to a single rotational representation is necessary to avoid massively complicating the runtime animation code.

Please note that this has been a very brief introduction to quaternions and why they are important. For further information on quaternions for game applications, consult [Lengyel04, Svarovsky00].

Animation versus Deformation

The two terms, *animation* and *deformation*, are often confused. The collective transforms of a skeleton at a certain moment in time is called a *pose*. *Animation* is the process of changing the pose over time. However, a pose cannot usually be rendered on-screen directly—it is simply a list of transforms. *Deformation* is the process of taking a single pose generated by animation and applying it to a mesh's vertices, moving them to the correct position so they are ready to be rendered. In general, animations do not know about vertices, they simply specify poses, whereas deformation does not know about the concept of time, simply transferring poses onto vertices.

Typically, the animation part of a game cares only about animations: playing them, sampling them, and blending them. It rarely, if ever, cares about actual mesh vertices and almost exclusively deals with skeletons and poses.

The low-level triangle rendering side of a game rarely cares about anything higher level than a skeleton's pose. Whatever animations are playing, it simply takes the pose on each frame, deforms the mesh into the given pose, and renders it.

This provides a clear separation between rendering and animation. This is useful since it allows the renderer to run at a different rate than the rest of the game, which is a vital part of many rendering engines. This is also a common place to make the split between a CPU and graphics hardware. Most current engines perform all animation on the CPU, but then hand the poses to graphics hardware to perform the actual deformation (and subsequent rendering) of a mesh.

Models and Instances

A single model is a description of an object. This usually consists of a mesh with vertices, triangles, textures, and so on. Most importantly for an animation system, it includes a skeleton that holds the properties of each bone, and how they are linked together. A single model can be used multiple times in a given scene, and there is no need to replicate it for each object in that scene. For example, each bird in a flock of seagulls will use the same vertices, the same texture, and the same skeleton, and thus they will all use the same seagull model.

However, each seagull will need some unique data: its position and orientation, the state of any animations playing on it, and the current positions of its bones. In addition, there will be game-specific data such as how hungry the seagull is, who its friends are, and whether it has picked up the rocket launcher.

All this data is particular to that one seagull, and lives in an *instance*. An instance stores all the unique information about a certain item in a scene, and holds references to shared data that describe the item.

Animation Controls

When you play an animation on a particular instance in the scene, certain things need to be stored: the animation, when it started, what speed it is playing at, what blending weight it is playing at, and so on. You also need to be able to later stop the animation or change its speed. Thinking of the flock of seagulls again, many of the birds will be playing the same "flap wings" animation, but they will be playing them at different speeds, and start them at different times. Thus, this data cannot be held in the animation itself, since there is only one of those shared between all the seagulls. In addition, you certainly do not want to make a copy of the animation for each seagull, because animations are quite large objects, and you would quickly run out of memory.

However, this data cannot be held directly in the instance. A particular instance will often have many animations playing on it, all blending together, or playing on different sets of bones. Each of these sets of data is usually independent, and you need a way to stop or change the speed of a particular animation without affecting the rest. It is also moderately common to have the same animation playing on a given instance more than once, but with different values. For example, when a soldier fires his automatic rifle once, he may play the "recoil" animation, which may last a second. If the soldier fires the weapon on automatic, he will play the animation once for each bullet fired, and may fire tens of bullets a second. Thus, at any one time, he may have 10 or more of the same recoil animation playing, but offset in time. If his aim is good, his target may also be playing the "hit by bullet" animation a lot, too.

This leads to the concept of an *animation control*, which is a data structure that links a particular instance in the scene with a particular animation, stores information such as the animation's speed and start time, and can be told to stop, pause, or change speed. Since each instance may have many controls hanging from it (one for each animation playing on that instance), and each animation may have many controls pointing to it (one for each instance playing that animation), controls usually live in two linked lists: one for instances, and one for animations.

Animation Storage

It is always useful at the planning stage of a system to throw estimates around, just to check how feasible certain ideas are going to be. This is a sanity check, before you start all the programming to see whether your scheme is going to work easily, or whether it is "pushing the back of the envelope." Even with rough calculations scribbled on the back of something handy, you will likely find that you are going to have to work hard to fit within processor and memory constraints.

Therefore, let us do some quick calculations on the simplest animation system we can think of: a scheme where we store a 4×3 matrix for each bone, one for each frame of each animation. This allows us to do very little work when replaying the animation. Simply pick your frame, and use the 4×3 matrix directly.

Let us assume some fairly typical numbers for a game, such as 30 frames per second, 5 major characters with 100 animations each, 15 minor characters with 20 animations each, each animation lasting an average of four seconds. All characters have 50 bones. These are very rough figures, of course, and probably underestimate many values, but we are mainly interested in order-of-magnitude results.

$$\text{TotalSpace} = 30 \cdot 4 \cdot 50 \cdot (4 \cdot 3) \cdot \text{sizeof}(\text{float}) \cdot ((5 \cdot 100) + (15 \cdot 20)) = 220 \, \text{Mb}$$

Well, that is not going to go down well with the project lead. It does not even come close to fitting on any next-generation consoles, let alone current ones.

To give an idea of the numbers we should be aiming for in these discussions, a PlayStation 2 console has 32 MB of memory. The animation system, if it is lucky, will get perhaps a quarter of that, usually less. On a good day, you have 8 MB to play with. Other platforms and newer consoles have more memory, but then you will also want higher bone counts and more animations. The previous numbers are quite conservative.

So, what can we drop? You cannot reduce the number of characters, the number of animations, or the number of bones, since those decisions are made by the design and art department. Of course, if they are asking the impossible, you need to tell them this, but these types of numbers have been done by other games, so it can be done. With these numbers in mind, let us look at various ways of solving the space problem.

Decomposition and Constant Elimination

The first step is to look at what is being stored for each bone. A 4×3 matrix is a good, complete description, but as previously mentioned, it encodes four quite separate concepts: translation, orientation, scale, and shear. Many bones in many animations do not perform some of these motions. Only a tiny minority of bones has any shear at all, and some animation systems do not even support the concept. Most bones will not perform scaling, with the main exception being "bones" that represent muscles (e.g., the large muscles in the chest, upper arm, thigh, and calf, and the complex systems of facial muscles). Bones representing actual skeletal bones with fixed joints, such as the knee, hip, and elbow, will not have any translation change during their animation either. Many mechanical systems (such as weapons) have parts that only slide relative to their parents; they do not change orientation, only position.

In addition, some animations simply do not move all bones. An animation of a character sitting at a bar will mainly move parts of the body above the waist. The character may tap one foot, or shift in position slightly, but most animations will not move most of the bones of the legs. These can therefore be stored as constant values, rather than storing the same value at every frame.

Therefore, for each bone, we can decompose the 4×3 matrix into its four components, and check which components are constant or identity over the lifetime of the animation. For each animation, we can store constant values just once, and eliminate identity values completely. Translations require three values, scales require three values, shears require three values, but orientations, as we have seen, are slightly annoying, and it is probably best to use a quaternion, which is four values.

That is going to save quite a bit of memory. Assuming that the constant values are a trivial amount of storage, and effectively insignificant, let us again examine our rough numbers.

Assume that only 10 percent of bones have shears, 20 percent of bones have scaling, 50 percent of bones have changes in translation, and 90 percent of bones have changes in orientation. Of course, the type of game and the characters used in it will change these figures quite a bit, and these are slightly pessimistic, but again, this is a back-of-the-envelope calculation. Therefore, the average space required for one bone for one frame is:

$$bytesPerBonePerFrame = \text{sizeof}\left(\text{float}\right) \cdot \left(\left(0.1 \cdot 3\right) + \left(0.2 \cdot 3\right) + \left(0.5 \cdot 3\right) + \left(0.9 \cdot 4\right)\right) = 24\,\text{bytes}$$

This is considerably better than the original 48 bytes, since we have halved the space required, although, 110 MB is still more than 10 times our budget. Additionally, we have introduced some runtime costs. For example, instead of simply reading a 4×3 matrix, we now have to look at the animation, read the data that is there, fill in the rest from animation constants or identities, and then reconstruct the 4×3 matrix result from the four separate pieces of information: translation, orientation, scale, and shear. However, this extra work is well worth the effort. This will form the basis for all the other optimizations we will discuss.

Keyframes and Linear Interpolation

The next most obvious step is to use fewer than 30 frames per second. Animations are, overall, smooth, and we can borrow a technique from the days of hand-drawn animation known as *keyframes*. Cinema film is 24 frames per second, but when animation was all drawn by hand, many animation houses would only draw 12 frames per second and show each frame twice. However, 12 frames per second is still a huge number for an hour-and-a-half-long movie (almost 65,000 frames). If your lead character appears in maybe half of those, they need 32,000 frames drawn. Even if these are drawn very roughly in pencil, and inked and colored by other artists later, this is a daunting number for one person to create. Typically, very few artists can draw a major character to a high enough quality, so farming the motion of that character out to hundreds of artists is not sensible, since you will end up with 100 characters that merely look similar, but move very differently.

The solution is to have the main character artist only do certain key, important frames of the character, such as static poses, the start, middle, and end of any motion, and more detail on any difficult and uncommon motions. These keyframes can be anywhere from one every quarter of a second, to many seconds apart, depending on the complexity of the motion. As you can see, this reduces the workload on the lead artist considerably.

These key frames are then passed to other artists, who draw the frames in between them. The idea is that all the essential characteristics of the motion are in these keyframes, and it is a much simpler task to draw the frames making up that motion once these guidelines have been drawn. These two roles have given rise to two important terms: *keyframe* and *tweening* (the process of drawing the frames in be*tween* the keyframes). Because the lead artist has already laid out the major facets of the motion, there is a limit to how much these "in between" frames can diverge from the original vision.

We can use these concepts in our animation code. We do not need to store animations at 30 frames per second; we can store them at a lower speed, and interpolate between the keyframes to produce the intermediate frames. This is one reason why quaternions are so much easier to work with than Euler angles. As discussed previously, quaternions interpolate far better, with no special poles where interpolation becomes difficult.

Therefore, we will use the simplest interpolation there is: linear interpolation. Given any two adjacent keyframes, to find the frame 25 percent of the way (in time) from the first to the second, we multiply the first frame's values by 0.75, the second frame's values by 0.25, and add the results together.

For translation, scale, and shear, this produces good results, but as usual, orientation is a special case. The problem is that when storing orientations either as a 3×3 matrix or as a quaternion, there is a constraint on the values. A 3×3 must be *orthonormal*, which means that the three column vectors must be of unit length (meaning the matrix is normalized) and at right angles to each other (meaning the matrix is orthogonal). Therefore, orthonormal = orthogonal + normal. A quaternion also needs to be normalized, which means that it is of unit length. Whenever you perform linear interpolation on either of these representations of an orientation, you will find that the result is frequently not normal or orthonormal, which leads to unwanted shear and scale effects creeping in.

Fortunately, there are good ways to renormalize orientations and prevent this. For quaternions, simply divide all four numbers by the quaternion's length, and for 3×3 matrices, perform a combination of normalization and moving the column vectors so that they are at right angles to each other. However, as discussed previously, interpolation of 3×3 or 4×3 matrices is not a good idea, since it is expensive and does not produce very good results. Notably, interpolating two 3×3s that represent rotations can introduce scales and shears that were not in the original matrices.

It is interesting to note that Euler angles do not suffer this problem; every possible triplet of values is a valid orientation and will never produce scale and shear effects. However, the problems with interpolation and poles make them so hard to use in other ways that quaternions are usually the better solution, and interpolating and renormalizing quaternions is not a difficult process. There is a note later in this chapter on the best way to interpolate quaternions; there is more than one. Before diving into the math libraries or textbooks, it is worth reading this brief discussion of the problem. The solution may be simpler than you expect.

So, just how much keyframing can we do? How many frames can we throw away and produce by interpolation rather than storing them? To answer this, we should first mention the problems associated with keyframes.

First, and most obviously, you are losing data. If the animation is complex with high-frequency components, this detail will be lost. Think of the animation of a two-bladed helicopter rotor. If it is spinning at 10 revolutions per second, and you store the animation at 30 frames per second, each blade will be sampled at three different orientations in each full revolution. For simplicity, let us measure the orientation in degrees and say that the three samples are 0°, 120°, and 240°. This is fine, since you can reconstruct the idea that the rotor is spinning, and playing the animation slowly using interpolation will show it moving smoothly in a circle. However, if we use keyframes and only store this animation at 10 frames per second, blindly assuming we can interpolate the rest, we will find that all the frames we store have the same value in them. From this, all the interpolation in the world will simply show that the rotor is not moving. We obviously need more than 10 keyframes per second in this case.

On the other end of the scale, if a person is asleep, his animation consists almost entirely of the rise and fall of his chest as he breathes. This motion has a repetition length of around five seconds, so storing only two keyframes, one with a risen chest and one with a fallen chest, over this period seems possible, and yet still produces good-looking animation. In practice, it is a little more difficult. What if the two frames you chose to use were both in the middle of the breathing cycle, with one as the chest is halfway through moving up and one as it is halfway through moving down? Both are the same, and again, the chest would not move. It is clear that as well as careful choice of frequency, it is important to choose carefully exactly which frames to store.

Another problem is that we are using linear interpolation, which assumes that given two keyframes, the motion between them is a straight line. This is a reasonable approximation in many cases. However, consider a bouncing ball. At no point is its motion that of a straight line. In fact it is (very nearly) a parabola between the bounces. As long as we have enough keyframes, approximating the motion as a series of straight lines between each keyframe is reasonable. However, as we take fewer keyframes, the approximation looks far worse, and you do not need to get as low as the previous examples of only having two or three keyframes per cycle before the motion looks very bad with linear interpolation. Often. having up to six keyframes per second still looks rather poor.

Even more of a problem is selecting which of the original frames to keep and which to throw away. For example, if we do not have a keyframe showing the instant the ball hits the ground, the linear interpolation will ensure that the ball never hits the ground, which will look very strange.

Therefore, there is a limit to how well keyframes can be used to reduce the amount of data stored. Of course, we can fairly easily change the number of keyframes used for each animation. Some require many keyframes and will tolerate very little interpolation; others require far fewer keyframes and can use a great deal of interpolation. To pick an extremely rough figure out of the air, most motions will start to look poor if fewer than five keyframes per second are used. However, note that having just one animation at double this rate takes up the same space as four animations at half this rate! Therefore, this cannot be taken as an *average* number for the sake of computing the space taken by animations. An average value around 10 keyframes per second is more realistic. This is still a good improvement from 30, which is a threefold reduction. Our memory use is now down to 37 MB, so it will just about fit inside a PlayStation 2, as long as you fill all of the graphics and sound memory with animation data as well.

Higher Order Interpolation

Many of the problems with interpolation are related to the way we reconstruct the in-between poses with straight lines. Most motions are not straight lines; they are some sort of curve. Therefore, it probably makes sense to use a curve rather than a straight line for reconstruction. However, which curve? This book is not nearly large enough to look at all the possible curves, nor to even introduce the mathematical basis behind curves and splines, so we will stick to a few simple case studies.

The simplest place to start is to replace each linear segment with a cubic Bézier curve. This is a very flexible and controllable curve that is also very simple to evaluate.

For linear interpolation between two stored frames F_1 and F_2, we define a purely conceptual time t that is 0.0 at F_1 and 1.0 at F_2. For linear interpolation to obtain a result R, the calculation is simple, as shown in Equation 5.2.1.

$$R = \left((1-t) \cdot F_1 \right) + \left(t \cdot F_2 \right) \qquad (5.2.1)$$

We can see that when t is 0.0, at the start of the segment, R is entirely F_1, and when t is 1.0 at the end, R is entirely F_2. For times above 1.0, we would instead switch to the next segment between F_2 and the next sample, F_3, and a new conceptual time t that again goes from 0.0 to 1.0.

For a curve, as well as defining the start and end points, we also need to be able to control the tangents of the curve at those end points (when t is 0.0 and when t is 1.0). We define two extra frames of data T_1 and T_2. These are not real frames since the animation does not go through them as it progresses. They simply define the shape of the curve. As you can see from Figure 5.2.2, as the curve leaves F_1, it is heading toward T_1, and as it arrives at F_2, it has been coming from T_2. The tangent of the curve at the end points F_1 and F_2 is defined by the values of T_1 and T_2, respectively.

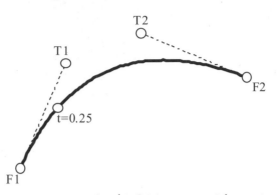

FIGURE 5.2.2 *A cubic Bézier curve with associated control points.*

The curve is evaluated using Equation 5.2.2.

$$R = \left((1-t) \cdot F_1 \right) + \left(t \cdot F_2 \right)$$

(5.2.2)

The cubic Bézier curve is quite good, as it gives explicit control over the two places the curve travels through, and also gives explicit control over the gradient of the curve at those two points. With this control, we can use Bézier curves to get some very good-looking approximations to the previously mentioned bouncing-ball case.

The main problem with Bézier curves is that for each section of the curve, you need three control points. Although each section uses four, we can assume that the final control point, F_2, is shared with the next curve and used as its F_1; thus, effectively, each segment only requires the memory to store three control points. However, this is still three times as many stored numbers as linear interpolation. One interesting variant of the Bézier curve is found by replacing T_2 with $F_2 - (T_2 - F_2)$ or $2F_2 - T_2$. In other words, pointing the F_2 to T_2 vector "the other way," so that it points beyond the end of the curve, not back into it. Note that you have not really changed the nature of the curve, you simply stored its control points in a different manner. So, if this has not changed the curve, why is it interesting? Because it allows you to share this new T_2 with the next curve's T_1 if you wish. In most cases, this is exactly the desired behavior, and reduces most curve sections to only requiring two control points instead of three.

There are a few other variants similar to this. For example, if you replace T_1 with the vector $(F_1 - T_1)$ and T_2 with the vector $(T_2 - F_2)$ in the formulation, you get another standard curve called a "Hermite" curve. The same trick of sharing adjacent tangent vectors can be done with this representation.

Note that with this version, we need to add a further refinement. Each section of the curve uses four control points—F_1, T_1, F_2, and T_2. Normally, F_2 and T_2 of one section can be used as F_1 and T_1 of the next section, but this is not always true. The bouncing-ball example shows this well. When the ball bounces, the T_2 of one section is not shared with the T_1 of the next, because the ball suddenly changes direction. This is called a *discontinuity*. In mathematical terms, this type of discontinuity is a "C1" discontinuity, because the slope or velocity of the curve changes abruptly. A "C0" discontinuity is one where the actual value suddenly changes, such as if the object is teleported somewhere, which are far rarer in animations, but they do happen. There is also a "C2" discontinuity (and of course the sequence continues to C3, C4, etc.), which is harder to see, and is where the acceleration changes suddenly. These happen often in animations, such as every time a muscle is tensed, there is a change in acceleration, and thus a C2 discontinuity. In general, preserving C2 continuity is not a terribly important feature of animation systems, and it is broken frequently.

By tying together curves by sharing end and control points like this, we easily achieve C0 and C1 continuity (we also happen to achieve C2 continuity in this case). However, where you do not want this continuity, you need to be able to specify multiple end points for adjacent curves, such as the place where the ball bounces. You can do this by having a list of indices that tell you, for each section of curve, which control point to use. Using this, each section will have four indices: one each for F_1, T_1, T_2, and F_2. However, adjacent curves will often have indices referring to the same controls, allowing for smooth interpolation in most cases, or discontinuities where not wanted.

Just how much memory can be saved by using Bézier curves instead of linear interpolation? The evaluation of the animation has become a little bit more expensive, since each section of the curve has actually increased from having a single sample to having two (and maybe a third for the occasional C1 discontinuity), and the index list has been added, which is small but still significant in size. However, this added size for each section is more than made up for by the reduction in the number of sections that need to be stored. A very general figure is that cubic curve interpolation can use roughly one-tenth the number of sections that linear interpolation can, and look just as good.

Therefore, the space required for each section has risen. We now need just over twice as many samples (let us assume 2.1 times as a reasonable modifier, if 10 percent of the curve sections require a C1 discontinuity), plus the index list, which is four integers per section. This puts the total per section at $(24 \cdot 2.1) + (4 \cdot \text{sizeof}(\text{int}))$, which is 66.4 bytes or 2.77 times as large per curve section. However, we are using one-tenth as many sections, so the real multiplier is a very encouraging 0.277 (which is around one-quarter) bringing the total space from 37 MB down to just over 10 MB. This is now getting very close to our target of 8 MB, but not quite.

There are plenty of other curve types out there, one interesting one being Catmull-Rom curves. Although more complex, they can further reduce the number of samples required by making the T_1 and T_2 tangent samples implicit, rather than explicit. Rather than storing them as separate entities, they can usually be stored as combinations of the surrounding F samples. This only works where you do not need explicit control over the exact value of the tangent at the control points, and only require the tangents to be reasonable and the curves to be C1 continuous. Since this is the common case, the saving in space is useful. This extra bit of saving now gets us into our target memory slot.

All the curve types introduced so far are *uniform* curves, which means that all sections of the curve represent the same amount of time. In practice, animations tend to have short periods of time with many changes, and long periods where the animation is smooth. It would be nice to store fewer curve sections for the smooth parts. This can be done by storing a time with each section of curve that says when the section starts. This way, some curve sections can refer to a long period of time, and others can refer to only a short period. The times are more properly called *knot values*, and these curve types are called *nonuniform* curves. Some of the uniform curves already mentioned also have nonuniform versions.

One interesting thing about nonuniform curves is that the index values are no longer strictly necessary. The curve sampler can always assume that the T_2 of one section is shared with the T_1 of the following section, meaning that the curve is always continuous. To introduce a discontinuity of any sort, one or more sections of the curve can be shrunk so that they take zero time, by setting the start time of the next section to be the same as this section's start time.

This allows curve types that are always continuous to be used, which opens up new possible types. One very powerful curve is the B-spline, which is a generalization of most of the curves already mentioned. The trickiest part about using B-splines is that although the curve is influenced and shaped by the control points, it does not necessarily travel through the control points because B-splines are a *noninterpolating* curve type. Despite this, B-splines are very quick to evaluate, have many elegant mathematical properties, and are what many commercial animation packages use.

Looping

Many animations loop. The loop must be continuous, with no pops, either in value (must be C0 continuous), or in velocity (must be C1 continuous). You should be able to rely on your animators to create animations like this, where the first and last frames match exactly and are smooth. However, it is important when considering questions such as compression, timing, and changing speed that you remember to consider the looping case, and ensure that whatever transformation you make to the data preserves any C0 and C1 continuity.

The more generalized case of looping one animation repeatedly is that of playing one animation directly after another. A very common example is that you have a walk cycle, and a run cycle, each of which loops properly. Then, you also have an animation that shows the transition from walk to run. The start of this animation joins seamlessly with the end of the walk cycle, and the end joins perfectly to the start of the run cycle. Again, animators are accustomed to creating animations that do this, and it is important that the animation code does not break this continuity or impose special conditions on that continuity. One constraint that is acceptable is to require that both animations be playing at the same speed, since maintaining C1 continuity is extremely difficult otherwise.

In practice, this simply means taking care when using curves to compress your animations, and ensuring that the tangent curves at each end are maintained wherever possible.

Playing Animations

When you want to sample an animation, you need to pick the time in the animation in which you are interested. This time is called the animation's *local time*. Local time typically begins at zero at the start of the animation, and ends at the original length of the animation (when played at normal speed). Thus, a five-second animation has local time going from 0.0 to 5.0.

The other time that games use is *global time*, which is the time that actually passes in the game. An animation's local time may pass at a different rate to global time because the animation is being played slower or faster than it was originally authored at, or it might even be played backwards, in which case local time will decrease rather than increase. However, forces such as gravity run on global time—you cannot (usually) speed them up or slow them down. There is a third time, known as *real-world time*, which is what the user perceives. This usually keeps lockstep with global time while playing, although the user can pause the game or watch a slow-motion replay, in which case they will go out of lockstep. Animation systems do not generally care about real-world time. It is mentioned simply to clarify what global time is and is not.

The speed of an animation is the ratio between the passing of global time and the incrementing of local time. If the speed is set to one, both will pass by the same amount each frame, and the animation will be played back at the same speed at which it was authored. If the speed is set to one-half, local time will progress at half the speed of global time, and the animation will play more slowly (it will last twice as long).

Some animation systems, especially those based on film and television tools, store local time not as a number of seconds, but as a number of frames, using 24 per second for film and either 50 or 60 per second for television. This is convenient for entirely keyframed systems, where every frame is stored in memory. To find which frame you need, simply take local time, chop off the fractional part leaving the integer, and look up that numbered frame. However, as soon as you have animations that are sampled at lower frequencies (which, as we have seen, is a huge space-saver), this system simply makes life more complex, since the 24 intervals per second now corresponds to no actual data concept at all, and simply makes development more confusing. For this reason, it is recommended that time be kept in seconds rather than frames.

Some systems "normalize" local time and say that it always starts at zero (the start of the animation) and ends at one (the end of the animation), and change the speed that the animation plays to stretch or shrink it to its required duration. An animation that was originally four seconds long, played at "original" speed, is actually played at quarter speed so that its one unit of local time lasts four seconds of global time. In practice, either arrangement is equally valid. The slight advantage of not normalizing is that most animations are played at the same speed they were authored at, which can make for easier debugging to be able to instantly see that an animation is four seconds long, and that at the moment, you are sampling it three seconds in.

Scrubbing

No matter how you deal with the question of "when is now," one thing that is important for an animation system is that it can deal with multiple global times simultaneously. This sounds like an odd requirement—there should surely be only one global time in a game at a time! Well yes, and you will usually be sampling animations at the global "current" time—usually the time being currently rendered. However, there are cases in which you will want to sample animations in the future or the past, without changing the concept of "now." An obvious example is when looking at a character's footsteps and deciding where they are walking to. As humans, when we walk, we look ahead and predict where our feet will be planted, and a good animation system must be able to do the same to a certain extent. Similarly, prediction is useful when doing animations for reaching for objects, throwing objects, jumping (typically, the game's jump happens the instant the takeoff animation *starts* not when it *ends*, to avoid "lag" on the controls), and is also used for motion extraction and compensation.

The ability to sample animations at any time (within a certain sensible range around the global time) is called *scrubbing*, which is a term borrowed from film and sound editing. It is obviously simple to sample a given single animation at any time you wish. After all, you need to be able to do this because multiple instances may be playing a given animation at different times. The important thing is to ensure that all the surrounding code does not rely on algorithms that do not cope well with multiple random accesses. For example, any technique that requires you go from frame A to frame B by having to perform some operation on all the frames in between is not going to be useable in a real game—the gap between frame A and frame B may be large, requiring many of these operations. Worse, frame B may be before frame A, which is tricky if the operations are hard to reverse.

One example is the practice of encoding animations as deltas from the previous frame. At first glance, this sounds great, since many animations have only very small frame-to-frame changes, which allows you to compress them to an extremely small memory size. Unfortunately, if you want to sample frame 200, you need to start at the beginning and apply all 200 deltas to get your result. In some cases, you can remember that last frame, you wanted to sample frame 198, and so you can start with the old result and apply only two deltas. In practice, storing this information rapidly spirals out of control and gets very complicated. It also does not help the worst case, which is still that of applying 200 deltas. There are various modifications to this scheme that make it less of an issue, but in general, it is unwise to use techniques that rely on persistence of data from a previous frame except in very specialized circumstances.

Blending Animations

One of the fundamental components of a good animation system is not just the capability to play back an animation, but also the capability to play back multiple animations and blend them together.

The Lerp

The fundamental unit of operation is the weighted blend between two transforms. This is usually called a *linear interpolation*, or *lerp*. Once you can do one of these, everything else builds on top of it. Although, in practice you can usually achieve multiway blends more efficiently than simply as a sequence of two-way lerps.

Blending two offsets is easy, requiring simple vector calculations. Blending two scales and shears is similarly easy. Blending two rotations is only slightly more work. Whether you are storing a rotation as a quaternion or as a 3×3 matrix, the principle is the same: perform a standard blend for each component (4 for a quaternion, 9 for a matrix), and then normalize the result. As mentioned earlier, normalizing a quaternion is considerably simpler than normalizing a matrix. However, in some cases, an animation system will need to blend matrices, such as when blending the results of an external system (such as physically simulated ragdolls) that does not use quaternions, so it is helpful to have code paths that blend matrices as well as quaternions.

In both quaternion and matrix cases, it is important that both source rotations are also normalized before performing the blend. Just normalizing the result will not ensure that the lerp actually looks good, since it will blend from one to the other, but not in a linear fashion. However, it is usually sufficient to only require that the sources be "moderately normalized." They do not have to be perfectly normalized/orthonormal for the blending to do the correct thing. Although this seems like a curiously fine distinction, in practice it is useful. The source rotations are typically obtained by sampling animations, which as we have seen also involves interpolations of rotations.

When interpolating the control points on an animation curve, we perform calculations on quaternions, and these operations themselves require normalization. One option is to fully normalize those results, then perform the blend between the two animations, and fully normalize again. However, even for quaternions, normalization is not cheap, as it involves a square root and divide (or, equivalently, a reciprocal square root, which some hardware finds just as easy). However, we can replace the postsampling normalize operations with a "mostly normalize" routine that uses an approximation to the square root instead of the fully correct result. Exactly what form this approximation takes varies according to the platform. Some platforms have a fast approximate square root built in, on some you will use a small lookup table, and on some you can do a (very) few Newton-Rapheson iterations on an initial guess.

For the two-way blend, this removes two of the three normalization operations, thus leaving only the last one, which usually does need to be to a high precision. This can result in good speed savings, with little or no loss in visual quality.

Quaternion Blending Methods

In the previous section, we blended two quaternions by simply adding their components together and normalizing. However, is this even valid for quaternions, since surely they are not normal vectors? Most texts say this is not valid and talk about *spherical interpolation* or *slerp* as being the only sensible way to blend two quaternions together. There are in fact at least three plausible ways to blend two quaternions, and possibly others yet to be discovered. The three methods considered here are:

Normalizing lerp, or nlerp: The simplest of the three. The four components of the two quaternions are simply blended together linearly, and the result renormalized.

Spherical lerp, or slerp: Middling complexity, and the one found most frequently in textbooks concerning quaternions.

Log-quaternion lerp (also known as *exponential map interpolation*):   Fairly complex. It involves "unwrapping" the quaternions into a locally flat space, and then performing interpolation.

Note that in all three cases, the two quaternions must be in the same hemisphere (strictly, the same hyperhemisphere, since it is a hemisphere in four dimensions), which means that we should take their dot-product, and if it is negative, negate one of them before applying any of the three methods.

For the interpolation of quaternions, a desirable property is for the interpolation to be along the shortest path. This is known as the path of "least torque," because the resulting rotation involves the least twist from one orientation to the other.

A second desirable property is that the interpolation occurs at a constant speed. In other words, as you smoothly interpolate from quaternion A to quaternion B, the result moves smoothly from one orientation to the other, rather than speeding up or slowing down along the way.

The third desirable property is whether three or more quaternions can be blended together, with the results independent of the blending order. This is similar to the property of associativity, although not identical. Ideally, the order in which the animations are specified should not be important.

To skip the lengthy and rather dull analysis, each of the three methods satisfies two of the desired properties, but not a third. It is in fact possible to prove that no method can ever provide all three. Nlerp does not have constant speed, slerp does not associate, and exponential map interpolation does not travel along the shortest path. Therefore, we need to compromise in some way, whichever method we choose to use. The question is, which involves the least-visible compromise?

The first thing to mention is that in animation, we will usually be interpolating between two (or more) quaternions that are quite close together. Over 45 degrees is extremely unusual, because we only need to interpolate when we are sampling a compressed animation (interpolating between subsequent frames, or control points in a curve, or whatever method you use), or we are trying to blend multiple animations that hopefully look moderately similar to each other. Either way, large interpolations are not likely to look very good, even with a mythical "perfect" interpolation scheme, simply because we are making up data that is not actually there. In the same way, no matter what clever tricks you use to enlarge a small image, it is still going to look like an indistinct mess since the data simply does not exist. Hopefully, such large interpolations will not be very common.

Conversely, when interpolating quaternions that are very close to each other (e.g., less than 1 degree apart), all three methods produce virtually identical results. In this case, we should naturally opt for the one that is simpler to execute.

So the question is, for interpolations of around 45 degrees, which looks best? The answer is somewhat surprising. Exponential map interpolation does not look very good, because it does not follow the path of least distance between the two. This effect is only slightly visible at small angles, but as the interpolation angle grows, becomes very visible.

Spherical interpolation looks the best, because it follows the path of least torque, and has constant velocity over the duration of the lerp. However, it has a big disadvantage in that it is not associative, so we may have some trouble using it. It is also moderately expensive to perform.

Normalizing linear interpolation is most obviously "hacky," so much so that it is not even mentioned in many textbooks about quaternions. It does follow the path of least torque, but the apparent speed of interpolation changes during the course of that interpolation. So, just how noticeable is the changing interpolation speed? The answer is, for practical angles: not at all. For an interpolation angle of 45 degrees, the difference between slerp and nlerp is tiny—only around 5 percent. In practice, this is almost impossible to detect, and far from objectionable. The best way to prove this is to write some actual interpolation code that works by either slerp or nlerp, blend some animations together, and toggle between the two methods on a key press. Not only is there only a tiny visible difference, but the real test (as with all questions of approximation) is to toggle between the two a random number of times, and then challenge 10 people to (separately) tell you which version is "correct."

The advantages of nlerp are that it is extremely obvious how it associates (simply add as many quaternions together as you like and normalize the result), and it is very fast to execute. You can even put the actual normalization off until later if you are going to blend it with more quaternions in the future. Therefore, given that the error is small and hard to notice, the default choice seems like it should be nlerp, unless slerp is actually required for a few special cases. The author has never found a case where exponential-map lerps looked better, yet their processing cost is considerable.

For fuller and more mathematically grounded discussion of blending quaternions, see [Blow04, Lengyel04].

Multiway Blending

The standard two-way lerp describes a linear interpolation between two bones, with a single weight determining the amounts of both bones.

If blending multiple animations together, there is a variety of ways to represent what fraction of the whole each source contributes. The simplest is to perform a sequence of two-way blends, starting with the first animation, and sequentially blending in each subsequent animation by the supplied amount. However, the results change according to the order of the animations. For example, if animations A, B, and C are blended together, each time having a blend weight of 0.5, you have:

$$result = 0.5A + 0.5B$$

$$result = 0.5\,result + 0.5C = 0.25A + 0.25B + 0.5C$$

Obviously, this is not a symmetrical result, since there is twice as much influence from animation C as the other two. If we perform the blending in the other direction, we get a different answer, with A having twice the influence. This seems an odd result, but possibly controllable. For example, we could change the weights to compensate. However, what if the animations A, B, and C have different durations, and animation B ends before the other two? When it ends, the influence of C (whatever that was) will be the same, but the influence of A will increase, taking over whatever influence B originally had. This is horribly counterintuitive, since it depends on concepts that should really be orthogonal to influence, such as animations starting and stopping.

A better method is to supply a weight for each animation. As well as multiplying each animation by its weight when summing, we also keep track of the total weight. Once all animations are summed, we divide the result by this total weight. For example, if we gave animations A, B, and C weights of 0.5, we would get:

$$totalWeight = 0.5 \qquad\qquad result = 0.5A$$

$$totalWeight = 0.5 + 0.5 = 1.0 \qquad\qquad result = result + 0.5B = 0.5A + 0.5B$$

$$totalWeight = 1.0 + 0.5 = 1.5 \qquad\qquad result = result + 0.5C = 0.5A + 0.5B + 0.5C$$

$$result = \frac{result}{totalWeight} = \frac{1}{3}A + \frac{1}{3}B + \frac{1}{3}C$$

This gives an even blend between all three, which is what you would expect if all were set to the same weight. A good thing about this method is that order does not matter. If one animation ends, the relative contributions of the other two depend only on their own weights, not on their position in the blending list. Remove animation B from the previous sequence and you will obtain half of each of A and C, which is logical if they both have the same weight.

One thing to notice is that if all three are the same weight, no matter what numerical value that weight is, you get the same result. If you change the 0.5 in the previous example to any value you wish, the result is the same. In fact, in any multi-way blend using this method, all weights are simply relative to each other and there is no absolute meaning to a weight of 0.5, 1.0, or 1000.0.

Fortunately, it is moderately intuitive that if animation X has twice the weight of animation Y, it will have twice the influence. However, it has one notable defect: there is no weight value that will allow a single animation to completely mask the others and cause them to have no influence at all. You can give the animation a very large weight such as 1 million, which will mostly work, but even then if another animation's weight is set to 1 million minus 1, it will have roughly the same influence. There are other ways to solve this, though, such as the masked lerp, which we discuss later.

The multiway blending operation can use approximate normalization operations on its sources in the same way the two-source lerp does, for even greater speed improvements. It should be noted that if performing multiway blending using the quaternion slerp operator, it is very hard indeed to get a blend that does not depend on blending order. Using nlerp, it is trivial.

Bone Masks

Frequently, you will want to apply an animation to only a few select bones, rather than to the whole skeleton. For example, you have a character walking along who wants to wave at someone. This animation involves only one arm; consequently, it does not involve the head, legs, or the other arm. Thus, the person could be sitting, walking, or running, and perhaps carrying something with the other arm or even pointing a weapon at someone (a fairly common past-time for computer game characters). Therefore, the "wave" animation will not have anything particularly useful to say about what the leg bones should be doing. However, if you play it, whatever data it has for the leg bones will still influence them in some way, which is not what you want. You need some way to say that an animation has no influence over some of the bones of the skeleton.

This is called a *bone mask*. It is simply a list of numbers, generally a value from 0.0 to 1.0, one for each bone in the skeleton, and it is applied to an animation. When the animation is blended with others, the mask is multiplied by the animation's overall weight when performing the blend. The result of this multiplication of the bone mask and the overall weight is called the *effective weight*, and is what is actually used when blending the multiple animations. Note that this means the weight for each animation changes from bone to bone—and this includes the total weight for each bone.

In this "waving" animation case, the bone mask would contain zeros for most of the bones, except for the bones in the arm and hand, which would contain ones. To produce a smooth blend between the body and the arm, the bones of the shoulder may have a fractional blend, such as 0.5. Fractional blends are especially common when blending lower-body animations such as runs and walks with upper-body animations such as firing with a rifle at a target. Fractional weights along the spine, increasing or decreasing as they progress up or down the spine, allow the ribs of the torso (and the clothing it wears) to blend incrementally, as they do in real life.

Bone masks can be created by naming convention, or by detecting which bones do not move during an animation. However, these are cumbersome methods, and poor at special cases (e.g., the animation for aiming and firing a rifle demands that the bones of the arm be stationary, but they are certainly part of the animation). The ideal solution is to allow the animator to author the weights directly. Sadly, most animation packages do not allow easy previewing of the effects of these weights, so this can also be a process of trial and error.

Naturally, it is a good idea to avoid storing bone data that will be entirely masked out by the bone mask—there is no point in storing data that will never be used.

Masked Lerp

This style of blending is almost identical to the standard two-way lerp, except that instead of a single blend value that applies to the whole of the two animations, a bone mask is used that gives the lerp value individually for each bone. Otherwise, the calculation for performing the blend is identical to the two-way lerp presented previously. The mask will be set to one to entirely use one animation, zero to entirely use the other, or a fractional value to produce a blend.

The important difference here is that the bone mask can allow one animation to entirely control a particular set of bones, while allowing the other animation to entirely control a different set of bones, and to blend between the places on the skeleton where they join. This type of blending can be performed by applying bone masks to a multiway blend, but the only way to do it properly is to apply the mask to one animation, and then the inverse mask to the other. This is cumbersome, so it is easier (and faster to execute) to have a specific binary lerp that performs this directly.

Hierarchical Blending

The techniques presented previously all take a series of animations and blend them together. However, it is frequently useful to take one set of animations, blend them together, then another set, blend them together, and then take the results of the two blending operations, and blend those together. One such example is when animating human figures. Frequently, you want to play an animation on the top half of the body, and a different animation on the bottom half. For example, the "animation" playing on the bottom half may actually be composed of many animations: you may be playing a run cycle, and want to transition smoothly into a walk cycle. During the transition, both run and walk cycle will be playing and being blended together. This blending must happen before being blended with the upper-body animations. Thus, we have a hierarchy of blending, which is frequently represented with a tree. Each frame, the tree of blends is traversed, sampling each animation and performing the necessary blends.

Typically, the leaves of the tree will be multiway blends used for the purposes of performing *time-based* blending, such as transitioning from a walk to a run. Moreover, the nodes of the tree, where the results of these time-based blends are combined, tend to be *area-based* blends, with each source corresponding to one section of the body, being blended together using bone masks. However, this is by no means the only way the blending tree can be used; it is simply a common example.

Motion Extraction

When the game is playing an animation of a stationary character, life is easy. The character stays in a fixed place, and animates. However, life gets trickier when the animation wants the character to move. Remember that two separate concepts are combined to make up what we see on the screen: the game's idea of where the instance is (typically a simple position and orientation), and the effect of whatever animations are playing on the instance. With a standing animation, the two are not that different, and there is no confusion.

However, if the instance plays a walk animation, things can get confusing. The animation may cause the character to walk away from where the game thinks it is, meaning that the character is not observing the correct physics—it may walk through walls, float in the air, and so on.

The obvious solution is for the game to move the origin of the character in the direction of the walk, and the walk animation to be authored so that the character does not actually move in the scene, but instead walks on the spot. This makes sure the game and the animation agree on where the character is. However, there are two problems with this. First, the speed of movement applied to the character must precisely match the speed at which the feet move backwards in the animation. If the two do not match, the resulting motion of the feet in world space will not be zero, and the feet will slip along the ground, which looks particularly bad.

The second problem occurs if the animation is more complex than a straight-line walk. What if the animation is that of a character climbing onto a ledge? The character first jumps up to grab the ledge, hauls itself up, then over the edge to a crouch, and then stands up. This is an extremely complex motion, but the game must somehow match it in some way so that the character actually moves during the process. The motion the game imparts must be removed from the motion that the animator puts into the character, or the various parts like the hands and feet will slide across the surface, which is something that is even more noticeable than slipping feet.

The process of taking an animation and deriving the overall movement of a character from it is called *motion extraction*, and there are a variety of techniques.

Linear Motion Extraction

Let us start with the simplest form of motion extraction, *linear motion extraction* (LME). Despite its simplicity, it is common, and very useful for many situations. First, look at the position of the root bone on the first frame of the animation. Then, look at its position in the last frame. Subtracting one from the other shows how the character moved during the animation, and dividing that motion by the duration of the animation gives the average velocity of the character during the animation.

In a preprocessing step, take this velocity, store it with the animation, and for each frame of the animation, subtract the cumulative effect of this velocity from the position of the root bone. Only after performing this subtraction on each sampled frame do you encode the root-bone's motion as compressed curves or whatever format your animation scheme chooses. This has now removed all the linear components of the root bone's movement from the animation. Naturally, the first and last positions of the root bone will now coincide, since that was how the velocity was defined, but the intermediate motions may still move around (what is termed the *residual* motion of the root bone). For example, in the ledge-climbing animation used previously, the motion is not linear at all. First, there is a sudden vertical motion as the character jumps, then a smoother one as it hauls itself up, a slower irregular motion as it stays crouched but moves onto the ledge (and moves in a horizontal direction for the first time), and then a quicker one as it stands up. However, the overall motion that is extracted is a straight line, and the animation encodes the difference between the real motion and this average motion.

At playback time, execute the reverse process. As the animation is playing, the game moves the character instance's position at the given velocity. The combination of the linear velocity applied by the game and the residual motion left in the animation is to play the animation back perfectly; except that this time, the character ends up in a different place, standing on top of the ledge instead of remaining where it started. This automatic extraction of motion is much better than using some hand-coded value on which both animator and game code need to closely agree. If the animation is later changed—for example, because the ledge height is changed—there is no need to update the code to match. The animation will still be in perfect sync with the velocity given to the instance, and there will still be no hand or foot sliding.

Composite Motion Extraction

The major problem with the previous technique is that it does not capture rotational movement. If you have an animation for a character turning on the spot, LME will simply say that nothing happened, since the position of the root bone did not change. However, you still need to rotate the instance, and the angle and speed of this rotation is important to make sure that the feet do not rotate while on the ground.

The same trick used in LME can be applied to the rotational component. Take the orientation of the first frame, the orientation of the last, find the axis of rotation, divide by the duration of the animation, and you have a rotational velocity. Subtract this rotation from the root bone's motion before encoding your animation. At run-time, as the animation is played, apply this velocity to the orientation of the instance, and you have both translational and rotational versions of LME.

You can, of course, do the same with scale and shear, but so few animations involve scale and shear of the root bone, and so few games understand the concept of scale and shear for a game entity, that it is unlikely to be important. Most motion extraction ignores these components.

So, this works fine, and the instance does end up correctly rotated and translated at the end of the animation, and the animation is played perfectly. The problem now is slightly more subtle. The question is "Where is the instance in the middle of the animation?" Imagine an animation where the character is running and turning left (you need to have animations like this, since the motion of running around a curve is very different from that used when running in a straight line), and that during this animation, the character turns through 90 degrees. The real movement should be along one-quarter of a circle. Unfortunately, LME plots a straight line between the start and end positions, and moves and rotates the instance along this line. It relies on the residual motion inside the animation to correct this linear movement, and render the character moving in a circle. However, the game logic does not know about the residual motion in the animation—it only knows about the instance's position and rotation.

There is no problem with the rotation, but the position at the middle of the animation is a long way from reality. What if the character were running around the edge of a curve in the road? In reality, the character should always stay a few inches from the edge of the road, and never be on the road itself. However, LME approximates the path during the animation as a straight line, which cuts across the corner. Thus, for part of the animation, the game logic would think the character was actually on the road, and would be hit by a car. Worse still, what happens if the player stops running in the middle of the animation and stands still—the character will actually pop to that position, no longer running on the edge of the road, but suddenly standing in the middle of it.

The secret is to encode the translational movement as always being relative to the current orientation of the instance. Of course, this had to be done anyway, since the translation component of even a straight walk cycle needs to know if the character is facing north, south, east, or west when it starts walking. However, that is only relative to the starting frame. The secret here is to make it relative to every intermediate frame, after the effects of rotation are taken into account.

The result is *composite motion extraction* (CME). The main difference in this example is that whereas with standard LME, the translation vector moved at 45 degrees to the starting orientation of the character, now we find that the translation is always exactly in the direction of the character's current orientation; the character's rotation on every frame means that the final resulting motion is a circle. In the example, we can see that this gives a result where the game's instance mirrors the motion of the animation precisely. This means that collision detection always works correctly, the motion can be stopped at any point, and the character is where the game expects it to be.

It is not that LME is "wrong" and CME is "right." Both correctly extract a component of motion from the animation and apply it to the game instance. It is simply that CME approximates many common motions with circular motion in a far more consistent manner than LME does.

Variable Delta Extraction

LME and CME are still not the end of the story. Both are pleasingly simple, and apply well to many common motions and animations. However, they still do not represent some motions adequately. Irregular motions such as the ledge-scaling example given earlier are poorly represented as either a linear or circular movement, and even smooth motions such as a bouncing ball are not represented well because it is a parabola, not a circle or a straight line.

The answer is not to find some more ever-better ever-more-complex approximations to the motion of the root bone and apply it to the motion of the instance, but to use the motion of the root bone directly. To do this, the root bone is ignored completely for the purposes of animation. Instead, each frame, the animation system samples the root-bone's transform at the current time, samples (or remembers) the root-bone's transform on the previous frame, and finds the difference between them, which is the *delta*. This delta is then applied to the instance's position and orientation.

Using this method, the instance always follows the motion of the root bone exactly, and there is never a mismatch between the rendered position of the object and the game's idea of where it is. This allows complex multipart animations such as the previous examples. However, it does require extra complication, since each frame, the root bone's motion must be sampled twice, and the delta from one to the other found. However, when playing back the animation, we can completely ignore the root bone's motion (we know it is all in the instance), so that is one less bone to sample there. Overall, the extra cost is usually unnoticeable (although there are other considerations, discussed later), and the extra fidelity in motion is extremely useful.

Finding Your Roots

In all this motion extraction discussion, one important fact has so far been glossed over. We have assumed that the instance should follow (to some variable degree of precision) the position of the root bone of the animation. However, this ignores one key question, "What actually is the root bone, and what does its position and orientation mean?"

The simple but naïve answer is that it is whatever the animator uses as the root bone, which for a humanoid character is usually the pelvis (although there are other conventions). However, this can cause complications when blending between animations, and when performing transitions. For example, imagine a cowboy of the Wild West walking down the road, saddle-sore from a long ride. Because of his aching hip joints and his wide gait, each step, his pelvis rotates to move his legs forward, so that its orientation swings by maybe 30 degrees either side of straight ahead. Since the pelvis is the root bone, this motion will be reflected in the game instance orientation, and it too will turn from side to side as he moves. This is counterintuitive, since he is (conceptually) walking in a straight line, but it is not actually a problem. Well, not yet at least.

Suddenly, a bandit jumps out in front of him, and being the fastest gun in the West, in an instant he transitions to his gun-fighting pose, draws his six-shooter, and fires. Sadly for him, he was just stepping out with his right leg, which means his game instance orientation was facing 30 degrees to the left. Transitioning instantly to his gun-fighting pose did not change that orientation (since it is a pose, not a motion, and therefore does not affect the root bone). He is now facing directly at the saloon, and the only thing he hits is a bottle of his favorite whiskey. The slim-hipped but wide-mustachioed bandit, who was careful to walk with pelvis always fixed directly ahead, fires back and mortally wounds our hero. The moral of the story is: choose your root bone carefully!

However, it is hard to think of a better bone in the skeleton to use than the pelvis. Sometimes, the shoulders are used, but they rotate even more than the pelvis. What is our hero to do? The real answer is to create a new root bone, one whose only purpose is to allow the animator to define exactly what he wants to happen to the game orientation of the object. This is called a *synthetic root bone* (SRB), since it does not actually correspond to a real place on the skeleton, and does not influence any vertex on the mesh. The most common version of SRB, standard in many animation packages, is the *ground shadow*. This bone sits at ground level, usually directly under the center of gravity of the character, and facing forward.

The exact position of the SRB is something that can be agreed on between the game programmer and the animators, since the SRB can in fact be anywhere they wish. Some people like to have the SRB at just below pelvis level (this helps when animating characters sitting down, since the SRB is then the bone they sit on, and the height can be directly matched to the height of the chair or ledge on which they are sitting). Others like to have it at shoulder level. The animation system does not care where exactly the SRB is, the important thing is that it makes sense from the game's point of view. With an SRB, the animator can do two things very easily. First, he can directly control how the character moves through the world in an animation, especially if using VDA rather than CME. Second, he can control the exact relationship between the graphical appearance of the mesh due to the animation of its physical skeleton, and where the game thinks it is.

When transitioning or blending between two animations, the position of the SRB in both is kept constant, and all the other bones in the skeleton are blended. This allows the cowboy with the white hat to always keep his SRB facing forward, and when he changes to his gun-slinging pose, he is still facing directly at the bandit—another one bites the dust.

If a Tree Animates in a Forest...

Motion extraction brings up an interesting problem that is not often discussed, and sometimes those writing an engine may not realize it is even a concern. This problem is the separation of game and graphics. In an ideal world, the game runs as an entirely self-contained system. It takes controller inputs in one end, processes the game world, and outputs the state of its world to the graphics (and sound) engine for display. It does not rely on the graphics system for anything, and in fact does not even care if the graphics system is there at all.

This system has many advantages, such as being able to display the graphics at any desired frame rate (especially important for the PC market), being able to transmit the graphics elsewhere (e.g., for a multiplayer game, where one machine is the host and the other is the client), or even having no display at all (the "headless" servers used for massively multiplayer games). The other advantage is that the game can process a large world, and the graphics system can increase its performance by only rendering the tiny fraction that the player can see.

However, when we talk about animation driving the movement of game objects, we break that model, and we now have graphics data feeding back into the game. Ideally, we should fix this. In a large world, it may mean animating everything in the world simply to find out how it moves around, and then for the vast majority of objects, simply throwing that animation data away, because the object was not visible.

It is therefore a good idea to separate the calculation of the motion-extraction of the root bone from the calculation of the rest of the bones. In addition, most animations do not (or should not) contribute to the movement of the root bone. Any action that is only played on a part of the body should be flagged as such, and ignored during motion-extraction replay. For the same reason, it can also be important that the animation sequencing code (that decides which animations to play and when to play them) should have a "light" version that ignores all animations that are purely graphical in nature and concentrates on the animations that change the motion of the game instance. In this way, the cost of instances that are not currently visible is minimized as much as possible.

Mesh Deformation

Once we have our looped, sampled, interpolated, and blended animation, what do we do with it? Well, we have a *local pose*, which is a sequence of transforms, each relative to a parent transform in a manner described by the connections in the skeleton. However, we cannot render that directly on the screen. We need to use this local pose to deform the vertices of a mesh that we can draw. This process is composed of several stages, as discussed next.

1. Transform Each Bone into World Space

The transforms are currently in a space relative to (or "local to") their respective parent bone, called a *local pose*. The first stage is to convert this to a *global pose* or a *world pose*, where each transform describes the bone's position in the world, without needing any other frame of reference except for the shared world origin and orientation (and fundamentally, everything has to be relative to that).

The procedure is simple. Start at the root node of the skeleton. Multiply its current transform by the instance's overall transform, which is the one that describes where the instance is in the world and which way it is facing. You now have the world-space transform of the root bone. Now, take each of the children of the root bone, and multiply each of their transforms by the root bone's world transform (the one you just calculated). You now have the world transforms of each child bone. Then, just keep recursing down the skeleton. For each bone, multiply its local transform by the world transform of its parent bone, and you now have the world transform of the bone.

For each bone, you must calculate the world transform of its parent before you can do this. It can be quite time consuming checking that this has been done, so a nice trick is to ensure that you keep your bone transforms (both local and world) in an array, ordered so that parent bones are always stored before child bones. This naturally implies that the root bone is always the first item in the array, since it is the only one without a parent. This way, you can process the bones in a linear fashion, and always be sure that a parent bone has been processed before any of its children.

The world pose is also the space in which most physics simulations or collision detection happens, and where inverse kinematics (IK) tend to happen, so it is almost always found as soon as the correct blending of the local pose has been performed.

2. Find the Delta from the Rest Pose

Now we have the bones in world space. However, we cannot simply apply those transforms to the mesh. This is because the mesh is already in a pose, which is the pose in which it was exported. This is called many things: the *binding, rest,* or *default* pose. What needs to be done first is to transform the mesh out of its rest pose (meaning that it is now in "no pose") before transforming it into the pose we want.

Therefore, we must first untransform by the rest pose, which is the same as transforming by the inverse of the rest pose, and then transform by the desired pose. Of course, we do not need to do two transforms per vertex; we can simply find the composite of these two transforms for each bone. Better still, since the rest pose is always the same for a given mesh, we do not have to find the inverse of its transforms every frame; we can calculate them just once—either when the model is exported, or when it is loaded into memory. Then, each frame, take the world-space transforms of the desired pose, multiply them by the precomputed inverse world-space transforms of the rest pose, and use the resulting transform to deform the mesh.

3. Deform the Vertex Positions

Each vertex in the mesh will have a certain number of bones that affect it. Depending on the type of mesh, the number of bones affecting a single vertex can be limitless. However, most animation systems pick a maximum number of bones per vertex that they will support. By far the most popular value is four. The reasoning is that most humanoid meshes require at least three to look good—areas where three bones all influence a single vertex include the crotch (the pelvis and both thighs), the shoulders (the upper arm, collar bone, and rib cage), and many parts of the face. However, three is not a power of two, and this causes programmers severe philosophical anxiety. Rounding up to four is much more agreeable. There is no strict reason why four is chosen, and many engines have optimized paths for three, two, and one, if the mesh allows. For example, most mechanical objects only need a single bone's influence for each vertex, since all the parts are rigid. However, if there is only one animation code path, four seems to work well as a balance between animation quality and performance.

Besides knowing which bones deform a vertex, we also need to know how much each bone influences that deformation relative to each other. This is a multiway blend, but this time the weights are fixed, and we can prenormalize them so that they strictly add up to 1.0.

The usual way of storing this information is to store, in each vertex, four indices into the array of bones, and four corresponding weights (sometimes only three weights are stored and the last is computed as one minus the others). This allows the vertex deformation code to do the following for each vertex:

```
vec3 FinalPosition = {0,0,0};
for ( i = 0; i < 4; i++ )
{
    int BoneIndex = Vertex.Index[i];
    float BoneWeight = Vertex.Weight[i];
    FinalPosition += BoneWeight *
        (Vertex.Position * PoseDelta[BoneIndex]);
}
```

Another advantage of using four bones is that the per-vertex data packs well into memory. The indices of the bones can easily fit into a byte each (256 bones are sufficient for most animation systems right now). The blend weights are strictly between zero and one, and eight bits of precision is sufficient, meaning they also fit into bytes. Thus, the total animation information fits into eight bytes.

4. Deform the Vertex Normals

This demonstrates the deformation of vertex positions, but vertices often include vectors used for shading as well: the normal, tangent, and binormal vectors. All three can be handled in similar ways, so we will look at only the normals for simplicity.

Whether animating or not, whenever you apply a transform to a vertex position, to ensure the normal is shaded appropriately, you need to transform it by the *inverse transpose* of the transform. That is, take the 3×3 matrix that represents the transform (the fourth column is the positional offset and is ignored, since normals are *vectors* and not *positions*), invert it, then transpose it, and then multiply the normal by it. Finally, for correct shading, the normal must be renormalized.

There are a couple of expensive operations in that sequence; notably, finding the inverse of a 3×3 matrix, and renormalizing the normal after the transformation. Performing these at every vertex is obviously undesirable. Therefore, many engines can take a few shortcuts. Naturally, these all reduce fidelity by a certain amount, but since these are vectors used for shading and not positions, a certain amount of error is acceptable.

The first optimization is more of an observation. If all the bone deformations are strictly rotations without scales or shears (translations are ignored), the transformation is *orthonormal*. That is, its basis vectors are of unit length and at right angles to each other. A feature of orthonormal matrices is that their inverse is their transpose. Thus, the inverse transpose is just the matrix itself, removing that chunk of work.

Starting with orthonormal matrices also has a second advantage. As long as the normals are unit-length before transformation, they will also end up unit-length, and thus do not need renormalization. This makes using transforms with only rotations and translations very cheap, and luckily, this is the case with most bones used in games today. Even in meshes where some of the transforms may involve scales or shears, it can still be worth having two code paths and only use the expensive one for the normals that require it.

The inversion of the matrix can be sped up in various ways. Some bones only have a uniform scale that is the same along all three axes. Not only are these simple to invert (simply multiply the whole matrix by a constant), but the scaling can be pushed until after the normal has been transformed, thus needing only three multiplies rather than nine.

Of course, even when the inverse transposes are needed, they do not need to be found at every vertex; they can be found once per bone instead, and a second array of inverse transpose delta matrices fed to the vertex deformation code. This does not reduce fidelity, but it does mean that the vertex deformation needs access to two bone arrays rather than one. In many architectures, this deformation is performed by custom hardware (such as a vertex shader), which requires the matrices to be uploaded to a certain area of memory with limited capacity. Doubling the size of the array halves the number of bones that can be uploaded at a time, which means that the mesh must be rendered in smaller pieces, decreasing efficiency.

Finally, one clever hack to increase speed is to always order the bone data in the vertices in decreasing order, with the bone with the largest weight being specified first. Then, only deform normals by the first few listed bones. Just using the first is quite common, and surprisingly effective. The effect of dropping bones for normals is far less visible than for positions.

Inverse Kinematics

So far, all the animation we have addressed so far is known as *forward kinematics*, or FK, where each bone determines where its child bones are, and they determine where their children are, and so on. At no point does the transformation of a child bone influence its parent.

However, animation in the real world is a complex interplay of influences both down and up the skeletal frame (indeed, there is of course no real-world concept of "child" or "parent" bones—we simply impose one because it is useful). When standing on one leg, the motion (or lack of it) of your foot is definitely being transferred upward to your pelvis and spine, and this type of animation is called *inverse kinematics*, or IK.

In fact, IK is more accurately defined as the part of "animation" that is not FK. As you can imagine, this is a huge topic, and the subject of much research, so this chapter can only introduce the basics. We will concentrate on moving a single child joint to a given position or orientation, and then allowing some small number of its parents to move to compensate for the motion. A good example is somebody picking up a cup of tea by the handle. Ideally, this motion would be animated by a human—the motion of the arm and wrist during this action is extremely complex. However, the game may not be able to control where on the table the cup is, or where the person is when he reaches for the cup, and so must do some runtime adaptation to make sure the two meet properly.

There is a wide variety of IK algorithms, and they are frequently used in combination to complement each other. Four algorithms will be introduced here, three of them being closely related, mathematically based bone operations, and one being a higher level method using animation input to guide its process.

Single-Bone IK

The simplest IK solution is almost trivial. It is the process of orienting a particular bone in a desired direction. This is commonly used to rotate eyeballs in their sockets to point at whatever a character is looking at, or to ensure that a camera is pointing at whatever the game designer wants it to. A secondary use is as a fix up for the variety of other IK solutions, such as ensuring that feet point in the correct direction and remain flat on the ground during a walk cycle, or that a hand holding a coffee cup keeps the cup level and upright as it moves it around.

First, find the vector along which the bone being rotated must point. For cameras and eyeballs, this is the normalized vector from the center of the bone to the point of interest. For feet and hands, the vector is defined by other methods (the normal to the ground for feet, or the vector opposite to gravity for a hand holding a coffee cup).

Then, find the vector along which the bone currently points. This is often as simple as taking a vector from the bone's transform matrix. With these two vectors, find the rotation that maps one to the other using standard matrix or quaternion methods, and apply this rotation to the bone.

A slight variation of this IK method is where you always start from some reference orientation of the bone, rather than the current orientation. Using the current orientation can lead to progressive rotation of the bone in some cases. This is commonly used for cameras, where the camera should always remain aligned vertically, rather than tilting over to one side or the other. If using the current orientation, this rotation along the camera axis happens a great deal. For example, tilt the camera down by 90 degrees, and then rotate to the side by 90 degrees until the camera is horizontal again. The camera will be pointing 90 degrees to the right of where it started, which is what you want, but it will also be tilted over to the left by 90 degrees. Although this example is extreme, the effect is very apparent even with small rotations. Starting from a known orientation each time will prevent this.

Multibone IK

Multibone IK is the term for the most general form of analytical IK. This is used where the application wants a given bone to end up in a certain place, and wants to allow movement of a certain number of bones higher up the skeletal tree to allow this motion. The number of bones allowed to move is typically constrained in some way, and the IK solver is informed which bones it may move and which it may not. Although the bones allowed to move typically form an unbroken chain in the skeletal hierarchy (i.e., each is a parent of the one before it), there are variations that allow any pattern of bones to be moved, and the fundamental nature of the solver does not need to change significantly.

To use a concrete example, we will use a fencer trying to hit a target with the tip of his fencing foil. The "lunge" animation has been played to the point where the fencer should have hit the target, but for various reasons the animation did not place the tip of the foil exactly on the target (perhaps the target moved, or perhaps it is slightly lower than the one for which the animation was authored). In this example, the IK algorithm may only move the bones of the arm and hand, and it might move the position of the shoulder by bending the spine (we assume this is a single bone for simplicity, although in many character rigs it is composed of multiple joints). The IK algorithm may not move the position of the hips or legs. The tip of the foil is called the *end effector* (a hangover from the fact that IK is derived from research on robot arms with some sort of tool, or effector, on the end), and the target it must hit is, naturally, called the *target*.

There are a number of algorithms for solving this type of general IK, but one of the simplest methods is called *cyclic coordinate descent*, which is the one presented here. It is by no means the best, but it is simple, easy to understand, and moderately useable.

The algorithm is iterative, and it is frequently possible that there is no solution. In this example, it may be that the fencer is simply too far from the target to reach, even with spine, arm, and sword fully extended. In this case, the iterations will go on forever, so a cap on the number of iterations is supplied by the calling routine. Additionally, the iterations can sometimes oscillate around the desired result, slowly getting closer and closer but never actually hitting, so a tolerance is supplied. Once the algorithm gets closer than this tolerance, it is declared "good enough" and the iteration stops. For this example, we declare that a centimeter of accuracy should be more than sufficient.

The principle is fairly simple. At each stage, pick one of the joints to move, and leave the other joints fixed in their current state. Measure the error between the current position of the end effector (the tip of the foil) and the target, such as the physical distance between them. Then, move the chosen joint to try to minimize this error. Typically, we start with the last bone in the chain. In this case, the wrist, which is the joint closest to the tip of the fencing foil, should be moved to minimize the error. Then, move up one link to the elbow joint, move that joint, then the shoulder, and then the spine. If the foil has still not hit the target, repeat, starting from the wrist again.

In practice, all of the joints we consider here are rotational joints, and most have fairly full rotational freedom (although the elbow joint itself can only hinge in one direction, the combination of the rotation of the upper arm and the bending of the elbow allow us to consider it as a joint with full freedom). For this type of joint, the details of the computation are simple. Find the vector from the rotation point of the joint (the point of the elbow, wrist, etc,) to the end effector. Then, find the vector from the rotation point to the target. Find the rotation that moves one vector to the other, just as with single-bone IK, and apply it to the joint. Repeat this operation for the different bones, until the solution is reached, or the number of iterations becomes too high.

One of the notable problems with cyclic coordinate descent is that it copes very badly if the chain of joints is already straight, or nearly so, but needs to be bent to make the end effector hit the target. The most common example is a leg that is nearly straight, but where the knee must bend significantly to make the foot hit a part of the ground that is higher than the animation thinks, as shown in Figure 5.2.3. Here, the foot is nearly in the right place horizontally, but is simply too far below the surface of the ground. Bending the knee to minimize this error results in only a very small bending motion. Bending the hip, again minimizing the error, also moves the foot only a small distance.

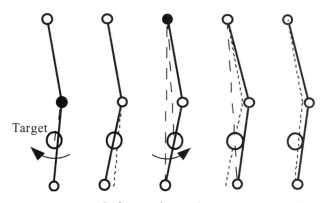

FIGURE 5.2.3   *Cyclic coordinate descent converging slowly.*

In Figure 5.2.3, the left frame shows how the middle joint rotates to move the line between the joint and the effector so that it goes through the target. The second frame shows how much the joint has moved the bone. The third frame shows the top joint rotating to move the line to the effector so that it goes through the target. The fourth frame shows how much this motion has moved the bones. The final frame compares the start and end poses, showing that the total system has changed only very slightly.

Because the leg has barely moved, this cycle can repeat for many iterations before converging on the correct solution. Note that for clarity, Figure 5.2.3 shows the leg already slightly bent. In practice, real animations can start the leg almost precisely straight, which results in far less movement per iteration than shown. In tests, 50 iterations were not uncommon, and sometimes even that was not sufficient. Lowering the error tolerance does not help much in this case, because once the knee starts to bend significantly, the algorithm converges very quickly. The problem is that it can take many iterations to get the knee to bend significantly in the first place.

The other problem is that if the knee is nearly straight, it is hard to predict which way the knee will bend. If the IK routine is required to move the foot slightly behind the person instead of slightly in front, and the leg is nearly straight, the most common solution that cyclic coordinate descent finds is for the knee to bend backwards. The algorithm can be modified to respect joint limits and prevent the knee from bending the wrong way; however, this can further increase the number of iterations required, and prevent the algorithm from finding a solution at all, even though one exists. In this case, the knee may simply keep trying to bend backward and being reset straight, time after time, never approaching a good solution, even though a perfectly good solution exists where the knee bends forward.

However, this specific case of a leg, where the hip may not move but the knee and ankle may, can be solved quickly and in a far more elegant manner.

Two-Bone IK

Two-bone IK is a special case of multibone IK, but it applies to a very specific, but also very common case—notably arms and legs. This is the special case where exactly two bones may rotate relative to their parents (the thigh and shinbones in the case of a leg), and where the middle joint (the knee) may bend in only one direction. In practice it is simple to constrain the joint to a single plane, which is the one defined by the two surrounding joints (hip and ankle) and another value such as a third supplied position. In the case of a two-bone knee IK, this third position may be derived from the position of the knee in an example pose supplied by the artist; one where the leg is bent in a reasonable manner with the knee pointing forward. If the knee is already bent in the current pose, a game may want to use that as the third reference position instead. This allows complex motions such as martial-arts kicks to be performed properly, even when the legs are highly rotated and the knee may be in a plane that is not straight ahead.

These three points then define a plane that the knee is confined to, which imposes one constraint on the knee position. The thigh and shinbones must remain constant length, and the angle and hip joints must not move. Each of these defines a sphere with a fixed radius around the respective joint that the knee must be somewhere on the surface of, which imposes another two constraints. Satisfying these three geometric constraints gives two possible positions for the knee, and one of them involves bending the knee backward, and can be ruled out.

IK by Interpolation

Performing IK by mathematically moving one bone at a time is all very well, but sometimes the motion you want to perform is more complex. A common example of this is a character standing still, but moving its head around to look at various objects in the scene. We would like to be able to find the vector between the center of the head and the object of interest, and then somehow point the head along this vector. The problem is that moving the head and neck is a complex biomechanical process involving many muscles, and can involve slight shoulder movement for the extremes of movement such as looking 90 degrees to either side or straight up. Using simple mathematical bone-based IK would not produce a natural result. Rather, the character would look robotic, with joints that can move unnaturally far, and do not influence their neighboring joints in a way that looks comfortable for a real human.

The solution is a primitive version of "Animation by Example" [Cohen00]. The artist supplies a number of example poses, and the animation system blends between them to create a composite pose. These poses can capture all the details of the complex movement of the neck, head, and shoulders that naturally happens as the character looks around.

The most common version uses nine different poses. One pose has the character looking directly ahead. One has the character looking directly upward, one 60-degrees downward, one 90-degrees left, one 90-degrees right, and four more for the corners (up left, up right, down left, down right). Note that it is extremely uncomfortable to move your head to look directly downward, so typically, the head will only move to around 60-degrees down and the eyes will look the rest of the way.

Each frame, the relative bearing and elevation of the desired view direction are found by simple trigonometry, and the angles used to derive interpolation values for the nearest four poses. Let us say that our target view direction is 54-degrees right and 15-degrees downward of the neutral pose. This is 60 percent of the way along the horizontal scale (54/90) and 25 percent of the way along the vertical scale (15/60), so the weights of the various poses are:

- **Look ahead:** $(1 - 0.25)(1 - 0.6) = 0.3$
- **Look downward:** $(0.25)(1 - 0.6) = 0.1$
- **Look right:** $(1 - 0.25)(0.6) = 0.45$
- **Look down and right:** $(0.25)(0.6) = 0.15$

The other five poses (left, up, left and up, right and up, left and down) are not used for looking in this direction.

As can be seen, these weights naturally sum to 1.0, so although they can be used in a traditional multiway blending, there is no need to divide by the sum, which can be a slight optimization in some cases.

This blending is performed for all the bones of the head, neck, and shoulders, and using this method, a character can look anywhere within the supplied blend space (often called a *gamut*) and still reflect the complex interactions of the muscles and bones in the shoulders and neck.

However, there are still two big problems with this method of using nine example poses and blending between them. The problem becomes immediately apparent as soon as we change the example from a person moving his head to the common game example of a soldier holding a rifle and moving his aim around.

The first problem is that the aim point is inexact. In both cases (a head looking, and a rifle being aimed), the end result, the direction of aim, is determined by a complex chain of rotations in a hierarchy. Although each individual rotation is being correctly interpolated, the way in which rotations and translations accumulate means that the final direction of aim is not going to be precisely correct. For a person looking in a certain direction, this small imprecision is perfectly acceptable as long as the eyeballs are pointed in the correct direction using a simple single-bone IK. It is in fact extremely rare for people to turn their heads to look precisely at something, since they typically move their head in the right general direction and move their eyeballs to zero in on the target.

However, in the case of the rifleman, such remedial action is trickier. The rifle will not point in the correct direction simply from the blending, and this deviation can be fairly visible. If the rifleman is firing directly at the player, the error in the aiming of the rifle barrel will be quite obvious, and the player may feel quite aggrieved to be hurt by a bullet apparently fired at the ground to his left.

The second problem is that the case of the rifleman involves a "loop" of bone dependencies, where each bone must precisely join the next. The loop in this case goes from the shoulders, down one arm to the hand, through the hand to the rifle it holds, to the other hand holding the rifle, back up the arm, and to the shoulder again.

This loop must remain unbroken as the rifle is moved around (hands should not slide along the weapon or wobble in space). However, animation systems only deal with nonlooping schemes such as the tree of bones in the standard skeletal arrangement. The way to fix this is to break the loop somewhere (usually between one of the hands and the rifle—typically the hand that rests on the barrel rather than the one holding the trigger grip), blend the animations as needed, and then rejoin the loop using IK to move the hand to the correct position. Fortunately, the errors are usually small, and using two-bone IK to place the wrist in the correct position and then single-bone IK to keep the hand in the correct direction is usually extremely effective.

To solve the first problem of the incorrect aim, we could do the same trick with the rifle as with the eyes—simply rotate the rifle to the correct direction. However, this will definitely mean that neither hand will automatically follow properly. Thus, we need to also IK the hands to the rifle as a secondary step. As previously, both arms perform a two-bone IK to place the wrists, and then a single-bone IK to orient the hands correctly.

The trouble with all this is that it is quite expensive, and we are overriding artist-created shape with machine-created shape using the individual IK fix ups. Unfortunately, this can only be done to a limited extent before the result starts to look poor. In this case, a small change in the rifle orientation can cause quite a large change in hand position (because the rifle is quite long), so the IK must work harder. Even if the IK works perfectly, the result can look quite unnatural, with the arms in cramped or over-extended positions that a real rifleman would never use.

A better solution would be to find the correct blend weights that result in the rifle pointing in the correct direction, and do as little remedial IK as possible. One method is to gradually iterate closer. First, guess some blend weights, perform the blend, see where the rifle ended up, measure the error, adjust the blend weights, and so on until the correct result is reached. This is quite effective, but the iteration is of course quite expensive. One way around this is to only perform one iteration per frame, so that the rifle approaches the ideal over time (this is in fact how our brains do the same thing), but in some cases the lag is undesirable.

Another clever trick is to do some precomputation to find where certain blend values will put the rifle, and to use this at runtime to fine-tune the first guess of the blend weights. This is well documented in a paper by Kovar and Gleicher [Kovar04], and is effective as long as the precomputation step is feasible. If the combinations of blends are hard to know ahead of time (e.g., if the soldier must also move from a stand to a crouch, will have a variety of differently shaped rifles, or if the operation must be performed on a wide variety of soldiers, all of different shapes and sizes), the number of combinations required in the precomputation phase is hard to compute and store.

A similar blending technique can be used for animations rather than static poses, and using more abstract variables than simply direction. A common example is walk cycles that must cope with uneven terrain. The animator creates three walk cycles: walking on the flat, walking up a slope, and walking down a slope. Then, when playing the walk cycles, measure the slope that the person is currently walking on, and use it to interpolate in the same way between the three walk cycles. The three walk cycles must be the same duration and their local times kept in sync, or else the footsteps will not be in phase.

Attachments

Frequently, animated characters carry objects. The most common example in games is, of course, a weapon. In some cases, the weapon is a separate object that is drawn separately from the character, and is moved each frame so that it is in the character's hands. In other cases, the weapon mesh is part of the character's mesh, or rather, there are two character meshes (one with weapon drawn, one without), and the appropriate one is chosen. However, if the character drops its weapon (e.g., because it is changing weapons, or because another character has just shot it dead), the game will switch instantly to the weaponless character mesh and place the weapon in the correct place. The weapon is then an autonomous object that will probably fall to the ground under gravity.

In either case, the game needs to know, for a certain pose, where the weapon needs to be placed. The obvious solution is make a bone in the character's skeleton that represents the weapon's root bone. In the case of the mesh that is both character and weapon in one, this bone is used to deform the combined mesh. In the case of separate character and weapon meshes, the bone will not be used by the mesh deformation routines, but its world-space transform will be used to set the root transform of the weapon mesh. As far as the animator is concerned, it is animated just like any other bone, and the mesh for the weapon follows correctly.

The slightly more complex case occurs when an animated object is being carried, or indeed the character is hanging off something (such as an airplane wing, dangling from a rope ladder beneath a helicopter, or clinging to the top of a speeding car—things that a surprising number of game characters seem to do on a regular basis). The world-space transform of one of the character's hands is defined by the object to which it is clinging. Given this, and the animation pose that the character is currently in, we need the world-space transform of the character's root bone. Walk the hierarchy from the hand up to the root, starting with the identity transform and each time transforming by the inverse of the usual parent-to-child transform that is extracted when sampling animations (i.e., the child-to-parent transform). The resulting composite transformation maps from "hand-bone space" to "root-bone space." Feed in the transform of the object being clung to, and you have found the "root-bone space" transform—in other words, the world position of the character's root bone. Then, proceed as normal, traversing the skeleton back down the tree, and draw.

Collision Detection

In many games, collision detection does not interface with animation at all, except in as much as the game asks the animation how the root bone moves. In these cases, approximating objects by a bounding box, sphere, ellipsoid, or other simple object oriented the same way as the game instance's world-space transform is perfectly adequate.

However, some games require far more accurate collision detection. Some need a bounding object for each bone, and to know which bone was hit. Others need pixel-perfect collision and must know exactly where on the triangle of the animated mesh a certain collision took place.

The simple and foolproof way is to do all mesh deformation on the CPU each frame, and to use the same data for both rendering and collision detection. However, this has some large performance and practical problems. The first is that where available, it is usually better to let vertex-processing hardware deform meshes, since that is what it was designed to do. The second is that this intimately links the rendering rate with the game rate—the two must be synchronized; otherwise, the data from one cannot be reused by the other. As discussed elsewhere, this is generally a bad idea for many reasons. Finally, the data format for rendering is typically very different from that for collision detection. Collisions do not care what texture the surface uses, and the rendering does not care whether the object is made from paper or steel.

So, let us assume that the rendering is doing what it does elsewhere and just think about collision detection in the most efficient way. Note that for simplicity, we will consider only intersecting a single ray against the deformed mesh. Polygon/polygon collisions and swept-body collisions use similar principles, but become complex quite quickly, and are beyond the scope of this chapter.

The first step is to store a bounding volume (box, sphere, ellipsoid, etc.), one for each bone, that bounds the vertices influenced by that bone during deformation. The ray being tested then checks for intersection against each of these bounding volumes, either by transforming the bounding volume by the world-space transform of the bone, or by transforming the ray by the inverse of the same transform, and then performing the intersection. Which of the two is performed depends on which is quicker for the particular type of bounding volume used.

For each bone, we now know that if the ray hit the bounding volume, there is a chance that the ray hit the mesh itself, but also that it will only have hit the part of the mesh deformed by that bone. In fact, this is not strictly true, but given the topology of the vast majority of meshes used in games, it is close enough to the truth to be useful. We can now perform software deformation of only that part of the mesh that is influenced by the bones whose bounding volumes were intersected, and the resulting collision polygons tested against the ray. The optimization is that usually only a few bone volumes will be hit by any particular ray, which means the portion of mesh that must be deformed and tested is relatively small.

Summary

This chapter introduced the basic components of most animation systems. Animations are encoded using a variety of compression methods, primarily to reduce the memory footprint, but also to support playing and sampling them in real time, while blending them together in various ways. The overall motion of the animation is transferred from the animation system to the game's instance, so that the game logic can keep track of the animated figure. IK corrects the animation to ensure that contact with other objects in the world is maintained even when blending and distorting the original animations. The pose is then transformed to world space, and finally the mesh is deformed using the animated bone positions and rendered on the screen.

These principles are shared by almost all animation systems. However, a real game's animation system will have many higher level systems layered upon these principles that are specific to the game, which is a juggling act between the needs of the animators and the needs of the game design. This demands flexibility and can result in many different methods for performing the same operation. As long as these are constructed using components of a single, shared, low-level animation system, the complexity of the code can be kept manageable, even when blending multiple techniques together.

Exercises

1. The differences between slerp and nlerp are discussed in this chapter. Make a library that can use either for blending between two quaternions, and compare the speed and accuracy of the two for various different rotations.
2. The general algorithm for a two-bone inverse kinematics solver was presented. Work out the actual code from the description given. The two solu-

tions, corresponding to the knee bending either forward or backward, are the two roots of a quadratic equation.

3. Experiment with the various keyframe and curve methods detailed in this chapter. It is easiest to visualize if this is done in a two-dimensional environment, and the extension to three or more dimensions is simple. Remember to include motions with discontinuities in them, and check how well the chosen method copes with them.

4. Evaluate a variety of nonuniform curve types and try placing single and multiple knots to see the effects. Try to re-create the same target shapes with different degrees of curve. It may be simpler to evaluate a quadratic curve than a cubic curve, but it may also require more control points to represent a given target shape. Find out the rough trade-offs between speed and storage space requirements.

5. As discussed, animations may be compressed by encoding them as curves rather than keyframes. Additionally, the control points of the curves may be quantized. For example, animation quaternions are always of length one, meaning that they do not need to be stored using four full 32-bit floating-point numbers. Try quantizing to a variety of fixed-point representations and see how few bits can be used while still obtaining acceptable results.

References

[Blow04] Blow, Jon, "Understanding Slerp, Then Not Using It," *Game Developer Magazine*, April 2004, available at *http://number-none.com/product/*.

[Cohen00] Cohen, Michael F.; Rose III, Charles F.; and Sloan, Peter-Pike, "Shape and Animation by Example," *Technical Report*, Microsoft Research, July 2000, available at *ftp://ftp.research.microsoft.com/pub/tr/tr-2000-79.pdf*.

[Kovar04] Kovar, Lucas, and Gleicher, Michael, "Automated Extraction and Parameterization of Motions in Large Data Sets," *Transactions on Graphics, 23, 3*, SIGGRAPH 2004, available at *www.cs.wisc.edu/graphics/Gallery/Kovar/ParamMotion/*.

[Lengyel04] Lengyel, Eric, *Mathematics for 3D Game Programming & Computer Graphics*, 2nd ed., Charles River Media, 2004.

[Svarovsky00] Svarovsky, Jan, "Quaternions for Game Programming," *Game Programming Gems*, Charles River Media, 2000.

5.3 ▪ Artificial Intelligence: Agents, Architecture, and Techniques

In This Chapter

- ▪ Overview
- ▪ AI for Games
- ▪ Game Agents
- ▪ Finite-state Machines
- ▪ Common AI Techniques
- ▪ Promising AI Techniques
- ▪ Summary
- ▪ Exercises
- ▪ References

Overview

In many video games, the quality of the experience depends on whether the game presents a good challenge to the player. One way to present a good challenge is to offer computer opponents, or sometimes even allies, that are capable of intelligently playing the game. In most cases, this is not a trivial problem to solve, but fortunately, there is an entire field of study that can help us out—*artificial intelligence* (or AI for short).

AI describes the intelligence embodied in any manufactured device. If we design a character or opponent in a video game that acts on its own, it is generally accredited with possessing AI.

Human-level AI is the stuff of dreams and science fiction. How do you take the accumulated common sense and expertise of a human and distill it into a computer?

Unfortunately, this problem is currently unsolved and it will likely be decades before we get close to understanding what it truly entails. Since general human-level intelligence is currently impossible to re-create, researchers chip away from dozens of different angles by solving much simpler problems. By sufficiently narrowing down the domain of an AI problem, it becomes possible to create behavior that is reasonable and believable, especially in the realm of video games.

This chapter first discusses the unique properties of game AI, and how it differs from other AI fields. With believable characters being the centerpiece of most game AI, the next section introduces the concept of a game agent. Game agents perceive the world, react in intelligent ways, and potentially adapt to the player. As the most widely used architecture for game AI, various flavors of finite-state machines are then examined and compared. The chapter finishes with a survey of the most common and promising techniques in game AI today. Intelligent movement for game agents is covered in-depth in Chapter 5.4, "Artificial Intelligence: Pathfinding."

AI for Games

Video game AI is very distinct from most other AI applications, such as military defense, robotics, or data mining. The core distinction is in terms of goals. The goal of an AI programmer is to create both entertaining and challenging opponents while shipping the product on time. These goals have the following five implications:

1. The AI must be intelligent, yet purposely flawed.
   - Opponents must present a challenge.
   - Opponents must keep the game entertaining and fun.
   - Opponents must lose to the player in a challenging and fun manner.
2. The AI must have no unintended weaknesses.
   - There must be no "golden paths" to defeating the AI every time in the same way.
   - The AI must not fail miserably or look dumb.
3. The AI must perform within the CPU and memory constraints of the game.
   - Most games are real time and must have their AIs react in real time.
   - Game AI seldom receives more than 10 to 20 percent of the frame time.
4. The AI must be configurable by game designers/players.
   - Designers must be able to adjust the difficulty level and adjust the AI.
   - If the game is extensible, players can tweak or customize the AI.
5. The AI must not stop the game from shipping.
   - The AI techniques employed must not put the game at risk.
   - Experimental techniques must be proved early in the development cycle during preproduction.
   - If the AI is given latitude to evolve or change, it must be testable to guarantee that it doesn't deteriorate when released to millions of consumers.

These requirements color a game developer's perception of the field of AI. An important distinction is that game AI doesn't need to solve a problem perfectly, only to the satisfaction of the player. For example, in pathfinding, the AI might need to calculate a path across a crowded room. Search algorithms exist to find the absolute shortest or cheapest path, but perfection is generally not a requirement for games. By relaxing the standards for many problems, shortcuts can be taken that make the problem tractable in real time or result in large computational savings.

Another consequence of game-specific AI is that the AI has access to perfect knowledge. For example, a given opponent doesn't need to sense the world the way a physical robot would need to. The game world is wholly inside the computer and the AI has the luxury of performing its analysis on these completely accurate representations. Much of robotics research concentrates on the problems of vision recognition and mechanical movement, both of which are rightfully ignored in games.

When designing game AI, considerable thought must be put into making the AI configurable by the game designers. Rather than making a perfect autonomous character or adversarial opponent, the goal is to make a highly customizable AI that can be adjusted for difficulty and individual attributes such as aggressiveness or accuracy. By creating a slightly more general AI that can be adjusted, the game can be balanced and tuned by game design experts to ensure that the game is enjoyable and fun.

Finally, an important consideration is that the product must ship on time. Experimental AI techniques are exciting and intriguing, but they have the potential to put the project unnecessarily at risk. Therefore, new AI techniques must be proven early in the development cycle. The promise that it will all come together three months before shipping is simply not acceptable.

Specialization

The last decade has seen a dramatic specialization of disciplines within game development. One of the more notable positions to fall out of this specialization is the role of the artificial intelligence developer. Once considered a side duty of general game programmers, AI has become complicated enough to warrant a deep understanding of the dozens of current and potential techniques. Even more interestingly, the skills of an AI programmer must vary dramatically between game genres. While strategy games require careful battlefield analysis and strategic planning, first-person shooter games require one-on-one tactical analysis and intelligent movement at the level of individual footsteps. There is no one-size-fits-all solution to game AI, which reinforces the tremendous specialization that takes place within this discipline.

Real-time strategy (RTS) games are perhaps the most demanding for an AI programmer, with current AAA titles typically requiring as many as three full-time AI developers. However, other titles like racing games, street fighting, or puzzle games might only need a part-time programmer for AI. Additionally, many companies are scripting more and more of their AI, which tends to push some of the AI work toward level designers.

Game Agents

With a firm grasp on the goals and purpose of game AI, let's now turn our attention to the *game agent*. In most games, the purpose of AI is to create an intelligent agent, sometimes referred to as a *nonplayer character* (NPC). This agent acts as an opponent, an ally, or as a neutral entity in the game world. Since the majority of game AI focuses around the agent, it is very helpful to study game AI from this perspective.

An agent has three key steps through which it continually loops. The steps are commonly known as the *sense-think-act* cycle. In addition to these three steps, there is an optional learning or remembering step that may also take place at the end of this loop. In practice, most game agents do not take this extra step, but this is slowly changing because of the added challenge and replayability that is leveraged as a result.

Sensing

The game agent must have information about the current state of the world to make good decisions and to act on those decisions. Since the game world is represented entirely inside the program, perfect information about the state of the world is always available. This means that there is no uncertainty about the world. The world offers accurate information to the game agent about the existence, location, and state of every opponent, barrier, or object. Unfortunately, while all of this rich information exists, it may be expensive or difficult to tease out useful and pertinent information.

At any time, the game agent can query the game world representation to locate the player or other enemies, but most players would consider this cheating. Therefore, it is necessary to endow the game agent with certain limitations in terms of what it can sense. For example, it might seem obvious, but game agents should typically not be able to see through walls.

Game agents are usually given human limitations. They are restricted to knowing only about events or entities they have seen, heard, or perhaps were told about by other agents. Therefore, it is necessary to create models for how an agent should be able to see into the world, hear the world, and communicate with other agents.

Vision

When modeling agent vision, it is important that the game engine provide fast methods for determining the visibility of objects. While game AI typically isn't very CPU intensive, visibility testing can be enormously expensive. Therefore, it is often limited to particular agents and performed only on a periodic basis.

In 3D games, vision usually starts with obtaining a list of pertinent game objects. For example, the agent might ask for a list of all enemies. Since agents are not concerned with most game objects that populate a world, it would be wasteful to consider every object in the game database. Once this pared-down list is constructed, a vector from the game agent to each game object is calculated. This toObject vector is then processed in the following ways to determine if the agent can see the game object. The order of these steps is important to minimize processing.

1. **Is the object within the viewing distance of the agent?**   Check that the magnitude of the vector is less than or equal to the maximum viewing distance. Note that it is computationally faster to compare the distance squared, since that eliminates having to perform a square root operation.
2. **Is the object within the viewing angle of the agent?**   Use a simple dot product between the toObject vector and the agent's forward vector to determine if the game object is within the agent's viewing angle. For example, if the dot product of the two normalized vectors is greater than or equal to 0.5, the object is located within an agent's 120-degree viewing angle.
3. **Is the object unobscured by the environment?**   The ray defined by the agent's position and the toObject vector must be tested against the environment. This test is expensive, so it is purposely performed after all other tests.

The preceding three steps are a reasonable approximation of human vision. However, the unobstructed test is rather coarse and will not detect if just a portion of an object is visible. This can be improved by testing if the extents of the agent's bounding volume can be seen. However, this added accuracy comes at a high cost since multiple ray casting tests will need to be performed.

Depending on the game, it might be advantageous to model vision that is more sensitive to movement. As most people have experienced, it's easier to see a moving object than a perfectly still object. Of course, this effect is related to how distant the object is, since close stationary objects are easier to see than distant ones. Movement sensitive vision can be modeled by ignoring stationary objects that are beyond a particular threshold distance, or by varying the recognition reaction time of stationary objects based on their distance.

Beyond visually sensing the simple existence of objects, many more aspects of the environment might be of interest. For example, it may be important to recognize hiding spots or high-risk areas that should be avoided. This advanced recognition about the topology of the world is critical for particular games such as first-person shooters. The existence of these interesting spots can be flagged by hand, or algorithms can be devised to discover them from the world representation [Lidén02, Tozour03b]. Once these areas of interest are marked, an agent should be able to sense them like any other object.

Truly understanding the topology of the world is so important for some games that Criterion, a middleware company, advertises a dynamic solution as one of their core technologies in their *RenderWare A.I.* product. Included on the companion CD-ROM are four *RenderWare A.I.* demos that illustrate their 3D Topology Dynamic Analyzer technology. These demos are quite fun to play with, so don't miss exploring this aspect of agent sensing.

Hearing

An interesting twist on agent awareness is to allow an agent to sense through hearing. For example, if the player tip-toes past a sleeping enemy, the enemy might not notice. However if the player runs past the same enemy, the enemy might hear the noise and wake up. Similarly, if the player starts wildly firing his gun, agents that can't see the player might rush to the scene because they heard the gunfire coming from that location.

Hearing is most commonly modeled through event-driven notifications. For example, if the player performs an action that makes a noise, the game will compute where that noise might travel to and inform any agents within that range. Rather than performing elaborate sound reflection calculations against the environment, this is usually accomplished through a simple distance calculation coupled with bounding areas. If a sound emanates inside area B and can be heard up to 10 meters away, all agents inside area B and within 10 meters are notified. This eliminates any computationally expensive sound modeling. See Chapter 5.5, "Audio Programming," for more details related to sound propagation.

Communication

Many types of agents are expected to communicate with each other, so it may be important to model the transfer of sensed knowledge between agents. Take, for example, guards. If a guard saw the player in a sensitive area, the guard could run away and alert others. The other guards can then use this information to make better decisions themselves, such as deciding to hunt down the player together, starting with the player's last known location.

Similar to the mechanism of hearing, information from communication will be event-driven in the form of notifications. When an agent has useful information and comes within a certain distance of other agents, the information will be sent directly to the other agents.

Reaction Times

When sensing the environment, it is important to build in artificial reaction times. Agents should not be able to see, hear, or communicate instantaneously. For example, it would look decidedly wrong to witness a guard take off running at the same instant the alarm is sounded.

Since agents do sense the world instantaneously, simple timers can be used to simulate reaction times. Typical reaction times for seeing and hearing might be on the order of a quarter to half a second. Communication reaction times would be longer to model speaking or gesturing between agents.

Thinking

Once an agent has gathered information about the world through its senses, the information can be evaluated and a decision can be made. This thinking step is the crux of what most people consider true AI, and can be as simple or elaborate as required.

Generally, there are two main ways in which agents make decision in games. The first is for the agent to rely on precoded expert knowledge, typically handcrafted through if-then rules, with randomness introduced to make agents less predictable. The second is for the agent to use a search algorithm to find a near-optimal solution.

Expert Knowledge

Many techniques exist for encoding expert knowledge. These include finite-state machines, production systems, decision trees, and even logical inference. By far, the most popular technique is the finite-state machine, to which a subsequent section is dedicated.

Encoding expert knowledge is appealing because it is simple and comes naturally to most people. It is quick and easy to write a series of if-then statements that ask "just the right questions," in order to make a good decision. For example, consider the rule, "If you see an enemy that is weaker than you, attack the enemy; otherwise, run away and get backup support." This simple rule embodies a great deal of common sense about knowing when to pick a fight. By accumulating knowledge in the form of if-then rules, elaborate decision-making processes can be modeled.

While expert knowledge can create a formidable AI, it is not a scalable solution. As the number of rules mounts, the system becomes brittle and bugs must be patched with more rules, which only exacerbate the inherent weakness in the system. Since expert knowledge is not a complete solution, it relies on game testers to uncover bugs so they can be repaired before the game ships. Since most agents only solve very narrow problem domains, limited expert knowledge is usually sufficient and the scalability problems generally aren't enough to cripple the technique.

Search

Search is another commonly used technique for making intelligent decisions. Search employs a search algorithm to discover a sequence of steps (a plan) that will lead to a solution or ideal state. Given possible moves and rules that govern moves, it is possible for an algorithm to explore the search space and find an optimal or near-optimal solution, if one exists.

In games, the most common use of search is in planning where the agent should move next. Game agent navigation is a tough problem that requires a great deal of programming effort in many games. As a result, a thorough discussion of pathfinding issues using search is detailed in Chapter 5.4.

Machine Learning

If imparting an agent with expert knowledge is not possible and search cannot efficiently tackle the problem, it is possible to use machine learning to discover systems for making good decisions. Potential machine learning algorithms include reinforcement learning, neural networks, and decision trees. These techniques show promise, but in practice they are almost entirely ignored by game developers. This may be due to their complexity, CPU requirements, effect on development time, the inexperience of developers, or simply the technique's inability to outperform various forms of expert systems.

Flip-Flopping

When decisions are made, there must be a mechanism to maintain that decision over some reasonable time period. If a decision is reevaluated every frame, it might flip-flop between two states and the agent will be paralyzed in a moment of indecisiveness.

Since agents should have reaction times built into their sensing and thinking, this should never happen at the scale of individual frames. However, flip-flopping might still occur every half-second and needs to be guarded against.

Acting

Until now, the game agent's sensing and thinking steps have been invisible to the player. Only in the acting step is the player able to witness the agent's intelligence. Therefore, this is a very important step in having the agent carry out its chosen decisions, and communicating its decisions to the player (if that enhances the game and the player's perception of the agent). In other words, if the agent is brilliant, and the player never realizes it, the effort making the agent intelligent was clearly wasted.

Depending on the game, there are numerous agent actions. Some common ones are to change locations, play an animation, play a sound effect, pick up an item, converse with the player, and fire a weapon. The adeptness and subtlety with which the agent carries out these actions will impact the player's opinion of the agent's intelligence. This places an enormous burden on the variety and aesthetic quality of the animations, sound effects, and dialogue created for the agent. In a very real sense, the agent can only express its intelligence in terms of the vocabulary afforded by these art assets.

In the early days of games, agents had very few animations with which to contend. Once 3D games emerged, the agent's repertoire expanded from several dozen animations to hundreds and thousands. This complexity resulted in a need to cope in a scalable manner with animation selection. Best practices in this area have moved the animation selection problem out of the code and directly into the hands of artists and game designers through data-driven design [Hargrove03a, Hargrove03b, Orkin02b].

As previously mentioned, the player is oblivious to any work the agent does during the sensing-thinking steps unless it is revealed during the acting step. Therefore, it is important to convey the hidden work to the player if it enhances gameplay. For example, if the agent has concluded that it's going to inevitably die in the near future, there might be nothing the agent can do to avoid this outcome. However, if the agent just sits there and dies, the agent will look dumb. A more entertaining outcome would be for the agent to use that information to either cower or shout "Oh no!" as it is about to die. This way, the players don't see a dumb agent getting killed—they instead see a smart agent who comprehends the situation. So, even though the outcome is the same, the agent and the game are greatly enhanced by exposing the intelligence.

Learning and Remembering

Learning and remembering together form an optional fourth step to the sense-think-act cycle. Without it, the agent will never get better, will never adapt to a particular player, and will never benefit from past events or information it witnessed or was told.

Interestingly, learning and remembering aren't necessarily important in many games, simply because agents might not live long enough to benefit from anything they might have learned. However, in games in which the agent is persistent for longer than 30 seconds, a significant advantage can exist when learning and remembering is incorporated.

For game agents, learning is the process of remembering specific outcomes and using them to generalize and predict future outcomes. Most commonly, this can be modeled with a statistical approach. By gathering statistics about past events or outcomes, future decisions can leverage these probabilities. For example, if 80 percent of the time the player attacks from the left, the AI would be smart to expect and prepare for this likely event. Thus, the AI has adapted to the player's behavior.

Remembering can be as simple as noting the last place the player was seen to use that information during the think cycle. By keeping some bookkeeping information on observed states, objects, or players, the agent can leverage past observances at a later date. In order to not accumulate too much knowledge, these memories can fade with time depending on how important they are. Memory fading can be a way to model selective memory and forgetfulness.

It is important to note that past knowledge doesn't always need to be stored in the agent. Some types of knowledge can be stored directly in the world's data structures (this is related to smart terrain, as discussed later). For example, if agents consistently get slaughtered in a particular place, that area can be marked as more dangerous. You could almost conceptualize this as the smell of death in a particular spot. During the think cycle, path planning and tactical decisions can consider this information and prefer to avoid the area.

Making Agents Stupid

In many cases, it is actually very easy to create agents that will dominate and destroy the player. Simply make the agents faster, stronger, have more resources, or more accurate with their firing. Of course, that's not really the point of game AI. The point is generally to lose to the player in a fun and challenging way.

Dumbing down an agent can be accomplished by making it less accurate when shooting, having longer reaction times, engaging the player only one at a time, and unnecessarily making itself more vulnerable by changing positions often. These simple steps will bring agents down a notch and give the player ample time and opportunity to defeat them.

Agent Cheating

While agents can be made superior by making them faster, stronger, or omniscient, in many situations players consider this cheating. Ideally, agents don't need to cheat to make intelligent decisions or to represent a challenge, but there are situations in which it can be the best route to go. For example, in a real-time strategy game, it is often necessary to make the opponents cheat at the highest difficulty levels to provide a supreme challenge to the player. However, it is advisable to let the player know so he will not feel resentful of the AI. That way, the player is making an informed decision to play against an AI that has an unfair advantage.

The primary lesson with cheating is to be upfront with the players and never let them catch you cheating. If the players suspect that the AI is cheating, they will feel less compelled to continue playing, and it can ultimately hurt the success of the game.

Summary of Game Agents

The sense-think-act cycle of game agents is a simple conceptual framework for organizing intelligent behavior. It isn't intelligent in and of itself, but it provides a good foundation for creating intelligent and believable agent behavior. It's a guide that helps the programmer conceptualize what an agent needs to know and consider before the agent acts in the world. As we will see in subsequent sections, many more techniques need to be employed to achieve intelligent AI.

Finite-State Machines

Within game AI, it is generally recognized that *finite-state machines* (FSMs) are the most common software pattern. This kind of popularity doesn't happen by accident. Rather, FSMs are widely used because they possess some amazing qualities. They are simple to program, easy to comprehend, easy to debug, and completely general to any problem. They might not always provide the best solution, but they consistently get the job done with minimal risk to the project.

However, FSMs have a darker side as well. Many programmers look at them with distrust since they tend to be constructed ad hoc with no consistent structure. They also tend to grow uncontrollably as the development cycle churns on. This poor structure, coupled with unbounded growth, makes many FSM implementations difficult to maintain.

Yet with all of their warts, FSMs are still the most compelling way to structure most game AI implementations.

The Basic Finite-State Machine

Formally, a finite-state machine is an abstract model of computation that consists of a set of states, a starting state, an input vocabulary, and a transition function that maps inputs and current states to a next state. Computation begins with the starting state and transitions to new states as inputs are received. The FSM can perform work within a given state, known as a *Moore machine*, or on the transitions between states, known as a *Mealy machine*.

Game developers deviate from the strict FSM definition in many different ways. First, the states themselves are used to define behaviors that contain code specific to that state. For example, states can be behaviors such as wander, attack, or flee. Second, the single transition function is typically divided among the states so that each state knows exactly what will cause its transition to another state, which helps keep the relation between states and transitions easy to understand. Third, the line between Moore and Mealy machines is blurred, as work is often performed both inside of a state and during transitions. Fourth, leveraging probability and randomness is extremely common when transitioning to a new state. For example, after being attacked, an agent might have a 10 percent chance of transitioning to the flee state. Fifth, extra state information not directly represented in the FSM, such as agent health, is often used as a deciding factor for some state transitions.

Since FSMs can elegantly capture the mental states or behaviors of an agent, they are a natural choice for defining character AI. Figure 5.3.1 demonstrates how an agent's behavioral FSM might be diagrammed using UML (Unified Modeling Language).

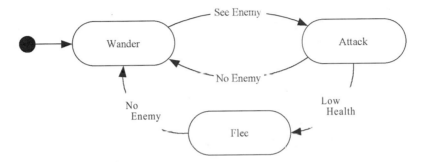

FIGURE 5.3.1 *An example of diagramming an agent's behavioral FSM in UML. The black dot points to the starting state.*

Defining an FSM

Having covered the basics, the next issue is how to define an FSM in the game. There are several different methods. The simplest and most straightforward approach is to directly code the FSM in the game's source language. Listing 5.3.1 shows an FSM defined in C/C++ using the `switch` statement construct. This is perhaps the simplest implementation of a finite-state machine.

Listing 5.3.1 An FSM coded directly in C/C++

```
void RunLogic( int * state )
{
    switch( *state )
    {
        case 0:  //Wander
            Wander();
            if( SeeEnemy() )     { *state = 1; }
            break;

        case 1:  //Attack
            Attack();
            if( LowOnHealth() ) { *state = 2; }
```

```
                            if( NoEnemy() )      { *state = 0; }
                            break;

                    case 2:  //Flee
                        Flee();
                        if( NoEnemy() )      { *state = 0; }
                        break;
                }
        }
```

The FSM in Listing 5.3.1 consists of three states and four transitions, identical to the diagram in Figure 5.3.1. Presumably, RunLogic is called each frame during the game while the agent is alive. Depending on the agent's current state, a single action will be carried out on that frame. After each action executes, potential transitions to new states are checked and possibly taken. The logic is simple and easy to understand. Debugging is also quite trivial with this implementation.

Unfortunately, there are several problems with this simple switch statement structure:

- The code is ad hoc, in that the language doesn't enforce the structure. There is nothing preventing another programmer from adding catch-all code outside the switch statement that further modifies states or executes actions.
- All transitions result from polling, which can be inefficient. In practice, it is better to be able to transition to a different state when an event occurs, such as being attacked by an enemy, rather than checking every frame if an enemy has attacked.
- There is no easy way to know that a state was entered for the first time. For example, upon entering the attack state, the agent might need to unsheathe his sword. One solution is to create a "preattack" state that prepares the sword and then immediately transitions to the proper attack state, but this can lead to an explosion of states that complicates the structure.
- The FSM is defined directly in the code and can't be specified by game designers. If the FSM is data-driven outside of the game code, the possibility for more parallel work exists, which might be important for larger games.

An alternative to directly hard coding an FSM in the game's source language is to create a scripting language that encapsulates the best features of an FSM and enforces a consistent structure. Such a scripting language might resemble Listing 5.3.2.

Listing 5.3.2   A fictional FSM scripting language that abstracts and enforces a consistent structure

```
AgentFSM
{
    DeclareState( STATE_Wander )
        OnUpdate
            Execute( Wander )
```

```
            if( SeeEnemy )
                ChangeState( STATE_Attack )
        OnEvent( AttackedByEnemy )
            ChangeState( Attack )

    DeclareState( STATE_Attack )
        OnEnter
            Execute( PrepareWeapon )
        OnUpdate
            Execute( Attack )
            if( LowOnHealth )
                ChangeState( STATE_Flee )
            if( NoEnemy )
                ChangeState( STATE_Wander )
        OnExit
            Execute( StoreWeapon )

    DeclareState( STATE_Flee )
        OnUpdate
            Execute( Flee )
            if( NoEnemy )
                ChangeState( STATE_Wander )
}
```

The fictional FSM scripting language in Listing 5.3.2 demonstrates several improvements over the hard-coded version:

- The structure of the FSM is enforced by what will be accepted by the script compiler.
- Events can be handled (via the OnEvent convention), as well as polling.
- When a state is entered for the first time, the OnEnter construct can be used to execute any special initialization. Conversely, there is an OnExit construct to carry out any cleanup code, regardless of what triggered the transition. The OnExit construct makes the script more explicit and reduces redundant code.
- A scripted, data-driven FSM can be specified by game designers and artists who are not familiar with traditional programming languages.

The Execute and if constructs indicate that a particular function should be called by the specified name. This requires the name within the parentheses to be bound to an actual function name in the game code. In the case of the if statement, the function will return a Boolean so that the script knows whether to execute the next statement. Note that this particular scripting language lacks curly brackets and semicolons, which is simply a language design choice.

Unfortunately, it is not trivial to create an FSM scripting language, and the decision to implement one should not be taken lightly. Typically, it can require several months of engineering work to design and implement the language. A custom compiler must be written that converts the scripted FSM into bytecode that can be interpreted "on the fly" by the game engine during runtime. This presents several problems in terms of usability and debugging, since compile-time errors in the script must be reported back by the custom compiler, and debugging the scripts during runtime will require extensive hooks and support. Unsurprisingly, it is not uncommon for a custom scripting language within a game company to be despised and hated by the people who must work with it on a daily basis. After all, it is extremely difficult and time consuming to create tools that approach the polish and robustness of commercial compilers and debuggers.

Since the difficulty is in the tools, at least one middleware company now offers FSM solutions that assist with creation (using visual diagramming) and debugging. However, since FSMs are trivial to implement directly in code and many companies already have proprietary scripting languages, it can be difficult to convince game developers that they can benefit from these outside solutions.

One possible solution to the dilemma is to develop a hybrid approach. Included on the companion CD-ROM is a "State Machine Language" that is implemented completely in C++. Through the use of several C-style macros and an FSM class, it is possible to achieve the abstraction and structure of many scriptable FSM languages. By existing entirely in the game's source language, namely C++, all of the compiling and debugging problems of scripting languages fall away. Listing 5.3.3 shows an example of the C++ State Machine Language.

Listing 5.3.3   A hybrid approach of coding an FSM directly in C++ using a supporting FSM class and C-Style macros

```cpp
bool AgentFSM::States( StateMachineEvent event,
                       MSG_Object * msg,
                       int state, int substate )
{
    DeclareState( STATE_Wander )
        OnUpdate
            Wander();
            if( SeeEnemy() )
                ChangeState( STATE_Attack );
        OnMsg( MSG_Attacked )
            ChangeState( Attack )

    DeclareState( STATE_Attack )
        OnEnter
            PrepareWeapon();
        OnUpdate
            Attack();
            if( LowOnHealth() )
                ChangeState( STATE_Flee );
            if( NoEnemy() )
                ChangeState( STATE_Wander );
        OnExit
            StoreWeapon();

    DeclareState( STATE_Flee )
        OnUpdate
            Flee();
```

```
             if( NoEnemy )
                  ChangeState( STATE_Wander );
}
```

The C++ state machine language example in Listing 5.3.3 conceals a great deal of functionality. However, the primary point is that the structure promotes a consistent format, good readability, and straightforward debugging. It supports the OnEnter and OnExit concepts, and event-driven triggers in the form of messages that get pumped into the state machine (captured by the OnMsg construct). What isn't supported is defining the FSM in a way that designers or artists can author it from outside the source code. However, this is the tradeoff to avoid creating tools and instead leverage the existing compiler and debugger.

Extending the Basic FSM

So far, we have seen several ways to extend the basic FSM. These include extending states to offer *OnEnter/OnExit* blocks and allowing event notifications to trigger transitions. As mentioned earlier, it's common to allow randomness and probability to influence transitions, and it's also common to refer to additional state information, such as health, when making state transition decisions.

Beyond these, there are several other important ways that FSMs can be extended. First, FSMs can have a stack-based history that tracks past states. As transitions are followed, states are pushed on and popped off the history stack. This is extremely useful if the agent becomes interrupted and later needs to return to a previous state. For example, if an agent was repairing a building (repair state), but subsequently got caught up in a firefight (attack state), once the fight is over, the attack state can pop itself off the stack and the FSM would return to the repair state. Therefore, once a state completes, it can choose to resume the last behavior without having to reexamine the situation.

A related stack-based extension is to allow a state to transition to a completely new FSM, pushing it onto an FSM stack. This results in a *hierarchical* FSM that can lead to better encapsulation of behaviors and tasks, thus keeping any one FSM from becoming too large and cumbersome [Houlette01]. Hierarchical FSMs can also reduce code duplication, since common subbehaviors can be referenced by many other FSMs.

Similar to hierarchical FSMs, a single FSM can potentially have substates that exist within a given state. Depending on the situation, this can be an effective way to break down behavior without resorting to a completely new FSM for just a couple of related states.

Multiple FSMs

So far, we have considered a single agent owning a single FSM, but there is no reason why an agent couldn't own several concurrently running FSMs. One model is to have an agent run both a "brain" FSM and a "movement" FSM. Another model is known as a *subsumption* architecture, where there are multiple levels of concurrently running FSMs [Brooks89]. The lowest level FSM takes care of rudimentary decisions such as obstacle avoidance, while the higher level FSMs focus on goal seeking and goal determination. A subsumption architecture remains robust because the lower levels must be satisfied before they allow the higher levels to influence the behavior.

Debugging FSMs

One of the chief benefits of working with FSMs is the ease with which they can be debugged. However, when there are dozens or hundreds of agents milling about, complex interactions can still be very difficult to debug. Therefore, it is prudent to build debugging facilities directly into your FSM architecture. At the very least, you should be able to log the states of each FSM over time. By capturing this data, particular logs can be examined after a bug has occurred and good clues will be available to help track down the cause.

Another way to facilitate debugging is to have agents display their current state above their heads. By being able to see the current state, you can quickly identify what each agent is "thinking," thus making it easy to visually spot errors. It might also help to display the last state as well so that it's clearer how the agent transitioned into the current state.

Summary of FSMs

Finite-state machines are general, simple, easy to understand, and easy to debug. They are much more useful than the formal definition might suggest, and can serve as the basis for almost any AI agent implementation. However, FSMs aren't capable of pathfinding, reasoning, or learning, so other techniques will most certainly have to be employed. Yet, it would be a mistake to not initially investigate whether FSMs could solve a portion of your AI needs.

Common AI Techniques

The following survey of common AI techniques is designed to provide an executive summary of the many tools that an AI programmer can wield. Since game AI is approached from so many diverse directions, a whirlwind tour of techniques is a good way to familiarize oneself with the diverse landscape of available solutions. The next section similarly provides a survey of promising AI techniques.

A* Pathfinding

A* pathfinding (pronounced A-star) is an algorithm for finding the cheapest path through an environment. Specifically, it is a directed search algorithm that exploits knowledge about the destination to intelligently guide the search. By doing so, the processing required to find a solution is minimized. Compared to other search algorithms, A* is the fastest at finding the absolute cheapest path. Note that if all movement has the same traversal cost, the cheapest path is also the shortest path.

Game Example

The environment must first be represented by a data structure that defines where movement is allowed [Tozour03a]. A path is requested by defining a start position and a goal position within that search space. When A* is run, it returns a list of points, like a trail of breadcrumbs, that defines the path. A character or vehicle can then use the points as guidelines to find its way to the goal.

A* can be optimized for speed [Cain02, Higgins02b, Rabin00a], for aesthetics [Rabin00b], and for general applicability to other tasks [Higgins02a]. Variations like D* attempt to make path replanning cheaper [Stentz94]. A* pathfinding is described in detail in Chapter 5.4.

Command Hierarchy

A *command hierarchy* is a strategy for dealing with AI decisions at different levels, from the general down to the foot soldier. Modeled after military hierarchies, the general directs the high-level strategy on the battlefield, while the foot soldier concentrates on individual combat. The levels in between deal with cooperation between various platoons and squads. The benefit of a command hierarchy is that decisions are separated at each level, thus making each decision more straightforward and abstracted from other levels [Kent03, Reynolds02].

Game Example

A command hierarchy is often used in real-time strategy or turn-based strategy games where there are typically three easily identifiable levels of decisions: overall strategy, squad tactics, and individual combat. A command hierarchy is also useful when a large number of agents must have an overall coherency.

Dead Reckoning

Dead reckoning is a method for predicting a player's future position based on that player's current position, velocity, and acceleration. This simple form of prediction works well since the movement of most objects resembles a straight line over short periods of time. More advanced forms of dead reckoning can also provide guidance for how far an object *could have moved* since it was last seen.

Game Example

In a first-person shooter (FPS) game, an effective method of controlling the difficulty level is to vary how accurate the computer is at "leading the target" when shooting projectiles. Since most weapons don't travel instantaneously, the computer must predict the future position of targets and aim the weapon at these predicted positions. Similarly, in a sports game, the computer player must anticipate the future positions of other players to effectively pass the ball or intercept a player [Laramée03, Stein02].

Emergent Behavior

Emergent behavior is behavior that wasn't explicitly programmed, but instead emerges from the interaction of several simpler behaviors. Many life forms use rather basic behavior that, when viewed as a whole, can be perceived as being much more sophisticated. In games, emergent behavior generally manifests itself as low-level simple rules that interact to create interesting and complex behaviors. Some examples of rules are seek food, seek similar creatures, avoid walls, and move toward the light. While any one rule isn't interesting by itself, unanticipated individual or group behavior can emerge from the interaction of these rules.

Game Example

Flocking is a classical example of emergent behavior in games, which results in realistic movement of flocks of birds or schools of fish [Reynolds87, Reynolds01]. Other emergent behaviors involving racecar applications and general-purpose creatures have been well documented [Darby03, Porcino03].

Flocking

Flocking is a technique for moving groups of creatures in a natural and organic manner. It works well at simulating flocks of birds and schools of fish. Each creature follows three simple movement rules that result in complex group behavior. It is said that this group behavior *emerges* from the individual rules (emergent behavior). Flocking is a form of artificial life that was popularized by Craig Reynolds' work [Reynolds87, Reynolds01].

The three classic flocking rules devised by Reynolds are:

- **Separation:**   Steer to avoid crowding local flock mates
- **Alignment:**   Steer toward the average heading of local flock mates
- **Cohesion:**   Steer toward the average position of local flock mates

Game Example

Games typically use flocking to control background creatures such as birds or fish. Since the path of any one creature is highly arbitrary, flocking is typically used for simple creatures that tend to wander with no particular destination. The result is that flocking techniques, as embodied by the three core rules, rarely get used for key enemies or creatures. However, the flocking rules have inspired several other movement algorithms, such as formations and swarming [Scutt02].

Formations

Formations are a group movement technique used to mimic military formations. Although it shares similarities to flocking, it is quite distinct in that each unit is guided toward a specific goal location and heading, based on its position in the formation [Dawson02].

Game Example

Formations can be used to organize the movement of ground troops, vehicles, or aircraft. Often, the formations must split or distort themselves to facilitate movement through tight areas. The game *Age of Empires 2: Age of Kings* pioneered several key techniques for formations [Pottinger99a, Pottinger99b].

Influence Mapping

An *influence map* is a method for viewing the distribution of power within a game world. Typically, it is a two-dimensional (2D) grid that is superimposed onto the landscape. Within each grid cell, units that lie in the cell are summed into a single number representing the combined influence of the units. It is assumed that each unit also has an influence into neighboring cells that falls off either linearly or exponentially with distance. The result is a 2D grid of numbers that gives insight into the location and influence of differing forces [Woodcock02].

Game Example

Influence maps can be used offensively to plan attacks; for example, by finding neutral routes to flank the enemy. They can also be used defensively to identify areas or positions that need to be strengthened. If one faction is represented by positive values and the other faction is represented by negative values within the same influence map, any grid cells near zero are either unowned territory or the "front" of the battle (where the influence of each side cancels each other out) [Tozour01].

There are also nonviolent uses for influence maps. For example, the *Sim City* series offers real-time maps that show the influence of police and fire departments placed around the city. The player can then use this information to place future buildings to fill in the gaps in coverage. The game also uses the same information to help simulate the world.

Level-of-Detail AI

Level-of-detail (LOD) is a common optimization technique in 3D graphics where polygonal detail is only used when it can be noticed and appreciated by the human viewer. Close-up models use large numbers of polygons, while faraway models use fewer polygons. This results in faster graphics processing since fewer polygons are rendered, yet there is no noticeable degradation in visual quality. The same concept can be applied to AI, where computations are performed only if the player will notice or appreciate the result [Brockington02a].

Game Example

One approach is to vary an agent's update frequency based on its proximity to the player. Another technique is to calculate paths only for agents that the player can see; otherwise, use straight-line path approximations and estimate off-screen movement. This technique becomes important when there are more than several dozen agents in a game and collectively they use too much processing power. This often occurs with RPG, RTS, strategy, and simulation games.

Manager Task Assignment

When a group of agents tries to independently choose tasks to accomplish, such as selecting a target in battle, the performance of the group can be rather dismal. Interestingly, the problem can be turned around so that instead of the individuals choosing tasks, a manager has a list of required tasks and assigns agents based on who is best suited for the job [Rabin98]. Note that this is very different from having the manager run through the list of individuals and assign tasks. Task assignment considers the tasks themselves first and uses them as the basis for prioritizing. This avoids duplication of tasks, and the best candidate for a task is always chosen. This type of tactical planning is more deliberate than the emergent coordination that can be achieved with a blackboard architecture. However, the resulting plan might not be as optimal as performing an exhaustive planning search [Orkin03a].

Game Example

In a baseball game with no runners on base, it might be determined that the first priority is to field the ball, the second priority is to cover first base, the third priority is to back up the person fielding the ball, and the fourth priority is to cover second base. The manager can organize who covers each priority by examining the best person for the job for a given situation. On a soft hit between first and second base, the manager might assign the first baseman to field the ball, the pitcher to cover first base, the second baseman to back up the first baseman fielding the ball, and the shortstop to cover second base, which is the correct play. Without a manager to organize the task assignment, it can be significantly harder to get coherent cooperation out of the players using other methods.

Obstacle Avoidance

A* pathfinding algorithms are good at getting a character from point to point through static terrain. However, often the character must avoid players, other characters, and vehicles that are moving rapidly through the environment. Characters must not get stuck on each other at choke points, and they must maintain enough spacing to maneuver when traveling in groups. *Obstacle avoidance* attempts to prevent these problems using trajectory prediction and layered steering behaviors [Reynolds99].

Game Example

In an FPS game, a group of four skeletons wants to attack the player, but must first cross a narrow bridge over a river. Each skeleton has received a route to the player through the navigation system. The skeleton closest to the bridge has a clear path across. The second skeleton predicts a collision with the first, but sees space to the right, which is still within the boundaries of the path across the bridge. The last two skeletons predict collisions with the first two, so they slow their rate of travel to correctly queue up behind the first two.

Scripting

Scripting is the technique of specifying a game's data or logic outside of the game's source language. Often, the scripting language is designed from scratch, but there is a growing movement toward using Python and Lua as alternatives. There is a complete spectrum for how far you can take the scripting concept.

Scripting influence spectrum:

- **Level 0:**   Hard code everything in the source language (C/C++)
- **Level 1:**   Data in files specify stats and locations of characters/objects.
- **Level 2:**   Scripted cut-scene sequences (noninteractive)
- **Level 3:**   Lightweight logic specified by tools or scripts, as in a trigger system
- **Level 4:**   Heavy logic in scripts that rely on core functions written in C/C++
- **Level 5:**   Everything coded in scripts—full alternative language to C/C++

Commercial games have been developed at all levels of this spectrum, with the oldest video games at level 0 and games such as the *Jak and Daxter* series at level 5 (with their GOAL language based on LISP). However, the middle levels are where most games have settled, since the two extremes represent increased risk, time commitment, and cost.

Game Example

Programmers must first integrate a scripting language into the game and determine the extent of its influence. The users of the scripting language will typically be artists and level designers. The written script will typically be compiled into byte code before actual gameplay and interpreted "on the fly" during gameplay.

The following are the advantages and disadvantages of scripting [Tozour02a].

Advantages of scripting:

- Game logic can be changed in scripts and tested without recompiling the code.
- Designers can be empowered without consuming programmer resources.
- Scripts can be exposed to the players to tinker with and expand (extensible AI).

Disadvantages of scripting:

- More difficult to debug.
- Nonprogrammers may be required to program.
- Time commitment and cost to create and support scripting language and complementary debugging tools.

State Machine

A *state machine* or *finite-state machine* (FSM) is a widely used software design pattern that has become a cornerstone of game AI. An FSM is defined by a set of states and transitions, with only one state active at any one time.

Game Example

In common practice, each state represents a behavior, such as `PatrolRoute`, within which an agent will perform a specific task. The state either polls or listens for events that will cause it to transition into other states. For example, a `PatrolRoute` state might check periodically if it sees an enemy. When this event happens, it transitions into the AttackEnemy state.

Stack-Based State Machine

A *stack-based state machine* is a technique and design pattern that often appears in game architectures. Sometimes referred to as *push-down automata*, the stack-based state machine can remember past actions by storing them on a stack. In a traditional state machine, past states are not remembered, since control flows from state to state with no recorded history. However, it can be useful in game AI to be able to transition back to a previous state, regardless of which state it was. This stack concept can be used to capture previous states, or even entire state machines [Tozour03c, Yiskis03a].

Game Example

In a game, this technique is important when a character is performing an action, becomes interrupted for a moment, and then wants to resume the original action. For example, in a real-time strategy game, a unit might be repairing a building when it gets attacked. The unit will transition into an attack behavior and might destroy the enemy. In this case, the conflict is over and the unit should resume its previous activity. If past behaviors are stored on a stack, the current attack behavior is simply popped from the stack and the unit will resume the repair behavior.

Subsumption Architecture

A *subsumption architecture* cleanly separates the behavior of a single character into concurrently running layers of FSMs. The lower layers take care of rudimentary behavior such as obstacle avoidance, and the higher layers take care of more elaborate behaviors such as goal determination and goal seeking. Because the lower layers have priority, the system remains robust and ensures that lower layer requirements are met before allowing higher level behaviors to influence them. The subsumption architecture was popularized by the work of Rodney Brooks [Brooks89].

Game Example

Subsumption architectures have been used in many games, including the *Oddworld* series of games, *Jedi Knight: Dark Forces 2*, and *Halo: Combat Evolved*. The architecture is ideally suited for character-based games where movement and sensing must coexist with decisions and high-level goals [Yiskis03b].

Terrain Analysis

Terrain analysis is the broad term given to analyzing the terrain of a game world to identify strategic locations.

Game Example

There are many strategic locations in a game that might be identified through terrain analysis, such as resources, choke points, or ambush points [Higgins02c]. These locations can then be used by the strategic-level AI to help plan maneuvers and attacks. Other uses for terrain analysis in a real-time strategy game include knowing where to build walls [Grimani03] or where to place the starting factions. In an FPS game, terrain analysis can assist the AI in discovering sniper points, cover points, or where to throw grenades from [Lidén02, Reed03, Tozour03b, van der Sterren00]. Terrain analysis can be viewed as the alternative approach to "hard coding" regions of interest in a level.

Trigger System

A *trigger system* is a highly specialized scripting system that allows simple if/then rules to be encapsulated within game objects or the world itself. It is a useful tool for level designers since the concept is extremely simple and robust. Often, it is exposed through a level design tool or a scripting language [Orkin02a, Rabin02].

Game Example

A designer might put a floor trigger in the middle of a room. When the player steps on the floor trigger (the condition), the designer might specify that a scary sound effect is played and a dozen snakes drop from the ceiling (the response). In this way, a trigger system is a simple way to specify scripted events without designing a complex scripting language. As an example, the level editor for *StarCraft* allowed users to define their own missions using a Windows-based trigger-system tool.

Promising AI Techniques

The previous section described many common techniques that are typically employed in current games. This next section examines techniques that show potential for the future. For some reason or another, each technique has found limited use or acceptance within the games industry. Some techniques are rather complicated or difficult to understand, some are not well known, and some solve niche problems and might never gain widespread use. Regardless, it is important to be aware of these promising techniques for games.

Bayesian Networks

Bayesian networks allow an AI to perform complex humanlike reasoning when faced with uncertainty. In a Bayesian network, variables relating to particular states, features, or events in the game world are represented as nodes in a graph, and the causal relationships between them as arcs. Probabilistic inference can then be performed on the graph to infer the values of unknown variables, or conduct other forms of reasoning [IDIS99].

Game Example

One particularly important application for Bayesian networks in games lies in modeling what an AI should believe about the human player based on the information it has available. For example, in a real-time strategy game, the AI can attempt to infer the existence or nonexistence of certain player-built units, like fighter planes or warships, based on what it has seen produced by the player so far. This keeps the AI from cheating and actually allows the human to deceive the AI by presenting misleading information, offering new gameplay possibilities and strategies for the player [Tozour02b].

Blackboard Architecture

A *blackboard architecture* is designed to solve a single complex problem by posting it on a shared communication space, called the *blackboard*. Expert objects then look at the blackboard and propose solutions. The solutions are given a relevance score, and the highest scoring solution (or partial solution) is applied. This continues until the problem is "solved."

Game Example

In games, the blackboard architecture can be expanded to facilitate cooperation among multiple agents. A problem, such as attacking a castle, can be posted, and individual units can propose their role in the attack. The volunteers are then scored, and the most appropriate ones are selected [Isla02].

Alternatively, the blackboard concept can be relaxed by using it strictly as a shared communication space, letting the individual agents regulate any cooperation. In this scheme, agents post their current activities and other agents can consult the blackboard to avoid beginning redundant work. For example, if an alarm is sounded in a building and enemies start rushing the player, it might be desirable for them to approach from different doors. Each enemy can post the door through which it will eventually enter, thus encouraging other enemies to choose alternate routes [Orkin03b].

Decision Tree Learning

A *decision tree* is a way of relating a series of inputs (usually measurements from the game world) to an output (usually representing something you want to predict) using a series of rules arranged in a tree structure. For example, inputs representing the health and ammunition of a bot could be used to predict the probability of the bot surviving an engagement with the player. At the root node, the decision tree might test to see whether the bot's health is low, indicating that the bot will not survive if that is the case. If the bot's health is not low, the decision tree might then test to see how much ammunition the bot has, perhaps indicating that the bot will not survive if its ammunition is low, and will survive otherwise. Decision trees are particularly important for applications such as in-game learning, because (in contrast to competing technologies like neural networks) extremely efficient algorithms exist for creating decision trees in near real time [Fu03].

Game Example

The best-known game-specific use of decision trees is in the game *Black & White* where they were used to allow the creature to learn and form "opinions" [Evans02]. In

Black & White, a creature will learn what objects in the world are likely to satisfy his desire to eat, based on feedback it gets from the player or world. For example, the player can provide positive or negative feedback by stroking or slapping the creature. A decision tree is then created that reflects what the creature has learned from its experiences. The creature can then use the decision tree to decide whether certain objects can be used to satisfy its hunger. While *Black & White* has demonstrated the power of decision trees to learn within games, they still remain largely untapped by the rest of the games industry.

Filtered Randomness

Filtered randomness attempts to ensure that random decisions or events in a game appear random to the players. This can be achieved by filtering the results of a random number generator such that non-random-looking sequences are eliminated, yet statistical randomness is maintained. For example, if a coin is flipped eight times in a row and turns up heads every time, a person might wonder if there was something wrong with the coin. The odds of such an event occurring are only 0.4 percent, but in a sequence of 100 flips it is extremely likely that either eight heads or eight tails in a row will be observed. When designing a game for entertainment purposes, it is desirable for random elements to always appear random to the players.

The technique involves keeping a short history of past results for each random decision that should be filtered. When a new decision is requested, a random result is generated and compared to the history. If an undesirable pattern or sequence is detected, the result is discarded and a new random result is generated. The process is repeated until a suitable result is accepted. Surprisingly, reasonable statistical randomness is maintained despite the deliberate filtering [Rabin03].

Game Example

Simple randomness filtering is actually very common in games. For example, if a character plays a random idle animation, often the game will ensure that the same idle animation won't be played twice in a row. However, filtering can be devised to remove all peculiar sequences. For example, if an enemy can randomly spawn from five different points, it would be extremely undesirable for the enemy to spawn from the same point five times in a row. It would also be undesirable for the enemy to randomly spawn in the counting sequence 12345 or favor one or two particular spawn points in the short term, like 12112121. Although these sequences can arise by chance, they are neither intended nor anticipated when the programmer wrote the code to randomly choose a spawn point. By detecting and filtering undesirable patterns or sequences with simple rules, a particular random decision can be guaranteed to always appear fair and balanced in the short term while still maintaining good statistical randomness.

Fuzzy Logic

Fuzzy logic is an extension of classical logic that is based on the idea of a fuzzy set. In classical crisp set theory, an object either does or does not belong to a set. For example, a creature is a member of the set of hungry creatures or is not a member of that set (it is either hungry or not hungry). With fuzzy set theory, an object can have continuously varying degrees of membership in fuzzy sets. For example, a creature could be hungry with degree of membership 0.1, representing slightly hungry, or 0.9, representing very hungry, or any value in between [McCuskey00].

Genetic Algorithms

A *genetic algorithm* (GA) is a technique for search and optimization that is based on evolutionary principles. GAs represent a point within a search space using a chromosome that is based on a handcrafted genetic code. Each chromosome consists of a string of genes that together encode its location in the search space. For example, the parameters of an AI agent can be the genes, and a particular combination of parameters a chromosome. All combinations of parameters will represent the search space.

By maintaining a population of chromosomes, which are continually mated and mutated, a GA is able to explore search spaces by testing different combinations of genes that seem to work well. A GA is usually left to evolve until it discovers a chromosome that represents a point in the search space that is good enough. GAs outperform many other techniques in search spaces that contain many optima, and are controlled by only a small number of parameters, which must be set by trial and error.

Game Example

Genetic algorithms are very good at finding a solution in complex or poorly understood search spaces. For example, your game might have a series of settings for the AI, but because of interactions between the settings, it is unclear what the best combination would be. In this case, a GA can be used to explore the search space consisting of all combinations of settings to come up with a near-optimal combination [Sweetser03a]. This is typically done offline since the optimization process can be slow and because a near-optimal solution is not guaranteed, meaning that the results might not improve gameplay.

N-Gram Statistical Prediction

An *n-gram* is a statistical technique that can predict the next value in a sequence. For example, in the sequence 18181810181, the next value will probably be an 8. When a prediction is required, the sequence is searched backward for all sequences matching the most recent $n-1$ values, where n is usually 2 or 3 (a *bigram* or *trigram*). Since the sequence might contain many repetitions of the n-gram, the value that most commonly follows is the one that is predicted. If the sequence is built up over time, by representing the history of a variable (such as the last player's move), it is possible to make a prediction of a future event. The accuracy of a prediction made by an n-gram tends to improve as the amount of historical data increases.

Game Example

For example, in a street fighting game, the player's actions (various punches and kicks) can be accumulated into a move history. Using the trigram model, the last two player moves are noted; for example, a Low Kick followed by a Low Punch. The move history is then searched for all examples where the player performed those two moves in sequence. For each example found, the move following the Low Punch and Low Kick is tallied. The statistics gathered might resemble Table 5.3.1.

Table 5.3.1 Statistics Gathered from Past Player Moves

Player Sequence	Occurrences	Frequency
Low Kick, Low Punch, Uppercut	10 times	50%
Low Kick, Low Punch, Low Punch	7 times	35%
Low Kick, Low Punch, Sideswipe	3 times	15%

The information in Table 5.3.1 can be used in two different ways. The first is to predict that the player's next move will be the one with the highest probability (the Uppercut with 50 percent likelihood based on past moves). The other is to use the probabilities as the chance that each will be predicted. Using this second technique, it is still possible to predict a Low Punch or Sideswipe as the next move, but it is less likely to make that prediction.

The statistics in Table 5.3.1 can be quickly calculated "on the fly" when a prediction is requested. A moving window into the past can be used so as not to consider moves that occurred too long ago [Laramée02b].

Neural Networks

Neural networks are complex nonlinear functions that relate one or more input variables to an output variable. They are called neural networks because internally they consist of a series of identical nonlinear processing elements (analogous to neurons) connected together in a network by weights (analogous to synapses). The form of the function that a particular neural network represents is controlled by values associated with the network's weights. Neural networks can be trained to produce a particular function by showing them examples of inputs and the outputs they should produce in response. This training process consists of optimizing the network's weight values, and several standard training algorithms are available for this purpose. Training most types of neural networks is computationally intensive, however, making neural networks generally unsuitable for in-game learning. Despite this, neural networks are extremely powerful and have found some applications in the games industry.

Game Example

In games, neural networks have been used for steering racecars in *Colin McRae Rally 2.0* and for control and learning in the *Creatures* series. Unfortunately, there are still relatively few applications of neural networks in games, as very few game developers are actively experimenting with them.

Perceptrons

A *perceptron network* is a single-layer neural network, which is simpler and easier to work with than a multilayer neural network. A perceptron network is composed of multiple *perceptrons*, each of which can either have a "yes" or "no" output. In other words, each perceptron either gets stimulated enough to trigger or it does not. Since a perceptron can classify things as "yes" or "no," it can be used to learn simple Boolean decisions such as attack or don't attack. They take up very little memory and are easier to train than a multilayer neural network or a decision tree. It is important to note, however, that perceptrons and perceptron networks have some limitations and can only learn simple (linearly separable) functions.

Game Example

In the game *Black & White*, every desire of a creature was represented by a different perceptron [Evans02]. For example, a single perceptron was used to represent the desire to eat (or hunger). Using three inputs (low energy, tasty food, and unhappiness), a perceptron would determine whether a creature was hungry. If the creature ate and received either positive or negative reinforcement, the weight associated with the perceptron would be adjusted, thus facilitating learning [Evans02].

Planning

The aim of *planning* is to find a series of actions for the AI that can change the current configuration of the game world into a target configuration. By specifying preconditions under which certain actions can be taken by the AI, and what the effects of those actions are likely to be, planning becomes a problem of searching for a sequence of actions that produces the required changes in the game world. Effective planning relies on choosing a good planning algorithm to search for the best sequence of actions, choosing an appropriate representation for the game world, and choosing an appropriate set of actions that the AI will be allowed to perform and specifying their effects.

Game Example

When the domain of a planning problem is sufficiently simple, formulating small plans is a reasonable and tractable problem that can be performed in real time. For example, in a game, a guard might run out of ammo during a gunfight with the player. The AI can then try to formulate a plan that will result in the player's demise given the guard's current situation. A planning module might come back with the solution of running to the light switch, turning it off to provide safety, running into the next room to gather ammo, and waiting in an ambush position [Orkin03a]. As game environments become more interactive and rich with possibilities, planning systems can help agents cope with the complexity by formulating reasonable and workable plans.

Player Modeling

Player modeling is the technique of building a profile of a player's behavior, with the intent of adapting the game. During play, the player's profile is continuously refined by accumulating statistics related to the player's behavior. As the profile emerges, the game can adapt the AI to the particular idiosyncrasies of the player by exploiting the information stored in his or her profile.

Game Example

In an FPS, the AI might observe that the player is poor at using a certain weapon or isn't good at jumping from platform to platform. Information like this can then be used to regulate the difficulty of the game, either by exploiting any weaknesses or by shying away from those same weaknesses [Beal02, Houlette03].

Production Systems

A *production system* (also known as a *rule-based system* or *expert system*) is an architecture for capturing expert knowledge in the form of rules. The system consists of a database of rules, facts, and an inference engine that determines which rules should trigger, resolving any conflicts between simultaneously triggered rules. The intelligence of a production system is embodied by the rules and conflict resolution [AIISC03].

Game Example

Many games use a simple version of a production system in the form of a series of rules constructed as if/else statements. However, true production systems are generally considered more structured and elaborate.

The academic community has had some success in creating bot AI for *Quake II* using the *Soar* production system [van Lent99], although the system requires upwards of 800 rules to play as a fairly competent opponent [Laird00]. Another applicable area is sports games, where each AI player must contain a great deal of expert knowledge to play the sport correctly. Microsoft's Sports Group experimented with some success using a production system to drive their team sports games, but the group has since been disbanded for unrelated reasons.

Reinforcement Learning

Reinforcement learning (RL) is a powerful machine learning technique that allows a computer to discover its own solutions to complex problems by trial and error. RL is particularly useful when the effects of the AI's actions in the game world are uncertain or delayed. For example, when controlling physical models like steering an airplane or racing a car, how should the controls be adjusted so that the airplane or car follows a particular path? What sequences of actions should a real-time strategy AI perform to maximize its chances of winning? By providing rewards and punishments at the appropriate times, an RL-based AI can learn to solve a variety of difficult and complex problems [Manslow03].

Reputation System

A *reputation system* is a way of modeling how the player's reputation in the game world develops and changes based on his or her actions. Rather than a single reputation model, each character in the game knows particular facts about the player [Alt02]. Characters learn new facts by witnessing player actions or by hearing information from others. Based on what the characters know about the player, they might act friendly toward the player or they might act hostile [Brockington03].

Game Example

In a cowboy gunfighter game, the player's reputation might be very important. If the player goes around killing people indiscriminately, others might witness the killings and relay the information to whomever they meet. This would give the player motivation to play nice or to make sure there are no witnesses.

Smart Terrain

Smart terrain is the technique of putting intelligence into inanimate objects. The result is that an agent can ask the object what it does and how to use it. For example, a smart microwave oven knows what it can accomplish (cook food) and how it should be used (open door, place food inside, close door, set cooking time, wait for beep, open door, take food out, close door). The advantage of such a system is that agents can use objects with which they were never explicitly programmed to interact.

The use of smart terrain is enlightened by *affordance theory*, which claims that objects by their very design allow for (or afford) a very specific type of interaction [Gibson87]. For example, a door on hinges that has no handles only permits opening by pushing on the nonhinged side. This is similar to letting the objects themselves dictate how they should be used.

Game Example

The term *smart terrain* was popularized by the very successful game *The Sims*. In *The Sims*, the objects in the game world contain most of the game's intelligence. Each object broadcasts to agents what it has to offer and how it can be used. For example, an agent might be hungry, and food on the table will broadcast "I satisfy hunger." If the agent decides to use the food, the food instructs the agent how to interact with it and what the consequences are. By using this smart terrain model, agents are able to use any new object that is added into the game through expansion packs or from Internet sites.

Speech Recognition and Text-to-Speech

The technology of *speech recognition* enables a game player to speak into a microphone and have a game respond accordingly. In the games industry, there have been a few attempts to add speech recognition to games. The most notable are Sega's *Seaman* for the Sega Dreamcast, and Nintendo's *Hey You, Pikachu!* for the Nintendo 64. While these first attempts were somewhat gimmicky, they serve an important role by feeling out the territory for viable speech recognition in games, both in terms of the current state of the technology and the possibilities for enhancing gameplay. New platforms such as the Nintendo DS have a microphone built-in, which encourages games to support speech recognition.

Text-to-speech is the technique of turning ordinary text into synthesized speech. This allows for endless amounts of speech without having to record a human actor. Unfortunately, currently, virtually no games use text-to-speech technology, perhaps because it sounds rather robotlike. In practice, it's more effective to record a human voice, especially since most games have access to enough disk space to store high-quality audio samples. The quality of voice acting in games has also risen in recent years, which makes bland text-to-speech less appealing. However, for some games, it can be quite entertaining for the player to enter his or her name and have the game speak it. For the right game, text-to-speech can be a novel technology that can set the game apart.

Weakness Modification Learning

Weakness modification learning helps prevent an AI from losing repeatedly to a human player in the same way each time. The idea is to record a key gameplay state that precedes an AI failure. When that same state is recognized in the future, the AI's behavior is modified slightly so that "history does not repeat itself." By subtly disrupting the sequence of events, the AI might not win more often or act more intelligently, but at least the same failure won't happen repeatedly. An important advantage of weakness modification learning is that potentially only one example is required in order to learn [van Rijswijck03].

Game Example

Within a soccer game, if the human scores a goal against the computer, the position of the ball can be recorded at some key moment when it was on the ground before the goal was scored. Given this ball position, the game can create a gravity well vector field that will subtly draw the closest computer players toward that position. This particular vector field is then phased in whenever the ball appears near the recorded position in a similar situation (and phased out when the ball moves away). This example lends itself well to many team sports games such as soccer, basketball, hockey, and perhaps football. However, the general concept is very simple and can be applied to almost any genre.

Summary

Game AI is distinctively different from many other related AI fields. The goal is to create intelligent opponents, allies, and neutral characters that result in an engaging and enjoyable experience for the player. Ultimately, the goal is not to beat the player, but rather to lose in a fun and challenging way.

Most games are populated by agents that sense, think, and act on their own; however, even a single opponent can be thought of as an agent. Advanced agents might also learn and remember in order to present a deeper challenge. It is important to realize that whatever an agent senses, thinks, or remembers, it is completely invisible and inconsequential to the player unless the agent can express the result through actions. An agent's outward appearance through movement, manipulation, animation, and dialogue is critical to making the agent appear intelligent. Typically, this requires tight integration and collaboration with the people who generate the art assets.

One of the most enduring techniques for endowing intelligence on agents is the ubiquitous finite-state machine. This simple computational model allows complex expertise to be expressed in a simple, easy-to-understand manner that is also convenient to debug. The actions and mindsets of an agent eloquently map to the states of an FSM, further allowing for simple, yet effective modeling of behavior. With the many enhancements developed for FSMs, it is easy to understand why they have become so universal within AI game development.

Finally, there are dozens of common and promising techniques for adding intelligence to games. Each game is unique and might require mixing and matching several different techniques. There is no single solution, and the resulting design is highly dependant on the exact requirements of the game. Therefore, it is critical that a developer becomes familiar with a broad range of techniques in order to experiment and make intelligent implementation decisions.

Exercises

1. Name several simple ways to make an AI opponent difficult to beat.
2. How could an agent apparently get better at playing a game over time without actually learning or remembering anything?
3. Design an FSM for a patrol behavior. For example, a patrol behavior might visit three different locations in an endless loop. Compose your answer as a UML diagram.
4. Design an FSM for a smart patrolling guard. Consider how the guard might detect intruders and what his reaction might be over his lifetime. Compose your answer as a UML diagram.
5. Take the FSMs you designed in the previous two exercises and convert them to the fictional FSM scripting language as described in Listing 5.3.2.

ON THE CD

6. Using the State Machine Language included on the companion CD-ROM, investigate the messaging scheme that allows agents to communicate with each other. Write a short explanation of each messaging function (starting with SendMsg). Give examples of how each might be useful.
7. Research a recent game that has received acclaim for its AI. What does the game do particularly well with regard to AI? What AI techniques are likely being used?
8. The game *Black & White* was hailed for its interesting and innovative use of AI. Research this game and comment on how the game design allowed the AI to be showcased.
9. Write a one-page essay on the future of game AI. What will it look like in 10 or 20 years? How about 100 years?

References

[AIISC03] "Working Group on Rule-Based Systems Report," *The 2003 AIISC Report*, AIISC, 2003, available online at *www.igda.org/ai/report-2003/aiisc_rule_based_systems_report_2003.html*.

[Alt02] Alt, Greg, and King, Kristin, "A Dynamic Reputation System Based on Event Knowledge," *AI Game Programming Wisdom*, Charles River Media, 2002.

[Beal02] Beal, C., Beck, J.; Westbrook, D.; Atkin, M.; and Cohen, P., "Intelligent Modeling of the User in Interactive Entertainment," *AAAI Stanford Spring Symposium*, 2002, available online at *www-unix.oit.umass.edu/~cbeal/papers/AAAISS02Slides.pdf and www-unix.oit.umass.edu/~cbeal/papers/AAAISS02.pdf*.

[Brockington02a] Brockington, Mark, "Level-Of-Detail AI for a Large Role-Playing Game," *AI Game Programming Wisdom*, Charles River Media, 2002.

[Brockington03] Brockington, Mark, "Building A Reputation System: Hatred, Forgiveness, and Surrender in Neverwinter Nights," *Massively Multiplayer Game Development*, Charles River Media, 2003.

[Brooks89] Brooks, Rodney, "How to Build Complete Creatures Rather than Isolated Cognitive Simulators," *Architectures for Intelligence*, Lawrence Erlbaum Associates, Fall 1989, available online at *www.ai.mit.edu/people/brooks/papers/how-to-build.pdf*.

[Cain02] Cain, Timothy, "Practical Optimizations for A* Path Generation," *AI Game Programming Wisdom*, Charles River Media, 2002.

[Darby03] Darby, Alex, "Vehicle Racing Control Using Insect Intelligence," *AI Game Programming Wisdom 2*, Charles River Media, 2003.

[Dawson02] Dawson, Chad, "Formations," *AI Game Programming Wisdom*, Charles River Media, 2002.

[Evans02] Evans, Richard, "Varieties of Learning," *AI Game Programming Wisdom*, Charles River Media, 2002.

[Fu03] Fu, Dan, and Houlette, Ryan, "Constructing a Decision Tree Based on Past Experience," *AI Game Programming Wisdom 2*, Charles River Media, 2003.

[Gibson87] Gibson, James, *The Ecological Approach to Visual Perception*, Lawrence Erlbaum Assoc., 1987.

[Grimani03] Grimani, Mario, "Wall Building for RTS Games," *AI Game Programming Wisdom 2*, Charles River Media, 2003.

[Hargrove03a] Hargrove, Chris, "Simplified Animation Selection," *AI Game Programming Wisdom 2*, Charles River Media, 2003.

[Hargrove03b] Hargrove, Chris, "Pluggable Animations," *AI Game Programming Wisdom 2*, Charles River Media, 2003.

[Higgins02a] Higgins, Dan, "Generic A* Pathfinding," *AI Game Programming Wisdom*, Charles River Media, 2002.

[Higgins02b] Higgins, Dan, "How to Achieve Lightning-Fast A*," *AI Game Programming Wisdom*, Charles River Media, 2002.

[Higgins02c] Higgins, Dan, "Terrain Analysis in an RTS—The Hidden Giant," *Game Programming Gems 3*, Charles River Media, 2002.

[Houlette01] Houlette, Ryan; Fu, Daniel; and Ross, David, "Towards an AI Behavior Toolkit for Games," *AAAI Spring Symposium on AI and Interactive Entertainment*, 2001, *www.qrg.northwestern.edu/aigames.org/2001papers.html.*

[Houlette03] Houlette, Ryan, "Player Modeling for Adaptive Games," *AI Game Programming Wisdom 2*, Charles River Media, 2003.

[IDIS99] "Bayesian Networks," *IDIS Lab*, 1999, available online at *http://excalibur. brc.uconn.edu/~baynet/.*

[Isla02] Isla, Damian, and Blumberg, Bruce, "Blackboard Architectures," *AI Game Programming Wisdom*, Charles River Media, 2002.

[Kent03] Kent, Tom, "Multi-Tiered AI Layers and Terrain Analysis for RTS Games," *AI Game Programming Wisdom 2*, Charles River Media, 2003.

[Laird00] Laird, John, and van Lent, Michael, "Human-level AI's Killer Application: Interactive Computer Games," AAAI, 2000, available online at *ai.eecs.umich. edu/people/laird/papers/AAAI-00.pdf.*

[Laramée02b] Laramée, François Dominic, "Using N-Gram Statistical Models to Predict Player Behavior," *AI Game Programming Wisdom*, Charles River Media, 2002.

[Laramée03] Laramée, François Dominic, "Dead Reckoning in Sports and Strategy Games," *AI Game Programming Wisdom 2*, Charles River Media, 2003.

[Lidén02] Lidén, Lars, "Strategic and Tactical Reasoning with Waypoints," *AI Game Programming Wisdom*, Charles River Media, 2002.

[Manslow03] Manslow, John, "Using Reinforcement Learning to Solve AI Control Problems," *AI Game Programming Wisdom 2*, Charles River Media, 2003.

[McCuskey00] McCuskey, Mason, "Fuzzy Logic for Video Games," *Game Programming Gems*, Charles River Media, 2000.

[Orkin02a] Orkin, Jeff, "A General-Purpose Trigger System," *AI Game Programming Wisdom*, Charles River Media, 2002.

[Orkin02b] Orkin, Jeff, "A Data-Driven Architecture for Animation Selection," *AI Game Programming Wisdom*, Charles River Media, 2002.

[Orkin03a] Orkin, Jeff, "Applying Goal-Oriented Action Planning to Games," *AI Game Programming Wisdom 2*, Charles River Media, 2003.

[Orkin03b] Orkin, Jeff, "Simple Techniques for Coordinated Behavior," *AI Game Programming Wisdom 2*, Charles River Media, 2003.

[Porcino03] Porcino, Nick, "An Architecture for A-Life," *AI Game Programming Wisdom 2*, Charles River Media, 2003.

[Pottinger99a] Pottinger, Dave, "Coordinated Unit Movement," *Game Developer Magazine*, January 1999, available online at *www.gamasutra.com/features/ 19990122/movement_01.htm.*

[Pottinger99b] Pottinger, Dave, "Implementing Coordinated Movement," *Game Developer Magazine*, February 1999, available online at *www.gamasutra.com/features/19990129/implementing_01.htm.*

[Rabin98] Rabin, Steve, "Making the Play: Team Cooperation in Microsoft Baseball 3D," *Computer Game Developers Conference Proceedings*, 1998, available on the *AI Game Programming Wisdom 2* CD-ROM, Charles River Media, 2002.

[Rabin00a] Rabin, Steve, "A* Speed Optimizations," *Game Programming Gems*, Charles River Media, 2000.

[Rabin00b] Rabin, Steve, "A* Aesthetic Optimizations," *Game Programming Gems*, Charles River Media, 2000.

[Rabin02] Rabin, Steve, "An Extensible Trigger System for AI Agents, Objects, and Quests," *Game Programming Gems 3*, Charles River Media, 2002.

[Rabin03] Rabin, Steve, "Filtered Randomness for AI Decisions and Game Logic," *AI Game Programming Wisdom 2*, Charles River Media, 2003.

[Reed03] Reed, Christopher, and Geisler, Benjamin, "Jumping, Climbing, and Tactical Reasoning: How to Get More out of a Navigation System," *AI Game Programming Wisdom 2*, Charles River Media, 2003.

[Reynolds87] Reynolds, Craig, "Flocks, Herds, and Schools: A Distributed Behavioral Model," *Computer Graphics, 21(4)* (SIGGRAPH '87 Conference Proceedings), pp. 25–34, 1987, available online at *www.red3d.com/cwr/papers/1987/boids.html*.

[Reynolds99] Reynolds, Craig, "Steering Behaviors For Autonomous Characters," Game Developers Conference Proceedings, 1999, available at *www.red3d.com/cwr/papers/1999/gdc99steer.pdf*.

[Reynolds01] Reynolds, Craig, "Boids," available online at *www.red3d.com/cwr/boids/*.

[Reynolds02] Reynolds, John, "Tactical Team AI Using a Command Hierarchy," *AI Game Programming Wisdom*, Charles River Media, 2002.

[Scutt02] Scutt, Tom, "Simple Swarms as an Alternative to Flocking," *AI Game Programming Wisdom*, Charles River Media, 2002.

[Stein02] Stein, Noah, "Intercepting a Ball," *AI Game Programming Wisdom*, Charles River Media, 2002.

[Stentz94] Stentz, Tony, "Original D*," *ICRA 94*, 1994, available online at *www.frc.ri.cmu.edu/~axs/doc/icra94.pdf*.

[Sweetser03a] Sweetser, Penny, "How to Build Evolutionary Algorithms for Games," *AI Game Programming Wisdom 2*, Charles River Media, 2003.

[Tozour01] Tozour, Paul, "Influence Mapping," *Game Programming Gems 2*, Charles River Media, 2001.

[Tozour02a] Tozour, Paul, "The Perils of AI Scripting," *AI Game Programming Wisdom*, Charles River Media, 2002.

[Tozour02b] Tozour, Paul, "Introduction to Bayesian Networks and Reasoning Under Uncertainty," *AI Game Programming Wisdom*, Charles River Media, 2002.

[Tozour03a] Tozour, Paul, "Search Space Representations," *AI Game Programming Wisdom 2*, Charles River Media, 2003.

[Tozour03b] Tozour, Paul, "Using a Spatial Database for Runtime Spatial Analysis," *AI Game Programming Wisdom 2*, Charles River Media, 2003.

[Tozour03c] Tozour, Paul, "Stack-Based Finite-State Machines," *AI Game Programming Wisdom 2*, Charles River Media, 2003.

[van der Sterren00] van der Sterren, William, "AI for Tactical Grenade Handling," *CGF-AI*, 2000, available online at *www.cgf-ai.com/docs/grenadehandling.pdf*.

[van Lent99] van Lent, M., Laird, J.; Buckman, J.; Harford, J.; Houchard, S.; Steinkraus, K.; and Tedrake, R., "Intelligent Agents in Computer Games," *AAAI*, 1999, available online at *hebb.mit.edu/people/russt/publications/Intelligent_Agents_in_Computer_Games(AAAI99).pdf*.

[van Rijswijck03] van Rijswijck, Jack, "Learning Goals in Sports Games," *Game Developers Conference Proceedings*, 2003, available at *www.gdconf.com/archives/2003/Van_Ryswyck_Jack.doc* or *www.cs.ualberta.ca/~javhar/research.html*.

[Woodcock02] Woodcock, Steven, "Recognizing Strategic Dispositions: Engaging the Enemy," *AI Game Programming Wisdom*, Charles River Media, 2002.

[Yiskis03a] Yiskis, Eric, "Finite-State Machine Scripting Language for Designers," *AI Game Programming Wisdom 2*, Charles River Media, 2003.

[Yiskis03b] Yiskis, Eric, "A Subsumption Architecture for Character-Based Games," *AI Game Programming Wisdom 2*, Charles River Media, 2003.

5.4 Artificial Intelligence: Pathfinding Overview

In This Chapter

- Representing the Search Space
- Pathfinding
- Summary
- Exercises
- References

Pathfinding is a problem that has to be dealt with in just about every game. If an agent cannot find its way around the level, it will seem quite incompetent. Pathfinding is not a trivial task. This is in part because the resources that a pathfinding system consumes can quickly get out of hand. Even though there are many search algorithms to choose from for pathfinding, the A* algorithm (pronounced A-Star) is by far the most popular. In this chapter, we will look at a few different algorithms and work our way up to A* to give you a complete understanding of how A* works and why it is so popular. There are also two applications on the companion CD-ROM that correspond to this chapter. The first one, *PathPlannerApp*, is designed to help you implement the algorithms covered in this chapter. The second application performs the algorithms implemented in the *PathPlannerApp* on an alternative common representation know as waypoint graphs.

ON THE CD

Representing the Search Space

To perform pathfinding, an agent or the pathfinding system needs to understand the level. An agent does not need a fully detailed model of the level. In fact, even humans don't keep track of every little detail about a level when trying to find a path in a building. For example, we typically do not pay attention to details such as the exact shape of every room, the color of the walls, and all the objects in each room. Similarly, an agent only needs a representation of the level that takes into account the more important and relevant information.

There are numerous ways to represent the relevant information of a level for an agent. The knowledge representation technique and the amount of information about the level directly affect the efficiency and quality of paths that an agent can find. The more information, the better paths the agent can potentially find. However, more knowledge is not always better. If you give the agent an overly detailed model of the level, it will waste precious memory space and CPU cycles to store and process unnecessary data.

Grids, waypoint graphs, and *navigation meshes* are among the most common representation schemes, each of which has its own advantages and disadvantages. The genre of a game, the type of levels, the number of agents, and many other constraints can make one scheme more appropriate than the others. In the following section, we cover the advantages and disadvantages of these representation schemes.

Grids

Two-dimensional grids are an intuitive way of representing the level for many games. In fact, RTS games such as *Age of Empires* and *Warcraft III* use a grid. Each cell is flagged as either passable or impassable. Each object in the world can occupy one or more cells. A building might occupy several cells, whereas a tree might occupy a single cell. Just because a grid is 2D does not mean that it cannot be used for a 3D RTS game such as *Warcraft III*. Even though *Warcraft III* levels are 3D, for any point on the terrain, a unit can be at only one elevation. For example, *Warcraft III* levels do not have bridges where the unit is allowed to go over the bridge and under the bridge. In essence, the elevation can be ignored, which reduces the 3D level to a 2D level.

A grid has several advantages. Given an arbitrary location in the world, you can immediately find the exact cell that corresponds to that position. In addition, for any cell in the world, you can easily access the neighboring cells. Grids can work quite well for levels that can be reasonably aligned to grid cells. Figure 5.4.1 shows a level that has been estimated using a grid despite the fact that everything is not perfectly aligned to a grid.

Waypoint Graphs

Instead of specifying passable and impassable parts of the level, a waypoint graph specifies the lines in the level that are safe for traversing. An agent can choose to walk along any of these lines without having to worry about running into major obstacles or falling into ditches or off a ramp. The waypoint nodes are connected through links. A link connects exactly two nodes together, indicating that an agent can move safely

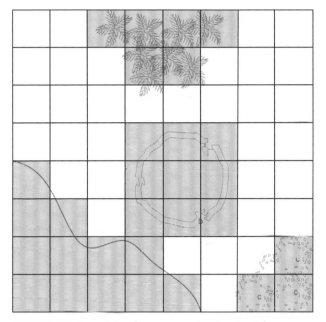

FIGURE 5.4.1   *A level represented using a grid.*

between the two nodes by following along the link. Figure 5.4.2 shows a waypoint graph for a level that would be harder to estimate using a grid. In addition, the classes in Listing 5.4.1 can be used to represent a waypoint graph.

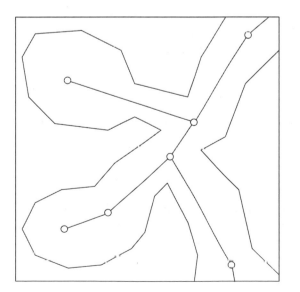

FIGURE 5.4.2   *A level represented using a waypoint graph.*

Listing 5.4.1   Waypoint graph node and waypoint graph link

```
class GraphNode
{
public:
    int                 m_id;
    Vector3             m_position;
    std::vector<int>    m_linkIds;
    ...
};

class GraphLink
{
public:
    int     m_id;
    int     m_beginId;
    int     m_endId;
    float   m_weight;
    ...
};
```

A typical grid cell is connected to its eight surrounding cells, whereas a graph node can be connected to any number of nodes. This makes waypoint graphs much more flexible than grids. In fact, for every grid, an equivalent waypoint graph can be created by placing a waypoint at the center of the passable cells, and connecting it to its eight immediate neighbors. However, this does not mean that using graphs is necessarily better. When a level is represented as a grid, there is no need for additional data to keep track of the neighboring cells. Instead, the indices of a cell can be used to compute the indices of the neighboring cells. Representing certain levels as a grid can save orders of magnitude of memory space, while using a waypoint graph can be a far better approach for levels such as the one in Figure 5.4.2.

The nodes of a waypoint graph can store additional information such as a radius. The radius can be used to associate a width with the links so that the agents do not have to follow the links very closely. By doing so, the agents can have plenty of room to deviate from the links without having to worry about running into obstacles or falling into a hole. However, many games do not associate a width with the links. Instead, they allow the agents to loosely follow the links and rely on additional runtime collision detection to save the agents from running into obstacles or falling into a hole. To rely on runtime collision detection to help an agent avoid holes, the level designer will have to provide additional collision information such as invisible planes or bounding volumes.

One of the biggest advantages of waypoint graphs is that they can easily represent arbitrary three-dimensional levels. Many FPS games such as *Unreal Tournament* and *Half-Life* use waypoint graphs.

Navigation Meshes

Navigation meshes have been gaining more and more popularity over the past few years. This is because they bring the best of both grids and waypoint graphs together. Figure 5.4.3 shows the equivalent navigation mesh representation for the level presented in Figure 5.4.2.

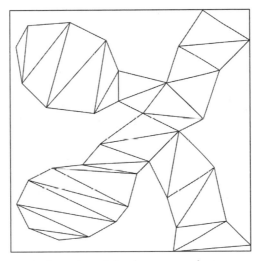

FIGURE 5.4.3   *A level represented using a navigation mesh.*

Navigation meshes are in many ways similar to waypoint graphs. The major difference is that every node of a navigation mesh represents a convex polygon or area as opposed to a single point. The advantage of a convex polygon is that any two points inside it can be connected without crossing an edge of the polygon. This means that if an agent is inside a convex polygon, it can safely move to any other point inside the polygon without leaving the polygon. An edge of the polygon is either shared with another polygon, indicating that the two nodes are linked, or not shared with any other polygon, indicating that the edge should not be crossed. Edges that are not shared with other nodes can be used to stop the bots from running into obstacles or falling off a cliff.

There are different variations of navigation meshes. One of the major distinctions is whether the nodes store a triangle or an n-sided convex polygon. Figure 5.4.3 is a mesh that is made of triangles.

As mentioned previously, waypoint graphs tend to emphasize the points and lines in the level that are safe for traversing. Unlike grids and navigation meshes, a waypoint graph does not specify passable and impassible regions. A waypoint graph is considered an incomplete representation of the level, whereas a navigation mesh is inherently a complete representation.

Another advantage of navigation meshes is that they tie pathfinding and collision detection together. When using a waypoint graph, an agent has to rely heavily on run-time collision detection to help it navigate the level. The cost of the collision detection can easily add up, especially as the number of agents increases. With navigation meshes, simple 2D line intersection tests against the edges of the polygons can determine whether an agent is hitting a wall, or when it is safely crossing into another polygon.

Pathfinding

Now that we have seen different ways of making a small-scale model of a level that an agent can use for pathfinding, let's look at how we can enable the agent to find paths around the level. The pathfinding algorithms we discuss here can be used on any of the representations that we covered in the last section. For the sake of simplicity, we will assume that the level is represented as a grid.

Let's start with the definition of a *path*. A path is a list of cells, points, or nodes that an agent has to traverse to get from a start position to a goal position. In most situations, a large number of different paths can be taken to reach the goal. Some paths are better than others are. One of the important criterion of a pathfinding algorithm is the quality of the path it finds. Some algorithms guarantee that they find the most optimal path, while others do not guarantee to even find a path. Plenty of algorithms can be misled in certain situations and ultimately fail to find a path. Algorithms that guarantee to find a path are referred to as *complete* algorithms, and algorithms that guarantee to always find the most optimal path are known as *optimal* algorithms. The amount of CPU cycles and memory needed to find a path is another important criterion of an algorithm.

In the upcoming sections, we will analyze five different algorithms. The first, which we will refer to as the Random-Trace algorithm, is a very simple algorithm that will be used as a basis to explain why A* is such a popular algorithm. To understand A*, you have to fully understand the Breadth-First, Best-First, and Dijkstra algorithms.

Random-Trace

Given a map such as the one in Figure 5.4.4a, how would you get an agent from the start cell to the goal? Assume that the map only contains relatively small convex obstacles. Unlike concave obstacles, convex obstacles do not have any cavities. For example, a square, line, or triangle is convex, whereas a U- or L-shaped obstacle is concave.

Consider the following solution: Allow the agent to move toward the goal until it reaches the goal or runs into an obstacle. If it runs into an obstacle, it can randomly choose to trace around the object in a clockwise or counterclockwise manner. It can then trace around the object until it can head toward the goal without immediately running into an obstacle. The agent can repeat this procedure until the goal is

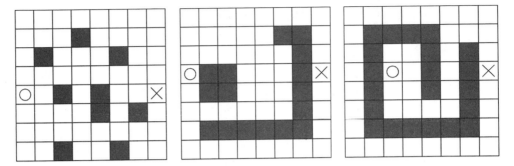

FIGURE 5.4.4 *Three different levels: a) trivial, b) nontrivial, and c) difficult.*

reached. This simple algorithm can work very well as long as the map only has relatively small convex obstacles. What is the weakness of this algorithm if the map has concave or even large convex obstacles? As you can see from Figure 5.4.4b, larger objects can have a substantial effect on the quality of the path. It would be much better for the agent to trace clockwise when he runs into the obstacles in Figure 5.4.4b, rather than trace counterclockwise. Note that a high-quality path would not even go into the concavity.

One of the fundamental problems with this algorithm is that it is incapable of considering a wide variety of paths. To get a good idea of how limiting this algorithm is, think about how many potential paths this algorithm can take for the map in Figure 5.4.4b. It can only pick between four paths even though there is an infinite number of paths between start and goal. This shortcoming is why this algorithm is not a complete algorithm. The Random-Trace algorithm does not even guarantee to find a path from start to goal in a finite amount of time for the map in Figure 5.4.4c.

Understanding the A* Algorithm

In this section, we look at why A* is such a popular algorithm for pathfinding. A* is a combination of two other algorithms—Best-First and Dijkstra. Best-First and Dijkstra are both derivatives of the Breadth-First algorithm. To get a complete understanding of A*, we will study these other algorithms and work our way up to A*. As you will soon see, these algorithms have a lot in common.

One of the most important characteristics of these algorithms is that they consider a wide variety of paths. In fact, they keep track of numerous paths simultaneously, and if they have to, they will consider every possible part of the map to find a path to the goal. To do so, they need a way of keeping track of the paths. A path can be described as an ordered list of subdestinations. Instances of the `PlannerNode` class presented in Listing 5.4.2 can be used to represent a path.

Listing 5.4.2   PlannerNode class for representing a node

```
class PlannerNode
{
public:
    PlannerNode    *m_pParent;
    int            m_cellX, m_cellY;
    ...
};
```

The PlannerNode class stores the position of a cell and a pointer to another PlannerNode that specifies which of the neighboring cells has led us to the cell. By chaining these nodes together using the parent pointers, we can represent a path between a starting cell and a goal cell. Given a path, additional PlannerNodes can be concatenated to the end of the path to create other paths. By creating additional paths that extend existing paths, an algorithm can work its way through the map in search of the goal.

All of the algorithms we are about to cover use two lists known as the *open* list and the *closed* list. The open list keeps track of paths that still need to be processed. When a path is processed, it is taken off the open list and checked to see whether it has reached the goal. If it has not, it is used to create additional paths, and it is then placed on the closed list. The closed nodes (or paths) are those that do not correspond to the goal cell and have been processed already.

Figure 5.4.5 shows the state of an algorithm that has completed the search process. In the case of this particular algorithm, the search started in the center and worked its way outward until it found the goal represented by the X. At the completion of the search, the light gray nodes are on the open list and the dark gray nodes are on the closed list. Again, each node on the open list represents a path between that cell and the starting cell, and the closed list contains paths that used to be on the open list. The arrows in Figure 5.4.5 represent the parent pointer of the PlannerNodes. The parent pointers that are part of the path between the start and the goal appear in bold and represent the solution path pointing from the goal back to the start. Breadth-First, Best-First, Dijkstra, and A* algorithms all follow the pseudocode in Listing 5.4.3.

Listing 5.4.3   The overall structure of the algorithms

```
1)create a node for the start point and push it onto
   the open list
2)while the open list is not empty
        A)pop a node from the open list and call it
           currentNode
        B)if currentNode corresponds to the goal,
           break from step 2
        C)create the successors of currentNode and
           push them onto the open list
        D)put the currentNode onto the closed list
```

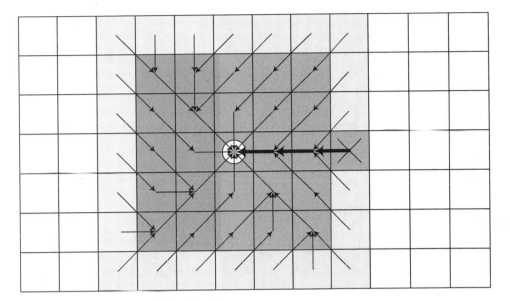

Figure 5.4.5   *Open and closed nodes.*

The pseudocode first creates a node and pushes it onto the open list. It then loops until it has examined every node on the open list. In the first iteration of the loop, the only node on the open list is the root node. Once it is popped from the open list, it is used to create additional nodes for neighboring cells. These successor nodes are then pushed onto the open list, and the current node is pushed onto the closed list. This process is repeated until either the goal is reached or the open list is empty. The node that reaches the goal is part of the path between the start and the goal. Once the goal has been reached, the path between start and goal can be obtained by traversing the parent pointer of the `PlannerNodes` starting from the node that reached the goal and ending with the root node. If the open list becomes empty without finding the goal, it means the goal cannot be reached. Unlike the Random-Trace algorithm, all four algorithms are considered complete algorithms because they guarantee to find a solution if one exists, regardless of how complicated the map is.

Before creating a successor node, the algorithms make sure there is no more than one node for any given cell of the grid. This is to prevent unnecessary reexploration of the map. The idea is that there is no need to store more than one path between the start and another single cell of the grid. If we come across another path to a cell to which we already have a path, we can either disregard the new path or pick the better of the two and disregard the other. To make sure we never have more than one path to any single cell of the grid, before creating a successor node, we have to see if we have already made a node for that cell. This means that we need to check the open list and the closed list. Even though this step can be very expensive, it is still better than unnecessarily reexploring parts of the map. Not catching redundant nodes can result in substantial consumption of memory and substantially more time to find the goal. Using a data structure that offers fast lookups, such as hash table or hash map, can have a significant effect on the performance on the algorithm.

The main difference between Breadth-First, Best-First, Dijkstra, and A* is in which node on the open list they decide to process every iteration of the loop. Breadth-First always processes the node that has been waiting the longest, Best-First always processes the one that is closest to the goal, Dijkstra processes the one that is the cheapest to reach from the start cell, and A* chooses the node that is cheap and close to the goal.

Breadth-First

Breadth-First tries to find a path from the start to the goal by examining the search space ply-by-ply. That is, it checks all the cells that are one step (or ply) from the start, and then checks cells that are two plies from the start, and so on. This behavior is because the algorithm always processes the node that has been waiting the longest. Breadth-First uses a queue as the open list. Every time a node is created, it is pushed to the back of the queue. By doing so, the node at the front of the queue is always the one that has been waiting the longest. The algorithm used to search for the goal in Figure 5.4.5 was actually the Breadth-First algorithm. The pseudocode in Listing 5.4.4 shows the details of the algorithm.

Listing 5.4.4   Breadth-First pseudocode

```
1)create the rootNode
   - set its x and y according to the startPoint
   - set its parent to NULL

2)push the rootNode onto the open list

3)while the open list is not empty

   A)pop the node that has been waiting the longest
     from the open list and assign it to currentNode

   B)if currentNode's x and y correspond to the
     goalPoint then
      - break from step 3

   C)for every nearbyPoint around the currentNode
      a)if this nearbyPoint is in a spot that is
        impassable then
         - skip to the next nearbyPoint

      b)if a node for this nearbyPoint has been
        created before then
         - skip to the next nearbyPoint
```

```
        c)create the successorNode
           - set its x and y according to nearbyPoint
           - set its parent to currentNode

        d)push the successorNode onto the open list

      D)push the currentNode onto closed list

   4)if the while loop exits without finding the goal,
      goalPoint must be unreachable
```

This algorithm is not the best pathfinding algorithm for several reasons. One of its major issues is that it consumes a lot of memory and CPU cycles to find the goal. If you place the goal five cells away from the starting cell, Breadth-First will create 100 nodes to cover the 10-by-10 region. More nodes means more memory consumption, and more CPU cycles are needed to allocate them and search the open and closed lists. Breadth-First does not take advantage of the location of the goal to focus the search effort. In fact, it searches just as hard in the direction away from the goal as it does toward the goal. It is important to note that Breadth-First finds the most optimal solution in terms of plies. Since it searches in a ply-by ply fashion, when it reaches the goal, it has found a path that has the fewest number of nodes in it. However, Breadth-First has no concept of distance. If you run Breadth-First for different coordinates, you might see unnecessary diagonal steps in the path. The path that Breadth-First finds heavily depends on the order in which the successor nodes are created. We will come back to this point when we talk about the Dijkstra algorithm.

Best-First

Unlike Breadth-First, which is an exhaustive search, Best-First is a *heuristic* search. Best-First uses problem-specific knowledge to speed up the search process. It tries to head right for the goal. The only difference with Best-First code would be to compute the distance of every node to the goal and use a priority queue that is sorted by the heuristic cost. Through every iteration of the loop, the node that is closest to the goal is processed. Figure 5.4.6 shows how Best-First compares to Breadth-First.

On average, Best-First is much faster than Breadth-First and uses significantly less memory. It typically creates very few nodes and tends to find "good quality" paths. However, Best-First has a rather noticeable shortcoming. Because it only cares about getting close to the goal, it can end up heading in a direction that does not necessarily result in finding an optimal path. The distance-to-goal measure is a heuristic or rule-of-thumb that can pay off quite often. However, it is not always the right thing to do. Figure 5.4.7 shows a map that was built to exploit the weakness of Best-First and causes it to head in a doomed direction and find a terrible path.

It is important to note that Best-First is still a complete algorithm. That is, in the worst-case scenario, it will exhaust all the nodes on the open list and find a path to the goal. However, it might not find a high-quality path.

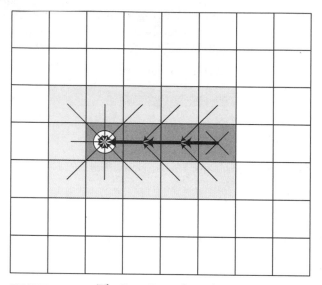

FIGURE 5.4.6   *The Best-First algorithm.*

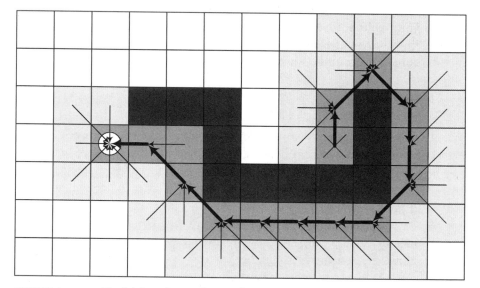

FIGURE 5.4.7   *Exploiting the weakness of Best-First.*

Dijkstra

The Dijkstra algorithm is similar to Breadth-First but always finds the optimal solution. The problem with Breadth-First was that as it went along, it only cared about plies. Dijkstra goes a step further and keeps track of the cost of the path from start to any given cell. By doing so, it always processes the cheapest path in the open list. This means that every `PlannerNode` needs to store the accumulated cost that was paid to get to it from the start node. When Dijkstra generates a successor node, it adds the cost of the current node to the cost of going from the current node to the successor node. If the move from the current node to the successor node is a diagonal move, some additional cost should be added since a longer distance is traveled. This is a major distinction from Breadth-First, since Breadth-First only thinks in terms of plies.

An advantage of Dijkstra is that it can understand regions that are weighted differently. Breadth-First and Best-First only understand passable and impassible regions and basically assume that the passable regions have a uniform weight or cost to travel through. Different terrain weights can be used to help an agent avoid certain parts of the map. The weighted region can represent costs such as additional resource consumption, or risks such as the risk of being seen by the enemy in certain parts of the map.

A complication occurs in Dijkstra that needs special consideration. Unlike Best-First and Breadth-First, it cannot simply say, "If a node has been created already for a cell of the map, there is no need to consider that cell again." Instead, it has to find out if the new path to that cell is better than the previously created path. Since the given cost of a node represents the accumulated cost that was paid to get to that node from the start node, the given cost can be used to decide which node is better. If the new path is better, the algorithm can get rid of the old path. If the old path is better, the algorithm can disregard the new path. Note that if Dijkstra does not perform this check, it cannot guarantee to always find the optimal solution. Listing 5.4.5 is an example of Dijkstra pseudocode.

LISTING 5.4.5 Dijkstra pseudo-code

```
1)create the rootNode
   - set its x and y according to the startPoint
   - set its parent to NULL
   - set its givenCost to 0

2)push the rootNode onto the open list

3)while the open list is not empty

   A)pop the node with the lowest givenCost from the
     open list and assign it to currentNode

   B)if currentNode's x and y correspond to the
     goalPoint then
           - break from step 3

   C)for every nearbyPoint around the currentNode
       a)if this nearbyPoint is in a spot that is
         impassable then
           - skip to the next nearbyPoint
```

```
b)create the successorNode
    - set its x and y according to nearbyPoint
    - set its parent to currentNode
    - set its givenCost to currentNode's
      givenCost + cost of going from
      currentNode to successorNode

c)if a node for this nearbyPoint has been
  created before then
    - if successorNode is better than oldNode
      then
        - pop the oldNode and delete it
    - else
        - skip to the next nearbyPoint

d)push the successorNode onto the open list

D)push the currentNode onto the closed list

4)if the while loop exits without finding the goal,
  goalPoint must be unreachable
```

It is important to emphasize that no other algorithms can find paths more optimal than the ones found by Dijkstra. Just like Breadth-First, Dijkstra is an exhaustive search and therefore consumes a lot of memory and CPU cycles to find a path. Exhaustive searches do not take advantage of the location of the goal, which results in not directing the search toward regions that are more likely to pay off.

A*

A* resolves most of the issues with Breadth-First, Best-First, and Dijkstra. It tends to use significantly less memory and CPU cycles than Breadth-First and Dijkstra. In addition, it can guarantee to find an optimal solution as long as it uses an *admissible* heuristic function (a function that never overestimates the true cost). A* combines Best-First and Dijkstra by taking into account both the given cost (the actual cost paid to reach a node from the start) and the heuristic cost (the estimated cost to reach the goal). A* keeps the open list sorted by final cost, which is computed by the following:

$$\text{Final Cost} = \text{Given Cost} + (\text{Heuristic Cost} * \text{Heuristic Weight})$$

Figure 5.4.8 shows how A* handles the map that was used to exploit the weakness of Best-First. The given cost that is incorporated into the final cost prevents A* from falling into the trap that we had made for Best-First.

Heuristic weight can be used to control the amount of emphasis on the heuristic cost versus the given cost. In other words, the weight can be used to control whether A* should behave more like Best-First or more like Dijkstra. For example, if the heuristic weight is set to 0, final cost will be exactly the given cost, which means that the algorithm will behave just like Dijkstra. On the other hand, if the heuristic weight

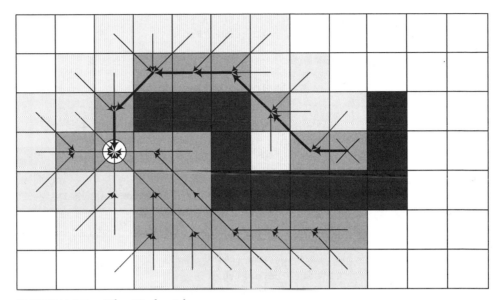

FIGURE 5.4.8 *The Λ^* algorithm.*

is set to an extremely large value, the algorithm will behave just like Best-First. In general, a number greater than 1 will put more emphasis on the heuristic cost, and a number less than one will put more emphasis on the given cost.

To guarantee that A* finds the optimal solution, the heuristic function used to compute the heuristic cost should never overestimate the actual cost of reaching the goal. Fortunately, by nature, the distance formula is a nonoverestimating heuristic function for pathfinding. For example, if the goal is two cells away from the current node, the distance formula will return 2, which is the least amount of cost that will have to be paid to reach the goal. However, if there is an obstacle between the current node and the goal or the cells in between have a higher weight, then the true cost of reaching the goal will be more than 2. Listing 5.4.6 is an example of A* pseudocode.

Listing 5.4.6 A* pseudocode

```
1)create the rootNode
    - set its x and y according to the startPoint
    - set its parent to NULL
    - set its finalCost to givenCost + heuristicCost

2)push the rootNode onto the open list

3)while the open list is not empty
```

```
    A)pop the node with the lowest finalCost from open
       and assign it to currentNode

    B)if currentNode's x and y correspond to the
       goalPoint then
             - break from step 3

    C)for every nearbyPoint around the currentNode
        a)if this nearbyPoint is in a spot that is
           impassable then
             - skip to the next nearbyPoint

        b)create the successorNode
             - set its x and y according to nearbyPoint
             - set its parent to currentNode
             - set its finalCost to givenCost +
               heuristicCost

        c)if a node for this nearbyPoint has been
           created before then
             - if successorNode is better than oldNode
               then
                 - pop the oldNode and delete it
             - else
                 - skip to the next nearbyPoint

        d)push the successorNode onto the open list

    D)push the currentNode onto the closed list

  4)if the while loop exits without finding the goal,
     goalPoint must be unreachable
```

Summary

To perform pathfinding, an agent needs to understand the level. This can be accomplished by providing the agent with a small-scale model of the level that encompasses its more important features. We discussed the strengths and weaknesses of grids, waypoint graphs, and navigation meshes, which are the most popular representation techniques. A search algorithm is executed on the small-scale model of the level to find paths between a start and a goal point. A* is by far the most popular algorithm for pathfinding. In this chapter, we showed the superiority of A* by comparing and contrasting it to other algorithms. Please note that there are many optimizations that can improve the performance of A* and other algorithms presented here. However, such optimizations can significantly reduce the readability of the algorithms and make them harder to understand. Refer to [Cain02] and [Higgins02] for examples of such optimizations.

Even though we spent a lot of time on A*, it is important to note that simpler algorithms such as Random-Trace can be very effective for simple levels. Despite the fact that Random-Trace is not a complete algorithm and cannot guarantee to find high-quality paths, it does not consume any memory. In addition, if the map is trivial, it will run significantly faster than even A* and Best-First.

You should also know that there is more to pathfinding than a representation technique and a search algorithm. For example, once an algorithm returns a path, the path might have to be modified a bit to make it seem more humanlike. In addition, avoiding movable obstacles in the level is an issue that needs to be dealt with as well. For interesting path following and steering algorithms, refer to [Reynolds97].

Performing searches on massive levels or multiple searches simultaneously can be very expensive. Hierarchical path planning and preplanning are two approaches of dealing with these situations. Hierarchical path planning uses multiple representations, each at a different level of detail. Paths are first resolved on the lower resolution layer and the details are then worked out on the higher resolution layers. For additional information on hierarchical path planning, refer to [Botea04]. Preplanning is a technique where the most optimal path between every two cells of the level is computed ahead of time and stored. During runtime, the precomputed paths are simply looked up without the need to perform a pathfinding search. For more information on preplanning, refer to [Surasmith02].

Exercises

1. For every algorithm covered in this chapter (Random-Trace, Breadth-First, Best-First, Dijkstra, and A*), answer the following questions: (a) Is the algorithm an exhaustive or a heuristic search algorithm? (b) Is the algorithm resource (CPU and memory) intensive? (c) Does the algorithm always find the optimal path? (d) Is the algorithm a *complete* algorithm?
2. Explain the difference between heuristic cost that is used by Best-First and given cost that is used by Dijkstra.
3. Why is A* typically preferred over Breadth-First, Best-First, and Dijkstra algorithms?
4. Use the *PathPlannerApp* application provided on the companion CD-ROM to implement Breadth-First, Best-First, Dijkstra, and A*.
5. The *WaypointGraph* application on the companion CD-ROM has two functions that perform A* and Dijkstra on a graph. Add a function that performs Best-First.
6. There are many other search algorithms such as Depth-First, Iterative-Deepening-Depth-First, Iterative-Deepening-A*, and Hill-Climbing. Research an algorithm that was not covered in this chapter and discuss its characteristics.

ON THE CD

ON THE CD

References

[Botea04] Botea, Adi; Müller, Martin; and Schaeffer, Jonathan, "Near Optimal Hierarchical Path-Finding," *Journal of Game Development*, Charles River Media, March 2004.

[Cain02] Cain, Timothy, "Practical Optimizations for A* Path Generation," *AI Game Programming Wisdom*, Charles River Media, 2002.

[Hancock02] Hancock, John, "Navigating Doors, Elevators, Ledges, and Other Obstacles," *AI Game Programming Wisdom*, Charles River Media, 2002.

[Higgins02] Higgins, Daniel, "How to Achieve Lightning Fast A*," *AI Game Programming Wisdom*, Charles River Media, 2002.

[Reynolds97] Reynolds, Craig, "Steering Behaviors for Autonomous Characters," available online at *www.red3d.com/cwr/steer/*, September 5, 1997.

[Surasmith02] Surasmith, Smith, "Preprocessed Solution for Open Terrain Environments," *AI Game Programming Wisdom*, Charles River Media, 2002.

[Tozour02] Tozour, Paul, "Building a Near-Optimal Navigation Mesh," *AI Game Programming Wisdom*, Charles River Media, 2002.

[Tozour03] Tozour, Paul, "Search Space Representations," *AI Game Programming Wisdom 2*, Charles River Media, 2002.

5.5 Audio Programming

In This Chapter

Overview

The role of the audio programmer has become increasingly important as games have evolved to feature more complex sound and musical components. Rather than just supporting real-time playback of audio content, the audio programmer must also support the creation and integration of sound within the game engine. In some sense, programming success can be measured by the degree to which an audio designer can integrate audio without the direct need for programmer support. In most situations, audio events are triggered by in-game events: a character plays a specific animation, a weapon fires, an explosion occurs, and so forth. Others are triggered by locality, such as ambient effects. Still others may be launched via scripts—such as dialogue in a cut-scene.

As with visual rendering technology, audio programming has moved past the simple basics of vanilla sound mixing and playback. However, every audio system should be built on top of a fundamental understanding of these basic principles and systems. On most modern gaming platforms, the capabilities of mixing and rendering audio data on hardware is a given. Moreover, these platforms typically have a reasonably robust API to program these capabilities. It is rare for an audio programmer to have to write a low-level mixer or filter in software. Instead, this chapter will focus on mid-level programming; that is, how one should make use of existing APIs and hardware to create an audio engine.

As with any other specialty, audio programming has its own standards and vocabulary. Since each platform has unique hardware and APIs, we will forgo any one specific API and instead provide the essential concepts and vocabulary necessary to understand audio programming. Once the groundwork has been laid, we'll explore some of the more advanced issues being faced by modern audio programmers [Boer02]. When you are ready to implement game audio, there are many places online to easily obtain APIs for Windows, Mac, and Linux PC platforms, and instructions on how to use them [MSDN, OpenAL].

Programming Basic Audio

To effectively program audio in modern computer games, it is important to have a basic grasp of the physics involved in the processing and reproduction of audio on modern computer hardware. We'll examine the fundamentals of sound in the real world and how it is stored digitally in a computer. Audio processing hardware works in a fundamentally similar manner, offering standardized operations, such as pan, volume, and pitch control on individual sound channels. In addition, we'll examine some fundamental aspects of sound manipulation, such as ADSR envelopes.

API CHOICES FOR WINDOWS, MAC, AND LINUX

There are currently two free audio rendering APIs that you may choose from to experiment with. The first, and by far the most popular, is the DirectX component known as DirectSound. It is freely available as part of the DirectX SDK, and is available for all currently supported Windows operating systems for the PC. DirectSound is, unfortunately, a rather antiquated API with many fundamental faults and problems. As a simple example, there is no basic support code for loading and parsing audio data from a wave file. As such, a significant effort must be expended to use this API, which explains some of the popularity of licensed third-party sound APIs on the Windows platform. However, there is a good deal of support and example code out there.

The other viable API, OpenAL, is a relative newcomer to the scene, but is a much better designed system (except for the puzzling lack of support for basic 2D sound rendering). OpenAL was designed to be the aural equivalent of OpenGL.

As you might expect, OpenAL is a cross-platform solution, making this an attractive option for game programmers looking to port their games to other platforms.

In addition to these free audio rendering APIs, numerous commercial APIs on nearly every platform may be licensed for a fee. These APIs are either easier to use or simply offer the convenience of a single API that will work across all platforms.

It's probably not a bad idea to examine as many APIs as possible to become familiar with their similarities and their differences. A potential employer looking to hire an audio programmer will be more impressed with someone who has familiarity with several systems, regardless of which API is ultimately used.

Basic Audio Terminology and Physics

In simple terms, a sound is nothing more than compression waves transmitted through a medium, such as air or water. A physically vibrating object, such as a piano string or a speaker cone, causes the initial vibrations. These vibrations are then transmitted across the medium until they reach a listener's ears, at which time they are converted back into physical vibrations by an eardrum. The eardrum converts the vibrations into nerve impulses, which our brains then translate into what we perceive as "sound."

The important information to remember is that sounds can be represented as a scale of wave pressure over time. Figure 5.5.1 shows a common representation of a sound wave.

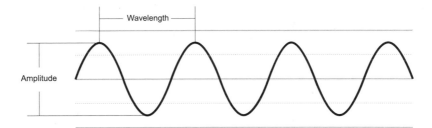

FIGURE 5.5.1 *Characteristics of a simple sine wave.*

The plotting of a sound wave is actually a measurement of the sound's *amplitude* over time. Amplitude is the measurement of a sound wave's pressure, either in a positive or negative direction. The perceived sounds we hear are not actually generated by amplitude, but rather, changes in amplitude. Most sounds tend to have a natural oscillation of repeating pressure patterns. You will note that Figure 5.5.1 looks very similar to a sine wave. This demonstrates the property of *frequency*. Frequency may be defined as the interval between wave cycles, and is usually measured in Hertz—the number of cycles that occur in a second. Human hearing ranges from approximately 20 Hz to 20,000 Hz.

Frequency is related to *pitch*, but is not necessarily synonymous with it. Pitch may be described as the perception of frequency. Humans tend to perceive high notes at a slightly lower frequency and lower notes at a slightly higher frequency. However, for the purposes of audio programming, this distinction is often incorrectly ignored, and the two terms are used interchangeably.

Tuning may be defined as a musical distribution of frequency over keys. In modern Western music, each octave is divided into 12 keys. An octave represents a doubling or halving of frequency, depending on whether you are traveling up or down in pitch. A system of tuning called *equal tempering* divides the 12 notes between each octave equally, so that no particular key is favored. This is the tuning that nearly all contemporary music uses. Table 5.5.1 shows the frequencies in Hertz for 12 keys through 9 octaves.

Table 5.5.1   Frequencies in Hertz for Equal Tempering Tuning

	0	1	2	3	4	5	6	7	8
C	16.352	32.703	65.406	130.81	261.63	523.25	1046.5	2093.0	4186.0
C#	17.324	34.648	69.296	138.59	277.18	554.37	1108.7	2217.5	4434.9
D	18.354	36.708	73.416	146.83	293.66	587.33	1174.7	2349.3	4698.6
D#	19.445	38.891	77.782	155.56	311.13	622.25	1244.5	2489.0	4978.0
E	20.602	41.203	82.407	164.81	329.63	659.26	1318.5	2637.0	5274.0
F	21.827	43.654	87.307	174.61	349.23	698.46	1396.9	2793.8	5587.7
F#	23.125	46.249	92.499	185.00	369.99	739.99	1480.0	2960.0	5919.9
G	24.500	48.999	97.999	196.00	392.00	783.99	1568.0	3136.0	6271.9
G#	25.957	51.913	103.83	207.65	415.30	830.61	1661.2	3322.4	6644.9
A	27.500	55.000	110.00	220.0	440.00	880.00	1760.0	3520.0	7040.0
A#	29.135	58.270	116.54	233.08	466.16	932.33	1864.7	3729.3	7458.6
B	30.868	61.735	123.47	246.94	493.88	987.77	1975.5	3951.1	7902.1

A sound's amplitude is a measure of its power. This power corresponds to its perceived loudness. In Figure 5.5.1, this corresponds directly to the maximum changes in height from the bottom to the top of the waveform. Amplitude is often measured in *decibels*. A decibel is one-tenth of a *bel*, which is less commonly used in measurements. Decibels (and bels) actually measure the perceived difference in loudness between two sounds, not an absolute loudness. Since perceived loudness increases linearly as power increases logarithmically, this is reflected in the scale. In other words, if a sound is twice as loud as another sound, it is $10 \log_{10}(2)$, or approximately 3.01 dB louder. It is important to understand the logarithmic nature of the decibel scale, because sound hardware often implements volume control as *attenuation* (reduction) in decibels. Generally speaking, hardware volume controls cannot actually *amplify* (increase) volume.

To measure absolute sound volume, a standard pressure (20 micropascal) has been defined as the approximate quietest average sound a human can hear transmitted through the air. All other human-audible sounds are compared against this measurement, resulting in an absolute scale. When decibels are used to describe a sound in terms of its perceived loudness, it is likely that this is the scale against which it is being measured. However, in audio programming, we're typically much more interested in relative sound volumes. After all, the player ultimately has the final control over the volume of the audio being rendered.

Inside your own sound-system layer, it is often far more practical to store sample volume as a ratio (0.0 to 1.0) rather than attenuation in decibels (–100 to 0). Combining volumes and interpolation are much more practical on a linear scale. You may use the functions in Listing 5.5.1 to convert between a decibel scale and a linear ratio.

Listing 5.5.1 Code to convert between a decibel scale and a linear ratio

```
float linearToLog(float fLevel)
{
   // Clamp the value
   if(fLevel <= 0.0f)
      return -100.0f;
   else if(fLevel >= 1.0f)
      return 0.0f;
   return (-2000.0f * log10f(1.0f / fLevel)) / 100.0f;
}

float logToLinear(float fLevel)
{
   // Clamp the value
   if(fLevel <= -100.0f)
      return 0.0f;
   else if(fLevel >= 0.0f)
      return 1.0f;
   return powf(10, ((fLevel * 100.0f) + 2000.0f) /
               2000.0f) / 10.0f;
}
```

Digital Representation of Sound

For a sound to be reproduced by a computer, we must first examine how digital audio is stored. The most common (and simplest) technique is known as *sampling*, which means measuring and storing the amplitude of a sound wave at discrete time intervals. The rate at which the samples are collected is known as the *sampling rate*, and is measured in samples per second. Typical sample rates range from 4,000 to 96,000 samples per second. The amplitude of the wave file is stored in a discrete value, typically represented by a value from 4 to 24 bits. This is known as the sample's *bit depth*. In general, it is agreed that most people cannot perceive quality improvements beyond CD-quality samples, which uses 16-bit samples measured at a frequency of 44,100 samples per second. Figure 5.5.2 shows how the sine wave from Figure 5.5.1 can be represented digitally.

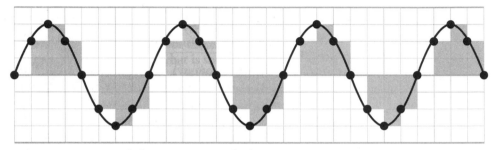

FIGURE 5.5.2 *Sampled representation of a basic sine wave.*

As is intuitively obvious, the greater the combination of bit depth and sampling rate, the more accurately a waveform can be represented. Figure 5.5.3 demonstrates a phenomenon known as *quantization error*. You can see how the amplitude of the waveform cannot be perfectly represented by the sampled data due to the low bit depth. The lower the bit depth, the more noise will be introduced into the signal. The amount of unwanted noise is directly related to the sample size. An 8-bit sample allows 128 discrete values, and sample error is limited to one-half the size of the sample step. Therefore, with 8-bit samples we have a 256:1 *signal-to-noise ratio* (SNR), which translates to 48 dB. Keeping in mind that a decibel is actually a measurement of the difference in sound volume, this measurement in decibels represents the difference in volume between the average noise level and the maximum volume of the signal. A 16-bit sample, on the other hand, offers a much more impressive SNR of 65,536:1, or 96 dB. Since the human range of hearing is approximately 100 dB, an optimally mixed 16-bit recording will have very little discernable noise introduced by quantization artifacts.

Just as low bit-depth creates quantization error resulting in a worse signal-to-noise ratio, sampling rate also has a dramatic effect on sound quality, but in different ways and for different reasons. The frequency of the sampling rate, as you might expect, has the most dramatic effect on how accurately high-frequency waveforms can be represented. Figure 5.5.4a demonstrates how a digital representation of a high-frequency sound wave using a low-frequency sampling rate has no chance of accurately representing the original sound. For the sake of this demonstration, keep in mind that we're using an unsophisticated algorithm (closest point) for sample placement, and a low bit depth, both of which tend to exaggerate the final outcome.

Quantization Error

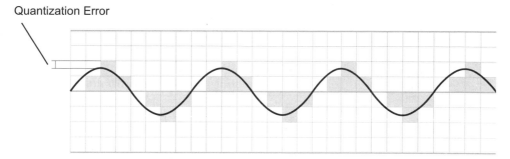

FIGURE 5.5.3 *Waveform showing maximum quantization error.*

Original Analog Sample

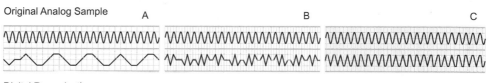

Digital Reproduction

FIGURE 5.5.4 *Demonstration of sampling error based on sampling frequency.*

Notice how by doubling the sampling rate in Figure 5.5.4b we get a much-improved digital version of the original waveform. However, this version still has obvious flaws.

Doubling the sampling frequency again in Figure 5.5.4c finally yields a digital waveform that matches reasonably close to the original.

This exercise demonstrates a phenomenon known as the *Nyquist limit*, which states, in part, that a specific sampling rate can only represent frequencies of one-half that sample rate. However, the differences between Figure 5.5.4b and Figure 5.5.4c demonstrate another property of the Nyquist limit, which states that the closer a frequency approaches its theoretical maximum, the worse the representation will be. It is for this reason that 44.1 kHz was chosen as a sampling rate for CD audio, even though humans have a nominal hearing range of 20 Hz to 20 kHz.

Audio Hardware Features

Modern audio hardware typically has very similar capabilities. We will examine how this hardware works in principle, and what you need to know as a programmer to effectively use these resources.

Figure 5.5.5 shows the pipeline that all audio data must flow through in a typical audio rendering system.

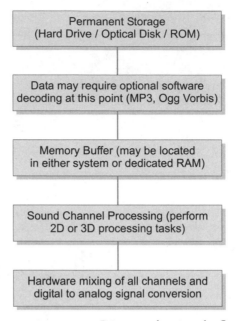

FIGURE 5.5.5   *Diagram showing the flow of audio data through a typical audio processing and rendering system.*

Data must first be retrieved from a permanent storage medium, such as an optical or magnetic hard drive, and stored in memory. From there, audio data is transferred or assigned to hardware *sound channels*. Once data is sent to a hardware channel, it is then manipulated according to a common set of parameters, controls, and settings (we'll discuss these later). After all the channels have been individually processed, they are then mixed together into a single audio signal. Finally, the mixed data is then converted from a digital stream of data back into an analog steam of audio for speakers to play.

There are several variations on this theme, of course, depending on the hardware platform. Some platforms, such as Sony's PlayStation 2 and Nintendo's GameCube, have dedicated audio memory. The PS2 has 4 MB of audio memory, while the Game-Cube has 16 MB. Microsoft's Xbox and PC, however, use a unified memory architecture, so any percentage of available memory can be allocated for sound samples from the global pool.

Additionally, it may be even more complicated than this on some platforms. For instance, developers may decide to swap memory allocations as well. On the PS2, some developers have opted to use the dedicated 4 MB of memory as a streaming destination for audio data from main memory. This allows more than 4 MB of total memory to be used, but comes at the cost of the PS2's main memory pool (32 MB).

Because of the abundance of audio memory (16 MB) compared to the main memory pool (24 MB), programmers of the Nintendo GameCube will often sacrifice portions of audio memory to be used as a swap file for main memory. These two techniques are sometimes used to equalize some of the differences in system memory, which may be important to those developing cross-platform titles. As you can see, memory allocation and usage can be a somewhat complicated affair.

There are also different ways of transferring the audio data depending on the volume of data to be transferred. For smaller sized samples, it is typical to store the entire sample in memory at once. However, for playing extremely long samples (such as music tracks or lengthy tracks of recorded dialogue), there is simply not enough memory to load the entire sample. This means that streaming will be required, where a small portion of the sample is loaded at any one time. As more data is required, it is fetched from the permanent storage system, while previously played data is discarded.

The core of an audio system, like so many other aspects of game programming, is really about asset management. The data to manage comes in the form of sampled waveforms. These audio files, once loaded into memory, are called *samples*. This dual use of the term *sample* is slightly unfortunate, but it is typically clear which meaning of the word is appropriate based on context. Typically, anywhere from several dozen to several thousand samples can be loaded at once, depending on how much memory is available. Often, the memory allocated to load the sample is called a *buffer*.

The other managed aspect is the hardware channels used to process and mix the sound data. A channel can mix a single sample at one time. Thus, the number of channels is equal to the number of individual samples that can be mixed and played at one time. Again, the number of available channels varies greatly from platform to platform, but you can expect anywhere from 16 to 128 individual channels on modern systems, and even more in future hardware.

Mixing and playback is generally as simple as assigning a sample buffer to a hardware channel, and instructing the channel to mix (play) the sound.

THE DIRECTSOUND EXCEPTION

Microsoft's DirectSound has made the unfortunate decision to use a mechanism whereby a single COM object (called a DirectSoundBuffer) represents both a sound buffer and a sound channel. This has the result of making it much more difficult to store more sounds in memory than one has buffers for. This necessitates some complications in design. Either a buffer and memory management scheme must be employed, or a more complex system of decoupling DirectSound buffers from sample data can be implemented by streaming all data from memory buffers to the DirectSound buffers. In this way, the DirectSound buffers can then be used as channels. Regardless of the solution chosen, the result is a more difficult task of audio programming when using the DirectSound API.

Sample Playback and Manipulation

Once a digital audio sample has been assigned to a channel, the hardware (or in some cases, the software) then takes over the job of processing the audio data in real time. This involves first manipulating the individual audio data, and then sending the audio data to a final mixing buffer, where it is combined into a single audio stream. Next, the audio hardware must convert this single digital audio signal back into an analog waveform for playback on speakers.

Before each channel is mixed together, there are certain common operations that you may perform on the channel. Three of these common operations are *pan*, *pitch*, and *volume* controls.

Panning is a simple operation that directs the relative position of a sound in a stereo field by attenuating the left or right mix. Panning is an operation that often can only be performed on nonstereo data. For hardware that does not support true 3D positional sound mixing, a simple pan (combined with the volume control) can be used as a simple substitute method for placing sounds in 3D space.

Pitch control is typically performed by simply processing more or fewer samples per second. This has the result of manipulating pitch, but as you can surmise, the side effect of this operation is to affect the sample's playback time.

Volume control, as described earlier, is typically implemented via an attenuation control measured in decibels. For instance, a volume setting of −3 dB will sound approximately half as loud as when set to full volume (0 dB).

Streaming Audio

As mentioned earlier, one important variation of audio playback is known as *streaming audio*. This is a general term used to describe the concept of reading data in real-time for playback directly off the bulk-storage medium (such as the disk) instead of storing the entire sample in memory. This is typically done for large audio tracks, such as music or recorded dialogue, where the size of the sample prevents it from being efficiently stored in memory all at once.

To prevent the audio stream from being susceptible to the intermittent skips that would occur if it literally tried to read audio data in real time, it is necessary to pre-buffer a small amount of audio data. Typically, these buffers range in size from half a second to perhaps two seconds in length. There are essentially two types of buffering methods: *circular buffers* and *double buffering (or buffer chaining)*. Figure 5.5.6 demonstrates these two methods.

Circular buffers use a single buffer for their buffering operations. The buffer contains a read and a write pointer. The read pointer will wrap around from the end of the buffer back to the beginning of the buffer when it exceeds the total buffer length (hence the name). The application must track how much data is pushed into the buffer, and must make sure it pushes data into the buffer well ahead of the read buffer, but not so far that it wraps around and interferes with the read buffer from behind. This is the method that DirectSound uses for streaming audio.

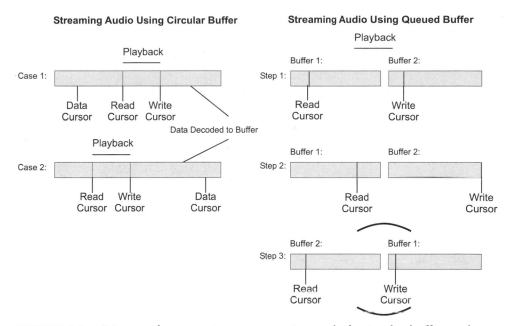

FIGURE 5.5.6 *Diagram demonstrating two streaming methods: circular buffers and buffer chaining.*

Double buffering is a slightly less complex method that makes use of two (or more) buffers. While one buffer is being played, the other buffer is filled with data. The application is notified that the next buffer in the chain is being used. The user can now begin streaming data into the previously playing buffer, and the cycle begins again. This is the method OpenAL uses for streaming audio.

Compressed Audio Formats

Because digital audio data requires so much memory, intensive efforts have been made to find ways to compress audio data to reduce this memory load. Generally speaking, nearly all audio compression formats are *lossy* compression formats (unlike *lossless* formats that preserve every bit, such as ".zip"). Because digital audio data is already an approximation of an analog signal, there is no need to preserve every single bit of data. Rather, the only important factor is the final acoustical result.

There are, in general, two classes of compression schemes you are likely to be working with in the game programming world: *bit-reduction* schemes and *psycho-acoustic compression* schemes. These encoding/decoding algorithms are also known as *codecs*, which is derived from the words *co*mpress and *dec*ompress.

Bit-reduction schemes are by far the simpler of the two methods. They employ techniques to reduce the number of bits that each sample is required to store. One of the most popular schemes of this type is known as ADPCM compression. ADPCM is designed to reduce the number of bits stored in a file from 16 to 4. Because of this, it always has a fixed compression ratio of 4:1. It employs a more sophisticated method of encoding numeric movement from sample to sample so that fewer bits are required to encode a reasonably high-fidelity sound. Although this method of encoding has been surpassed in recent years by other formats, there are still reasons why you should understand this more simplistic compression. First, ADPCM compression schemes are much less computationally expensive than high-compression psycho-acoustic techniques such as MP3 compression. The simplicity of the algorithm means that it is much easier to implement this compression in hardware. The PS2, Xbox, and Game-Cube all use ADPCM compression in hardware. This simple compression immediately quadruples the effective audio memory for no additional CPU cost. On the PC side, however, ADPCM is typically not supported in hardware, and so must be decoded via software codecs. Generally speaking, because of the abundance of memory on the PC, most games on this platform do not use ADPCM compression.

The most famous audio compression scheme, MP3, is in the psycho-acoustic compression class. Two other formats useful for game developers are Ogg Vorbis, an open-source format, and Windows Media, a format developed by Microsoft. This type of compression scheme uses sophisticated algorithms to encode sound, and saves space by discarding audio data that our ears would not typically be able to hear. These schemes can compress audio data in a variable manner, depending on the desired final quality of the reproduction. As such, you can expect anywhere between a 5:1 and 25:1 compression. Most current-generation psycho-acoustic codecs can emulate CD-quality audio at a 10:1 compression ratio. Unfortunately, advanced compression techniques such as this come at the cost of CPU time. It would still be impractical to encode every single sound file using psycho-acoustic compression techniques. However, the high-compression ratio makes this a perfect fit for encoding a single track of audio, such as game music or a dialogue track.

THE MP3 FORMAT AND LICENSING FEES

Why would game developers want to look at compression formats other than MP3? Simple: putting MP3 support in your game legally requires you to pay licensing fees to Franhofer-Thompson, the MP3 patent owners. Ogg Vorbis and Windows Media both are high-quality formats, and both have well-documented APIs for use in games. More importantly, neither of these formats requires paying a licensing fee for including this technology in your game. Ogg Vorbis, as the only open-source, high-compression codec on the market, is making considerable in-roads in the games industry.

ADSR Envelopes

One volume-control technique that you should be familiar with is the basic *ADSR envelope*. ADSR is an acronym for Attack, Decay, Sustain, and Release. As indicated, these four parameters can be used to define a standardized volume envelope. Let's look at a standard ADSR envelope in Figure 5.5.7.

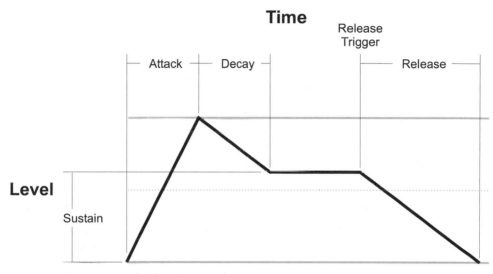

FIGURE 5.5.7 *A standard ADSR envelope.*

The attack parameter (Λ) is a measurement of time between the initial volume of zero and the final, full volume. The decay parameter (D) is a measurement of the time from full attack volume to the sustain volume. The sustain parameter (S) is a measurement of the volume of the envelope held between the decay and release phases. Finally, the release parameter (R) is a measurement of time from the release point to the zero volume point.

You may have noticed that one significant measurement has been omitted—the length of the sustain. This is simple to explain: The ADSR envelope was originally designed for applications such as electronic synthesizers. The envelope was triggered when a key was pressed, and the sustain was defined by the time the key was held down. In other words, this envelope should be used in a real-time environment.

When implementing a musical synthesizer, a real-time ADSR envelope is an absolute necessity for creating more realistic sounding instruments with smaller sized samples. However, the benefits of this type of envelope can also be seen with sound effects. Consider implementing ADSR envelopes into your basic sound-system design if you have an opportunity to do so.

3D Audio

In the world of interactive computer entertainment, everything has moved into the third dimension, including audio. Most modern audio hardware today has the capability to process 3D audio. A big part of an audio programmer's job involves understanding how sounds work in the real world, and then reproducing those sounds in a digital world. To start, let's examine how 3D audio works at a fundamental level.

In the real world, our two ears allow us to spatially locate sounds in 3D space, somewhat analogously to the way our two eyes help visualize a 3D environment. Our brain discerns the slight timing and acoustical differences between our two ears to locate sounds. Figure 5.5.8 demonstrates how the spatial difference between our ears creates a slight timing delay that helps to determine a sound's relative position.

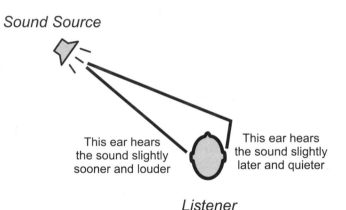

FIGURE 5.5.8   *How a listener determines a sound's position in the world.*

The process of reproducing 3D audio in games revolves around providing these types of aural cues for the game player to immerse them more fully into our simulated world. One of the biggest problems, however, is the wide variety of speaker arrangements for a given set of hardware. While some computers and home theater systems have surround-speaker capabilities, the majority of these systems have only a pair of stereo speakers. How, then, do we represent sounds in a 3D world with only a pair of speakers in front of the listener?

The simplest solution involves panning sounds between the left and right speakers to position the sound source around the listener, and attenuating the volume to simulate distance from the listener. This yields decent results for sounds originating in front of the listener, but is obviously deficient in that there is no good way to create a sound originating from behind the listener. In fact, it is troublesome to represent any sound outside of a rather limited arc directly in front of the listener.

While simple pan-volume schemes work well enough, there are better solutions out there. A technique called *HRTF* (Head Relative Transfer Function) encoding allows more realistic sounding 3D audio using only two speakers. This is accomplished by encoding into the left and right channel the types of aural cues that occur with sounds based on the natural shape of your ears. For instance, sounds that originate from behind the listener have their high frequencies slightly attenuated, just as it happens in real life.

While in theory this does work quite well (especially with headphones on), the practical matter is that HRTF in the real world is only partially successfully in fooling the listener's ears. This is due to the unavoidable problems of different speaker systems, room configurations, and even differences in the physical dimensions of different listener's ears.

The best solution is perhaps the most straightforward: place speakers all around the listener. The most common surround-sound speaker solution today is a 5.1 speaker arrangement. This is a six-channel system: left, right, center, left rear, right rear, and subwoofer (low frequency) channels. Other arrangements add or subtract high-frequency speakers to make 4.1, 6.1, and even 7.1 systems.

Fortunately, the complexity of converting a position in 3D space to a multichannel panning mapping is not one that we as game developers have to solve. This sort of functionality is typically provided in hardware. Our task is to provide two different sets of data to the audio hardware so that it knows how to mix the desired audio streams into a final multichannel mix. The first set of data is, oddly enough, not any type of audio data at all.

The *listener* is simply a position and an orientation (sometimes defined as two orthogonal vectors) in 3D space. The listener represents the physical head of a virtual person in the virtual world. The listener acts much in the same way as the camera does for 3D graphics. It is important that your listener is oriented to the world in a similar fashion to your engine's graphics, as they will be likely using the same set of positional coordinates and properties to render.

Each sound in the world is defined as a *source*, and is positioned and oriented in *world space*. Just as polygons are transformed from world space to camera space by the camera's transformation matrix, so are sounds transformed from world space to *listener space*.

While the listener represents a fairly simple set of data, the source is a bit more complex, and often has more data associated with it. Some of this data includes velocity (used to apply Doppler shift), min and max cone angles for directional sounds, and min and max distances (to define a source's gain).

Environmental Effects

Perhaps one of the greatest benefits to modern hardware-accelerated audio systems is the ability to create programmatically generated *environmental effects*. Simply put, environmental effects are an attempt to mimic the natural coloration of sound that occurs in the real world due to geometry and materials. For instance, we all know the different ambience that occurs in a large church versus a small hallway. By re-creating these subtle effects in our virtual world, we give the user a more immersive experience.

In essence, environmental effects describe the nature of sound propagation. Much like a wave in a calm pool of water, sound waves will reflect off surfaces in the world. The amount of reflection is dependent upon what the material is made of. Hard, smooth surfaces will tend to reflect most of the signal, while soft, porous materials will tend to absorb much of the sound.

Sound transmission, when dealing with environmental effects, is categorized three ways: direct transmission, early reflections (or echo), and late reflections (or reverberation). Figure 5.5.9 shows how these sounds are transmitted from a source to a listener.

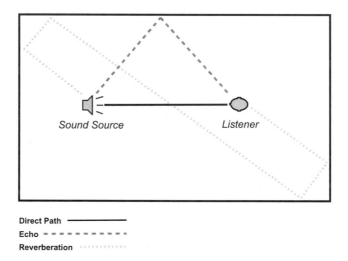

FIGURE 5.5.9   *Demonstration of direct path, echo, and reverberation.*

Although sound propagation through complex structures in real life is quite complex, there are two substantial contributions that we can focus on that contribute the bulk of the reverberation effect: *environmental geometry* and *material composition*.

To demonstrate how environmental geometry can affect sound propagation, we can see in Figure 5.5.10 how a wall blocks the direct transmission of sound from the source to the listener. This will leave only indirect transmission of sound from source to listener, and so the sound will be affected by the frequency absorption of the materials off which the sound must bounce. This phenomenon is known as *obstruction*.

Material composition is the other factor that affects sound propagation. Certain materials will cause specific frequencies (both high and low) to be absorbed. In addition to absorbing sound, specific materials will also cause sounds to be scattered. This is known as *diffusion*.

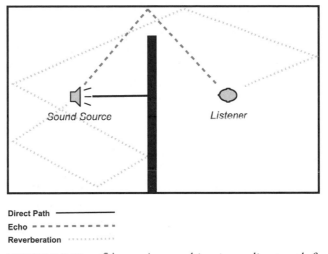

Direct Path ——————
Echo = = = = = = = = = =
Reverberation · · · · · · · · · ·

FIGURE 5.5.10 *Obstruction resulting in no direct path for the sound.*

You may be familiar with how material can also act to block specific frequencies while allowing others to pass through at reduced volume. Generally speaking, low frequencies can be transmitted through many types of material, while high frequencies tend to be reflected and absorbed by walls. This phenomenon can be noticed by listening to the differences in transmission of sound by a stereo system in another room. If you close the door, you only hear the muffled bass part of the music. If the door is opened, the high frequencies, now unblocked, flow freely out of the room and to the listener's ears. This phenomenon is known as *occlusion*.

Environmental Effects Standards: I3DL2 and EAX

There are currently two competing standards that define environmental extensions for modern hardware implementation. I3DL2 (Interactive 3D Audio Rendering Level 2) is a standard established by the Interactive Audio Special Interest Group (IA-SIG) to define a reverberation model and API for use in games and other interactive applications. EAX is a reverberation model invented by Creative Labs that started fairly simply with 1.0, allowing preselected reverberation models with several parameters. It then grew into 2.0, which is still the most widely supported of today's standards. EAX 2.0 is, in fact, nearly identical to the I3DL2 specification in both form and function. More recently, Creative Labs released EAX 3.0, officially dubbed EAX Advanced HD. Because this particular version of EAX is exclusive to Creative Labs' Audigy cards, we still see EAX 2.0 and I3DL2 as a reasonable baseline standard for audio solutions in the foreseeable future. The specifications for these standards can easily be found on the Internet [EAX, IA-SIG].

In truth, the I3DL2 specification is suitable for quite advanced reverberation modeling. Further advances in the reverberation model, such as EAX HD, provide good marketing bullet points on the back of a game box, but in truth, most listeners would likely not be able to tell the difference between the two reverberation models unless it was specifically pointed out to them.

These reverberation models all work in a similar manner. A set of global reverberation parameters is set on the listener. These parameters are intended to describe the listener's environment in a general sense. Some of these parameters include settings that describe the overall room size, decay rate, reverberation volume, air absorption settings, and so on.

This provides a reasonable baseline for the environmental reverberation engine to apply reverberation settings on any sound. However, each source also has its own set of unique parameters. This allows each sound to have a unique reverberation signature. Why would each sound source need unique properties if the listener were in a single location? The answer is simple: the unique properties are, in fact, more of a reflection of the difference in location between the source and listener. Properties such as obstruction and occlusion are not inherent in any particular location. Rather, they are, in some sense, a calculation describing the properties of how the world affects sound traveling from the source to the listener, given those two unique positions in the world.

Programming Music Systems

Depending on the type of game and platform you work on, you might find yourself having to create a music playback system. In general, music systems on modern hardware will be one of two basic types of flavors: a *sampled-based MIDI player* or a *digital audio stream player*. These two types of systems both have strengths and weaknesses, and both continue to be used on today's platforms.

A MIDI-based Music Player

A MIDI-style player is based on the simple concept of storing information as discrete musical notes, and using a sound engine to play particular instruments. MIDI is an acronym for Musical Instrument Digital Interface, and represents a long-established method of communicating common musical data in real time between electronic instruments [MIDI]. The standard encodes music in the form of musical notation, not as digitally encoded sound. This provides a tremendous saving of space, but it limits the acoustic quality of the music to the device that is rendering the music in real time. Modern audio hardware now has the capabilities of general-purpose synthesizers with only a small amount of programming work. Most of this work involves decoding MIDI and sample data, as well as some basic work in real-time envelope control (such as the ADSR envelope described earlier). Another significant disadvantage is the limited repertoire of instruments, which must be sampled and stored in memory.

MIDI music has two primary advantages over digital audio streams. The first advantage is greater control. Because each note of music is a discrete event and played electronically, the program has great control over every aspect of the music. For instance, a player could actually have a musical riff change keys, control looping points, or even dynamically switch instruments on one or more tracks to create different musical moods. Other capabilities inherent in this format include the ability to synchronize music to a specific beat pattern, speeding up or slowing down the musical tempo to a desired rate. Musically themed games or puzzles could benefit greatly from this type of control.

The other advantage MIDI-based players have is a small storage footprint. A MIDI song requires the use of a set of sampled instruments (or even algorithmic instruments in some cases), but the actual song data is almost negligible in size. Literally hours of music can be stored in just kilobytes of RAM. As such, MIDI-based music is very common on platforms where storage space is at a premium, such as downloaded games or cartridges/flash card-based platforms such as the Nintendo Game Boy and DS.

DLS

The MIDI format is not the only standardized format useful for MIDI-based players. Perhaps the most important other format to understand is the DLS (DownLoadable Sound) format. The DLS format is essentially a collection of MIDI-ready instruments in a single file format package. By extracting and using this set of sampled data, MIDI instruments can essentially be programmed at will to match whatever set of sounds is required for a given piece of music. DSL essentially provides a convenient, standardized package of instrument samples, playback instructions, and envelope data.

iXMF

One of the newer developments in the world of game audio has been the creation of the iXMF (Interactive eXtensible Music Format) specification. The XMF is essentially a container system for encapsulating MIDI files, DSL files, and custom meta-data. This provides a convenient and robust method for a game to package these types of files together into a single, unified package. iXMF is an extension of this format designed to address the needs of interactive content. If you want to develop an interactive music system, it would be wise to at least read the iXMF specifications to see what ideas you can glean from its pages.

A Digital Audio Stream Player

Digital audio streams are the opposite of MIDI in almost every way. These types of audio streams are simple to produce and create. Because a digital audio stream is simply a digital recording, there are no limitations on the ultimate quality of the original material being recorded. This has given rise to licensed soundtracks, and even live recording of symphonic scores, Hollywood style, all for games. Because of the ease of use and high-quality sound of digital audio streams, it is the most popular choice of today's high-end gaming systems, and will likely continue to be so in the future.

However, this type of fidelity comes at the cost of both size and flexibility. Unless a game is using a high-compression scheme, music alone will amount to a large percentage of a game's total footprint in disk space. In terms of flexibility, it is much harder to manipulate the data stream in any meaningful manner, save for queuing or looping discrete segments of music. Keep in mind, though, that it is still possible to create an adaptive music system using only looping and queued segments of pre-authored music.

A Conceptual Interactive Music System

Although there are nearly an infinite number of ways to create an interactive music system, we will demonstrate a simple conceptual system that can be created given nearly any type of audio content and/or platform capabilities.

To start, we must assume several factors—our audio content must have the capability to queue individual chunks of music end to end. We will call these discrete chunks *segments*. Our player also must have the capability of recognizing and sending a notification when a segment is about to end playing—with enough lead time to choose and queue another segment. This is the backbone of building an interactive music system, and can be built effectively with either MIDI-based or streaming audio players.

So, we now essentially have a map of short musical segments (each a couple bars long) that are designed to flow together to form a cohesive piece of music. If we allow random branching, we can introduce interesting variation into the piece with minimal effort. Let's call this map structure a musical *theme*. To provide true interactivity, we can create multiple music themes and define transitions from one theme to another. However, it won't typically work to simply map any currently playing segment in one theme to the starting segment of another theme. Instead, we must ensure that we can explicitly map the segment transitions depending on the originally playing segment when switching from one theme to another. This way, we have complete control over every segment switch. Obviously, the number of specialized transition segments grows exponentially with each theme and the number of segments in each of those themes, so it is important to place realistic limitations on these numbers. Figure 5.5.11 demonstrates how the music path can flow from theme to theme through custom transition segments.

The result of this system, while a significant investment in both programming and composing effort, can be truly remarkable: a completely seamless musical score that contains automatic and internal variation within a single musical theme, and can even switch between different musical themes as required by the game environment.

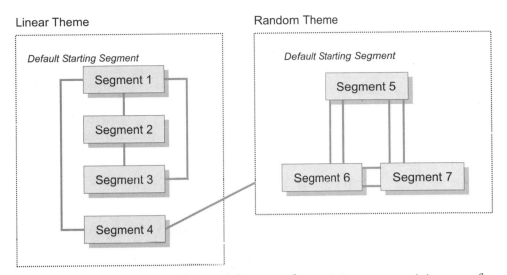

Linear Theme

Random Theme

FIGURE 5.5.11 *The concept of musical themes, each containing a connectivity map of music segments forms the basis for this interactive music system. Here we demonstrate two sample themes and their internal segment maps.*

Programming Advanced Audio

Audio programming in today's and tomorrow's computer games will be much more than creating a simple, low-level audio API. In the following pages, we'll discuss some of the most advanced audio-related issues facing the industry. Some of these issues are only now being effectively addressed in modern games, and some of them are still waiting for practical solutions to come with the next generation of game developers.

3D Audio Environmental Effects Integration

With the advent of hardware-based environmental effects, the next logical question is: How do we integrate this feature into a game engine? Unfortunately, this question, in many ways, has still not been definitively answered. Let's first define the problem.

We first have to create the environmental effects based on specific locations in our game world. In general, environmental effects change continuously based on your position in the world. In practice, we will define areas in which the overall effect should be relatively similar, such as the interior of a single room. The effect can be set manually or generated by scanning the geometry and material types found in the world and creating reverberation settings based on this input. These generated reverberation settings must be stored along with the geometry that defines its boundaries, so that the reverberation settings may be retrieved in real time based on a positional value in the world. Figure 5.5.12 illustrates this process.

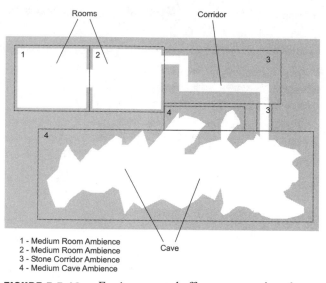

FIGURE 5.5.12   *Environmental effects per area based on room acoustics.*

While this is a considerable task already, there's still more complexity to consider. Unfortunately, the nature of any particular sound involves the positions of both the source and the listener, which is why there are typically settings to apply to each of these programmatic elements. Detecting sound obstruction means determining in real time if an object is blocking the line of sight between a sound source and the listener. For this, you will likely have to rely on a physics component of your engine to perform this type of ray-casting test.

Even more complicated is the proper detection and application of the obstruction parameter. In some ways, this is something of a pathfinding problem for sound. If a sound is completely blocked off from the listener by solid objects (such as walls), the obstruction rating should be the lowest component among those obstacles (such as a door). However, if the door is opened, the door can no longer obstruct the sound, and this should no longer be a factor. This type of dynamic audio pathfinding problem is much tougher to solve. In fact, many games still do not attempt to solve the problem at all. Figure 5.5.13 illustrates how a sound must essentially "pathfind" to the listener position to determine the proper occlusion settings.

Obviously, the ideal solution is one in which the audio phase is completely automated, and the designer has to do nothing at all to get realistic reverb settings from anywhere in the game environment. As game worlds become bigger and more complex, it will be important for programmers to figure out ways of streamlining the development process. This will allow game content creators to build these bigger and better game worlds with ever-increasing efficiency.

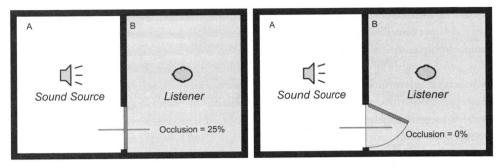

FIGURE 5.5.13 *Occlusion data that is dynamically affected by a door.*

Audio Scripting and Engine Integration

One of the most important jobs of an audio programmer does not involve any low-level audio programming. Rather, it is the integration of an existing audio API into a toolset designed for streamlined content creation. Audio in games typically does not exist in a vacuum. It is nearly always triggered by some event, locale, script, effect, character, or animation. It is the job of the audio programmer to ensure that there is a seamless methodology regarding the placement and real-time control of all audio content in a game.

Just as visual rendering is moving beyond using single-pass basic texture rendering (e.g., using bump and/or normal maps, dynamic shadows, specular highlights, environment maps, etc.), it is no longer acceptable for an audio system to just play simple wave files (or whatever the platform's native sample format is). The next level of audio programming is the concept of *audio scripting*.

The essential premise behind audio scripting is this: game programmers should rarely have to think about audio. At the game level, mundane audio programming should be minimal. All audio events are triggered via engine-level mechanics. In addition, in the rare case they do have to trigger some type of audio playback from game code, programmers should never, ever reference or have to deal with wave files. Instead, programmers should trigger an audio script or an audio event.

Now, instead of simply playing back a small, linear track of audio (represented by a single audio file), audio designers have the freedom to define any type of behavior that can be represented by our data script format. How extensive this audio script should be is ultimately up to the audio programmer. Audio scripting involves simple sample playback commands in addition to programmatic elements. It should be built on top of an existing low-level API and encapsulate common programmatic elements into a user-defined data format. However, this format should be efficient enough to be used for each sound event in the game without a lot of runtime or memory overhead. Let's examine a number of common audio-related problems that must be solved in a typical game.

Sound variation. When a common sound (such as a footstep) is played over and over again, the player quickly memorizes every nuance of the sample. A sound script allows the audio designer to choose from a set of similar samples to add basic variation. In addition, it may add a small amount of pitch and volume variation on each playback. The script may even use input, such as ground type values, to choose from entirely different sample sets. The script may even choose multiple layers of sounds to combine in layers, further adding to the variation. By adding this functionality to the audio script format, we can ensure that even small sample sets don't become repetitive sounding too quickly.

Sound repetition. Often, a single sound is used in many different places simultaneously. For instance, a sword clanking may be used on one of your in-game creatures. If you have 30 creatures on the screen at once, though, it may be advantageous to limit the number of simultaneous sword clanks that occur at any one time. After all, sounds tend to reach a saturation point after a certain number of repetitions. Additionally, this will help to conserve sound channels for other types of game sounds.

Complex sound looping. A simple looping sound is often not sufficient. Machinery often has unique starting and stopping sounds, and it is cumbersome to program this type of mechanism using basic playback mechanisms. A sound script, however, can define discrete starting, looping, and ending samples that are triggered at scripted intervals. Imagine an elevator that can travel to several different floors. A single sample is triggered when the elevator starts, and the looping sample fades in shortly as the start sample fades out. When the elevator finally stops, the loop is stopped and the stopping sample is played. However, to the client, this was as simple as playing and then stopping a single sound event.

Background ambience. To produce convincing background ambiences, an audio designer may combine a number of elements that merge together to form a seamless *soundscape*. This may involve playing several looping elements that shift pitch and volume randomly over time (this is great for wind effects). Additionally, one-shot elements may be periodically played at randomly timed intervals surrounding the listener in 3D space to provide additional interest. This type of background ambience would be tedious to program for each locale, but a dedicated scripted system could easily provide the capabilities of performing such tasks.

As you can see, the concept of audio scripting allows an audio system to become much more than a rudimentary sample playback engine. Modern sound programming should allow much more intricate playback of component elements and parameter control, combined through a unified data scripting mechanism. An important aspect of game development is optimizing the pipeline for efficient creation of game assets. By allowing audio content creators to have more control over aspects of audio performance, you facilitate the creation of more interesting and immersive audio content, and free up game programmers to concentrate more on programming game logic and less on triggering and playing samples here and there.

Lip-Sync Technology

Many of the advances in rendering technology have allowed hyperrealistic rendering of the human form, including faces. One of the more challenging aspects of facial rendering is how to animate the mouth in perfect synchronization with a character's speech. This technology is generally known as *lip-sync*.

At a basic level, simply moving a mouth open and closed based on a wave file's amplitude provides a surprisingly good approximation. If your budget is limited or your characters will only be viewed from far away, this is a reasonable solution. However, modern games are pushing the envelope with full phonetic representation and animation. There are at least two approaches currently being pursued. One method scans a text transcript of the voice performance, and the expected phonemes and syllables are then matched up to the actual performance. The second approach is based on pure sound analysis. While a trickier problem to solve, this approach has the advantage of being language-neutral—a considerable advantage for games that must be shipped in many different languages.

The game-side rendering of lip-sync data has its own challenges. Based on the set of phonetic data, artists must manipulate bones or textures (or a combination of the two) to create realistic facial and mouth animations to match the expected phonemes.

A number of excellent articles both in print and on the Internet describe the basics of rendering human phonemes.

Advanced Voice Playback

Many games, especially sports titles, involve a lot of human dialogue commenting on real-time action being performed in the game. Because it is simply not possible to pre-record every conceivable play, it often falls on the audio programmer to find ways of cleverly stringing together logical phrases. Initially, fairly rudimentary techniques were used, but tomorrow's games will be using much more sophisticated techniques to blend phrases and words together.

As a simple example, one common problem is how to insert a player's name into a phrase. Without proper timing and inflection cues, it will sound like an obvious cut-and-paste job. However, by properly blending one phrase into another (much in the same way that real speech occurs), the chopping effect can be minimized.

As the sports game genre advances, gamers will demand more realistic and entertaining commentary. There are still plenty of advances to be made in this category of audio programming.

Voice Recognition

Audio programming is not exclusively devoted to real-time rendering of audio events. One emerging specialization of audio programming is *voice recognition*. Simply put, voice recognition is the capability for a computer to identify and recognize commands spoken by the human player. This gives a level of interactivity beyond the somewhat clumsy mechanism of choosing commands in real time from a menu using a game controller. Several tactical shooters are already using this technology to good effect, and it is likely we will continue to see developments in this area.

Summary

As you can see, audio programming from the perspective of a game developer is certainly no longer about fine-tuning some low-level audio mixing routines. Modern hardware and rendering libraries now take care of the basics. Instead, the lowest-level job will typically be integration of a complete audio scripting system into a game engine. As an audio programmer, your job is to give as much power and control as possible to the audio content creators, while minimizing the time any programmer must think about low-level programming tasks. That leaves a world of much more advanced and exciting audio-related research topics to investigate and implement in tomorrow's games.

Exercises

1. How is a sound typically represented in computer memory?
2. How does a sample's bit depth affect its final signal-to-noise ratio?
3. What are two basic properties of the Nyquist Limit?
4. How does streaming sound differ from normal sound playback?
5. What are the two essential interfaces (data sets) required to render a sound in three-dimensional space?
6. What are the two most prominent characteristics of a sound that occlusion affects?
7. Design a pseudocode function that computes the attenuation and pan for a given sound source in a two-speaker configuration. The function accepts a sound position in 3D space and the listener's forward and up vectors. The function returns the attenuation (in the range of [0.0, 1.0], with 1.0 being full volume) and the pan (in the range of [−1.0, 1.0], with −1.0 being full left speaker and 1.0 being full right speaker). This function will require the use of a cross product, a dot product, and a trigonometric function. Document any design assumptions, such as the threshold for deciding when a sound is too far away to hear.
8. Describe all of the events in a game that require sound, and what events trigger them. Given this information, design a rough conceptual system allowing audio content creators and artists to incorporate all sound content into the game without any programmer support. How can sounds be attached to or triggered by all of these events?
9. Choose one of the following themes: sports game, squad-based network-enabled shooter, or role-playing game. Describe any potential audio tasks a programmer will be asked to solve for the game type you have chosen. Then, describe briefly how you would attempt to research and solve these tasks.

References

[Boer02] Boer, James, *Game Audio Programming*, Charles River Media, Inc., 2002.

[EAX] For information about EAX, visit *www.eax.creative.com*.

[IA-SIG] For information about I3DL2 or iXMF, visit *www.iasig.org*.

[MIDI] For more information about the MIDI, DLS, and XMF formats, visit *www.midi.org*.

[MSDN] DirectSound & DirectMusic: DirectX 9 documentation, *msdn.microsoft.com/directx*.

[OpenAL] OpenAL is a 3D cross-platform audio-rendering standard: *www.openal.org*.

5.6 ■ Network and Multiplayer

Overview

This chapter introduces the concepts and terminology involved with network and multiplayer programming. It begins with an assessment of multiplayer game modes, followed by an exploration of network programming fundamentals, including network protocols, real-time data transfer, asynchronous environment guidelines, and game security.

Multiplayer Modes

Multiplayer games share a generic set of concepts, in addition to mode-specific details. This section surveys the common ground, describing three key differentiating factors of multiplayer design/implementation: *event timing*, *shared I/O*, and *connectivity*.

Event Timing

Games follow either a turn-based or a real-time *event-timing* model. Some games contain a mixture. In such cases, turn-based events take precedence due to their lock-step nature. Consequently, timing models influence design and implementation paths of various components.

Turn Based

Turn-based games restrict movement to a single player, making all other players wait for their turn; also referred to as *round robin*. Most board games and card games exhibit turn-based gameplay. These games tolerate high and/or variable latency and low-bandwidth conditions.

Real Time

Real-time games support simultaneous player interaction, often requiring arbitration to handle *race conditions*. Examples of such conditions include determining the first to cross the finish line, grab an object in the game world, or lose all health. A special category of real-time games, known as "twitch" games, relies on a constant flow of race conditions. All real-time games design around a rigid set of latency and bandwidth requirements, but twitch games tend to degrade with latencies above 150 ms, and become unplayable above 500 ms (0.5 seconds).

Shared I/O

Games run on a single computer often facilitate multiple players by sharing input and display systems. Players may share a single input device such as assigning different keys on a keyboard to each player, or simply passing the entire keyboard between turns in a turn-based game, or plug in additional input devices for exclusive use by each player. One could consider this a form of connected multiplayer. In fact, multiple input devices provide a good means to simulate players on a low-latency network. The next few sections describe models for sharing the displays.

Full Screen

A full-screen multiplayer game normally requires one of the following conditions:

Complete playfield visibility.   Card games show the entire table. A checkers or chess game shows the entire board. A game with a virtual world such as a soccer playfield or a war game's battlefield must display the entire field. Without this constraint, one or more players may not see their game entities and subsequently fail in efforts to control them.

Player funneling. To facilitate multiple players in a snapshot of a larger game world, *player funneling* restricts players to stay within a virtual cage the size of the screen display. It's as if four people were each holding one corner of a blanket. If they all pull in opposite directions, the blanket stays put. If one person decides to move in the same direction of the person opposite him, the blanket moves in that direction. The popular role-playing game *Gauntlet* uses this technique to arbitrate player movement while scrolling through the game world.

Turn-based screen control. Since turn-based games only allow one person to move at a given time, the display only necessitates showing the current player's viewpoint. In this scenario, the display simply switches to the active player's camera.

Split Screen

With split-screen multiplayer, each player is allotted separate portions of the display to show personalized views of the game world. The following are common component separations required for each player:

- **Camera** (each player's point of view)
- **Cull data** (one for each screen since the point of view differs for each player)
- **Heads-Up Display, or HUD** (game stats relevant to each player)
- **Map data** (centered on current player)
- **Audio effects** (mixing required since normally only one audio system)

Splitting the screen incurs a performance hit due to the multiple render cycles. Updating each view during the render phase of the game loop keeps the display state consistent, the importance of which becomes relevant when two or more players exist in close proximity. One possible optimization, which breaks this consistency, involves round robin rendering. Only one view updates per render phase, and the updated view changes to the next player on the next render phase. In a four-player game, a hybrid of this could update two views each render phase. This helps keep the view consistent in the close proximity case; otherwise, each player will be three updates out of sync with one of the other views.

There are two standard methods for dividing the screen real estate: *viewports* and *render destinations*. Viewports render directly to the back buffer, and render destinations render to a texture placed on geometry, which then renders to the back buffer. Due to their performance benefits over render destinations, viewports experience greater acceptance. However, render destinations offer unique capabilities over viewports. The created textures map to geometry of any shape. This geometry may freely move in the virtual display, thus allowing varied size, rotation, translation, and overlap with transparency.

A hybrid option known as *windowed mode* may use either viewports or render destinations to display the contents within the window. This adds further performance degradation to the base modes, but on a PC, it allows players to drag their view onto separate monitors, or otherwise customize their window layout. Usability studies suggest it is best to offer the player a few predesigned and playtested layouts to choose from; otherwise, the customizability tends to detract from gameplay because a new player doesn't necessarily know how to form a good layout to deal with particular game features.

Connectivity

The connection type determines latency and bandwidth. These two constraints then dictate game timing, number of controllable game entities (including players), and other game design elements. However, connected multiplayer games reuse many ideas from nonconnected multiplayer games. Some connected games use split-screen displays or player funneling. Others pass input data as if additional input devices were connected to the same computer.

Due to the lack of latency requirements, turn-based games work over a greater variety of connection mediums. In this case, data transfer need not be fast; the data just needs to get there intact eventually. For example, game moves saved to a file and then transferring that file by e-mail, FTP, or even saving it to a removable disk and walking it over to another computer are all acceptable means of turn-based game connectivity. The following categories offer real-time connectivity:

Direct link: Linking computers over a short connection normally guarantees low latency, while bandwidth depends on the medium. Popular cable links include a modified serial cable (a null modem cable) and a USB cable. Popular wireless links include infrared and Bluetooth. Each harbors specialized protocols to facilitate communications that tend to restrict to peering.

Circuit-switched network: The public phone networks provide an unshared direct connection or circuit. This maintains a consistent, low-latency medium, but is short on bandwidth and player distribution (only two player; call conference modem games never really took off). An Internet service provider (ISP) allows the circuit to attach to an Internet conduit (the modem at the ISP), which places the packet data traffic on the Internet. This solves the player distribution problem, but takes away the low-latency benefits of the direct circuit.

Packet-switched network.   Data networks share virtual circuits that are created and released for each data packet. Network configurations vary in hardware, transmission medium, and protocols, and the Internet combines these smaller physical networks into a single large logical network, allowing people to play anybody from anywhere, at any time. However, the Internet suffers from a wide variance in bandwidth and latency. It is also less reliable than the public phone system.

Protocols

A *protocol* is an agreed-upon format for transferring data between devices. This format specifies some or all of the following methods:

- Packet length conveyance
- Acknowledgement methodology
- Error checking
- Error correcting
- Compression
- Encryption
- Control packet description

Packets

The logical transmission units of a protocol, otherwise known as *packets*, consist of two parts: a header section and a payload section. The header contains the format elements of the protocol. A protocol considers the payload as a Binary Large OBject (BLOB), which it does not modify; rather, it simply delivers it according to the terms of the protocol. The following demonstrates a simple packet structure:

```
struct packet
{
    // Header
    short PacketLength; // Length of this packet
    short PacketType;   // Control Information
    int   Checksum;     // Error checking

    // Payload
    char [256] Blob;    // Higher layer protocol data
};
```

When creating packet structures, the structure may be formed such that it requires no special *serialization* (reformatting the data into a serial form). The following factors determine whether a packet structure requires serialization:

Pointers: Since pointers refer to local memory, the data pointed to needs to be serialized into a byte stream.

Abstract data types: ADTs commonly contain references, which require their extraction and placement in an array.

Byte alignment linkers: Default to word alignment for processor performance. To avoid this byte padding, use the following preprocessor directives:

```
#pragma pack (1) // Byte aligned, no padding
  // Add packet structures here
#pragma pack () // Set back to default alignment
```

Endian order: When building a game that connects across platforms, multibyte intrinsic types require *endian* synchronization. The Sockets API provides the following macros to place multibyte in the standardized *network order* (since routers need to inspect address variables): ntohs, ntohl, htons, and htonl. Following the same standard for endianess reduces confusion.

Specific intrinsic types: Use intrinsic types that have a specified width. For example, use "__int32" rather than "int," since the size of "int" differs on 32-bit and 64-bit CPUs.

Unicode strings: Start out using Unicode character strings at the beginning of a game development project to make localization easier at the end of the project. Otherwise, an additional conversion/serialization step needs to occur for cross-language packet exchange where one language uses 1-byte ASCII strings and the other uses 2-byte Unicode strings.

Request for Comments

Protocol specifications require distribution to get used. They also need to be constructively criticized or otherwise commented on to identify imperfections. From this need arose the Request for Comments [RFC] repository for new and existing protocol specifications. Most public Internet protocols have an associated RFC specification number associated with a detailed description on the RFC Web/FTP site.

Protocol Stack

The Open System Interconnect (OSI) specification formalizes interoperability between devices and software entities into logical layers. Figure 5.6.1 illustrates the flow of data between layers, pointing out common protocols that reside in each layer.

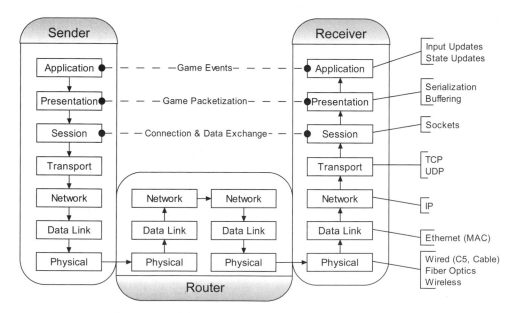

FIGURE 5.6.1   *The OSI model.*

The Internet model provides a variation of the OSI model that combines the Application, Presentation, and Session layers into one layer and calls it the Application layer. This simplifies the model for workers in the lower layers, but the core work in multiplayer game development takes place at the higher layers.

Physical Layer

The *physical layer* streams bits of data over a communication medium. Popular mediums include category-5 twisted-pair wire, coaxial cable, and various wireless frequencies. The game developer's primary concern at this layer regards latency, bandwidth, and reliability of the media.

Bandwidth and Latency

Bandwidth represents the data transfer rate from source to destination, commonly measured as bits per second and often confused with the more useful measurement of bytes per second due to its abbreviation "bps." *Latency* represents the delay a single bit of data experiences traversing from a source computer to a destination computer, commonly measured in millisecond time units. Bandwidth calculations must account for the initial latency cost; otherwise, the initial latency becomes amortized in the bandwidth calculation. Amortized bandwidth approaches actual bandwidth when line latency and total transfer time deviate, thus making line latency insignificant. The following demonstrates a not-so-deviant case:

Data (δ)	= 240 bits
Transfer Time (θ)	= 4 s
LATENCY (λ)	= 500 ms
BANDWIDTH (β)	= unknown
$\beta_{Amortized}$	= δ / θ
	= 240 b / 4 s
	= 60 bps
β_{Actual}	= $\delta / (\theta - \lambda)$
	= 240 b / (4s – 500 ms)
	= 240 b / 3.5s
	= 68.5 bps

With bandwidth increasing and latency decreasing, it may seem pointless to even consider these calculations. Realize that initial line latency is included only once, but packets normally transmit in intervals. This requires adding in the line latency time multiple times throughout the session. If 32 packets are delivered each second, the calculation must multiply the line latency by a factor of 32.

Media

Designing a connected game requires setting a minimum bandwidth. Determining the supported media dictates the bandwidth. Otherwise, designing the packet model and arriving at a minimum bandwidth will determine the media over which it may be played. Either way, one must know the bandwidth saturation of each medium. Table 5.6.1 lists some common bandwidth specifications.

Table 5.6.1   Max Bandwidth Specifications

Media Connection Type	Speed (bps)
Serial	20K
USB 1&2	12M, 480M
ISDN	128K
DSL	1.5M down, 896K up
Cable	3M down, 256K up
LAN 10/100/1G BaseT	10M, 100M, 1G
Wireless 802.11 a/b/g	b=11M, a=54M, g=54M
Power Line	14M
T1	1.5M

Note that both DSL and cable download 2 to 12 times faster than they upload data. The serial specification describes the uncompressed transfer rate a null modem experiences. Phone modems use the serial chip (UART), so the serial chip theoretically limits phone modems. Both 28.8K and 56K modems acquire the extra transfer rate through additional compression schemes. Direct serial transfers also contain smaller headers, which increases their bandwidth relative to TCP/IP, for example. The actual delivered bandwidth of any given medium tends to reliably hit about 70 percent of its advertised theoretical maximum.

Data Link Layer

The *Data Link layer* serializes the data for the Physical layer and manages the transmission to its neighboring node. The Ethernet adapter or network interface card (NIC) handles this serialization. Each NIC contains a MAC address to identify it as a unique node on the local network. Not all NICs contain unique MAC addresses; however, for a subnet to communicate, all NICs on that subnet must contain a unique MAC address.

Network Layer

The *Network layer* handles packet routing. Its most popular resident, Internet Protocol (IP), contains both the source and destination IP address for a packet. Richard

Stevens' book [Stevens94] provides clear, in-depth coverage of IP and its companion protocols TCP and UDP.

IP Addresses

Two common versions of IP exist on the Internet today: the popular old IP version 4 (IPv4), and IP version 6 (IPv6), also referred to as the next generation (IPng). The header formats differ in all but the first 4 bits of data that specify the IP version used. The major difference between these protocols centers on the size and format of the IP address entries. An IPv4 address contains 4 bytes, commonly displayed in 8-bit decimal sections:

$$255.000.255.000$$

An IPv6 address contains 16 bytes, commonly displayed in 16-bit hex sections:

$$FFFF:FFFF:0000:0000:FFFF:FFFF:0000:0000$$

IP entry GUIs should be designed to accept both forms of addresses. The Sockets API, responsible for passing the IP address to this layer, provides a generic means of dealing with either address. For further details, see the discussion on binding a socket to an IP address in the "Session Layer" section of this chapter.

Unicast

An individual's IP address, or unicast address, comes from one of the following sources:

Static (user assigned):   The static assignment of an IP address is usually reserved for servers that require a well-known presence.

Dynamic Host Configuration Protocol (DHCP):   Routers commonly use this protocol to assign IPs to a specific NIC. The DHCP server maintains an IP lease list containing the IP address assigned, the NIC MAC address assigned to, and the lease expiration time. When an IP address lease expires, it may automatically renew with the same IP or a different IP depending on the policy in place.

Automatic Private IP Addressing (APIPA):   The fallback when a DHCP service is not available.

Special Addresses

The following commonly used IPv4 addresses have special meaning and may not be used as a unicast address.

Multicast

Range: *.*.*.{224-239}

Special "multicast" routers allow multiple IPs to enter a group. When a member of the group sends a packet, he sends one packet to the group address on the router, and the router redirects that packet to all members. Multicasting provides excellent bandwidth savings, but the hardware costs make this technology sparse.

Local Broadcast

Range: 255.255.255.255
Socket macro: INADDR_BROADCAST

Local broadcast packets deliver themselves to all adapters on the local subnet, reaching up to 222 IPv4 adapters.

Directed Broadcast

Range: *.*.*.{240-255}

Similar to local broadcasts, but instead of broadcasting on the local subnet, it broadcasts on the specified subnet. Although a nice feature, directed broadcasts are usually discarded by firewalls.

Loop Back

Range: 127.0.0.1
Socket macro: INADDR_LOOPBACK

Packets sent to this address never reach the physical layer. Instead, they are transferred from the send queue to the receive queue at the IP layer.

Address Any

Range: 0
Socket macro: INADDR_ANY

Computers with single adapters often use this address as the source address when setting up a listening socket, because it selects the IP associated with the only NIC on the computer. Computers with multiple NICs may also use this address to allow automatic selection of any available NIC for the socket to listen on.

Domain Name

A domain name provides a human-readable form of the IP address, and a layer of indirection through the Domain Name Service (DNS). For example, the Web server located at 16.15.32.1 provides less description than the domain name *www.gamedev.net*. The DNS indirection allows the gamedev.net site to move to another IP address at any time, but clients can use the same domain name. The DNS is a server infrastructure dedicated to fast domain name resolution. While DNS often meets its service goals, it has its downsides.

First, it adds a layer of complexity to the socket connection process if an address requires resolution, which takes some time since it must contact one or more DNS servers to do so. Working with an IP address directly would save connection time.

Second, the DNS server may be unreachable, leaving one unable to connect even with an active network. Again, using an IP address directly avoids such dependencies. Another problem with DNS centers on the changing of a domain name's associated IP. Moving a domain name to point to a new IP takes time to propagate through the DNS server infrastructure. Moving a domain to a new server may take hours or even days before all DNS nodes reflect the change. Caching the most recent IP resolution provides a good fallback solution if the DNS fails for some reason, although it's not 100 percent reliable.

The Sockets API contains methods to resolve a domain to an IP and look up all domain names associated with an IP, `getaddrinfo()`, and `getnameinfo()`, respectively.

Transport Layer

The *Transport layer* ensures data delivery between endpoints. It recovers from errors and controls the flow of data. It also provides the notion of "ports" as a logical extension to the IP address.

Ports

A *port* number works similar to an apartment number, where an IP address works similar to the address of the apartment complex. To deliver a piece of mail, the mail carrier needs both numbers. Network connections also require a complete "Net Address":

$$\text{Net Address} = \text{IP Address} + \text{Port}$$

Ports range between 0 and 64k. Common network services such as FTP, Telnet, and HTTP use "well-known ports" in the range of 0–1024. Historically, RFC 1700 maintained port specifications. Now, these numbers are maintained by the Internet Assigned Numbers Authority [IANA]. Additional, but less common, services map to the 1k–5k port space. While entirely valid, using port numbers below 5k may clash with other servers running on a LAN. For example, creating a server that listens on port 80 may never receive any traffic due to the router forwarding all port 80 traffic to the LAN's Web server.

TCP and UDP packet headers contain both a source and destination port entry. The listening port must be agreed upon by both endpoints before attempting a connection. If a connector lacks this information, it will require connection attempts on all 64k ports to find which port the host chooses to listen on. The connector must also specify the return port, but due to its inclusion in the packet, it may be selected at random.

Transmission Control Protocol

TCP works best for large data transmissions and data that must reach its destination. The following sections highlight the most-used features of TCP.

Guaranteed In-Order Delivery

TCP will not deliver data to the session layer out of order. If two bytes, byte "A" and byte "B," are sent in respective order, TCP guarantees that byte "A" will be delivered to the session layer before byte "B," even if byte "B" arrives before byte "A."

TCP supports a special flag in the header called "Out of Band," which allows sending/receiving of priority packets. However, the architecture required to use this facility is frowned upon. The recommended alternative entails the creation of a separate TCP connection to handle high-priority data.

Connected

TCP requires a connected state between endpoints that supports the following features:

Packet window: Although data flowing between the Transport and Session layers is considered a stream, TCP-to-TCP data transmission occurs through packets. This allows for a window of N outstanding packets, each with a window sequence number used for stream reconstruction, packet acknowledgment, and resending when necessary.

Packet coalescence: Also referred to as the Nagle algorithm or packet nagling, this combines smaller packets into a single larger packet to reduce network congestion caused by many small packets. If 1 byte of data were sent in a packet, 41 bytes would actually be sent: 40 for the header and 1 for the data. The downside to this is that data may sit in the TCP stack waiting for more data, causing unacceptable latencies. Nagle, on by default, may be turned off with the TCP_NODELAY socket option.

Connection Timeout: Off by default, this facility sends a simple "Timeout" packet after the line remains idle (no transmissions) for a specified period of time. The receiver of the heartbeat must reply with an acknowledgment in a given amount of time, or the TCP session closes. Use socket option SO_KEEPALIVE to configure TCP timeouts.

Streaming: Data transmitted over TCP comes as a stream to the Session layer rather than individual packets. Internally, TCP sends/receives data in packets, but these packets do not necessarily reflect the size of the data buffers made at the Session layer through a call to send(). TCP may split or combine individual send commands depending on TCP settings. This requires that the Presentation layer provide facilities to reconstruct data into packets if needed.

User Datagram Protocol

UDP communicates in a send-and-forget manner, not guaranteeing order of delivery or even delivery at all since no direct connection is made. Data transmits in packets instead of a stream, which assumes a connection. The lack of connection maintenance also reduces the UDP header size. The reduced header size in conjunction with the absence of resends and packet coalescence provides a better latency/bandwidth model than TCP.

Avoid writing a guaranteed layer on top of UDP, which bypasses all the time and effort built into TCP. Firewalls tend to render such solutions useless anyhow, because they commonly block all incoming UDP traffic. The policy to block all incoming UDP traffic stems from the security issue introduced by not verifying the return address. Stopping a network attack involves identifying its source—a difficult journey without a confirmed return address. Design the game to allow TCP as a fallback for denied UDP traffic.

Broadcasting

All broadcasting over IP networks takes place with UDP packets. This makes perfect sense with the connectionless nature of UDP. However, broadcasting floods network bandwidth, and firewalls normally drop incoming broadcast packets. This restricts its use to LANs where it provides an excellent method of player/game discovery. Lobby servers, such as GameSpy, replace actual UDP broadcasting on the Internet with a logical subscription-based broadcast in which one must connect to the server to receive TCP packets sent to all connections.

Session Layer

The *Session layer* manages connections between applications. Its responsibilities include establishing connections, terminating connections, and coordinating data exchange. The Sockets API provides a cross-platform Session layer model to handle these tasks.

Sockets

The *Sockets API* supports several basic implementation models, each simple at the outset to implement. The complexity emerges when maintaining multiple sockets, setting options for lower layers in the protocol stack, and ultimately using high-performance socket extensions. While sticking to the standard socket API methods promotes cross-platform portability, this model generally limits itself to client development. Servers often push connectivity limits and/or data throughput, which necessitate use of OS-specific socket extensions. About a dozen extensions exist that obscure the best approach to achieving high performance. The "Sockets Programming" references at the end of this chapter contain reams of information on both basic and high-performance sockets. Although not listed in the references, most modern programming languages support the Sockets API, including Java, C#, C/C++, and Visual Basic. The remainder of this section presents a general overview of sockets, and more importantly, the high-level differences in the ways to use sockets. The code snippets use WinSock defines, which occasionally differ ever so slightly from their Unix equivalents.

Origins

Sockets originated as an extension to the file I/O paradigm, which explains why the file descriptor "fd" abbreviation is scattered throughout sockets. To this day, serial

[Camp93], socket, and other connection types maintain file descriptor compatible handles. These handles pass to file I/O interfaces such as read() and write(), allowing data transfers to follow the standard reader/writer design pattern. Unix hosted the first Sockets API, which provided additional functionality to deal with the latent data transmissions and protocol control. Many years passed before third-party ports were made available on the Microsoft Windows platform, but soon after these first ports became available, Microsoft released its own implementation of the WinSock Sockets API.

WinSock

All the standard socket interfaces exist in WinSock, with specific extensions containing the "WSA" function name prefix. Microsoft provides nonstandard, briefly documented socket extensions external to the Winsock specification that allow for socket reuse and additional high-performance features.

All WinSock programs must use two such extension functions to allocate/free system resources; Unix sockets do not require such initialization:

- **WSAStartup()**:   Call this before using any Winsock API methods.
- **WSACleanup()**:   Call this to release all socket handles after closing them.

Socket Modes

Sockets are either *blocking* or *nonblocking*. By default, sockets use blocking mode. In a game that requires an active user interface, blocking sockets should only be used in separate threads, because blocking calls puts their thread to sleep until the action completes. To hack around the blocking problem in a single thread, one can "peek" for data available to read, since a socket read() call often blocks waiting for data. Setting nonblocking mode provides a better alternative to peeking because it actually completes the operation if possible or returns an error that it would have blocked if it were in blocking mode. In contrast, a successful peek polls for arrived data, and still requires an additional read operation to clear the data off the stack. This double read of kernel memory buffers degrades performance considerably in server applications.

To switch between blocking and nonblocking mode:

```
unsigned long arg = ?; //0=blocking 1=non-blocking
int status = ioctlsocket( fd, FIONBIO, &arg);
```

Once in either blocking or nonblocking mode, it remains in that mode for the duration of the process. If WinSock is shut down and reinitialized, it will be set back to blocking mode. To force a blocking call to return, either close the socket or make a call to WSACancelBlockingCall().

Standard Socket Models

The sockets specification provides two socket models: standard and select. The select model provides a mechanism to handle sets of up to 64 sockets each. The following sections briefly cover the simplest form of the standard socket model and common usage patterns.

Socket Creation

This line of code creates a TCP socket descriptor:

```
SOCKET tcpSocket =
socket(PF_INET, SOCK_STREAM, IPPROTO_TCP);
```

This line of code creates a UDP socket descriptor:

```
SOCKET udpSocket =
socket(PF_INET, SOCK_DGRAM, TPPROTO_UDP);
```

TCP Connecting

To connect to a remote listening host socket, a destination net address is required. The following code creates an IPv4 compatible address structure and attempts a TCP connection:

```
SOCKADDR_IN addrV4;
addrV4.sin_family          = AF_INET;
addrV4.sin_port            = htons(4000);
addrV4.sin_addr.s_addr = inet_addr("10.2.15.89");

int error =
connect(tcpSocket,(SOCKADDR*)&addrV4,sizeof(addrV4));
```

The following code uses the preferred `getaddrinfo()` method to create an IP address compatible with both versions 4 and 6:

```
PADDRINFOT info = NULL;
ADDRINFOT            hints;
hints.ai_flags      = AI_NUMERICHOST;
hints.ai_family     = PF_INET;
hints.ai_socktype   = SOCK_STREAM;
hints.ai_protocol   = IPPROTO_TCP;

char strPort[10] = "4000";

int result =
getaddrinfo("10.2.15.89",strPort,&hints,&info);

int error =
connect(tcpSocket, info->ai_addr, info->ai_addrlen);

TCP LISTENER
```

The TCP host must bind the socket to a port and a local adapter with the `bind()` call. Next, the host must listen for incoming connections, and finally sit and wait to accept the connection.

```
int status =
getaddrinfo(htonl(INADDR_ANY),strPort,&hints,&info);

status =
bind(tcpSocket, info->ai_addr, info->ai_addrlen);

int connectionBacklog = 1;
status = listen(tcpSocket, connectionBacklog);

int addrLen=0;
PADDRINFOT remote = NULL;

SOCKET newSocket =
accept(tcpSocket, &remote.addr, &remote.ai_addrlen);
```

Stream Transmissions

After connection, the client and host may freely send and receive data. Among other error conditions, the send operation may error if the TCP buffer is too full to accept data, in which case the send should succeed once the buffers have time to transmit their contents.

```
#pragma pack (1)
struct Packet
{
        short    length;
        char             username[10];
};
#pragma pack ()

Packet pkt = {12,"testpkt"};
int flags = 0;  // No flags, rarely used

int err = send(tcpSocket,(char*)&pkt,sizeof(pkt),flags);
```

TCP receive operations may look very different between implementations due to its streaming nature. The following sample provides a common solution for packetizing the data stream. It assumes the first 2 bytes of all application layer packets contain the length of the packet. This allows the system to determine how big a buffer to create for the complete packet read operation.

```
// Handle Endian order if used cross platform
short pktLen;

// a short is used to represent packet length
short lenSize = sizeof(short);
```

```
int bytesToRead = lenSize;
int flags = 0; // ignore

// Read the packet length first
int bytesRead =
recv(tcpSocket, (char*)&pktLen, bytesToRead, flags);

// Allocate buffer for to read in entire packet
char* buffer = new char[pktLen];
memcpy( buffer, &pktLen, lenSize );

// Read remainder of packet
bytesToRead = pktLen – lenSize;
bytesRead =
recv( tcpSocket, &buffer[lenSize], bytesToRead,flags);
```

Datagram Transmissions

UDP's `sendto()` method acts similar to the combination of TCP's `connect()` and `send()` methods. UDP's `recvfrom()` method combines even more functionality in comparison to TCP's, with `recvfrom()` taking the place of `bind()`, `listen()`, `accept()`, and `recv()`. The following shows UDP's send method with previously declared parameters:

```
int status = sendto( udpSocket, (char*) &pkt, sizeof(pkt),
info->ai_addr, info->ai_addrlen );
```

In addition to combining so much functionality into one method, `recvfrom()` also avoids the two-step read of packet length followed by a read of the remaining packet. This is due to `recvfrom()` only reading one packet at a time. Simply create a buffer the size of the largest possible packet, and call `recvfrom()` with the buffer and its length:

```
int flags = 0; // ignore, not very useful
char buffer[MAX_PACKET_SIZE];

int bytesRead =
recvfrom(udpSocket, buffer, MAX_PACKET_SIZE, flags
&remote.addr, &remote.ai_addrlen);
```

The `recvfrom()` will only fill up to the size of a single packet and return. The method will never combine packets, as TCP would, because it does not stream data as TCP does.

High-Performance Socket Models

Standard socket models fall short with respect to performance in several areas, most notably in event notification and memory buffer copies. Additional shortcomings exist in the `accept()` architecture and in socket reuse. For implementation details on each of these subjects, search for the following keywords: WSAEventSelect, I/O Completion Ports, poll, and Kernel Queues. The following provides an overview of the issues involved with each problem.

Event notification entails use of multiple threads, and kernel level signaling of a blocking application thread waiting for an operation to complete, such as data arriving, data sent, or a socket closed. "Standard" sockets need a thread for each outstanding operation, and "select" sockets require a thread for every 64 sockets. Event notification requires only one main socket processing thread that receives the signals for all sockets. Once signaled, the processing thread can handle the operation or place the operation in a signaled queue to process in a worker thread from a thread pool.

Standard sockets copy data from kernel buffers to user-supplied buffers during a read call. Asynchronous I/O solves this performance issue by allowing the application or user thread to pass the kernel some number of buffers to use instead of its own. After a buffer fills, the kernel then signals the user thread about the readied data. This greatly reduces overhead with data transfers—critical for maximizing data throughput.

The Listen/Accept role of a TCP connection host using the standard socket model requires the host to accept a socket connection before receiving any data from the connector. Accept creates a socket that requires the lengthy process of the kernel allocating a descriptor. Two solutions exist for lessening the impact of this problem. One solution allows the passing of a created but unconnected socket descriptor to the accept method, thus bypassing the expensive socket creation hit at runtime. This still requires the connection to happen before any authentication. The other solution allows the connect method to send an initial data packet with the connect request. This allows the host to authenticate a connection request before the TCP connection request returns accepted.

Creating a socket descriptor consumes valuable resources. Reusing socket descriptors after they close allows servers to handle many transient connections with faster response times. This requires connections to confirm closure and that closed sockets not release their descriptor handle. The standard socket `close()` method frees socket descriptors in addition to closing the connection. Note that this only applies to TCP sockets, since UDP sockets inherit reuse since they never connect and thus never require closure.

Three methods exist in the Sockets API to control TCP, UDP, and IP protocol options and session layer I/O: `getsockopt()`, `setsockopt()`, and `ioctlsocket()`. These take a socket, a predefined operation code, and the arguments associated with the operation (plus other overhead parameters). Refer to the references at the end of this chapter for a thorough explanation of all these options and sockets programming at large.

Presentation Layer

The Presentation layer provides generic data conversion by preparing data for transmission and converting incoming data back into a format recognized by the Application layer.

Compression

Real-time data packets are relatively small compared to file transfers, normally on the order of 10–1000 bytes. They should not exceed the network's Maximum Transmission Unit (MTU), which dictates the largest size of a single packet. Packets larger than the MTU, normally around 2k bytes, must be split over multiple packets. Dealing with such small data sizes makes it counterproductive to use generic compressors such as Huffman encoding, due to their table overhead. A better generic alternative would be a custom encoder built into the packet serialization process. Such an encoder may implement the following data reduction methods:

Pascal strings: C/C++ commonly follows the NULL terminated string convention. This poses two problems. First, the containing buffer is normally created at a static maximum string length, which often wastes space, including the space required by the NULL terminator. Second, a packet stream works best if the length of the pending data comes first. With NULL terminated strings, the length remains a mystery until reaching the NULL terminator. Pascal strings reserve the first byte or two of the string to place the string length, and forego the NULL terminator.

String tables: Some strings are set once during a game and continuously used, such as a username in chat rooms. Keep a table of strings and associate an integer key with each string. Introduce a string to all players as a string/key pair, and then only send the key in all future references. New players need to receive a copy of the entire table upon entering the game.

Bit fields: Placing small enumerations and Boolean variables into bit fields conserves bandwidth. Implement this at the structure level to avoid having to serialize the data. Placing bit fields consecutively also reduces gaps of unused byte space.

Float to fixed: Often, floating-point accuracy is overkill for certain data representations, such as percentages. A fixed-point number commonly uses a single 2-byte integer and logically splits it into a two parts: the whole number and the fraction. This saves 2 bytes over the common 4-byte floating-point representation. Save more memory by splitting a short or char if precision requirements permit.

Matrix to quaternion: 3D orientation is commonly represented in matrix form for any number of reasons. A quaternion provides the same information and accuracy with fewer bytes.

Encryption

The most likely person to hack a game packet is the person running the game. Never pass sensitive data to a DLL, as they are easy to chain, allowing the user to replace the authentic DLL with his own to change the data, which it then passes on to the authentic DLL. This chaining process is also referred to as *shimming*. The WinSock

DLL may also be shimmed, rendering IP Security vulnerable to local data tampering. The best method to keep data from the gamers' prying eyes involves encrypting within the executable module.

Serialization

Structures may contain integer alignment padding, pointers, or other data not intended to leave the local computer. To solve this problem, serialize the data by using a secondary buffer and filling it with the exact byte stream to pass to the Session layer.

When using TCP, data is sent to and received from the Session layer as a stream. To work in packets over TCP, this layer must provide the logic to identify the size and type of packet as such:

```
struct packet
{
        ushort Length;  // Size of this packet
        ushort ID;      // Predefined packet type
        ...                     // Additional header info
        char   Data;    // Data from Application Layer
};
```

The positioning of the Length variable as the first variable works well in the receiving architecture. First, post a 2-byte socket read operation. Create a buffer to hold the size of the packet. Then, post a second read operation to receive the remainder of the packet. Repeat for the next packet.

Buffering

The following sections describe different types of buffering found in the Presentation layer.

Packet Coalescence

Although supported by TCP, turn it off and create a customized coalescence system to avoid excessive latencies. Since UDP doesn't support this feature, such a system at the Presentation layer could be used with UDP. Game clients normally abandon all coalescence in lieu of absolute lowest latency. Game servers may actually lower overall latency through coalescence by freeing up processing time and bandwidth. The effects are most noticeable in servers with large numbers of clients.

Induced Latency

Ideally, all players act on the same input data from all users at the same time. The induced latency technique sends input as soon as it latches locally, and then stores it for some prescribed amount of time (the induced latency) before using it, as shown in Figure 5.6.2.

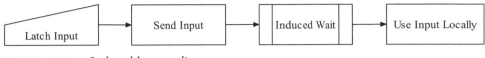

FIGURE 5.6.2 *Induced latency diagram.*

Adding a server that sends local input back at a steady rate allows the server to send previous input when current input does not arrive in time for the server sendoff. In this case, the local machine never stores their input and acts only on input received from the server. Of course, this runs the risk of stopping and waiting for input to arrive from the server, but the intent is to use this on a synchronous model, which must stop and wait for remote input as well.

Dead Data

Since UDP packets may be received out of order, a real-time game may not use old data, allowing the Presentation layer to discard such older packets. A more complex system uses old data to either confirm paths or help provide more accurate interpolation. Old data may also be entered into replay queues for smoother transitions and a more accurate original path. The game designer must decide whether the replay shows actual paths or viewed paths. Since actual paths may conflict with local paths, running the replay system should warp to discrete position/orientation nodes rather than rerun through a simulation with collision detection.

Large Packets

Data packets larger than UDP's MTU or larger than the TCP's send buffer must be split into multiple packets. The Presentation layer handles this subdivision and reconstruction. Such a system involves the addition of a new packet type ID for "large packets," a unique instance ID to differentiate it from other large packets, and a sequence number. A given large packet must either transmit the total number of packets in the first packet, or provide a special sentinel number for the final packet.

Application Layer

The *Application layer* deals directly with game data and game logic. While the Session and Presentation layers often contain generic implementations replaceable with middleware, the Application layer is always part of the game. Here, the update model and synchronization code form the core of a networked game.

Version Verification

When a quality assurance (QA) team starts testing, especially during development when many versions of game components exist, always run a sanity check on all component versions. This check includes comparing size, version, and checksums of all executable files and dynamic link libraries (even system DLLs used), data, and art files. One risks a constant chasing down of nonbugs without using a robust validation system.

Update Models

The game's *update model* guides the design of the most intense packets in the game. The *input reflection model* presents packets sent over the network as if they were another input device attached to the computer. The *state reflection model* processes the input locally and sends the processed data, such as new positions, orientations, velocities, and accelerations.

Input Reflection

This model usually sends slightly processed input data, processed enough to make the input generic rather than deal with specific device nuances. The generic input for a single player using a mouse, joystick, and keyboard can usually fit in a packet less than 32 bytes in size, depending on the controls used. Such a small payload turns out smaller than the combined protocol headers of TCP/IP at 40 bytes. Expending more bandwidth on header data than on the actual packet payload data is generally frowned upon as an inefficient use of bandwidth. The low packet latency mandate overrides general network bandwidth efficiency, and in this respect, input reflection excels.

Human perception of delay plays a critical role in establishing the latency requirements of input reflection. The average person will notice anything more than approximately $1/10^{th}$ of a second delay in hand/eye coordination tasks. Frame rate also plays a role, since ideally each new frame changes with respect to player input. With human perception and average maximum frame rates capping at around 60 fps, an acceptable packet send rate ranges between 16 to 64 input packets per second.

Input reflection might use a synchronous or asynchronous play model. Synchronous play, where the game stops and waits until it receives input data from all users, looks horrible and plays jerky when latencies vary or rise, but it always remains 100 percent in sync. Asynchronous play, where the game predicts remote player input when not available, produces difficult game synchronization problems when wrong predictions result in dramatic in-game events such as a crash, death, or anything else that produces a "rising of the dead" on a resynchronization. Even without catastrophic events, the resynchronization of input reflection requires a complicated, comprehensive, and potentially memory-intensive state save for each input simulation past a prediction point until the actual input arrives. This allows recovery at any point past the prediction, so that the game goes back to a save point, discarding all future state (or in this case, current state), and resimulates the game from that point. Asynchronous play is better suited to the state reflection model or hybrids thereof, which may use input reflection as hints.

Pure input reflection works well with the synchronous "stop & wait" model. The prime directives of this model keep:

- Latency low
- Latency consistent
- All clients in sync

The last item requires rigid rules on randomness. The following tips help avoid unintentional randomness.

- The function rand() must use the same seed on all clients if used in simulation calculations. There should be no actual randomness between clients. Since only one rand() instance exists for a given process, consider creating a custom randomizer for the game if multiple systems need it.
- Use rand() in a reproducible manner; avoid sharing it between the physics system, which is consistent, and the graphics system, which introduces variance across clients.
- Fix all uninitialized variables. Clear all stack and heap variables to remove residual contents before setting. Partial initialization of dirty structures and arrays are very difficult bugs to locate.
- Fix all freed pointer reads. Rely on heap tools for this.
- Validate versions of all files between clients. Note that art files may affect physics calculations.
- Avoid using client system time for calculations, as they rarely match 100 percent.

State Reflection

The *state reflection model,* also known as the *positional update model* for passing object positions and other locality variables, provides a flexible environment geared toward prediction and synchronization at will. The data packets normally require much more information, but object prioritization allows distant objects to update less frequently. The simplified synchronization of this model eases the production of a "drop-in" game where players can join a game in progress; a common method of game entry for role-playing games (RPGs).

Synchronization

One of the most artistic tasks of a network game programmer revolves around keeping all clients in sync with minimal visual or game event related anomalies.

Dead Reckoning

Dead reckoning is a basic prediction method that uses the last known position, orientation, momentum, and acceleration to determine the most plausible current position. The object undergoes simulation over time assuming no changes to acceleration factors. The results work well for all but drastic changes in acceleration, which should be capped in the game's design.

AI Assist

Standard AI design involves setting waypoints for nonplayer characters (NPCs). Positional updates provide such waypoints but lack the smooth transition between waypoints. Leveraging the AI to control the transition works well as long as the waypoints don't change too often. To achieve this, give waypoints a commitment time, and refrain from removing the waypoint for a tunable amount of time. This causes the game to run slightly out of sync, but avoids the distracting "bee wiggle" that results from wavering waypoints.

Arbitration

As in real life, some things just don't work out as planned and require unbiased third-party *arbitration* to rectify a situation with no clear outcome. Fuzzy logic helps build a weighted decision as to the correct outcome based on affected clients and the server's view of a situation. A simplified, dictator-style approach ignores the client views and forces clients to take the game server's view. Most games instantiate the dictatorship role in the server, but design the game with incremental states. The client may lessen the impact of dictation by delaying critical events, such as a dying sequence that starts with a badly wounded sequence while it waits for the final word from the server/arbitrator.

Real-Time Communication

Real-time networked games require a great deal of coding effort to efficiently handle waiting for data to arrive. Properly crafting multithreaded constructs to avoid spinning, dead lock, lock contention, and excessive context switches help to reduce the wait. These constructs grow in complexity with the number of interactions.

Reducing wait time often requires a judgment call on the following data-related issues:

Priority: Certain types of data impact the feel and fairness of gameplay, while other types of data merely support the game through added flair. Data that impacts gameplay needs to arbitrate outcome with other players.

Security: Encrypting all data traffic costs both CPU time and extra bandwidth, which in turn cause additional delivery delay. One encryption algorithm doesn't necessarily fit all. Consider the following optimizations:

- Lower bit strength encryption on less-sensitive data.
- Use *secret key* instead of *public key* for high-frequency transmissions.
- Use *message digest* instead of secret key if the intent is to tamperproof without hiding contents from prying eyes.
- Encrypt every other packet (or even less often) on high-frequency transmissions, and then use the encrypted packets to sanity check data in nonencrypted packets.

Compression: Converting, packing, or otherwise compressing data comes at a CPU cycle cost. While bandwidth reduction often takes priority over CPU cost, a very small bandwidth saving may incur a large CPU cost.

Reliability: Does the data need to arrive? If so, use a guaranteed protocol. If not, use a nonguaranteed protocol. Games often require data on time or not at all. Using UDP avoids resends, freeing bandwidth, socket buffers, and CPU cycles for required and on-time data.

Synchronicity: Will the game adopt a "stop & wait" policy on latent data? If so, the simulation may need to freeze, but the graphic subsystem should continue to update. Stopping graphical updates appears as if the system hung. The user needs fluent access to chat and menu systems to communicate with connected parities or take action on the latency issue by booting a player or simply exiting the game.

Connection Models

The connection models described in this section should not be confused with connection- and connectionless-oriented protocols such as TCP and UDP, respectively. Even though UDP is considered connectionless, a packet follows a path considered a pseudoconnection for this discussion.

Broadcast

Broadcasting simplifies player discovery, but should never be used for normal packet delivery. To receive a broadcast packet requires actively listening for all broadcasts. Broadcast packets must contain some special identifying mark to distinguish them from broadcasts sent by other applications (which you have no choice but to weed through). A Globally Unique IDentifier (GUID), built from a hash of unique numbers—IP address, MAC address, and current date/time—handles such circumstances. Creation usually occurs outside the application, followed by embedding it as a constant within the source code. Microsoft provides "guidgen.exe" to create these numbers, and similar tools exist on other platforms.

A GUID established for game broadcasts solves the problem of game discovery. To use broadcasting for all game packets during gameplay requires a second GUID for the game instance. While broadcasting provides a useful mechanism for game discovery on LANs, avoid its use for high-frequency game packets. If say 10 four-player games were played on the same LAN, each person would have to weed through 39 packets for each game event, while only three are of concern to any given player.

Peer to Peer

Peer-to-peer connectivity means every player connects directly to every other player, as shown in Figure 5.6.3. This model experiences the least amount of latency because packets avoid the additional scenic trip to a server. This latency benefit comes at the cost of increased bandwidth requirements and connection maintenance complexity as the number of players increases beyond two. Since two-player games are not affected by the adversities of peering, they normally use this model unless the game architect requires a server.

Client/Server

The *client/server* model suits most games over two players, better than peering, due to the easier connection maintenance and lower bandwidth.

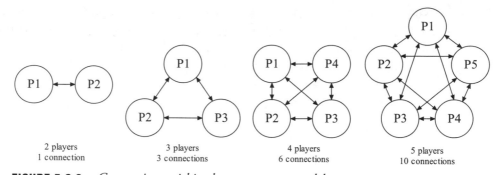

FIGURE 5.6.3   *Connections within the peer-to-peer model.*

Having a server in the connection model, as shown in Figure 5.6.4, offers many benefits over peering arrangements. Packet coalesce works best with on servers. "Lossy TCP," a construct that requires a server, works as follows. UDP packets are commonly refused by secure firewall configurations. If your game relies on high packet through-put in the absence of UDP, you must resort to TCP. TCP tends to back up, trying to redeliver packets that become outdated if not delivered immediately. A server can implement a "Lossy TCP" for clients that cannot accept UDP traffic by maintaining a buffer of size two; one slot for the item currently being sent, and the other slot for the latest packet. An incoming packet simply replaces the second slot item if one exists.

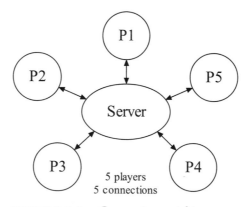

FIGURE 5.6.4   *Connections within a client/server model.*

Connection Complexity

Maintaining a connection requires monitoring the line for input, outputting data (duplicating effort for each additional player), keeping silent connections from closing with "keep alive" packets, and handling dropped connections either by ending the game or attempting to reconnect. Table 5.6.2 illustrates the number of connections required using different connection models.

Table 5.6.2 Number of Connections Required Using Different Connection Models
(N = number of players)

	Broadcast	Peer to Peer	Client/Server
Connections	0	$\sum_{x=1}^{N-1} x$	Client = 1 Server = N

Bandwidth

Bandwidth costs increase linearly with the number of players. With bandwidth at nearly the same premium as latency, peering tends to fail beyond the simplest two-player game. In a fully connected game, going from two to three players more than doubles the bandwidth requirements. That is more than just application data, since each packet comes with the transport's header. Table 5.6.3 illustrates the number of times a single packet must be transmitted for each player using the different connection models.

Table 5.6.3 Number of Times a Single Packet Must Be Transmitted for Each Player
(N 5 number of players)

	Broadcast	Peer to Peer	Client/Server
Send	1	$N-1$	Client = 1 Server = N
Receive	$N-1$	$N-1$	Client = 1 Server = N

Asynchronous Environments

An asynchronous environment exists where two or more branches of code run simultaneously. This section assumes a basic understanding of threads, signals, and critical sections. The following information provides tips for network game programming in a multithreaded environment.

Set network thread priority above or equal to the main render thread, but always below the audio thread. Make sure all network threads exit before exiting the main thread, or shared data will likely cause a null pointer exception.

Use signals and events to wake up or otherwise communicate the availability of new information across threads. The alternative, polling for state change, also goes by the name "spinning" because of the time wasted accomplishing nothing. Both events and signals are limited system resources, so plan accordingly. Remember that events notify all subscribers, where signals usually notify one of N subscribers. Expect to run into signals with thread pools that contain multiple subscribers, but only one available thread should receive a wake signal to process the work item.

System timers signal a high-priority thread, so refrain from lengthy activities in the timer thread or risk skewing time. Choose a reasonable timer resolution; no need to go above 128 Hz for most cases. Make sure to use the proper high-resolution timer, as more than one timer may exist on the OS. Use the multimedia timer for Windows.

Use critical sections sparingly. Try to design with the least amount of critical sections, and always keep the amount of time in a critical section to a minimum. Always match a critical section entry with an exit. Avoid entering in one method and exiting in another, as this complicates the design. All shared data writes require critical sections if more than one thread writes to the data. Avoid calling another critical section within a critical section at all costs; otherwise, deadlocks may occur. For incremental data modifications, use `interlockedincrement()` and `interlockeddecrement()` in Windows or their OS equivalent rather than using a critical section. Precede all shared data definitions with the `volatile` keyword; using data in a critical section does not relieve the possibility of shared data getting stored in registers between context switches.

Security

As soon as someone starts boasting about his perfectly secure system, he gets hacked. One-hundred-percent security does not exist. Keys and passwords can always be compromised at some level. Security takes development time and affects game performance. Instead, make a great game and provide an environment *secure enough* against all but the most diligent delinquent. The best way to go about securing a system involves using multiple security mechanisms. Start with standard security measures, and then add some creative convolution to make breaking security a hands-on affair rather than leaving the system open to automated cracking. The remainder of this section describes security mechanisms, what they do, and where to use them.

Encryption

The three goals of encryption are:

Authentication: Verification of an entity's claimed identity
Privacy: Prevent unauthorized viewing of data
Integrity: Assurance that data was not tampered with after leaving its source, although it does not prevent tampering

Atomic security elements commonly address one or two of these goals, but not all three. Higher level security layers combine the atomics to meet additional goals.

Public Key (Asymmetric—Key Pairs)

The *public key encryption* algorithm creates two keys: one public and one private. The public key is made public so others may encrypt data with it. The encrypted data requires the private key to decrypt. This algorithm is stronger than secret key encryption, but requires much more computational time. Both symmetric and asymmetric key encryptions provide privacy only.

Secret Key (Symmetric—Same Key)

The *secret key encryption* algorithm creates one shared key used to both encrypt and decrypt data. Use this algorithm to encrypt real-time data, as it requires less computation time. To share a secret key, encrypt it with the remote end's public key and send it to the remote end.

Ciphers

Block and *stream ciphers* describe how the key mechanism interacts with the plain text to produce the cipher text. Block ciphers work with a fixed-size data block. If the plain text does not fill the data block, the block cipher adds padding. Plain text larger than the block is split across multiple blocks. Stream ciphers work with any size data. The simplest cipher, called Electronic CookBook (ECB), combines the key and the plain text to produce the cipher text. Other variations use the output from the previous cipher operation in addition to the key and plain text, providing stronger encryption [Sch96].

Message Digest

The relatively fast *message digest algorithm* produces a checksum to verify message integrity, but does not encrypt the data or provide authentication.

Certificates

Certificates, also known as *digital IDs*, provide authentication through a trusted third party [VeriSign]. The third party stores public keys associated with a verified entity and delivers them on request, encapsulated in certificates that confirm the key owner's identity.

Copy Protection

Stopping game software pirating may not work entirely, but several reasons make it a worthwhile endeavor to at least delay the inevitable. A chart-topping game makes a large percentage of its lifetime sales in the first month of its release. Consider purchasing a copy protection system as an insurance policy on these initial sales. Even though professional criminals will break the protection, many more would not think twice about burning a copy for their friends.

An old form of copy protection involved the use of a code sheet distributed with the game. The code sheet contained numerous entries that did not photocopy. The game would randomly ask for codes from the code sheet to be entered in order to continue play. A similar approach was to request words from specified sections of the manual. The deterrence here was to ship a very large manual. Both code sheets and digital copies of the large manuals started popping up all over the Internet.

CD-ROM copy protection combines tricks using valid data in sectors marked as invalid on a CD-ROM, and encryption [Safedisc].

Watermarking

While not preventing illegal copying, digital watermarks make nonvisible alterations to art assets that can prove theft if such art appears in other works; for example, another game using artwork without permission from the creator.

Execution Cryptography

The following sections detail measures to take against attacks on the game execution modules.

Code Obfuscation

Stripping the code of its symbol names complicates reverse engineering. While not possible with interpreted languages, a code obfuscator changes all variable and method names to nondescriptive names. For example, a variable named "WorldPosition" would change to "v0001," leaving a hacker to figure out the intended purpose. Code obfuscators do not affect the actual byte code.

Heap Hopper

Tools are available that take snapshots of the heap before and after an event takes place, such as moving a player entity forward. After taking several snapshots between moves, certain variable locations consistently show change. A hacker can narrow in on the movement variable and change it manually, or make a program to automate changes. *Heap hopping* moves sensitive data around in the heap to make it more difficult to associate an action with a specific variable change. This may be done in numerous ways, but one strategy creates several heap buffers of the same size, copies data from one location to the next, and modifies the variables in the new location, thus preventing a hacker from narrowing in on the sensitive data.

Stack Overrun Execution

Stack overrun execution hacks take advantage of deficient packet data validation by the game. If a user sends malformed data that causes a function in the game to overrun its stack, the hack can modify the return instruction pointer to point another location, be it in the code or a data buffer the user sent in a packet. Such a hack usually requires a great deal of code analysis to craft, but there are determined hackers willing to spend the effort to make such an attack.

No Op Hacks

One of the easiest hacks involves changing the executable file by replacing method calls with "No Operation" byte codes. A hacker could use this to bypass certain validation checks, allowing further tampering of the code.

Timer Hacks

Many games use the computer's timers to regulate the game physics or otherwise control movement. Changing the system clock is very simple. To counter such hacks, verify that the timer never goes back in time or never takes unreasonable forward leaps.

DLL Shims

Game DLLs have method entry points. A shim DLL mimics these entry points and provides replacement code for each entry point so it silently replaces the original DLL. This allows monitoring of data passed to the methods of the DLL and often the changing of code execution. Several viable counters to this attack include using numeric entry points (ordinals) instead of method names, or providing only one entry point that returns class object pointers. Using a DLL with named method entry points makes the shim builder's job much easier, while a single entry point makes the hacker work harder.

User Privacy

Breaching a player's right to privacy creates headaches ranging from bad public relations to legal trouble. An online subscription game typically collects very personal data for billing purposes. Never divulge the following critical pieces of information:

- Real name
- User password
- Address
- Phone number(s)
- E-mail address
- Billing information
- Age (especially of minors)

Use strong cryptographic measures for both transmission and storage of such information. In addition, limit access to this secured data within the development team.

While not a listed element in the critically private information, a user's IP address justifies a fair degree of privacy. Peered connection architectures make sharing IP addresses unavoidable, but not their display. Displaying a user's IP allows even the nontechnical person to simply enter someone's IP into a program that could perform various network attacks.

Username and Password Interception

Using public key encryption for transmission of username and passwords, and not showing the users password as it is typed are sufficient standard practices to secure this information. Problems with username/password theft normally stem from impersonation over chat or e-mail channels, and fake utilities. Prevention by educating the user is the best step to take on both accounts. Fake game-specific utilities often require the user to enter in his username and password, which it sends to the hacker through some untraceable means such as a hotmail e-mail account. To reduce the impact of such a breach, all changes to the account and access to billing should require confirmation through the user's e-mail.

Firewalls

A *firewall* either inspects packets to determine if they should pass through the firewall, or provides an encrypted session.

Packet Filter

Stateful protocol inspection, or *packet filtering*, looks at protocol headers to determine whether a packet should be allowed to pass. A port filtering device inspects the port entry of a TCP or UDP packet and either accepts or rejects the packet based on user settings for a given port. Users should keep ports blocked in case they inadvertently acquire a malicious program that attempts to communicate data from their computer. This applies twofold to computers running a game server, which should block every port not explicitly in use. Games that require certain ports be made available should allow configuration of exactly which port(s) the game uses.

Similar filters inspect IP address entries in IP packets and accept/reject packets based on the source. Such filters provide a way to ban specific IPs from access to the network. Entry of IP addresses into the banned table provides the most benefit when done by an automated process that detects numerous denied connection requests to elements on the network behind the firewall.

Proxies

Application *proxies* inspect the data within the packet. Such a proxy server could check MIME or FTP traffic for viruses.

Circuit Gateways

Circuit gateways set up secure sessions, and ignore packet contents.

Network Address Translation (NAT)

The NAT protocol allows routers to share a single WAN IP address between all network adapters connected to the router. It accomplishes this by sharing the 64 K port space of the WAN IP between them. To share the port space, the router maintains a NAT table that maps LAN addresses, IP:Port, to WAN ports. This process hides LAN IPs from the Internet side of the router, which only sees the WAN IP. This indirection makes it more difficult to direct attacks on a specific address.

The NAT algorithm determines whether requested ports actually map directly to the WAN port. In the case of two requests for the same port, from separate adapters, one request will either be offered a different external port or return with an "in use" failure. Figure 5.6.5 illustrates this process.

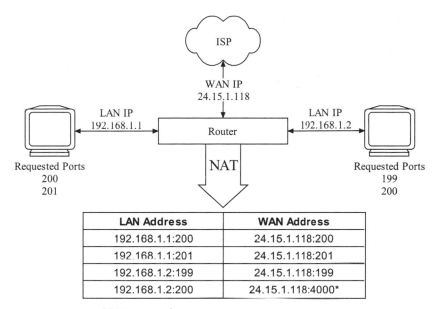

FIGURE 5.6.5   *NAT at work.*

Port Forwarding

Hosting socket connections requires a preagreement between client and server as to the IP and port on which the server listens for client connections. When a computer behind a NAT listens on a port, there is no guarantee the WAN port is the same such port. To compensate for this problem, most routers allow the forwarding of specific ports or ranges of ports to a specific LAN IP. This in essence places a static entry into the NAT table.

Port Triggering

Port triggering enables transient port forwarding. Some routers enable port triggering with a table of process names and ports to forward, when requested, to the requesting computer. After the socket closes and the port is subsequently released, the port returns to the pool of ports available for translation by the NAT. This reduces the vulnerability caused by the static nature of port forwarding. It also allows the game, requiring the specific port(s), to work on different computers without the need to manually update port forwarding.

DMZ

Adding a LAN IP to the demilitarized zone (DMZ) setting on a router forwards all ports to that particular computer. This bypasses the NAT, and its security feature of hiding the computer's IP. A computer in the DMZ shares the WAN IP with the router.

Determining WAN IP

When a computer behind a router uses conventional means to determine its own IP address, it receives the LAN IP issued through the DHCP service. No clear-cut method exists to reliably retrieve the WAN IP programmatically. The most reliable, cross-platform-friendly and router-brand-agnostic method is by third party:

Third party: Send a packet to a third party requesting a response containing the IP address they see in the sender portion of the IP packet. Such a third-party tool may be written as a server dedicated to this purpose, or a simple server-side script built for access through HTTP.

UPnP: Universal Plug and Play contains methods to gain the WAN IP for newer routers that support it.

Parse router admin page: Routers have different ways to access this information through administration tools. The Web page admin interface is popular, and a developer could write code to parse the IP from the admin page. The problem is that each router admin page hierarchy and page format differ, thus requiring time-consuming vender-specific special-case code support.

Summary

This survey of multiplayer development began by looking at different multiplayer categories, from split-screen to real-time network connections. The core material focused on dissecting the OSI layers in an average network game. The OSI layers contained mediums, IP, TCP and UDP, sockets, packet presentation, and game logic related to controlling latency. Next, the real-time communication models of broadcasting, peer-to-peer, and client/server were analyzed for strengths and weaknesses, followed by tips for working in multithreaded environments. The chapter concluded with a glimpse into the necessary evils of game security.

No single book covers all the technical details of multiplayer development. Complete coverage would entail a discussion of all the dirty details on numerous platforms on the following subjects: serial communication, server design, network gear and infrastructure, socket programming, voice over IP (VOIP), tools of the trade, unit and beta testing, available middleware analysis, database development, Web development, asynchronous programming, and much greater depth in latency hiding/recovery for every game genre.

 ## Exercises

Protocol Search

Use the RFC Web site (*www.rfc-editor.org/*) and the IANA Web site (*www.iana.org/ assignments/port-numbers*) to answer the following questions:

1. What protocols do the following RFCs cover: RFC 791, RFC 792, RFC 793, RFC 768, RFC 2616, RFC 10, and RFC 9?
2. What protocols are associated with the following ports: 80, 3074, 20/21, 1433, and 3306?

Throughput Calculations

Assume the following conditions for problems 3 through 5:

- 256 kbps DSL connection on all endpoints
- Eight clients sending to a dedicated server
- Each client sends at 32 Hz
- Application packet data is 64 bytes per packet

3. Determine client sending saturation given a TCP protocol, packet, and send rate.
4. Determine bandwidth saturation using UDP.
5. How many clients could a server support with a bandwidth of 1 Mbps?

Packet Construction

6. Rewrite the following Packet so it does not need to be serialized and is as small as possible. Assume the following conditions:

- System supports a maximum application packet length of 300 bytes.
- Packets will be exchanged between varieties of platforms, including 64/32 bit systems and Windows/Unix.

```
typedef enum PktCode
{
    Pkt0=0,
    ...                        // Other IDs
    PktMax=65000
};

struct Packet
{
    PktCode    ID;
    BOOL       Lights;
    int        HourOfDay;      // 0-23
    short      DayOfWeek;
    int        Health;         // 0-100%
    int        PacketLength;
    char       UserName[64];
};
```

WinSock

ON THE CD

Complete Exercise 7 using the ServerMon application server (on the companion CD-ROM) running on a remote system, preferably running Windows Server 2003 or greater with 2 GB of RAM. Client computers should also run with at least 2 GB of RAM for the "Critical Mass" tasks. Lower RAM will limit the system resources required for 30,000 connections due to the kernel page locked memory limitation of Windows.

7. Blackbox:
   a. (optional) If the instructor supplies a Web page containing the IP:Port of the server, acquire that information from the Web page using either the WinINet SDK or MFC HTTP reader class. A more advanced alternative entails reading the HTTP protocol RFC to format a page request and implement a simple HTTP protocol to acquire the Web page.
   b. Connect to that IP:Port given for the Blackbox server, and wait for a Pkt_Message (defined in the header file "PacketDefs.h" on the companion CD-ROM) packet containing further instructions. This program will test your ability to host and connect using TCP and UDP, and send and receive data using both protocols.

ON THE CD

8. Critical mass:
   a. Make and maintain 30,000 TCP connections.
   b. Listen for, accept, and maintain 30,000 TCP connections (not supported in the provided ServerMon.exe).

Encryption

Use Microsoft's Crypto API to perform the following:

9. Implement public key encryption with a certificate:
   a. Generate a certificate using makecert.exe.
   b. Extract the public key from the certificate to encrypt some plain-text message.
   c. Get the private key associated with the certificate, which was placed in a key container you named during the creation of the certificate. Use this private key to decrypt the cipher text generated in Step b.
10. Implement symmetric key encryption:
    a. Generate a symmetric/secret key.
    b. Encrypt a plain-text message.
    c. Save the secret key to a file.
    d. Load the secret key from the file and use it to decrypt the cipher text generated in Step b.

References

Protocols

[Hind95] Hinden, Robert, "IP Next Generation Overview," available online at *http://playground.sun.com/pub/ipng/html/INET-IPng-Paper.html.*

[IANA] Internet Assigned Number Authority, "Well Known Ports," available online at *www.iana.org.*

[NSIP04] Network Sorcery, "IP, Internet Protocol," available online at *www.networksorcery.com/enp/protocol/ip.htm.*

[NSIP604] Network Sorcery, "IPv6, Internet Protocol version 6," available online at *www.networksorcery.com/enp/protocol/ipv6.htm#Version.*

[NSTCP04] Network Sorcery, "TCP, Transmission Control Protocol," available online at *www.networksorcery.com/enp/protocol/tcp.htm.*

[NSUDP04] Network Sorcery, "UDP, User Datagram Protocol," available online at *www.networksorcery.com/enp/protocol/udp.htm.*

[RFC] Internet Society, "The Request for Comments," available online at *www.rfc-editor.org/.*

[Stevens94] Stevens, Richard, *TCP/IP Illustrated, Volume 1, The Protocols*, Addison-Wesley, 1994.

Communication APIs

[Camp93] Campbell, Joe, *C Programmer's Guide to Serial Communications, Second Edition*, Sams Publishing, 1993.

[Darcy] Darcy, Jeff, "High-Performance Server Architecture," available online at *http://pl.atyp.us/content/tech/servers.html.*

[Jones02] Jones, Anthony, *Network Programming for Microsoft Windows, Second Edition*, Microsoft Press, 2002.

[Kegel00] Kegel, Dan, "Micro benchmark comparing poll, kqueue, and /dev/poll," available online at *www.kegel.com/dkftpbench/Poller_bench.html.*

[Lemon] Lemon, Jonathan, "Kqueue: A generic and scaleable event notification facility," available online at *http://people.freebsd.org/~jlemon/papers/kqueue.pdf.*

[Provos00] Provos, Niels, "Scalable network I/O in Linux," available online at *www.citi.umich.edu/techreports/reports/citi-tr-00-4.pdf.*

[Stevens04] Stevens, Richard, *UNIX Network Programming, Volume 1, Third Edition: The Sockets Networking API*, Addison-Wesley, 2004.

Middleware

[DirectPlay] Available online at *http://msdn.microsoft.com* keyword DirectPlay.

[Quazal] Available online at *www.quazal.com.*

Latency Compensation

[Aronson97] Aronson, Jesse, "Dead Reckoning: Latency Hiding for Networked Games," available online at *www.gamasutra.com/features/19970919/aronson_01. htm*.

[Caldwell00] Caldwell, Nick, "Defeating Lag with Cubic Splines," available online at *www.gamedev.net/reference/articles/article914.asp*.

[Haag01] Haag, Chris, "Targeting: A Variation of Dead Reckoning (v1.0)," available online at *www.gamedev.net/reference/articles/article1370.asp*.

Security

[Coleridge96] Coleridge, Robert, *The Cryptography API, or How to Keep a Secret*, available online at *http://msdn.microsoft.com/library/en-us/dncapi/html/msdn_ cryptapi.asp*, August 19, 1996.

[Gibson02] Gibson, Steve, "Distributed Reflection Denial of Service," available online at *http://grc.com/dos/drdos.htm*.

[RSALabs00] RSA Laboratories, *RSA Laboratories' Frequently Asked Questions About Today's Cryptography*, Version 4.1, May 2000.

[Safedisc04] MacroVision, "Safedisc Copy Protection," available online at *www. macrovision.com/products/safedisc/index.shtml*.

[Sch96] Schneier, Bruce, *Applied Cryptography: Protocols, Algorithms, and Source Code in C, 2nd Edition*, John Wiley & Sons, 1996.

[TwoFish96] Schneier, Bruce, *The Twofish Encryption Algorithm*, John Wiley & Sons, 1996.

[Veri04] VeriSign, "Digital ID, A Brief Overview," available online at [VeriSign].

[VeriSign] VeriSign, "Protect Your Digital ID; Protect Your Private Key," available online at *www.verisign.com/repository/PrivateKey_FAQ/*.

AUDIO VISUAL DESIGN AND PRODUCTION

6.1 Visual Design

In This Chapter

- Overview
- Graphic Design Principles
- Color Theory
- User Interface Design
- Summary
- Exercises
- References

Overview

Visual design can be described as the management and presentation of visual information. It encompasses many forms of communication, in both the two-dimensional and three-dimensional realms. Many fields of endeavor such as cinema, theater, and architecture owe their success or failure to strong visual design. This is also true in the more traditional design fields such as graphic design, illustration, typography, and symbol creation. These disciplines use visual design to communicate with the viewer through the practical application of basic principles. Although new, as a form of entertainment, computer and console games still rely on these same basic principles to communicate information.

The "Look and Feel"

During the early concept stages of a project, there is usually no real technology or code base. The game is simply an idea on paper. The programming code has yet to be written, so a more traditional method of utilizing imagery to convey the idea is used. During this preproduction process, the designer and art director begin to explore the look and feel of the game. Preliminary sketches and concept drawings help to visualize what the game may look like. Early design concepts can be tested and rejected with a minimum of effort and very little wasted manpower. These early drawings or paintings help define the vision of a game, and begin to set expectations for all those involved. They are used to define qualities such as tone, mood, and style. Often, these concepts are collected into what is sometimes referred to as an Art Bible, a document where all of the best ideas and imagery are kept. It helps the project leads of the team to maintain a common reference point from which they can begin to create a game.

For the artistic vision to maintain a strong presence throughout the development cycle, the game artist must understand and use some basic design principles.

Graphic Design Principles

Graphic design is a communication process through which ideas and concepts are presented in a visual medium. Using graphic elements, composition, layout, color and typography, information can be presented in a very powerful and compelling way. Good graphic design is often invisible to the user. The information is understood with a minimum of effort and can be acted upon easily. Bad design, on the other hand, can interfere with the presentation of information to the point where the intended audience comes away with little or no useful data. In game development, this translates to user frustration, negative game experiences, and bad reviews.

Graphic design can be broken down into several basic principles. By understanding each and with proper use, a cohesive design that is both pleasing and informative will result. These principles are *balance*, *rhythm*, *emphasis*, and *unity*.

Balance is the visual equilibrium in a composition. Opposing forces cancel one another out and give the image stability. *Symmetrical balance* is where objects of equal weight are placed on either side of a central point or fulcrum. *Asymmetrical balance* is where objects of nonequal weight are balanced around a point or fulcrum. Examples of each are shown in Figure 6.1.1.

Rhythm is the pattern created by repeating various elements within a design. This rhythm produces order and predictability. It also gives movement to a composition, allowing the artist to control the visual energy. Figure 6.1.2 shows an example of rhythm.

Emphasis is created when the pattern of movement is interrupted. The rhythm is broken and forms a focal point, usually drawing the eye to it first. Emphasis can also be created through repetition and contrasts in elements such as color, size, shape, or texture. The right image in Figure 6.1.2 demonstrates emphasis.

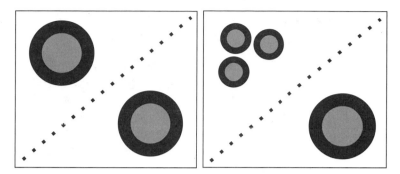

FIGURE 6.1.1 *Symmetrical and asymmetrical balance.*

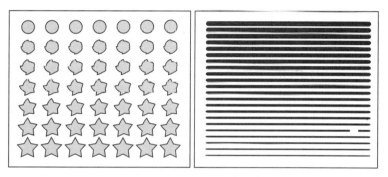

FIGURE 6.1.2 *A rhythmic pattern is predictable. To create emphasis and focus the eye on a specific location, the pattern can be interrupted.*

Unity is the harmony of all parts. It forms a cohesive whole within a design. Elements that are in unity look like they all belong together.

Elements of Graphic Design

Elements are the parts of a design that can be isolated and defined. The principles are applied to these elements to form a cohesive design. These elements are *line, shape, space, texture, size,* and *color,* as shown in Figure 6.1.3.

A *Line* is any mark that connects two points. It can be curved or straight, have weight, and emphasize direction. Lines can be combined to form textures and patterns.

Shape refers to anything that has height and width. This can include characters, symbols, and forms. Three basic primitive shapes form the building blocks for all other shapes: the rectangle, the circle, and the triangle. Shapes, and the forms they create, can be either two dimensional or three dimensional. A two-dimensional form has width and height. By adding depth, the third dimension is achieved.

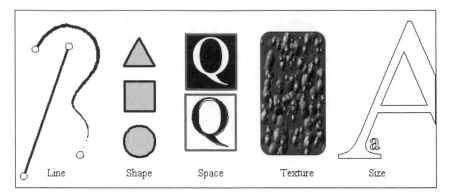

FIGURE 6.1.3   *The basic elements of graphic design.*

Space is the area around or between elements and can be thought of as positive or negative. In most two-dimensional designs, the background is considered negative space, while objects form the foreground and compose the positive space.

Texture is the look and feel of a surface. We relate all textures to our previous experiences of touch. A texture can also be imaginary and not necessarily tied to a known touch experience. All surfaces can be described in terms of a texture. Examples of a texture might be rough, soft, smooth, or cold.

Size is how large or small something is. It is the comparative relationship between things. Size can be used to create a sense of importance or make objects appear closer to the viewer. Size relationships can be used to create a sense of depth or perspective. A good example of size relationships can be found in a mathematical ratio called the "Golden Mean" or "Golden Rule." It is often found in nature and considered aesthetically pleasing.

Color is a generic term that covers a broad array of areas. To use color effectively, it is important that some of the basic science behind it is also understood. The first area we will explore is *color theory*.

Color Theory

We see color in a small portion of the electromagnetic spectrum known as *visible light*. Other types of radiation found above and below visible light in the electromagnetic spectrum are radio waves, microwaves, infrared, ultraviolet, x-rays, and gamma rays. When we see a color, it is the reflection of light off a surface. All of the other colors are absorbed by the surface, allowing only the color we see to be transmitted.

The reflected colors we see all fall within the *visible spectrum*. A beam of sunlight can be broken into this spectrum by passing through a prism. The result shows the visible spectrum broken down into individual colors. They always follow a specific order—red, orange, yellow, green, blue, indigo, and violet. Just prior to red on the electromagnetic spectrum is infrared light. Just after the violet, it transitions into ultraviolet light.

To help define how colors appear, they are broken into several qualities such as hue, saturation, and value.

Hue: Refers to the name of a color within the visible spectrum.

Saturation: Refers to the amount of a color. The less saturated a color is, the more gray value is visible.

Value: The amount of white or black that is present in a color. This is often referred to as the lightness or darkness of a color.

When we look at the world in sunlight, we see only the colors that are reflected into our eye. This is known as *subtractive color*. Print graphics, paintings, and drawings all use subtractive color. See Color Plate 1 for an example.

Primary colors: Within the subtractive color wheel, there are three primary colors: red, yellow, and blue.

Secondary colors: These colors are formed by mixing the primary colors. They are green, orange, and violet.

Tertiary colors: These colors are formed by mixing one primary and one secondary color. They are yellow-orange, red-orange, red-purple, blue-purple, blue-green, and yellow-green.

By mixing one or more sources of light, colors can be achieved using *additive color*. Because the colors are emissive rather than reflective, they behave and blend differently. A common example of something that uses additive color is a television or computer monitor. Within the games industry, most artwork is created with software that uses the additive color chart. See Color Plate 2 for an example.

Primary colors: The three primary colors of the additive chart are red, green, and blue.

Secondary colors: Equal portions of any two primary colors will yield a secondary color of magenta, cyan, or yellow.

White: Equal portions of all primaries (red, green, and blue) will yield white.

Color harmony: This categorizes colors and determines harmonious groups such as complimentary, split complimentary, triads, and analogous colors. The order, amount, and combination of these colors are where the "art" comes in.

User Interface Design

The amount of effort devoted to the design and implementation of the interface in a game can be staggering. How people interact with computers, extract information, and use this knowledge is now a critical element in the development of software. The user interface (UI) design is an important link between the programming code and the end user. For a successful interface between man and machine to occur, a UI must be predictable, consistent, and informative.

Underlying any good UI design are the fundamentals of graphic design. As defined earlier, graphic design is nothing more than presenting information in a strong, consistent, visually appealing format. The text and visual elements are organized in such a way as to provide the viewer with an easy way to retrieve, sort, and store the information. Composition, layout, and typography are all balanced to provide the strongest visual presentation possible. However, graphic design, in the traditional sense, is a one-dimensional medium for conveying information. It is targeted to a non-interactive, one-way presentation.

UI design adds many new elements to the basic equation. Sound graphic principles are needed, and consideration has to be given on a whole new set of design elements. User interaction, navigation, the impacts of sound, animation, and time all affect the end experience. The designer must consider how he will be controlling the user experience. What type of feedback mechanisms will be in place, and how will all of these elements tie together to form a positive user experience?

Often, the best UI is the one that is most transparent to the user. Depending on the needs of the game, a minimalist approach to the user interface design might prove to be the most appealing. It's always best to start with the simplest solution first, and add more complexity as needed. With all of this to consider, it's easy to see why creating a solid, well thought-out design can have a major impact on the time of a game development artist.

Design Considerations

First, consider some basic graphic design principles and how they can be expanded on for use within an interface design.

Simplicity: Artists, as a rule, have a tendency to over design or overwork game graphics. In interface design, the simplest solutions are generally the easiest to use, and most effective. Sometimes, more information and greater impact can be gained from a minimalist approach.

Consistency: Humans are creatures of habit. We learn through repetitive actions and are quicker to respond to events if we can predict the behavior. Once a user has learned the function or placement of an interface element, he will use that knowledge on new screens in an attempt to find consistency in the structure. If the consistency isn't there, the user will be frustrated by having to relearn new paradigms from screen to screen. Consistency also makes design seem simpler to use. By setting up consistent placement of repetitive elements such as where the Cancel button is found, it is possible to create an environment where the user feels empowered and comfortable to explore.

Know the target user: In the broadest strokes, this means understanding and predicting how the product will be used by the target demographic group. The UI design for a children's product will be radically different from one targeted at adults. Consideration must be given to how knowledgeable the user is, how he perceives the information presented, what types of feedback mechanisms will be used, and how simple the navigation requirements are. Products that are targeted at an international audience must consider the cultural implications of design elements. For instance, a color can have very specific connotations in one country, and entirely different ones in another.

Color usage: A UI should not rely on color alone to convey critical information. Approximately 8 percent of the male population have either color blindness, or color perception deficiencies. Additional feedback mechanisms will insure that the user understands what the designer intended. Using value contrast between the foreground and background elements, especially when text is concerned, can avoid readability issues. It is also advisable to avoid large amounts of light text on a dark background. It is more difficult to read and causes visual fatigue or eyestrain.

Feedback mechanisms: These visual and auditory elements help the end user understand his interaction with the UI. A common example of this is standard buttons in most computer applications. They usually have a rollover state that indicates when the user is over a "hot spot" on the button. The feedback mechanism can take the form of a visual highlight change, a special effect, an animation, or a sound. It also tells the user that he has accomplished a task. Because of the nature of computers and the tendency for them to lock up or crash, it is usually wise to let the user know when the program is performing a task. A progress bar can satisfy this need easily and prevent user frustration. If loading a file takes longer than about 5 to 10 seconds, it is a good idea to show some form of a progress bar or percentage feedback.

Design Elements

A flow chart of the design is an invaluable tool for spotting errors in design or functionality. This is especially critical when the functional design and the aesthetic design are being done by two different people. It is fairly common for the game designer to come up with the functional requirements of the menuing system, while the artist comes up with how it will look. Often, a flow chart will flush out flaws in the logic of the design well before any time and effort has gone into creating art assets. Creating a UI while the design is still in a major state of flux will lead to rework and wasted art. An example flow chart is shown in Figure 6.1.4.

Usually, the simplest design is the most efficient. Human short-term memory stores only five to seven items before it begins to lose focus. Many of the most successful designs rely on this basic idea. The user is never more than three to five clicks away from accessing the information he wants. Of course, this is sometimes impossible to maintain, but keeping the navigation to a minimum will increase the user's comfort with the menus. Grouping multiple functions or options in one area is also a good practice. This allows the user to make decisions that are more efficient and keeps him within the same area of the screen. If the user is given the impression that he is jumping from screen to screen with each menu navigation, he may have a tendency to feel lost within a large menu system.

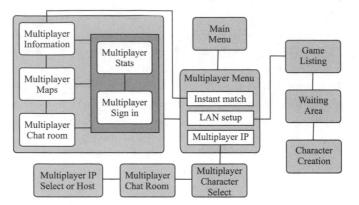

FIGURE 6.1.4   *A flow chart helps to visualize a design.*

Establishing a grid: Underlying all good design is a grid. This is a visual structure that provides the framework for the design and gives it balance and rhythm. By observing any magazine, newspaper, or advertisement, a grid can be found that all images and text fall within or on. From a design standpoint, the grid gives the artist a logical structure for the layout. A well-designed grid will give the UI screens consistency and allow the user to better understand and predict the behavior of the menu. It also provides a good basis for narrowing down design decisions and establishing a set of rules or style guides that can be applied to new screens. Figure 6.1.5 shows an example of how grids can be used.

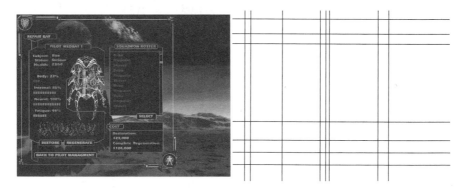

FIGURE 6.1.5   *Grids will help tie a design together.*

Tiered menu system: The most powerful menu system is one that can adjust to the needs of the user. For the novice, it may only contain the most basic commands. For the advanced user, the interface can be made to reveal more complexity, allowing for greater control. By allowing the user the ability to control the amount of data he is given access to, he will be more apt to explore.

Localization considerations: Overseas sales make up a substantial part of the target market for many of today's games. Converting a title to a different language is generally referred to as *localization*. By keeping in mind some of the simpler localization rules, a game artist can avoid additional rework when it comes time to localize a product.

First, do not embed text directly into the artwork for the game or menu. If possible, text should be handled via the programming code as either a TrueType font or a bitmap font. However, if it is embedded in the art (such as a sign or logo), it is a good idea to separate the text onto a unique layer in the base art file. This will allow the artist easy access to only the artwork that is affected by the translation. Next, allow for 30 percent of additional space around any text. Some languages, such as German, have a tendency toward much longer translated words that take up more space in the UI. Lastly, avoid small font sizes and test them often against the target output device (TV or computer monitor). As a general rule of thumb, don't go below 12 pixels in font height. Below that size, there are not enough pixels to form some of the basic letterforms, especially with languages such as Japanese. When creating fonts for console platforms, it is critical that they be previewed on the target system. A font that reads very well on a PC can often become unreadable on an NTSC television.

Typography Fundamentals

Choosing the right font will add solidarity and elegance to a design. There is no exact science or formula that will yield good results every time. However, understanding some of the basic typographical rules can significantly reduce the time it takes to create a solid design.

Humans recognize letters and words as shapes, which are memorized as a meaning or concept. Consider how a page of text is read. Each letter isn't sounded out in the reader's head. Instead, combinations of letters have been memorized as a shape recognition unit, forming a word. When text is written in all uppercase letters, it is much more difficult to read, since the pattern recognition is reduced to simple rectangles instead of unique groupings found in a mix of upper- and lowercase letters. A good test of this is to take any paragraph of text in a word document, switch it to all uppercase, and read it. The time it takes to read a single sentence is slowed significantly since the brain can't use its natural ability to recognize shapes as efficiently.

Serif versus san serif fonts: A serif font is distinguished from a san serif font by the addition of small strokes at the ends of each character stroke, as shown in Figure 6.1.6. In large bodies of text, serifed fonts are generally considered easier to read. The serifs provide horizontal structure for the eye to follow. Although the same rules apply when designing computer or game typography, it is usually less of an issue. It isn't often that large amounts of text are structured in a page format. In addition, the resolution limits of the output screen will often restrict the amount of text that can be displayed at one time. Even though hardware continues to evolve, designs must target the lowest common denominator in terms of screen resolution.

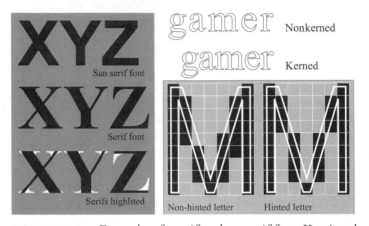

FIGURE 6.1.6 *Examples of a serif and san serif font. Kerning shows the spacing between letters. Hinting allows text to be reduced and still maintain legibility.*

International font considerations: Games are often localized to major languages such as French, German, and Spanish. To minimize the amount of work involved to convert from one language to another, fonts usually contain a specific set of specialized characters. Most of the Western Europe translations can be accomplished by using a font that has a single-byte character set that provides 256 characters. This set generally contains the Latin letters, Arabic numerals, punctuation, and some drawing characters. The recognized standard for these 256 character codes is the ANSI (American National Standard Institute) Character Code set, used by most large computer companies. However, 256 characters falls well short of what is necessary in a single font for translations that involve some of the Far Eastern languages. In some cases, these fonts may need as many as 12,000 characters to cover the language properly. To provide the needed character codes, double-byte or multibyte (MBCS/DBCS) character sets are used. These sets are a mixture of single-byte and double-byte character encoding that provides over 65,000 characters.

Kerning: Kerning is the adjustment of space between characters so that part of one letter extends over the body of the next, as shown in Figure 6.1.6. We see this letter spacing every day, but don't really notice its presence. An example would be the narrow spacing between two circular letters such as a "c" and an "o." This spacing or kerning would be much narrower for two parallel letters such as two lowercase "l's." Most computer or TrueType fonts have the spacing information built into them. Kerning makes the word forms more solid and readable. Without it, text appears disjointed, lacks cohesion, and is more difficult to read.

Hinting: Hinting is a mathematical instruction added to the font that distorts the character's outline before it is converted to a bitmap for display on the screen. These modification hints allow the designer to have a fairly high level of control over the resultant bitmap shape of the letter, especially at smaller sizes. Without this control, features that define the font (line weight, widths, serif details) can become inconsistent, irregular, and sometimes even disappear at smaller sizes. This can have a dramatic effect on legibility. An example is shown in Figure 6.1.6.

TrueType versus Bitmap Fonts

Although TrueType fonts have kerning built into them, some game engines don't necessarily support their use. Because these fonts require more memory and special programming code to use, they are often replaced with a simple bitmap font. A bitmap font is a texture map with all of the necessary letters spaced out in a grid of cells. With this cell-based approach, the letter spacing is often defined by the width of a specific cell. This usually doesn't allow for kerning and can lead to a more simplistic look to the font.

Creating a Font

The creation of a custom game font is no small undertaking. By creating a font, creative control over a major visual element in the game is gained; however, there is a tremendous amount of work involved. Generating a proper TrueType font entails creating the base alphabet and numbers, and the international characters necessary for European translations. In addition, creating the kerning and hinting information can add unexpected time to the schedule. One distinct advantage with generating a font from scratch is from the copyright and licensing standpoint. It is no longer necessary to get copyright and license agreements for use within the game and on the packaging.

Rapid Prototyping

Rapid prototyping allows the UI designer to quickly work through the logic and flow of a menu system without the need to involve the programming team. A number of programs and methods allow the design to be fleshed out and tested easily. At the simplest level, a flow chart can be used. Another popular way is to generate HTML pages with simple hyperlinks between them that mimic the navigation. More advanced programs such as Macromedia's Director or Flash can be used to show functionality, and to begin to test out elements such as animation and sound. These prototypes serve to solidify artistic elements and provide programmers and other team members with a very clear, concise vision of the artistic direction.

Summary

Because of the content-rich environment provided by game development, a whole new set of art-related disciplines have emerged. When personal computers first began to reach the mass market, they were a relatively simple communication device. Little or no visual design was needed to help present the information. Monochromatic screens were used to display low-resolution text. The personal computer had yet to be considered a form of entertainment, so there was little need to go beyond the utilitarian. In the few short years since then, hardware capabilities have gone through an exponential growth curve. Now, full-color, photo-realistic 3D environments and movie-quality cut scenes are commonplace. Along with this explosive evolution in the technology has been a corresponding maturation in the expectations and sophistication of the users. Now, more than ever, strong visual design helps mold the experience of the user and makes the human-machine interface successful.

Exercises

1. List the principles and elements of graphic design. Show an example of each.
2. Create an example graphic showing the electromagnetic spectrum, and principle ranges within it.
3. Create an example of an additive and a subtractive color chart. Describe the differences between each color model.
4. List the design elements that should be considered when beginning to create a UI design.
5. Generate a layout design for a menu system. Show the underlying grid system on which the design is based.
6. Show an ANSI Character Code set that includes international character sets. Describe how it is used when a product is localized to a different language.
7. Design a game font. This font should contain uppercase characters, lowercase characters, and numbers. Extra Credit: Create international characters needed for localization.
8. Design an interactive menu system for a fictitious game. Using rapid prototyping techniques, create a functional user interface that shows menu navigation.

References

[Beaumont87] Beaumont, Michael, *Type—Design, Color, Character and Use,* Quarto Publishing, 1987.

[Hamlin 96] Hamlin, J. Scott, *Interface Design with Photoshop*, New Riders Publishing, 1996.

[IBM04] "IBM Design fundamentals," IBM, 2004, available online at *www-3.ibm.com/ibm/easy/eou_ext.nsf/publish/561*.

[Johnson04] Johnson, David, "Psychology of Color," *Infoplease,* 2004, available online at *www.infoplease.com/spot/colors1.html*.

[Knobler71] Knobler, Nathan, *The Visual Dialogue,* Holt, Rinehart and Winston, Inc., 1971.

[Marcus92] Marcus, Aaron, *Graphic Design for Electronic Documents and User Interfaces,* ACM Press, 1992.

[Mayer04] Mayer, Roger, "Color Theory," Brown University, 2004, available online at *www.cs.brown.edu/courses/cs092/VA10/HTML/start.html.*

[Microsoft04] "Microsoft Typography," Microsoft, 2004, available online at *www.microsoft.com/typography/default.mspx.*

[MundiDesign04] "Web color studies," Mundi Design Studios, 2004, available online at *www.mundidesign.com/webct/.*

[NASA04] "Electromagnetic Spectrum—Introduction," NASA, 2004, available online at *http://imagine.gsfc.nasa.gov/docs/science/know_l1/emspectrum.html.*

[Swann89] Swann, Alan, *How to Understand & Use Grids,* Quarto Publishing, 1989.

6.2 ▌ 3D Modeling

In This Chapter

- ■ Overview
- ■ Introduction to 3D Modeling
- ■ Box Modeling with Polygons
- ■ NURBS
- ■ Subdivision Surfaces
- ■ 3D Sculpting
- ■ Reverse Engineering
- ■ BSP Modeling
- ■ Common Approaches to Constructing Geometry
- ■ Modeling Methodology
- ■ Critical Analysis
- ■ Summary
- ■ Exercises

Overview

In this chapter, you will learn about the process of creating 3D models. Some methods discussed are standard day-to-day work for a modeler, and some are less used or special-purpose methods, but are still worth mentioning. This chapter begins with a step-by-step example of how a 3D character model is created to familiarize you with basic workflow. Later, we will examine a few typical gaming models and how they are created, including a car, an environment, and a low-polygon character.

Introduction to 3D Modeling

A professional 3D modeler is a sculptor and a technician. He is an artist and an engineer. He must be concerned with the form, expressiveness, and style as well as the polygon count, topology, and efficiency of his models.

Although there are many methods and types of modeling, in gaming today polygon modeling is king.

Box Modeling with Polygons

Box modeling is just as the name implies. You start with a polygon box, and cut, extrude, and refine until you have a finished model. This is a freeform approach to modeling, and somewhat mimics the process of sculpting with clay. Let's dive right in to creating a simple character using box modeling techniques.

Concept Sketch

If possible, begin with turnaround sketches of the character you are modeling, as shown in the two right-hand sketches in Figure 6.2.1. A posed sketch is great for showing the personality and attitude of the character, but it is not ideal as a modeling reference. Turnaround sketches provide nearly exact proportions and show form that may be confusing on a posed sketch. These turnaround sketches can be scanned in and imported into your modeling program. When seen directly in the viewport, turnaround sketches will make the modeling process much easier. Note that it helps to make your image a square, power-of-two resolution, like 256 × 256, 512 × 512, or 1024 × 1024. Otherwise, the video card may have to resample the sketch to one of these resolutions, reducing the fidelity of the image.

FIGURE 6.2.1 *A posed concept sketch of a character, along with two turnaround sketches.*

Before you begin any modeling, a few technical requirements should be defined. Most important at this stage is the polygon count you are targeting. In games today, character polygon counts can range anywhere from 200 polygons to 15 million polygons (when using normal maps). Your polygon count budget will depend on the game platform (PC, PS2, Xbox, Game Cube), game engine, number of characters onscreen simultaneously, level of detail method, and so forth. Generally, the total polygon budget for a scene, including polygon budgets for the environment and individual characters, are decided jointly by the management (art director, lead programmer, and producer) during the preproduction phase. For the purposes of this chapter, we'll target under 4,000 polygons, which is typical of a main character for a PS2 street fighting game or hero for a third-person action game. Other technical questions to define include: what is the desired scale, what unit should equal one game engine unit, how many segments are desired around joints, can semitransparent (alpha channeled) textures be used for hair or other elements, and what angle will the model be viewed from most of the time?

There are two main phases to box modeling. First, you rough out the character. Second, you refine the model so that it has correct proportions, all of the necessary topology, and fine detail.

Roughing Out the Character

To rough out the character, begin by adding a polygonal box to the scene (Figure 6.2.2a). The fundamental techniques from here are *cut*, *extrude*, and *adjust*. Cutting subdivides faces and adds new faces. Extruding adds more volume to the model, like adding a chunk of clay to a sculpture. Adjusting is the artistic part of modeling. You are trying to capture the form, profile, and character of your model by moving vertices around in 3D space.

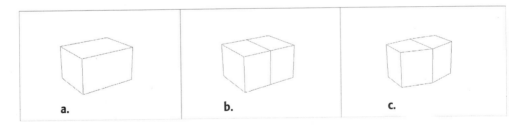

a.   b.   c.

FIGURE 6.2.2   *Start with a box, cut a centerline, and then approximate the torso shape.*

The box we are starting with will eventually be the torso of our character. A front, back, and two sides are not enough faces to define the basic shape of a torso, so we will cut the box in half (Figure 6.2.2b). Having a centerline is also extremely helpful in modeling, because it allows you to create only half the model, and mirror it. However, whenever possible, show both halves of the model, because it helps in visualizing correct proportions.

Next, adjust the box so that it more closely reflects the shape of a human torso (Figure 6.2.2c). Move the vertices such that the box is wider than it is deep, and tweak the center vertices (the ones that were added down the centerline) so that the middle is slightly bulging.

Now extrude the top face three times and the bottom face once (Figure 6.2.3a). This gives us enough cross-sections to define the rough contour of a torso. Adjust the vertices using *move*, *rotate*, and *scale*, so that spinal curvature is reflected and the volumes represent a human body.

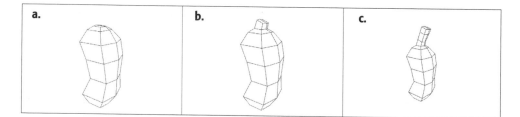

FIGURE 6.2.3   *Extrude and form the torso, and then extrude and adjust the neck.*

Create the base of the neck by selecting the face that is on the top of the torso and extrude it a small amount (Figure 6.2.3b). Scale this new face smaller so that it approximates the base of the neck. Extrude again to create a short neck. Move it forward and rotate it to approximate spinal curvature.

Once the neck is created, it's time for the head. Select the top of the neck and extrude twice. The first extrusion will be at eye level and the second will be at the top of the head. It now looks more like a longer neck than a head. Grab all of the faces around all four sides of the new head protrusion and extrude again to create some head volume (Figure 6.2.4a).

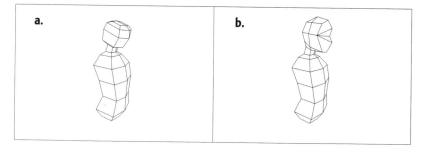

FIGURE 6.2.4   *Neck extruded and cut to approximate a head.*

Now, adjust until you have a rough approximation of the head. Add a cut directly above the eye line for the brow and under the eye line for the nose. Add a cut down the side of the head. Adjust vertices until the head is recognizable (Figure 6.2.4b).

After the head is roughed out, create the arms. Model the arms in the standard "Da Vinci Pose," meaning that the arms will be outstretched with elbows slightly bent and the wrist at about the same height as the shoulder, and the legs straight down with knees slightly bent. Hands will be palms facing downward.

It is easier and faster to create only one of the arms; in this example, the right arm is modeled. Select the upper two polygons on the right side of the torso, and extrude slightly. Scale and position this so that it mimics the base of the shoulder (Figure 6.2.5a).

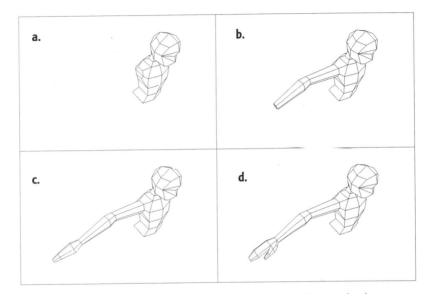

FIGURE 6.2.5   *Right arm constructed through extruding and adjusting.*

Extrude again to create the upper arm, ending at the elbow. Adjust the vertices to represent the size of the elbow, and rotate around the "up axis" to give a slight bend in the elbow. Extrude twice and adjust to create the bulging forearm, and small wrist (Figure 6.2.5b).

For the hand, extrude three times to form the widest area of the hand, the fingers, and the fingertips (Figure 6.2.5c).

Extrude the two polygons above the inner wrist for the thumb base. Select the side of this extruded box (nearest the fingertips) and extrude twice. Adjust this mass into a thumb shape (Figure 6.2.5d). Look at your own body for reference. Notice that in a relaxed position, the thumb is about an inch or two under the other fingers.

After the arm is roughed out, move to the leg. Don't worry about the opposite arm for now; it will be mirrored after one of the legs is modeled. Creating the rough leg is basically the same process as creating the arm; just extrude and adjust.

Select one of the faces underneath the torso. In this example, the polygon for the right leg is selected (Figure 6.2.6a). Extrude and adjust four times to represent the thigh and knee, down to the ankle (Figure 6.2.6b). The foot is created by extruding once from the ankle, creating a "nub." Then, select the front of this nub, and extrude (Figure 6.2.6c).

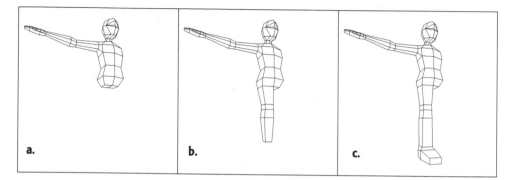

FIGURE 6.2.6   *Right leg constructed through extruding and adjusting.*

When the right arm and right leg are completed, mirror half of the body to create the other side (Figure 6.2.7).

FIGURE 6.2.7   *Mirror half of the body to create the left arm and left leg.*

Refining the Model

Now, on to the second phase of box modeling. In this step, you refine the model so that it has all of the basic topology and correct proportions. The rough model that has been created doesn't much resemble the sketch of the character yet. More detail will need to be added for smoothness and contour. New polygons will be created for elements like the cuffs and belt. The hair and headphones will be modeled as a separate object.

The first thing to do is a proportions match—the head isn't big enough, the torso is too large, and so forth. Now that we have a very simplified humanoid mesh, it's time to start making it look more like the character in Figure 6.2.8.

FIGURE 6.2.8 *Compare the rough model to the turnaround sketches.*

By placing the turnaround sketches behind the model, we can see how much the rough model varies from the original sketches. Push and pull points until you have a decent representation of the proportions and volumes of the drawings. Don't worry too much about the details at this point. Important things to check for are head size, shoulder height, extremity lengths, and eye level (Figure 6.2.9).

FIGURE 6.2.9 *Proportions matched.*

Notice that the legs and arms seem somewhat to the left of the sketch. A drawing is generally not perfectly symmetrical. Try to approximate an average of what you see on the left and the right. More importantly, attempt to capture the contour and character of the model.

Now that the model is starting to resemble the sketch, it's time to start adding detail. The squared-off legs and shoes do not have enough resolution to hold up in a game engine, especially since they are so exaggerated and prominent. Cut an additional row of faces up the center of each foot and leg (Figure 6.2.10). Continue cutting and adjusting until enough detail is present to represent better curvature. Pay particular attention to the profiles (the edge, viewed from the side), and constantly compare the model to the turnaround sketches.

FIGURE 6.2.10   *Adding detail in the leg.*

The cuffs are created by selecting a row of faces around the lower leg and extruding (Figure 6.2.11).

Hands are often one of the most complex parts of a character model. General problems to solve are how to transition from a relatively low-detail arm to a more dense hand, where and which direction lines should flow to support all of the muscles and structures of the hand, and accurately reflecting the form and shape of a hand.

Begin by cutting the rough hand volume (Figure 6.2.12a) just behind where the knuckles will be (Figure 6.2.12b). This should leave you with a "stump hand." Divide the face of the stump so that there are enough faces to extrude four fingers (Figure 6.2.12c). Extrude slightly for the knuckles, and adjust the vertices so that the finger

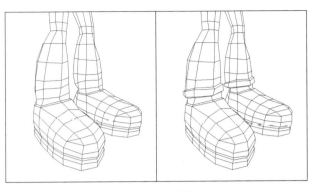

FIGURE 6.2.11   *Extrude the cuffs out.*

bases are roughly circular (Figure 6.2.12d). Extrude the fingers out, with enough segments for the knuckles (Figure 6.2.12e). Tweak vertices until a nice hand shape is obtained, and cut as needed to support the various structures and muscles of the hand (Figure 6.2.12f). Once the form of the hand is correct, cut additional segments around the joints (Figure 6.2.12g). When joints are animated, two or three segments are necessary so that the joint maintains its form. In this example, two segments per joint are used. Reference Figure 6.2.13 to follow the buildup of the hand from the underside.

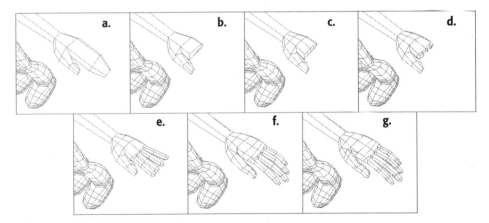

FIGURE 6.2.12   *Sequence showing the buildup of a hand.*

The entire time during modeling, compare the hand model that you are designing to your own hand at as many angles as possible to help troubleshoot proportional problems. It is best to model the hand in a relaxed, slightly bent posture. This makes it a bit more difficult to add a skeleton to, but will result in a more realistic hand in the end. Pay particular attention to the back of the hand and how it curves. The back

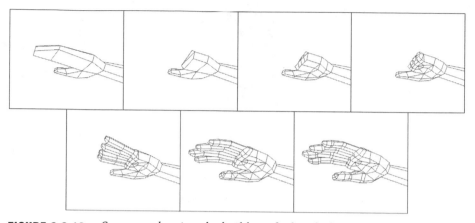

FIGURE 6.2.13   *Sequence showing the buildup of a hand, shown from the underside.*

hand is not flat. You will find that the middle finger knuckle (when in a relaxed posture) is higher than the pinky knuckle. Also, notice the mounts and valleys of the palm. Try to represent the meatiness of the thumb base, hand edge, and below the knuckles. Pay attention to the angle and facing of the thumb. It is facing across the hand more than downward.

The arm is more of the same. Cut additional cross sections and adjust vertices until the model matches the form and contours of the sketch (Figure 6.2.14).

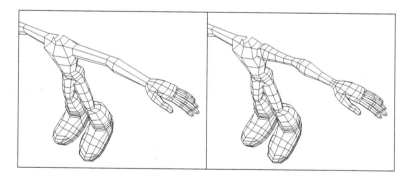

FIGURE 6.2.14   *Sequence showing the buildup of an arm.*

The torso presents some complications. Here is where a good sense of anatomy is important. Start by subdividing the main chest polygons to be more circular, as a frame for the breasts (Figure 6.2.15a). Extrude twice for breast polygons, and adjust vertices until proper breast form is achieved (Figure 6.2.15b). Bevel the edge where the bottom of the shirt will be, and flare it out (Figure 6.2.15c). Cut polygons to support skeletal structures like the ribcage and shoulder blades (Figure 6.2.15d). Add rows of polygons surrounding the center of the back to support the spinal indentation (Figures 6.2.15e and 6.2.16b). Add an additional row of polygons surrounding the shoulder joint to support animation deformation (Figure 6.2.15f).

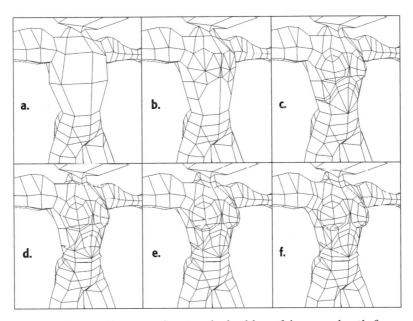

FIGURE 6.2.15   *Sequence showing the buildup of the torso detail, from the front.*

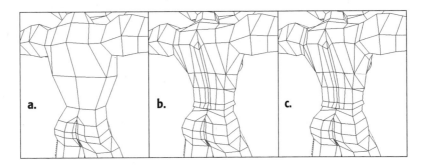

FIGURE 6.2.16   *Sequence showing the buildup of the torso detail, from the back.*

The head is finished in a few phases. Begin by adding a few sections to support the major structures of the face, including the brow line, eye line, cheekbone line, mouth, nose, and hairline (Figure 6.2.17b). Select all of the faces above the hairline, and extrude a volume for the hair (Figure 6.2.17c). Adjust some of the faces toward the bottom of the hair, where the ponytails will be to accommodate extruding.

Extrude and adjust verts to create the ponytails. An additional cut on the largest volume is added to simulate the hair curling back up (Figure 6.2.17d). Add additional detail to support all of the curvature and structures of the face. Cut in polygons that follow the shape of the eyes. Add more polygons to the cheekbone, and check the face from all angles to ensure cheekbone curvature and volume. Add more segments around the nose and mouth (Figure 6.2.17e). Once you are happy with the face and head, add some asymmetry. Move the part of the hair slightly off center, and cut in a part that zigzags back toward the crown of the head (Figure 6.2.17f). Figure 6.2.18 shows the completed character in wireframe.

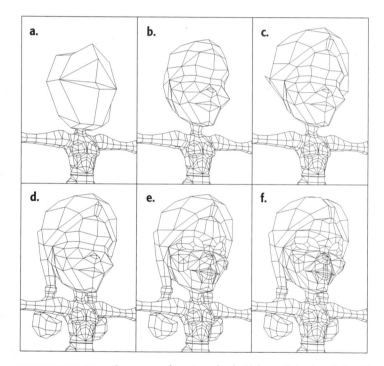

FIGURE 6.2.17   *Sequence showing the buildup of the head detail.*

In this section, we covered the basics of box modeling. We used a character in this example, but the same methodology applies to modeling anything. Start with a rough object, whether it's a box, cylinder, or even a generalized loft. Then, cut, extrude, refine, and adjust until you have rough structures for the entire object. Once you have a roughed-out model, check for topology problems and address them now. Correct any proportion issues. Once you are happy with the rough model, refine until the model is detailed and complete.

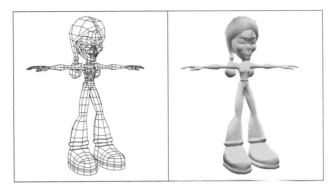

FIGURE 6.2.18 *The completed character in wireframe and shaded. Images courtesy of WildTangent, modeled by David Johnson.*

NURBS

NURBS is an acronym for "Non Uniform Rational Basis Spline," and is a form of modeling that uses curved surfaces based on relatively few data points. NURBS have been used extensively in the film industry for quite a while, and have limited use in the gaming industry.

A NURBS spline is made up of *control vertices*, often referred to as CVs. A NURBS spline is essentially a 3D line. Notice that the spline does not pass through the CVs, except for the first and last points. The CVs create a *hull* that influences the spline (Figure 6.2.19a).

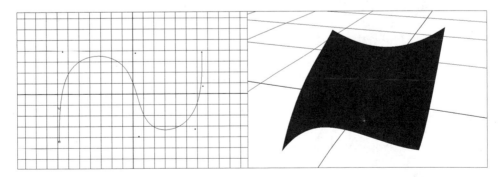

FIGURE 6.2.19 *a) A NURBS spline defined by control vertices. b) A NURBS surface.*

A NURBS surface is a curved 3D mesh that is defined by multiple NURBS splines and is often referred to as a *patch* (Figure 6.2.19b). NURBS surfaces generally have four sides. When modeling with NURBS, you must decide how various surfaces can be connected to form shapes that are more complex. For instance, an arm can be modeled by wrapping the NURBS surface into a basic cylindrical shape and then refined to add support for joints, muscle bulges, and other definition. A face is divided into sections with a patch circling the mouth, a patch circling the eyes, and additional patches to support the remaining facial structures and to bridge the other patches.

Advantages of NURBS include:

- Resolution independent
- Can tessellate "on the fly"
- Curved surfaces
- Inherent mapping coordinates

Disadvantages of NURBS include:

- Build using only square patches. Not ideal for complex objects such as hands.
- Tangency between patches can be difficult to solve.
- Topology problems (lining up isoparms).
- Difficult to change between high- and low-density areas.
- Can result in an unwieldy number of isoparms.
- Not supported by all game engines.

Subdivision Surfaces

Think of *subdivision surfaces* as a hybrid somewhere between polygon modeling and NURBS modeling. Subdivision surfaces are created using standard polygon modeling techniques, but the result is a smoothed surface, like a NURBS model. Subdivision surfaces offer the best of both worlds in polygon and NURBS modeling. You have the infinite resolution of a NURBS model and none of the topology headaches.

Hierarchical subdivision surfaces are a subset of subdivision surface modeling. A subdivision surface model is a low-resolution mesh that is smoothed a number of times when rendered. Hierarchical subdivision surfaces allow the artist to enter each level of smoothing and adjust vertices. This is useful because it allows you to work very rough, and rig and animate a very efficient model, yet render with as much detail as needed. This is an improvement over standard subdivision surface modeling because otherwise, your low-resolution model must contain all of the detail.

3D Sculpting

Another method for creating game models is a category called *3D sculpting*. Programs like ZBrush from Pixologic allow you to push, pull, and sculpt high-resolution models without worrying about topology. This type of product works more like a paint program (Adobe Photoshop, for instance) than a 3D modeling program. You use brushes to add minute details and refine models beyond what is practical using traditional modeling methods.

Three-dimensional sculpting is by far the best technique for creating high-quality *normal maps*. A normal map is a texture that is applied to a low-resolution model that gives the illusion that there is much more detail than actually exists. Typically, lighting is calculated at every vertex of a model, but with normal maps, the lighting is processed at each texture pixel. For instance, a medium resolution model may have 3,000 lighting calculations (3,000 vertices), whereas a model with a 512×512 pixel normal map will receive about 260,000 lighting calculations.

To sculpt a normal map, you start by creating a low- to medium-resolution model in any modeling program (Figure 6.2.20a). Then, bring the model into a 3D sculpting package. The model is tessellated to an extremely dense, high-resolution mesh (Figure 6.2.20b). You can then sculpt fine detail, such as scales, veins, musculature or clothing wrinkles in a relatively short time (Figure 6.2.20c). Once the sculpted model is complete, a utility can be used to create a normal map by comparing the low-resolution and high-resolution maps. The normal map is applied to the original low-resolution mesh (Figure 6.2.20d).

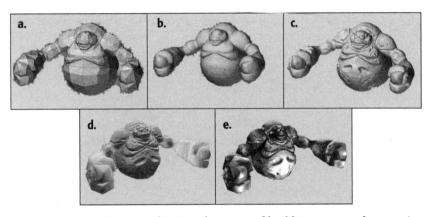

FIGURE 6.2.20   *Sequence showing the stages of building a normal map. a) Original low poly mesh. b) Tesselated high-resolution mesh. c) Sculpted detail. d) Low-resolution mesh with normal map applied. e) Final rendering, low-resolution model with normal map and texture.* Images courtesy of Pixologic.

Reverse Engineering

Another way to create models, although less common in gaming than the previous techniques, is a category of modeling called *reverse engineering*. Reverse engineering means digitizing a real-world "physical model." Laser scanners, optical scanners, and 3D point digitizers are a few examples of technologies that are used to capture real objects. In gaming, you have probably witnessed a 3D character whose head was "cyberscanned" or a car in a racing game that was point digitized (Figure 6.2.21).

FIGURE 6.2.21   *A car being laser scanned using a FARO Laser ScanArm.* Images courtesy of FARO Technologies, Inc.

Laser scans are another way to generate normal maps. A sculpture, or maquette, is laser scanned to create an extremely dense mesh from a "point cloud," generally based on many millions of polygons. An artist uses a reduced version of the scan to build a game-ready low-polygon model. The normal map is generated by comparing the original scan to the artist-created model.

We will not cover specific reverse-engineering techniques in this book because each of the many technologies has individual and specific workflows. Suffice to say that if you work at a company that uses any of these technologies, they will generally train you in the related techniques and software.

BSP Modeling

Many game levels are created using a technique called *BSP modeling* or "Brush modeling." *Counter-Strike, Unreal Tournament,* and *Quake III Arena* are common examples of games that contain BSP levels. BSP is an acronym for "binary space partitioning." It's a programming term that describes a way to organize data. From an art standpoint, BSP modeling is essentially a way to cut away chunks of the world using primitive volumes such as boxes and cylinders.

In typical BSP modeling, the scene starts with a solid world. The artist selects a brush from a preset list of primitives (box, sphere, cylinder, etc.) and subtracts the volume to create an open room. Think of this as a miner inside a mountain. The mountain is solid rock, and the miner blasts away to carve out rooms and tunnels.

Creating BSP environments can be very fun and gratifying. An artist can very quickly carve out a rough level, and play it instantly. Brushes are easy to adjust and reform without worrying about topology and mesh editing. BSP environments have inherent mapping, so basic texturing can be applied with great ease.

BSP is common in indoor first-person shooter levels. Every game engine that employs BSP levels has an associated editor that is used to design the BSP brushes. For example, *Unreal Tournament* has UnrealEd, *Half-Life* has the Valve Hammer Editor, and *Quake III Arena* has Q3Radiant. Generally, when you purchase and install any of these games, the editor is included. You will need to check the documentation or online resources to learn any of these editors.

Common Approaches to Constructing Geometry

Modeling a character is perhaps the most fun subject to sculpt, but in gaming, characters are only one of many responsibilities of a modeler. Vehicles, environments, weapons, props, and sometimes user interfaces will require modeling.

Case Study: Final Drive Nitro

We'll now look at the issues involved with modeling cars and levels for a racing game.

Racing games are a great example of a non-character-based genre where the structure of the game puts many requirements on the modeling.

Creating a car model is much the same as creating a character. Start with a reference, like a photograph of a car, or a high-resolution CAD mesh. Create a low-resolution roughed-out car, and refine and adjust until the car has sufficient resolution. Note that the most common view of a car is of its rear, so spend extra attention and polygons on this area of the car. Figures 6.2.22 and 6.2.23 show the wireframe model of a car and how it appears in the online game *Final Drive Nitro*.

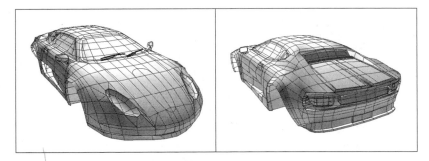

FIGURE 6.2.22   *Wireframe of a car model. Modeled by Zhang Changhua at Gamestar. Images courtesy of WildTangent.*

Car modeling has some other specific considerations. Positions must be defined for wheels, glows, and upgrade attachments. This is commonly specified with *locator objects* or *point objects*, or perhaps defined in text files. You may be required to model the interior of the car. Damaged versions of panels, and sometimes underlying structures may be necessary.

Many games, including car-racing games, require the use of level-of-detail (LOD) meshes to keep the frame rate consistent. LOD meshes are multiple versions of the

FIGURE 6.2.23   *The same car, seen in the car select screen and during gameplay. Images courtesy of WildTangent.*

model at progressively lower resolutions. Up-close models are rendered at higher LODs while distant models are rendered at lower LODs. As a model recedes into the distance, it will switch between LODs. Therefore, several LODs of a character or vehicle must be modeled. Generally, a modeler will construct the most-detailed LOD first, and then create the less-detailed LODs either automatically through a modeling package plug-in or by manually reducing it.

Level modeling is performed using the same basic methods as other types of modeling, but there are unique technical goals for environments. Polygon counts are important, but harder to define with environments. Since it is generally impossible to render an entire level, it is broken into smaller chunks, so that pieces can be *culled*, or removed from the rendering pipeline. You are mainly concerned with how many polygons are rendered at any given time, after culling. Although, the entire polygon count of the level is important because it impacts memory consumption and loading time. On consoles, there should be a fixed polygon density that you are targeting. However, PC games often have to support a range of machines, so it is common to support several clipping distances (how far out the scene is rendered), or simply model the environments with the lowest common denominator in mind.

Texture usage is important to keep in mind while modeling environments. For instance, in the example racing level (Figure 6.2.24), each lane was cut to provide rows for tileable textures. The method of lighting used will have an impact on how the model is set up. If vertex colors are used (as in the racing example), you must have enough vertices to support large washes of light and dark areas, but shadows are generally not possible, as they would require too many vertices. If light maps are used (textures that define lighting), vertex count is not a concern, as lighting is based on textures, not vertices.

Depending on the type of level, the way you will go about modeling will vary. For any level, it is common to start with a sketch of the map, including notes for important visual or gameplay elements.

For racing levels, you will start with a spline that follows the rough shape of the entire track, and loft a profile of the road, with a curb. From the base profile, create a large set of variations, including different road widths, split roads, banks, and so forth,

FIGURE 6.2.24   *a) Wireframe model of a level. b) Model with vertex lighting. c) Textures and effects added. Images from Final Drive Nitro, courtesy of WildTangent. Modeled by Luo Jun and Feng Yuhui at Gamestar.*

and apply these over the course of the track. This will start you off with a roughed-out, playable track. Continue to refine the banking, turns, jumps, and overall gameplay until you are satisfied that you have a fun driving experience. It may be necessary to add rough road textures, and major buildings or structures to give you a sense of scale.

Low-Polygon Modeling

Although polygon counts increase exponentially with each generation of hardware, and normal mapping makes high-polygon modeling a valuable skill to master, low-polygon modeling isn't going away any time soon. The extra power will often be used to push greater numbers of low-polygon characters on screen rather than just display a couple of high-resolution characters.

When modeling low-resolution characters, especially if they will be seen from a distance, common in many real-time strategy games, there are a few special considerations. Pay particular attention to profiles. Spin your character to every conceivable angle, and see if the forms hold up. Define large muscle and structural forms. Exaggerate bulges. Don't worry about tiny details, as they will probably be rendered by only a few pixels. Fine detail should be painted into the texture, not modeled in. Paint in shadows and accentuate highlights in the texture (see Figures 6.6.25 and 6.2.26).

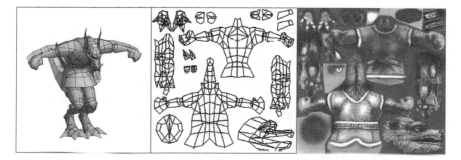

FIGURE 6.2.25   *a) Wireframe low-polygon monster. b) Mapping coordinates for the monster. c) Texture map. Images courtesy of WildTangent. Model and texture by David Johnson.*

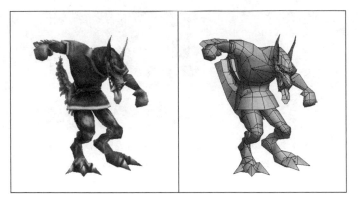

FIGURE 6.2.26   *Finished and posed model. Images courtesy of
WildTangent. Modeled by David Johnson.*

Modeling Methodology

As a professional modeler, you will need to be able to look at an object or sketch, and
visualize how it can be represented as a game model. Just as a 2D animator starts with
rough gesture "line of action" and adds volumes to visualize and begin a sketch, a 3D
modeler starts with simplistic volumes for major structures of a model. The rest of this
section presents other techniques to help you work efficiently, and evaluate the quality of your work.

Use Reference Material

The better reference material you are working from, the more accurate your model
will be. If you are modeling a real-world object, take orthographic photographs from
as many angles as possible. If you have access to scan data, it can be difficult to work
with, but it is the best reference without question. If you are working from a sketch,
try to work from turnaround sketches.

It is extremely effective to have your reference material in context. Create textures
from your reference material, and show them in the viewport of your modeling package. If you are working from a sketch, use the black line as the alpha channel, and you
have a great "sketch wireframe" that is very easy to model on top of. Apply some
transparency to your model so you can see the mesh superimposed over the reference
material to constantly check proportions and positioning. If you are working from
scan data, snap vertices to the scan mesh to ensure exact volumes. If you are modeling
a car, you can generally do a search online to obtain useful specification data such as
height, width, length, and wheelbase.

Work Rough and Refine

Start models by blocking out major structures with rough shapes. It is easy to identify
and solve problems when your model is still rough. Once you start subdividing and

the polygon count gets unwieldy, it becomes increasingly difficult to make broad changes. Working rough also establishes a basic structural topology. It will give you lines that run the length of your model and provide an excellent basis from which to refine.

Critical Analysis

It's easy to look at a model and know that it is not quite right, but it is considerably more difficult to identify exactly what's wrong, and how it should be corrected. Here are a few tools for you to use in the critical analysis of your models.

Profiles

Too many head models suffer from "flat face" syndrome. The cheekbone doesn't protrude enough or the eye socket isn't concave enough. To help solve problems like this, check your profiles. Rotate the model to all angles, and compare them to an actual person. How far does a head have to turn for an eye to be obscured by the bridge of the nose? When modeling a nose, check it from the side, front on, top down, three quarter, and upshot. Does it hold up from all these angles? Turnaround sketches can ensure that front and side profiles are relatively good, but the 45-degree angles will have to come from your artistic sensibility. If something seems off, compare it to a real-world person or object.

Topology

Topology, as it relates to 3D modeling, is how the vertices, faces, and edges are laid out and arranged to form the various structures of a model. A good topology will have just enough detail to support a structure, and in an even, well-distributed manner. Arms and legs should have nice rows and columns, and if there is strong muscle definition, polygons will be present to frame these muscles, and provide good profiles. Avoid long, skinny polygons wherever possible. It is preferable to have a vertex sharing four or less faces. More are acceptable and even necessary at times, but try to avoid extremes where many faces are connected by a single vertex.

Distribution of polygons is very important. Generally, the hands and face will have the greatest number of polygons. Consider what angle the model is going to be seen from and at what scale in the game. If the model will be seen from a distance, all that facial detail may be unnoticeable, and would have been better spent smoothing larger profiles.

Objective Opinion

As an artist, it can be uncomfortable to accept criticism about your work, but it is necessary in the team environment of game development. Get someone else to look at your model and offer his or her initial reaction to your work. Modeling can be a technical endeavor at times, and it's easy to lose track of the artistic element. Having a second set of eyes look at your work can often give you a fresh look at what is right and wrong about your model.

Expressiveness and Essence

This is difficult to articulate, but is the most important thing to consider while modeling, particularly with characters. Does your model capture the character, personality, and emotion of the reference sketches? Do the eyes have the same spark; does the smile or grimace look convincing, or flat and lifeless? Does the model look inviting, or intimidating enough? You may have to deviate from the sketches, and exaggerate these important features to get them to read in a 3D model.

Summary

Since a vast majority of game modeling is done with standard polygon editing, most of this chapter was spent discussing techniques specific to polygons. NURBS, subdivision surfaces, 3D sculpting, reverse engineering, and BSP modeling were also introduced. A step-by-step demonstration of how to model a character using polygons was presented. Finally, we discussed what makes a good model, and how to analyze and improve your models.

3D modeling is both a technical and artistic endeavor. As you become more familiar with the tools, processes, and methods of creating models, the more the technical side will become second nature and the more you can focus your attention on the much more important, artistic side.

Exercises

1. Using box modeling techniques, create a character of your own design, or find reference for an existing character.
2. Using NURBS surfaces, create an underwater creature; for example, a fish, dolphin, or whale.
3. Using subdivision surface techniques, create of a monster of your own design, or find reference for an existing character.
4. Import one of your creatures into a 3D sculpting program, and sculpt in fine detail.
5. Use a BSP level editor such as UnrealEd or Worldcraft to create a rough level with four rooms.

6.3 | 3D Environments

Overview

The task of the 3D artist is not much different from that of the classic oil painter. The tools have become a little more complex, but the intent is the same. All artistic work (except sculpture) seeks a way to take a 2D space (canvas, computer screen) and convincingly turn it into a visceral world or altered experience. Basic techniques for conveying light, distance, and form have been used throughout the centuries to manipulate the human perception of space and volume. The 3D artist uses these same techniques and brings them one-step closer to reality in a game space by allowing the player to interact with the world the artist has created.

Careful attention to constructing a world that is within technical specification will assure the game runs smoothly. Careful attention to consistency of style, lighting quality, color schemes, texturing, and volume enhancements will ensure a convincing and positive gameplay experience. This chapter provides some of the key tactics used in creating compelling 3D environments.

Preplanning

Building games is a team process, and one driven by economics. The entire team must keep in mind the game's aesthetic appeal to the target audience, and make that aesthetic fit into the technical restrictions of the target platform.

Typically, the target platform, game style, and artistic implications have already been determined by the publisher in conjunction with the art director by the time an art team begins environment production. The technical rules vary from project to project, and it is the artist's task to work within these limits to create a compelling, dynamic, and exciting 3D environment.

Artistic Approach

A successful 3D environment will maintain consistent style, enhance the volume of the 3D space through judicious use of distance effects, and fake detail whenever possible (to enhance frame rate). It is not enough for a game to *be* 3D; it must also *look* 3D.

Setting and Style Consistency

The art director will work with the art team to ensure that all assets are created in line with the goal of the game. Each artist should, on an individual basis if necessary, review similarly styled games, and consider what has succeeded and failed in these game environments. Consider the artistic approach used in games that have a feel similar to what you want to design. While wild strokes of creative and artistic genius are desirable, the reality is that much creativity is based on the work of prior artists. Use successful prior work as a starting point and try to improve on it for the benefit of the current project.

Style consistency should be guided by the art director, and the artist will save much rework by adhering to the set style. It would, for example, be inappropriate to place palm trees in a landscape destined to go into a Northern European first-person shooter, or use a surreal mountain landscape in a contemporary outback race setting. Similarly, color palettes should reflect the intent of the game. For example, World War II games are generally expected to have a certain palette, and unless the game specifically deviates from that genre, it is wise to stay within expectations. A player who is a fan of World War II genres would expect greens, browns, grays, and typical military color schemes.

Camera Viewpoint

Different camera views are used throughout the games industry. First-person cameras show the world as if the player has the camera attached at eye level; it is the view with which we currently see our world. *CounterStrike* (Valve) and *Doom3* (Id Software) are examples. Third-person cameras show the world from an over-the-shoulder view. The player can typically see his character in the camera view. *Diablo 2* (Blizzard Entertainment), *Warcraft* (Blizzard Entertainment), and *Dark Orbit* (Figure 6.3.1) [WildTangent01] are examples of this view. Side-scrollers show the world from the side, and are more common as 2D games but are being reinvented for the 3D world as processors become more powerful. *R-Type Final* (Irem) and *Phoenix Assault* (Color Plate 3) [WildTangent04a] are fine examples of the side-scroller revolution.

FIGURE 6.3.1 *Dark Orbit is built using the third-person view.* © *WildTangent, Inc. Reprinted with permission.*

Volume Enhancements

The environment viewed through the computer screen is necessarily flat, and it is the artist's task to exaggerate the 3D aspects when necessary to help lend credibility to the environment and differentiate it from a 2D setting.

The players should feel fully immersed in the fantastic world that has been created for them, and clever environmental construction will help reinforce that. The layout of the game environment will, in part, be set by the level designer. The artist then has the task of manipulating the level design into something visually compelling.

Some environmental components work well with some camera views, and do not work with others. For example, a towering rock spire has a different visual impact in a first-person perspective, where it might disappear into the upper clouds or environmental fog. In a third-person view, the tip of the spire might sweep near the camera, greatly enhancing the 3D effect. Tunnels, tubes, spires, pits, towers, cliffs, and so forth all have something in common: they enhance the perceived volume of the 3D world.

Figure 6.3.1 shows this method of terrain exaggeration in practice [WildTangent01]. Gameplay in *Dark Orbit* is restricted to a 2D plane, so emphasizing the surrounding terrain became important for conveying depth and scale of the world. Notice how the tip of the spires sweep dramatically past the camera, and the pits plunge deeply into the planet. Deep pits are emphasized with colorful fog to reinforce our perception that faraway or deep objects become obscured by haze with distance. This "distance effect" is a powerful weapon in the environmental artist's arsenal and will be discussed further.

These concepts are best understood by first reading about them and then experiencing them. The reader is strongly encouraged to play these free game demos at the Web links listed in the "References" section [WildTangent01, WildTangent04a]. Beyond the games listed there, think critically about what you see in each game you play, and try to analyze what makes an environment seem large, scary, cold, friendly, warm, and so forth. As an artist creating environments, you will be, in large part, responsible for shaping the player's emotions to fit the purpose of the game.

Distance Effects

Another method of lifting the flat 2D game screen into compelling 3D space is to over-exaggerate colors and contrast. The player's acceptance of what is real (more popularly known as "suspension of disbelief") is flexible when playing a game. A playing experience can be "enhanced" by exaggerating colors beyond what can typically be seen in the "real" world. An example of this is seen in photography. Underwater photography done without special lighting typically looks drab and monochromatic. Professional underwater photographers use light enhancements to bring out the colors of the underwater world. Other professional photographers will frequently enhance the color intensity and contrast of their photographs by using polarizing filters to remove reflected light. Try looking around outside through a set of polarized sunglasses. Observe that direct light is more colorful, shadowed areas are darker, and contrast is increased overall. Colors reflected off objects will depend on the color of the polarized lens.

Rules in the "real" world can be used in games to convey distance and depth. For example, near objects will be higher in contrast, more detailed, and typically darker than similar objects seen farther away. Fog is a good way to convey this depth.

Human perception of color can also be manipulated to convey depth. Warm colors such as reds, yellows, and browns are perceived as being closer to us in space than cool colors such as blues or greens. This principle is frequently used in interface design, but can also be used in world building.

The environmental artist can use rules from both the "real" world and the "enhanced" world to manipulate how the player will view the environment. Color Plates 1 and 2 illustrate these concepts and show how a classically 2D environment has been transformed into 3D space, with the perception of depth greatly enhanced by using both rule sets. Color Plate 3 shows a first-pass attempt at the environment details. While the first pass is reasonably good, if we apply the previously discussed principles to the scene we will get a much more convincing portrayal of depth and space.

First, let's discuss geometry. In Color Plate 3, note the large water-tower-like structure in the background, and the large rock in the foreground. These objects seem to stand alone, and since the water tower is an alien object and a rock can be any size, we need to add additional objects into the scene so the player has some sense of their scale. In Color Plate 4, we have added an additional tower and moved it closer to the player, and added a rock in the background. The proximity of these objects and their relative sizes give the player a more visceral sense of the scale of the world, and the scale of the alien objects in the scene. Also, note in Color Plate 3 that the water layer almost looks like a cloud or some glowing fog. In Color Plate 4, the objects have been reflected in the water below them, most notably the foreground rock. This reflection detail defines the water plane and gives the player a more solid sense of playable space.

Next, we consider contrast level and fog throughout the scene, and how to add visual intensity to objects and add volume to the environment. The most obvious change is the addition of detail and contrast to the near-ground rock in Color Plate 4. As mentioned previously, near objects will in general be darker and higher in detail than far objects. Far objects will, in the real world, be affected by haze in the air, and details will be obscured by light reflecting off this haze. All objects receive less "haze" treatment as they appear closer to the camera. Starting from back to front, we see the sky in Color Plate 3 has been fogged a bit in Color Plate 4. The contrast level of the large background planet has been reduced (as has color, but that will be discussed in the next section). The rear water tower has been hazed out, as has the rear rock. In Color Plate 4, the near tower is higher in contrast and darker than the rear tower, and the near rock is subsequently higher in contrast and darker than the near tower. The most near-ground objects are the player ship and enemy ships. These have received the highest contrast level. In this case, one could argue that the contrast has been taken too far, and that color values are suffering as a result, but it is instructive to see the result nonetheless. For final production, the ship contrast levels would be toned back a bit so color values are not so garish, and every other object's contrast level would be scaled back proportionately. Finally, the water surface has been given higher contrast in the near-ground and less contrast along the distant horizon.

Now we will briefly discuss color. The major object throwing the color out of balance in Color Plate 3 is the large background planet. In Color Plate 4, the planet has been given a cooler bluish tone to show the effect of light scattering in the blue haze of our planet's atmosphere. This has the added benefit of seemingly pushing the distant planet farther into the background. It is now less distracting to the player and seems to fit more naturally into the 3D environment.

Faking Detail

Regardless of development platform, there are always limitations on usage of texture space and polygon count. A "realistic" environment cannot contain all the details that we see in real life, regardless of setting. Video cards are also limited in the number of textures they can hold without affecting performance. One way to circumvent texture and polygon limitations is to use vertex coloring in the scene. Vertex coloring is the process of painting the vertexes in your mesh. Any texture applied in the area between two differently colored vertexes will adopt their color gradient. Vertex coloring is a popular and cheap (does not require much processing power) method of adding color to a mesh. Vertex coloring can be added in areas where shadows are needed, depth or a depression must be implied, or just to add color variety to a heavily tiled texture. Color Plate 5 shows an image of a scene from the game *Polar Bowler* [WildTangent04b]. The ice tunnel relies heavily on vertex coloring to add interest and variety to the ice. Only one texture is used on the ice walls throughout the scene. By adding blues, purples, and the occasional yellow vertex color, the perception of depth and variety is greatly enhanced, and varying degrees of warmth and coolness are spread throughout the tunnel. If additional vertex coloring detail is desired, a polygon face may be tessellated to add vertices to an area (as long as performance allows).

Scheduling

Game production is an economic endeavor, and as such is schedule driven. Start by building the largest-scale components of the environment, with the intent of revisiting your work or handing it off to another artist for a different phase (work structure varies for every shop). This approach is analogous to painting the large background parts of a canvas and then going back later to fill in details. In addition, the art director will have set a technical limit on how detailed a scene may be, so part of efficiently constructing a complete set of game environments is getting one scene as complete as possible near the start of the project. By completing one scene, you will have an understanding of how quickly the remaining scenes will be built, and what pitfalls to avoid along the way.

Summary

The principles introduced in this chapter are only a starting point in creating compelling and beautiful environments. The actual creation of 3D environments will vary in each software application, but the theory of the environment's display in a game is the same: create the perception of 3D space on a flat 2D computer screen. A 3D game will by definition use geometry to attempt to create the perception of volume, but the best implementation will not ignore the basics of proper color use, contrast levels, and real-world distance principles. Lastly, color theory and enhancements of real-life observation have been used throughout the centuries to convey depth on a flat canvas and can be used today to bring a 3D world to life.

Exercises

1. Find a screenshot of an environment in one of your favorite games. Create a written critique documenting what works and what doesn't work about the environment in the scene. Specifically address the emotion that is created in the scene. Consider whether the color schemes work well, and how these or other color schemes are used in different parts of the game. How would changing the lighting, color schemes, and contrast levels affect the player's perception?

2. Compare an environment from a first-person game with an environment in a third-person game. What elements have a powerful impact in the first-person perspective that does not work as well in the third-person, and vice versa?

References

[WildTangent01] *Dark Orbit,* available online at *www.wildgames.com,* 2001.
[WildTangent04a] *Phoenix Assault,* available online at *www.wildgames.com,* 2004.
[WildTangent04b] *Polar Bowler,* available online at *www.wildgames.com,* 2004.

6.4 ■ 2D Textures and Texture Mapping

Overview

Much like covering this book with a paper cover, or wrapping a football in gift wrap, or painting a ceramic sculpture of a horse with glaze paints, even a 3D model in a game needs the equivalent of a cover, a wrapper, or color coating. A successfully completed 3D model usually means that an artist has worked through a few necessary steps in the assembly process to give the model a colorful custom skin. Such steps include the creation of well-prepared digital images, referred to as *texture maps*, and a method of meticulously getting these 2D images to show up directly onto the surface of a 3D model. In this highly artistic phase that occurs between the modeling and lighting of an object, the artist will create digital images, usually within a popular 2D paint program using more traditional art skills. In the relating steps that follow, however, certain technical skills must be developed before knowing how the artist can go about preparing the final art or texture map for the best use by the model's geometry. This seemingly complicated process is called *texture mapping*, or *UV mapping*. All environmental objects in a 3D game, as well as the avatars, automobiles, certain effects, and even the sky, rely on these steps to give polygonal geometry color values. During production of all such objects, this step of assigning texture coordinates has to happen before the artist can actually see his or her texture on the model.

This chapter discusses the kinds of texture maps that are often used, and demystifies the technical process of how an artist tells the computer how to apply a texture to a particular polygon on a model and explicitly how to display it on-screen. Although there are many ways of "skinning this cat," the discussion of creating texture maps and the approaches for texture mapping techniques will focus more on those that a professional game artist will commonly use in the creation of real-time video games.

While wearing the hat of "texture map artist," these people are responsible for creating the texture maps, which may also be known as *color maps* or *diffuse maps*, depending on the 3D application used. Looking at Figure 6.4.1, notice that upon the involvement of these steps in the production workflow, the textured model can be exported and begin to make its way into the game engine for the purpose of evaluating the appearance and impact it has on gameplay. Generally speaking, the sooner art can be critiqued while in the game alongside other environmental art, special effects, properly scaled characters, and so forth, the better off the team will be to make critical changes sooner during development.

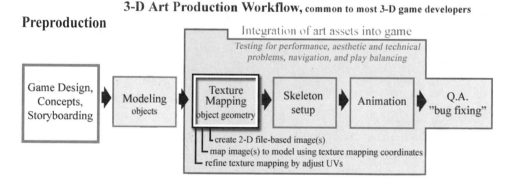

FIGURE 6.4.1   *Texture mapping is a midproduction component with several steps.*

After the mapping step is completed, even a temporarily assigned texture on a model can be changed several times to improve it aesthetically. These revisions can be updated on the model quickly for further ongoing evaluation. This phase is where most texture artists would rather spend their time—past the more technical stuff and well into the creative part of making it look ideal for their game. A fast and proven method of texture mapping a model will be demonstrated in detail in the case study at the end of this chapter.

2D File-Based Images Used for Texture Mapping

Even though many types of 2D images can be used for real-time game art, below the surface they all share certain physical attributes. To help the artist get past some of the more technical aspects of this process, and so that the language between team members is understood, here is a brief description of these attributes. Each image or texture map is a two-dimensional array of color values called *texture elements* or *texels*. These are pixels in the texture map. Each texel occupies a specific location and has a unique physical address. This address in the texture space is also represented by a column and row number. As shown in Color Plate 7c, the U direction represents texture elements and their values along the horizontal axes, and the V represents texture elements along the vertical axes of the texture space.

An artist will use many types of texture maps, and they all share this makeup. They can be used either alone or in combination. A few of these texture maps are essential to all 3D games, and so have been illustrated in Color Plate 6 and will be described in more detail in the following paragraphs. A texture artist may at some point make color maps, transparency maps, bump maps, normal maps, environment maps, and light maps, to name a few. Each has a unique visual affect within the game. However, until such a texture map is assigned to a model to give it more character, color, and depth, it will have a generic machine perfect "skin," as in Color Plate 8b.

Color maps: This texture map gives basic color, or diffuse color, to a model by way of a file-based texture map. *Diffuse* colors are those we refer to when an object is evenly lit, not oversaturated, too bright, or in shadow. In a 3D program like 3DS max, this is assigned via the Diffuse Color channel from within the Material Editor. In another program, like Maya, this would be the Color Channel. This image can be of any one solid color, combination of colors, drawn by hand using a digital paintbrush, or scanned from a painting or a photograph.

Depending on the look of the game, any source used can provide this color information for a model. When creating such a color/diffuse map from a photograph, there are ideal images and not so ideal or poorly lit images. An artist should avoid using photos that already show evidence of a light source in the scene, perhaps from afternoon sun or an overhead stadium light. If the photo has such highlights, pronounced directional shadows, or other captured lighting information, the artist must take care to eliminate them in the final image. Sometimes, the artist will first need to even out the lighting throughout the image using photo manipulation tricks in a paint program. The texture in Color Plate 7a has even lighting with just enough shadow to convey that the surface isn't flat throughout.

Transparency maps: This is a file-based color or grayscale image that is used in combination with the color map to control the transparency of the surface. Such maps are also referred to as *opacity maps*, or just *alpha maps*. The shades of gray will control the amount of transparency, with black being 100 percent transparent and white being 100 percent opaque, or no transparency (see Color Plate 6a). A computer interprets the pixel values not as color, but in a way that describes the transparency of the surface at each texel. A transparency image designed for a tree or houseplant, for example, will have a random-looking pattern of solid-white leaf-shaped patterns against black, whereas one for a lacy see-thru window curtain will have a wider range of grays with a lighter shade background for a less-transparent decorative design pattern (see Color Plate 6c).

Bump maps: To enhance the often flat inherent look found in 3D games, a bumpier surface appearance for things like castle rock walls and lumpy alien skin can be achieved on a surface level with this type of texture map. Use of a bump map produces results that simulate a bumpier, 3D relief surface. The model's geometry isn't altered by this and only appears to have more detail in the mesh (see Color Plate 6b). Before considering this type of texture map in your game design and art production, however, this should be a known supported feature of the graphics chip on the target system.

The way a bump map works is similar in principle to the grayscale alpha maps used for transparency, except that the grayscale information is now used to control the amount of "bump" that appears on the model's surface. What often gives this trick away is when the same model's profile is seen. It will seem flatter than the bumps, lumps, and divots suggest it should. This is an acceptable tradeoff. For a real-time game, to achieve a similar level of 3D detail with only slightly better visual appeal would cost the artist a ton of extra time to model such detail and consequently will slow the game's performance because of the added polygons.

What You Should Know Before Creating a Texture Map

In the development of the latest cutting-edge game, there will likely still be technical constraints an artist must be aware of that will determine how he or she approaches the construction of images. Such constraints won't affect the final look or style, but the size and position of image subjects, and the scale of the finer details within the texture map. This kind of upfront planning will save artists much time and frustration once they are well into the workflow. Learning as much as one can during preproduction about the game design, the specific objects to be texture mapped, and how they are to be used within the game environment will help during production. The following are several recommended questions that should be asked to get the artist better prepared for a successful mapping job.

A few of the technical questions that an artist should ask his or her art director, game or level designer, and programmer beforehand are things like, how much file space in the final product will be allocated for all texture maps? What resolution size should the final texture maps be? In an effort to reduce the number of images used by the game overall, or by a specific level, is tiling of textures acceptable? For example, a large Olympic field or airplane runway may have large surface areas of repeating grass and asphalt, respectively. A *tiling texture* is a cleverly designed texture map that provides a seamless repetition of a single texture map that covers a large span of ground surface. Another question may be, are areas of a model to have interchangeable textures? An example of this would be a design feature in a racing game that supports having interchangeable decals on a racing car that a gamer can then specify. What about optimization of all textures to reduce file size? For real-time games, there typically is a need to optimize by reducing the size and color space to be compatible with the intended game platform. You can expect this step in every game studio.

The level of importance of various 3D objects and their surfaces in the game is another important consideration that the texture artist should know beforehand. An example would be a prominently placed object in a level or main hero character. What is the look of the game? Before designing and painting the one or more images for a model, understand the game's design, the style, and the target audience for which it is intended. For example, is it stylized or photorealistic? Are the potential players teens or middle-aged women? Are objects to appear to have lighting and shadows, meaning are the textures to be created with an implied light source evident? Answers to questions such as these can affect what technical decisions you make along the way, and guide how you call attention to significant objects and surfaces while playing down the less-important ones.

Texture Mapping Coordinate System

To place 2D textures onto 3D models, the texture artist will use a *texture mapping coordinate system*. This will help establish a direct correlation between the 2D image and the *texture space* of the 3D model. It is like a set of instructions that define which areas of the texture image are mapped to certain parts of the model. The basic method of texture mapping is to specify the coordinates of each texel in the texture map (U,V) that map to a unique point across the model's surface. The UV coordinates are specified at the polygon vertices and are interpolated across each polygon's surface by the graphics chip. Although other types of model geometry can have texture coordinates, such as spline models, patch models, or NURBS, polygon models are typically the type of geometry that is exported for use in game engines. Moreover, unlike NURBS that have an inherent set of such texture mapping coordinates, polygon models always need to have texture coordinates applied to them. As shown in Color Plate 7c, the texture coordinates are on the range of 0 to 1 in the U and V directions. In the case of tiling textures that are to repeat more than once across the surface of a model, it is expected to have texture coordinates outside the range 0 to 1.

Every texture artist should know that achieving perfect UV mapping in game development is nearly impossible. They should, however, strive for the ideal UV mapping while being mindful of other important objectives during this process. UV mapping involves tradeoffs that an artist learns to accept and balance in the pursuit of efficiency and continuity. Such goals will make more sense after the case study at the end of this section. Figure 6.4.2 compares two scenarios, demonstrating both bad and ideal "packing" of UV geometry. The two UV editor windows show the results of two differently mapped organic models used by the company WildTangent. Although both have used all areas of the texture space well, example b has fewer continuously mapped geometry groups and will be easier to paint. The UV clusters are grouped and positioned in a logical fashion for easier recognition.

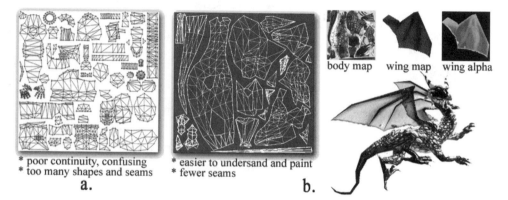

FIGURE 6.4.2   *UV mapping results of a human character and a dragon body.*

Methods for Mapping UV Coordinates

Several common systems for mapping UV coordinates are available from within 3D applications. Each uses one of two methods for placing images on a model by way of projecting or wrapping them onto the model. *Image projection mapping* is a technique where an image is projected onto geometry. It would be like having a slide projector aimed at your model while projecting a static image onto the surface of a few of the model's polygons or through all of them. An example of such a method is *planar projection mapping*. Although this is an easy way to get mapping coordinates on the model quickly, it is less desirable for certain shapes because of problems it creates, such as streaking along the sides of the model. Depending on the shape of the model, other methods are more suitable and produce better results. As the names imply, other methods such as *spherical mapping* coordinates, *cylindrical mapping* coordinates, and *box mapping* coordinates are also used. These are like tools, with each being suitable for geometry forms that resemble the name. For example, a spherical mapping method is commonly used for shapes like planets and eyeballs, whereas box mapping will be used when the object is a crate, a box train, or a building. The best way to learn their strengths and weaknesses is to try each on several models of different shapes. With time and experience, each will become familiar to the texture artist. And like specialized tools, knowing when and how to use them will save time and produce more predictable results.

After these UV mapping systems are used, some adjustments are often still needed to smooth out any wrinkles. Things get more challenging when the model's form is a combination of several of these simpler shapes. For example, how one might assign mapping coordinates for a simple shape like a cylinder or a sphere should differ from the method used to map a human figure's arm that is attached to a torso. This more complex shape blend is like having a cylinder attached to another cylinder, as in Figure 6.4.3c. Now attach a head on top of both the arm and torso and then try to map it all with one texture map. The case study at the end of this section provides such an example.

To help simplify this work, today's 3D packages offer ways of applying and controlling the placement of UV coordinates with real-time visual feedback, using gadgets and gizmos that show the 3D placement of textures. Fortunately, unlike texture mapping objects for film or broadcast production, the advantage of creating content for real-time games is that an artist already has a good idea of what the mapping is going to look like from within the 3D application. In film work, to check the actual results of what the freshly mapped surfaces will look like, a test render has to be done in software. In Color Plate 7b, two images show examples of the tool's 3D placement icon for spherical mapping and one for the box mapping tools.

Because the coordinate system is like a set of instructions that define which areas of the texture are mapped to certain parts of the model's polygons, how one controls this assignment of UV mapping coordinates becomes an important skill for any texture artist. How the artist manipulates these UV points (see Color Plate 7c) is ultimately accomplished within this texture space. Within the 3D application, this is done using a UV editor window that exposes the mesh's UV control points within the texture space. The control points (or UV points) are the mesh's vertex points, only laid out flat in a 2D area represented in a space between 0 and 1. Moving these control points in the texture space along the U direction adjusts texture pixels along the horizontal axes, and along the V direction adjusts them along the vertical axes of the model's surface.

After assigning a file-based texture map to a UV mapped object, the final refinement pass is testing and editing the UV points. This manual adjustment of UVs into a more uniform configuration can take much time and practice. A temporary image or *test image* that has a busy pattern or some discernable visual noise, as shown in Color Plate 8c and 8d, can be used for the texture map as a visual aid. The checker pattern on a 3D model is a visual indicator of how well the UVs are being adjusted. The following case study describes how to use a test image and evaluate the results.

Case Study: Texture Mapping a Character

The following case study is designed to give you a better understanding and appreciation of the concepts and practices discussed in this section. It steps you through the process of analyzing and preparing a complex model for mapping, assigning several different mapping coordinate systems, and manually adjusting and packing UVs within the texture space for optimal use of a texture map. Although this flexible approach isn't the only one available to a texture artist, it relies only on tools and features available in 3D applications used by the gaming industry. Due to evolving methods and tools available within the latest 3D applications, other approaches are becoming obsolete. The techniques demonstrated here also focus on getting artists through the technical aspects of the process quickly and efficiently so that more of their budgeted time can be spent on the creative process of refining the finalizing the texture.

If you want to follow along with this case study, you can load the model from the companion CD-ROM called "sister.max" into 3DS max. It is a full-body, single-mesh female polygon model created for a WildTangent game. Due to its intricate form and curvy shape, an organically shaped character model represents a greater challenge to texture map. Moreover, because character models are often viewed from 360 degrees in most games, the difficulty is further compounded by the need to consistently apply the UV mapping coordinates without stretching or distorting texels.

During this case study, expect to work interactively between the 3D application and a paint program. Throughout the texture mapping process, the more interactive it is for the artist, the faster and more intuitive it becomes with more control over the desired results. With time and practice, artists can define their own way of working that is best for them. For future reference, several third-party software products are also written to support this notion of working interactively by allowing the user to import and export 2D and 3D data back and forth between popular 2D and 3D programs, while specializing in the process of assigning UV mapping interactively and painting onto 3D objects in real time.

The following five steps will texture map the character model. These steps can sometimes overlap and can be revisited at any time during production.

Step 1: Evaluating the Model's Mesh Design and Edge Placement

As the texture map artist in the assembly process of creating 3D objects, someone may hand you a model, as shown in the example model in Color Plate 8a and 8b. This is a single continuous polygon mesh with no UV mapping since they do not occur on polygon surfaces automatically. The first thing an artist should do is analyze the construction of the mesh and check for areas in the model's design where mapping can be difficult. In this example, these are the areas where polygons meet at acute angles, like the armpit, the crotch area, and the top of the neck. Since a polygon model can consolidate large areas of the model into one texture map, and because the need to optimize texture space and to usually maintain a low total count of textures used, the texture for this entire character will be represented in a single texture map, as shown in Color Plate 8e. In anticipation of the next step, the artist will also evaluate the placement of polygon edges that will define simpler groups of polygonal shapes, as shown in Figure 6.4.3b.

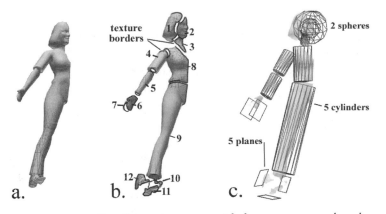

FIGURE 6.4.3 *Duplicate parts are avoided or even removed and remaining geometry is sectioned and grouped, based on their resemblance to simpler, more primitive shapes.*

Step 2: Delete Duplicate Elements and Dissect What Is Left

To save time by reducing the amount of surfaces you will have to map, identical geometry should be identified and deleted. As in this example, a character model often has a symmetrical design throughout the body. During the construction process of such a model, it is likely that the modeler constructed only half of the final model in an effort to save time. For this reason, many characters are seamed right down the middle. An edge down the center is a good place to dissect and eliminate half the body, as shown in Figure 6.4.3a. The benefit is that after mapping one of the duplicate elements or body parts, the texture artist can easily copy, flip, and move it back to where the original was before he deleted it. This step will eliminate the possibility of duplicating UV mapping work that wastes time, especially if the identical part is a complicated shape that was hard to map. This consolidating of geometry also improves how much area of the valuable texture space the duplicate parts would have taken up unnecessarily. Wasted texture space, unused or used by identical parts, is inefficient to production and wasteful to the product's performance and image quality.

Again, the fewer pieces of geometry that are left to represent the entire model, the fewer surfaces there are to map, and therefore the more texture space real estate the artist can devote to mapping them. In the end, this means more pixel resolution and better image quality in the game.

Next, the artist will divide the entire model into smaller groups of more primitive-like shapes, as if separate objects but not move them apart. The separation of geometry shown in Figure 6.4.3b is an added optional step after deleting symmetrical parts. It was done here only to show more clearly the different groups of geometry. The artist can leave the mesh intact and do a face-level subobject selection instead as many times as needed and apply separate mapping coordinates for each selection set of polygons. This step makes the steps that follow easier by breaking the model into more manageable parts. Mapping coordinates can now be applied more quickly and intuitively by using a combination of planar, spherical, or cylindrical mapping coordinates. The narrow cylinder-like shape of the arms and legs can be mapped separately from the even larger cylinder or capsule-like shape of the torso. The head shape in Figure 6.4.3c is similar to a sphere in form. Isolating the head at the neckline from the rest of the model makes it so that a spherical mapping method can be used for this group of polygons. This approach also reduces the amount of subdivisions needed to map fairly large sections of this female character.

When subdividing geometry into mapping groups as in Figure 6.4.3b, edge boundaries called *texture borders* are created. These are potentially unsightly seams in the texture-mapped model and are best placed at locations that are easily concealed, much like the inseam of a pair of pants. As mentioned previously, by separating the head at the neckline, there is a better chance that something in the model's design will provide a more natural and expected transition at the neckline. Tricks like these play down seams that are inevitably created at texture borders. If the concept drawing of the character has been provided, reference it for a better idea of seam placement based on clothing design.

In addition during this step, there may be times when existing polygon edges and/or vertex points should be moved to a better location on the model for optimal results. In all attempts to improve the efficiency of the texture mapping process and final outcome, you should be careful to not change the intended design of the model's form. Doing so will sometimes offend the modeler or alter the concept artist's original design. To avoid changing the shape or profile of a model, further dividing an edge or polygon face for better placement of a texture border is a good alternative. This solution, of course, will increase the polygon count with each new division and potentially exceed the model's specified "polygon budget."

Step 3: Assigning a Texture Map and Applying UVs

The texture artist is finally at a good place to assign a bitmap to the model. This could have been done as a first step, but would be less useful since steps 1 and 2 require that the artist work in wireframe mode to see the polygon edges and vertices. For this step, the artist first creates an image file using a filename that coincides well with the model's name, and places it in the directory it needs to be in for the game. The artist then assigns it to the model from within the 3D program using a simple drag and drop method. The image file is usually a .bmp, .jpg, or .png that is 512 pixels $\times$ 512 pixels in size, or smaller, but usually of a number that is a factor of 2. In creating the texture map initially, the highest possible resolution is always recommended. This can be reduced or downsampled to a smaller image later, like a 256 $\times$ 256 or a 128 $\times$ 128 pixel dimension. The larger resolution also enables the texture artist to design and evaluate textures at their most optimal level. The final image size will depend on resolution limitations imposed by the minimum specified system or file optimization requirements.

When testing the model for texture coordinates, a common practice is to create and assign a temporary *test image* that has a consistent pattern. A checker pattern of small black and white squares, as in Color Plate 8d, is a good one to use. This enables the UVs to be visualized and aids the artist through the decision process of selecting mapping tools and adjusting their controls during the next two steps. Other test images can have numbers and color squares, as used in Figure 6.4.4. More than one can be used sequentially to help expose problem areas for seams, stretching, distortion, and inconsistent resolution or pixel distribution. A few test images have been provided on the companion CD-ROM in this section's folder.

ON THE CD

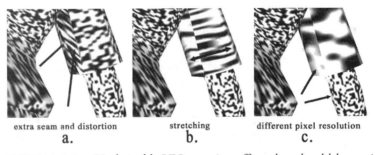

extra seam and distortion   stretching   different pixel resolution
       a.   **b.**   **c.**

FIGURE 6.4.4   *Undesirable UV mapping effects that should be avoided.*

To see the assigned texture map or test map on the model, UV coordinates must be applied. Although not ideal in all cases, a planar mapping system can be used by default just to get the newly assigned texture map to show up on the model. To apply the initial UV mapping, select a group of faces to planar map. Find and use the planar mapping tool within your 3D program. Perfect placement of the projected image is not important since it is only temporary. Later, more time, experimentation, and precision can be devoted to improving the final UV mapping using any one or combination of other mapping systems. The idea is to see the results in real time and to be able to work interactively while visualizing the effect on the model. For this case study, more than one mapping coordinate type will be needed for the character. Figure 6.4.3c should guide the artist in the selection of the mapping type and where to use them. For most bipedal characters, mostly cylindrical, spherical, and planar mapping are used in combination.

Step 4: Evaluate the Texture Space and Adjust UVs

In this final and somewhat technical phase of texture mapping, the texture artist will be refining his work. While evaluating the appearance of the test image on the model, the artist should try to avoid any situation resembling the problems shown in Figure 6.4.4. For example, while looking at the checkered squares on the surface of the model, the artist should ensure that there is good consistency in the pixel resolution throughout the model's surface. If the checkers in some areas appear to be larger or smaller than most, the artist can adjust the scale of individual UV points or groups of polygons from within the editor until the checkers more closely resemble the other checkers on the surface. Alternatively, if areas appear to have rectangular instead of square checkers, this indicates that stretching is occurring in the direction of the longer side of the black and white rectangles. To correct this, the artist will select and move the points that define the offending faces and move them vertically or horizontally in the editor. Again, this is like modifying mesh geometry but on a 2D plane instead. As the UV points and polygons are moved around in the editor, the changes should be updating the results on the surface of the 3D model. The preferred arrangement of checkers throughout the model should ultimately resemble Color Plate 8d. This will produce optimal results for the final texture map that will respond to this mapping.

For efficient use of the texture map, the artist should also ensure that each unique area of the model is referencing a unique area of the texture space. Within the UV editor, there are numerous ways to change the placement and packing of polygon groups by moving, rotating, and even flipping them. When packing the shapes into the texture space, it isn't very important to use up all of the space. Depending on desired texture map detail, contrast, and complexity, maintaining a consistent pixel resolution and distortion-free surface detail may be more important than using up every possible area. With time and experience, a dedicated texture artist will get better at deciding which is more important.

Step 5: Let the Real Fun Begin—Creating the Texture Map

Since a correctly named texture is already assigned to the model and the mapping coordinates are properly applied, the artist can now move forward and focus only on improving the texture map. If a test image is still showing on the model, the artist can choose to paint over it or assign a differently named texture map altogether and view this on the model. With all UV mapping completed, the missing duplicate areas of the model can also be re-created and welded back together to reconstruct the original single-mesh model. For this example model, the final texture map and mapping are shown in Figure 6.4.5.

Additional reference information for this example can be found at *www. titopagan.com*.

These five steps are all that a texture artist will need to know to improve his texture mapping process and get up to speed with professionals. By eliminating the majority of guesswork during the mapping stage, artists can save themselves and their team lots of time and frustration. If an artist or team of artists clearly understands how to execute each of the steps, the final art will reflect their knowledge and technical control over their craft, and allow the original idea for the game to shine through.

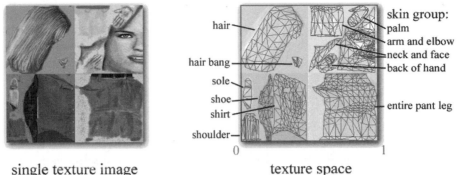

single texture image   texture space

FIGURE 6.4.5 *The final texture map with the various body parts labeled.*

Summary

The result of any 3D art asset for a real-time game is the product of all the steps one takes to design, model, texture map, and animate objects. Even if an artist isn't dead set on becoming a texture artist, this kind of work is a much-needed task in any game production environment. Texture maps are the color component of 3D models, and UV texture mapping is an intrinsic part that can make or break an object's close-up appearance in a video game. Because teams are generally smaller in the games industry than art production studios for other industries, more tasks have to be accomplished per individual team member. The topics covered in this chapter represent a large and valuable portion of any 3D artist's employable skill set. A professional texture artist will learn all that he can about his program's UV mapping tools, the UV editor, and the controls within the editor window.

References

[Capizzi02] Capizzi, Tom, *Inspired 3D Modeling and Texture Mapping*, Premier Press, 2002.

[Demers02] Demers, Owen, "Axel's Face: Texturing Polygons," *[Digital] Texturing and Painting*, New Riders, 2002.

[Pagan02] Pagan, Tito, "Efficient UV Mapping of Complex Models," *Game Developer Magazine* (August 2002): pp. 28–34.

6.5 | Surface Effects

Overview

In Chapter 6.4, "2D Textures and Texture Mapping," texture maps were applied to 3D models to give flat surfaces detail. However, single textures can only go so far toward simulating the complexities of a surface. This chapter will look at various surface effects that go beyond single textures and add visual pizzazz to a game. Motion blur, explosions, water, blinking neon signs, and glow are examples of surface effects that will make a game look more detailed and feel alive.

There are three fundamental techniques on which all surface effects are based: modifying the lighting algorithm, layering multiple textures, and changing the UV mappings. Some of these effects are done by artists, and some require the assistance of programmers.

Vertex Coloring

During the lighting phase of rendering, each vertex is assigned a *vertex color* by the lighting calculation. Vertex colors can also be assigned or painted by an artist. This can combine with the lighting or completely replace it, depending on the engine you are using.

Painting vertex colors can be used to break up tiling textures by subtly changing their hue. For instance, if you were running around in a rocky desert landscape, the dull browns of the texture would feel very flat and uninteresting. Painting reds and lighting/darkening regions can add some variation and break up the monotony of the scene. You may also paint in lighting effects that may not be generated by your lighting renderer. Bounced light from a skylight streaming into a room may not be calculated by your renderer, but you can simulate it by painting it into the vertex colors.

Many games with outdoor 3D environments use vertex colors instead of real-time lighting. In this case, you are completely throwing out the entire lighting phase during rendering, and using the vertex colors that the artist set up in the art package. It is common to start the vertex colors by putting lights in the scene, and *baking* or assigning the rendered results into the vertex colors. From there, the artist can hand paint to add more complexity, color, or touch up areas where the basic lighting was not interesting enough. An example of vertex coloring is shown in Figure 6.5.1.

FIGURE 6.5.1   *a) An ice texture used throughout this level.*
b) Vertex colors were used to add color and vibrancy to the level.
Images from Polar Bowler, courtesy of WildTangent. Environment by Jeff Selbig.

Alpha

An *alpha channel* is a grayscale texture map that specifies the transparency of a texture. Generally, pixels that are black result in complete transparency, white pixels result in completely opaqueness, and gray pixels cause semitransparency. Artists paint alpha channels to make a car's glass see through, to sparkles of magic for their see-though glow, or to simulate branches on a tree, as shown in Figure 6.5.2.

FIGURE 6.5.2 *A tree texture and its alpha channel.* Images courtesy of WildTangent.

Reflection

There are three common approaches to reflection maps in 3D games: *camera-projected reflections, cubic reflection maps,* and *dynamic cubic reflection maps.*

A camera-projected reflection map uses a texture map, and it wraps it around the model. This is a pretty fast method for reflections (compared to the other two), but it has the disadvantage of being somewhat unrealistic, because as the camera moves around an object, the reflection also follows, as opposed to showing what would be reflected on the backside. These can be created by photographing a chrome ball in a place that mimics the general lighting of the game environment in which it will be used (Figure 6.5.3).

FIGURE 6.5.3 *A reflection map for using the camera projection technique.*

A cubic reflection map or *cubemap* is created by creating six textures—for up, down, left, right, front, and back. These are combined into a *cubic reflection map.* As the 3D model is rendered, the cubic reflection map is invisibly placed within a box that has these six textures assigned to it, and the reflection is calculated perfectly from whatever angle the model is seen. This method has the disadvantage of being preset. As the reflective model moves throughout the world, the reflection doesn't change to represent the changing lighting and areas that the model will be passing through. Cubemaps can be created using Microsoft's texture tool, which is included in Microsoft's DirectX SDK and saved in the .dds format. An example is shown in Figure 6.5.4.

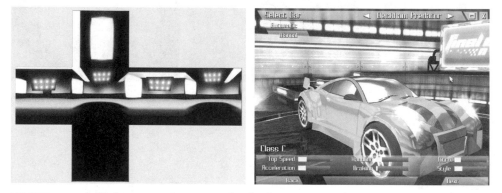

FIGURE 6.5.4   *Cubemap and an example of it being projected onto a car model. Images from Final Drive Nitro, courtesy of WildTangent. Car model by Yin Yi at Gamestar. Cubemap by David Johnson.*

Dynamic cubic reflection mapping is similar to a cubemap, but the six textures are not created by an artist ahead of time. Instead, they are created "on the fly," by rendering the environment through six cameras as the model travels throughout the world. This creates accurate reflection, but is very computationally intensive.

Static and dynamic cubic reflections can also add the possibility of a *reflection mask*. This is a grayscale texture, similar to an alpha channel, but instead of specifying transparency, the reflection mask specifies how reflective the model should be. This can allow the artist to make cars have highly reflective glass windows and chrome, matte bumpers and tires, and the body panels somewhere in between.

Bump Mapping and Normal Mapping

During the lighting phase, each vertex is compared to the lights to determine a vertex color. The problem with this is that you cannot have very detailed and realistic lighting because there are not enough vertices to support subtle lighting changes, like wrinkles in clothing or stucco on a wall.

Bump mapping and normal mapping allow you to have a lighting calculation at every pixel, instead of every vertex. They provide the illusion of much higher polygon models than you are actually using.

A bump map is essentially a height map. Black pixels are recessed and white pixels are protruding. Bump maps can be painted in any standard paint program. It is common to make bump maps tileable, to match environmental tiling textures. An example of a bump map is shown in Figure 6.5.5.

FIGURE 6.5.5 *A bump map for a dirt ground texture.*

Normal maps are similar to bump maps, but differ in how they are encoded and authored. You can instantly spot a normal map by its light-bluish tone. Normal maps use the red, green, and blue components of a color image to encode a vector or normal. This is used by a shader to modify the normal that would have been used. Because normal maps use an encoded image, they are virtually impossible to paint by hand. Normal maps are created by modeling a low-resolution model, and a high-resolution model, and using one of many utilities to compare the two models and *bake* a normal map. The finished normal map is then applied to the low-resolution model for in-game rendering. Figure 6.5.6 shows a normal map.

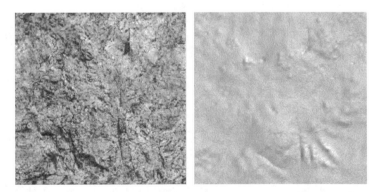

FIGURE 6.5.6 *A rocky ground texture and its normal map.* Image *courtesy of WildTangent. Texture and normal map by David Johnson.*

Multitexturing

A *multitexture*, as the name implies, means the use of more than one texture. Multiple textures can be combined to cover different scale (or detail) levels, for lightmaps, or for compositing effects.

Blend Modes

When more than one texture is combined, you must specify how they are to be combined. Replace, Add, Modulate, and Modulate2X are common examples of different blend modes that can be used on multitextures. Different game engines may have additional blend modes. With a multitexture shader, you start with a base layer; a tileable dirt road texture, for example. In most game engines, this is considered layer zero. Then, you add an additional texture in layer one, a road cracks texture, for instance. The road cracks texture must have a blend mode assigned to it, and in this instance multiply would be used.

Modulate is generally the default blend mode for textures, and is sometimes called *multiply*. Essentially, modulate will darken the texture and is often the mode used for lightmaps or shadow maps. What really happens is that pixels in the first texture are multiplied by the pixels in the second texture to produce the result. For example, any pure white pixels in the modulate texture will leave the original texture unchanged (1.0 * pixel color = pixel color). Likewise, 50 percent gray pixels will darken the result by half (0.5 * pixel color = ½ pixel color), and black pixels will completely black out the result (0 * pixel color = 0). Figure 6.5.7 shows an example.

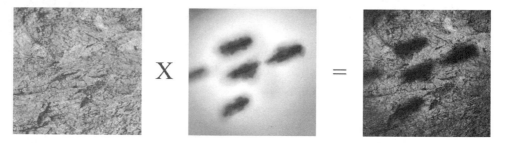

FIGURE 6.5.7   *Modulate blending of the original texture against a texture with shadows painted in. The result is a darker version of the original.* Image courtesy of WildTangent. Rocky texture map by David Johnson.

Replace overrides everything that has come before it. When used on the initial layer of a shader, it will override the lighting, resulting in a *fullbright* texture.

Add effectively brightens the texture. Add is used for glowing elements or lights themselves. This makes sense because the pixels from each texture are being added together to get the resulting texture, as shown in Figure 6.5.8.

Modulate2X is similar to modulate, but it is followed by multiplying the resulting pixels by two (Figure 6.5.9), which effectively brightens the image and gives it more range (the difference between the lightest and darkest pixels). Initially, begin Multiply2X textures with a 50 percent gray, and then paint in lighter and darker areas. Anything lighter than mid gray brightens the image; anything darker than mid gray darkens. This mode is sometimes used for lightmaps because it can result in a richer dynamic range than modulate lightmaps can.

FIGURE 6.5.8 *Add blending of the original texture against a texture with pools of light painted in. The result is lighter than the original. Image courtesy of WildTangent. Rocky texture map by David Johnson.*

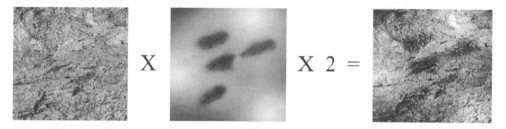

FIGURE 6.5.9 *Modulate2X blending of the original texture with a texture of both shadows and pools of light painted in. The result is a texture with a nice range of dark and light areas. Image courtesy of WildTangent. Rocky texture map by David Johnson.*

When designing multitextures, you can simulate the results using Adobe Photoshop. Each layer in Photoshop can have blend modes assigned to it, just like a game engine's multitexture layers. The naming convention in Photoshop is different, so Table 6.5.1 lists the nearest equivalents.

Table 6.5.1 Photoshop Equivalents to Game Engine Blend Modes

Game Engine	Photoshop
Replace	Normal
Add	Screen
Modulate	Multiply
Modulate2X	Overlay

There are many more blend modes that various game engines often support, but the ones discussed are the most common, and should be well understood by any effects artist.

UV Animations

The mapping coordinates on a *sprite* (a camera-facing polygon) or model can be animated to create moving effects. Scrolling the mapping coordinates can be used to create a waterfall. Flipbook animations use a texture that has been divided up into rows and columns, with progressing imagery in each *cell*. The mapping coordinates flip through each cell to create a short animation. Explosions and progressing neon signs are created with flipbook animation, as shown in Figure 6.5.10. In addition to these types of UV animations, sine wave functions can warp the mapping coordinates to create the illusion of waving water. When combined with multitextures, a shifting lower layer can simulate a color or intensity animation from a light source.

Figure 6.5.10   *A flipbook animation, used to animate a neon sign lighting up gradually. Image from Final Drive Nitro, courtesy of WildTangent. Painted by Luo Jun at Gamestar.*

Lightmaps

Lightmaps are used to create high-quality lighting for environments. Lightmaps, sometimes also called *shadowmaps,* are a use of multitexturing. A base layer provides the texture of the surface, like stucco, brick, or carpeting. An additional multitexture layer (the lightmap) is added to provide shadows and highlight, therefore simulating realistic lighting.

When using BSP editors, the lightmaps are created by the editor, and the artist doesn't need to worry about how they are created. When using a 3D authoring package, the artist will be responsible for setting up and creating the lightmaps.

There are a few phases to creating lightmaps. First, the environment must be modeled and textured. Next, an additional set of mapping coordinates must be laid out to support the lightmaps. This is often done with an automatic UV generation utility that will provide mapping coordinates for every surface. Then, the artist lights the scene. Using the built-in renderer of the software, tune the color, intensity, and shadow of the lights as you see fit. Lastly, the lights are rendered or *baked* into the lightmap. This means that the renderer calculates the lighting of the environments and draws it into the lightmap texture.

Multitexture Blending versus Framebuffer Operations

Multitextures are created by taking multiple textures and combining them together in various ways, but once this is complete, the object that this multitexture is applied to must be added to the scene being rendered. This is where framebuffer operations come into play. A *framebuffer operation* is the method that will be used to blend an object with whatever is behind it. Framebuffer operations use many of the same blend modes that multitextures use; for example, replace, modulate, and add are commonly used framebuffer operations.

Replace is often the default framebuffer operation. A replace framebuffer operation will result in the object being rendered as a solid object, with nothing visible behind it. All of the other framebuffer operations will result in the object having some transparency, whether it is a darkening effect (modulate), a glowy magical effect (add), or using a simple alpha channel (blend). Any object with alpha channel transparency must use the blend framebuffer operation (or one of the blend variants).

Vertex and Pixel Shaders

Beginning with DirectX 8, vertex and pixel shaders have been available to PC game developers. Vertex and pixel shaders allow developers to write custom effects programs that modify how an object will be rendered. Before vertex and pixel shaders, you didn't get much more than textures, lights, alpha, and reflection. Now, sophisticated effects can be applied to objects or the entire scene.

Vertex shaders are programs that can be used to modify a model's shape and/or its mapping coordinates. One common use for this is skeletal animation. This allows the bone deformations of a character to be processed much faster than alternative methods because it is offloaded to your video card's GPU, or *graphical processing unit*. Vertex shaders can also simulate waves in water, fisheye lens effects, and toon rendering.

Pixel shaders or *fragment shaders* allow you to modify the pixels that are rendered. Pixel shaders are commonly used to create reflections, refractions, blurring, glows, custom lighting, and other visual niceties.

Compositing

In most 3D authoring packages, a shader or material is something that you apply to an object. While this is also often the case with 3D game engines, you can also apply shaders to the entire rendered scene, as if it were an object. This is how depth of field, motion blur, heat distortion, and other effects are implemented.

When compositing, the entire scene is rendered, but instead of being displayed on your monitor, the results are sent to a *render target*. A render target is a temporary texture that can have filters or shaders applied to it. Colorization filters can create night goggle effects. Depth detection and blur filters can create depth of field blurring. Edge detection can result in a toon shading look.

HDRI

HDRI is an acronym for "high dynamic range image." It was created because standard image formats like .jpg have a limited "dynamic range" of intensity that can be represented, from 0–255 in each color channel (red, green, and blue). If you take a photograph inside a room in your house on a sunny day, you will get detail in the room and shadows, but anything outside the window might be entirely white. HDRI images solve this by storing a much larger range of lights and darks.

In games, high dynamic range rendering can be used to create *light blooms* around light sources because they are known to be *brighter than white*.

HDRI images can also be used instead of a traditional light source for creating lightmaps. As an example, an outdoor scene can be lit with a main directional sunlight, and some ambient blue to simulate the light being contributed by the sky itself. However, this usually looks pretty terrible, so additional lights are added to fill in the scene. Alternatively, an HDRI image can be used to map all of the light being contributed from every angle. Using an image to light a scene, rather than point lights (whether or not the image is an HDRI), is called *image-based lighting*. HDRI images can also be used instead of light sources in some game engines.

HDR images can be created by taking several photographs of the same subject, often a chrome ball, at many different exposure settings to capture all the detail from the darkest shadows to the brightest lights. These are combined into a single HDRI image file. HDR images are often created and processed using HDR Shop by Paul Debevec [Debevec]. HDR Shop is also useful for converting a reflection map into a luminance map for image-based rendering.

Common Effects

We've looked at the technical details of surface effects, but how do you make amazing looking effects? The following is a case study in a few examples of effects that are common in games.

Depending on the game, there will be different pipelines for designing effects. In some circumstances, the artist will hand off textures to a programmer. In others, the artist will mock up the effect in a 3D package and render a small movie, as an example for how the programmers should try to implement the effect. In other circumstances, the artist will create the entire effect in an editor.

Dust

Dust being kicked up from the tire of a skidding car is a pretty basic effect, but one that you are bound to see in any racing game. The look of this effect will be different, based on the type of surface on which the car is driving. When on a dirt road, a giant cloud of brown dust can be formed, while skidding on asphalt will result in a smaller white smoke cloud. Figure 6.5.11 shows an example of a dust texture.

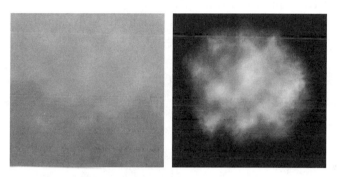

FIGURE 6.5.11 *Dust and the alpha channel for the dust particle.*

It is effective to add some amount of variation to the color texture for dust, rather than a solid brown. As multiple layers of particles build up, this perturbation adds separation between the layers of dust.

Bullet Hole

A bullet hole left in a wall after it's been shot up is a very common effect in first-person shooters. Figure 6.5.12 shows a sample texture of a bullet hole and its associated alpha channel. A programmer will stick a polygon to an environmental surface and apply this texture to create the bullet hole effect.

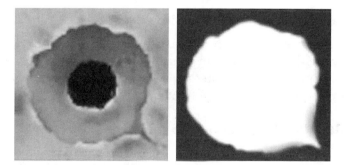

FIGURE 6.5.12 *Bullet hole and its alpha channel.*

Weapon Trail

When your hero slashes a bad guy with his sword, you may want a trail of glow behind the weapon. To do this, you will simply provide the coder with a bitmap that has glowy stuff in it. The hero model must be implemented with points defined at the tip and hilt of his sword. The programmer will implement a polygon mesh that will lag behind the sword points so that as the sword moves faster, the polygonal trail will lag and create the glowy effect.

The framebuffer operation of the shader applied to this trail should be *add* so that it glows brightly against the background. Note that when you are using add framebuffer operations, the texture itself should be somewhat darkened, generally under 50 percent brightness to allow some headroom when added against the environment. Otherwise, the effect will quickly blow out too bright. Figure 6.5.13 shows an example of a glow trail texture.

FIGURE 6.5.13   *Glow trail as painted, and resized to a game ready bitmap.*

Notice that the texture in Figure 6.5.13 was resized to 64 × 64. Square, power-of-two-sized textures (16, 32, 64, 128, 256, 512, 1024, 2048) are generally preferable, so this texture was shrunk to a 64 × 64 size. Since there is no tiny detail in the trail, the resized texture will be indistinguishable from the original.

Explosion Flipbook Animation

Flipbook animations are created by laying out several frames of animation on a single texture sheet, as shown in Figure 6.5.14. The code places a sprite in the scene, and moves the UV coordinates to play back the cells like an animation. This is efficient, because it can be stored in memory like any other texture.

Multilayered Particle Systems

A particle system can be many things, ranging from missile trails to fairy dust to dirt kicked up by a car's tire. Particle systems are probably the most common effect that you are likely to encounter. For this example, we will analyze all of the details that go

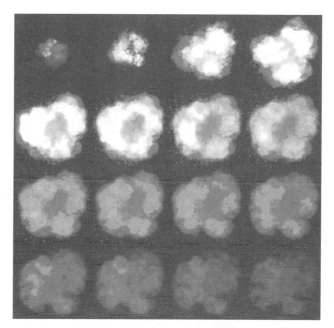

FIGURE 6.5.14 *A 16-frame explosion flipbook animation.*
Image from Phoenix Assault, courtesy of WildTangent and Wanako Games.
Created by Edmundo Bordeu using Particle Illusion by Wondertouch.

into a missile launch and explosion, as shown in Figure 6.5.15. First, you must identify the stages. The missile is launched, the missile flies though the air, and the missile
explodes and dies on impact. Each of these three stages will require several layers to
the effect.

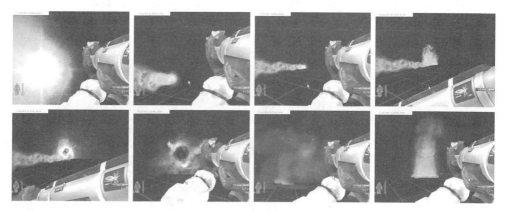

FIGURE 6.5.15 *A series of frames showing a multilayered missile launch and explosion
effect. Effect designed by Javier Ojeda. http://thefxman.com/.*

The launch has several considerations. The launch must take place from a specific position in the game. This is commonly flagged by a text file, a bone in a model, or other point locator relative to the launching device. The missile and its various effects will start here. The visual components that you will need are a missile model, a flash of light, some fire that shoots out of the barrel, one or more layers of smoke spewing from the launch, perhaps a dust shockwave, and depending on the circumstances, maybe some camera shake.

The second phase, flying though the air, has substantially fewer elements. You will need a flipbook animation of a dissipating smoke cloud and flaming thruster texture.

The third phase, impact, needs another flash, an explosion, smoke, and some debris. You may use additional particle systems for debris and secondary smoke trails.

Magic Spell

Magic can look like many different things. In this example, we will use some common elements. The layers that we will use are some glowing, rising, twirling particles, a streaking "teleporter" rim, a main glow, and some multilayered spinning runes on the ground. The textures used for this effect are shown in Figure 6.5.16, and the final effect is shown in Figure 6.5.17.

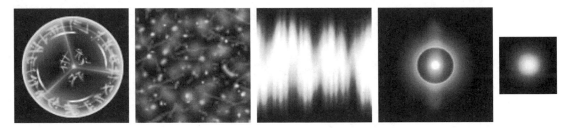

FIGURE 6.5.16   *Textures used in the magic effect. a) Runes, rotating. b) Streaks, which are stretched and shifted. c) Alpha to mask the top and bottom of the streaks. d) Particle. e) Glow.*

FIGURE 6.5.17   *A composite of the magic effects.*

Most of the layers in this are pretty straightforward, but the streaking effect may not be so obvious. The streak texture is applied to a cylinder (Figure 6.5.18a), and the shader's vertical tiling parameter is set to 0.001. This has the effect of stretching the texture vertically by an extreme amount, resulting in a one-pixel row of the texture stretching all the way up the cylinder (Figure 6.5.18b). The shader is also set to quickly shift this texture upward, so the lines will evolve, appear, and disappear in a random fashion. Interestingly, diagonal lines painted into the streak texture result in a streak moving around the cylinder, while dots or vertical lines result in streaks that are stationary. Then, the mask is applied (Figure 6.5.18c), with a multiply blend mode to fade the effect toward the top and bottom. Lastly, the entire shader is told to use an add framebuffer operation so that all of the elements glow against one another and the background.

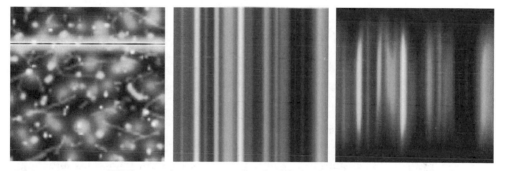

FIGURE 6.5.18   *(a) The streak texture, with a highlight demonstrating the row of pixels that will be stretched over the height of the cylinder. (b) The stretched streak texture. (c) After the mask is multiplied.*

Effects Editors

There are a few tools of which any effects artist should be aware. Render Monkey, FX Composer, and Effect Editor are tools that aid in developing pixel and vertex shaders. Effect Editor is more targeted at programmers, while Render Monkey and FX Composer are more artist friendly.

ATI's Render Monkey can be downloaded for free at their Web site [Render-Monkey]. NVIDIA's FX Composer is available for free at their developers' page [FXComposer].

Microsoft's Effects editor is free and is included in the DirectX SDK [Microsoft-Effects].

Particle Illusion by Wondertouch does not create game-ready art, but it is a valuable tool in rapidly prototyping effects and how they will look. After an effect is designed in Particle Illusion, it can be rendered out to an .avi file, and used to communicate the layers and prototype sprites that will be used for in-game effects. Wondertouch's Particle Illusion can be purchased at their Web site [ParticleIllusion].

There are many other editors for creating effects, and depending on the game engine you are using, there may be a system for editing effects specific to that engine. Unreal Ed and Havok both have custom effects-editing systems.

Summary

Complex surfaces are difficult, if not impossible, to re-create with a single texture and basic lighting. This problem is made even worse since textures are repeated many times in a scene due to limited texture memory. Surface effects are designed to add detail back to the surfaces and deal with repetition by breaking up and disguising these repeating textures.

The three main techniques for surface effects are:

- Modifying the lighting algorithm (vertex coloring, bump mapping, normal mapping)
- Layering multiple textures (multitexture blending, lightmaps)
- Changing the UV mappings (flipbook animations, scrolling or waving textures, reflection, refraction)

Vertex and pixel shaders are advanced tools for manipulating the three main techniques. Since shaders are programmable, they can create a wide variety of effects. Effects like distortions, toon rendering, reflections, refractions, blurring, and custom lighting are all possible with these shaders. Artists can experiment with many of these surface effects by using the effects editors provided by Microsoft and the major graphics card manufacturers.

Exercises

1. Use Photoshop's layers and blend modes to simulate a lightmap.
2. Create a normal map and preview it on a low-resolution 3D model.
3. Create an eight-frame flipbook animation, laid out in a single 256×256 texture.
4. Download and run a shader editing program. If you are using ATI hardware, get Render Monkey; if you are running NVIDIA hardware, get FX Composer.
5. Load a pixel shader onto an object into the viewport of your 3D authoring package.
6. Create a multilayered particle system effect. Simulate a missile 1) being launched, 2) flying through the air with a smoke trail, and 3) exploding on a target. Use your 3D authoring package for this exercise.

7. Create a small room environment and decorate it with some furniture. Lay out base mapping coordinates and texture the scene. Lay out an additional set of mapping coordinates for lightmaps. Light your scene. Render lightmaps and preview the results in the viewport of your 3D application.
8. Create an .hdr image from multiple images using HDR Shop.
9. Create a cubic reflection map.

References

[Debevec] Debevec, Paul, HDR Shop, *www.hdrshop.com.*

[FXComposer] FX Composer, NVIDIA, available at *http://developer.nvidia.com/ page/tools.html.*

[MicrosoftEffects] Effects, Microsoft, available as part of DirectX, *www.microsoft. com/downloads/* then click the DirectX category.

[ParticleIllusion] Particle Illusion, Wondertouch, available at *www.wondertouch.com/ default.asp.*

[RenderMonkey] Render Monkey, ATI, available at *l.*

[St-Laurent04] St-Laurent, Sebastien, *Shaders for Game Programmers and Artists,* Thomson Course Technology, 2004.

6.6 Lighting

Overview

Whether you are creating a prerendered cinematic, a level for a first-person shooter, or prerendered 3D assets for a top-down three-quarter view game, lighting will play a critical role in defining the look of the game. More than just making objects visible, lighting has the ability to reveal or conceal details in your scene. It can be used to make an object stand out from the background, define the irregularity of a surface, or even through shadow define objects that are out of frame or obscured by a wall in the scene. Light can define the mood of a scene, or focused, light can even be used to direct the attention of the player.

To use light effectively, it is important to understand how light interacts with the surfaces in your scene and how that interaction affects the other visual components of the composition. Understanding light requires that you look at both the aesthetic qualities of light and the technical components that guide its use within the digital RGB system.

Seeing Dimension in a Flat World

The single most important role that lighting plays in games, whether for cinematics or in level design, is to help define the three-dimensional form of your scene on the two-dimensional plane of your television or computer monitor. This two-dimensional medium strips away important stereoscopic cues that your eyes are designed to collect and send to the brain. As a result, an artist must rely on the use of lighting to enhance and emphasize the three-dimensional aspects of the game world.

Light and Surface

In the real world, we can only see a surface when light bounces off (or emanates from) the surface and hits our eyes. What we see is a result of the qualities of the light revealing the qualities of the surface. With our eyes, we collect the combined information to be interpreted by the brain, giving us an understanding about that surface. Humans are very adept at distinguishing between infinitely subtle differences in light and how it plays off surfaces. For example, the slightest blemish or ding on a brand new car is instantly recognizable.

In the digital realm, a surface has no visual quality at all until you define it. Given the complexity of real-world vision, it should not be surprising that even computer-generated sets and actors in film, created and rendered by the best artists with the most powerful computers, will often look artificial. It is the complex play of light on the physical world that is so hard to re-create, and both light and surface are insepara-bly intertwined.

Luminance

An often-overlooked factor in digital lighting is that a light's apparent brightness is actually due to its contrast with surrounding elements in the scene. On the computer, the brightest object in a scene will never be more than the RGB value of R:255, G:255, B:255, which is pure RGB white. Once a light is as bright as it can be (without the tex-tures looking washed out), the only option for making it appear brighter is to reduce the brightness of surrounding areas. Furthermore, if a light source is directly visible in the scene, such as a bare light bulb, being pure white is not enough to make it look *real*. Our understanding of how lights look is largely informed by our experience of film and video. To get the light to have a cinematic look, effects such as glowing must be artificially replicated in the game. These lens effects can be as simple as adding a glow texture to a polygon in front of the light object. A common technique is to have code rotate the glow polygon to always face the camera. Many of these effects are much sim-pler than they look on screen, but they are necessary to sell the scene.

Accent on Form

One of the effects of translating three-dimensional space into a two-dimensional image is the loss of typical stereoscopic depth cues. To help bring out foreground and midground subjects from the background, lighting techniques can be borrowed from the film and video industries. The classic lighting scheme for shooting a subject is the three-point light setup. This setup uses three lights: a key light, a fill light, and a kicker light or back light. With these three lights, most subjects will exhibit well-defined form and remain clearly defined within their environment.

Directing the Focus with Light

In cinema, there is an often-used technique where an actor's eyes seem to be glowing from a beam of light (with no apparent source). The motivation for such lighting is simple; it is to direct the audience's attention to the actor's eyes to draw the audience into the actor's emotional state. Although this example of using light to focus attention can be heavy handed if it draws attention to itself, it is an important compositional tool for helping the audience read a scene. For example, if you want to lead your player to a different part of a game level, you can accent the preferred passage with lighting that helps it stand out from the other details in the scene. Avid gamers will look for such clues, but even the novice gamer will be unconsciously drawn toward this highlighted detail.

Setting the Mood

Lighting can help define the texture of a surface, accent form, and direct attention, but it is also crucial for setting the mood of a scene. A bright scene with sharp black shadows is reminiscent of a sunny day and conveys a sense of alertness and cheerfulness, much like the world of Nintendo's *Mario*. A dark night scene lit with blue moonlight and yellow torches that cast long wavering shadows is much more sinister or spooky, and was used quite effectively in the *Thief* series. In each case, lighting is critical to conveying the mood of the game and setting the player deep inside both the emotional and physical world.

Light Models

In the real world, light can emanate from a wide variety of sources. A scene might be lit by sunlight, moonlight, incandescent bulbs, red neon lights, car headlights, or torches. Additionally, in the real world there is a lot of indirect light that bounces off various surfaces, which will change the color and dispersion of the original light. In the digital realm, your options are limited to four common light models: point, spot, directional, and ambient.

Each model has different parameters that can be adjusted, but they have one parameter in common: the color of the light. Normally, we envision light as being white or yellow, but a light source in the real world or in a game can be of any color, from neon red to moonlight blue. Keep this in mind as you examine each light type.

Point Light

A *point light*, sometimes referred to as an *omni light* because it casts lights in all directions, is useful for a wide variety of lighting situations. As indicated in Figure 6.6.1, the point light radiates out evenly from a single point. This light tends to work well for lighting areas where a specific source is not apparent. There are certain types of light sources such as torches or unshaded light bulbs where a point light is an obvious choice, but even some shaded lights are easier to emulate with a point light. While you can't focus a point light, it can cast shadows, so it can be directed by obstructing the light with surrounding objects. As with most of the light types, you can *attenuate* (or reduce the intensity of) a light by adjusting the falloff parameters. Depending on the sophistication of the point light model, you may even be able to adjust the near attenuation, a parameter that allows the light to fade in as it travels from its source. Used together, near and far attenuation parameters can be adjusted to finely control the area affected by the light.

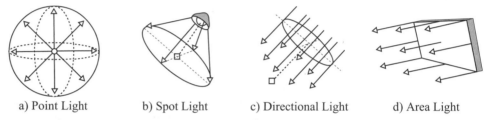

a) Point Light   b) Spot Light   c) Directional Light   d) Area Light

FIGURE 6.6.1   *Common light models used to light three-dimensional environments.*

Spotlight

Spotlights have all of the parameters of point lights (position and attenuation) with the addition of being able to focus the light like a flashlight or car headlight. In Figure 6.6.1, the spotlight is differentiated from the other light types in that it casts a cone of light, controlled by changing the cone width and orientation (direction). Because there is a directional nature to spotlights, there are two common ways that its direction is often controlled interactively. One way is for a spotlight to lock on to a target object, thus constantly changing its direction to follow an object. The second way is for a spotlight to emanate from a source that is actively moving in the scene. An excellent example of the second technique is in *Doom 3*, a game where the darkness plays a strong role in both the mood and the gameplay. In *Doom 3*, the player holds a flashlight object that shines a spotlight in whatever direction the player faces. This interactive nature of the light source is critical to gameplay and helps the player connect and explore the environment.

Directional Light

Both point lights and spotlights radiate from a single point in 3D space, thus the rays of light fan out as they get farther from the source. To emulate sunlight with a spotlight, the light source would have to be infinitely far away, which isn't practical. The nature of sunlight is that the light rays are essentially parallel because the sun is so far away from the earth. The concept of a *directional light*, with its parallel light rays, was created to simulate light sources such as the sun. Directional lights are the simplest to use since they are specified by a direction, intensity, and color. In some directional light models, there are parameters for adjusting the area or range affected by the light, but these parameters are not commonly implemented in most game engines. The directional light is usually placed in the role of the key light when lighting an outside environment, and therefore must be combined with other lights to achieve a well-lit scene.

Area Light

An *area light* is a specialized light that is used to simulate light coming from a large surface area. Typical office lighting, with the large rectangular ceiling boxes, gives a unique quality of light that can be emulated with an area light. Recent advances in 3D art packages may even allow an object to be used as a light source. It is important to understand that these complex area light shapes can be very calculation intensive. Because of the complexity of the calculation, area lights are generally not implemented in graphics hardware for consoles or PCs; however, some 3D art packages do offer them for prerendered scenes. In real-time game engines, area lights can be simulated with several point lights or spotlights.

Ambient Light

Ambient light represents the color and intensity of light that affects every surface of every object in a scene. You might think of this as the light that allows you to see detail in the shadows where the direct light is being blocked. Unfortunately, the way that a digital ambient light works does not have a real-world equivalent. In the real world, ambient light is created by indirect light sources, such as sunlight that is reflected off objects. A digital ambient light is a single RGB value that is applied to everything in the scene.

It is important to understand that the look of reflected light is substantially different from bumping up the value of all rendered pixels in a scene. The digital equivalent, *radiosity*, is a way to mathematically simulate this phenomenon, but the calculations make it impossible to currently do in real time. However, if the light sources and 3D models don't move relative to each other, radiosity effects can be *baked* into the vertices of a 3D model. This is done by precalculating the radiosity light value for every model vertex (the reflected ambient light that would strike each vertex), and using these values at runtime to color (light) the model's vertices. Another technique is to bake the radiosity values into separate material (texture) layers to be rendered at runtime. With either technique, radiosity can add very subtle and accurate ambient lighting to any static models within a scene, such as street environments or interior architecture.

Shadows

Shadows are critical for spatially orienting objects and characters in a scene. An object without a shadow will appear to float above the floor, so it is crucial to ground objects with shadows. When lighting a scene for film or video, one of the more problematic aspects of lighting a scene is controlling the shadows, because every light casts a shadow. In digital lighting, this task is much more controllable, since shadows can be turned on or off for each light. However, the drawback of digital lighting is that real-time shadows are not cheap to compute, so you generally want to limit what shadows in the scene are calculated in real time. The art of working with shadows in a real-time environment is to find a balance between adding shadows to the texture layers of your objects and using a limited amount of real-time projection.

The relative dispersion of shadows will be affected by the hardness or softness of the light. Hard lights project crisp shadows that are well defined and have sharp contrast. Soft lights create soft, diffused shadows with deemphasized surface contours and reduced contrast. Since the shadows are what tie the object to the ground, it is important to have consistency between any shadows baked into the textures or vertices and the real-time shadows projected from the lights in the scene.

Lens Effects and Atmosphere

The blooming or glow that we are familiar with around very bright areas in film and video is caused by a variety of phenomena. For example, lens flare is caused by reflections within a lens, and the star-like glow around lights is caused by reflections on a camera's aperture blades (a five-blade aperture will create five streaks in the flare). A heavy atmosphere, such as fog, can also create glows or visible beams of light. If you are creating prerendered cinematics, all of the current 3D packages have rendering effects that can be added to your scene to achieve a wide variety of lens and atmospheric effects. In real-time game engines, you can still achieve many of the common effects either by faking the effect with special halo objects or light cones. These can be usually rendered with an additive effect, or occasionally some effects can be done programmatically either to the entire frame or based on special glow or light maps applied to the shaders.

Illuminated Textures

There is one more lighting technique to add realism to your scene that, while not actually a light model, is critical to accurately representing elements that are casting or emanating light. For example, many light sources have translucent physical features, like light shades, frosted glass, or textured glass, which are in effect glowing or emanating light. The most direct way to emulate an illuminated material is to add self-illumination to that material. In this case, the lighting calculation for the surface takes into account that it is giving off light, not just reflecting it. It is important to understand that in the most common type of self-illumination, it is not actually making the material brighter; it is reducing the effect of lights on the texture by bringing up any pixels that are in shadow up to the full intensity of the original texture. By adding self-illumination with the use of a grayscale image, you can selectively control the brightness of each pixel with a corresponding bitmap.

Summary

This chapter introduced the uses and techniques of digital lighting. Lighting is critical to defining the surface texture and form of 3D objects. It is important for conveying a mood or atmosphere, and can even be used to direct the player's attention. As far as implementation, there are four main types of lights used in real-time games: point, spot, directional, and ambient. Shadows are an integral part of lighting and are crucial for grounding objects in a scene. However, shadows can be expensive to calculate in real time, so a game will use a combination of baked-in shadows and real-time projected shadows.

As you proceed to light your game levels or cinematic scenes, make sure to do extensive research into your genre. Analyze how films in similar genre use lighting in telling a story; observe the use of lighting in a variety of games to see how lighting can create moods and enhance the gaming experience; observe real-world light and find ways to simulate that effect in your three-dimensional level designs.

Exercises

1. Find a scene in a computer-animated film that used light as a strong visual element. Break down the role of lighting in the scene and describe the following aspects: colors, brightness, contrast, shadows, atmospheric lighting, or lens effects. Approach this exercise as if you were writing instructions to an artist responsible for the lighting in the scene.
2. Describe how the light is used in defining the mood of the scene.
3. Create a diagram of the position of each light in the scene, along with qualities such as light type, color, brightness, use of shadow casting, and any other unique quality or technical characteristics.
4. How the lighting fits into the compositional structure. Describe the two-dimensional composition of the lighting and how the lighting helps the readability of the three-dimensional space.

References

[Birn00] Birn, Jeremy, *[digital]Lighting & Rendering,* New Riders Publishing, 2000.

[Hill04] Hill, Steve, "Hardware Accelerating Art Production," *Gamasutra,* 2004, available online at *www.gamasutra.com/features/20040318/hill_01.shtml.*

[Jackman02] Jackman, John, *Lighting for Digital Video & Television,* CMP Books, 2002.

[James04] James, Greg, and O'Rorke, John, "Real-Time Glow," *Gamasutra,* 2004, available online at *www.gamasutra.com/features/20040526/james_01.shtml.*

[O'Rourke03] O'Rourke, Michael, *Principles of Three-Dimensional Computer Animation, Third Edition,* W. W. Norton & Company, Inc., 2003.

6.7 ∎ Animation

Overview

This chapter discusses the process of creating animated 3D art for real-time games. Animation for these games is the art of capturing a series of individual movements in digital form and then playing them back in real time. Just about everything in a game—from the user interface, to atmospheric effects, to characters and walking critters—will need to be animated. Even the camera may need to be animated through a 3D environment in a predictable and controlled manner. Animation establishes the character and personality of humanoid figures and both real and imagined creatures.

Becoming an animator in the games industry has become one of the more highly sought-after positions. It is also among the most complicated tasks that a digital artist can undertake in a production studio. Because 3D animation takes place in time, having the freedom to artistically manipulate both time and space for expressing actions and moods is very rewarding. In creating a suitable motion for a never-before-seen creature, an animator can play God and invent—as long as it works and looks believable in the game. The return for such artistic work is the opportunity to contribute significantly to a game's distinctly different style and unique feel. Being the competent animator that earns a living creating such original work can feel like a bonus.

Basically, all things set in motion require thought about how to design their movement on a frame-by-frame or pose-to-pose basis. Thought must also be given to how to evaluate the results and how to feed the data to the game's animation system. Due to the popularity of character-based animation in games, and the overlap with motion for other inanimate 3D objects, this chapter intentionally focuses on the creation of motion for real-time characters.

Responsibilities and Expectations of the Animator

An animator in the games industry is predominately a character animator, since moving and talking characters are commonly needed in most game genres. The animation of many different kinds of characters is an art form that takes much time and practice to perfect, thus making character animation more of a specialization. As competent game animators, it is their job to understand the meaning behind an expression and how to get the body posed and moving to accurately or stylistically convey the action for playback in real time. An animator should also be knowledgeable in anatomy, since creating believable motion requires an understanding of the underlying mechanism, like rotating joints and bulging muscles. Character work is a tall order and usually calls for seasoned animators. Moreover, as the saying goes, you do get what you pay for when a game company is in search of experienced talent.

In practice, a common mistake many game companies make is to not clearly understand the difference between a trained animator and an experienced technical artist. Both are essential and needed for a successful 3D game, but they are not the same person. An animator who is trained in traditional animation understands the fundamental principles of animation and proper timing and how to use them to his advantage. With a 3D package in hand, this individual can learn the specialized tools-of-the-trade quickly that will allow him to create and control expressive performances. However, a good technical artist or "tools jockey" who masters the software first and foremost isn't necessarily capable of producing compelling animations that are not run of the mill, robotic, or poorly timed. The concepts and principles behind fluid and convincing motion aren't yet a button push away.

Any industry-savvy computer artist, given a chance, will at least attempt to animate characters. The result of his effort, and lack of experience, is more obvious than one would think to any member of their team. At a glance, it either looks or feels correct or it does not. No one ever asks what the animator did to get where he did, or how much time it actually took to complete a character animation. However, almost anyone is a good critique for convincing and appropriate motion. Consider the fact that at an early age, even children quickly develop the ability to read body language or posture and facial expressions. As a result of daily observation of others, people understand the basics of believable human motion and can be acceptable judges of one's work. They may not be effective in describing the problem with the motion they see, but will know intuitively that there is a problem. A computer artist embarking on a career as an animator will need to be open to ideas that are different from his own. Taking criticism constructively is another essential trait of a successful animator.

The artistic versus the technical are two different disciplines that inevitably come together when animating in 3D. Requiring the use of both sides of the brain, each discipline calls upon different skills and approaches that command special attention and ongoing determination by the animator or "all-purpose" game artist. During this marriage of art and code, producing desired results for complex game characters is undoubtedly a technical challenge. Fortunately, improved features and workflow in today's top 3D applications continue to make the process of learning animation tools visually interactive and a more intuitive process with every new release of software. To stay well informed of such improvements, there are literally hundreds of tutorials and examples on the Internet that can walk an animator through the steps of learning the new and improved tools of each application. User group forums and product-sponsored sites are also good sources for learning the tricks and techniques used by game developers. Industry trade shows are planned events where many animators participate for continuing their specialized knowledge. Historically, however, many startup game companies do not typically budget time or money for such ongoing training of their animators.

For creating animation by hand, most game companies will expect that an industry animator is proficient in the use of at least one of the primary 3D packages. These are usually the same 3D software products used for all other facets of creating 3D objects and characters, such as modeling, texturing, and exporting. The tools for animating characters are common to all popular packages, and although their workflow, names, and visual appearance may be slightly different, the concepts are generally the same.

Learning to Animate for Real-Time Playback

Learning the art of animation is simple and affordable to anyone who takes the time to observe the way things around them move, react, and behave. For animators, the world is like a textbook for studying the anatomy of all living things. Study how the human body moves on its own or in response to other physical objects and forces, like the wind or gravity. Learning to animate well requires knowing what important elements to observe and lots of practice and patience in trying to simulate them.

Two basic and fundamental elements of animation common in all motion are *timing* and *space*. To give life to an otherwise static object or statuelike character is to understand the role that time and space play in the illusion of movement. A good way to demonstrate this is to study a simple bouncing ball. If one were to observe the motion frame by frame, one could see how different the spacing of the ball is at the top of its arc (or parabola), compared to its spacing during acceleration both before and after a bounce. The timing is such that the ball feels suspended in place just a bit longer at the top of the arc it travels than it does at any other place while it moves in free flight. Conveniently, this example also illustrates another important effect in timing: *ease-in* and *ease-out*.

There are many proven techniques and principles common to 2D animation that can and should be considered for 3D. Unfortunately, there are too many to cover in detail, but here are a few examples of which any animator should be aware. With a little creative thinking, these principles can enhance any motion. Figure 6.7.1 shows a *squash and stretch* technique that can be used when creating more rubbery cartoon-like gag-based animation for a kid's game. It can also be used to help "sell the idea" of an expression with *emphasis* and *exaggeration*. Other examples are *anticipation*, *follow-through*, *reaction and takes*, *weight shift*, and *timing* to suggest weight and force. In Figure 6.7.2a, a good sense of body weight is conveyed between two versions of the same simple 3D character (a biped skeleton). Time and space are used well to capture the varying rate of movement (or travel) of the more solid character as it impacts the platform below it, compared with the lighter feeling character that is transported by a lifting force. If one were to animate a character that can fly or jump about, the concept of lift can also help "sell" the animation.

FIGURE 6.7.1   *Squash and stretch technique applied to a character. Courtesy of George Henion. © George T. Henion. Reprinted with permission.*

Since game characters usually do not exist in an empty world devoid of objects, interaction with furniture, doors, and weapons, for example, can be expected. Figure 6.7.2b demonstrates *anticipation*, in the subtle stepping movement as he prepares to lift a heavy object.

Think of what should be present in the motion to help make the animation believable. It isn't enough to just satisfy the requirement by having the motion complete. Think of other things about the character that should be conveyed within the

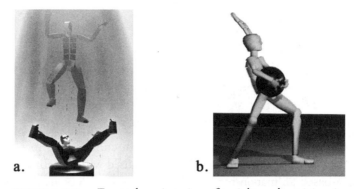

FIGURE 6.7.2 *Example animation of weight and anticipation. See the file* *heavyobject.mov on the companion CD-ROM. Courtesy of Martin Bartsch.*

ON THE CD

motion as it interacts with things. Is the character heavy or small? Is the character strong or perhaps frail? Are they wearing special gear that enhances or hinders their movement? Are they traversing across a terrain that is smooth, bumpy, or slippery? Are they injured and favoring a particular side of their body?

Another technique called *overlapping action* is often used by traditional animators for adding life to an otherwise bland design of a simple character. This technique can make a very ordinary and dull move more interesting by breaking the action into different parts. For example, the drawing in Figure 6.7.3 shows the yo-yo in a hand moving forward first, with the fingers of the hand dragging behind for a bit, and then *follows through* after the hand releases the yo-yo.

FIGURE 6.7.3 *Overlapping action. Courtesy of George Henion. © George T. Henion. Reprinted with permission.*

In a realistic oil portrait, attention to even the smallest detail is often present. In the case of motion, more detail can be captured by studying the subtle nuances in a move that are less apparent at a casual glance. Capturing the subtleties in an animation brings more life and personality to a character. Animation that appears dynamic, natural, and conveys weight and realistic movement often has what animators call *secondary action.* This is the movement of smaller parts or details of a character; for example, things like hair, clothing accessories, cloth, and a tail that continue to move and linger after the primary motion has stopped. For example, a woman wearing long dangling earrings turns quickly to her left. Even though her head, face, and short hair stops moving at the end of the head turn, the hanging earrings continue to swing beyond the turn of the head and move to and fro like a pendulum, just a bit longer in time. See the *secondary_action.avi* animation on the companion CD-ROM for a similar example.

To separate oneself from the mediocre or average character animation talent, an animator should take the time to learn the fundamentals of animation and borrow from them for his own work. A career 3D animator develops ways of incorporating proven traditional techniques within a 3D system, with the basic difference from 2D animation being that it operates by manipulating volume through genuine three-dimensional movements. The animator manages to capture in 3D what its long-standing 2D predecessor has already established to give the illusion of movement to much simpler flat shaded shapes common to cartoons. In addition, having learned how to use the tools available in a 3D software package for animation, an animator should develop his own approaches to animating that are less technical and more artistic. In general terms, this produces a less mechanical feel in favor of a more natural and fluid motion. Experimenting with tutorials found both online and within CG books and manuals will expose an animator to other methods that may be faster and more affective. An animator should try to not rely on software and features that claim to "auto animate." A seasoned animator or studio art director looking to hire an animator will see right through this approach.

Production Workflow of Character Animation

The development process for a good majority of real-time games requires the same basic steps. From initial concept to exporting into a game engine, the pipeline for creating these virtual actors follows the same paradigm. With a character mesh in hand, you must first attach the mesh to a structure that will enable the character artist or animator to deform the mesh into various poses. These poses are *keyframed* at different intervals through time, and recorded for playback within the real-time 3D game. The multiple frames that transition or blend the motion between the key poses, referred to by animators as *in-betweens*, are automatically generated by the computer. The established order and rate in which the hand-keyed motions are played is handled programmatically from within the game. In anticipation of "player control" of a game character, the animations are designed with the in-game transitions in mind. The exercise at the end of this chapter will help clarify many of the typical issues that an animator must address to prepare animation for a game engine. Following are the steps one takes in preparation of animation. This is often followed by an export process for getting the motion from the authoring 3D software to a file format that the game build process understands and supports. It is now ready for testing at run-time within the game engine.

To help demonstrate important production steps, we'll review a typical animation setup and workflow. The mention of software tools or features specific to any one of the 3D packages will be omitted intentionally to avoid confusing anyone not acquainted with product-centric features and terminology. The example model reviewed was for an actual RPG-style game created and published by WildTangent in 2004.

Planning Your Work

As with anything initially designed on a blank sheet of paper, animating objects for video games can begin an abstract thing with many possible directions. One can make certain basic assumptions, of course, about the motion for a game. For example, an animation can be designed to serve the purpose of giving a fox character or a floating puffy cloud personality, or to make an otherwise inanimate object more interesting. Before creating a single animation key, however, someone has to give thought to what the look, feel, and timing of this built-to-move piece will be. This creative vision may have originally been described in written form by a game designer, or illustrated visually in a storyboard, or at least implied in a model sheet. With even a model sheet in hand, besides being a series of sketches of your character design presented from several angles, an animator may glean some direction to begin constructing an animation. A well-detailed model sheet may explicitly show how a character stands, if it slouches, how it expresses certain feelings or attitude, is very uptight, or self-righteous. Perhaps the character appears to roll off knuckles when walking, drag its knuckles on the ground, or walk on its toes. A profile shot will show something about the proportions and posture of a character that the front view drawing may not. It can convey the size of a character relative to other characters or objects so that you can try to capture something in the motion to help support this important difference. The more specific a model sheet is, the less likely an animator will have problems when he gets to the animation. This may sound obvious, but there can be designs that have extraneous parts in the character, making them difficult or impossible to animate well. This in turn can make the work harder and less enjoyable. This can also mean that the result is often bland or boring. Planning ahead can prevent unnecessarily hard work and poor-quality animation.

In building a motion sequence, much like constructing a fence from a dimensioned and detailed blueprint, or rehearsing a dance choreography number, motion needs a way to visually communicate details of the design so that it can be carried out by the animator. For character animation, this previsualization of a performance is best done by physically acting out the move. Animation is a performance art, much like dancing, acting, or a martial arts kata. Before a dancer can perform a physically difficult solo dance routine, she must be well trained in the art of dance. She will need to know how to balance her weight, move through space, perform a high vertical jump, and land with great ease. A mime actor standing before an audience will know how to gesture with his body to convey emotion. Likewise, an animator needs to know how to convey the desired expression or mood before he can get a CG character to do the same. Good training for emoting and creating the right poses that read well may come from taking acting classes, studying actors or animals in film, watching skilled athletes perform highly trained maneuvers, or watching video-taped street performers mime. For example, the Web site *www.bbcmotiongallery.com* is a free library of motion imagery that has an extensive collection of domestic and wild animal videos one can download for free. Standing in front of a mirror, with no one watching, of course, is an excellent first stab at visualizing a move. Whatever the source of inspiration, animators should invest time in understanding the expected performance before they can re-create it.

As with any other visual art form, the more preproduction planning for animation before beginning the work, the easier the job is with fewer revisions later. Additionally, like building a stage set for a movie where the more one knows up front about what the camera sees during a shoot and from what angles, the better a decision can be made about where to spend valuable time during the construction phase. If the camera will pan back and forth from the left to the right in a computer or video game, and the characters or "actor" will also move from left to right, there will be less reason to be concerned for how the character's weight shifts to its own left and right side, thus saving the animator some production time. In contrast, a 3D game that allows for greater camera control enables seeing the character from all possible angles. Careful planning can again result in creating better animation that reads well without blowing the production budget.

Finally, an animator will also need to know what approach to take given the rig's design and capabilities, and which software features he should use before diving in to create the motion. He'll also need to give thought to whether he should build the motion sequence in a linear fashion as in *straight-ahead* animation, which is the process of designing each keyframe in order from first to last. Because the entire process is kept very creative and spontaneous, this usually produces action that has a fresh and slightly comical look. An alternate approach may be to establish *extreme* or *key poses* at the beginning and the end first. This is followed by "tweening" the character, or creating and sliding additional key poses between the extremes, to vary the timing and spacing and to progressively fill in more detail. The animator will also need to know if motions are cyclic in nature and if they are to seamlessly transition into other moves listed on the *move list*.

Modeling and Texture Mapping

For the modeling of low-polygon models that have to move and bend, here are several things a character artist should consider:

- Avoid having geometry edges or missing polygons that may show when the model moves. For example, a robed character with no geometry underneath may have to be animated to fall down, thus exposing the bottom area of the robe.
- When placing geometry near body joints, the modeler or *rigger* should make certain that the pivot points are well placed. Have enough subdivided geometry around them so that the mesh can bend nicely without flattening or collapsing the volume of the mesh. If needed, the animator may need to move vertices around or add more edges, as in Figure 6.7.4.

- To reduce the appearance of surface stretching, the modeler should try to avoid having too much detail granularity in the texture map around areas that will experience a considerable amount of stretch when animating.
- It is common to have to go back and refine areas of a texture that are mapped to parts that seemed unimportant or were hidden from view when the model was originally created.
- The more complicated the design of a character is, the more difficult and time consuming it will be to prepare for animation or animate. Beginners to animation may have to simplify their character designs and make sacrifices to keep the character simple enough to control and animate well.

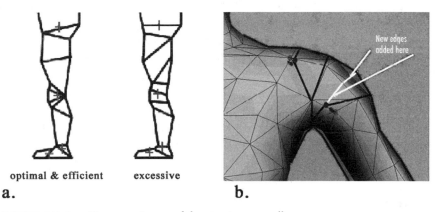

FIGURE 6.7.4 *Constructing models to animate well.*

In creating animation for real-time characters, an animator will need a way to deform the mesh so that it takes on expressive key poses. A commonly used method for manipulating the "only skin deep" surface uses a skeletal structure that can simulate the way living things are able to move in the real world. A skeleton or *rig* comprised of *bones* gives the animator a means to deform geometry in a more intuitive and predictable way. The use of a skeleton is much like outfitting a puppet with an armature rig made up of flexible wire or a rod-and-joint construction arranged in a hierarchical relationship. As with a puppet, this virtual rig is then inserted into the mesh object and moved to change its shape.

Creating a Skeletal Rig

An animator in the games industry will most likely be responsible for rigging the 3D characters. *Rigging* is the process of attaching or binding a mesh object to other *control objects* (such as a *skeleton*). These control objects will be used to deform or move the mesh. An animated skeleton is the underlying structure that drives the movement of characters created as either a single mesh object or as a segmented model.

Skeletal rigs can be custom made to fit any form, shape, or sized character. They can be constructed of any combination of parametrically created bone objects, helper objects, and mesh objects. The appearance of a bone can also vary considerably in appearance among different 3D packages or even within the same package. Whichever is used, they simply provide a visual aid to help the animator more intuitively control and manipulate his character. A bone can be a simple shape, such as a long narrow box, or an elongated diamond shape. In contrast, a bone can be a custom shaped mesh object that is designed to look like the human or animal bone it represents, like a hipbone, spine bone, or skull. Sometimes, a bone object can have extra fins or special handles extending from them to help the animator select the bone from within the character body mesh.

In the example shown in Figure 6.7.5a, the skeleton is made up of bones joined together, in a configuration that more closely resembles a human. This set of bones came prepackaged as a set from within a specific 3D package, and was then adjusted to a size and proportion suitable for the character's mesh. Figure 6.7.5b illustrates another human rig made up entirely of segmented mesh objects. For clarity, the segments in this image were intentionally separated with even more space between the various body parts. Again, they are linked together in a parent-child relationship with the hips at the top of the hierarchy. Lastly, a combination of both simple mesh objects and bones are used for the human rig in Figure 6.7.5c.

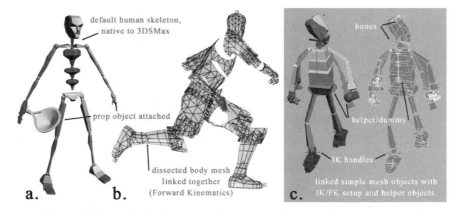

FIGURE 6.7.5 *Skeleton rig design can take on many forms with varying control. (Rig c. is courtesy of Nick Kondo).*

For the best animation possible, most character animators feel it is important to have good control over the rig. There are many devices available with each 3D program that offer control of linked bones. For optimal results, controls need to feel comfortable, respond quickly and predictably, and be easy to use. With complex characters, there can be as many as 100 controls for an entire body. These can be facial-animation target shapes (Figure 6.7.12a), controls for bone rotation and scale XYZ values, IK goal position XYZ values, and constraints. It's good practice to simplify controls whenever possible. Having to wrestle with a rig can hinder the creative process and often forces a frustrated animator to accept poor results.

There are trade-offs to having ideal controls. The more control for manipulating a complex rig, the more experimentation the animator will need to create full body expressions, with balancing and shifting of body parts that transition well between poses. A poorly designed rig that doesn't offer good control of large areas can mean it will take more work and time to establish the various poses, with more parts to move overall. Better gross control enables the animator to be more flexible and means that he doesn't have to commit to anything right away, making large area changes quickly. On the other hand, a highly specialized rig is often less interchangeable and harder to repurpose for use with other character types. To save the animator time and many steps, the individual responsible for constructing the rig should understand what the animator will need. Arguably, finding the right balance between complexity and control is a subjective call an animator should be allowed to make. This may take more time upfront to set up, but it can be well worth it in the long run.

The proper placement of each bone is also an important factor to good animation. A well-proportioned and detailed model will clearly convey the positioning of the body's underlying structure (see Figure 6.7.6). When placing bones, the animator should take care to understand the mesh topology and give thought to where deformation of the mesh will take place. It helps to see through the mesh object of the character's body, as in Figure 6.7.7, so that while placing bones, one can determine the proper centering of each joint. Using as few bones as possible is also a good practice because that would require less processing in-game for supporting and maintaining that character. A good rule of thumb when determining how many bones to use is to assume that the smaller the character is on screen, relative to other characters, the fewer bones will be needed to clearly articulate the entire body, since the more subtle nuances may not be noticed. In contrast, the more important the character and the larger it is displayed on screen, the more complex the rig can be with more effort needed to animate the subtle nuances for added realism.

Depending on the game's need for more subtle details, the hand is an example of a body part that may or may not require multiple bones. For any mesh object to have smaller independently moving parts (like a hand's three fingers and a thumb with two or more joints each), the skeletal structure within the hand must have enough bones to control each digit separately. The complexity for building the rig, as well as animating it, has just increased considerably. The so-called joint is the bone's pivot point at the end of each bone length and is where they rotate, along one or more axes (Figure 6.7.7b). Understanding the anatomy of a character is critical in determining where to put the start and end points of each bone. When a bone at the top of a chain is rotated about its joint or pivot point, all attached bones, or children bones, are also affected.

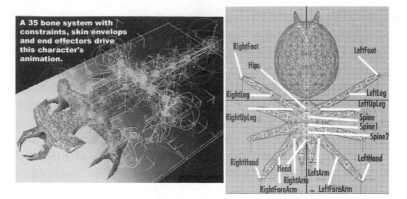

FIGURE 6.7.6   *Label all parts to avoid confusion.*

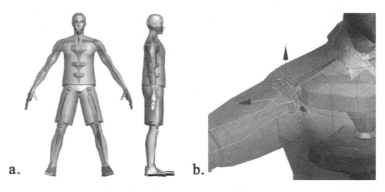

FIGURE 6.7.7   *A bind or figure pose, with a transparent mesh for evaluating placement of joints.*

Several rigs can be built to serve different purposes during the production of multiple animations for a single character. Differently configured rigs will provide more specialized controls for specific parts of the character's body. For example, for outfitting a character that walks and talks, a facial animation rig will facilitate the development of facial expressions and speech animation, while a separate full-body rig can focus on providing better control over body limbs and spine. The facial rig may stem from the neckline on up to the head and have branching bones that reach out to provide control over the surface of the face, as in Figure 6.7.12b.

Several things to consider when designing a rig:

• The best place to start building a skeleton is usually the base of the spine or the hip (*root*).
• The distance between pivot points directly determines the length of each bone. Place the start and end of each bone at the center of the point of rotation.

- When building a skeleton, it is best to view the model in wireframe or transparent mode (Figure 6.7.7a), viewing the model from as many angles or windows as possible. This will ensure the best placement in the body relative to the bone's pivot point and the polygon edges.
- A bone may have to pass through the outside of the mesh between joints to get proper placement of the joint. This is acceptable and doesn't introduce a problem.
- For real-time game development, it may be important to keep the bone count as low as possible. Check with a programmer about performance specifications.
- Proper naming of bones and other parts of a rig will help organize the setup. This also simplifies the process of selecting them when looking for them in a program's track view or schematic diagram.
- Use interactive controls when possible to help speed up the animation process. Setting them up can be quite involved. Getting everything to move naturally using controls will require reading the software manual and practicing with the various constraint options. An animator should take the time to do this before venturing into making an appropriate animation rig.
- Helper objects, dummies, or end bones are needed at the end of every extremity to terminate a chain. This ensures that a continuous link between bones during binding will reach the last child in the chain.

Vertex Weighting—Binding the Mesh to the Skeleton

The mesh will need to be attached to the skeleton using a method for binding it to all of the assigned bones. On a vertex level, one or more animated bones will control the amount of movement of each vertex point relative to each other. This process of assigning and adjusting the amount of influence each bone has for every vertex is called *vertex weighting*. The adjustment of vertex weight values is important to maintaining good form and volume of the mesh as it is being deformed by the moving bones. Properly weighted vertices will make the model's form look great during most, if not all, frames of animation, and not just at the pose that was used during the initial binding. To this end, every vertex point in a low-polygon model should be evaluated during the playback of every animation to see the full effect of each bone's influence during all animation sequences. The process of refining vertex weighting can and should be revisited often during the animation process. It is usually the more extreme sequences that stress the mesh to a point that reveals the less than ideal weight values in problem areas, such as the shoulders.

To speed up the process of vertex weighting, the rigger can use what are referred to as *envelopes* to assign a group of vertices to each bone. As shown in Figure 6.7.8, each bone that the mesh is bound to has its own adjustable three-dimensional envelope to control the amount of influence over vertices that it encompasses. There is an inside envelope, with a falloff to an outside envelope. The controls for adjusting the size and effect of the falloff are similar to those used to adjust the falloff of a spot light. Although finer and more precise adjustments of weight values can be addressed on a vertex level, the process of doing so is much more tedious and time consuming. For a faster workflow, using envelopes is a good place to start for defining the area of influence each bone has over often hundreds of vertices. Although finer control for each vertex is available, envelopes, as a first pass, should cover about 90 percent of the work with little fuss. After creating new animations or loading existing motions, the rigger can further test the vertex weighting. The dialing in of more optimal values for any questionable vertex point can begin. For a more intuitive and artist-friendly approach to adjusting the weight values, some programs even support "3D painting" of each bone's influence using a 3D paintbrush. The amount of influence can also be represented to the user in color for visual clarity.

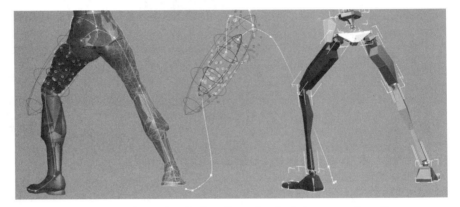

FIGURE 6.7.8   *A look "under the hood" at the thigh bone envelope for vertex weighting.*

Animation—Hand Keyframe

This is last step in the production workflow process for character animation. Learning how to animate any 3D object is to truly teach oneself by trial and error. Although the concepts and practices are simple to comprehend, the process of controlling and predicting the results of animation can seem daunting at first. The only way to overcome this is to work through various tutorials that walk a student through the process of animating something similar. Doing so is like following a recipe step by step in a cook book. Every major 3D program comes chock full of "How-to" tutorials and examples. They are written with the intention of revealing important tools and workflow issues specific to the task of animating an object or character in their 3D package.

This chapter does not provide a tutorial on how to animate. Instead, it is an overview of concepts, important terms, and common approaches all animators should know to build from. Workflow recommendations and tips are offered to help the new animator troubleshoot common problems when creating a character animation.

A common approach for creating motion for game characters and other environmental 3D objects is hand-keyed animation. This means the animator created the animation manually using keyframes, without the aid of any other existing motion data or animation plug-in. A trade term that is specific to creating keyed motion for characters is *pose-to-pose* animation. To better understand this approach, look at the opening art for Part 6 of this book as a visual reference. The multiple images of the running Jack Russell terrier resemble stop-motion animation. As in clay or flipbook animation, the incremental changes to objects or drawings together create movement or "life"—the key concept of animation. Traditionally, a movie film camera was started and stopped, one frame at a time. While the camera was stopped, an animator would adjust the figure or object to the next pose. The camera would film another frame—this would continue until all the animation was filmed. Playing the film at a predetermined frame rate creates the illusion of motion.

In the pose-to-pose approach to animating a character, the skeleton of the model is rotated and positioned into a key (or "extreme") pose, and then another, along a timeline. Each figure pose is keyed, or held in place using keys, for every bone on that frame. For example, Figure 6.7.9a shows several keyframes along a 70-frame animation. The time span between the poses is not important at first. Just capturing the action in a sequence of static poses is the initially creative focus of this approach. Once this is done, the animator can play back the animation in real time and review the timing between keys as the computer fills in the movement for all the frames between. When compared to manually drawn hand animation of each in-between frame, this is where the beauty and power of today's computer technology saves animators lots of time and money.

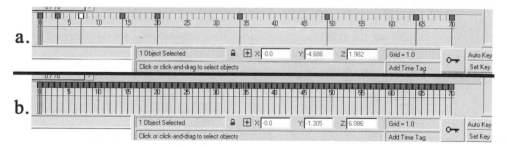

FIGURE 6.7.9   *(a) Key frames on a 70-frame timeline resulting from hand animation versus (b) motion capture data.*

Kinematics, the study of motion in its most basic form, plays a role in how an animator will manipulate a rig and how the hierarchical linking of bones from parent to children will be set up to form a system. Kinematics systems come in two varieties, *forward kinematics* (FK) and *inverse kinematics* (IK). When using FK, the order of the bones is important. The best place to start animating is with the root of the skeleton. FK, more commonly known as *keyframe animation*, is the most accurate way to animate and requires the least amount of time to set up. This makes it popular among new animators. However, it isn't necessarily the fastest way nor does it produce the most fluid results. The animator is essentially hand positioning each bone, in order from the root forward through the chain, in the exact position desired. Working with an FK system is like animating a jointed wooden stick figure or a hinge joint G.I. Joe® action figure or Barbie® doll. The pose-to-pose approach works best with this setup. Since the root bone is the parent of all other bones, its position and movement should be established before working on any other bone that the parent will affect. Later, the animator can create the movement of other bones from the root toward the head, hands, and feet. Should the animator work on the feet first, adjusting for how they touch the floor plane, they will undoubtedly be affected by any changes made to the root later on and will throw off the position for bones that are children of the root. Another disadvantage of this system is the constant time-consuming rekeyframing of all the bones in the chain.

A less time-consuming and easy-to-use kinematics system is IK. This is a goal-driven animation system that operates based on manipulating a single "goal object" to position an entire chain or object hierarchy. It is the opposite of FK. Instead of defining movement by moving and orienting the bones from the root out to the extremities, the opposite approach is taken. For example, the hand is placed in a pose, and the animation program will attempt to figure out how the other bones and joints should move or rotate to reach that pose. IK can produce more fluid movement, but can be harder to control with less accuracy.

A rig that is set up for IK takes much more time to configure and test. The significant savings in time during animation more than makes up for the extra steps involved in setting up an IK system. Because the movement resulting from IK more closely resembles the real world, experienced animators will use it often and in combination with FK for better results. Learning when to use IK over FK in the same rig is very much a creative process that requires a good understanding of the movement. Movement that is goal-driven works well with IK, while movement driven by an "internal force" works well with FK. Each system is unique and can be used to the animator's benefit if understood well.

Built-in features can help speed up the animation process considerably. In the straight-ahead animation approach mentioned previously, the use of *set key* mode via a user interface button or hot key is a good example of a valuable time saver. Starting with the first frame, adjust the character to assume the first position of the animation. Press a key to invoke this feature, and all bones are instantly keyed at that frame. Then, moving forward in time, various bones are rotated and translated to create the second pose. Set keys again. It is important to establish the main broad strokes first with the core central parts of the body, since they are the bones in the hierarchy that will inevitably affect all other bones in the chain. Later, once the broad strokes of the animation are in place, overlapping action can be added by animating the movement of things like hair or a long beard, staggering the keys after the rotation and positioning of the head is done. Sometimes, simply offsetting a single key can add much personality to an otherwise stiff-looking animation.

There are several things an animator should consider when creating animation for any kind of game character. Here are some helpful recommendations:

- Become familiar with the software's timeline and keyframe functions. These are the basis of animating all objects well in a 3D program.
- Practice with a single simple character first before working on more complex scenes and character setup. The software CD that comes with each 3D program may contain some models for this purpose. The Internet is also a good source for models.
- The start and end frames of a looping motion must often be the same for game characters. A copy and paste function may be available to the animator within his program of choice. For a perfectly seamless blend, it is best to view what the *function curve* looks like going in and out of the keys at both the beginning and the end of a sequence. As shown in Figure 6.7.10, look for the function curve editor in your program. Learn to use the controls to edit function curves. Familiarity with this editor will quickly advance a novice animator's control for adjusting keys and refining animation.
- With high-frequency motions that play back too fast in real time to evaluate properly, adjust the playback setting in the program so that it plays the sequence in slow motion. This will allow the animator to study the motion path of each bone for smoothness. Varying the playback speed also provides a better idea of what the final timing of the motion should be before actually adjusting the keys to affect the timing of the motion.
- Some programs will allow saving and loading of animation clips, even for use on different characters. You can later load this clip to replace or be added to the end of an existing animation clip. This file type is used only for merging and loading animations and can't be opened as a scene file. When copying and pasting keys, it is a good idea to see what is happening in graph form in a motion track that shows the function curves for the animated bones.
- In the pose-to-pose method, the motion generated between key poses may look mechanical or choppy. To smooth out the motion, the animator can add additional keys where needed. A good way to visualize the path of travel by each bone is to turn on *trajectory* in your 3D application. Figure 6.7.11 has the trajectory of the neck bones for the example Dragon model provided on the companion CD-ROM.
- For a more fluid and natural-looking animation, avoid having bones travel in a straight line. Prefer elliptical motion paths, as revealed using the trajectory path visual aid, as in Figure 6.7.11b.
- Avoid hyperextending joints.
- Avoid having sliding feet if possible. Explore any features the software may provide to lock down and release the feet and hands at each frame.

ON THE CD

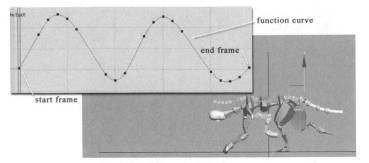

FIGURE 6.7.10   *A function curve is another vital aid to troubleshooting and editing keys. Here, the motion is expressed as a function curve on a graph.*

FIGURE 6.7.11   *Displaying a bone's trajectory shows the motion pattern as well as problems in the motion path. The left image reveals a pronounced stutter in the motion of the neck.*

Not all programs are alike when giving thought to important time-saving features. When making the selection of which production software to use for character work and animation, there are certain standard approaches and common expectations among professional game animators. For example, having the ability to easily remap motion data from one skeleton to another of the same or different bone count, as well as having a different configuration or naming convention. The support for repurposed content can save a team much valuable time and money. Saving the bind pose and other key poses separately for later use is another important feature. Animating with both IK and FK interchangeably offers more freedom of control during animation. Having a built-in parametrically configurable prenamed skeleton that can take on any shape or size is a bonus. Tools to lock feet down to the ground plane, attach hands to props and goal objects, is another huge benefit and time saver. Other devices for dynamically adjusting motion and animation controls, such as setting up joint constraints, prop linking, mirroring of motion, changing of orientation, and copy/ paste of poses are all attractive features to a tech-savvy producer art lead or production artist. When adjusting the timing of an animation, having access to function curves within a track view window is a must for finer control of all keys.

Facial Animation

Facial animation for in-game characters is another area of work that would fall within the responsibility of the animator. Although less common than body motion, the use of facial animation for expressing emotions and speech with audio dialogue is quickly becoming a vital component to passive story telling cut-scenes of newly released game titles. Facial animation is meticulous work that requires much attention to detail and a lot of time to set up and complete. Even so, highly ambitious PC and console games are going the extra mile to develop the best-looking and ever-engaging close-ups of their star characters.

Before an animator can jump in and start to set up a character for animating facial features and expressions, he must first have a clear grasp of how muscle movement can affect facial tissue. The animator will be able to simulate the appearance of a desired expression if he knows how muscles move over bone and each other, what their range of motion is, and how each affects the soft fatty tissue and skin attached to it. The animator can set up his underlying structure more accurately having a full understanding of the 11 major facial muscles that control facial expressions. For example: in a yawn, the jaw opens very wide by rotating downward from the rest of the head, and the facial muscles around the mouth would bring the corners of the mouth closer together (neither up nor down), with eyes made to squint or close and eyebrows drawn in. In keyframing such a pose, a good structure will allow the animator to focus on moving the areas of the face that are essential to making this expression read. Valuable time for experimenting would not be sacrificed by forcing the animator to wrestle with a less than ideal structure.

Setting up a face model for animation can be accomplished using one of two common methods. Both methods have their limitations and technical drawbacks, in conveying a wide range of facial expressions commonly needed to make a base face mesh appear to emote feelings. Sometimes, an animator can work around limitations and even use them as part of the design.

The first method is referred to as *morphing*, because a base mesh of a face or head changes shape by blending between other states or *target* shapes of the same model. The animator must create a library of key poses or facial expression targets to animate. Each target mesh is like a frozen version of an extreme state of every expression, or *phoneme* for lip-syncing. The set of targets are used by the game engine to deform the base mesh. In a predetermined order, it re-creates the detailed facial expression or appearance of speech in real time, sometimes, in combination with an audio file of spoken words, or human sounds. One of the technical drawbacks to creating the multiple target meshes is that the number and order of vertices must be carefully maintained throughout the various target versions in order to work.

The second method resembles the same workflow for setting up a full-body rig. The animator would first create a skeletal structure designed to deform the surface of the face that would enable him to simulate the underlying muscles of human facial features. Figure 6.7.12b, along with the example animation *secondary_action.avi* on the companion CD-ROM, shows how facial gestures and mouth movement have been created with keyed bones. For a potentially wide range of expressions, a high number of bones may be required. Limiting the number of bones that have to be rotated, as well as the points of the face that they control, is one way to help simplify this daunting task.

Using a rig, in order for specific parts of a face, such as the brow, to move independently from other parts of the mesh, the vertex points will need to be controlled with a single moving bone or a group of bones. This mesh deformation technique will move individual or groups of vertex points associated with facial features. To get the face to express a smirk, puzzled, or surprised look, the brow part of the face mesh can be moved to create such an expression. For example, in moving these subparts, the bones controlling the vertex points above the eye will have to be manipulated and keyed. For real-time game animation, the animation system used to deform the mesh in-game understands the additional bones that are different or in addition to the body rig, as in Figure 6.7.12b.

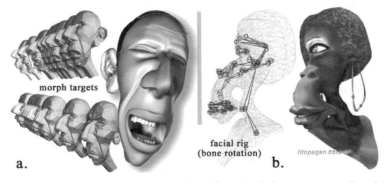

FIGURE 6.7.12   *Two commonly used methods for animating facial features and expressions. The models in the left image are courtesy of Nick Kondo, an animation created by Martin Bartsch.*

Other Important Considerations for Facial Animation

- The relationship between the inner structure (meaning how it's rigged) and the outer surface is a key component in facial animation with bones.

- When facial animation is used in a game, the character usually ends up being a big part of what audiences see on the screen, because the dialog lines that we hear are coming out of the character's mouth, and also because there is a wide range of nonverbal communication that can be achieved with facial expressions.
- When blocking out animations, it is useful to start by first animating the eyes, because audiences usually look at the eyes first. You can use a single null point to control the point of interest and direction in which the eyes look.
- It is also important to keep different timing for each of the different major components of a face, like the eyebrows, lips, and nose, blinking of eyelids, and the tongue. This often results in more engaging gestures and overlapping secondary motion. In addition, animating things like the jiggle of loose skin separately, for example, is a good way to convey secondary motion and a sense of mass.
- When syncing the lips to the dialogue, it's best to focus on animating the important intonations, which usually gives you better results than over-animating or exaggerating the lip positions. The open and closed mouth positions are the most important shapes because they are the extremes that show emotion.
- Facial animation is usually applied to the character after the body's primary motion has been blocked in.

Motion Capture

Another common way to provide character motion for a game is to use motion capture data, or *mocap*. In contrast to the hand animation approach, mocap is movement that was performed by a live actor and captured by a computerized system that records the performer's every twitch, sway, and bounce, all in real time. This motion data is then mapped onto a virtual actor, designed to carry out the same performance. A video clip from a motion capture session been provided on the companion CD-ROM, entitled *mocapmotion.avi*. This approach to animation is often a quick and precise way of getting realistic motion onto a noncartoon game character. Keep in mind that the expression of the motion is only as good as the performer's ability to carry out the desired motion, as instructed by the creative director. Therefore, a lot of preplanning and good direction is important to avoid buying costly motion data files that may require a lot of rework by a development team animator, or may even be cut from the project.

ON THE CD

In only a few days, mocap animation can be recorded and prepared for immediate use in a game engine. In contrast, it can take one or more animators weeks or months to hand animate a large amount of character motions. The cost of capturing such data may seem expensive initially to a cost-conscious project manager or producer developing a low-budget game. However, the long-term savings becomes apparent when comparing the cost of creating detailed and realistic moves that usually takes hours and hours apiece to hand animate. The trade-off in time saved by going this route can often offset the cost and preparation time. In addition, if the project calls for animation that must represent characteristic movements of real people or signature moves of celebrities, as in sports, mocap may be the only viable option.

Appropriate Use and Availability

Of course, mocap shouldn't be used in a product just because one can. Certain game genres may not prefer such realistic motion and require a hand animation approach to enhance their product's style. For example, in a more cartoonlike game filled with fun, goofy, or playful characters, hand animating them will give the character capabilities that not even the most flexible or athletic human possesses. Yet other game genres inevitably need to have such motion capture services in-house to make it cost effective for them due to the volume of moves needed and control over trained talent. A sports-oriented game can have a wide range of specialized moves, requiring precision to make them believable to a sophisticated audience. A high-frequency dance performance that exhibits great styles and time-based rhythm would also be best carried out by properly trained dancers, and not one or more animators.

The majority of game companies in the United States do not own their own mocap studio. Consequently, many have to send an art lead, or an art director and talent to a mocap studio for one to three days to capture their custom moves. Different studios will have different systems and equipment for capturing the motion data. There are advantages and disadvantages to each system. Game development leads should shop around and research for the studio that will best serve their project's specific needs and budget.

There are several things to consider when preparing for a motion capture shoot. Here is a preshoot checklist for review, in no particular order:

1. Before a trip to the studio, prepare and submit a well-planned move or shot list with a naming convention and description that can be easily understood by the studio technicians. The studio usually likes to see this as early as possible to optimize their system for the upcoming moves. The move list is closely tied to the final price in that the more complicated the motion is to capture, more time may be needed to both successfully capture and clean up the moves in postproduction before delivery to the client.

2. Use exceptional talent who can deliver the desired moves and take direction well. These individuals may charge more than the friend or cousin willing to do the work. Not paying the professional's price may cost more in the long run if the motions are inferior due to poor execution.

3. Have the talent bring comfortable shoes that are well broken in. The studio technicians may place markers on them that can potentially deface the shoes. Ask the studio about this beforehand.

4. Select a motion capture system and team that has experience troubleshooting problems.

5. Be well rested for the shoot and ready to make quick decisions and give direction.

6. Lunch needs to be thought about beforehand, so that valuable time is not lost during the day of the shoot. Make sure that the talent has lots of water nearby.

7. Have important props handy that the talent can interact with during a shoot. The proper weight and size can be important to an accurate performance.

8. For very physical moves and stunts, ask the studio to provide padding and/or landing mats. It's a good idea to have a stunt coordinator and/or paramedic on standby if the motions can cause bodily injury to the performer.

9. Before the capturing begins, be clear about instructions for the method and schedule of delivering approved motions. The person paying for the motion never leaves the studio with any captured data that is ready for use. Allow at least a couple of days before expecting the first batch of processed motion files.

FIGURE 6.7.13 *Having exceptional talent and choosing the right mocap system are key to producing optimal results.*

Simulation Animation

With today's 3D applications, another way to create realistic animation by a 3D artist or animator is to set up simulations that perform real-world effects, and then record the resulting animation of affected objects. These systems can create the effect of wind that blows particles around for creating smoke, fire, or waterfalls. An artist can set up a simulation with collision physics that can break a wall down into smaller parts by having a separate object thrown into it. Even cloth or moving hair can be simulated for real-time playback in a game. A falling person, a bouncing ball, or even a sliding car can be simulated using today's well-developed software and plug-ins that offer different systems for simulating physics. These may impose a bit of a learning curve to master the many subtle variations in their settings. Like motion capture, it is definitely worth the payoff in believability by producing complex and convincing results. Beside, this suspension of disbelief is what helps to sell an interactive 3D experience.

Summary

The scope of work that an industry artist or animator is expected to contribute on a project varies extensively. For character work and animation specifically, this chapter discussed the many facets of the production pipeline. It involves planning, modeling, texturing, rigging with vertex weighting, animating both body and face with keyframes, motion capture, or physics simulation. Animation is a tough job, make no bones about it. As the scope of design and the complexity of environments continue to increase for interactive games, the volume and variety of virtual inhabitants will also continue to increase. Learning the recommended workflow steps and approaches to setting up and animating this growing cast of digital actors will help secure more ongoing gratifying work for the art and animation staff. Newer tools of the trade will have to be learned and mastered to compete on all levels.

A seasoned animator's patience and devotion will continue to be challenged as he learns the use of professional tools and advanced methods for making both player avatars and nonplayer characters give grand performances. However, becoming comfortable with the software is still just a smaller part of the work requirement and knowledge base a successful animator must have. As a craft, there is still much to know artistically about animation for creating exceptional moves that compete well. Convincing and fluid animation is hard to create and requires an understanding of both the tools at hand and the performance arts. With enough time and determination, convincing motion can be achieved. Once the animator understands the principles for animating believable characters discussed here and with other sources, they can be applied to animating any other object.

Exercise

Hand-Animated Character Motions for a Real-Time Game

The following is a typical list of specifications common to first- and third-person games. It starts with a move list that can be used as a guide for creating a base set of character motion for an interactive PC or console game. A main character in a game can easily have requirements that exceed this number of moves. Other characters may start here, or have a few specialized moves that support their unique purpose in a game.

ON THE CD

A complete dragon model with textures has been provided on the companion CD-ROM in the file formats .dxf, .3ds, .max (version 6). A set of motions are also provided in the file *dragonMax6.max*. The motions can also be viewed in the provided movie file *dragon.mov*. With this set of example moves to guide the animator, he should try to create a set of his own. For the purpose of learning how to create a custom rig for this model, the files *dragon_mesh.3ds* and *dragon_mesh.dxf* have no keyframe data.

Technical Specifications

1. The artist responsible for rigging a character should know the desired scale of each particular character relative to each other beforehand, so that the overall height of the skeleton can be established before binding the mesh to it. The artist can use any available method for binding the mesh to the skeleton, but should try to create only rigid vertices in the process and avoid using or creating what are referred to as "deformable vertices."
2. Establish the correct orientation for all characters before animating. The game code will require this of all characters so that they face correctly in game.
3. All characters are to have a base set of moves, as in the following move list:
   a. A looping *walk* cycle in place
   b. A looping *run* cycle in place
   c. An *attack* the opponent cycle
   d. An *idle* or fidget cycle—to be used while standing in place and waiting
   e. A *die* sequence (not prolonged dying)
   f. A taunt cycle in place
      In addition to the preceding set of moves, different variations of attack, idle, and/or die may be required per character. See game specifications.
4. Animations can be constructed and maintained within a single scene file, or can be created in separate scene files. If separated into their own individual files for exporting, each animation will need to have a common base pose at frame 0 for each file. Animation keys can start at any frame afterwards.
5. Test the vertex weight values of all animations against all custom motions for the character before submitting. Motions maintained in separated files do not need to have the same final version of the character with the final vertex weight values. However, the file with the correct vertex weights must be identified for the export of the character mesh.
6. Create all animations with a playback setting of 30 frames per second.
7. All looping cyclic motions are to play back seamlessly, with no apparent hitching or slight pausing. Walk cycles are to have a consistent rate of travel in a straight direction without sliding of planted feet. Suggestion: create the walk or run with forward translation to ensure the proper planting of the feet, and then remove the forward motion keys of the root before submitting.
8. No motion sequence should have the character traverse the ground in any direction so that it moved too far off the original location.
9. All animations that imply interaction with another opponent assume that the opponent is immediately in front of the character.

10. If designing a motion that involves the use of a prop while "interacting" with an opponent—such as a sword weapon for melee combat, or a devise that carries the character such as a bicycle or baby carriage—make certain that you have an example prop to work with before creating the animation. This can be a placeholder prop that represents the final scale and volume of the worst-case object for the character (such as the longest sword). This will ensure the proper rotation of the arm and orientation of the weapon relative to the ground plane. With respect to a bike, for example, the correct vertical position from the ground plane can be established with the prop in place.

11. Because of the possible 360-degree viewing angle of all characters, make sure no body parts or props seemingly penetrate other body parts of the character. Likewise, avoid having the foot penetrate the ground plane.

References

[Fleming02] Fleming, Bill, *Animating Facial Features and Expressions*, Charles River Media, 1999.

[Pagan02] Pagan, Tito, "Rigging Beyond Bipeds," *Game Developer Magazine* (November 2001): pp. 23–34.

[Williams02] Williams, Richard, *The Animator's Survival Kit*, Faber and Faber Limited, 2001.

6.8 ■ Cinematography

Overview

In 1983, an interactive cartoon called *Dragon's Lair* hit the arcades, offering the first glimpse and inspiration for bringing the film experience to the world of video games. It is fitting that this early example borrowed a nonlinear technology from the film and video industry, the laser disc, and grafted a video game interface onto the front end to control the experience. It would be another decade before *Doom* would show up and gamers would see the first images that would hint at the potential for creating a cinematic experience in real time.

As computer graphics have come to dominate many aspects of movies, much of the supporting high-end computer technology for the film industry has trickled down and informed related technology in the computer games industry. This pollination from the film industry goes beyond technology to include cultural influences, and it is these cultural influences that have driven game developers to try to bring the cinematic experience to their craft.

Defining Cinematics for Games

At the beginning of the game design process, it is important to decide if and how cinematics will be used within the game. If the cinematics are not integrated into the design as part of gameplay (e.g., to move along the story), you should seriously consider eliminating them or at least relegating them to a small role outside of gameplay. Your design document should be as specific about the motivation for each cinematic or cut-scene as it is for each level or gameplay element. This will help the development of the game design, and help the team keep the scope of the project in check right from the start.

The Language of Cinema

Once you string images and action together in a cinematic sequence, you introduce an additional set of visual elements that if not constructed skillfully have the power to confuse the viewer and thus disrupt the flow of the gaming experience. Thankfully, for those tasked with creating cinematic sequences in games, the history of cinema brings with it a wealth of knowledge about the language and rules of making movies.

In 1895 when Auguste and Louis Lumiere previewed "Arrival of a Train at La Ciotat Station" (a film of a train coming into a train station toward the camera), history recorded that the audience jumped in fear of the train heading toward them on the screen. This first impression hinted at the emotional power of the new medium. It wasn't long before story entered the medium with Georges Melies' 1902 film, "Le Voyage dans la lune" (A Trip to the Moon). Melies' film even used special effects to complete the image of the fictional world, and he is considered a pioneer of special effects. However, the real breakthrough in cinema was to come shortly with the films of D.W. Griffith. It was Griffith who first expanded the language of film through the use of sophisticated editing techniques. The cinematic language that emerged from the silent era was fully dependent on the visual image. For the artist designing and building cut-scenes for games, the ability to deliver your message without a lot of dialogue will free up your resources and reduce or eliminate some of the biggest headaches in the production of cinematics.

Delivering Emotion

Film director Samuel Fuller once remarked that the motion picture industry isn't selling clothes or cars or wood, but rather it is selling "emotion." Fuller's comment points at the fundamental purpose of cinema, which translates equally to games as well. Even a simple win sequence, shown after successfully completing a level in a puzzle game, delivers an emotional narrative by reinforcing the accomplishment and heightening the excitement. Throughout this chapter, the art of creating cinematics for games will draw on the language of film, but there is a key difference between using the cinematic sequence within a game and the medium of the narrative film. In games, cinematic sequences are first and foremost elements of gameplay, and gameplay has its own set of rules wholly independent of the rules that govern the linear narrative of film.

Integrating Cinematics into Games

Understanding that the artistic purpose of the in-game cinematic is to guide or enhance the emotional state of the player lets you explore the specific roles that these sequences play in games. Almost every game has some kind of noninteractive cinematic sequence. These can range from the most basic flourish of fireworks, announcing your successful completion of a level in a puzzle game, to the elaborate dramatic interludes found in games like *Doom 3* where the cinematics are fully integrated into the gaming experience.

Offering a Reward: The Original Cut-Scene

The most basic type of cinematic is the classic win sequence. This may not even be a flashy graphic, for it can be as simple as the remaining pieces of a puzzle game dancing off the bottom of the screen followed by the next level configuring itself before your eyes. Obviously, the simple puzzle game example doesn't require much extra art or effort. Often, these sequences can be handled programmatically or with simple scripting by a level builder. For the most part, these sequences use the game engine to display in-game assets in a sequence created specifically as a climatic "exclamation point" at the end of a section of gameplay.

However, these types of sequences can be much more elaborate. For example, if there is a character associated with the player, you may want to show that character expressing satisfaction. Segments between levels might show new powers acquired or new dangers that lay ahead. The flipside of the win segment is the lose animation. These lose animations could show a simple "try again" message, or be more elaborate illustrations of lost powers or the consequences of failure.

Pacing

Pacing is a very important role for cut-scenes. For example, you can use the cut-scene to prepare the player for faster paced gameplay by signaling that a dangerous situation has erupted just ahead. Conversely, cut-scenes can give the players a breather between levels while they get ready for their next assault. Simple puzzle game cut-scenes, previously mentioned as a reward, are also used to allow the players to gather their focus and energy for the next challenge. Every gamer appreciates a moment to give his or her thumb and index finger a break.

Advancing the Plot: Intros, Finales, and Back Story

Since the early indulgent days of four-minute intro sequences, game designers have become more skillful at paring down the intro and cut-scenes into digestible segments that don't interfere too much with gameplay. If there is one place where cinematics can bog down a game, it is when they are used to create a back story or drive a plot in the game. Used effectively for this purpose, they have the potential to give your game world a boost of credibility, but these types of cinematics can be expensive and time consuming to produce. More importantly, they put gamers into a passive role with which they might become impatient. Unlike going to the movies where the viewer chooses to engage in a passive role, a person who picks up a game is choosing to play interactively. There are no hard rules about how extensive these sequences can be before they begin to work against the game, but it is best to generally err on the shorter side. Moreover, if you have a flexible design, you can make adjustments if early focus testing reveals game flow problems.

Hints, Clues, and Instruction

Cinematic sequences are a great way to teach the player important or subtle gameplay elements. As with all cinematics, it is important that they flow well with the gameplay. Therefore, it is a good idea to plan your hints with the pacing of the game in mind, by setting a mood or by advancing the plot. Using this technique, it is critical that important information is not buried in the middle of a long sequence of fluff. Many gamers get frustrated at long or frequent cinematic sequences, so plan cut-scenes with the gameplay pace in mind.

Technical Considerations

Once the role and scope of any cinematic sequences have been clearly defined, the cinematic designer must then determine how the game integration will be accomplished. There are several key technical issues to consider before working any further on the design of cut-scenes.

Prerendered versus In-Game

The most important logistical issue is how the cut-scene sequences will be executed. Every aspect of cinematic production, from the script to the final packaging of the product, will be affected by the fundamental decision of whether you will create these sequences to run independently of the game engine, or create them as runtime sequences to be rendered "on the fly" by the game engine.

Prerendering Cinematics

In the early 1990s, when the first relatively inexpensive 3D animation software came out, 3D game engines were far more primitive than what could be shown in a prerendered animation file. Even today, with a complete suite of the latest 3D animation and postproduction tools, the prerendered approach still has an edge, but the gap is closing rapidly. Great strides have been made with the latest generation of graphics cards and 3D game engines. The visual justifications for prerendered cinematics are rapidly disappearing.

However, other advantages to the prerendered approach aren't directly related to the final look. With prerendered graphics, cinematic production can begin immediately, which offers more flexibility in the scheduling and may help insure that the cinematics do not jeopardize critical milestones close to the end of the project. Additionally, some types of games, like the top-down three-quarter view games or side scrolling games, don't lend themselves well to in-game cinematics. While these games may use 3D art in generating the final game assets, the art is generally not set up to be seen up close. It may be possible to use some of the 3D elements created for these games, but in all likelihood, these objects will need some additional detail work to be used in a pre-rendered cinematic sequence.

Unfortunately, prerendered cinematics come with their own set of drawbacks. It is very common that the assets used for these cinematics will need to be created specifically for this purpose. It may be possible to share some of the models and animations with the game engine, in order to cut down on the workload, but expect to have a team creating unique assets for these productions. Another drawback is the access time when playing cinematics off a disc-based media or hard drive. For this reason, it is common to put the more involved cinematics at the transitions between levels where drive access is already occurring, and thus the pause will be less disruptive to gameplay.

Mechinima

Using a game engine to render out cinematic sequences, a method called *mechinima* for its reliance on the game engine, is really the original cinematic method used in games. A rudimentary form of mechinima is often seen in the "demo mode" that most games display when they are left running on the title screen or in store kiosks. Many early cinematics were nothing more than noninteractive sequences constructed out of preexisting game elements and scripted to run within the game engine.

A popular form of mechinima is the replay most commonly seen in sports and racing games. The beauty of replay cinematics is that the player scripts his own video, with the game engine adding elaborate camerawork based on a set of cinematic rules and principles. Since the player typically doesn't control the replay, special animations or effects can be created specifically to enhance these sequences. A nice example of this is in the Microsoft racing game *RalliSport Challenge*, where replay in the Sahara course might show a herd of zebra running near the track as if startled by your car, a detail not present during the race. This and other cinematic touches help create the look of a sports channel replay immediately familiar to anyone who has watched similar events on television.

Tools

An important part of any production is having the right tools. For prerendered cinematics, the tools are the same that a small video or postproduction house might have for creating 3D animation. The core tools are a 2D art package, like Adobe Photoshop, a 3D animation package, such as Discrete's 3DS max or Maya by Alias, and a compositing tool, such as Discrete's Combustion or Adobe® After Effects®. Lastly, you will need the addition of a nonlinear editing system for the final editing and marrying of image and sound.

For mechinima cinematics, the needed tools may not exist at the start of the project. This is critical to determine at the beginning of the project so that tools can be built. Ideally, a programmer can be assigned the task of working with the cinematic artist to come up with a method for scripting the action, setting up camera framing and moves, and even scripting edits between multiple cameras. For exporting levels directly out of a third-party 3D animation program, the simplest approach is to add camera and edit tag functionality to your exporter (the custom plug-in code that converts native tool info into game-specific info). Many of these programs allow notes to be entered on specific frames of animation. These notes can be used to add a wide variety of frame-specific information tags that the game engine can use for playback.

Scheduling

Even if you determine the ideal approach to integrating game cinematics, cinematic productions are riddled with technical surprises. The most important scheduling considerations are purely cost/benefit comparisons that weigh the time cost against the aesthetic value to the cinematic and game. The following are some variables to take into consideration:

Difficult animation.   Many types of animation are difficult to get right and should be avoided if possible. If you need to use complex animation, design the sequences using animation from the interactive portion of the game. It can be very cost effective to leverage the resources allocated to gameplay.

Full-shot character animation.   If you can convey a walking or running animation with a medium shot that doesn't show the lower body, you can get the point across with half the animation. Lower body animation, particularly when trying to maintain contact between the foot and ground, can be tedious and time consuming.

Close-up shots.   The closer you get to objects in your scene, the greater the level of detail you will need to put into your models, textures, and animation. Any elements that only have a brief screen time should probably be composed to avoid the necessity for excessive detail.

Inessential detail.   Determining what details are essential can be as straightforward as eliminating the shoe leather, those nonessential actions like getting from place to place, when or how you get there is not important. However, subjective decisions can be more difficult, such as determining what details are unimportant to moving the game along.

The Cinematic Language

Once the cinematic sequences have been integrated into the overall game design and it's been determined whether to use a prerendered or real-time approach, it's time to move into the preproduction stage and understand some of the fundamentals of the cinematic language. However, don't forget that creating clear, understandable cinematic sequences involves a complex set of visual communication skills beyond the fundamentals of composition and form familiar to the visual artist.

Framing

The fundamentals of composition still hold true with cinematic framing, but the addition of motion as a compositional element brings with it the potential for far more complex arrangements. By creating compositional structures that evolve, you can illustrate ideas that can only be expressed through motion and change.

A comprehensive study of cinematic composition would require the focus of an entire book, and there are already several good books available on the subject. What is important here is to form a common descriptive language to express your cinematic designs using universal terminology. From the extreme close-up to the long shot, every variation in the framing carries a different emotional impact and a different set of actions it can capture well. In film, all shots are considered when designing the final sequence. However, in game cinematics, every change in the framing opens up the potential that the framing might reveal detail that doesn't currently exist in the character models, textures, lighting, or other elements in the environment. The extreme close-up, for example, is used in film to create an intimacy with the character, whereas the same shot of a game character may reveal the simplicity of the model or texture, showing its flaws rather than the emotion you are trying to convey.

Movement: Action and Direction within the Frame

Understanding how to use movement and action to tell a story cinematically is a craft that requires both extensive study and practice. Within the frame, movement can sometimes convey meaning, such as witnessing a character performing a significant action or reacting to a significant event, but on a purely visual level, it also becomes part of the compositional structure. To control the emotion and meaning within a cinematic scene, you need to have command over how your subject moves and interacts with both the environment and other characters in the scene.

It is important to be aware that motion works on both a two-dimensional and three-dimensional level. At the most basic level, you are always working in a two-dimensional medium. As the creator of the cinematic, your understanding of the scene can easily be skewed by your detailed knowledge of the 3D layout. Storyboarding your action will help create dynamic two-dimensional compositions by forcing you to think two-dimensionally before you have a scene to put a camera into. As you develop experience, you will learn to see two-dimensionally through the lens of the camera, but this is a skill that is surprisingly difficult to do without training.

As a point of further study into what can be accomplished compositionally within the frame, it's helpful to look at the films of Akira Kurosawa. Kurosawa is a director who has pushed the use of deep focus, a film technique where everything from the foreground to the background is in focus at the same time. Kurosawa's mastery over composition using this technique provides some of the most dynamic examples of sophisticated cinematic compositions.

Editing: Creating a Seamless Experience

At the birth of film as a form of expression, the first films were all single takes of various actions or subjects. According to records of the time, the early filmmakers thought that the audience would be totally lost if the film cut to the same action shot from a different angle. It wasn't long before directors like D. W. Griffith were rapidly pushing the limits of the edit wildly beyond their predecessors. Many of today's top directors still credit Griffith with having laid the foundation for modern film.

The key to creating cuts or transitions between shots is to maintain spatial continuity. A common rule involves what is called the *line of action*. The line of action is the most important reference point in helping honor the spatial relationships of your characters or subject. Line of action refers to an imaginary line running between the left frame and right frame subject matter. For example, in a two-camera scene with two characters sitting at a table, the line of action travels from one character to the other. You would not want to cut between cameras placed on opposite sides of the line—choose only one side of the line to place the cameras. If you break this line of action with your camera cuts, the character will appear to jump to the opposite side of the frame. If the rule is followed, visually the two characters will always maintain their relative positions on the screen and the audience will not get the characters confused. Cutting between two cameras positioned on the same side of the action line will be smooth and the focus will remain on the action, not the cut.

This simple construct can be extrapolated to work with very complex problems of staging overlapping action, shifting action, or any choreographed sequence you can come up with. It is highly recommended to reference a good book on film directing to learn how to handle these complex staging scenarios. Additionally, reverse engineering a scene from one of your favorite movies can also teach you a lot about the art of staging complex scenes.

Planning and Preproduction

Whether you have decided to prerender your cinematics or have taken the real-time approach, some basic preproduction planning techniques are essential. While each approach will have unique scheduling requirements, the preproduction should get underway as soon as the team can be assembled. Script development is a separate topic that won't be discussed here other than to note that writing natural dialogue for characters does not come easily to most people without training. It is a deceptively complex art to do well and is often a core weakness in many story-driven games.

Research

Researching your subject matter is one of the most cost-effective preproduction tasks. Gathering reference material defining the exact visual look and feel of every aspect of your subject matter will save endless hours of floundering around for the look and feel of the game. Look at any of the readily available books or DVD extras on the preproduction material generated for any animated feature. While all feature films engage in this research and design, animated features like the works by Pixar, Disney, or Dream-Works provide the closest correlation to the games industry. Hopefully, now that some game production budgets are starting to look more like movie budgets, the preproduction process will be integrated at the beginning of the design process as it is in the film industry.

As you do your research, it is critical that you keep the reference material organized. There are several things you can do to help this. The most important organizing process is to get your materials scanned and backed up with the rest of the art assets. These materials should be easily accessible to all team members and updated as changes occur. Keep any documents you create for detailing design directions stored with the related materials.

Production Illustration and Storyboards

Storyboarding is an essential part of any production. *Storyboards* are visualization tools used to illustrate aspects of the story that can be described visually. You have probably seen examples of *editorial storyboards*, sequences of comic strip-like frames showing how the story will unfold, shot by shot, but this is just one form of production illustration that is used in preproduction. The following are some of the production illustration tools that are useful to insuring that the cinematics and the game in general match the common vision for the game:

Editorial storyboards: These storyboards are a complete layout of the cinematic sequence with all shots and transitions described with notes on dialogue, camera motion, framing, and timing. Editorial boards do not have to be elaborately illustrated, but they should indicate important content, framing, and action.

Key frame storyboards: These boards focus on single key moments in the story or action, rather than the shot-by-shot coverage of the editorial boards. Add enough detail to key frame boards to help describe the look and feel of key scenes as well as the cinematic framing with these illustrations. Where editorial boards describe the entire flow of the cinematic, the key frame board is used to sell the look and feel of key moments from the storyboards.

Concept and design illustrations: These boards are used for describing details in the environment such as sets, props, color details, and other directions in style. The detail depicted in these illustrations is used to elaborate on design elements to sell the design and give detailed visual direction to the production team. The illustrations usually are not finished pieces; rather, they are often a combination of sketchy lines with areas of highly detailed rendering that the modeler or level designer can extrapolate to the rest of the scene.

Layout: Layout illustrations are essentially blueprints for the levels, set pieces, camera staging, action paths, and any visual directions that will aid the cinematic team in executing the cinematic design. These can be floor plans of levels/buildings or top-down illustrations showing the position of props, characters, and cameras. It is a useful exercise to create these staging diagrams to indicate how characters and cameras will move during a given scene.

The more detail put into the storyboards and production illustrations, the more accurate the schedule will be. If the level of detail is sketchy in places, build more buffer time into the schedule, because there will certainly be more revisions as the details are worked out during production.

Production Practices

With storyboards in hand, a detailed schedule, and a team allocated to the project, it is time to get to work implementing your vision. By now, you will have noted many potential problem areas and done some initial technical tests to eliminate as many unwanted surprises as you can before production begins. However, the only certainty is uncertainty, so be prepared to make adjustments. Some of the potential problem areas will already be known, but there are more general problems that are not necessarily related to how much detail you put into your preproduction. An experienced production team understands that the game design is just a map and that the experience of the territory may be quite different. Once the first pieces come together and this map of fun and entertainment gets put to the test, there will certainly be aspects of gameplay that don't end up working as expected.

In-game art dependencies are another area to keep an eye on. This is of particular concern to those who are planning to use the mechinima approach, since the cinematics are fully dependent on in-game assets. Look for ways to work with partial assets. It's easier to make minor camera adjustments if assets get moved around, rather than rushing through the entire process once assets are complete. Finally, putting the polish on the sequence will eat up more time than anyone will expect. Rather than trying to guess when you need to move on to the next scene or cinematic, try to keep all of the cinematics at a similar stage of polish. Use an iterative approach by prioritizing issues and working through similar priority levels across the project as a whole.

Summary

It is clear that the complex issues of creating professional-quality cinematics brings with it the need for visual communication skills that are not necessarily required in the real-time interactive portions of the game. An artist experienced with the principles of the cinematic language will often bring an eye for filmic quality to the game environment that the general public will immediately find familiar. Unfortunately, an experienced modeler, game animator, or level builder does not inherently bring a comparable set of skills to the design of cinematic sequences.

To expand your game production skills to the creation of cinematics, it is imperative that you be informed of the unique cinematic vocabulary, and dedicate some focused time to the study and practice of this form of communication. If you possess a love of film, this learning process will become a lifelong passion and greatly enhance your enjoyment of going to the movies. It is likely that you are already fascinated by the amazing strides in computer graphics that are prominent in many new films, and this may even be driving your interest in the games industry with its ever-expanding ability to create fantastic worlds. If you want to become an effective cinematic designer, you will need to expand your study into the larger body of film and animation. The breadth of educational material on the topic of film is extensive. With the University of Southern California's School of Cinema and Television having celebrated its 75th anniversary in 2004, it should be clear that this is a very mature field of study.

Exercises

1. Choose a film that contains a scene that you find particularly memorable. When picking this scene, you will get more out of the exercise if you pick a scene from a movie that involves a subject matter or genre commonly found in popular games. Rent, purchase, or borrow a copy of the film, preferably in DVD format, so you can easily jump to the scene and step through the sequence. Go through the scene shot by shot and reverse engineer the sequence, creating the following preproduction materials:

    ON THE CD

    a. **Editorial storyboard.** Storyboard the scene that you have chosen by breaking down the sequence shot by shot. Include dialogue, description of action (both verbally and with visual cues such as directional arrows), and description of camera moves (with the type of transitions between the shots, such as cut or dissolve). There is an Excel sheet on the companion CD-ROM, *storyboard.xls,* which can be printed out for this exercise. You can adjust the column widths to match the aspect ratio of the film, or draw the top and bottom frame lines to indicate the letterbox framing.

    b. **A top-down layout diagram of the set or environment for the scene.** Figure out where all the cameras in the scene are and label them by shot. Be sure to indicate any camera moves, showing both the start and end position and a direction indicator for the path the camera follows. Actors and their movement within the frame should also be indicated.

    c. **An illustration showing the composition of tonality.** Pick a few frames that are characteristic of the play of light and dark in the scene. Do not use lines to sketch out the detail; rather, you should use shading techniques to indicate how dark and light break up the two-dimensional space within the frame.

2. Using the same scene you chose for Exercise 1, analyze the scene for what it would take to re-create the sequence as a cinematic for a game based on the same story and characters.
   a. Create an asset list that breaks down the scene into model and support animations or effects.
   b. Create a list of changes and optimizations that you can make to simplify the resources that would be required to re-create the cinematic without substantially changing the essence of the meaning conveyed by the scene. The types of changes to consider are simplifying the dialogue, reducing the number of camera angles, or changing the angles to eliminate complex animation. Finally, narrow the focus of the scene to one key idea.

References

[AFI90] *Hollywood Mavericks*, American Film Institute, 1990.

[AFI92] *Visions of Light: The Art of Cinematography*, American Film Institute, 1992.

[Barwood00] Barwood, Hal, "Cutting to the Chase: Cinematic Construction for Gamers," *Gamasutra*, 2000, available online at *www.gamasutra.com/features/20000518/barwood_01.htm*.

[Begleiter01] Begleiter, Marcie, *From Word to Image: Storyboarding and the Filmmaking Process*, Michael Wiese Productions, 2001.

[Hancock00] Hancock, Hugh, "Machinima Cutscene Creation, Part One," *Gamasutra*, 2000, available online at *www.gamasutra.com/features/20000930/hancock_01.htm*.

[Hancock00] Hancock, Hugh, "Machinima Cutscene Creation, Part Two," *Gamasutra*, 2000, available online at *www.gamasutra.com/features/20001006/hancock_01.htm*.

[Hancock02] Hancock, Hugh, "Better Game Design Through Cutscenes," *Gamasutra*, 2002, available online at *www.gamasutra.com/features/20020401/hancock_01.htm*.

[Katz91] Katz, Steven, D., *Film Directing Shot By Shot: Visualizing From Concept to Screen*, Michael Wiese Productions, 1991.

[Schnitzer03] Schnitzer, Adam, "GDC 2003: How to Build a Better Cutscene," *Gamasutra*, 2003, available online at *www.gamasutra.com/features/20030306/schnitzer_01.htm*.

6.9 ■ Audio Design and Production

Overview

Although audio in games has been around since the very first blip of *Pong*, there has been a dramatic evolution over the last 30 years in regard to its production. Back in "the old days" (the 1980s), programmers would tweak what they could of the crude audio chips and type in the most simplistic melodies for music. Most sound FX consisted of some type of electronic bleep or bloop, while the music was nothing more than three or four voices of short, repeating, merry-go-round-like tunes.

As the industry spread its wings into the mid-1990s, the CD-ROM became a viable storage device where "real" music could be stored on the disc. This brought in a new wave of talented musicians who no longer needed to know C++ or assembly language in order to create audio. On the sound design front, more channels of audio and storage became available for samples (.wav files), so that now when you fired a gun or witnessed an explosion, a movielike sound effect would trigger in place of the beloved bleep or bloop.

Increased storage for sound also allowed for voice-overs and dialogue to be present in games. Narrators and actors could now be used to help convey emotion and story-line, as opposed to the player just reading dialogue off the screen. As the new millennium rolled in, budgets grew to a point where live orchestras, choirs, union actors, mixers, engineers, live musicians, mastering engineers, and multichannel surround could be used to create realistic listening experiences that would rival the best of the film industry. DVDs could hold gigabytes of data, hours of music, thousands of sound effects, and tens of thousands of voice-over lines. Interactive 5.1 surround could be achieved, and effects like real-time reverb and occlusion could now be heard. Multiple audio streams of data could be passed through the processors, which enabled no limits on assets such as music, ambiences, and streaming dialogue. It can even be said that because of the interactivity, high rate of streaming, real-time 5.1 surround, and so on, that games have now *surpassed* film and television in regard to overall production.

Game audio would have to go through some pretty tough times and changes as the metamorphosis occurred throughout the 1990s. In the early days, game audio was always considered *post*production, probably because most film and television audio is exactly that. However, games are very different due to one major factor: technology. In film and television, a scene has to be completely finished before an audio engineer or composer can get his hands on it. In games, that is just not the case. Because of the technology involved, each game on every system could be (and usually is) handled a completely different way depending on the nature of the game and the engine surrounding it. For example, one programmer may be working on a driving game and using streaming to load in the track, level, and/or graphics data. This leaves less bandwidth available for audio. Because of the game-dependent technology and the diverse ways to incorporate game audio, the audio director, composer, sound designer, and so on need to be involved with a project from the *very* beginning to help map out a plan of attack in regard to the sound.

Today, budgets for audio production in games are up. Technology in game audio is some of the most advanced and exciting technology in audio overall. Game producers are gaining audio savvy; understanding the important role that sound and music have in the creation of an immersive gameplay experience. All in all, things are good and getting better in the game audio studio—even for the people pushing the faders and signing the licensing agreements.

So, just how does sound for games work? It's a lot of black magic! The good news is that, in today's game development environment, capable teams of audio professionals are a black box—the game producer provides the vision, and the audio professionals output results. This isn't to say there aren't complex challenges involved. Contributing to this is the fact that there is no one standard way of creating audio (or any other kind of asset) for games. With the exception of direct knockoffs, mods, and sequels, each new game works differently from other games, from design to core technology, making their respective development process as unique as they are.

To deal with this, game audio professionals have a number of options for developing audio for interactive media—streaming, sequenced playback, surround sound, adaptive scores, and more. Deciding just how a game should sound and how it will deliver those sounds is the combined responsibility of the producer, lead programmer, and audio director.

This chapter explores numerous aspects of audio design and production, including the different roles and teams, audio design fundamentals, sound/music/voice-over design, audio equipment, and audio business issues. First, we begin with the various roles and teams.

Audio Team

Modern game projects require an entire crew of audio professionals to get the job done well. Music supervisors, sound designers, audio directors, voice actors, implementers, audio software engineers, casting agents, orchestral contractors, dedicated music executives, and more. In this section, we'll look at the individual roles key to the development of game audio content and the solutions used in providing sound for games.

Game audio production is both a science and an art. There are business, technical, and creative elements involved, and professionals in each of these areas who are crucial to its development. In the early days of game development, one team member filled all three roles; however, things are different in modern game development. More and more audio professionals enter the game development industry every year, each wearing very specific "hats." Some are composers, others sound designers, and others are surround sound mixers. Whereas in 1984, the "sound guy" was responsible for writing the music, programming the sound engine, clearing any licenses of any kind, creating sound effects, and the company CEO, nowadays each unique task calls for a dedicated team member to provide expertise.

Producing audio for games takes skill and knowledge of music and sound, and the tools involved in creating those elements. Creating and producing good music is a craft that takes years to hone. The same can be said for great sound design. The role of the producer is to guarantee the best talent is working on the project—and therefore he should have a level of familiarity with what is involved in game audio production. This section provides an overview of the audio-specific skills and tools involved in the production of great game audio.

Music Team: Music Director

The *music director* oversees the high-level decision-making regarding what music will go into a game, including who will be contracted to create it. Like most job titles in the games industry, the actual responsibilities of a music director will vary from company to company. For instance, the largest game publishers have *music executives*, with a team of *music supervisors* working under them. They usually bring a large rolodex of music industry contacts with them, have access to the top artists and composers, and understand the ins and outs of music contracting and licensing. Other smaller companies may have a music director who licenses songs from whatever band happens to be in the producer's CD player at the time. Other companies don't even have a music director, with all decisions going through the production or design departments.

Music Team: Composer

Composers write custom music to be placed in games. Sometimes, game companies have in-house writers who create music for their games, but this is becoming more uncommon. Instead, talent is contracted on a per-project basis to help manage a particular project's specific music needs. The production of the music can be done entirely by one person writing, recording, mixing, and so forth. With larger budgets becoming more common, composers often have a team including assistants, orchestrators, orchestral contractors, musicians, and such who all work together to create the finished product.

Music Team: Music Producers

Music producers are hired to maintain the creative vision of a musical recording. In the recording industry, they are hired by the recording artist or label to ensure that the recording process goes smoothly and that the artists, musicians, and engineers are giving their best to the project. Traditionally, it's been uncommon for a game company to contract a dedicated music producer to direct the music creation process, although it has happened. Usually, only larger budget projects can contract a music producer. As custom theme songs for games by pop musicians become more common, however, there will be more accomplished producers entering the fray, to create hit tracks to accompany games, as is common practice in feature films.

Music Team: Recording Engineer

The *recording engineer* is a staple of the music production process. They get the best possible sounds out of each performance on the project. If your audio production process consists of one or two sound designers producing music in a closet at your house, then chances are that one (if not both) will wear the hat of recording engineer. In fact, with the evolution of the recording studio moving into the home, most composer/producers have some basic engineering chops. However, truly professional music demands a truly professional team, which of course includes a dedicated recording engineer.

Music Team: Mix Engineer

The *mix engineer* takes the completed recorded tracks put together by the recording engineer and balances their sonic characteristics and volumes (i.e., "levels") relative to one another. Mixing is an essential phase in the production of music. Although the temptation may exist to cut corners and use the same person to do the recording as the mixing, often a dedicated mix engineer can bring recorded music to a new level.

It's common practice in the recording business to use a separate engineer for mixing, recording, and mastering.

Music Team: Mastering Engineer

Mastering, as it pertains to music in games, is the final stage of music production. The *mastering engineer* typically has superhuman hearing, and listens for any subtle imbalances, mistakes, or other problems in the mixed-down recordings. In addition, the mastering engineer makes certain that the volumes of every piece of music are matched relative to one another. For example, stick a major recording artist's album in your music player and you'll notice that each track exists in the same place regarding loudness and character—that's the work of a mastering engineer. Mastering is essential if the music files are coming from many different sources (i.e., producer/composers).

Music Team: Assistant Engineer

Recording and mix engineers, like composers, are traditionally hired on a per-project basis for their particular flavors they bring to the finished music product. They are used to working in different studios, for different projects. *Assistant engineers* are hired by recording studios to help visiting engineers find their way around particular rooms containing gear and setups that may otherwise be alien to them. The cost of an assistant is factored into the cost of the studio hired to host the recording project.

Sound Design Team: Audio Director/Manager

Audio directors manage sound design teams. They keep track of resources and schedules, and attend meetings with the production and design teams. Audio directors execute the vision of the producer on the sound and dialogue front. They sit in production meetings, work with the producer to set realistic goals, tackle problems, and make certain that above all else, the audio assets are created to spec and delivered on time.

Sound Design Team: Sound Designer

The *sound designer* is a critical member of a game development team. With audio being one-third of the gaming experience, sound designers bring the world on the screen to life. Sound design as a craft has been around since the inception of "talkies" (i.e., movies with soundtracks). Sound in games began as a modest affair, with limited processing and nearly prehistoric (but downright cool-sounding) sound chips as the only weapons in the sound designer's arsenal. The current and future state of sound playback in games is much more advanced, with systems supporting CD-quality sample playback. This means that sound designers can capture sounds from the real world, exaggerate them, and import them into the game environment. This gives games the Hollywood edge, larger-than-life quality audiences have come to expect from visual entertainment.

Sound Design Team: Implementer

Implementers work in the sound design department with various production tools to attach sounds designed by sound designers to environments, events, and characters. They are, in a sense, the level designers of the audio department. Implementers, as dedicated audio team members, are the most recent introduction to the game audio circle. Only the largest companies will have a dedicated audio implementer, instead relying on sound designers, or in worse cases, programmers, to get the sound into games. The reason we say "worse" is simply because programmers are, in general, not audio professionals. They aren't trained to understand the subtle methods involved in placing and balancing sounds in virtual environments. The best-case scenario is to dedicate a team member to getting the job done right.

Dialogue Team: Casting Agent

Casting agents are contracted by game companies to line up talent for voice acting parts. Good casting agents have a wide network of voice talent, both union and nonunion, for game companies to use. They know the best people for the jobs, the professional actors who can get the script read right, in little time. Good casting agents will create a demo free of charge, for the audio team to review in deciding who gets a part in their project.

Dialogue Team: Voice-Over Director

A *voice-over director's* job is identical to that of a film director: to coax the best and most appropriate performance out of the talent acting the role in a production. It's common for a game production to contract a dedicated voice-over director to work on dialogue recording sessions. That's not to say it's mandatory yet—which is often reflected in resultant subpar dialogue found in many games. The temptation exists to allow the audio director or producer to direct the voice talent. This is only advisable if the individual has experience doing so; otherwise, the quality of the performances may suffer considerably, and often without anyone noticing until it's too late. The importance of a good director cannot be emphasized enough.

Dialogue Team: Voice Actors

Voice actors come in one of two flavors: union and nonunion. Union talent is expensive, but the quality of their work is unmatched. Nonunion professionals are less expensive than union talent, but can usually only do one voice very well. It is common for games to use a mix of both types of actors, relying on union talent for the main characters and nonunion for secondary and tertiary roles.

Dialogue Team: Dialogue Editor

Once voice actors' performances are captured, the files must be cut up and organized. A *dialogue editor's* job is to do just that. They master the files, check for errors, and submit the assets to the audio director. The job is often tedious but critical, and goes to a junior member of the audio team.

Audio Design Fundamentals

There are three main elements to a video game that are all equally important to the entire experience. First, there are the visuals, including art, video, and animation. Second, there is the design, which incorporates the visuals, plus game design, programming, feel, and movement. Finally, there is the audio, which includes everything you hear.

Unfortunately, most companies don't take audio as seriously as visuals and design. Often, there should be a bigger percentage of the budget dedicated to audio, to allow for union voice acting, intelligent script writing, or even live orchestras. Audio in games is sometimes looked at as postproduction, similar to the film industry. However, for video games, the composer and sound designer need to be working from day one, figuring out technically how everything will be incorporated into each phase or level of the game. In recent years, the situation has become progressively better, with more and more live musicians and talented voice acting being incorporated in games. It's very important to know this kind of information. You may find yourself trying to explain how important audio is and why certain creative and technical aspects need to be focused on.

Two key points to concentrate on are creativity and integration. Creativity speaks for itself. The tricky part is how to get sounds into the game world. Integration with the programmers and/or designers/producers is half the work. Once the sound has been created, it is important to make sure the sound is properly being triggered at the right time, volume, pitch, and pan. Deciding on how the audio will be triggered should be discussed very early in the project. Keep in mind that almost every project you will ever work on will be set up and handled differently.

On the creative side, you want your work to stand out from anything anyone has ever heard in a game before. Using elements such as ambiance, as opposed to music, can sometimes create a more realistic and enjoyable atmosphere. The key is to think outside the box and to bravely bring your audience to unexplored shores in terms of sound, music, and dialogue.

One of the most difficult parts of audio in games is trying to make everyone happy. There are many different people on a team, and almost every one is a music critic. It's funny; people can generally look at a piece of art in a game and tell whether it is good. People can move a character on screen and tell if it feels good or not. But put a tune in a game!?!? Everyone has different music tastes! It's hard to find two people who agree on every single piece of music! Take country music, for example. Some people love it, and others can't stand it. A game designer or producer shouldn't choose what kind of music he likes for the game, but what type of music fits and enhances the game the best.

When writing music, it's getting harder and harder to be original, but something that stands out will catch people's attention. Don't try to have your music sound like "video game music." Write a great tune! Sometimes people get caught up in "exactly" what the look or feel of the game is. If you just write a great tune, players will remember and like it.

The best instrument to learn is the piano/synthesizer/keyboard. With the knowledge of that instrument, you can pretty much re-create any instrument in the world (through devices known as *samplers*). It also allows you to record your compositions into midi files, which can be edited and recorded easily on a computer.

There are three huge things that, to become successful, you will need to focus on: 1) the creative element; 2) the technical aspects; and 3) the business/networking aspects. If you can study and master those three things you will be well on your way to becoming a success in the video game audio world.

Audio Implementation

One of the biggest transformations that game audio has gone through recently is the creation of audio tools that enable the power of interactivity to be put back into the audio creator's hands. It is widely said in the games industry that creating a sound effect or music track is merely only *half* the work.

The other half is the integration and implementation; yet another huge difference that the games industry has over film and television. A sound designer could create the greatest gunshot sound in the world. However, if it is integrated incorrectly it could quickly become the most *annoying* sound in the world. Things like randomization of samples, pitch, and volume variations are all very important when creating game audio. Knowing when and where to cross-fade a particular music track or the use of a well-placed "musical sting" could mean all the difference in the overall enjoyment of the game experience.

Back in the 1980s and 1990s, a sound designer or musician had to sit down for hours and days upon end with programmers, painstakingly integrating each and every sound heard in a game. Each 3D volume, pitch variation, and randomization had to be set to ensure nonrepetitiveness. If the programmer or audio designer didn't have the time, knowledge, experience, or energy to do this, the audio would lack greatly.

Finally, the industry got smart and decided to make games data-driven, in which the assets (audio, models, textures, and such) are not part of the code, but rather data that drives the behavior of the game. This development put most of the power back into the audio designer's hands by creating amazing integration audio drivers that the audio folks could now interact with on their own, without needing to spend the programmer's precious time. Audio designers could now set up banks with randomization, control 3D volume positioning, and integrate effects like reverb, randomization of different samples, and pitches. All the programmer has to do is provide an audio event trigger, and the sound designer can now go behind the scenes and tweak to his heart's content.

With the proper equipment and tools, many audio drivers even offer "real-time" tweaking "on the fly" while the game is being played. Simply stated, this means that if the audio designer is playing a particular level and hears that the explosion sound is too loud, he can simply turn it down in real time in the audio engine while playing the game to get the exact volume he prefers. Again, not only volumes, but pitch, 3D positioning, randomization, reverb effects, and so forth can all be controlled by the audio engineer.

One important aspect of game audio is the "audio/sound driver." This is the software program or tool that enables sound designers, composers, and so on to interface with the game and what the programmer is doing. Simply stated, it's the tool that you will put all of your sounds in so that the programmer can easily trigger them from within the game.

There are many different sound drivers that are capable of doing many different things. Some may only be set up to simply trigger sounds. Other more complex drivers could have complete interactivity built-in that would enable the sound designer or composer to set up exactly how he wants the audio to perform without working with programmers to implement every single nuance of sound.

A good example of how sound drivers have changed the workflow would be the footstep sound. "In the old days," one may have had to provide the programmer four to six different ".wav" files of footstep sounds, and then sit down with him as he wrote code to randomly trigger one of the footstep sounds each time a foot hit the surface. Then, the programmer would have to tweak or write code to get the proper random pitch range and volume. Needless to say, this was quite time consuming, and the final audio quality relied on the audio programmer as opposed to the audio designer. These days, most sound drivers enable the audio designer to go in and set (as well as audition in real time) all of these nuances. The audio programmer is now more focused on creating audio event triggers (play sound scheme 42 when foot hits surface) instead of having to deal with all the behind-the-scenes tweaking that should be put in the audio designer's hands in the first place. Bottom line, the better you know and understand your audio/sound driver system, the more effective you will be as an audio designer.

Every console or platform is a little different, but all have memory, storage, and bandwidth constraints. Even though a platform like the PlayStation 2 has four times more memory for sound than the original PlayStation, you will still find yourself running out of space quickly. Instead of sacrificing sampling quality, the challenge today is to try to keep everything at an extremely high level of quality. Included in this is creating many more sounds and variations, since games are getting increasingly larger each year. All of this of course takes up more memory and media storage.

Another constraint issue is how the code is handling the console's resources (such as memory and disc) within any given level. Many times, a game may need to access the disc to load in level or graphic information. When this happens, the sound designer or composer needs to figure out how the music being streamed off the disc will be affected, since the disc resource may be tied up during the loading. Either the music must fade out, transition to ambient sound held entirely in memory, or perhaps the code can be modified to minimize the impact of loading. There are many different ways to engineer audio even within the same machine, and it's the biggest audio challenge that must be faced.

More information about audio for specific platforms can be found on the Game Audio Network Guild (G.A.N.G.) Web site [GANG] at *www.audiogang.com.*

Sound Design

Sound design is an extremely important element of game development. It is easily the most interactive element of the soundscape and one of the most focused on technical aspects of game audio. Implementation is key when presented with a sound design challenge. Creating a really great explosion, gunshot, or footstep sound is merely only a small percentage of what needs to happen to get the sound effect to sound good. Multiple and dynamic versions of each sound create a more realistic environment that will not sound as repetitive. When creating sound effects for games, one of the hardest challenges is to make the game sound dynamic without being too repetitive. To accomplish this, a sound designer must create numerous variations of the same sound. For example, you wouldn't want to record just one footstep sound and keep playing it over and over for the entire game (although some games still do that, unfortunately). It is better to record lots of footstep sounds, pick out anywhere from 6 to 20 different ones (depending on space constraints), and randomly trigger them within the audio/ sound driver. Once in the driver, you can set effects like randomization, pitch, volume, 3D, and so forth. Dynamics and being nonrepetitive are the keys to successful audio design within games.

As far as creating unique sounds, it's always best to combine preexisting sound libraries with going out and recording/editing your own sounds. Sound designers shouldn't just rely on stock sound libraries. Sound libraries are great for certain aspects but not for everything. Preexisting sound libraries are great for layering in with sounds you've created. With all of the great audio software and tools available, it is easy to take a sound and manipulate it into something completely different. You can get some pretty amazing sounds just by pitching it down a few octaves. The key is to be creative and think of things that you normally may not do. It's more than likely that every sound you need could be recorded with objects right in your own home. For example, need lots of wet mucky squishy sounds? For this, you could use a thick Jell-O® mix about halfway before it gets hard. This makes a nice, thick, liquid sauce. Need a rumbling or rolling huge metal crate? Try hitting and wobbling a metal bowl or pan back and forth on a vent or air-conditioning unit. Being creative is not only an important part of sound design, it is also the most fun!

Another issue to remember is that different types of microphones will produce different outcomes. A good suggestion is to use a few different mics placed at different areas for the sound you are trying to record. Once you get it back in your studio, you can then decide which sounds (or layer of sounds) work best. When in doubt, add a little low-end equalization to your sound. It will always bring up the presence and make it sound a little bigger.

If doing a sports-related game, make sure to ask the publisher to get you into an event to record the sounds (i.e., crowds, chants, cheers, ambiance, etc.). Many times, the publisher is paying a great deal of money to secure professional sports licenses, and it is very easy to get into special events if you just ask the publisher to ask the licensor.

Sound Design Example: Street Basketball

To better realize the amount of work and thinking that goes into a game, let's look at an example of exactly what needs to be done to create sound design. Let's take a street-styled basketball game for our example. For this game, you would want to create the exact audio experience you would hear if you were actually on the court. To accomplish this, you would have many different in-game sound effects and multiple audio streams constantly being triggered. Here's how it may work:

Footsteps would be one of the key sound effects. In this particular game, there would be many different court surfaces such as concrete, wood, asphalt, and dirt. There would also be many different types of backboards such as wood, metal, fiberglass, and acrylic. In addition, there would be different types of nets such as nylon, chain, or no net at all. Each court could have any combination of these sounds, so they must all be recorded individually. You would typically record a bunch of different footsteps sounds on all of the different surfaces, and then pick your favorite ones that are different enough from each other. Along with footsteps, you will also want to record foot squeaks and foot scuffs. Once you record and then put these sounds into your audio editing tool (e.g., Sound Forge, Wavelab), you will then have to insert them into the audio/sound driver. In the audio/sound driver, you'll want to trigger the footsteps randomly and never repeat the same footstep twice. You will also vary the pitch randomly and can control the volumes depending on where the player is in 3D space. Throw in a few random scuffs and squeaks here and there and you have an elaborate footstep soundscape.

One thing to note: all of the in-game sound effects are put into the driver as mono files. This is done so that the programmer can whip the sound around in 3D. Having a stereo file for a static sound would not work. Each player has his own set of footsteps that are being triggered in a multichannel environment. The player who you have control of is usually in the center of the screen, so you would want to keep him straight up the middle and in the center. Everyone else, however, is running all around the player. Because there may be 10 players, each with a full set of footsteps, you would have to prioritize certain more important sounds over the footsteps because of a limit of voice allocation or too many sounds playing all at the same time. Volume control in this instance becomes very important.

Some of the other needed sounds are actions such as ball hits, passes, rebounds, jumps, lands, player "oofs," ball slaps, ball off backboard, ball off rim, baskets, swishes, and so on. These sounds must all play in surround, with dynamic pitch, volume, randomizing, and 3D. Most sound engines and programmers are already calculating 3D space based on position and volume, so in essence, the sound designer only needs to concentrate on integrating the proper space, volume, and pitch positioning.

Ambience

Another extremely important and often overlooked element in sound design is ambience. Ambiences can sometimes create a mood even more than music can. Even a small hum coming from a computer or distant waterfall or wind through trees enhances the experience tenfold. Many times, depending on space and limits of the machine, you will want your ambiences in full, complete surround sound. This can be accomplished by creating a stereo ambience *bed* and mirroring the image in the back speakers. These ambience beds could consist merely of wind, room hums, distant ocean waves, and so forth. Aside from a stereo bed, there will also be specific 3D objects within the environments that should have sounds as well (such as streams or machinery).

Music

How is music for games created? Technically, you can do it a thousand different ways. Every project might be approached completely differently because of the technology, the creative aspect, and the audio or game engine/tools. It's part of the composer's job to figure out how exactly to pull off what you're trying to accomplish both technically and creatively.

Interactive Music

Interactive music is music that changes based on what the player is doing. Movies vary the music to match the action or moods of the story, but since games are not statically fixed in time, they must adjust the music "on the fly" to match how the player is driving the game. If the player is fighting zombies, then the music might be intense. As the last zombie is killed, the music might transition into a more relaxed score. There are several ways to create this interactive music.

Sometimes, you may choose to use MIDI branching for complex nonlinear interactive music. This is where the score is set up with specific branching points that are able to transition into several other specially designed scores. Another simpler method is to take one piece of music and transition it to another piece of music at a certain time in the game when a certain event is triggered. It can be as simple as that, or as complex as adaptive audio, in which every little thing in the game is hooked up to a MIDI channel. Because some game hardware supports multiple streams and a large hard drive, you're able to take a great deal of data and have it all be streaming at the same time, even in 5.1 surround sound. For example, you could write different variations and different intensity levels of the same song, record it all with a live orchestra, and then crossfade in between the different intensity levels. This can be accomplished by setting up flag points so that the programmer always knows the current part of the song, so that when the scene changes or the action gets more intense, you can then crossfade into different variations and intensity levels of the song. Another interactive music technique is to use short and quick musical stings as an effective way to relay emotion and intensity. Opening a secret door and hearing a "reveal" type sting may give the player joy. Opening that same secret door and hearing an eerie and scary sting may bring about hesitation.

Streaming Music

Streaming music is a simple yet powerful method of providing high-quality music. The music is stored on a disc-based media or hard drive and is read a bit at a time (as opposed to trying to load the entire song into memory at once). This allows for fully produced tracks of CD (Redbook) quality audio to be used in games. Streaming music is by far the most widely used method of providing music, now and for the foreseeable future.

Creating Music

When creating music, you normally receive an early version of the game with no audio whatsoever. Most of the time you will discuss music styles with the designers or producers. During some game productions, a level may not be completely finished, so sometimes you will have to go just on storyboards and art. A good rule of thumb is to provide a few different 30-second demo versions of the music to see which one the designers/producers like best. It is a good way to get an idea of what they are thinking, and saves you the time of creating a great two- or three-minute piece, only to have it rejected because it wasn't exactly what they wanted. For the audio professional, it's nice when the designers and producers trust the composer's expertise. However, keep in mind that every project, producer, designer, developer, and publisher works differently for each and every game.

Listening and referencing movie soundtracks is a very good way to get a taste of the styles for certain games. Many times, a producer or designer may come to you and say, "We want it to sound like *Conan the Barbarian*," or whatever movie they feel best represents the feeling they are trying to convey. Keep in mind that most movie music is incidental or *background* type music, whereas video game music, for the most part, is *foreground* music. Video game music is often in-your-face, heart-pounding, adrenaline-kicking stuff. A good way to create music that matches a particular environment or feel is by referencing and using certain instruments in the music to help convey a scene. For example, a didgeridoo will instantly put you in Australia. Big tubular bells or a low male choir may give you a sense of spookiness. Wind in trees and a high female choir may give you an underwater or icy feel.

Scoring for picture is a valuable craft in the world of entertainment production. Regardless of whether composers deliver music for a film, a television show, or a game, their role remains the same. They are responsible for conveying subconscious and emotional information to the audience. Without music to guide them, the audience may be unsure how to feel about what they see on screen. Carefully crafted musical cues convey feelings and messages that are essential to experiencing the full production.

Film is linear, whereas video games are interactive, so you don't know what the player is going to do next. It's much more challenging and much more rewarding as a player to hear music change when you do something.

As with many things, timing is everything, and the triggering of musical cues to picture is no exception. Imagine what would happen if the score to *Star Wars* were set to play two minutes behind the action on the screen? It would be confusing to see Luke Skywalker staring at his uncle's house in ruins with the cantina music playing in the background. Fortunately, timing cues for linear media, like film, are simple since the playback sequence is the same with every play session. When the action is hot on the screen, the score is excited. When a scene is suspenseful, so is the music. The music matches the mood.

Games don't work this way, since they are nonlinear. Theoretically, the sequence of events in a game could occur in a different order during each play session. A linear soundtrack can quickly become disjointed in relation to the action on the screen.

Game music's legacy is repetition. Repetition in game soundtracks has an upside and a downside. The upside is that, just like a pop song on heavy rotation on the radio, the music for a game can quickly become memorable and a strong element in the title's brand. The downside is that the music can quickly become annoying and turned off by the audience, which is an undesirable result.

When creating video game music, it is important that the composer is aware of not being too repetitive. For example, if you are creating a two-minute song, the main motif shouldn't repeat unless it changes a bit or other instruments are added, subtracted, changed, and so forth. The thing to remember is that the player will be hearing your song over and over again, so you want to make sure you deliver something unique and different each time before the loop happens.

Adaptive Audio System

The key to creating music and sound effects for an ever-evolving game experience is to adopt an *adaptive audio system*. On the music front, an *adaptive music system* handles the problem of repetition. Most games feature music that repeats over and over. While the music can be of very high quality, some players find the repetition distracting and opt to turn the volume off. Adaptive music systems introduce the ability for the music team to create musical content that never plays back the same way twice.

Another advantage to using an adaptive score is the ability to more accurately deliver valuable information to the player about the state of the game. Since the state of a game can be in flux, it's impossible for a linear soundtrack to stay updated and synced to the context of the game. An adaptive score, however, can inform the players about their health, impending danger, or the distance between their character and their goal. Thus, adaptive music can be a powerful design tool for communication.

Adaptive music puts more control in the hands of the designer to convey emotion in context with the current happenings in the game. Since the score reacts in time to specific events, the music can swell with emotion during appropriate moments, or pull back as necessary. With a repeating linear score, the music could be at any point in its cycle—missing opportunities to deliver emotional impact.

The key is to develop audio systems that can create music, sound, and dialogue objects that have adaptive traits programmed in. The audio programmer on the team can develop tools to the audio director's specs to do just that. There are also third-party game audio tools available, such as Creative ISACT, which have the capability to introduce variation and adaptation to music, sound effects, and dialogue. Introducing these properties to a game's soundscape and soundtrack will improve believability and immersion.

Not every score has to be nonlinear. It is okay to use full songs for certain sections. If the section or scene changes, you can go into another new song altogether that reflects the current mood. It is important to note that every project is going to be different and require a different approach to audio. This is the challenge, and "the fun part" of doing game audio. Keeping an open mind to all of the technical possibilities is very important. Don't be afraid to speak up and try new ideas.

Voice-Over Production

An area in which games sometimes drop the ball in audio is the voice-over production. Having the proper budget and talent becomes very important when trying to achieve high production quality for games. Every effort should be made to hire talented union actors. You will quickly find that the extra money spent is worth it in the end. It is much harder to find talented nonunion people to act. Although it may seem cheaper to go nonunion in the beginning, it could end up costing much more because of the amount of time, takes, and retakes you'll need to record.

It is important to keep up to date on the rules and regulations of recording union actors. For example, a union actor can only record up to three different characters within the four-hour time frame you are paying for. You will have to pay extra if you want them to do other character voices, even if it is only a few lines. The other thing to know is that you cannot mix union and nonunion talent on a project in certain states within the U.S.

You must have all of your bases covered for the game when going into a voice-over session. At the end of the session, you'll want to incorporate many different voice elements for the actual gameplay, so it's good to grab as much as you can. The following is a good list of situations and reactions that would be smart to record for each character. For each of the items on the list, you will want to record at least five or six of each; *plus*, you should do subtle, medium, and loud/large versions of each. You can quickly see how one "jumping" sound turns into 15 to 20 different sounds and variations. You will want to record these last, because some of them contain screaming or stress of the vocal chords. Take your time and have the actor improvise some of these.

They are *very* important to the game, and only having one or two "getting hit" sounds for 20+ hours of gameplay will get annoying very quickly!

Utterances: Taunts, vocal self-reflection ("What was that?")
Bodily functions: Breathing (subtle and heavy), coughing
Physical exertion: Jumping, landing, throwing a punch, pushing, pulling
Emotions: Crying, scared, startled, upset, relieved
Pain: Hit in face, hit in stomach, on fire, electrically shocked
Death noises: Falling to death (short and long), violent death (scream), subtle death (last breath), drowning

Spatialized Audio

Spatialized audio is a perfect tool for video games. Imagine playing a driving game and hearing an opponent's car engine coming up from behind on your right before you see the car on-screen. The player then quickly moves to the right to cut off his opponent without ever seeing him. That's interactive audio, and that is the future of video games.

The film industry uses multichannel audio, but often it's rare that movies really take advantage of the technology. Of course, there are exceptions, like the bullet whizzing in *Saving Private Ryan* and *The Matrix*. Unfortunately, a common argument in Hollywood is that the picture is in front of you and the action is in front of you so the sounds for the most part should be in front of you. While this may be the case with many movies, games put the player in the midst of the action, and it's crucial for game developers to surround the player with an immersive soundscape.

If there is a scene in a jungle, every bit of that jungle should surround the player. The reality is that this takes much more time and energy to record and mix, but the result is worth it.

So, as you can hear, in the real world, sound occurs 360 degrees around us. It comes at us from every direction. Developers seek to mimic the experience of the real world in their virtual worlds and require solutions for realistic sound playback. Proper sound placement in game worlds falls on the shoulders of the audio director and the sound team to deliver realistic sound behavior.

Spatialized audio involves reproducing recorded sound in such a way that it is perceived to possess a particular location in space relative to the listener. The most popular form of spatialized audio is stereo.

Putting "space" into a soundtrack for a linear production like film or television is fairly straightforward, as the technology and techniques have been around for nearly a century. These techniques and tools translate flawlessly into the linear component of nonlinear entertainment (i.e., in-game cinematics, CGI cut-scenes, FMVs). The real trick comes in bringing these elements to life during gameplay. Since events take place in real-time during gameplay, playing back a linear sequence of recorded sound effects just doesn't work. Instead, the game engine must generate spatial and environmental characteristics of sounds "on the fly." These characteristics are based on location information provided by the objects in the game world.

Mono

Mono is short for monophonic sound. This format refers to one-channel soundtracks. Mono is used for systems that have only one speaker allocated for sound playback. Since there is only one speaker in a mono system, there are no controllable spatial characteristics. Even though mono hasn't been the main format for sound playback on home systems for quite some time, consoles usually support a mono output mode, so this might need to be considered. In addition, sounds effects are normally recorded in mono so that they can be placed dynamically around the player with stereo or surround sound.

Stereo

Stereo is the preferred playback format that has been around for decades and is a standard in music production today. Stereo music production involves two tracks, played back over a left and a right speaker channel. Differences in the volumes of individual instruments in each speaker create the illusion of those instruments existing in a space between the two speakers. For instance, if the vocals in a particular song are at full volume in the left speaker but not in the right speaker at all, the vocals will sound as if they are to the "left." If, however, the vocals are at full volume in both speakers, they will sound as if they are in the "center." Gradual changes in volume between the two speakers will cause the vocals to sound as though they are "moving" to the left or right.

Multichannel Surround

Surround sound, ever prevalent in movie theaters, involves using more than two speakers. The most common configuration is referred to as 5.1, where the "5" represents the number of full-bandwidth speakers in the system, and the ".1" represents the subsonic bass channel, or *subwoofer*. In a 5.1 system, there are three forward channels (left, right, and center) and two channels in the rear (left and right). 5.1 mixes are generally created such that all on-screen dialogue takes place in the center channel, music and front sound effects are in the left and right front channels, and special sound effects and ambience are in the rear left and right channel. Multichannel surround formats can be created in many configurations, with some semipopular options being 6.1 and 7.1.

After a failed attempt at a four-channel consumer surround format in the 1970s, the home theater industry backed away from multichannel in the home. Consumers today are savvy, however, and the hunger for cutting-edge technology and the most immersive game experience possible has created a market for surround sound systems among gamers.

To get the massive amount of uncompressed audio data onto a fixed delivery medium like film or a digital medium like DVD (six channels of uncompressed audio is a huge amount of data), the audio data must be encoded. The two major formats for surround encoding are Dolby and DTS. For more information on each of these technologies, visit their respective Web sites [Dolby, DTS].

3D Spatialized Audio

One limitation of stereo and conventional multichannel surround configurations is the notable lack of a vertical component. Using these systems, sound can be made to seem as though it is coming from in front, behind, or to either side, but it cannot be made to sound as though it is coming from above or below. Another limitation involved with multichannel surround systems is the cost, in which more speakers mean a greater cost to the consumer purchasing the system. A third limitation lies in the placement of the speakers by the listener. Proper playback of multichannel surround requires proper placement, and for many people, proper placement of the six speakers involved in 5.1 is not always convenient, if they even have the space to place them at all.

To combat these limitations, audio engineers have developed 3D spatialized audio. Using 3D spatialized audio technology, a game audio engine can create the illusion of a sound coming from anywhere in space around the listener. This implies the full 3D space around the listener: up, down, left, right, front, back, and all around.

The technology involves a technique using special frequency filtering that mimics the way sound interacts with a human's head, ears, and chest. These filters are called *head-related transfer functions*, or HRTFs for short.

3D spatializing software solutions have found a home in the games industry on all major consoles and the PC market, thanks to companies such as Microsoft, Creative Labs, Sensaura, and the legacy of the now defunct A3D. These groups poured a great deal of money and research into the development of middleware software capable of delivering 3D audio environments for game developer's virtual worlds.

Unfortunately, 3D spatialization has its limitations. Much like multichannel surround, proper speaker placement is necessary to enjoy the full effect the technology offers. For this reason, 3D spatialized audio is best experienced on headphones.

Environmental Audio

Direction is only part of the picture to consider when modeling the behavior of sound in games. Certain environmental properties are equally critical in the transmission of sound. Qualities like air pressure, humidity, room size, room shape, and room material all have a profound impact on how a listener hears a sound. Creating these varying environmental effects has become an important aspect of game audio development. Modeling the interaction of sound as it would actually occur in a real environment would take an excessive amount of processing power to complete. Instead, modern solutions need to somehow cheat to create a realistic reproduction of the behavior.

As sound travels through the air, it will bounce off, bend around, and penetrate objects in its path. The objects encountered can be anything from walls, to people, to dense air pockets. Compounding the situation, objects in the real world are made from varying types of materials, such as wood, stone, flesh, and plastic, all of which absorb and reflect frequencies with various measures of aptitude. Temperature, wind gradients, and humidity all have a profound effect on the tonal characteristics of sound, as does room size, room contents, and the physical materials used to build the room.

All of these factors combine to create truly complex sonic interactions that affect the listener perceived quality of sound. For instance, a shout occurring on the opposite side of a brick wall from the player's in-game character should sound markedly different than if the shout occurred in same room as the character.

Games require special audio solutions to model the effect that different environments have on sound. Most modern audio systems for games have some inherent ability to deliver environmental effects for real-time, in-game modeling of realistic sound behavior. Of particular note are the solutions offered by Creative Labs. Their work has been most extensive in the development of environmental audio synthesis solutions. Their solution is named EAX for Environmental Audio eXtensions. EAX allows game audio designers to model the effect of the environment on sound. EAX has the ability to give different material characteristics to the walls of a room. Creative has an extensive program for developers interested in integrating EAX into their productions, including tools, training, and support [CreativeLabs]. It truly is the most comprehensive solution for environmental audio effects in the business.

Studio Savvy

Like animators, artists, and software engineers, audio professionals have their own suite of tools they use to produce content. In fact, audio professionals use more tools, both software and hardware, than any other professional in the development process. While an animator and programmer can get away with a few pieces of key software and a high-powered PC, audio pros need a varied pallet of sounds, processing devices, recording equipment, and other gear to reach their full potential. This section looks at the key tools in the audio production world.

Every musician needs a good sequencer for composing music. Both Macs and PCs have great sequencing software. The best advice would be to go online and download the different demos for each. Whether it's Cakewalk for the PC or Digital Performer or Cubase for the Mac, a comfortable sequencer to create music is very important. Aside from the sequencer, you'll need a strong set of sounds and instruments. Programs such as GigaStudio or VST plug-ins enable the musician to have thousands of different and unique sounds at their fingertips. There really isn't any one style for video game music; therefore, you may be asked to incorporate many different sounds, styles, and techniques in your music writing. A good set of instruments and sound will enable you to do this.

Many video game audio professionals use the program Sound Forge for the PC. This is one of the most versatile, easy-to-use, and affordable audio software programs on the market. There are tons of plug-ins available to make it even more powerful. Another piece of equipment a sound designer will definitely need is a portable DAT machine or digital recording device with a great microphone for grabbing all of those in-the-field sound effects.

When putting everything together for prerendered game cinematics, such as music, sound effects, and dialogue, a good postproduction tool becomes important. Whether it's Digital Performer or Pro Tools on a fast Mac or Nuendo or Vegas on the PC, a good software program for mixing takes the level of quality and convenience to the next level.

Hardware

Modern studios center around computer production environments, limiting the historic reliance on hardware audio professionals had for decades. This isn't to say that specific pieces of hardware aren't necessary in a quality recording environment. There are many great mixers, effects boxes, and other tools that audio designers can use to create cutting-edge audio assets for games. Audio directors know what they need and what can be replaced with software. There are some critical hardware components that are a must for a great audio production studio.

The Triad

Arguably, the three most important components in an audio production suite are the microphones, A/D converters, and monitors (i.e., speakers), which are all hardware components. These three devices are necessary to get the best possible sound into the computer environment and to monitor it once inside. These devices are deceptively expensive but critical to the creation of great sound. If your goal is to have an in-house sound studio, don't flinch when you see the prices attached to these line items.

PC versus Mac

The ever-raging debate over platform superiority is no stranger to the world of audio production. There was a time when high-end music production could only be done on a Mac. This is no longer true, and now PCs are extremely popular platforms for audio production.

One thing to keep in mind is that game audio tools like SCREAM and XACT will only run on a PC, so at some point, if you're going to be implementing sound into a game, a PC is required. Roughly 99 percent of all audio implementation lives in the PC world, so plan to have some PCs in the audio development environment.

Software

The cornerstone of modern audio production is the software recording/editing environment. Software options for production are far more cost effective than the overhead-heavy production facilities of the twentieth century. While some of the old guard believe that software is no replacement for tried-and-true hardware devices, changes in the media production landscape dictate that, at least for the moment, that software is the dominant solution, and the audio world is no exception.

Applications for Audio Production

There are many great software tools for recording/producing music, editing sound clips, and for tweaking sound effects. There are two main types of production software: multitracking software and stereo editing/mastering software. Audio production software is fairly standard from one industry to another, although there are some noncommercial applications we will discuss that are specific to the game audio field.

Multitrack recording software is used primarily for producing music, although these packages are useful for creating complex sound effects from multiple sources. Stereo editing/mastering software is used to cut up dialogue, tweak sound effects, and to put the finishing touches on music files.

Popular multitracking software packages include:

- Cakewalk Sonar
- Steinberg Cubase SX
- Steinberg Nuendo
- Digidesign Protools
- MOTU Digital Performer
- Apple Logic

Popular software packages for editing/mastering include:

- Sony Sound Forge
- Steinberg Wavelab
- Adobe Audition

Chances are your audio team will employ one or more of these packages in the development of audio assets. It may be valuable to familiarize yourself with the names of these programs, as they come up often in audio talk.

Virtual Instruments and Effects

Virtual instruments, which are software programs that create sound, are replacing hardware workstation synthesizers and samplers. This recent surge in popularity is bringing down the cost of the audio production studio. Some believe that the sound of a virtual instrument cannot match that of its actual counterparts, and in some cases, this seems to be true. However, the quality of these tools increases every year, and in some cases, even the most well-trained ear can't tell the difference between actual and virtual.

Software samplers are particularly useful in game audio production. Systems like Gigastudio, Kontact, and Mach 5 can load mammoth sample files that, when programmed correctly, can be made to sound just like a real-life full orchestra. Orchestral libraries from Vienna Symphonic Library, Sonic Implants, and Garritan Orchestral Strings deliver sound quality that is near-lifelike. These tools are perfect for creating mock scores that will later be referenced when the actual score is recorded. They are also useful when a project is faced with extremely limited resources for the music budget. Nothing replaces the sound of an actual orchestra performing a piece of music, but the fidelity of high-quality orchestral samples is truly amazing.

Sound Effects Libraries

Once upon a time, game audio sound effects consisted of sound chips programmed to mimic real-life sounds. Today, game systems feature memory capable of playing back sampled bits of recorded sound. The difference in realism has improved the quality of games markedly.

One challenge in producing sound effects for games lies in where to get recordings of certain sounds. It's not always easy to record the sound of a volcano, a WWII attack plane, or a llama. The solution is the sound effects library. Sound effects libraries are collections of sound recordings spanning a variety of sources, like animal sounds, vehicle sounds, city sounds, and so forth. There are many commercial libraries available, including The SFX Kit from Sound Ideas, the first sound library created specifically for use in games and other media.

The Business

Just having talent and technical chops is not enough. Networking is also about 50 percent of the game for any aspiring game musician. VPs, producers, designers, and programmers change jobs often, so if you can impress them initially, they will keep coming back and your list of potential clients will become huge within a short period of time.

Game Audio Network Guild

If you are serious about becoming an audio professional in the games industry, it will be extremely helpful to join the Game Audio Network Guild [GANG]. The Game Audio Network Guild is a nonprofit organization established to educate the masses in regard to interactive audio by providing information, instruction, resources, guidance, and enlightenment to its members and content providers and listeners throughout the world. G.A.N.G. empowers its members by establishing resources for education, business, technical issues, community, publicity, and recognition. G.A.N.G. also supports career development for aspiring game audio professionals, publishers, developers, and students.

G.A.N.G. is a resource for composers, sound designers, programmers, musicians, actors, engineers, producers, designers, directors, and others who have a genuine interest in interactive audio. By banding together and providing one voice, members can better articulate, discuss, and confront issues inside the interactive entertainment community. One of the focuses and goals of G.A.N.G. is to encourage and promote the creation of better sounding audio, which advances interactive industries by helping produce more competitive and entertaining products. G.A.N.G. promotes and recognizes quality through the annual G.A.N.G. Awards Show. The G.A.N.G. Web site (*www.audiogang.org*) provides a wealth of information pertaining to the interactive audio universe and the people working in or aspiring to be a part of it.

Passion and Location

If you are passionate enough, you should never give up. Passion drives everything! The will to succeed, to do better, and to survive becomes very important in any industry. Another important element is being in the right place. If you are looking to get into the video games industry, you need to move to a place that has many opportunities for game development. Los Angeles is the hub of the entertainment industry at large, including the games business. San Francisco, Seattle, and parts of England are rife with games industry activity as well. Vancouver, Boston, and parts of Texas are also growing.

Talent and determination are the two biggest assets you could have. With enough determination, you can achieve/find/create luck. Put together your best-written songs on a CD and go to the E3 convention in Los Angeles and/or the Game Developers Conference. Pass out CDs, make friends, learn, and network with people. Take your demo and send it out to all the game companies. It's all about being in the right place, and it's hard to be discovered if you're sitting in your bedroom. That goes for getting into any part of the industry; it's all about working your way up and who you know.

A CD with about five or six of your best songs or sound effect demos will become your résumé. It's always best to present the stuff you love writing the best. Don't send out a demo that has lots of different varieties of music. Just send the style you love to write. It's always the best-sounding music because it comes from your heart.

A study of audio is always helpful, but learning software tools and being an apprentice to someone who is already working in the field is much more advantageous. It's a great idea to go to all of the trade shows to meet people in the industry. Going to the Game Developers Conference and E3 is also very important [GDC, E3]. Learn about the industry through G.A.N.G., Gamasutra, and organizations like the IGDA [GANG, Gamasutra, IGDA]. A few great books on game audio include *The Complete Guide to Game Audio* [Marks01], *DirectX 9 Audio Exposed* [Fay03], *The Fat Man on Game Audio* [Sanger03], and *Audio for Games: Planning, Process, and Production* [Brandon04].

Summary

Audio production is of vastly growing importance to the overall game experience. In recent years, the process of creating and implementing audio into games has gone from being an afterthought to a forethought. Budgets have increased, and dedicated audio professionals are core members of production teams. With its subtle but important emotional and informational contribution, audio provides the subconscious underpinning to the gameplay experience that makes gaming seem "real."

For games to deliver the quality experience audiences have come to expect over a great century of movie-going, game creators must be serious about preplanning, creating, and implementing audio content into their game worlds.

Exercises

1. Why is interactive audio, as opposed to static audio, important for games?
2. Choose a popular game and study the music sound design. How does the music influence the mood or pace? Does the music match the tension level at all times? What's the ratio of real music to ambiance? How does the game handle switching music tracks?
3. Choose a popular game and study the sound design of the sound effects. Make a list of every sound effect you hear during five minutes of gameplay and what action or event causes it. Mark which ones are placed in 3D space around the player. What is the maximum number of sound effects that ever play at one time? For a given sound effect, like footsteps, how many different variations can you detect?
4. Choose a popular game and study the voice-over sound design. How many different voices are there? Are phrases stitched together or recorded as a single piece? Critique the acting quality of the voice-overs.
5. Design the soundscape for a sports game of your choice. List the types of sound effects along with what triggers them. List the types of music and ambiance.

References

[Brandon04] Brandon, Alexander, *Audio for Games: Planning, Process, and Production*, New Riders, 2004.

[CreativeLabs] Creative Labs, *http://developer.creative.com/*.

[Dolby] Dolby, *www.dolby.com*.

[DTS] DTS, *www.dtsonline.com*.

[E3] Electronic Entertainment Expo, *www.e3expo.com*.

[Fay03] Fay, Todd M.; Selfon, Scott; and Fay, Todor, *DirectX 9 Audio Exposed: Interactive Audio Development*, Wordware Publishing, 2003.

[Gamasutra] Gamasutra, *www.gamasutra.com*.

[GANG] Game Audio Network Guild, *www.audiogang.com*.

[GDC] Game Developers Conference, *www.gdconf.com*.

[IGDA] International Game Developers Association, *www.igda.org*.

[Marks01] Marks, Aaron, *The Complete Guide to Game Audio: For Composers, Musicians, Sound Designers, and Game Developers*, CMP Books, 2001.

[Sanger03] Sanger, George A., *The Fat Man on Game Audio: Tasty Morsels of Sonic Goodness*, New Riders, 2003.

PART
7

GAME PRODUCTION AND THE BUSINESS OF GAMES

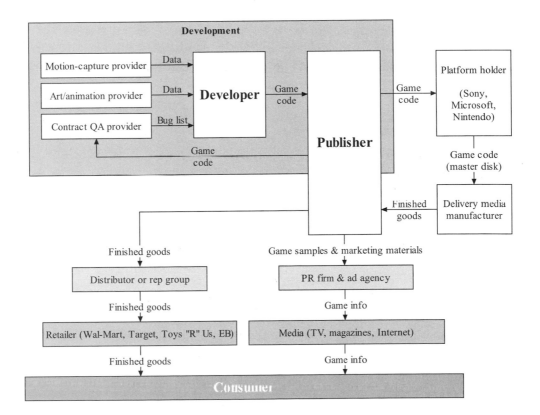

7.1 Game Production and Project Management

In This Chapter

- Overview
- Concept Phase
- Preproduction Phase
- Production Phase
- Postproduction
- Summary
- Exercises
- References

Overview

Today, mainstream video games and computer games are made by large teams of people. These are big, expensive, time-consuming projects. It's not a simple or obvious process. This chapter reveals the process, from the point of view of the person who manages it: the producer.

Some companies may refer to the producer by a different job title (director or project manager, for instance, rather than producer), and may ascribe a different job description to the job title of producer, but herein the project manager is referred to as the producer.

There are producers who work for game publishing companies, to manage the making of games to be published by the employer. There are producers who work for game developers, managing the developer's team in fulfilling a game development contract for the publisher producer. This chapter, and the others in this section, cover both internal production and external production, as managed by the publisher producer.

There are five phases in the process of making a game: concept, preproduction, production, postproduction, and aftermarket. Herein, the first four phases are fully discussed. The reader may learn about the aftermarket phase in [Sloper02].

Concept Phase

The first phase of a game project (preceding the preproduction phase) is the concept phase. In any of a variety of ways, the publishing company (employer) has decided to pursue a game concept. The producer is often the first person assigned to work on a new project.

Where Concepts Come From

Game concepts are usually not the brainchild of a game designer. They are usually logical or obvious business decisions based on past successes or business deals. For example, it often happens that a publishing company already owns a successful game franchise, and desires to make a sequel. Or, the publisher has negotiated a deal with a film studio to make a game based on a movie. Or, the publisher owns game technology, a game engine, and desires to make a new game using that existing technology. Occasionally, new original concepts come along, either designed by internal creative personnel or submitted by an external developer.

For the purposes of this chapter, orders have come down that the producer must produce a game based on the company's successful game franchise, *Ultimatt Combatt.* The producer's job is to produce *Ultimatt Combatt III.* Certain guidelines are usually handed down to the producer with the assignment. For instance, the game should be an RTS, should use at least a few of the characters from *Ultimatt Combatt II,* should include an online component, and should add new features inherent in other games that are currently gaining wide consumer acceptance. The producer can't simply write down a few sentences parroting these guidelines. Much more than that must go into the writing of a conceptual design document.

Producing the Conceptual Design

Before serious work can begin on the game, the central concept of the game must be written down. Form follows function, which means that the purpose of the concept document dictates what form the concept document will take. The concept document serves a number of purposes, but at this stage, its primary purpose is to communicate a vision of the game so that all involved parties may agree on it.

The concept document might be written by the producer or a game designer. The producer can use an internal game designer (a designer who is employed full time by the publishing company), or might hire an external game designer, after first having executed a contract that swears the designer to secrecy. Moreover, sometimes, the concept paper is submitted by an external development company.

The creation of the concept document probably requires several meetings to achieve consensus.

The conceptual design must briefly describe the specific story and character developments that will occur in *UCIII*. The conceptual design must briefly outline the specific improvements that will be made in the game, the user interface, and the level design. In addition, the document should address specific ways in which *UCIII* will reclaim users who have been stolen away by competing products, citing research on the user base, customer support findings, and magazine reviews. If the game is to be published for a console (Xbox or PlayStation, for example), then additional feedback should be obtained from the platform holder (Microsoft or Sony) and incorporated into the concept document.

In the case of a licensed concept, the producer would also discuss the concept with the licensor. However, since *UCIII* is an internal IP, an outside meeting isn't necessary in this case. If the *UCII* team is internal, the producer would want to brainstorm with the people who worked on that game. Every person who worked on a game that was released has pet features he or she wishes had been included. Worthwhile features have a second chance for consideration in *UCIII*. The sales team who moved *UCII* into store chains probably also has some suggestions, and those need to be considered as well.

The conceptual design also needs a "working title" for the game. It might seem a simple matter; the designer chooses a name for the game and that is that. However, in reality the game's title is an important marketing tool, and the title chosen at the beginning is subject to change as marketing activities heat up prior to the game's release. In the case of *Ultimatt Combatt III*, all that's needed is a subtitle. The producer and designer agree to call it *Ultimatt Combatt III: Extreme Warfare*. For at least the duration of pre-production and some (or much) of the production phase, that is the title by which everyone will refer to the project. The final title will be determined later.

Having collected ideas and wish lists from a variety of sources, the producer distills it all down into a short document. It has to be short because of its intended audience: busy executives. You've heard of "executive summaries?" Executives want to hear the highlights first. Once their interest is piqued, they may stick around to hear a few details as well. In addition, they will certainly come to the table with questions. The concept document needs to be brief, yet provide satisfactory answers to the big questions.

Green Light Committee

Each publishing company does things differently. However, before permitting a producer to commit the company's resources to a big project, the company needs to be in complete agreement as to the details and direction of the project.

The producer brings printed copies of the conceptual design document, as well as a PowerPoint presentation. The games *Ultimatt Combatt* and *Ultimatt Combatt II* are installed on the machine in the meeting room in case anyone wants to have a quick look.

Present at the green light meeting will be executives of the publisher's studio, distribution, licensing, sales, marketing, financial, and international divisions. The executives of the publisher's overseas operations may not be physically present in the room, rather participating by means of teleconference or videoconference. Each executive has his or her own views and concerns. Although they already know that they want to make a sequel to *Ultimatt Combatt II,* they won't necessary all agree as to what form that sequel should take. The devil is in the details. Green light meetings can go smoothly or can produce surprising twists.

Publishing executives may say, in oblique ways, that they do not disagree with the idea of proceeding with a project. However, they often prefer not to put their official seal of approval on proceeding with a risky project, in case it might go badly. However, if the publisher has a solid green light process in place, it needn't always be the producer who will have to shoulder all the blame if a project doesn't go well. The green light process is for the benefit of both sides of the table (the producer and the studio on one side, and the executives on the other).

If all goes well in the green light meeting, the producer is given the approval (a "green light") to proceed, and to use the publishing company's resources: money, personnel, equipment, office space, and its internal network, among other things. Typically, the producer is given platform, territory, scheduling, and budgetary guidelines at this time, if not before.

Once the concept phase is over, the production process can be broken down into three phases.

Preproduction: This is the phase during which planning and team building take place.

Production: During this phase, the game is actually created.

Postproduction: Bugs are identified and fixed, the game is tweaked, and the package and manual are created.

Preproduction Phase

Once the concept is fleshed out, and the producer has the go-ahead to put a project together, serious work begins. The producer needs to have a full game design document (GDD) written, and must select a development team. Work can progress on both fronts simultaneously.

The GDD

If the game is to be developed internally, and the company has one or more game designers on staff, the GDD can be written internally (by a company employee). If the game is to be developed externally, and/or the company does not have a full-time game designer on staff who can write the GDD, then the GDD could be written by a freelance designer, or by a designer who works for the development house that will create the game. In the case of *UCIII,* it is decided that the bulk of the new programming work will be done by an external development house, yet to be selected. In-house programmers will also be needed because the game's online functionality will use existing technology created and owned by the publishing company. Moreover, because the company has game designers on staff who are already intimately familiar with the *Ultimatt Combatt* universe, the GDD will be written internally.

Team Selection

When a game is developed internally, the first document the producer must create is a staffing plan. When a game is developed externally, a bid package must be created to facilitate developer selection. Since *UCIII* is to use both internal and external resources, both a staffing plan and a bid package have to be created.

Internal Staffing Plan

The producer must determine what personnel are needed, and must create job descriptions for each different type of job. Job descriptions detail the duties and pay ranges for each individual on the internal team.

To staff an internal team, a producer has three choices:

- Use existing employees, in roles they've performed before.
- Promote or transfer existing employees from other departments, like QA.
- Hire new employees.

The first of these seems like the simplest way to go, but it can be quite a management challenge to keep creative personnel working year round. It is rarely smooth or easy to have another project ready for a programmer who has just finished one project. Each programmer on a project is finished with his responsibility on that project at different times, which exacerbates the problem. Consequently, assigning internal personnel to a new project is very much like a juggling act.

Transferring or promoting from within is not without its own challenges. The producer might want to bring in a talented lead tester from QA to train to become an assistant producer. The tester might be willing, but his manager might not. Conversely, the manager might be delighted to give the deserving tester an opportunity—but the tester might not want to work on the particular game being staffed.

Hiring new employees can be an exhausting and time-consuming task for the producer. So many résumés to read, so many interviews to conduct. A good H.R. department can help smooth out the bumps, by filtering the candidates and arranging for interview sessions. When a promising candidate comes in, not only the producer will need to be involved. Other project leaders will also need to meet potential new hires. New staffers need to be able to do the required duties, and fit in with the existing team.

Selecting an External Developer

The producer probably has a selection of external developers with whom he or she has worked before, and would like to work with again. The producer can widen the field by asking other producers for recommendations, and by checking out developers via other resources, such as the IGDA and Gamasutra.com.

It sometimes happens that a desirable developer cannot make a bid on a project. Perhaps the developer is already booked up, working to capacity. Or, perhaps the particular project is outside the developer's expertise (the genre, the subject matter, or the platform). In such a case, the developer may suggest another developer that the producer can contact.

If a developer is interested in bidding on a project, the producer has to provide fairly detailed information so the developer can make a realistic estimate. In an ideal world, the developer would like to have a complete GDD. However, this isn't always possible. Whether or not there's a full GDD, another document, a bid package, is usually needed at this point. However, before the producer can send this to the external developer, a contract called a Confidentiality Agreement or an NDA (Non-Disclosure Agreement) usually needs to be signed.

Confidentiality and Nondisclosure Agreements

The games industry is famous for its cutthroat competitiveness and secrecy. It takes a long time to make a game, so if too much information about the game leaks out early on, a competing company could steal the publisher's thunder by beating them to the punch with a similar game.

Consequently, before sharing such important and valuable information with an outside company, the publisher asks the developer to sign an NDA. The contract says that the developer recognizes the value and importance of confidentiality and will not reveal the publisher's plans to any uninvolved parties.

It's standard operating procedure for developers to sign confidentiality agreements and NDAs when asked to bid on a project, even when they've done projects for the publisher previously. Once the NDA is signed, the producer can share the information with the developer. The producer can tell the developer about the concept verbally, but the developer needs detailed information.

The Bid Package

The developer needs to know the game's genre, platform, and target audience, and what products the game must compete against. The developer needs to know the publisher's target ship date. Is this to be a triple-A game, or a budget title? How many levels, characters, or missions will the game entail? What special technologies or features will be included? Is the developer expected to create all the assets and technology, and if not, exactly which aspects of the project are to be handled by the developer? Must a demo be created, and if so, what are its specs and due date?

The producer will be contacting several developers to get several bids. Each developer will have different questions, so the producer collects all the developers' questions, and then writes a single bid package so all developers can bid based on the same package.

The bid package includes information for the developer, and questions for the developer to answer. The developer needs to be told when the bid is needed, what format the bid should take, and what information is needed in the bid.

For the developer, bidding is an art more than a science. If the bid price is low, the developer could well win the project...but then might go broke before the project is finished. If the bid price is high enough that the developer will make a good profit, the project might go to another developer with a lower bid.

Some developers ask for royalties on the game's sales. The producer will usually want to see a lower upfront cost (advance) if royalties are to be part of the picture. However, increasingly, these days, royalties are on the decline [Rogers04].

A good developer will respond with a bid on the requested date, in the requested format, and with all requested information. A great developer will also provide a breakdown, so that the producer can make more informed choices. On the opposite side of the coin, a developer whose bid is late, or doesn't provide all the requested information, doesn't make a good impression on the producer, and thus may lose the project.

Having collected bids, the producer can select the developer(s) who will create the game. Now a contract is needed.

The Development Agreement

The producer and the developer can't just shake hands and get to work. No smart developer will begin spending resources on a project without a contract and an initial payment.

It is usually the larger, more powerful entity in a venture that is responsible for writing the contract. That means it is usually the publisher's responsibility. The publisher typically has a "boilerplate," a standard development contract that contains the terms that the publisher prefers. The producer works with the publisher's legal counsel to fill in the blanks in the contract. The game's working title and the developer's business name and address are plugged in.

The developer's specific duties are spelled out. The developer is to create a game and a demo for one or more specific platforms. The game must meet certain design criteria, per the design document, which is attached. The developer will provide source code with the deliveries, which are to occur per a detailed schedule.

The publisher's specific obligations are spelled out. Payments are to occur within X days of acceptance of a delivery. If the publisher is responsible for creation of assets for use by the developer, those are to be delivered in the specified format according to a detailed schedule.

The agreement details ownership of intellectual property. In the case of *UCIII*, the developer owns no IP. However, the developer may own the technology or engine. The publisher warrants that it has the right and authority to make games based on the *Ultimatt Combatt* universe, including places, characters, and objects therein. The developer warrants that it is not using technology patented by other parties without having secured full right and authority to do so. Both parties typically hold the other party harmless. For example, if a third party sues the developer because the third party claims ownership in some part of the *UC* universe, the publisher will be the responsible party in the suit. Alternatively, if a third party sues the publisher for the use of their patented source code in *UCIII,* the developer is supposed to be responsible in that suit.

The agreement describes the circumstances under which the contract could be terminated, and what would happen in the event of termination.

One could write an entire book about development agreements. For the purposes of this chapter, though, the most important aspects of such agreements are the milestones and the milestone approval cycles.

Milestones

The developer is going to do a lot of work for the publisher, and in exchange is going to be paid a lot of money. The publisher can't just fork over the money and wait two years to see what the developer will deliver. That's much too great a risk. The developer might never finish the game, or might deliver a game that isn't satisfactory. In addition, the developer can't work for two years, hoping to get paid upon completion. The publisher might be unhappy with the way the game turned out, or might decide that it no longer suits their evolving business plan, and refuse to pay. The solution is to break the project down into chunks, called *milestones*.

The milestones call for the developer to do specific things in a specific order. The features that are due in a milestone are called "deliverables." To avoid disagreements as to whether a deliverable has been satisfactorily fulfilled, the producer and the developer have to work together to write clear, concise milestones into the development agreement.

For example, it wouldn't do to have a milestone that simply says, "Level 1." The developer and the producer might interpret this differently. The developer could deliver a version of the game that contains nothing more than the game world's first level, and that permits the user to move a "camera" through it, without any characters or items being therein. If the producer wanted the deliverable to include a fully functioning player character, able to run, jump, pick up items, and interact with NPCs, and to encounter all the NPCs and objects called for in the GDD for Level 1, then the producer should make sure that this expectation is fully described in the milestone.

Terms like "alpha" and "beta," if used in milestones, should be for reference purposes only, not as definitive terms. Neither term has a universally agreed definition. It can be useful to name milestones something like "developer's beta," for instance, to mean, "the developer has implemented all features and has, to the best of the developer's knowledge, identified and fixed all known bugs." If the publisher's QA department has their own working definition of beta that differs from the contractual milestone, it would be unfair to withhold payment for milestone delivery for that, unless the QA definition of beta were to be used in the writing of the milestone. The developer wants its milestone approvals to come from the producer directly, not from another entity such as a QA lead.

Milestones need to be written very clearly, so that anyone reading the milestone would have no doubt as to what is expected. Poorly written milestones can hurt both the developer and the publisher. Disagreements as to whether a milestone has been met, and a payment due, can result in production delays and bad feelings. The developer can suffer damage or even go out of business if payments are not made. The publisher can suffer by loss of an important project and a poor public image when the news gets out. The importance of clear milestones cannot be overstressed.

Milestone Approvals

While the writing of the milestones is of tremendous importance to both parties, the approval of milestones is of importance primarily for the developer, whose very livelihood is at stake. The developer's business plan calls for payments to come in within a reasonable time after acceptance of milestone deliveries. The development agreement then must include a clause covering the approval of milestones by the producer and the publisher. Milestones are typically not payable upon delivery, but rather upon approval and acceptance. The well-written contract says this explicitly.

Typically, the producer contractually agrees to review a milestone delivery and accept or reject it within seven days. Contracts have to be very clear, so even the term "seven days" needs to be defined. Does it mean seven calendar days regardless of weekends and holidays? Or does it mean seven business days? Unless the milestone is extremely large or the producer is severely overworked, there is rarely a reason why a milestone couldn't be reviewed within five business days, or even less.

The well-written milestone serves as a checklist for the producer to review the milestone. If the milestone calls for a player character to be fully implemented, running, jumping, ducking, and shooting, then that is very quick and easy for the producer to check. If the milestone calls for the game to include a very large playing area that could take the producer days to explore due to a sizable amount of interactions and difficult fighting, the developer might want to build in cheats of various types to facilitate the producer in running through the deliverables.

The first two milestones are usually (1) contract signing, and (2) the technical design document (TDD). Upon signing the contract, the developer needs a payment to begin work. The first task is to write the TDD.

The Technical Design Document

By this time, if the GDD is not yet fully complete, there should be enough from which the developer can begin work on the TDD. If one regards the GDD as a statement of the problem, the TDD can be viewed as a statement of the solution [Blair93]. The purpose of the TDD is to lay the foundation for the programming work; identify the technical challenges and put into place a plan for dealing with them; and to specify what technology will be used, what equipment is needed, and what personnel will be employed in creating the game's code. And, most importantly, to make a detailed task list.

To some extent, there are interdependencies that make it difficult to create a detailed list of milestones without first having the TDD in place, so it may be that the detailed milestone descriptions are written after the TDD is accepted and the schedule is finalized. The exact order of events is subject to the specifics of the project, the concept, and the working style of the companies and managers involved.

Scheduling

One of the true black arts of the game producer is the writing of a schedule. It's part science and part wishful thinking. With a GDD and TDD in hand, the producer can get to work.

In making the game's schedule, the producer plans for everything—the more detail the better.

- The programming milestones
- Creation of all visual assets
- Creation of all audio assets
- Creation of demo version and/or E3 demo
- Delivery of assets for marketing materials
- Creation of package and manual
- Creation of strategy guides
- Licensor approvals
- Platform holder approvals
- Green light meetings
- ESRB rating
- Vacations
- Holidays

Some producers use a project-scheduling tool like Microsoft® Project™, and others write schedules in a spreadsheet like Microsoft® Excel®. Scheduling-specific tools like Project facilitate the use of interdependencies in the plan, so that tasks that cannot be done until other tasks are finished can be scheduled. Whichever planning tools the producer uses, the experienced producer always starts by planning backwards from the target ship date.

The Golden Spike and Game Scheduling

On May 10, 1869, the tracks of the Union Pacific railroad were joined to those of the Central Pacific Railroad at Promontory, Utah, with a golden spike to symbolize the importance of having crossed the entire North American continent by rail [SFMuseum]. The builders of the cross-continental railroad didn't start at one end and work their way to the other. They started at both ends, and worked their way toward the middle. Building a game schedule is a lot like that.

The back end (from beta to the target ship date) cannot be compressed. The finished goods can not be moved from the manufacturer's warehouse to the stores' warehouses any faster than the trucks can drive. The manufacturer requires a certain amount of time to make the finished goods, and they can't be cajoled into making them faster. The console platform holder (in the case of *UCIII*, an Xbox game, that would be Microsoft) requires a certain amount of time to test and approve the game after the publisher's QA team has certified it. Don't even think about asking Microsoft to speed that up! In addition, the QA team needs a certain amount of time to fully test the game. Therefore, the producer begins by scheduling backwards from ship to beta.

Given the desired ship date, and the firm and unchangeable tasks that must occur just prior to shipping the finished product, the producer then knows when the game must be at beta. Let's call this the "target beta date."

Scheduling from the present, forward through the programming task list, the producer then needs the game's assets to all be completed and implemented before that date. All the game's features need to be implemented and (to the best of the developer's knowledge) debugged by that date. The game's levels need to be designed, built, and incorporated by that date. If all goes well, the forward track does not overlap with the backward track, and the Golden Spike can be driven in. The real world, however, doesn't always work out that cleanly.

Using the TDD and working with the developer, the producer can determine when the game will actually be at beta. When it is determined that the actual beta date will be later than the target beta date, there are two options the producer can explore. The first is to reduce development time so that the target beta date (thus the target ship date) will be met. The second is to push back the ship date.

To the uninitiated, it would seem that it might be simpler to push back the ship date. However, the producer will meet stiff resistance to this option from the publishing company executives. The publisher's business model requires the timely shipping of new products. Requests to spend more time and money are, therefore, fiercely resisted.

Therefore, the first thing the producer has to explore is how to reduce development time to meet the target beta date.

Reducing Development Time

To a certain extent, it's possible to add people to reduce workload. However, as described in *The Mythical Man-Month,* adding people adds complexity to a project and at some point becomes counterproductive. If it has been estimated that it will take two programmers one month to implement a particular bit of code, it is not necessarily true that four programmers could get it done in half a month. The existence of the "man-month" concept does not mean that men and months are interchangeable [TMMM82].

Up to this point, we have discussed the project schedule in terms of programming, with little if any mention of the time it takes to create graphics, animation, 3D models, sounds, voice, story text, or music. The reason for this apparent oversight is simple: programming is the single most time-intensive task in making interactive electronic entertainment. Creation of the assets to be used by the programmers can occur in parallel, and asset deliveries can be made to dovetail with the requirements of the programmers. That said, it often happens that programmers have a need for place-holder assets to make features work. If a programmer is spending time creating place-holder assets, that isn't the best use of the programmer's time. When looking for ways to reduce programming time, the producer is well advised to find ways to have assets ready well before the programmers anticipate needing them.

When adding programmers and revising the schedule does not result in a comfortably realistic Golden Spike, the next thing the producer has to reexamine is the game design. The initial GDD invariably lists features that are essential, features that add to the perceived value of the game, and features that are nice but unnecessary. The producer should look at the GDD as a wish list, and should reevaluate the importance of the game's features.

Prioritizing the Feature Set

The producer must first consider anew the central premise of the game, in order to prioritize the features in light of that premise. In the case of *UCIII*, it has already been determined that the game should be an RTS, should use at least a few of the characters from *Ultimatt Combatt II,* should include an online component, and should add new features inherent in other games that are currently gaining wide consumer acceptance. If, in the writing of the GDD, the designer has added other features that go beyond those basic requirements without significantly adding to the marketability of the game, those features can go on the chopping block. Then, subtracting the time it would take to implement those features, the producer can see if the target beta date and the projected beta date can be joined with a Golden Spike.

Looking for Bottlenecks

In addition to prioritizing the feature set, the producer should reexamine the programming schedule as broken down by task. The goal is to determine anew which features are taking the most time. Typically, the features that take the most time are also the most important. However, perhaps there are multiple lower priority features that, taken together, can be cut to save development time. It often happens that very low-priority features are quick and easy to implement. When time is tight, it's best to schedule those for later in the project, to be implemented only if the project is running on schedule.

It sometimes happens that cutting features to achieve the desired schedule results in greatly reducing the game's marketability. In such a case, the producer has no choice but to ask for more time. And as we all know, time is money.

Budgets

The budget is essentially a spending plan. It's desirable to anticipate all costs in advance, so that by the time the game is finished, the planned amount of money is not exceeded.

Most producers use a spreadsheet program like Excel to make budgets. In building the budget, the producer starts with the schedule. The budget is typically broken down by the month. Therefore, the first thing is to build a grid with each column representing a month of the project. The rows are then used to delineate the various types of expenses to be incurred during the project. Again, the more detail the better. For each month of the project, the producer inputs:

- Salary for each internal employee
- Payments to each external developer or vendor
- Cost for equipment purchases or rental
- Cost for software purchased
- Cost for supplies purchased
- Travel and meals
- Shipment costs

When making a budget, the producer quickly realizes that a dollar amount is often just an estimate, based on an assumption or based on an estimate made by another individual. The producer annotates all assumptions to justify all estimates or amounts that might be subject to interpretation or disagreement by a reader of the budget. In the example budget, the leftmost column is reserved for assumptions, which are numbered and listed in detail at the bottom of the worksheet.

For the sake of busy executives who just want to know the bottom line without wading through all the details, the budget should include an overview sheet that breaks down the budget to the essential factoids.

Each publishing company calculates budgets differently. Some may go so far as to require the producer's budget to include the use of office space and amortization of equipment and furniture that already is owned by the publisher. Alternatively, some publishers may simplify this by requiring the producer to include a flat overhead cost in the budget. Or, if these overhead costs aren't included in the budget, perhaps they're included in the P&L.

Profit and Loss Analysis

Certain things not covered in the budget still need to be accounted for to determine whether the cost of making the game will be covered. The producer, or perhaps the marketing manager assigned to the project, will create a Profit and Loss Analysis, also called a P&L. The P&L might alternatively be called an ROI (Return On Investment analysis).

The P&L weighs all costs associated with the game versus all anticipated revenues, so that it can be determined in advance whether a game should be made.

On the costs side:

- Production costs (those costs covered in the game's budget)
- Cost of goods (manufacturing cost, including platform holder licensing)
- Marketing costs

- Licensor royalties
- Developer royalties

On the revenues side:

- Projected sales
- Anticipated wholesale price
- Ancillary sales (OEM, strategy guides)

Part of the number crunching that needs to be done, whether the producer works for the publisher or the developer, is a break-even analysis. Having collected estimates from various parties involved, it isn't difficult to determine how many units need to be sold for the venture to be profitable. Many publishers have a target profit percentage requirement. Below a certain profit margin, a project should not be undertaken.

Kickoff Green Light

Once the producer has made a schedule, a budget, a GDD, and a TDD, the preproduction phase is complete. Once more, the producer goes before the green light committee. If the executives approve the plan for the game, the producer gets a green light to proceed, committing the publisher's resources to production of the game.

In the case of a licensed game, the licensor's approval of the plan is needed at this point. In the case of a console game, it would be unwise to proceed without the platform's approval as well.

Summary

Preproduction is all about planning. Preproduction is vital. If the producer plans thoroughly in preproduction, production should go smoothly—or at least as smoothly as anything can, given the vagaries of the real world. In addition, the most unpredictable element in any game project is the people working on it.

Production Phase

In the production phase, actual work begins. Think of it as analogous to building a skyscraper. No earthmoving equipment or construction equipment is fired up until the blueprints are finished, funding is secured, and permits are obtained.

Programming a mainstream console or PC videogame usually does not produce any visible/playable code for the first few months. Again, consider the construction of a skyscraper. The construction company doesn't begin by putting girders up. Rather, construction begins by digging a hole in the ground. Similarly, programmers have to create the game's foundation before they can start putting visible gameplay up on the screen.

For the producer, this means a couple of things. First, he or she doesn't have anything to show for the money being spent. Second, the producer now has more time to turn his or her attention to getting assets made. Producers (and producers' bosses) like to have something they can see.

Show Me

As mentioned previously, milestones are both a way of measuring progress and (in the case of external development) a key to unlock payments. Because there is little that the developer can show the producer during the first few months, the producer may have to sign off on payments based on nothing more than progress reports and trust. The producer, having worked closely with the development manager, may feel a certain amount of comfort and trust in the progress reports. However, the producer also must have check requests signed by his superior. Therefore, the producer must feel trust for the developer manager, and must convince superiors to trust the development manager—and the producer.

The good news is that the producer can now focus attention on getting the visual and audio assets created. Art is created faster than code, so the producer will have something to show fairly quickly.

Art assets might be created internally or externally. Externally created art might be created by a full-service developer (a company that makes both code and art), or it might be created by an art house. Regardless of where or by whom the art is to be created, the first step has to be the creation of an art list.

Art Lists

Art lists are generated from the game design document. The designer (the writer of the GDD) might create the art list, or perhaps the game's art director creates the art list from the GDD and then runs it by the designer for a reality check.

The art list must include every art asset that has to be created, from the introductory cinematic, to each character and all items they can use, all the way down to the "start" button on the title screen.

An art list is much more than a simple "grocery list" of what graphics are needed for a game. The art list must include quite a lot of information. Therefore, an art list usually is more like a table or spreadsheet than a grocery list.

At a minimum, the art list needs to provide the following information about each art asset:

- Descriptive name
- Asset filename
- Asset type or format
- What level or scene the art asset is used in
- Brief description

Once work on the art has gotten under way, even more information will be needed. A spreadsheet is a good tool to use for making art lists and taking them one step further and turning them into tracking tools. Microsoft Excel is widely available to all members of the team (even those using Macintosh computers), which makes it a useful tool for this purpose. Some projects may use other tools to list or track the art assets.

Asset File-Naming Conventions

It makes the programmer's job easier if the assets are named according to a logical system or convention. If one artist names one of his graphic files "knight_left_arm.3dt" and another names one of her files "Kyra's-eyelid-for-blink.bmp," then a directory listing of the files will look like a mess. They're all different lengths and there is no coherent naming methodology. Worse, the programmer has to be mindful of whether he's typing a dash or an underscore when inputting the filenames into the code.

It's standard operating procedure for each project to establish a convention for file naming. The filename is specified in the art list (or sound list, etc.), and the team member who creates the asset must give the asset file the preassigned name upon asset completion. An incorrect filename can be grounds for asset rejection.

The first few characters of an asset filename might be based on asset type, world location, and/or character name. For example, perhaps the game has a location called "Old West Town" and a character called "Lefty." Lefty has a unique walk, which means his footsteps sound must be different from the footsteps sound of the other character(s) in the location. If Lefty is encountered only in the Old West Town, the filename for his footsteps sound might be SOWLF001.WAV. S for Sound, OW for Old West Town, LF for Lefty, and this is the first asset in the list of sounds for Lefty in the Old West Town. The filename for the raw form of the texture for Lefty's face might be TOWLF010.BMP. The filename for the third spoken line of Lefty might be VOWLF003.WAV.

A logical and coherent file-naming convention smoothes the process for the programming team and neatens the directories containing assets. In the event a bug occurs in which a problem file's name is given, anyone reading the error message will know what type of file caused the problem and where in the game the problem occurs. There are other benefits as well. The importance of file-naming conventions is a frequent topic of discussion among developers at game conferences.

Asset Tracking

The producer must be able to closely monitor the progress of all aspects of the project. The producer needs to keep track of the following information about each art asset:

- Who is responsible for creating the asset
- Date work assigned
- Date first draft of asset completed
- Date asset delivered to producer for approval
- Date asset reviewed by producer
- Whether asset was approved or rejected
- Reason for rejection if asset rejected
- Date rework assigned
- Date second draft of asset completed
- Date asset redelivered to producer for approval

- Date asset rereviewed by producer
- Whether asset was approved or rejected
- Reason if asset rejected
- Date asset delivered to programming team
- Date asset implemented in game

Hopefully, an asset won't be rejected more than once before implementation. Additional columns may need to be reserved for additional approval turnarounds.

Asset Approval Cycles

As seen previously, it isn't enough for an asset to be created and delivered. Before it can be passed on to the programmers and implemented, art, sound, or music assets need to be reviewed and accepted by the producer. A clearly defined asset approval procedure facilitates rapid payment (in the case of external art creation) and (whether the art is created internally or externally) prevents many potential problems.

Typically, the manager of the art team delivers assets for approval in batches. The producer might designate someone to review the assets (art director, lead designer, etc.) or might do the review himself. In any case, the reviewer should conscientiously review the assets and provide clear and detailed feedback within the contractual review period, or sooner. Then, the art house needs to have, and should take, a reasonable timeline to rework and redeliver. All of this is so milestone checks can be paid in a timely manner so the project can progress smoothly.

Of course, another reason for reviewing and approving art, sound, and music assets is to ensure the quality. If a piece of art or animation doesn't look good enough, or doesn't fit stylistically, detailed commentary should be provided along with the rejection, so that the asset can be redone appropriately and smoothly.

Asset Delivery Formats

The TDD should specify the format of all game assets. The programming team's engine needs 2D graphics to be in a particular format, and that goes as well for 3D models, textures, and animations. Sound and music assets likewise need to be in a particular format for use by the game's engine. The asset creator must deliver assets in those forms. It would be a waste of the programming team's time to have to convert assets into the proper format. To keep overall development time to a minimum, the programming team's time has to be used efficiently and productively.

The producer (or whomever is reviewing assets for approval) needs to have software tools for viewing assets to approve them. Everyone has easy and ready access to utilities for viewing JPGs, BMPs, and TIFFs, or for hearing WAV or MP3 files or playing AVI or MPG files. However, specialized tools are needed if less commonly available asset formats are used in the game. It's not difficult for a producer or art director to get and use these specialized programs, but when it comes to marketing managers, these programs can present a problem. It is often desirable for a marketing manager to be able to show off game assets. If the specialized program is difficult to obtain, clunky to use, or too expensive, that could be a problem for marketing presentations. It is not unreasonable for the producer to request that some assets be provided in common formats for marketing purposes.

Red Flags

The most important job of the producer during the production phase is to spot "red flags." The producer's job is to keep the game project on track. After all, there's a schedule to meet. Many things can go wrong. Occasionally a catastrophe will occur without warning, taking everyone on the team by surprise. However, most problems build slowly over time, and usually there are warning signs. The experienced producer learns to recognize these red flags early on, and to deal with them before things get worse.

The most obvious sign of a problem is schedule delays. When a milestone is late, or is missing deliverables, the experienced producer starts digging to find the root cause.

Red flags usually start flying because of design problems, personnel issues, money trouble, or technical glitches. Moreover, there is a certain amount of synergy between the four. That is to say, personnel problems can lead to technical problems, design problems can cause personnel problems, and so on.

Team Dynamics

By the time assets are coming in, the project team has been working together long enough for interpersonal dynamics to come into play. Some team members develop respect for each other. Other team members may start to show signs of dissatisfaction due to jealousy or envy. Some personalities may simply not go well together.

In general, programmers, being engineers, can seem "cold." They value facts and technical solutions. Sometimes, programmers aren't fully aware of the way their words and opinions can affect the sensibilities of those around them. When engineers write, their i's are always dotted and their t's are always crossed, but their words often come across as dry and without emotive impact.

To make another sweeping generality, artists can sometimes seem "warm." They value colors, lines, and feelings. Artists might communicate using emotional ideas, and sometimes exaggerate for effect. When artists are forced to write, it can be colorful and dramatic, but there may be spelling or grammatical errors. Artists might omit necessary detail or provide too much unnecessary detail.

There are exceptions to every rule. Not every programmer is like the *Star Trek* character Data, and not every artist is destined to move to Tahiti or to chop his ear off. Certainly, programmers have emotions, and artists are not functionally illiterate. Within a particular profession, there is a spectrum of personalities and attitudes. However, it is well established that certain personality types tend to exist within specific professions. Programmers and artists are the classic "oil and water" mixture of the game business. The best technical directors are those who can both command the respect of the technical team and communicate and coordinate smoothly with the nonprogrammers around them. Likewise, the best art directors are those who have a great eye for design and can lead their artists, and can also communicate and coordinate smoothly with the nonartists who depend on their work.

When the art and code are being created at different locations, the natural discomfort of this sometimes uneasy mix is minimized. However, when everyone's under one roof, team meetings or encounters can sometimes be contentious.

However, conflicts can arise in a game team for other reasons as well.

Programmer A is assigned to work on a part of the code that depends on the work of Programmer B. Programmer A may disagree with the coding structure used by Programmer B, or may resent the fact that Programmer B has been assigned the more prominent role. One or both of those programmers may have a less than ideal way of handling the disagreement or resentment.

Artist T, assigned to do textures for the 3D models in the game, may envy Artist M who is assigned the more glamorous job of creating the 3D models. Feelings might simmer for a while until something occurs that causes the pot to boil over.

In general, squabbles increase when development is not going well (when there are delays, when things aren't working, and when the game isn't fun). Tempers can flare over problems with the gameplay. Staffers' differing opinions on a game's features can escalate into shouting matches.

A lead programmer might have issues with authority figures. An artist with game design aspirations might be jealous of the game designer's "sexy" job title. A longtime employee might covet a new hire's larger cubicle, or (even worse) office—with a view and a door.

Specific techniques for resolving these types of conflicts go beyond the scope of this chapter. These problems aren't unique to the games industry. There are many books on management and even on how to deal with personality differences in the workplace. The producer, the lead designer, the technical director, and the art director all have to manage productivity and workplace matters, and all sorts of interpersonal issues that may arise—with their staff, and with each other.

Some common morale-boosting tactics used in the games industry are to have networked game sessions after hours or paintball events offsite, to order in free pizza or Chinese food, to enact flex time and lax dress codes, and to permit a playful office décor. Game offices usually look like fun places to work. It is work to make games, but it is enjoyable work, for the most part—and for most people.

Personnel Issues

Sometimes, problems cannot be resolved by managing them away. No amount of free pizza and game nights can fix problems caused by someone who isn't pulling his weight or who stirs up trouble.

It's not unusual for a game company to use flex hours. For example, an employee might be permitted to come in any time between 8:00 A.M. to 10:00 A.M., as long as he puts in a full eight-hour day, gets his tasks done on schedule, and comes in earlier for team meetings once a week. Most of the time, and for most staffers, that type of loose schedule works fine. However, there is the occasional person who abuses the privilege. He comes rolling in around 11:00 A.M. and/or leaves without having put in his eight hours. When pressed, he says he took his work home and did it there. This person seems to believe that he has earned the right, as though being in the games industry inherently gives him perks beyond those given by his supervisor.

The mainstream video game project depends on teamwork. The prima donna attitude is insidious. It can be infectious, diminishing the team's strength like termites eating the heart out of the supporting timbers of a house. If one person is permitted to take liberties, others will follow.

Another type of troublemaker is the rabble-rouser. A member of the team might have strongly held opinions about game features, working conditions, or management style. He is free to have opinions and to express them, but when he embarks on a relentless campaign to enlist allies and to sway the opinions of others, he isn't contributing fully to the team effort, and is in fact undermining it.

Large companies have a Human Resources department, with firm guidelines on how to handle problem employees. The producer coordinates with H.R. to make sure that the proper procedures are used. The producer meets with the problem employee. The employee is informed that there is a problem, and is told what he must do to continue his employment. The meeting is memorialized (i.e., the producer makes a written record of the discussion) and both parties sign it.

H.R. may require the producer to keep the employee until at least three such warnings have been issued on paper. Then, if the employee has not remedied the disruptive behavior, the employer can terminate the employee. The paper trail is an important legal record that informs the employee of the seriousness of the issue and protects the employer in case the employee sues after having been let go. The paper trail establishes that there was just cause for the termination.

Yearly personnel reviews are another tool used by large companies to track the performance of the employees. Some companies even have employees write reviews of their supervisors.

Design Problems

Depending on the type of game or the project plan, it often happens that the game's fun is not self-evident until the project is fairly well along. A game team needs to see the fruits of their labors, and the longer it takes, the more opportunity for dissension to arise. Those who sailed with Christopher Columbus, months at sea with no land in sight, were near mutiny when the shores of the American Indies were finally seen.

When the game eventually becomes playable, if it isn't very fun or isn't yet particularly impressive, morale could well take a dive. If Columbus' men had touched down at barren desert islands devoid of plant life, animal life, gold, or water, a full mutiny would surely have erupted.

This underscores the importance of building the fun right into the detailed GDD (as opposed to building in the fun later). Moreover, it behooves the producer to make sure that the fun is self-evident as early in the project as possible.

Money Troubles

A developer might underbid a project, resulting in money troubles even when milestone payments come in on time. When this happens, there are a few possible solutions. The publisher might have to agree to pay additional money to the developer (amending the contract). The publisher might pull the project and sue the developer for breach of contract. The publisher might farm out some of the tasks to in-house staff or another developer to get the project finished.

A publisher might be slow in making milestone payments, for a variety of reasons. Perhaps an inexperienced producer doesn't appreciate the importance of timely milestone reviews. Perhaps the publisher's accounts payable department has a habit of delaying all payments as long as possible. Perhaps a young publishing company simply hasn't yet come to grips with the need to streamline payments to important vendors. Sometimes, a large publicly held publisher, faced with poor quarterly results, will tighten its belt and slow down payments in general, just to make the books look better. When any of these things results in significant delays of milestone payments to an external developer, there is a range of possible outcomes.

If the developer is well managed and has enough money in the bank (and enough concurrent projects with different publishers), the developer may be able to continue working on the project. The developer is nevertheless likely to file a complaint with the producer and request that the publisher tighten up its act, making payments more promptly.

If the developer is operating dependent on the income from the publisher, milestone payment delays can be disastrous, for both the developer and the project (and thus for the publisher). If development personnel are not getting their paychecks, they might resign. The developer might tell the producer that all work on the project is stopping until payment is received. The developer might have to file for bankruptcy and lay off its staff.

The producer must keep a sharp eye out for any financial red flags at all times throughout the project. The producer must make sure that developer payments are made promptly.

Technical Glitches

Everything depends on the technology working. Sometimes, a game requires that some new technology be developed from scratch. It doesn't always go perfectly and according to schedule.

Sometimes, a technical problem can be worked out, after which the team can manage to make up for lost time. And sometimes lost time is just lost. And sometimes a technical problem cannot be fixed. The producer might have to ask his superiors for more time, perhaps bring in different programmer(s) to save the day, or the project might have to be canceled.

The usual sign of a technical glitch is a milestone delay (or a milestone missing an important deliverable). The experienced producer will be on the lookout for technical problems before they become evident through project slowdowns.

Change Requests

Developers hate it when the publisher asks for changes. The experienced producer hates to ask the developer for changes. However, for games to compete in the marketplace, they have to be better and cooler than the other games out there. Therefore, change requests are an uncomfortable fact of life in the game business.

Requests for significant changes to the original design can come from a variety of sources. Publishing executives might review the game (during a green light review, for example) and determine that improvements or new features are needed. Marketing might hear about a new game coming out and ask the producer to add features to compete with the upcoming game. A tester in QA might enter a suggestion for changes into the bug-tracking database.

When the executives decree that a change is needed, the producer discusses the change with the external developer or internal development team to determine what the schedule and budget impact will be. It may be that the changes entail extra costs and/or push the schedule back. Sometimes, the producer might look for a tradeoff, a way to delete previously planned features in exchange for the new requested features. That isn't always feasible. The producer can then present the new information to the executives and get approval for a contract amendment (in the case of an externally developed project) and/or a schedule extension.

When marketing asks for changes, the producer explains to marketing the impact on the budget and schedule. If marketing is adamant, the producer can research the schedule and budget impact as mentioned previously. If marketing and the executives are then in agreement that the requested changes are worth the budget and schedule hit, the producer has an official green light to proceed with making the changes.

When a tester suggests a significant change, the producer usually simply rejects it, due to schedule and budget impact.

Minor change requests from anyone may be passed along to development by the producer, and, if easy and worthwhile, may well be implemented into the game. Numerous such requests, however, could result in a complaint from the developer. If the developer is an external company, there may even be a request for additional money to cover the changes. A formalized change request process would be a useful way to filter, track, and quantify change requests, and producers are advised to implement such a process in their projects.

Schedule Delays

As seen previously, delays in the schedule might be caused by a variety of factors: technical glitches, personnel problems, money issues, excessive change requests, or perhaps someone simply underestimated how long it would take to learn a technology or to perform a task.

Each of these factors is tightly woven with the others in an intricate tapestry. There is synergy between all the aspects of a game project. Regardless of what causes a schedule delay, a schedule delay will cause money problems.

Anything that happens late in the schedule is, in the experienced producer's eyes, the reddest flag of them all.

When a red flag pops up, the producer gets into gear. He confers with his generals, both those who report to him and those to whom he reports. He finds out what caused the flag to go up, and how bad it is. He considers what can be done to solve the problem and puts things into motion as quickly as possible.

Kicking Off Tasks

Throughout the course of the game project, there are several different things going on, usually simultaneously. Once programming has been kicked off and is underway, the producer kicks off the creation of graphical (visible) assets. Then, once the art effort has been kicked off and is underway, the producer kicks off the creation of audio assets, including music and recorded voice-overs.

The experienced producer has made a schedule that includes even more than that. He keeps a close eye on the calendar and makes sure that thorough preparation is made for each planned event on the schedule, in time for each event to occur when it's scheduled to occur. The better prepared the producer is for the planned events, the better he will be able to deal with unplanned events.

Audio Kickoff

The audio task is kicked off in much the same way as the programming and art tasks are kicked off. The game designer and/or the sound designer go through the GDD with a fine-toothed comb to identify each sound effect, musical cue, and voice cue. Then, a sound list and music spec can be created. The voice-over script is a much more involved matter, as will be seen shortly.

Sound List

There must be a sound for each action in the game. In creating the sound list, the game designer and/or sound designer must consider what actions are possible and define a sound that would be appropriate for that action. Some sounds might be reusable (suitable for multiple different actions).

Music Specification

The game designer writes a list of each place in the game where music is desired. Each piece of music has to be specified as to genre, mood, length, and whether the music will loop. Sometimes, it is useful to indicate examples, artists, or composers. The result is a document that tells the music composer exactly what kind of music is desired, how each piece of music is used in the game, and how long each piece should run.

Story Text and Voice-Over Script

Story text and voice dialogue should not be fully contained within the GDD, but rather must be defined separately.

Story text and other in-game text is a collection of assets for use in the game. Each block of text that will be displayed may have to be given an asset name just like any other asset. The game designer should consult with the programmer who will work with the text to determine this. The programmer will also need a systematic presentation detailing how (under what circumstances) each discrete block of text is used in the game. Someone (probably the art director) will make a determination about fonts and font sizes of in-game text.

Dialogue that is to be spoken aloud is written in the form of a radio script, with the exception that each discrete speech has to be given an asset filename.

The game designer might not be the one to create the final voice-over script. The producer might hire a professional writer to write dialogue that has color, life, and character. Screenwriters have experience and training in "emotioneering," a term coined by David Freeman for the use of techniques to make an audience become emotionally connected to characters through dialogue, gestures, lighting, camera angles, and symbols [Freeman04]. Most game designers, on the other hand, have experience playing games, and their training is in the testing or making of games.

The game designer might write a functional or working script of the game that the screenwriter can use as a starting point. However, the smart producer will bring in the screenwriter sooner than that, during the creation of the GDD, to maximize the benefits of having a professional storyteller involved.

The final voice-over script includes the lines to be spoken, information about the characters, and how (under what circumstances) each line is used in the game.

Creation of Sound Effects

Sound list in hand, the sound engineer might create the sound effects from scratch, or might cobble them together from a sound effects library. The sound engineer delivers the assets with the proper file-naming conventions, and in the formats specified in the TDD. The producer and/or design director review, approve, and track the sound effects using the same kind of approval cycle as described for art assets previously.

Creation or Licensing of Music

For most low-budget or low-profile games, music is created from scratch by a freelance musician who makes game music. Music specification in hand, the musician may want to see the game to get a deeper appreciation of the atmosphere and mood desired. He or she usually composes and performs the music in a home studio, delivering the music in the form of WAV files. The producer and/or lead designer review, approve, and track the music. Unless he or she is very much in demand and has the clout to demand otherwise, the freelance musician is usually paid on a work-for-hire basis, per minute of music contracted.

Increasingly, high-profile games have come to use recorded music or newly commissioned music from popular artists. Recent video games have featured music by Outkast, MC Hammer, Mark Mothersbaugh (Devo), LL Cool J, INXS, and Sarah McLachlan, to name a few [IGN04].

When the producer plans to use popular music in the game, deals must be struck and contracts must be signed through the musicians' agents. If the music has been published on CDs through a recording company, the recording company also has to be dealt with and credited. In addition, all musicians' compositions are protected by associations like ASCAP (the American Society of Composers, Authors, and Publishers). Each of these entities may have different requirements for how their rights are to be respected and how they are to be compensated from game sales. Royalties are likely to be required rather than a flat payment. Further information about how producers license music can be found in [D'Arcy04].

Recording of Voice-Overs

Many large game publishers have signed contracts with the Screen Actors Guild (SAG), and are required to use union actors for their voice-overs. Union actors are usually represented by an agent. The game's producer can call some agencies and get numerous demo reels of available voice actors.

Sometimes, the producer or director might want to provide a few lines of dialogue so an actor could audition for a part. However, because game voice-over work doesn't enjoy as broad an audience as commercial, film, or TV work, voice actors don't necessarily want to go through the bother that a game audition can entail. Some voice actors might have a home recording setup, which could make such requests easier to fulfill.

In the case of games based on films or TV shows, the voices of the show's actual cast are usually desired. No auditions required! Working with big name stars can be a real thrill for the team.

Some game companies have internal voice recording facilities. If not, the producer can rent time at a recording studio. As actors perform their roles, there is SAG paperwork that must be completed. The producer and/or director and the lead designer and/or screenwriter may be needed at the recording session to ensure that each speech has the proper inflection and meaning appropriate to its use in the game. The sound engineer delivers the recorded assets, properly named according to conventions and in the format specified in the TDD, and they are reviewed, approved, and implemented in the game.

Payment to union actors is often done through a payroll company rather than through the publisher's Accounts Payable department directly to the actors.

First Playable—Proof of Concept

The first major turning point in the production of a mainstream console game or PC game is when the assets are implemented and the game starts to look, sound, and play the way it's supposed to. If there had been any doubt about whether the design is feasible, this stage might be called "Proof of Concept." Many producers call this the "First Playable" milestone. As seen previously, a lot of hard work has resulted in bringing the game to this stage of development, so many people have been waiting expectantly for this moment.

The producer has been waiting for this moment to gauge the project's progress. He or she has seen and approved the graphics and sounds, but now the pieces are to be joined together and made interactive. He or she profoundly hopes that the resulting whole will be considerably more than merely the sum of the various parts. It also has to be entertaining and enjoyable.

The experienced producer knows that significant judgments about the game will be made when the most important decision-making parties see the game at this stage. Those parties are the licensor, the platform holder, and publishing company executives and marketing.

Decision makers are accustomed to making rapid judgments. When they see the game, if it looks impressive and lives up to or exceeds their expectations, they'll be happy. If anything is missing and has to be explained or apologized for, they won't. If one of the key features that the producer had hyped to get the decision makers excited about the game is not yet implemented, there could be trouble for the project.

In pitching the hypothetical *Ultimatt Combatt III* project, the art director had created an image of Napoleonic era armies doing anachronistic battle against flying saucers. The decision makers had been excited by that image in particular. It exquisitely conveyed the essence of *UCIII*, which would permit players to set up imaginary battles between armed forces of all nations and eras.

If the first playable build of *UCIII* has Napoleonic armies but no flying saucers, or does not yet enable these differing forces to battle one another in an interesting way, the decision makers may well conclude that they had been led down a primrose path. After the presentation, they might start expressing doubts that the project will turn out well. They might start to find fault with the job that the producer is doing.

Therefore, if the first playable milestone is less than spectacular, the experienced producer will want to hold off showing it to the decision makers a while longer, if possible.

Keeping Everyone On Board

Even when the first playable build looks and plays wonderfully, politics are bound to begin taking an important role in the project at this point. It is the producer's job to control the impact of politics on the project. The best tactic for this is "divide and conquer." When the decision makers are brought together for a major green light meeting, the producer is less able to control events. It's best if the producer meets each of the parties, individually, beforehand and lobbies for their support by addressing their concerns.

Licensor(s)

When the project is based on a licensed property, the producer develops a working relationship with the IP owner's licensing contact. The producer needs to have easy access to this person. A formalized approval process is important, so that all submissions, approvals, and reasons for rejections are clearly understood. When the producer has a first playable build that looks and plays great, it needs to be shared with the licensor. Although there is a formal approval process, perhaps the new build is simply sent for informal comments or just to get the licensor excited about the game's progress. Any comments that come back should be noted and taken into consideration. Licensors appreciate being kept in the loop throughout the project.

Platform Holder(s)

When the *UCIII* producer has an exciting first playable Xbox build, he calls his contact at Microsoft and offers a look. The Xbox account representative will most likely be enthusiastic and will want to see it. Any resulting feedback should certainly be taken into consideration. Platform holders appreciate being kept in the loop.

Executives

When the producer is satisfied that the build makes an excellent first impression, he can simply wander over to the executives' offices and tell them he has something to show. The executives may be too busy to follow the producer back and have a look, and that isn't a bad thing. It's best if executive sneak peeks are given on an individual basis, so that the "divide and conquer" tactic can be put into use. When executives review a game together, one person's comment can have a subtle yet profound impact on the thinking of the others. The wise producer listens and responds to the comments of each executive, individually, establishing rapport and mutual respect on a personal level.

The Team

On a daily basis, the successful producer establishes rapport and mutual respect with each member of the team on a personal level. The producer listens to the team members' thoughts and suggestions about the game, the features, the project, and the working conditions.

Achieving the first playable build is a major milestone, and the team deserves special acknowledgment of the fact. The producer might organize an offsite lunch or dinner, perhaps as an adjunct to a bowling or paintball outing. An important part of such a gathering would be a short speech by the producer and perhaps one or two of the other team leaders. The producer acknowledges the teamwork that brought the project to this point and energizes the team to take it the rest of the way. The producer addresses any doubts or concerns, and offers a plan for dealing with them. The producer restates the primary objectives: to make the game fun, and to get it done.

An Alternate Method

Sometimes, the plan from the beginning is to build the game as a series of iterative prototypes. This approach to production, sometimes called "the Cerny method," recognizes that although a design feature might sound good on paper, it can be difficult to implement and have it turn out to be fun [Fristrom04, Price03].

When this method is used, the team pushes in a series of efforts, each building on the last, somewhat like the steps in a stairway. It is natural for a bit of an emotional dichotomy to occur when a leveling off occurs in the upward push.

Keeping the Momentum Going

Having attained a first playable build or an interim prototype, the team can experience two opposing impulses. One is to relax and take a break because something has been accomplished. The other is to pour on more coal because although the game is starting to look cool, it doesn't have everything in it yet. The former impulse has to be discouraged so that the latter impulse can prevail. Both impulses are contagious, so the producer can encourage the desirable impulse by setting an example and pouring on more coal.

Phases within Phases

Just as game production can be broken into three phases (preproduction, production, and postproduction), the production phase can be thought of as occurring in three parts (early production, midproduction, and late production). Each part of the production phase has its own character. The first part, discussed previously, ends when the game has started to come together. The second part, midproduction, is largely a frenetic buzz of activity as asset creation is fully underway while the programming effort continues, and marketing activities begin.

The terms *alpha* and *beta* are often heard, but precise definitions of those terms vary from company to company. Alpha might mean that most or all of the assets are implemented, and most or all of the features are functioning. Beta might mean that all of the assets are implemented, all of the features are functioning, and the development team believes that there are no serious bugs remaining. Alpha might mark the transition from midproduction to late production, and beta usually marks the transition from production to postproduction.

The Multitasking Producer

The producer is in high demand from many directions during midproduction. He is in the middle, fielding information requests, problem reports, and meeting requests. There are assets to approve, milestones to pay, and numerous paperwork demands. These attempts to get some of the producer's precious time come from developers, platform holders, licensors, agencies, and numerous internal departments. He is also besieged with calls from new developers pitching their services, applicants seeking jobs, recruiters waving job offers, kids with game ideas, and even the media wanting information or an interview.

While the producer is on the phone, someone drops in with a piece of paper. While he's talking to one person, another is standing nearby waiting for an opening. The phone is ringing, the pager is beeping, the computer is saying "You've got mail," and papers are emerging from the fax machine and the printer.

The producer learns quickly how to manage his time. He sets priorities in the morning and resets them in the afternoon. He may occasionally close the door and put up a Do Not Disturb sign. He might seek a location where he can get some work done without interruption, if such a thing is possible as long as cell phones and Black-berries exist. It's a wonder that he manages to get things accomplished, but he finds a way.

Managing Midproduction

Two factors can help the producer in this difficult phase.

First, on a very large project, there are managers handling various aspects so the producer doesn't have to do it all himself. The more people there are to manage, the more managers are needed. In the case of an internal project, there would be a leader of the programming team, a leader of the graphics team, a leader of the design team, and someone in charge of getting all the audio created. In the case of an external project, the producer manages the managers at the external sites.

Second, midproduction doesn't last forever. As the keeper of the schedule, the producer knows where the end of the tunnel is. When the assets are finished, approved, and in the can, the pressure on the producer will reduce in intensity—a little, maybe.

Expecting the Unexpected

The experienced producer knows that no matter how well planned the project, unforeseen events will crop up. There's an old saying that advises, "roll with the punches." The producer deals with surprises as a matter of due course, confident in the team's ability to handle just about anything. That isn't to say that all unexpected events are equal, no matter when they occur. The later in the project a surprise occurs, the more difficult it can be to deal with.

Red Flags in Midproduction

By midproduction, the project is "snowballing" [Sloper03]. With the project's target beta date now being much closer, things going wrong at this point can be more difficult to remedy. Delays at this phase are likely to cause delays at the end. As discussed previously, the most common causes of delays and red flags are design problems, personnel issues, technical glitches, and money troubles.

Design problems at this phase may be fixable, but the risk to the ship date and product quality is increased. There is still some time to take up the slack. Missing the ship date is not necessarily certain at this point. Design challenges should have been identified and addressed in earlier phases.

Personnel problems in midproduction (especially the loss of a key team member in programming or project management) can jeopardize the ship date. If someone new has to be brought in, there will be downtime while the new person is hired and comes up to speed. Hopefully, someone experienced and already familiar with the technology and the design can step in to fill the gap.

Technical glitches at this phase would be unusual, especially if the iterative prototypes method of production is being used. It's good development practice to tackle the hard stuff earlier in the project.

Money troubles at this stage are (perhaps counter intuitively) the easiest to fix. The publisher simply has to determine whether the project is worth spending the extra money. If it is, the money will be spent. If it isn't, the project may be canceled.

Design by Committee—Another Name for Consensus?

As the game comes together, everyone who looks at it seems to experience a sudden burst of creativity. New ideas spring forth from every quarter. The producer's suggestion box overflows with change requests: new directions, new features, new characters, new missions, and new worlds. For the producer to reject them all might be politically unwise. Team members might feel that they are getting the mushroom treatment. Moreover, suggestions from marketing and executives cannot be ignored. The producer may have to make a plan to incorporate significant changes, including the time and money to implement the changes. To make midstream course corrections will probably require a high-level green light meeting.

It's likely that some changes will be green-lighted. And it sometimes happens that the changes feel like a kludge. Some type of shortcoming of the design had been identified, and because a lot of money had already been spent, it was decided to put a patch over the hole. The fix sometimes seems inelegant, but the decision makers agree that it's the best way to deal with the situation and move forward.

Late Production

Late production is that phase of production in which all the assets have been created, but coding has not yet been completed.

At this point, depending on the type or genre of game, the level designers might still be working (making new levels, but without generating any need for new assets). The game is not yet at beta, but QA should be in the picture by now. Marketing has probably been started before this, or gets going in earnest at this point.

This period can be challenging for a producer who isn't knowledgeable about marketing, and/or who is working with a marketing person who isn't knowledgeable about game development.

The Working Title Is Dead— Long Live the Final Title

Many game projects are started with the game having only a "working title." The designer or the producer may have chosen what to call the game, and the team has become accustomed to referring to the game by that title. Then, one fine day, the marketing department says they need a title that will sell the game better.

In the case of our hypothetical *UCIII* project, the producer and designer had agreed early on to call the game *Ultimatt Combatt III: Extreme Warfare*, and the green light committee had not objected. Marketing has now done some focus testing and has gotten some unfortunate feedback. It seems that the term "extreme" has been overly used in the marketplace, and has been tacked onto everything from racing to skating to fishing. Marketing now proposes that the focus of the game is warfare that crosses historical eras, the present day, and hypothetical future times. Thus, the new title recommendation is *Ultimatt Combatt III: War of the Ages*, or perhaps *Ultimatt Combatt III: Beyond the Bounds of Time*. Marketing suggests trying one on for size for a while, and then perhaps trying on the other one. The wise producer knows, however, that the team will not take kindly to even one name change, much less two. Since marketing would be happy with either title, the team is permitted to decide between the two.

The title now being finalized, title art can be created for *Ultimatt Combatt III: War of the Ages*. The press blitz can begin.

Screen Shots and More

Marketing needs to have exciting imagery from the game. Each magazine needs images that are unique. Therefore, someone, perhaps the art director or the game designer, sits down with marketing and works to make a set of screen shots. It may be necessary to have a cheat-enabled version of the game to make the screen shots, or level design tools that permit the creation of any desired combination of game characters. The art department has to create high-resolution images for use on magazine covers.

The magazines want interviews. They don't want the producer, of course—he or she is just a manager. They ask to interview the game designer, but marketing wants someone more photogenic. One of the artists or one of the programmers is good-looking, so that person is enlisted for the photo shoot. Somebody tells the interviewer some stuff and the interviewer has what is needed.

A few short interruptions like that and the P.R. machine is off and running.

E3 Demo

E3 (the Electronic Entertainment Expo, an important games industry trade show) happens in the spring. The producer cannot schedule when E3 will happen, but can plan to have a demo ready for E3, depending on what phase of development the game is in at that time. The team may well be working on the game throughout two E3 shows. If the first E3 happens during preproduction, there won't be a demo that year.

If the next E3 happens during the project's production or postproduction phase, management would be unlikely to forego having a demo of the game at E3.

When the programming team is focusing on making a solid demo of the game for a trade show, it is not necessarily able to continue working toward getting the game finished. Code that goes into a demo doesn't necessarily all go into the final product. Therefore, any demo is, in effect, an interruption of the overall effort. However, when the demo makes an excellent impression on the trade show attendees, the morale boost can counteract the interruptive effect.

It's important to schedule the demo into the project early on, so that the team knows well in advance that this interruption will occur. The exact specifications of the demo should be worked out with marketing during the preproduction phase. As the time to work on the demo approaches, there are likely to be some new thoughts about the demo specs. If marketing requests changes that affect the ship date, the producer explains the schedule impact to marketing. The producer rolls with the punches and adapts the demo spec insofar as is feasible, keeping an eye on the ultimate ship date throughout the creation of the demo.

Magazine Demo

Another type of demo often needed is the magazine CD demo. The timing of this demo varies from the E3 demo. The best time to have a demo appear in a magazine is during the month prior to the date that the game will be appearing in the stores. Typically, the game is to appear on store shelves in November, in time for the Christmas peak selling season. The issue that circulates in October, confusingly, usually says "November" on it. Magazines have about a three-month lead time, so the demo probably has to be out of QA and at the magazine's office in July, if not sooner. Typically, that is a very busy month for the programming team, feverishly working to fix a large list of bugs found in QA.

Magazine demos create user demand for the full game, so although the timing of the demo comes at an awkward time, it's important to get the demo done. Fortunately, the E3 demo can be largely repurposed. Any bugs or shortcomings of the E3 demo can be addressed and thoroughly tested before going to the magazine.

Platform Holder Promotional Demo

Sometimes, the platform holder will request a demo to put on a promotional disc. In the case of *UCIII*, Microsoft might request a demo to put on a disc that would ship with new Xbox units or in an Xbox magazine. The platform holder provides requirements and due dates. The schedule hadn't included a promotional Xbox demo, but such a demo will enhance the publisher's relationship with the platform holder and enhance sales of *UCIII*. The E3 demo provides a solid framework for an Xbox demo, so producing this demo won't be as bad an interruption as making the E3 demo was. Therefore, the producer rolls with the punches and makes sure that this unexpected demo goes out. It has to be tested by the publisher's QA department, and will be thoroughly tested by the platform holder's QA department as well.

Red Flags in Late Production or Postproduction—Big Red Flags

Any red flags that had been ignored previously, in the hope that they might go away over time, have not done so. Rather, they have only grown bigger or redder. At this point in the project, things are bound to catch up with the unwise producer who tried to ignore red flags.

By late production, any unfortunate events can have serious consequences indeed. Design problems at this phase are not fixable without pushing back the ship date. Personnel problems (especially the loss of a key team member in programming) likely spell doom for the ship date. Technical glitches at this phase could be fatal for the ship date. Money troubles at this stage might coincide with serious publisher-developer relationship problems, spelling big trouble for the ship date.

At this point in the project, the wise producer immediately hammers red flags the instant they try to pop up.

Postproduction

When all assets have been created and integrated, and all features have been implemented, the production phase has ended and postproduction begins. In the film industry, postproduction refers to the activities that go into finalizing a movie after the cameras have been put away and the actors have gone home: editing, dubbing, titling, general cleanup, and the marketing and distribution of the film. In the games industry, postproduction is that period in which QA tests the game, identifying bugs and places where adjustments are needed. Marketing creates the box and paper materials ("box & docs") and arranges broadcast, online, print, and in-store advertisements and promotions. The sales department forecasts how many units will be needed. The operations department arranges to have the game manufactured.

The artists and design personnel are all gone, having moved on to other projects, but the programmers and production staff are working just as hard as ever. The sound engineer might still be at work, recording foreign-language voice-overs.

Personnel Transfers

As the game project nears completion, some team members' talents are no longer needed after their tasks are finished. When a game is developed internally, and when the personnel structure is such that the personnel report to a project team, this means that some personnel need to be transferred to different projects.

The producer then meets with HR, department heads, and other producers to determine how this shift should take place—not just for one or two people, for dozens.

The producer also meets with each individual to discuss that person's career development and to do a performance review. Performance reviews aren't always pleasant to give or receive, but they are necessary to chart an individual staffer's growth within the company and to inform the staffer's next supervisor.

Even when a project is developed externally, personnel shifts often coincide with the completion of a project or phase.

Localizations

At one time, games were merely translated. However, users complained about the poor use of their language. Sometimes, just translating the words doesn't result in an enjoyable play experience. Most American gamers are familiar with butchered English in games (or films) coming from other countries, particularly Asian countries. A classic example is the line "All your base are belong to us," from the game *Zero Wing*, published by the Japanese publisher Toaplan for the Sega Genesis [Bradk].

However, American games that are merely translated (rather than localized) for non-English-speaking territories can also generate such snickers. The wise producer doesn't short-shrift the localization process [Swartz04].

It's always ideal to ship localized versions simultaneously with the primary language version of a game, but for a variety of reasons, it's easier to build and tweak the primary language version first. Easier doesn't mean better, so the experienced producer strives for "sim-ship" (simultaneous shipment of versions for various territories).

To begin, the international department determines which territories the game should be localized for. In the case of a game developed externally, the contract usually specifies that the developer will be responsible to develop localized versions. Typically, a publisher's contract specifies the publisher's standard territories, or perhaps simply mentions a specific number of localizations. Localizations requested beyond those called for in the initial contract probably require a contract amendment. Hopefully, new localization requests made late in the production process do not require sim-ship. The team members can only crunch so much and still get the main SKU (the main version, usually the English version) finished on schedule.

Some territories are more challenging to localize for than others are. German text uses more characters than English text, which means that when there are text boxes, the translated text often won't fit. Japanese and Chinese use fewer characters but the characters are more complex, so the text sometimes needs to be larger. However, even enlarged text for Asian languages may not adequately fill a text box that had been sized for English text.

Voice-overs should be recorded in the localized language as well. It wouldn't do to hire an actor who learned to speak in that language, however. People in a country can tell when they hear their language spoken by someone who isn't a native speaker. In addition, of course, the writing of the dialogue needs to be artful. It wouldn't do to simply have a translator write the voice-over dialogue. Translators aren't necessarily trained in the art of screenwriting.

Cultural aspects also must be considered when localizing a game. Many games created in America or Asia might use swastikas for an evil-looking enemy symbol, especially if the game takes place during World War II or its story involves latter-day Nazis. However, if such a game is to be marketed in Germany, where people are still sensitive about this regrettable part of their history, swastikas cannot be used. Some countries also have laws against realistic blood. The localizing producer needs to be aware of these things, and in fact, the designer should be aware of these things when writing the initial GDD.

Artful writing, coupled with well-informed cultural awareness, marks the difference between localization and mere translation. A full discussion of game localization goes beyond the scope of this chapter. For more on this topic, see [Chandler04].

ESRB Rating

Marketing or the producer does the necessary ESRB paperwork to obtain the rating to put on the box, manual, and disc printing (or cartridge label). This paperwork has to be done prior to finalizing the *box & docs*.

The publisher usually knows what rating the game will have, since the ESRB guidelines are clearly stated. Some companies might desire a rating that indicates that the game is suitable for older audiences only, in order to generate controversy. There's a saying in marketing, "there's no such thing as bad press." This isn't strictly true, of course, but it is true that some controversy can increase awareness, which can sometimes lead to increased sales.

If the ESRB were to assign the game a higher rating (a rating for an older audience than anticipated by the publisher), and if marketing or sales had concerns about the effect on sales, the game would have to be changed to achieve the desired rating.

Box & Docs

As the game nears completion, marketing creates the packaging and manual. Marketing might ask the creative services people (be they an internal department or an outside vendor) to prepare *box comps* (composites of different packaging ideas). Several of the best ones then might be circulated among the team to get their reactions. Marketing might bring in some gamers to get their reactions. Such *focus groups* can be used to get feedback on the packaging, the ads, the game's overall concept, its title, platform, features, and even the bullet points that go on the package.

The package front typically includes an artist's rendition of an exciting moment from the game. It always includes the logo of the publisher, and sometimes the logo of the developer (if the developer is one who has brand name recognition). It also includes some "selling points," which may be a descriptor of the game's genre or primary features and perhaps a superlative quote from a game reviewer. And, of course, the ESRB rating symbol.

The package front also includes an indication of the platform for which the game is intended. If the game is, like our hypothetical *UCIII* game, an Xbox game, the package is in the standard Xbox format, with Xbox packaging design elements. These design elements are strictly enforced by Microsoft and by Sony and Nintendo for games on their platforms.

If the developer's logo is not shown on the package front, it's usually on the package back, unless the developer is a new unknown entity who didn't have the clout to negotiate having its logo on the package. Sometimes, the publisher's creative services people might not know that they are supposed to put the developer's logo on the package back, especially if the producer didn't tell them. Console platform holders regulate the number of logos that can be on a game package. If a game uses IP owned or controlled by numerous parties, requiring numerous logos on the package back, then some parties' logos simply cannot be on the console game package. Sometimes, the owners of technology used in making the game (the engine, the audio system, other middleware) also require that their logos be on the box. The lucky producer gets to be the one to negotiate these details.

The most important things about the back of the box are the descriptions and the screen shots. The goal of the box front is to get a consumer to pick it up and look at it. A bad box front (one that is just good enough for a consumer to pick it up) would result in the consumer putting the box back on the shelf. A good box front would make the consumer want to turn the box over and look at the back. A bad box back would result in the consumer putting the box back on the shelf. A good box back should make the consumer want to put the box in his shopping basket and take it to the cashier.

The way to make a good box back is to show numerous exciting scenes from the game, with each scene looking markedly different from the others. In addition, it should include lots of information about the game's best features, described in such a way that the consumer sees that this game should be purchased instead of another game.

For a PC game package, system requirements need to be shown. This goes on the box bottom or on the back. System requirements can be a subject of interdepartmental contention. QA won't permit the system requirements to list systems they weren't able to test, while sales wants as broad a range of systems as possible.

The back of the box also includes all legal language to cover copyright and trademark ownership, and sometimes even liability declaimers. The game's rating is explained more fully on the back than it was on the front.

The instruction manual must be written and laid out attractively. Some PC games don't include a paper manual, but it's standard and expected to make an instruction manual for console games. As with the package, the manual for console games must adhere to the platform holder's standards.

The game designer or the producer might write the first draft of the manual, and then it might be rewritten by creative services. Development provides images and screen shots as needed.

The box and the manual (and any other printed materials, including the design to be printed on the disc or on the cartridge label) circulate among production, QA, development, marketing, and creative services until all parties agree that no errors, inaccurate claims, or omissions remain.

As will be seen shortly, all these paper materials have to be finished at least two weeks before the game is released by QA. If QA were to find a problem that necessitated a change after the manual went to press, that could be a headache for the producer.

Strategy Guide

Many publishers have a department, sometimes called "New Business," that looks for alternate methods of making money from the company's games. New business might make a deal with a company that makes strategy guides. One challenge for the producer is that the effort to make a strategy guide for a game often can't take place until the game is in QA and the strategies for playing the game are fully known. The game designer is the ideal person to coordinate this effort. If the game designer wears just one hat (one that says "game designer" on it), this is a reasonably good time in the project for this task to occur. However, if the game designer wears another hat, especially that of lead programmer or producer, this timing can be a challenge.

Quality Assurance

Other than marketing, the biggest effort underway during postproduction is the massive testing push that goes on in QA. Depending on the scope of the game, the number of testers might number in the dozens.

Each tester plays the game and writes reports on the problems found. Testers have to be patient, computer-literate workers capable of clear written communication. It isn't enough to simply find a bug; the tester has to describe how the bug occurred and, if possible, how to replicate it. The tester may even have to explain what was expected, what occurred instead, and why it's a problem. Sometimes, the tester might even have to suggest some possible solutions to fix the problem.

The lead tester (sometimes called the QA lead) creates the test plan, a budget for the game's QA effort, and the customized database for tracking, reporting, and analyzing the bugs.

Test Plan

The lead tester analyzes the game, using the GDD, TDD, and the current build of the game. The lead needs to determine how many testers will be needed, what kind of test techniques or procedures are appropriate, and how long the test process is likely to last. From this, the lead can determine a test budget.

A single-player game with a few different play modes is easier to test than a large, multiplayer game with many play modes, user selectable options, and player characters. A game that is played offline on a single console requires a different test process than a game played online on a wide variety of PC hardware configurations and operating systems. The lead incorporates such considerations into the test plan.

The QA Database

Different game publishers use different software packages to track bugs found in QA. Commercially available packages include PVCS Tracker (Serena Software), TestTrack (Seapine Software), Raid (Catalytic Software), FogBUGZ (Fog Creek Software), and Bugzilla (Mozilla). Some publishers create their own bug-tracking systems from database software. Bug-tracking systems may reside on an internal network or external server and/or may have a Web-based front end.

The bug-tracking database offers a click-and-type interface for testers to report bugs. A bug report form typically includes fields used for all games, and fields that are specific to one game.

Generic fields for a PC game might include, for example:

- Tester name
- Build number (date)
- Version or SKU
- Computer ID (which machine)
- Operating system
- Bug status (new, open, closed)
- Bug severity (fatal, severe, mild, suggestion)
- Bug type (crash, unfriendliness, graphic glitch, etc.)
- Replicability (can the bug be replicated)
- Location of bug (where in program the bug occurred)
- Name of bug (a one-line description akin to an e-mail subject line)
- Detailed description of bug

Most of these should be self-explanatory. Bug status is always "new" when the bug has just been written and has not yet gone through the filtration process with the QA lead and the producer. A bug awaiting work is said to be "open." A bug that has been fixed or is not going to be fixed is said to be "closed."

The bug severity field gives the tester a chance to give his or her opinion as to how bad the bug is. The lead and the producer will also be providing input in this regard. Should their judgment of the bug's severity differ from the tester's, the field is likely to be changed (usually by the lead).

When a tester has found a problem in a particular part of the game, depending on the specifics of the problem found, the tester tries to make the problem happen again. A replicable bug is a bug that can be fixed. It sometimes happens that a sharp-eyed tester may spot something that happened once, but he or she isn't able to make it happen again. A one-time event might never happen again, but the fact that a problem was seen has to be reported. The report may be left open for a while (perhaps weeks) until the lead determines that it is unlikely to happen again.

The tester's choice of a name for the bug is important. It might sometimes suggest greater or lesser severity. Moreover, because there are many ways to express a thought, the wording of the bug's name might mask the fact that the problem has already been reported.

The most significant field is also the hardest one to write. The tester has to clearly communicate the problem so that all readers can understand it clearly.

- What the problem is.
- Where in the game the problem was spotted.
- What the tester and/or player character was doing just prior to the incident.
- What was supposed to happen.
- What happened instead.
- Why it's a problem.
- What might be the cause of the problem.

It might be possible or desirable for the bug description field to be broken down into separate fields for each of the preceding, but often it's unnecessary to fill in each of them. When the game crashes, everybody knows what was supposed to happen instead—that the game not crash.

Some teams might prefer that testers not speculate as to the cause of the problem. However, sometimes the tester could have valuable insights into causes.

It can be a little irritating to the tester to have to write each of these out (and it can be a little irritating for the development team to have to read each of them), so it is common practice that the tester uses his or her discretion to write a detailed description.

Some games may, by their very nature, require special fields or radio button labels. For our hypothetical *Ultimatt Combatt III* game, for instance, the "location" field might instead be labeled "era," and to fill in the field, the tester might click a radio button or select an entry from a drop-down list.

Era:
- Old Testament
- Greek Empire
- Roman Empire
- Crusades
- Napoleonic

In addition, when testing *UCIII*, the tester probably also has to specify which army types were involved in the bug.

Attacking Force:
- Ancient Egyptian
- Trojan
- Roman
- Crusaders
- Hessians

Defending Force:
* Minutemen
* Doughboys
* Confederacy
* Nazi storm troopers
* Green aliens

The lead, in setting up the bug-tracking database, takes into consideration the fact that some bugs might exist solely when one type of army clashes with another type of army, and only in a particular level of the game.

The QA lead can use the database to perform an analysis. Which parts of the game are the most buggy? Which programmer's code is the most buggy? Are bugs being fixed quickly? Will the game be released in time? The QA lead needs to have a firm grasp on the forest, not just the trees, especially if he or she is called to participate in an operations or green light meeting.

QA—The View from Inside

Testers are the grunts of game production. Their pay is at the bottom of the scale. Their opinions about the game design aren't sought until it's far too late. The result of their work is sometimes resented by the programmers whose work is called into question.

Despite the outsiders' frequently held notion of testers as people who just play games all day, testers exhibit technical expertise when they have to reconfigure a PC to perform a specific test. They exhibit patience and fortitude when they play the same game hour after hour, day after day, to test and retest specific modes, features, and bugs. They exhibit clarity of communication when they write detailed bug reports.

Throughout the testing of a game, testers endure the humdrum grind of the workaday world, especially if they work for a large publishing company. The tester clocks in early in the morning and clocks out at the end of the day. There are meetings to attend; lunch hours and break times are tightly controlled. Coworkers wander by to chat while the tester is trying to concentrate on his task. Overtime pay goes to the test budget's bottom line, so overtime is tightly controlled. When overtime is demanded, the tester's private time is shortened. When the project is over, if the tester isn't needed for another project, the tester may be let go.

The producer's response to the tester's bugs can add to the tester's frustration. Often, the producer simply dismisses a bug as WNF (will not fix), CNR (cannot replicate), WAD (works as designed), or NAB (not a bug). Moreover, later in the QA process, the producer may refuse to even look at bugs of severity below "severe."

Many testers see these frustrations and shortcomings of the tester's life as justification for doing no more than what is demanded of them. For these testers, QA can be a dead-end job.

However, for many other testers, the QA job is a fascinating challenge because each game is unique. These testers grow to become QA leads. With solid QA lead experience, the step up to the studio is a natural progression. A large number of producers, designers, and executives got their start in QA.

The QA-Producer Relationship

Because QA's job seems to be to find reasons why a game is not yet ready to release, it sometimes occurs that an adversarial relationship develops between QA and production. It is unnecessary for this relationship to become adversarial. The experienced producer recognizes the vital service performed by each tester who reports bugs found in the game. QA and production both share a common goal for the game: they both want the game to be good so it will sell well. The wise producer works to smooth the communication and the relationship between QA and the development team. When the development team is internal, it's a good idea for team members (especially the designer and the producer) to test the game alongside the testers, entering bug reports and participating fully in the QA effort.

Even so, the producer often has to play the role of "bad cop," rejecting some bugs rather than letting them pass on to the development team. Some testers might be overly zealous in reporting minor shortcomings that can't be fixed without delaying release. Sometimes, a new tester will come on board the test cycle and not know that a particular problem has already been reported. The lead tester might be filtering the bugs before they go to the producer, but because ideas can be described using different wordings, it might not be realized that a bug has been duplicated.

On the other hand, a producer might reject a bug, saying that it isn't a bug at all. The tester has perhaps merely misunderstood a feature. The game works as designed, so the "bug" will not be fixed.

As the QA cycle nears its scheduled completion, the producer and lead tester work out a bug prioritization system. For example, "A" bugs might be those that absolutely must be fixed. The game crashes, a highly visible feature doesn't work, or a virus is present in the code, for instance. Releasing the game with an "A" bug not fixed would be catastrophic for the product and for the publisher.

"B" bugs might be those that are highly desirable to fix, because left unfixed they would be noticed by many users. For example, there might be a visible graphical glitch, or a desirable feature might be left out. An unfixed "B" bug might generate some negative comments, but the game is still enjoyable.

If someone describes a problem by starting with the words, "it would be nice to fix," that can be classified as a "C" bug. If someone talks about a feature and says, "it would be nice if we could add it," that could be classified as a "D" bug.

Nearing the scheduled completion date, the producer and lead tester could first agree to reject all "D" bugs out of hand, and then a week or two later, all "C" bugs. If severely pressed for time, they might agree to fix nothing but "A" bugs so the game can be finished and released.

The publisher is in business to sell games. If the game is never released, the game can't be sold. If games aren't sold, the testers, programmers, artists, and producers can't continue receiving paychecks. "Ship it" becomes a catchphrase heard throughout QA when the code release date comes nigh.

Operations

Operations is the department that coordinates manufacturing (some publishers may use a different nomenclature for this department). Console games are usually manufactured by the platform holder, but PC game manufacturing is handled by the publisher. Operations coordinates both.

Operational planning for a new product kicks off once the game hits QA. A bill of materials (BOM) is created to determine exactly what goes into a particular product. Operations coordinates with sales to determine how many units are to be manufactured. The game's progress through QA is closely monitored to make sure the game will release and ship on time. Operations coordinates with marketing and creative services to make sure that the circulation of the paper materials is on schedule.

The paper materials take longer to manufacture than the game media does. A CD manufacturer can churn out hundreds of thousands of copies of a CD in a day (including inserting all paper materials, and then shrinkwrapping and boxing the assembled product). However, the printed materials usually take two weeks to produce. Besides the manual and the package cover art (usually a sheet of paper that slips under the clear plastic skin of the CD case), the publisher may want to include other paper materials in the package. There may be a user registration card (collected for marketing research), an insert that advertises the publisher's other games, or a poster that the enthusiastic player can hang on the wall.

Sometimes, new information comes along after the package has already been put to rest, necessitating putting a sticker on the shrinkwrapped product. This costs only a couple of cents per unit, but a million units times 2¢ is $20,000.00. Therefore, it's desirable to plan things thoroughly so stickers are not necessary.

Most new game releases occur during the Christmas selling season. The most important sales weekend is the weekend just after Thanksgiving (the last weekend in November). The game has to be in the store warehouses in early November so the stores can include the game in Sunday newspaper supplements before Thanksgiving. CD manufacturers are understandably, then, under a lot of pressure in the months of September and October. Operations coordinates with the manufacturer to get a slot in the manufacturer's very tight schedule. A PC game might be manufactured between a music CD and a movie DVD, since the manufacturing process is largely the same.

Operations takes care of getting the printing done, and then the materials delivered to the disc manufacturer. Operations also handles getting the finished product shipped to the warehouses of the stores that will sell the finished goods.

OEM and Bundled Versions

PC games can be bundled (shipped together) with new PCs or new PC peripherals or accessories. The company that makes the PCs or accessories is known as an original equipment manufacturer, or OEM. Requests for OEM versions typically come through the new business department.

The timing of a new business request for an OEM or bundled version of a game can vary. Usually, such requests occur after a game has been released and has been on the market for a while, which means that the producer is asked for the new version while he or she is busy working on a later project. However, sometimes new business might request an OEM version while the game is in production. The timing of these requests is usually not under new business' control. Rather, the OEMs themselves might be looking for products to bundle with a device they're releasing on their own timetable. If the producer cannot meet the request, this moneymaking opportunity is lost.

Post Mortem

It's a common practice, after completion of a project, to write a detailed report called a *post mortem*. "Post mortem" means, literally, "after death," so the name isn't entirely apropos (usually, no furry programming creatures were killed or injured in the making of a game), but that's what they're commonly called, and we're stuck with it. The project is dead; long live the game itself.

The post mortem typically has three sections:

- What went wrong?
- What went right?
- What we can learn from the experience?

There are good reasons for writing a post mortem.

The team managers can learn valuable lessons that they can apply to future projects. Moreover, post mortems can put a lesson into clear sharp focus, further strengthening the learning.

Managers of other projects can also learn from the experiences of the team who shares their lessons in a post mortem. Typically, the post mortem is written for the benefit of others who work for the same publishing or development company. Sometimes, a post mortem is published, in a print publication for game developers or as a speech at a conference for game developers. Hard-won knowledge should be shared, so that others can get the benefit without sharing all the pain.

Summary

This chapter discussed the job of the producer, especially his or her role in creating a game. From concept to preproduction, through production to postproduction and even into after-market, the producer manages and pushes and cajoles. The producer is the man or woman in the middle, under pressure from all directions and communicating outward, upward, and downward. It's a tremendous amount of work, but the reward is the satisfaction of seeing a finished product on the store shelf.

Exercises

1. Research a list of the top 100 games of the past year. What percent are sequels, what percent are licenses, and what percent are original concepts?
2. Write a one-paragraph description of the current best-selling video game (no less than 90 words, no more than 110). Use your own words.
3. Distill your paragraph down to four or five short bullet points intended to make a consumer buy the game. Use your own words.
4. Distill it down further, to one short sentence. Use your own words.
5. Research Web sites where lists of game developers may be found. Make a list of all developers within a 100-mile radius of your present location. If there is none, list the five developers nearest to your location.
6. Research game contracts at the IGDA Web site. Write a clause for a milestone approval cycle.
7. Schedule the phases of a fictional game project from start to finish given that the game must be on shelves by Thanksgiving of next year. Create a list of questions that must be answered to make your schedule more accurate.
8. Since the completion date is nonnegotiable, how can the schedule be tweaked to meet the deadline?
9. Research what programs exist for making a schedule and managing tasks. Briefly compare features and price.
10. Budget a fictional game project to be developed internally using the most recent salary survey from gamasutra.com.
11. Write a milestone description for a "first playable" build for a game of your choosing. Make the description detailed and specific, quantifiable, and measurable.
12. Research books on time management and dealing with difficult personalities in the business world.
13. Research the finances of a recent hit video game. Considering the game's unit sales (at a known retail price) versus the game's gross take, determine the average wholesale price. For extra brownie points, research how much the publisher spent to produce the game to determine a rough net profit.
14. Research what programs exist for tracking bugs and briefly compare features and price.

References

[Blair93] Blair, Gerard M., "Planning a Project," available online at *www.see.ed.ac.uk/ ~gerard/Management/art8.html*, 1993.

[Bradk] "History of 'All Your Base,'" available online at *www.planettribes.com/ allyourbase/story.shtml#hist*.

[Chandler04] Chandler, Heather M., *The Game Localization Handbook*, Charles River Media, 2004.

[D'Arcy04] D'Arcy, Keith, "Music Licensing for Videogames: How Popular Music & Artists Can Make Games Pop," available online at *www.gdconf.com/archives/2004/darcy_keith_01.doc*, 2004.

[Freeman04] Freeman, David, *Creating Emotion in Games*, New Riders, 2004.

[Fristrom04] Fristrom, Jamie, "Postmortem: The Swing System of Treyarch's Spider-Man 2 Game," *Game Developer Magazine* (September 2004): p. 28.

[IGN04] IGN Insider, "Music," available online at *http://music.ign.com/gamemusic.html*, 2004.

[Price03] Price, Ted, "Postmortem: Insomniac Games' Ratchet & Clank," available online at *www.gamasutra.com/features/20030613/price_pfv.htm*, 2003.

[Rogers04] Rogers, Dan Lee, "Necessary Evil; The Rapid Retreat of Advanced Royalties," *Game Developer Magazine* (June–July, 2004): p. 44.

[SFMuseum] The Virtual Museum of the City of San Francisco, "Driving the Last Spike," available online at *www.sfmuseum.org/hist1/rail.html*, 1996.

[Sloper02] Sloper, Tom, "Following Up After The Game Is Released: It's Not Over When It's Over," *Game Design Perspectives*, Charles River Media, 2002: p. 261.

[Sloper03] Sloper, Tom, "Managing the Development Process," *Secrets of the Game Business*, Charles River Media, 2003: p. 262.

[Swartz04] Swartz, Bill, "There's No Excuse for Bad Localizations," available online at *www.gamedaily.com*, October 6, 2004.

[TMMM82] Brooks, Frederick P., Jr., *The Mythical Man-Month; Essays on Software Engineering*, Addison-Wesley, 1982: p.16.

7.2 Games Industry Roles and Economics

Overview

Delivering a game into a consumer's hands is an increasingly complex, lengthy, and costly process. Games industry veterans constantly debate the relative importance of developers as creative auteurs versus publishers as soulless businesspeople, or retailers as channel arbiters versus media as opinion-mongers. However, each "driver" entity on the highway to the consumer—developer, publisher, platform owner, retailer—is essential to the transaction, as the industry's economic structure demonstrates. "Adjunct" entities that feed into the channel also offer a plethora of service alternatives that reduce cost, save time, or improve quality.

In this chapter, we examine the economics and roles of 11 entities that collaborate to bring a game to market (Figure 7.2.1).

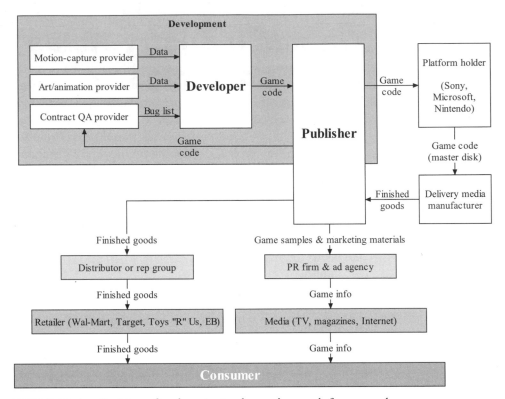

FIGURE 7.2.1   *Position of each entity in the product path for a console game.*

Game Developers

Without game developers, entertainment would no doubt be a duller and more complacent activity. Whether independent companies of 15 to 200 people or subsidiaries of larger publishers, developers create the immersive experiences that inspire millions to forego reality for fantasy. Game development involves the very technical disciplines of programming, including code optimization for target hardware, physics and artificial intelligence simulations, camera and interface development, and creation of tools to improve development efficiency. The art of game development lies with designers who envision everything from game balance to placement of doors in a level, artists who realize previously unimagined characters and worlds with an eye toward technical efficiency, and animators who marry a character's appearance and personality through motion. Producers keep the train on the track, identifying roadblocks before (or as) they occur and negotiating solutions among all stakeholders.

Full-Service Game Developers

Game developers in this category incorporate all the disciplines necessary to create millions of lines of game code from a single idea. Projects range from six-month, tightly focused opportunistic releases to three years of complex asset integration into a whole that is vast in scope. More than one recent project has exceeded five years and $50 million to complete. The current cost for a multi-SKU console release (PS2, Xbox) now ranges from $3 to $8 million, with team sizes of 20 to 50 people. However, major publishers already project development costs of $25 million or more on next-generation marquee titles, and team sizes for such titles can reach a staggering 350 people.

Given such financials, the proverbial brainstorm-turned-million-seller is rarer than industry aspirants care to believe. The majority of best-sellers are based on existing intellectual property owned or controlled by the publisher, initiated by the publisher with a team whose qualifications (not the least of which is cost) complement that IP.

Publishers can initiate "surefire" projects based on a blockbuster movie or book license, or "questionable" pet projects of a particular executive. Larger publishers can mine the seam of past releases for remakes, due to the hotly debated publisher practice of acquiring intellectual property rights to a promising developer's original game idea. Two truisms unite all these methods: a "no-brainer" concept does not guarantee a great game, and an offbeat idea, well executed, sometimes sells spectacularly.

Developers interact primarily with their publisher and, on occasion, with the platform provider, who provides them with direct technical assistance for the target platform. Developers also promote themselves and their titles to the media, frequently in conjunction with their publisher.

Independent development companies work with publishers on a contract basis. The publisher pays the developer upon completion of various development milestones. These are technically advance payments against a negotiated royalty based on unit sales; however, the royalty is only paid after the publisher's advance payments have been recouped. In one recent example, a publisher and developer negotiated $4/unit royalty, but recoupment against significant development advances ensured the developer would only receive royalties after the 900,000th unit sold. Scenarios like this feed ongoing industry debates about more equitable revenue sharing for developers. Many developers have quietly resorted to building their profit margin into their milestone payment schedule.

Another tightly negotiated contractual term is "net receipts." Simply, this is the amount of money a publisher actually receives from the sale of the game; net receipts are the basis upon which royalty is calculated. In practice, it can be extremely difficult for developers to figure out exactly how much royalty is due, since each publisher deducts different items from gross receipts to arrive at net receipts. For example, a "generous" (for the developer) definition of net receipts could be limited to actual costs, could be capped at a particular percentage, and could cover only cost of sales, cost of goods, and a reserve for retail markdowns. However, publishers have been known to claim marketing and overhead charges as well—and to deduct all items as fixed percentages, without the necessity of proving actual outlays. Wise developers always work with legal counsel on such negotiations.

Development groups also exist as wholly or partially owned subsidiaries of publishers. As employees of either the parent company or the subsidiary, internal team members draw corporate salary and benefits. Stock options, bonuses for achieving sales targets, and profit-sharing programs vary widely by publisher; the development community generally acknowledges that the relative stability of working for a major publisher goes hand in hand with a smaller piece of the profit pie on momentous successes.

Other funding alternatives such as venture capital, completion bond funding, and angel financing play a small but growing part in game development.

Historically, many development groups have gotten their technological start creating PC games. Wide availability of technical information and a small but active engineering community supported many of today's marquee developers as they created early hits such as *Doom*. Today, developers such as Bioware, id Software, Valve, and 3D Realms include user-creation modules in their games, with which their player communities can modify parts of their games. Many entry-level designers or programmers in the industry today earned their position through a compelling "mod" presented as part of their portfolio.

Development for today's consoles—Sony's PlayStation 2 computer entertainment system, the Nintendo GameCube, and the Xbox video game system from Microsoft—is harder to break into. The expense of proprietary development kits—up to $10,000—and the requirement of a preexisting relationship with a publisher closes the door to all but the most organized and connected startup groups with previous platform experience. Consequently, many developers earn their credentials in PC gaming, and then make the leap to console on the strength of proven technology, design, and relationships.

Motion-Capture Service Providers

As hardware platforms follow Moore's law of increasing computing power, consumers and publishers have demanded increasing realism in their games. In particular, developers can now replicate the uniquely identifiable characteristics of human motion with great accuracy for the first time in gaming. Mechanical leg movements on a football player gliding as if on ice have been replaced by true running steps with the inherent force, momentum, and style of the original human player. To be sure, we cannot ignore the stunning contributions of painstaking manual animation to this advancement. However, for the speed and efficiency of achieving realism in human movement, we have motion-capture technology to thank.

Motion capture is the technological process by which scripted movements of human actors are "captured" by magnetic or optical sensors, yielding data that is then inserted into the game engine. *Mocap* is usually used when lifelike human movement is essential to the game concept. For example, a perfectly replicated signature move in a football video game is a selling point to consumers playing as their favorite wide receiver, while a cartoon character might benefit from manual exaggeration of certain animations to emphasize its unreality. A mocap session is similar to a movie shoot, usually involving a director, a script or "moves list," an engineer manipulating the software that processes captured data, and actor(s) selected for their ability to repeat the desired action sequence accurately. Once the session is complete, the animation team works through the raw data, tweaking an elbow position or sword arc until the model behaves exactly as desired in-game.

Developers access motion capture facilities in two ways: the publisher makes its onsite studio available, with costs allocated internally to the project, or directly sub-contracts an external mocap service provider. As with any marriage of the subjective with technology, mocap works best with trained specialists at every level. Publishers with key franchises requiring mocap (such as football games) can recoup on the investment and training for an in-house studio; for most others, mocap is contracted out at costs exceeding $150,000 for a full-service session.

As demand has increased for motion-capture services, the competition among independent mocap studios has led to price pressure. Some leading providers have honed their service-side offering as a result, providing shoot management and data processing, animation tuning, assistance with engine integration, and post-shoot troubleshooting. One provider has productized their data processing software, offering it for license independently of its services. All providers continue to refine the accessibility of data throughout their processes, so developers can benefit from the efficiency of mocap without sacrificing the artistry of keyframe animation.

Art and Animation Service Providers

The increase in computer processing capability in game hardware has provoked an exponential increase in the quantity of art assets required. Onscreen processing limits of several characters comprising a few hundred textured polygons have exploded to millions of polygons making up a main character, several AI characters, a 3D deformable environment with actionable objects, extensive special effects, and realistic environmental lighting. The resulting productivity demands sometimes require outsourcing of the art production process.

Generally, the publisher and developer agree upon the outsourcing of art at contract. A full-service developer might bring an art group to the table based on a previous working relationship, or a publisher might specify a group on its vendor list. In either case, the cost of outsourcing is factored into the project cost and paid during the advance period. Developers generally list contracted art as a separate line item in their proposal.

Art production is one way for fledgling developers to build their reputation on a console platform, particularly if the group's members have a PC background. The developer not only gains access to the proprietary development systems, but also learns the constraints of art production for the target platform and game engine—from simpler matters such as per-character polygon count to the bedeviling issue of limited texture memory. Art production teams who master these issues build impeccable working relationships with their partner publishers, and carefully hire top-flight programmers that have the best chance at breaking through to full-service independent development.

The cost of art production varies wildly with desired quality level, quantity of assets requested, duration of project, and extent of process/logistical integration with the full-service development team. In addition, art production houses run the gamut from long-established, full-time art houses charging top dollar for experience, to startup groups and offshore companies looking to break in at any price. Billing can be per man-month, per minute of cut-scene animation, or flat-fee, and can include royalties if the artwork is integral to the project's brand identity. For the pressured development team who receives a perfectly executed art asset delivery in time to hit a key milestone, and for the publisher whose high expectations for graphic quality were met in that milestone, every dollar is worth it.

Publishers

If developers are the artistic brain behind video games, publishers are the muscle and nerve that coordinate all aspects of bringing a game to a consumer. The publisher's role is so extensive and influential that publishers have taken on the aura of medieval fiefdoms, where money flows in mysterious directions and decisions are made by cabal. Acting as the "suits" to developer "geeks," publishers make up the second half of the classic "art versus commerce" conflict that inspires hyperbolic excesses on games industry message boards. If we step back from the rhetoric, we see wide variation within the category: global conglomerates with multiple regional divisions covering internal and external development, marketing and sales, quality assurance, finance and licensing for any viable delivery platform; smaller companies specializing in marketing and sales of certain genres for certain territories; groups specializing in specific platforms such as PC or mobile phones; entities focusing on discovering gems in one territory for distribution in another; and Web sites offering pay-per-play downloads. To choose the best partner, developers must extensively research prospective publishers' strategic priorities, business model, and execution strengths and weaknesses—much of which can be inferred from publicly available information. Mismatched expectations on any of these fronts can doom the best-executed game to the bargain bin.

Console and PC Publishers

For brevity, and because the vast majority of packaged games wind up in consumers' hands through this model, we will focus on "traditional" console/PC publishers such as Electronic Arts, Activision, THQ, Atari, and Sega. We examine the role of publishers who also control a hardware platform (such as Sony or Nintendo) in a later section. Finally, since we reviewed game development previously, for this overview we will set aside that function of a publisher's role.

Traditional publishers sit in the conceptual center of the video game industry, primarily because they bear the executional and financial burden of every process between code creation and game purchase. Responsibilities and accountabilities include:

Management of the game development process: Publishers are involved in everything from time-to-market scheduling to creative input. The foundation of a publisher's relationship with retail partners is a good product shipped on time in the right quantities.

Debugging, playtesting, and other quality assurance: Publishers are legally liable for the game's quality to both consumers and the platform holder.

Securing all necessary licenses: These include in-game music; creative properties, trademarks, or technologies controlled by other companies; athletic leagues and players; and the right to publish on controlled platforms (consoles). Experienced developers obtain an indemnity from the publisher against any licensing omissions the publisher might make.

Manufacturing and shipping the finished game: This responsibility includes writing and printing the manual, designing the cover, buying the case, placing orders with media manufacturers, assembling all the elements into a game package, and shipping it to the channel. Aside from the QA implications of an unstable assembly process, lackluster packaging encourages consumers to look elsewhere on the store shelf.

Maintaining good relationships with retailers via cooperative channel inventory management: More than just the "schmooze" of golf and expensive dinners, publishers' sales efforts must include in-store merchandising programs, funding for product placement in retail circulars ("white space"), joint assessment of a title's sales potential, and markdowns or returns at publisher cost if the title does not perform as expected.

Communicating title features and availability to the consumer: Whether via "meta-channels" such as press events for games industry media, or direct communication with gamers via television, print, demo opportunities, Web site, or Internet/direct mail, publishers are responsible for letting the public know what's out there.

Housekeeping: This responsibility includes all the human resource, tax and finance, investor relations, and legal services issues involved in running the company.

Industry voices frequently criticize publishers for "unfairly" sharing revenue with their developer, without whose creativity there would be nothing to sell. Since revenue sharing is established at contract, a knowledgeable and firm negotiating stance goes far in ensuring fairness for the developer; the many factors that can strengthen a developer's negotiating position are covered elsewhere in this book. In pure financial terms, however, the market law of risk versus reward explains why publishers keep the lions' share of revenue, if not of profit. Table 7.2.1 answers the gamer's frequent question: "Where does my $50 go?"

Table 7.2.1   Generalized Breakdown of Revenue from a $50 Console Game

Amount	Purpose	Paid By	Paid To
$3	Cost of goods	Publisher	Media manufacturer
$7	Publishing license royalty	Publisher	Platform holder
$13	Retailer profit	Consumer	Retailer
$3	Markdown reserve	Publisher	Retailer
$8	Development cost	Publisher	Developer
$10	**Operating cost**	Publisher	Internal (overhead, freight, co-op, bad debt)
$6	**Marketing**	Publisher	Ad agencies and media

Items in **bold** can be converted to profit through careful publisher cost management.

Quality Assurance Service Provider

Occasionally, a publisher will decide not to maintain quality assurance (QA) as an internal core competency. Companies such as Absolute Quality or Beta Breakers provide complete debugging and gameplay evaluation to such publishers on a contract basis. The clear advantage is peace of mind about product quality without the necessity of managing the significant human-resource issues and financial overhead of an in-house test team.

Contracted QA has a long history of success with PC publishers, who bear the unique burden of ensuring that their latest release works within a range of hardware specifications. Depending on the publisher's defined compatibility set, the contract QA house can be asked to test hundreds of variants on PC game software + operating system software + hardware + peripherals, and project results for configurations not tested. Such companies can recoup the significant investment in equipment representing the current gaming market (the "test bed") over multiple projects.

Console publishers are gradually warming up to the idea of contract testing. One obstacle to date has been the expense and proprietary nature of development and debugging systems for controlled platforms. If the publisher provides such equipment to its external QA partner, the platform holder holds the publisher responsible for proper security and authorized use. Another more emotional than factual objection is the perceived risk of code leaks from sources beyond the publisher's own walls; if a game is to be pirated, better to control the leak internally than pursue legal remedies against a partner. During the most recent console transition, contract QA houses made great strides in accommodating these issues, and have since worked closely with both publishers and platform holders to ensure that the figurative firewall includes rather than excludes their services.

Public-Relations Firms, Advertising Agencies, and Merchandising Teams

Although marketing departments at some publishers look as populated as E3 on opening day, few heads of marketing deny the efficiencies of contracting external firms for public relations, advertising generation, and in-store merchandising assistance. Much more than additional heads and hands, such companies combine effectiveness through relationships, the creativity that comes from time to brainstorm, and a reach that falls just short of handing a game directly to the consumer.

Publishers occasionally learn to their dismay that some brand-name PR firms specializing in national media such as *USA Today* and *Newsweek* can fail miserably at communicating their message to the video games industry media such as *Electronic Gaming Monthly* and *Edge*. The best games industry communications managers successfully pitch the latest role-playing game to a sophisticated news outlet while, on the other phone line, explaining this year's business plan to the local game journalist. The publisher gives the PR firm complete access to its game's development, while the PR firm coaches the publisher on speaking skillfully and consistently to all of its constituencies.

Similarly, a lack of alignment between publisher and ad agency on the creative vision for the marketing plan directly impacts sales. Many top-shelf ad agencies approach the video games industry as a creative soul mate, believing that innovative interactive entertainment requires bleeding-edge advertising. Experienced games industry marketing executives, on the other hand, know that their audience wants to see in-game footage. (Such creative tension results in either a memorable commercial or a new ad agency.) Agency partnerships range from a fully retained relationship covering all software releases, to different agencies retained for distinct product lines, to per-title arrangements.

In-store merchandising assistance is a luxury best afforded by platform holders. With anywhere from 4 to 24 linear feet devoted to its hardware and software in key retailers, for example, Nintendo is legendary for its merchandising team's deep relationships with store managers, enabling them to update signage, straighten displays, restock empty shelf slots, and chat up the electronics section manager on upcoming releases. Publishers whose key releases are integral to a platform holder's lineup can obtain preferential placement and subsequent coddling of their titles by the platform holder's in-store team. Publishers have been known to maintain merchandising teams for shorter or longer periods, but the justification for such cost begins with shelf space; sending staff to straighten up just a few facings is desirable in principle but questionable in financial practice.

Platform Holders

"Platform holders" are companies that manufacture the hardware (and in some cases, the software) on which game software runs. As with publishers, a wide variety of companies comprise game platform holders: cell phone providers, personal digital assistant (PDA) and other handheld device manufacturers, PC makers (both the boxes and the chips inside them), video game console manufacturers, development software/tools providers such as Microsoft and Silicon Graphics, and Web-based development and delivery services such as WildTangent. Such companies share the characteristic of owning, controlling, or influencing the software that appears on their platform, whether by providing application programming interfaces (APIs) to help developers access the features of their hardware, or by outright permission-based control of anything that involves the platform. Frequently, platform holders also create software for their own hardware; in this section, we review the platform holder's role exclusive of publishing functions.

Platform holders derive their revenue from any of the following sources:

- Sales of the hardware itself
- Sales of (or licensing fees from) any peripherals compatible with the hardware
- Sales of their own games compatible with the hardware ("first-party games")
- Licensing fees from compatible games made by other companies ("third-party games")
- Licensing of development tools or APIs necessary to create games for the hardware
- Manufacturing proprietary delivery media for the hardware (such as game cartridges)

Consoles and PCs differ fundamentally in that console makers strictly regulate access to their platform via various licensing permissions, while PC makers provide their APIs for free to any interested developer. For this reason, we categorize the PC platform as "open" and consoles as "closed." Handhelds such as PDAs and to a certain extent cell phones follow the "open" PC model, while proprietary handhelds such as Nintendo's Game Boy Advance and DS are just as "closed" as Nintendo's GameCube.

PCs as a Platform

The "PC platform" is in fact a conglomeration of intersecting partnerships among CPU manufacturers, development software/tools providers, graphics chip manufacturers, and box assemblers. Look in the manual for your new PC and you might see:

- Intel Pentium 4 primary processor (CPU)
- ATI Radeon graphics processor
- Microsoft DirectX
- Assembled and sold by Dell

Each of these categories provides support to game developers, mostly for free, with the intent of making money from compatible software or hardware sales.

As the most visible example of successful "ingredient marketing," Intel has spent years courting game developers to maintain its image as provider of the fastest CPUs available. It provides sample boards and technical assistance to game developers, and will even work closely with leading game developers on R&D for its future generations of chips. The objective, of course, is for gamers to specify "Intel Inside" when they purchase their next gaming PC.

Graphics chip companies such as NVIDIA and ATI have built a healthy complementary market to CPUs by creating graphics chips customized for multimedia and, of course, games. In addition to the developer benefits already listed, graphics chip companies will secure cutting-edge games under development on an exclusive basis, paying the developer to incorporate the technological bells and whistles that set their chip apart from the rest. Graphics chipmakers also create APIs that allow developers to take advantage of their chip's unique features. Once "hardcore" gamers realize that their longed-after new releases look best when run on a particular graphics chip, they gladly upgrade.

Two well-known technology companies have made names for themselves in the development software/tools space. Microsoft, with its DirectX API, has succeeded over the years in stabilizing the technological risk of game development on PCs, much as it has standardized its operating system for the user. Silicon Graphics has created a less widespread, but popular among game developers, API called OpenGL. Both companies give their APIs away to qualified engineers for free, encouraging information sharing among their developer communities and placing as few limits as possible on use. The advantage for developers is learning a software platform that is invisibly compatible with the multiple hardware combinations available in the market.

PC "box-makers" such as Dell and HP play a less active part in promoting game development on their PCs, since the tough work is done by their "ingredient" companies. However, to the extent they target gamers as potential customers, they might secure an exclusive set of games to preload on the PC before it's sold to consumers.

One important factor in PC publishing for developers and publishers is the lack of royalty paid to the hardware company for the privilege of platform compatibility. The beneficial effects are lower cost-of-goods and higher profit margins for publishers, and easier access to both development and self-publishing for developers. However, since nearly any competent and inspired PC development group can complete and ship a PC game at relatively low cost, many groups do so. The resulting competition among thousands of titles for shelf space at retail has created a cutthroat sales channel for PC games, where retailers return units unsold after eight weeks to publishers, and only the top 30 games sell more than 300,000 units.

Consoles as a Platform

In direct contrast to the open and loosely affiliated PC game development scenario, development for game consoles such as Sony's PlayStation 2, Nintendo's GameCube, and Microsoft's Xbox is tightly controlled at all levels by the respective companies. To create and sell games on these platforms, a developer/publisher requires the following licenses and permissions:

License to use development software and hardware: Only provided after the console platform holder's favorable evaluation of the applicant's potential for bringing quality games to market. For developers, a publisher's recommendation carries great weight in obtaining development systems.

License to conduct general marketing and sales activities: Again, granted only if the platform holder believes the company has the structure and resources to succeed. Smaller publishers without a direct sales force or consistent product flow struggle to establish credibility on a console platform, sometimes signing its products over to a licensed publisher for distribution.

License to use the platform holder's trademarks and logos in-game, on packaging, and in advertising:　Platform holders provide templates for all logo and trademark use, and review all materials for correct use before the product can be assembled.

Permission to create a game:　Granted after platform holder review of the game concept early in the development process. Instances in which platform holders reject a concept, although rare, cause great vexation, as usually the publisher has already sunk funding into the project.

License to release the game to the channel:　After extensive testing by developer, publisher, and platform holder. Platform holder certification is a tense part of the process, as the game can be rejected any number of times for bug fixes or standards violations.

According to industry logic, the company that creates the console, engineers the APIs that developers use to build games for the hardware, and incurs the cost for marketing and selling the hardware to consumers is entitled to royalties from game sales—generally around $7/unit—to cover those costs. At launch, the retail price of the console rarely covers its actual component cost, and that cost doesn't include R&D amortization. Many millions of units later, after multiple reengineering efforts to reduce the actual bill of materials ("BOM"), successful console platforms can generate vast software-side profits while the platform holder breaks even on the hardware. Over a successful console's lifespan of five to seven years, the platform holder recoups the current console's R&D costs over the first few years, and invests in R&D for the next-generation console during the last few years. An imbalance of software revenues against hardware costs has driven console platform holders such as Atari, 3DO, and Sega out of the hardware business entirely.

Delivery Media Manufacturers

An often-overlooked cog in the publishing machine is the actual game manufacturing and assembly company. With the exception of Nintendo's Game Boy Advance and DS, today's platforms are disk-based; this welcome change reduced cost of goods for publishers and cut manufacturing time dramatically, enabling (almost) just-in-time inventory management. Manufacturers obtain a license from console platform holders to work with the proprietary disk medium and/or other antipiracy technology on the disk, and pay a nominal per-unit royalty for that technology to the platform holder.

Historically, console platform holders have always controlled manufacturing directly, with Sony and Nintendo continuing this model. Publishers submit their orders directly to the platform holder, or simultaneously to the platform holder and the manufacturer. The publisher pays both manufacturing cost and royalty directly to the platform holder, sometimes on a cash-in-advance basis. During busy seasons when manufacturing capacity is strained, the platform holder has final say over which products receive priority. However, in general the manufacturer adheres to a certain turnaround time as part of its terms of service. All the same, for an AAA title release date when every day in the schedule counts, even one day over "the standard turnaround time" can cause urgent telephone calls up and down the publishing chain.

With its Dreamcast, Sega was the first to offer complete publisher control of the manufacturing process. Microsoft has continued this trend with its Xbox. In this scenario, once the platform holder releases tested game code to the manufacturer, the publisher is free to negotiate turnaround times and pricing based on the strength of its relationship with the manufacturer. In practice, the cost of goods does not vary widely, but the licensing of three or four manufacturing companies ensures an alternative supplier.

To save additional time or cost, publishers often receive their goods from the licensed manufacturer as unpackaged disks on spindles, and ship them to a separate facility to assemble. Since such "pack-out houses" are not licensed or controlled by the console platform holder, the publisher is free to pursue the most advantageous partnership based on cost, turnaround time, proximity to the publisher's distribution center, or expertise with different kinds of packaging. Such processes must be managed carefully to prevent Murphy 's Law from afflicting the extra shipping and handling steps.

Retail

As the most visible part of the video game publishing trail to the consumer, retail is rewarded handsomely with as much as a 30 percent margin on a game sale. Many routes a game takes to a consumer's hands are not visible to the consumer, but certainly influence the game choices with which he's presented. For the purposes of this discussion, we examine primarily brick-and-mortar stores; online sales of packaged goods have steadily increased but are largely controlled by brick-and-mortar establishments. Long download times and insufficient storage on the client device continue to hamper commercial downloading of games over the Internet, excluding casual games with smaller file sizes. In practice, mass-market online distribution of games awaits greater penetration of broadband connections and a business model that adequately compensates all participating entities.

Distributors

Although it might seem odd to begin a discussion of retail with the middleman, it's useful to know that distributors enable smaller regional store chains, individual "mom and pop" stores, and other niche retail outlets to service their customer base uniquely in the face of stiff competition from national discount chains. Distributors buy nearly every game a publisher releases; their strengths are breadth of selection, close cost management, and the ability to sell to stores whose size or business practices preclude dealing directly with the publisher. In short, the distributor brings the publisher incremental sales more efficiently than if the publisher were to service those accounts directly.

Distributors might specialize in differing product lineups. Some distributors located closer to major population centers claim the advantage of quickest delivery of the latest releases. Although publishers frown upon the service, distributors also try to boost their allocation of high-demand titles to supplement national retailers' supply in the critical days between sellout of the first shipment and arrival of the next. Others might focus on "closeouts"—marked-down or discontinued games that make their way from the publisher or retailer's warehouse to the bargain bin at a loss for the publisher but profit for the distributor and retailer. Some distributors focus on making games "rental-ready," repackaging games in sturdy cases for small rental chains. Some distributors act as publishers on import or other low-visibility titles, taking the financial risk on the hope that one might turn out a gem.

In its role of making the market for games more efficient, the distributor itself must be extremely efficient to secure its roughly 3 percent margin on sales. Generally, distributors secure massive warehouse space in low-rent areas, depend on the publisher for sales materials rather than creating their own, and pay their salespeople with heavy emphasis on commission. The cliché of "making it up on volume" is possible for a distributor that works every angle to its benefit.

Manufacturers' Representatives

Manufacturer's representatives, or "rep groups," are a testament to the power of relationships in a high-tech world. Usually small companies of just a few people, rep groups secure agreements allowing them to act as contracted salespeople on the publisher's behalf. They're responsible for knowing the product line, the target retailer's operation, publisher practices, and when to sell more versus mark down (although they must recommend the latter to their publisher first). For these services, the publisher pays them a percentage of net sales (all sales minus any returns).

Rep groups are usually of most value in situations where the rep group's relationship and credibility with a retailer is stronger than the publisher's is. This includes launches of new product lines, a new publisher's entry into the market, or reaching out to a retailer not yet included in the publisher's existing retailer base. The rep group acts as go-between, advising both publisher and retailer on how to work through new processes on each side. Despite hard work and sincere commitment by leading rep groups, publisher sales executives constantly reexamine the wisdom of contracting external companies for such a vital task. Perhaps disappointing sales on a key product prompts the initial questioning, or cost watchers eyeing the rep group's commission percentage. The result in either case, and the bane of every rep group, is the publisher's call informing them, "we've decided to go direct."

Regional Retailers

Despite the increasing standardization of the retail experience nationwide, successful regional retailers have learned the keys to survival: know your customer, provide exactly what he wants, give great service, and offer occasional surprises. These precepts apply perfectly to the game market, where smaller video game–only retailers and mom-and-pop stores can't compete on price or speedy availability of new releases. The smaller retailer can provide detailed knowledge on the latest game or on an obscure release from years back—and if the store manager or buyer is very good, he will know where to lay his hands on both.

The key to regional retailers' success is good relationships with both their distributor and, ideally, with each publisher. Although economies of scale prevent a publisher from servicing regional retailers directly, solid chains with several stores can attract the publisher's notice, either through the grapevine or via distributor's advocacy with the publisher on their behalf for things such as in-store merchandising items and, rarely, markdowns. Since hardcore gamers frequently staff regional chains, publishers can use such chains to create word-of-mouth recommendations from "experts" for their latest releases.

Rental Retailers

Rental retailers such as Blockbuster and Hollywood Video have emerged from relative obscurity as a retail category to major drivers in the channel. Until recently, publishers treated rental retail with respect but not much attention; although the sell-in quantity "per door" was less than at traditional retailers, those units were never returned or marked down. Recently, however, industry market research from many sources has shown that the primary driver behind consumer purchase intent is hands-on experience with the game. As rentals can encourage sales of a good game, so can they stop a bad game's sales dead at launch. As a result, publishers now work out their lineup carefully with rental retailers, evaluating rental retailers' value in advance promotion side by side with actual units sold.

Rental retailers, in turn, have identified the game market as a potential growth segment of their business. Some chains are experimenting with revenue-sharing models. Other rental retailers are moving into sales as well; having created a potential buyer for a game through rental, such retailers have stopped sending the buyer to a competitor for the purchase. In short, rental retailing is transforming into a new service model for gaming consumers.

National Retailers

Finally, we come to the names that consumers know: Wal-Mart, Target, Best Buy, Toys "R" Us, and Electronics Boutique. The lineup varies slightly from publisher to publisher, but this group of national retailers makes up the core of the industry's sales efforts, and represents the most direct way for publishers to get a game into a consumer's hands.

National retailers have direct relationships with the publisher, which means that the publisher provides them with:

- Games shipped directly to the retailer's warehouse, or direct to store if the retailer can accommodate.
- In-store merchandising materials, such as standees, posters, shelf talkers, and box fronts for display.
- Extensive sales materials on each title, usually including a direct pitch by the publisher's marketing and sales staff to the buyer.
- Generous terms on sales (average net 60, although retailers with clout stretch this as desired).
- Hands-on inventory management, including publisher sales staff poring over store-by-store inventory to increase sales efficiency.
- Various relationship-building perks, such as tickets to a local sports event or an expensive dinner after the sales call. (Wal-Mart is notably strict in its policy of "no freebies" to its buyers.)
- Credits against existing invoices or free goods to help the retailer mark down and move through stagnant inventory.
- Unique sales programs customized by retailers, whether a gift-with-purchase, in-store event or celebrity appearance, or sales contest for in-store staff.

The retail buyer has tremendous influence in the process of getting a game to consumers. The buyer is usually responsible for the entire video game category, but depending on the relative importance of video games to the retailer's revenue, video game buyers might also be responsible for related categories such as video, electronics, or toys. The best buyers listen to the salespeople but also conduct their own research, accepting the publisher's stance but listening to the wants of their own customers. The worst buyers pay little attention to video games, failing to keep abreast of trends or failing to pass information along to store-level employees. Frequently, the difference between a coherent, well-stocked video game department at one retailer and a disorganized jumble of last year's games at a different chain is directly attributable to the buyer.

For publishers, the buyer controls several elements that can mean sales success or failure: whether to stock a game at all, how deeply to stock it, "white space" or co-op advertising in retail circulars, and in-store pricing. The decision to pass on a game can mean forecast deficits of thousands of units if that retailer is responsible for 40 percent of a game's launch volume. Smaller publishers suffer from buyers "cherry picking" their best titles only, while larger publishers and platform holders can benefit from the buyer's courtesy in taking the entire product line. A buyer's decision to stock a game in "gamer-heavy" stores in key locations, but not in minor secondary locations, is a strong sign to a publisher to redouble its in-store efforts to achieve chain-wide distribution. A buyer's decision to show a title in the retailer's "white space" circulars (usually bundled with the daily newspaper) creates a measurable sales spike the week the ad is viewed by millions of avid gamers watching for the next release. Finally, buyers have the authority to designate a key title as a loss-leader, pricing it below the usual $49 at launch to drive store traffic to higher margin purchases. For hot releases, publishers designate a manufacturer's advertised price ("MAP") program, in which any retailer who reduces their advertised price below a certain level is denied co-op funding for the offending ad.

However, this relatively weak penalty is only effective when combined with a strong buyer-salesperson relationship that neither party wishes to damage.

Much as "going direct" are two words rep groups dread, "no open to buy" are four words that bedevil publishers. "Open to buy" is the amount of money the buyer can spend buying games within a certain period, usually quarterly or 30 days. Essentially a budget, it's calculated from a combination of cost of inventory on hand, sales rate or "turnover" of that inventory, and revenue expected against that inventory for the period. Open to buy is very restricted around the Thanksgiving–Christmas holiday interval, when large numbers of games are expected to sell huge quantities. A publisher salesperson pitching an excellent game who receives the response "no open to buy" is chastised by his or her management for not pitching the buyer earlier on the game's quality. A salesperson hearing the phrase in response to a poor-quality game should understand this message: Your game isn't good enough to compete with the other releases during this time period. In short, if the publisher manages its retail relationships well, open-to-buy issues should be no surprise.

To manage such relationships to this degree, publishers require voluminous data quickly and frequently. Publishers can derive sales data of their own games from internal sales information, of course, but sales data on competitive games or titles released during the same period puts an important context around one's own sales. For example, poor sales of a publisher's franchise platform title can mean anything; poor sales of the next platformer to appear might mean that that console's audience doesn't look for the platform genre; and poor sales of all games during that period might indicate overall industry softness, or poor supply of the hardware platform at retail. For such data, a company called NPD offers a subscription service called TRSTS (Toy Retail Sales Tracking Service) [NPD]. Major retailers report their weekly sales, which then are aggregated and sent back to subscribing publishers on a monthly or weekly basis.

Summary

The video games industry is now in its third decade of providing interactive entertainment to the consumer market. Through the years, although industry entities have largely retained their roles in the channel, the balance of power (and flow of money) among them has fluctuated widely. All major industry players forecast a skyrocketing of project costs for the 2005–2006 platform generation. Given the amount of money in play, a major stumble by any company in the value chain will not only affect the title in question, but could also turn the entire industry balance of power on its head.

Exercises

1. Using Microsoft Excel and the data in Table 7.2.1, construct a basic spreadsheet modeling the relationships among cost, unit sales, and profit.
2. Using the cost structure in Table 7.2.1, how many units of this game would you need to sell to break even? To make $1 million in profit?

3. Using the breakeven sales quantity in the preceding exercise, manipulate the values given you in Table 7.2.1 to reduce your breakeven number.

4. Discuss the advantages and disadvantages of making the following games. Consider budget, project management, marketing, technology, sales forecast, profitability, risk, and quality.
   a. An NFL football game.
   b. A game based on an original idea from your company's most famous designer.
   c. A sequel to last year's game from your company's most famous designer.

5. You are the president of a small development company under contract to a publisher for a game based on your original idea and on your custom-developed technology. You're located in Austin, Texas, and you've been together as a group for five years. The project budget is fairly generous. You realize that you don't have enough artists and animators on staff to achieve your next five art milestones. Do you hire or outsource? Discuss in terms of schedule, technology, budget, company culture, and quality.

6. You are the manager of a video game store in Seattle, Washington. Your store is one of four within a regional retailer selling console and PC games; you order titles for your store through corporate HQ. You know your games and you've been careful to hire staffers who know the industry and pay attention to regular customers' desires. A Best Buy has just opened in the local mall, and last weekend you saw to your shock that they are selling this year's #1 console game at $10 below your price. What do you do to ensure your shop's continued success? Consider short- and long-term strategies.

References

[Bethke03] Bethke, Erik, *Game Development and Production*, Wordware Publishing, 2003.

[Gibson03] Gibson, Elizabeth, and Billings, Andy, *Big Change at Best Buy: Working Through Hypergrowth to Sustained Excellence*, Davies-Black Publishing, 2003.

[IGDA03] IGDA Contract Walk-Through—Second Release, 2003, available at *www.igda.org/biz/contract_walkthrough.php*.

[Kent03] Kent, Steven, *High Score!: The Illustrated History of Electronic Games*, 2nd ed., McGraw-Hill Osborne Media, 2003.

[Kushner03] Kushner, David, *Masters of Doom: How Two Guys Created an Empire and Transformed Pop Culture*, Random House, 2003.

[Menache99] Menache, Alberto, *Understanding Motion Capture for Computer Animation and Video Games*, Morgan Kaufmann, 1999.

[NPD] NPD Funworld, *www.npdfunworld.com*.

[Sheff93] Sheff, David, *Game Over: How Nintendo Zapped an American Industry, Captured Your Dollars, and Enslaved Your Children*, Random House, 1993.

7.3 ■ The Publisher-Developer Relationship

In This Chapter

Overview

It's unlikely you will have failed to notice the increasingly frequent comparisons being drawn between video games and the traditional entertainment superpowers of music and film, most notably the record-breaking first-day sales of Microsoft and Bungie's Xbox epic: *Halo 2*. What may come as more of a surprise is that the processes and costs involved in taking a modern video game from abstract concept to the shelves of your local retail store are becoming equally comparable to and even sometimes eclipse those of the latest blockbuster Hollywood films. In this chapter, we explore exactly how a game is commissioned, what the deal will consist of, and the key stages of development thereafter.

Just as the games we play today are dramatically different from those 20 years ago—from the look, feel, and content to the multidigit ergonomics of the modern game controller—the makeup and complexion of the companies, individuals, and processes involved in the production of games has evolved. Of course, much of this is simply a result of the extraordinary growth of the leisure software industry, from its roots in university activity clubs, arcades, and bedrooms to the $20 billion entertainment giant that exists today.

Hopefully, this chapter will go some way toward helping you to build a basic understanding of the delicate and not so delicate power struggles that occur on a daily basis in game development.

Sowing the Seeds

The first playable video game, *Spacewar,* was a university club project completed in 1962 by MIT student Steve Russell. Russell could not have possibly known that, less than half a century later, his simple space rocket duel controlled with toggle switches and stored on tickertape would be superseded on a mass-market scale by globally connected miniature supercomputers smaller than a shoe box, with gigabytes of storage, responsive analog control, and 3D visuals approaching photo-realism.

It is possible, however, that "godfather of the video game industry" Nolan Bushnell did have this vision. The University of Utah undergraduate trumped *Spacewar* with his own *Computer Space*, the first coin-operated video game, in 1971, but it was alongside Al Alcorn with their now-legendary startup company, Atari, that Bushnell practically invented the games industry as we know it with the 2D bat and ball game, *Pong*, and subsequently taking digitized "TV games" from the arcades and into people's homes in the form of cartridge-based consoles.

However, it was the advent of programmable home computer systems such as the Sinclair Spectrum, BBC Micro, and Commodore 64 (and subsequently the Commodore Amiga and the Atari ST) that transformed the video game development industry. A legion of technically minded teenagers turned their attentions to creating wonderfully abstract light and sound shows. Most importantly, these systems gave them the means to develop their own fully playable videogames, with recognizable characters, structured levels, and rudimentary sound samples and effects.

What began as an underground scene soon developed into a bedroom industry. The combination of a uniquely level and relatively inexpensive technological playing field, healthy peer competition, growing consumer penetration and (unlike previous home entertainment systems that required expensive specialist cartridges) simple recordable magnetic tape and disc media, a new industry grew almost overnight.

Of course, unlike today where global data transfer is an everyday phenomenon thanks to the Internet, back then these often one-man development teams needed to get their lovingly crafted games to a paying audience through more traditional retail distribution methods.

And here is where the lines were (and still are) drawn between developer and publisher.

The Developer/Publisher Divide

In the very simplest of terms, where a developer of a game was able to conceive and subsequently implement their abstract ideas into a piece of accessible software that was entertaining, exciting, and engaging, the same people rarely possessed the requisite commercial knowledge or ability to then successfully package, promote, and sell the title through the retail channels. And so began the complex rights, financing, and power struggle between creative talent and commercial savvy.

There are many variations on this theme, some of which are discussed later in this chapter, but as a rule the developer conceives, documents, and prototypes game ideas to a stage where the creative and commercial merits can be tangibly assessed, at which point a publisher will be sought to option the right to fund, market, and distribute the title. The complications begin when it comes to agreeing to the structure of the deal. How much will the game cost to develop? How long will it take? How many people are likely to buy it? What percentage of profits will the developer receive? How much and which kinds of marketing should publisher commit to?

All these points and many more need to be thought out, discussed, and agreed on before a game can be added to a release schedule, and even then, issues during development can (and do) sometimes mean that even a complete game may not actually reach the shelves, regardless of the time and money already invested.

One of the most important parts of this chain of events and a starting point for most is the pitching process, which is the single most important initial factor in getting a game from the developers' collective mind to the hands of the consumer.

In this next section, we look at the different stages of a modern-day game pitch, and the various interactions that take place along the way.

The Pitching Process

With mainstream videogame titles now costing upwards of $2 million to develop, and often more than that again to distribute and market, publishers have to be completely convinced of the ability of a title to perform commercially before committing it to their portfolio. However, with development timescales now averaging around 14–18 months (and sometimes several years), and the nebulous nature of "good gameplay," it's extremely difficult to judge these factors at a sufficiently early stage in a title's gestation. This is one of the key factors in the recent trend for licensed titles and high-profile sequels.

What this all means is that even before a contract has been signed, there is an immediate power struggle between the (comparatively) cash-poor developer, who is unable to sustain the cost of developing a game to completion without the security and financial incentives of a guaranteed publishing deal, and the risk-averse publisher who must be careful not to back an unsuccessful title, but who also does not want to miss out on signing the next potential *Grand Theft Auto* or *Tomb Raider* super-franchise.

These factors have developed over the years into a fairly standardized pitching process, and an independent development team looking to pitch a new concept to a publisher would usually be expected to provide the following assets as part of their presentation:

- Game prototype
- Pitch presentation
- Outline game design
- Technical design
- Project schedule AND budget

Let's look at each of these in turn.

Game Prototype

In many respects, the games industry has come full circle. In the early days, publishers were often approached with completed or near complete titles, practically ready to put on the shelves. As the industry grew, and flush with success and money, a period of time elapsed where developers and publishers seemed to believe they could do no wrong, and developers were able to get new ideas commissioned over a game of pool and a beer with little or no documentation or technology. (This isn't idle industry folklore; this author has personally been responsible for at least three such titles!)

Of course, development costs and team sizes have now spiraled dramatically, and the game prototype has become one of the most important factors in showing *proof of concept*.

The publisher will normally look for the following features in a prototype:

- Core gameplay mechanic or key gameplay points of difference
- Demonstration of control method/camera system
- Demonstration of team proficiency with proposed technology and tools
- A good approximation of "final quality" proposed visual styling

Many developers today aim to complete a full working level of the game to give the best facsimile of how the finished game will look and play. For example, a racing game would likely include a full track and at least one car to demonstrate the handling, styling, and type of racing, or an action adventure title would have a fully textured and animated character negotiating a single game level, including the key control or game features that make it different from other action adventure titles, as well as some example adversaries displaying rudimentary AI (artificial intelligence).

Larger developers will also often use a separate smaller team to create the prototype so that clever shortcuts can be used to produce the necessary results without affecting the development schedule of the full game.

Pitch Presentation

The role of the pitch presentation is to deliver a complete yet brief overview of the critical factors of the game in the most attractive and exciting way possible. Aimed at the marketing department, this is usually delivered as a PowerPoint presentation and should contain the following:

- Concept overview and genre profile including target market
- Concept USPs (unique selling points—what makes it stand out from its competitors)
- Proposed technology and target platform(s)
- Team biographies and heritage
- Outline marketing information, including potential licensing opportunities

The developer will also include any marketing-focused visuals such as game logo, high-detail renders of key characters, and an exciting promotional video, preferably including early gameplay footage.

Outline Game Design

The *outline game design* documentation is much more thorough than the pitch presentation, and focuses on intimate design detail such as storyline, control dynamics, camera system, user interface, inventory, and so forth. This documentation is primarily for the core development team to reference their work from, but is often given to the producers and technical workers at publishers so they can see the substance behind the glossy prototype.

As well as detailed written descriptions, the game design document will also include representative diagrams, schematics, and concept visuals to ensure no room for misinterpretation of features between the design team and the programmers and artists who will create the content.

Technical Design

The *technical specification* appendix is usually broken into two sections; one section written by the lead programmer who will cover the technical and code-specific aspects of the concept, with the other section written by the lead artist covering the technical art and content requirements of the concept. Whereas the design document focus is very much on the core concept idea and how gameplay and the associated components will fit in with the plot or storyline, the technical design will cover the practical details on how the proposed design will use the various platforms, development tools, and technologies.

From the programming side, the content of this document will cover topics such as AI requirements, special effects, the proposed rendering and animation technology, any tools or middleware that are going to be used, and what kind of programming needs and skill sets will be required by the technical team.

There will also be some indication on how version management will be maintained and what processes will be put into place to achieve this, such as Microsoft Source Safe or NXN Alien Brain (code/asset management tools), and backup procedures to ensure vital assets do not get destroyed as a result of unforeseen data loss disasters.

The technical design will also be used to outline the structure of the proposed game systems that are required for the project. At this stage, this information only needs to be "top level," but with sufficient detail that a programming schedule could be ascertained. Taking the time to produce this structure at this stage can also be used as a heads-up to help identify any requirements that differ from the norm or may need special skills.

Project Scheduling and Budget

As you would expect, this is the most important element of any pitch.

A developer may have a fantastic and original idea for a game, complete with a killer prototype, but if the publisher suspects for one second that the development team is unable to manage the product to strict schedule and budgetary constraints, while maintaining the originally proposed vision, it's extremely unlikely the game will get signed.

The publishers' main aim when viewing this part of the pitch documentation will be to look for considerable detail and transparent accounting in the proposed budget, alongside detailed schedule information. Publishers are particularly keen to see that the budget and schedule will allow for contingency scenarios. They look for these indicators to ascertain how realistic a concept timeline/budget really is. Often, publishers will use similar in-house and third-party projects as benchmarks to help validate this, so if a title is considerably more or less expensive than they usually experience, they will want a good reason as to why that is the case.

Discrepancies between what the developer has pitched and what the publisher believes is attainable are often the cause for much negotiation and alteration at this stage. To try to alleviate such a situation, developers will usually have several sets of budget figures and schedules that have been specifically tailored to match typical project spends and portfolio profiles of the publishers in question. It is also worth mentioning again that while the overall cost is obviously important, it's actually the developer's ability to deliver the product to the agreed quality on time that is most critical, as even small schedule slippages can be enough to cost the publisher dearly.

In this super-competitive market, publishers book advertising space, in-store point-of-sale, OEM deals, and press coverage months in advance of release. Therefore, missing the original release slot for a title can have catastrophic consequences, as it may not be possible to rebook these activities to accompany the new launch date, and the carefully timed press and PR activities will be wasted as the fickle game-buying public focuses on the next big launch.

It's situations like these where already borderline releases may be cancelled, as the extra costs on top of duplication and distribution simply no longer make commercial sense.

The Deal

Once a publisher expresses interest in a product, this is simply the start of the process and is by no means a guarantee that they will take it on board. It merely shows their intent to enter into commercial negotiations.

Unlike the early days of video game development where publishers were little more than duplication and distribution companies, today's mass-market climate demands a much more integrated and global operation, and with such significant budgets and potential market scope, it is crucial that the deal is structured fairly and leaves no room for interpretation on any aspect of the agreement.

In this section, covering the deal, it is assumed that the publishing agreement is being signed between a global publisher and an independent developer for a single product that is not using any existing IP (intellectual property), and that it is to be developed for one or more of the main gaming platforms.

The publisher in this instance will be marketing and distributing the product across all of their applicable territories. A publisher who operates at this level will usually allocate a much larger marketing budget for the game to maximize awareness and promotion across all available forms of media, which in turn should be reflected in the consumer awareness and purchasing of the game, and therefore the gross returns for both the publisher and the developer. By working with a single global publisher, the developer can also usually expect streamlined communication, consistent product marketing and messaging, and clearly defined street dates in each territory.

Deal Dynamics

The following section covers the main considerations and actions at the contract stage of negotiations.

Research

An often-overlooked part of the deal stage is researching the prospective publishing partners thoroughly. Many developers are just looking to get a deal signed quickly so that funding for their project is secured, relying on good faith and lawyers to ensure that contractual obligations are met. However, research carried out at this stage into how the publisher runs their business can be invaluable when it comes to the final negotiations.

The majority of independent developers in today's climate belong to local, national, and international bodies and forums such as the IGDA, who encourage community and information sharing within the development network as well as working directly toward a more sustainable environment and business model. Therefore, this is a great way for developers to find out this kind of information directly from their peers.

It doesn't take much networking to find somebody that is either working with or has previously worked with any given publisher, and the questions developers should seek answers for as a minimum include:

- What type of publishing deal was it (multiterritory, multiplatform, licensed)?
- Did the publisher give prompt and accurate invoice payments (milestones)?
- Were prompt, detailed, and accurate royalty reports/payments given?

- Was marketing and PR support delivered as agreed?
- Did the publisher force any unwanted/unnecessary game changes?
- Would the developer recommend the publisher?

The other method is to ask the publisher for this information directly. Many developers won't do this, as they feel that they are not in the position to make such a request, and certain publishers will rely on this fact to ensure the contracts are drawn up entirely in their favor. Asking for such basic information of any business partner is essential regardless of the industry and should never be skipped.

IP Rights

It was historically often the case with developers' proprietary ideas that the work done to build a game world, its characters, and unique gameplay mechanics should remain the property of the developer. Generally, a publisher is expected to pay an additional fee and increased royalty to purchase the rights to this IP from a developer, if at all.

In today's climate, however, many publishers will no longer sign a publishing agreement unless they are able to acquire these rights, as they risk spending millions building a valuable new franchise only for the developer to take it elsewhere. When this happens and the developer decides to sell the rights to its IP as part of a publishing deal, they need to ensure that they will be the team responsible for developing all future games based on this IP, or at the very least ensure there is an option that they will have first refusal if the opportunity arises.

While developers are always adamant that they will never give their IP to a publisher, it is important to bear in mind that a publishing partner will have more to gain when they are promoting a franchise in which they have a long-term stake. If this route is taken, the developer will need to ensure that if the IP is no longer being used by the publisher, it should revert back to the developer so they can market it to other potential partners.

Within the agreement, the following areas of IP should be covered and clarified:

- Ownership of game name
- Trademarking
- Logos
- Who owns the Web URL
- Who will run the online presence for the game
- Unique characters
- Source code including artwork and associated assets
- Music (if relevant)

The creation and ownership of IP is one of the hardest parts of the negotiation process, and the publisher will usually want to entirely own the franchise to maintain their total control over the project. From a developer's perspective their IP is the most valuable asset they have, and where possible they should try to retain the rights or at least allow for a reversion of rights against some form of payment from the publisher.

In the situation where a developer is selling their entire IP to a publisher, the developer should always research similar franchises to better estimate the potential "value" of this IP to the publisher to give them a stronger hand at the negotiating table.

Of course, with new and untested IP, it will take some effort to try to convince a publisher that it is worth as much as a title already established on the market; another catch-22 scenario.

Future Products

It's unlikely that you haven't noticed the game market becoming flooded with licenses, sequels, and ports (conversions from a different game platform) of popular IPs in recent years. This is where publishers expect to capitalize on previous calculated risks, be it with a new game franchise or the purchase of game rights for a film or sports license.

Most publishers expect every project they sign to have potential for extra exposure, and developers need to be aware of this to be able to make good any opportunity to extend the life of their concept, and therefore its value with a publisher. Being able to talk to a publishing partner about ideas that a developer has for potential expansion packs or sequels, even at the pitch stage, will demonstrate to the publisher that the developer is aware of the way the market works and may even plant the seed for future projects.

Future Products: Ports

When a publisher decides to port a product to a platform that wasn't part of the original agreement, they may choose not to use the original development team, or depending on how successful the title is, the original development team may choose to focus on the sequel or a completely new franchise. Even if this is the case, the original developer should always be entitled to some form of royalty payment from the publisher— if only at a nominal rate. Moreover, while the exact amount of this royalty may not be stated at the start of a project, if it is included in the contract it will be something that can be addressed at a later date should the situation arise.

Future Products: New Franchises

In a situation in which a partnership between a publisher and developer worked well, it is common that the publisher will want to work with that developer again.

Although this situation is not guaranteed and may be months or years in the future, the terms of such a situation will increasingly be laid out in the initial publishing agreement. While there may not be a great deal of information pertaining to such a situation, the publisher and developer will usually agree to a first refusal or an exclusive "first pitch" period before the developer is allowed to seek an alternate publishing partner, even for completely new titles.

In the case of one well-known development studio, the publisher asked for first refusal on any future project that the developer should produce over a five-year period, and in this instance the developer was paid a rather large one-off sum for this privilege. This is known as an *exclusivity clause*, and is becoming increasingly popular among publishers who have learned expensive lessons from buying up lots of development houses in the 1990s.

Future Products: Technology

When a developer is creating proprietary technology for their game, the publisher will almost certainly want to own the code entirely and have free access to all software tools for unrestricted use. This allows a publisher to take over development should the publishing agreement be breached by the developer. Ownership of the tools and core technology will also allow the publisher to contract with third parties to complete ports of the original game; for instance, when the original developers are not being used.

This becomes a largely moot point when developers are using middleware during production, although any tools that a developer may create to supplement or enhance the middleware still need to have rights clarified in the agreement to protect both parties from misunderstandings or confusion. This is especially important in the case of a breach of contract from either side, and can mean the difference between the game being finished and spending the rest of eternity on a backup tape.

Payment Negotiation

Of course, what every commercial agreement boils down to is money, and video games are no exception. In terms of pure development cost, the amount paid to developers varies dramatically. For instance, the current top tier of major global publishers will generally pay around $2–$3 million for an AAA (highest expected quality) PS2 game, and around $4–$5 million for the same game if it is to be developed on all main platforms (PC, Xbox, and PS2) in the six key languages (English, Japanese, Spanish, French, German, and Italian).

Some of the smaller publishers, by contrast, will only pay around $1 million for an A-grade PS2 game title, and others still will only take completed titles; such is the saturation of the market and increasing competition from abroad (in particular, Eastern Europe, India, and Asia).

These figures are of course dependent on the individual product, and they do not take into account any licenses or associated talent, which may significantly drive up the development cost of the product. From the outset, it should be clear who is responsible for payment of these services, and some developers will even insist that these are accounted for separately from the main project, and paid for directly by the publisher.

Projected budgets can also rise and fall depending on the technology being used. For example, developers who use middleware ("off-the-shelf" third-party technology) can sometimes receive discounted rates for licensing by going through the publisher—who may already receive preferential rates by bulk-buying licenses—instead of approaching the vendor directly.

As previously mentioned, developers are always recommended to have several sets of budgets and even a scalable game design document that is tailored for such varied situations, as these that will allow them to modify their idea to meet the publisher's requirements. However, it always makes sense to pitch initially with a single vision, only reverting to the other options if necessary.

Deal Structure

Once a budget and schedule is agreed in principle between a developer and the publisher, certain decisions can be made about the type of deal a developer wants to structure, and this will determine how negotiations proceed.

For example, if the projected cash flow generated from milestone payments during the development period looks strong, and the developer is sure there is enough contingency throughout the schedule to ensure that the game can be taken to completion, the developer may decide to concentrate on negotiating a stronger royalty rate with the publisher. They may also look to secure fixed guarantees and clearly defined and agreed levels of marketing and PR support.

If the developer is concerned about the schedule and budget, especially if their milestones are tightly packed, they may decide to focus their contract negotiations on securing guaranteed payments at defined stages (on signature of the contract and then alpha, beta, gold, primary territory launch, subsequent territory launches, etc.). Either way, developers should always look to secure as much of the overall development cost in the form of an initial advance payment from the publishers as possible. (More information on payment definitions later in this chapter.)

Developers also need to consider the prospects and benefits of royalties versus larger milestone payments. Generally, this equates to the smaller the milestone payments, the higher the royalties (although even this metric only operates within a certain window).

Avoiding Contract Breach

What should be at the forefront in all developers' minds throughout the contract signing process is that any slippage caused by poor scheduling or lack of contingency by the developer that is the result of projections agreed upon at this stage (financial or product feature) will almost always result in a breach of publishing contract. This will more often than not result in the publisher withholding milestone payments until the project hits the agreed timetable or feature list. It cannot be emphasized enough how important it is for developers to be realistic about scheduling and budgets rather than just trying to get a deal signed and worrying about it later, as countless developers have found out to their detriment in recent years.

Such is the level of publisher control that even when the issues that caused slippage or feature reduction are overcome, the publisher may still not pay the developer the full amount of money owed to them because of the breach. As a result, it is important for developers to build in contingency "burn" to their entire budget so that if the worst should happen, they (hopefully) won't go out of business.

While the process may conform to a template, the actual detail of the deal never will, so having as much data available will allow the developer to enter into negotiations on a stronger footing. Once the budgetary details have been agreed on, the developer must then use the agreed information and their own individual scenario to decide the best payment model to negotiate toward.

Advance Payment against Royalties

An *advance royalty payment* is usually the agreed royalty rate multiplied against a percentage of the total unit guarantee decided on by the publisher via their retail and distribution channels. Advance royalties will generally fit in around the 60 to 100 percent mark of the predicted first year unit guarantee. Some development teams aim to recoup most of the actual development cost or at least six months team "burn" at this stage to give them a comfort zone in which to operate. This upfront payment is used to cover setup costs and any required preproduction phase.

Guarantees

Guarantees usually come in two forms; a figure that is contractually guaranteed by the publisher and must be paid for regardless of how well the game actually sells, or a guarantee that is based on an amount of units sold necessary to maintain exclusivity with that publisher. If the game fails to sell the units that the publisher has agreed, the developer is free to try to secure a new publishing partner. Option two is generally the most common guarantee used by a publisher.

Milestones

Milestone payments represent the rate of release for development funding that was agreed on between the publisher and developer during the contract negotiation stage. The exact content of each milestone is always agreed on in advance by both the developer and publisher. It is vitally important that the developer raise any potential issues at this negotiation stage rather than trying to get a publisher to change a milestone specification after the initial agreement or when a situation arises, as practically no publisher will accommodate this kind of action.

When a publisher verifies that a milestone has been reached, they will check to the very letter of the original agreement before releasing any monies to the developer. A single point missed by the developer can result in payment being withheld until the point in question is addressed.

The developer will need to keep in mind that a publisher can usually cancel (known in the industry as "canning") or suspend a project at any point. The one and only concern of a publisher through the development timeline is to protect their investment—the game project—so slippage and features cut through poor scheduling and bad management will all work against a developer when it comes to milestones.

Publishers as a rule want the relationship between themselves and the developer to be profitable, and developers should be transparent on what can and cannot be delivered at the earliest possible stage so corrective action or rescheduling can take place.

Milestone Payments

In almost all publishing agreements, the milestone payments are viewed as an advance against royalties, and are recouped out of the profits that would otherwise be payable to the developer once the game has shipped.

For example, when a publisher signs a $3 million project, the developer may be given $400,000 by the publisher in the form of an advance royalty payment and the first milestone as a combined payment—this will help the developer meet any setup costs that came about because of the project. The remainder of the development funding would likely then be divided into equal monthly payments across the production cycle, with the final payment being slightly larger than the normal milestone payments to "encourage" the developer to supply a gold master candidate on time, and to give the developer a small reserve of money to hopefully see them through until the next project or further royalties being realized.

As already mentioned, developers will need to have on hand several sets of figures that will allow them to adjust the schedule to match the milestone payments so they can meet the requirements of development. These figures need to cover all of the teams' salaries and an amount set aside to cover potential areas of risk, and when the worst happens and the schedule needs to be reworked to take into account an unforeseen event.

In addition, it is recommended that a developer have a working document that keeps track of ongoing project costs. The developer needs to be aware of this "bottom line" throughout the duration of the project and use the internal document to chart progress and see what changes need to be made on a daily, weekly, or monthly basis to remain successfully on target. This document will also be a vital for creating the next budget and schedule for any future projects, and much of the reason that established teams are generally given precedence over new "startups."

Completion Bonus

Dependent on the publisher, the completion bonus is paid at either the gold master or when the product ships to its primary launch territory. Most developers will look to generate one or two months' "burn" from the completion bonus—this is usually to keep the developer in business until their next project is signed.

The completion bonus is still largely looked at as a "potential" bonus rather than a fixed amount, as there will usually be conditions laid out by the publisher as to whether the developer is entitled. These conditions will usually include hitting all deadlines, which most importantly would include the street date, early project completion, and providing the right assets for sales and marketing such as demo materials and other promotional assets.

Most developers will try to load the milestone payments across the development period to cover any potential completion bonus in case they do not meet any criteria for such a payment.

Royalty Negotiation

Typically, the royalty rates used by publishers are arrived at as a percentage of the wholesale price of the product. While royalty rates can be up to 40 percent of the wholesale price, they more often than not sit somewhere around the between 18 to 25 percent area.

To put this into perspective, a game project that costs $2 million to develop will need to sell around 350,000 units to start generating any kind of royalty for the developer—the so called "break-even" point—so it is very important that a developer considers fixed rate guarantees in place of royalties if they feel that this level of sell through may not be realistically achievable for their product. In terms of what this usually means, in a per-unit situation a publisher will typically receive $24 for every unit sold, so the developer usually receives around $4 for every copy sold (past the break-even point).

An increasingly common model that can be negotiated is to offer a step-up rate of royalty payments on volume of units sold. For example, a project that has been signed with an agreed base royalty rate of 15 percent may increase the royalty to 20 percent if the product sells more than 100,000 units over the break even point, and then increase again to 25 percent when the product sells a further 150,000 units past the break even point. This is a much fairer way of dealing, as it ensures that the developer shares in any significant or unexpected success, such as happened with the development team behind the original *Tomb Raider* game.

In the PS2 project example outlined previously, the milestone payments from a publisher will essentially be financing development to the projected total of $3 million. In this case, the developer's royalty would be set at 15 percent by the publisher, meaning that the developer would not see any royalty income until 15 percent of the publisher's net sales revenue matched the $3 million advance. By this time, the publisher will have already received nearly $14 million in net sales and therefore has made a considerable profit from the title.

An important aspect of negotiating the correct royalty rate is to have a clear definition and understanding of what the publisher considers the wholesale price. Most developers will start at 40 percent and work down to a royalty rate that is agreeable to both parties. Some publishers will simply arrive at the wholesale price as the full retail cost of the product less the costs of materials such as box, disc, manual, and so forth (this is sometimes referred to as *COGS* or cost of goods sold), while others will have very broad definitions and may incorporate deductions such as marketing spending, promotional costs, and sample/review copies on top of the COGS.

As the earlier section on research outlined, it's important for the developer to understand the publisher's individual business to ensure they get the best possible deal for their game. Many developers will never see a royalty payment due to the way in which the wholesale price is calculated by their publisher, and since no two publishers work in quite the same way, it is recommended that the developer clarifies any issues with a good lawyer or agent before signing the publishing contract.

Royalty Payment

Most developers will have royalties paid to them in their native currency rather than in the currency of the publisher. This is not so much an issue for European developers who largely are now paid royalties in the Euro, but with the majority of Western publishers based in the United States, exchange rates still often come into play.

When negotiating, the developer should always make clear what currency is being referred to for each territory, and if possible, request that royalty payments are made to the developer in their preferred currency rather than in numerous types of different currencies from different territories. Another factor to take into account that relates to Europe in particular is that all video games will be subject to VAT (Value Added Tax) that ranges from 13–25 percent depending on the country. It should be clear in the royalty agreement how this is being calculated against the wholesale price, and therefore what impact it will have against the royalty the developer will receive.

Contractually, a developer should also ask for the right to audit the financial records of the publisher to verify that the correct royalty payments are being made. If the publisher refuses access to these books or upon audit are found to be in breach of the royalty agreement, they could be open to legal action from the developer. However, a publisher's resources are much greater than almost any developer's and it can often be the case that the developer will go bust or be forced to cut their loses rather than fight royalty rights through the courts.

Tellingly in recent years, a large number of developers in the UK, Europe, and the United States have been forced into liquidation due to royalty payment issues with their publishers.

Development Milestones

In this final section, we look at the main stages of the game development process once full development has begun.

Development Timeline

The development period for a game project varies wildly between companies (and per-platform), and there is nothing set in stone to dictate how long any specific project should take to complete.

Projects can vary in length from 10- to 12-month movie license titles or annual sports title updates, to the "common" 18- to 24-month cycle for an original PlayStation 2 game.

Here are some example development periods for different platforms:

- 4–6 months for a high-end mobile phone game
- 18–24 months for a PlayStation2, Xbox, or GameCube game
- 10–14 months for a film-licensed game
- 16–20 months for an original IP PC game

Of course, there are projects that constantly push the boundaries at either end of the spectrum, such as Valve's five-year opus, *Half Life 2*.

Almost all projects share the same milestones described in this chapter, and generally share the same proportionate amount of time in each stage. Figure 7.3.1 shows an average timescale of 20 months from the creation of the core concept document through to duplication:

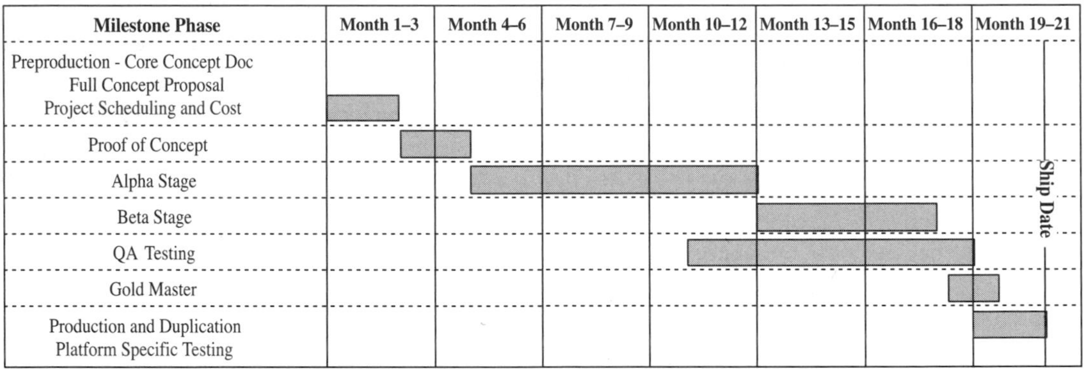

Milestone Phase	Month 1–3	Month 4–6	Month 7–9	Month 10–12	Month 13–15	Month 16–18	Month 19–21
Preproduction - Core Concept Doc Full Concept Proposal Project Scheduling and Cost	▧						
Proof of Concept		▧					
Alpha Stage			▧	▧			
Beta Stage					▧	▧	
QA Testing					▧	▧	
Gold Master							▧
Production and Duplication Platform Specific Testing							▧

FIGURE 7.3.1 *Amount of time spent in each milestone phase of game development.*

Alpha Stage

The definition of the *alpha stage* varies from developer to developer; however, in general it usually means that the game's "functionality" is complete. This usually translates to all of the required features of the design having been implemented, but not all necessarily working exactly in the desired manner.

From the start of development to reaching the alpha stage is the longest part of the development cycle. This is usually where some slippage can occur as features take longer to implement than planned, or the chosen technology either doesn't deliver the necessary requirements or demands more work to bring to the expected state.

It is during alpha that most gameplay feedback from focus groups (including QA), the design team, and the publisher can be incorporated without too much of an impact to the schedule. This is largely due to the core gameplay features not being totally completed and therefore more open to modification and tweaking. However, this can also be a double-edged sword and needs to be closely managed by the producer to ensure that the project is kept on track and doesn't start to take on slippage due to lots of additional (unplanned) features being added to or changed from the original design specification.

During alpha development, some of the sounds, language localization, music, and voice talent (if applicable) may still consist of temporary placeholders, with final content in these areas implemented in the *beta stage*. However, artwork should be largely final during this stage with all placeholder graphics removed before beta.

The alpha stage can also be a great sounding board for the design team to validate gameplay mechanics, and the publisher's QA department can assist in functionality testing and feedback. This can help refine control methods and the user interface ahead of formal bug testing. It is sometimes the case that what looked great on paper can often prove too difficult or not practical when executed. In addition, ideas that were written off during the core concept or full proposal stage, which looked too difficult or unattractive, can suddenly be realized and incorporated due to the technology being in place.

It is also at the alpha stage that the world at large will start hearing about the game in greater detail via magazine and Internet Web sites through "first look" articles, interviews, and PR by the publisher.

Quality Assurance—QA

The role and methodology of QA testing varies from company to company; most developers don't have full-time "in-house" QA departments and rely on various self-moderated ways of bug-fixing their own code, often leaving most of the shortfall or noncritical minor bugs to the QA departments of their publisher to pick up during the beta stage.

During the beta stage and through to the completion of the project, the game will be under constant test from the publisher's QA department (or increasingly by dedicated "professional" test teams at testing service outsourcing companies). Most feedback given to the team will come in the form of gameplay flaws, difficulty issues, and technical bugs relating to graphics, sound, or hardware incompatibility, the latter of which being particularly important for PC products.

For developers of console products such as the Microsoft Xbox and Sony PlayStation systems, there will be an additional layer of QA at the platform holder's location (sometimes in several different countries) where further *guideline* or *technical requirement checklist* (TRC) testing is carried out to ensure the game adheres to the various quality control standards that platform holder has put into place.

The testing procedures for console products are much tighter than developing for any other platform, since console games cannot generally be patched. Therefore, console games have to reach a much higher standard before release, whereas PC developers can often fall into the habit of leaving minor bugs to fix until after launch, because they know that they can always patch the problem later. This is often done with an additional download from a support site or specialist online game sites and magazine cover disks.

The timeline for platform TRC testing varies slightly, but Sony final approval (or *submission* as it's referred to) takes between four to six weeks to complete, with a further two to four weeks added if the game "fails" submission and needs to be fixed/sent back.

The producer and the publisher's external producer will act as the buffer between QA and the development team to ensure they are not flooded with haphazard bug reports.

Most companies use bug-tracking programs, automated spreadsheets, or Oracle database systems to manage and prioritize bug feedback from QA. Key team members will also have periodic bug update meetings to ensure that fixed bugs are being removed from the project and the reports from QA are focusing on the immediately important areas.

Beta Stage

The beta stage is effectively when all of the features that were delivered during the alpha stage are now working and locked down so no core functionality at this stage is changed. Since all of the proposed gameplay mechanics and technological features have been implemented, the testing department is largely spending its time trying to "break" the game and providing minor gameplay tweaking feedback on areas such as difficulty settings, scoring or points systems, and so forth.

During beta, the final sound effects, musical score, voice talent, and localization are all added and completed, with constant testing and feedback from QA to ensure that all content is up to the desired standard, and in the right places. These tasks are usually handled during beta simply due to the developers being able to focus more on content-driven issues over the technical tasks that dominate alpha.

During beta, the press and public will be given more information about the game in the form of in-depth "hands-on" features, and as the game nears completion, preview reports.

For PC titles featuring an online component, it is becoming increasingly common for developers to release reduced content "beta test" builds of their game for controlled public testing. This helps with nailing down hardware compatibility issues unique to PC titles, and gives the development team genuine consumer feedback to supplement that provided by QA. Public beta tests can also help developers see their content in a real-world setting that is impossible to re-create in all but the largest corporate QA departments. Factors such as stress testing can be viewed with the appropriate action to fix problems or issues before release.

It is also during beta that games are under the biggest threat of being leaked illegally to the public. Usually, this happens through an internal company leak (e.g., by unscrupulous freelance QA testers) or through rogue journalists and sometimes even hardware partners. In most cases, developers and publishers have internal procedures to help try to prevent this, such as digital watermarking, although there are still numerous unauthorized releases of beta code each and every quarter, often on the highest profile titles.

Gold Master

The *gold master* is named after the gold-colored recordable discs originally used to send final mastering assets to the publisher for mass duplication.

It is at this final development stage for PC titles that copy protection is added, installation software is integrated, and device drivers can be added to the game.

Once all of the critical bugs have been removed from the game and all parties are in agreement that the requirements of the beta definition have been met, the game is declared a gold candidate and is sent for duplication.

It is usually at this point that work will be finalized on a specific demo for magazine cover mounts or Internet distribution, although increasingly teams are building specific demo content and trade show previews into the original schedule and cost breakdown, especially in the case of console developers, due to the long lead times on magazines.

Production Summary

Throughout these processes are many regular mini-milestones, as it's often necessary for publishers to have some means of ensuring targets are being hit and the project is moving at the rate indicated in the schedule and on budget, and for the developers it generally dictates them getting paid.

These mini-milestones usually happen once a month at most companies with senior management and key development team members being present. While they can be annoying to the development team, who largely just want to get on and develop their game, they are a vital way of making sure that everything is on track. This ensures that all the components of the team are communicating and any change in the status of the project is known or problems are highlighted with the appropriate action taken.

Badly managed projects that have irregular milestone meetings often slip. Slippage results in budget overspends, so it is vital that development management and the publishers or investors involved have a process in place that is adhered to. This protects the investment, and ensures that the game project hits its target and makes retail.

Summary

While few people outside of senior management will ever need to apply the full range of knowledge given in this chapter, regardless of your chosen game development role or level you will inevitably be a part of this process in one way or another as it represents the framework for game development itself. The better your understanding of the process as a whole, the more effective you can be when operating as part of a team involved in an occasionally difficult but often hugely rewarding industry.

It is clear from this chapter that the game development process, particularly project funding and the developer/publisher relationship, has evolved considerably during the market's transition from niche hobby to mass-market entertainment industry. Game prototypes and the pitching process as a whole have become critical and costly core competencies for developers, and many companies too slow to add business talent to their creative teams, regardless of their talents, have paid the ultimate price.

However, it is also important to remember that this evolution is still happening. The more proactive developers are learning to take advantage of this changing climate, from giving up developing of new IP and focusing on fast, reliable, and cost-effective work for hire partnerships with publishers developing ports and licenses, through to the opposite end of the scale working with film-style investment funds, allowing them to fund development of their new titles through to completion, and thus retaining ownership rights and maximizing their royalty share. Some analysts also predict a gradual move to film-style production, where development teams are assembled specifically for each title according to their respective skills, and this is already starting to happen on a modest scale.

We are also working in industry that never sits still. With each new hardware generation, the average development timescale, budget, and team size can be expected to increase, putting further pressure on independent developers. However, with the new handheld consoles and even mobile phones fast approaching the fidelity of current-generation console platform titles, smaller developers will at least have the opportunity to transfer their relevant and proven skills to these platforms.

Hopefully, this reinforces the importance of further reading and research throughout your study and into whichever role you choose to pursue in game development. The following exercises will help to give you a more practical understanding of the topics covered in this chapter.

Exercises

1. Take either your own game design idea or your current favorite video game and create a pitch presentation as described earlier in the chapter. If using an existing video game, use the Internet to find existing promotional assets such as concept art, screenshots, and gameplay movies to add substance to your presentation.

2. Using the same game, list the *key* gameplay features that will need to be developed for the prototype to convince the publisher of proof of concept. Remember, the prototype stage must be rapid and cost effective, so don't get carried away! Really think about what the game in question does differently or better that would need to be conveyed in a playable demo. Taking the aforementioned *Halo* series, for example, you might list:
   a. The rechargeable shield health system
   b. Dual weapon wielding

    c. Cutting-edge graphics engine details like shaders and bump mapping.

    d. One or two active enemy types

    e. One or two weapon types

    f. A single fully detailed area of the environment showing visual styling

    g. Some basic animations/physics like running, jumping, firing, and reloading

3. Taking a development schedule of 14 months and a headcount of 22 people for a single platform title, use the information in the development milestone section, as well as the rest of this book and the Internet, to split the team into relevant departments, devise a basic schedule, and calculate an approximate budget. The Web site *www.igda.org* is a good place to start researching average department salaries for the video games industry.

4. Using the information you created in Exercise 3, formulate a chart as shown in Figure 7.3.1 to show the game development stages as a percentage of total project time.

7.4 ▌ Marketing

Overview

Game developers have a tremendous number of tools to use to promote their companies and the video games they create. For one thing, the sheer number of different media—print, broadcast, and online—allow for marketing at all levels of the spectrum, from high-budget TV ads to online game site ads.

Moreover, that doesn't include the literally thousands of Internet sites that have been set up by players themselves for further discussion between gamers. These "fan" sites, offering news and views for the hardcore gamer, offer specialized advice on a certain current or upcoming platform or title or might drill down to every aspect of play in a single game.

There are dozens of ways to market games, brands, and even the companies themselves to obtain maximum visibility for a video game. This chapter explains how each of these advertising channels works and how they can be leveraged. Being heard above the noise is difficult, especially with the intense competition among games, but this chapter discusses both traditional and innovative ways that this can be achieved.

The Publisher's Marketing Promise

Most marketing activities are carried out by the publisher. Before a developer signs on with a publisher, the terms for promoting the game during development and after completion should be clearly understood by both parties, and spelled out in the contract. The developer and publisher should agree on a list of marketing activities, along with who is responsible for each activity. While some publishers may not want to guarantee such activities, it is important for each side to clearly understand what the other party intends to do to promote the game.

Usually, publishers have "template" programs for their third-party titles. An A-tier title—a big franchise game like *Harry Potter*, for example—might get considerable support: promotion to the consumer media and the game media and perhaps even a kick-off event, but most will not. A game considered a B-tier title might get a very thorough push to the game media including a media tour, but may not enjoy much consumer media coverage. Finally, C-tier titles might only have a preview/review program to game writers. The following are some questions that should be posed before a development contract is signed.

- What kind of PR will the publisher perform?
- Will the publisher need the participation of the developer for interviews, attending trade shows, and so forth?
- Will the developer be mentioned in all of the releases?
- Will the developer be able to view and fact check press releases?
- What advertising (magazine or TV ads) is being planned for the title?
- How does the title compare to the other games the publisher will be releasing during the same fiscal quarter?

These questions will give a developer a sense of where they stand and how their title will be marketed. Even if the publisher doesn't intend to put much marketing muscle behind the title, there are many things a developer can do to help promote the title, as discussed in this chapter.

Traditional Advertising and Retailers

The video games industry is in the business of selling products, and there is no denying that traditional advertising is important and effective, albeit expensive. Unfortunately, only the top games will warrant this kind of marketing support. Traditional advertising consists of television ads, magazine ads, in-store promotions, placement on retail ad flyers, and tie-ins with other products such as cereal and fast food or promotions with celebrities such as musicians or actors.

If a high-profile game targets a particular console, such as the PS2, there are possible marketing opportunities with the console maker itself. In cases like this, the console maker might choose to help promote the game as a way to promote their own console. These higher profile games can also be placed on demo kiosks inside stores for shoppers to try out. Often, these kiosks will offer a playable demo or sometimes a movie preview of a hot new game, depending on what the developer can offer the console maker. With thousands of kiosks at retail stores, this is a very effective way to get potential buyers to sample a game.

Publishers pay a good deal of money to retailers to ensure that their games are advertised in the retailer's ads and prominently displayed within the store. It is no accident that particular games are clustered at the ends of aisles, known as *end caps*. Another place where high-profile games are featured is in cardboard standup displays, which also cost additional dollars. Even getting a game to be at eye level on a shelf can cost more money at many retailers. Other advertising at the retailer can be seen in the form of posters, cardboard standup promotions, and oversized empty boxes of a future title.

Getting Heard in the Media

To maximize visibility for a game, all media categories should be evaluated and a plan should be created that brings each into the know about the game at the right time.

The enthusiast media consists of several categories: publications that focus on console games like *GamePro*, *Electronic Gaming*, and *Game Informer*; magazines that cover only PC titles like *Maximum PC*, *PC Gamer*, and *PC World*; online sites catering to the game fan, such as *Gamespot*, *IGN.com*, and *The Adrenaline Vault*; and the cable channels that feature games all the time or in concert with covering hardware and software for the early adopter: *G4/Tech TV* and *Game Nation*. A few radio shows cover games, such as David Graveline's syndicated "Into Tomorrow" and Craig Crossman's "Computer America." There's also a radio show on the *Online Gaming Network* and both *C/Net Radio* and *CNN Radio* have game segments.

The enthusiast media offers developers and publishers one of the best ways to develop early interest in a title. This process can be started as much as two years before launch.

Phone and E-Mail versus Face-to-Face Visits

The quality of a game accounts for about two-thirds of the reason a title is covered. One-third is based on a PR or marketing person's knowledge, creativity, and persistence.

E-mail works at first as a contact medium. News releases can be sent as an e-mail blast. Brief, friendly cover e-mails (usually described as pitch letters) should accompany them. Once a game is pretty far along, it is best to have a face-to-face meeting with editors to demonstrate the game and let them try it.

This involves requesting an appointment, preparing for the meetings, and then traveling to editor offices. Most of the writers for the enthusiast media are in the San

Francisco Bay Area; Los Angeles, or New York. Minneapolis and Richmond, Vermont would also be stops for the thorough approach.

Covers, Ears, and Top Lines

Magazine covers are tough to obtain; the game has to be a big license or a blockbuster. Ears are a better bet (a brief teaser line on the cover), and, of course, ideas for a bigger feature can be pitched. For example, is the technology developed for a game going to have an impact on future titles in its genre? Does the developer "own" a big designer whose comments on the future of games would be worth an interview? The key is emphasizing what is different about a game.

Working with Fan Sites

One of the more interesting ways to create interest in game titles is through the fan sites. With the growth of the Internet, game fans have found a voice, building their own sites where endless news, rumor, and discussion rules.

Gamers, in particular, seem to love engaging in discourse about anticipated titles and discussing every aspect of a published game, down to strategies on how to get past a tricky level or complete a mission in a game. As a result, thousands of bulletin boards and Web sites have sprung up where fans can have discussions.

With some searching, title-specific communities or sites focused on a category of games (e.g., first-person shooters (FPS) or massively multiplayer online role-playing games (MMORPGs)) can be located.

The most dedicated fan sites will post stories that most traditional gamer media wouldn't consider newsworthy. For instance, patch changes, online server status, competitions, and so forth give marketing people the opportunity for constant visibility.

The fan sites can definitely help spread the buzz, but they can be even more helpful when provided with free stuff as payback. For instance, perhaps the developer or publisher has produced swag (T-shirts, mouse pads, key chains, posters, or other branded merchandise or giveaways for the game). These gifts can go a long way toward generating fan site coverage. Fan site writers do their own reviews, so they will take beta copies and gold masters (or free subscriptions for a MMORPG). However, the main media should be served first. If there is enough swag, multiple items or other freebies to give away, banners or other promotions for the game can be negotiated in return for these items.

While fan sites are great free advertising, games with particularly dedicated fans need a dedicated in-house employee to deal with fan questions. FPS titles and MMORPG games attract fanatical communities whose inquiries and questions need to be answered.

Publicity Opportunities

PR for a game should start very early and take advantage of each stage of development. The following outlines most of the opportunities to promote a game.

Announce the product in development: This would be a medium-length press release, mentioning the developer (and publisher if known). If the lead designer is a known entity, he should be mentioned, as well as previous games he has designed. The press release should end with a paragraph each for the developer and the publisher. This paragraph, a general description of the company, should be well thought out. It's referred to as the "boilerplate," because, once developed, it is used on every release.

Provide early screen shots: Once development is underway, the developer/publisher team may want to distribute early screen captures to the game media.

Demo an alpha version: Alpha versions are tricky. However, if there is good interest in the game and a member of the marketing team can demo the alpha level, the game can be taken on the road to editor offices to show it off. It is not recommended to blindly send such an early version directly to an editor.

Send more screen shots and character art: Once the title is well underway, the developer will be able to provide more screens and perhaps character art. It's recommended to create an "Asset Calendar" grid that lists the items that can be doled out to the media. Everything should not be given to everybody. Select the best screens and art and offer these on an exclusive basis to the top print books and sites. Have a group of assets that can be sent to everyone else. The offerings should be spaced out so the top media is continually receiving new material to use to publicize the game.

Provide a beta version: Now that the media is primed, beta product for review can be sent to editors. The media should be followed up on once they receive the product to be sure they are not encountering problems. A technical person might be required to talk them through any problems.

Offer developer Qs and As: Fans are always interested in stories behind the game—anything particularly interesting or unusual. Several select media outlets should each be offered an interview on a unique topic.

Distribute a gold master: When the game is finally ready to go to the mastering house (or a digital distributor), there is another opportunity. By this time, several key writers will be waiting for an early chance to see the final game. The master should be given to long-lead publications first (like magazines), so the game sites don't scoop them.

Reviews: Reviews of the game are the bread and butter of the industry. The writers should be checked in with occasionally to be sure everything is going well.

Tips & tricks: After the title is launched, fans are interested in ways to conquer the game. Game and fan sites will post tips and tricks, offered exclusively.

Promote any award the game wins: A short, not too commercial release can be issued if a game receives a site's publication or retailer award. These awards should be distributed to fan sites only. The icon for the award can also be posted on the game's promotional Web site and the developer's Web site.

Contacting the Media

Most of the visibility achieved for a title will be done through media relations.

Create an Editor Database

A PR agency that specializes in games can be hired or a developer can buy a basic media guide. *Bacon's Media Directories* are some of the best, and they now come in an online version. This resource will need to be supplemented by research and updated constantly. Editors often change beats, or assignments, and move around between publications. New media start and go away.

Armed with a list of editors, some Internet research should be done on the editors. It's important to know who reviews particular genres. Eventually, the editors should be separated into categories. For example, it's best to separate the enthusiast press from consumer editors. It may also be helpful to specify editors by game genre, traditional media versus fan sites, and so forth.

News Releases

The standard form for distribution of information to journalists is a *news release*, which implies it contains something "new" or "news." It's important to know that news is generally made *when* it is announced. Therefore, if the "new" information is known only in-house, it can be planned when to release it (governed only by Security & Exchange [SEC] regulations if the company is public).

Releases are becoming more and more formatted, consisting of a lead paragraph of 35 words or less announcing the "news" followed by short paragraphs giving more detailed information (this is called the *inverted pyramid* format). A quote or two are usually also included. This is the place—and the only place—for opinion. The rest of the release should be factual.

Short declarative sentences with active verbs are best. Without journalism training, it's best to find a worthy competitor and copy the style of their releases. It's also worth picking up a copy of the writing stylebook issued annually by the Associated Press (AP), because journalism writing calls for capitalizations and abbreviations not taught in high school.

It is important to learn journalism style and not be overcommercial. The goal should be to write such scintillating copy that much of the material is used word for word. An evaluation of what does happen to previous releases is often a good lesson in how to improve.

It's a good idea to space out news, about four to six weeks apart. The most fervent media will not likely take more news than that, preferring to give other companies a chance for space in their publication. Fan sites might be an exception, especially when working on an exceptionally hot property.

Pitch Letters

News releases are usually sent through e-mail and are accompanied by a short cover letter or a *pitch letter* that sums up the key points more succinctly. The subject line should give a hint of the topic to make the editor open the e-mail. Clever is good, as long as it conveys a brief message; for example, "Harry Potter Title to Include New Technology" or "Harry Potter Technology Enhances Game Wizardry."

After a simple salutation, the e-mail should immediately list what differentiates the title (most editors will only read the first paragraph). For important editors, the pitches should be personal, perhaps referencing other stories or reviews the editor has written. Everyone is flattered to know someone has paid attention to his or her work.

The news release should be in plain text within the body of the e-mail. Editors prefer not to get attachments. Screens and artwork should be offered rather than attaching them to the e-mail. One option is to use a subject line like, "Hit Reply for new Harry Potter Screens."

A follow-up call should be done three or four days after the e-mail is sent to check that they received it. Only one message (even if several calls have been made) and one e-mail should be left. If there is no reply, assume the writer is not interested. Be ready to "pitch" again on the phone, instead of stupidly asking, "Did you get my e-mail?" Editors get dozens, if not hundreds of e-mail pitches in a day.

If the writer does answer and gives a "No thanks," it doesn't help to argue. A better answer is the question, "Can you tell me what I need to make our releases more appealing to you?" Some writers will be kind enough to help determine how to get their attention in the future. By reading up on the editor before the call, the success rate can be dramatically improved.

Media Tours

Face-to-face meetings with editors are better for building relationships, so when there is something really important to impart, it might be worth seeking the budget to travel. Fortunately, for the games industry, more and more of the key enthusiast press are located in San Francisco or Los Angeles, which means fewer days on the road, especially if appointments are scheduled back to back. Generally, about 45 minutes should be allowed for each meeting (restrict the demo to 10 minutes and use the rest of the time to let the press play the game and ask questions). If the title is not far enough along, explain that at the beginning. At the conclusion of the meeting, it's a good idea to leave behind a PowerPoint presentation giving basic background on the company. Renting a car is best to move quickly from one office to another.

Reviews

Positive game reviews are, of course, the primary goal of any developer/publisher. It's not possible to control what the reviewer thinks, but it helps to direct attention toward areas of the game that shine.

Reviewer's guides for a complicated game might be in order. These are designed to suggest how the writer approaches the review. The guide highlights certain aspects of the game and suggests how the editor can get more enjoyment out of playing, and can be useful in avoiding startup confusion if the title is more complicated.

One MMORPG company offers reviewers "virtual tours," a chance to ride along with a game master as he gallops invisibly through the game/story line. This is a great way for new players and reviewers, who don't have the time to play through the enormously complicated MMORPG genres, to learn more about the title. The writer and game master (who visits the game frequently all day to monitor play) can be hooked up over a phone line with the editor following on his or her own PC.

Beyond Reviews: Pitch Feature Stories

This advanced PR technique offers a way to get even more coverage. The idea is to give the writer a new angle. However, features must be offered on an exclusive basis. A writer isn't going to go to much trouble developing a longer piece, only to find that his or her competitor has the same story. If this occurs, it will burn bridges forever with that writer.

For the enthusiast press, look at how the title might be advancing the industry or is part of a trend. For example, when video game companies first started contracting with Hollywood celebrities to star in their games, the industry rags, and later the consumer media, heavily covered the story. When claymation was first used for games (and movies), it was covered as much as the titles were. Key questions are, What is unique about the game or the development of the game? Is there a good "behind the scenes" angle to the title?

Consumer Media

Feature stories show up most often in the consumer publications, because these publications feel their readers are less interested in the nitty-gritty play of the game. These publications may be intrigued by a broader story on how a certain title breaks ground or how an interesting feature or technology element is used in a title, such as speech recognition. Often, these publications will also showcase several new games in a particular category. For example, a *USA Today* might do a roundup on new movie-based games or a story on titles for kids K–8. The large consumer publications are also very competitive, so they look for a story that no one else has done. Key in on what makes a title different or how it fits into a trend, and then develop an enticing pitch for a single writer.

The following are some of the different media categories that could be interested in a particular game title. They run the gamut, and require a more sophisticated approach.

Consumer Print Opportunities

One of the more prestigious media categories in the consumer area is the long-lead magazines, most of which cater to males. These generally reach out to an older gamer, someone with the affluence to buy what he wants. Some of these magazines, like *Wired* (and its online site *www.wired.com*), focus heavily on technology topics. A publication like *Playboy, Rolling Stone*, or *Maxim* will have a writer who covers games, but that will be just one of the topics included for readers, so space for games is limited.

In the short-lead space, there is *Newsweek, Time*, and *U.S. News & World Report*, and the larger daily newspapers like *The New York Times, USA Today*, and the *Los Angeles Times*.

Another great way to generate mass audience visibility is by pitching to a reporter who covers games for a newspaper syndicate like Gannett or Knight Ritter or, better yet, a wire service like AP or Reuters. If successful, the story will run in dozens or even hundreds of newspapers all at once.

Broadcast Opportunities

The larger cities also have TV and radio talk shows, which sometimes feature a reporter who covers games, consumer electronics, and other tech products. Many of these reporters are not listed in media source guides.

The key thing for any reporter, but especially for consumer writers, is to emphasize what differentiates a particular title:

- Is it the first title to . . . ?
- Is it based on a new engine/technical breakthrough?
- Is it a hot franchise?
- Does it have celebrity tie-ins: author, actor, voice actors?
- Does it have an unusual story line?
- Does it launch a great, original character?

In working with consumer editors, always provide great art. High-quality art makes a huge difference in generating coverage; however, it is better to provide concept art rather than in-game screenshots. While screenshots accurately provide a single frame of the game, they generally don't convey the action, excitement, or characters very well. The consumer writer might also be interested in pictures of celebrities involved with the game.

Broadcast coverage is trickier, but well worth the effort because TV provides the opportunity for mass exposure. As a visual medium, TV also brings a game to life.

The TV station should be offered B-Roll (professionally shot film footage) of the development studio, showing people at work and the game in development. In addition, a few practiced sound bites with the game designer should also be filmed. Make an articulate spokesperson available for in-studio interviews. Think visual, talking heads are boring; suggest a prop—a peripheral such as a driving wheel or a flight jacket representing the military branch in an aviation title.

Ideally, the reporter should get involved in the demo, so it's critical to prebrief him on game features. Arrive at the studio early enough to engage him in conversation and cover the main points of the game. Send ahead to the producer a list of some good questions that the reporter might want to ask about the game. Find out the reporter's own interests and game knowledge in order to mention something of particular interest.

Events: Generating Mixed Media Coverage and Buzz

Events can be expensive; choose the titles to promote, carefully. As an example, an event staged in New York in Central Park for a Game Boy Advance title starring Bugs Bunny helped Atari win the PC license for Warner Bros. *Looney Tunes* titles.

Pick a media capital to generate many attendees. New York is best for consumer media coverage. San Francisco and Los Angeles have become the centers for the game press. Alternately, do your event in a small city and send B-Roll to the other markets.

Marketing at Trade Shows

The largest and most important trade show for the games industry is the Electronic Entertainment Expo, better known as E3. This tradeshow takes place every year in Los Angeles in May. All of the major game publishers pay for prominent booths to promote their products for the coming year. This is the place where games are showcased and sold to buyers from major retailers such as Wal-Mart, Toys "R" Us, and Electronics Boutique.

While the main purpose of E3 is to promote games for retailers, there is a secondary opportunity in that an enormous amount of press and hundreds of magazine and Web site editors also attend. This creates a tremendous opportunity for free publicity. Unfortunately, participation is costly, so every dollar spent must be effective.

The best way to promote a game with many editors is to have a booth or be part of someone else's. For example, an unknown MMORPG company was able to manage 125 interviews by hanging off one island in a larger booth.

Within E3, location is key. A booth (or station) adjacent to the booth of a large or hot company is helpful, because PR people can be stationed in the aisles to catch the writers and TV crews that wander by.

Generating PR as a Developer when the Publishing Partner Fails to Deliver

Many developers lament that their publisher, after promises to the contrary, is not mentioning them in the game's publicity, or the game is not getting much coverage because the publisher has other titles considered more important to promote.

One solution is for the developer to hire his or her own PR agency. The developer can then offer to have their agency supplement the publisher's efforts. Since the publisher's PR team usually does not have the budget or time to do more than reviews with the core enthusiast media, this supplemental PR agency can focus on all of the other opportunities with peripheral media.

A developer's PR agency can:

- Help expand the editorial contacts made by the publisher's in-house team at the time of launch.
- Identify weaknesses in the publisher effort and tactfully offer to make some calls to writers the publisher's staff does not know or hasn't been able to interest in the title.
- Help edit press materials submitted by the publisher and check to see that the publisher gives the developer credit for their work in all materials.
- Support the publisher for press events. Extra contacts can be added to press lists used by the publisher, increasing attendance.

Another way to supplement publisher activities is for the developer to contact editors who decline an event invitation to see if they have time for an appointment the next day. Unfortunately, some writers rarely attend off-site events. In one example, Vicarious Visions, a developer, was able to schedule a full set of interviews within editor offices the day after a publisher event. That gave Vicarious Visions the full attention of magazine editors, and it wouldn't have occurred if the developer relied solely on the publisher.

Magazine Promotions

If there is money to promote a title, one opportunity is to pack a promotion within a traditional game magazine. For example, a recognizable or unique central character in a game can be placed on a poster and packed with the magazine.

Much less expensive than advertising within big game magazines is purchasing the opportunity to have a title featured on a demo disk that is affixed to the cover of the publication that month. With this type of promotion, either an AVI or a playable level can be offered. This provides an easy way for many potential customers to focus and spend time with a new game.

Online Advertising

For most developers, advertising in the major game print or consumer publications is out of the question, because of the expense. However, running advertising on the online gamer sites is still relatively inexpensive in terms of how many people can be reached. One good way to obtain advertising is in "trade"—giving something to the medium in exchange for the space.

The fan sites are a particularly good place to start. Many of these online sites are run by game lovers in their spare time. The Webmasters can use any kind of support, including small fees or even free product they can give away, because it helps them attract traffic.

Corporate PR: How to Build a Brand for the Company

Once a developer gains some stature in the industry (usually after they've completed a few contracts or sold their first original title), they start to be concerned about building the reputation of the company. Fortunately, a number of publications cater to company news.

First, there is the media that are concerned specifically with developer topics.

The lead publication here is *Game Developer* magazine and its accompanying online news site, *gamasutra.com*. Other online news sites for the developer/publisher include *shacknews.com*, *flipcode.com*, *gamedev.net*, and *joystick101.org*. If the developer has strong artist skills on staff, they might also be able to appeal to *Computer Graphics World* or *Animation* magazine.

A number of industry newsletters also sprang up in the last few years: *Game Daily*, *Electronic Gaming Business*, *Game Industry News*, and *Digital Media Wire*.

When a developer is covered in these trade publications, it gets their name out in the community. This can help a developer be known as an innovator or as a hot company. It might also help get partnerships, attract top talent, or be acquired.

At the top of the food chain are the business publications: *Business 2.0*, *Fortune*, *Forbes*, and *BusinessWeek*. These service publications are looking for stories that appeal to top management.

Positioning Discussion

Before a developer invests money in a corporate PR effort, they must get their company positioning down. This usually involves a full-day discussion, led by a senior PR professional, designed to help articulate what is unique about the company, and the priorities for moving the reputation of the organization ahead. In this type of session, the following should be considered:

- What is the best way to describe the company? Does everyone on the executive team use the same words? Is the company described the same way with various audiences?
- Who are the target audiences that the company needs to reach and influence to move the company ahead? Just publishers? Specific publishers?
- How important is the company's reputation in the industry? Is it important for peers to recognize the company's talents?
- Do the company's audiences associate the reputation of the company with one or a few individuals? Is this a problem, or something to build on?
- Are any other audiences important in building the business of the company?
- What differentiates the company's work from other developers?
- Would the target audiences currently associate differentiating factors with the company?

- Where should the company be in five years? Will that require any changes to the company?
- Considering all these things, what are the key messages the company wants to get across to their target audiences?

PR companies, such as The Bohle Company, typically offer a one-day positioning meeting that gets everybody thinking and all executives on the same page. A corporate PR plan can then be structured, with these goals in mind.

The following are some tactical corporate activities that might be considered.

Technical Articles

If a developer is willing to share information on how an interesting technology challenge was met, *Game Developer* magazine or *gamasutra.com* might be interested. In addition to these, several journals and books are published regularly that accept these types of technical articles: *Journal of Game Development* (*www.jogd.com*), the *Game Programming Gems* series (*www.gameprogramminggems.com*), and the *AI Game Programming Wisdom* series (*www.aiwisdom.com*).

Speaking Opportunities

Game developers can raise the visibility of their company through speaking opportunities. Within the developer community, the best place to start is with the Game Developers Conference (GDC), where developers and publishers from all over North America come to the greater San Francisco area usually during the month of March (*www.gdconf.com*). Regional gatherings, like the Austin Game Conference (*www.gameconference.com*), can also be effective as well as the smaller monthly IGDA gatherings all over the world (*www.igda.org*). For exposure to publishers and retail buyers, the Electronic Entertainment Expo (E3, *www.e3expo.com*) can also be worth pursuing.

The big conferences book a minimum of nine months in advance. Being accepted is not guaranteed, so a great abstract is key. If the speaker is a respected industry expert or the developer has put out a recent hit game, a one-hour presentation may be best. Otherwise, it is advisable to suggest a panel, where a company's spokesperson would be one of the participants.

Generating Business Press

While the national business press focuses on large, public companies, opportunities exist for the small company with a clever way of doing business.

To get the attention of a business reporter, stories must be proposed that have a business or economic angle. Reporters need to be told what is different about how a company operates or what was done to make the company successful that might be helpful for other small businesses. These stories must also be offered exclusively, since these magazines are highly competitive.

Summary

As seen in this chapter, an effective marketing strategy for video games is a comprehensive web of getting the right people to see and talk about the game at the right time. It begins early in the development process by building buzz with magazines, online game enthusiast sites, and amateur fan sites. It then progresses to playable demos for trade shows, magazines, and other enthusiast media. Meanwhile, it helps to promote the company and people developing the game by obtaining additional media coverage in related media. Near completion of the game, the rounds must be made with editors to obtain magazine publicity and reviews. Finally, traditional media kicks in with magazine advertising, television advertising, and in-store promotions. Then, to maintain the momentum once the game is released, fan sites and enthusiast media must be serviced.

Exercises

1. Pick a high-profile game, like EA Sports' *Madden 2005*, and search the Internet for all related press releases distributed by the publisher. For example, Electronic Arts has a database of their press releases at *http://info.ea.com/news/news.php*. For each press release you find, what purpose does it serve?

2. Visit a game retailer and inventory what kinds of game product promotions are being displayed in the store. What games are stored on the end caps and standup displays? What posters or other promotional material exist? What demo kiosks are there and what demos/movies are available on them? Given each game platform, what percentage of shelf space does each have?

3. Go to the E3 Website (*http://www.e3expo.com*) and obtain the exhibitor floor plans for the next conference. Based on examining the floor plans and companies listed, which two halls are the most desirable? Name the top five companies that probably spent the most money for their space.

4. Pick a high-profile MMORPG game, like *EverQuest 2*, and create a list of Internet fan sites. What percentage of these sites have advertising? What products are being advertised?

7.5 Intellectual Property Content, Law, and Practice

In This Chapter

- Overview
- Categories of IP Protection
- The IP Content of Video Games
- Patents
- Copyrights
- Trademarks
- Trade Secrets
- Transfers of IP Rights
- Avoiding IP Infringement
- Summary
- Exercises
- References

Overview

To the creative, technological, managerial, and financial layers of video game study, add another: the law of intellectual property. Where a player sees seamless onscreen interactive game play, and a developer sees original characters, artwork, backgrounds, storylines, dialogue, music, and sounds brought to life by software game engines and tools, a lawyer sees an amalgam of patents, copyrights, publicity rights, moral rights, trademarks, and trade secrets. To an increasing extent, video game development choices, and ultimately what appears on the player's screen, are shaped by the web of rights and remedies the legal system collects under the heading of "intellectual property." Intellectual property often is abbreviated IP, and that designation will be used here.

A working definition of intellectual property is the bundle of rights to the intangible creations and inventions of the human intellect.

It is useful to think of IP rights as a bundle because it is possible to subdivide rights based on factors such as use, duration, exclusivity, transferability, and geographic scope. IP rights have complementary parts: the right to exploit and the right to control exploitation by others. For example, a developer's right to prevent others from reproducing a game is fundamental to the developer's right to be compensated for the assignment of the game IP to a publisher. IP is intangible. IP is not the book or CD, but rather ownership rights to the written expression contained in the book or audiovisual recording on the CD. A book and CD can be physically possessed and have a finite presence. The written expression or audiovisual recording can be perceived through an expanding array of technology, including the Internet. Consequently, they can have virtually limitless presence. This combination of factors, the intangible nature of IP rights and technological advances in IP reproduction and distribution, presents a great challenge to the enforcement of IP rights today.

In North America, Western Europe, Japan, Australia, and to a lesser degree in the remainder of the world, the allocation and enforcement of IP rights is governed by national and sometimes local laws, government agencies, and international treaties that pertain to patents, copyrights, trademarks, and trade secrets. These laws, primarily the IP laws of the United States, are the focus of this chapter. The emphasis will be on video game IP. However, the application of these laws extends far wider, to all manner of scientific, technological, literary, artistic, and commercial creations, discoveries, and inventions.

This chapter is a distillation of what are complex and evolving IP laws and principles. It should be noted that the description of particular laws and principles may be subject to unstated qualifications or omissions. IP laws and principles can and do change and can vary significantly among different jurisdictions. This chapter does not constitute legal advice, which should be obtained through consultation with an attorney in the context of specific facts.

Categories of IP Protection

It will be useful to start with an introduction to the principles that govern the major forms of IP protection and to consider their interrelation.

A patent protects certain novel, useful, and nonobvious inventions having a utilitarian function.

The owner of a United States patent has rights superior to all subsequent inventors, but for a limited term that is currently 20 years. Rights to an invention are not protected from use by others unless a patent is obtained from the United States Patent and Trademark Office (USPTO). In exchange for the monopoly IP rights granted to the patentee during the patent term, the patentee must make a full public disclosure of the invention in the patent. This disclosure may be freely exploited by anyone once the patent expires. Patents permeate the hardware technology on which video games are played. So-called method patents are increasingly used to secure a monopoly in particular forms of gameplay or software functionality.

Conversely, exclusive IP rights to an invention, discovery, or other confidential and commercially valuable information can be maintained indefinitely as a trade secret. The owner of a trade secret can preclude others from disclosing nonpublic information obtained from the owner, but the owner cannot stop independent discovery and use of such information. A patent does not protect ideas, only the functional embodiment of an idea in a new and useful device or method. A trade secret can be used to protect the idea itself from use by others. The protection accorded trade secrets is a matter of federal and individual state laws, the latter of which often are modeled on the Uniform Trade Secrets Act.

A copyright protects creative expression in any fixed medium such as books, film, CDs, videotape, records, and computer hard drives. As with patents, copyrights do not protect ideas, only their expression. This limitation applies to so-called *scenes a faire*—stock literary devices like plots, incidents, scenes, and characters. In the field of video games, this concept is captured in the term "genre." It enables such similar games as *Street Fighter*, *Virtua Fighter*, and *Mortal Kombat* to coexist without copyright infringement. Copyright protects against only actual copying; therefore, another person can claim rights to identical expression as long as it was not copied. Theoretically, two people working without knowledge of each other could paint the same picture, write the same software, or take the same photograph. Each could copyright his or her creative work. The concept of copyright "expression" does not include individual words, names, or titles. The duration of a copyright currently is the life of the author/artist plus 70 years, or a fixed period, as discussed later, for anonymous or corporate authors. It is not necessary to register a copyright, although important enforcement benefits are conferred by doing so. Copyright registration is the statutory responsibility of the United States Library of Congress.

A trademark is any word, symbol, or device that serves to identify the source or origin of particular goods or services. ATARI, INSOMNIAC GAMES, and MICROSOFT are examples of famous word marks of their respective companies. RATCHET & CLANK is the trademark for Insomniac Games' popular video game. Sega's "Sonic the Hedgehog" graphic is an example of a widely recognized design trademark. The stylized SEGA lettering is a combined word and design mark. The nonfunctional trade dress of a product—the product's "total image"—is also capable of serving as a trademark. An example is the case design of the Microsoft Xbox. Unlike a copyright, a trademark can be obtained for a word or title, as long as the word or title signifies the source of the product or service. For example, the words "star wars" and "Harry Potter" cannot be copyrighted as the title of a single book or film, but can serve as a trademark for a series of books or films and for merchandise related to the book or film that originates from one source. Moreover, the creative content of the *Star Wars* and *Harry Potter* stories, including the text or screenplay and such subcomponents as characters, costumes, dialogue, scenes, and plot, is protectable by copyright. Ownership of a trademark is established by first use. It is not necessary to register a trademark to secure exclusive rights, but, as with a copyright, registration confers significant benefits. The USPTO registers trademarks, as do the individual states. The federal trademark law is known as the Lanham Act. The duration of a trademark potentially is perpetual. It lasts as long as it is in use to identify the source of goods or services. A federally registered trademark is renewable every 10 years as long as the mark continues in use in interstate commerce.

The IP Content of Video Games

The typical video game is protected by an umbrella of patents, copyrights, trademarks, and trade secrets that may be owned by different parties. Because copyright covers creative expression fixed in a tangible medium, it is the most prevalent form of IP protection in video games. Software in the form of game engines and tools, software documentation, artwork, storyline, backgrounds, characters, costumes, weapons, dialogue, text, sound effects, and music are among the forms of copyrightable expression found in games. Copyright ownership originates with the author or creator. This can be the employee who draws the artwork or an independent contractor who scores the music. Under "work-for-hire" principles later discussed, employee contributions normally become the property of the employer by operation of law. Independent contractors must assign their rights in a written agreement to the party who commissions the work. Copyrights are subject to transfer by assignment or license. An assignment conveys all rights to the copyrighted IP. A license conveys less than all of such rights; for example, the nonexclusive, nontransferable, perpetual right to sell the copyrighted work throughout North America. Independent developers typically assign rights to those portions of the game that are experienced by a player to the publisher that funds development of the game. They grant an irrevocable and nonexclusive license to the publisher for the software that enables the game to run. The game may be based on a copyright license, such as when a film, book, or comic is made into a video game.

Patents may apply to the technology embodied in the hardware on which the game is played, on the media (diskette, CD, cartridge, hard drive) on which the game is recorded, and on software that enables the game to perform particular functions. Hardware patents are owned or licensed by the manufacturer, who also may be the publisher—in the case of Sony, Microsoft, and Nintendo—and at times, also the developer of the game. Because patents are expensive to acquire and to enforce, they are rarely sought by independent developers.

Video games also provide a fertile environment for trademarks. The publisher and developer of the game, often separate parties, may each trademark their business name as a word mark and may create a design such as fanciful lettering or a graphic as a further source of their identification. The title of the game may be the separate subject of trademark protection. If a particular feature of the game also acts as a designation of the source of the game, it may function as a trademark. Sega's adoption of Sonic the Hedgehog as its corporate mascot, Nintendo's similar display of Mario the Plumber, and Sony's *de facto* use of Crash Bandicoot in connection with PlayStation games serve as recognized brands of these companies.

Lastly, confidential aspects of the know-how used to program the game, budgets and financial statements, and the terms of the agreements between the developer and its publisher, its employees, and its independent contractors, may be secured from use by others as trade secrets. Prior to the release of a much-anticipated game to the public, the entire contents of the game may be maintained as a trade secret to build interest and thwart simultaneous-release knockoffs.

Patents

American patent law is based on the United States Constitution and a federal statute, the Patent Act, as amended. There is no applicable state law.

Works Protected

Patent law protects inventions and processes ("utility" patents) and ornamental designs ("design" patents). Inventions and processes protected by utility patents can be "any new and useful process, machine, manufacture or composition of matter, or any new and useful improvement thereof. . . ." In general, laws of nature (e.g., $E=mc^2$), physical phenomena, and abstract ideas lacking a practical application are not patentable.

Recently, inventors have applied for so-called "method" patents covering computerized processes and functions. In one widely followed lawsuit, Sega of America sued Fox Interactive, Radical Games, and Electronic Arts for infringement of United States Patent No. 6,200,138 entitled "Game Display Method, Moving Direction Indicating Method, Game Apparatus and Drive Simulating Apparatus." Sega claims its patent covers the gameplay in Sega's *Crazy Taxi*, in which the player races his taxi around obstacles and pedestrians and careens through a tortuous road course in an effort to deliver his passenger as fast as possible. The defendants are the licensor, developer, and publisher of *Simpson's Road Rage*, which Sega asserts involves much the same gameplay. Concern about the proliferation of method patents that appear to involve "obvious" inventions resulted in the passage of the American Inventors Protection Act of 1999. It provides enhanced defenses in method-patent lawsuits.

The patentability of computer software, which is comprised of "mathematical algorithms," is now settled. A mathematical algorithm is not patentable subject matter to the extent that it is merely the embodiment of an abstract idea. However, the practical application of a mathematical algorithm to achieve a useful, concrete, and tangible result is patentable subject matter. Hence, software that enables a processor to convert data into animated figures on a screen—for example, a video game engine—comprises patentable subject matter.

The Patent Act also provides for design patents. In contrast to utility patents, design patents cover only nonfunctional aspects of a tangible object, such as the features of action figures based on the characters and costumes appearing in a game.

Standards

To qualify for a utility patent, an invention must be (1) new, (2) useful, and (3) nonobvious to a person of ordinary skill in the art to which the invention pertains. To satisfy novelty, the invention must not have been known or used by others in this country before the patent applicant invented it, and it must not have been patented or described in a printed publication in the United States or a foreign country before the applicant invented it. The utility criterion is easily met; the invention must have some practical use and not be merely frivolous. Efforts to secure a patent for the ever-illusive perpetual motion machine fail because they have yet to achieve perpetual motion. To meet the nonobvious requirement, the invention must be sufficiently different from existing technology and knowledge so that, at the time the invention is made, the invention as a whole would not have been obvious to a person having ordinary skill in that field. Much of the determination of patentability of an invention relates to whether it was known in the "prior art." Often, this determination is made based on whether the invention is disclosed in one or a combination of prior patents. For this reason, a patentability opinion from patent counsel based on a comprehensive search and analysis of prior patents is commonly the first step to determine whether to proceed with a patent application.

Procedure

Patent protection is obtained by demonstrating in an application filed with the USPTO that the claimed invention meets the stringent standards for grant of a patent. Even if an invention or process appears to satisfy the requirements of novelty, utility, and nonobviousness, a patent will not be granted if the invention was patented, described in a printed publication in the United States or abroad, or in use prior to the application date. This is true even if the inventor was unaware of the publication or use. Pursuant to the on-sale bar, if the invention was in public use or on sale in the United States more than one year before the application date it is ineligible for patent.

As of this writing, it is common for a patent application to take more than two years to be processed by the USPTO. The cost in processing and legal fees for the typical software patent exceeds $10,000, and can easily increase to several times that amount for complicated subject matter.

Ownership

In general, the inventor is the owner of the patent. There may be multiple inventors, each of whom must be identified as a coinventor on the patent application. Employee ownership of an invention raises a number of issues. An employee may be the absolute owner of a patentable invention if the invention occurs outside the scope of the employee's employment and on the employee's own time, and does not involve use of the trade secrets, property, or facilities of the employer. A patentable invention created by an employee within the scope of his or her employment is still "owned" by the employee for purposes of listing on the patent. However, an employee may have a legal obligation to transfer complete ownership by assignment to an employer under patent law's "hired to invent" doctrine. In the absence of a contract specifying the respective rights of employer and employee to inventions made by the employee within the scope of employment, an employee may have a legal obligation to assign all rights to the employer if the employee was hired for the specific purpose of creating the invention. In a second category are employees hired for their general creative or inventive skills, but not specifically to create an invention. Provided the skills and duties are sufficiently related to the invention, courts have upheld a duty to assign the invention rights to the employer. In a third category is an employee whose job duties are unrelated to invention. This employee has no duty to assign rights in inventions to the employer. Nonetheless, the employer may be entitled to a royalty-free, nonexclusive, nontransferable license to use the invention if it was created on the employer's time and using the employer's property and facilities. This is commonly referred to as a "shop right." In view of the uncertain interpretation a court may give to particular employment facts, the subject of ownership of employee inventions, as well as ownership of other forms of IP, should be addressed in a written employment agreement signed by the employee at the outset of employment. In states such as California, employers are statutorily limited in the waiver of invention rights they may demand from employees by contract.

Inventors have used a variety of devices, short of incurring the expense of a formal patent application, to establish the priority date of their invention. Common are notarized notebooks and diaries. The ineffectual practice of mailing a sealed self-addressed envelope containing the invention description to obtain the post office date stamp remains popular. The Patent Act was amended to allow for a provisional application to address this issue. The provisional application enables an inventor to claim as the filing date of a subsequently filed formal application the date of the provisional application provided it properly discloses the subject matter. The fees for a provisional application are less than a formal application, it does not require claims or a declaration, and it is subject to less-stringent USPTO review. There are limitations to a provisional application that should be understood before it is undertaken. One drawback of a provisional patent application is that the scope of disclosure cannot be later expanded to claim additional inventive subject matter.

Exclusive Rights

A patent owner has the right to exclude others from making, using, or selling the patented invention or design in the United States during the term of the patent. A person can infringe the patent even if he did not copy the patented invention or even know about it. A utility patent covers the exact invention claimed and its functional equivalent that achieves the same result by comparable means. A design patent covers designs that are substantially similar to the patented design.

Duration

A utility patent is granted for 20 years from the date the patent application is filed. The previous period was 17 years from the date the application was granted for patents issued prior to June 8, 1995. There are statutory provisions to extend the duration of a patent for applications whose approval is delayed by certain USPTO or Food and Drug Administration (in the case of pharmaceuticals) action. A design patent is granted for 14 years. Once the patent on an invention expires, anyone is free to make, use, or sell the invention or design. Moreover, the patent supplies a detailed description of the invention, facilitating its lawful copying once the patent expires.

Notice

Although not required, notice of a patent may be indicated on a product by the statement that it is patented or by printing the patent number and date on the article or affixed label. There is no official patent notice symbol as such.

International Patent Law

The oldest and most important international treaty relation to intellectual property is the International Convention for the Protection of Industrial Property originally signed in Paris in 1883 (Paris Convention). The Paris Convention covers patents, industrial designs, trademarks, trade names, and unfair competition. It requires each signatory nation to protect the IP of foreign nationals to the same extent and under the same conditions as that nation protects the IP of its own citizens. The Paris Convention also provides priority rules that enable a filing in one signatory nation to relate back to an earlier filing in another. The Patent Cooperation Treaty goes further and creates an international patent filing system under which patents filed in national and certain regional patent offices may eventually mature into patents in any one or more of the signatory countries. The European Patent Convention establishes a European Patent Office as a single place to file patent applications for member countries.

Copyrights

American copyright law is based on the United States Constitution and a federal statute, the Copyright Act of 1976, as amended. There is no applicable state law.

Works Protected

Almost any original expression can be the subject of copyright protection. The Copyright Act refers to "original works of authorship," specifically including literary works; musical works, including any accompanying lyrics; dramatic works, including any accompanying music; pantomimes and choreographic works; pictorial, graphic, and sculptural works; sound recordings; and architectural works. Software code is considered a work of authorship. The subject matter of copyright includes compilations and derivative works. Copyright protects multimedia works such as video games under the copyright categories of audiovisual works, compilations, or derivative works, or a combination of these. Original music in a game may be separately published and copyrighted as a musical work. Copyright protection extends to the underlying computer software that implements a multimedia work, as well as the "look and feel" of the user interface in a multimedia work.

Equally significant is what copyright does not protect. The Copyright Act expressly states: "In no case does copyright protection for an original work of authorship extend to any idea, procedure, process, system, method of operation, concept, principle, or discovery. . . ." Titles and names standing alone are not copyrightable. Even renowned titles like "Star Wars" and "The Wizard of Oz" are not subject to copyright protection. It also is impossible to copyright facts apart from the original expression of the facts. For example, telephone numbers are "facts" that cannot be separately copyrighted. A directory of telephone numbers arranged alphabetically by customer cannot be copyrighted for the additional reason that it lacks originality. However, a directory listing telephone numbers in a novel manner that requires effort to create, perhaps arranged by customer age, nationality, or type of dwelling, may be granted "thin" copyright protection. The copyrightable subject matter would be the arrangement of the telephone numbers in a new way. It would not include the telephone numbers ("facts") themselves.

Standards

Two criteria must be met for copyright protection: originality and "fixation in a tangible form." The originality threshold is low. The work merely must be the author's own work product and not be copied. A federal appeals court has ruled that the "modicum of creativity" embodied in the classic video game *Breakout*, in which players move a "paddle" to hit a "ball" against a "wall" of rows of rectangles, was sufficient to warrant issuance of copyright registration.

To satisfy the requirement of fixation, there must be a physical embodiment of the work. The fixation test is met even if images only can be perceived with the aid of a device, such as a computer or CD. Unfixed works, such as an untaped live broadcast, are not subject to federal copyright protection. The text of Martin Luther King's "I Have a Dream" speech is copyrighted because it was written in advance. His actual delivery (performance) of the speech is separately copyrighted as a film and separately as a recording. Had it not been fixed on film, the delivery of the speech could not be copyrighted. The publications and official speeches of government officials are public works that cannot be copyrighted. Thus, President Lincoln could not copyright "The Gettysburg Address."

Procedure

If a work meets the minimum requirement of originality and is fixed in a tangible or perceptible medium, it is automatically the subject of copyright protection. It is no longer necessary to obtain a copyright registration from the Library of Congress to claim copyright protection. However, suit to enforce the copyright through injunction and recovery of damages may not be brought until the copyright is registered. Registration also enables the copyright holder to seek statutory damages (no less that $750 or more than $30,000 for each violation as the court determines is just; up to $150,000 for willful infringement in the court's discretion) in lieu of proof of actual damages. Attorney fees and litigation costs may be awarded to the prevailing party, whether plaintiff or defendant, at the discretion of the court. Registration requires completion of a copyright registration form along with a small registration fee and two copies of the work. Criminal penalties are available in cases of willful infringement·brought by the government. It should be noted that software publishers are banding together to bring enforcement actions against companies large and small that use their software without valid licenses. A copyright registration may be filed with the United States Customs Bureau to protect against the importation of illegal copies.

Ownership

Ownership of copyright initially belongs to the author or authors of the work. The "author" is generally the individual who created the work, but there is an exception for works made for hire. The author of a work made for hire is the employer or hiring party for whom the work is prepared. A work created by an employee within the scope of his or her employment is a work made for hire. If outside the scope of employment, the author is the employee unless there is a written agreement giving the employer rights. For a specially ordered or commissioned work created by an independent contractor, the commissioning party is the author only if there is a written agreement expressly providing and the work falls within one of eight special categories of commissioned works (e.g., translations, compilations, part of a motion picture or other audiovisual work). Where there are two or more authors, and in the absence of a written agreement, each is a joint owner and can use or license the work without the consent of the other owner provided the use does not destroy the value of the work.

Exclusive Rights

A copyright owner has five exclusive rights in the copyrighted work: reproduction right (copy, duplicate, or imitate); modification right; distribution right; public performance right; and public display right. A visual artist's moral right to object to improper attribution of authorship and to require others to respect the integrity of the work is recognized in the Visual Artists Rights Act of 1990. Moral rights are given considerably more prominence in European countries where such rights cannot be surrendered or sold. Nonvisual artists, including creators of literary, musical, and audiovisual works, are not covered by this law. They must find protection through other means such as contract. The fair use of a copyrighted work, including use for purposes of criticism, comment, news reporting, teaching, scholarship, or research is not an infringement of copyright. A parody of a copyrighted work such as portraying children's cartoon characters engaged in adult entertainment also does not constitute infringement. What is a fair use or legitimate parody depends on a balancing of factors applied to the particular facts of each case. Another exception to copyright infringement is the so-called first-sale doctrine that terminates the copyright of the author in a specific embodiment of the work, such as a book, upon the initial sale of the work. The new owner is thereafter free to use, lend, display, or sell the work. Thus far, only two states (Maryland and Virginia) have enacted versions of the Uniform Computer Information Transactions Act (UCITA) relating to licensing of computer software. More states have laws expressly limiting application of UCITA. UCITA significantly limits the first-sale doctrine by permitting copyright owners to restrict the rights transferred to a revocable "license" rather than outright sale. It now appears UCITA will be of limited effect.

Electronic publishing rights and the right to share copyrighted works online is hotly debated and the subject of increasing Congressional and judicial attention. A common thread in court rulings is that conventional copyright protection is not lost merely because the medium may be Internet transmission instead of a tangible text or recording. Congress has attempted to update the Copyright Act to keep pace with technological advances, most notably with the Digital Millennium Copyright Act in 1998. The DMCA makes significant changes in U.S. law affecting Internet-related practices and businesses and bans circumvention of technological measures employed to prevent infringement. Copyright holders are now focusing on industry-wide development of such technological measures. Well-publicized lawsuits have been filed to prevent the unauthorized downloading of music. Sony has brought suits in several countries seeking to stop the proliferation of so-called "mod chips" enabling console games to be run on unauthorized hardware.

Duration

The duration of a copyright depends on the date the copyright was created, because statutory changes over the years have created differing rules. Under present law, the copyright term for works created by an individual on or after January 1, 1978 is the life of the author plus 70 years. Anonymous works and works made for hire have a term of 95 years from the date of first publication, or 120 years from the date of its creation, whichever is sooner. Pre-1978 copyrighted works in their first term of copyright under the prior statute are granted a 75-year copyright term from the date of registration of the work. The current duration periods were upheld recently by the Supreme Court against the claim that they extended copyrights beyond the constitutionally permissible "limited times."

Notice

The use of copyright notice is optional for works distributed after March 1, 1989. Copyright notice is beneficial to establish willful infringement. It can take any of these three forms: © followed by a date and owner's name; "copyright" followed by date and name; or "copr." followed by date and name. It is also customary, but not required, to add such words as "all rights reserved."

International Copyright Law

The United States is a member of The Berne Convention for the Protection of Literary and Artistic Works, an international copyright treaty for the protection of works of authorship administered by the UN World Intellectual Property Organization (WIPO). The Berne Convention is based on principles of national treatment with the result that copyright registration is done on a country-by-country basis. At present, the United States is the only treaty member to require copyright registration as a condition to commencement of an infringement action. Signatory nations to the Berne Convention agree to uphold the copyright of foreign authors pursuant to their respective national copyright laws. Nonetheless, enforcement vigor varies considerably among member nations. The North American Free Trade Agreement (NAFTA) provides multilateral copyright protections among the United States, Canada, and Mexico.

Trademarks

American trademark law is based on common (judge-made) law, the federal Lanham Act, and various state laws.

Works Protected

Any word, symbol, name, slogan, picture, design, shape, color, sound, or smell that serves to identify the source or origin of goods or services can be a trademark. There are actually four types of trademarks. A trademark is a mark (brand, logo) used on goods (e.g., GAME BOY ADVANCE for Nintendo of America's handheld video game player). A service mark simply is a mark used in connection with services (e.g., GOOGLE as the service mark for an Internet search engine). A certification mark is used by the owner to certify qualities or characteristics of the goods or services of others (e.g., the EC/EARLY CHILDHOOD, K-A/KIDS TO ADULTS, E/EVERYONE, E+10/EVERYONE+10, T/TEEN, M/MATURE, and AO/ADULTS ONLY game rating logos of the Entertainment Software Rating Board). A collective membership mark is used by the owner to signify membership in a group or organization (e.g., TEAMSTERS for a labor union). Only trademarks and service marks are considered here, and following conventional usage, they are referred to collectively as trademarks.

Standards

The word, name, symbol, or device must be capable of distinguishing the owner's goods or services from the goods or services of others. Trademarks are commonly classified based on the degree of protection they are accorded. In descending order of enforcement strength, they are:

Arbitrary or coined: A term that bears no relationship to the product or service and often has no meaning other than as a designation of source of the product, such as ION STORM, SHINY, EIDOS, and NAUGHTY DOG for games, KODAK for cameras and film, and EXXON for gasoline.

Suggestive: A term that subtly suggests something about the product, such as ELECTRONIC ARTS, 3D REALMS for games, GAMECUBE and PLAYSTATION for game consoles, STAPLES for office supply stores, and FEDERAL EXPRESS for national overnight delivery service.

Descriptive: A term that describes something about the product, such as RENDERWARE for rendering software, GATHERING OF DEVELOPERS for games, ELECTRONIC ENTERTAINMENT EXPO for an annual game exposition (E3), VISION CENTER for optical clinics and eyeglass stores, and QUIK PRINT for fast printing and duplicating services.

Generic: The common name for the kind of product, such as Greatest Hits, Handheld and ThreeDee for games, Super Glue for strong and fast bonding glue, and Lo-cal for reduced-calorie foods and beverages.

Arbitrary and suggestive marks can perform as a trademark immediately upon use. A descriptive mark only serves a trademark after some period of exclusive use in which the mark acquires a "secondary meaning" in the minds of consumers apart from its descriptive connotation. It is on this basis that the highly descriptive mark TV GUIDE qualifies for registration for a television programming publication. Generic terms can never serve as a trademark, no matter how long in exclusive use. An example is the unsuccessful effort by Miller Brewing Co. to register "Lite" as a trademark for its low-calorie beer. When Microsoft Corporation, owner of the WINDOWS mark for a user interface system, sued Lindows.com, owner of the LINDOWS mark for a computer operating system, the defense presented is that "windows" was a generic term for a user interface system at the time of Microsoft's adoption and cannot be transformed by use into a trademark. After years of litigation, Microsoft settled with Lindows.com by payment of a large cash settlement in exchange for Lindows.com abandonment of its mark. Conversely, a term originally valid as a trademark can become generic through indiscriminate public use. Cellophane, nylon, aspirin, thermos, yo-yo, Murphy bed, refrigerator, and escalator are among examples of once-famous trademarks lost through "genericide," the transformation of a mark through indiscriminate public use into the common name of a product or service. XEROX, FEDEX, and FRIGIDAIRE thus far have avoided this fate through extensive promotional effort.

Procedure

Trademark rights are created by adoption and use of a distinctive mark or brand. The most effective trademark protection is obtained by filing a trademark registration application in the USPTO. Federal law also protects unregistered trademarks, but such protection is limited to the geographic area in which the mark is actually used. To qualify for federal protection, the trademark must be used in interstate commerce. Federal registration is available not only for trademarks in current use in interstate commerce, but also for trademarks whose owners have a bona fide intent-to-use the mark at a future date in commerce. Registration will not be granted until the trademark is in actual use. The current fee for federal registration for each category (class) of goods or services is $335, but is subject to revision. State trademark protection exists under common law simply by adoption and use. Protection is limited to the area of actual use within the state. State statutory registration is also available.

Ownership

A trademark is owned by the first party to use it in connection with goods or services, or the first to apply to register it under the federal intent-to-use procedure if the mark was not previously in use.

Exclusive Rights

Trademark law in general, whether federal or state, protects a trademark owner's commercial identity (goodwill, reputation, and investment in advertising) by giving the trademark owner the exclusive right to use the trademark in connection with specific goods or services. Any person who later uses the same or similar trademark in connection with goods or services in any way that is likely to cause confusion or mistake or to deceive is an infringer. Similarly, the law provides a right of action for "unfair competition" to protect against a wide variety of deceptive commercial practices causing product or service confusion, the two most common being false designation of origin (trademark or trade dress infringement) and false description or representation (false advertising). The general test for likelihood of confusion is said to be whether an ordinary consumer, exercising due care under the circumstances, is likely to regard a trademarked product or service as coming from the same source as the product or service of the challenged trademark. Among factors courts will consider in making this determination are (1) the degree of similarity between the marks in appearance, pronunciation of the words used, meaning and overall impression; (2) the intent of the later user in adopting the trademark, including evidence of the intention to trade on the good will of the earlier user; (3) relatedness of the goods or services; (4) similarities in marketing and channels of distribution; (5) evidence of actual confusion; (6) public awareness or "fame" of the earlier trademark; and (7) the degree of care likely to be exercised by purchasers. Application of the test is unavoidably subjective and fact specific. As just one example, similar pronunciation of differently spelled trademarks may be a significant factor when the marks are used in connection with goods that are ordered orally over the counter, such as cigarettes, but may be insignificant when used on goods sold exclusively through self-service outlets, such as candy sold through vending machines. A likelihood of confusion standard is applied by courts to determine infringement and unfair competition, and by the USPTO to determine whether to grant registration of an application that is found to be similar to an existing registered mark or a mark for which an earlier application is pending.

In cases of proven infringement, the trademark owner can obtain injunctive relief and damages against the infringer. If the trademark is not registered, the geographic area of exclusivity is the actual area of use and any adjacent area of natural expansion. A key advantage of federal registration is that it expands the geographic area to nationwide protection regardless of the area of actual use. State registration extends the borders of protection statewide. Federal registration also confirms advantages of additional enforcement remedies, including up to three times actual damages and attorneys' fees in appropriate cases. A federal trademark registration may be filed with the Customs Bureau to protect against the importation of misbranded goods. Congress enacted the AntiCybersquatter Consumer Protection Act in 1999 to afford protection to the owners of trademarks from the bad-faith registration of the same or confusingly similar designation as a domain name.

As stated, actions for trademark infringement and unfair competition require proof of the likelihood of confusion. The Lanham Act was amended by the Federal Trademark Dilution Act of 1995 to provide a federal right of action for trademark dilution. Owners of "famous" marks may now sue those who use a mark that "causes dilution of the distinctive quality of the mark" without the requirement of demonstrating a likelihood of confusion between the marks. The focus of a dilution action is not to protect consumers from confusion, but to protect the investment of owners of famous marks from "blurring" or tarnishment by other businesses. In a recent Supreme Court decision, the seller of lingerie, adult novelties, and gifts using the mark VICTOR'S LITTLE SECRET was found not to have diluted the famous VICTORIA'S SECRET registered trademark for lingerie. Although consumers might "mentally associate" VICTOR'S LITTLE SECRET with VICTORIA'S SECRET, the Supreme Court held there was no evidence that the owner of the VICTORIA'S SECRET mark had lost any ability to distinguish its products from those sold by others. Actions for trademark dilution are also provided under state law. The standard to prove dilution varies from state to state.

Duration

A trademark continues as long as it remains in use. Federal registrations are subject to renewal every 10 years from the date of issuance. The duration of state trademark registrations varies by state.

Notice

While notice of trademark ownership is not required, it is advisable and aids in the establishment of willful infringement. Only a trademark for which a federal certificate of registration has issued may use the notice symbol ®. All other trademarks, including state-registered trademarks, use the superscript letters "TM" for trademarks and "SM" for service marks.

International Trade Law

The United States became a signatory to the Madrid Agreement Concerning the International Registration of Trademarks (Madrid Protocol) on November 2, 2003, becoming the 59th member country. The Madrid Protocol promises to effect a major change in the feasibility of international registrations for American trademark owners. Briefly, the owner of an application or registration in the USPTO can submit one international application to the USPTO. The application permits the designation of the Madrid Protocol member nations to which it will apply. The USPTO reviews the international application for compliance and then forwards it to the International

Bureau of WIPO (World Intellectual Property Organization), a United Nations agency. After resolving any deficiencies, WIPO issues an International Registration with a registration date and number. WIPO then forwards the International Registration and "extension applications" to the trademark office in each of the nations designated by the applicant. The extension application is subject to examination in each country designated. If no refusal is issued within a stated period, the trademark is automatically registered in that member country. Besides permitting one filing in the home country, a streamlined procedure and lower filing fees, the Madrid Protocol provides for a uniform 10-year renewal cycle. For transnational products such as video games that are often localized for North American European and Asian markets, the ratification of the Madrid Protocol by the United States is a major advance. In addition to the Madrid Protocol, the Paris Convention has long provided for reciprocal treatment of trademarks and priority filing dates among signatory countries, including the United States. However, it is necessary to apply for trademark registration in each country in which the trademark is in use at a typical cost of several thousand dollars for each country. As a general proposition, a single trademark application can be submitted to the European Union and, if approved, is effective within EU members. The North American Free Trade Agreement (NAFTA) provides multilateral trademark protections among the United States, Canada, and Mexico.

Trade Secrets

Trade secret law is governed by the individual states. A growing number of states have enacted versions of the Uniform Trade Secrets Act.

Works Protected

The Uniform Trade Secrets Act (UTSA) defines "trade secret" as: "...derives independent economic value, actual or potential, from not being generally known to, and not being readily ascertainable by proper means by, other persons who can obtain economic value from its disclosure or use, and is the subject of efforts that are reasonable under the circumstances to maintain its secrecy."

The few states that have not adopted the UTSA commonly apply the definition appearing in the Restatement of Torts: "A trade secret may consist of any formula, pattern, device or compilation of information which is used in one's business, and which gives him an opportunity to obtain an advantage over competitors who do not know or use it. It may be a formula for a chemical compound, a process of manufacturing, treating or preserving materials, a pattern for a machine or other device, or a list of customers."

Standards

Under the UTSA definition, economically valuable information in any format can be a trade secret. Unlike copyright, there is no requirement that information exist in some "fixed" form in order to be a protectable trade secret. Nor does the trade secret have to be novel, original, or creative. Instead of novel, the information must be secret. Secrecy is the determinant in most cases; commercial value is a minimal requirement. Most clearly, information generally known to the public is not entitled to trade secret protection. The general business experience, memory, and skill that inure to an individual over the course of employment also cannot be claimed as a trade secret. Employees who acquire such knowledge in the course of their work for a game company typically are free to use the experience when they leave. Matters that are completely disclosed by the nature of the goods or services are not deemed secret if determinable upon inspection. Customer lists present a special case. They are likely to constitute trade secrets in situations in which the trade secret owner can demonstrate that customers are not generally known and that the customer list is not one that may be compiled easily from a telephone directory, trade association member list, or other readily available public documents.

The owner of a trade secret may disclose it to others, as long as disclosure is accompanied by an enforceable pledge of secrecy. The secrecy test has two prongs: (1) whether the information is generally known or available; and (2) whether the trade secret owner takes affirmative steps to safeguard the confidentiality of the information. Companies using trade secret protection should adopt a trade secret protection plan; put the secrecy policy in writing and have it acknowledged by all employees; clearly identify the information as secret; and provide for secure storage and restricted access. Transmission of unencrypted trade secrets over the Internet presents particular risks of interception or misdirection and should be avoided.

Procedure

There is no registry or other direct government regulation of trade secret information.

Ownership

An employer or hiring party generally owns trade secrets developed by employees and by independent contractors who are hired to invent or create such information. Explicit language protecting the employer's trade secrets in employment contracts is highly recommended.

Exclusive Rights

The UTSA protects trade secrets from "misappropriation." Misappropriation is defined in the Act to cover situations in which the information is knowingly acquired, disclosed, or used by improper means. "Improper means" is not defined in the UTSA, but would include acting without the consent of the trade secret owner and using the information in a manner adverse to the interests of the owner. Suits alleging misappropriation under the UTSA must be brought by the trade secret owner within three years of actual discovery or of an obligation to know due to surrounding circumstances.

Duration

A trade secret lasts as long as it meets the definitional test. The UTSA provides a three-year statute of limitations in which to sue for misappropriation.

Notice

There is no notice practice in view of the secret nature of the trade secret. Internal procedures within an organization to assure maintenance of trade secret treatment are advisable by stamping documents and restricting access.

International Trade Secret Law

There are no multinational treaties or agreements specifically pertaining to trade secret law.

Transfers of IP Rights

The value inherent in IP is realized by the ability to transfer a portion or all of the IP rights to others. A publisher contracting with an independent developer wants to own the developer's game IP free of the claims of others so that it might be sold to end users. The developer must convey title to the IP, and must represent that the IP does not infringe the patents, copyrights, trademarks, and trade secrets of others. Developer employees or independent contractors may assert IP claims based on their contributions to the game. The developer must capture these rights through employment or contractor agreements to solidify its own rights and to satisfy the publisher's demand for complete IP ownership. This transfer of rights by employees and contractors to the developer is an implicit part of their compensation, absent of which they are unlikely to be hired. If the game embodies third-party IP such as software, characters, story, or music, the developer or publisher must secure licenses or releases to these. The third parties realize the value of their IP by granting such rights in exchange for commissions, royalties, or fees.

The owner of IP has the right to transfer all rights by assignment, or a portion of the rights by license. The rights may be placed in the public domain, either intentionally, through IP misuse or neglect, or as the result of expiration of a registration. Alternatively, the owner may elect to make no use of the IP rights and to prohibit others from use. It has been charged that some patents are procured not to protect the owner's use, but to prevent use of the invention by competitors.

There are three issues to be resolved in evaluating the transfer of IP rights: identification of the owner; the nature of the rights transferred; and the form of the transfer.

The law presumes that the person who creates the IP is the owner. Because multiple parties can contribute to the creation of IP, as is the norm in video game development, it is necessary to analyze who has made a contribution and what they have contributed. In the case of a popular song, for example, the composer, lyricist, vocalist, and the musicians may be different people, all of whom may claim some portion of the bundle of rights in the song. The composer and lyricist do not have rights to the performance of the vocalist and musicians unless they contract for those rights. Conversely, the performers do not own the music and lyrics. Moreover, one or more of these parties may have assigned or licensed their rights to others. Tracking down all of the rights holders can be an arduous task, particularly if a large number of owners is involved and considerable time has elapsed. As the purchaser of IP created by others, the game creator must be in a position to assess ownership rights and assure that all necessary rights are being transferred.

An assignment is the contractual device used to irrevocably transfer all rights in particular IP. Any transfer of less than all rights is deemed a license. A licensor, the person granting the license, retains one or more rights to the IP such as the right to license others or to use the IP itself, to approve quality, to limit quantity, to restrict geographic area, to collect royalties, or to reacquire the rights at license termination. In most instances, an assignment is not enforceable unless in writing. In the case of patents, copyrights, and trademarks, all of which are listed in government registries, an assignment can be submitted to the relevant government agency for recordation. A recorded assignment serves as notice to future purchasers that ownership rights have been transferred.

Most transfers of IP rights take the form of a written agreement. In some employment contexts, IP rights may transfer by operation of law. This is true of the limited shop rights acquired by an employer in an employee's patentable invention and the copyright acquired by an employer in the work-for-hire of its employees. IP rights also are capable of transfer by inheritance where the right is owned by an individual. Inheritance has an important place in copyright transfers. For example, the period of statutory copyright protection for works created after 1978 extends 70 years beyond the life of the individual author or artist. This requires particular diligence when undertaking to identify ownership of a longstanding copyright. IP rights may be transferred from private control to the public domain by the owner's intention, inattention, or mistake. There are many opportunities for this to occur, such as the failure to file a patent application before the end of the on-sale period, failure to enforce a trademark against infringing users, failure to maintain the confidentiality of trade secret information, and failure to secure copyright ownership in publisher or employment contracts. The services of an attorney skilled in IP law are a necessary adjunct to IP ownership to avoid these and many other pitfalls.

Avoiding IP Infringement

The vast amount of IP that is created makes it inevitable that rights of two or more creators will overlap. Anyone who has sought to name a company or game, secure a domain name, or create original characters, stories, or gameplay has experienced the frustration of discovering someone has gotten there first. Even worse is investing substantial effort and funds to create IP only to learn, after the fact, and perhaps in the form of a complaint seeking significant damages, that what was thought to be original in fact clearly infringes another person's patent, copyright, trademark, or trade secret. This revelation is all too common in the games industry and elsewhere in the entertainment and technology fields. With a contested patent infringement lawsuit costing each side a million dollars in legal fees alone, it is a risk that must be avoided. With some effort, it can.

By their nature, trademarks are the most visible form of IP; trade secrets are the least. The Internet now provides a means to search federal trademark registrations and applications through the official USPTO Web site (*uspto.gov*). Microsoft would have been better served if it had understood in advance that its proposed title *Mythica* for a multiplayer online role-playing game was too similar to the registered trademark MYTHIC ENTERTAINMENT, developer of a similar game *Dark Age of Camelot*. Microsoft settled a trademark infringement lawsuit brought by Mythic Entertainment and abandoned its game. Domain name registries are also searchable. Many game companies maintain Web sites or can be located through Internet search engines. Commercial services are available that will conduct searches of proprietary and public trademark, business name, and domain name databases for a fee. Consequently, before adopting a trademark it is both possible and prudent to determine whether the same or a similar mark is in use in connection with substantially the same goods or services. To illustrate, adopting the trademark "Hims" for a simulation game in which male characters interact in daily "guy" activities would produce legal howls from Electronic Arts, owner of the registered trademark THE SIMS for a simulation game. Intentional infringement carries enhanced penalties. In instances in which the trademark similarities are not free of doubt, an attorney familiar with trademark practice should be consulted. Attorney clearance may avoid exposure to damages tied to willful violation.

Trade secrets cannot be researched, but infringement occurs in rather predictable contexts. Recall that trade secrets are only violated if they are misappropriated. Independent knowledge from an untainted source is a complete defense. Workers can be the knowing or unwitting transmitters of infected trade secrets when they change employers. The new employer should take measures to block the use of trade secrets previously acquired by the employee by written policy and contract. In many cases of misappropriation that find their way to court, an employee has been hired precisely because of the valuable trade secrets acquired from a rival company. The new employer will be hard pressed to mount a defense. Publishers and developers face a different side of this issue. To begin a game, the developer must pitch confidential concepts and ideas. The developer wants all of this information, as broadly construed as possible, to be treated as trade secrets. The publisher wants to hear the pitch, but does not want to be prevented from considering similar concepts and ideas from others if a deal is not struck. A well-drafted nondisclosure agreement (NDA) is the solution, but the parties may struggle with the scope of protected information and the publisher's permitted uses. Publishers commonly have the greater leverage in negotiating an NDA. Developers may be put to the choice of complete protection by making no disclosure, and therefore no deal, or taking their chances by disclosing their creative ideas with less than perfect safeguards.

Copyrights, like trademarks, are searchable in a government registry. In this case, it is maintained by the Library of Congress (*loc.gov*). The dilemma presented by copyright infringement analysis is that the accused infringer is only liable if there is copying of a commercially significant portion of a copyrighted work. Ignorance, while not bliss, may be a perfectly effective defense. Conversely, knowing infringement of a copyrighted work subjects the infringer to substantial enhanced penalties and costs if prosecuted. In cases in which a copyrighted work "influenced" or is the "inspiration" for a new work, it is important to avoid copying material portions of the prior work and prudent to avoid any duplication. What was plagiarism in high school can be an expensive copyright lawsuit in game development. If a prior copyrighted work is the known basis for a new work, and a license or other permission is not sought, the author or artist must assure that the new work will be viewed as an original creation, or that it satisfies the fair use or parody exceptions to copyright enforcement, or relies on those portions of the prior work that constitute uncopyrightable ideas or *scenes a faire*. The statutory penalties imposed for copyright infringement are sufficiently severe to render any degree of copying of a protected work foolhardy. Recently, Robert Crais, author of the best-selling crime novel *L.A. Requiem*, sued Activision after the lead designer of its best-selling game *True Crime: Streets of L.A.* volunteered that he was "inspired" by Mr. Crais' book.

Like copyrights and trademarks, the federal government maintains a registry of searchable patents (*uspto.gov*). Other Web sites, such as Delphion (*www.delphion.com*), contain useful patent search capabilities and resources. In addition, like copyrights and trademarks, knowing infringement of a patent subjects the infringer to enhanced damages. However, unlike copyright, the absence of copying is not a defense to infringement of patented subject matter. This raises the dilemma of whether to conduct a search of prior patents to determine if the proposed invention is the subject of existing patents. One school of thought counsels against a search to avoid a later charge of willfulness if a patent is discovered and then ignored. The other school of thought advises conducting a search to understand what patents may present a problem and to work around them. In fact, general knowledge obtained from patents may facilitate the invention effort. Overlaying these conflicting approaches is the fact that patent infringement searches are difficult to properly conduct and may be inconclusive in outcome. An opinion from patent counsel that an invention does not infringe prior art patents may be used to counter a charge of willfulness in a later lawsuit, but such opinions can cost thousands of dollars depending on the complexity of the subject matter. Moreover, to a greater degree than copyrights and trademarks, patents are subject to challenge. In the case of method patents, a substantial number fail to be upheld by courts. As with the other fields of IP law, sensitivity to the possibility of infringement is essential. Caution in avoiding the more obvious opportunities for infringement is crucial to the successful development of video games.

Summary

As multimedia combinations of the creative and inventive efforts of diverse contributors, video games are a case study in the nature and scope of intellectual property. Games are entertainment. However, they would not be made, especially at the huge budgets required, were it not for the fact that IP ownership can be acquired and enforced, rights can be transferred, and value can be received. The impact of effective IP laws can be seen in the state of technological development in countries that honor IP rights and those that do not. It is not happenstance that the strongest world markets for video game creation and sales are North America, Europe/Australia, and Japan, all nations with a long tradition of IP rights registration and enforcement.

Exercises

1. A game developer has an idea for a role-playing game (RPG) that he believes involves highly original characters and scenes. The title for the game, the names of the lead characters, a preliminary design document sketching the plot and the first few levels, and several screens of computer artwork have been created. The developer is concerned about protecting the ownership of his idea when he makes presentations to potential publishers. What protections are available to the developer under IP law?

2. The developer in Exercise 1 has now obtained a contract from a publisher. In the contract, the developer assigns all of his rights to the game to the publisher. Because the developer is the creator of the game, can the developer later sell the film rights to the game to a film producer?

3. The developer in Exercise 1 is about to hire his first employee. What IP rights belonging to the employee should the developer secure in the employment contract?

4. Immediately after the release of the game, the developer in Exercise 1 receives a letter claiming the RPG gameplay infringes the patent of the letter writer. On what grounds may the developer challenge the validity of the patent?

5. When the game is released, the developer in Exercise 1 notices that there is no mention of the developer on the box; only the publisher's name and logo appear. The publishing agreement is silent on the matter of developer credits. Does the developer have the right to be listed on the box?

6. Search the patent database (*uspto.gov*) for the title "Sanity System for Video Game," which is currently in the "Published Applications" database. Read the full application and determine the game and company to which it applies. (Hint: use pertinent keywords in Google, use *mobygames.com* to locate games people worked on, and/or use *gamespot.com* to track down reviews.)

7. Search the federal trademark database (*uspto.gov*) for the game title "Dead Ringer." Is "Dead Ringer" available for use as a video game title based on your search? What additional searches could you undertake before determining the availability of "Dead Ringer" for use as a game title?

References

[ALI95] *Restatement of the Law Third: Unfair Competition*, American Law Institute, ALI, 1995.

[CopyrightAct76] *Copyright Act of 1976*, as amended, 17 U.S.C. §§ 101–810, 1001–1010; 1101; 1201–1205; 1301–1332 [United States].

[Hirtle04] Hirtle, Peter B., *Copyright Term and the Public Domain In the United States*, available at *www.copyright.cornell.edu/training/Hirtle_Public_Domain.htm*.

[IGDA03a] *Contract Walk-Through*, Business Committee, International Game Developers' Association, 2003, available at *www.igda.org/biz/contract_walkthrough.php*.

[IGDA03b] *Game Submission Guide*, Business Committee, International Game Developers' Association, 1st ed., 2003, available at *www.igda.org/biz/submission_guide.php*.

[IGDA03c] *White Paper*, Intellectual Property Rights Committee, International Game Developers' Association, Final Draft, 2003, available at *www.igda.org/biz/ipr_paper.php*.

[PatentAct] *Patent Act*, as amended, 35 U.S.C. §§ 1–136 [United States].

[TrademarkAct46] *Trademark Act of 1946 ("Lanham Act")*, as amended, 15 U.S.C. §§ 1–46 [United States].

[ULC85] *Uniform Trade Secrets Act*, Uniform Conference of Commissioners on Uniform State Laws, *www.nccusl.org* (Final Acts and Legislation).

7.6 ▪ Content Regulation

In This Chapter

- Overview
- A Brief History of Censorship in America
- Congress Takes a First Look at Video Games
- The Advent of Industry Self-Regulation
- Criticism of the ESRB Rating Program
- Video Game Content Regulation in the Courts
- Content Regulation in Other Countries
- Summary
- Exercises
- References

Overview

Video games have passed many mileposts on their path to becoming a financial and cultural powerhouse of the entertainment industry. Somewhere between *Pong* and the latest console game, technology and creativity combined to enable games to reach a level of realism and expressiveness as immersive and as popular as the books, plays, motion pictures and television that came before. Just when this milestone was reached is hard to pinpoint. Arcade games no doubt led the way, but increasingly powerful PCs beginning in the early 1980s, followed by game consoles later in the decade, established video games as an engaging interactive medium for character portrayal and story telling.

By the early 1990s, Nintendo and Sega were battling for the mass market with games featuring cute and cuddly Mario and Sonic. The medium was now in place. Along with it came the message, and the subject matter of this chapter. In 1993, the realism and gore of *Mortal Kombat* made it an overnight sensation. It and a then-obscure PC game featuring vampires and scantily clad women called *Night Trap*, were sensationalized by those enduring elements in society dedicated to rooting out what, by their lights, is offensive, indecent, obscene, degenerate, and subversive expression. The battle over video game content had begun.

A Brief History of Censorship in America

Video games are only the latest medium of expression to be subject to public outcries for regulation, if not outright censorship. The battle over game content is being waged in a legal arena whose rules reflect more than two centuries of changing public mores and evolving attitudes toward government control. The touchstone of analysis, the First Amendment to the United States Constitution, was adopted with the other nine "Bill of Rights" in 1791. As relates to the suppression of speech, it provides in 10 protean words: "Congress shall make no law . . . abridging the freedom of speech. . . ." The Fourteenth Amendment extended this prohibition to state and local government abridgment of speech in 1868.

The notion of free expression is engrained in American political philosophy. However, implementation of the seemingly absolute protection of the First Amendment by the courts, and most particularly by the Supreme Court of the United States, has been anything but absolute, or even consistent. Indeed, for most of the Amendment's history, only conventional forms of political expression were deemed constitutionally secure; many other forms of speech were deemed beyond the First Amendment's shield. These included sedition (speech intended to undermine the government), fighting words inciting to violence, defamation (libel and slander), group libel (hate speech), and obscenity. Books, plays, and films were truly "banned in Boston," and in other jurisdictions large and small across the country. Church leaders often were at the forefront of censorship campaigns. High water marks were reached when state censors attempted but failed to ban James Joyce's *Ulysses* in 1934 and Henry Miller's *Tropic of Cancer* 30 years later. Propelling this censorship effort was an encompassing definition of obscenity, which extended beyond explicit sexual content to include profanity and sacrilegious language that are taken for granted today. The depiction of violence *per se* received little attention during this period. Judges gave "smut" censors wide range. Obscenity was deemed by the courts as utterly without redeeming social importance, and therefore not entitled to First Amendment safeguards.

A profound liberalization in public values and tolerance for social differences after World War II eventually influenced the Supreme Court to extend First Amendment protections to nonpolitical forms of speech, but in a gradual and halting manner. Profanity and sacrilegious language are now protected, but sexually explicit forms of expression found to be "obscene" continue to be outside the constitutional protection. The Supreme Court continues to uphold bans on the dissemination or exhibition of sexually explicit material, particularly "when the mode of dissemination carries with it a significant danger of offending the sensibilities of unwilling recipients or of exposure to juveniles."

The current position of the Supreme Court is that sexually obscene expression can be suppressed, but only if the material, taken as a whole, appeals to the prurient interest in sex, portrays sexual conduct in a patently offensive way, and does not have serious literary, artistic, political, or scientific value. Whether such material appeals to a "prurient interest" or is "patently offensive" is measured by the moral standards of the local community where the trial court happens to be located. Only "hard core" materials are deemed outside the First Amendment protection. The Supreme Court has given these examples: "(a) Patently offensive representations or descriptions of ultimate sexual acts, normal or perverted, actual or simulated. (b) Patently offensive representations or descriptions of masturbation, excretory functions, and lewd exhibition of the genitals."

Supreme Court Justice Potter Stewart's cynical definition of pornography "I know it when I see it"—distills for critics the unchanneled nature of the inquiry. To be sure, not all sexually explicit expression is obscene. In fact, the depiction of nudity or the use of offensive language is not even presumptively obscene, and it cannot be prohibited by government merely because it offends someone somewhere. Yet, sexually explicit but nonobscene expression can be regulated in a variety of ways, such as restrictive zoning of "adult" theaters or prevention of retail access to sexually explicit material by children.

In the 1920s, the popularization of the new medium of motion pictures gave rise to a wave of local censorship laws that threatened to overwhelm the fledgling studios. The First Amendment as then interpreted by the Supreme Court provided no sanctuary from this onslaught. Questions were raised whether an Amendment adopted in the age of print to protect political expression even applied to the medium of moving pictures intended for amusement. Rather than fight the censorship laws of each city and village, the film industry sought to side-step them by adoption in 1930 of a Motion Picture Production Code. The Code was voluntarily administered by the Motion Picture Producers and Distributors of America under its imposing chairman, Will Hays. By most accounts, the idiosyncratic regulation of the Hays Office, as it was known, traded decades of film banality for immunity from unchecked government censorship. In one famous example, the Hays Office fined the producer of *Gone With the Wind* the then substantial sum of $5,000 for Clark Gable's signature utterance of the word "damn." The successor to the Hays Office is the Motion Picture Association of America (MPAA). The MPAA functions today in a very different First Amendment environment, one that accepts all mediums of expression as equal and places a substantial burden on the government to justify limitations on expressive content claimed to be objectionable.

Congress Takes a First Look at Video Games

Much like the film studios in the 1920s, video game publishers confronted threats of wide-scale censorship following release of more realistic and more violence-dominated games in the early 1990s. However, the focus was different. Then, concern was mainly the sexual immorality of motion pictures viewed by a mainly adult audience. Now the concern was the marketing of violence to minors. The conventional wisdom is that Senator Joseph Lieberman (D. CT), then chairperson of the Subcommittee on Regulation and Government Information, scheduled hearings on video game violence in late 1993 and early 1994 after receiving complaints and then personally viewing *Mortal Kombat* and *Night Trap*. While violent games constituted only a small percentage of game sales at that time, and video games increasingly were being marketed and sold to an older audience, the public perception of video games was that they were children's toys and that fighting games like *Mortal Kombat* and *Street Fighter II* dominated sales.

Joined by Senator Herb Kohl (D. WI), chairperson of the Subcommittee on Juvenile Justice, Senator Lieberman called to testify the executives of Nintendo and Sega, then two of the leading game publishers, representatives of the Software Publishers Association and Amusement and Music Operators Association, and a panel of "experts" involved in the effects of media on children. While one member of the expert panel testified that video games are overwhelmingly violent, sexist, and racist, the main concern throughout the hearings appeared to be the impact on children of the depiction and interactive commission of violent and gory acts on realistic characters, particularly digitized human images, in games like *Mortal Kombat* and *Night Trap*. None of the expert panelists offered evidence that violent games had any adverse effect on children, but all decried the exposure of children to such violence and some presumed such an adverse effect.

The most compelling testimony was offered by executives of the two dominant publishers and archrivals, Nintendo and Sega. Sega was the first to publish *Mortal Kombat*, and *Night Trap* also was released on its system. While Nintendo later published a version of *Mortal Kombat*, much of the gore had been removed to comport with Nintendo's view of itself as a marketer of games to children. In fact, the Nintendo licensing system required games developed for its systems to be screened for blood, nudity, and religious content. Nintendo used this difference to attack Sega, and in the process gave credence to the charge that publication of the Sega version of *Mortal Kombat* and *Night Trap* were harmful to children. In its defense, Sega noted that its games were sold to an older audience, and that it had adopted a rating system to identify violence and other features in its games that might be inappropriate for younger players. However, this did little to appease critics.

While the hearings did not result in proposed legislation, their impact on the video games industry was both immediate and lasting. Coincidentally, the hearings transformed *Night Trap* into a best seller.

The Advent of Industry Self-Regulation

The Senate hearings on the effects of video game content were unexpected and taught industry leaders the necessity of organization and public relations. It was obvious that the industry needed its own trade group to monitor the expanding efforts to regulate game content at the national, state, and local levels, to present a united and coordinated response to such efforts, and to promote the positive aspects of games. The Interactive Digital Software Association, recently renamed the Entertainment Software Association (ESA), was formed in the aftermath of the hearings to serve these functions.

Game publishers then set about to create a voluntary rating system, much as the MPAA had done, to forestall government-imposed regulation, and to blunt the criticism that consumers, especially parents, could not exercise informed choice in avoiding games that are violent, sexually explicit, profane, or in some other manner personally offensive. The Entertainment Software Rating Board (ESRB) was established in 1994 to formulate a system for rating video games based on the age appropriateness of their content and to implement voluntary adoption and use by the video games industry. Today, the ESRB independently applies and enforces ratings, advertising guidelines, and online privacy principles adopted by the industry. The rating system that was devised has two parts: *rating symbols* (on the front of the game box) suggest age appropriateness for the game, and *content descriptors* (on the back of the game box) indicate elements in a game that may have triggered a particular rating and/or may be of interest or concern. In its first 10 years, the rating system has become ubiquitous on console games and on most PC games.

The rating symbols are comprised of stylized alphabetical letters intended to capsulate a game's suitability for one of six age groups, with a seventh symbol for pending ratings.*

EARLY CHILDHOOD

Titles rated **EC** (**Early Childhood**) have content that may be suitable for ages 3 and older. Contains no material that parents would find inappropriate.

EVERYONE

Titles rated **E** (**Everyone**) have content that may be suitable for ages 6 and older. Titles in this category may contain minimal cartoon, fantasy or mild violence and/or infrequent use of mild language.

EVERYONE 10+

Titles rated **E10+** (**Everyone 10 and older**) have content that may be suitable for ages 10 and older. Titles in this category may contain more cartoon, fantasy or mild violence, mild language, and/or minimal suggestive themes.

TEEN

Titles rated **T** (**Teen**) have content that may be suitable for ages 13 and older. Titles in this category may contain violence, suggestive themes, crude humor, minimal blood and/or infrequent use of strong language.

MATURE

Titles rated **M** (**Mature**) have content that may be suitable for persons ages 17 and older. Titles in this category may contain intense violence, blood and gore, sexual content, and/or strong language.

ADULTS ONLY

Titles rated **AO** (**Adults Only**) have content that should only be played by persons 18 yrs and older. Titles in this category may include prolonged scenes of intense violence and/or graphic sexual content and nudity.

RATING PENDING

Titles listed as **RP** (**Rating Pending**) have been submitted to the ESRB and are awaiting final rating. (This symbol appears only in advertising prior to a game's release.)

*Please be advised that the ESRB Ratings icons, "EC", "E", "E10+", "T", "M", "AO," and "RP" are trademarks owned by the Entertainment Software Association, and may only be used with their permission and authority. For information regarding whether a product has been rated by the ESRB, please visit *www.esrb.org*. For permission to use the Ratings icons, please contact the ESA at *esrblicenseinfo.com*.

There are currently 32 content descriptors, such as "*Blood and Gore*—depictions of blood or the mutilation of body parts; *Cartoon Violence*—violent actions involving cartoonlike situations and characters. May include violence where a character is unharmed after the action has been inflicted; *Fantasy Violence*—violent actions of a fantasy nature, involving human or nonhuman characters in situations easily distinguishable from real life; *Intense Violence*—graphic and realistic-looking depictions of physical conflict. May involve extreme and/or realistic blood, gore, weapons, and depictions of human injury and death; *Nudity*—graphic or prolonged depictions of nudity; *Sexual Violence*—depictions of rape or other sexual acts; *Strong Lyrics*—explicit and/or frequent references to profanity, sex, violence, alcohol, or drug use in music; *Strong Sexual Content*—graphic references to and/or depictions of sexual behavior, possibly including nudity; *Use of Drugs*—the consumption or use of illegal drugs; *Use of Alcohol*—the consumption of alcoholic beverages; *Use of Tobacco*—the consumption of tobacco products." The ESRB Web site contains the full list and explanation of content descriptors at *ESRB.org*.

Ratings are determined by a consensus of at least three raters trained by ESRB. The raters are of various ages and backgrounds, have no ties to the computer and video games industry, and to assure diverse views are not expert game players. To obtain a rating, publishers fill out a questionnaire describing in detail what the game contains. They also submit actual videotaped footage of the game, showing the most extreme content and an accurate representation of the context and product as a whole. The raters then separately view the game footage and recommend the rating and content descriptors they believe are most appropriate. ESRB then compares the recommendations to determine if there is consensus. When the raters disagree, ESRB may enlist additional raters to review the game to reach broader consensus. Once consensus on a rating and content descriptors is reached, ESRB issues an official rating certificate to the publisher. When the game is ready for release to the public, publishers send copies of the final product to the ESRB. The game packaging is reviewed to make sure the ratings are displayed in accordance with ESRB standards. Random checks are conducted to verify that the information provided during the rating process was accurate and complete. Over 1,000 video games are subject to the ESRB rating system each year.

Criticism of the ESRB Rating Program

While the ESRB rating system enjoys wide adoption today, even receiving praise from Senator Lieberman, it continues to generate criticism. There are, of course, groups that would prefer outright censorship of video games and other forms of expression they find offensive. To them, a voluntary rating system can never eliminate the possibility that games will slip through the net and reach inappropriate players. The National Institute On Media and the Family and the Interfaith Center On Corporate Responsibility are among private organizations that publish their own lists ranking the "best" and "worst" games for children. At the opposite pole are groups that believe the current ratings are a form of indirect censorship and go too far. As in the movie industry, an "M—Mature" or "AO—Adults Only" game rating can restrict the potential market for a game. A publisher may feel compelled to make concessions to avoid the potential loss of sales. Indeed, to the extent that the ESRB ratings may be incorporated in government regulations, implicit censorship becomes explicit.

There also is the issue of the accuracy of the ratings. Quite apart from the obvious subjectivity of the rating categories themselves, the element of player interactivity can materially alter the game experience between different players. The ESRB explicitly acknowledges this gap by requiring the notice "Game Experience May Change During Online Play" to warn purchasers that player-generated content has not been rated. In addition, the duration of gameplay can extend over 50 or more hours, making it questionable whether any reviewer can absorb the entire content and accurately rate it, despite the fact that submitted material must include the most extreme content.

Enforcement of the rating system at retail is another area that has drawn repeated criticism. While some retail chains such as Wal-Mart are reported to have a policy to check the age of young purchasers and not sell "M—Mature" rated games to minors under 17, many others do not. Legislation that would impose penalties on sellers of variously defined mature-content games to minors continues to be introduced across the country. Congressman Joe Baca (R. CA), author of a bill to impose federal penalties on those who sell or rent video games to minors that depict nudity, sexual conduct, or content harmful to minors due to graphic violence, sexual violence, or strong sexual content, declares on his Web site (*house.gov/baca*): "Video games with violent and sexually oriented material are brainwashing and conditioning our kids to violence." California just enacted a statute that penalizes sellers of "M—Mature" rated games to minors. It requires video game retailers to post signs about the ESRB rating system and the availability of explanatory material. There is also indication that retail chains are cracking down. Acclaim's liberal depiction of topless nudity in *BMX XXX* prompted Wal-Mart, Toys "R" Us, and a few other major outlets to refuse to stock the game.

Yet another area of condemnation is the industry practice of marketing adult games to children. The ESA has promulgated an Advertising Code of Conduct to eliminate this practice, followed by creation of the Advertising Review Council in 1999, and ESRB's *Principles and Guidelines for Responsible Advertising Practices* in January 2000. But in a report to the President and Congress in 2000 entitled *Marketing Violent Entertainment to Children: A Review of Self-Regulation and Industry Practices In the Motion Picture, Music Recording & Electronic Games Industries*, the Federal Trade Commission found widespread marketing of "M—Mature" rated video games to children under 17. The same FTC report found only limited consumer awareness of the ESRB rating system, citing a 1999 ESRB study that only 45 percent of survey parents had any awareness of the ratings. This compares with 94 percent of parents who claimed familiarity with the MPAA movie rating system. Other studies cited at the time by the FTC showed that an equally low percentage of parents actually use the ESRB rating system. In three updates, the most recent in 2004, the FTC concluded the ESRB had made progress in increasing awareness and use of the game rating system, and in enforcement of its advertising code. However, the FTC continues to find lax enforcement among retailers of their policies not to sell "M—Mature" rated games to minors.

Video Game Content Regulation in the Courts

What the FTC Report and follow-up reviews did not find, indeed what no authoritative source has yet to find, is of equal importance. There is no scientific study that shows a credible link between the violent or sexually explicit content of video games and harm to children or others who play them. Anecdotal evidence is offered in the form of events such as the Columbine High School shootings in 1999. Instances in which avid teenage players of violent games are involved in real-life violent crimes do make headlines, often become lawsuits, and may inspire legislation and ordinances to suppress game content or distribution. Each time a new game breaks sales records by ratcheting up the depiction of violence, nudity, or some other perceived vice—most notably of late *Grand Theft Auto: Vice City* and its progeny—the advocates of control are reinvigorated.

Thus far, the courts have rebuffed government attempts to censor video games. Three recent federal court decisions address, in different contexts, attempts to regulate game content. They cast light on the future of censorship efforts.

In the first of these cases, *American Amusement Machine Association v. Kendrick*, decided in 2001, the Court of Appeals for the Seventh Circuit granted a preliminary injunction to manufacturers and distributors of arcade machines and their trade association blocking enforcement of an Indianapolis ordinance that limited the access of minors to games that depict violence. The ordinance forbids any operator of game machines to allow a minor unaccompanied by a parent, guardian, or other custodian to use "an amusement machine that is harmful to minors." It also requires warning signs, and, in the case of locations with five or more machines, the screening of the machines from observers. The ordinance defines "harmful to minors" as "an amusement machine that predominantly appeals to minors' morbid interest in violence or minors' prurient interest in sex, is patently offensive to prevailing standards in the adult community as a whole with respect to what is suitable material for persons under the age of eighteen (18) years, lacks serious literary, artistic, political or scientific value as a whole for persons under that age," and contains either "graphic violence" or "strong sexual content." In this case, only "graphic violence" was at issue.

Judge Richard Posner, a noted federal jurist, wrote the opinion of the Court. He first observed that the ordinance imports traditional First Amendment sexual obscenity standards to the regulation of content that depicts violence. For obscenity, which is unprotected speech, the test is its appeal to prurient interest and patent offensiveness to community moral standards. "But offensiveness," Judge Posner concluded, "is not the basis on which Indianapolis seeks to regulate violent video games. Nor could the ordinance be defended on that basis. The most violent game in the record, "The House of the Dead," depicts zombies being killed flamboyantly, with much severing of limbs and effusion of blood; but so stylized and patently fictitious is the cartoon-like depiction that no one would suppose it to be 'obscene' in the sense in which a photograph of a person being decapitated might be described as 'obscene.' It will not turn anyone's stomach. The basis of the ordinance, rather, is a belief that violent video games cause temporal harm by engendered aggressive attitudes and behavior, which might lead to violence."

Hence, to regulate speech on grounds that it is harmful to minors requires Indianapolis to show a compelling government interest. "Children," Judge Posner wrote, "have First Amendment rights, and Indianapolis has a heavy burden to justify their restriction." Indianapolis offered "social science studies" in support. Judge Posner responded: "There is no indication that the games used in the studies are similar to those in this case or other games likely to be marketed in game arcades in Indianapolis. The studies do not find that video games have ever caused anyone to commit a violent act, as opposed to feeling aggressive, or have caused the average level of violence to increase anywhere." Absent such a showing of compelling state interest, the Indianapolis ordinance was unlikely to withstand First Amendment scrutiny and a preliminary injunction blocking enforcement was ordered.

Concern about the link between violent video game content and the commission of a violent act by a minor was also present in the second case, *James v. Meow Media, Inc.*, decided in 2003 by the federal Sixth Circuit Court of Appeals. The parents and estate of students killed by Michael Carneal during a shooting rampage at Heath High School in Paducah, Kentucky sued video game, movie production, and Internet content-provider firms for the deaths. They alleged Carneal regularly played video games, including *Doom*, *Quake*, *Castle Wolfenstein*, *Resident Evil*, and *Final Fantasy*, watched movies, and viewed Internet sites that "desensitized" Carneal to violence and "caused" him to kill the students at Heath High School. Although the lawsuit was brought as a civil wrongful death action to recover damages, the Court of Appeals recognized that the imposition of civil liability on protected speech can violate the First Amendment. Citing among others the *American Amusement Machine Association* decision, the Court stated: "most federal courts to consider the issue have found video games to be constitutionally protected."

The parents of the dead students argued that they were not seeking to regulate all speech, but only violent speech directed to young, impressionable children, or even more specifically at Carneal. The Court of Appeals found some merit in this position. "The protections of the First Amendment have always been adapted to the audience intended for the speech. Specifically, we have recognized certain speech, while fully protected when directed at adults, may be restricted when directed toward minors. . . . We have also required, however, that such regulations be narrowly tailored to protecting minors from speech that may improperly influence them and not effect an 'unnecessarily broad suppression of speech' appropriate for adults." Such narrow tailoring was more properly the task of a legislature, and not litigants in a private action seeking to recover damages. The Court of Appeals said the parents could not proceed with their private claims in such circumstances.

In the final decision, decided in 2004, the United States District Court for the Western District of Washington permanently enjoined enforcement of a Washington law that penalized distribution of video games to minors that contain "realistic or photographic-like depictions of aggressive conflict in which the player kills, injures, or otherwise causes physical harm to a human form in the game who is depicted, by dress or other recognizable symbols, as a public law enforcement officer." The plaintiffs in this case, *Video Software Dealers Association v. Maleng*, were game creators, publishers, and distributors who asserted the Washington statute infringed their First Amendment rights. The District Court observed that "[s]imilar disputes have erupted across the country as state and local governments have attempted to regulate the dissemination of violent video games to children. As of this date, no such regulation has passed constitutional muster." The Washington law would prove no exception. With earlier cases showing the way, the District Court rejected the legislature's characterization of speech depicting violence as obscenity, and thus entitled lesser constitutional protection. The District Court held that "obscenity" in the context of the First Amendment means material that deals with sex. Finding the video games at issue are expressive speech entitled to the full protections of the First Amendment, the District Court said content-based regulations are presumptively invalid. They will only be upheld if the legislature can show regulation is necessary to serve a compelling state interest, and that it is narrowly tailored to achieve that interest. The legislature, the District Court explained, "must do more than simply 'posit the existence of the disease sought to be cured.'" While the state has a legitimate and compelling interest in safeguarding the physical and psychological well-being of minors, it must show the legislation will accomplish the intended remedy.

As in *American Amusement Machine Association*, the expert reports and studies offered to show this connection in the *Maleng* case were found to be insufficient. The District Court explained that most of the studies relied on by the state had nothing to do with video games. None was designed to test the effects of such games on the player's attitudes or behavior toward law enforcement officers, the specific harm the legislature sought to address. Nor was the statute narrowly tailored. Having rejected the Washington law, the District Court said: "Given the nationwide, on-going dispute in this area, it is reasonable to ask whether a state may ever impose a ban on the dissemination of video games to children under 18. The answer is 'probably yes' if the games contain sexually explicit images . . ., and 'maybe' if the games contain violent images, such as torture or bondage, that appeal to the prurient interest of minors. . . ."

Several principles can be derived from these decisions and others addressing the First Amendment protections afforded video game content.

1. Video games are entitled to the same First Amendment protections as traditional forms of expression such as books, plays, art, and motion pictures. The First Amendment protects entertainment and political and ideological speech. The interactive nature of video games is immaterial to the protection of their content.

2. Only video games challenged on the basis of sexual content will be evaluated under the lower First Amendment safeguards applicable to obscenity. In such cases, the test is whether the game, taken as a whole, appeals to the prurient interest in sex, portrays sexual conduct in a patently offensive way, and does not have serious literary, artistic, political, or scientific value.

3. Government efforts to suppress video game content based on violent content are subject to a higher "strict scrutiny" burden. The government must show a compelling interest in regulation and that the means chosen are the least restrictive means to achieve the objective. It is not enough to "posit the existence of the disease"; theoretical or anecdotal links between exposure to violence in video games and harm to minors will not suffice. A connection must be shown by unbiased, authoritative, and relevant analysis.

Content Regulation in Other Countries

As can be seen, content regulation of video games in the United States is shaped by political, legal, and cultural forces that are unique to this country. While video games have become a global phenomenon, individual nations react differently to the censorship issues surrounding game content. Germany, for example, has general laws banning public displays of the swastika and other Nazi symbols. *Wolfenstein 3D* and *Return to Castle Wolfenstein*, although anti-Nazi in content, fell under this prohibition. The Chinese Ministry of Culture has banned a foreign game that depicts Manchuria and Tibet as sovereign nations. Japanese video games tend to be less bloody than elsewhere, but more than make up in brutal sexually explicit content that generates calls for regulation. Australia initially banned *Grand Theft Auto: Vice City* due to its depiction of violence against prostitutes, until the offending material was removed. Neighboring New Zealand bans *Manhunt*. The Greek Parliament went so far as to ban all video games in 2002, which it substantially narrowed under pressure from the European Union and the United States.

Many countries have adopted self-regulatory rating systems for reasons similar to those motivating the ESRB. Canadian companies voluntarily apply the ESRB ratings although they are not members of the ESA of Canada. China and Australia have adopted government-run rating systems. Germany promulgates a "banned list" of video games that depict the gory killing of people or showing cruelty to humans. South Korea has similar "no blood" regulations.

Summary

Game developers and publishers who intend to push the envelope of acceptable content must take careful note of the laws and culture in which the games will be played. They face choices based on the economic and the creative costs of triggering censorship. Sex and violence may indeed sell games, but only if the sex and violence are permitted to reach consumers. By and large, publishers have bent content to the dictates of local markets, modifying or removing content to avoid outright censorship or a restrictive rating.

Exercises

1. In what ways does regulation of video game content differ from regulation of books, art, plays, and motion pictures?
2. How does the ESRB ensure that its reviewers fairly and effectively evaluate the entire content of a video game? Is the procedure successful? What are the possible problems with requiring reviewers to play the games they review?
3. Should online games that rely on player content be rated by the ESRB?
4. Does self-regulation such as the ESRB rating system constitute censorship? What are the negative effects of an industry rating system on game creativity?
5. Should major retail outlets like Wal-Mart be permitted to refuse to sell a video game simply because they disagree with its content? What legal defenses do you anticipate will be presented by Wal-Mart if it were to be sued by a publisher for refusing to sell its video game? Should Wal-Mart be able to assert that it has a First Amendment right not to sell a game whose content it finds objectionable?
6. In what ways does the First Amendment analysis applied by the courts differ for sexually explicit and graphically violent video game content? Do you believe there should be a distinction between the two? What is the best argument for treating violent games under the less protective standard for sexually explicit games?
7. Is private self-regulation always preferable to government mandatory regulation? Can you make the argument that self-regulation is potentially more suppressive of free speech than public controls?

References

[AAMA01] *American Amusement Machine Association v. Kendrick*, 244 F.3d 572 (7th Cir.), certiorari denied, 534 U.S. 994, 2001.

[ESRB04] Entertainment Software Rating Board, *http://esrb.org*, December 1, 2004.

[FTC00] Federal Trade Commission, *Marketing Violent Entertainment to Children: A Review of Self-Regulation and Industry Practices In the Motion Picture, Music Recording & Electronic Game Industries*, September 2000.

[FTC04] Federal Trade Commission, *Marketing Violent Entertainment to Children: A Fourth Follow-up Review of Industry Practices in the Motion Picture, Music Recording & Electronic Game Industries*, July 2004.

[GameDaily04] GameDaily, *Developing for a Mature Audience, http://biz.gamedaily. com/features.asp?article_id=8179§ion=feature* (November 30, 2004).

[IDSA03] *Interactive Digital Software Association v. St. Louis County*, 329 F.3d 954 (8th Cir.), 2003.

[IGDA04] International Games Developers Association, *Anti-Censorship*, *http://igda.org/censorship* (December 1, 2004).

[James02] *James v. Meow Media, Inc.*, 300 F.3d 683 (6th Cir. 2002).

[Kent01] Kent, Steven L., *The Ultimate History of Video Games*, Ch. 25, 2001.

[Miller73] *Miller v. California*, 413 U.S. 15, 1973.

[NIMF04] National Institute on Media and the Family, *Ninth Annual Mediawise Video Game Report Card*, *http://mediafamily.org/research/report_vgrc_2004*, November 25, 2004.

[Reno97] Reno v. American Civil Liberties Union, 521 U.S. 844, 1997.

[VSDA04] *Video Software Dealers Association v. Maleng*, No. C03-1245L, W. D. Wash., July 15, 2004.

[Wikipedia04] Wikipedia, *Video Game Controversy*, *http://en.wikipedia.org/wiki/Video_game_controversy*, December 1, 2004.

About the CD-ROM

This CD-ROM contains source code, demos, art files, and other material that is described in the book. Every attempt has been made to ensure that the source code is bug-free and will compile easily. Please refer to the Web site *www.introgamedev.com* for errata and updates.

Contents

The content of the CD-ROM is organized within three main directories: Chapter Content, Figures, and Presentations.

Chapter Content: Contains all files referenced within the chapters. For example, files referenced within Chapter 6.7 can be found in the directory "Chapter Content\Part 6 AV Design and Production\6.7 Animation."

Figures: Source images of the figures in this book.

Presentations: PowerPoint presentations that complement each chapter.

System Requirements

Intel® Pentium®-series, AMD Athlon or newer processor recommended. Windows XP (64MB RAM) or Windows 2000 (128MB RAM) or later recommended. 3D graphics card required for some of the sample applications. DirectX 9 or newer also required. The following software is required in order to take advantage of all the files provided on the CD-ROM: Microsoft Visual Studio .NET 2003, 3ds max 6, Microsoft Word, Microsoft Excel, Microsoft PowerPoint, Adobe Reader, and QuickTime Player.

INDEX